www.wadsworth.com

wadsworth.com is the World Wide Web site for Wadsworth and is your direct source to dozens of online resources.

At *wadsworth.com* you can find out about supplements, demonstration software, and student resources. You can also send email to many of our authors and preview new publications and exciting new technologies.

wadsworth.com
Changing the way the world learns®

Of Children

AN INTRODUCTION TO CHILD AND ADOLESCENT DEVELOPMENT

NINTH EDITION

GUY R. LEFRANÇOIS

UNIVERSITY OF ALBERTA

WADSWORTH
™
THOMSON LEARNING

Australia • Canada • Mexico • Singapore • Spain
United Kingdom • United States

WADSWORTH

THOMSON LEARNING ™

Psychology Publisher: Edith Beard Brady
Development Editor: Sherry Symington
Marketing Manager: Marc Linseman
Marketing Assistant: Megan Hansen
Project Editor: Lisa Weber
Print Buyer: Mary Noel
Permissions Editor: Joohee Lee
Production Service: Patti Zeman, Hespenheide Design
Text Designer: Stephanie Davila, Hespenheide Design
Art Editor: Hespenheide Design
Photo Researcher: Jennifer Lawson, Hespenheide Design

Copy Editors: Brenda Koplin and Christianne Thillen
Proofreader: Bridget Neumayr, Hespenheide Design
Illustrator: Randy Miyake, Hespenheide Design
Cover Designer: Hespenheide Design
Cover Image: Nhi Chu, *Stand and Be Counted* (detail), April 2000, acrylic on canvas, $5' \times 15'$ mural; courtesy of Nhi Chu (student, Toolworks Specialized Deaf Services, San Francisco) and David Rio Tea Company, San Francisco.
Cover Printer: Phoenix Color
Compositor: Hespenheide Design
Printer: R. R. Donnelley Willard

Library of Congress Cataloging-in-Publication Data
Lefrançois, Guy R.
    Of children : an introduction to child and adolescent development / Guy R. Lefrançois—9th ed.
        p. cm.
    Includes bibliographical references and indexes.
    ISBN 0-534-52605-5 (alk. paper)
    1. Child development. I. Title.
RJ131.L38 2000
305.231—dc21   00-047724

Wadsworth/Thomson Learning
10 Davis Drive
Belmont, CA 94002-3098
USA

For more information about our products, contact us:
Thomson Learning Academic Resource Center
1-800-423-0563
http://www.wadsworth.com

International Headquarters
Thomson Learning
International Division
290 Harbor Drive, 2nd Floor
Stamford, CT 06902-7477
USA

UK/Europe/Middle East/South Africa
Thomson Learning
Berkshire House
168-173 High Holborn
London WC1V 7AA
United Kingdom

Asia
Thomson Learning
60 Albert Street, #15-01
Albert Complex
Singapore 189969

Canada
Nelson Thomson Learning
1120 Birchmount Road
Toronto, Ontario M1K 5G4
Canada

1976

1980

1988

1994

This book is
affectionately
dedicated to
Laurier,
Claire,
and Rémi,
and to Elizabeth,
Liam,
and Zachary,
beautiful children,
and to all things beautiful.

2000

BRIEF CONTENTS

TABLE OF CONTENTS

PART FIVE: ADOLESCENCE

ABOUT THE AUTHOR

Guy R. Lefrançois holds an appointment at the University of Alberta, where he also received his Ph.D. He is the author of another bestseller in developmental psychology: *Lifespan*, Sixth Edition (1999), published by Wadsworth. He is also widely known for his education texts: *Psychology for Teaching*, Tenth Edition (2000), published by Wadsworth, and *Theories of Human Learning: What the Old Man Said*, Fourth Edition (2000), published by Brooks/Cole.

PREFACE

'Tis strange—but true;
For truth is always strange;
Stranger than fiction
—Lord Byron, *Don Juan*

Dear Reader,

When she read the first edition of this book, my grandmother shook her head more than once. Often, when I'd describe a finding or a theory that did violence to her beliefs, she would mutter, "Sounds pretty strange to me, Guy. You sure you're not writing fiction?" Hey, as Lord Byron tells us, truth *is* strange—*stranger than fiction*! And complex, too, he might have added.

Over the years, the study of child and adolescent development has become increasingly complex, with even more theories, more findings, and more speculation. *Of Children* has been completely revised to reflect these changes in the field, and to assist students in capitalizing on this wealth of material. I also have tried to communicate how fascinating the subject of child development can be and how provocative, challenging, and sometimes controversial. To achieve these goals, this new edition has the following new emphases:

New to This Edition

Greater Emphasis on Context and Diversity

This edition recognizes more clearly than the previous edition the importance of the contexts (relationships) within which we develop. As a result, it makes more use of cross-cultural research, and is more sensitive to the fact that our increasingly multicultural societies don't provide all children with the same experiences—or opportunities. Every chapter includes one or more inserts titled *Across Cultures*. These look specifically at how different contexts might contribute to different developmental outcomes.

More Real-Life Connections and Internet Resources

The book emphasizes throughout the extent to which topics and issues in child and developmental psychology relate to real life. In addition, every chapter includes inserts entitled *In the News and on the Web*. These high-interest and high-relevance inserts are built around news items gleaned from some of the world's newspapers. Each includes one or more URLs that direct readers to important Internet sources for more information and clarification. The student is guided further by a list of Internet resources at the ends of chapters, and suggested subject headings for conducting online research.

Stronger Focus on Biopsychology

This revision reflects more clearly psychology's increasing interest in biopsychology. Accordingly, there are major expansions and additions dealing with the growth and functioning of the brain, behavior genetics, and the relationship between brain and behavior.

More Tools for Active Learning

Many features in this ninth edition are designed to involve the student more actively in the reading-learning process. For example, many of the tables and figures are *interactive*: They ask questions, present dilemmas, pose problems, and suggest activities. Similarly, most of the *Across Cultures* and *In the News and on the Web* inserts present the reader with suggestions for things *To Do* or *To Think About*. Every chapter also begins with questions designed to focus attention on the most important features of the chapter; and every chapter concludes with a series of applied questions.

New Thought Challenges to Encourage Critical Thinking

Finally, also reflecting the goal of actively involving the student, every chapter includes a number of *Thought Challenges*, brief presentations of intriguing and highly relevant problems and questions. Possible answers for each of these are given at the end of the chapter.

Topics Thoroughly Updated

This edition contains a large number of new or significantly expanded topics including coverage of:

▲ children who leave home early and street children in North America and throughout the world

▲ the methods and ethics of assisted reproduction

▲ behavior genetics

▲ stunting, wasting, and infant mortality in North America and the world

▲ parent and infant attachment

▲ emotional intelligence and social competence

▲ gender identity, including homosexual gender identity

▲ ethnic identity formation

▲ nutrition and physical fitness at all ages

▲ bullies and child victimization

▲ effects of the new media, including VCRs, video games, and the Internet

▲ loneliness and solitude in childhood and adolescence

▲ gang violence

▲ trends in drug use, including "date-rape" drugs

New Special Features

These new pedagogical features in this revision are designed to reinforce the goals for this new edition:

▲ **Across Cultures:** boxed inserts that present views of development in different contexts and emphasize the extent to which developmental outcomes depend on context.

▲ **In the News and on the Web:** discussions of highly current issues based on newspaper and Internet sources which serve to underline the relevance of developmental topics and issues to everyday life. These also include search terms for exploring the online database offered with the text, *InfoTrac® College Edition*.

▲ **Online Resources and *InfoTrac College Edition*:** Web site suggestions and access to an online database of relevant articles. Throughout the text are suggestions for Web sites to consult for more information as well as search terms to aid online research. Also, with the online database that accompanies this text, *InfoTrac College Edition*, students are able to access from their home computers the full text of articles in more than 900 periodicals and scholarly journals. At the end of each chapter are detailed descriptions of suggested readings as well as search terms to aid in online exploration of major concepts.

▲ **Concept Summaries:** tables that provide summary information for major topics.

▲ **Thought Challenges:** brief boxes scattered throughout each chapter that present problems, issues, and dilemmas that ask students to think critically. Suggestions for possible answers to stimulate further thought appear at the end of each chapter.

▲ **Running Glossary:** definitions of key terms at the bottom of the page where they first appear. In addition, a list of study terms at the end of each chapter and full glossary at the end of the text help students master key terms.

▲ **Focus Questions and Applications:** pre-chapter questions and end-of-chapter exercises. A brief list of introductory *Focus Questions* precede each chapter to help students watch for key ideas. There are also follow-up application questions at the end of each chapter that encourage students to reflect on the material they've just read. These have been thoroughly updated.

▲ **At a Glance:** boxed inserts that present brief, current, and highly graphic data reflecting some important feature of life for North American children, some now with full-color illustrations.

New Supplementary Aids: Print, Multimedia, Online

This edition has more aids to help students and instructors than ever before. The book now includes supplements that are offered in traditional print as well as multimedia and the Internet.

Study Guide: Written by George Semb, University of Kansas, this complete Study Guide for students includes study questions and a review for each chapter, important terms and concepts, practice tests in both multiple-choice and true-false formats, and activities to accompany each chapter (ISBN 0-534-52607-1).

Instructor's Manual: The Instructor's Manual contains chapter learning objectives, lecture notes, discussion questions, suggestions for teaching, and suggested activities for students. It also includes general information about course objectives, procedures, and how to plan the course. Included is a list of film, videotapes, and computer software, as well as a sample student survey. Transparency masters are provided for each chapter (ISBN 0-534-52608-X).

Test Bank and *ExamView*®: The test bank for *Of Children* includes approximately 100 multiple-choice, 150 true/false, 40 fill-ins and 40 essay questions per chapter. All answers are located in the back of the chapter with page references to the main text (ISBN 0-534-52609-8).

The test bank is also available in computerized form, using *ExamView*. The *ExamView* software offers both a Quick Test Wizard and an Online Test Wizard that guide instructors step-by-step through the process of creating tests that can be delivered in print or online. Instructors will be able to see the test they are creating on the screen exactly as it will print or display online. Tests of up to 250 questions can be built using up to 12 question types. Using *ExamView*'s complete word processing capabilities, instructors can enter an unlimited number of new questions or edit existing questions.

Web Tutor 2.0 for *Of Children*: This Web-based learning and course management tool helps instructors take the course beyond the classroom boundaries. Professors can provide virtual office hours, post syllabi, set up threaded discussions, track student progress with the quizzing material, and more. *Web Tutor* provides rich communication tools, including a course calendar, asynchronous discussion, real time chat, a whiteboard, and an integrated email system. For students, *Web Tutor* offers real-time access to a full array of study tools, including flashcards (with audio), practice quizzes, online tutorials, and Web links. Available either on a WebCT platform (ISBN 0-534-52612-8) or Blackboard (ISBN 0-534-52613-6).

PsychLink for Child Development: A CD-ROM that includes figure art and lecture slides in PowerPoint for classroom presentations. Instructors can customize this by adding, deleting, or rearranging the PowerPoint slides (ISBN 0-534-52611-X).

Wadsworth Psychology Resource Center Web Site: A sophisticated student Web site complete with student activities, Internet resources (including links to *InfoTrac College Edition*), practice quizzing and discussion forums offering students yet another option for greater exploration beyond the classroom. Also, a complete website for instructors offering these same options plus additional features such as Hot Topics, Research and Teaching Showcase, Teaching Tips, and classroom activities are provided through the password-protected Faculty Lounge.

InfoTrac College Edition, **an Online Library on Your Home or Office Computer:** A free four-month subscription to this extensive online library is enclosed with every copy of the book. This allows instructors and students easy access from home or office computer to the latest news and research articles online. This is updated daily and spans four years. This database features thousands of full-length articles (not abstracts) from hundreds of academic journals as well as popular sources.

CNN Today: Child and Adolescent Development: Videos featuring CNN news clips are provided with this text. Organized by topics covered in a typical child and adolescent development course, these videos are divided into short (2- to 5-minute) segments perfect for introducing key concepts or launching lectures. There are yearly updates in the form of a new video and recent news reports. *CNN Today: Child and Adolescent Development*, Vol. 1 (ISBN 0-534-36705-4); *CNN Today: Child and Adolescent Development*, Vol 2 (ISBN 0-534-36937-5).

Lifespan Video: This video includes 23 clips that range from 2–3 minutes and portray important developmental milestones and concepts across the lifespan (ISBN 0-534-36915-4).

Lifespan Human Development Video Series: Adopters can choose from a variety of continually updated film and video options including selections from *Films for the Humanities and Sciences*, the Annenberg CPB *Discovering Psychology* series, The Pennsylvania State University's *PCR: Films and Videos in the Behavioral Sciences and Services* and many others.

A Personal Note

"So why did you write this book?" asked my grandmother.

The truth is, it had to do with the chickens. It all started the day I left the chicken coop open and our senior hen, never very bright, led her entire brood into the swamp willows where an opportunistic coyote feasted grandly. My punishment was time alone in the cellar of the country schoolhouse where my father taught. In this dank basement, while the coyotes licked their chops, I discovered hundreds of old library books long forgotten. I wasn't old enough to read very well, but I loved the look and feel of these wonderful volumes—biographies, romances, myths, legends, dog stories, poems—even textbooks. Many were mildewed and musty, some with edges nibbled by mice, but that just added to their mystery.

As I write to you today, I know that my dream for *Of Children* is a dream that was born in that distant cellar. Part of that dream is that this might be a book that, even if you happened upon it years from now in a cold and gloomy cellar, its pages yellowed by age and fungus, it might still strike a spark in your mind. Or heart.

Thank You

Writing the many editions of *Of Children* strikes me as being a little like climbing mountains. Success requires the efforts of a staggering number of people. Sadly, there is space to name only a few. They include:

▲ A succession of editors of previous editions, whose influence on the author, as well as on the book, continues, and who have made climbing the mountains a joy: Dick Greenberg, Ken King, Suzanna Brabant, and Sabra Horne.

▲ Edith Beard Brady, Publisher, the editor for the current edition, for whose guidance toward new peaks I am deeply thankful.

▲ Sherry Symington, Senior Development Editor, and Lisa Weber, Senior Project Editor, whose patience, intelligence, and thoroughness made the climb so much easier.

▲ Brenda Koplin and Christianne Thillen, copy editors, who looked for—and often found—clutter that they could take away to pretty the landscape.

▲ Leslie Krongold, Technology Project Manager, who led us with her technical expertise.

▲ Annie Berterretche, Assistant Editor, and George Semb, study guide and testbank author, who masterminded our support systems.

▲ Gary Hespenheide and Patti Zeman at Hespenheide Design who always made sure that everything would be in place for the ascent.

▲ Mr. Nhi Chu of Toolworks Specialized Deaf Services Program in San Francisco, California, who rendered the perfect cover image.

▲ Marc Linsenman, Marketing Manager, who ensured that our communication from the field was accurate and compelling.

▲ A legion of Wadsworth reps, past and present, who let the world know what we were doing.

▲ My maternal grandmother with whom I lived in early adolescence, who taught me how to stew a rabbit, which helps one survive on the mountain.

▲ The several hundred reviewers who have helped me continue to refine and improve this text through the years. I am especially grateful for the recent help of the following reviewers for the ninth edition: Dana Albright, Clovis Community College (New Mexico); Ted Barker, Okaloosa-Walton Community College; Glen Bradley, Pensacola Junior College; Elizabeth Rellinger, Illinois College; Harriette Richard, North Georgia College and State University; Elisabeth Shaw, Texarkana College; Colleen Stevenson, Muskingum College; and Doug Strauss, State Fair Community College.

My hope that you will enjoy this book and learn from it remains unchanged, as does my conviction that each is necessary for the other. And I would love to hear your suggestions and reactions: guy.lefrancois@ualberta.ca.

Yours,

Guy R. Lefrancois

Edmonton, Alberta

PART ONE

Grown-ups love figures.
Antoine de Saint-Exupéry, *The Little Prince*

The Beginning

Camille Tokerud/Tony Stone Images

When you tell them [grown-ups] that you have made a new friend," the little prince quoted on the opposite page continues, "they never ask you any questions about essential matters. They never say, 'What does his voice sound like? What games does he love best? Does he collect butterflies?' Instead, they demand: 'How old is he? How many brothers has he? How much money does his father make?' Only from these figures do they think they have learned anything about him."

Science, too, asks "grown-up" questions that are impersonal and objective. It asks, "How do average 4-year-olds think?" "How can they be made to understand reality?" "In what ways must they change to be more like adults?" It seldom asks questions such as "What does Marilyn feel about rainbows?" "What does Cindy know of spiders and sugar and silver strings?" "Why does Robert sometimes cry in the middle of the night?"

As is made clear in the four chapters that make up Part I, the grown-up science that studies children deals mainly with the composite, *average* child. But in this text, we pause often to remind ourselves that there is no average child—that the concept is simply an invention made necessary by our need to make sense of children. And although we ask many questions that require figures as answers, we do stop occasionally to notice that Marilyn sings when she sees rainbows, and that Cindy has dreamt the magic that binds spiders and sugar and silver strings. And we ask, too, what it is that makes Robert cry.

"Will you walk into my parlour?"
    said the spider to the fly.

Mary Howitt, *The Spider and the Fly*

Little Miss Muffet sat on a tuffet
Eating some curds and whey,
Along came a spider and sat
    down beside her
And frightened Miss Muffet away.

Anonymous: Nursery Rhymes, "Little Miss Muffett"

Studying the Child

CHAPTER 1

Myrleen Ferguson Cate/PhotoEdit

During circle time in Marie's kindergarten class, when it was Jason's turn to share, he brought out something the children had never seen before: a live black widow spider. His uncle had given him this prize. "Where my uncle's house is," he informed the class, adjusting his glasses, "there's things that can kill you, like snakes and black widows."

Jason is a solemn little guy, deadly serious about most things. When he wears his glasses, he looks like a small professor.

It was a large female black widow spider in a glass jar; the entire class crowded in for a closer look. "Just the lady ones can kill you," Jason explained. "See the red thing on her belly? That means she can kill you if she wants. My uncle got bit by one and he nearly died."

"Is there anything else you want to say about your spider before we put her away?" the teacher asked. "Oh yes," Jason announced solemnly. "My uncle keeps my aunt under his bed."

There were gasps of amazement; nobody laughed.

"I'm sure he was just joking, Jason," said Marie. "Nobody keeps his wife under the bed."

"My uncle does," said Jason, gravely. "I heard her talking under the mattress."

Later that week at the parent-teacher meeting, Marie checked with Jason's mother about the story. Apparently, Jason's uncle wanted to discourage the children from playing under the bed so he pretended he was hiding their aunt there. When the children tried to peek under the bed, he projected his voice and, in a high-pitched tone, said, "If you come any closer, little ones, I'll eat you!"

FOCUS QUESTIONS

1. What is this book about?

2. How have ideas about childhood changed?

3. What are the rights of children? The responsibilities of parents and societies?

4. What are the most basic current beliefs about children and their development?

5. How do we study children?

6. How reliable are our conclusions?

ORGANIZATION OF *OF CHILDREN*

You and I are grown up; we're not scared of things under the bed, are we? Unlike little children, we know that there's nothing there. We can look all we want and nothing will eat us. You can't fool us just by projecting your voice. We recognize lies and we know that magic isn't real.

Little children don't know these things. Part of growing up is learning what to expect, becoming familiar with what's out there, and sorting fact from fancy, reality from wishes.

Describing differences among infants, children, adolescents, and adults, and explaining how these differences come about, is mostly what this text is about.

Of Children is divided into six parts (see Table 1.1). Part I is an introduction consisting of four chapters. Chapter 1 explains what developmental psychology is and how psychologists study children; Chapter 2 introduces some of the most important theories used to explain developmental change; Chapter 3 deals with our genetic origins; and Chapter 4 looks at systematic changes that occur from conception through birth and at important influences on the unborn child. Parts II through V look at physical, intellectual (cognitive), and social and emotional changes and processes during each of the major pre-adult periods: **infancy**[1] (birth to age 2); early childhood (2 to 6 or 7); middle childhood (6 or 7 to 11 or 12); and adolescence (11 or 12 to 19 or 20). Part VI is an ending.

---

infancy A period of development that begins a few weeks after birth and lasts until approximately 2 years of age.

---

[1] Boldfaced terms are defined in the glossary at the end of the book and on the page where they first appear.

TABLE 1.1
Organization of *Of Children*

PART	AGES	CHAPTER
I The Beginning	—	1 Studying the Child
		2 Theories of Development
		3 Conception, Heredity, and Environment
		4 Prenatal Development and Birth
II Infancy	Birth to 2 years	5 Physical and Cognitive Development in Infancy
		6 Social and Emotional Development in Infancy
III Early Childhood	2 to 6 or 7	7 Physical and Cognitive Development in Early Childhood
		8 Social and Emotional Development in Early Childhood
IV Middle Childhood	6 or 7 to 11 or 12	9 Physical and Cognitive Development in Middle Childhood
		10 Social and Emotional Development in Middle Childhood
V Adolescence	11 or 12 to 19 or 20	11 Physical and Cognitive Development in Adolescence
		12 Social and Emotional Development in Adolescence
		The End

⌐ HISTORICAL AND CURRENT VIEWS OF CHILDHOOD

Strange as it may seem, the concepts that define "childhood" are not universal in all social groups. Of course, as James and Prout (1997)[2] point out, the biological immaturity of infants is universal. Also, patterns of biological maturation—such as learning to walk or sexual maturation during adolescence—are highly similar in all social groups.

But the experience of being a child can vary dramatically across social contexts, as highlighted throughout this text. For example, in *Across Cultures:* "Mari, A Mayan Child; Liam, A North American Kid," we see how Mari's life is unlike the lives of most children in the industrialized world. Much of the reason for this difference, explains Gaskins (1999), is that this Mayan society has different views of childhood than are typical in many industrialized nations. Among other things, these Mayans believe that adult work activities are so important that all childhood activities must be structured around them. They believe, too, that the development of children into adults is something that is preprogrammed and simply happens naturally with no need for parental involvement. As a result, play is given little importance in the Mayan world, and is in fact often discouraged. Similarly, parents spend little time speaking with their children other than to admonish them or give them directions. This is in sharp contrast with the predominant North American view that emphasizes and caters to the child's wishes and interests, and that stresses the importance of play as well as the importance of verbal and social interaction. Nor, as we see shortly, does this Mayan view reflect the current North American preoccupation with the rights of children.

It is partly because the experience of childhood is not universal that our views of childhood, and the theories that we use to explain human growth and development, are often valid only for children of our own social groups—or perhaps from highly similar social groups.

---

[2] References in this text are cited in the style recommended by the American Psychological Association (APA). Thus, authors' names are followed by the year of publication. The alphabetical list of references at the end of the book gives all the information necessary for locating each source.

Snapshots of Childhood

Not surprisingly, much of this text reflects North America's contemporary attitudes toward childhood—attitudes that are warm, positive, sympathetic, concerned. Many of the beliefs implicit (or sometimes explicit) in these pages express what Greene (1999) describes as the "currently fashionable Vygotskian emphasis on socially supported learning" (p. 262).[3] That she shares this implicit belief is partly why Liam's mother so willingly abandons her chores to read to him, to play with him, to let him determine when she will speak on the phone and when she will take him to the beach and to the zoo and perhaps even to Disneyland or the moon—or maybe just into the backyard.

It has not always been so. In fact, even today it isn't always and everywhere entirely so, as the following historical snapshots of children show.

We should note at the outset that historical snapshots are not always accurate. For one thing, there are few records of what life might have been like before the "print cultures"—those societies that regularly produce written artifacts. When Ariès (1962) attempted to uncover what the lives of medieval European children were like, he was forced to put together fragments gathered from many sources: historical paintings, school and university regulations, and Doctor Heroard's description of the upbringing of the French king Louis XIII. Relying on records such as this, claims Pollock (1983), results in a biased view of what childhood was really like for medieval children.

Snapshot 1: Antiquity Our view of childhood during antiquity is even less reliable than that relating to medieval times. Nevertheless, some writers have concluded that prior to the Middle Ages, and perhaps even prior to the eighteenth century, children were not really considered human beings. In antiquity, we are told, **infanticide** was not altogether uncommon (deMause, 1975; Ajuriaguerra, 1988).

---

infanticide The killing of an infant.

[3] Vygotsky was a Russian psychologist. His theories are discussed in Chapter 2.

Mari, a Mayan Child; Liam, a North American Kid

Mari is 18 months old. During a typical morning of a typical day, explains Gaskins (1999), Mari spends all her time in or close to the small compound where her family lives. Her parents are both busy, as are all her older siblings. No one plays with her; no one even speaks with her except to tell her not to do things—like going into the mud or dropping a rock into her sister's washtub. To stop her from interfering with important household chores, she is told to feed the chickens. She takes a gourd filled with dried corn and scatters it near the house. For a while she watches as the chickens eat. Later her mother tells her and her 3- and 5-year-old siblings to go and feed themselves. They spend most of the next hour picking, cleaning, and slowly eating the fruit that grows in and around the compound. "From the beginning to the end of this scene," writes Gaskins (1999), "Mari has said nothing to anyone" (p. 32).

Liam is also 18 months old. During his typical morning, his father is away at work, but his mother is at home. She too, like Mari's mother, has important household chores to perform. While she works, Liam plays with his toy car, driving it around the kitchen floor. When he bangs into his toy box, a book falls out. He picks it up and toddles over to his mother.

"Read it," he says, and his mother cheerfully puts her work aside and sits to read the book to Liam. But she doesn't just read: She asks questions; she explains and elaborates; she fills her reading with startling visions of magic. "What's this?" "What's that?" "Is that a blue fish or a red fish?" "What would you do if you had a truck like that?" "Let's pretend you're the tiger."

While they're reading, Liam's father phones. "I wanna talk," Liam says. His mother hands him the phone. When Liam tires of his dad, his mother takes the phone again, but Liam will not wait. "Read," he says. "I have to go," Liam's mother explains on the phone, "Liam wants me to read to him." Smiling, she returns to the book.

To Think About: Young Mayan children, says Gaskins (1999), spend very little time in imaginative or "pretend" play. Most of their play time involves large-motor activities such as climbing trees, chasing each other, or chasing bugs. In contrast, as we see in Chapter 8, North American children spend a great deal of time in various forms of pretend play.

What sorts of beliefs do you think these cultural differences reflect? How important are cultural beliefs about childhood?

Snapshot 2: The concept of childhood in medieval Europe By the Middle Ages there had been some improvements in the treatment of children. But McFarland (1998) notes that these improvements required centuries, and in retrospect were sometimes not all that significant. In contrast, improvements in how the world currently treats its children can now be measured in decades rather than in centuries.

That improvements in the treatment of children were not all that dramatic is implicit in Ariès's dramatic account of medieval childhood. For example, he describes a mother who has just given birth to her fifth child and who is very depressed at the thought of having one more mouth to feed, one more body to clothe. A neighbor consoles her: "Before they are old enough to bother you," she says, "you will have lost half of them, or perhaps all of them" (p. 38).

What is most evident in this little vignette is the callous attitude that both the mother and her friend seem to have toward children; their deaths are preferable to the burden of caring for them. Many of Ariès's readers were quick to infer that the medieval mother must have cared less for her children than does today's mother. If you are not strongly attached to your children, there is little need to worry that they might suffer or die.

But that isn't at all what Ariès meant to illustrate. "In medieval society," he informs us, "the idea of childhood did not exist." But he immediately adds: "This is not to suggest that children were neglected, forsaken or despised. The idea of childhood is not to be confused with affection for children" (1962, p. 128).

That the *idea* of childhood was still largely undeveloped is evident in the many ways in which children appeared to be viewed as nothing more than

THOUGHT CHALLENGE: *The main point of Ariès's account of the lives of medieval children is that childhood is a concept that is invented and elaborated by societies. What sort of evidence is there in the painting to the right that the concept of childhood had not yet been invented?*

Please see Possible Responses to Thought Challenges *at the end of this chapter.*

What we know of how children were regarded and treated in the past is often based on highly unreliable records, such as mothers' diaries, school regulations, the laws and judgments of the courts—even paintings such as this, in which the dress, the activities, and the facial expressions of children often seem more adultlike than childlike.

miniature adults. Thus they were seldom given toys designed especially for them. And they were quickly sent to work or given adult-like responsibilities whenever necessary. Perhaps, suggests Ariès, parents and society didn't see them as innocent and helpless creatures in need of nurturing and guidance.

Snapshot 3: Childhood in eighteenth-century Europe

Historical accounts of the lives of eighteenth-century European children are often shocking descriptions of abuse and cruelty—perhaps because, like today, the most flagrant and horrible abuses are the most sensational and the most likely to have been recorded. In 1761, for example, the British courts sentenced one Anne Martin to two years in Newgate prison. Her crime? She habitually poked out the eyes of the children she took begging with her; it increased their incomes—and hers.

Aha, you say, the courts did offer some protection to children! True, but it was skimpy protection indeed. As Pinchbeck and Hewitt (1973) point out, Anne Martin's case was unusual in that the children whose eyes she removed weren't her own. Had they been her own children, it's likely that no one would have paid any attention because parents could generally treat their own children any way they wanted.

But that wasn't always true, says Hanawalt (1993). She reports the case of a group of neighbors who came to the rescue of a boy who was a stranger to them, but who was being beaten by a clerk and a cook. Because the cook and the clerk continued to insist that they had a right to beat the boy, the neighbors beat them up. And the cook and clerk went to court, suing the neighbors who had deprived them of their rights. But the judge felt the two men deserved the beating, and they lost their case.

Nevertheless, British courts weren't above severely punishing children for infractions of laws. Siegel and White (1982) report the case of a 7-year-old girl who stole a petticoat—which doesn't seem like that terrible a crime. Still, she was brought to trial, convicted, sentenced—and hanged!

Eighteenth-century European attitudes toward children were reflected not only in the ways children were treated by the courts, but also in the ways many were treated by their parents. Kessen (1965) reports that in the crowded and disease-riddled slums of eighteenth-century European cities, thousands of parents abandoned unwanted children in the streets or on the doorsteps of churches and orphanages. Foundling homes sprang up all over Europe in an attempt to care for these children, but the majority died in infancy (before the age of 2 years). Kessen (1965) reports that of 10,272 infants admitted to one foundling home in Dublin in the last quarter of the eighteenth century, only 45 survived. (Indeed, before 1700, even if a child were not abandoned, its chances of surviving till the age of

5 were less than one in two; most died of diseases, including the plague.)

The high mortality rate of abandoned children was not restricted to eighteenth-century Europe. It was characteristic of the other side of the Atlantic as well, even into the nineteenth century. With few exceptions, children in infant homes (asylums) in the United States before 1915 died before the age of 2 (Bakwin, 1949).

Snapshot 4: Child labor in the nineteenth century

The nineteenth century brought some improvement in the status of children in Europe, and abandonments decreased drastically. Sad to say, this appears to have been at least partly because of children's increasing economic value as workers. In thousands of factories and mines, both in Europe and in the United States, children as young as 5 or 6 years, male and female, worked 10 hours a day or more at grueling labor in conditions so hazardous that many became ill and died (Kessen, 1965).

In Britain, for example, children were employed extensively in the coal mines. They were especially valuable workers because most of the mines were underground and had to be worked by means of tunnels that were often too small for grown men. Many of these tunnels were barely more than 2 feet across, were very poorly ventilated, and often had 3 or 4 inches of water in them as well. Children had to crawl through the tunnels, dragging baskets loaded with coal behind them by means of a "girdle and chain." The seventh earl of Shaftesbury (his name was Anthony Ashley Cooper) described the blisters and wounds resulting from this device, the illnesses children suffered in the mines, the physical and mental abuse, and the beatings. He begged the British House of Commons to pass a bill that would establish the minimum age for employment of males in the coal mines at 13 and that would completely prohibit the employment of females underground. Following considerable debate and in spite of strong opposition, a bill prohibiting females from working underground was passed. However, many members were convinced that children whose fathers were miners were more likely to profit from an education in the mines than from a "reading" education; as long as they had reached the age of 10, boys could continue to be employed in the mines.

Conditions in North America were, in some instances, not very different from those that prevailed in parts of Europe. Clement (1997) reports that in cities and industrialized areas, large numbers of children were employed in factories and cotton mills. In rural farm families, female children were expected to sew and cook and clean even when they were only 4 or 5. And male children were expected to work around the barn and in the fields as soon as they were physically able.

Snapshot 5: The developing world today

The twentieth century, too, still has its share of ignorance, of cruelty, of needless pain and suffering. Seventy of the world's developing nations have **under-5 mortality rates (U5MR)** greater than 70 per 1,000 children born alive—a rate many times higher than is common in developed countries (Bellamy, 1999a). In Afghanistan, for example, about 257 infants of every 1,000 born alive subsequently die before age 5, a rate 32 times higher than that of the United States or Canada. (See *At a Glance:* "Survival of the World's Infants.")

The United Nations reports that as recently as 1990, some 4,500 infants died each day from measles, tetanus, and whooping cough, and another 7,000 from diarrheal dehydration (Grant, 1992). Pneumonia added significantly to this total, and starvation more than doubled it. As a result, even in 1990 more than 30,000 children died each day from preventable causes. That was about 10 million preventable child deaths a year, almost 2 million of them from vaccine-preventable diseases.

Have conditions for the world's children improved very much in the past decade? In some ways, yes. Henderson (1999a) reports that following massive worldwide efforts, coverage rates for immunization have increased from 5% in 1980 to more than 80% currently. As a result, deaths from the six major diseases for which children are immunized (measles, tetanus, whooping cough, tuberculosis, polio and diphtheria) have been reduced by 3 million a year. Yet each year more than 12 million children

---

under-5 mortality rate (U5MR) Death rate for children under 5 who are born alive. U5MR is used by the United Nations as an indicator of how well nations treat their children.

Survival of the World's Children

In many parts of the world, infant mortality—defined as deaths before the age of 1 year—exceeds 100 for every 1,000 live births (it's at 191 in Niger and 170 in Angola [Bellamy, 1999a]). Preventable or treatable conditions such as diarrheal dehydration and pneumonia account for the vast majority of those who die. In Canada and the United States, infant mortality is less than 8 per 1,000 live births— although it was as high as about 100 per 1,000 at the turn of the century (Figure 1.1). Infant mortality rates in the United States are more than twice as high for blacks (17.7 per 1,000) as for whites (8.2 per 1,000) (U.S. Bureau of the Census, 1998; *Canada Yearbook, 1999*).

Shocking disparities among the world's nations are evident in:

- Under-5 mortality rates as high as 320 out of every 1,000 live births in Niger—and rates as low as 4 per 1,000 in Sweden, Singapore, Norway, and Finland (Bellamy, 1999a. See Figure 1.2)
- Maternal death rates ranging from 0 to 1,800 per 100,000 live births (Way, 1998)
- Primary school enrollment ranging from a low of 24 to a high of 100% of children (Way, 1998)

FIGURE 1.1 (right) Changes in infant mortality rates (under age 1, per 1,000 live births) in the United States, 1915–1995. Sources: Based on U.S. Bureau of the Census (1991), p. 77, and (1998), p. 98.

FIGURE 1.2 (below) Under-5 mortality rates for selected countries. Number of deaths per 1,000 live births, for children under age 5. Source: Based on Bellamy, 1999a, pp. 94–97.

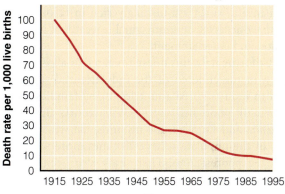

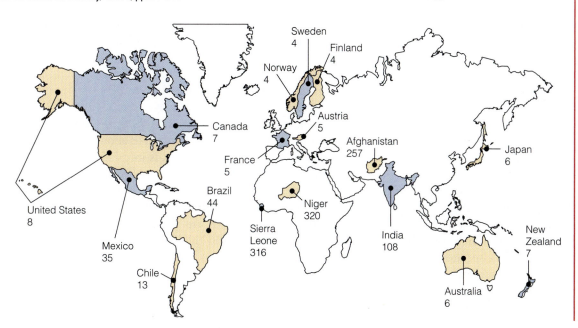

under age 5 die (Bellamy, 1999a). That is partly because there are still more than 26 million children who are not vaccinated each year (Henderson, 1999). This means that 1 out of every 5 of the children currently being born each year is not being immunized against the major vaccine-preventable diseases.

Children being born today, explains Bellamy (1999b), have only about 1 chance in 10 of being born in a relatively affluent home, but they have a 30% chance of being born in extreme poverty and a 40% chance of finding themselves only slightly better off. A shocking 50% of the world's poor are children! (See *In the News and on the Web:* "Gypsies of Svinia.")

Snapshot 6: The industrialized world today The vast majority of the 1 in 10 children who are born into relative affluence are born to parents living in the world's industrialized countries. These children are born into a world astonishingly rich in resources; they have access to an unimaginable wealth of information and entertainment.

Unfortunately, this doesn't mean that all is perfect with the children of the industrialized world. Even in industrialized countries, many families are shockingly poor. Bellamy (1999b) reports that in Australia and England, for instance, the wealthiest 20% of the population have 10 times more wealth than the poorest 20%. There have also been dramatic social changes in recent decades. For example, the percentage of never-married 20- to 24-year-old women increased from 30 in 1960 to more than 70 in 1997 (U.S. Bureau of the Census, 1998). Divorce rates have also increased enormously in recent decades, so that close to half of all children spend an average of six years in a one-parent family. In both Canada and the United States, in about 85% of these families, the mother is the single parent (U.S. Bureau of the Census, 1998; *Canada Yearbook, 1999*). In addition, demographic (population) changes have resulted in smaller families, reduced birthrates, more childless couples, and greater proportions of young adults (resulting from previous increases in birthrates) and elderly people (resulting from medical advances). Another important change, the effects of which are discussed in detail in Chapter 10, is associated with the role of television in people's lives, especially children's.

Some observers argue that the net effect of these changes is that in recent decades families are less child-centered than had been anticipated. In fact, says Bullock (1993), childhood may be a terribly lonely and often frightening experience for many. "Divorce rates are increasing," writes Bellamy, "overwork blights family life, human contact shrinks and the young, increasingly alienated, are treated more as consumers than as children" (1999b, p. 2).

Among other things, childhood in our industrialized times brings with it a high probability of being looked after by a series of strangers, most likely outside the child's home. It includes, as well, the probability of losing a father or a mother during much of the time of growing up—or at least of losing some of their interest and attention, and perhaps some of their affection as well. Childhood now brings the possibility of major adjustments if one or the other of the parents remarries, particularly if stepsiblings are brought into the family. There was a time, not long ago, when the things that most children feared were highly predictable: pain, death, spinach, supernatural beings, and things that go bump in the night. Recent decades have added some new fears: concerns over whether parents will divorce, fears related to being left alone, fears associated with the likelihood of having to make new adjustments, and, too often, fears associated with wars.

But all this paints too bleak a picture. The challenges and the changes of recent decades don't overwhelm all children and are not always a source of loneliness or despair. For many children, these are challenges and changes that result in strength rather than in weakness, in a sense of community rather than alienation, in joy rather than sadness.

Why Look at History?

These historical snapshots are important not so much for what they tell us about the lives of children (although that, too, is interesting and important in its own right), but more because they emphasize the extent to which we are products of our particular social, cultural, and historical realities. In today's jargon, we are products of our **contexts**. So, to understand the lives of children, we need to know

context That which surrounds and influences. In psychology, the term is used to include the totality of environmental and circumstantial influences on development and behavior.

IN THE NEWS AND ON THE WEB

Gypsies of Svinia

"White" Svinia is a typical, picturesque Serbian village of several hundred inhabitants, one store, and one school.

On the outskirts of white Svinia, perhaps 300 meters beyond the last house, is "black" Svinia—a miserable mass of mud-and-stick huts huddled against squalid, half-completed apartment buildings. Here live the Gypsies of Svinia, called "people of the Roma." They live in conditions worse than many in the Third World, without bathrooms, their only drinking water from a polluted pool, and with little hope of education or employment. When they send their children to the school in Svinia— which they must if they are to receive the monthly relief money that the government grants them—most are immediately classified as mentally retarded. This is apparently because the children speak Romani, the Gypsy language, and know little Slovak. When they enter school, they are given intelligence tests in Slovak. Six years later, laments one mother, they leave school still in first grade, still not knowing how to read or write.

But perhaps even more chilling than the misery they live in is the racism Gypsies are subjected to. In Svinia, they are referred to as "blacks" by the "white" Slovaks, some of whom speak openly of the need to exterminate them. In some parts of Europe, they are forced to live in garbage dumps, in huts made of trash and tin. Throughout most of Europe, they make up a far larger percentage of the prison population than would be expected based on their numbers.

B. Pilon, "Invisible victims: Relief agencies have ignored the plight of Serbia's Gypsies." *Edmonton Sun,* 26 December 1999, p. 72.

The Gypsies of Svinia, film produced by the National Film Board, Ottawa, Canada, 1999.

To Think About: One of the antiracist websites indexed below points out that much of what we think about groups of people is determined by what we hear and see on the news media. For example, it's common for the European news media to report unsolved crimes as having been committed by people of "gypsylike" appearance. Where I live, too, it has been normal practice to specify the ethnic membership of those suspected or accused of criminal actions—unless they are part of the white majority.

Are there similar instances of racist reporting where you live? What difference do you think this might make?

Resources: For more information on racism against the Serbian Gypsies, see the following website, which is dedicated to fighting discrimination. It also offers support and advice, publishes a journal in Romani, and otherwise disseminates information on Roma history and culture:

http://www-gewi.kfunigraz.ac.at/romani/vereine/centro/

Here are two of the many websites devoted to antiracism:

http://members.aol.com/POARAR/indexa.html

http://www.ecri.coe.int/

For additional readings, explore *InfoTrac College Edition*, your online library. Go to http://www.infotrac-college.com/wadsworth and use the passcode on the card that came with your text. Try the following search terms: Gypsies, Romani, and racial prejudice.

something of their contexts—that is, something of their families, their schools, the economic and political realities of their times, their place in history and in culture. Each of us is the product of an absolutely unique assortment of genetic material (unless we have an identical twin), but we are also products of experiences that are influenced more than a little by the social-cultural contexts of our lives.

CONCEPT
SUMMARY

Historical and Current Views of Childhood

Historical Period	Some Probable Characteristics of Views of Childhood
Antiquity	Selective infanticide; immature infants perhaps viewed as something less than fully human.
Medieval Europe	High infant and child mortality; no clear view of childhood as a vulnerable period, or of children as needing nurturance and guidance.
Eighteenth-century Europe	Poverty and perhaps emotional indifference lead to widespread abandonment of infants; continuing high infant mortality rates.
Nineteenth-century Europe and North America	Industrialization contributes to widespread use of children as manual laborers in factories, mines, fields, shops, and so on; ambivalent attitude toward children.
The developing world today	Relatively high under-5 mortality rates, often due to preventable causes; increasing recognition of children's rights; increasing use of immunization prevents many needless deaths.
The industrialized world today	Accelerating social and technological changes present new risks and challenges; preoccupation with the rights, the needs, and the desires of children.

Note: Although these trends and attitudes are descriptive of some cultures and of some families during the periods in question, they sometimes were not very widespread. Clearly, not all children risked infanticide during antiquity. And even at the height of child labor exploitation in the eighteenth century, there were many well-cared-for children who played and went to school and had carefree childhoods in loving homes.

Ponder, for example, how different your life might have been had you been born in medieval times. (See *Concept Summary*.)

CHILDREN'S RIGHTS

Had you been born in medieval times, there is a chance that you might have been used as the plaything in one of the sports used by the gentry to amuse itself: baby tossing. Basically, baby tossing involved throwing infants from one gamesman to another (basketball and football had yet to be invented). One of the unlucky babies was King Henry IV's infant brother, who was killed when he fell while being tossed from window to window (deMause, 1974).

Throughout history, children have died not only in sport but from other causes, too. Had you lived in Massachusetts in 1646, you would not have had to put up with unruly offspring. Say you had a son who wouldn't listen to you, who was making your life miserable. You could drag him before a magistrate, establish that here was a defiant and rebellious kid, and, as long as he was 16 or more, they'd put him to death for you! That was the law (Westman, 1991b).

By the twentieth century, the courts would no longer hang or shoot problem children; the once-absolute control that parents and various agencies had over the lives of children had been weakened considerably. Yet it was still possible for parents and teachers to get rid of the worst troublemakers. One way of doing this was to "voluntarily" commit them to mental institutions—voluntarily, because parents and guardians simply "volunteered" them (Farleger, 1977). Until recently, such children had no legal recourse, no matter how badly they felt they had been treated. Now, however, the courts have determined that children cannot be brought in for "treatment" without their "informed consent" (Halasz, 1996).

Evidence of increasing concern about the rights of children is apparent not only in court decisions but also in two other important events: (1) the adoption of ethical principles to guide research concerning children; and (2) the formulation and widespread international acceptance of a code of children's rights.

Research with Children

In 1973, the Society for Research in Child Development published its *Ethical standards for research with children* (1973). These principles recognize that research is unethical when a child is coerced into participating, when a child is exposed to stress or other potentially damaging conditions, when a child's privacy is invaded, and so on. The principles specify that permission of parents and children alike must be obtained before conducting child research. Furthermore, consent must be "informed" in the sense that children and their parents are fully aware of any aspect of the research that might affect their willingness to participate.

United Nations Convention: Children's Rights

A United Nations convention held in 1989 on the rights of the child culminated in the formulation of an extensive charter of children's rights. In September 1990, summit meetings on children's rights led to the signing by 105 nations of this Charter of Children's Rights (Balke, 1992). By 1996, almost all countries had signed the charter into law. As Bellamy put it, "A century that began with children having virtually no rights is ending with children having the most powerful legal instrument that not only recognizes but protects their human rights" (1996b, p. 1).

The Charter of Children's Rights The international Charter of Children's Rights is based on four general principles:

▲ The rights are to apply to all of the world's children equally, without discrimination or distinctions of any kind.

> **THOUGHT CHALLENGE:** *Despite the wide-scale acceptance of the Charter of Children's Rights, perhaps as many as 30,000 children die each day—mainly of vaccine-preventable diseases, starvation, diarrheal dehydration, and wars (Grant, 1992; Bellamy, 1999b). What should be done about this situation? What can be done?*
>
> *Please see* Possible Responses to Thought Challenges *at the end of this chapter.*

▲ In all actions that involve children, their best interests shall be the most important consideration.

▲ All of the world's states shall do their utmost to ensure child survival and optimal development.

▲ Children have the right to be heard.

These four principles are reflected in the specific rights discussed in the charter (see Table 1.2).

Rights of Protection versus Rights of Choice As de Winter, Baerveldt, and Kooistra (1999) point out, the rights of children are geared toward providing optimal, growth-fostering conditions for them. That is, not only must children be protected from the dangers to which their immaturity exposes them, but their access to a stimulating social environment must also be safeguarded. Note that these are essentially rights of protection rather than rights of choice. According to Saidla (1992), giving children choices as though they were mini-adults is a misuse of the concept of children's rights. In many instances, children lack the maturity and the knowledge required for making the best choices in their own lives. Elizabeth, my 5-year-old granddaughter, has the right to adequate nutrition, medical care, and education. But, understandably, she does not have the right to make all her own nutritional, educational, and medical choices. Many of those choices are her parents' responsibility. And even if her parents are unable to convince her that she should eat her spinach because it's good for her, they can at least ensure that she doesn't eat only candy bars.

This does not mean, of course, that children have no responsibilities. As Caldwell (1989) points

TABLE 1.2
The Charter of Children's Rights

A universally accepted proclamation of the United Nations asserts that, among other things, every child (meaning all individuals below age 18) has specific birthrights.

CATEGORY OF RIGHTS	SPECIFIC EXAMPLES OF RIGHTS
Civil rights and freedoms including the right to	• A name and a nationality from birth • Freedom of thought, conscience, and religion • Protection of privacy • Protection from torture or other degrading treatment or punishment • Protection from capital punishment and life imprisonment
A family environment	• In which parents have a primary, but state-assisted, responsibility for the child's care and upbringing • From which the child cannot be taken unless it is clearly in their best interests • Whose responsibilities will be assumed by the state should the child be deprived of a family
Safeguarding of health and welfare including	• The right to life • The right to the highest attainable standard of health • The provision of special care for those with special needs • The right to an adequate standard of living
Education, leisure, and recreation rights reflected in	• Free and compulsory education for all children • School discipline that respects the child's dignity • School programs geared toward social and physical as well as mental development
Special protection measures including	• The assurance that no child under 15 shall take direct part in war or be recruited into armed forces • Special treatment by courts of law, taking into consideration the child's age and directed mainly toward rehabilitation rather than punishment • Freedom from fear of exploitation

out, society expects its children to assimilate dominant cultural values and eventually to foster the continuation of the culture. In addition, society expects its children to take advantage of their rights and the opportunities provided for them—that they will mature and learn. (See Figure 1.3 for a summary of the relationships among the rights and responsibilities of parents, society, and children; Figures 1.4 and 1.5 for a look at child poverty; and *Across Cultures:* "Children and War" for examples of horrendous violations of children's rights.)

⌐ THE STUDY OF CHILDREN

Psychology is a general term for the science that studies human behavior and thought. **Developmental psychology** is the division of psychology

psychology The science that examines human behavior (and that of animals as well).

developmental psychology That aspect of psychology concerned with the development of individuals.

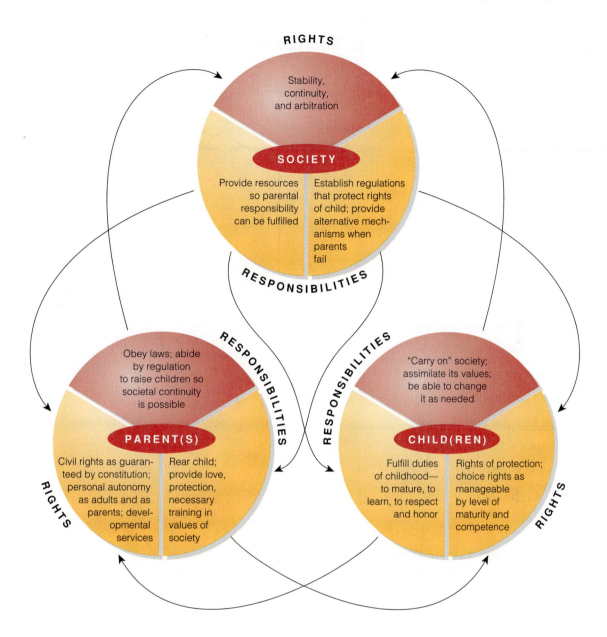

RIGHTS

Stability,
continuity,
and arbitration

SOCIETY

Provide resources
so parental
responsibility
can be fulfilled

Establish regulations
that protect rights
of child; provide
alternative mech-
anisms when
parents
fail

RESPONSIBILITIES

RESPONSIBILITIES

RESPONSIBILITIES

Obey laws; abide
by regulation
to raise children so
societal continuity
is possible

PARENT(S)

Civil rights as guaran-
teed by constitution;
personal autonomy
as adults and as
parents; devel-
opmental
services

Rear child;
provide love,
protection,
necessary
training in
values of
society

RIGHTS

"Carry on" society;
assimilate its values;
be able to change
it as needed

CHILD(REN)

Fulfill duties
of childhood—
to mature, to
learn, to respect
and honor

Rights of protection;
choice rights as
manageable
by level of
maturity and
competence

RIGHTS

concerned specifically with changes that occur over time and with the processes and influences that account for these changes. In other words, development refers to changes in behavior with the passage of time. The task of the developmental psychologist is twofold: to describe changes and to discover their underlying causes. A third, closely related task is to advance theories that organize and interpret observations and that are also useful for making predictions.

Three important concepts in the study of children are *growth*, *maturation*, and *learning*. To *develop* is to grow, to mature, and to learn.

FIGURE 1.3 Caldwell's triadic model of the rights and responsibilities of parents, children, and society in relation to each other. Source: B. M. Caldwell (1980). Balancing children's rights and parents' rights; in R. Haskins & J. J. Gallagher (eds.), *Care and education of young children in America: Policy, politics and social science.* Norwood, N.J.: Ablex, p. 37. Reprinted by permission of the publisher.

Growth ordinarily refers to physical changes. These are mainly quantitative changes because they involve addition rather than transformation.

growth Ordinarily, such physical changes as increasing height or weight.

| AT A GLANCE | **Poor Children in North America** |

Children's rights, proclaims the United Nations, should assure them of medical care, nutrition, education, and special care if required—and the right to a peaceful environment and to affection, love, and understanding. But even in the wealthiest and most child-centered of the world's nations, millions of children are poor. For example, although the proportion of U.S. citizens over age 65 living in poverty declined from 24.6% to 10.8% between 1970 and 1996, during that same period the proportion of U.S. children below the poverty level increased from 14.9% to 19.8%. About 13.8 million children in the United States live in poverty. In Canada, the situation is similar. In 1996, more than 1 child in 5 lived below the poverty level.

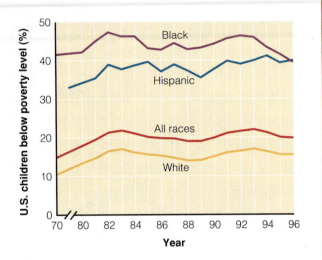

FIGURE 1.4 Children living in poverty in the United States. These figures include only children under 18 who live at home. *Source:* Adapted from U.S. Bureau of the Census (1998), p. 477.

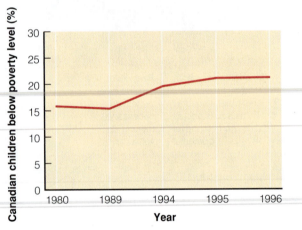

FIGURE 1.5 Children under 18 years living in poverty in Canada, 1980 to 1996. Source: Adapted from *Canada Yearbook 1999.* Ottawa, Ontario: Minister of Industry, Communications Division, Statistics Canada, 1998, p. 207.

Changes such as increasing height or enlargement of the nose are examples of growth.

Maturation describes changes that are more closely related to heredity than to a child's environment. Sexual unfolding during pubescence is an example of maturation. Although these changes follow a genetically programmed timetable, in almost all aspects of human development, maturation and learning interact. Learning to walk, for example, requires not only that the child's physical strength and muscular coordination be sufficiently mature but also that there be an opportunity to practice the different skills involved.

Learning involves relatively permanent changes that result from experience rather than simply from

maturation A developmental process defined by changes that are relatively independent of a child's environment. Although the nature and timing of maturational changes are assumed to result from genetic predispositions, their manifestation is at least partly a function of the environment.

learning Includes all changes in behavior that are due to experience. Does not include temporary changes brought about by drugs or fatigue or changes in behavior resulting simply from maturation or growth.

ACROSS CULTURES

Children and War

My good friend, Joseph Minimoto, died in 1987. He died largely as a result of World War II, although he was only a child when that war started and he lived in California, where none of the fighting took place. But when the Japanese bombed Pearl Harbor in 1941, President Franklin D. Roosevelt, caught up in the general hysteria that swept the United States, issued order number 9066. That order gave the U.S. military the right to exclude from certain areas and activities all U.S. citizens of Japanese ancestry; it also gave the right to detain them, without legal recourse, in what Roosevelt termed "relocation centers." Ten such camps were established in the United States, and some 120,000 people of Japanese ancestry—some no more than one-eighth Japanese—were imprisoned in these remote concentration camps surrounded by barbed wire. Joe and his family were sent to Heart Mountain Camp in Wyoming. It opened on August 12, 1942, and didn't close until November 10, 1945.

Joe remembered these as sad, frightened, hungry years. Both his Japanese grandparents as well as his father died in the camp. All three suffered from tuberculosis. His mother, a descendent of the Cheyenne Dog Soldier tribe of Wyoming, was heartbroken and never recovered. She died a few years after their release from the camp.

Joe survived another four decades. He spent his last years fighting the ravages of a long-undiagnosed case of tuberculosis. The doctors guessed he had contracted the disease in the camp.

One year after Joe died, the U.S. Government passed the Civil Liberties Act of 1988—popularly referred to as the Japanese-American Redress Bill. It provided for a written apology, signed by the president of the United States, to every person of Japanese ancestry who had been interned during the war. It also awarded monetary compensation of $20,000 per person.

Joe received neither.

Harland, D. (1989). *Children on the front line: The impact of apartheid, destabilization, and warfare on children in Southern and South Africa.* New York: United Nations Children's Fund. A UNICEF report on the impact of war on children.

Weglyn, M. (1976). *Years of infamy: The untold story of America's concentration camps.* New York: Morrow. An account of the American internment of people of Japanese ancestry during World War II.

To Think About: During the twentieth century, more than 60 million people have been killed in wars—of which approximately 30 are ongoing as of this writing. In medieval times, wars typically killed only soldiers. Even as recently as during World War I, 95% of those killed were armed, fighting personnel. But now, wars kill about four times more civilians than fighters, and most of those killed are women and children (Bellamy, 1996). During the last decade of the twentieth century, for example, more than 1.5 million children have been killed by wars. Furthermore, research indicates that even if they are not killed or physically wounded, many children who are exposed to war or interned in war camps subsequently manifest a variety of psychological symptoms including depression and behavioral problems (Paardekooper, de Jong, & Hermanns, 1999; Berman, 1999).

To Think About: The United Nations has decreed that children have a right to "a peaceful environment." What, if anything, should the world's nations do about wars that kill children? What *can* they do?

Resources:

http://www.cnn.com/US/9703/24/internedorphans/ A 1997 CNN news item describing a war camp established specifically for orphans of Japanese ancestry.

http://www.children-of-the-camps.org/ A history and a description of the impact on children of the wartime internment of citizens of Japanese ancestry.

http://www.warchild.org/ An account of the global impact of wars on children. A website maintained by an organization dedicated to alleviating the suffering of children in war zones.

maturation or growth—or from influences that have temporary effects such as drugs or fatigue.

Development itself includes all the processes and changes whereby individuals adapt to their environment. Because adaptation involves growing, maturing, and learning, all these processes are aspects of development. (See Table 1.3.) The main difference between learning and development is that learning is concerned with immediate, short-term adaptation, whereas development refers to gradual adaptation over a period of years. In addition, development includes the effects of growth and maturation; learning is limited to the effects of experience.

Accordingly, the subject of developmental psychology is the human from conception to death (although in this text we don't deal with the entire life span but stop instead at adolescence). Developmental psychology undertakes two important tasks: observing children and their progress in adapting to the world, and trying to explain that adaptation.

The study of children is a relatively recent enterprise, closely tied both to the social changes that occurred in seventeenth- and eighteenth-century attitudes toward children and to intellectual movements reflected in the writings of philosophers and early scientists. In addition, advances in biology and medicine and the increasing availability of elementary education contributed significantly to the development of child psychology.

---

development The total process whereby individuals adapt to their environment. Development includes growth, maturation, and learning.

Early Observers of Children

Closely associated with the beginnings of the study of children were people such as the British philosopher John Locke and the French philosopher Jean-Jacques Rousseau.

John Locke The child is basically a rational creature, Locke informed his late-seventeenth-century colleagues. The child is born with a mind that is a little like a blank slate (**doctrine of the tabula rasa**). At first there is nothing on it; but experience changes that, said Locke, because children quickly absorb the knowledge, information, and habits that are given to them. Furthermore, he said, children are highly responsive to rewards and punishments, and must be carefully and firmly disciplined. In Locke's (1699) words, "If you take away the Rod on one hand, and these little Encouragements which they are taken with, on the other, How then (will you say) shall Children be govern'd? Remove Hope and Fear, and there is an end of all Discipline."

Jean-Jacques Rousseau Rousseau's child, described in his book *Emile* (1762), is not at all like Locke's child. This is not a child who is a "blank slate," neither good nor bad until the rewards and punishments of experience exert their influence. Instead,

---

doctrine of the tabula rasa The belief, associated with John Locke and with behaviorists such as Watson, that children are born with no (or few) predetermined characteristics, tendencies, or habits. Developmental outcomes are thought to result primarily from the effects of experience.

TABLE 1.3
Some Important Definitions

Psychology	The science that studies human thought and behavior
Developmental psychology	Division of psychology concerned with changes that occur over time and with the processes and influences that account for these changes

Development involves:
  Growth
  Maturation
	Physical changes; primarily quantitative
	Naturally unfolding changes, relatively independent of the environment (for example, pubescence—the changes of adolescence that lead to sexual maturity)

Learning	Relatively permanent changes in behavior that result from experience (rather than from maturation, fatigue, or drugs)

Rousseau recognizes the "natural" goodness of the child and the corrupting influence of certain kinds of education (Hendrik, 1997). Rousseau insists that if children were allowed to develop in their own fashion, untainted by the corruption and evil in the world, they would undoubtedly be good when grown: "God makes all things good; man meddles with them and they become evil."

Although both Locke and Rousseau are closely associated with the beginning of the study of children, their ideas led to different conceptions of childhood. Locke's description of the child as a passive creature, molded by the rewards and punishments of experience, closely parallels the descriptions of development in learning theory, particularly as exemplified in the works of B. F. Skinner (described in Chapter 2). Rousseau's view of an active, exploring child developing through deliberate interaction with the environment finds an important place in the work of Jean Piaget (also described in Chapter 2).

Later Observers of Children

Although the science of child psychology owes much to early "child philosophers" such as Rousseau and Locke, its beginnings are usually attributed to the first systematic observations and written accounts of children, such as William Preyer's (1888–89) detailed observations of his own children and Charles Darwin's (1877) biography of his son (Cairns & Valsiner, 1984).

G. Stanley Hall Hard on the heels of these European pioneers followed the American, G. Stanley Hall (1891), who became the first president of the American Psychological Association. Hall was profoundly influenced by Charles Darwin's theory of evolution. "**Ontogeny** recapitulates **phylogeny**," Hall insisted, summarizing in one short phrase his conviction that the development of a single individual in a species parallels the evolution of the entire species (an idea now largely discredited). As evidence for this theory, Hall described the evolution of children's interests in games, noting how these games seem to correspond to the evolution of human occupations and lifestyles. Notice, said Hall, how a child is, in sequence, interested in games corresponding to each of the major, sequential human lifestyles: an arboreal existence (for example, climbing on chairs and tables); a cave-dwelling existence (crawling into small spaces, making tiny shelters with old blankets); a pastoral existence (playing with animals); an agricultural existence (tending flowers and plants); and finally an industrial existence (playing with vehicles).

One of Hall's most important contributions to the study of children was his pioneering use of **questionnaires**, lists of questions designed to uncover the thoughts, the emotions, and the behaviors of children. Often, too, he presented his questionnaires to adults to try to get them to remember what they had felt and thought as children. Always, he tabulated, summed, averaged, and compared the results of his questionnaires, a true pioneer of the application of scientific procedures and principles to the study of human development. Also, Hall wrote extensively for the lay public, and was highly regarded as one of the important "popularizers" of psychology (Fried, 1998).

John B. Watson Another American pioneer of child psychology was John B. Watson (1914), who introduced an experimental, learning-theory-based approach to the study of development. His influence, as well as that of Skinner, shaped a model that came to dominate child study through the early part of the twentieth century. This model looked for the causes of developmental change among the rewards and punishments of the environment and viewed the child as the passive recipient of these influences, much as had Locke.

The contributions of Watson and Skinner, along with other important contributors to the study of children such as Sigmund Freud, Erik Erikson, and Jean Piaget, are discussed in Chapter 2, which deals with theories of development.

---

ontogeny Systematic changes that occur in the lives of individuals. Changes that define life-span development.

phylogeny Changes that occur in a species over generations. Evolutionary changes.

---

questionnaires Sequences of carefully structured questions. Questionnaires are often used in social science research.

Why Study the Development of Children?

Economic and social changes have done much to change our attitudes toward children. Advances in medicine and hygiene have saved many children from early deaths and made it less traumatic for us to love them. Legislation has begun to grant them legal rights and protection from various forms of abuse. Children, for most people in our society, are no longer either an economic burden or a necessity. We, and they, have the advantage of a wealthier and perhaps kinder age. As a result, today's industrialized societies can aptly be described as child centered.

In this child-centered age, we study children for a variety of reasons, not least because we want to understand how we become what we are. Our hope is that with greater understanding, we will be better able to ensure the development of happy, productive, healthy individuals.

To simplify, our study of developmental processes is intended to provide us with information about (1) the sorts of behaviors we might expect from children at different ages, (2) the optimal experiences for children at different developmental levels, and (3) the nature of developmental problems and the best treatments for them. As a result, the study of children provides a wealth of information that is of tremendous practical importance for teachers, nurses, counselors, physicians, child welfare professionals, clergy, and parents. (See *Concept Summary*.)

⌐ RECURRING ISSUES AND BELIEFS

A number of important questions have served as recurring themes in developmental psychology. The issues that underlie these questions have guided much of its research and theorizing, and are reflected in the most important of developmental psychology's beliefs. The issue explored by Locke and Rousseau is one of these recurring questions.

▲ Is it best to view the child as an active, exploring organism, discovering or inventing meaning for the world, as Rousseau argued? Or is it more useful to emphasize, as did Locke, the effects of rewards and punishments on a more passive recipient?

Today, Rousseau's is the predominant view—of an active, exploring child deliberately attempting to create meaning out of the world (Greene, 1999). At the same time, most psychologists recognize the important influence of reward and punishment (Locke's view).

▲ What are the relative effects of genetics and of environments on the developmental process?

This question has been the source of one of the main controversies in psychology: the **nature-nurture controversy**. Extreme points of view on this issue maintain either that the environment is mainly responsible for whatever children become (nurture) or that genetic back-

---

CONCEPT SUMMARY   Pioneers in the Study of Children

Pioneers	Identifying Belief
Locke	*Tabula rasa:* Children are like empty vessels, passive recipients of the effects of experience.
Rousseau	*The natural child:* Children are active, inquiring, and basically good unless society corrupts them.
Hall	*Ontogeny recapitulates phylogeny:* The development of the individual mirrors the development of the human race.
Watson	*Give me a dozen healthy infants and I will make of them what I will:* Children are shaped by the rewards and punishments of their environments.

ground (nature) determines the outcome of the developmental process. The dominant position today is that, as Eisenberg (1998) puts it, nature and nurture aren't forces that act in opposition. That is, it isn't a question of one or the other having its way and determining the outcome of development. The important question, says Anastasi (1958), is not *which* of these two forces is most important, but rather *how* each is effective. Still, as we see in Chapter 3, the nature-nurture issue continues to be hotly debated.

▲ Is development a continuous, relatively uninterrupted process, or does it consist of separate stages?

As is true for most of the recurring questions in human development, there is no simple answer. **Stages** in developmental psychology are defined as separate, sequential, age-based steps in the development of abilities, understanding, or competencies. Many important developmental theories are stage theories (for example, those of Piaget or Freud). But, as we see in Chapter 2, it has been difficult to identify abilities or competencies that invariably appear at a predetermined age and develop in a fixed, predictable sequence. Many of our characteristics appear to be subject more to continuous development than to stages. We don't develop like caterpillars—cocoon to butterfly to egg to caterpillar to cocoon to butterfly, each stage undeniably different from the one that precedes or follows it. Nevertheless, stage theories are useful in organizing the facts of human development and in helping us understand and talk about them.

None of these issues has been completely resolved. Perhaps they cannot be, and perhaps history will show that they weren't particularly important in any case. What is important, however, is to keep in mind that what we think and say about children—indeed, the questions we ask and sometimes the answers we are prepared to accept—is strongly influenced by our assumptions and beliefs. Many of the most important current beliefs about children and their development relate to the questions and issues that have recurred in the field. Some of these beliefs are summarized in the following *Concept Summary*.

METHODS OF STUDYING CHILDREN

As we see in Chapter 5, which looks at the minds of infants, most of us are victims of a curious phenomenon labeled **infantile amnesia**: We remember virtually nothing—at least consciously—of our infancies or even of our early preschool days. So powerful and general is infantile amnesia that Newcombe and Fox (1994) found that 9- and 10-year-old children were generally completely incapable of recognizing photos of their preschool classmates. Yet most adults can, years later, identify photos of over 90% of their elementary school classmates.

As a result of our infantile amnesia, when we try to make sense of the mind and emotions of infants, we can't rely on what we remember of what it was like to be an infant. Nor can infants tell us in words. Hence, much of what we know of the private lives of preverbal children is based on inferences we make. However, these inferences are *scientific* inferences: They are based not on speculation, inspiration, or the prejudices of grandparents, but on careful, controlled, and replicable observations.

Observation

Observation is the basis of all science, so the study of children always begins with observation. Child development researchers use two types of observation: naturalistic and nonnaturalistic.

---

nature-nurture controversy A very old argument in psychology about whether genetics (nature) or environment (nurture) is more responsible for determining development. Also called the heredity-environment question.

stages Identifiable phases in the development of human beings. Such developmental theories as Jean Piaget's are referred to as stage theories because they describe behavior at different developmental levels.

infantile amnesia A mysterious but apparently universal human phenomenon evident in the fact that most people do not remember events of infancy or of the early preschool period.

CONCEPT SUMMARY — Recurring Issues and Beliefs in Developmental Psychology

Recurring Issue	Dominant Current Belief
Active-passive	Children engage actively in exploring and in trying to create meaning. They are not simply the passive recipients of information, responding blindly to the rewards and punishments that life provides.
Nature-nurture	The causes of development are to be found in the interaction of environmental and genetic forces, rather than in their separate effects.
Social-historical	Development is profoundly influenced by the interaction between a person's characteristics and the historical, social, and cultural context in which the person develops.
Similarities in development	Some common threads appear to run through the developmental paths that different individuals take. These developmental similarities allow psychologists to describe developmental stages or phases.
Uniqueness in development	At the same time, there are pronounced differences among individuals, even among those having similar contexts and genetic histories. The differences become even greater when context and genetic history are more dissimilar.
Predictability of development	Change is what human development is all about. The quest to describe and understand changes that occur with age and experience is based on the belief that some of the factors that influence change, and some of the processes involved, are identifiable and their effects predictable.

Naturalistic Observation When children are observed without interference in natural (rather than contrived) situations—for example, at home or on the playground or in school—that is **naturalistic observation**. Psychologists who observe children and write **diary descriptions** of their behavior (sequential descriptions of behavior at predetermined intervals) are using naturalistic observation. Similarly, psychologists who describe continuous sequences of behavior (**specimen descriptions**), behaviors observed during specified time intervals (**time sampling**), or specific behaviors only (**event sampling**) are also using naturalistic observation (Wright, 1960; see Table 1.4). Note that in each of these methods, children's behavior remains unaffected by the observation.

---

naturalistic observation The study of children in natural settings; an investigation in which the observation has little effect on the behavior of those observed.

diary description A method of child study that records sequential descriptions of a child's behavior at predetermined intervals (daily or weekly, for example). Sometimes useful for arriving at a better understanding of general developmental patterns.

specimen description A method of child study in which detailed specific instances of a child's behavior are recorded. Useful for in-depth studies of individual children.

time sampling A method of child observation in which behavior is observed during specific time intervals, frequently with the aim of recording instances or frequency of specific behaviors.

event sampling A method of child study in which specific behaviors are observed and recorded and unrelated behaviors are ignored.

Michael Newman/PhotoEdit

Naturalistic observations of children involve as little interference with ongoing activities as possible and occur in "natural" environments such as playgrounds, homes, or, as shown here, in schools.

The methods of naturalistic observation may be used in combination. For example, time and event sampling are often used together. Time sampling specifies when observations will be made; event sampling specifies what behavior will be observed. Thus, in a study of children's playground behavior, an investigator might use a checklist to record instances of specific behaviors such as laughing, yelling, fighting, or cooperating (event sampling), and observe each child for 5-minute periods at 2-hour intervals (time sampling).

Nonnaturalistic Observation Nonnaturalistic observation involves methods and situations designed to have an effect on children's behavior—in contrast with naturalistic observation where children are observed in *natural* settings, and where the investigation is designed not to affect ongoing behavior. Nonnaturalistic observations are sometimes termed

nonnaturalistic observation The study of children using questionnaires or interviews (clinical investigations) or when the environment is manipulated or changed (experimental investigations).

TABLE 1.4
Naturalistic Methods of Observing Children

METHOD	DESCRIPTION	MAIN USES	EXAMPLE
Diary description	Fairly regular (often daily or weekly) descriptions of important events and changes	Detecting and understanding major changes and developmental sequences	Investigator makes occasional, dated notes of child's interesting language expressions
Specimen description	Detailed description of sequences of behavior, detailing all aspects of behavior	Studying individual children in depth; not restricted to only one or two predetermined characteristics	Investigator videotapes sequences of child's behavior for later analysis
Time sampling	Behaviors are recorded intermittently during short but regular time periods	Detecting and assessing changes in specific behaviors over time	Investigator records what child is doing during 30-second spans, once every 30 minutes
Event sampling	Specific behaviors (events) are recorded during the observational period; other behaviors are ignored	Understanding the nature and frequency of specific behaviors (events)	Investigator notes each time child bangs her head on the wall

Source: Based in part on Wright, 1960.

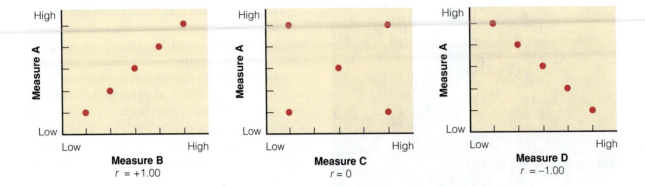

FIGURE 1.6 Representations of correlation (*r*), indicating the extent to which two measures tend to vary together: The *direction* of the relationship (positive or negative) is shown by the *sign* of the correlation coefficient (plus or minus). The *strength* of the relationship is indicated by the *magnitude* of the correlation coefficient: The closer *r* is to ±1, the stronger the observed relationship; the closer it is to 0, the weaker the relationship. In this example, scores on Measure A correlate perfectly with scores on Measures B and D and not at all with scores on Measure C.

clinical if they involve the use of interviews or questionnaires. When investigators attempt to manipulate or change a child's environment, the resulting studies are called experimental. Experiments are described later in this chapter.

Correlational Studies

Many studies of child development proceed as follows: Researchers decide to investigate the sources (causes) of specific characteristics in a group of children; children with these characteristics are identified; a comparison group of otherwise-similar children without these characteristics is also identified. An attempt is next made to obtain historical information about these children (for example, home environment, presence or absence of a father, intelligence, presence of similar characteristics in biological ancestors, and so on). Researchers then compare the two groups with respect to these historical variables. In the end, either a relationship—a **correlation**—will be found to exist between specific historical variables and present characteristics, or no relationship will be found.

Some Examples   Suppose you look at the relationship between sexual abuse and eating disorders, and you find, as did Deep and associates (1999), that almost half the women with eating disorders in your sample were sexually abused before they developed an eating disorder. This would be an example of a **positive correlation**: As incidence of sexual abuse increases, incidence of eating disorders also increases (see Chapter 11 for a discussion of this study).

Now suppose you look at the relationship between obesity and dating in adolescence, and you find, as did Halpern and associates (1999), that the fatter girls in your sample are significantly less likely to have dates. This would be an example of a **negative correlation**: As amount of fat increases, number of dates decreases (this study, too, is discussed in Chapter 11). (See Figure 1.6.)

Many correlational studies in psychology are **retrospective studies**. They are called retrospective because they try to identify relationships by looking back at a child's history (*retro* means backward) to

correlation   A mathematical measure of a relationship among variables. It is usually expressed as a number ranging from +1.00 (a perfect positive relationship) through 0 (no relationship) to −1.00 (a perfect inverse relationship).

positive correlation   A relationship where increases or decreases in one variable are associated with corresponding increases or decreases in another.

negative correlation   A relationship where increases or decreases in one variable are associated with opposite changes in another.

retrospective studies   Studies that attempt to identify causes and precursors of current situations by looking at preceding historical conditions.

see how factors in the past are related to present behavior. The Deep et al. (1999) study, which looked at the relationship between sexual abuse and eating disorders, is an example of a retrospective study.

The Correlational Fallacy A common error in interpreting studies such as this arises from the apparently logical (but false) assumption that if two events are correlated, one causes the other. Thus we might easily assume, following Deep and associates' study, that sexual abuse causes eating disorders. This is the **correlational fallacy**. As Deep and associates point out, there is no proof of causation here. Consider, for example, that a large number of women who are sexually abused *don't* develop eating disorders—and that many who do were not sexually abused.

As an extreme example of the occasional absurdity of the correlational fallacy, consider that in the isolated rural area where I was raised, there was a high correlation between total number of outhouses and number of teachers in local villages. That one caused the other seems unlikely. But that each is related to a third, important variable—namely population—is clear, and serves as a more likely explanation of the correlation between the two.

By the same token, if we find that measures of home background (socioeconomic indicators such as family income, parental education, and so on) are correlated with school achievement, can we conclude that parental income and education cause high or low achievement? No. Correlational studies show relationships or their absence; they do not establish causation.

Even though correlational studies cannot establish that one thing causes another, it's still true that the presence of a correlation is a *necessary* condition for inferring causality. However, a correlation alone is not a *sufficient* condition. If, as my grandmother believed, it's true that having freckles causes people to have violent tempers, then there must be a correlation between presence of freckles and bad tempers. If there is no such correlation, then my grandmother is dead wrong: Freckles do not cause bad tempers. Unfortunately, however, even if this correlation exists and is strong, she might still be wrong. Freckles might simply be the work of the same fairies who mischievously hand out uncontrollable tempers—or they might be nothing more than genetic accidents in my grandmother's sample.

So, identifying a correlation between two things is necessary if we are to determine whether one causes the other. But a correlational relationship is still not proof of a causal relationship, although a carefully controlled experiment might strongly suggest causality.

Experiments

The **experiment**, an example of *nonnaturalistic observation*, is science's most powerful tool for gathering useful observations. An experiment is distinguished from naturalistic observations in that it requires the systematic manipulation of some aspect of a situation to detect and measure the effects of that manipulation. In an experiment, the observer controls certain **variables** (characteristics that can vary)—called **independent variables**—to investigate their effect, or lack of effect, on other variables, termed **dependent variables**. For example, in an experiment to investigate the relationship between two teaching methods and the development of language skills, the experimenter can manipulate (control) the variable "teaching method" by using teaching method A with one group of students and method B with a second group. In addition, if we are to have faith in the results of the experiment, subjects must be randomly

---

experiment A procedure for scientific investigation requiring manipulation of some aspects of the environment to determine what the effects of this manipulation will be.

variable A property, measurement, or characteristic that is susceptible to variation. In psychological experimentation, such qualities of human beings as intelligence and creativity are referred to as variables.

independent variable The variable in an experiment that can be manipulated to observe its effect on other variables.

dependent variable The variable that may or may not be affected by manipulations of the independent variable in an experimental situation.

---

correlational fallacy The apparently logical but often false assumption that if two events are related (correlated), one causes the other.

assigned to the two methods to guard against the possibility that students in one group might have some systematic language-acquisition advantage over students in the other group.

In this illustration, "teaching method" is the independent variable; it is under the experimenter's control. The various measures of the subjects' language skills are dependent variables. The experimenter's **hypothesis** (scientific prediction) is that the independent variable (teaching method) will affect the dependent variables (language skills).

Experimental procedures often use experimental groups and control groups. **Experimental groups** are ordinarily made up of participants who are treated in some special way. The object is usually to discover whether the special treatment (independent variable) has a predictable effect on some outcome (dependent variable). To ensure that any changes in the dependent variable are in fact due to the treatment, it is often necessary to use a second group—the **control group** (also called no-treatment group)—for comparison. This second group must be as similar as possible to the experimental group in all relevant ways except that it does not experience the special treatment. The effect of the treatment is then assessed by comparing the two groups with respect to some outcome (dependent variable) after the experimental group has been given the treatment.[4]

It's important to recognize that the results of experiments can be believed with confidence only when those results have been replicated—that is, when the same outcome can be observed in repetitions of the same experiment. A single experiment does not prove anything. In fact, a whole battery of related experiments is not likely to prove much either—that is, to prove it absolutely, beyond the shadow of any doubt. Absolute proof is a rare luxury in science.

Still, carefully controlled and replicated experiments are science's only reliable way of investigating cause-and-effect relationships. They are science's best source of information, the foundation for its most logical and useful conclusions. But in many situations, experiments are not possible or would be quite unethical. In some of these situations, correlational studies can be highly informative. Consider, for example, an experiment designed to investigate the effects of poverty on young children. Such an experiment would require that investigators assign randomly selected children to precisely defined conditions of wealth or poverty at a critical stage in their lives and that these children be examined and compared later—hardly an ethical undertaking.

Longitudinal and Cross-Sectional Research

There are two approaches to studying human development: A **longitudinal study** observes the same subjects over a period of time; a **cross-sectional study** compares different subjects at one point in time. For example, there are two ways of investigating differences in the rules used in games played by 2-year-olds and 6-year-olds. One way is to observe a group of 2-year-old children at play, and then four years later observe the same children again. This is the longitudinal approach, which, for these purposes, is more time-consuming than necessary. Similar results could be obtained by simultaneously

---

hypothesis An assumption, prediction, or tentative conclusion that may be tested through the application of the scientific method.

experimental group A group of subjects who undergo experimental manipulation. The group to which something is done in order to observe its effects.

control group Consists of subjects who are not experimented with but who are used as comparisons to the experimental group to ascertain whether the outcomes were affected by the experimental procedure.

---

[4] This is only one of a large variety of experimental designs that are used in psychological research. For others, see Ray (1997).

---

longitudinal study A research technique in the study of child development that observes the same subjects over a long period of time.

cross-sectional study A technique in the investigation of child development that involves observing and comparing different subjects at different age levels. A cross-sectional study would compare 4- and 6-year-olds by observing two groups of children at the same time, one group consisting of 6-year-old children and the other of 4-year-old children. A longitudinal study would require that the same children be examined at the age of 4 and again at age 6.

A longitudinal study of development follows the same subjects over a period of time. It is highly useful for providing information about changes that occur within individuals over time. However, longitudinal studies can be highly time-consuming and therefore very expensive. To study the development of this little girl through the time span represented by these photos would have taken about a decade.

observing several groups of 2- and 6-year-old children and then comparing them directly.

Cross-sectional and longitudinal approaches are both essential for studying human development. Each has some strengths, and some weaknesses and limitations as well. For some questions, a longitudinal approach is necessary even though it is time-consuming. If investigators want to discover whether intelligence test scores change with age or remain stable, they must do this by observing the same children at different times; this question cannot be answered using a cross-sectional approach. A cross-sectional approach cannot give us information about changes that occur over time within a single individual, because it looks at each individual only once.

Among the problems associated with longitudinal research are its higher cost, the fact that instruments and methods may become outdated before completion, the possibility that some of the research

questions will be answered in some other way before the project is finished, and the tremendous amount of time that is sometimes required. Often an experiment must be designed to continue beyond the lifetime of a single investigator (or team of investigators). This is the case with the Terman study of giftedness, which began in the early 1920s and continues today (Terman et al., 1925). This kind of study encounters an additional problem related to subject mortality. The death of subjects not only reduces the size of samples but also may bias the results. If, for example, individuals of a certain personality type die younger than do others, a longitudinal assessment of personality change might reveal some significant changes with old age when such change is, in fact, not the case. As a purely hypothetical illustration, if aggressive people die before those who are nonaggressive, we might be led to believe that people become less aggressive as they age.

One of the most serious limitations of longitudinal studies is that they usually assume that currently valid measures will be equally valid in the future. This problem is particularly evident in longitudinal studies of vocabulary growth, intelligence, and related variables for which rapidly changing conditions may significantly affect the appropriateness of measures used.

Cross-sectional studies sometimes suffer from a similar problem, stemming from their assumption that children now at one age level are comparable to children at that age level at another time. With respect to intelligence, for example, drastic improvements in educational experiences and in exposure to television can affect children to the extent that measures of intelligence obtained at one time cannot meaningfully be compared with measures obtained some years earlier.

It should be noted that many of the problems associated with longitudinal research (for example, subject mortality, higher cost, greater time requirement, changing contexts in the lives of subjects) apply only to longer-term research. But not all longitudinal research is long-term. For example, longitudinal studies of infant development might span only weeks, or perhaps only days or hours. However, because human development spans a huge spread of years, much of our longitudinal research necessarily is long-term.

Sources of Developmental Variation: Age, Time, and Birth Cohort

Human development is defined as change over time. Hence developmental researchers are mainly interested in changes related to age. However, the results of research can often be misleading, because change in human development isn't always related only to age. It can also be related to influences that are specific to the time of testing, or to the individual's birth cohort.

Influences of Time of Testing For example, let's say I gave a vocabulary test to eight large groups of 5-year-olds in 1970. These groups represent all geographic, ethnic, and social dimensions in my country. Then, 10 years later, I give the same eight groups the same test (a longitudinal study). I find that there has been a 300% increase in size of vocab-ulary during this 10-year span. Can I conclude that vocabulary typically increases 300% between ages 5 and 10?

The simple answer is perhaps not. Maybe something has happened between 1970 and 1980 to account for this 300% increase in vocabulary (like the proliferation of computers, of television sets, religions, or other factors). Perhaps if I had tested 5-year-olds in 1980, they, too, would show a significant increase when compared with 5-year-olds in 1970. Perhaps the observed changes are at least partly a function of time of testing rather than simply of increasing age.

Influences of the Birth Cohort A birth cohort is a group of individuals who have in common the fact that they were born within the same time period. The "1970 birth cohort" includes all individuals who were born during 1970; the "December 1970" birth cohort includes all individuals born during December 1970; and the "birth cohort of the eighth decade in the twentieth century" includes all individuals born in the 10-year period between January 1, 1970 and December 31, 1979. A birth cohort is therefore of a specific initial size and composition. It does not normally increase in size, but rather decreases as members die. Finally, it disappears completely. But before it disappears, its composition gradually changes. For example, because men die at an earlier age than women, the male-female ratio of a birth cohort usually changes over time. Similarly, racial composition might also change as a result of different mortality rates.

What is most important for the developmental psychologist is not so much that individuals of a single birth cohort are of the same age, but that they may be subject to a variety of experiences that are different from those to which members of other birth cohorts are exposed. For example, my grandmother's birth cohort dates to the turn of the twentieth century and includes people who were born into a world without electricity, television, computers, and airline travel. These rather obvious cohort-related influences might be important in attempting to understand why an 8-year-old in 1978 might be quite different from an 8-year-old in either 2028 or 1928.

birth cohort A group of individuals who have in common the fact that they were born within the same range of time.

Less obvious cohort-related influences also include changes in medical practices (including the widespread use of a variety of inoculations), in nutrition, in leisure-time activities, in work roles, in morality, and so on. Because of these influences, birth cohorts that are scarcely separated in time might turn out to be different in some important ways.

Separating the Effects of Age, Time, and Birth Cohort
One of the most serious problems that developmental researchers face is the difficulty of separating the effects of age, time, and birth cohort. Often these sources of variation cannot be distinguished. In a cross-sectional study it may be impossible to determine whether differences between two age groups are age-related, or whether they are due to cohort-related factors because two different birth cohorts are being examined. In a simple longitudinal study it may be impossible to separate the effects of time of testing from those of age. In addition, generalizations derived from a longitudinal study might be applicable only to the specific birth cohort under investigation.

One way of overcoming these important research problems is to use what are termed **sequential designs** (Tudge, Shanahan, & Valsiner, 1997). Essentially, these studies involve taking series of samples at different times of measurement. One well-known sequential design is the **time-lag study** in which different birth cohorts are compared at different times. For example, a time-lag study might compare 10-year-olds in 1995 with 10-year-olds in 1997, 1999, and 2001 (see Figure 1.7). Because subjects are of the same age when tested but were born in different years, they belong to different birth cohorts. Consequently, observed differences among the groups might reveal important birth cohort-related influences.

(The following *Concept Summary* lists the various methods of studying child development.)

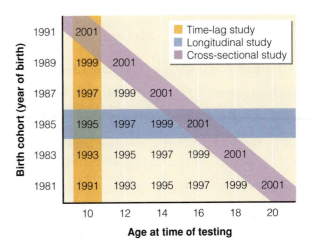

FIGURE 1.7 Schematic representation of three research designs. Years inside the figure indicate time of testing. Vertical columns represent possible time-lag studies (different birth cohorts; different times of measurement; same ages). Horizontal rows represent possible longitudinal studies (same birth cohort measured at different times). Diagonals represent possible cross-sectional studies (different birth cohorts examined at one point in time).

than one approach. If you are interested in knowing whether children have more affection for cats than for dogs, you might simply compare the number of children who have dogs with the number who have cats (naturalistic observation). Alternatively, you might ask a sample of children which they like best (interview technique). Or you might arrange for different children, alone and in groups, to meet different cats and dogs—also alone and in groups (experimental approach)—and assess the children's reactions (perhaps through simple visual observation, or by measuring their heart rates and other physiological functions).

Note that each of these approaches might lead to somewhat different answers for the same questions. Even if there are more cats than dogs in the

EVALUATING DEVELOPMENTAL RESEARCH

In practice, the methods child development researchers use are determined by the questions they want answered. Some questions can best be answered by one approach; others, by another. And some questions, of course, lend themselves to more

sequential designs Research strategies that involve taking a sequence of samples at different times of measurement in order to reduce or eliminate biases that may result from confounding the effects of age with influences relating to the time of testing and the subject's birth cohort.

time-lag study A developmental study in which subjects of one age are compared to other groups who are also the same age, but at a different point in time (for example, comparing 12-year-olds in 1995 with 12-year-olds in 1990 and in 1985).

Methods of Studying Children

Method	Main Characteristics
Observation	The basis of all science. Observation is naturalistic when children are observed without interference in natural rather than contrived situations (time or event sampling, diary descriptions, or specimen descriptions [see Table 1.4]). Nonnaturalistic observation may involve structured interviews or questionnaires, and may be experimental.
Correlational study	Looks for relationships between two (or more) variables. A correlation exists when changes in one variable are accompanied by systematic changes in another (for example, during early childhood, increasing height is correlated positively with increasing vocabulary). The existence of a correlation is necessary but insufficient for inferring causality.
Experiment	Involves systematic attempts to manipulate the environment to observe the effects of specific independent variables on given dependent variables. Science's most powerful means of gathering observations.
Longitudinal study	A study in which the same subjects are followed over a period of time.
Cross-sectional study	A study in which subjects of different ages are studied at one point in time.
Time-lag study	A study in which subjects of the same age are compared to each other at different points in time (hence comparisons of different birth cohorts when they are of the same age).

homes of your subjects—many parents think cats are less demanding—children might really like dogs better. And maybe, even if they do like dogs better, more would be afraid of dogs than of cats because strange dogs are somewhat more frightening than strange cats. Thus an important point to keep in mind as you evaluate some of the studies described in this text is that answers are sometimes partly a function of research methods used.

Truth in psychology, as in most disciplines, is relative. The validity of research conclusions can seldom be judged as absolutely right or wrong, but must instead be evaluated by how useful, clear, consistent, and generalizable they are. Of all these, perhaps **generalizability** is most important. Too often, results of a specific research project apply only to the

situation in which they were obtained; they cannot be generalized to other, similar situations. The value of conclusions that can't be generalized is limited.

As an intelligent consumer of psychological research, there are a number of important things that you have to keep in mind.

Sampling

As we just saw, the conclusions of developmental research are usually intended to be generalizable to an entire population—that is, to an entire collection of individuals (or objects, or situations) with similar characteristics. For example, the entire collection of North American fifth-grade children defines a population; all left-handed, brown-eyed 4-year-olds make up another population. In most cases, the populations that are of interest to a researcher are too large to be investigated in their entirety. What

generalizability The extent to which conclusions can be applied (generalized) from one situation to others; the generality of conclusions.

the investigator does, instead, is select a **sample** from this larger population. Ideally, the sample is carefully chosen to be representative of the entire population.

For example, if the object is to obtain valid information about the moral beliefs and behaviors of American children, a sample (a portion) of American children is interviewed. But if the results are to be generalizable, the sample cannot comprise subjects from San Francisco or Boston alone. Rather, subjects must represent all major geographical areas in the nation. In addition, care must be taken to ensure that all nationalities, major religious groups, socioeconomic levels, occupations, and ages are represented in proportions similar to those in the entire population. One of the simplest and most effective ways of ensuring this is to select subjects at random from the entire population.

Ecological and Cross-Cultural Validity

There is a large body of research indicating that Japanese students perform better than American students on measures of mathematics achievement (see, for example, Westbury, Ethington, Sosniak, & Baker, 1993). Several conclusions can be based on this observation: Japanese students are more intelligent, or at least more capable, in mathematics; the Japanese school system is more effective than the U.S. school system; or both.

Are any of these conclusions valid? No, says Westbury (1992). A more careful analysis of the data suggests that the Japanese mathematics curriculum fits the tests used in the study more closely than does the U.S. curriculum, giving Japanese students an unfair advantage. When students are compared only on what they have been taught, American students do about as well as the Japanese.

But not all researchers agree that American students do about as well as the Japanese when they are tested only on what they have been taught. Recent international studies of achievement in mathematics and science continue to suggest that the educational systems in Japan and Taiwan produce higher achievers in mathematics and science (U.S. Depart-

Alan Oddie/PhotoEdit

Children from different cultures sometimes perform very differently on various tests, a fact whose meaning is often completely unclear. Researchers need to ask not only whether the tests are suitable for different cultures, but also what some of the other causes of observed differences might be. Conclusions based on research conducted with only one cultural group cannot easily be generalized to other groups.

ment of Education, 1997). Findings such as these have led to considerable controversy about (a) whether such differences are real, and (b) what the reasons might be for any real differences. Those whose minds are already made up, says LeTendre (1999), often use negative, culturally biased stereotyped images to bolster their conclusions—images such as that of Japanese schools as "repressive, exam driven," and North American schools as "harmonious, child centered" (p. 38).

THOUGHT CHALLENGE: *How many plausible explanations can you think of for apparent international differences in achievement—such as in mathematics? How might you attempt to determine whether these differences are real?*

sample A subset of a population. A representative selection of individuals with similar characteristics drawn from a larger group.

A similar situation exists when comparing children from different cultures—or even when comparing children within single multicultural nations. We can never be certain whether observed differences reflect real differences (in underlying capacities, for example), or whether they result from the influences of different environments (different contexts). For example, according to Stevenson (see Coulter, 1993), the finding that Japanese (and Taiwanese) students do better than North American students in mathematics may also be due to a combination of the following facts: North American students spend about 20 hours per week with friends, whereas Japanese and Taiwanese students spend closer to 10; more than 75% of students in North America are dating but fewer than 40% of students in Japan and Taiwan are dating; and 60% of North American students have jobs but only 20% of students in Japan and Taiwan have jobs.

The fact that children from different cultures often perform differently on various tests and in different situations underlines the importance of asking two questions: (1) Are the tests and assessment procedures we're using suitable for different cultures? and (2) What might be the underlying causes of observed differences? Conclusions based on research conducted only with North American samples may not be valid in Western Europe or in Third World countries. Similarly, research conducted only with white middle-class subjects in North America should not be generalized to the entire population.

Subject Memory

When Hampsten (1991) studied the diaries and letters of American pioneer women, she found that life had been harsh and difficult for their children. Most children had to work hard at young ages, many were exposed to a variety of physical dangers, and many died or were maimed. But when, as adults, they wrote accounts of their childhoods, they described mainly happy experiences—and almost no bad times. Autobiographical memory, claim Brewin, Andrews, and Gotlib (1993), is highly unreliable.

Hence researchers who use people's recollections to understand the past must take into consideration the possibility of unintentional distortions.

Subject Honesty

Researchers must also consider whether subjects might distort the facts intentionally, especially when personal matters are being researched. Comparisons of adolescent sexual behavior today with behavior characteristic of adolescents several generations ago are typically unreliable, at least partly for this reason. Given prevailing attitudes toward sexual behavior, it is reasonable to suppose that today's adolescents would be more willing to reveal their sexual activity than adolescents of the 1920s.

Experimenter Bias

Some research indicates that investigators sometimes unconsciously bias their observations to conform to their expectations. One effective means of guarding against experimenter bias is the **double-blind procedure**. This technique requires simply that experimenters, examiners, and subjects remain unaware of either the expected outcomes of the research or of the assignment of subjects to experimental or control groups.

When we consider all these possibilities, it's clear that we must be careful when interpreting the results of developmental research. Among the important questions to ask are those listed in the *Concept Summary*. And then, of course, it's important to ponder whether the questions posed by any developmental research project are important—whether the answers obtained really matter in our understanding of children.

---

double-blind procedure An experimental method in which neither subjects nor experimenters involved in data collection or analysis are aware of which subjects are members of experimental groups and which are not. Double-blind procedures are used as a safeguard against experimenter and subject bias.

CONCEPT SUMMARY · Evaluating Developmental Research

Issues	Checklist of Important Questions
Sampling	Is the sample a good representation of the population to which the observations and conclusions are meant to apply?
Ecological validity	Is there something special or unique about the social, cultural, or historical context in which observations are made? Do the characteristics of the context in interaction with the characteristics of the individuals reduce the generalizability of the findings?
Subject memory	Must the investigation rely on human memories? Has the possibility of systematic or random distortion been taken into account?
Subject honesty	Does the validity of the observations depend on the honesty of participants? Do they have a reason to consciously or unconsciously distort facts?
Experimenter bias	Is there a possibility that experimenters' or subjects' expectations have influenced observations?
Ethical issues	Have the rights of all participants been considered and safeguarded?

MAIN POINTS

Organization of *Of Children*

This text deals with human development, the process whereby children adapt to their environment. Development includes maturation (genetically programmed unfolding), growth (quantitative changes), and learning (changes due to experience).

Historical and Current Views of Childhood

The idea of childhood is not universal. There is evidence of selective infanticide during antiquity. In medieval times infant mortality was high, and the idea of childhood as a distinct state was not widely developed. During the eighteenth and nineteenth centuries, child labor flourished and child-rearing practices were often harsh. The twentieth century has brought increasing concern with the social, physical, and intellectual welfare of children, especially in the industrialized world. However, in many nonindustrialized, underdeveloped areas of the world, millions of children die each year—primarily from malnutrition, vaccine-preventable causes such as measles and tetanus, and diarrheal dehydration.

Lower birthrates, greater numbers of childless couples, delayed marriages, increasing numbers of one-parent families, and the impact of television have altered the experience of childhood.

Children's Rights

Children's rights include assurances of ethical standards for research with children, as well as the nearly universal adoption of a United Nations Charter of Children's Rights. The legal rights of children in today's industrialized societies are primarily rights of protection (the right to adequate medical and educational care, to affection and love, to a peaceful environment, to the opportunity to develop) rather than adult rights of choice that entail adult responsibilities.

The Study of Children

Psychology is the study of human behavior and thought; developmental psychology is concerned with systematic changes over time. Development includes growth (physical changes), maturation (biologically based changes) and learning (changes due to experience).

Among early pioneers of the scientific study of children were John Locke (tabula rasa) and Jean-Jacques Rousseau ("noble savage"). Later pioneers included Charles Darwin (baby biography; evolution), G. Stanley Hall ("ontogeny recapitulates phylogeny"), and John B. Watson (we become what we are as a function of our experiences).

Recurring Questions, Themes, and Beliefs

Recurring questions in human development ask about the relative influence of heredity and environment, whether development is continuous or occurs in discrete stages, and whether we should view children as primarily active or passive. Common basic beliefs are that children are active and create meaning, that causes of development are complex interactions between the environment and specific characteristics of an individual, and that in spite of marked individual differences, there are some commonalities in the developmental patterns of different individuals.

Methods of Studying Children

The basis of the science of child development is observation. Naturalistic (nonintrusive) observations of children include diary descriptions (regular descriptions of interesting events), specimen descriptions (continuous sequences of behavior), event sampling (recordings of predetermined behaviors), and time sampling (recordings during predetermined time intervals). Nonnaturalistic observations may be clinical (questionnaires or interviews) or experimental.

Correlational studies look at relationships among variables, and are often retrospective (go back in time). High positive correlation does not prove that changes in one variable cause changes in another.

In an experiment, an investigator randomly assigns subjects to groups and controls independent variables to determine whether they affect dependent variables (outcomes).

Studies of child development can be longitudinal (comparing the same children at different periods in their lives), or cross-sectional studies (comparing different children at the same time).

Developmental psychologists are mainly interested in changes associated with age rather than with cohort effects (related to historical influences specific to people born during the same time span) or time of testing. One way of separating these effects is to use sequences of samples, thus permitting different combinations of longitudinal, cross-sectional, and time-lag studies. In a time-lag study, different cohorts are compared at different times (for instance, 7-year-olds in 1991 are compared with 7-year-olds in 1995, 1999, and 2003).

Evaluating Developmental Research

The value and generalizability of research results are subject to the influences of sample representativeness, subject memory and honesty, experimenter bias, **ecological validity**, and other factors. Truth, here as elsewhere, is relative.

---

ecological validity An expression sometimes used to refer to the fact that psychological phenomena are highly dependent on environmental factors. For example, cultural, social, and other systems affect our behavior. A generalization is said to be ecologically valid to the extent that it takes environmental circumstances into account.

Focus Questions: Applications

1. What is this book about?
   - Define the terms listed in the "Key Terms" section.
2. How have ideas about childhood changed?
   - Compare inferred medieval attitudes toward children (as reflected in sports such as, say, "baby tossing") with the most common current North American attitudes. Compare these attitudes with those reflected in instances of wartime atrocities against children (child beatings, starvation, rape, murder, and so on).
3. What are the rights of children? The responsibilities of parents and societies?

- When, if ever, should the state interfere in the home with respect to the care and upbringing of children?
4. What are the most basic current beliefs about children and their development?
   - What are your personal beliefs about the most important influences in development? On what evidence are these beliefs based?
5. How do we study children?
   - Ask a simple, specific, important question about the development of children. How might you find an answer for your question?
6. How reliable are our conclusions?
   - Referring to question 5, how would you evaluate your answer?

Possible Responses to Thought Challenges

Thought Challenge, page 7

Ariès notes that there seemed to be a tendency for early European artists to portray children as miniature adults rather than as children. This is evident in the clothing artists painted on children, which was often identical to that worn by adults (but smaller, of course!). Also, it was almost as though no one had yet noticed that the heads of young children are larger than those of adults relative to the rest of their bodies, that their legs and arms are somewhat shorter, that their expressions are often less serious, less preoccupied.

In fact, however, using the way children were depicted in old paintings as evidence of a lack of appreciation of childhood would probably not convince a judge in a court of law. Science, too, needs more evidence.

Thought Challenge, page 13

What *should* be done is a matter for our consciences; what *can* be done is clearer. Each of these causes of child mortality can be prevented or reversed through a combination of global immunization, distribution of food supplies, and oral rehydration therapy (ORT). (ORT involves an attempt to increase the dehydrated child's fluid intake and replace essential salts. ORT solutions can be made by dissolving specially prepared mixtures in water, or they can be made from salts, sugar, or rice powder dissolved in the correct proportions.) Further, the effects of each of these causes of infant and child death—vaccine-preventable diseases, diarrheal dehydration, infection, and poor nutrition—can be lessened enormously through something as simple as breast-feeding.

Thought Challenge, page 31

The group that achieves at the highest level might do so for one or a combination of the following reasons: they are more intelligent; they have higher levels of the specific ability or talent being measured; their teachers are better; they spend more time studying the tested subjects; their motivation is higher; parents help them more; they spend less time watching television; they spend less time working outside of school; they have developed better test-taking skills; the tests are biased . . . and on and on. There are always many plausible reasons for believing, or not believing, what we think (want?) to be correct.

Key Terms

birth cohort, 28

context, 10

control group, 26

correlation, 24

correlational fallacy, 25

cross-sectional study, 26

dependent variable, 25

development, 18

developmental psychology, 14

diary description, 22

doctrine of the tabula rasa, 18

double-blind procedure, 32

ecological validity, 34

event sampling, 22

experiment, 25

experimental group, 26

generalizability, 30

growth, 15

hypothesis, 26

independent variable, 25

infancy, 4

infanticide, 5

infantile amnesia, 21

learning, 16

longitudinal study, 26

maturation, 16

naturalistic observation, 22

nature-nurture controversy, 21

negative correlation, 24

nonnaturalistic observation, 23

ontogeny, 19

phylogeny, 19

positive correlation, 24

psychology, 14

questionnaires, 19

retrospective studies, 24

sample, 31

sequential designs, 29

specimen description, 22

stages, 21

time-lag study, 29

time sampling, 22

under-5 mortality rate (U5MR), 8

variable, 25

Further Readings

The major changes of childhood seem to us to be pretty universal. But the idea of childhood is not, explain James and Prout, editors of the following collection of articles. The main point of these articles is to illustrate how our ideas of childhood are molded by our beliefs and our social realities.

James, A., & A. Prout, eds., (1997). *Constructing and reconstructing childhood: Contemporary issues in the sociological study of childhood*. Washington, D.C.: Falmer Press.

Fascinating descriptions of changes in the status of children throughout history are provided by:

Ariès, P. (1962). *Centuries of childhood: A social history of family life* (R. Baldick, trans.). New York: Alfred A. Knopf. (Originally published 1960.)

Kessen, W. (1965). *The child*. New York: John Wiley.

A booklet containing all the Children's Rights articles of the U.N.'s Convention on the Rights of the Child can be obtained free from:

United Nations Children's Fund
UNICEF House, H-9F
United Nations Plaza
New York, NY 10017
telephone: (212) 326-7072

The following short book on the methods of science includes useful suggestions for conducting and evaluating psychological research, as well as for writing research articles:

Ray, William J. (1997). *Methods toward a science of behavior and experience* (5th ed.). Pacific Grove, Calif.: Brooks/Cole.

An annual UNICEF publication, *The state of the world's children* presents an up-to-date summary of important indicators of the well-being of children throughout the world. The publication can be accessed without charge at http://www.unicef.org/.

Bellamy, C. (1999). *The state of the world's children: 1999*. New York: Oxford University Press.

Online Resources

For additional readings, explore *InfoTrac College Edition*, your online library. Go to http://infotrac-college.com/wadsworth and use the passcode that came on the card with your book. Try these search terms: children's rights, parenthood, developmental psychology.

If everybody rode a horse
There'd be no smog, of course,
But then there'd be something worse.

Red Skelton, American comedian

Theories
of Development

Myrleen Ferguson Cate/PhotoEdit

CHAPTER 2

Not only would we have less smog if everyone rode a horse, as suggested in the quote on the opposite page, but we'd also have much nicer potatoes if my grandmother's theory is correct.

I learned this when my parents had sent me to Victoire, Saskatchewan, to live with my grandmother so I could continue school. We were sitting on her porch one June evening, gazing out over the garden.

She pointed to a long row of lush green leaves. "Nice potatoes," she said in French, her native language.

I spotted a thick cluster of fernlike foliage. "Nice carrots too," I responded, which would have been the wise thing to say even if it weren't true.

"Horse manure," she said. The French word she used—*merde*—is only slightly less offensive than its four-letter counterpart in English. "I use horse manure."

"But your neighbor, Boutin, uses manure too and his potatoes aren't nearly as good as yours."

"Cow manure. That's what he uses," said Grandma. "All wrong for potatoes."

"Why?" I asked.

"I have a theory," said my grandmother.

That's when I was given my first lesson on Grandma Francœur's theory of wastes (My cousins and I were less polite then; we called it Grandma's ____ theory.) Among other things, the theory explained why horse manure favors potatoes and carrots; why chicken droppings—though not those of roosters—invigorate cabbages; why flattened and dried patties of cow dung excite flowers.

FOCUS QUESTIONS

1. What's a theory? What's its purpose? How can you tell whether a theory is a good one?
2. How does Freudian psychoanalysis relate to child development?
3. What are the principal assumptions and explanations of behaviorism?
4. Do children learn through imitation?
5. What are the basic ideas underlying Piaget's theory?
6. What are some of the roles of biology and culture in development?
7. What is self-actualization?

THEORIES IN PSYCHOLOGY

My grandmother's ramblings were a lesson in theory making—a lesson that I now pass on. A theory need not be an exotic collection of obscure pronouncements; nor does it substitute for the absence of facts. In its simplest sense, a **theory** is an *explanation* of facts. As Thomas (1999) explains in his discussion of theories of child development, to theorize is to suggest "(1) which facts are most important for understanding children and (2) what sorts of relationships among the facts are most significant for producing this understanding" (p. 4).

Purposes and Characteristics of Psychological Theories

As an explanation of facts, a theory is a collection of related statements intended to make sense of observations (of facts). It does so by organizing and explaining observations. And in psychology, as in other sciences, explanation is important. For one thing, if we can explain something, we can not only make predictions about it but also control it. For example, if my grandmother understands why specific manures affect certain crops in given ways, she can predict these effects and exercise control over her garden (barring such acts as severe storms, locust infestations, or small boys chasing cats among the turnips).

Similarly, if a theory explains why some children are happy and others are not, then it should be possible to predict which children will be happy. And if the circumstances affecting happiness are under our control, it should also be possible to bring happiness to saddened lives. Thus theories can have practical aspects. At the same time, they are one of science's most important guides for doing research. In large part, it is a theory—sometimes crude, sometimes elegant and refined—that tells the medical researcher where to look for a cure for cancer, what the cure will look like when it is found, and how it might be used. In the same way, psychology's theories tell the psychologist where and how to look for change in the course of development. They suggest, as well, some of the causes of change and how change might be predicted, and perhaps even controlled.

Origins of Theories Theories are seldom handed to philosophers and scientists carved in pieces of rock—or stored electronically in computers. Instead, they arise from making observations that are important enough to need explanation. Because what different theorists consider to be important and in need of explanation may vary a great deal, there are many different theories in most areas of psychology.

The types of observations on which scientific theories are based are seldom of the kind that were of such interest to my grandmother. **Science**, if nothing else, insists on a kind of objectivity, precision, and **replicability** (repeatability) that was not characteristic of my grandmother's garden. In fact, science is as much an attitude as a collection of methods. The classical "scientific method" (state the problem, make a prediction, select methods and gather required materials, make observations, and reach conclusions) is simply a way of ensuring that observations are made under sufficiently controlled

---

science An approach and an attitude toward knowledge that emphasize objectivity, precision, and replicability. Also, one of several related bodies of knowledge.

replicability A crucial quality of valid scientific or experimental procedures. A procedure is said to be replicable when it can be repeated and the results of so doing are identical (or highly similar) with each repetition.

---

theory An organized, systematic explanation of observations useful for explaining and for predicting.

circumstances that they could be made by anyone—that, in short, they can be replicated and confirmed. The attitude that defines science's search for explanation emphasizes the replicability of observations and demands precision in measuring and observing; hence the importance of the research methods described in Chapter 1. Clearly, if the facts on which a theory is based are suspect, the theory is not likely to be useful.

How Expectations Affect Observations   If a theory is simply an explanation of facts, why, you might ask, are there so many theories? One reason is that different theories may be used to explain quite different facts. Even very general theories of development—those that attempt to explain all of development—are not all based on the same observations. That's at least partly because theorists select the observations they think require explanation. Furthermore, even when psychologists try to be scientific—that is, very precise and very replicable—their observations may be quite different. Observations are often more or less accurate depending on the precision of our measurements, they are often relevant only in specific circumstances and sometimes for specific individuals, and they are colored by our expectations—in other words, by our theories and our assumptions.

As an example of how theory-based expectations color observations, Hunt (1961) reports how, in the seventeenth century, a man named Joseph DeAromati noticed that it's possible to see parts of plants in bulbs or in seeds. "Ha ha," said DeAromati. "This means that plants are fully formed in the seed!" This conclusion was quickly generalized to humans, leading to the theory of *preformationism*. This theory maintained that if your eyes were good enough to see the detail inside a sperm or an egg, you would see a fully formed but stunningly miniature little human there—a sort of extreme human bonsai. There then arose a heated controversy between the *animalculists*, who were absolutely convinced the complete little person would be found inside the sperm, and the *ovists*, who thought it far more likely the little person would be inside the egg (the ovum).

Then Antonie van Leeuwenhoek invented the microscope, which should have resolved the controversy once and for all. But it didn't! For a time, the battle seemed to go to the animalculists: "The little

person is inside the homunculus," declared a prominent scientist named Hartsoeker, peering through his microscope. "I've seen it." And to prove he had, he drew it in exquisite detail. But these crude, early microscopes allowed the ovists, too, to see a complete little person inside the egg!

Even today, with astonishingly good microscopes and the best of intentions, we sometimes see what isn't there at all. Imagine how much poorer is our sight when our microscopes are not so strong.

Characteristics of Good Theories   We cannot easily determine whether a theory is right or wrong—whether it is accurate and truthful or not. But we can at least decide whether it is useful. The best theories, says Thomas (1999), are those that (1) accurately reflect the facts, (2) are expressed in a clearly understandable way, (3) are useful for predicting future events as well as explaining past ones, (4) can be applied in a practical sense (have real value for counselors, teachers, pediatricians, and so on), (5) are consistent within themselves rather than self-contradictory, (6) are not based on a great number of assumptions (unproven beliefs), (7) can be proven wrong (and, therefore, can also be shown to *probably* be correct), (8) are based on convincing evidence, (9) are able to take new observations into consideration, (10) provide a stimulating and unusual view of development, (11) provide reasonable answers for the questions they address, (12) stimulate new research and discovery, (13) continue to attract attention over a long period of time, and (14) are satisfying in that they explain development in ways that make sense.

Models Underlying Theories of Child Development

Theorists don't all share the same views of people and of human nature. Sometimes they make different assumptions about what is involved in human development. For example, some theorists think it useful to view people as though they were machines. This **mechanistic model** suggests that in the same

---

mechanistic model   A model in human developmental psychology based on the belief that it is useful to view human beings in terms of their reactive, *machinelike* characteristics.

way machines are highly predictable, so too might it be possible to predict—and control—human behavior given sufficient knowledge about the external environmental conditions that affect behavior.

Other theorists insist that it is more useful to emphasize the biological, highly active, self-directed aspects of humans. This **organismic model** describes development as resulting from internal, biological and psychological determinants. It looks for regularities in behavior to understand the uniqueness of the individual.

A third model, the **contextual model** (sometimes labeled the *ecological model*), emphasizes the role of society, culture, and family in shaping the outcomes of development.

The organismic model is reflected in theories such as those of Freud, Erikson, and Piaget; the mechanistic model is evident in early behavioristic learning theories, such as that of Watson; and the contextual model is apparent in the theorizing of Bronfenbrenner, Bandura, Vygotsky, and behaviorists such as Skinner. These theories are summarized and explained in the remaining pages of this chapter. (See *Concept Summary*.)

A PSYCHOANALYTIC APPROACH: FREUD

One of the best known and most influential of all psychological theories is that of Sigmund Freud— the **psychoanalytic** approach. This theory is based on the assumption that the most important causes of human behavior and personality are deep-seated, usually unconscious forces within individuals. Freud believed that these forces, some of which are in conflict with one another, are at the root of mental disorders. Hence psychoanalysts (Freudian thera-

---

organismic model A model in human development that assumes people are active rather than simply reactive, and they are therefore more like biological organisms than like machines.

contextual model A developmental model that emphasizes the importance of the individual's interaction with environmental context. It looks at the historical period in which individuals are raised, as well as at the unique experiences they have.

psychoanalytic General label for Freudian theory. Also used to describe clinical or therapeutic procedures based on Freudian ideas, and especially on ideas related to the subconscious.

---

pists) can help restore mental health, argued Freud, by helping patients understand their unconscious drives and resulting conflicts.

Among the techniques that Freud found useful for therapy—techniques that soon became part of standard psychoanalytic practice—were free association; the analysis of dreams and of the unintended use of expressions and words (popularly termed Freudian slips), both of which were assumed to reflect unconscious desires or fears; the use of hypnosis; and painstaking analysis of childhood experiences, especially those that were sexual or traumatic (intensely frightening).

Although Freudian psychoanalytic theory has been used mainly for treating mental disorders, it is basically a theory of human development. This theory has had an enormous influence on later theorists and practitioners—even though the most important beliefs and concepts of psychoanalytic theory are no longer an important part of current developmental theories. The following sections present a brief account of this incredibly complex, sometimes bewildering, but always fascinating view of the development and machinations of human personality.

While reading about Freud, it is worth keeping in mind that his theory is very much a product of the Victorian era in which it was developed—an era that by today's standards was one of extreme sexual repression and male domination. These cultural factors greatly influenced Freud's theory and are reflected in both the importance he gave sexual motives and behaviors and the masculine orientation of the theory. Much of what Freud initially thought about development applied primarily to male children—and to females only as a sometimes hasty and incomplete afterthought (de Fiorini, 1998).

Basic Freudian Ideas

Perhaps the most basic of all Freudian ideas is the notion that human behavior is driven by two powerful tendencies: the urge to survive and the urge to procreate (Schmidt-Hellerau, 1997). Because the urge to survive is not usually threatened by our environments, but the urge to procreate is constantly being discouraged and prevented, sexual urges assume such enormous importance in Freud's description of human development that they are given a special term: **libido**. The libido is the source of energy for sexual urges; accordingly, the urges themselves are referred to as *libidinal* urges. Sexuality is a very broad term in Freud's writings. It means not only activities that are clearly associated with sex but all other activities that may be linked with body pleasure, however remotely (for example, behaviors such as thumb sucking or smoking).

Three Levels of Personality

There are three broad, sequential stages of personality development, says Freud. These are manifested in the development of id, ego, and superego.

Id The Freudian infant is all **instincts** (unlearned tendencies) and primitive reflexes, a bundle of unbridled psychic energy seeking almost desperately to satisfy urges that are based on the drive to survive and to procreate. These urges, labeled **id**, are a lifetime source of energy; they are the basic, underlying motive for all we do. But, unlike older children and adults, the infant has no idea of what is possible or impossible, no sense of reality, no sense of right and wrong, no internal moral rules that govern conduct. As a result, says Freud, the infant is driven by an almost overwhelming urge to obtain *immediate* satisfaction of impulses. An infant who is hungry does not wait; right now is the time for the nipple and the sucking!

Ego But life is not always so kind to the infant. Almost from birth, there is an abrupt clash between these powerful libidinal urges and reality. For example, hunger, perhaps the most powerful of the survival-linked drives, can't always be satisfied immediately. The reality of the situation is that the

Freud's theory was profoundly influenced by the male-dominated, sexually repressive beliefs and customs of the Victorian era in which he lived. Paintings and photographs of Freud's era often depict the family very formally, with the stern-faced father typically in a position of command.

American Museum, Bath, Avon, UK/Bridgeman Art Library

mother is often occupied elsewhere, and the infant's satisfaction must be delayed or denied. Similarly, the child eventually learns that defecation cannot occur anywhere and at any time; parental demands conflict with the child's impulses. This constant conflict between id impulses and reality results in the development of the second level of personality, the **ego**.

The ego is the rational level of human personality; it grows out of a realization of what is possible and what is not. The ego develops directly as a result of a child's experiences. Its evolvement includes the realization that delaying gratification is often a desirable thing, that long-term goals sometimes require the denial of short-term goals. Although the id wants immediate gratification, the ego channels

---

libido A general Freudian term denoting sexual urges. The libido is assumed to be the source of energy for sexual urges. Freud considered these urges the most important force in human motivation.

instinct A complex, species-specific, relatively unmodifiable pattern of behaviors such as migration or nesting in some birds and animals.

id One of the three levels of the human personality, according to Freudian theory. The id is defined as all the instinctual urges to which humans are heir and is the source of all human motives. A newborn child's personality, according to Freud, is all id.

ego The second stage of the human personality, according to Freud. It is the rational, reality-oriented level of human personality, which develops as children become aware of what the environment makes possible and impossible, and therefore serves as a damper to the id. The id tends toward immediate gratification of impulses as they are felt, whereas the ego imposes restrictions that are based on environmental reality.

CONCEPT SUMMARY   **Theories in Psychology**

Definition Of Theory	A systematic, organized collection of statements intended to organize and explain important observations
Purposes	• Explanation • Prediction • Control • Guiding further research

Criteria for Evaluating Theories	**Illustrated by Grandmother Francœur's Theory of Manures**
Does it accurately reflect the facts?	Yes, if carrots and other vegetables behave as expected under specified conditions.
Is it expressed in a clearly understandable way?	It is stunningly clear, except to the very stupid.
Is it useful for predicting future events as well as explaining past ones?	Yes. It allows the gardener to predict in the spring what will happen in the fall. In the fall, it presents explanations for what happened during the summer.
Can it be applied in a practical sense?	By gardeners, absolutely.
Is it consistent within itself rather than self-contradictory?	In general, yes, although my grandmother has sometimes contradicted herself with regard to chicken manure.
Is it based on a great number of assumptions (unproven beliefs)?	No.
Can it be shown to be wrong?	Yes. Its predictions can easily be confirmed—or denied.
Is it based on convincing evidence?	Perhaps not. Convincing evidence would require planting other gardens, as well as her own, with all possible combinations of vegetables and fertilizers over a number of years—in other words, controlled experimentation.
Can it take new observations into consideration?	That depends on the observations. Tremblay's bigger spuds in 1979 presented a problem.
Does it provide a stimulating and unusual view of development?	Of the development of vegetables? Yes.
Does it give reasonable answers for the relevant questions?	In reality, it doesn't answer the key question: Why do different manures affect vegetables in different ways?

Theories in Psychology (continued)

Criteria for Evaluating Theories	Illustrated by Grandmother Francœur's Theory of Manures
Is it likely to stimulate new research and discovery?	It could.
Does it continue to attract attention over a long period of time?	Yes. The theory is now many, many decades old. And we still talk about it.
Is it satisfying? Does it make sense?	It makes sense.

Models Underlying Developmental Theories	Related Metaphors	Representative Theorists
Mechanistic	People as machines, highly reactive to the environment	Early behaviorists such as Watson
Organismic	People as biological organisms, responding to inner drives	Piaget, Freud, Erikson
Ecological	People as plastic, strong, resilient, adaptive to a range of environmental and inner factors	Bronfenbrenner, Vygotsky, Bandura, Skinner

these desires in the most profitable direction for the individual.

Superego There is no opposition, no conflict, between the levels of personality represented by the id and the ego. Both work toward exactly the same goal, according to Freud: satisfying the **needs** and urges of the individual. But the third level of personality—labeled the **superego**—sets itself up in direct opposition to the first two. The superego is essentially the person's **conscience**. Like the ego, it develops from repeated contact with reality, but it reflects social rather than physical reality. As such, it is concerned with right and wrong, with "shoulds" and "should nots."

The superego (or conscience) begins to develop in early childhood says Freud, and results mainly from the child's *identifying* with parents, and especially with the same-sex parent. **Identification** involves attempting to become like others—adopting their values and beliefs as well as their behaviors. By identifying with their parents, children learn the religious and cultural rules that govern their parents' behaviors; these rules then become part of a child's superego. Because many religious, social, and cultural rules oppose the urges of the id, the superego and the id are generally in conflict. Freud assumed that this conflict underlies many mental disorders and accounts for much deviant behavior.

need Ordinarily, a lack or deficiency in the organism. Needs may be unlearned (for example, the need for food and water) or learned (the need for money or prestige).

superego The third level of personality according to Freud. It defines the moral or ethical aspects of personality and is in constant conflict with the id.

conscience An internalized set of rules governing an individual's behavior.

identification A general term referring to the process of assuming the goals, ambitions, mannerisms, and so on of another person—of identifying with that person.

Freud's Psychosexual Stages

Freud's description of the development of these three levels of personality—the id, ego, and super-ego—provides a unique account of child development. It's an account that traces the child's progression through a series of five **psychosexual stages**—a theory of **psychosexual development**. Because Freud believed that the major underlying source of energy for human behavior and development is sexual, stages in psychosexual development are identified and distinguished mainly through the objects or activities necessary for the satisfaction of basic urges during that stage. The labels for each stage reflect changes in matters of sexual satisfaction as the child matures (see Table 2.1).

The Oral Stage The **oral stage** as defined by Freud lasts through most of infancy (approximately to the age of 18 months). It is characterized by the infant's preoccupation with the mouth, with sucking, and with eating.

During this first stage, a child's personality consists mainly of id. Children constantly seek to satisfy their urges and are incapable of deliberately delaying gratification. Not surprisingly, psychoanalytic therapists sometimes attribute later eating disorders, such as **bulimia nervosa**, to developmental problems that originate during the oral stage (Urzua Moll, 1998).

The Anal Stage During the second year, the area of sexual gratification shifts from the oral region to the anal region. In the early part of the **anal stage**, says Freud, the infant derives pleasure from bowel movements. But later, as the child acquires control of sphincter muscles, pleasure may come from withholding bowel movements to increase anal sensation. Both of these behaviors oppose the mother's wishes. As a result of conflicts such as these, the child begins to develop an ego—a sense of reality, an awareness that some things are possible whereas others are not, coupled with the ability to delay gratification to some extent.

---

psychosexual A term used to describe psychological phenomena based on sexuality. Freud's theories are psychosexual in that they attribute development to sexually based forces and motives.

psychosexual development A Freudian term describing child development as a series of stages that are sexually based.

oral stage The first stage of psychosexual development, lasting from birth to approximately 8 months of age. The oral stage is characterized by preoccupation with the immediate gratification of desires. This is accomplished primarily through the oral regions, by sucking, biting, swallowing, playing with the lips, and so on.

bulimia nervosa Significant preoccupation with body shape and weight manifested in recurrent episodes of binge eating often accompanied by self-induced vomiting, use of laxatives or diuretics, strict fasting, or vigorous exercise.

anal stage The second of Freud's psychosexual stages of development, beginning at approximately 8 months and lasting until around 18 months, and characterized by children's preoccupation with physical anal activities.

TABLE 2.1
Freud's Stages of Psychosexual Development

STAGE	APPROXIMATE AGES	CHARACTERISTICS
Oral	Birth to 18 months	Sources of pleasure include sucking, biting, swallowing, playing with lips. Preoccupation with immediate gratification of impulses. Id is dominant.
Anal	18 months to 2 or 3 years	Sources of sexual gratification include expelling feces and urination, as well as retaining feces. Id and ego.
Phallic	2 or 3 to 6 years	Child becomes concerned with genitals. Source of sexual pleasure involves manipulating genitals. Period of Oedipus or Electra complex. Id, ego, and superego.
Latency	6 to 11 years	Loss of interest in sexual gratification. Identification with same-sex parent. Id, ego, and superego.
Genital	11 and older	Concern with adult modes of sexual pleasure, barring fixations or regressions.

Freud believed that development sometimes becomes stuck at a particular level (termed **fixation**) or goes back to a more primitive level (termed **regression**). The **anal-retentive** personality (stingy, self-centered) is one possible manifestation of fixation or regression at the anal stage. Similarly, the **oral-aggressive** personality (loud, boorish, insistent) might result from developmental problems linked with the oral stage (Agmon & Schneider, 1998).

The Phallic Stage In the Greek legend, King Oedipus, who has been abandoned by his parents and then adopted, ends up unwittingly killing his father and marrying his mother. Each of us who is male, claims Freud, is a little like Oedipus: As we progress through the third developmental stage, the **phallic stage** (roughly from ages 2 to 6), our increasing awareness of the sexual meanings of our genitals leads us to desire our mothers (and to wish to replace our fathers)—all unconsciously, of course. This is our **Oedipus complex**. Healthy resolution of this complex depends on being able to identify closely with our fathers, at the same time renouncing the lust we sense unconsciously for our mothers (Ikonen, 1998).

For girls, too, there is a similar developmental progression marked by what Halberstadt-Freud (1998) describes as vehement rejection of the mother based on an unrecognized jealousy of her. This jealousy, says Freud, results from the girl's sexual feelings for her father, and is labeled the **Electra complex**.

The Latency Stage The resolution of the Oedipus or the Electra complex marks the transition from the phallic stage to a period of **sexual latency** (from age 6 to 11). This period is marked by a loss of sexual interest in the opposite-sex parent and a continued identification with the same-sex parent. The process of identification is very important in Freud's system because it involves attempts not only to behave like the parent with whom the child is identifying but also to be like the object of identification regarding beliefs and values. In this way, the child begins to develop a superego. Note that identification, like many other significant phenomena described by Freud, is largely an unconscious rather than a conscious process.

The Genital Stage At about age 11, following a lengthy period of sexual neutrality, the child enters the stage of adult sexuality labeled the **genital stage**. The hallmark of this stage is typically the beginning of heterosexual attachments, says Freud. Also during this last developmental stage, the superego (conscience), which has previously been very rigid, becomes progressively more flexible as the adolescent matures.

Defense Mechanisms

In both normal and abnormal development, explains Freud, the id constantly strives for gratification. At the same time, the superego wars against the impulses of the id, raising moral and cultural objections to unbridled gratification. And through all this, the ego struggles to find some way of finding the gratification that the id craves, but within the constraints imposed by the superego.

---

fixation A Freudian term for the arresting of development at an immature developmental stage. Thought to be evident in personality characteristics and emotional disorders relating to the earlier stage.

regression A psychoanalytic (Freudian) expression for the phenomenon of reverting to some of the activities and preoccupations of earlier developmental stages. Evident in abnormal personality characteristics and emotional disorders.

anal-retentive Freudian term for a personality type described as stingy, hoarding, selfish, and linked with fixation or regression at the anal stage of development.

oral-aggressive Freudian label for personality characterized as loud, obnoxious, demanding, and thought to be associated with fixation at or regression to the oral stage of development.

phallic stage The third stage of Freud's theory of psychosexual development. It begins at about the age of 18 months and lasts to the age of approximately 6 years. During this stage children become concerned with their genitals and may show evidence of the much-discussed complexes labeled Oedipus and Electra.

Oedipus complex A Freudian concept denoting the developmental stage (around 4 years) when a boy's increasing awareness of sexual feelings leads him to desire his mother and envy his father.

Electra complex A Freudian stage occurring around the age of 4 or 5 years, when a girl's sexual feelings lead her to desire her father and to become jealous of her mother.

sexual latency A Freudian developmental period during which sexual interest is dormant (latent). Assumed to last from about ages 6 to 11.

genital stage The last of Freud's stages of psychosexual development, beginning around the age of 11 and lasting until around 18. It is characterized by involvement with normal adult modes of sexual gratification.

In its attempt to compensate for failures in satisfying all the id's urges, the ego often resorts to one or more **defense mechanisms**, according to Freud. Basically, defense mechanisms are ways of channeling urges and of reinterpreting (and often distorting)

defense mechanism A relatively irrational and sometimes unhealthy method used by people to compensate for their inability to satisfy their basic desires and to overcome the anxiety accompanying this inability.

reality. The ego is successful, explains Freud's daughter, Anna Freud (1946; Sandler & Freud, 1984), when it eliminates or reduces the anxiety that accompanies the continual struggle between the id and the superego. In a sense these mechanisms are the ego's attempt to establish peace between the id and the superego, so that the personality can continue to operate in an apparently healthy manner. Thus at one level, defense mechanisms are normal, healthy reactions to the world (Porerelli et al., 1998). What sometimes happens, however, is that the individual comes to rely too heavily on defense mechanisms. The result may be a dramatically distorted view of self, of others, and of objective reality, and may be evident in various personality disturbances.

Several dozen distinct defense mechanisms have been described by Freud and his followers. As a result, notes Vaillant (1998), definitions are often vague, overlapping, and sometimes contradictory. The most common of these defense mechanisms are summarized and illustrated in Table 2.2.

TABLE 2.2
Some Freudian Defense Mechanisms

Defense mechanisms are common methods of refocusing the demands of the id and of reducing anxiety associated with unwanted urges. They are invented by the ego as it tries to establish peace between the id and the superego. Defense mechanisms are very common in the lives of those who have no clearly recognizable disturbances. It is only when people rely on them excessively that defense mechanisms become a problem.

MECHANISM	EXAMPLE
Displacement Undesirable emotions are directed toward a different object.	A man who is angry at his wife kicks his dog.
Reaction formation Behavior is the opposite of the individual's actual feelings.	A woman loves an unobtainable man and behaves as though she dislikes him.
Intellectualization Behavior motivated by anxiety-provoking emotions is stripped of its emotional meaning.	A football player who enjoys hurting opponents convinces himself he is moved by the desire to win for his coach and his teammates and not by his desire to inflict pain.
Projection Undesirable feelings or inclinations are attributed to others.	A man who is extremely jealous of a competitor convinces himself it is the competitor who is jealous of him.
Denial Unpleasant, anxiety-provoking aspects of reality are distorted.	A heavy smoker, unable to give up the habit, concludes that there is no substantial evidence linking nicotine with human diseases.
Repression Unpleasant experiences are buried deep in the subconscious mind and become inaccessible to waking memory.	A person who was sexually abused as a child remembers nothing of the experience.

Questions: Can you think of an additional example of each defense mechanism? How likely is it that you would recognize defense mechanisms in your own life? Why?

Review of Freudian Theory

Freud's theory is one of the most comprehensive and influential of all psychological theories. It continues to have an enormous influence on psychotherapy. For example, research and writing on Freudian topics such as defense mechanisms continue at a very high rate (Cooper, 1998). Also, Freudian theory has tremendously influenced our attitudes toward children and child-rearing. More than anyone else, Freud was responsible for making parents realize how important the experiences of the early years can be.

The importance of Freudian theory is not limited to its direct effects on parents, educators, physicians, and others but includes its vast influence on the development of other theories (such as those of Erikson and John Bowlby). However, many of Freud's students and followers have rejected much of Freudian theory. For many, Freud paints too dark and cynical a picture of human nature: Primitive forces over which we have no control drive us relentlessly toward the satisfaction of instinctual urges and bring us into repeated conflict with reality. From the very moment of birth, our most basic selves—our ids— react with anxiety and fear. We fear that our overpowering urges to survive (and eventually to procreate) will not be satisfied, and we suffer from the anxiety accompanying that fear. According to Freud, this trauma of birth leads to all our adult anxieties.

Freud's theory is clearly weak from a scientific point of view, based as it is on a limited number of observations collected by a single individual (Freud himself) and not subjected to any rigorous analysis. Further, as Thomas (1999) notes, the data that Freud used in attempting to explain child development was far from reliable. In fact, he didn't interview or test children at all, but relied instead on his interpretation of the dreams, the fantasies, and the recollections of his neurotic adult patients. Also, the theory has often been criticized because it places excessive emphasis on sexual and aggressive impulses. (See Table 2.1 for an overview of Freud's developmental theory.)

⌐ A PSYCHOSOCIAL APPROACH: ERIKSON

Of the theories inspired by Freud's psychoanalytic views, that developed by Erik Erikson (1956, 1959, 1961, 1968) is the most important for the field of child development. The elaboration of this theory spanned a huge portion of the twentieth century (Erikson was born in 1902 and died in 1994 at the age of 92). Erikson not only witnessed dramatic changes in psychology during this period, says Weisberg (1996), but he contributed enormously to them as well.

Although Erikson's theory draws heavily from Freud's work, it also departs from it in several important ways. Recall that Freud emphasized the role of sexuality (libido) and the impact of conflicts between the id, ego, and superego. In contrast, Erikson downplays the role of sexual conflicts and instead emphasizes the importance of children's social environment. His theory is a theory of **psychosocial development** rather than of psychosexual development.

A second departure from Freudian theory is Erikson's concern with the development of a healthy ego (or **identity**, in Erikson's words) rather than with the resolution of powerful internal conflicts. As a result, the theory is far more positively oriented: It emphasizes "emotional wellness" rather than emotional illness (Weisberg, 1996).

A third important difference between Freud and Erikson, notes Eagle (1997), is that Erikson expanded his view of human development to include the entire life span. Development doesn't end at adolescence, notes Erikson; the reality of our social environments is that new challenges and new competencies are required throughout life. And the unfolding of these competencies can be described as a series of stages.

Psychosocial Stages

There are eight broad developmental stages that span our lives, says Erikson. The first five of these stretch from infancy through adolescence; the final three cover the period from adulthood to death.

psychosocial development A term used by Erikson to describe human development as a sequence of stages involving the resolution of crises that are primarily social.

identity In Erickson's theory, a term closely related to self. To achieve identity is to arrive at a clear notion of who one is. It includes the goals, values, and beliefs to which the individual is committed. One of the important tasks of adolescence is to select and develop a strong sense of identity.

Each of Erikson's stages is defined by a basic conflict resulting from the need to adapt to a changing social environment—hence the label *psychosocial* rather than *psychoanalytic*. And at each level, new competencies are required of the individual. In fact, resolution of the conflict that labels each stage requires a specific new competency.

Trust versus Mistrust For example, in the first year of life, according to Erikson, the infant has to develop competencies related to being able to trust. Trust is one of the basic components of a healthy personality. But in the first year of life, says Erikson (1959), there is a strong tendency to mistrust the world because so little is known about it. This presents a conflict with the infant's inclination to develop a trusting attitude and to become more independent. Hence the label for this stage: **trust versus mistrust**.

The most important person in an infant's life at this stage is the primary caregiver—usually the mother. Successful resolution of the conflict between trust and mistrust depends largely on the infant's relationship with this caregiver, and on the gradual realization that the world is predictable, safe, and loving. According to Erikson, if the world is unpredictable and the caregiver rejecting, the infant may grow up to be mistrustful and anxious.

Autonomy versus Shame and Doubt At first, infants can't intend to do something and then deliberately do it; they have no sense of themselves as authors of their own actions. They react rather than act, says Erikson. But during this second stage, corresponding to Freud's anal stage, they gradually begin to realize that some intentions can be acted upon—that, for example, the nipple can *deliberately* be sucked. With this realization, they begin to develop a sense of autonomy. However, this autonomy is threatened by children's inclination not to accept responsibility for their own actions, but instead to return to the comfort and security that characterized the first stage—hence the **autonomy versus shame and doubt** conflict (Erikson, 1961). If children are to resolve this conflict and develop a sense of autonomy, says

One of an infant's first important tasks, says Erikson, is to develop a sense of trust. Not falling too often helps.

Erikson, it's important that parents encourage attempts to explore and that they provide opportunities for independence. Overprotectiveness can lead to doubt and uncertainty in dealing with the world later. What the child needs, according to Erikson (1959), is a balance between parental firmness and flexibility.

We should note that here, as in all of Erikson's stages, the resolution of the psychosocial conflict is never absolutely final. For example, as Baltes and Silverberg (1994) note, the conflict between the urge to be both dependent and autonomous continues throughout the life span.

Initiative versus Guilt By the age of 4 or 5, children have resolved the crisis of autonomy, according to Erikson. In short, they have discovered that they are autonomous and independent, that they are somebody. They will now spend much of the remainder of their childhood trying to discover exactly who it is that they are (Erikson, 1959).

---

trust versus mistrust   The first of Erikson's stages (to age 2), marked by a conflict between the infant's need to develop trust and an urge to remain dependent.

autonomy versus shame and doubt   The second Erikson stage, about ages 18 months to 2 or 3 years, when the preschooler faces the challenge of developing a sense of mastery and control (autonomy) but has to give up some of the security of relying on parents.

True to his Freudian orientation, Erikson assumes that children initially try to discover who they are by attempting to be like their parents—that is, by *identifying* with them. During this stage they establish a wider physical environment, made possible by their greater freedom of movement. Their language development is sufficiently advanced for them to ask questions, understand answers, and also imagine all sorts of possibilities. In fact, says Erikson (1959), they can now imagine things that frighten them.

With their increasing exploration of the environment, children develop a sense of initiative. Not only are they autonomous, but they are also responsible for their behavior. Because the central process involved in resolving the **initiative versus guilt** conflict is one of identification, parents and family continue to be the most important influences in a child's development. It is important for them to encourage young children's sense of initiative and to nurture a sense of responsibility, says Erikson.

Industry versus Inferiority The fourth developmental stage, **industry versus inferiority**, corresponds to Freud's **latency stage**. Recall that in Freudian theory, this period is marked by an absence of heterosexual interest. Reflecting his Freudian orientation, Erikson describes this stage as one in which children manifest an increasing need to interact with and be accepted by peers—mainly same-sex peers. It now becomes crucial for children to discover that their selves, their identities, are significant; that they can do things; in short, that they are *industrious* and competent. Children now avail themselves of all opportunities to learn those things they think are of importance to their culture, hoping that by so doing they will become someone. Successful resolution of this stage's conflict depends to a large extent on the responses of significant social agencies—especially schools and teachers—to children's efforts. If the child's work is continually demeaned and seldom praised, the outcome may be a lasting sense of inferiority.

Identity versus Identity Diffusion Perhaps the most highly researched and widely discussed of all of Erikson's ideas relates to his fifth developmental stage. During this stage, which corresponds to Freud's genital period and spans adolescence, the child is faced with the daunting task of developing a strong sense of identity.

At its most basic level, the formation of an identity appears to involve arriving at a notion not so much of who one is, but rather of who one can be—in other words, of developing one of several potential selves. The source of conflict lies in the various possibilities open to adolescents—possibilities that are magnified by the variety of cultural models in the environment. Conflict and doubt over choice of identity lead to what Erikson terms **identity diffusion**. It is as though adolescents are torn between early acceptance of a clearly defined self and the dissipation of their energies as they experiment with a variety of roles. One of the primary functions of adolescence is to serve as a period during which the child need not make a final decision concerning self (as a *moratorium*, in Erikson's words). The development of identity during adolescence is discussed in detail in Chapter 12.

Adult Stages Erikson's description of development does not end with adolescence but continues throughout the entire life span. He describes three additional psychosocial conflicts that occur during adulthood and old age and require new competencies and adjustments. The first of these, **intimacy and solidarity versus isolation**, relates to the need to develop intimate relationships with others (as opposed to being isolated) and is especially important for marriage and parenthood. The second,

initiative versus guilt The third of Erikson's stages (2 or 3 to 6 years), marked by a developing sense of self and of responsibility, and a greater independence from parents.

industry versus inferiority Erikson's label for a developmental period spanning middle childhood, characterized by emphasis on interaction with peer.

latency stage The fourth of Freud's stages of psychosexual development, characterized by the development of the superego (conscience) and by loss of interest in sexual gratification. This stage is assumed to last from the age of 6 to 11 years.

identity diffusion Marcia's term for an adolescent state devoid of commitment or identity crisis; common in early adolescence.

intimacy and solidarity versus isolation Erikson's label for the developmental stage that spans early adulthood, marked by the need to develop close, caring relationships with others.

generativity versus self-absorption, describes a need to assume social, work, and community responsibilities that will be beneficial to others (that will be generative), rather than remaining absorbed in self. The third, **integrity versus despair**, concerns facing the inevitability of death and the need to realize that life has meaning—that we should not despair because its end is imminent.

Review of Erikson's Theory

Erikson's theory is sometimes referred to as a theory of the life cycle, of ego psychology, of psychosocial development, or as a psychoanalytically oriented theory concerned mainly with the development of healthy personality. Contrasted with Freud's views, Erikson presents a highly positive and optimistic picture of human development.

As just described, the development of children according to Erikson involves resolving a series of conflicts and crises. These developmental crises involve a conflict between new abilities or attitudes and inclinations that oppose them. Resolving the conflict results in the development of competence in some primarily social capability; hence the concept of psychosocial development. The resolution of conflicts is never perfected during one developmental phase but continues through succeeding stages; hence the concept of life cycle. Perhaps the most crucial crisis involves developing a strong sense of identity; hence the concept of ego psychology.

Although Erikson assigns ages to each of these psychosocial stages, the ages do little more than provide a very general guide. This is especially true during adulthood, when important social, physical, and emotional events such as retirement, children leaving home, illness, and death occur at widely varying ages and sometimes in a totally unpredictable sequence. Some of the important social and physical

changes of childhood are more predictable; hence the ages assigned to the psychosocial crises of childhood are more accurate.

Erikson's theory, like Freud's, does not lend itself well to experimental validation. What Erikson's theory provides is a very general framework for describing and interpreting some of the major changes that occur in the human life span. Its usefulness rests largely in the insights that may result from examining the lives of individuals within the context of the theory. (See *Concept Summary*.)

BEHAVIORISTIC APPROACHES

Freud and Erikson's psychoanalytic approaches have a number of important things in common: First, they are **developmental theories** (they are concerned with changes that occur in individuals over time); second, they are stage theories (development consists of progression through sequential stages); and third, they make important assumptions concerning the biological (inherited) aspects of behavior and personality.

Basic Assumptions of Behavioristic Approaches

Behavioristic approaches do not share any of the preceding characteristics to any important extent. They make few assumptions about biological predispositions (and certainly none about unconscious forces), and they don't describe sequential stages of increasing capabilities and competencies.

As the term implies, **behaviorism** focuses on actual behavior. Behavioristic theory is especially concerned with relationships between experience and behavior; consequently it makes extensive use of concepts such as *reinforcement* and *punishment*,

---

generativity versus self-absorption The Erikson stage spanning middle adulthood, marked by a need to be productive and useful to society despite tendencies to be highly concerned with the self.

integrity versus despair Erikson's label for the last developmental stage in the life span, marked by a need to make sense of one's life despite increasing tendencies toward despair in the face of old age and imminent death.

developmental theory Psychological theory concerned with systematic changes that define human development. Child developmental theories deal with changes from birth to adolescence; life-span developmental theories deal with the entire span of life (birth to death).

behaviorism A general term used to describe approaches to learning and development that are concerned primarily with the observable, objective components of behavior (such as stimuli and responses).

Erikson's Psychosocial Stages Compared to Freud's Psychosocial Stages

Erikson's Psychosocial Stages	Corresponding Freudian Psychosexual Stage	Principal Developmental Task	Important Influences for Positive Developmental Outcome
Trust vs. mistrust	Oral (0–18 months)	Developing sufficient trust in the world to explore it	Mother; warm, loving interaction
Autonomy vs. shame and doubt	Anal (18 months–2 or 3 years)	Developing feeling of control over behavior; realizing that intentions can be acted out	Supportive parents; imitation
Initiative vs. guilt	Phallic (2 or 3–6 years)	Developing a sense of self through identification with parents and a sense of responsibility for own actions	Supportive parents; identification
Industry vs. inferiority	Latency (6–11 years)	Developing a sense of self-worth through interaction with peers	Schools, teachers; learning and education; encouragement
Identity vs. identity diffusion	Genital (11 years through adolescence)	Developing a strong sense of identity—of ego (self); selecting among various potential selves	Peers and role models; social pressure
Intimacy vs. isolation	Genital (young adulthood)	Developing close relationships with others; achieving the intimacy required for long-term commitment	Spouse, colleagues, partners, society
Generativity vs. self-absorption	Genital (adulthood)	Assuming responsible adult roles in the community; contributing; being worthwhile	Spouse, children, friends, colleagues, community
Integrity vs. despair	Genital (older adulthood)	Facing death; overcoming potential despair; coming to terms with the meaningfulness of life	Friends, relatives, children, spouse, community and religious support

Myrleen Ferguson Cate/PhotoEdit

> **THOUGHT CHALLENGE:** *Erikson was optimistic and positive in his analyses of contemporary societies, notes Smelser (1996). He had visions of a highly ethical, peaceful, harmonious world.*
>
> *Phrase the contemporary world's (or your nation's) developmental stage as an Eriksonian type of conflict. As in the* Concept Summary *on Erikson and Freud, specify what **developmental tasks** and competencies might be involved in resolving this conflict, and what influences might be important for a positive outcome.*

Rewards and punishments, behaviorism insists, shape our behaviors. If the dog feels soft and warm and snuggles close when Holly hugs him, she is likely to reach and hug again. But if her reach and hug become too much a grab and yank and the dog tumbles her over in his haste to get away, she might be less likely to yank at the dog next time.

which describe how behavior may be encouraged or discouraged.

Behavioristic approaches to development (also referred to as learning theory approaches) make two fundamental assumptions: First, behavior can be reduced to responses or actions that can be observed, measured, and analyzed. Second, behavior is highly responsive to reinforcement (usually **rewards**) and punishment. Accordingly, the main goals of behavioristic theorists have been to discover the rules that govern relationships between a **stimulus** (plural, *stimuli:* conditions that lead to behavior) and a **response**, and to learn how responses can be controlled through the administration of rewards and punishments.

Note that many of these assumptions are also assumptions of the mechanistic model described earlier. According to the behavioristic model, experiences and circumstances—especially those that are reinforced or punished—are among the most important factors in shaping the course of our development. In some ways, this model asserts that our behavior is like the functioning of a machine. As long as we understand how the machine works, we are in a

position to predict its actions, given sufficient knowledge of immediate circumstances. The goal of the behavioristic theorist is to understand the human machine so well that by knowing enough about past functioning and immediate circumstances, it would be possible to predict behavior accurately and, in some instances, to control it as well.

The behavioristic approach is not only mechanistic but also highly contextualist in its emphasis on the importance of environmental influences. The rewards and punishments that are the causes and consequences of behavior are, in fact, context.

The behavioristic approach was introduced into American psychology through the work of John B. Watson (1878–1958) and B. F. Skinner (1904–1990) and led to a dramatic upheaval in psychology. Both theorists believed strongly in the importance of the environment as the principal force in shaping development. Both were convinced that development could be understood through an analysis of specific behaviors, the circumstances leading to them, and their consequences. Watson is associated with a

developmental tasks Sequential, age-related developmental milestones usually evident in new abilities or changes in attitudes or interests. Although many developmental tasks are common across cultures, some are specific to particular cultures.

reward An object, stimulus, event, or outcome that is perceived as pleasant and may therefore be reinforcing.

stimulus (plural *stimuli*) Any change in the physical environment capable of exciting a sense organ.

response Any organic, muscular, glandular, or psychic process that results from stimulation.

learning theory based on a model of **classical conditioning**; Skinner developed a model of **operant conditioning**. **Conditioning** refers to a process whereby certain behaviors are affected by the environment. Classical and operant conditioning are described and illustrated in the following sections.

Classical Conditioning

The name of the Russian physiologist, Ivan Pavlov (1927), will probably be forever associated with classical conditioning—and with introductory psychology courses. Ironically, however, he stumbled upon his most famous observation almost by accident. At the time, he had been conducting experiments on the digestive processes of dogs—work for which he was awarded no less than the 1904 Nobel prize in medicine and physiology! But while studying digestion, Pavlov noticed that the more experienced dogs in his laboratory began to salivate even before they had any food in their mouths. In fact, they began to drool as soon as they saw their keeper approaching. Because none of the dogs had ever eaten any of their keepers, Pavlov reasoned that they were salivating because they had formed some association that linked the sight of the keeper to the presentation of food. This observation led Pavlov to a series of investigations of a simple form of learning now called classical conditioning.

In the best known of these investigations, illustrated in Figure 2.1, meat powder is presented to the dog. The powder is termed an **unconditioned stimulus** (US) because it leads to a response (salivation) without any learning having to take place—in other

words, without *conditioning*. Because the salivation occurs in response to an unconditioned stimulus, it is labeled an **unconditioned response** (UR). Now the food powder is paired with another distinctive stimulus, such as the sound of a bell. The sound of the bell is initially a *neutral* stimulus: It does not lead to salivation by itself. But after the sound of the bell has been paired often enough with the meat powder, it becomes a **conditioned stimulus** (CS) which now leads readily to salivation—now termed a **conditioned response** (CR) because it occurs in response to a conditioned stimulus.

A Classical Example: Little Albert Watson believed that in the same way behaviors can be conditioned in animals, so, too, might they be in humans. For example, he reasoned, infants typically react with fear when they hear a sudden, loud noise. The noise is an unconditioned stimulus for an unconditioned fear response. It follows from what we know about classical conditioning that if a frightening noise were paired often enough with a neutral stimulus, the neutral stimulus might eventually become a conditioned stimulus that would reliably lead to a conditioned fear reaction.

In a widely known demonstration of this possibility, Watson and his assistant, Rosalie Rayner (Watson & Rayner, 1920) exposed an 11-month-old infant they called Little Albert to a white rat. In the beginning, Little Albert played fearlessly with the rat as he sat on his mattress. But then Watson (or Rayner, the point isn't clear from Watson's notes) pounded a 3-foot-long, 1-inch steel bar just behind

---

classical conditioning Also called learning through stimulus substitution, because it involves the repeated pairing of two stimuli so that a previously neutral (conditioned) stimulus eventually comes to elicit the same response (conditioned response) that was previously evoked by the first stimulus (unconditioned stimulus). This type of conditioning was first described by Pavlov.

operant conditioning A type of learning in which the probability of a response changes as a result of reinforcement. Much of the experimental work of B. F. Skinner investigates the principles of operant conditioning.

conditioning A term used to describe a simple type of learning whereby certain behaviors are determined by the environment.

unconditioned stimulus (US) A stimulus that elicits a response before learning. All stimuli capable of eliciting reflexive behaviors are examples of unconditioned stimuli. For example, food is an unconditioned stimulus for the response of salivation.

unconditioned response (UR) A response elicited by an unconditioned stimulus.

conditioned stimulus (CS) A stimulus that elicits no response—or elicits a global response initially, but as a result of being paired with an unconditioned stimulus and its response, acquires the capability of eliciting that same response. For example, a stimulus that is always present at the time of a fear reaction may become a conditioned stimulus for fear.

conditioned response (CR) A response that is elicited by a conditioned stimulus. A conditioned response resembles its corresponding unconditioned response. The two are not identical, however.

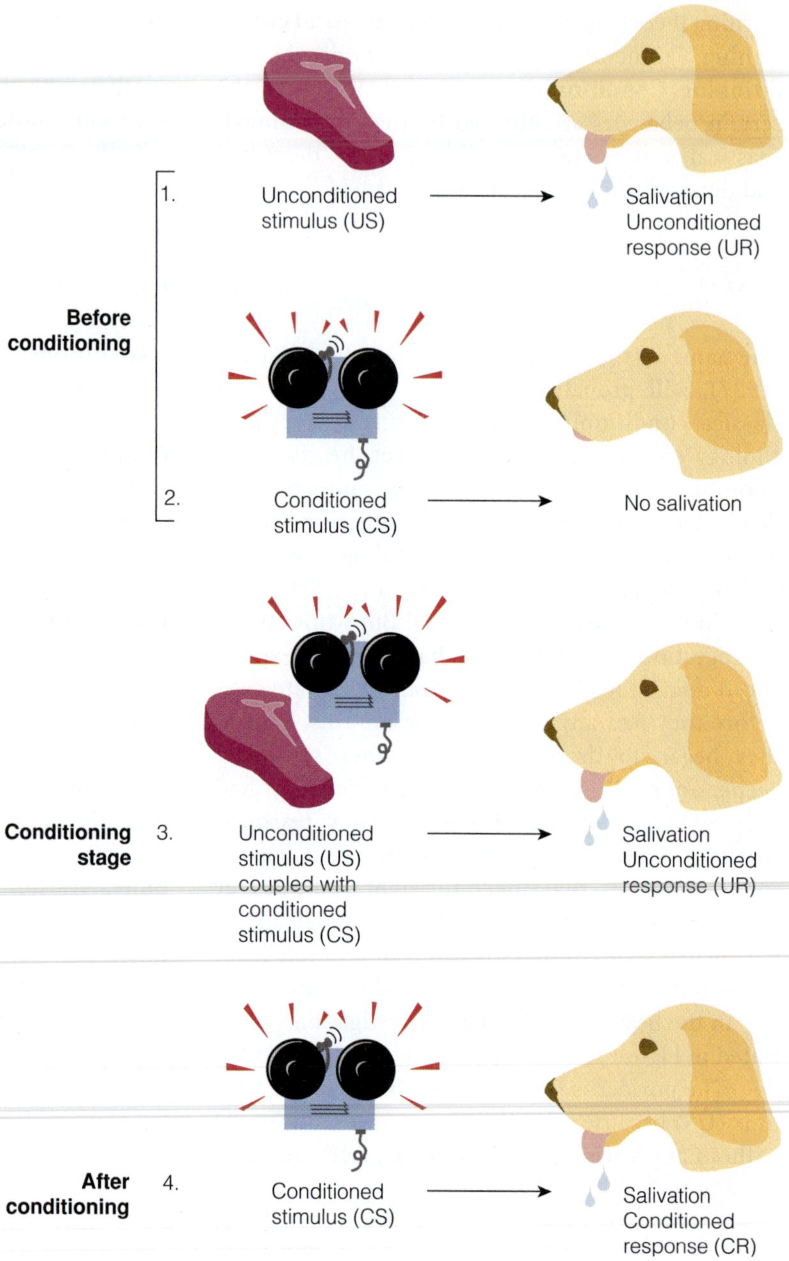

FIGURE 2.1 Classical conditioning. In (1), an unconditioned stimulus leads to an unconditioned response, whereas in (2) a conditioning stimulus does not lead to the same response. In (3), the unconditioned stimulus is paired with the conditioning stimulus a number of times so that eventually the conditioning stimulus alone elicits the original response, as in (4).

Before conditioning

1. Unconditioned stimulus (US) → Salivation Unconditioned response (UR)

2. Conditioned stimulus (CS) → No salivation

Conditioning stage

3. Unconditioned stimulus (US) coupled with conditioned stimulus (CS) → Salivation Unconditioned response (UR)

After conditioning

4. Conditioned stimulus (CS) → Salivation Conditioned response (CR)

Albert. But Albert was a stout little fellow; he didn't immediately burst out crying. So again, someone pounded on the bar. And this time, Albert began to whimper. "On account of his disturbed condition," wrote Watson, "no further tests were made for one week" (1930, p. 60).

A week later, Albert was brought into the lab once more and the banging and the rat were paired a total of five times. After that, whenever Albert saw the rat, he started to cry and tried to crawl away. "Surely," claimed Watson, "this is proof of the conditioned origin of a fear response. It yields an explanatory principle that will account for the enormous complexity in the emotional behavior of adults" (1930, p. 161).

Although Watson and Rayner's demonstration with Little Albert is more systematic than most situations in which we acquire emotional responses, Watson clearly believed that the results could be generalized, and that classical conditioning accounts for much of our emotional learning. Perhaps I am a case in point. When I was 5 years old, my grandfather's dog attacked me. I remember a tall, gaunt, wolflike creature with slobbering lips and huge fangs and a growl such as I now hear only in my nightmares. But in fact, it might have been a smallish dog, since I was only a small child. And perhaps it didn't rip me apart as savagely as I recall: The skin was broken in only two places. Yet when my car broke down on the way to the cabin last week, and I had to walk into a farmyard for assistance, the farm dog came bounding and barking toward me and, again, I had to fight back a strong feeling of fear—even though I have never been bitten again, and I have owned and raised and loved several of my own dogs. Perhaps I am conditioned to fear strange dogs more than most people do. That is, my intense fear of the dog that attacked me as a child has spilled over into an exaggerated fear of all strange dogs.

Operant Conditioning

Classical conditioning is sometimes useful for explaining simple learning such as my heightened reaction to strange dogs—in which my response is related to stimuli that precede it. But as Skinner (1953, 1957, 1961) points out, many human behaviors do not fit this description. Instead they are related to their possible consequences. Skinner coined the phrase "operant conditioning" to describe a type of learning in which an organism "operates" on the environment instead of simply reacting to stimuli.

Although he expressed considerable respect, and even admiration, for Pavlov and his discoveries, Skinner didn't agree that classical conditioning was useful for explaining many important human behaviors (Skinner, 1996). It seems clear, says Skinner, that an organism (whether rat, pigeon or human being) will repeat a response that has been rewarded and will suppress a response that has been punished (see Figure 2.2).

Reinforcement and Punishment Anything that increases the probability of a response occurring is said to be reinforcing. Reinforcement is *positive* when the *addition* of something, such as a reward, leads to an increase in behavior. It is negative when the *removal* of something, such as an aversive stimulus, leads to an increase in behavior. The important point is that both **positive reinforcement** and

positive reinforcement A stimulus that increases the probability of a response recurring as a result of being added to a situation after the response has occurred. It usually takes the form of a pleasant stimulus (reward) that results from a specific response.

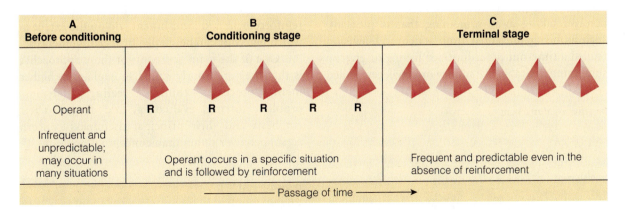

A Before conditioning	B Conditioning stage	C Terminal stage
Operant Infrequent and unpredictable; may occur in many situations	R R R R R Operant occurs in a specific situation and is followed by reinforcement	Frequent and predictable even in the absence of reinforcement

————— Passage of time —————▶

FIGURE 2.2 Schematic model of operant conditioning. In (A), the operant behavior alone is not rewarded. In (B), conditioning begins. The operant behavior takes place by chance; it is immediately reinforced. It occurs again, by chance or deliberately, and the reinforcement is repeated. As the timeline in the figure shows, repetition becomes more and more frequent as the learner catches on. Eventually, the operant behavior continues even without reinforcement at the terminal stage (C).

negative reinforcement increase the probability of a response occurring. A simple way of remembering the difference between the two is to recall that positive reinforcement involves a *reward* for behavior, whereas negative reinforcement involves *relief* from something unpleasant.

Unfortunately, real-life situations are more complicated than this black-and-white terminology suggests. Subjective terms such as *reward* and *relief*, although they aid our understanding, are misleading. Reinforcement and **punishment** have to do with effects rather than perceived pleasantness. Whereas reinforcement, whether positive or negative, serves to make a response more likely, punishment does not. Thus a parent or teacher who keeps "punishing" a child but who observes that the punished behavior becomes more rather than less frequent may well be reinforcing that behavior—or something (or someone?) else is. Similarly, sometimes a teacher's praise of a student's behavior leads to a drastic reduction of that behavior. Reinforcement? No. By definition this is punishment. The point is that pleasantness and unpleasantness are subjective; in contrast, reinforcement and punishment are objective phenomena defined by increases or decreases in the frequency of behavior.

In the same way as there are two kinds of reinforcement, there are two corresponding kinds of punishment. One kind involves an unpleasant consequence, like being beaten with a hickory stick. This is sometimes referred to as *presentation punishment* because it involves presenting an aversive stimulus (scolding). Another kind of punishment involves taking away something that is pleasant, such as being prevented from watching television (called a **time-out** procedure), or having to give up something desirable like money or privileges (called

response-cost punishment). This type of punishment is sometimes labeled *removal punishment*.

Extinction Another possibility, of course, is that the behavior will be neither reinforced nor punished, that it will simply have no consequences and will stop occurring—a phenomenon termed **extinction**.

Distinctions among the various kinds of reinforcement and punishment are illustrated in Figure 2.3. As the illustration makes clear, both may involve stimuli with pleasant or aversive effects, but whether these stimuli are added to or removed from the situation determines whether they are reinforcing or punishing. It is worth emphasizing again that both reinforcement and punishment are defined by their effects. Many types of **reinforcers**, some of which are described in Table 2.3, can be used systematically in childrearing and in the classroom. (See *In the News and on the Web:* "Fido Learns to Beg.")

Review of Behavioristic Approaches

Behavioristic theory explanations of human development emphasize the role of the environment in shaping our personalities and behaviors. Unlike psychoanalytic approaches, they are not concerned with psychodynamic conflicts and other hidden causes of behavior; and unlike the more cognitive approaches, which we discuss next, they don't often pay much attention to concepts such as understanding and knowing. Instead, they focus on the role of reinforcement and punishment and on the extent to which behavior can be shaped by its consequences.

One of the main criticisms of these approaches is that they are poorly suited to explaining higher mental processes—thinking, feeling, analyzing, problem solving, evaluating, and so on. Their emphasis and their principal usefulness concern actual behavior rather than conceptual processes.

---

negative reinforcement A stimulus that, when removed from the situation, increases the probability of occurrence of the response that precedes it. A negative reinforcer is usually an unpleasant or noxious stimulus that is removed when the desired response occurs.

punishment Involves either the presentation of an unpleasant stimulus or the withdrawal of a pleasant stimulus as a consequence of behavior. Punishment should not be confused with negative reinforcement, because punishment does not increase the probability of a response occurring; rather, it is intended to have the opposite effect.

time-out A form of punishment in which the transgressor is removed from ongoing (and presumably rewarding) activities.

---

response-cost A form of punishment involving the loss of a previously earned reward.

extinction In operant conditioning, the cessation of a response as a function of the withdrawal of reinforcement.

reinforcer A reinforcing stimulus. The effect of a reinforcer is reinforcement —an increase in the probability of a response recurring.

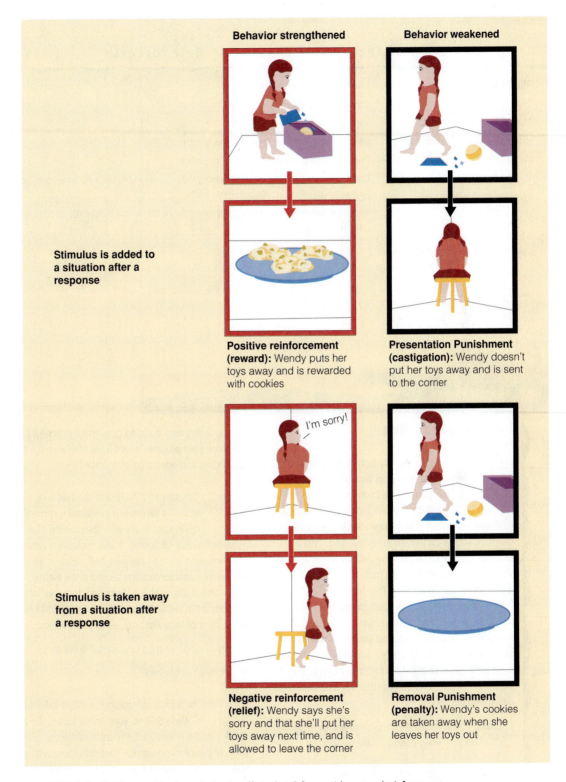

FIGURE 2.3   The four combinations of stimulus effects that define punishment and reinforcement.

TABLE 2.3
Examples of Classes of Reinforcers

REINFORCERS	EXAMPLES
Consumables	Candy, drinks, chocolates, fruit
Manipulatables	Toys, games, puzzles
Visual and auditory stimuli	Bells, buzzers, smiling puppets, green lights
Social stimuli	Praise, a pat on the back, a smile, applause
Token reinforcers	Coins, counters, points, or other tokens that can be exchanged for other reinforcers
Premack principle	Activities that occur frequently—and that are presumably pleasant (reading; watching television)—can be used to reinforce other, less frequently occurring activities (studying)

Sources: Bijou and Sturges (1959), Premack (1965).

IN THE NEWS AND ON THE WEB

Fido Learns to Beg

In exclusive and expensive Manhattan, aspiring apartment purchasers who own dogs and other pets are often turned away. Or, reports Tracie Rozhon, their pets are required to successfully audition for the building canine interview committee. Psychologist Susan Freedman heads up such a committee in her building. "We want to make sure they'll sit on command for the doorman," she says. "Then perhaps we'll have them interact with another dog, just to see how they handle it."

Interviews can be quite traumatic for owners and their pets, reports Rozhon; sometimes both need to pop tranquilizers to calm down. One couple, desperate to purchase a $400,000 apartment, admitted that they went so far as to switch dogs for the interview, substituting their dog's better-behaved sister for their own more delinquent pooch.

T. Rozhon "Fido is meeting the Co-op board and learning to beg." *The New York Times,* 9 January 2000, section 1, pp. 1, 39.

To Think About: How would you go about designing a training program, using operant conditioning principles, to train a dog for a building committee interview? Do you think your program might have relevance for the upbringing and education of children?

Resources: The first of the following two sites is a privately maintained website that deals specifically with the training of dogs, using operant conditioning. It also includes a variety of information on the principles and variables involved in operant conditioning. The second is the website of a national organization, *Behaviorists for Social Responsibility,* dedicated to increasing applications of the science of behavior analysis to social issues:

http://mmg2.im.med.umich.edu/~kleung/training.html

http://www.bfsr.org/

For additional readings, explore *InfoTrac College Edition,* your online library. Go to http://www.infotrac-college.com/wadsworth and use the passcode on the card that came with your text. Try the following search terms: operant conditioning, classical conditioning, and reinforcement.

A second criticism of behavioristic approaches is that by emphasizing the machinelike qualities of human functioning, they rob us of what we consider most human—namely, our ability to think and imagine, and our ability (real or imagined) to exercise significant control over our own behavior. Critics have claimed that in its attempts to reduce behavior to observable stimuli and responses, behaviorism dehumanizes us.

Although these criticisms may be reasonable and fair with respect to older and more extreme interpretations of behaviorism, they are less pertinent for more recent positions. Bijou (1989a), for example, notes that whereas Watson's theory describes an essentially passive organism, today's behaviorism sees the individual "as always being in an interactive relationship with the environment" (p. 68). In his words, the individual is "adjustive" rather than simply "reactive." However, Bijou's contemporary behaviorist does not view our ability to think, to imagine, or to feel as a cause of behavior. Bijou labels these cognitive activities implicit interactions. The primary concern of the behaviorist is not so much these implicit—hence, unobservable—interactions as it is the more observable interactions between stimuli and responses. Bijou cautions, however, that insofar as the contemporary behaviorist views people as adjustive rather than simply reactive, the environment is given a less important role in determining behavior. The causes of behavior, he claims, are not found in the environment alone, but rather in all the factors that are involved in a person's interactions, including history of past interactions.

On a more positive note, Skinner's theory, says Travis (1992), reflects that he was not only a scientist, a psychologist, and a philosopher, but also a poet. Operant theory continues to have a tremendous influence not only in theory and research but also in practical applications. Behavioristic approaches to development are sometimes very useful not only for understanding developmental change, but also for controlling it. The deliberate application of conditioning principles to change behavior (termed **behavior modification**) has proven extremely useful in a variety of settings, including the classroom and psychotherapy.

Theories, we should remember, are inventions whose purpose is to simplify, to explain, and sometimes to predict. Unlike orthodox views of traditional religions, they need not be accepted or rejected in their entirety. Elements from different theories can sometimes be combined to produce new theories—new insights—that go far beyond the original theories. A case in point is Albert Bandura's social cognitive theory, which in some ways serves as a transition between behaviorism (a concern with behavior) and cognitivism (a concern with more *cognitive* or intellectual matters). This theory is discussed in the next section. (See *Concept Summary* for an overview of behavioristic explanations of development.)

THOUGHT CHALLENGE: *Watson firmly believed that what we become is mainly a result of the experiences we have as we develop. "Give me a dozen healthy infants," he said in what may well be his most widely quoted (and longest) sentence, "well-formed, and my own specified world to bring them up in and I'll guarantee to take any one at random and train him to become any type of specialist I might select—doctor, lawyer, artist, merchant-chief and yes, even beggar-man and thief, regardless of his talents, penchants, tendencies, abilities, vocations, and race of his ancestors" (1930, p. 104).*

Elsewhere he wrote, somewhat less optimistically, "The world would be considerably better off if we were to stop having children for twenty years (except for experimental purposes) and were then to start again with enough facts to do the job with some degree of skill and accuracy" (Watson, 1928, 16).

What is your reaction to each of these statements?

SOCIAL COGNITIVE THEORY: ALBERT BANDURA

Operant learning might be a highly inefficient, and perhaps somewhat ineffective, way of learning if all we could do is wait for a correct and desirable

---

behavior modification A general term for the application of behavioristic principles (primarily principles of operant conditioning) in systematic and deliberate attempts to change behavior.

CONCEPT SUMMARY   Behavioristic Approaches to Development

Behavioristic approaches to development look at the relationship between the individual's experiences and behavior, paying special attention to antecedent conditions (stimuli) and to the consequences of behavior (reinforcement or punishment, for example). These approaches are illustrated in classical and operant conditioning.

Important Terms in Behaviorism	Capsule Definitions
Stimulus	Any change capable of eliciting a response
Response	A reaction resulting from stimulation
Unconditioned stimulus (US)	Stimulus that elicits a response prior to learning
Unconditioned response (UR)	Response to an unconditioned response
Conditioned stimulus (CS)	Stimulus that is effective after learning (conditioning)
Conditioned response (CR)	Response to a conditioned stimulus
Reinforcement	An increase in the probability of a behavior; the effect of a reinforcer
Reward	Consequence that is added to a situation and is reinforcing
Punishment	Presentation of an unpleasant stimulus or withdrawal of a pleasant one; has an effect opposite to that of reinforcement
Respondent	Behavior *elicited* by a stimulus
Operant	Behavior *emitted* by an organism

Classical Conditioning	Operant Conditioning
Associated with Watson and Pavlov	Associated with Skinner
Deals with responses that are elicited by stimuli as reactions *to* the environment	Deals with operants that are emitted by the organism as actions *upon* the environment

behavior (**operant**) to be emitted, and then hope that subsequent circumstances might prove reinforcing. Consider, for example, the problem of learning how to drive a car. Would it be reasonable to expect that a totally inexperienced adolescent, given a set of keys and a car, would quickly learn to drive simply as a result of, by chance, emitting the right sequence of operants and being sufficiently reinforced by the sound of the motor starting and the sensation of moving in some desired direction without running up against a tree?

In fact, it would be difficult to learn to drive in this way. But the point is that there aren't a lot of 15-year-olds with no experience of cars. Almost all of them have seen their parents and others driving; some have even read instruction booklets describing rules of the road; they've listened to peers and siblings talk about

operant The label used by B. F. Skinner to describe a response not elicited by any known or obvious stimulus. Most significant human behaviors appear to be operant. Such behaviors as writing a letter or going for a walk are operants, if no known specific stimulus elicits them.

model A pattern for behavior that can be copied by someone else.

how you start and drive cars. In Bandura's terms, they have been exposed to many different **models**.

Much of our learning, says Albert Bandura, is **observational learning** (or learning through **imitation**). It results from imitating models. But learning through imitation, Bandura (1977, 1997) points out, is really a form of operant learning. That's because an imitative behavior is much like an operant; it's not just a response to a specific stimulus (as is the case for a **respondent**), but rather an **emitted response**. And imitative behaviors, say Bandura and Walters (1963), are often reinforced in one of two ways: **Direct reinforcement** occurs when the consequences of an imitative behavior lead to reinforcement—as, for example, when a child learns to say *milk* as a result of imitating a parent, and is then given a flagon of that liquid; **vicarious reinforcement** involves a kind of second-hand reinforcement—as when observing someone else being rewarded leads to further imitation.

The Processes of Observational Learning

In addition to being based on the principles of operant conditioning, and perhaps even more important, Bandura's (1997) theory recognizes the tremendous significance of our ability to anticipate the consequences of our actions, to symbolize, to ferret out cause-and-effect relationships. The power of models, he insists, is largely due to their *informative* function.

Ian Shaw/Tony Stone Images

Models do not all have the same influence on children. Children are most likely to imitate people who are important to them and with whom they identify (such as parents, siblings, and close friends); similarly, they are most likely to imitate behaviors that are highly valued.

---

observational learning Learning through imitation.

imitation The complex process of learning through observation of a model.

respondent Used by Skinner in contrast to the term *operant*. A respondent is a response elicited by a known specific stimulus. Unconditioned responses of the type referred to in classical conditioning are examples of respondents.

emitted response A response not elicited by a known stimulus but simply emitted by the organism. An emitted response is an operant.

direct reinforcement Reinforcement that occurs as a direct consequence of a behavior—like getting paid to work.

vicarious reinforcement Reinforcement that results from observing someone else being reinforced. In imitative behavior, observers frequently act as though they are being reinforced when in fact they are not being reinforced; rather, they are aware, or simply assume, that the model is being reinforced.

From observing models we learn not only how to do certain things but also what the consequences of our behaviors are likely to be. Accordingly, four distinct processes are involved in observational learning.

Attention First, we have to pay attention. Children aren't likely to learn very much from a model if they pay no attention to important aspects of that model's behavior. Whether they attend, Bandura informs us, depends a great deal on the value of the model's behavior. (Is it important for the observer to be able to swear like that? Throw a ball in that way? Cock his head in just that fashion?) Also, behavior that is not very distinctive, that occurs only rarely, or that is complex and difficult to perform is less likely to be attended to. Not surprisingly, the most effective models—those commanding the greatest attention—are those that are most attractive, most trustworthy, and most powerful (in terms of social power, which can come from knowledge, money, or prestige) (Brewer & Wann, 1998). It's one of the reasons that actors and sports stars can be such effective models.

Retention Second, children must not only attend, but must also be able to remember. This, explains Bandura, implies being able to represent mentally the behavior to be imitated, either in words or images.

Reproduction Third, the observer must be able to reproduce the behavior that has been attended to and retained (represented mentally). This might require certain motor and physical capabilities, as well as the ability to monitor and correct ongoing behavior, says Bandura.

Motivation Finally, in observational learning as in all learning, there must be **motivation** (reasons for behavior), explains Bandura. Without motivation, many behaviors that are observed and potentially learned will not be performed. There is an important distinction between *acquisition* and *performance*: Much is acquired (learned, in other words) but does not become part of behavior (is not performed).

Manifestations of Observational Learning

A model may be an actual (perhaps very ordinary) person whose behavior serves as a guide, a blueprint, an inspiration for somebody else; a model might also be symbolic, says Bandura. **Symbolic models** include book characters, oral or written instructions, pictures, mental images, cartoon or film characters, television actors, and so on. Also, computer-based models are used extensively for various kinds of training programs, such as pilot training with computer-controlled simulators

(Shebilske et al., 1998). Nor are models always examples of more advanced skills and competencies displayed by older people, as might be the case when children imitate adults. Abravanel and Ferguson (1998) report that even 2- and 3-year-olds imitate and learn from each other. In contrast, Lindberg, Kelland, and Nicol (1999) report a fascinating study in which horses did not learn to open a feed bin as a result of watching other "model" horses who already knew how to open the bin! If nobody had opened the bin for them, they would have starved.

Bandura and Walters (1963) describe three different effects of imitation on learning in children: the modeling effect, inhibitory-disinhibitory effects, and the eliciting effect.

The Modeling Effect The **modeling effect**, according to Bandura and Walters, is the learning of novel behavior through imitation. That Eskimo children learn Inuit rather than Greek is evidence that they model the language that surrounds them. (That, however, is not the whole story with respect to language learning; see Chapter 5.)

The Inhibitory-Disinhibitory Effects The **inhibitory effect** is the suppression of deviant behavior, usually as a result of seeing a model being punished for a similar behavior. The **disinhibitory effect** is the opposite: It's the appearance of previously suppressed deviant behavior, often as a result of the model's being reinforced. For example, if Edward, who is deliberately drug-free, has friends who begin to use marijuana, the amount of reinforcement he thinks they receive (in terms of the "fun" they seem to be having, their apparently increased social prestige, acceptance by the group, and so on) may disinhibit his use of drugs. If, as a result, Edward begins to smoke dope, it won't be that he has learned something new, as in modeling, but that his previously suppressed "deviant" behavior has been disinhibited. But if Edward later sees his friends apprehended and

---

motivation Our reasons for behaving. What initiates behavior, directs it, and accounts for its cessation.

symbolic models Nonhuman models such as movies, television programs, oral and written instructions, or religious, literary, musical, or folk heroes.

modeling effect Imitative behavior involving the learning of a novel response.

inhibitory effect The suppression of deviant behavior as a result of observing a model.

disinhibitory effect The appearance of previously suppressed deviant behavior as a function of observing a model.

punished, or perhaps if he sees them experiencing ill effects from the drug (like a frightening drop in school grades, or failure to make the football team), he might then stop using marijuana. Again, there is no new learning involved, although there is a change in behavior resulting from the influence of models; this change illustrates the *inhibitory* effect.

The Eliciting Effect The **eliciting effect**, say Bandura and Walters, is illustrated when the model's behavior leads to *related* but not identical behavior in the model—behavior that is neither novel (as in the modeling effect) nor deviant (as in the inhibitory-disinhibitory effect). It's as though the model's behavior suggests some response to the observer and therefore elicits that response. A child "acting up" in school may elicit misbehavior in his classmates. They may not imitate his behavior precisely, but may simply engage in the same general type of behavior or misbehavior.

The three effects of imitation are summarized in Table 2.4.

Judgments of Self-Efficacy

As we have just seen, Bandura's theory is a *behavioristic* theory of imitation: It's based on the assumption that much important learning involves various models that act as social influences on children, and that imitative behavior becomes more or less probable as a function of its consequences.

But at another level, the theory is a *cognitive* one: As we saw, it gives a central role to children's ability to symbolize—that is, to reason, to imagine, to anticipate the outcomes of behavior. There is no doubt, Bandura (1977) assures us, that reinforcement controls much of our behavior, but it doesn't control us blindly. Its effects depend largely on our awareness of the relationship between our behavior and its outcomes. As Bruner (1985) points out, reinforcement often occurs a long time after the behavior it follows, as happens, for example, when you study for an examination. In such cases, it isn't reinforcement (or the possibility of punishment) that affects behavior directly so much as your ability to anticipate the long-term consequences of behavior.

Recently, Bandura's increasingly cognitive orientation has become even more evident in a series of studies and books that deal with what is termed **self-referent thought**—thought that has to do with our selves, with our own mental processes (Bandura, 1986, 1993, 1997). Among other things, self-referent thought deals with our estimates of our abilities, with our notions about how capable and effective we are in our dealings with the world and with others. A

---

eliciting effect That type of imitative behavior in which the observer does not copy the model's responses but simply behaves in a related manner.

self-referent thought Ideas or thoughts that have to do with the self and, specifically, with self-knowledge. Self-referent thoughts are often evaluative; they deal with our personal estimates of how effective we are in our dealings with the world and with others.

TABLE 2.4
Bandura and Walters's Three Effects of Imitation

TYPE OF EFFECT	DESCRIPTION	EXAMPLE
Modeling Effect	Learning novel behavior as a result of observing a model.	After watching a cartoon, Karen whips her little brother with her aquatic "noodle," yelling, "I have the power!"
Inhibitory-Disinhibitory effect	Stopping or starting some deviant behavior as a result of seeing a model punished or rewarded for similar behavior.	Ralph gets rid of all his cigarette butts after his brother is caught shooting butts at the cat.
Eliciting effect	Engaging in behavior related to that of a model.	Robin takes voice lessons after her cousin becomes a hero by playing a trumpet solo at the family reunion.

very specific term has been coined to describe our estimates of our own effectiveness: **self-efficacy**.

Efficacy means competence in dealing with the environment. The most efficacious people are those who can most effectively deal with a variety of situations, even when these situations are ambiguous or highly stressful. Thus self-efficacy has two separate but related components: the skills that are required for the successful performance of a behavior and an individual's beliefs about personal effectiveness. From a psychological point of view, it is not so much the skills component that is important, but rather a person's own perceptions of self-efficacy.

Developing Notions of Self-Efficacy Not long ago my oldest son said something that surprised and alarmed me. We were talking about the various foolish things each of us had done when we were very young. I didn't have that much to say. He did.

"I thought I'd be able to fly from the upstairs window if I held a really clean sheet over my head like Superman's cape," he said. "One day I decided to fly but I couldn't figure out where the clean sheets were. I thought about taking one off the bed, but I was worried it wouldn't work with a dirty sheet. So I didn't jump."

Young children don't have very good notions of their personal capabilities, says Bandura (1986). Their self-judgment, and their corresponding self-guidance, is less than perfect. As a result, without external controls they, like my son, would often be in danger of severely hurting themselves. Since they cannot impose the internal self-judgment, "I can't do that," they require the external judgment, "*You* can't do that." As Harter (1988) reports, most young children have an exaggerated and unrealistic notion of self. For example, when asked if they think they are "smart" or "not smart," there is a definite bias in the direction of "smart."

The sense of personal control over behavior that is essential for judgments of personal efficacy begins to develop very early in infancy, according to Bandura (1986). Some of its roots lie in an infant's

discovery that looking at the mother makes her look back in return; that smiling or crying draws her attention; that waving a hand makes her smile. Later, as infants begin to move around freely, they begin to learn more about the effects of their behaviors—and also more about their own effectiveness. The direct effects of an individual's behavior, Bandura suggests, are one of four important sources of influence on judgments of self-efficacy. He labels these influences *enactive* because they result directly from *action*.

Interestingly, however, the individual who is mostly successful doesn't invariably arrive at highly positive judgments of self-efficacy—although that is more likely to be the case than not. Nor does lack of success always correspond to negative judgments. As Weiner (1980a) points out, there are different factors to which we can attribute success or lack of success. Some of these, like ability and effort, are under personal control and reflect directly on the efficacy of the individual. Others, such as luck or the difficulty of the task, are not under personal control and do not, therefore, have very direct implications for judgments of self-efficacy.

A second influence on the development of notions of self-efficacy is *vicarious* (second-hand); it comes from observing the performance of others. Even as children we arrive at notions of how effective we are partly on the basis of comparisons we make between ourselves and others. And, as Bandura (1981) suggests, the most informative comparisons we can make are those that involve others whose performance is similar to ours. A 12-year-old who trounces his 6-year-old brother in a game of skill and intelligence learns very little about his personal effectiveness. Similarly, if he, in turn, is soundly defeated by his father, he may not have learned much more—except, perhaps, a touch of humility.

A third source of influence on self-judgments, Bandura (1986) argues, is *persuasion*. "You can do it, Guy. I know you can. Sing for us. We love the way you sing." (This is a totally fanciful illustration; even dumb animals don't much like the way I sing.) Persuasion, depending on the characteristics of the persuader and on the relationship between persuader and "persuadee," can sometimes change an individual's self-efficacy judgments and lead that person either to attempt things that would not otherwise be attempted or not to attempt them ("Guy, they're just flattering you. Please don't sing").

self-efficacy Describes our estimates of our personal effectiveness. The most efficacious individuals are those who deal most effectively with a variety of situations, especially those that are ambiguous or stressful.

The fourth source of influence on self-efficacy judgments is a person's level of **arousal**, according to Bandura. The word *arousal* can have a lot of meanings; in this context, its most important meaning has to do with intensity of an immediate emotional reaction. Situations that produce very high arousal are shocking, sudden, frightening, intensely exciting, deeply moving—in short, situations that lead to profound positive or negative emotions. High arousal can significantly affect self-judgments in either direction. For example, extreme fear might conceivably lead to specific judgments of high or low efficacy. A mountain climber might, because of fear that threatens to turn his legs to jelly, decide that he is not capable of completing a climb. In contrast, a mother who finds her child trapped beneath an overturned automobile might, in a sudden surge of emotion, believe that she is capable of lifting the vehicle off the child.

In summary, four separate sources of influence can affect an individual's judgments of self-efficacy, according to Bandura. Bandura calls these sources enactive (based on the outcome of the individual's own actions), vicarious (based on comparisons between the person's performance and the performance of others), persuasory (the result of persuasion), and emotive (the result of arousal or emotion).

The Importance of Self-Efficacy Judgments As Bandura phrases it, "Perceived self-efficacy refers to beliefs in one's capabilities to organize and execute the courses of action required to produce given attainments" (1997, p. 3). This aspect of self-knowledge is critical, says Bandura. Among other things, it's an important determiner of what we do and don't do. In fact, in some situations, self-efficacy judgments may be a better predictor of behavior than relevant skills are (Caprara et al., 1998). That's because under most circumstances, children (and adults, too) don't seek out and undertake activities in which they expect to perform badly. "Efficacy beliefs," says Bandura (1993), "influence how people feel, think, motivate themselves, and behave" (p. 118).

Judgments of personal efficacy affect not only our choices of activities and settings, but also the amount of effort we are willing to put out when faced with difficulties. The stronger our beliefs about our efficacy, the more likely we are to persist and the greater will be the effort expended. But if our notions of self-efficacy are not very favorable, we may abandon difficult activities after very little effort and time.

Perceived self-efficacy influences our thoughts and emotions as well as our behaviors. Those who judge that their effectiveness is low are more likely to evaluate their behaviors negatively and to see themselves as being inadequate. Not surprisingly, negative evaluations of personal effectiveness have been shown to be related to depression and emotional problems in children (Bandura et al., 1999).

Finally, notions of self-efficacy are intimately linked with what we think and feel about ourselves. As Kegan (1982) puts it, we want to *mean* something. We want others to think we are worthwhile, important, effective. And we're not likely to believe that is the case if we don't have positive evaluations of our personal effectiveness. That's why parents, schools, and peers are so important: Each tells us a great deal about how well we can do things—or how badly.

And so it continues throughout life. In adolescence we are faced with new tasks, new challenges—as we are, too, throughout adulthood and into old age. At every step these new challenges require new competencies and new behaviors—and new judgments of personal effectiveness.

Review of Social Cognitive Theory

Bandura's social cognitive theory is an important bridge between behavioristic theories, which try to explain development entirely through observable, nonmental events like stimuli and responses, and cognitive theories, which are mainly concerned with mental events. The behavioristic roots of Bandura's theory are apparent in the notion that certain social behaviors (notably, imitative behaviors) are reinforced in various ways and are therefore more likely

---

arousal As a physiological concept, arousal refers to changes in functions such as heart rate, respiration rate, electrical activity in the cortex, and electrical conductivity of the skin. As a psychological concept, arousal refers to degree of alertness, awareness, vigilance, or wakefulness. Arousal varies from very low (coma or sleep) to very high (panic or high anxiety).

to recur. The theory's cognitive orientation is evident in its recognition of the power of our ability to imagine the consequences of our actions. It is our anticipation of the weight of our pay packets—or of the taste of ice cream—that keeps us running at the wheel or trying to climb the ladder, not just a blind reaction to external stimulation.

Bandura's theory is also a good example of how theories need not be static and unchanging, but rather can change with new information and new beliefs. Thus his recent writings deal with self-efficacy and with the notion that what we think, feel, and do is profoundly influenced by our judgments of our personal effectiveness.

Although the theory provides a useful way of looking at some aspects of development, especially at social motivation, it is not a comprehensive theory meant to account for most of the important observations in human development; in contrast, Jean Piaget's theory of cognitive development, discussed next, attempts to be comprehensive. (See the *Concept Summary* for an overview of Bandura's social cognitive theory.)

A COGNITIVE APPROACH: PIAGET

Psychoanalytic theorists are concerned primarily with personality development; behavioristic theorists emphasize behavior and its consequences; a third group of theorists focus on the intellectual (cognitive) development of children.

CONCEPT SUMMARY

Bandura's Social Cognitive Theory

Important Concepts	Explanations, Illustrations, Examples	
Observational learning	Learning through imitation of models that can be *symbolic* (like fictional heroes or written instructions) or real-life	
Effects of imitation are evident in	• Modeling effect—the acquisition of novel behavior • Inhibitory-disinhibitory effect—appearance or suppression of deviant behavior • Eliciting effect—engaging in *related* behavior that is neither novel nor deviant	
Self-efficacy	Private judgments about personal effectiveness and competence; fundamentally important in determining what we do; important influences on our sense of well-being (or of unhappiness)	
Important sources of information that shape judgments of self-efficacy	**Sources of Influence**	**Information that might lead Joan to positive self-evaluations**
	Enactive	Her professor invites her to apply for the more advanced horseshoeing program.
	Vicarious	She knows that Guy studied really hard, but will not be admitted into Horseshoeing 307.
	Persuasory	Her boyfriend tells her she can probably win any scholarship she wants.
	Emotive	She becomes extremely excited as she contemplates her future as head ferrier in the stables at the track.

Cognition is the art or faculty of knowing. Cognitive theorists are concerned with how we know—that is, with how we obtain, process, and use information. For many decades, the most widely cited and most influential of all theories of cognitive development has been that of Swiss theoretician Jean Piaget (Stanton, 1993). His is a complex, far-reaching theory developed over a career spanning more than half a century (he was born in 1896 and died in 1980, still highly active at the age of 84). By one count, Piaget produced more than 52 books and almost 500 articles (Smith, 1993). His work continues to be influential although neo-Piagetians now seek to refine his findings, and some researchers largely dismiss his stage theory.

Some of the main aspects of Piaget's theory are introduced briefly in the following sections. More specific details of the theory, and the contributions of other theorists to cognitive development, are discussed in the chapters that deal chronologically with children's intellectual development (Chapters 5, 7, 9, and 11).

Piaget's Basic Ideas

Probably the most basic of all of Piaget's ideas, says von Glasersfeld (1997), is this: *Human development is a process of adaptation. And the highest form of adaptation is cognition* (or knowing). This idea stems directly from the fact that Piaget was trained as a biologist rather than as a psychologist. Consistent with his early training, he began his study of children by asking two of the most fundamental questions of biology: (1) What is it that enables organisms to adapt to their environments and survive? and (2) What is the most useful way of classifying living organisms? Rephrased so that they apply to the development of children, these questions become: (1) What are the characteristics and capabilities of children that allow them to adapt to their environments? and (2) What is the most useful way of classifying or ordering child development? Piaget's answers for these two questions are the basis for his theory: *assimilation* and *accommodation lead*

to adaptation is his highly abbreviated answer for the first question; *development can be ordered in stages* answers the second. We look at the meaning of these answers in the next two sections.

Assimilation and Accommodation Lead to Adaptation

The newborn infant, says Piaget, is in many ways a helpless little organism, unaware that the world out there is real, lacking any storehouse of thoughts with which to reason or any capacity for intentional behaviors, and having only a few simple reflexes. But these helpless little creatures are also remarkable sensing machines. Furthermore, they seem to be naturally predisposed to acquiring and processing a tremendous amount of information. They continually seek out and respond to stimulation. As a result, the sucking, reaching, grasping, and other reflexes that are present at birth become more complex, more coordinated, and eventually purposeful. The process by which this occurs is adaptation. And, as the answer to the first of the questions of biology states, **assimilation** and **accommodation** are the processes that make adaptation possible.

Assimilation involves making a response that has already been learned, or that was present at birth; to accommodate is to *change* a response. For example, an infant is born with the capability to suck—what Piaget calls a sucking **schema** (also *scheme*, plural: *schemata* or sometimes *schemas* or *schemes*). The sucking schema allows the infant to assimilate a nipple to the behavior of sucking. Similarly, a child who has learned the rules of addition can assimilate a problem such as 2 + 2 (can respond appropriately because of previous learning). Often, however, our understanding of the world is insufficient to deal

---

cognition Mental processes such as thinking, knowing, and remembering. Theories of cognition attempt to explain intellectual development and functioning.

assimilation In Piaget's theory, the act of incorporating objects or aspects of objects to previously learned activities. To assimilate is, in a sense, to ingest or to use something that is previously learned; more simply, the exercising of previously learned responses.

accommodation The modification of an activity or an ability that a child has already learned, to conform to environmental demands. Piaget's description of development holds that assimilation and accommodation are the means by which an individual interacts with the world and adapts to it.

schema (also scheme) The label used by Piaget to describe a unit in cognitive structure. It usually labels a specific activity: the looking scheme, the grasping scheme, the sucking scheme.

First is the nipple, a bulbous thing that, from birth, infants know what to do with—in Piaget's terms, they can assimilate to the activity of sucking. But even a well-practiced activity (Piaget calls it a schema) like sucking a nipple needs to be changed if it is also to accommodate fingers—and sometimes even toes or entire feet. Assimilation and accommodation are the two drivers of cognitive growth.

Laurence Monneret/Tony Stone Images

with the current situation. The newborn's sucking schema is adequate for ordinary nipples but does not work quite as well for fingers and toes; the preschooler's understanding of numbers is sufficient for keeping track of toys but is inadequate for impressing kindergarten teachers. The changes in information and behavior that are required by these new situations define accommodation. In short, assimilation involves reacting on the basis of previous learning and understanding; accommodation involves a change in understanding. And the interplay of assimilation and accommodation leads to change and adaptation. (See Chapter 5 for further illustrations of these concepts.)

Development Can Be Ordered in Stages According to Piaget, cognitive development occurs in four distinct stages, each marked by the child's strikingly different perceptions of the world and different adaptations to it. Each stage is the product of learning that occurred in earlier stages, says Piaget, and each is a preparation for the next stage.

Four Stages of Development

Piaget's four major stages of cognitive development are listed in the *Concept Summary* on page 73 and are briefly discussed next. (They are covered in greater detail in Chapters 5, 7, 9, and 11.)

Sensorimotor Period In the very beginning, says Piaget, infants understand the world only in the here and now; it is real only when it is being acted on and sensed. When the ball is no longer being touched, looked at, or chewed, it doesn't exist. It isn't until toward the end of the second year that children finally realize that objects have a permanence and an identity of their own—that they continue to exist when they are not in view. By the end of the **sensorimotor period**, children have also begun to acquire language and are progressing rapidly from a sensorimotor to a more cognitive intelligence.

Preoperational Thinking Following the acquisition of language, children enter the period of **preoperational thought** (ages 2 to 7). At this stage, says Piaget, children rely excessively on perception rather than on logic. He used what he called "conservation experiments" to support his claim. In one of these experiments, children are presented with two glasses

sensorimotor period The first stage of development in Piaget's classification. It lasts from birth to approximately age 2 and is so called because children understand their world primarily through their activities toward it and sensations of it.

preoperational thought The second of Piaget's four major stages, lasting from about 2 to 7 or 8 years. It consists of two substages: intuitive thinking and preconceptual thinking.

that contain equal amounts of water. The experimenter then pours the contents of one glass into a tall, thin tube—or, alternatively, into a wide, shallow dish. The child is then asked whether each of the containers still has the same amount of water or whether one container has more than the other. So-called preoperational children, relying on the appearance of the two containers, now believe that the tall tube has more because it is higher (or less because it is thinner)—or that the shallow dish has more because it is "fatter" (or less because it is shorter). Even when they realize that the water could be poured back into its original container so that both glasses would again appear equal, preoperational children continue to rely on perception (on actual appearance) rather than on reasoning. (See Chapter 7 for more details.)

Concrete Operations During the next major stage, children begin to rely less on perception and to think more logically, using what Piaget labels **concrete operations** (ages 7 to 11 or 12). An operation is a thought—what Piaget called an *internalized action*. In this sense, it is a mental action or, more precisely, an operation performed on ideas according to certain rules of logic. These rules of logic permit the concrete operational child to scoff at the ridiculous simplicity of a conservation problem: Of course there is the same amount of water in both containers because none has been added or taken away, because one misleading dimension is compensated for by the other (it is taller but thinner), and because the act of pouring the water from one container to the other can be reversed to prove that the quantity of water has not changed. Concrete operational children are capable of this kind of logic, but it is a logic that is tied to real, concrete objects and events.

Formal Operations In time, many children will finally be able to reason logically about hypothetical situations or events. When they can go from the real to the merely possible or from the possible to the

actual, finally free from the restrictions that once bound them to the concrete world, they are in the last stage of cognitive development, described by Piaget as **formal operations** (beginning about age 11 or 12). During this stage, thinking may be characterized by the ability to manipulate abstract ideas and to reason using advanced laws of logic. Piaget believed that during this stage children's thought has the *potential* of becoming as logical as it will ever be. Note the emphasis on the word *potential*; many of us remain strangers to the deductive logic of formal operations throughout our lives. However, as Ricco (1993) argues, the logic of formal operations is a logic concerned with hypothetical states of affairs. It is the kind of logic that might be very useful for the sorts of problems that schools and universities present. But for many of life's problems, other forms of logic—especially those dealing with meaning, and those that are more sensitive to doubt, relativity, and probability—are more appropriate. Piaget recognized this, and in some of his more recent writings he discusses a formal operations logic of meanings (see Piaget & Garcia, 1991).

Review of Piaget's Theory

Child development, in Piaget's view, is best described as the emergence of progressively more logical forms of thought—that is, as the development of ways of thinking that become increasingly more effective in freeing children from the present and allowing them to use powerful symbol systems to understand and manipulate the environment. According to Piaget's theory, the major characteristics of thinking in each of the four developmental stages influence all aspects of children's understanding of the world, including their notion of space, time, numbers, reality, causality, and so on.

Piaget's theory has been one of the most influential child development theories of the twentieth century. As Beilin (1992) suggests, trying to assess its influence is a little like asking about Shakespeare's

---

concrete operations The third of Piaget's four major developmental stages, lasting from age 7 or 8 to approximately 11 or 12, characterized primarily by children's ability to deal with concrete problems and objects, or objects and problems easily imagined in a tangible sense.

formal operations The last of Piaget's four major developmental stages. It begins around the age of 11 or 12 and lasts until about 14 or 15. It is characterized by children's increasing ability to use logical thought processes.

impact on English literature. Writers such as Elkind (1996) and Flavell (1996) suggest that Piaget actually founded the field of cognitive development, introduced some of its most important concepts, shaped the direction of an enormous percentage of its research, and gave us some of the most useful conclusions that characterize the field.

At the same time, however, Piaget's theory has been widely criticized. For example, Piaget has often been criticized for using small samples, for conducting uncontrolled investigations, for being the sole investigator, and for not using sophisticated measuring instruments or advanced statistical analyses (Thomas, 1999). Supporters argue that the fact that the ages at which different children reach specific stages can vary considerably does not invalidate the basic metaphor of the theory—a biological/philosophical metaphor that tries to explain intellectual adaptation.

Still, there is considerable evidence that Piaget underestimated the information-processing capabilities of infants and young children (Wellman & Gelman, 1992). This probably is related to Piaget's lack of tools and instruments with sufficient sensitivity to detect infants' cognitive capacities. Recent studies of infants' responsiveness to stimulation often make use of sophisticated instruments that measure changes in heart and respiration rate, movements of the eyeballs, changes in pupil size, brainwave activity, and so on—all devices not available to Piaget in the 1920s and 1930s.

Some critics argue that Piaget overestimated the importance of motor activity in infants' cognitive development and underplayed the importance of perception, most especially of visual perception (Bullinger, 1985). Others criticize Piaget because his theory says relatively little about individual differences among children, about the factors that might account for these differences, or about what can be done to promote intellectual development. In addition, the language and concepts of the theory are sometimes difficult, and it is not always clear that terms such as *assimilation* and *accommodation* add significantly to our understanding of human behavior.

One additional weakness of Piaget's theory is that it appears to assume that development ceases with adolescence. Although Piaget recognized that the abilities characterizing formal operations, the final developmental stage, are not always achieved during adolescence (or even in adulthood), he described no further developmental stages—as have a number of others, including Erikson and, later, Labouvie-Vief (1986) and Basseches (1984).

Despite these criticisms, Piagetian theory has clearly been a major cognitive developmental theory, and it continues to have an influence on current research and practice. (See *Concept Summary*.)

A BIOLOGICAL APPROACH: ETHOLOGY

Biological approaches to understanding human development emphasize innate behavior patterns or tendencies. These approaches are often based on research with nonhuman animals, in which genetic influences are sometimes more readily apparent than among humans.

The role of biology (of heredity) in determining nonhuman animal behavior has long been accepted. I fully expect my English setter to be reasonably adept at sniffing out ducks, because she has the genetic ancestry of all English setters. I would not expect the same talents or interests of Tigger, our prematurely retired cat. Even if Tigger's and the English setter's early experiences had been identical, I still would not expect Tigger to enjoy walking at my heels or to drool at the prospect of a cold swim in a reedy pond. We know that many of the behaviors and habits characteristic of animals aren't acquired solely as a function of experience. A moth doesn't fly into a flame because it has learned to do so; dead moths don't fly. We can therefore assume that the attraction light has for a moth, like the overpowering urge of a Canada goose to fly south in the fall or a salmon to swim upriver, is the result of inherited tendencies.

Are we, in at least some ways, like moths and salmon? If so, what are our flames, our rivers?

Ethologists and Imprinting

Ethologists (scientists whose principal concern is **ethology**, the study of animal and human behavior,

CONCEPT SUMMARY

Piaget's Developmental Theory

Main Ideas	Piaget's theory explains intellectual adaptation as progressive change resulting from the interaction of *assimilation* (the use of previously learned responses) and *accommodation* (the modification of behavior). Infants are predisposed to acquire information; they construct progressively more logical and useful representations of reality as they interact with the world. Their representations, understanding, and competencies can be described as a series of four stages.

Piaget's Four Major Stages	Approximate Ages	Some Major Characteristics
Sensorimotor	Birth to 2 years	• Intelligence in action • World of the here and now • No language, no thought, no notion of objective reality at beginning of stage
Preoperational	2 to 7 years	• Egocentric thought • Reason dominated by perception • Intuitive rather than logical solutions • Inability to conserve
Concrete operations	7 to 11 or 12 years	• Ability to conserve • Logic of classes and relations • Understanding of numbers • Thinking bound to concrete • Development of reversibility in thought
Formal operations	11 or 12 to 14 or 15 years	• Complete generality of thought • Propositional thinking • Ability to deal with the hypothetical development of strong idealism

Some Contributions and Criticisms of Piaget

Contributions	• Highly influential developmental theory • Founded current conceptions of cognitive development • Stimulated an enormous amount of research and theorizing
Criticisms	• Underestimated information-processing capacities of young children • Overestimated capacities of adolescents (and even adults) • Used small samples, inadequate controls, and poor experimental procedures • Is sometimes obscure and difficult • Failed to recognize that development continues throughout the life span

---

ethologists Scientists who study the behavior of animals (including humans) in their natural habitats.

ethology The science of animal behavior. Involves the study of animal forms (including humans) in their natural environments.

especially under natural conditions) think that yes, we are a little like moths. And although the flames that entice us might be less obvious than those that attract the moth, they are perhaps no less powerful.

Our mothers, says British researcher John Bowlby, might be one of those flames, because in some ways, we are a little like baby ducks or chickens who almost inevitably imprint on their mothers (Bowlby, 1969). **Imprinting** is the tendency of newly hatched geese (or chickens, ducks, and some other birds) to follow the first moving object they see. They do this, says pioneering animal behaviorist Konrad Lorenz (1952), as long as they are exposed to this moving object during a **critical period** of time. If they are exposed to the same moving object (a **releaser**) before or after this *critical* period, imprinting does not ordinarily result (Figure 2.4).

imprinting An instinct-like type of learning that occurs shortly after birth in certain species and that is seen in the "following" behavior of young ducks or geese.

critical period The period during which an appropriate stimulus must be presented to an organism for imprinting to occur.

releaser A biological term for the stimulus that first gives rise to instinct-like behaviors such as the "following" behavior of newly hatched chicks. In this case, the *releaser* is generally the mother hen.

Imprinting among newly hatched birds is clearly important for survival. A gosling's chances of survival are far better if it, along with all its fellow goslings, follows its mother. But the gosling follows the mother goose not because it is aware of a genetic relationship between this big bird and itself; it follows her simply because she happened to be the first moving object it saw during the critical few hours following hatching. Ethologists have repeatedly demonstrated that if some other object—like a big balloon, for example—replaces the mother goose, the young gosling quite happily follows the balloon instead. When Lorenz substituted himself for the mother goose, the young goslings followed him much as they would have their mother.

Among animals, attachment, too, appears to be an imprinting phenomenon, subject to the all-important *critical* period. Many animals, both wild and domestic, appear to form strong mother-infant bonds *providing mothers and infants are exposed to each other during a critical period of time* (which, not surprisingly, is almost invariably very shortly after birth). Thus, a lamb that is removed from its mother

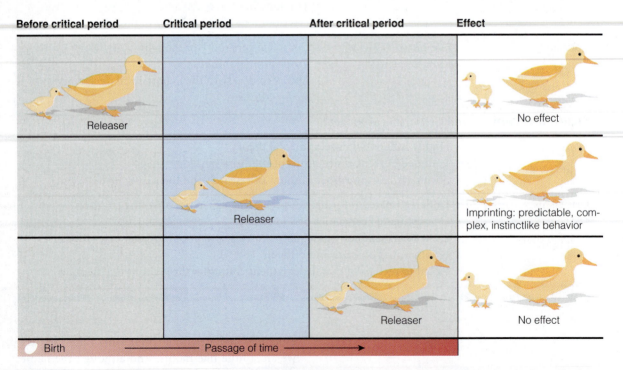

Before critical period	Critical period	After critical period	Effect
Releaser			No effect
	Releaser		Imprinting: predictable, complex, instinctlike behavior
		Releaser	No effect

Birth — Passage of time →

FIGURE 2.4 A model of imprinting. Under appropriate environmental conditions, exposure to a releaser during the critical period leads to imprinting, which is manifested in predictable behaviors. Imprinting does not occur in the absence of a releaser or if the releaser is presented too early or too late.

Imprinting among birds clearly has survival value, even when it is directed toward an experimenter such as Konrad Lorenz. Bowlby suggests that attachment between infant and mother may have a similar genetic underpinning.

Nina Leen/TimePix

at birth and not brought back for a week or more doesn't ordinarily show any evidence of attachment to her. Perhaps even more striking, ewes do not appear to be attached to their lambs under these circumstances and will sometimes butt them out of the way if they insist on coming too close (Thorpe, 1963).

Bowlby's Attachment Theory

Although the search for imprinted behaviors among humans has not led to the discovery of behaviors as obvious as "following" among geese, some theorists, such as Bowlby (1979, 1980, 1982), suggest that there are important parallels between the findings of ethologists and the development of attachment between human mothers and their infant. As we see in Chapter 6, Bowlby's research with young infants indicates that we have a natural (inherited) tendency to form emotional bonds with our mothers or with some other permanent caregiver during what he terms a **sensitive period**. Such bonds, Bowlby argues, would clearly have been important for an infant's survival in a less civilized age. The need for bonds is evident in an infant's attempts to maintain physical contact, to cling, and

---

sensitive period A period during which specific experiences have their most pronounced effects—for example, the first six months of life, during which an infant forms strong attachment bonds to the mother or caregiver.

to stay in visual contact with the mother (Bowlby, 1979). It is evident as well in the effects of separating mother and infant—effects that are marked, in Bowlby's (1979) words, by "emotional distress and personality disturbance, including anxiety, anger, depression, and emotional detachment" (p. 127).

In Bowlby's theory, not only are strong and secure infant-mother attachments important for positive and happy emotional development and the avoidance of psychological distress, but they are also closely implicated in the developing infant's eagerness to explore. As we see in Chapter 6, a parent to which an infant is securely attached is one that infants can leave to explore, confident that the parent will still be there to protect and save them (both literally and metaphorically) if they need to come running back (Bretherton, 1997).

Review of Bowlby's Theory

Bowlby's ethological theory is not a very general theory of human development; its main purpose is to explain early emotional development, and especially early mother-infant attachment—for which it provides an intriguing biological explanation. We look at this attachment theory in more detail in Chapter 6.

Some critics argue that Bowlby has overemphasized the role of the mother and neglected that of the father. But as Ainsworth (1979) notes,

Bowlby has focused on the role of the mother primarily because she is typically the principal caregiver. In the absence of the mother, the father or some other caregiver may substitute for her.

Another point of controversy is Bowlby's assertion that failure to form strong attachments during infancy subsequently causes adjustment problems and difficulties in establishing loving relationships as an adult. The long-term consequences of attachment quality are still unclear, and the subject of ongoing research (Thompson, 1998).

It seems clear that the concepts and language of animal imprinting are not entirely appropriate for understanding human behavior. Human attachment is not as predictable a behavior as "following" in geese; nor is there as definite a critical period during which the appropriate stimulus must be presented if the relevant behavior is to appear. In addition, the implications of not forming an attachment bond with a primary caregiver early in life are not as clear for an infant as for a gosling. The gosling that fails to imprint on its mother is likely to become lost and perish; the long-term consequences for infants are not so clear. (See *Concept Summary.*)

ECOLOGICAL APPROACHES: VYGOTSKY AND BRONFENBRENNER

Biological approaches look at genetically based (hence biological) influences in development; in contrast, ecological approaches emphasize the importance of the individual's context—hence the importance of the environment. In developmental psychology, **ecology** deals with relationships between human behavior and the social contexts in which behavior and development occur (Bronfenbrenner, 1989).

Vygotsky's Cultural-Historical Approach

The Russian psychologist Lev Vygotsky was a major force in Soviet psychology by the time he was 28;

ecology The study of the interrelationships between organisms and their environment. In developmental psychology, ecology relates to the social context in which behavior and development occur.

CONCEPT SUMMARY **Bowlby's Biological Approach**

Main emphasis	The importance of innate (biological) tendencies or patterns of behavior as an explanation for mother-infant attachment
Important Related Terms and Concepts	**Explanation**
Ethology	Science that looks at the behavior of animals in their natural habitats
Bonding	Biologically based attachment between mother and infant
Imprinting	A type of learning involving complex, species-specific behaviors that typically occurs shortly after birth, usually in response to a specific stimulus. For example, "following" in young ducks.
Releaser	Stimulus that elicits (releases) an imprinted behavior
Critical period	Period during which a releaser must be present for imprinting to occur
Sensitive period	Period during which a specific type of learning is most likely to occur, given specific, appropriate experiences

that was in 1924. Unfortunately, 10 years later he died of tuberculosis. Yet many of his ideas, old as they are now, still seem fresh and important. In recent decades, Vygotsky's work has become immensely popular in writings on human development and education (Popkewitz, 1998).

Vygotsky's Three Most Basic Ideas Vygotsky was "the Mozart of psychology," its "child genius," writes Davydov (1995). At the age of 28, he had assimilated all of the relevant theories then current and had begun to map out a theory of development that dominated the field in the former Soviet Union for more than 70 years—and probably still does today (Thomas, 1999).

This theory is unified by three main themes: first is the importance of culture: second is the role of language; and third is the concept of *zone of proximal growth.*

The Importance of Culture We are not like other animals, says Vygotsky. Why? Because we can use symbols and tools; as a result, we create cultures, and a **culture** has a vitality, a life of its own. Cultures grow and change and exert a powerful influence on their members. They determine the end result of competent development—the sorts of things that its members must learn, the ways they should think, the things they are most likely to believe. As Bronfenbrenner (1989) puts it, we are not only culture-producing beings, but also culture-produced. Culture is what permits humans to have a history—and perhaps a future as well (Vygotsky, 1986).

The importance of culture in Vygotsky's system is evident in the distinction he makes between **elementary mental functions** and **higher mental functions**. Elementary functions are our natural, unlearned capacities. They are evident in a newborn's ability to attend to human sounds and to discriminate among them, and they are apparent in its ability to remember the smell of its mother, or in the capacity to goo and gurgle and to scream and cry.

With exposure to a human culture, however, and especially with the learning of powerful symbol systems such as language, elementary mental functions are eventually transformed into higher mental functions. These are sophisticated mental functions, not evident in nonhuman animals. They are apparent in our use of language and in the ability to think and reason. The transformation from elementary to higher mental functioning is absolutely fundamental to human development. And, insists Vygotsky (1986), it requires social interaction with adults and competent peers. As Abecassis (1993) puts it, "For Vygotsky, biology alone cannot explain the development of higher mental functions; it is necessary to add culture" (p. 48). And one of the most important features of culture is language.

The Role of Language Language, after all, is what makes thinking possible. Language is not only the basis for human culture, but is essential for **consciousness**. Thus, during the preverbal stage of development, children's intelligence is much like that of an ape, says Vygotsky (1986). It is purely natural, purely practical—*elementary,* in other words. But language changes all that. Why? Because language makes human social interaction possible. With language comes the possibility of what Vygotsky terms "upbringing and teaching" (Davydov, 1995).

Language takes three sequential forms, each of which has a different purpose (see Table 2.5), explains Vygotsky (1986). The most primitive form of speech, social speech (or external speech), is common until around the age of 3. Its main function is to control the behavior of others (as in, "I want milk!") or to express simple concepts.

Egocentric speech dominates children's lives approximately between ages 3 and 7. This type of speech, says Vygotsky, is a sort of bridge between the social speech of the preceding period and the more internal (inner) speech of the next period. Egocentric speech often serves to control children's own behavior, but may be spoken out loud. For

---

culture Signifies the customs, beliefs, achievements, art, and literature that are particular to a distinct group of people.

elementary mental functions In Vygotsky's system, simple, unlearned behaviors like reflexes. Present in both animals and human infants.

higher mental functions In Vygotsky's system, learned behaviors such as are evident in thinking and speaking. Highly dependent on language.

---

consciousness Awareness of one's self and surroundings; awareness of one's existence; awareness of one's awareness.

TABLE 2.5
Stages and Functions of Language: Vygotsky's Theory

STAGE	FUNCTION
Social (external) speech (to age 3)	Controls the behavior of others; expresses simple thoughts and emotions
Egocentric speech (3 to 7)	Bridge between external and inner speech; serves to control own behavior, but spoken out loud
Inner speech (7 onwards)	Self-talk; makes possible the direction of our thinking and our behavior; basis of consciousness; involved in all higher mental functioning

example, young children often talk to themselves as they are trying to do something: "Push. Okay, now turn. Turn. Tu . . . push. . . ."

Inner speech is our private self-talk—what James (1890) called our *stream of consciousness.* According to Vygotsky, inner speech is what makes thought possible. It is the basis of all higher mental functioning.

Zone of Proximal Development According to Vygotsky, language is one of the most important ways in which cultures influence and shape the course of development. For Vygotsky, development is a function of the interaction between culture and children's basic biological capacities and maturational timetables. But, insisted Vygotsky, it is the environmental context (the culture) that is most important, not biological maturation (Valsiner, 1987).

Development (or growth) takes place when environmental opportunities and demands are appropriate for the child. In a sense, culture instructs the child in the ways of development. But the instruction is effective only if the child's biological maturation and current developmental level are sufficiently advanced. For every child, says Vygotsky, there is a **zone of proximal development**—a sort of

potential for development. In a sense, this zone of development spans what the child can do alone and what might be accomplished with the help and guidance of others. Davydov (1995) explains the concept as follows: "What the child is initially able to do only together with adults and peers and then can do independently, lies exactly in the zone of proximal development" (p. 18). The challenge is to present children with tasks that lie within this zone, and then to provide them with the help they need to learn and to accomplish tasks successfully. Demands that are beyond children's capacities—in other words, that are beyond their zone of proximal development—are ineffective in promoting growth; similarly, demands that are too simple are wasteful. Thus, one of the important techniques for teachers and parents is what is labeled **scaffolding**—providing support through guidance, demonstrations, explanations, provision of models, explanation of objectives, and so on (Ukrainetz, 1998.)

Review of Vygotsky's Theory

For Vygotsky, the driving force in development is found in the demands and requirements of the culture. In contrast, Piaget's child is more solitary, working alone to discover and create meaning; the driving force in this system is cognitive uncertainty

inner speech Vygotsky's final stage in the development of speech, attained at around age 7, and characterized by silent "self-talk," the stream-of-consciousness flow of verbalizations that give direction and substance to our thinking and behavior. Inner speech is involved in all higher mental functioning.

zone of proximal development Vygotsky's phrase for the individual's current potential for further intellectual development, a capacity not ordinarily measured by conventional intelligence tests. He suggests that hints and questions might help in assessing this zone.

scaffolding A Vygotskian concept to describe the various types of support that teachers/upbringers need to provide for children if they are to learn. Scaffolding often takes the form of directions, suggestions, and other forms of verbal assistance and is most effective if it involves tasks within the child's zone of proximal growth.

The "average" child, who is typically the subject of most child development studies and textbooks, shares many aspects of life's important realities with other "average" children. But there are important aspects of every child's context that are unique, and often very private.

ate practical value to child-care specialists, teachers, or even psychologists, they are absolutely fundamental to our understanding of the complexity and variety of the human experience. The average children of which our textbooks speak are always average only in their culture. Other cultures have different norms— different averages. (See *Concept Summary.*)

Bronfenbrenner's Ecological Theory

The importance of cultures and of changing social environments is the central theme of an important theory presented by American psychologist Urie Bronfenbrenner (1979, 1998). The emphasis in this theory is on understanding development as the product of interactions between the person and the environment. Hence Bronfenbrenner's model has three components: the person, the context in which behavior occurs, and the processes that account for developmental change. It is, in Bronfenbrenner's words, a *process-person-context* model, and development is simply the process through which "properties of the person and the environment interact to produce constancy and change in the characteristics of the person" (p. 191).

One of Bronfenbrenner's most important contributions to our understanding of how children develop is his description of the various levels of context in which a developing child interacts. Children's environments—the ecological systems in which development occurs—insists Bronfenbrenner, go far beyond the activities and events that affect them directly. Many things happen in the wider community, in the country, perhaps even in the world, that influence development in important ways. One way of looking at the child's ecology, suggests Bronfenbrenner, is to look at the characteristics of the different ecological systems that define the child's total environment.

The Microsystem For example, many important interactions occur at an immediate, face-to-face level. These define the **microsystem**. The complex patterns of behaviors, roles, and relationships

and contradiction (disequilibrium is Piaget's term). And Bandura's child learns through social imitation; the driving force is a need to learn through observation.

Vygotsky's theory describes development as a social process. Cognitive development, claims Vygotsky, results from interactions of a child with adults and more competent peers. By participating jointly in various activities, children develop and practice cognitive skills that were initially beyond their abilities, but fall within their zone of potential development (Davydov, 1998).

One of Vygotsky's most important contributions is his recognition of the importance of culture in shaping children's development. And although the concepts of culture and language as determiners of development are perhaps too vague to be of immedi-

---

microsystem Defined by immediate, face-to-face interactions in which everybody affects everybody (for example, child and parent.)

CONCEPT SUMMARY **Main Ideas in Vygotsky's Theory**

Three Main Themes	Explanations
Culture	Cultures make us human; without cultures, we would be like animals, relegated to *elementary* mental functions, incapable of *higher* thought.
Language	• Language is the most important tool of human cultures. • Language makes thinking possible; thought is dependent on *inner speech.* • *Inner speech* is self-talk. Developmentally, it appears last. Without inner speech, says Vygotsky, we could not contemplate a future. • *Egocentric speech* bridges internal and external speech, and is common between ages 3 and 7. • *Social speech* is external speech. It is the earliest and most primitive form of speech.
Zone of proximal development	• Vygotsky's phrase for the child's potential for further development, given appropriate cultural experiences. • In a sense, the *zone* includes the range of tasks that the individual is capable of, given appropriate assistance (in the form of suggestions, models, hints, questions, and so on). Tasks *below* this zone are too simple and of little value; those above the zone are too difficult to be very useful.

within the home, the school, the peer group, the workplace, the playground, and so on, that include the individual in actual interactions, are all microsystem components of the individual's ecological system. Everybody in the individual's microsystems influences the individual, says Bronfenbrenner.

The Mesosystem In turn, microsystems may influence each other in important ways. For example, how Ronald's mother treats him may be influenced by her interactions with his father. Perhaps she is less likely to be gentle and loving with her son if she has just had an argument with her husband. Similarly, how Ronald interacts with his sister, Nan, may reflect how his mother interacts with Nan. According to Bronfenbrenner, interactions among microsystems that include the developing person define what is meant by the **mesosystem**.

The Exosystem The home does not exist in isolation, however, explains Bronfenbrenner. How parents treat children is influenced by schools, by teachers, perhaps by the church, and by employers and friends. In short, it is influenced by all the relationships that exist between members of a child's microsystems and others. For example, interactions between Ronald and his father may be influenced by the father's relationships with his colleagues or his fishing buddies. Interactions between an element of the microsystem that ordinarily includes the developing child and an element of the wider context that does not include the child define the **exosystem**.

The Macrosystem All the interactive systems— micro-, meso-, and exosystems—that characterize

mesosystem Interactions among two or more microsystems (for example, family and school).

exosystem Interactions between a system in which a child is involved (microsystem) and another system that does not ordinarily include the child (father's relationships with employers, for example).

cultures define the **macrosystem**. Macrosystems are describable in terms of beliefs, values, customary ways of doing things, expected behaviors, social roles, status assignments, lifestyles, religions, and so on, as these are reflected in interactions among systems. In Bronfenbrenner's (1989) words, the macrosystem "may be thought of as a societal blueprint for a particular culture, subculture, or other broader social context" (p. 228).

Chronosystem All the ecological systems in which children develop change over time. **Chronosystem** is the term Bronfenbrenner uses to describe this concept. Many of these important changes will occur in microsystems. They might involve events such as the birth of a sibling, parental divorce, loss or introduction of pets, and so on. Sometimes changes involve wider aspects of the macrosystem. For example, within the last few decades of the twentieth century there have been profound changes in family employment patterns (from one to two wage earners), in family structure (from two- to one-parent families), in child-rearing styles (from home-rearing to other child-care options), in age of marriage (from younger to older), in age of childbearing (also from younger to older), and in

---

macrosystem All interactive social systems that define a culture or subculture.

chronosystem Bronfenbrenner's term for his recognition that important aspects of environments (of ecologies) change over time.

range of expected school attendance (from quasi-compulsory kindergarten to quasi-expected post-secondary). Clearly, many of these macrosystem changes directly affect the microsystems of which the child is a part—the family, the home, the school.

These concepts are abridged in Table 2.6 and Figure 2.5. For an illustration of how contexts are shaped by cultural expectations and beliefs, and of how important they can be in the life of a developing child, see *Across Cultures:* "Ellen de Luca, the Fat Girl."

Review of Bronfenbrenner's Ecological Theory

Although most contemporary developmental theorists pay lip service to the importance of taking context, person, and interaction into account, many researchers continue to operate within one of the two models that have dominated much of our thought and research. One model says that the causes of developmental change are to be found primarily within the individual; the other insists that the individual's environment is a more important cause of change. It's the old nature-nurture debate (about which we say more in Chapter 3).

The model that underlies our thinking is tremendously important to our research and our conclusions. One model says that if Johnny turns out to be an unmanageable scoundrel, we should

---

TABLE 2.6
Ecological Systems in Bronfenbrenner's Theory

LEVEL	DEFINITION	EXAMPLE
Microsystem	Child in immediate, face-to-face interaction	Mother singing to child
Mesosystem	Relationships between two or more microsystems	Mother and father interacting
Exosystem	Linkages and relationships between two or more settings, one of which does not include the child	Father's relationship with employer
Macrosystem	The totality of all other systems, evident in the beliefs, the options, the lifestyles, the values, the mores of a culture or subculture	Society's child-care legislation; expectations and requirements of culture
Chronosystem	Changes, over time, in ecological systems that affect the child	Parental divorce; birth of new sibling

FIGURE 2.5 Bronfenbrenner's ecological view of influences on the developing child. At the center is the child in immediate, face-to-face inter-actions in a variety of *microsystems*. Microsystems also interact and affect one another to define *mesosystems*, which are themselves affected by wider social realities (*exosystems*). All of these ecological systems reflect the dominant cultural values and beliefs of wider society (*macrosystem*). And all of them change over time (*chronosystem*).

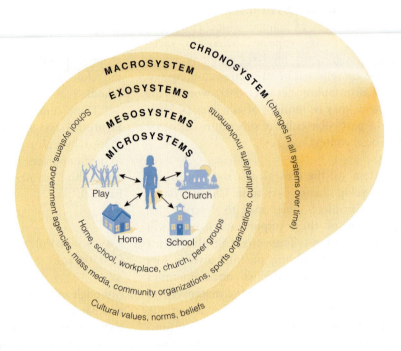

Ellen de Luca, the Fat Girl

"Her name was Ellen De Luca. But I never thought of her with a name until the day I made her cry," says Jeff of the girl who arrived at his first high school ceramics class at the same time as he did (Sachs, 1984). The girl was easily twice as wide as Jeff, so he had to stand back and let her through first. "What a butt!" said the guy behind him.

The girl moved off to a corner, away from the others, and Jeff promptly fell in love with Norma, a slim, beautiful blond, the kind of girl, he says, "I had been dreaming about ever since I started dreaming about girls."

In the class, the beautiful Norma threw exquisite pots and vases; Ellen's were clumsy and ugly. It seemed that she kept bumping into things, breaking pottery, slamming doors—and also watching Jeff, wistfully catching him kiss-ing Norma or rubbing her back. But Jeff didn't even know Ellen's name, noticing only how big she was as she walked down the aisles, or how she would sometimes eat two cheeseburgers in the school cafeteria and then maybe as many as six chocolate bars. And she threw the wrappers under the table.

"Somebody should tell her," said Jeff.

"Tell her what?"

"That she'd do herself and the rest of us a big favor if she'd go bust up another class. It's a real drag having her around."

Ellen de Luca, standing alone and unobserved behind Jeff, heard every word. Crying, she turned and shuffled away. Next day, and the next, and the one after that, she didn't return to class. In the end, Jeff went to her home and tried to apolo-gize, but Ellen de Luca would hear none of it. "I'm going to kill myself," she said.

"I didn't mean it, Ellen. Honestly," Jeff insisted.

"It's everybody else too." she answered. "Nobody likes me. I'm going to kill myself."

Based on Sachs, M. (1984). *The fat girl*. New York: Dutton.

To Think About: Norma and Ellen share many important aspects of context: They attend the same school and classes, they know many of the same people, and their families live in the same neighborhoods and have similar lives and values. What is it that makes their lives so different? Can you think of other situations in which cultural rules and expectations interact with people's characteristics to determine important aspects of context?

look for the cause and the explanation in his temperament and his personality characteristics; the other says we should look to his environment. But neither of these models says that we should look at how Johnny's characteristics influence his environment, and at how, in turn, his environment influences him. Neither insists that the cause is at least partly to be found in the changing interactions that occur between Johnny and his alcoholic mother, his overworked and indifferent teachers, or his peers (the microsystem). Neither suggests that the aborted affair between Johnny's father and his kindergarten teacher is of consequence (the mesosystem). Neither is concerned with interactions that might have occurred between Johnny's mother and her employer, leading to a reduction in her pay and chronic, irrepressible disgruntlement (the exosystem). Neither asks the researcher to look at how society's encouragement of the changing structure of the family affects Johnny's well-being (the macrosystem and the chronosystem). That neither model asks these questions is a weakness of some of our traditional approaches to understanding child development; that Bronfenbrenner's ecological systems theory does is among its strengths.

But it is one of its weaknesses as well. Explanations based on ecological systems theory require the analysis of an almost infinite number of highly complex interactions. Identifying these interactions; observing and quantifying them; sorting out relationships among them; teasing out reciprocal influences between individuals and their micro-, meso-, and exosystems; and determining how changing cultural values and options impinge on the individual—all these are difficult tasks. But perhaps if we mull them over long enough, we may find that they are not impossible tasks to achieve. Bronfenbrenner's ecological systems theory at least suggests where we should begin.

⌐ DYNAMIC SYSTEMS APPROACHES

Human behavior and development is dynamic, insist a number of theorists such as Fischer and Bidell (1998) and Thelen and Smith (1998): Development can be understood only through continuous, mutual interaction among all levels of the developing system. With children, according to this view, any change in one aspect of the system—rapid

biological growth, for example—leads to disequilibrium and a readjustment in other aspects of the system—in social reactions, for instance. The result is a continual process of reorganizing behavior to make it more effective and more appropriate. But within this variability, there is nevertheless some order and predictability. **Dynamic systems approaches** look for order in this variation.

Detecting Order in Variation

The explicit use of dynamic systems theory approaches is relatively new in developmental psychology; the research is still in its infancy. However, recognition of the variability of human behavior and of the importance of interaction is not at all new. The cornerstone of both Bronfenbrenner's and Vygotsky's theories, for example, is their recognition of the importance of the individual's interactions with changing social environments, and their emphasis on the variability of human experiences as well as of developmental outcomes. But recognizing the complexity of development is not the same thing as analyzing it. As Fischer and Bidell (1998) put it, "Dazzled by all this complexity, scientists often retreat into oversimplification and stereotyping" (p. 468).

Dynamic systems approaches are complex approaches, most often based on advanced mathematical models and predictions. Such models have been applied in studies of how children develop intention (Mascolo, Fischer, & Neimeyer, 1999), representation (Mascolo & Fischer, 1999), empathy (Fishman, 1999)—even how bullying and victimization are developed and promoted (Pepler, Craig, & O'Connell, 1999). These models aren't directed toward describing stages or developmental achievements; rather, they are geared toward understanding "the self-organizing processes of continually active living systems" (Thelen & Smith, 1994, p. 44). As Fischer and Bidell (1998) explain, they involve doing research that is sufficiently complex that it can provide new insights about the variability among humans. Its objective, as we noted, is to find order in this variability.

dynamic systems approaches Approaches that emphasize the dynamic (changing) nature of human development, and that view development as a complex and highly variable interaction of processes involving all aspects of development. Often based on complex mathematical models.

Review of Dynamic Systems Theory

Dynamic systems theories, notes Thomas (2000), emphasize changes within interacting components of a system. They recognize that physical, emotional, social, and intellectual growth are linked in complex ways, that changes in functioning in one area can have profound effects on functioning in other areas. They agree, as well, that the human organism carries its own sources of motivation and energy, that it doesn't simply respond to external forces. Dynamic systems theories introduce new metaphors for human development. These metaphors replace machine models that see humans as highly reactive to external forces. They also replace metaphors that view development as a series of steps or stages, or perhaps as a mountain to climb—(and then perhaps to tumble down?). One of the new metaphors, described by Thelen and Smith (1998), compares development to the patterns of water flow in a mountain stream, with its constantly changing eddies and whirlpools, its currents, its riffles, its responsiveness to storms and droughts and melting snows and winds and maurauding bears, and geological changes over many eons.

It is a complex—and wonderful—thing to understand the patterns of water movement in a stream; so too, is it complex—and wonderful—to understand the interwoven patterns of development among children.

⌐ A HUMANISTIC APPROACH: ABRAHAM MASLOW

Had I spoken of Piaget or Freud, of Skinner or Vygotsky, of ethology or ecology, in my 75-year-old grandmother's kitchen, she would have listened politely. But in the end she probably would have said, "That's theory. It's all very nice, but what about Frank?" Why Frank? Simply because he was a unique 9-year-old. And although there is little doubt that Freud, Skinner, and Piaget might each have had something very intelligent, and perhaps even useful, to say about Frank's habits of stealing chicken eggs, writing poetry, and dancing little jigs in mudholes, they would have been hard-pressed to convince my grandmother that they knew more about Frank than she did. My grandmother was a humanist.

Humanistic psychologists are concerned with the uniqueness of the individual child. A basic humanistic belief is that it is impossible to describe the environment, much less a child, in a truly meaningful way because what constitutes the important features of the environment varies among individuals. Humanism emphasizes the importance of each person's view of the world and of themselves. To understand the behavior of children, this view says, we must try to perceive the world as they see it—from the perspective of their knowledge, their experiences, and their goals and aspirations (Rogers, 1951). This orientation, sometimes labeled **phenomenology**, underscores again that the individual is unique rather than average.

Because of its emphasis on the individual's uniqueness, humanism doesn't easily lead to theories that are both highly specific and widely applicable. But it does suggest an attitude toward children and toward development that is of tremendous potential value to those concerned with the welfare of children. Humanistic orientations tend to personalize (to humanize) our attitudes toward children; they restore some of the dynamism of the developmental process that our more static and complex theories might otherwise remove.

Maslow's Humanistic Need Theory

Perhaps the best known and most influential of all humanistic theories is that described by Abraham Maslow (1970). We are moved by two hierarchical systems of needs, Maslow informs us. The **basic needs** are physiological (food, drink) and psychological (security, love, esteem). These needs are also labeled *deficiency* needs because, when they are not satisfied, we try to remedy what we lack. For example, hunger represents a deficiency that can be satisfied by eating.

phenomenology An approach concerned primarily with how individuals view their own world. Its basic assumption is that each individual perceives and reacts to the world in a unique manner, and that it is this phenomenological worldview that is important in understanding an individual's behavior.

basic needs Unlearned physiological requirements of the human organism; specifically, the needs for food, drink, and sex.

The **metaneeds** are higher-level needs. Metaneeds show themselves in our desire to know, in our appreciation of truth and beauty, and in our tendencies toward growth and fulfillment—qualities termed **self-actualization** (Figure 2.6). The metaneeds are termed *growth* needs because activities that relate to them don't fulfill a lack but instead lead to growth.

Our needs are hierarchically arranged, says Maslow, in the sense that the metaneeds will not be attended to unless the basic needs have been reasonably well satisfied; that is, we pay attention to beauty, truth, and the development of our potential when we are no longer hungry and unloved (at least not terribly so).

Self-Actualization The most important of Maslow's metaneeds is self-actualization—a troublesome concept. Even Maslow (1970) admitted that "the exploration of the highest reaches of human nature and of its ultimate possibilities and aspirations is a difficult and tortuous task" (p. 67). Leclerc and associates

metaneeds Maslow's term for higher needs. In contrast to basic needs, metaneeds are concerned not with physiological but with psychological functions. They include the need to know truth, beauty, justice, and to self-actualize. Also termed *growth needs*.

self-actualization The process or act of becoming oneself, developing one's potentiality, achieving an awareness of one's identity, fulfilling oneself. The term *actualization* is central to humanistic psychology.

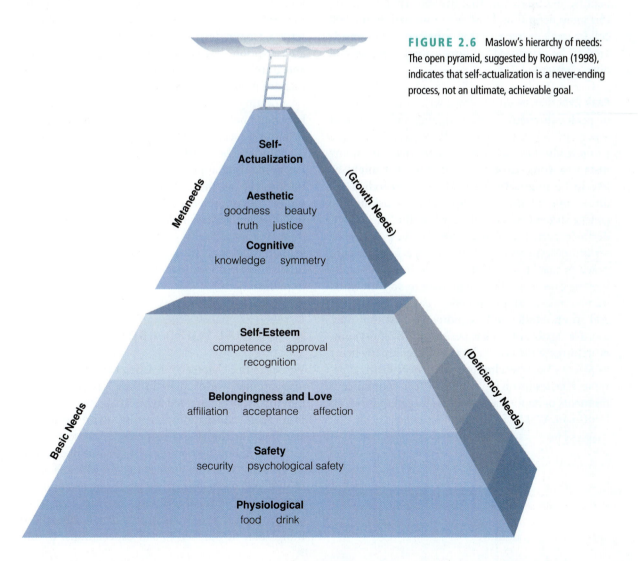

FIGURE 2.6 Maslow's hierarchy of needs: The open pyramid, suggested by Rowan (1998), indicates that self-actualization is a never-ending process, not an ultimate, achievable goal.

(1998) report that even decades later, the concept still remains unclear. Their survey of "experts" indicates that self-actualization is most often viewed as a process rather than a state. It is a process of growth, of becoming, of fulfillment. Because it is a process, suggests Rowan (1998), the triangle that has typically been used to illustrate the hierarchy of needs is misleading. "What is wrong with the triangle," he says, "is that it suggests that there is an end point to personal growth" (p. 88). But we never reach that end point.

Maslow (1970) suggests that self-actualization is characterized by absence of "neurosis, psychopathic personality, psychosis, or strong tendencies in these directions" (p. 150). On the more positive side, he claims that self-actualized people "may be loosely described as [making] full use and exploitation of talents, capacities, potentialities, etc." (p. 150). Using this loose definition, Maslow's examination of 3,000 college students revealed only one person he considered to be actualized (although there were several dozen "potentials").

Peak Experiences In Maslow's writings, the concept of **peak experience** is an intriguing and important aspect of self-actualization. Peak experiences are profoundly moving experiences that, in many instances, come close to defining what it might be like to be fully actualized. Maslow researched the dimensions of the peak experience by asking 190 college students to describe for him the "most wonderful experience of your life" (1970, p. 67). The resulting composite picture of a peak experience suggests that it is a relatively rare but profoundly moving experience that might have to do with work, human relationships, athletics, nature, mysticism, and so on. Studies with children suggest that they, too, are capable of peak experiences. The most common of these include feelings that accompany being in places of overwhelming beauty, near-death experiences, crises involving danger or fear, spontaneous moments of euphoria, or even unforgettable dreams (Hoffman, 1998). (See *Concept Summary*.)

---

peak experience Label introduced by Maslow to describe an intensely moving and unforgettable experience that has a profound effect on an individual's life. Peak experiences might involve what are interpreted by the individual as supernatural experiences, profound mystical revelations, startling insights, and other events closely related to the process of self-actualization.

Review of Maslow's Humanism

Maslow's is a highly optimistic, positively oriented theory of human development. It stresses the worth and uniqueness of the individual, and it describes development as a process that is guided by our need to achieve "full humanness" (Maslow, 1970, p. iii). *Full humanness*, says Maslow, is another way of saying self-actualization. The view that children are directed by a need to become (to actualize) and that the process of actualization is essentially positive and self-directed presents a subtle but important contrast to some of the more mechanistic, more passive, and less inner-directed theories we considered earlier.

Critics have been quick to point out that humanism does not present a scientific theory in the sense that, say, behaviorism does. Instead, it presents a general description of the human condition, a description that is viewed by some as too vague and unreliable to contribute much to the development of psychology as a science. Humanists counter by pointing out that science is only one way of knowing, that there is value in the insights provided by more subjective approaches.

Among the most important contributions of the humanistic approach are its recognition of the importance of the self and its emphasis on the uniqueness of each child. Although humanistic theory does not address well the specifics of the developmental process, it might in the end serve to explain facts that are not easily accounted for by other theories. (See Chapter 13 for more about humanism.)

A FINAL WORD ABOUT THEORIES

We began this chapter by insisting that facts and theories are not worlds apart in their "truthfulness"— that theories are intended to be explanations of facts. From these explanations, scientists strive for understanding, for the ability to predict, and sometimes for control. But theories do more than explain facts. As Thomas (1999) notes, they suggest which facts we should look at. In effect, they guide our invention of "facts" and give them meaning. Theories lead us to accept certain things as true—specifically, those things that fit our beliefs and expectations. By the

CONCEPT SUMMARY **Basic Concepts of Maslow's Humanism**

Humanistic orientation	An orientation that emphasizes the uniqueness and worth of humans as individuals, and that encourages the fullest possible development of human potential.
Phenomenology	Reflects the assumption that each person's world is individual, unique, and not fully knowable by anyone else.
Basic needs	• Also called *deficiency needs* because when unsatisfied, they are manifested in a sense of a lack of something, and give rise to behaviors designed to remove the deficiency. • Include physiological needs (for food, drink, and sex, for example) as well as psychological needs (the need for security, for acceptance and affection, for approval).
Metaneeds	• Also called *growth needs* because they are expressed not in a lack or deficiency so much as in a person's desire to grow, to become more than they now are. • Include aesthetic and cognitive needs expressed in the need to find such intangibles as truth, beauty, justice, goodness, order, symmetry, and so on. • Also include the highest of all human needs, the need for *self-actualization.*
Self-actualization	• The process or act of becoming, of developing, of enhancing potential, of achieving self-awareness, of growth, of fulfillment . . . • A tendency toward "full humanness." • The most central concept in humanistic psychology.
Peak experience	An intensely moving, unforgettable, life-changing experience. Peak experiences might involve what are interpreted by the individual as supernatural experiences, profound mystical revelations, startling insights, and other events. Closely related to the process of self-actualization.

same token, theories also lead us to ignore contradictory or apparently irrelevant observations.

Theories also tend to "normalize" the child, explains Greene (1999). That is, theories give us a picture of what a "normal" or average child is like, and then we compare real children to this sometimes very unreal picture. Greene also points out that the pictures our theories draw for us vary enormously, that they "fractionate" the child. Thus learning theories give us a picture of a highly malleable, moldable, "conditionable" child; Piaget draws a picture of the child as a thinker; and Freud shows us the "instinctual" child.

The following *Concept Summary* lists the approaches to developmental theory discussed in this chapter. History, as is so often its custom, may one day inform us about the fruitfulness of these approaches.

Approaches to Developmental Theory

Approach	Representative Theorist	Main Underlying Model	Major Assumptions (theoretical beliefs)	Key Terms
Psychoanalytic	Freud	Organismic	Individual is motivated by instinctual urges that are primarily sexual and aggressive.	Id, ego, superego, psychosexual, fixation, regression
	Erikson	Organismic	Child progresses through developmental stages by resolving conflicts that arise from a need to adapt to the sociocultural environment.	Competence, social environment, developmental tasks, psychosocial
Behavioristic	Watson, Skinner	Mechanistic/ Organismic	Changes in behavior are a function of reinforcement and punishment.	Reinforcement, punishment, stimuli, responses
Social cognitive	Bandura	Contextual/ Organismic	Observational learning leads to developmental change; our ability to symbolize and to anticipate the consequences of our behavior is fundamental, as are our estimates of our self-efficacy.	Imitation, modeling, eliciting, inhibiting-disinhibiting, self-efficacy
Cognitive	Piaget	Organismic	Child develops cognitive skills through active interaction with the environment.	Stages, assimilation, accommodation, adaptation, schema
Biological	Bowlby	Organismic	Social behaviors have a biological basis understandable in evolutionary terms. The formation of attachment bonds is one example.	Attachment bonds, imprinting, sensitive period

Approaches to Developmental Theory (continued)

Approach	Representative Theorist	Main Underlying Model	Major Assumptions (theoretical beliefs)	Key Terms
Ecological systems	Vygotsky, Bronfenbrenner	Contextual	The ecology of development is the study of accommodations between a person and the environment (culture), taking the changing characteristics of each into account.	Culture, language, ecology, microsystem, mesosystem, exosystem, macrosystem, chronosystem
Dynamic systems	Fischer, Bidell	Organismic/ Contextual	A change in any part of the system (mind, body, environment) leads to disequilibrium and readjustment.	integrated systems, interactions and relationships, variability, order, mathematical models
Humanistic	Maslow	Organismic/ Contextual	All individuals are unique but strive toward the fullest development of their potential.	Self, positive growth, metaneeds, basic needs, self-actualization, peak experiences

MAIN POINTS

Theories in Psychology

A theory attempts to organize and explain observations, and provide possibilities for predicting future outcomes. Ideally, theories should reflect "facts," be understandable, be useful for both predicting events and explaining the past, be practical, be internally consistent, be stimulating, provide reasonable answers for important questions, and lead to further research and discovery. Models are metaphors that underlie and guide theories. Mechanistic models emphasize our machinelike predictability; organismic models emphasize the active, exploring nature of children; and contextual models underline the influence of historical variables and culture.

A Psychoanalytic Approach: Freud

Freud's theory assumes that among the important causes of behavior are deep-seated, unconscious forces that can be discovered through dream analysis, hypnosis, free association, and the analysis of childhood experiences. Chief among these forces are sexual urges (libido), which define the first level of personality, the id. The second level is the ego (reality-based and typically in conflict with the id); the third is the superego (conscience; social and cultural taboos). Freud describes five developmental stages (oral, anal, phallic, latency, and genital) differentiated from each other by the areas of a child's body that are the main source of sexual gratification at the time.

A Psychosocial Approach: Erikson

In contrast with Freud's theory, Erikson's psychosocial theory of child development is concerned mainly with healthy development and does not concede an important role to subsconscious, sexually based forces. He describes development as progressing through a series of stages, each marked by a basic conflict whose resolution results in the manifestation of some new social competence: trust versus mistrust (birth to 18 months); autonomy versus shame and doubt (18 months to 2 or 3 years); initiative versus guilt (2 or 3 to about 6 years); industry versus inferiority, (around 6 to 11 years); identity versus identity diffusion (11 years through adolescence); intimacy versus isolation (young adulthood); generativity versus self-absorption (adulthood); and integrity versus despair (older adulthood).

Behavioristic Approaches

Behavioristic theories make no assumptions about unconscious forces or deep-seated instincts; instead, they focus directly on children's immediate behavior and on the environmental forces that affect behavior. In classical conditioning, illustrated by Pavlov and Watson, repeated pairing of stimulus or response events leads to learning. In operant conditioning, described by Skinner, the probability of a response occurring changes as a function of its consequences (positive or negative reinforcement increases the probability of a response occurring; punishment does not). Operant conditioning deals with operants (emitted responses); classical conditioning deals with respondents (responses to stimuli).

Social Cognitive Theory: Albert Bandura

Observational learning (learning through imitation) involves four types of processes, relating to, paying attention, remembering, being able to perform, and being motivated to do so. Through imitation, children learn new responses (the modeling effect); they suppress or engage in deviant responses (the inhibitory or disinhibitory effect); or they are encouraged to do things related to the behavior of a model (the eliciting effect).

Self-efficacy refers to private judgments about personal effectiveness and competence. These judgments are important in determining what we do and don't do, the amount of effort we expend, and our feelings about ourselves. Sources of information that affect our judgments of self-efficacy are enactive (reflect the results of our behavior); vicarious (based on comparisons between ourselves and others); persuasory (reflect the effects of others persuading us); and emotive (affected by our level of arousal).

A Cognitive Approach: Piaget

Piaget's biologically based theory of cognitive development describes adaptation through assimilation (using activities that are already in children's repertoire) and accommodation (changing activities to conform to environmental demands). The four major developmental stages are sensorimotor (world of here and now; intelligence in action); preoperational (egocentric thought; perception-dominated; intuitive rather than logical); concrete operations (more logical but tied to real objects and events); and formal operations (potentially logical thought; hypothetical, idealistic reasoning).

A Biological Approach: Ethology

Biological approaches to development look at the role of biology (heredity). Ethologists are biologically oriented scientists who study behavior in natural situations. Bowlby uses principles of ethology (specifically, of imprinting) to explain the development and importance of the attachment bonds that form between mothers (or other principal caregivers) and their infants during a *sensitive period.*

Ecological Approaches: Vygotsky and Bronfenbrenner

Ecological approaches emphasize the importance of interaction in changing contexts. Vygotsky's cultural-historical approach emphasizes the importance of culture and especially of its main invention, language. The zone of proximal development, an expression of Vygotsky's belief in the interdependence of development and social environment, is a child's potential for development in a given context. It's reflected in what the child can accomplish with help and guidance from more competent peers and adults.

Bronfenbrenner's ecological systems theory looks at the interaction between the growing child and environmental contexts. It describes four levels of context ranging from those closest to the child to those farthest away: the microsystem (the child in face-to-face interaction); the mesosystem (interactions among elements of the child's microsystem); the exosystem (interactions between one of the child's microsystems and another context with which the child does not ordinarily interact); and the macrosystem (the totality of all contexts relevant to the child's life). A fifth system, the chronosystem, recognizes that these systems change in important ways over time.

Dynamic Systems Approaches

Dynamic systems approaches look for order in the tremendous variability found in human behavior. They view behavior as the result of relationships and interactions among components of various systems where changes in one component affect all other components. Dynamic systems approaches are often based on complex mathematical models.

A Humanistic Approach: Abraham Maslow

Humanistic theory is concerned with uniqueness and human potential (self-actualization—a never-ending process tending toward the development of "full humanness"). Maslow describes two sets of needs that motivate us: deficiency (basic) needs, which are psychological (safety, esteem, love) and physical (food, drink); and metaneeds (growth needs), such as the need to self-actualize. These are hierarchical in that lower-level needs must ordinarily be satisfied before higher-level needs are attended to. Peak experiences (monumental, life-changing events) may be an important part of the process of self-actualization.

Focus Questions: Applications

1. What's a theory? What's its purpose? How can you tell whether a theory is a good one?
   - Describe what an ideal theory of child development might tell us.
2. How does Freudian psychoanalysis relate to child development?
   - Can you identify examples of children's behavior that illustrate each of Freud's psychosexual stages? Or Erikson's psychosocial stages?
3. What are the principal assumptions and explanations of behaviorism?
   - Devise a classroom procedure that applies some of the principles of conditioning theory for either teaching a specific lesson or reducing a behavior problem.
4. Do children learn through imitation?
   - Observe children with a view to identifying examples of each of the three principal effects of imitation.

5. What are the basic ideas underlying Piaget's theory?
   - Illustrate the twin processes of assimilation and accommodation in a child's behavior.
6. What are some of the roles of biology and culture in development?
   - Identify the most important characteristics of the type of culture you think would be best for fostering optimal human development. Or do you believe culture makes little difference—that we would be what we are no matter what?
7. What is self-actualization?
   - Analyze your own life in terms of the extent to which you think you have reached your "full humanness."

Possible Responses to Thought Challenges

Thought Challenge, page 48

There are at least two reasons for men's fear of women, explains Goldwater (1998). One is the historic fact that women can create life, and the fear that they can (and perhaps do) control men's sexuality for their own life-creating purposes. The other is a much more recent fear based on the possibility—should that be *probability*?—that men will soon no longer be necessary for creating life.

Did you think of other reasons? Do you agree with these?

Thought Challenge, page 54

Possibilities include developmental conflicts such as advanced morality versus violence and destruction; global altruism versus "me first"; fair distribution of national wealth versus economic dominance, etc. Resolving each of these implied conflicts requires different actions, different competencies. Their resolution, says Smelser (1996), and the realization of Erikson's vision of a peaceful and harmonious world seems improbable given inescapable evidence of humanity's propensity for violence and destruction.

Thought Challenge, page 57

It's possible that Little Albert grew up with a debilitating fear of rats, of people wearing white, of loud noises, of steel bars, of mattresses, of psychologists, of female assistants . . . It's possible, too, that he suffered from none of these conditions.

The fact is we really don't know what happened to Little Albert. But an impressive number of psychologists have reported that Albert was later *deconditioned* (or, more precisely, *counterconditioned*) by Watson and Rayner so that he would no longer be afraid of rats. But the truth is that Little Albert was taken away from the hospital before Watson could cure him of his fear. That he would have attempted to do so is clear from the original article (Watson & Rayner, 1920; see also Prytula, Oster, & Davis, 1977). A conditioning procedure could have been used for that as well, as Jones, Albert, and Watson (1974) later demonstrated with Peter, a boy who was afraid of rabbits.

Watson and Rayner were later strongly criticized for failing to ensure that Little Albert suffered no lasting ill effects. It's unlikely that this experiment would be approved today, given our contemporary strict ethical guidelines for research.

Thought Challenge, page 61

Both these statements are clear examples of Watson's *environmentalism*, the belief that what we become is entirely a function of environmental forces. While psychologists continue to accept that environmental forces are critical in shaping developmental outcomes, and while many continue to debate (sometimes very emotionally) the relative contributions of heredity and environment in human development, it's likely that none would agree completely with either of Watson's statements.

Key Terms

Further Readings

Because Freud, Erikson, and Piaget were voluminous—and sometimes difficult—writers, it is often easier and more valuable to use secondary sources for information about their theories. The following are especially useful starting points:

Singer, D. G., & T. A. Revenson (1997). *A Piaget primer: How a child thinks.* Madison, Conn.: International Universities Press.

Thomas, R. M. (1999). *Comparing theories of child development*, 5th ed. Belmont, Calif.: Wadsworth.

Langer, J., & M. Killen, eds. (1998). *Piaget, evolution, and development.* Mahwah, N.J.: Erlbaum.

Wadsworth, B. J. (1996). *Piaget's theory of cognitive and affective development*, 5th ed. New York: Longman.

For a clear account of Vygotsky's life and theories, see:

Kozulin, A. (1990). *Vygotsky's psychology: A biography of ideas.* New York: Harvester Wheatsheaf.

For more detailed information about Bronfenbrenner's ecological systems theory, see the following book:

Bronfenbrenner, U. (1979). *The ecology of human development.* Cambridge, Mass.: Harvard University Press.

The first of the next two references is an excellent summary of Bandura's social cognitive theory; the second is a simple summary of his imitation-based theories; and the third gives a clear account of his work on self-efficacy:

Bandura, A. (1986). *Social foundations of thought and action: A social cognitive theory.* Englewood Cliffs, N.J.: Prentice-Hall.

Bandura, A., & R. Walters (1963). *Social learning and personality development.* New York: Holt, Rinehart & Winston.

Bandura, A., ed. (1995). *Self-efficacy in changing societies.* New York: Cambridge University Press.

Maslow's humanistic psychology is well explained in:

Maslow, A. H. (1970). *Motivation and personality*, 2nd ed. New York: Harper & Row.

 Online Resources

For additional readings, explore *InfoTrac College Edition*, your online library. Go to http://www.infotrac-college.com/wadsworth and use the passcode on the card that came with your text. Try the following search terms: Piaget, Freud, behaviorism, developmental theory, psychoanalysis.

I'm afraid you've got a bad egg,
   Mr. Jones.
Oh no, my Lord, I assure you! Parts
   of it are excellent!

Punch, 1895

Conception, Heredity, and Environment

Robert Brenner/PhotoEdit

CHAPTER 3

The quote on the opposite page talks of eggs. That's what you and I were in the beginning—an egg. Not a big, oval chicken egg such as Mr. Jones had on his plate; instead, a microscopic egg—and, of course, a sperm, infinitely tinier. Of the millions that began the journey, this was the only sperm to finish, the only one to butt its tiny head hard enough, long enough, to succeed in penetrating that tough eggshell.

Those were our biological beginnings, you and I.

But what if we had a bad egg? Or a bad sperm, for that matter? Is that possible?

As we'll see in this chapter, science says that yes, it's sometimes possible for an egg or a sperm to be defective. And it's possible, too, for what started out as a good egg to be spoiled by drugs or bad nutrition or radiation or other things.

But most of the time we can, like Mr. Jones, claim that our eggs—or at least some parts of them—are most excellent!

FOCUS QUESTIONS

1. What are some of the mechanics, and the marvels, of what our elders called "the birds and the bees"?

2. What is the nature-nurture controversy?

3. What is the likely outcome of a child being raised by a chicken? A wolf? Alone in an attic?

4. What are the most common genetic defects and problems?

5. How can we diagnose genetic problems?

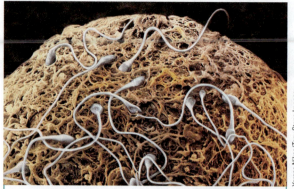

Yorgos Nikas/Tony Stone Images

Conception, the biological beginning, occurs when a sperm cell succeeds in penetrating an ovum's relatively tough outer shell. The 23 chromosomes of which it is composed then unite with the ovum's 23 chromosomes to form the 23 pairs of chromosomes that compose an individual's entire genetic complement.

▢ THE MECHANICS OF HEREDITY

The mechanics of **heredity** are complex and sometimes bewildering; its marvels, astounding. The marvels are best left to poets, but the mechanics can be simplified—although nature yields simplicity only very stubbornly.

Conception: Sperm Meets Ovum

Imagine one of the tiniest of all human cells, the **sperm**, a fragile thing swimming desperately against horrendous currents, using whiplike motions of its enormously long tail to propel itself. Its tail is fully 12 times the length of its body. It, along with perhaps another 3 or 4 hundred million sperm that have been produced in a man's **testes** and released at **ejaculation** during sexual intercourse, has undertaken an immense journey, given its size. If completed, this journey will bring it across the colossal expanse of the **uterus** and up a gigantic **fallopian tube**.

There, should this sperm reach its goal, it will encounter the largest cell in the human body, an **ovum** (plural, *ova*; also referred to as the **egg cell**). The ovum measures about 0.15 millimeters in diameter (about half the size of each period on this page). Interestingly, all of a woman's ova are present in her **ovaries** at birth—perhaps as many as a million of them. They are primitive and immature, and more than half of them atrophy before **puberty** (the beginning of sexual maturity). Of those that remain, about 400 will mature and be released between puberty and **menopause** (cessation of menstrua-

---

heredity The transmission of physical and personality characteristics and predispositions from parent to offspring.

sperm cell The sex cell produced by a mature male. Like egg cells (ova), sperm cells consist of 23 chromosomes rather than 23 *pairs* of chromosomes.

testes Spherical male organs in mammals, of which there are normally two. Produce sperm, but, strangely, are termed eggs (*huevos*) in Spanish.

ejaculation Seminal emission. The sudden and usually forceful discharge of semen, a liquid containing sperm, by the male.

uterus A term for the womb.

---

fallopian tube One of two tubes that link the ovaries and the uterus. Fertilization (conception) ordinarily occurs in the fallopian tubes. From there the fertilized egg cell moves into the uterus and attaches to the uterine wall.

ovum (plural, **ova**) The sex cell produced by a mature female approximately once every 28 days. When mature it consists of 23 chromosomes, as opposed to all other human body cells (somatoplasm), which consist of 23 *pairs* of chromosomes. It is often referred to as an egg cell.

egg cell (See *ovum*.)

ovary A female organ (most women have two of them) that produces ova (egg cells).

puberty Sexual maturity following pubescence.

menopause Cessation of menustruation.

tion), one every 28 days. In contrast, a man produces sperm at the rate of several billion a month and usually continues to produce them from puberty until death.

Battered, and perhaps close to exhaustion, the sperm nears the end of its journey. But even if it happens to be one of the three or four hundred surviving sperm that have made it to this point, the goal is not yet in hand (figure the odds! about one in a million of even getting this far). Even if the sperm reaches this point, there is a high probability that no ovum will be here to fertilize, and the odyssey will all have been for nothing. Remember that an ovum is released only once every 28 days. And, unlike the sperm cell, which can live 4, 5, or even 6 days, thus lying in wait for a time if need be, the ovum generally dies within about a day of having been released.

But if there is an ovum at the end of the journey, it will be found about halfway up one of the fallopian tubes (many of the other sperm have foolishly gone up the wrong tube). Having reached the ovum, the sperm now butts up against it, its tail whipping wildly, seemingly almost frantic to penetrate the tough outer shell. If it succeeds in perforating that membrane and entering the egg, it will be the only sperm to do so. The egg immediately releases enzymes to harden the covering, making it virtually impenetrable to any other sperm that might still be bent on conquest. Those that are left outside are doomed!

The stage is now set for the next phase of this incredible drama. Within a short time, the very matter of which the sperm is formed fuses with that within the ovum and, voilà, we have **conception**—the creation of a single new living cell that is the beginning of human life. This new cell, termed a **zygote**, now begins its journey down the fallopian tube. And as it drifts *down* the current (hey, it doesn't have a tail to swim with), the genetic material within the cell duplicates itself to form two identical copies of this material. Following duplication, the two identical copies of genetic material within

the zygote ease over to opposite sides of the cell, and the cell pulls apart and re-forms, creating two identical cells—a type of cell division termed **mitosis**. The process is repeated, so that there are now four identical cells, and mitosis now begins to accelerate. Two days after conception, perhaps only four cells have been formed, but by the end of the first week, there may be several hundred. By the time we are born, there will be tens of trillions; when we die, should we live a while, there will be hundreds of trillions of cells in our bodies. And each of them will contain an identical copy of the entire genetic blueprint we were born with.

That mitosis produces duplicate cells is an important feature of cell division; it explains why every one of the cells in our bodies has exactly the same genetic makeup—why the forensic investigator can nail the criminal with a single cell from a fingernail clipping as easily as with a cell from her blood, her hair, her skin, or her tooth. And it explains why the paleontologist dreams, with some reason for optimism, of recreating a woolly mammoth from a microscopic bit of its 10,000-year-old frozen carcass.

What's in the Sperm and the Ovum?

Mitosis, the duplication of cells to form trillions of identical cells, is one of two ways in which our cells divide. You see, we have two kinds of cells in our body: **sex cells**, which consist of ova in the female and sperm in the male (these sex cells are also labeled **gametes**); and body cells (called **somatic cells**). As we saw, all normal somatic cells contain identical genetic information—the same genetic code.

In contrast, each gamete is different from every other. That's because gametes result from a special

---

conception The beginning of life. Also called *fertilization*, conception occurs with the union of a sperm cell with an egg cell.

zygote A fertilized egg cell (ovum). A zygote is formed from the union of a sperm cell and an egg cell; it normally contains 46 chromosomes (a full complement).

mitosis The division of a cell into two identical cells. Occurs in body cells as opposed to sex cells.

sex cells Sperm and ovum. Mature sex cells each contain 23 chromosomes rather than 23 pairs and are different from each other.

gametes Mature sex cells. In humans, the egg cell (ovum) and the sperm cell.

somatic cells Also called body cells; all cells in our body other than sex cells. Normal somatic cells each contain 23 pairs of chromosomes. All our body cells normally contain identical genetic information.

kind of cell division termed **meiosis**. Meiosis results in daughter cells that have only half the genetic material found in the parent cell. This genetic material is found on rodlike structures called **chromosomes**, of which there are 23 pairs in every human cell. But in meiosis, each of these 23 pairs of chromosomes separates to form gametes (sperm cells in the male; ova in the female) that have only half of each pair—hence 23 single chromosomes rather than 23 *pairs* of chromosomes. Furthermore, when chromosome pairs in the parent cell divide to form gametes, they do so randomly, and genetic material crosses over from one chromosome to another. As a result, individual components of chromosome pairs wind up in any of a mind-boggling number of possible combinations. And because two parents are involved, the total number of different individuals that can result from a single human mating is some almost meaningless number larger than 60 trillion.

So should we be amazed that we are so much like our parents and siblings? Not really. You see, in these over 60 trillion theoretically possible combinations there is a vast amount of redundant information, much of which is absolutely fundamental to our humanity. That pretty well every one of us has a single head, two eyes, an astonishingly developed brain, functional digits, and on and on, lies in the secrets of our genetic code.

Why You Are Female or Male

Of the 23 chromosomes contained in each sperm and each ovum, one, termed the **sex chromosome**, determines whether the offspring will be male or female. (The other 22 chromosomes are called **autosomes**.) As shown in Figure 3.1, the father produces two types of sperm, one type with a larger sex chromosome labeled the **X chromosome** and one type with a smaller sex chromosome labeled the **Y chromosome**. If the sperm that fertilizes the ovum contains an X chromosome, the offspring will be a girl; if the sperm cell contains a Y chromosome, the result will be a boy. Because the mother produces only X chromosomes, it is accurate to say that only the father's sperm can determine the sex of the offspring.

The ratio of males to females at birth is about 105 to 100 (U.S. Bureau of the Census, 1998). But males are more susceptible to various illnesses and diseases, so that by the age of 5 there are almost as many girls as boys. By age 75, women outnumber men by about 2 to 1.

The Genetic Code

That you are male or female is a biological accident, a fortuitous happening determined by a single pair of tiny chromosomes. In that pair of chromosomes, together with the other 22 pairs of chromosomes you inherited, lies your genetic code—your own, absolutely unique genetic blueprint.

Your genetic blueprint is coded in the form of arrangements of **deoxyribonucleic acid (DNA)**

---

meiosis   The division of a single sex cell into two separate cells, each consisting of 23 chromosomes rather than 23 pairs of chromosomes. Meiosis therefore results in cells that are completely different, whereas mitosis results in identical cells.

chromosome   A microscopic body in the nucleus of all human and plant cells containing the genes—the carriers of heredity. Each mature human sex cell (sperm or ovum) contains 23 chromosomes, each containing countless numbers of genes.

sex chromosome   A chromosome contained in sperm cells and ova responsible for determining the sex of the offspring. Sex chromosomes produced by the female are of one variety (X); those produced by the male may be either X or Y. At fertilization (the union of sperm and ovum), an XX pairing will result in a girl; an XY pairing will result in a boy. Hence the sperm cell is essentially responsible for determining the sex of the offspring.

autosomes   All chromosomes in mature sperm and ova other than the sex chromosome. Each of these cells therefore contains 22 autosomes.

X chromosome   One of two types of sex chromosomes, produced by both males and females. It is the only sex chromosome produced by females. An XX pairing of chromosomes determines that the offspring will be female.

Y chromosome   One of two types of sex chromosomes, produced only by the male (who also produces X chromosomes). An XY pairing determines that the offspring will be male.

deoxyribonucleic acid (DNA)   A substance assumed to be the basis of all life, consisting of four chemical bases arranged in an extremely large number of combinations. The two strands of the DNA molecule that compose genes are arranged in the form of a double spiral (helix). These double strands are capable of replicating themselves as well as crossing over from one strand of the spiral to the other and forming new combinations of their genetic material. The nuclei of all cells contain DNA molecules.

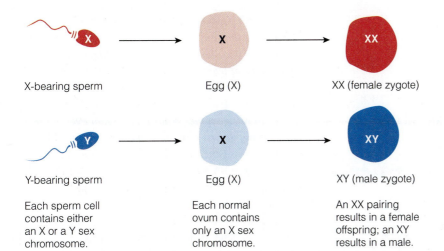

X-bearing sperm

Egg (X)

XX (female zygote)

Y-bearing sperm

Egg (X)

XY (male zygote)

Each sperm cell contains either an X or a Y sex chromosome.

Each normal ovum contains only an X sex chromosome.

An XX pairing results in a female offspring; an XY results in a male.

FIGURE 3.1 In this figure there is a clue to a fact of which Henry VIII was sadly ignorant as he beheaded a succession of wives for failing to give him a son. Can you figure it out before continuing? Only the male sex cell, the sperm, can contain either an X or a Y sex chromosome; the ovum always contains only the X chromosome. Because an XY pairing determines that the offspring will be male (XX is female), the "failure" of Henry's wives to produce sons was really his fault.

molecules that are located on your chromosomes. These are highly complex molecules, explains Sinclair (1998a), although each consists of arrangements of only four chemical bases. These chemicals, or *nucleotides*, are *adenine, guanine, thymine, and cytosine*, abbreviated AGTC, respectively. Not only are there only four of these chemical bases, but they invariably occur only in the pairs T–A or C–G (and the reverse, A–T and G–C). But because they occur in long interwoven strands (the shape, shown in Figure 3.2, is called a **double helix**), the number of variations possible is almost limitless.

Genes Our genetic instructions, the most basic units of our genetic blueprints, are segments of these DNA molecules. These segments are called **genes**. In total, our chromosomes contain about 70,000 genes (Wahlsten, 1999). These genes, either in pairs or in complex combinations of pairs, determine our potential for inherited characteristics. That's because the instructions coded into the genes that we inherit provide our cells with directions for synthesizing the thousands of different enzymes and proteins that are the basis of the living, functioning cells of which we are composed. Whalsten (1999) reports that there are more than 11,000 known human proteins. It is these instructions that deter-

mine that a cell will become part of the liver, that another will be part of the brain, and so on. As Sinclair (1998a) puts it, "Brain is distinguishable from muscle because of brain-specific proteins, and the differentiation and development of specific tissue is therefore dependent on the control of protein synthesized by the cells within that tissue" (p. 24). (See Figure 3.3.)

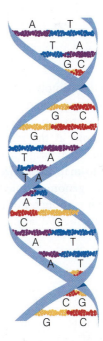

double helix The natural state of DNA molecules; essentially, two spiraling, intertwining chains of corresponding molecules.

genes The carriers of heredity—of which we have perhaps 70,000 or 100,000.

FIGURE 3.2 DNA molecules are arranged in sequences of pairs in a spiraling, double-helix structure. Genes, the units of heredity, can be thought of as locations or addresses on a segment of DNA molecule.

One human
body cell

Contains 23 pairs of chromosomes

For a total of about 70,000 genes

That are segments of DNA

Which, in the total human genome,
comprise about 3.3 billion pairs of the
chemical bases
A–T, T–A, C–G, and G–C

FIGURE 3.3 What's in a human cell? Mapping the human genome means determining the entire sequence of the more than 3 billion pairings of the chemical bases that make up DNA. Knowing the chemical sequence of a gene allows scientists to deduce its corresponding protein.

How Genes Interact

The goal of **genetics**, simply put, is to identify and understand the relations and functions of genes. Especially relevant to psychology is **behavioral genetics**, which looks at the relationship between genes and human behavior. A massive, worldwide project designed to map the entire complement of human genes, the **genome** project, has now succeeded in identifying, though not fully understanding, the human genome (Pollack, 2000).

---

genetics The science that studies heredity.

behavioral genetics The branch of genetics whose goal is to understand the functions, the identity, and the interactions of genes that are relevant to behavior.

genome The complete set of genetic instructions contained in our genes.

THOUGHT CHALLENGE: *Even what appears to be among the simplest of organisms, a single-celled yeast, has been found to contain a staggering 6,297 genes and at least as many proteins (Wahlsten, 1999). We humans, far more complex with our more than 3 trillion cells, have perhaps 70,000 genes in our genome. What might seem even more surprising, at first glance, is that almost one-third of the yeast's genes have homologs in humans (meaning that they are identical or nearly identical—that they share long sequences of duplicate chemical bases).*

The common house mouse has about the same number of genes as we do. And we share a far greater percentage of genes with the mouse than we do with the single-celled yeast.

What might this mean?

Mendelian and Molecular Genetics The human genome project uses complex, highly sophisticated techniques and enormous computer power. These techniques now make it possible to examine chromosomes directly, to look at sequences of DNA molecules, to identify their specific chemical components, to locate chemical segments that correspond to genes, and even to modify and to duplicate genes (see, for example, Peakman & Page, 1998).

As we noted, as a result of the human genome project, our genes have now been identified and assigned to specific locations, although scientists are still some distance from fully understanding how genes determine human characteristics, or which characteristics are affected by a given combination of genes. The implications of more fully understanding gene functioning are staggering. Correcting genetic defects might be possible, as might the alleviation of disorders and diseases caused by cell malfunctions. We might also eventually be able to predict accurately the outcome of different gene pairings.

In contrast, the first scientific studies of inheritance required only a magnifying glass (or even just a good pair of eyes), a generous allotment of intelligence as well as of inquisitiveness, and the patience of a monk.

The monk was Gregor Mendel, a nineteenth-century Austrian monk who bred, counted, and sorted generations of peas. By noting which peas had wrinkles and which didn't, and by relating them

THOUGHT CHALLENGE: *We have begun to be able to detect genetic defects before birth, to cure or prevent genetically linked disorders, to engineer our offspring in whatever direction we think perfection lies.*

What comes next? Does medicine play God? Do governments engineer genes to produce the kinds of people they want? Do chromosomal tests become mandatory? Do such tests become part of who we are, like our Social Security numbers?

to parent plants as well as to offspring, Mendel discovered some of the first, and perhaps most important, secrets of genes—secrets having to do with dominance and recessiveness. Not surprisingly, the study of genetic dominance and recessiveness by looking at family resemblance is referred to as **Mendelian genetics**.

Gene Dominance and Recessiveness Recall that genes come in pairs. Each member of a corresponding pair is called an allele. One **allele** has been inherited from the mother; the other member, from the father. Recall, too, that during meiosis, when the gametes are being produced, cells from both the mother and the father divide and are sorted randomly. What this means is that although the mother received half her genes from her father and half from her mother, her offspring might receive a preponderance of genes from one grandparent rather than the other.

The functioning of genes, as we learned, is responsible for our physical characteristics. For example, there are pairs of genes that correspond to eye color, hair characteristics, and virtually every other physical characteristic of an individual. In addition, other combinations of genes appear to be related to personality characteristics such as intelligence—although the ways in which genes affect personality are not as obvious or as easily measured as the ways in which they affect physical characteris-

tics. Among the many characteristics known to be largely determined, or at least influenced, by genes are a variety of disorders, illnesses, and defects, including some forms of blindness and baldness, hemophilia, and Down syndrome. Some of these conditions are discussed later in this chapter.

The secret that Mendel discovered from his studies of peas is that in some situations, one member of a pair of genes—that is, one allele—may be dominant over the other. In such situations, if an individual inherits different alleles from each parent (is **heterozygous** for that gene), the characteristics corresponding to the dominant form of the gene will appear in the individual (**dominant inheritance**). We know, for example, that the allele for normally pigmented skin is dominant over the allele for albinism (unpigmented skin) (McKusick, 1998). Hence an individual who inherits an allele for normal skin from one parent and one for albinism from the other will nevertheless have pigmented skin. A true albino (completely unpigmented skin) would need to be **homozygous** with respect to skin pigmentation. That is, such a person would need to have inherited recessive alleles for unpigmented skin from each parent (**recessive inheritance**). It follows as well that two albino parents will inevitably produce albino children. Figure 3.4 illustrates another characteristic related to the presence of a dominant allele: the ability to roll the tongue in a particular way.

Nondominant Interaction If human genetics were limited to the effects of single pairs of genes and their dominance or recessiveness, genetics would be relatively simple. In fact, however, many characteristics

Mendelian genetics The study of heredity through an examination of the characteristics of parents and offspring.

allele Each of the two corresponding forms of a gene, one being inherited from each parent.

heterozygous Having inherited different forms of corresponding alleles for a gene.

dominant inheritance The expression of traits related to a dominant allele. Occurs in individuals who are homozygous for the dominant form of the allele (have inherited identical *dominant* forms of the allele) and in individuals who are heterozygous for that trait (have inherited competing dominant and recessive forms of the allele).

homozygous Having inherited identical forms of alleles for a gene.

recessive inheritance The expression of traits related to a recessive allele. Occurs in individuals who are homozygous for the recessive form of the allele (have identical recessive alleles for the gene in question).

THOUGHT CHALLENGE: *Hemophilia, a blood-clotting disorder, is discussed later in this chapter in At a Glance: "Hemophilia among European Royalty." It is a genetic disorder linked with a recessive gene. It was first discovered during the second century in the Middle East, where, in a small community, increasing numbers of male babies were bleeding to death following circumcision. And throughout history, the disease has continued to appear among highly interbred groups such as, for example, European royalty (Tuddenham, 1997).*

Why is the incidence of genetic disorders linked with recessive genes more common among closely related individuals?

determination is the most common form of transmission among humans, notes Wahlsten (1999). Also, the effect of alleles is often additive rather than competitive. Thus the expression of many genetic characteristics, such as hair characteristics, for example, is often a sort of additive function of the action of corresponding alleles.

To further complicate matters, the DNA that genes consist of occasionally undergoes **mutations**—changes that may be brought about through x-rays, chemicals such as mustard gas, some drugs, or other causes. (See *Concept Summary*.)

---

polygenic determination The determination of genetically based characteristics as a function of the interaction of groups of genes.

mutations Changes in genetic material as a result of a mutagen (agent such as x-rays or certain drugs capable of altering genetic codes).

are a function of an undetermined number of pairs of genes acting in combination. This **polygenic**

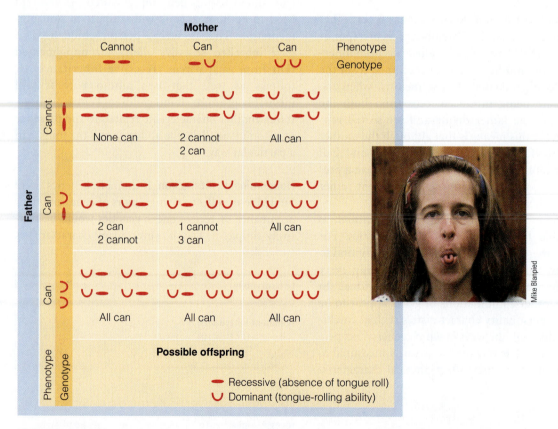

FIGURE 3.4 Can you roll your tongue as shown? Because tongue-rolling ability is determined by a dominant gene, if you can roll your tongue, then either your mother or your father can, because one of them must have the dominant gene for tongue rolling. If you cannot, one or both of them might still be able to roll their tongues. All possibilities are shown in the figure.

CONCEPT SUMMARY **Important Concepts in Heredity**

Terms and Concepts	Explanations
Conception	The union of gametes to form a zygote (a fertilized cell)
Gametes	Sex cells: The ovum (egg cell) for females; sperm cells for males. Production of mature sex cells begins at puberty and continues indefinitely for males; it ends at menopause for women.
Mitosis	Process by which body cells (somatic cells) divide, resulting in genetically identical cells.
Meiosis	Process by which sex cells divide to form gametes (ovum and sperm) that are genetically unique.
DNA	Deoxyribonucleic acid. Found in the nuclei of all human cells. The basis of organic life. Consists of four chemical bases arranged in an intertwined spiral pattern (double helix) in an enormous number of potentially different combinations.
Chromosomes	Microscopic, gene-containing bodies, of which there are 23 pairs in every normal human body cell, one pair inherited from each parent.
Sex chromosomes	One of the 23 pairs of chromosomes in cells (the others are called autosomes). Determine our sex. Males produce either an X or a Y sex chromosome; females, only an X. An XY pairing results in male offspring; an XX pairing, in female.
Behavior genetics	Science that looks at the relationship between genes and behavior.
Genes	Units of heredity, of which we have about 70,000. Segments of DNA molecules.
Human genome project	A massive, long-term, international project designed to map the entire human genetic structure.
Allele	One of two corresponding forms of a gene. Individuals who possess identical alleles for a gene are said to be homozygous; those who don't are heterozygous.
Dominant inheritance	Where a genetically based characteristic is determined mainly by the presence of the dominant form of a gene.
Recessive inheritance	Where the characteristics associated with a recessive allele are manifested only if both corresponding alleles are recessive.
Polygenetic determination	Where a genetically based characteristic is determined by the interaction of groups of genes.

GENOTYPE AND PHENOTYPE

Your genetic makeup is your **genotype**; it consists of all the genes you have inherited from your parents, including those whose effects are not expressed. Your manifested characteristics are your **phenotype**. Phenotype can often be observed directly (color of hair, for example); genotype is hidden and must either be inferred from phenotype or determined through an examination of the matter of which genes are composed.

It's possible to make accurate inferences about genotype for characteristics determined by **recessive genes**, but not for those determined by **dominant genes**. Normally, for example, the gene for nonred hair is dominant over that for red hair. Therefore we can infer that individuals whose phenotype (manifested characteristics) includes red hair must have two recessive genes for red hair (genotype). On the other hand, we can't be certain about the genotype for dark-haired individuals because they might have either two dominant genes for darker hair or a dominant gene for dark hair and a recessive gene for red hair (see Figure 3.5).

genotype Our inherited chromosomal or genetic makeup.

phenotype Manifest characteristics related to genetic makeup.

recessive gene A gene whose characteristics are not manifest in the offspring unless it happens to be paired with another recessive gene. When a recessive gene is paired with a dominant gene, the characteristics of the dominant gene will be manifest.

dominant gene The gene (carrier of heredity) that takes precedence over all other related genes in genetically determined traits. Because all genes in the fertilized egg normally occur in pairs of corresponding genes (termed *alleles*—one from the male and one from the female), the presence of a dominant gene as one member of the pair of genes means that the hereditary characteristic it controls will be present in the individual.

In reality, the effects of genotype on phenotype are not quite so simple as the hair-color illustration implies. As we saw, most human characteristics, including hair color, are usually polygenic, the result of combinations of genes. Often, as well, they are additive, meaning that phenotype results from the combined effects of alleles. As a result, the effects of polygenetic determination are not either/or (for example, either red or nonred), but include a whole range of possibilities. Thus it is that individuals are not simply red or nonred-haired, but can also have hair that is auburn, golden, black, mousy, even purple or blue.

The issue is further complicated by the fact that many human characteristics are not only polygenic but also **multifactorial**. That is, they result not simply from the influences of many genes, but rather from **interactions** among genes and a variety of environmental influences. As we see later in this chapter, these influences can include social experiences, drugs, injury, disease, and so on.

Genotype-Phenotype Relationships

Plomin (1987) summarizes the relationships between genotype and phenotype as follows:

▲ First, it is clear that genotypic differences lead to phenotypic differences. If you are homozygous with respect to the allele for the inability to roll

multifactorial Affected by or resulting from the combined or interactive effects of more than one factor—for example, the combined effects of genes and environments.

interaction A condition that exists when two or more forces influence each other, sometimes in very complex ways; also relates to how two or more forces act together (*coact*) to affect certain outcomes.

FIGURE 3.5 Phenotype (manifested characteristics) is influenced by genotype (genetic makeup). But genotype cannot always be inferred from phenotype. A brown-eyed person might have two genes for brown eyes or just one with a recessive gene for blue eyes.

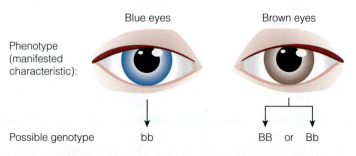

B: Gene for brown eyes; dominant
b: Gene for blue eyes; recessive

Blue eyes   Brown eyes

Phenotype (manifested characteristic):

Possible genotype   bb   BB   or   Bb

your tongue as shown in Figure 3.4, it is extremely unlikely that you can demonstrate that particular trick—although never entirely unlikely given the possibility of mutations.

▲ Second, characteristics that are influenced by more than one gene (polygenic) tend not to be dichotomous (either/or) but are distributed in a manner that approximates what is referred to as the **normal curve** (a bell-shaped curve in which the majority of cases cluster near the average, with fewer and fewer cases occurring farther and farther from the average). For example, height tends to be widely distributed, with most people being about average and few people being extremely tall or short.

▲ The environment also has important effects on manifested characteristics. Thus, height is not simply polygenic but rather multifactorial; it is clearly affected by environmental factors such as nutrition and health.

Canalization

For some characteristics, such as being able to speak two languages, a person's environment makes a great deal of difference; for others, such as hair color, it makes no difference. That is, some aspects of phenotype seem to correspond much more closely to underlying genetic material than do others. Characteristics that are less affected by environmental forces are said to reflect a higher degree of **canalization** (Waddington, 1975). Put another way, such characteristics are said to have a high degree of **heritability**. High heritability for a trait means that

genotype contributes significantly to the variations that might be seen in a population.

For characteristics that are not highly canalized, phenotype may be very different from what might have been predicted on the basis of genetic makeup alone. In evolutionary terms, canalization may be seen as a genetic tendency toward a predictable regularity that ensures that individuals of one species will be much more similar than dissimilar.

Reaction Range Even for highly canalized characteristics, however, phenotype (manifested characteristics) usually is influenced both by genetic and environmental factors. That is, **epigenesis**, the unfolding of genetically influenced characteristics, is brought about by the interaction of genes and environment. In a sense, it's as though genetic influences (genotypes) make possible a range of different outcomes, some more probable than others. Gottesman (1974) labels this range of possibilities **reaction range**. Simply stated, the reaction range for a particular characteristic includes all the possible outcomes for that characteristic given variations in the nature and timing of environmental influences. For example, your genetic makeup at birth might have been such that your most probable adult height would be 6 feet (1.83 meters). But, given exceptional nutrition—and maybe as a result of hanging upside down with weights dangling from your ears, you might conceivably succeed in growing to 6 feet 8 inches (2.03 meters) and be a sought-after apple picker. Or, given poor nutrition and a long-term bout of diarrhea, you could end up somewhat more stunted at 5 feet 6 inches (1.67 meters)—and content yourself with picking raspberries.

The Epigenetic Landscape Thus does the environment interact with genotype to determine which of the many possible outcomes—that is, which reaction from the range of all possible reactions—will be manifested. But which reaction is most likely to be expressed? Will you be tall, short, or average?

The answer, says Waddington (1975), depends on the relationship of relevant environmental

---

normal curve A mathematical function represented in the form of a symmetrical bell-shaped curve that illustrates how a large number of naturally occurring or chance events are distributed.

canalization Waddington's term to describe the extent to which genetically determined characteristics are resistant to environmental influences. A highly canalized trait (such as hair color) remains unchanged in the face of most environmental influences; less highly canalized characteristics (such as manifested intelligence) are highly influenced by the environment.

heritability An estimate, often expressed as a percentage, of the extent to which variations in a characteristic are determined by the individual's genetic makeup (genotype).

---

epigenesis The developmental unfolding of genetically influenced characteristics.

reaction range All the possible outcomes for a particular characteristic given variations in the nature and timing of environmental influences.

forces with genetic forces during the course of your development. To represent this relationship, Waddington presents the analogy of the **epigenetic landscape**, shown in Figure 3.6. In this model, genetic forces are represented by the valleys and contours that run down the landscape; the tilt of the landscape represents environmental forces; and the ball represents some characteristic, such as height. Where the ball ends up represents the final state of that characteristic.

The analogy makes several important points. First, given a normal environment (without dramatic shifts such as might result from earthquakes in the analogy), the most likely outcome is, quite predictably, that represented by the deepest grooves and valleys. Second, shifts (different tilts) in the environment can change the ball's path and dramatically affect the final outcome; third, for highly canalized traits (deeper channels), far greater environmental forces (changes in tilt) will be needed to influence the final outcome; and fourth, subtle environmental forces are more likely to affect the course of development early (at the top of the figure) rather than late in development (at the bottom of the figure, where all channels are deeper).

The concepts of reaction range and epigenetic landscape recognize that for human characteristics that are multifactorial, the same genotype can give rise to very different outcomes. As Wahlsten (1999) points out, "Most psychologically interesting behaviors are multifactorial, involving numerous genes whose actions are influenced by diverse features of the environment" (p. 612). Hence most behaviors of interest to the psychologist may be thought of as having a reaction range with some outcomes being more probable than others. (See *Concept Summary*.)

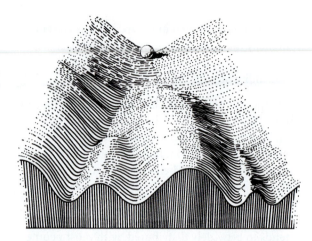

FIGURE 3.6 Waddington's epigenetic landscape is a graphic analogy depicting the interaction between environmental and genetic forces. The ball represents some characteristic of a developing organism, such as intelligence. The valleys and contours of the landscape represent genetic forces; they make certain outcomes more probable than others. Changes in the tilt of the landscape represent environmental forces, such as schooling and parenting. The analogy implies that changes in the environment are more influential earlier than later in a person's life (tilting the landscape only slightly is more likely to send the ball down a different course when it has just begun to roll, rather than later when it finds itself in deeper contours). Source: Based on Waddington (1975).

STUDYING GENE-ENVIRONMENT INTERACTION

One of the psychologist's important tasks is to discover the nature and timing of experiences that are most likely to have a beneficial influence on phenotype. Doing so requires understanding how genes and **environment** interact to determine the outcome of development. Of course, things would be far simpler if we weren't dealing with interactions, if we could actually separate the effects of environments and of genes in order to understand them better.

Feral Children

What do you suppose would happen, for example, if you were to conduct an experiment in which children would be taken from their parents at birth or very soon thereafter and raised by—or at least in the company of—wild animals? What human traits would they show as adults? Would this experiment reveal that what we think of as "human nature" is mainly genetic, robust enough to persist even in such an environment? Or would it reveal that human nature is the product of being reared in human cultures?

---

epigenetic landscape   Waddington's graphic analogy used to clarify the relationship between genetic and environmental forces.

environment   The significant aspects of an individual's surroundings. All the experiences and events that influence development, including the prenatal environment, social interactions, health, education, and so on.

CONCEPT SUMMARY Important Concepts in Genetics

Terms and Concepts	Explanations
Genotype	The individual's underlying genetic makeup.
Phenotype	The individual's manifested characteristics.
Multifactorial	Describes traits that are influenced by a variety of environmental influences as well as by genes.
Canalization	Describes the extent to which genetically influenced characteristics are resistant to environmental influences. Highly canalized traits (traits with high heritability) are less affected by environmental forces.
Reaction range	All the possible outcomes for a particular characteristic given variations in the nature and timing of environmental influences. Reaction range is greatest for least-canalized traits.

Stories of Feral Children Of course, we can't conduct such an experiment. But there are stories of **feral children** (wild children), children ostensibly abandoned by their parents and brought up by wolves or wild dogs or tigers, that might provide a "natural" experiment of this kind. Singh and Zingg (1942) describe 30 of these stories, and Armen (1974) reports that at least 54 such children have been found in the world. One of these stories is that of Amala and Kamala, two children reportedly dug out of a wolf's den in northern India. They had supposedly been abandoned as infants and raised by a she-wolf. When they were dragged from the den, claim Singh and Zingg (1942), they were as wild as any wolf. And when they had been tamed somewhat, they continued to scurry about on all fours, growling at people, refusing cooked food, gnawing on bones, and devouring raw meat. Eventually they languished and died. Similarly, McNeil, Polloway, & Smith (1984) report that when found, most feral children walk on all fours rather than upright, and that many are unable to learn to speak, or experience great difficulty in doing so.

But maybe we shouldn't take these stories too seriously; the evidence is not very convincing. In fact, Dennis (1941, 1951) claims he couldn't find a

single documented case of a child actually having been raised by a wild animal. The evidence, he says, is based solely on reports of children who apparently were found with animals or in animal lairs. The identity of these children usually has been unknown, so the length of time they spent in isolation can only be guessed; and in no case has anyone actually observed them with their supposed "adoptive parents." Dennis suggests it is likely that the so-called wild children were initially brain-damaged or had other developmental disabilities, and that this might explain why they were abandoned by their parents in the first place.

The Story of Genie But the literature has more recently reported several stories of abandoned children that are more believable. One is the story of Genie—a less dramatic story, perhaps, but no less sad. Unlike Amala and Kamala, Genie was not abandoned in the wilds. Instead, at the age of 20 months she was abandoned in a small, upstairs bedroom in her own home. Except for brief periods when she was still a toddler, Genie would not leave her room from age 20 months to 13 years.

Curtiss (1977) describes how Genie's room contained only a small crib entirely covered with wire mesh, and an infant potty. Nothing else. Day after day after day, she was left alone in this room, naked except for a leather harness that strapped her to the potty so that she had to sit on it for hours at a time.

---

feral children Wild children; children allegedly abandoned by their parents and raised by wild animals.

Corbis/Bettmann

Although there are no fully documented cases of children actually being raised by animals, some children have been neglected by parents and raised in almost total isolation. Such cases can provide researchers with important information about the interaction of heredity and environment, and about critical periods for learning things such as language.

Sometimes they forgot her on the pot at night; other times, they stuffed her into a straitjacket type of sleeping bag and threw her in the crib, completely imprisoned within the wire mesh. Her father or, more rarely, her brother, would occasionally come in and feed her—almost always either baby food, soupy cereal, or a soft-boiled egg. Her father permitted no other contact with her and allowed no one to speak to her. Whoever fed her simply stuffed as much food as possible into her mouth as quickly as possible. If she spit some of it out, her face would be rubbed in it. And if she cried or whimpered or made some other noise, even if only with her potty or her crib, her father would come in and beat her with a stick. He never spoke to her, but sometimes he pretended he was a dog, barking and growling at her and sometimes scratching her with his fingernails. If he wanted to threaten her, he would stand outside her door and make his most vicious dog noises.

When Genie was 13 years old, following an especially violent fight with the father, the mother finally took her and left. Shortly after that, Genie was discovered, charges were filed against the parents, and Genie was admitted to a hospital. Genie's father committed suicide on the day he was to be brought to trial. Although Genie made some progress, her language and social development remained far below normal (see Curtiss, 1977, and Rymer, 1993, for more complete details; see Chapter 7 for a discussion of the relevance of Genie's story for understanding the development of language; see also photo on page 439).

Historical Family Studies

From a psychological point of view, stories like Genie's might be important to the extent that they shed light on the heredity-environment issue. The argument is that whatever characteristics these children share with others who are brought up in more "normal" environments result from genetic influences, and that whatever "human" characteristics they failed to develop are more sensitive to environmental forces. Thus we might begin to separate the relative contributions of each to human development. But in truth, the study of feral children is not a very scientific way of investigating gene-context interaction; it doesn't allow the sorts of controls that science demands.

Another approach to the same puzzle is to look at differences and similarities among members of a family. Why? Simply because family members share genes. As Plomin (1987) points out, there is 100% genetic similarity between identical twins, approximately 50% similarity among siblings who share both parents, and somewhere around 25% similarity among siblings who share only one parent.

It is the high degree of genetic relatedness among family members that led Francis Galton, Charles Darwin's cousin, to conclude that intelligence is largely hereditary. He had noticed that most of England's outstanding scientists came from just a few families. But this isn't very good research, surely. Even if Galton's observations were entirely accurate, they don't prove his point because it could be argued, for example, that the reason these families produced outstanding scientists was simply that they provided their children with environments that led to the development of genius. Still, Galton was convinced of the heritability of intelligence, and he argued that parents should be selected for favorable genetic characteristics—a practice termed **eugenics**.

Animal Studies

Gene-environment interactions can sometimes be studied more easily with animals than with humans. First, certain anatomical measurements are sometimes possible with animals but not with humans (brain dissections, for example). Second, animals'

environments can be controlled far more completely than can humans' environments (in terms of environmental stimulation, food, social contacts, and so on). Third, animal matings can be controlled precisely, and many generations can be produced and studied over shorter periods of time. And fourth, as Wahlsten (1999) points out, we share an enormous number of genes even with animals as different from us as the ordinary house mouse.

Still, there are some serious limitations of animal studies, not the least of which is the difficulty of generalizing findings from animals to humans. Because this text is about children, we mention rats and other animals only in passing.

Breeding Animals for Intelligence Animal studies have demonstrated that it is possible to breed different strains of the same species that are predictably different in some identifiable characteristics. For example, in only a few generations mice can be bred for aggression, emotionality, or preference for alcohol; and rats can be bred for intelligence (see Figure 3.7). In much the same way, various "personality" characteristics have been developed in different breeds of dogs: fierceness and fighting ability in pit bull terriers, vigilance in German shepherds, and obstinacy and contrariness in the Lefrançois hound.

Experience Interacting with Genes But even in rats, dogs, and other nonhuman animals, genetics by itself seldom tells the whole story. Consider, for example, the case of the song thrush, an absolute glutton for snails. Because the snail invariably comes wrapped in a hard shell, eating it might pose a problem for a stupid bird. But not for the song thrush. Grabbing the snail's foot in its beak, the bird whips its head sideways, back and forth, back and forth, smashing the snail against a rock until the shell is demolished (Weisfeld, 1982). This appears to be a genetically influenced behavior because the European blackbird, a close relative of the song thrush that also dines on snails, doesn't seem to be able to learn the same shell-smashing behavior. However, it is also an environmentally influenced behavior because, in the beginning, the young song thrush doesn't know how to smash a snail shell. It learns to do so largely by trial and error during a critical period early in its life. If it's not given an opportunity to learn during this critical period, it

---

eugenics A form of genetic engineering that selects specific individuals for reproduction. Applying eugenics to humans raises a number of serious moral and ethical questions. It is widely accepted and practiced with animals, however.

FIGURE 3.7 An approximate representation of Tyron's (1940) successful attempt to breed maze-bright (intelligent) and maze-dull (dumb) rats. He kept track of how many errors rats made as they learned to run a maze and then mated the fastest learners with other bright rats and the slowest learners with other dull rats. After only 18 generations, there was no longer any overlap between the groups. The dullest rats among the bright group had become brighter than the smartest of the dull group. Source: Based on Tryon (1940), p. 113.

Unselected parental strain

Second-generation rats

Fifth-generation rats

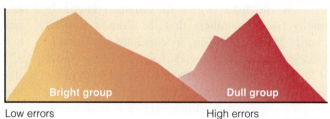

Eighteenth-generation rats

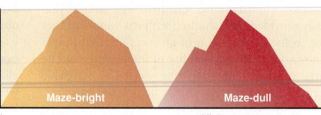

goes through life never knowing how to eat a snail the way other song thrushes do it.

What investigations such as these illustrate most clearly is the complexity of gene-environment interaction, even for behaviors we might assume to be entirely genetically based. In addition, animal studies suggest that behaviors with important adaptive functions become more probable through succeeding generations. Because these behaviors concern biological adaptation and the survival and propagation of species, they are typically related to feeding, rest, defense, reproduction, or elimination (Weisfeld, 1982).

Are there similar, genetically ordained behaviors among humans? Some researchers think so. These behaviors, they argue, are common to all members of the species—and hence to all human cultures. In addition, they occur in the absence of experiences that might otherwise explain their acquisition. Weisfeld (1982) suggests that these genetically programmed behaviors might include such things as infants' distress at being separated from their mother or other caregiver (more about this in Chapter 6); the tendency of mothers in all cultures to hold their infants on the left side, whether or not they are right-handed; various facial expressions that have identical meanings everywhere (such as the human smile, which occurs in blind as well as in sighted infants); and human vocalizations, which are initially identical in deaf and in hearing infants.

Studies of Twins

"If I had any desire to lead a life of indolent ease," Gould (1981) tells us, "I would wish to be an identical twin, separated at birth from my brother and raised in a different social class. We could hire ourselves out to a host of social scientists and practically name our fee. For we would be exceedingly rare representatives of the only really adequate natural experiment for separating genetic from environmental effects in humans" (p. 234).

Why is this so? Because identical twins are genetically identical; they result from the splitting of a single fertilized ovum (zygote). This segmentation results in two zygotes with an identical genetic makeup (hence **monozygotic** or **identical twins**). The other type of twins, **dizygotic twins**, (or **fraternal twins**) results from the **fertilization** of two different egg cells by two different sperm cells. This is possible only when the mother's ovaries simultaneously

release more than one egg, and the result is twins who are no more alike genetically than ordinary siblings.

Frequency of Multiple Births Unfortunately for researchers, the incidence of twins is relatively low—approximately 1 in every 86 births. Furthermore, identical twins are much rarer than fraternal twins—about 1 in every 250 births worldwide (Segal, 1999). Identical triplets occur only about once in every 50,000 births; quadruplets and quintuplets are, of course, even rarer ("The Guinea Pigs," 1997).

The precise causes of twin births are not known. Interestingly, however, it doesn't seem that the tendency to produce identical twins is genetic. In fact, Segal (1999) suggests that the chances of identical twins occurring in any given family are about the same as in any other, and that the event appears to be highly random. That, however, seems to be less the case for fraternal twins. Much more is known about the factors that may be involved in such births. For example, the probability of having fraternal twins is higher among women above age 35. Also, fraternal twins are more common among certain ethnic groups than others (about 1 in 22 births among the Yoruba tribe in Nigeria compared with 1 in 700 in Japan; Gall, 1996; Segal, 1999). Other factors sometimes associated with the probability of having fraternal twins are listed in Table 3.1.

monozygotic Resulting from a single egg. Twins and higher multiples whose origins are the division of a single fertilized ovum are genetically identical.

identical (monozygotic) twins Twins whose genetic origin is a single egg. Such twins are genetically identical.

fraternal (dizygotic) twins Twins whose genetic origins are two different ova and who are therefore no more alike genetically than any other pair of siblings.

fertilization The union of sperm and ovum; the beginning of life.

TABLE 3.1
Factors Correlated with Incidence of Fraternal Twin Births

Note that these are simply correlations, not causes. Also, many of the relationships described here are considered speculative rather than conclusive.

Mothers are most likely to have fraternal twins if:
- They are over 35.
- They have intercourse frequently.
- They have had many children previously.
- There is a higher incidence of twins among ancestors, especially on the mother's side.
- Conception occurred after intercourse that followed a period of sexual abstinence.
- Parents are not subjected to undue stress.

Source: Based on information in Segal, 1999, pp. 4–5.

Intelligence Many studies of twins have looked at correlations for intelligence test scores. Recall from Chapter 1 that a correlation coefficient is a measure of strength of relationship, usually expressed as a number ranging from −1 to +1. A high positive correlation—say, +0.75 to +1.00—means that if one twin has a low intelligence test score, the other twin is likely also to have a low score (or both are likely to have high or mediocre scores). A high negative correlation means that a low score for one would be associated with a high score for the other.

In general, the median correlation coefficient for intelligence test scores for identical twins is above +0.80, whereas that for fraternal twins is below +0.60 (Bouchard & McGue, 1981). This observation appears to be true even for very young children. For example, Reznick, Corley, and Robinson (1997) report a correlation of .83 for intelligence test scores of a group of 2-year-old monozygotic twins. Correlation for comparable dizygotic twins was .61.

If members of identical and fraternal twin pairs have had similar environments, these correlations may be interpreted as evidence that measured intelligence is influenced by heredity. With decreasing genetic similarity there is a corresponding decrease in the correlation in intelligence scores; the correlation for cousins is less than that for twins. This, too, is evidence of the influence of heredity.

But these data also support the belief that the environment influences measured intelligence. Because most sets of identical twins have more similar environments than do cousins or siblings, the higher correlations between various intelligence measures for identical twins may be due at least in part to their more nearly identical environments. The difference between identical twins reared together and those reared apart is additional evidence that environment influences development. Median correlations of intelligence test scores of identical twins raised together and apart were +0.85 and +0.67, respectively. Because these twins are genetically identical, environmental forces are clearly important. It's also revealing that as identical twins grow up, their phenotypes (manifested characteristics) become less similar while their genotypes remain identical—additional evidence of the importance of gene-environment interaction (McCartney, Bernieri, & Harris, 1990).

Studies of Adopted Children

Like studies of twins, studies of adopted children provide an important source of information about interactions among genetic and environmental influences. When it's possible to obtain information about both biological and adoptive parents, and about natural and adopted children, studies of adopted children permit a wide range of comparisons—for example, among individuals who share genes only (like adopted children and a biological parent), who share environment only (like adopted and natural children), or who share both (like siblings in the same family).

For example, in the Minnesota-Texas Adoption Project, which began in 1973, investigators have had access to data that include physical as well as cognitive measures of the adopted children's biological mothers (and sometimes fathers as well), the adopted children themselves, the adoptive parents, and the adoptive parents' biological children in the adoptive home (for example, Loehlin, Horn, & Willerman, 1997; Beer, Arnold, & Loehlin, 1998). The Colorado Adoption Project provides similar opportunities (for example, Cherney, Fulker, & Hewitt, 1997).

As Figure 3.8 shows, the highest correlations for intelligence test scores are for those who share genes; the lowest are for those who share environment but not genes. Perhaps even more striking, correlations between adopted children and their biological mothers are higher than those between adopted children and their adoptive parents. In fact, the correlation between adopted children and their biological mothers is about the same as that between adoptive parents and their own children, in spite of the fact that the adopted children, unlike the biological children, are not raised by their own mothers (Plomin et al., 1997).

These findings have also been corroborated in the Colorado Adoption Project. For example, Alarcon and associates (1998) analyzed data from 175 adopted children and their adoptive parents as well as their biological mothers, and data from another 209 non-adopted children and their parents. Consistent with other findings, they also report that different environments appear to have far less effect on intellectual abilities than biological factors.

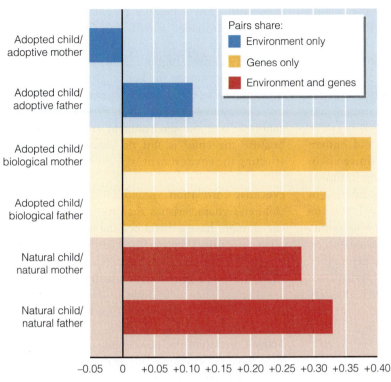

FIGURE 3.8 Correlations for general cognitive ability from a 20-year longitudinal study of adopted and natural children. Source: R. Plomin, D. W. Fulker, R. Corley, and J. C. DeFries (1997). Nature, nurture, and cognitive development from 1 to 16 years: A parent-offspring study. *Psychological Science* 8: 442–447.

So, how do we now evaluate the nature-nurture question? The issue is still not a simple one. And although the question has been posed since the beginnings of psychology, the answers that psychologists accept have changed dramatically over the years. Sternberg (1991) points out that in the 1960s, psychology accepted the idea that the reason some children were more intelligent than others was that they had inherited more "intelligence" from their parents. However, by the 1970s, many had come to believe that intelligence is determined mainly by a child's experiences, and there was a surge of emphasis on providing children with stimulating experiences, especially early in life. The 1980s brought the conviction that both heredity and environment are important, but not as isolated forces—that rather it is the interaction between the two that is important. In Gottlieb's (1992) words: "The cause of development—what makes development happen— is the relationship of the two components, not the components themselves. Genes in themselves cannot cause development any more than stimulation in itself can cause development" (p. 161). The only

logical conclusion, insists Harris (1998), is that the causes of human variation are to be found in interactions among our genes and our environments.

Gene-Environment Interaction

To understand the conclusion that developmental outcomes are the product of interactions among our genes and our environments, we have to understand what is meant by interaction.

What Is Interaction? Interaction is not a simple concept; nor are its outcomes always highly predictable. Consider, for example, something as simple as changes in temperature as a way of changing water into ice. We know that water and temperature can interact to form ice. It seems a simple interaction—although we would be hard pressed to understand the texture of ice, its taste, or its effect on our skin solely by understanding temperature and water. Also, the effect of temperature on water is not always ice: It can also be steam. But that, too, appears to be a relatively simple, highly predictable interaction: More heat eventually equals steam; less heat eventually equals ice. But the interaction is not quite so simple because there are other variables involved, other interactions at play. For example, with changes in air pressure, the interaction of water and temperature changes so that now, more or less heat is required for the same effect.

So too, with genes, environment, and human behavior; interaction is not a simple additive affair. Relative contributions of heredity and environment may change with a person's age, may be different in different environments, and may vary from one individual to another. As Eisenberg (1998) points out, nature and nurture are not opposing forces. Children don't just inherit their parents' genes; they also inherit the parents themselves, perhaps an assortment of siblings and other relatives, the very places in which they live, and on and on.

Gene-Environment Correlation: The Scarr-McCartney Model

"The dichotomy of nature and nurture has always been a bad one," write Scarr and McCartney (1983). Why? Not simply because both influence the outcomes of development, but because they can also influence each other directly. For example, what we know of evolution makes it clear that those gene combinations that underlie adaptive behaviors are more likely to survive in our gene pools; those that are maladaptive have a poorer chance of surviving. Thus does the environment influence genes.

It is perhaps not so obvious, but no less true, that genes can also influence environment. For example, a study of 700 pairs of twins reported by Plomin (1989) provides strong evidence of a close relationship between genetic influence and measures of environmental factors. Similarly, O'Connor and associates (1998) report a correlation between genes and environment in studies of adopted children.

Scarr and McCartney (1983) summarize many of these concepts in a model that attempts to explain the observation that genes and environments are often very closely correlated.

Passive Correlation To begin with, say Scarr and McCartney, there is a sort of **passive** correlation between children's genes and the environment. This

correlation results because parental characteristics that are themselves genetic influence the sorts of environments they provide for their children. For example, Sandra's highly intelligent parents might provide more books for her, might enroll her in a variety of courses, might take her on safaris, and so on. This source of correlation between the child's genotype and the environment is termed passive because the child is not deliberately involved in affecting the environment.

Evocative Correlation Second is the observation that children's characteristics that are genetically influenced might have a direct bearing on their environments because they elicit certain responses from others. For example, Robert's teachers might go out of their way to provide stimulating and expensive experiences (hence a different environment) for Robert because he seems to be a little **prodigy**.

Active Correlation As they develop, children deliberately look for environments that reflect genetically influenced interests and abilities. This gives rise to what Scarr and McCartney label **active correlation**—*active* because the child purposely selects and shapes aspects of the environment. Thus Martha, who is athletic, fast, and strong, looks for opportunities to play organized sports and to work physically; and Alfredo, who comes from a long line of concert pianists, surrounds himself with music, and constantly begs his parents to buy him music teachers. Both Martha and Alfredo actively strive not only to select environments compatible with their genotypes, but also to shape those in which they find themselves. The active selection of environments is labeled **niche-picking**.

passive correlation Scarr and McCartney's label for the observation that genetically influenced parental characteristics sometimes determine important aspects of a child's environment—thus explaining some of the correlation often observed between genotype and environments.

prodigy Somebody who displays exceptional talent for something at an early age.

active correlation Scarr and McCartney's label for the observation that people often deliberately select, or try to shape, environments to conform to genetic predispositions—a phenomenon that accounts for genotype-environment correlation.

niche-picking Scarr and McCartney's term for the active selection of environments highly compatible with personal interest, skills, and other personal characteristics.

An Illustration of Gene-Context Interaction We can't always pick our niches, however. Sometimes forces more powerful than those we control shape our worlds and determine many of our experiences. But even in these cases, our genes can nevertheless affect our environments.

As an example, during the Great Depression of the 1930s, thousands of fathers lost their jobs and could no longer look after their families. One of the effects of this dramatic change in father's environments, explain Elder, Nguyen, and Caspi (1985), was also a very significant change in the environments in which children found themselves. Some fathers became harshly punitive toward their children; others became exploitive; still others became more rejecting and indifferent. In contrast, mothers, for whom loss of the husband's job would be an economic but not a personal blow, seemed relatively unaffected, and their relationships with their children changed little.

These changes, notes Elder (1979), were especially difficult for adolescents, whose relationships with parents changed in systematic ways. Boys' perceptions of the power and attractiveness of their fathers tended to decline, whereas the influence of the boys' peers increased. Interestingly, however, adolescent boys did not appear to suffer in terms of confidence, aspirations, and positive self-concept. In contrast, girls tended to lower their aspirations and their self-esteem and to experience increased moodiness and unhappiness. These negative effects, claims Elder, were linked not so much to economic hardships as to the rejecting behavior of the fathers. And, in general, the negative effects were more serious for girls than for boys.

But what is most striking, and most relevant for our understanding of how genes can affect environments, is the observation that the least attractive girls suffered most. In Elder, Nguyen, and Caspi's (1985) words, "If girls were unattractive, family hardship accentuated fathers' overly demanding, exploitive behavior . . . [but] only when girls were rated as unattractive" (p. 371). In fact, in some cases economic hardship actually increased the extent to which fathers were warm and supportive of their attractive daughters, sacrificing and going out of their way to provide for them. It seems that girls' genetic characteristics (physical attractiveness) had a marked effect on their environments (at least with respect to father-daughter relationships).

One lesson to be learned from studies such as these is clear: If we are to understand the development and the lives of people, it is essential that we take into account the contexts in which they are born and live. In Bronfenbrenner's terms, we need to look at the microsystem (in this study, the adolescent in interaction with father, mother, and peers); the mesosystem (family interactions with school or with adolescents' workplaces); the exosystem (the father's changed relationship with his work setting); and the macrosystem (the dramatic social and economic changes of the Great Depression). An ecological approach to understanding development provides a framework for beginning to understand how characteristics that have a strong genetic basis (physical appearance, for example) can influence interactions in systems that are also influenced by environmental factors (such as economic conditions, for instance).

Human Plasticity: Reaction Range Revisited

When Snyderman and Rothman (1987) questioned 1,020 American psychologists, they found that most believed that intelligence is inherited to a significant degree. At the same time, virtually all recognize that human characteristics are profoundly influenced by the interaction of genes and changing contexts.

In spite of this, the old nature-nurture question—the question of whether certain traits are influenced primarily by heredity or by the environment, the question of how important each is—has not gone away. It's a controversy that stems from an extreme and often emotional belief that all of us are, or at least should be, equal. And if we are equal, then it cannot be that Frances has an assortment of genes highly likely to lead to charm, intelligence, and grace while Francis starts his life with an assortment of genes that propel him blindly toward stupidity or schizophrenia.

Or can it? Science suggests that yes, our genes are different and yes, we have different probabilities of reaching certain outcomes. But science also tells us that, in Gottlieb's (1992) words: ". . . the persistence of the nature-nurture dichotomy reflects an inadequate understanding of the relations among heredity, development, and evolution . . ." (p. 137). Science also tells us that genes, by themselves, determine little.

They simply underlie potential, making some outcomes more probable than others. Even in the face of highly probable (highly canalized) outcomes, environmental forces can lead to surprising and wonderful things.

That is the essence of Gottesman's (1974) concept of reaction range (discussed earlier). It is also the basis of Stern's (1956) **rubber-band hypothesis** (Figure 3.9). In this model plasticity, or reaction range, is likened to the stretchability of a rubber band. Some of us were born with short, unstretched bands (limited inherited potential for intelligence), others with longer bands. Some environments stretch bands a lot, others hardly stretch them at all, and some perhaps even shrivel them. Long bands, of course, stretch more easily.

rubber-band hypothesis Stern's comparison of human intelligence to a rubber band, the original length of which is genetically determined. The final length of the band is determined by the interaction of environmental forces with the band's elasticity.

Do highly demanding environments break bands? Do old bands become frayed and brittle? Do bands stretch more easily when new? Unfortunately, analogies are simply comparisons; they provide no answers for questions like these. (see *Concept Summary* on pp. 118–119.)

GENETIC DEFECTS

To continue with the rubber-band analogy, not only are there long and short bands, but there appear to be some that are brittle—and others that are astonishingly elastic. In this section, we look at brittle bands, at those that have defects. But we consider only a very small fraction of the thousands of conditions that are now known to be genetically linked, and that are catalogued in the most recent edition of McKusick's (1998) compendium—currently contained in three very large volumes.

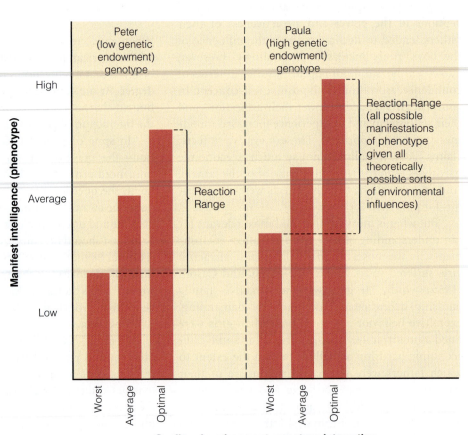

FIGURE 3.9 The Stern rubber-band hypothesis, a model of gene-environment interaction and of reaction range. Individuals with different inherited potentials for intellectual development (genotype) can manifest a wide range of measured intelligence (phenotype) as a function of gene-environment interaction

In most cases, serious disorders are linked with recessive rather than dominant alleles. Recall that an allele is one of two corresponding forms of a gene, and that these can be homozygous (the same form) or heterozygous (of different forms). The reason most severe abnormalities are linked with recessive forms of a gene is simple: Any abnormality that is linked with a dominant allele will always be manifested in all individuals with that form of the gene, and will have relatively little chance of being passed on to offspring (especially if it leads to early death). For example, a disorder that is fatal in childhood and that is linked with a dominant gene should disappear from the human gene pool after a single generation. In contrast, abnormalities that are linked to the recessive forms of a gene will be manifested only in individuals who have not inherited the normal allele from at least one parent. Many individuals may be carriers of a single recessive gene for some abnormality, without manifesting the abnormality. Their offspring will likewise not manifest the abnormality, unless both parents carry the relevant recessive gene and each passes it on to the offspring.

Huntington's Disease

One exception to the general rule that most serious or fatal disorders are linked to recessive alleles is **Huntington's disease** (also called Huntington's chorea). In fact, Huntington's disease is one of the few examples of a genetic disorder that shows *complete* dominance—meaning that carriers of the gene almost invariably manifest the disease (McKusick, 1998). For most other genetically linked disorders, dominance is often incomplete. This means that sometimes the disorder is not manifested; other times, it manifests itself in different, or weaker, forms.

Despite being linked with a completely dominant allele, Huntington's disorder is still present in the human gene pool because it does not ordinarily manifest itself until the age of 30 or 40, thus giving carriers an opportunity to pass the gene on to their offspring. When Huntington's does appear, it leads to rapid neurological deterioration and eventual death.

Until recently there was no way of determining whether an individual carried the dominant gene for Huntington's disease. Thus people whose grandparents, parents, uncles and aunts, or siblings had cases of Huntington's could only wait to discover whether the disease would eventually strike them too. Now, however, using the new techniques of molecular genetics, geneticists have succeeded in locating the gene for the disorder, making it possible to determine relatively accurately the probability that an individual will be affected. However, Huntington's disease is still incurable—and fatal (van Vugt & Roos, 1999). As a result, more than half of those who might be carriers of the gene prefer not to be screened (Jacopini et al., 1992).

Sickle-Cell Anemia

Sickle-cell anemia is a genetic disorder linked to a recessive gene (Figure 3.10). In the United States, approximately 10% of all African Americans, and a much lower proportion of whites, carry the recessive gene for sickle-cell anemia (Thompson, Gil, & Abrams, 1992). These 10% are heterozygous for this gene (having one normal and one abnormal allele); another 0.25% of the African American population are homozygous recessive individuals (carrying two defective genes). Effects of the defective gene are clearly apparent in abnormally shaped red blood cells (sickle-shaped, rather than circular), which multiply with lack of oxygen. Sickle-shaped cells tend to clot together and thus carry even less oxygen, thereby increasing in number and reducing oxygen still more. Individuals who are homozygous recessive for this gene often die in childhood or are severely ill throughout life (Famuyiwa & Akinyanju, 1998). Those who are heterozygous for the gene are ordinarily healthy except in conditions of low oxygen, such as at high altitudes; there they may become quite ill, indicating that the normal gene is not completely dominant.

The fact that sickle-cell anemia is so common among blacks, particularly in Central African coastal areas (40% heterozygous and 4% homozygous recessive), would, on the surface, appear to be a

---

Huntington's disease An inherited neurological disorder characterized by neural degeneration, typically beginning between the ages of 20 and 40 and usually leading to death.

sickle-cell anemia A blood-cell disorder associated with a recessive allele, far more common among blacks than whites.

Studying Gene-Environment Interaction

Type of Investigation	Observation
Feral children	Largely anecdotal evidence of animal-like traits among children ostensibly raised by wild animals.
Historical family studies	A handful of families have produced most of England's most brilliant scientists. (Galton)
Animal studies	After 8 generations, even the dullest of the "bright" rats is "brighter" than the brightest of the dull rats. (Tryon)
	The thrush eats snails by smashing their shells against rocks, but must learn to do so through a period of trial and error during a critical period early in its development. (Weisfeld)
Studies of twins Studies of adopted children	The higher the degree of biological relatedness, the higher the correlation for measures such as intelligence, some manifestations of mental disorders, and a number of other characteristics. At the same time, shared environments are reflected in higher correlations in many of these same characteristics.

Main Conclusions	Reliability
"Human nature" is largely a function of being raised by humans in a human environment.	Very low: unreplicable, unverifiable anecdotal evidence
Intelligence among humans is largely inherited.	Very low: no control for similarity of environments
Intelligence—or at least maze-brightness—among rats is largely inherited.	Problems of establishing generalizability from rats to humans
Context and genetic influences interact in complex ways to determine even what seem to be highly "instinctual" behaviors.	Problems of relevance to human behavior
• Genes clearly contribute to measured intelligence—as do environmental influences. • In a sense, genes determine potential; the interaction of genes and context determines outcomes. • While we have different probabilities of reaching certain outcomes, we are remarkably plastic within a range of possible outcomes (rubber-band hypothesis). • Environments are often correlated with genotype. In the Scarr-McCartney model, the sources of correlation may be passive (parents' genetic makeup determines both their children's genotype and the environments they provide for them), evocative (children's genotypes influence people's reactions to them), or active (children's genotype influences their selection and shaping of environments)	High reliability; well-controlled, frequently replicated studies

Parents

Phenotype normal (don't manifest sickle-cell anemia); genotype heterozygous (each possesses both the normal and the defective allele for sickle-cell anemia)

Normal gene   Defective gene

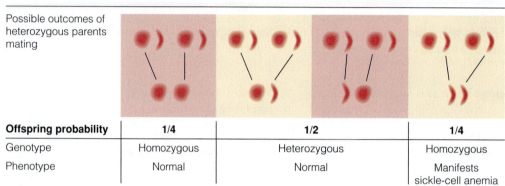

Possible outcomes of heterozygous parents mating			
Offspring probability	1/4	1/2	1/4
Genotype	Homozygous	Heterozygous	Homozygous
Phenotype	Normal	Normal	Manifests sickle-cell anemia

FIGURE 3.10 Sickle-cell anemia is linked to a recessive gene. In this illustration, parents are heterozygous (each possesses both the normal gene, which is dominant, and the sickle-cell gene, which is recessive) and therefore neither parent suffers from the disease. As shown, there is a 1 in 4 chance that the offspring of such parents will inherit two defective genes and suffer from the disease.

contradiction of evolutionary theory. We would expect the presence of the sickle-cell gene to have disappeared over generations. However, following the discovery that individuals who are heterozygous for sickle-cell trait are also resistant to malaria, it becomes clear that the high incidence of this defective gene in malaria-prone areas is, in fact, a dramatic example of ongoing evolution. Not surprisingly, incidence of the disease is now decreasing among African Americans.

PKU

Phenylketonuria (PKU) is a genetic defect associated with the presence of two recessive alleles. In individuals suffering from this disease, the liver enzyme responsible for breaking down the amino acid phenylalanine into usable substances is absent or inactive. Infants who inherit two recessive genes for PKU appear normal at birth, but with the con-

tinued ingestion of phenylalanine (which makes up about 5% of ingested protein by weight) their nervous system deteriorates irreversibly, and they become increasingly mentally retarded (Dennis et al., 1999). Fortunately, however, PKU is easily detected at birth; and its onset can be prevented by providing children with diets low in phenylalanine from infancy (Brown & Guest, 1999). Here, then, is a disorder that is clearly genetic, but that does not become manifest until the occurrence of specific environmental events (ingestion of phenylalanine). Furthermore, in the absence of these environmental influences (that is, given a diet low in phenylalanine), the individual's genotype (presence of relevant recessive alleles) will not be reflected in the phenotype (manifested characteristics).

Tay-Sachs Disease

Another disorder caused by a recessive gene is **Tay-Sachs disease**, an enzyme disorder that results in the brain's inability to break down certain fats. Eventually these build up, preventing neural transmission and leading to the degeneration of brain cells. Affected individuals commonly die before the age of 3. In some cases, however, symptoms of Tay-Sachs disease develop in adolescents or even in adults

phenylketonuria (PKU) A genetic disorder associated with the presence of two recessive genes.

Tay-Sachs disease A fatal genetic enzyme disorder that can be detected before birth, but that cannot yet be prevented or cured.

(MacQueen, Rosebush, & Mazurek, 1998). Although the gene for Tay-Sachs disease can be detected, the disease cannot yet be prevented or cured.

Muscular Dystrophy (MD)

Muscular dystrophy (MD) is a degenerative muscular disorder of which there are various forms. Some forms have been linked to a recessive gene (Funakoshi, Goto, & Arahata, 1998). It sometimes involves an inability to walk and may lead to death. Also, it is often associated with lower mental functioning (Cotton, Crowe, & Voudouris, 1998). Some forms of MD (for example, Duchenne MD) can be detected in **fetuses** by genetic screening. In addition, parents can be tested, which would result in an estimate of the probability that their offspring will be affected.

Neural Tube Defects

Among the most common congenital malformations are **neural tube defects**, which occur at a rate of 1 for every 500 to 1,000 births (Miller et al., 1990). Neural tube defects may take the form of spina bifida, in which the spine remains open at the bottom, or of anencephaly, in which portions of the skull and brain are absent. Such defects often lead to severe retardation or death. Although genetically linked, the causes of these defects are multifactorial. For example, certain drugs (such as lithium) used in treating mental illness (Kennedy & Koren, 1998) and starvation as in times of famine (Susser et al., 1998) are associated with higher incidence of neural tube defects. It is known, for example, that folic acid deficiency in the mother is closely associated with an increased risk of neural tube defects. As a result,

many physicians recommend that mothers take folic acid supplements prior to conception. Good natural sources of folic acid include peanuts, organ meats such as kidney and liver, and green leafy vegetables. In addition, folic acid is added to most vitamin supplements and, in the United States, is now a required additive in enriched white flour.

Neural tube defects generally develop very early in pregnancy (as early as the first week) and can be detected by means of an **AFP test**—a standard test conducted at about the thirteenth week of pregnancy to ascertain the level of *alpha-fetoprotein* in the mother's blood (Ormond, 1997). If this substance is present in higher-than-normal concentrations, additional tests (such as *ultrasound* or *fetoscopy*, which are described later) are performed to determine whether there is a neural tube defect. In some jurisdictions, AFP screening is routine or even mandatory (as are tests for PKU).

Diabetes Mellitus

Some forms of **diabetes**, an insulin-deficiency disease, are associated with recessive genes, as well as with other factors. Children born to mothers with diabetes mellitus have a 2 to 3 times higher risk of birth defects, which can include limb deformities, cardiac problems, neural tube defects, and other problems (Friedman, 1992).

Other Genetic Defects

Thousands of genetic defects have now been identified and catalogued (McKusick, 1998). A few, like Huntington's disease, are associated with a dominant allele; others, like sickle-cell anemia, result from the presence of two recessive alleles. The vast majority, however, are polygenic as well as multifactorial: They result from interactions among a number of genes and are also affected by

---

muscular dystrophy (MD) A degenerative muscular disorder, most forms of which are genetic, usually manifested in an inability to walk and sometimes fatal.

fetus An immature child in the uterus. Fetal development begins eight weeks after conception and lasts until the birth of the baby.

neural tube defects Spinal cord defects often linked with recessive genes, sometimes evident in failure of the spine to close (spina bifida) or in the absence of portions of the brain.

AFP test A screening test designed to detect the likelihood of a fetal neural tube defect by revealing the presence of *alphafetoprotein* in the mother's blood.

diabetes Disease associated with deficient secretion of insulin resulting in abnormally high sugar levels in the blood and urine. Some forms are linked with a recessive gene.

other factors such as aspects of the prenatal or postnatal environment (for example, the ingestion of phenylalanine by individuals who carry the recessive alleles for PKU).

CHROMOSOMAL DISORDERS

As we have seen, genetic defects may be linked to specific recessive or dominant genes, or to a combination of genes; many are also affected by environmental conditions. In addition, there are genetic defects that appear to be related primarily to chromosomal errors. These are often referred to as **chromosomal disorders**. Many of these disorders result from improper divisions and recombinations during meiosis (when sex cells divide to form sperm and ova).

Down Syndrome

Down syndrome is the most common chromosomal birth defect. About 1 out of every 680 live births has Down syndrome, but about twice that many fetuses are affected by the condition, approximately half resulting in spontaneous miscarriages during the first third of pregnancy (Dill & McGillivray, 1992).

Some children with Down syndrome have characteristic loose folds of skin over the corners of the eyes; others don't. Mental retardation is common among children with Down syndrome, and their language development is often retarded (Kumin, Councill, & Goodman, 1999). Kent and associates (1999) report that a minimum of 7% of children with Down syndrome also manifest symptoms of **autistic disorder** (often marked by social withdrawal, restricted interests, repetitive behaviors, and limited or absent communicative skills). Not all children are equally affected.

Most cases of Down syndrome appear to be due to failure of the twenty-first pair of chromosomes to separate during meiosis (a phenomenon termed nondisjunction). Hence the resulting gamete (sex cell) has an extra copy of the twenty-first chromosome. When this gamete is combined with the other gamete during fertilization, the zygote (fertilized egg) has an extra twenty-first chromosome (thus the alternative medical label, **trisomy 21**). A smaller number of cases are due to translocation of chromosome 21 material to another chromosome; others appear to be related to a gene mutation on the twenty-first chromosome (Lendon, Ashall, & Goate, 1997).

Mother's Age and Down Syndrome Because nondisjunction of the twenty-first chromosome typically occurs during meiosis of the ovum rather than of the sperm, Down syndrome is usually associated with the mother rather than the father. Increased probability of producing a child with Down syndrome is closely associated with the age of the mother, with the incidence ranging from 1 in 1,420 for women in their early 20s to about 1 in 30 for women aged 45 (Dill & McGillivray, 1992; see Figure 3.11). Also, fathers aged 50 to 55 have a 20% to 30% greater chance of fathering children with Down syndrome (Erickson & Bjerkedal, 1981). In these instances, disjunction failure would usually occur during meiosis of the sperm, rather than of the egg.

Because medical science knows precisely what the genetic cause of Down syndrome is, it is possible to detect its presence in the fetus before birth. Procedures for doing so are discussed later in this chapter.

Down Syndrome and Alzheimer's Disease Individuals with Down syndrome who live beyond age 40 have a very high probability of developing **Alzheimer's disease**—a disease that usually appears at a later age in the normal population (Lendon, Ashall, & Goate, 1997). Its principal

---

chromosomal disorders Chromosomal errors sometimes evident in the presence or absence of extra chromosomes or portions thereof.

Down syndrome The most common chromosomal birth defect, related to the presence of an extra twenty-first chromosome (technically labeled *trisomy 21*) and sometimes evident in mild to severe mental retardation.

autistic disorder A serious childhood mental disorder usually apparent by 30 months, characterized by social unresponsiveness, poor or nonexistent communication skills, and bizarre behavior.

---

trisomy 21 (See *Down syndrome*.)

Alzheimer's disease A disease associated with old age (but also occurring as young as 40), marked by progressive loss of memory and brain function, and eventual death.

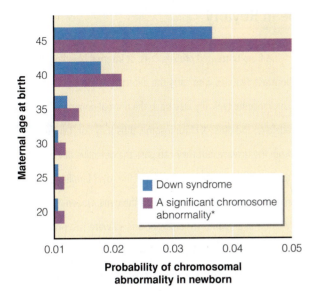

*Excludes unbalanced translocation and XXX.

FIGURE 3.11 The probability of Down syndrome or some other chromosomal abnormality increases dramatically with age. Source: Based on Friedman et al. (1992).

symptoms include progressive loss of memory and eventual deterioration of brain function, leading to death. Research in **molecular genetics** reveals that individuals with Down syndrome and those with Alzheimer's disease often share a defective gene. Not surprisingly, this gene is located on the twenty-first chromosome (Labudova and associates, 1998). Interestingly, Down syndrome males with this allele have a 3 to 4 times higher probability of developing Alzheimer's than do Down syndrome females with the same allele (Schupf et al., 1998). It seems clear that at least in some cases, Alzheimer's may result from a defective gene on the twenty-first chromosome.

Abnormalities of the Sex Chromosomes

A number of chromosomal defects involve the sex chromosomes (labeled X and Y). Some involve the absence of a chromosome; others involve the pres-

ence of an extra chromosome, some involve a compressed or fractured chromosome, and some involve a defective gene, most often on an X chromosome.

Defective genes on an X chromosome are sometimes referred to as **X-linked** (or as *sex-linked*). This chromosome is the site for genes relating to defects such as fragile X syndrome (a highly common cause of mental retardation, discussed shortly), night-blindness, baldness, and hemophilia. Each of these defects is associated with recessive genes, and each is more often manifested among males than females. Why? Simply because females who inherit the defective gene on one of their two X chromosomes typically have the corresponding normal allele on the other chromosome. As a result, they are carriers of the defective allele, but they do not manifest it (because it is recessive). Males, on the other hand, have only one X chromosome; the other sex chromosome is a Y. Because X-linked defective alleles are found only on the X chromosome, the normal dominant allele that would counter the effect of the recessive gene for one of these disorders is never present on the Y chromosome. Accordingly, males manifest conditions such as hereditary baldness and fragile X syndrome far more often than do females. Yet the gene is passed on from mother to son—not from father to son—because it is the father who always passes on a Y chromosome to his sons, and the mother who always passes on the X chromosome. (See *At a Glance:* "Hemophilia among European Royalty" and Figure 3.12.)

Fragile X Syndrome Fragile X syndrome is one of the most common causes of inherited mental retardation. In fragile X syndrome, the X chromosome is abnormally compressed or even broken. Although the condition can also occur in females, it is far more common among males and is one of the reasons why there are more mentally retarded males than females in the general population. Interestingly, over half of females with fragile X syndrome are of normal

molecular genetics The study of genetics based on the structure of chromosomes.

X-linked Refers to genes that appear only on the X sex chromosome. Typically used to describe certain genetic defects that, because they are on the X chromosome, are far more common in males than in females.

fragile X syndrome A sex-linked primarily male disorder that increases with the mother's age and is often manifested in mental retardation.

Hemophilia among European Royalty

Queen Victoria and her two daughters.

© Corbis/Bettmann

Hemophilia-A is a sex-linked recessive genetic disorder. Males who carry the recessive form of the gene on their X chromosome are always affected. That's because the Y chromosome (which all males possess) does not carry the corresponding normal allele. The blood-clotting mechanisms of males who are so affected don't work properly, and they run the risk of dying from untreated bruises, cuts, or internal bleeding. In contrast, females who carry the defective allele on one X chromosome typically also have the normal dominant allele on the other X chromosome; thus they don't suffer from the disease, but they can pass the defective allele on to their children. Many members of the royal families of nineteenth-century Europe carried the gene. Queen Victoria of England was a carrier, and so were two of her daughters (Figure 3.12).

Recent advances in molecular genetics have led to the identification of genes that are involved in about half of severe cases of hemophilia, and has also led to the production of an agent (labeled *factor VIII*) that is effective in its treatment. Tuddenham (1997) speculates that effective gene therapy will soon be available for hemophilia.

FIGURE 3.12 Descendants of Queen Victoria, showing female carriers and affected males.

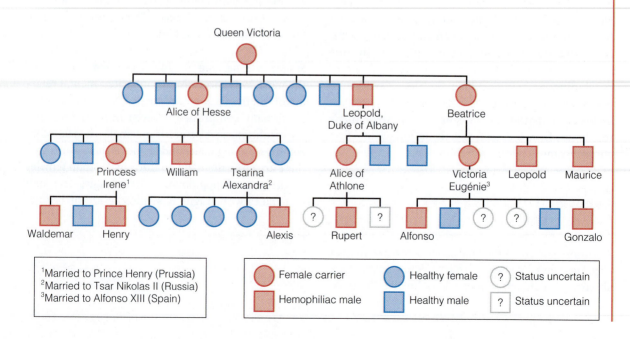

[1]Married to Prince Henry (Prussia)
[2]Married to Tsar Nikolas II (Russia)
[3]Married to Alfonso XIII (Spain)

○ Female carrier ○ Healthy female ○ Status uncertain
□ Hemophiliac male □ Healthy male □ Status uncertain

intelligence; this is the case for only about 20% of affected males (Mazzocco et al., 1998). However, there is a very wide range of intellectual performance and developmental level among individuals with fragile X syndrome (Bailey, Hatton, & Skinner, 1998). Severe restlessness and hyperactivity are also often characteristics of males with fragile X syndrome (Turk, 1998).

Unlike Down syndrome, in which mental retardation is typically apparent very early in life, fragile X individuals often manifest no symptoms of retardation until puberty, after which there is frequently a marked decline in intellectual functioning. Because of this, fragile X syndrome has historically been underdiagnosed, or diagnosed very late. Furthermore, its diagnosis remained very uncertain until the discovery of its genetic causes, coupled with recent advances in genetic testing (Carmichael et al., 1999).

Turner's Syndrome Turner's syndrome is a chromosome disorder that affects about 1 out of 2,500 female children (Dill & McGillivray, 1992). These children are born with one sex chromosome completely or partially missing. The condition is given the shorthand notation 45, X (or 45, XO). (The number indicates the total number of chromosomes; the letters refer to the sex chromosomes present. Thus a normal male is denoted 46, XY.)

Most fetuses with a missing X chromosome are aborted spontaneously; those that survive typically have underdeveloped secondary sexual characteristics, although this is not evident until puberty. Possible signs of the disorder include (1) swelling in the extremities that disappears with age, leaving loose folds of skin (webbing), particularly in the neck region, fingers, and toes, and (2) short stature. Gargan (1997) suggests that these physical alterations, especially when they're severe, often present serious adjustment problems for these girls. Mental ability is usually normal, although there are some indications of higher impulsivity, occasional attention problems, and sometimes learning problems (Temple & Marriott, 1998; Romans et al., 1997). Injections of the female sex

hormone estrogen before puberty are often helpful in bringing about greater sexual maturation, although Turner's syndrome females remain sterile (Emery & Mueller, 1992).

Klinefelter's Syndrome Klinefelter's syndrome is a chromosomal aberration that involves the presence of an extra X chromosome in a male child (hence 47, XXY). It is considerably more common than Turner's syndrome (1 out of 1,000 males; Dill & McGillivray, 1992) and is marked by the presence of both male and female secondary sexual characteristics. Children suffering from this disorder typically have small, undeveloped testicles, more highly developed breasts than is common among boys, high-pitched voices, and little or no facial hair after puberty. Therapy with the male sex hormone testosterone is often effective in improving the development of masculine characteristics and in increasing sex drive. Incidence of schizophrenia appears to be higher among males with Klinefelter's syndrome (Bekaroglu et al., 1997; Pinabel, Gorwood, & Ades, 1997).

Supermale Syndrome Supermale syndrome is the label sometimes applied to males with an extra Y chromosome (47, XYY). Such males are typically tall; sometimes they are also of lower than average intelligence. Some research has linked this syndrome with criminality, but the conclusion remains tentative and premature (Emery & Mueller, 1992). However, XYY males are often less mature and more impulsive than normal. (See *Concept Summary*.)

BEHAVIOR GENETICS

The type of genetics that is of greatest interest to psychologists, says Wahlsten (1999), is that which links genes with behavior. This largely explains why it is, for example, that research on the genetic basis of intelligence has been of such lasting interest. As

---

Turner's syndrome A chromosomal abnormality in which a female child is born with a missing sex chromosome (one rather than two X's); characterized by underdeveloped secondary sexual characteristics that can sometimes be improved with injections of estrogen before puberty.

Klinefelter's syndrome Results from the presence of an extra X chromosome in a male child; marked by the presence of both male and female secondary sexual characteristics.

supermale syndrome A chromosomal disorder affecting males with two y chromosomes (hence XYY), sometimes, though not always, linked with greater than average height, lower intelligence, and higher impulsivity.

CONCEPT SUMMARY — Genetic Defects and Chromosomal Disorders

Genetic Defect	Some Characteristics
Huntington's disease	• Linked to a *dominant* gene but not manifested until age 30 or more • A serious neurological disorder that is usually fatal
Sickle-cell anemia	• Linked to a recessive gene • Far more common among blacks than among Caucasians • Varies in severity; can lead to serious illness with lack of oxygen
Phenylketonuria (PKU)	• Linked to recessive genes • Associated with severe retardation developing early in life • Easily detectable at birth • Effects preventable through dietary means
Tay-Sachs disease	• Linked with recessive gene • An enzyme disorder usually leading to early death
Muscular dystrophy	• Some forms linked with recessive genes • Degenerative muscular disorder
Neural tube defects	• Genetically linked defects of spinal tube • May be manifested in *spina bifida* or *anancephaly* • Detectable by means of AFP test
Diabetes mellitus	• Some forms linked with recessive gene • An insulin deficiency disease, often controllable

we saw, studies of twins and of adopted children leave little doubt that our genes are instrumental in our manifestations of intelligence. The same research also indicates that in addition to the several thousand known medical conditions that are clearly genetically linked, there is convincing evidence of a genetic basis for at least some manifestations of emotional and behavior problems such as alcoholism, depression, obesity, anorexia nervosa, infantile autism, and schizophrenia. For some of these conditions, specific gene locations have been identified. But, cautions Rall (1998), science has not yet been successful in identifying any single gene that is a major cause of any mental disorder or personality characteristic. That, he explains, is because the underlying causes for most of our behaviors and characteristics are usually multifactorial; accordingly, they are highly susceptible to environmental influence.

Physical and Personality Characteristics

We know that physical traits such as eye color, hair and facial characteristics, body type, and so on are, to a large extent, genetically based. And research with twins, as well as with mice, also makes it clear that obesity is strongly genetically linked (Leibel, 1997; Giraudo, Billington, & Levine, 1998). We also know that these characteristics can affect how people relate to us, how we feel about ourselves, and ultimately how we behave. Hence, genetic contributions to at least some of our personality characteristics may be highly indirect.

The Search for Specific Genes Still, one of the major emphases in behavior genetics is the search for specific genes that contribute significantly to a characteristic or a behavior. "The classical approach,"

CONCEPT
SUMMARY **Genetic Defects and Chromosomal Disorders (continued)**

Chromosomal Disorders	Some Characteristics
Down syndrome	• Often associated with *nondisjunction* of the 21st chromosome, so that offspring has 3 (hence *trisomy 21*) • Common cause of mental retardation • Closely associated with parental (especially maternal) age • Sometimes linked with autistic disorder; often associated with *Alzheimer's disease* after age 40
Fragile X syndrome	• X-linked disorder (as is hemophilia, some forms of color blindness, male hereditary baldness, and other conditions) • Linked with an abnormally compressed or broken X chromosome • Far more common among males than females • Highly common cause of mental retardation, often not manifested until adolescence
Turner's syndrome	• Female disorder linked with absence of an X chromosome • Sometimes apparent in underdeveloped secondary sexual characteristics • Symptoms sometimes alleviated through injections of estrogen at puberty
Klinefelter's syndrome	• Male child with an extra X chromosome (XXY) • Treatment often involves injections of testosterone
Supermale syndrome	• Male child with extra Y chromosome • Often tall • Tentative but poorly established link with criminality

explains Wahlsten (1999), "begins with a noteworthy difference in phenotype and then asks whether inheritance follows Mendelian rules and whether the hypothetical gene is linked to a marker at a known location on a chromosome" (p. 603). Once researchers know the DNA sequence of the **marker gene** in question, they can create a mutation of it that, in effect, blocks its functioning. These mutants, termed **knock-outs**, can be used to study the contributions of specific genes to a wide range of characteristics.

Among the characteristics most often studied using this *knock-out* approach, and other tools of molecular genetics, are the many personality characteristics for which some genetic contribution is suggested by studies of human twins and of laboratory animals. For example, many studies have found that

identical twins have very high **concordance** for personality characteristics such as anxiety, depression, conservatism, introversion/extroversion, obesity, and schizophrenia. Concordance is a measure of the probability that if one twin has a specific characteristic, so will the other twin. For example, numerous studies indicate that the concordance rate for schizophrenia is about 50% (that is, of all members of twin pairs who were schizophrenic, about 50% had a schizophrenic twin). The concordance between fraternal twins is only about 10% (Plomin, 1997).

knock-outs Custom-made genetic probes consisting of a DNA sequence that has been altered so as to block the synthesis of a specific protein in a target gene. Also termed *null mutants*.

concordance A measure of the probability that both individuals of a twin pair will share the same characteristic. A concordance rate of 50% for schizophrenia means that half of all individuals who have a schizophrenic identical twin would also be expected to be schizophrenic.

marker gene A gene whose presence on a chromosome is associated with a known characteristic.

Using techniques of molecular genetics, researchers have succeeded in identifying genetic effects for characteristics sometimes described as *pre-schizophrenic*—for example, neuroticism and insensitivity (Kampen, 1999), high anxiety (Katsuragi et al., 1999), and aggressiveness (Manuck et al., 1999). But there is yet no single "schizophrenia" gene. Schizophrenia, like most human characteristics, is clearly multifactorial. If it weren't, the concordance rate for identical twins for schizophrenia wouldn't be 50%; it would be 100%!

Obesity Not surprisingly, family and twin studies suggest that some forms of obesity, too, have a strong genetic basis. But, caution Faith, Johnson, and Allison (1997), it's clear that human obesity is also environmentally determined, that it has much to do with what, when, and how much is eaten as well as with physical activity.

The new techniques of molecular genetics have been used extensively in investigations of obesity, where much of the research has been conducted with rats and mice. And although no single "fat gene" has been discovered, there are indications that certain types of obesity are at least partly controlled by certain **proteins** and neurotransmitters (Giraudo, Billington, & Levine,1998). And researchers have succeeded in inducing, or preventing, obesity by genetically altering animals' biochemistry. The next step in the treatment of obesity, predict Campfield, Smith, & Burn (1998), may well involve genetically engineered drugs that inhibit food intake, inhibit fat absorption, enhance the utilization of energy, and stimulate the expulsion of fat—or do all of these.

Alcoholism There are at least three lines of evidence to suggest that the propensity toward alcoholism has a significant genetic basis. We know that children of alcoholics are about four times more likely to be alcoholics than are members of the general population; studies of twins have found very high concordance rates for alcoholism; and certain racial groups appear to be more prone to alcoholism, whereas others are less likely to become alcoholic (Vallee, 1998).

Although environmental influences (social and cultural factors and family habits and values, for example) may account for some of the higher inci-

dence of alcoholism for some people, a fourth source of evidence is even more convincing: There appear to be detectable, biologically based differences between alcoholic-prone and "normal" individuals. Differences have been found with respect to certain liver enzymes involved in metabolizing alcohol (Emery & Mueller, 1992), and with respect to specific brain receptors that might be associated with responses to alcohol (Blum et al., 1990).

In spite of this evidence, most of the research that has tried to find specific genetic links for alcoholism has not succeeded in doing so (for example, Sander et al., 1999; Itoga et al., 1999).

Some Conclusions and Cautions

News media provide our most common source of information on genetics. Unfortunately, says Conrad (1997), they tend to sensationalize and to exaggerate: "Obesity gene discovered!" "Gay gene identified!" "Scientists finds gene for schizophrenia!" Furthermore, they tend to ignore subsequent disconfirmations; these are seldom very exciting. As a result, discredited ideas often remain part of public knowledge long after science has abandoned them.

Still, there is little doubt that the field of behavior genetics is advancing at an astonishing rate.

GENETIC RISK AND GENETIC COUNSELING

Recent advances in genetics have enormous implications for assessing genetic risk. For a disorder that is linked directly to the presence or absence of known genes or to known chromosomal abnormalities, it is often possible to identify affected children before birth, or to determine the probability that parents will produce children with the disorders. For disorders whose origins are only partly genetic or for which the genetic contributions are complex and not completely known, it is nevertheless often possible to determine the probability that a child will be affected.

Prenatal Diagnosis

Prenatal diagnosis, the assessment of aspects of the condition of the unborn, is an extremely important

---

protein A molecule made up of chains of one or more amino acids. In a sense, proteins are the basis of organic life.

tool in assessing genetic risk. There are six principal techniques for fetal diagnosis: amniocentesis, chorionic villus sampling (CVS), ultrasound, fetoscopy, radiography, and preimplantation diagnosis.

Amniocentesis In **amniocentesis**, a hollow needle is inserted into the **amniotic fluid** surrounding the fetus, allowing a physician to obtain 15 ml to 20 ml of fluid. This fluid contains fetal cells, which are then examined to reveal the absence of chromosomes or the presence of extra chromosomes. In addition, the blood type of the fetus, the chemical composition of the amniotic fluid, and the genetic characteristics of the fetal cells may be determined. These can provide evidence of other diseases that might affect the unborn child. Because the procedure involves a slight risk of infection and leads to miscarriages in from 0.5% to 1% of cases, it is commonly used only when the pregnant woman is older and when there is a probability of fetal abnormality or other complications (Vergeer, van Balen, & Ketting (1998). Amniocentesis is not usually performed until week 11 to 14 of a pregnancy.

One of the most common uses of amniocentesis has been for the detection of trisomy 21 (Down syndrome). Because of the moderate risks associated with the procedure, and because incidence of trisomy 21 increases dramatically with age (see Figure 3.11), the procedure is most commonly used when the mother is 35 or older or when a younger mother is known to be at risk. However, because about 95% of pregnant women are under 35, initial screening by age alone misses about 80% of Down syndrome fetuses (Kloza, 1990).

Fortunately, there is now another way of identifying women who are at higher risk of bearing a child with Down syndrome. Specifically, it has been discovered that the level of alpha-fetoprotein (AFP) in the pregnant woman's blood is significantly lower than normal. (Recall that AFP levels are routinely assessed to detect the likelihood of neural tube defects, with higher than normal levels indicating a higher probability of problems.) Thus AFP tests can significantly increase detection of Down syndrome babies among mothers of all ages (Rose et al., 1994).

Chorionic Villus Sampling (CVS) Chorionic villus sampling (CVS, or chorion biopsy) is a medical procedure for obtaining and examining fetal cells. In CVS, a plastic tube is inserted through the vagina (or a fine needle through the abdomen) to obtain a sample of the **chorion** (Vergeer, van Balen, & Ketting, 1998). The chorion is a precursor of the placenta and contains the same genetic information as the fetus. The advantage of a chorion biopsy over amniocentesis is that it can be performed as early as 7 weeks after conception. Also, because it provides enough fetal cells, chromosomal examination can usually be performed the same day. Amniocentesis, on the other hand, requires a 2- to 3-week period of tissue culture. If the results lead to a decision to terminate the pregnancy, this can be accomplished more simply and more safely in the first trimester of pregnancy. (Amniocentesis does not provide results until well into the second trimester of pregnancy.) Chorion biopsy procedures are somewhat more experimental than amniocentesis and carry a slightly higher risk of complications—including loss of the fetus in about 3% to 4% of cases (Green, 1994).

Ultrasound Ultrasound (sometimes called sonogram) uses sound waves to provide a computer-enhanced image of a fetus in real time. It is among the least harmful and least traumatic of techniques currently available, and is also the method of choice for demonstrating that a fetus is alive. In addition, it

prenatal diagnosis Assessment of the unborn, typically aimed at detecting the presence of disorders and abnormalities.

amniocentesis A procedure whereby amniotic fluid is removed from a pregnant woman by means of a hollow needle. Subsequent analysis of this fluid may reveal chromosomal aberrations (Down syndrome, for example) and other fetal problems.

amniotic fluid A clear or straw-colored fluid in which the fetus develops in the uterus.

chorionic villus sampling (CVS) A procedure in which samples of the membrane lining the uterus are used to permit prenatal diagnosis of potential birth defects.

chorion Part of the placenta, the flat membrane on the inside of the uterus, to which the umbilical cord is attached.

ultrasound A diagnostic technique in medicine that uses high-frequency sound waves to provide images of internal body structures. Ultrasound recordings are used extensively to evaluate the condition of the fetus.

is the most exact means for estimating fetal age, detecting the position of the fetus, discerning changes in fetal position, detecting multiple pregnancies, and identifying a variety of growth disorders and malformations. In fact, says Abramsky (1994), it is not only the most common prenatal diagnostic technique used but also the one that detects most fetal abnormalities.

Ultrasound images of the fetus make it possible to see the beginnings of fetal activity, including behaviors such as thumb sucking. They also allow the physician to examine bone structure, to assess length of bones, to determine relationships among the size of various body structures, and even to count fingers and toes. Ultrasound is always used with amniocentesis or CVS to guide the physician, but is not a substitute for these procedures because it cannot provide samples of fetal cells.

Fetoscopy Fetoscopy is a surgical procedure that allows the physician to see the fetus by means of a light-equipped probe inserted through the vagina. It is used mainly to obtain samples of tissues from the fetus itself, the most important being blood. Fetoscopy can furnish the physician with important information about the status of the fetus, especially when there is a possibility of disorders such as hemophilia. However, it carries higher risks than amniocentesis—about a 3% to 5% higher probability of miscarriage (Emery & Mueller, 1992).

Radiography Some inherited disorders and malformations can be diagnosed through **radiography**—that is, with x-rays of the fetus. However, because of the possibility that x-rays may harm the fetus, sonograms are used instead whenever possible.

Preimplantation Diagnosis All the fetal diagnostic techniques discussed so far can be carried out only after the fetus has begun to develop. However, it is now possible to determine the chromosomal structure of the fetus before the fertilized egg has implanted. One way of doing this is to remove a mature egg and fertilize it with the father's sperm (in vitro fertilization) (Evers-Kiebooms & Decruyenaere, 1998). The zygote is allowed to multiply to the 8-cell stage, and then a single cell is removed and examined for the presence of specific genetic disorders—all within a matter of hours. Removal of a single cell apparently does not affect subsequent development. If no defects are found, the zygote can then be implanted in the uterus.

Preimplantation diagnosis brings with it the great advantage that it can identify problems before a therapeutic abortion would otherwise be necessary. (See *Concept Summary*.) However, its use is still limited to a handful of advanced, highly specialized medical centers. (See *In the News and on the Web:* "Embryo Screening.")

Treating Genetic Disorders

Not all genetically based disorders are equally serious. Many can be treated and controlled; some can be cured. For example, the effects of PKU, as previously noted, can be prevented through diet. And in Chapter 4 we see how the effects of Rh incompatibility in the fetus, once a usually fatal condition, can be prevented through inoculation of the mother, or reversed through blood transfusions. For other conditions, it is sometimes possible to replace deficient enzymes, proteins, vitamins, or other substances (the use of insulin to control diabetes, for example). Similarly, various drugs or even surgery may be used to control and sometimes to cure genetic diseases (cancer, for example).

In addition to these (and other) medical treatments, there are several other possible treatments. One involves using clones (identical copies) of normal genes to replace those that are defective; a second uses modified genes that "knock out" a specific aspect of the functioning of a defective gene; another uses viruses or even antibiotics to eradicate bacteria or other agents involved in the development of genetically linked diseases (Fisher, 1997; Campfield, Smith, & Burn, 1998).

---

fetoscopy A surgical procedure that allows the physician to see the fetus while obtaining samples of tissue for determining its status.

radiography The use of x-rays; occasionally used as a tool in prenatal diagnosis.

preimplantation diagnosis A fetal diagnostic technique in which fertilization typically occurs in vitro and a cell from the fertilized ovum is removed and examined for abnormalities prior to implantation in the mother.

CONCEPT SUMMARY   **Methods of Prenatal Diagnosis**

Prenatal diagnosis refers to the examination of the fetus prior to birth. It can assess normal fetal development as well as provide information relating to possible fetal problems, and is used extensively in genetic counseling.

Method	Procedure	Advantages/disadvantages and Uses
Amniocentesis	Hollow needle inserted through abdomen into amniotic sac to withdraw fluid containing fetal cell	• Not usually performed until week 11 to 14 of pregnancy • Useful for detection of chromosomal abnormalities such as Down syndrome
Chorionic villus sampling (CVS)	Fetal cells obtained from the chorion (precursor of the placenta) by inserting a tube through the vagina	• Possible as early as 7 weeks after conception • Provides much the same information as amniocentesis, but much earlier • Higher risk of infection and miscarriage
Ultrasound	Sonogram of fetus provides real-time, computer-enhanced image of fetus	• Noninvasive, painless, low risk, without known side effects • Provides actual image of fetal morphology (shape) and movement • Useful for detecting normal (and abnormal) fetal development and for determining fetal position and age
Fetoscopy	Surgical procedure involving insertion of instrument that allows physician to "see" fetus and obtain actual samples of fetal tissue	• Provides fetal cells for analysis • Useful for detecting disorders such as hemophilia • Higher probability of miscarriage than CVS or amniocentesis
Radiography	X-ray procedure	• Can detect certain malformations • Possible fetal damage from x-ray effects; hence ultrasound typically used instead
Preimplantation diagnosis	Genetic examination of cells prior to implantation, typically following in vitro fertilization	• Permits detection of specific genetic disorders prior to pregnancy • May eventually be useful for correcting genetic disorders

Embryo Screening

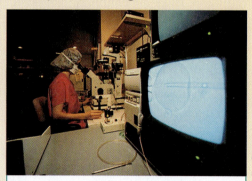

Microassisted fertilization. As the computer image shows, this technician is about to insert a single sperm into an ovum. The fertilized ovum may be allowed to go through several cell divisions, following which a single cell can be removed and examined for defects. The resulting embryo might then be implanted directly into a prospective mother or might be preserved frozen to be implanted at a much later date.

A Ms. Carole Craig of Manitoba is the first Canadian woman to give birth to a so-called designer baby. Ms. Craig suffers from a genetic defect evident in an abnormal chromosome. Preimplantation diagnosis was used to reject those among several potential embryos containing the defect, and to select an apparently healthy embryo. In vitro fertilization was then used to implant the embryo. Without this procedure, it is extremely unlikely that Ms. Craig would ever have borne a child; if she had gotten pregnant, most of her embryos would have been defective and her body would have rejected them.

Dr. Yury Verlinsky, director of the Reproductive Genetics Institute in Chicago, reports that more than 200 such babies have now been born at his clinic, and that all were free of genetically linked medical conditions carried by their parents (for example, Huntington's chorea, Tay-Sachs disease, and cystic fibrosis).

M. Stevenson, "Canada's first child from embryo screening due soon." *National Post, Toronto*, 29 November 1999, p. A1, A5.

To Think About: These procedures, says Dr. Patricia Baird, head of the Canadian Royal Commission on Reproductive Technologies, carry a tremendous risk of abuse—and the possibility of significant financial gain for those who sell the services. For example, some clinics have closed apparently because an overwhelming number of prospective parents want to use them solely to select the sex of their offspring. Also, some practitioners have been accused of selling their services to people indiscriminately, even when the conditions these people want to avoid in their children are not known to be genetic. At present, few countries have any laws governing the use and sale of reproductive technologies. Do you think there should be such laws? What might they stipulate?

 Resources: The U.S. National Health and Medical Research Council has a comprehensive document on ethical guidelines for assisted reproduction, available at: http://www.health.gov.au/nhmrc/publicat/synopses/e28syn.htm

 For additional readings, explore *InfoTrac College Edition*, your online library. Go to http://www.infotrac-college.com/wadsworth and use the passcode on the card that came with your text. Try the following search terms: embryo screening, assisted reproduction, surrogate mothers, cloning.

Genetic Counseling

Although prenatal (and preimplantation) diagnosis, along with techniques for monitoring changes in the mother, provides powerful tools for detecting potential problems, many genetically based problems cannot always be detected with absolute certainty. In many cases, however, it's possible to estimate the probability of a given outcome. In such cases, parents and physicians may be faced with difficult decisions involving serious ethical questions. In these situations, genetic counseling offers a needed service.

Genetic counseling is a branch of medicine and of psychology that attempts to provide counsel to

genetic counseling Medical/psychological assistance with decisions regarding the initiation or termination of pregnancy when there are known or suspected genetic risks involved.

physicians and parents. Such counseling typically strives to assess the probability of a defect's occurrence, its likely seriousness, the extent to which it can be treated or even reversed, and the best courses of action to follow once a decision has been made about whether to have a child. In many instances, genetic counseling takes place before conception and takes into account the age and health of the mother and the presence of genetic abnormalities in the mother's and father's families. In other cases, genetic counseling occurs after conception (see Table 3.2).

Providing genetic counseling, says Barr (1999), is a key strategy in reducing the number of children born with disabilities and disorders. But, as Williams (1995) points out, this gives rise to some serious ethical issues. Not everyone agrees that prenatal diagnosis should be used to identify children with Down syndrome or other conditions so that they might be aborted. This is partly why, despite the availability of genetic counseling in numerous medical, research, university, and community centers, it is not always

widely used. Also, there is still a relatively widespread lack of knowledge about such counseling on the part of physicians and potential clients alike. Further, psychological barriers such as fear, social stigma, religious values, and financial considerations can limit the use of genetic counseling and reduce its effectiveness even when it is available.

Prenatal diagnosis can also present some potential for abuse. (See *Across Cultures:* "Chang Yu-ju, an Only Child.")

GENETICS AND THE FUTURE

Genetic counseling has traditionally been limited to advising prospective parents about the likelihood of their having a child with a given problem and providing them with information about their options. And the options have typically consisted of deciding to try to conceive or not to, or of deciding to have a therapeutic abortion or not to. The application of genetic information may be very different in the near future.

TABLE 3.2
Probability of Some Common Multifactorial Defects

GENETIC DEFECT	INCIDENCE (PER 1,000 POPULATION	SEX RATIO (M:F)	NORMAL PARENTS HAVING A SECOND AFFECTED CHILD (%)	AFFECTED PARENT HAVING AN AFFECTED CHILD (%)
Autism	0.2	3:1	2	—
Cleft lip and/or cleft palate	1–2	3:2	4	4
Club foot	1–2	2:1	3	3
Congenital heart defects	8	1:1	1–4	2 (father affected)
				6 (mother affected)
Diabetes mellitus (juvenile, insulin-dependent)	.2	1:1	6	1–2
Congenital dislocation of hip	1	1:6	6	12
Epilepsy ("idiopathic")	5	1:1	5	5
Hydrocephalus	.5	1:1	3	—
Manic-depressive psychosis	4	2:3	10–15	10–15
Mental retardation (of unknown cause)	3	1:1	3–5	10
Profound childhood deafness	.1	1:1	10	8
Schizophrenia	10	1:1	10	14

Source: Adapted from R. F. Mueller & I. D. Young (1998). *Emery's elements of medical genetics,* 10th ed. Edinburgh and London: Churchill-Livingstone. Used by permission.

* — means no data.

Chang Yu-ju, an Only Child

Chang Yu-ju is the first, and only, son of a Chinese family living in an industrial town just west of Beijing. On the wall of his parents' house hangs a contract they have signed with the local health station. The contract is a promise that they will have only one child. The state thanks them for their promise; more than that, it helps them keep their promise and rewards them for doing so.

The state helps them by providing free sex education and advice, free contraceptives, free sterilization for both men and women, even a free contraceptive pill for men that has been available in China since 1970 (Liljeström, 1982). The state helps them as well with praise, good examples, and many posters extolling the virtues of one-child families.

The state rewards them in material ways as well. Yu-ju's parents received a bonus when he was born; parents of subsequent children get no such bonuses. Yu-ju's parents will also receive a monthly supplement until he reaches the age of 14. Had they been peasants, they would have been given an additional allotment of land (twice as much as usual) for their personal use. Instead, when Yu-ju was born his mother received additional maternity leave, and the family was given larger living quarters.

Yu-ju, too, will be rewarded for being the first child. He'll receive priority for entry into nursery schools, hospitals, even universities. In fact, many hospitals have special beds reserved for first children, both to ensure that they will be well cared for and to minimize the risk that parents might be left childless should they lose their only one. Nor will Yu-ju ever be forced to work in the country if he doesn't want to.

Occasionally the state bends the rules to accommodate conditions in remote rural areas. Thus, it might allot several hundred "second" children to be distributed among a rural town's couples. Also, couples who have a handicapped child might be permitted to have another child, as would be two people who remarry, even if each has previously had a child.

Some Results of One-Child-Only Policies

Although these policies are not universally applied in China, they have resulted in a dramatic decline in population growth (from 2.3% per year between 1965 and 1980 to 1.3% between 1980 and 1990). In addition, under-5 mortality rates have dropped from 203 per 1,000 in 1960 to 47 per 1,000 in 1997, with complete immunization rates of more than 98% (Bellamy, 1999a).

Another result of these policies is a sometimes alarming increase in the ratio of male to female children in areas where prenatal diagnosis allows parents to determine the sex of the child and to arrange for the abortion of female fetuses ("China fears sexual imbalance," 1983). Although Mao Tse Tung insisted that "girls are just as good as boys," not everyone truly believes this is so.

Christopher Arnesen/Tony Stone Images

China's one-child policy has led to a preponderance of male children in some regions where parents have access to prenatal diagnosis, allowing them to determine the sex of the fetus and to abort those that are female.

To Think About: What are some of the possible implications of growing up an only male child under these circumstances? Of growing up an only female child?

We now appear to be on the threshold of a new age. Almost daily there are new discoveries in genetics. Scientists are now able to detect genetic weaknesses, and strengths, from the very earliest moments of life. Our mushrooming knowledge of cell biology at the molecular level is opening new doors into the vast and almost uncharted world of genetic engineering. Science is breaking the genetic code; it's learning to read the codes that direct the structure and function of the protein molecules that are the fundamental units of our biological lives. Science has begun to discover ways of altering genetic messages, of rewriting the code either to enhance the possibilities implicit in our genes or to correct errors. Scientists can now reproduce sequences of genetic material and duplicate them. The results include new medications, new refining and manufacturing processes, new foods, even new lives.

What other possibilities do the genetic sciences open up? Pergament (1990) suggests that among other things, it may soon be possible to separate X- and Y-bearing sperm, to inactivate one or the other, and therefore to select the sex of children before conception. It might also be possible to analyze chromosomes simply and accurately. And, now that the human genome has been mapped (Becker, 2000), chromosome analysis and modification might conceivably lead, in some distant future, to "designer babies." In fact, speculates Pergament (1990), we may eventually perfect the artificial womb. Then, if we don't want to be bothered with the events described in the next chapter, we might simply purchase some gametes from a catalog and have them incubated.

Ethical Issues Important ethical issues are involved here. Some concern the potential dangers of experiments that can, theoretically, produce new forms of life, the consequences of which cannot really be imagined because the nature of that life may be unknown before its creation. Other issues concern the morality of altering genetic codes, the ethics of decisions relating to creating or ending life, the legal-

ity and morality of surrogate mothering and artificial insemination, maybe even the very definition of life. Responding to these concerns, a Canadian commission (the Royal Commission on Reproductive Technologies) has proposed 293 recommendations to govern genetic research and its applications (Kondro, 1992). The commission advocates jail sentences or fines for researchers trying to clone human **embryos**, produce human-animal hybrids, or sell human eggs, sperm, embryos, or fetal tissue ("Tough curbs urged for reproductive medicine," 1993). "This is not a medical policy but a social matter," explained Patricia Baird (1994), chair of the commission. "We must be careful not to commodify human beings, and commercialize human reproduction" ("Baird sounds off at Snell," 1994, p. 3).

Still, a large number of clinics now buy and sell ova, sperm, even frozen embryos (see, for example, http://www.creatfam.com/applicat.htm). Court fights over their legality, and over cloning, genetic engineering, and other reproductive technologies will be the "legal frontier" of the next century, predicts Antonio Lamer, chief justice of the Supreme Court of Canada (Tibbetts, 1999). For example, a recent Chicago court case saw an estranged husband and wife in court battling over a frozen embryo. She wanted it implanted; he was seeking a court injunction to prevent the implantation so that he would not be forced into being a father (Tibbetts, 1999).

Perhaps by 2050 issues such as these will have become more important than the science that gave them birth, and another new discipline will have arisen to deal with them.

But we have not yet reached the year 2050, and we continue to struggle with questions whose answers are not at all clear. Although we know vastly more now than we did even 10 years ago, there is still much about our beginnings that we do not understand.

---

embryo The prenatal organism between 2 and 8 weeks after conception.

MAIN POINTS

The Mechanics of Heredity

Conception results from the union of the two gametes (sex cells), sperm and ovum, each with their 23 chromosomes, to form the zygote with its 23 pairs of chromosomes. Presence of two X chromosomes in the zygote results in a female; presence of an X and a Y (which can only be produced by the father) results in a male. The genetic code is found in arrangements of DNA molecules on the chromosomes, segments of which define our 70,000 genes. The code is contained in specific arrangements of the nucleotides adenine (A), guanine (G), thymine (T), and cytosine (C) arranged in long sequences of A–C, C–A and T–G, G–T pairs.

The first scientific studies of genes compared family resemblances among generations (Gregor Mendel) and discovered the phenomenon of gene recessiveness and dominance (Mendelian genetics), implicit in the fact that some genes may have two different forms (alleles) at corresponding locations on specific chromosomes (the individual is said to be heterozygous for that gene, rather than homozygous), and that in such cases, an allele might be dominant over the other—meaning that the characteristic it represents will be manifested in the individual. Most genetic transmission is polygenic (involves more than one gene) and multifactorial (involves other factors in addition to genetic ones).

Genotype and Phenotype

Genotype is genetic makeup; phenotype is manifested characteristics. Manifested characteristics (phenotype) that typically correspond closely to underlying genetic makeup (genotype) are said to be highly canalized—have high heritability. Reaction range refers to the range of possibilities implicit in genotype. The outcome of development is usually highly dependent on the nature and timing of environmental influences in interaction with genotype.

Studying Gene-Environment Interaction

Studies of feral (wild) children are poorly controlled and tell us relatively little about the interaction of nature and nurture. Historical family studies suggest that many human qualities are influenced by genotype. Animal studies indicate that sometimes complex behaviors in animals are highly influenced by genes (like maze-learning in rats). Studies of identical twins reared together suggest the same conclusions, as do studies of adopted children, which typically report higher (though modest) correlations between biological mothers and their children than between adopted children and adoptive parents. Some observations from each of these kinds of studies also demonstrate the importance of the environment (for example, twins reared together resemble each other more than those reared apart).

We tend to think of our genes as being within us, and of contexts as being outside of us, each separate from the other. But each changes as a function of the other. Developments made possible by our genes (for example, language) nevertheless depend on context (for instance, our not being abandoned). Thus genes and contexts interact to determine the course and outcomes of human development. Furthermore, genes and environments are often correlated rather than distinct. The Scarr-McCartney model suggests this is because parents' characteristics that are genetically based influence both their children's genotypes and the environments they provide for them (passive correlation); the child's genotype influences how others interact with them (evocative correlation); and children actively select and shape aspects of the environment to conform with and enhance genetically based interests and talents (active correlation).

Elder's study of the differential effects of the Great Depression on the lives of attractive and less attractive girls illustrates how biology (attractiveness) and the environment can interact to influence development. It, like Stern's rubber-band hypothesis, is useful to emphasize the plasticity rather than the limits implicit in our genes (interactive rather than additive).

Genetic Defects

Many genetic defects are associated with recessive genes and will therefore not be manifested unless the individual inherits the genes (or gene combinations) from both parents. Huntington's disease is associated with a dominant gene and is a usually fatal neurological disorder not manifested until later in life. Other genetic defects include sickle-cell anemia (a blood-oxygenation disorder); PKU (a metabolic disorder leading to mental retardation but preventable through diet); and other conditions such as Tay-Sachs disease, muscular dystrophy, some forms of diabetes, and neural tube defects.

Chromosomal Disorders

Chromosomal disorders result from errors in chromosomes. They include Down syndrome, which results from an extra chromosome 21 (trisomy 21; marked by varying degrees of developmental retardation and associated with a higher probability of Alzheimer's disease).

X-linked disorders are caused by defective genes, the recessive allele being on the X chromosome. Because males have only one X sex chromosome (the other is a Y), they don't have the corresponding normal allele and therefore manifest the disorder (hemophilia, night blindness, color blindness, and hereditary baldness, for example). Because girls have two X chromosomes, they most often have the normal allele to counteract the defective one. Thus females can be carriers of X-linked disorders they don't manifest but pass on to their children.

Fragile X syndrome, linked to a compressed or broken X chromosome, is a common cause of mental retardation. Turner's syndrome affects girls only and is linked to an absent sex chromosome (XO rather than XX). It is usually treated with hormones at puberty. In Klinefelter's syndrome, males have an extra X chromosome (XXY—underdeveloped secondary sexual characteristics). XYY syndrome, which affects men only, is labeled the supermale syndrome and may be associated with lower impulse control.

Behavior Genetics

Behavior genetics attempts to link genes with behavior. It uses studies of twin concordance, as well as more advanced techniques of molecular genetics (such as the use of custom-made knock-out mutations of genes that control specific instances of protein synthesis). It provides evidence of genetic linkages for intelligence, obesity, autism, schizophrenia, and many other conditions. No single gene has yet been identified as a major cause of any of these characteristics and conditions. Most genetically linked human characteristics (such as the propensity toward alcoholism) are clearly multifactorial.

Genetic Risk and Genetic Counseling

Prenatal diagnosis permits the detection of genetic abnormalities and fetal diseases prior to birth. Its main techniques are amniocentesis (analysis of amniotic fluid withdrawn through a needle), chorionic villus sampling (CVS; analysis of a sample of the chorion), fetoscopy (a surgical procedure used to obtain fetal blood or skin samples), ultrasound (use of sonar techniques to detect physical characteristics as well as fetal movement), radiography (x-rays), or preimplantation diagnosis (examination of zygote cells before implantation in the uterus).

High genetic risk frequently presents alternatives other than therapeutic abortion, including drugs, enzymes, surgical procedures, blood transfusions, surgery, dietary control, and various other procedures to prevent, alleviate, or cure genetically influenced conditions. Genetic counseling advises parents about the probabilities (or the certainty) of genetically based problems, about available options, and about the most likely outcomes.

Genetics and the Future

Scientists can now detect genetic problems before an infant's birth; they can duplicate sequences of genetic code; they have begun to learn to read—and to rewrite—the codes that direct the structure and function of the protein molecules that are the fundamental units of our biological lives. The new genetic sciences are yielding astonishing new products in medicine, in refining, in manufacturing. They are also producing significant ethical dilemmas.

Focus Questions: Applications

1. What are some of the mechanics, and the marvels, of what our elders called "the birds and the bees"?
   - Describe what happens in human conception.
2. What is the nature-nurture controversy?
   - What, in your opinion, is the most reasonable one-paragraph resolution of this controversy?
3. What is the likely outcome of a child being raised by a chicken? A wolf? Alone in an attic?
   - Would a fully documented case of a feral child tell us anything important? What? Why?
4. What are the most common genetic defects and problems?
   - Explain why most serious genetic disorders are associated with recessive alleles.
5. How can we diagnose genetic problems?
   - Develop a decision tree of test outcomes, options, and most reasonable choices given relevant factors such as religious beliefs, age, and so on.

Possible Responses to Thought Challenges

Thought Challenge, page 100

That we have so many genetic homologs with the mouse means at least two things: (1) from a practical point of view, it means that the mouse is an extraordinarily useful ally in the search to understand the structure and function of human genes; and (2) from a scientific/philosophical point of view, it means that we and the mouse share a common ancestry.

Thought Challenge, page 101

All possible responses to any of these questions are highly controversial. There is clearly a need for well-thought-out, socially motivated, ethical principles to guide—perhaps even to control—genetic research and applications.

Thought Challenge, page 102

Recall that many genes come in two forms—two alleles—one of which may be dominant over the other. Most genetically based defects are associated with recessive alleles. This means that if an individual inherits that allele from one parent, as long as the normal allele is inherited from the other parent, the person will be normal (although a carrier of the defective allele). But if the parents are closely related, they are far more likely to carry the same defective alleles than are unrelated individuals (because they have common ancestors, they share far more genes). Hence the reason for the higher incidence of genetic disorders among highly inbred groups.

Key Terms

Further Readings

The following two references are good introductions to many of the topics discussed in this chapter:

Mueller, R. F., & I. D. Young (1998). *Emery's elements of medical genetics,* 10th ed. New York: Churchill-Livingstone.

British Medical Association (1998). *Human genetics: Choice and responsibility.* New York: Oxford University Press.

A highly readable account of the nature-nurture issue is the following:

Harris, J. R. (1998). *The nurture assumption: Why children turn out the way they do.* New York: The Free Press.

For fascinating, tragic, and contemporary accounts of an abandoned child, see:

Curtiss, S. (1977). *Genie: A psycholinguistic study of a modern-day wild child.* New York: Academic Press.

Rymer, R. (1993). *Genie: A scientific tragedy.* New York: Harper Perennial.

The following is a well-written, easily understood account of molecular genetics and, specifically, of the human genome project.

Bodmer, W., & R. McKie (1995). *The book of man: The human genome project and the quest to discover our genetic heritage.* New York: Scribner.

Intriguing accounts of sometimes astonishing similarities that have been reported among identical twins separated at birth, and other important findings from studies of twins, are provided in:

Segal, N. L. (1999). *Entwined lives: Twins and what they tell us about human behavior.* New York: Dutton.

Wright, L. (1997). *Twins and what they tell us about who we are.* New York: John Wiley.

 Online Resources

For additional readings, explore *InfoTrac College Edition,* your online library. Go to http://www.infotrac-college.com/wadsworth and use the passcode on the card that came with your text. Try the following search terms: conception, nature-nurture, genetic defects, genome.

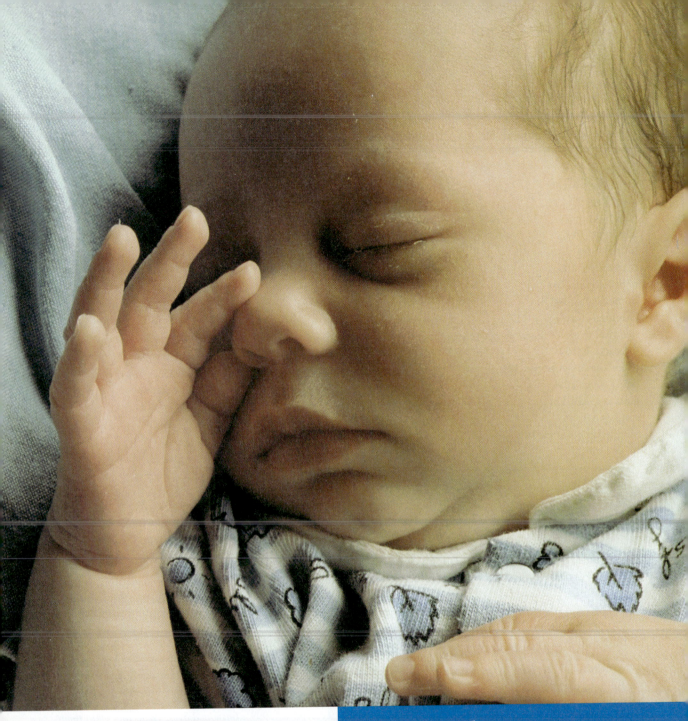

You praise the firm restraint with
which they write . . .
But where's the bloody horse?

Roy Campbell Adamastor, *On Some South African Novelists*

Prenatal Development and Birth

SuperStock

CHAPTER 4

One day Paul Charpentier ran to our house from his, about a mile away, and said, breathlessly, "Larocque's horse is colting." Then Paul and I, along with my older brother, Maurice, scrambled across the river on the rocks, up the bank, down past the sheds, over the railroad track, under the barbed-wire fence, and up to Larocque's barn where we could see into the corral.

But there was no horse. Not one. Just then, Old Man Larocque emerged from the chicken coop with a pail of mash and about 20 chickens clucking behind, and Paul asked, "Where's the horse?"

"There," said Old Man Laroque, waving vaguely toward the pasture behind the barn. "But you ain't in time." I guess we weren't, because the newborn colt was already frisking about. But I, at age 6, wasn't sure what we had been expecting to see.

So Maurice told me to ask our mother where babies come from, acting like he already knew himself. Those things were a big deal in those days. And, in keeping with the spirit of the times, my mother tossed my question aside and distracted me with a couple of chores.

But eventually, other colts were born and our questions were finally answered. The answers were simple, straightforward, universal, and timeless—which is not something you can say about many answers. It seemed that babies had always been made in pretty much the same way and that we could expect that this would never change—well, at least not in our lifetimes.

ASSISTED REPRODUCTION

We were wrong. Reproduction is no longer always a simple, clear-cut thing; sometimes it's *assisted*. Assisted reproduction includes a variety of approaches. For example, it might involve **artificial insemination**, typically a clinical procedure wherein the father's sperm is introduced directly into the mother (sometimes using anonymous donor sperm, in which case the identity of the biological father may never be known). Assisted reproduction also includes the use of **drugs**, perhaps to stimulate ovulation, perhaps to increase the probability of the fetus coming to term. Another possibility involves inserting an ovum from a donor into a woman whose fallopian tubes are blocked. Using **surrogate mothers**, in which one woman bears a child for another, is a further possibility. Still another possibility involves conception completely outside the mother's body, either in another woman's body or by in vitro fertilization (IVF) (literally meaning "in glass"). In vitro fertilization typically refers to a process in which sperm penetrate and unite with ova on their own, although in a laboratory. Fertilization can also be *microassisted* in the sense that the sperm is artificially inserted into the ovum. This is termed **intracytoplasmic sperm injection** (ICSI). The fertilized egg is typically allowed to go through several cell divisions, and the resulting embryo can then be implanted in the mother to develop as it normally would (embryo implanta-

---

artificial insemination An artificial breeding procedure often used in animal husbandry and sometimes with humans. This procedure eliminates the necessity for a physical union between a pair of opposite-sex individuals.

drugs Chemical substances that have marked physiological and sometimes psychological effects on living organisms.

surrogate mothers Surrogates are substitutes. In assisted reproduction, a surrogate mother is a woman who carries a child for someone else.

tion—also termed *zygote implantation*). Alternatively, the embryo might be frozen to be thawed and implanted at a later date. Macas and associates (1998) report that close to 90% of all embryos survive freezing and thawing. (See *In the News and on the Web:* "Issues in Assisted Reproduction.")

DETECTING PREGNANCY

No matter whether it's assisted or natural, reproduction always begins with conception, the details of which are described in Chapter 3. Recall that when an ovum is fertilized by a sperm cell, the resulting zygote contains the individual's entire genetic endowment in the arrangement of the DNA molecules that make up its 23 pairs of chromosomes. Normally, all changes that take place in this cell's development will result from the interaction of genetic predispositions with the environment, both before and after birth. As noted in Chapter 3, it is difficult to separate these two effects; they are not, in fact, separate and additive, but combined and interactive. Nevertheless, it is possible to isolate and describe the effects of specific experiences at certain times and under certain circumstances. For example, during prenatal development, some drugs and chemicals and other environmental conditions can have markedly harmful effects on the fetus. This chapter looks at some of these possible effects as it traces the normal course of prenatal development from conception through birth.

Probable and Positive Signs of Pregnancy

Barring the use of chemical tests or a medical examination, there are very few absolutely certain signs of pregnancy before the later stages of prenatal development. However, there are some less certain signs, most of which also occur later in pregnancy. For example, cessation of **menses** (menstruation) is one

---

intracytoplasmic sperm injection (ICSI) Microassisted fertilization. Involves the mechanical insertion of sperm into ova in the laboratory.

menses A monthly discharge of blood and tissue from the womb of a mature female. The term refers to menstruation.

IN THE NEWS AND ON THE WEB

Issues in Assisted Reproduction

There are now some astonishing new ways of reproducing. And some unexpected problems and issues as well. For example, recent news items report:

- Women far beyond normal childbearing ages having children. A 60-year-old European woman recently gave birth to a baby girl ("Mom, 60, Delivers Healthy Girl," 1994). She lied about her age so that the doctor would agree to implant a zygote in her. He says he would have refused had he known her age. "One has to set a limit," said he. "I think age 50 is enough."
- Couples hiring surrogate mothers to "carry" zygotes that might be the result of the union of their own gametes, or that might be gametes purchased (or stolen) from someone else. For example, Mark and Crispina Calvert paid Anna M. Johnson $10,000 so that she would have a zygote (resulting from Mark's sperm and Crispina's ovum) implanted and bear a child for the Calverts. Ms. Johnson later changed her mind and decided to keep the child. A court case ensued. The decision: Under California and New Jersey state law, because surrogate mothers are not biologically related to the fetus, they cannot be considered either legal or natural mothers ("Court to Decide Right of Surrogate Mother," 1992). Under English law, however, the birth mother is the legal mother even if she isn't the genetic mother (Lockwood, 1997).
- People fighting over frozen embryos, sperm, or ova. For example, a man and woman in Chicago are in court battling over frozen embryos. The couple are estranged; she wants one of the embryos implanted so that she can have a child; the embryos are the product of his sperm and her ova; he doesn't want to be forced into fatherhood (Tibbetts, 1999).
- A woman attempting to give birth to her own grandchild. Pamela Reno's son lost a game of Russian roulette ("Mom Had Son's Sperm Removed Before He Died," 1999). While he lay near death in an intensive care unit, Pamela had her son's sperm removed. "It's the only way I can be a grandma," said Reno (p. 41). Her plan? Find an egg donor and have her son's child—that is, her grandchild—implanted in her own body.

- Clinics that readily sell "custom-made" frozen embryos—custom-made in the sense that the ova and sperm are selected from individuals with known characteristics so that buyers can decide whether they want to spend their money on brains, beauty, athletic prowess, musical talent, or exotic skin colors (Langton, 1997).
- Lesbian mothers selecting the fathers of their children. Lesbian singer Melissa Etheridge has now revealed that the father of her two children is veteran rock star David Crosby. Etheridge chose Crosby because, in spite of his well-known drug and health problems, she is a fan of his music ("Etheridge Chose 'Musical' Crosby," 2000).

To Think About: Consider just a few of the many moral, ethical, and legal dilemmas implicit in assisted reproduction: Who should have access to reproductive technologies? Should there be age limits? Should there be financial or educational requirements for prospective parents? Should gametes and embryos be available for purchase like any other commodity? What rights should surrogates have? Should parents be allowed to select the sex of their offspring? What are some ethical issues involved in what medicine labels embryo reduction in the case of multiple pregnancies?

 Resources: Many websites are devoted to this rapidly expanding area. The first of the two listed here is a British site that describes itself as a resource for the latest information and technology relating to assisted reproduction; the second is the site of a fertility clinic at Presbyterian Hospital in Charlotte, North Carolina:

http://www.reproduction.net

http://www.ivfsuccess.com/

 For additional readings, explore *InfoTrac College Edition*, your online library. Go to http://infotrac-college.com/wadsworth and use the passcode that came on the card with your book. Try these search terms: surrogate mothers, artificial insemination, frozen embryos.

of the first signs of pregnancy, but it wouldn't normally be noticed until at least two weeks of pregnancy have passed because conception ordinarily occurs approximately two weeks after the last menstrual period. Nor is this a certain sign of pregnancy; many other factors may cause it (like anorexia, undernutrition, overexercise, or certain medical conditions).

Morning sickness, although it affects approximately two-thirds of all pregnant women, does not ordinarily begin until about two weeks after the missed period and can easily be mistaken for some other ailment. Changes in the breasts (enlargement, darkening of the aureoles, increased sensitivity) are also common, but are highly subjective and therefore quite unreliable. And **quickening**, the movement of the fetus in the womb, is not usually noticed by the mother until the fourth or fifth month, and by then most women have realized for some time that they are pregnant.

In addition to these probable indications of pregnancy, there are some more positive signs, such as the fetal heartbeat, which can be heard with the aid of a stethoscope. Similarly, fetal movements can be detected by feeling the abdomen or sometimes simply by observing it. X-rays and ultrasound are two other methods of ascertaining the presence of a fetus.

Pregnancy Tests

Several decades ago, the surest early medical test of pregnancy was the so-called rabbit test. It required the use of a rabbit, a frog, a mouse, or some other creature—which had to be both female and virgin. The animal would be injected with a small amount of urine from the possibly pregnant woman. And if she were, in fact, pregnant, the effect would be a rupturing of small sacs on the animal's ovaries. Sadly, the animal had to be killed to complete the test.

Fortunately for virgin rabbits and mice, chemical pregnancy tests are now widely available, and can be purchased over the counter for use in the home. Similar tests are also used by physicians. These test kits detect the same changes in a woman's urine as did the rabbit test. Specifically, they react to the pregnancy hormone, human chorionic gonadotropin (HCG), and are effective as early as two weeks after conception. Positive indications in early pregnancy tests are highly reliable, although sometimes there are *false* positives (Ikomi et al., 1998). Negative readings are less accurate, however, and should be followed by a second test a week or so later if the menstrual period has still not begun (Neinstein & Harvey, 1998). Physicians also have access to more accurate tests that examine the woman's blood for the presence of a subunit of HCG, labeled *betaHCG*. This highly reliable test also allows relatively accurate prediction of expected time of delivery (*Health Guide: Pregnancy, 1999*).

STAGES OF PRENATAL DEVELOPMENT

The **gestation period** (the time between conception and birth) varies considerably for different species: Cows take about as long as people; elephants need 600 days; dogs come to term in approximately 63 days; asses need about one year (365 days); but hamsters get it all done in only 16.5 days (*Compton's Online Encyclopedia*, 2000).

The human gestation period is usually calculated in **lunar months**, each month consisting of 28 days; hence a typical pregnancy lasts 10 lunar months, or 280 days, when these days are counted from the onset of the last menstrual period, as they usually are. However, the actual gestation period is approximately 266 days because fertilization normally occurs when ovulation takes place, about 12 to 14 days after the onset of the last menstrual period.

The American College of Obstetrics and Gynecology has standardized the terminology used to describe prenatal development by identifying

---

quickening The name given to the first movements of the fetus in utero. Quickening does not occur until after the fifth month of pregnancy.

gestation period The period of time between conception and birth (typically 266 days for humans).

lunar month The length of a complete moon cycle—from full moon to full moon, for example; hence, 28 days.

three developmental periods with clear time boundaries. The **germinal period** (also called the **fertilized ovum stage**, or *zygote*) begins at fertilization and ends two weeks later, shortly after implantation in the uterus. The **embryonic period** follows and terminates at the end of the eighth week. The **fetal period** lasts from the end of the second lunar month until the birth of the baby.

Germinal Period

Except in certain cases of assisted reproduction (such as *in vitro fertilization*), fertilization usually occurs in one of the mother's two fallopian tubes, each of which links an ovary to the uterus (Figure 4.1). After fertilization, the zygote (fertilized ovum) is carried toward the uterus by currents in the fallopian tubes, a process requiring between 5 and 9 days. Cell divisions occur during this time. Nevertheless, the zygote is hardly larger at the end of the first week than it was at the time of fertilization, mainly because the cells it consists of are considerably smaller than they originally were. This is not surprising because the ovum has received no nourishment from any source other than itself.

One week or so after fertilization, the ovum is ready to implant itself in the uterine wall. At this stage, many potential pregnancies terminate due to implantation failure. For those that continue, the ovum facilitates implantation by secreting certain enzymes and producing tiny, tentacle-like growths, called **villi**, that implant themselves in the lining of the uterus to obtain nutrients from blood vessels.

---

germinal period The first two weeks of prenatal development.

fertilized ovum stage (also called *germinal period*) The first stage of prenatal development, beginning with fertilization and lasting until the end of the second week of intrauterine development.

embryonic period The second stage of prenatal development, lasting from the end of the second week through the eighth week after conception.

fetal period The final stage of prenatal development, which begins at the end of the eighth week after conception and lasts until the baby's birth.

villi Tiny, tentacle-like growths emanating from the fertilized egg, allowing it to attach itself to the uterine wall to what will become the placenta.

At the same time, the lining of the uterus engulfs the uterus and prepares to nourish it—which is why menstruation, the monthly shedding of the uterine lining, doesn't occur after successful implantation. This is the beginning of the **placenta**—the organ that allows nutrients to pass to the **fetus** and waste materials to be removed, while keeping the blood of the mother and of the fetus separate. In time, the placenta and the fetus are connected by the **umbilical cord**, a long, thick cord that is attached at one end to the placenta and at the other to what will be the child's navel. The umbilical cord consists of two arteries and one large vein and will eventually be approximately 20 inches (50 cm) long. It contains no nerve cells, so that there is no connection between the mother's nervous system and that of the child in utero (in the uterus). Note that the placenta serves as a link between mother and fetus, whereas the umbilical cord links the fetus to the placenta.

The Embryonic Period

The embryonic period begins at the end of the second week of pregnancy, following implantation of the fertilized ovum in the wall of the uterus. The normal course of physiological development in the embryonic and fetal stages is highly predictable and regular.

At the beginning of this stage, the embryo is still only a fraction of an inch (2.54 centimeters) long and weighs much less than an ounce (28.35 grams). Despite its tiny size, not only has cell differentiation into future skin cells, nerves, bone, and other body tissue begun, but the rudiments of eyes, ears, and nose have also begun to appear. In addition, some of the internal organs are beginning to develop. In fact, by the end of the first lunar month, a primitive heart is already beating. By the end of the second lunar month, the embryo is between 1.5 and 2 inches (3.8

---

placenta A flat, thick membrane attached to the inside of the uterus during pregnancy and to the developing fetus. The placenta connects the mother and the fetus by means of the umbilical cord, through which the fetus receives nourishment.

umbilical cord A long, thick cord attached to what will be the child's navel at one end and to the placenta at the other. It transmits nourishment and oxygen to the growing fetus from the mother.

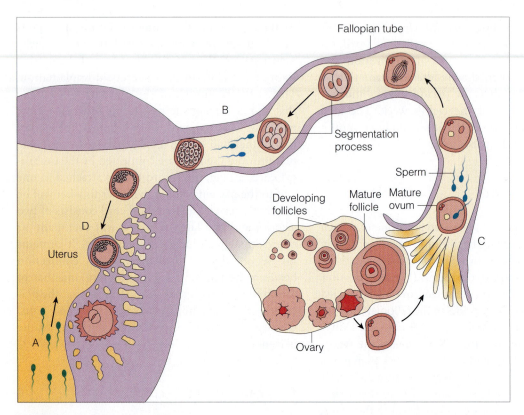

FIGURE 4.1 Fertilization and implantation. At A, millions of sperm cells have entered the vagina and are finding their way into the uterus. At B, some of the spermatozoa are moving up the fallopian tube (there is a similar tube on the other side) toward the ovum. At C, fertilization occurs. The fertilized ovum drifts down the tube, dividing and forming new cells as it goes, until it implants itself in the wall of the uterus (D) by the seventh or eighth day after fertilization.

and 5 cm) long and weighs close to two-thirds of an ounce (19 gm). All the organs are now present, the whole mass has assumed the curled shape character-istic of the fetus, and the embryo is clearly recogniz-able as human. Arm and leg buds have appeared and begun to grow, resembling short, awkward paddles. External genitalia (sex organs) have also appeared.

The Fetal Period

By the end of the eighth week of pregnancy, which marks the beginning of the fetal period, the absolute mass of the fetus is still quite unimpressive. By the end of the third lunar month (10 weeks of preg-nancy), it may reach a length of 3 inches (7.5 cm) but will still weigh less than an ounce (20 gm). The

head of the fetus is one-third of its entire length; this will have changed to one-fourth by the end of the sixth lunar month and to slightly less than that at birth (see Table 4.1 and Figure 4.2).

During the third month of pregnancy, the fetus is sufficiently developed that if it is aborted it can make breathing movements and give evidence of both a primitive sucking reflex and the **Babinski reflex** (the infant's tendency to fan its toes when tickled on the soles of its feet) if stimulated appropriately. However,

---

Babinski reflex A reflex present in newborn children but disappear-ing later in life. The toes fan out as a result of being tickled in the cen-ter of the soles of the feet. Normal adults curl their toes inward rather than fanning them outward.

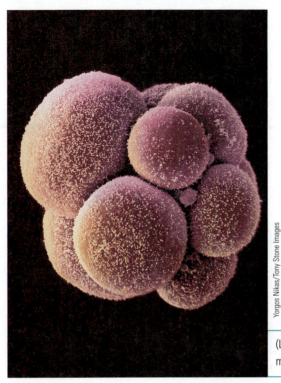

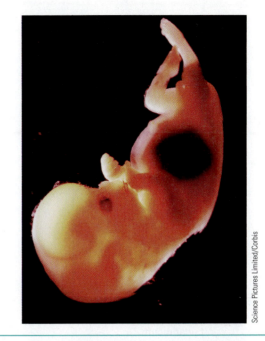

Yorgos Nikas/Tony Stone Images

Science Pictures Limited/Corbis

(Left) The fertilized ovum at three days after conception, color enhanced and magnified 992 times, and (above) the fetus in the womb at 10–12 weeks.

TABLE 4.1
Prenatal Development by Lunar Month
(weight and length are approximate)

LUNAR MONTH	WEIGHT	LENGTH	CHARACTERISTICS
1	Negligible	Negligible	Cell differentiation into those that will be bones, nerves, or other cells
2	2/3 oz. (19 g)	1½ to 2 in. (3.75 to 5 cm)	All organs present; leg buds and external genitalia just appearing
3	7/8 oz. (24.5 g)	3 in. (7.5 cm)	If aborted, will make primitive breathing movements and suck; bones forming, organs differentiated
4	4 oz. (112 g)	6 in. (15 cm)	
5	11 oz. (308 g)	10 in. (25 cm)	Fetal movement (quickening); lanugo appears
6	20 oz. (560 g)	12 in. (30 cm)	Heartbeat clearly discernible; eyelids present
7	2.6 lb. (1.2 kg)	15 in. (37.5 cm)	
8	4 lb. (1.8 kg)	16 in. (41 cm)	All major changes have now occurred; development is largely a matter of increasing weight and length
9	4.7 lb. (2.1 kg)	17.5 in. (44 cm)	
10	7.5 lb. (3.4 kg)	20 in. (50 cm)	

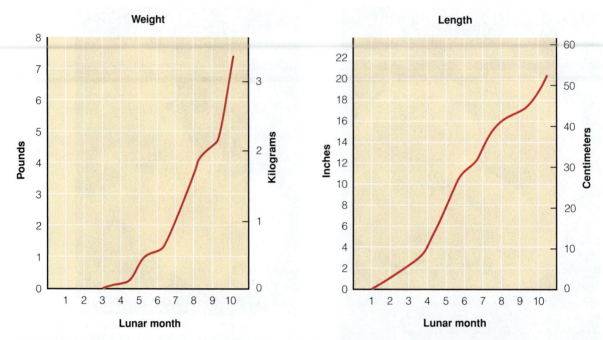

FIGURE 4.2 Approximate weight and length of the fetus at the end of each lunar month of prenatal development. Note the extraordinarily steep growth curves. These decline somewhat in early infancy—and even more dramatically later. Otherwise, most of us would not fit in our beds.

the fetus will have no chance of survival if born at this stage of development.

During the fourth lunar month of pregnancy, the fetus grows to a length of 6 inches (16 cm) and weighs approximately 4 ounces (113 gm). The bones have begun to form, all organs are clearly differentiated, and there may even be evidence of some intrauterine (within the uterus) movement. During the fifth month a downy covering, called **lanugo**, begins to grow over most of the fetus's body. This covering is usually shed during the seventh month but is occasionally still present at birth. The fetus weighs approximately 11 ounces (311 gm) and may have reached a length of 10 inches (25 cm) by the end of the fifth lunar month.

Toward the end of the sixth month, it is possible to palpate (feel by touch) the fetus through the mother's abdomen. The heartbeat, already discernible in the fifth month, is now much clearer. The

lanugo Downy, soft hair that covers the fetus. Lanugo grows over most of a fetus's body sometime after the fifth month of pregnancy and is usually shed during the seventh month. However, some lanugo is often present at birth, especially on the infant's back.

eyelids have now separated so that the fetus can open and close its eyes. It is approximately a foot (30 cm) long and weighs close to 20 ounces (567 gm). If born now, it would have some chance of surviving in a modern hospital with sophisticated care to compensate for the immaturity of its digestive and respiratory systems.

The fetus's growth in size and weight becomes more dramatic in the last few months of the final stage. Brain development is also particularly crucial during the last three months of pregnancy, as it will continue to be after birth, especially for the first two years of life. The unborn child's sensitivity to malnutrition is assumed to be related to neurological growth during the late stages of fetal development (Morgane et al., 1993). This sensitivity is sometimes evident in lower developmental scores during infancy and impaired mental functioning among children born to malnourished mothers.

Most of the physical changes that occur after the seventh month are quantitative It is now a matter of sheer physical growth: from 15 inches and 2.6 pounds (38 cm; 1,180 gm) in the seventh month, to 16 inches and 4 pounds (41 cm; 1,816 gm) in the eighth month, to 17.5 inches and 4.7 pounds (44 cm; 2.1 kg) in the ninth month, and to 20 inches and 7.5 pounds (50 cm; 3.4 kg) at the end of the tenth month.

Two terms that are sometimes used to describe the general pattern of fetal development are **proximodistal** and **cephalocaudal**. Literally, these terms mean "from near to far" and "from the head to the tail," respectively. They refer to the fact that among the first aspects of the fetus to develop are the head and internal organs; the last are the limbs and digits (Robson & Hughes, 1996).

After approximately 266 days of intrauterine development, most fetuses are ready to be born, although some appear to be ready earlier and some later. But before we look at birth, we turn to a discussion of the factors that may be important to the normal or abnormal development of the fetus. (See *Concept Summary*.)

proximodistal Literally, from near to far. Refers to a developmental progression in which central organs develop before external limbs and in which the infant acquires control over muscles closer to the center of the body before acquiring control over those more peripheral.

cephalocaudal Referring to the direction of development beginning with the head and proceeding outward toward the tail. Early infant development is cephalocaudal because children acquire control over their heads before acquiring control over their limbs.

EFFECTS OF DRUGS AND OTHER AGENTS ON PRENATAL DEVELOPMENT

A wide range of influences can have significant effects on the developing fetus. Influences that cause malformations and physical defects in the fetus include **teratogens** and **mutagens**.

Teratogens affect the embryo or fetus directly, and include various maternal illnesses, drugs, chemicals, and minerals. The name is derived from *teras*, the Greek word for "monster." Teratogens are so-called because such substances were thought to be capable of producing monsters—and can in fact produce monstrous deformities. Drugs such as *thalidomide* and *quinine* are known teratogens. Environmental hazards, such as those associated with the production and use of various chemicals, may also be powerful teratogens. For example, Czeizel, Hegedus, and Timar (1999) report frightening levels and patterns of **congenital** abnormalities

teratogens Drugs and other substances that cause fetal defects.

mutagens Substances capable of causing changes in genetic material.

congenital Present at birth, although not necessarily inherited. For example, a birth defect would be congenital if it is due to the influence of drugs, and *genetic* if it is a condition determined by genetic makeup. It might also be *multifactorial*.

CONCEPT SUMMARY   **Stages of Gestation (Prenatal Development)**

Stage	Description
Germinal period	Also termed the period of the zygote; begins at fertilization and ends two weeks later, after implantation of the zygote (fertilized egg) in the uterine wall. Still microscopic.
Embryonic period	From end of second to end of eighth week of intrauterine development. During this stage most of the important morphological (pertaining to form) changes occur. Teratogens (influences that cause malformations and defects) are most influential during this period. At the end of this period, the embryo is close to 2 inches (4.5 cm) long and weighs about one-sixteenth ounce (19 grams).
Fetal period	From the end of eighth week until birth. Accelerating growth curves toward the end of this period.

among children born to mothers living within 25 kilometers (15 miles) of an acrylonitrile factory in Hungary. These abnormalities included undescended testes in boys, chest structure abnormalities, and clubfoot. Risk of abnormalities decreased with increasing distance from the factory. Note that the effects of teratogens are not passed on from one generation to another.

In contrast, the effects of mutagens can be transmitted from one generation to another because mutagens cause changes in genetic material and these changes can then lead to malformations and defects. Thus, deafness caused by a mutated gene (resulting from exposure to a mutagen such as radiation, for example) may be passed on to offspring; deafness caused by a virus (such as the teratogenic cytomegalovirus) will not be.

Note that the effects of many teratogens and mutagens often depend on a variety of factors, both environmental and genetic. That is, the occurrence and severity of a defect associated with a particular agent are often determined by a fetus's genetic background, the timing of the exposure, and the stresses that might result from the additional presence of other harmful agents—not to mention the moderating effects of other positive external influences. Accordingly, the effects of any given teratogen or mutagen can vary widely from one fetus to another.

Prescription Drugs

About 90% of all pregnant women take one or more drugs, says Gillespie (1998); in fact, 10% take between 10 and 19 different drugs, and an astonishing 6% will have taken more than 20 drugs while pregnant.

We know that many drugs can affect the fetus; but about many others, we are still uncertain. Because it is clearly unethical to use human subjects in controlled investigations of chemical substances whose effects may be injurious to the fetus, our information about the effects of drugs on the fetus is often based on studies of animals or on observations of human infants under poorly controlled conditions. In the case of prenatal exposure to drugs, generalizing results from studies of animals to humans presents an additional problem, because certain drugs have dramatically different effects on

members of different animal species as well as on children relative to adults. Also, normal adult doses of a drug might well represent huge doses for a fetus weighing only ounces, particularly if the drug crosses the placental barrier easily.

Known Teratogenic Prescription Drugs Among the better-known teratogenic prescription drugs are *thalidomide*, which causes severe physical changes in the embryo; *quinine*, which is associated with congenital deafness; *barbiturates* and other painkillers, which reduce the body's oxygen supply, resulting in varying degrees of brain damage; and various anesthetics that appear to cross the placental barrier easily and rapidly and cause depression of fetal respiration and decreased responsiveness in the fetus. Other prescription drugs that also appear to be teratogenic include *acitetrin*, which is associated with a higher risk of miscarriage as well as malformations, and *tetracycline*, which is associated with dental staining (Coustan & Mochizuki, 1998). Accutane (isotetrinoin), a synthetic vitamin A used to treat acne, is a known teratogen (Gillespie, 1998).

Suspected Teratogenic Prescription Drugs Other *suspected* teratogens include *lithium*, which is used in the treatment of manic-depression, and *benzodiazapines* (mild tranquilizers such as Valium® and Librium®) as well as amphetamines (stimulants, sometimes called "ice" in street talk) and some antihistamines (Coustan & Mochizuki, 1998). When these are used therapeutically, their effects on the developing fetus may be very small. However, the effects of habitual use and of overdosing are less clear, with some research reporting increases in the risk of abnormalities such as cleft palate (Friedman & Polifka, 1996; Coustan & Mochizuki, 1998).

The prescription drugs mentioned in this section are only a few of the drugs that are thought to be harmful to the fetus. There are many others that do not seem to have any immediate negative effects, but whose long-term effects are negative, or still unclear. This is the case for estrogens, for example, one form of which—*diethylstilbestrol (DES)*—was heavily prescribed through the 1940s and 1950s for

diethylstilbestrol (DES) A drug once widely prescribed to lessen the probability of miscarriages. It has been linked with medical problems in offspring.

women who were at risk for spontaneous abortions. It is still prescribed in some parts of the world (Palmlund et al., 1993). Not until several decades later did medical researchers discover a link between DES use by pregnant women and vaginal cancer among girls subsequently born to these women. Similarly, use of other forms of estrogens by pregnant mothers has now been linked with significantly higher rates of infertility among their daughters (Coustan & Mochizuki, 1998). Because these effects occur so long after use of the drug, and because they are manifested in only a small percentage of the offspring, they are extremely difficult to detect. For this reason, many medical practitioners discourage the use of any prescription drugs by pregnant women unless absolutely necessary.

Over-the-Counter Medication

Among nonprescription drugs that may also have negative effects on the fetus are *aspirin* (*acetylsalicylic acid*), which may increase the tendency to bleed in both mother and fetus. Coustan and Mochizuki (1998) report evidence that a normal dose of aspirin *doubles* bleeding time for anywhere from 4 to 7 days. Hence even relatively low doses of aspirin may be associated with a higher probability of intracranial hemorrhage in infants, especially those who are premature (Friedman and Polifka, 1996). In addition, a variety of animal studies with rats, monkeys, dogs, cats, and mice have found that aspirin, used in doses comparable to those that might be used when treating rheumatic disease among humans, is associated with a significantly higher probability of fetal malformations as well as subsequent behavioral problems.

Acetaminophen (Tylenol®, Anacin 3®, Datril®, or Tempra®, and many other combinations) appears to pose little risk to the unborn fetus in normal therapeutic doses. But in the case of an overdose during pregnancy, the risk of fetal death may be quite high, although the evidence is still tentative (Coustan & Mochizuki, 1998). Over-the-counter *antihistamines* appear to pose no great risk to fetal development, although their use during the first trimester of pregnancy may be associated with fetal death or malformations. A very common over-the-counter antacid and laxative, *magnesium hydroxide* (milk of magnesia), does not appear to pose any known risk to the fetus (Gillespie, 1998).

There has been some question concerning the effects of megadoses of common vitamins. Evidence suggests that vitamin C (*ascorbic acid*) in usual therapeutic doses poses little risk to the fetus. Similarly, normal doses of vitamin A (*retinol*) do not appear to have measurable negative effects. There is a slight chance, however, that very high doses may increase the risk of anomalies. Vitamin B_6 (pyridoxine), even in very high doses, is not associated with fetal problems. Finally, evidence suggests vitamin D deficiency may be associated with delayed bone calcification (hardening) in the fetus. On the other hand, severe overdoses of vitamin D may result in fetal problems (Coustan & Mochizuki, 1998).

Although not exactly an over-the-counter drug, the effects of aspartame, the increasingly common sugar substitute in diet products (common trade names include Equal® and NutraSweet®) may be of interest. Aspartame, too, seems unlikely to be a teratogen. However, animal studies indicate that it may be associated with a somewhat higher risk of fetal harm if the mother suffers from phenylketonuria (PKU). This is a genetic disorder that, as we saw in Chapter 3, involves the inability to metabolize phenylalanine, and that often leads to mental retardation in children whose diets contain phenylalanine. Because aspartame contains phenylalanine, PKU mothers who ingest a great deal of it may expose their fetuses to some risk.

Importance of Timing and Other Factors

At least five separate factors determine the potential effect of a drug (or other agent) on the fetus, and make the task of determining likely effects highly complex: (1) the mother's reaction to the drug; (2) drug dosage and frequency of use; (3) interactions with other drugs the mother is taking or might have taken in the past; (4) the conditions for which the mother is taking the drugs; and (5) the timing of drug use. How these factors interact, and their importance, is often unclear. This is why, for a vast number of substances reviewed in their detailed examination of the effects of drugs on the fetus, Friedman and Polifka (1996) repeatedly include the caution: "A small risk cannot be excluded." Further, in their words, for many drugs "the quantity and quality of data on which risk estimate is based," is "poor," "very poor," "poor to fair," or just "fair." The data are considered "good" in far fewer than half of all instances.

What has been clearly established, however, is that the timing of exposure to possible teratogens is critical. Thus, exposure during the first two weeks after conception may be associated with implantation failure and lead to **abortion**. In fact, about 30% to 40% of all potential pregnancies are lost before they are recognized—that is, in the first two weeks (Simpson, 1991). Exposure during the embryonic stage (weeks 2 to 8) is generally associated with the most serious structural changes (physical deformities and abnormalities). This is because the embryonic period is marked by the most rapid development of organs. After this stage, the fetus's basic structure has already been formed and is not as vulnerable to external influences.

The period that is most *critical* for different teratogenic agents depends a great deal on precisely what part of the fetus they affect. Thus thalidomide led to missing limbs in the fetus only if the mother took it between the 34th and 50th day of her pregnancy (Abel, 1998). (See Figure 4.3.)

Exposure to Chemicals

There are so many chemicals in our environments that it is extremely difficult to separate their potential effects one from the other. In fact, tens of thousands of chemicals are currently in use in the world, and several thousand new ones are introduced each year. Combined in various ways, these chemicals make up the more than 2.5 million compounds in existence in the world (Gillespie, 1998). Although most of these are "contained" in one way or another—that is, they do not find their way into our air, our water, or our food—and are essentially harmless, others are not so benign. Many chemicals that are "endocrine-disrupting" may have very subtle, long-term consequences that cannot easily be attributed to a specific causal agent (Colborn, vom Saal, & Soto, 1993). Some of these chemicals tend to

accumulate in body fat, and their negative effects can be transmitted to the fetus either directly or through the mother's milk. Other chemicals have more direct effects, sometimes causing serious fetal malformations or death.

One example of a highly toxic chemical is **methylmercury**, whose effects received worldwide attention following the births of a large number of severely deformed and retarded infants in Minimata Bay, Japan. The deformities subsequently were traced to the presence of high levels of mercury in the fish that inhabitants of this community consumed in great quantities; the mercury was, in this case, an industrial waste. The effects of mercury are now known as **Minimata disease**.

Another teratogenic group of chemicals whose effects are well known are the **polychlorinated biphenyls** (PCBs) and related chemicals such as *dioxin*, often used in manufacturing herbicides or insecticides. These chemicals appear to be associated with a higher incidence of miscarriage and with physical deformities. For example, following the leak into the air of the gas *methyl isocyanate* (used to manufacture pesticides) in Bhopal, India, the rate of spontaneous abortions quadrupled (Bajaj et al., 1993).

In addition to the chemicals known to be harmful to the fetus, there are many toxic chemicals whose effects on fetal development are unknown, although we know how they affect children and adults. Lead is one example. It is present in some fuel emissions, in some paints, in certain metal products, and elsewhere. It accumulates slowly in the body; and when it reaches sufficiently high concentrations, it can lead to serious physical and mental problems in children and adults. Gillespie (1998) suggests that all pregnant women should either refrain from painting or wear gloves when they do so, not only because many paints contain lead, but also because most contain mercury as well.

---

abortion A miscarriage occurring usually before the twentieth week of pregnancy when the fetus ordinarily weighs less than 1 pound.

methylmercury Mercury compound that tends to accumulate in fatty tissue, and that is associated with birth deformities and malformations in offspring.

Minimata disease Disease linked with the presence of methylmercury. Affects prenatal development, typically causing severe deformations, mental retardation, blindness, and even death.

polychlorinated biphenyls (PCBs) Group of chemicals, such as dioxin, that may be associated with miscarriage and deformities in offspring.

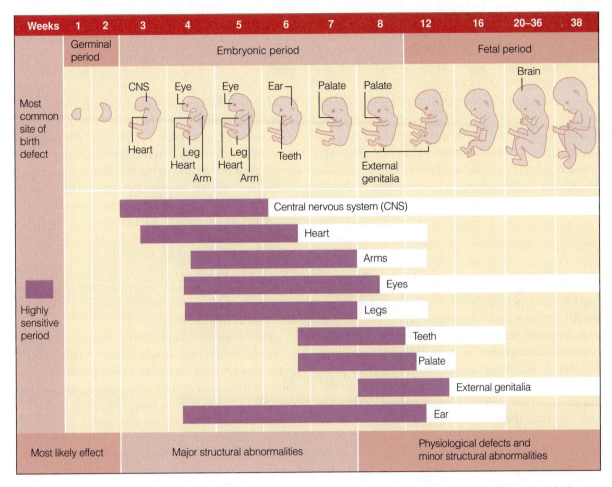

Weeks	1	2	3	4	5	6	7	8	12	16	20–36	38

FIGURE 4.3 The most serious structural defects in prenatal development are most likely to develop during the embryonic period, when all the basic organs and limbs are being formed (during the first eight weeks). Periods of highest sensitivity to teratogens are shown in purple; periods of lower sensitivity are indicated in white.

Nicotine

The harmful effects of maternal smoking on the fetus have been well documented: These include a significantly higher probability of fetal death or stillbirth, often associated with placental problems in which the placenta becomes detached from the uterine wall. Maternal smoking is also associated with **ectopic pregnancy**, a condition in which implantation occurs outside the uterus (most often in a fallopian tube, but also sometimes in an ovary or even in the abdomen) (Castles et al., 1999a).

Maternal smoking is also a highly significant contributor to premature births as well as to significantly lower birth weight, both of which, as we see later in this chapter, can be associated with a variety of problems in infants (Sherwood et al., 1999). There are also indications that maternal smoking may be linked with developmental problems that become evident later in life—for example, a slightly higher risk of childhood cancers (Sasco & Vainio, 1999); somewhat lower scores on some measures of cognitive ability (Trasti et al., 1999); a

ectopic pregnancy A pregnancy in which the zygote implants and develops anywhere outside the uterus—most often in a fallopian tube (a *tubal pregnancy*), though sometimes elsewhere as well.

higher risk of **sudden infant death syndrome (SIDS)** (Dybing & Sanner, 1999); and a higher probability of middle-ear disease (Stathis et al., 1999).

Although there has been some decline in the number of mothers smoking while pregnant, a vast body of research now indicates that environmental tobacco smoke (ETS) ("secondhand" smoke) may have much the same effects on the fetus as maternal smoking (for example, Hanke et al., 1999). The carcinogen (cancer causing) content of ETS is, in fact, frequently higher than that in smoke inhaled directly by smokers (Sasco & Vainio, 1999).

Caffeine

The effects of caffeine on the fetus remain somewhat unclear, perhaps because the effects are different for different individuals and because they do not appear to be very dramatic. Nevertheless, some research indicates that the probability of premature delivery is somewhat higher among mothers who consume higher levels of caffeine (Smigaj, 1999). Similarly, summaries of large numbers of studies indicate that there is a somewhat higher risk of lower birth weight with high caffeine consumption, usually defined as 400 milligrams of caffeine a day, about equivalent to four or more cups of coffee (Santos et al., 1998).

Alcohol and FAS

Alcohol consumption by pregnant women may be associated with premature birth and with various defects in their offspring. The classical collection of alcohol-related effects in the newborn is labeled **fetal alcohol syndrome (FAS)**; less serious effects are sometimes labeled *fetal alcohol effects (FAE)*. Some writers argue that because of its vagueness, because of the danger that it can easily be misapplied, and because of the stigma attached to it, the label FAE should not be used at all (Halamek, 1997).

Medically speaking, FAS should be diagnosed only when there are abnormalities in three areas: retarded physical growth; central nervous system problems evident in neurological problems, developmental retardation, or intellectual impairment; and characteristic cranial and facial malformations. These malformations typically include a low forehead, widely spaced eyes, a short nose, a long upper lip, and absence of a marked infranasal depression (the typical depression in the center of the upper lip, extending upward toward the nose) (Coustan & Mochizuki, 1998). FAS now appears to be one of the major causes of mental retardation in the western world, say Murphy-Brennan & Oei (1999). And because it does not occur naturally, but results from well-known causes, it is potentially entirely controllable. In fact, however, prevention programs have not been very successful in changing maternal behavior in significant ways.

With humans it is difficult to conduct the types of experiments that would allow researchers to determine precisely the amounts of alcohol and the timing of intake that result in these effects. Nor is it possible to separate completely the effects of alcohol from those of other drugs that might accompany alcohol use, or from the effects of malnutrition, also a possible corollary of alcohol use. The current consensus is that even in small amounts, alcohol may be harmful to the fetus, although it may not necessarily lead to fetal alcohol syndrome, but only to some of its effects. For example, Day and associates (1999) report that even among the offspring of mothers who are light to moderate drinkers, there is a significant correlation between size at the age of 10 (head circumference, weight, and height, for example) and prenatal exposure to alcohol.

The evidence is not all in, and the conclusions are still tentative. However, in summarizing the effects of alcohol on the developing fetus, Brendt and Beckman (1990) conclude that consuming six drinks or more of alcohol per day constitutes a high risk, but that fewer than two drinks per day is not likely to lead to fetal alcohol syndrome. But, as Newman and Buka (1991) point out, a single binge

---

sudden infant death syndrome (SIDS) Unexplained and unexpected infant death. The leading cause of infant death between the ages of 1 month and 1 year (not really a *cause*, because the *cause* remains unknown; rather, a *label*).

fetal alcohol syndrome (FAS) A collection of symptoms in newborns associated with maternal alcohol consumption during pregnancy and sometimes evident in varying degrees of neurological, mental, and physical problems.

of heavy drinking at a critical period in embryonic development might do significant harm. Given these findings, corroborated by a large number of other investigations, it should come as no surprise that an increasing number of medical practitioners recommend that pregnant women refrain completely from alcohol use. In Friedman and Polifka's (1996) words, "no safe amount of alcohol drinking during pregnancy has been determined" (1996, p. 15).

Illegal Drugs

As we have seen, various prescription and nonprescription drugs used for medicinal purposes can harm the developing fetus, as can various legal recreational drugs such as alcohol, nicotine, and caffeine. In addition, many illegal recreational drugs—narcotics, marijuana, and cocaine—can also affect a fetus adversely. Studying their effects is especially difficult, however, given that controlled investigations are not generally possible. Thus, there is often no way of ensuring that a cocaine user, for example, has not also used other drugs. As Smigaj (1997) points out, cocaine users often take tranquilizers and barbiturates to ease their periods of abstinence, heroin users often turn to alcohol between hits, and marijuana users often smoke nicotine as well.

Narcotics

Still, it seems clear that babies born to narcotics addicts are themselves addicted, and they subsequently suffer a clearly recognizable withdrawal, labeled the **neonatal abstinence syndrome (NAS)**. Its symptoms may include tremors, restlessness, hyperactive reflexes, high-pitched cries, vomiting, fevers, sweating, rapid respiration, seizures, and sometimes death (Khan & Chang, 1997). Often these symptoms don't reach a peak until the infant is 3 or 4 days old. Treatment, which typically involves giving the newborn low doses of morphine sulphate or barbiturates, sometimes lasts for several

weeks (Coghlan et al., 1999). Some physicians recommend methadone or morphine maintenance for the mother during the later stages of pregnancy and then gradual weaning of the infant from the drug after birth (Fischer et al., 1999). Interestingly, when mothers who breast-feed are also on methadone, abrupt cessation of breast-feeding can also lead to symptoms of NAS (Malpas & Darlow, 1999).

Marijuana There is some uncertainty about the effects of marijuana on the fetus. The results of much of the research are ambiguous, says Smigaj (1997). This may be partly because of difficulties in obtaining reliable information about drug use. It may also be due to the confounding of effects that results because the fetus is seldom exposed to only a single, clearly identifiable agent. There is, nevertheless, some tentative evidence of lower birth weights and a higher risk of prematurity for children born to heavy marijuana users (Sherwood et al., 1999). Coustan and Mochizuki (1998) conclude that marijuana use should be avoided completely during pregnancy, for several reasons: Its carcinogenic effects appear to be even more serious than those of nicotine; it crosses the placental barrier easily, reducing fetal heart rate and affecting fetal brain activity; and there is tentative evidence that its use might be linked to prematurity, malformations, and other fetal problems.

Cocaine Two more recent and perhaps increasingly common drugs abused by pregnant women are cocaine and **crack**. (Crack is easily manufactured from cocaine, is less expensive, and has far more intense and immediate effects than cocaine used more conventionally; see Chapter 12.) Cocaine addiction is reportedly about five times more common than heroin addiction in the United States. Some reports claim it has reached "epidemic proportions" (Food and Nutrition Board, 1990). However, estimates of illegal drug use are seldom very reliable.

Once thought to be relatively harmless, cocaine is now considered not only highly addictive, but also

neonatal abstinence syndrome (NAS) Neonatal symptoms associated with the mother's use of narcotics that has resulted in the newborn also being addicted. Severe cases may be fatal.

crack Name given to the drug that results when cocaine is "cooked down" with bicarbonate of soda to produce freebase cocaine (also called rock). It is usually smoked rather than snorted and produces a much stronger and more immediate rush than cocaine.

potentially very harmful to the unborn. Like most mood-altering drugs, it crosses the placental barrier easily. And because it is fat-soluble, it remains in the placenta and in amniotic fluid, where the fetus continually ingests it. A dose of cocaine lasts about 48 hours in the adult; in the fetus it may last a lot longer (Smigaj, 1997).

Infants born to cocaine and crack users are significantly smaller than average, have lower head circumference, and are more likely to be premature (Richardson et al., 1999). Pregnant cocaine users are also more likely to abort their fetuses (Miller & Boudreaux, 1999). And, notes Smigaj (1997), such mothers are also at risk of effects leading to their deaths as well to that of the fetus. In fact, much of the published research indicates that cocaine use is associated with risk of serious pregnancy complications and congenital (present at birth) problems. For example, infants born to cocaine and crack users manifest more startle reactions and more tremors than children of nonusers. They are also more likely to manifest disturbances in sleep patterns, feeding difficulties, diarrhea, fever, and increased irritability. On average, they are smaller and may show evidence of growth retardation—for example, delayed age of standing, pulling up to a sitting position, and developing visual and auditory orientation (Mullin, 1992). And they are not only more likely to be stillborn or to abort spontaneously but also more likely to die of sudden infant death syndrome (described in the next chapter) (Kandall et al., 1993). There is evidence, too, that children of cocaine-addicted mothers are more likely to suffer emotional and physical abuse, and the disadvantages of more disorganized and chaotic child-rearing environments (Miller & Boudreaux, 1999).

Some researchers suggest that because of the widespread use of cocaine by pregnant women, and because of its range of negative effects on infants, labeling its consequences the *fetal cocaine syndrome*—as has been done with alcohol—might be useful. The most common characteristics of this syndrome include growth retardation, low birth weight, prematurity, irritability, and several physical features such as small toenails, a short nose, and microcephaly (a small head). However, Friedman

and Polifka (1996) note that the meaning of this syndrome is still not clear.

Currently, close to 1 million children have been born to crack-addicted mothers, claims Hutchinson (1991). Because crack has been available since 1985, many of these children are now in school. The most seriously affected of them are, in Hutchinson's words, "a new breed, unlike other children with histories of drug exposure. They are in constant motion, disorganized, and very sensitive to stimuli. Crawling, standing, and walking take longer to develop. They are irritable and hard to please. It is hard for them to make friends. They respond less to the environment" (p. 31). (See *Concept Summary*.)

EFFECTS OF MATERNAL CHARACTERISTICS ON PRENATAL DEVELOPMENT

The large variety of drugs and chemicals to which the mother is exposed can have important consequences for the well-being of the fetus. So can various other maternal characteristics, such as her age, the quality of her nutrition, and her health. All of these factors need to be taken into consideration by physicians.

Maternal Health

A wide range of diseases and infections are known to affect the fetus. The best known is probably rubella (German measles); others are syphilis, gonorrhea, and poliomyelitis, each of which can cause mental deficiency, blindness, deafness, or miscarriages. Cretinism (subnormal mental development, undeveloped bones, a protruding abdomen, and rough, coarse skin) may be related to a thyroid malfunction in the mother or to an iodine deficiency in her diet. If the deficiency is not too extreme, it can sometimes be alleviated in the child through continuous medication after birth.

Diabetes Diabetes is a maternal condition that can have serious consequences for the fetus (Buchanan & Kjos, 1999). Before the discovery of insulin, fetal

CONCEPT SUMMARY

Drugs and Chemicals That Might Affect Prenatal Development

For any given individual, the occurrence and severity of an effect may be influenced by (1) the fetus's genetic background; (2) the timing of the influence (often more serious during the embryonic period—weeks 2 to 8); (3) the interaction of more than one influencing factor; (4) the mitigating effects of other positive influences.

Influence	Some Possible Effects
Prescription drugs	
thalidomide	Severe morphological changes in the embryo; limb reduction
quinine	Congenital deafness
acitetrin	Risk of miscarriage
tetracycline	Dental staining
accutane	Fetal malformations
lithium	Higher risk of cardiac defects
benzodiazapines (Valium)	Minimal effect in therapeutic doses
amphetamines	Little effect in therapeutic doses
diethylstilbestrol (DES)	Higher risk of cervical cancer
Over-the-counter drugs	
acetylsalicylic acid (aspirin)	Little risk at normal doses; risk of hemorrhaging with high doses
acetaminophen (Tylenol)	Little risk at normal doses; risk of fetal death with overdosing
antihistamines	No known negative effects
milk of magnesia	No known negative effects
Vitamins	Little apparent risk in normal doses; may be some risk with massive doses
Aspartame	Unlikely to be a teratogen
Chemicals	
methylmercury	Minimata disease; mental retardation; blindness; death
PCBs	Higher incidence of miscarriage and deformities; coffee-colored skin pigmentation
lead	Serious physical and mental problems in adults
nicotine	Occasional placental problems and ectopic pregnancy; lower birth weight; prematurity; higher risk of fetal death; higher risk of SIDS; similar risks associated with ETS (environmental tobacco smoke)
caffeine	Little effect in normal doses; excessive consumption may be more toxic
Alcohol	Mild to extreme fetal alcohol syndrome; growth retardation; mental retardation
Illegal drugs	
narcotics	Neonatal abstinence syndrome (withdrawal symptoms); sometimes fatal
marijuana	Unlikely to be teratogenic, except in massive doses
cocaine; crack	Neurological problems, growth retardation, increased susceptibility to SIDS, increased likelihood of fetal death

and maternal death were very common. Now, however, mortality rates among diabetic mothers are about the same as those among nonpregnant diabetic women. And with timely diagnosis and proper medical management, fetal deaths are generally low (Pearson & Copland, 1999). Management involves careful monitoring of mother and fetus to assess and control sugar levels (glycemic control). Simple self-monitoring procedures are available for in-home use.

Although fetal death as a complication of maternal diabetes has been greatly reduced, the rate of birth defects among these infants is still 2 to 4 times higher than normal. The most common defects include limb, heart, lung, and neural tube defects (Piazze et al., 1999). Most of these birth defects result from influences that occur early in pregnancy—hence the importance of careful monitoring from the outset.

Herpes   *Herpes simplex type 2* (**genital herpes**) is the most common of all sexually transmitted diseases. Although its effects on the mother are typically more annoying than debilitating, it can have serious effects on the fetus, particularly if the mother's infection is active at the time of delivery. The probability that infants will contract the virus during birth is extremely high. Because the newborn does not possess many of the immunities that are common among older children and adults, the herpes virus may attack the infant's internal organs, leading to visual or nervous system problems or death in about 50% of cases (Eden et al., 1990). As a result, infants born to mothers infected with herpes virus are often delivered through cesarean section to prevent infection, especially if the mother is suffering from an outbreak of herpes at the time of delivery (Marks, Fethers, & Mindel, 1999). However, the use of the drug acyclovir (and, more recently, *valacyclovir* and *famciclovir*) appears to be effective in reducing outbreaks of herpes in the mother, thus often eliminating the need for a cesarean delivery (Scott, 1999).

Another form of herpes virus, **cytomegalovirus** (CMV), affects the salivary glands and can also be passed on to the fetus during birth. It is one of the main infectious causes of mental retardation, and an important cause of deafness. Although more than half of all pregnant women appear to have been exposed to CMV, the risk of affecting the fetus appears to be relatively low. At present, there appears to be no way of reducing it further (Krew & Gill, 1997).

AIDS   Acquired immunodeficiency syndrome (AIDS) is another sexually transmitted disease that is of considerable current concern. First reported in the United States in 1981, the disease remains incurable and thus ultimately fatal. In 1996, more than 66,000 new cases of AIDS were reported in the United States (U.S. Bureau of the Census, 1998)—about 1000 new cases were reported in Canada in 1996 (*Canada Yearbook, 1999*). Estimates are that worldwide, more than 20 million are now infected, including as many as 1 out of every 10 people in southern and eastern Africa. And the prognosis is that virtually all will eventually die from resulting complications (Painter, 1997). In industrialized countries, the death rate has declined dramatically, largely as a result of powerful new drugs. (See *At a Glance:* "AIDS in the United States and Canada.")

AIDS is caused by the **human immunodeficiency virus** (HIV), which is transmitted through the exchange of body fluids, primarily through blood/blood exchange or through semen/blood exchange. Accordingly, transmission occurs mainly through anal intercourse (because of the thinness of rectal tissues, which frequently tear during intercourse), through blood transfusions involving infected blood, and through the communal use of hypodermic syringes. In North America, AIDS has been most common among homosexual males and among intravenous drug users. In countries such as South Africa, transmission is primarily heterosexual,

---

genital herpes   An incurable sexually transmitted viral disease that usually includes sometimes painful or itchy lesions in the genital area.

cytomegalovirus (CMV)   A herpes virus affecting the salivary glands; can be transmitted from mother to infant during birth. An important cause of mental retardation and deafness.

acquired immunodeficiency syndrome (AIDS)   An incurable and fatal disease, transmitted through the exchange of body fluids, caused by HIV (*human immunodeficiency virus*).

human immunodeficiency virus (HIV)   The presumed cause of *acquired immunodeficiency syndrome (AIDS);* a virus that appears to be able to mutate rapidly, and whose control has proven difficult.

AT A GLANCE   ## AIDS in the United States and Canada

AIDS is a fatal disease caused by the human immunodeficiency virus (HIV), which is transmitted primarily through the exchange of body fluids. Infants and young children with AIDS have almost invariably been infected by their mothers while in the womb. Hence there are relatively few new AIDS cases among children before the age of 12. With increasing sexual activity at adolescence, however, incidence of AIDS increases dramatically. Of the approximately 620,000 cases of AIDS reported in the U.S. between 1981 and 1997, almost 85% have been male. However, incidence among females has risen enormously in recent years so that now more than 25% of all new cases are female (U.S. Bureau of the Census, 1998).

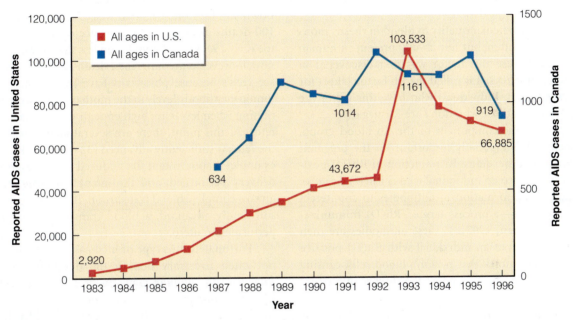

FIGURE 4.4 AIDS cases reported in the United States (1983–1996) and Canada (1986–1996). (From U.S. Bureau of the Census, 1998, p. 146 and *Canada Yearbook, 1999*, p. 34.)

and the disease is about as common among women as among men. In North America, too, incidence is also increasing among heterosexual men and women (see Chapter 12 for more information).

Most infants and children who are infected acquire the virus directly from their mothers through blood exchange in the uterus or during birth. With the use of powerful new drugs during pregnancy (zidovudine, for example), the risk of transmission from infected mother to fetus has been reduced by about 70% (Hanson et al., 1999). Cesarean deliveries reduce transmission even more. In one study, the use of both drug therapy and cesarean delivery reduced transmission rates to only

2% among 196 mothers. For 1,255 mothers who delivered without cesarean section but who were undergoing drug therapy, transmission rates were 7.3% ("The Mode of Delivery," 1999).

In the absence of prenatal drug therapy and cesarean deliveries, transmission of AIDS from mothers to infants remains high. For example, Jean and associates (1999) report a transmission rate of 27% in a study of 81 HIV-infected women. But the prognosis for infants of infected mothers has improved dramatically with the use of *zidovudine* with pregnant mothers who are infected, and its use with newborns after birth (Brockmeyer, 1999). Whereas, prior to these drug therapies, most infected infants died before the age of 1, now many are surviving 8 or 10 years or even longer ("AIDS Kids Beat Odds Against Survival," 1994).

Clearly, high-risk women (current or past intravenous drug users and those whose sexual partner(s) include bisexual males and/or men who have been or are intravenous drug users) should be tested for antibodies for the AIDS virus before considering pregnancy.

Rh(D) Immunization

There is a particular quality of blood in rhesus monkeys that is often, but not always, present in human blood. Because this factor was first discovered in Rhesus monkeys, it is called the **Rh factor** (short for *rhesus factor*). Individuals who have this factor are Rh-positive; those who don't are Rh-negative.

A specific component of the Rh blood group, labeled D, is especially important for the pregnant mother and her fetus. Introduction of Rh(D)-positive blood into an individual who is Rh(D)-negative leads to the formation of antibodies to counteract the D factor—a process termed **Rh(D) immunization** (Bowman, 1997). If these antibodies are then introduced into an individual with Rh(D)-positive blood, they attack that person's blood cells, causing a depletion of oxygen and, in the absence of medical intervention, death.

Unfortunately, this situation can occur in the fetus (termed **fetal erythroblastosis**) when the fetus has Rh(D)-positive blood and the mother is Rh(D)-negative. Because the Rh factor is a dominant genetic trait, this situation can occur only when the father is Rh(D)-positive and the mother is Rh(D)-negative. If blood from the fetus gets into the mother's blood-

stream—termed *transplacental hemorrhage*—the mother's blood will begin to produce antibodies. These are usually not produced early enough or in sufficient quantities to affect the first child, but subsequent fetuses may be affected. Transplacental hemorrhage occurs in approximately 75% of all pregnant women, either during pregnancy or immediately after birth (Bowman, 1997). Hence the chances of Rh(D) immunization are very high—if, of course, the mother is Rh(D)-negative and the father Rh(D)-positive.

At one time, this condition was always fatal. Bowman (1997) reports that it accounted for about 100 deaths per year in the province of Manitoba in the early 1940s (total population less than 1 million); now, however, it accounts for 1 death every 3 years or so. That's because physicians have learned how to monitor antibody levels in the mother's blood, determining when levels are high enough to endanger the fetus. At this point, there are several alternatives. If the fetus is sufficiently advanced (32 or 33 weeks, for example), labor might be induced or a cesarean delivery performed, and the infant is immediately given a complete blood transfusion. If the fetus is not sufficiently advanced, a blood transfusion may be performed in utero.

Fortunately, this type of medical intervention is not often necessary due to the development of *Rhogam (Rh Immune Globulin or RhlG)* in 1968. Rhogam contains passive antibodies that prevent the formation of additional antibodies. It has become routine for physicians to ascertain whether a pregnant woman is Rh(D)-negative and whether she is at risk of Rh(D) immunization; this information should be gathered at the time of the first prenatal visit. Husbands or partners of Rh(D)-negative women should then be screened as well. If they too are Rh(D)-negative, there is little chance of fetal erythroblastosis. However, because of the possibility of an extramarital conception, mothers who are Rh(D)-negative and their fetuses should be monitored closely throughout pregnancy.

When an expectant mother is at risk of immunization (that is, she is Rh(D)-negative and the father is Rh(D)-positive), Rhogam is sometimes administered during the seventh month of gestation, even though the incidence of immunization before delivery is low (approximately 2%). Current medical guidelines are that all such women be

Rh factor A blood protein found in some individuals but not others. When present in the fetus's blood but not in the mother's, it can cause birth complications.

Rh(D) immunization Process in which the introduction of the Rh(D) factor into the blood of someone who doesn't already possess this factor leads to the formation of antibodies to counteract the D factor. These antibodies can be fatal to someone with the Rh(D) factor.

fetal erythroblastosis A medical condition in the newborn marked by lack of red blood cells. Can be fatal if sufficiently serious and not attended to in time.

administered Rhogam within no more than 72 hours of delivery, as soon as it has been determined that the fetus is Rh(D)-positive and that the mother is therefore at risk of Rh(D) immunization. Similarly, Rhogam should be administered in the event of the abortion or miscarriage of an Rh(D)-positive fetus if the mother is Rh(D)-negative. The drug must be administered after the termination of every Rh(D)-positive pregnancy (Hartwell, 1998). (See Figure 4.5 for an Rh(D) decision flowchart.)

Maternal Emotions and Stress

A once-common folk belief was that the mother's emotional states could be communicated directly to her unborn child. If the pregnant woman worried too much, her child would be born with a frown; if she were frightened by a rabbit, the result might be a child with a harelip; if she had a particularly traumatic experience, it would mark the infant, perhaps

for life. Accordingly, she must try to be happy and have pleasant experiences so that the child could be born free of negative influences.

Most of these beliefs about pregnancy are simply tales. However, because of the close relationship between the mother and the fetus, a number of investigators have pursued the idea that stimuli affecting her will also have some effect on the fetus, however indirect. One theory is that because of the close connection between mother and fetus, changes in the mother's chemical balance accompanying intense emotions and stress might affect her unborn child. There is very tentative evidence, for example, that mothers who are anxious during much of their pregnancy might have infants who are more irritable and more hyperactive and have more feeding problems (Spezzano, 1981). Similarly, Webster, Chandler, and Battistutta (1996) report poorer fetal outcomes for women who are victims of abuse while pregnant.

These findings are highly uncertain, however. Not only is it extremely difficult to arrive at valid and

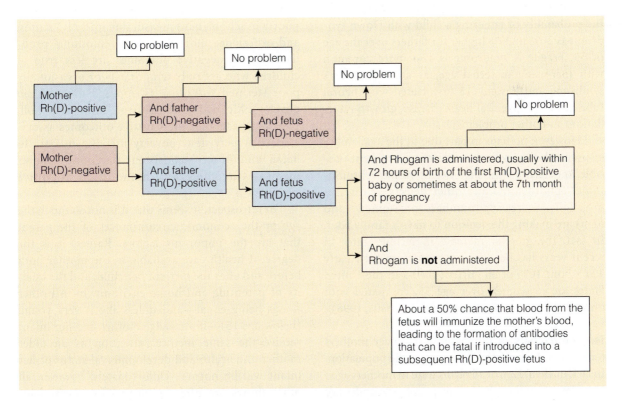

FIGURE 4.5 Rh(D) immunization flowchart. Immunization occurs when the Rh(D) factor is introduced into an Rh(D)-negative mother's blood, leading to the formation of antibodies which, if they are later introduced into the bloodstream of an Rh(D)-positive fetus, attack the fetus's blood cells in a potentially fatal condition termed *fetal erythroblastosis*. An injection of the drug *Rhogam* can prevent this condition.

useful measures of emotional states in mother and infant, but it is also often impossible to control a variety of other factors that might be related. For example, in the Webster, Chandler, and Battistutta (1996) study, abused women also tended to smoke more cigarettes, take more drugs (including antidepressants), and have more medical conditions. Any of these factors alone, or in combination, might account for more negative fetal outcomes. Hence conclusive statements about the influence of maternal emotional states on the unborn are not warranted.

Maternal Age

A mother's age can also be related to the well-being of the fetus. Infants of both older and younger mothers are sometimes at a disadvantage.

Older Mothers We know, as was pointed out in Chapter 3, that the incidence of trisomy 21 (Down syndrome) is about 40 times higher for women over age 40 than for women age 20. We know, as well, that the probability of fathering a child with Down syndrome is 20% to 30% higher for fathers over the age of 55. Fragile X syndrome is also more common with increasing maternal age, as are Klinefelter's syndrome and trisomy 18 (associated with neural tube defects, congenital heart disease, growth retardation, and other problems).

However, perhaps in part due to the availability of prenatal diagnostic procedures that make it possible to determine the presence of various chromosomal abnormalities and other defects or diseases prenatally, increasing numbers of women (and men) are making the decision to have a family later. In fact, the greatest increase in fertility rates in recent years has been among women in their early 30s. About 10% of all current births in the United States are to women over age 35, compared with only 6% in 1970 (U.S. Bureau of the Census, 1998).

Teenage Mothers Birthrates among teenage mothers remain very high relative to the rest of the population. In fact, in 1996, 12% of all births were to mothers aged 15 to 19—even though of all pregnant girls under age 19, 80% of black teenagers, 40% of Hispanics, and 28% of non-Hispanic whites underwent an abortion (U.S. Bureau of the Census, 1998).

Children born to younger teenage mothers are often at a physical, emotional, and intellectual disadvantage relative to children born to older mothers. There are more miscarriages, premature births, and stillbirths among teenage mothers, and surviving infants are more often the targets of abuse and neglect (Stier et al., 1993). These children's developmental scores on various measures are often retarded, and incidence of low birth weight is about 2 times higher for teenage mothers (U.S. Bureau of the Census, 1998).

Maternal Poverty

As Dean, Ducey, and Malik (1997) point out, however, much of this research fails to take into account the social circumstances of teenage parenthood—the poverty and the lack of social, educational, and medical assistance. Persistent poverty, says McLoyd (1998), is clearly associated with more negative developmental outcomes. In fact, children who live in poverty tend to do more poorly in school, have measurably lower IQ scores, and experience more social and emotional problems. These negative outcomes are less true of children who are only temporarily or occasionally poor (termed *transitory* as opposed to *persistent* poverty). McLoyd (1998; Huston, McLoyd & Coll, 1997) suggests that the negative outcomes associated with persistent poverty are due in part to harsh and often inconsistent parenting, poorer medical care, and less home-based cognitive stimulation.

In retrospect, it seems that it is not so much the age or the economic circumstances of the parent that are the important factors. Rather, it is the degree of health care available to the mother both before and after the birth of her child, and the quality of parenting and home environment. All other things being equal—and unless she is very young (below age 15)—if a teenage mother and her infant receive the same medical attention as an older mother, the health and developmental status of her infant will be normal. Unfortunately, however, all other things are often not equal for the teenage mother. (See Chapter 12 for a more detailed discussion of teenage pregnancy. See, also, *In the News and on the Web:* "Child Fathers Twins.")

IN THE NEWS AND ON THE WEB

Child Fathers Twins

"Child fathers twins!" sounds a little like the headline you might see on a tabloid at a grocery store checkout stand. But no, the story is not invented. Twin girls have been born to a 17-year-old mother, who claims to be "thrilled to bits." The father, Britain's youngest-ever father of twins, is an unnamed 13-year-old boy. The boy, who is described as a "regular truant" from school, claims he was happy when he found out. "It's all a nice shock," he said, puffing on a cigarette, explaining how he felt his mates were maybe a little "jealous of his situation." About raising the babies, he said, "We'll learn what to do as we go along." He is now planning on leaving school. "I want to earn a few quid to see my babies right," he said.

N. Bunyan, "Fathering Twins at 13 'a nice shock,' Boy Says." *The National Post* (*Toronto*), 4 December 1999, p. A1.

To Think About: Two things are striking about this news item: (1) the shockingly low age of the father, and (2) the father's eagerness to be involved in the care and upbringing of the twins. That he thinks his mates are "jealous," and that the mother is "thrilled to bits" says

much about their immaturity. How many reasons can you think of not to be jealous of the boy's situation, or thrilled to bits for the mother?

 Resources: The first of the following two websites is dedicated to teen pregnancy prevention. It describes a variety of related programs and published information, and it provides recent statistics on incidence of teen pregnancy in the United States. It also provides culturally specific information on teen pregnancy and pregnancy prevention. The second site includes a wealth of information on teen pregnancy and on nutrition, health, and drug use among pregnant teenagers, as well as information on the care of newborns:

http://www.advocatesforyouth.org/pregnanc.htm

http://www.bu.edu/cohis/teenpreg/teenpreg.htm

 For additional readings, explore *InfoTrac College Edition*, your online library. Go to http://infotrac-college.com/wadsworth and use the passcode that came on the card with your book. Try these search terms: teen pregnancy, pregnancy prevention.

Michael Newman/PhotoEdit

Incidence of twin births among teenage girls is only slightly lower than that among older women. But that the father of twins should be only 13, as was recently the case in Britain, is extremely rare.

Maternal Nutrition

Nutrition is one of the most important external influences on the developing fetus.

Effects of Serious Malnutrition During the German siege of Leningrad in World War II, many Russians lived near starvation in bitterly cold, unheated homes. Many died. But perhaps most striking, in one clinic that had seen an average of 3,867 births a year for the preceding three years, only 493 infants were born in 1942 (Shanklin & Hoden, 1979). Most of these babies were born in the first half of the year and had been conceived before the famine was at its height; only 79 were born in the second half of the year.

Similar outcomes have been reported far more recently in parts of the world suffering from famine. For example, Mattson (1998) reports very high fetal death associated with nutritional deficiencies in Zimbabwe following a prolonged drought. And Agarwal and associates (1998) report that over a 5-year period, 18% of all pregnancies terminated in "pregnancy wastage" (meaning spontaneous abortions or stillbirths) in an impoverished rural community in India.

Effects of Less Serious Malnutrition Investigating the effects of less dramatic forms of malnutrition is difficult. Investigators can't always separate the effects of malnutrition from the effects of other factors that often accompany malnutrition (poor sanitation, poor medical care, drug use, and so on). Effects sometimes attributed solely to malnutrition might also be at least partly related to these other factors. In addition, malnutrition is seldom limited to the prenatal period but usually continues into infancy and even childhood.

Nevertheless, studies with animals, as well as with humans, leave little doubt that malnutrition, especially protein deprivation, has serious negative consequences for the developing brain (Rizzo et al., 1997). We also know that deficiencies in folic acid are linked with the development of neural tube defects, and that iron and calcium are especially important for fetal development. Unfortunately, says Gillespie (1998), most women have inadequate stores of iron, folic acid, and calcium. For affluent, middle-class mothers, these nutrients are readily available in supplements as well as in natural foods sources; sad to say, for those who are less affluent, and perhaps less well educated, their availability may not be nearly so ready.

Nutritional Requirements during Pregnancy During pregnancy, the mother's energy requirements and her metabolism change. The presence of a growing fetus means that the mother requires somewhere between 10% and 15% more calories. And metabolic changes include an increased synthesis of protein, which is important for the formation of the placenta and enlargement of the uterus; a reduction in carbohydrate consumption, the effect of which is to provide sufficient glucose for the fetus; and increased storage of fat to satisfy the mother's energy requirements (Gillespie, 1998).

Pregnant women must increase intake not only of protein but also of important minerals (for example, calcium, magnesium, iron, and zinc) and vitamins (mainly B_6, D, and E). Recommended dietary allowances for pregnant women range from 25% to 50% above those for nonpregnant women (Recommended Dietary Allowances, 1980).

Research indicates that average intake of these nutrients is often less than recommended for American women. Hence current medical advice emphasizes that what the woman eats is more important than how much. For fetal brain growth, protein appears to be among the most important ingredients of a good diet.

Optimal Weight Gain in Pregnancy Physicians now use the concept of **body mass index** (BMI), rather than weight alone, to determine if an individual is obese, excessively thin, or ideal. Body mass index reflects the relationship between height and weight. It's calculated by dividing your weight in kilograms by the square of your height in meters. (To get exactly the same index using pounds and inches, multiply your weight in pounds by 703, then divide by the square of your height in inches.) For adults, a

---

body mass index (BMI) The ratio of height to weight, computed by dividing weight in kilograms by the square of height in meters. Normal BMI is between about 20 and 27 (somewhat higher with increasing age). Indexes above and below these cutoffs indicate obesity or excessive thinness.

During pregnancy, protein and mineral needs increase greatly, as does need for caloric intake (by about 10% to 15%). Current recommended weight gain during pregnancy for an initially average-weight woman is 25 to 35 pounds; for women who are initially underweight, it is even higher.

Amy Etra/PhotoEdit

BMI somewhere between 20 and 26 is considered most ideal. Those above BMI 27 or 28 would be considered somewhat obese; 32 is severely overweight, and above 45 brings high risks. For younger children, considerably lower BMI scores indicate being overweight (in the low 20s), depending on age (Sizer & Whitney, 1997).

Current medical advice contradicts the long-held belief that women should be careful to minimize weight gain during pregnancy. Infant mortality rates are often lower in countries where pregnant women gain significantly more weight than do pregnant women in the United States or Canada. Maternal weight gain leads to higher fetal weight

and reduces the risk of illness and infection. Accordingly, doctors who once cautioned women to limit their weight gain to about 10 pounds now suggest that the optimal weight gain for a woman who begins pregnancy at an average weight (BMI between 19.89 and 26) is somewhere between 25 and 35 pounds (11.5 to 16 kg); it is even higher for women who are initially underweight. For women who are initially overweight, recommended gains are correspondingly lower (15–25 lbs.; 7–11.5 kg) (Gillespie, 1998). Total recommended weight gain for women carrying twins is 35 to 45 pounds (16–20.5 kg).

Unfortunately, these recommendations are probably most relevant for those least likely to be exposed to them and least able to comply with them. Malnutrition and starvation are seldom a deliberate choice. (See *Concept Summary*.)

CHILDBIRTH

Childbirth is something that happens almost 4 million times a year in the United States, and slightly under 400,000 times a year in Canada—although fertility rates (proportion of women having children) have declined considerably in both countries. In China, childbirth is estimated to happen more than 20 million times a year. (See Figure 4.6 in *At a Glance:* "Births and Deaths in the United States and Canada.")

Birth in today's industrialized nations is largely a medical procedure. Doctors and other medical personnel work to ensure the safety of the newborn as well as the safety and comfort of the mother. They have at their command techniques and procedures to induce labor, to accelerate it, to delay it, even to stop it if necessary. They can administer drugs to lessen the mother's pain, perform blood transfusions on the infant, or effect a **cesarean delivery**.

In earlier times (and even today in less developed parts of the world), people's experiences of birth were sometimes very different. Birth often

birth The process whereby the fetus, the placenta, and other membranes are separated from the mother's body and expelled.

cesarean delivery A common surgical procedure in which the fetus is delivered through an incision in the mother's abdomen and uterus.

CONCEPT SUMMARY

Maternal Characteristics That Might Affect Prenatal Development

Influence	Some Possible Effects
Maternal health	
Diabetes	• Two to 4 times higher rate of fetal defects
	• Careful monitoring and control of sugar levels important
Herpes	• Highly contagious during birth
	• Nervous system problems including mental retardation
	• Fetal death
	• Cesarean section recommended, especially if outbreak present at birth
	• Use of acyclovir often suppresses symptoms in mother
AIDS	• Often transmitted to fetus by infected mother
	• Zidovudine and other drugs have significantly increased survival rate in childhood
Rh(D) immunization	• Can occur only if mother is Rh(D) negative, father Rh(D) positive, and fetus Rh(D) positive
	• If untended, may lead to fetal death in the absence of a blood transfusion
	• Can be prevented through injection of Rhogam within 3 days of birth of first Rh(D)-positive child
Maternal emotions	• No direct neurological link between mother and fetus
	• Some speculation that maternal chemical changes accompanying intense emotion might affect fetus
	• No conclusive statements

occurred in birthing huts, in fields, in forests, or perhaps most often, in homes. These "primitive" (or perhaps "more natural") births were sometimes a solitary experience; sometimes there were midwives, healers, or other attendants. In general, it was believed to be far simpler, shorter, and less painful than birth often is today. Goldsmith (1990a) quotes a nineteenth-century traveler who had been trekking with the Guyana women of South America: "When on the march an Indian is taken with labor, she just steps aside, is delivered, wraps up the baby with the **afterbirth** and runs in haste after the others" (p. 22). (See *Across Cultures:* "A !Kung Woman's First Child.")

But we know too that in earlier times birth was often a tragic experience: Infant mortality was high, and the death of the mother too was not uncommon. A century ago, more than 100 of every 1,000 infants died; that number has now been reduced by almost 90% (U.S. Bureau of the Census, 1998). The decline in infant mortality rates is due not only to medical advances but also to improved sanitation and a consequent reduction in maternal and infant infections. Through the Middle Ages, high risk of death during childbirth (or of subsequent infections) made childbearing a relatively dangerous undertaking. Even as recently as 1960, of every 100,000 women giving birth in the United States, an average of 37 died (75% of these were nonwhites). Now, maternal mortality rates have been cut by more than 80% (still twice as high for black as for

---

afterbirth The placenta and other membranes that are expelled from the uterus following the birth of a child.

**CONCEPT
SUMMARY**

Maternal Characteristics That Might Affect Prenatal Development (continued)

Influence	Some Possible Effects
Older mothers	• Higher risk of some chromosomal problems, including Down syndrome • Modern health care has reduced age-related risks considerably • Increasing frequency of childbirth to older mothers
Teenage mothers	• About 12% of all births • Social, physical, intellectual disadvantages linked not with the mother's age, but with other conditions such as poverty and associated disadvantages
Socioeconomic disadvantages	• Persistent poverty (more than transitory poverty) associated with poorer developmental outcomes (lower IQ, poorer school achievement, emotional problems) • Effects mediated by often inconsistent and harsh parenting, lack of cognitive stimulation, and lower expectations
Maternal nutrition	• Serious malnutrition sometimes associated with miscarriages and decline in birthrate • Less serious malnutrition may have negative effects on physical and neurological development • Increased nutrition requirements for pregnant women • Optimal weight gain for normal-weight women, 25 to 35 pounds (11.5 to 16 kg)

white mothers). In the same period, infant death rates were more than halved, from 26 per 1,000 live births to less than 8 (see Figure 4.7).

The Initiation of Childbirth

What causes the childbirth process to begin remained a mystery for many years. Hippocrates, writing some 2,400 years ago, thought he knew. The child starts the whole process, he informed his readers. When the fetus has grown too big, there simply isn't enough nourishment available, so it becomes agitated, it kicks around and moves its arms, and it ruptures the membranes that hold it in. And then it forces its way out, head first because the head part is heavier than the bottom part (Liggins, 1988).

Hippocrates was at least partly wrong, although many people believed his speculation right into the eighteenth century. We now know that it isn't the size of the fetus or its agitation that leads to childbirth. Rather, it is changes in brain activity of the fetus—specifically, increases in adrenal activity. This increased activity results in the production of the hormone **oxytocin** by the mother, as well as producing other chemical changes in both mother and fetus, leading to the initiation of labor (Hull et al., 1997). As well, prior to the initiation of labor, normally the fetus has turned one final time so that the head is pointing downward.

oxytocin A hormone that brings about contractions and leads to childbirth. Synthetic oxytocin is often used to induce labor.

Births and Deaths in the United States and Canada

At the height of the baby boom in 1960, almost 4.3 million babies were born in the United States. Only 1.7 million people died, leaving a natural population increase of about 2.6 million. Similarly, in Canada, where the population is about 1/10 that of the U.S., an average of 400,000 children were born each year between 1946 and 1966. Now, however, although our populations are considerably higher, the number of births has actually declined during the '90s. This means that the fertility rate (number of births per 1,000 population) has dropped—partly because of more effective contraception and partly because of changed attitudes toward conception and childbearing. Thus in Canada, fertility rate has declined from 15.3 per 1,000 in 1975 to 12.0 per 1,000 in 1997. In the United States, it has declined from 18.4 in 1970 to 14.8 in 1996.

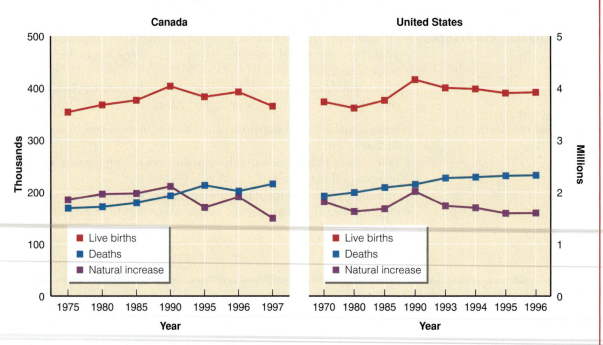

FIGURE 4.6 Births and deaths in Canada and the United States, 1970–1997. Source: Based on data from *Canada Yearbook, 1999,* p. 86 and from *Statistical Abstract,* U.S. Bureau of the Census (1998), p. 76.

Stages of Labor

Labor, the process by which the fetus, placenta, and other membranes are separated from the mother's body and expelled, usually begins gradually and proceeds through three stages. That there are exceptions to the normal process has been substantiated by the many others who didn't quite make it. Birth may also be induced by the physician. Sometimes there are medical reasons for doing so; at other times, it is done primarily for the convenience of physicians or mothers. This typically requires breaking the amniotic sac and injecting the mother with a synthetic form of the hormone oxytocin. Induced labor is sometimes more difficult than labor that begins naturally.

labor The process during which the fetus, placenta, and other membranes are separated from the woman's body and expelled. The termination of labor is usually birth.

ACROSS CULTURES

A !Kung Woman's First Child

When she felt the contractions were sufficiently strong and frequent, Sanyo, a woman of the !Kung, hunter-gatherers of the Kalahari, rose silently from her bed. She didn't awaken her husband—or even her parents, although they, too, slept in the same hut. Among the !Kung, a marriage is not considered consummated before the birth of a child; until then, the couple lives with the wife's parents. This would be Sanyo's first child.

For a moment, Sanyo considered waking her mother; the first birth is sometimes assisted by the mother. But !Kung women are strong and independent, and Sanyo scarcely hesitated. Alone, she walked out into the veld, smelling the rich earth smells of the land, the excitement of another dawn. Silently, she gathered handfuls of sedges and grasses, laying them in a soft bed at the foot of a tree. Then she leaned back against the tree, caught up in the mounting sensations of the contractions, excited that she, too, would soon be a mother, anticipating the pride with which she would walk back to the village, carrying her newborn.

Did Sanyo sense any fear, even a twinge of apprehension? No. She knew that some births were longer than others, that some were sometimes difficult. If hers were like that, she would walk back to the village and the women would massage her back while her husband, using his walking stick, would draw a fine line in the sand, straight away from the hut, out through the village and beyond, praying all the while: "Come out, come out, come to the village, everyone is waiting for you" (Fried & Fried, 1980, p. 29).

Sanyo had no need for mother or husband. When she sensed the baby's head emerging, she squatted over the grassy mound, delivering it easily onto the soft bed. A girl! She, like all first-born girls, would be named for her father's mother.

Sanyo wiped the baby clean with the grasses, cut the umbilical cord with a stick, wrapped the baby in the blanket she had brought, and quickly erased all traces of the delivery, burying the stained grasses and carefully marking the spot with a stick so that no man would accidentally step on it and lose his sexual potency or his hunting skills.

Quickly, she hurried home. Tonight there would be a feast and a dance for the new baby.

Goldsmith, J. (1990a). *Childbirth wisdom: From the world's oldest societies.* Brookline, Mass.: East-West Health Books. Also see the book upon which this account is based: Fried, M. N., & M. H. Fried, (1980). *Four rituals in eight cultures.* New York: W. W. Norton.

To Think About: To what extent might the pain and fear sometimes associated with childbirth be influenced by cultural expectations? Can you think of other reactions and expectations that are typical in your cultural group—and that you therefore assume to be "natural" but that might be quite different elsewhere?

Anthro-Photo File

Anecdotal evidence suggests that unassisted "primitive" births are easier than many hospital births. But the fact is that chances of infant and maternal death were far higher for this !Kung woman and her child than is the case for most medically assisted births.

Stage 1: Dilation and Effacement of the Cervix The first stage of labor is the longest, lasting an average of 12 hours for a first birth, and about half as long for subsequent births. It consists of initially mild contractions that are usually spaced quite far apart (like butterflies in my stomach, said one woman). Contractions become more painful and last consid-

erably longer toward the end of the first stage of birth (like a bear cub in my guts, said another).

In the first stage, the **cervix** (the opening to the uterus) dilates to allow passage of the baby from the

cervix The small circular opening to the womb (uterus) that dilates considerably during birth to permit passage of the baby.

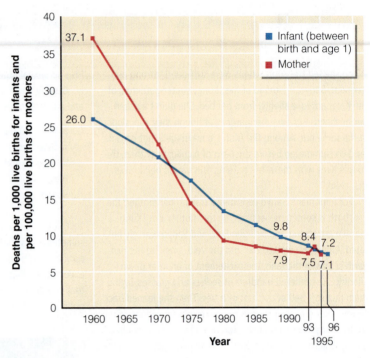

FIGURE 4.7 Declining maternal and infant mortality rates from delivery and complications of pregnancy and childbirth, 1960 to 1996. Source: U.S. Bureau of the Census (1998), p. 99.

uterus, essentially erasing (*effacing*) itself (hence the label, **dilation and effacement of the cervix**). Contractions are involuntary spasmlike actions that exert a downward pressure on the fetus as well as a distending force on the cervix. If the amniotic sac (the sac filled with amniotic fluid in which the fetus develops) is still intact, it absorbs much of the pressure in the early stages and transmits some of the force of the contractions to the neck of the cervix. However, if the sac has ruptured or bursts in the early stages of labor, the baby's head will rest directly on the pelvic structure and cervix, serving as a sort of wedge.

Stage 2: Delivery The second stage of birth, **delivery**, begins when the cervix has dilated to about 10 centimeters (about 4 inches). It starts with the baby's head emerging (in a normal delivery) at the cervical opening and ends with the birth of the child (Figure 4.8). The second stage usually lasts no more than an hour and often ends in a few minutes. The fetus ordinarily presents itself head first and can usually be born without the intervention of a physician. On occasion, however, complications arise that require some sort of intervention. For example, the head of the fetus may be too large for the opening provided by the mother. In such a case the physician may make a small incision in the vaginal outlet (an **episiotomy**), which is sutured after the baby is born. Complications can also arise from abnormal presentations of the fetus: **breech** (buttocks first), **transverse** (crosswise), or a variety of other possible positions. Some of these can be corrected before birth by turning the fetus manually in the uterus (**version**). Sometimes the fetus is delivered just as it presents itself.

---

dilation and effacement of the cervix The first stage of labor, during which the cervix dilates until, having reached a diameter of about 10 cm. (4 in.), it is large enough to permit passage of the fetus.

delivery The second stage of labor, beginning with the baby's head emerging (in a normal delivery) at the cervical opening and terminating with the birth of the child.

episiotomy A small cut made in the vaginal opening to facilitate the birth of a child. An episiotomy prevents the tearing of membranes and ensures that once the cut has been sutured, healing will be rapid and complete.

breech birth An abnormal presentation of the fetus at birth: buttocks first rather than head first.

transverse presentation A crosswise presentation of the fetus at birth.

version The act of turning. In obstetrics, refers to turning the child in the uterus to facilitate birth.

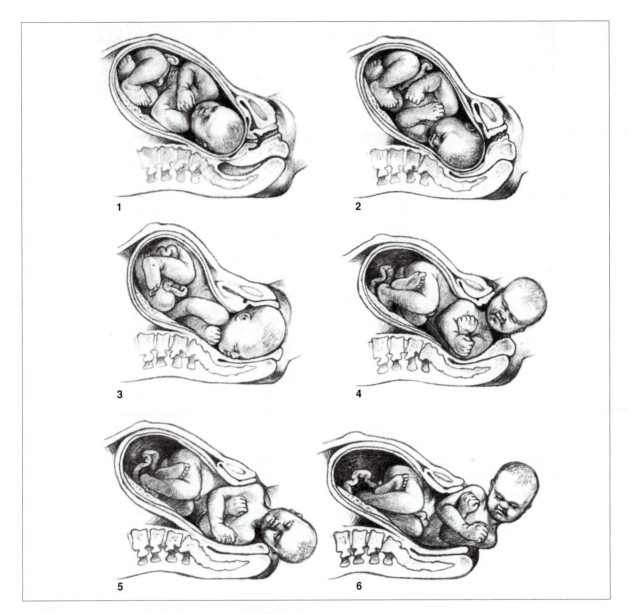

FIGURE 4.8 These cross sections show the first two stages of a normal presentation and delivery of a baby. The first stage (*dilation and effacement of the cervix*, illustrations 1 and 2) lasts an average of 12 hours for a first birth, and terminates with sufficient dilation of the cervix (the opening to the womb) so that the actual delivery can begin. The second stage (*delivery*, illustrations 3–6) seldom lasts more than an hour. The third stage (*afterbirth*; not shown) is the delivery of the placenta and other membranes.

Toward the end of the delivery stage, the attending physician or nurse severs the newborn's umbilical cord; places silver nitrate or antibiotic drops in its eyes to guard against gonococcal infection; and checks to see that its breathing, muscle tone, coloration, and reflexive activity are normal. Following this, the physician assists in the third and final stage of birth and evaluates the condition of the neonate, or newborn, perhaps by means of the Apgar scale (discussed later in this chapter).

Stage 3: The Afterbirth In the third stage, the afterbirth—the placenta and other membranes—is expelled. This process usually takes less than 5 minutes and seldom more than 15. The physician examines the afterbirth carefully to ensure that all of it has been expelled. If it is incomplete, surgical procedures—frequently **dilation and curettage (D&C)**, a scraping of the uterus—may be performed to remove remaining portions. At the end of the third stage of labor, the uterus should contract and remain contracted. It is sometimes necessary to massage the abdominal area or administer various drugs to stimulate contraction and to guard against the danger of postpartum (after birth) hemorrhage.

Cesarean Delivery

In an increasing number of instances, medical intervention bypasses these three stages of birth through cesarean deliveries, which constitute almost one-

---

obstetrics A sophisticated medical term for midwifery; the medical art and science of assisting women who are pregnant, both during pregnancy and at birth.

dilation and curettage (D&C) A surgical procedure that involves scraping the walls of the uterus. It is occasionally necessary after birth if all of the placenta has not been expelled.

---

third of all births in the United States (see Figure 4.9 in *At a Glance:* "Cesarean Delivery in the United States"). In such cases, birth is accomplished by making an incision through the mother's abdomen and uterus and removing the baby. Cesareans are most often indicated when the mother's labor fails to progress, if previous cesareans have been performed, when the fetus is in a breech presentation, or if the physician detects signs of fetal distress. Cesarean deliveries are ordinarily undertaken before the onset of labor, but they can also be performed after labor has begun. Epidural analgesia (commonly termed an *epidural*), an injection of anesthetic sometimes used to relieve pain in childbirth, appears to increase the risk of insufficient dilation of the cervix, sometimes requiring a cesarean delivery (Thorp et al., 1994).

Although cesarean deliveries have clearly saved the lives of many mothers and infants and alleviated much pain and suffering, the rapid increase in the proportion of cesarean births relative to nonsurgical births has been a source of some concern (*ACOG practice bulletin*, 1999). Although much of this increase clearly results from dramatic improvements in the physicians' ability to monitor the fetus during labor, critics assert that not all cesarean deliveries are necessary. When unnecessary, such surgery presents potential disadvantages and dangers not inherent in a routine delivery, including greater medical risk to the mother, a longer recovery period, and higher risk of infection. In addition, the use of anesthetics during surgery may depress neonatal responsiveness and may be related to the occasional respiratory problems of infants delivered by cesarean section. In some jurisdictions, significant reductions in rates of cesarean deliveries have been attained with no increase in fetal or maternal problems (Main, 1999.) Reductions are accomplished largely by reviewing the need for a

AT A GLANCE	**Cesarean Delivery in the United States**

Cesarean section deliveries in the United States have quadrupled in frequency since 1970 (see Figure 4.9). Not surprisingly, the highest rates are for women in older age groups, where almost one-third of all births are cesarean deliveries. Although cesarean deliveries have clearly saved the lives of many mothers and infants, some critics argue that they are used too frequently. While the procedure is routine and low risk, it entails a somewhat higher risk of infection, medical problems for the mother, and respiratory problems among infants.

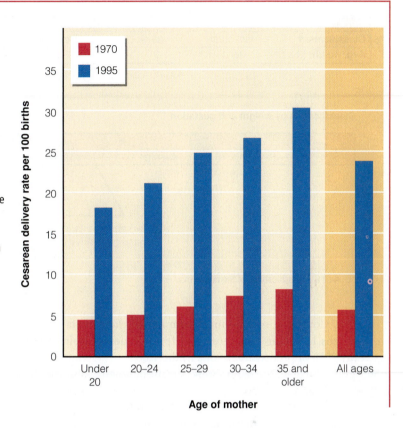

FIGURE 4.9 Increases in percentage of cesarean deliveries in the United States, 1970–1995. (Based on U.S. Bureau of the Census, 1994, p. 79; 1998, p. 83.)

cesarean delivery in cases in which they might simply have been done routinely, as sometimes happens for breech births, twins, or patients who have had previous cesareans. However, in the case of infections such as HIV, cesarean sections appear to decrease transmission rate by half (*The mode of delivery,* 1999).

Classification of the Newborn

The physical status of the newborn has traditionally been classified according to the length of time spent in gestation and by weight (see Figure 4.10). A fetus expelled before the 20th week and weighing less than 500 grams (about 1 pound) is termed a spontaneous abortion (sometimes simply an abortion or a miscarriage). A fetus delivered between the 20th and 28th week and weighing between 500 and 999 grams (between 1 and 2 pounds) is an **immature birth**. At

one time, infants born immaturely invariably died; the majority still do, most of them from respiratory failure. For example, 81% of a sample of 808 infants who weighed less than 1,000 grams died at birth or were stillborn (Bottoms et al., 1999). But with modern medical procedures, an increasing number survive, some born as much as four months prematurely and weighing as little as 750 grams (1 pound) or less.

The birth of a baby between the 29th and the 36th weeks is called a **premature birth**, provided the child weighs between 1,000 and 2,499 grams (between 2 pounds, 3 ounces, and 5 pounds,

immature birth A miscarriage occurring sometime between the 20th and 28th weeks of pregnancy and resulting in the birth of a fetus weighing between 1 and 2 pounds.

premature birth The birth of a baby between the 29th and 36th weeks of pregnancy. A premature baby weighs somewhere between 2 and 5 pounds and is less likely to survive if less than 2 pounds.

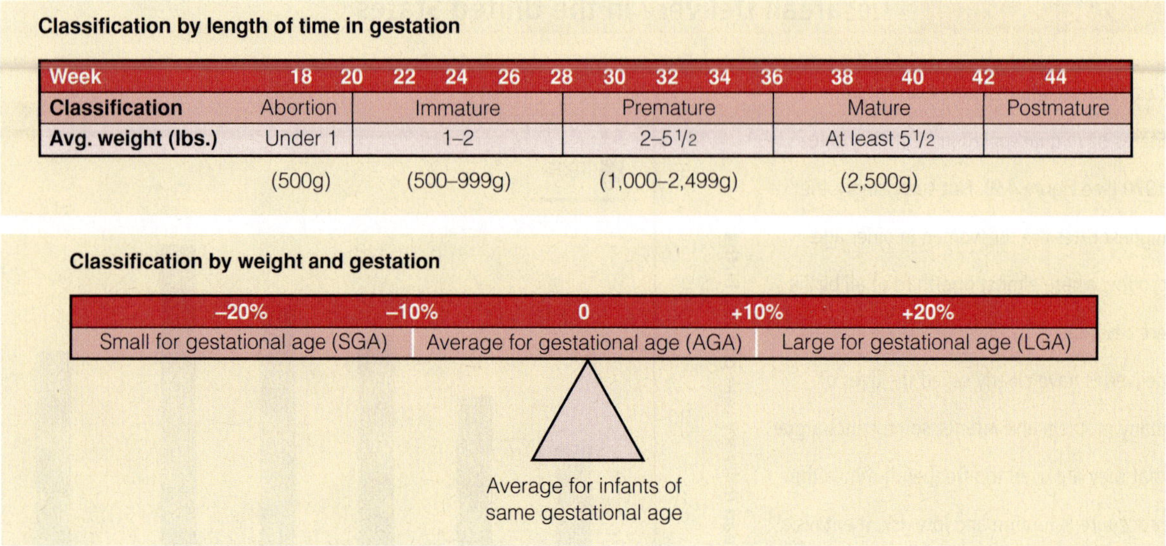

Classification by length of time in gestation

Week	18	20	22	24	26	28	30	32	34	36	38	40	42	44
Classification	Abortion		Immature				Premature				Mature		Postmature	
Avg. weight (lbs.)	Under 1		1–2				2–5½				At least 5½			

(500g)   (500–999g)   (1,000–2,499g)   (2,500g)

Classification by weight and gestation

−20%	−10%	0	+10%	+20%
Small for gestational age (SGA)	Average for gestational age (AGA)		Large for gestational age (LGA)	

Average for infants of
same gestational age

FIGURE 4.10 Classifications of the newborn.

8 ounces). Complications are more common if the child weighs less than 1,500 grams. A few decades ago, only 20% of premature infants in the 1,000- to 1,500-gram range (2.2 to 3.3 pounds) survived; now between 90% and 95% survive.

A **mature birth** occurs between the 37th and the 42nd weeks and results in an infant weighing over 2,500 grams (5.5 pounds). A late delivery is called a **postmature birth**.

All newborns, regardless of whether they are premature, are also classified as small for gestational age (SGA) when they weigh less than 90% of the weight of newborns of the same gestational age; as large for gestational age (LGA) when they weigh above the 90th percentile (that is, in the top 10%); or as average for gestational age (AGA) (see Figure 4.10).

Medically, it's important to distinguish between prematurity and being SGA, because the implications of being SGA may be more serious than the implications of being simply premature. The premature but AGA infant has been developing at a normal rate and, unless very premature, may suffer no negative consequences. However, the SGA infant, regardless of gestational age, has been developing less rapidly than normal. The most common causes of growth retardation are chromosomal abnormalities, maternal infections and diseases, and maternal substance use (like smoking). As we saw, each of these can have serious negative consequences for a fetus.

Neonatal Scales

In almost all North American hospitals it is routine to evaluate the condition of newborns by means of the **Apgar scale**. The scale, shown in Table 4.2, is almost self-explanatory. Infants receive scores (0, 1, or 2) according to whether each of five appropriate signs—appearance (color), pulse (heart rate), grimace (reflex irritability), activity (muscle tone), and respiration—is present. Maximum score is 10; average score is usually 7 or better; a score of 4 or less indicates that the neonate must be given special care immediately. The Apgar evaluation is administered at least twice: at 1 minute after birth and at 5 minutes after birth (and sometimes at 10 minutes after birth). Five- and 10-minute scores are often higher than 1-minute scores.

---

mature birth The birth of an infant between the 37th and 42nd weeks of pregnancy.

postmature birth The birth of an infant after the 42nd week of pregnancy.

Apgar scale Widely used standardized evaluation procedure for newborns that looks at their heart rate, respiration, muscle tone, color, and reflexive responses.

TABLE 4.2
The Apgar Scale

When the midwife grabbed Zachary Fish, he kicked out strongly enough that she was barely able to hang on. Then, recalls his mother, he opened his eyes, black as night in his little red face, and he let out a yell that scared the cat right out of the room. What would you guess Zachary's Apgar score might have been?

SCORE	HEART RATE	RESPIRATORY EFFORT	MUSCLE TONE	COLOR	REFLEX IRRITABILITY
0	Absent	Absent	Flaccid, limp	Blue, pale	No response
1	Slow (less than 100)	Irregular, slow	Weak, inactive	Body pink, extremities blue	Grimace
2	Rapid (over 100)	Good, crying	Strong, active	Entirely pink	Coughing, sneezing, crying

A second important scale for assessing the condition of a newborn infant is the **Brazelton Neonatal Behavioral Assessment Scale (NBAS)** (Brazelton, 1973). Like the Apgar scale, it can be used to detect problems immediately after birth. In addition, it provides useful indicators of both central nervous system maturity and social behavior. The Brazelton scale involves evaluation of 26 specific behaviors, including reaction to light, to cuddling, to voices, and to a pinprick; it also includes the strength of various reflexes. The scale is particularly useful in identifying infants who might be prone to later psychological problems. For example, parents of infants who are less responsive to cuddling and to other social stimulation might be alerted to this from the very beginning and might be able to compensate by providing the infant with more loving contact than might otherwise have been the case.

The Mother's Experience: Prepared Childbirth

The preceding discussion of the delivery of a human child is admittedly clinical and perhaps a little like the cold, antiseptic hospitals in which most North American babies are born: It fails to uncover and transmit the magic of the process. We can recapture some of the wonders, however, by looking more closely at mothers' experiences of childbirth.

The inexperienced mother sometimes approaches birth with some degree of apprehension; there is often some pain associated with childbirth. However, advocates of prepared childbirth (also called **natural childbirth**) claim that through a regimen of prenatal exercises and adequate psychological preparation, many women experience relatively painless childbirths.

Natural childbirth, a phrase coined by a British physician, Grantly Dick-Read (1972), refers to the process of having a child without anesthetics. The Dick-Read process involves physical exercises, relaxation exercises, and psychological preparation for the arrival of the child, all directed toward delivery in

THOUGHT CHALLENGE: *Several years ago, I sought out a handful of women whose personal experience with childbirth qualified them to make subjective comments more valid than those my imagination might supply.*

"What's it like, having a baby?" I asked.

"It's a piece of cake," my first expert assured me in her characteristic, cliché-ridden way. "It's as easy as rolling off a log."

"It hurts like *@#$%<" my second expert insisted, in her typically profane manner. "It's a hell of a big log!"

Which impression do you suppose is most accurate?

Brazelton Neonatal Behavioral Assessment Scale (NBAS) A wide-ranging assessment scale for newborns that looks at many different reflexes and several dozen different types of behaviors.

natural childbirth Childbirth with little or no use of drugs such as painkillers.

which painkillers are unnecessary. Natural childbirth is based on the assumption that alleviating the fear of pain, together with training in relaxation, will result in less pain. And, in fact, the conclusions of research that has looked at the effects of relaxation training on both the mother and the newborn are almost invariably highly positive (for example, Janke, 1999).

Lamaze, Leboyer, and Bradley Methods Various methods of prepared childbirth have been developed and are widely taught and used. The **Lamaze method** and the **Bradley method**, for example, teach expectant mothers breathing and relaxation exercises. These are practiced repeatedly, often with the assistance of the father, until they become so habitual that they will be used almost "naturally" during the actual process of birth. The Bradley method also encourages mothers to find what is "comfortable" for them, to "tune in" to their bodies. Both of these approaches emphasize proper nutrition, relaxation, and exercise—all of which have been shown to be related to maternal and infant well-being (for example, Horns et al., 1996; Mackey, 1998). Monto (1996) suggests that the Bradley method may be somewhat more critical of the conventional medical model than is the Lamaze method, that it is more likely to encourage mothers to question their doctors.

The **Leboyer method** is concerned more with the delivery of the infant than with advance preparation of the mother. Leboyer (1975) advocates delivering the baby in a softly lit room, immersing the infant almost immediately in a lukewarm bath, often for a relatively long time, and then placing the baby directly on the mother's abdomen without clamping the umbilical cord immediately. These procedures are designed to ease the infant's transition from the womb to the world; thus the need for soft lights that do not contrast as harshly with the darkness of the womb as does conventional delivery-room lighting, and for a lukewarm bath to approximate the feeling of being supported by amniotic fluid. Leboyer claims that his procedures eliminate much of the shock of birth and result in better-adjusted individuals. Critics suggest that birth in dimly lit surroundings might contribute to the physician's failing to notice important signs of distress or injury and that the dangers of infection are greater under these circumstances than when more conventional hospital practices are used. Also, research by Nelle et al. (1996) indicates that not clamping the umbilical cord when it stops pulsating may be associated with short-term changes in blood pressure.

Hospitals or Homes, Doctors, Doulas, or Midwives? I and all my biological siblings were born at home. My mother was attended by my grandmother and another highly experienced old lady. Neither would have qualified as midwives, but they had a pretty good general idea of what to do. And, fortunately for *moi*, they weren't called upon to do anything really creative. It wasn't that my mother consciously chose this *natural childbirth at home with old ladies* approach; it's simply that where we lived, she had no choice.

Many mothers now have a choice. And many choose to have their babies by natural means—which, as we saw, doesn't usually mean having them at home with assorted relatives, or in the corn field or potato patch. More often, it means that they will enroll in prenatal classes and learn a series of exercises and breathing skills, and perhaps acquire a few reassuring notions about the process.

Many of today's mothers also have a choice about where the birth will occur. For some, home is that choice; others choose hospital birthing rooms—a homier and more comfortable alternative to a conventional operating or delivery room—or hospital family suites where father and other siblings can actually stay. Although most North American births still occur in hospitals, length of hospitalization is considerably shorter than it once was (often only a matter of hours).

Traditionally, in countries such as Great Britain the majority of births were attended to by **midwives**

Lamaze method A method of natural childbirth based on a variety of breathing and relaxation exercises designed to remove, or at least reduce, the need for anesthetics and other medical intervention.

Bradley method A method of prepared childbirth emphasizing relaxation training and tuning in to the mother's body to find what is most comfortable.

Leboyer method A method of prepared childbirth emphasizing birthing conditions rather than preparation of the mother (for example, birth occurs in a softly lit room, and the infant is immersed in a lukewarm bath and later placed directly on the mother's abdomen).

rather than by physicians, a practice less common in North America (Jenkins, 1995). However, with the medicalization of birth, the use of midwives has declined, even in Europe, and their role has changed. An increasing number of births are attended to by physicians, and when midwives are used, they are often part of a medical team.

In North America, a **doula** may also be used in childbirth. *Doula* is a Greek word for a woman who helps other women. Doulas are typically women, unrelated to the mother, who are hired (or, in some cases, volunteer) to provide emotional and physical support during childbirth, as well as to provide information. Unlike midwives, doulas do not ordinarily perform any clinical tasks. Often, they also assist the mother after childbirth, helping her with breast feeding, care of the newborn, and perhaps even an assortment of household tasks. Research by Manning-Orenstein (1998) suggests that the use of doulas can contribute significantly to a new mother's sense of confidence and security.

Sedatives in Childbirth For one mother, childbirth may be quite painful; for another it may be a slightly painful but intensely rewarding and satisfying experience. Although the amount of pain can be controlled to some extent with anesthetics, the intensity of the immediate emotional reward will also be dulled by the drugs. In addition, sedatives given to the mother may affect the infant. Finally, as we saw earlier, the use of *epidural anesthesia*, especially in the early stages of labor, can impede dilation, sometimes making a cesarean delivery necessary (Thorp et al., 1994).

Postpartum Depression As many as 10% of all women suffer from depression after giving birth (Campbell & Cohn, 1991). It isn't clear whether this **postpartum depression** is due to hormonal changes, to the effects of sedating drugs that might have been used in labor, to disruptions in lifestyle, or to other factors. Bryan et al. (1999) report that in a sample of 403 women, those who were most likely to experience postpartum depression were those who were youngest, who were single, who had a history of substance abuse, and who had experienced previous emotional disorders.

Nahas, Hillege, and Amasheh (1999), who studied 45 mothers who had experienced postpartum depression, describe its predominant symptoms in terms of feelings of loneliness, helplessness, fear of failure, and inability to cope with overwhelming tasks. Meighan et al. (1999), who looked at postpartum depression from the husband's point of view, report that even after they have recovered, mothers who experienced postpartum depression often seem very different from who they were, and that fathers typically feel afraid and helpless. The condition often takes a heavy toll on the fathers, and on the relationship. Unfortunately, too, depressed mothers may be a risk factor for newborns, especially if their depression leads them to neglect or reject their babies. Fortunately, the prognosis for postpartum depression is excellent, with most cases improving quickly with time and disappearing completely within a year (Campbell & Cohn, 1991).

The Child's Experience

How do children, the heroes of this text, react to the process of birth? We can only guess. Still, it seems likely that they are largely indifferent to the process. After all, they cannot reason about it, they cannot compare it with other more or less pleasant states, they can do nothing deliberately to alter it, and they will not even remember it. But consider the incredibly dramatic difference that birth makes. Up to now, the child has been living in a completely friendly and supportive environment. Receiving nourishment, getting oxygen, eliminating wastes—everything has been accomplished without effort. The uterus has been kept at exactly the right temperature, the danger of bacterial infection has been relatively

---

midwife In many jurisdictions, a licensed professional, generally female but occasionally male, who assists in childbirth—but who is generally neither a doctor nor a nurse.

doula A birth assistant. May be involved before, during, and after birth. Sometimes plays a role similar to that of a caring partner.

postpartum depression A form of depression that affects about 10% of all women and begins shortly after childbirth. In some cases, postpartum depression can be serious and dangerous, but it usually ameliorates and disappears with time.

insignificant, and there have been no psychological threats—so far as we know. Now, at birth, the child is suddenly exposed to new physiological and perhaps psychological dangers. Once mucus is cleared from its mouth and throat, the newborn must breathe unassisted for the first time. As soon as the umbilical cord ceases to pulsate, it is unceremoniously clipped an inch or two above the abdomen and tied off with a clamp. And the child is now completely separate—singularly dependent and helpless, to be sure, but no longer a physiological parasite on the mother.

Dangers of Birth Birth is not without danger for the newborn. Throughout the world, 40% of all births are not attended by a trained health professional (Bellamy, 1999a). Injuries, including brain damage, sometimes occur during the birth of a child. This is often the result of tremendous pressure exerted on the head during birth—especially if labor is long and if the amniotic sac has been broken early, in which case the head, in a normal presentation, has been repeatedly pressed against the slowly dilating cervix. In addition, the infant must pass through an opening so small that deformation of the head often results. (For most infants the head usually assumes a more normal appearance within a few days.)

An additional source of pressure on the child's head may be forceps, clamplike instruments sometimes used during delivery. Although the fetus's head can withstand considerable pressure, the danger of such pressure is that it may rupture blood vessels and cause hemorrhaging. In severe cases, death may result; otherwise, brain damage may result because cranial hemorrhage can restrict the supply of oxygen to the brain.

Perhaps the greatest danger of birth is from **anoxia**, a shortage of oxygen to the tissues, and especially to the brain. The term asphyxia is often used interchangeably with anoxia. Strictly speaking, asphyxia refers to unconsciousness resulting from too little oxygen and too much carbon dioxide in the blood. Obviously, anoxia can lead to asphyxia.

The causes of anoxia can be fetal (for example, they might result from the umbilical cord being lodged between the fetus's body and the birth canal,

or being twisted and effectively blocked, disrupting the flow of oxygen through the cord—a situation referred to as **prolapsed cord**). They can also be maternal (for example, due to cardiorespiratory problems in the mother, resulting in inadequate blood flow via the placenta). Or they might be placental (for example, resulting from **placenta previa**, a condition in which the placenta detaches prematurely from the uterine wall, often necessitating an emergency delivery) (Sunshine, 1997).

Anoxia may be evident in impaired neurological, psychological, and motor functioning associated with brain damage (sometimes including serious mental and physical problems evident in cerebral palsy, seizures, and even death). But, say Holbrook and associates, (1997), the fetus appears to be more resilient to anoxia than the adult; as a result, the outcome of anoxia is sometimes barely noticeable.

Psychological Birth Trauma In addition to the physiological trauma, or shock, that accompanies birth, there is a remote possibility of **psychological birth trauma**. Rank's (1929) theory of the **trauma** of birth maintains that the sudden change from a comfortable, relatively passive existence to the cold and demanding world creates great anxiety for a newborn child, who is plagued forever after by a desire to return to the womb. Evidence of this unconscious desire is supposedly found in the position assumed by many children and adults while sleeping or in times of stress—the characteristic curled "fetal position." However, there is no substantial evidence to support the theory of psychological birth trauma.

---

anoxia A condition in which there is an insufficient supply of oxygen to the brain.

prolapsed cord A condition that sometimes occurs during birth when the umbilical cord becomes lodged between the infant's body and the birth canal, cutting off the infant's supply of oxygen. The effect may be brain damage of varying severity, depending on the length of time until delivery following prolapsing of the cord.

placenta previa A condition in which the placenta detaches from the uterine wall prior to the birth of the infant, leading to anoxia and fetal distress, in the absence of rapid intervention.

psychological birth trauma The supposed shocking effects of the transition from the comforts of the womb to the cold, cruel world, evident in our abiding, albeit subconscious, desire to return to the safety of the womb—especially in times of great stress.

trauma An injury or nervous shock. Traumatic experiences are usually intense and unpleasant.

▣ PREMATURITY

Prematurity is defined by a short gestation period (36 weeks or less) and low birth weight (small for gestational age, or SGA—less than 90% of average weight for term, usually less than 2,500 grams (or 5.5 pounds). It is one of the more serious possible complications of birth, affecting approximately 10% of all infants born in the United States, and almost one quarter of all children born in the world's least developed countries (Bellamy, 1999a). Prematurity accounts for between 60% and 80% of all neonatal deaths. In addition, it is a major factor in conditions such as **cerebral palsy**, seizures, and lung disease (Collins, 1997).

Causes of Prematurity

Despite dramatic advances in western medicine, incidence of premature births seems not to have changed for at least 40 years. Part of the reason for this is that we do not know the precise causes of premature delivery, although research has identified several factors that are related to its

occurrence (see Table 4.3). These include poverty, malnutrition, mother's age, smoking and other drug use, and the presence of various infections and diseases such as **gonorrhea** and **chlamydia**. In addition, infants from multiple births are more frequently premature than are infants from single births.

In the United States, social class and race appear to be correlated with incidence of prematurity, with premature deliveries being about twice as common among black women. Note, however, that factors such as social class and race have no inherent explanatory value. Certainly, neither causes prematurity any more than they cause the environmental conditions of poverty, ill health, and lower socioeconomic opportunity with which they are often associated. Finally, a number of infants are preterm in the absence of any of these negative influences and despite excellent maternal care, nutrition, and health. (See *At a Glance:* "Birth Weight and Prenatal Influences.")

---

cerebral palsy Label for a collection of congenital problems associated with brain damage and manifested in motor problems of varying severity, and occasionally in other problems such as convulsions or behavior disorders.

gonorrhea A relatively common STD, most strains of which are easily treated with antibiotics. Usually results in painful urination and a mucuslike discharge in males, but is not so easily detected in women.

chlamydia A highly common STD, especially among women, often asymptotic (without apparent symptoms), especially in its early stages, and therefore often undetected and unreported. A common cause of infertility among women.

TABLE 4.3
Factors Associated with Higher Risk of Prematurity

Prior premature delivery

Multiple gestation (the presence of more than one fetus)

Incompetent cervix (the cervix has a tendency to dilate and efface prematurely)

Anomalies of the uterus

Cocaine abuse

Smoking tobacco

Regularly standing or walking for prolonged periods

Vaginal bleeding

Maternal vaginal infections such as gonorrhea, chlamydia, or trichomonas vaginalis

Birth Weight and Prenatal Influences

Prematurity and low birth weight are among the most serious complications of birth. Low birth weight accounts for about three-quarters of all neonatal deaths; among survivors, it accounts for various conditions including motor problems, medical problems, general developmental retardation, and lower intelligence. Factors implicated in low birth weight include smoking and use of other drugs, maternal age, and inadequate nutrition and prenatal care. The relationship of social class and race to low birth weight and prematurity is probably due primarily to other associated factors such as poorer nutrition and prenatal care. In some of the world's least developed countries, such as Bangladesh, about half of all infants weigh less than 2,500 grams (about 5.5 pounds) at birth. In fact, 17% of all infants born in the world are underweight. In the United States, the percentage of infants born underweight is 7; in Canada, it's 6; and in the Cook Islands, it's only 1 (Bellamy, 1999a).

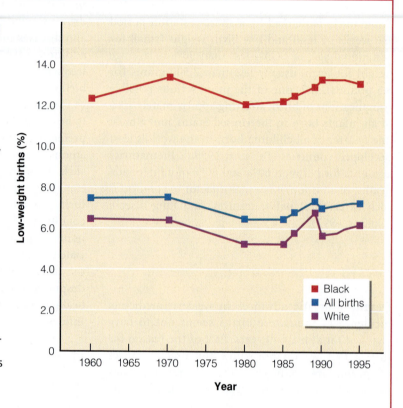

FIGURE 4.11 The relationship of race to low birth weight (less than or equal to 5 lb., 8 oz. (2,500 gm) before 1970; less than 5 lb., 8 oz. (2,500 gm) for subsequent years). Source: U.S. Bureau of the Census (1998), p. 832.

Consequences of Prematurity

One of the most obvious possible effects of prematurity is death. Indeed, only a few decades ago the likelihood of death for a premature infant weighing between 2,000 and 2,500 grams (4 pounds, 6 ounces and 5 pounds, 8 ounces) was approximately six times greater than for an infant weighing 3,000 grams (6 pounds, 10 ounces) or more. Now, however, the majority of premature infants weighing 2,000 grams (4 pounds) or more survive. In fact, more than 90% of infants who weigh as little as 1,000 to 1,500 grams survive; and an astonishing 76% of those who weigh between 751 and 1,000 grams (1 pound, 10 ounces and 2 pounds, 3 ounces) also survive (Collins, 1997). Most of these preterm infants spend the first two to three months of their lives in intensive care nurseries, often in incubators (also called *isolettes*). Chances of survival decrease 10% to 15% for each 100 grams below 1,000 grams.

(Goldsmith, 1990b). However, half or more of neonates who weigh less than 1,250 grams suffer adverse consequences; one-third or more suffer from severe physical or mental handicaps (Beckwith & Rodning, 1991).

Hack and colleagues (1992; 1993; 1994) have been following a group of 249 very low birth weight infants (under 1,500 grams; about 3 pounds) through the first decade of their lives. Comparisons of these children with controls of average birth weight reveal lower weight, height, and head circumference at age 8, significantly higher incidence of various illnesses and surgical procedures, and significantly poorer performance on most measures of intellectual functioning including intelligence, language, reading, mathematics, spelling, and motor abilities. A subgroup of these low birth weight infants who weighed less than 750 grams at birth (about 1½ pounds) were at even greater disadvantage. Almost 25% were mentally retarded, about half were in special education classes, 25% had vision problems, and 25% suffered from measurable hearing loss.

Although survival rates of preterm infants have increased dramatically since the days of our grandparents, Hack and Fanaroff (1999) report that there have been no significant changes through the 1990s. Survival rates and rates of mild as well as serious developmental and health problems are about the same for infants born at the beginning of the decade as for those born at the end. With current methods of care, say Hack and Fanaroff, we have reached the limits of viability. Mounting incidence of infant and child developmental and medical problems associated with prematurity are a cause of serious concern.

Prevention of Prematurity

"We still aren't fully aware of all the events that occur to elicit this [birthing] reaction," says Dr. David Olson (quoted in "Shortening the Time," 1993, p. 4). If we were, he adds, we might be able to figure out how to prevent premature delivery. At present, all we can do is try to identify women who appear to be at greater risk. This can't be done with certainty, because the precise causes of premature delivery are not always known. However, it's possible to estimate degree of risk given knowledge of a woman's status with respect to the factors listed in Table 4.3. It's also possible to monitor uterine activity and sometimes to detect an increase in activity before the onset of preterm labor.

There are several different approaches to preventing preterm labor: bed rest, avoiding sexual intercourse, using antibiotics and other drugs, and suturing the cervix. None of these has been clearly proven to be effective, although there is some evidence that each might sometimes be helpful (Goldsmith, 1990b).

Care of Premature Infants

Survival rates for premature infants born in the 23rd to 25th week of pregnancy range from 17% to 58% in various studies; up to 85% of those born between the 26th and 28th week survive (Hack & Fanaroff, 1999). Nor is prematurity inevitably linked with physical, psychological, or neurological inferiority. With adequate care, many premature infants fare as well as full-term infants.

Nutrition and Medical Care What are the dimensions of that care? First they include advances in medical knowledge and technology. Ventilators, for example, make possible the survival of infants whose hearts and lungs are not sufficiently developed to work on their own; so does intravenous feeding. The content of intravenous feeding is especially important, because it substitutes for nutrients that the infant would ordinarily have received as a fetus. Certain fatty acids appear to be crucially involved in brain growth and neuron development during the last trimester of pregnancy—roughly the period of intrauterine growth that a 27-week preterm infant would miss. Accordingly, premature infants' nutrition must include these nutrients at the appropriate time and in the appropriate form. Not surprisingly, hospital care of premature infants is sometimes enormously expensive ("Shortening the Time," 1993).

Psychological Care In addition to important medical advances in the care of premature infants, a tremendous amount of research in the past 20 years has investigated the possibility that at least some of the adverse psychological consequences of prematurity might be due to the lack of stimulation the preterm infant receives in an intensive care nursery—or, perhaps more accurately, the inappropriateness of the stimulation.

Harrison (1985) summarizes 24 studies that have evaluated various forms of "supplemental" stimulation for preterm infants. Some investigated the effects of tactile stimulation (stroking, holding); others looked at auditory stimulation (taped recordings of the mother's voice, for example), vestibulary stimulation (oscillating hammock or water bed), and gustatory stimulation (pacifier). The studies indicate clearly that additional stimulation of preterm infants is beneficial to their development. Positive effects include greater weight gains, shorter hospital stays, greater responsiveness, and higher developmental scores on various measures (for example, Bradley et al., 1994). The evidence is clear that the traditional hands-off treatment once given most premature infants is not the best form of care for them.

A REASSURING NOTE

It is often very disturbing for nonmedical people to consult medical journals and textbooks in search of explanations for their various ailments. Inevitably they discover that they have all the symptoms for some vicious infection or exotic disease. So if you happen to be pregnant at this moment or are contemplating pregnancy, you might find yourself a little apprehensive. I draw this to your attention only to emphasize that by most accounts, pregnancy and delivery are positive experiences. The intrauterine world of the unborn infant is less threatening and less dangerous than our world. And it might be reassuring to note that in many cases when the fetus would have been grossly abnormal, nature provides for a spontaneous abortion. In most cases, when a fetus comes to term, the probability that the child will be normal and healthy far outweighs the likelihood that it will suffer any of the defects or abnormalities described in this chapter.

MAIN POINTS

Assisted Reproduction
Assisted reproduction might include artificial insemination, the use of drugs to stimulate ovulation, surrogate mothering, in vitro fertilization, which can also be microassisted, and embryo implantation.

Detecting Pregnancy
Early signs of pregnancy are not always clear, but simple urine tests can be performed very early in pregnancy—at home or by physicians. The gestation period for humans is about 9 calendar months (10 lunar months, or 280 days, beginning from the onset of the last menses).

Stages of Prenatal Development
Prenatal physiological development occurs in three stages: During the germinal period (first two weeks), the fertilized ovum moves down the fallopian tube and implants itself in the uterine wall; in the embryonic period (weeks 3 through 8), the embryo, including all major organs, develops; in the fetal period (week 9 to birth), the fetus grows mainly in size and weight and develops neurologically.

Effects of Drugs and Other Agents on Prenatal Development
A wide range of prescription drugs can act as teratogens (including thalidomide, associated with underdeveloped or absent limbs, and lithium, linked with cardiac defects). Over-the-counter drugs such as aspirin pose little risk in normal doses but are associated with a risk of hemorrhaging at higher doses. Harmful chemicals include mercury (Minimata disease), hydrocarbon compounds like dioxin and PCB (higher incidence of spontaneous abortions and physical deformities), and lead (serious physical and mental problems in children and adults).

Cigarette smoking increases fetal heart rate and activity and is associated with significant retardation of fetal growth, much higher incidence of premature births, smaller birth weights, higher probability of placental problems, higher risk of miscarriage and fetal death, and higher incidence of childhood respiratory diseases.

Alcohol consumption may lead to fetal alcohol syndrome (FAS), symptoms of which may include mental retardation, retarded physical growth, and characteristic cranial and facial malformations (low forehead, widely spaced eyes, short nose, long upper lip, absence of a marked infranasal depression). Infants born to narcotics addicts are themselves usually addicted at birth (neonatal abstinence syndrome). Infants of cocaine users are more likely to abort, be stillborn, die of SIDS, or suffer from behavioral problems later in childhood.

Effects of Maternal Characteristics on Prenatal Development

Diseases such as rubella, syphilis, gonorrhea, and diabetes can lead to mental deficiency, blindness, deafness, or fetal death. Herpes can be transmitted to the fetus during birth and can lead to serious complications, including death. Use of *acyclovir* reduces probability of transmission, as does a cesarean delivery. AIDS can also be transmitted from mother to fetus and is fatal. Transmission rates can be reduced considerably with the use of drugs.

In the absence of medical intervention (injections of Rhogam), mothers who are negative for the Rh blood factor would be at risk of giving birth to infants suffering from fetal erythroblastosis when the father is Rh(D)-positive.

For older mothers there is a higher probability of some chromosomal defects (trisomy 21; trisomies 13 and 18; Klinefelter's syndrome; fragile X syndrome). Infants born to teenage mothers are at higher risk of physical, emotional, and intellectual disadvantage (more miscarriages, premature births, and stillbirths, and more emotional and physical abuse among those who survive)—usually because of the less advantageous social and medical circumstances of teenage parenthood.

Socioeconomic disadvantages, especially persistent poverty, are closely associated with poorer developmental outcomes (lower IQ scores, poorer school achievement, more socioemotional problems)—often mediated by poor parenting and lack of cognitive stimulation in the home.

Maternal malnutrition, often associated with poverty, may lead to higher fetal mortality, lower fertility, and poorer brain development.

Childbirth

Birth (ordinarily 266 days after conception) occurs in three stages: dilation and effacement of the cervix (9 to 12 hours), delivery (usually accomplished within an hour); and afterbirth (expulsion of the placenta and other membranes, lasting several minutes).

Newborns are classified as small for gestational age (SGA; more than 10% below average for date); average for gestational age (AGA); or large for gestational age (LGA; more than 10% heavier than average for date). Newborns are routinely evaluated at birth by means of the Apgar scale—a scale that looks at their appearance (color), pulse (heart rate), grimace (reflex irritability), activity (muscle tone), and respiration (respiratory effort).

Cesarean delivery is accomplished through a surgical incision. Natural, or prepared, childbirth refers to the preparation for and process of having a child without anesthetics (for example, the Lamaze and Bradley methods).

Prematurity

Prematurity appears to be linked to social-class variables such as diet and poorer medical attention, the age of the mother, smoking, drugs, multiple gestations, and previous history of preterm deliveries. Its most apparent effects are the greater possibility of death, physical defects, medical problems, and impaired mental functioning. Medical advances have made it possible for over 90% of premature infants weighing as little as 1,000 to 1,500 grams (2.2 to 3.3 pounds) to survive. Both medical care and cognitive stimulation are important to the well-being of premature infants.

Focus Questions: Applications

1. How early can pregnancy reliably be detected?
   • What are some advantages of early detection?
2. How does a fetus grow?
   • Describe the major changes that occur during each of the three stages of prenatal development.
3. What sorts of influences can harm or nurture a fetus's development?
   • Using library resources, write a brief summary of recent research dealing with the consequences of mother's age, drug use, or nutrition on the fetus.
4. What is prepared childbirth?
   • To impress your professor with your dedication and enthusiasm, arrange to attend the birth of an elephant, a giraffe, or some other animal (zoos, veterinarians, farmers, and pet owners might be helpful). Compare this animal birth with a human birth.

Possible Responses to Thought Challenges

Thought Challenge, page 172

In our recent past, childbirth was evidently primarily a female affair. In addition, the process seems to have been shrouded in mystery, in secrecy, and in superstition.

Thought Challenge, page 172

An unattended birth might, gravity being what it is, be somewhat easier in an upright or squatting position. Also, a squatting woman might more easily be able to tend to the newborn during birth. However, the mother's lying down presents certain advantages for an attended birth—not the least of which is that physicians and midwives don't have to stand on their heads,
or lie on the floor, to see what's happening. Strangely, Gillespie (1998) informs us, the change in positions may have had nothing to do with convenience or medical expediency. Medical historians attribute this change to King Louis XIV, who wanted to see his mistress give birth. Presumably, he didn't want to lie on the floor or stand on his head, so he had her lie down instead. Thus the whole thing began as a sort of royal command!

Thought Challenge, page 175

Almost invariably, some pain and discomfort are associated with natural childbirth. But its intensity and duration vary tremendously. Furthermore, the pain of the event seems to be quickly forgotten by many women.

Key Terms

abortion, 152
acquired immunodeficiency syndrome (AIDS), 158
afterbirth, 165
anoxia, 178
Apgar scale, 174
artificial insemination, 142
Babinski reflex, 146
birth, 165
body mass index (BMI), 164
Bradley method, 176
Brazelton Neonatal Behavioral Assessment Scale (NBAS), 175
breech birth, 170

cephalocaudal, 148
cerebral palsy, 179
cervix, 169
cesarean delivery, 165
chlamydia, 179
congenital, 148
crack, 155
cytomegalovirus (CMV), 158
delivery, 170
diethylstilbestrol (DES), 150
dilation and curettage (D&C), 172
dilation and effacement of the cervix, 170
doula, 177

drugs, 142
ectopic pregnancy, 153
embryonic period, 145
episiotomy, 170
fertilized ovum stage, 145
fetal alcohol syndrome (FAS), 154
fetal erythroblastosis, 160
fetal period, 145
genital herpes, 158
germinal period, 145
gestation period, 144
gonorrhea, 179
human immunodeficiency virus (HIV), 158

Further Readings

The following short book is a look at some of the ethical issues involved in assisted reproduction:

Shenfield, F., & C. Sureau, eds. (1997). *Ethical dilemmas in assisted reproduction.* London: Parthenon.

A simple, highly informative, straightforward description of fetal development is the following:

Gillespie, C. (1998). *Your pregnancy: Month by month.* New York: Harper Perennial.

For those concerned about the potential effects of prescription drugs on the fetus, the following provides an alphabetically organized description of the effects, recommended dosages, and mechanisms of action for many of the most commonly prescribed drugs:

Coustan, D. R., & T. K. Mochizuki (1998). *Handbook for prescribing medications during pregnancy,* 3rd ed. New York: Lippincott-Raven.

FAS is sometimes described as the main cause of mental retardation in the western world. The following short book is a thorough look at this significant social problem:

Abel, E. L. (1998). *Fetal alcohol abuse syndrome.* New York: Plenum.

Those interested in an account of birth in primitive tribes throughout the world might consult:

Goldsmith, J. (1990a). *Childbirth wisdom: From the world's oldest societies.* Brookline, Mass.: East-West Health Books.

The following are some original sources for information about natural childbirth:

Bradley, R. A., & M. Hathaway (1996). *Husband coached childbirth,* 4th rev. ed. New York: Bantam, Doubleday, Dell.

Dick-Read, G. (1972). *Childbirth without fear: The original approach to natural childbirth,* 4th ed., H. Wessel & H. F. Ellis, eds. New York: Harper & Row.

Lamaze, F. (1972). *Painless childbirth: The Lamaze method.* New York: Pocket Books.

Leboyer, F. (1975). *Birth without violence.* New York: Random House.

Online Resources

For additional readings, explore *InfoTrac College Edition,* your online library. Go to http://infotrac-college.com/wadsworth and use the passcode that came on the card with your book. Try these search terms: assisted reproduction, childbirth, midwives, fetal alcohol syndrome.

PART TWO

Infancy

> I cannot abide that passion for caressing new-born children, which have neither mental activities nor recognizable bodily shape by which to make themselves lovable, and I have never willingly suffered them to be fed in my presence.
>
> Michel de Montaigne, *Essais*

SuperStock

How dramatically Montaigne's sixteenth-century attitudes clash with those of our times! And how strenuously might today's mother defend the mental activities, the bodily shape, the lovableness of her child!

Which is not to say that the newborn infant is capable of the sorts of mental feats that might be involved in pondering problems of quantum physics or Boolean algebra. Not likely. You see, the world is an amazing, bewildering, and largely unfamiliar place for the newborn. Much of the business of growing up is a matter of becoming familiar with things. That is mostly what occupies the first two years of life: becoming familiar with breasts and bottles, with cups and cats, with doors and dragons; learning when to cry, when to be afraid, when to laugh and smile; learning about mothers and fathers, and about strangers too; and learning to speak. This is what the next two chapters are about.

While reading these chapters, keep in mind that the infant, whom Montaigne would not suffer to be fed in his presence, is a real *person* and not just a compilation of science's hard-earned facts and speculations. Try to remember—or at least to imagine—some of the feelings of being an infant. Is the world bewildering and frightening? Exciting and marvelous? Astonishing and delightful?

"Who was your mother?"

"Never had none!" said the child, with another grin.

"Never had any mother? What do you mean? Where were you born?"

"Never was born!" persisted Topsy.

"Do you know who made you?"

"Nobody, as I knows on," said the child, with a short laugh. "I 'spect I grow'd."

Harriet Beecher Stowe, *Uncle Tom's Cabin*

Physical and Cognitive Development in Infancy

Jennie Woodcock; Reflections Photolibrary/Corbis

CHAPTER 5

"Growing" kids such as Topsy describes in the quote on the opposite page would have been a convenient way of doing things in remote northern Saskatchewan, where we lived. There were no doctors or hospitals close by; pretty well everybody was born at home. Just "growing" like Topsy might have been simpler.

I, too, was born at home. I remember nothing of my birth, but I was reminded of it as I worked my way through the previous chapter. In Goldsmith's (1990a) *Childbirth Wisdom*, I read how normal pregnancies and births in preindustrial tribes involve little stress and little disruption in daily routines. "The vast majority of Tlinget women," she quotes an observer of this Alaskan tribe, "suffer very little and some not at all when their children are born."

A little like picking a ripe cabbage? My mother says no, that's not the way it is, even for kids born at home.

I remember that one hot August morning when I was 7, they sent my three siblings and me to Delisle's, where we played in the barn loft, climbing into the rafters and jumping down into the new hay, until some time in mid-afternoon my father came for us.

"Come see your new sister," said he. I can still picture the scene: My mother didn't look like she had just strolled to the garden and plucked a cabbage. Or maybe the cabbage had gotten to her first. And my new sister didn't look like she had just sprouted in the garden. There she lay, fresh-born, her skull flattened a little on one side, her skin mottled blue and red, her eyes screwed shut, little fists clenched, whimpering. And I remember my other sister saying, like only a 4-year-old can, " She's soooo ugly. Are you sure she's ours?"

FOCUS QUESTIONS

1. How important is nutrition for a newborn?
2. What are some important physical and intellectual characteristics of neonates?
3. What can a newborn see? Hear? Smell? Taste? Feel?
4. Can newborns think?
5. How can an infant manage to learn something as complicated as a language?

THE DESIGN OF A NEWBORN

Neonates—newborns—are often like the new sister just described, or worse if they haven't been cleaned up yet and they still have remnants of their stay in the womb clinging to them. Often, too, their features are deformed from the pressures of passing through the birth canal.

Newborns are remarkably helpless creatures. They have little physical and motor control, and unlike the young of many animals, they surely wouldn't survive very long if left on their own.

What is it like to be a newborn? Does the world mean anything? Does the newborn have primitive ideas, budding concepts, some sort of pattern that will govern its intellectual growth? What does it feel? Is there joy in the beating of its little heart? Is it capable of ecstasy? Does sadness drive its cries? Does purpose inform its movements?

THOUGHT CHALLENGE: *Imagine for a moment that you've been asked to design an organism that begins life in as primitive a condition as a neonate—that is, with as little physical and motor control as an infant has and with as unsophisticated an understanding of self and world. But you must design this organism in such a way that within two years it will be able to walk, talk, recognize its grandmother, ride a tricycle, laugh, sing, and smear chocolate pudding on its face—or on the dog if it wants to.*

So what are the details of your design?

neonate A newborn infant. The neonatal period terminates when birth weight is regained.

These are not easy questions to answer. In fact, it will take us the remainder of this chapter, and most of the next, to consider the answers that science (and sometimes good sense) has begun to provide.

Blueprint for a Neonate

If you needed to design an organism that would change from the helplessness and ignorance of the newborn to the sophistication of the 2-year-old—and eventually that of the 6-year-old, the adolescent, the adult—you would need to pay attention to biophysical development, to the development of the mind, and to social development. Biologically, you would need to design a creature that is capable of converting raw proteins, carbohydrates, minerals, vitamins, and other foodstuffs into nutrients. And you would have to schedule the effects of these nutrients into a sequence of biological growth and maturation that would, among other things, eventually lead to the organism's control of its own movements. And if you were something of a poet, you might put some grace, some exuberance, into those young movements.

Intellectually, you would need to design your little organism to process an absolutely astonishing amount of information. And it would want to process this information regardless of whether it received any immediate and tangible reward (such as food or a caress) for doing so. The information-processing system you give it would be automatically geared toward focusing on the most informative aspects of the environment. Accordingly, your little organism would react strongly to surprise and novelty; it would search out the unexpected and invent ways of organizing the information it gathers, thus building concepts and ideas.

Socially, you would want to program into the organism a wide range of emotions to serve as motives for its actions. These emotions would lead it to establish complex relationships with other organisms of the same species (and sometimes even with members of other species). Socially, your organism would be built to be gregarious and to love. And you would mark it with an overwhelming urge to procreate when mature, thus contributing to the survival of its species. Perhaps you would design it, as well, to defend things that might be related to its survival and to that of others of its kind.

And as a crowning achievement in your design of this creature, you pretune it to attend to speech; you wire it so that it is capable of inventing language.

What Is a Neonate?

Our bare-bones answer to the question "What is a neonate?" is this: A neonate is a self-driven little sensing machine designed to mature and grow physically in a predetermined way, programmed as an extraordinarily capable information-processing system, endowed with powerful emotions and gregarious tendencies, and prewired to develop language. And that is some piece of work!

In this chapter we look at the newborn's growth and behavior, at motor development, and at perceptual and cognitive development. In the next chapter we look at infants' social relationships and attachments, at personality and emotional development. These two chapters cover infancy, a period that lasts from the first few weeks of life to the age of 2.

NUTRITION, HEALTH, AND PHYSICAL GROWTH IN INFANCY

In the beginning, infants are almost completely helpless physically. They can't move to new places; they have no way of ensuring that their environments are neither too cold nor too warm; they can't clean themselves; they have no protection against wild dogs, vultures, or one-eyed cats. They can't even find food unless it is put under their very noses. Once they find it, though, they suck. Sucking is one of those primitive reflexes present at birth in virtually all mammals.

Breast-Feeding

The sucking reflex is what ensures the infant's survival—that and the presence of a lactating mother. In fact, physicians pretty well universally recommend that the infant needs nothing other than a willing, and lactating, mother for 6 months or longer (Scott & Binns, 1999). One of the year-2000 goals of the U.S. surgeon general was that 75% of all mothers attempt to breast-feed their infants, and that at least 50% con-

tinue until the infants reach the age of 6 months (Report of the Surgeon General's Workshop, 1984). The surgeon general felt called upon to urge women to breast-feed their infants because there had been a dramatic reduction in its popularity following the wide-scale marketing of commercial infant formulas in the 1940s and 1950s (Wagner & Wagner, 1999). By the 1970s, fewer than one mother in 4 breast-fed. In the past several decades, breast-feeding has again increased in popularity, but remains well below year-2000 goals in North America. About 50% or so of mothers in the United States initiate breast-feeding (Pediatric Nutrition Handbook, 1997). Of these, perhaps fewer than half will still be breast-feeding 4 months later (see Figure 5.1). Among the various reasons why a mother might stop breast-feeding are the belief that she isn't producing enough milk for her infant, painful breasts, the infant rejecting the breast, or other personal reasons (Thompson, 1998). In the United States, breast-feeding is most common among the more educated mothers. It is also almost twice as common among whites as among blacks. (See *At a Glance:* "Breast versus Bottle.")

Advantages of Breast Milk

Mothers's milk, science tells us, is the best of foods for most newborns. Not only is it species-specific, it is even infant-specific. It contains just about the right combination of nutrients, the right proportion of fats and calories, and the almost-perfect assortment of minerals and vitamins (Kunz et al., 1999). Furthermore, it is easier for infants to digest than cow's milk, and less likely to lead to allergic reactions. It provides infants with a measure of immunity against infections and diseases—especially against diarrhea, which as we saw in Chapter 1 is one of the principal causes of infant mortality in the developing world. There are indications, too, that the effects of the infant's increased immunity might be apparent in a greater resistance to a variety of diseases, including cancer, in adulthood (Rodriquez-Palmero et al., 1999). And, not least important, human milk contains nutrients that are essential components of tissues such as the brain and the retina (Rodriquez-Palmero et al., 1999).

Not surprisingly, researchers have found that human milk is highly beneficial in the care of

| AT A GLANCE | **Breast versus Bottle** |

It seems that for many years there has been a quiet battle over breast-feeding—a breast-versus-bottle battle. On one side are the mothers who, for a variety of reasons, choose not to breast-feed their infants. On the other are a legion of physicians and philosophers. Their arguments for breast-feeding have varied through history, notes Kessen (1965). In early times, many insisted that breast-feeding is something all animals do; it is therefore natural and good. Others appealed to religion and duty, convinced that suckling is the child's sacred birthright and the mother's solemn duty. Still others believed that maternal virtues and morals might be transmitted through breast milk. (So, do the virtues and morals of cows get transmitted through cow's milk?)

More recently, physicians invoke an impressive list of medical reasons to support their recommendations. And, reports Bellamy (1999a), some 51% of the world's women are still breast-feeding their infants at the ages of 20–23 months, and 44% of infants are exclusively breast-fed until the age of 3 months.

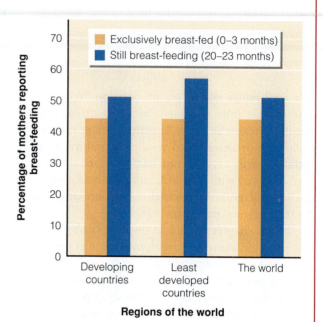

FIGURE 5.1 Percentage of mothers breast-feeding in the world. Source: Based on Bellamy (1999a), page 101.

premature infants, although it often needs to be fortified with essential components to ensure that the infant is receiving enough nutrition (Schanler, Hurst, & Lau, 1999).

Some research indicates, as well, that breast-feeding might present some medical and psychological advantages for mothers. For example, Labbok (1999) reports that breast-feeding reduces the risk of blood loss in the mother after birth, that it also appears to reduce the risk of ovarian and of breast cancer, and that it may reduce the incidence of spinal and hip fractures in later life.

Despite these compelling arguments for breast-feeding, it would be misleading not to emphasize that in much of the industrialized world, where sanitation and nutrition are excellent, bottle-fed infants thrive. In addition, it is worth noting that breast milk is affected by the mother's intake of food and drugs, as well as by chemicals to which she is exposed. Alcohol, nicotine, barbiturates, stimulants such as caffeine, sedatives, and prescription drugs can each have an effect on breast-fed infants (Howard & Lawrence, 1999). Clearly, in some circumstances an infant might fare much better with cow's milk or goat's milk.

Nutrition and Brain Development in Infancy

The newborn's central nervous system is functionally immature at birth. Although the brain is relatively large (approximately one-quarter the size of the rest of the body, compared with an adult ratio of about 1 to 8), much of it is not yet functioning (except for the brain stem, which is involved in activities such as breathing, sleeping, and temperature control). Activity in the association areas of the brain (the cortex, where most brain-wave activity occurs in adults) increases very rapidly during the first months of life.

Optimal brain development appears to be influenced by two important factors. One is sensory and cognitive stimulation; the other is nutrition. Protein and certain fatty acids (which are present in milk—and especially in human milk—but not ordinarily in infant formulas) are especially important to normal brain development, both during the prenatal period and in the first year or so of life (Willatts et al., 1998). Deficiencies in iron, in iodine, and in vitamin A may also be implicated in poorer mental development (Wasantwisut, 1997).

Although very severe malnutrition can lead to poor mental development, the often-quoted conclusion that moderate malnutrition leads to lower IQ and retarded mental development is overstated and premature, claims Guesry (1998). In fact, the human brain appears to be remarkably resistant to the effects of nutritional deficiencies—providing the infant receives adequate stimulation. Similarly, the belief that these effects can be prevented or perhaps even reversed through improved nutrition and various nutritional supplements is more a statement of social policy than of scientific fact. As Wauben and Wainwright (1999) note, brain development is such a complex process that changes that might occur at the cellular level—say as a result of nutritional deficiencies or enrichment—will not necessarily be evident in observable and measurable behaviors.

Note, too, that the apparently negative effects of malnutrition on intellectual functioning should probably not be attributed to malnutrition alone. These effects are likely due to a combination of factors related to poverty. For example, undernourished infants tend to become apathetic and listless and to withdraw from environmental and social stimulation. The effects of this withdrawal are often compounded because many undernourished infants are born into families with little or no formal education, and they experience a serious lack of stimulation in the first place. The effects of these circumstances, together with the possible contribution of protein deficiency to less than optimal development of brain cells, may constitute a significant developmental disadvantage.

The point is not that malnutrition has no harmful effects on mental development, or that optimal nutrition is not important. Quite the contrary. Severe malnutrition can clearly be detrimental—especially when it is combined with other negative influences. However, we cannot confidently say that *moderate* malnutrition is also significantly harmful. Nor can we easily separate the effects of moderate malnutrition from those of other facets of poverty. Hence, as Ricciuti (1991) suggests, social programs should be directed toward improving poor children's developmental environments (in homes, day-care centers, and schools), rather than simply improving their diets.

Nutrition and Physical Growth in Infancy

Physical growth in infancy is relatively predictable given adequate nourishment. However, because of our different genetic programs, identical nourishment will not make all infants exactly the same at all ages. Average physical development during infancy is shown in Figures 5.2 and 5.3. Note that these are median, or midpoint, values. What this means is that 50% of all infants of a given age are expected to be taller than the indicated measurement, and 50% will be shorter. There is nothing intrinsically valuable or "normal" about being at or near these "**norms**"; conversely, there is nothing negative about being moderately above or below the norm. Only when an infant is significantly above or below the median might there be cause for concern.

How much below average is a cause for concern? The answer is about 2 **standard deviations** below average—or in about the bottom 2.27%. Children who are more than 2 standard deviations below average for height are, by definition, suffering

---

norm An average or standard way of behaving. Cultural norms, for example, refer to the behaviors expected of individuals who are members of that culture.

standard deviation A mathematical measure of the distribution of scores around their mean (average). In a *normal distribution*, about 68% of all scores fall within 1 standard deviation of the mean; 95% fall within 2 standard deviations of the mean.

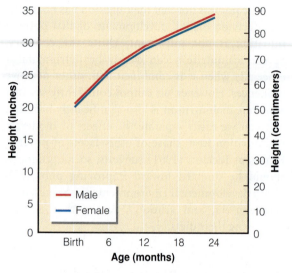

FIGURE 5.2 Height at the 50th percentile for U.S. infants, birth to 24 months. Source: Adapted from Health Department, Milwaukee, Wisconsin; based on data by H. C. Stuart and H. V. Meredith, prepared for use in the Children's Medical Center, Boston. Used by permission of the Milwaukee Health Department.

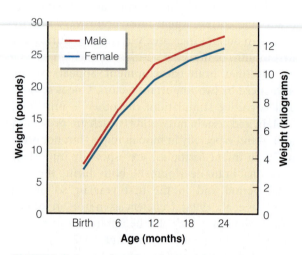

FIGURE 5.3 Weight at the 50th percentile for U.S. infants, birth to 24 months. Source: Adapted from Health Department, Milwaukee, Wisconsin; based on data by H. C. Stuart and H. V. Meredith, prepared for use in the Children's Medical Center, Boston. Used by permission of the Milwaukee Health Department.

from **stunting**; **wasting** is defined as being in the bottom 2.27% for weight. Unfortunately, in the world's most undeveloped countries, 40% of children under age 5 are significantly underweight, and 47% are moderately or severely stunted (Bellamy, 1999a). This represents an enormous number of children, given that over 85% of the world's children are born in Third World countries (Lozoff, 1989). Not surprisingly, the mortality rate for many of these countries is well over 150 per 1,000 children under age 5 (Bellamy, 1999a). In contrast, the under-5 mortality rate for the world's most developed countries is only about 9 children per 1,000, and the percentage of children who are underweight is negligible. (See Figure 5.4.)

The World Health Organization estimates that well over half of all children born in Third World countries suffer from malnutrition. Most serious is protein undernutrition, which as we saw may have long-term negative effects not only on physical growth, but also on cognitive functioning. Serious protein deficiency in infancy is sometimes evident in the condition labeled **kwashiorkor** (or a related condition, *marasmus*) (Sefa-Dedeh, 1992). In serious cases, kwashiorkor is marked by extreme wasting and stunting, listlessness, unresponsiveness, and sometimes death. In less severe cases, its effects are nevertheless still sometimes apparent in smaller physical size as well as in cognitive deficits later in childhood (Galler & Ramsey, 1989). Kahn and associates (1999) report that communicable diseases and malnutrition, evident primarily in diarrhea and kwashiorkor, are responsible for over half the under-5 deaths in parts of South Africa.

Malnutrition is, of course, far less common in industrialized countries—even though significant numbers of mothers and children live in poverty,

stunting Severe growth retardation, defined as more than 2 standard deviations below average height relative to normal children of the same age.

wasting Defined as more than 2 standard deviations below average weight for average children of that age—hence in the bottom 2.27% of the population.

kwashiorkor An infant nutritional deficiency disease related primarily to lack of protein; marked by stunting, listlessness, apathy, failure to thrive, and sometimes death. Physical symptoms often include swollen bellies and feet, and loss of hair.

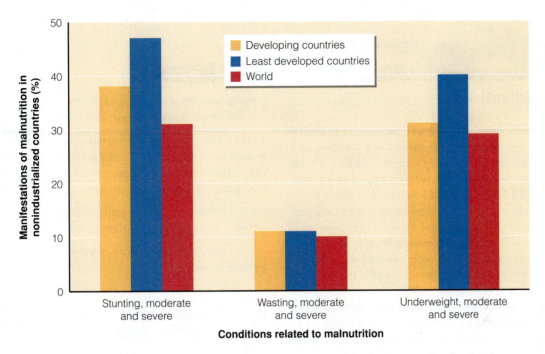

FIGURE 5.4 Manifestations of malnutrition in nonindustrialized countries. Source: Based on data from Bellamy (1999a), p. 101.

and many children don't have enough to eat. While few of these children suffer from kwashiorkor, many might be far more likely to reach their full human potential, both physically and intellectually—not to mention lead happier lives—if their bellies were always as warm and full as they should be.

SUDDEN INFANT DEATH SYNDROME

A local newspaper recently ran the story of a 3-month-old infant who had apparently been vigorous and healthy, but who had been found lifeless in his crib one morning. Police described the death as "suspicious" and were investigating. (See *In the News and on the Web*: "Infanticide.")

Several days later, the newspaper again reported on this death. Medical authorities had determined that the infant had died of sudden infant death syndrome (SIDS), sometimes referred to as "crib death" or "cot death," and all suspicions had been abandoned. In fact, however, a diagnosis of sudden infant death syndrome is really not a diagnosis at all; it is an admission that the cause of death is unknown. And, as Meadow (1999) points out, sometimes all suspicions should not be abandoned. (See *At a Glance*: "Sudden and Less Sudden Infant Deaths.")

This mysterious cause of infant death accounted for approximately 1.5 deaths for every 1,000 live births—as recently as 1980. But now, following important discoveries about ways of preventing SIDS, that figure has been reduced to below 1 death per 1,000 (Figure 5.5). However, SIDS is still a leading cause of death of older infants.

Definition

First formally defined in 1969, SIDS is simply "the sudden and unexpected death of an infant who has seemed well, or almost well, and whose death remains unexplained [later]" (Valdes-Dapena, 1991, p. 3). For a long time, SIDS could neither be predicted nor prevented. But concerted medical efforts have succeeded in reducing SIDS deaths in the United States by about 33% since 1980 (U.S. Bureau of the Census, 1998).

Infanticide

In December of 1996, Brian C. Peterson, then 18, and his pregnant girlfriend, 16-year-old Amy S. Grossberg, went to a motel in New Jersey. There she gave birth to a baby boy. Desperate to keep her pregnancy from her mother, Amy Grossberg and Brain Peterson then stuffed the infant into a plastic bag and tossed it into a dumpster where it was found, dead, the next day. Because the mother suffered post-birth hemorrhaging and sought medical attention, the police eventually traced the infant to its parents. At first, both claimed that the child had been stillborn. An autopsy contradicted their story, both plea-bargained, and both were sentenced to 8 years in prison. As part of the plea bargain, all but 2$\frac{1}{2}$ years were suspended for her; all but two years were suspended for him. In early January 2000, Brian C. Peterson was released from prison.

R. Hanley, "Man Is Freed after Serving 18 Months in Baby's Death." *Washington Post*, 5 January 2000, p. A21.

To Think About: Some people feel that given the help-lessness and dependence of infants, those who commit crimes against them should be punished more severely than is often the case. What do you think?

Resources: Comprehensive information about children's rights can be found at:

http://its2.ocs.lsu.edu/guests/wwwlawl/human/children.htm

http://www.courttv.com/trials/grossberg/070998.html

For additional readings, explore *InfoTrac College Edition*, your online library. Go to http://infotrac-college.com/wadsworth and use the passcode that came on the card with your book. Try these search terms: infant murder, infanticide.

Common Characteristics of SIDS Victims

Although research hasn't yet determined precisely what causes SIDS, it has succeeded in identifying some characteristics shared by many SIDS victims. The most common of these, surprisingly, is age. SIDS occurs during a far narrower age span than almost all diseases. Specifically, it is extremely rare in the first several weeks of life, peaks between 2 and 4 months, falls rapidly to age 6 months, and then declines more slowly until the age of 1. SIDS deaths are uncommon (fewer than 5% of the total) after the age of 1 (Hillman, 1991).

Other than age, there are several nonspecific risk factors for SIDS. One is sex, with males accounting for about 60% of cases. There is evidence, too, that SIDS may be slightly more probable among infants whose siblings have been victims. This should not be taken as evidence of a genetic link, however, because a comprehensive survey of SIDS deaths in the United States over a 5-year period showed that infants who had an identical twin who died of SIDS were at no greater risk than anybody else (Malloy & Freeman, 1999).

Other risk factors include bundling infants in layers of clothing; maternal smoking and, to a lesser extent, fathers smoking as well; and, perhaps most important for SIDS prevention, sleeping in a **prone** (facedown) rather than a **supine** (faceup) position (Jeffery, Megevand, & Page, 1999). The evidence seems clear that infants who are put to sleep on their sides or on their backs are at far lower risk for SIDS than infants who sleep on their stomachs. Also, SIDS is more common among infants born prematurely, and among those who have recently suffered from upper respiratory infections.

There is some speculation, as well, that maturation of the brain may be delayed or abnormal in some SIDS victims. Thus SIDS has sometimes been

prone On the belly; a sleep position. Or sometimes not a sleep position.

supine On the back; a sleep position. Or sometimes just a way to look at clouds.

| AT A GLANCE | ## Sudden and Less Sudden Infant Deaths |

Between 6 and 8 of every 1,000 children born alive in Canada and the United States die before the age of 1—about half the number who died only a few decades ago. Of these, the majority die very early, primarily of congenital (present at birth) abnormalities or of being excessively premature and underweight. For those who die later, the most common cause of death is SIDS—a still mysterious and largely unpredictable event. SIDS deaths are often treated as suspicious. But the opposite also happens, explains Meadow (1999); some deaths that should be suspicious are treated as SIDS. Meadow studied the cases of 81 infants who, the courts decided, had been murdered (43 of them by their mother, 5 by the father, and 2 by both!). Of these 81 victims, an astonishing 42 had initially been judged to have died of SIDS, and another 29 were given some other "natural" cause of death. (See Figure 5.5).

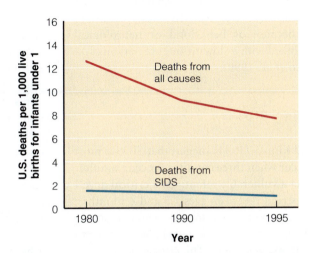

FIGURE 5.5a Decline in infant mortality rates from all causes and from SIDS for infants under 1 year, 1980–1995. Source: Based on U.S. Bureau of the Census (1998), p. 99.

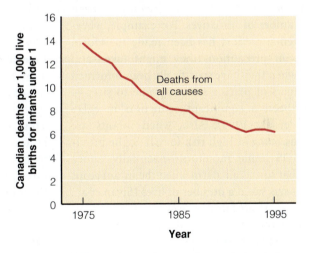

FIGURE 5.5b Decline in infant mortality rates in Canada from all causes, 1975–1995. Source: Based on *Canada Yearbook, 1999*.

associated with **apnea**, a temporary cessation of breathing that generally causes the person to wake up. Hunt (1991) suggests that SIDS may result from an infant's inability to learn the voluntary behaviors

that eventually replace defensive breathing reflexes. "There is a critical at-risk period for all infants when reflexive defensive responses have faded, but voluntary defensive responses are not yet sufficiently strong," says Hunt (1991, p. 185). Young infants reflexively stick out their tongues when a piece of plastic is put over their mouths. If the object is not dislodged, they typically move their heads from side to side; and if that doesn't work, they swing their

apnea A temporary paralysis or collapse of throat muscles during sleep. Victims typically awaken at once and again breathe normally. Apnea is involved in about 5% of all insomnia complaints. Severe apnea can endanger life.

arms toward their faces. Eventually these behaviors are replaced by more voluntary behaviors. Perhaps SIDS victims have not learned these voluntary behaviors because of behavioral or neurological problems linked with a slow-to-mature nervous system (Franco et al., 1999).

Preventing SIDS

Filiano and Kinney (1994) suggest that SIDS is most likely to occur when three conditions occur simultaneously: (1) a vulnerable infant; (2) a critical developmental period (between ages 1.5 and 4 months); and (3) some external stressor (like parental smoking, temperature fluctuations, being placed prone to sleep, or infant infections). The critical period cannot be prevented from occurring, but parents can exercise some control over the other factors.

The significant reduction in SIDS deaths that has taken place in the last several decades has been due to a number of initiatives. For example, wherever a systematic effort has been made to inform parents about precautions they might take—and especially when they have specifically been informed of the dangers of placing infants prone to sleep—there has been a significant reduction in SIDS (Mehanni et al., 1999). Also, when infants are identified as being at high risk for SIDS, the provision of SIDS home monitors—essentially, apnea detectors that sound an alarm when the infant stops breathing—has saved a number of lives (Sivan et al., 1997). Research indicates, as well, that having an infant share a room with parents reduces the risk of SIDS (Scragg et al., 1996).

It's important to emphasize that in many SIDS cases, apnea does not appear to be involved. In these cases, a monitor can neither predict the occurrence of SIDS nor, of course, prevent it. The use of a monitor, suggests Ranney (1991), may add stress in an already stressful household, especially when, as is not uncommon, the machine emits false alarms, further terrifying parents. At the same time, use of a monitor for at-risk children might reassure parents that they are doing everything they can to ensure their child's survival.

SIDS remains unexpected, unexplained, unpreventable, and—by definition—fatal. It occurs throughout the world and appears to have existed many centuries ago, although it would not have been as easily recognized or considered as important because infant mortality from other causes was so high. None of the factors sometimes associated with SIDS has been shown to cause it. Many SIDS victims are apparently thriving infants who seem completely normal and healthy, and who simply die, usually silently in their cribs at night. Small wonder that physicians and parents remain baffled and saddened, and law enforcement agencies, suspicious.

BRAIN AND BEHAVIOR IN NEWBORNS

At birth, the newborn's brain is about one-quarter the size of its body—which, of course, is why newborns always seem to have such big heads. The normal adult body-to-head ratio is closer to 1 to 10, rather than 1 to 4 (see Figure 7.4 in Chapter 7). Why is the newborn's head so large? Simply because it must accommodate an inordinately large brain. Interestingly, however, the skull in the newborn isn't a solid bony case, as it is in the adult. If you feel the top of a newborn's skull, you can easily detect a soft spot roughly in the center, a little toward the front. This is one of six **fontanels**, gaps that allow the bones of the skull to close in on each other and even to overlap slightly while the baby's head is being forced through the narrow birth canal. After birth, the fontanels close up and harden. But by the end of the second year, infants are still not as hard-headed as we adults are. The closing of the fontanels forms *sutures* that permit the skull to expand as the brain continues to grow. The skulls—and brains—of adults do not continue to grow.

During the final several weeks of fetal development, the absolute weight of the brain increases dramatically. At birth, the brain weighs about 25% of what it will weigh at adulthood. Contrast that with the fact that the newborn's total weight at birth is only about one-twentieth of what it will be in adulthood.

---

fontanels   Six gaps, detectable as soft spots, in the skull of a newborn.

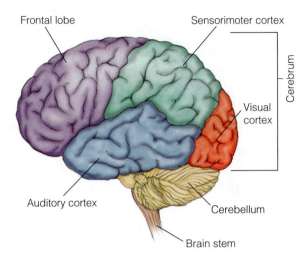

Frontal lobe

Sensorimoter cortex

Cerebrum

Visual cortex

Auditory cortex

Cerebellum

Brain stem

FIGURE 5.6 The main structures of the brain. The various sub-structures of the cerebrum are intimately involved in "higher" mental functions. In particular, the frontal lobe is associated with speech and reasoning. The cerebrum's ⅛-inch-thick covering, the cerebral cortex, is so convoluted that its surface area is actually much larger than the space it occupies.

Development of the Brain

The very large brain of the newborn consists essentially of three main parts—as does the adult brain (Figure 5.6). The **brain stem**, which is an extension of the spinal cord, is the most highly developed brain structure at birth. It is concerned mainly with physiological functions such as breathing and heart functioning. The **cerebellum**, a structure found low at the back of the brain behind the brain stem, is concerned with balance and with sensory and motor activity. The **cerebrum** is the convoluted and wrinkled mass that would be immediately visible if the skull were to be opened. It makes up about 75% of the total mass of the brain, and its functions are

among the most important in determining what it is to be human. Thus, the various structures of the cerebrum are responsible for sensation (vision and hearing, for example), for body movement and coordination, and perhaps most important, for thought and language. It is the most recent brain structure from an evolutionary point of view, and also the latest to develop in the fetus. In fact, those parts of the cerebrum that are concerned with thought continue to grow and develop into early adulthood. The outer covering of the cerebrum is labeled the **cerebral cortex**. The cerebral cortex is only about 1/8th of an inch thick.

The major early developments in the brain after birth have to do mainly with its communication system—that is, with its system of interconnections. The brain, as well as the rest of our nervous systems, is composed of billions of **neurons** (nerve cells). These are highly specialized cells whose function is to store and transmit impulses in the form of electrical and chemical changes. Transmission occurs through interconnections that form among neurons. Each neuron consists of a **cell body** from which several arms extend. One of these is typically larger and longer than the others, and is termed an **axon**. The others are hairlike extensions termed **dendrites**. Neural transmission ordinarily proceeds from the cell body outward along the axon, at the end of which the impulse (message) jumps the gap—termed a **synaptic cleft**—to the dendrites of adjacent neurons (Figure 5.7).

The brain continues to grow very rapidly during the first two years, reaching about 75% of adult weight at the end of that period. The very rapid development of the brain that occurs during this

---

brain stem Brain structure at top of spinal cord, involved mainly in functions essential for physiological survival (respiration, heart action, temperature control).

cerebellum Brain structure at base of skull, at the rear of the brain stem, closely involved in coordinating motor activity and maintaining balance.

cerebrum Most highly developed part of the brain. A wrinkled mass of brain tissue whose principal functions relate to sensation, thinking, speech, and other higher mental processes.

cerebral cortex Outer covering of the cerebrum, only about one-eighth inch thick.

neurons Nerve cells, the basic building blocks of the human nervous system. Each neuron consists of a cell body, axon, and dendrites.

cell body The main part of a cell, containing the nucleus.

axon Elongated, trunklike extension of a nerve cell. Nerve impulses are ordinarily transmitted from the nerve cell outward along the axon.

dendrites Hairlike tendrils found on a neuron's cell body; their function is to receive neural impulses.

synaptic cleft Space between terminal buttons at ends of axons and dendrites of adjoining neurons. A gap that must be bridged if neural transmission is to occur.

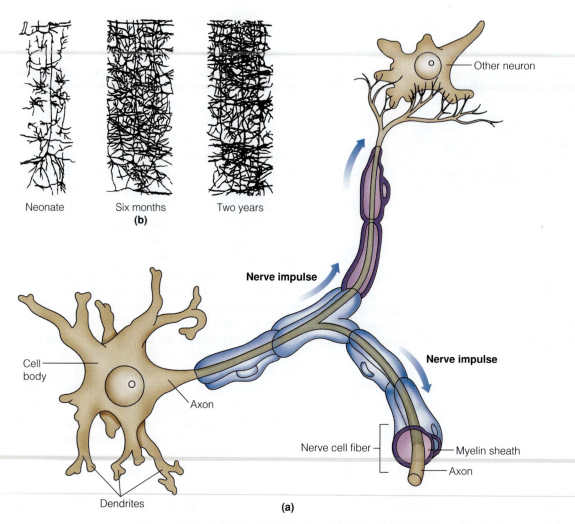

(b)

Neonate   Six months   Two years

Nerve impulse

Nerve impulse

Other neuron

Cell body

Axon

Nerve cell fiber

Myelin sheath

Axon

Dendrites

(a)

FIGURE 5.7   (a) The main components of a single neuron. (b) The increasing complexity of synaptic connections during the first two years of life. Much of the increase in brain weight that occurs during the first two years is due to the formation of dendrites leading to new connections among existing neurons, as well as to the *myelination* of neural pathways—their encasement in fatty tissue that both protects them and improves their ability to transmit impulses. Reprinted with permission of the publisher from *The Postnatal Development of the Human Cerebral Cortex*, vol. I-VIII by Jesse LeRoy Conel, Cambridge, Mass.: Harvard University Press, Copyright © 1939–1975 by the President and Fellows of Harvard College.

time does not involve the formation of new neurons, but rather the development of new connections among them, as well as the development of protective coatings (**myelin sheaths**) that enhance neural transmission. What this **brain proliferation**

myelin sheath   Fatty covering that surrounds nerves and nerve cells, protecting them and enhancing neural transmission.

brain proliferation   Expression used to describe the rapid development of a staggering number of increasingly complex neural connections in the first two years of life.

means is that by the age of 2, the infant brain has an enormous number of potential connections among brain cells. These connections are what make it possible for 2-year-olds to learn so much so rapidly. And perhaps nowhere is the staggering potential of this brain more evident than in the learning of language.

Interestingly, the brain of the 2-year-old may contain more potential connections than it will ever contain again. What happens, explain Fischer and Rose (1996), is that the billions of connections that aren't used eventually disappear.

The Role of Experience

This is where experience comes in. The human brain is extraordinarily dependent on experiences if it is to develop normally (Rumbaugh, 1998). It seems that in the absence of appropriate stimulation early in life, far more of these billions of connections will be lost than would otherwise be the case. Environmental events, such as exposure to language, for example, are critical to the development of the brain (Fox, Calkins, & Bell, 1994). This is clearly illustrated in experiments with animals. For example, Rosenzweig (1984) found that rats who are raised in enriched environments have significantly heavier brains than rats raised in impoverished environments. And kittens who are blindfolded for the first several weeks of their lives lose most of the neural connections usually associated with vision and never do learn to see normally (Hubel, 1988).

For ethical reasons, experiments such as these can't be conducted with humans. However, examinations of brain functioning of Romanian orphans exposed to highly deprived environments during their first years of life also reveals dramatic differences between the functioning of their brains and that of normal children (Kaler & Freeman, 1994). As a result of findings such as these, some researchers suggest there are distinct periods of very rapid brain growth, which are *critical* in the sense that exposure to appropriate environmental stimulation during these periods is translated into very rapid learning and is evident, as well, in measures of intelligence (Fischer & Rose, 1996). Not surprisingly, the most dramatic of these spurts in brain growth occurs early in the first year of life. Other spurts are evident around ages 7 or 8, again at the onset of adolescence (11 or 12), and again in late adolescence (18 or 19).

The Brain and Infant States

An important function of the brain during early infancy is to control the infant's general condition—that is, the infant's physiological arousal or infant state. Following a careful study of the behavior of infants, Wolff (1966) describes six distinct infant states: *regular sleep, irregular sleep, drowsiness, alert inactivity, alert activity,* and *crying* (these last two

states are sometimes grouped together and termed *focused activity*). (See Figure 5.8.) Note that they are essentially descriptions of *central nervous system* activity. It is interesting to find there is evidence that these states are present in the fetus, although they are less easily detected at that time. We know, for example, that toward the end of the prenatal period, the fetus spends alternating periods of time asleep and awake (Groome et al., 1997).

Newborns vary consistently in the amount of time spent in each state, some sleeping more than half the day, others sleeping for only a few hours (Brown, 1964). Similarly, some cry as much as 40% of the time and others hardly at all. With increasing age, expected changes include a decline in the amount of time spent sleeping and an increase in alert activity.

The average neonate sleeps as much as three-fourths of the time. It isn't clear whether infants dream while they sleep, but an extremely high proportion of their sleeping time (as much as half) is characterized by **rapid eye movement (REM) sleep**. And we do know that in children and adults, most dreams occur during REM sleep. Amount of REM sleep declines gradually during infancy. By the age of 2 years, approximately 25% of the infant's sleep is of the REM variety—very similar to that of an adult.

◤ MOTOR DEVELOPMENT IN INFANCY

Within hours of birth, beavers are able to dive, hold their breath, and swim; young antelope can run with their mothers; baby geese can follow a goose, or a person, to a pond and across it. These animals are **precocial**: They are born with highly developed motor capacities.

---

rapid eye movement (REM) sleep A stage of sleep characterized by rapid eye movements. Most of our dreaming occurs during REM sleep, which accounts for approximately 25% of an adult's sleep time and as much as 50% of an infant's.

precocial In biology, refers to birds and animals whose motor capacities are highly developed at or within a short time of birth.

State	Description	Responsiveness
Regular (deep) sleep	Largely motionless, eyes closed, regular breathing	No response to mild stimuli
Irregular sleep	Twitching motions, eyes closed, irregular breathing	Sounds or bright light can elicit grimace or smile
Drowsiness	Moderately active state precedes or follows sleep, eyes may be closed or open	Responsive to stimuli
Alert inactivity	Relative inactivity, eyes open, breathing more rapid than regular sleep, examining environment	Highly responsive; maintains examination of world
Alert activity	High activity, eyes open, rapid breathing	Moderate responsiveness to stimuli
Crying	High activity, eyes open, low alertness, rapid breathing	Low responsiveness to stimuli

Regular (deep) sleep 33.3%
Irregular sleep 33.3%
Crying 5%
Alert activity 8.3%
Alert inactivity 10%
Drowsiness 10%

Relative distribution in newborn

FIGURE 5.8   The infant's state reflects level of alertness or responsiveness to the environment. States are closely related to the infant's level of brain activity (arousal). Source: Based on Wolff (1966).

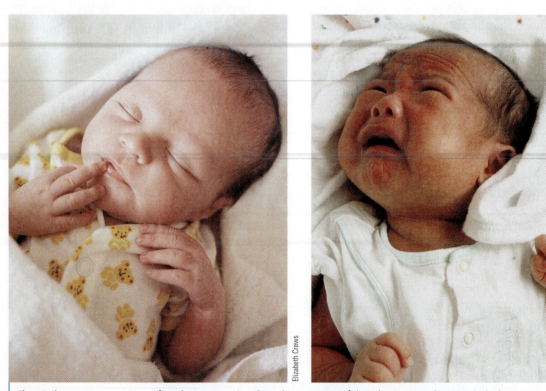

Elizabeth Crews

Elizabeth Crews

Sleep is the most common state of newborns, occupying about three-quarters of their day. Fortunately, crying is the least common state.

In contrast, human infants are **altricial**: They are born with relatively undeveloped motor capacities. They cannot walk; they can't even control the movements of their hands and heads. As a result, they remain physically helpless for a prolonged period of time.

Reflexes

In fact, in the very beginning, the newborn is incapable of intentional behaviors. That's because the newborn's responses are reflexive. Recall that **reflexes** are very simple behaviors that don't have to be learned. They are behaviors present at birth, responses that are essentially unavoidable, inescapable reactions to stimulation. Reflexes can easily be elicited in a normal child by presenting the appropriate stimulus.

Some reflexes, such as the breathing reflex, are **survival reflexes**. Survival reflexes are essential for survival, and include the **vegetative reflexes**—so called because they have to do with finding and obtaining nourishment. The **sucking reflex** is probably the best known of the vegetative reflexes, and can easily be elicited by placing an object in a child's mouth. The rooting reflex (sometimes called the head-turning reflex) is also a vegetative reflex, as are swallowing, hiccuping, sneezing, and vomiting; each can be elicited by the appropriate nourishment-related stimulation. The rooting reflex, for example, can be elicited by stroking a baby's cheek or the corner of the mouth. This reflex is evident in breast-fed babies, who turn readily toward the nipple when the breast touches their cheek.

Some common motor reflexes in newborns have no apparent survival value today but might have been useful in humanity's early history. These reflexes include the **moro reflex**, a generalized startle reaction that involves throwing out the arms and feet symmetrically and then pulling them back toward the center of the body. This reflex, some speculate, might be important for tree-dwelling primate infants. If they suddenly fall but throw out their arms and legs while so doing, they might be lucky enough to catch a branch and save themselves. If this happened to some very distant relative of mine, that may be why I am here writing to you today. The moro reflex can be useful in diagnosing brain damage because it is sometimes present later in life among people with impaired motor function. In normal infants it ordinarily disappears with the development of the brain and increasing control over motor actions (Mandich et al., 1994).

Other reflexes that disappear with time are the **palmar reflex** (also called the *Darwinian* or *grasping* reflex), which is sometimes sufficiently pronounced that a neonate can be raised completely off a bed when grasping an adult's finger in each hand; the *swimming reflex*, which occurs when a baby is balanced horizontally on its stomach; and the stepping reflex, which occurs when an infant is held vertically with its feet lightly touching a surface. Another highly interesting reflex that disappears with age is one first noticed and described by Joseph Francois Felix Babinski more than 100 years ago (Estanol, Huerta, & Garcia, 1997). Not surprisingly, it's called the Babinski reflex. This reflex is evident in the typical fanning of the toes when an infant is tickled in the middle of the soles of the feet. The Babinksi reflex is useful in diagnosing certain types of brain injury, and is also occasionally an indication of cerebral palsy (Ghosh & Pradhan, 1998). The *Concept Summary* lists some common reflexes of newborns.

---

altricial Born with highly undeveloped motor capacities. Requiring a relatively lengthy period of care.

reflexes Simple, unlearned, genetically based, unconscious, and largely unavoidable reactions to specific stimuli—such as blinking the eye in response to a puff of air.

survival reflex One of several reflexes in the newborn that are closely linked to physical survival—for example, the breathing reflex and the sucking reflex.

vegetative reflexes Reflexes pertaining to the intake of food (for example, swallowing and sucking).

sucking reflex The automatic sucking response of a newborn child when the oral regions are stimulated. Nipples are particularly appropriate for eliciting the sucking reflex.

---

moro reflex The generalized startle reaction of a newborn infant. It characteristically involves throwing out the arms and feet symmetrically and then bringing them back in toward the center of the body.

palmar reflex The grasping reflex that newborn infants exhibit when objects are placed in their hands.

Although reflexive behaviors appear to be highly rigid and unmodifiable reactions, an infant quickly begins to exercise a limited degree of control over some of the circumstances that lead to reflexive behaviors. When not hungry, an infant may avert its head or purse its lips tightly, thus avoiding the stim-ulation that might lead to the sucking response. Second, also beginning very early in life, an infant is capable of modifying some reflexive responses, including sucking (perhaps by changing the shape of the mouth or the placement of the tongue to increase the behavior's effectiveness) (Widstrom &

C O N C E P T S U M M A R Y

Some Reflexive Behaviors in the Newborn

Reflex	Stimulus	Response	Approximate Age of Appearance	Approximate Age of Disappearance
Sucking	Object in the mouth	Sucks	2–3 months in utero	Becomes voluntary during first year
Rooting (head turning)	Stroking the cheek or the corner of the mouth	Turns head toward side being stroked	Neonate	Becomes voluntary during first year
Swallowing	Food in the mouth	Swallows	Neonate	Becomes voluntary during first year
Sneezing	Irritation in the nasal passages	Sneezes	4–6 months in utero	Present in adult
Moro reflex	Sudden loud noise	Throws arms and legs out symmetrically	Neonate	Disappears by 3–4 months
Babinski reflex	Tickling the middle of the soles	Spreads and raises toes	Neonate	Diminishes by 1 month; disappears by 5–6 months
Toe grasp	Tickling the soles just below the toes	Curls toes around object	4–6 months in utero	Disappears by 9 months
Palmar grasp	Placing object in the infant's hand	Grasps object tightly	4–6 months in utero	Weak by 8 weeks; gone by 4–5 months
Swimming reflex	Infant horizontal, supported by abdomen	Coordinated swimming movements	8–9 months in fetus	Disappears after 6 months
Stepping reflex	Infant vertical, feet lightly touching flat surface	Makes coordinated walking movements	8–9 months in fetus	Disappears after 2–3 months

Thingstrom-Paulsson, 1993). The human organism—programmed to process information, to learn, to change—is capable of change very early.

Locomotion and Motor Control

The development of the infant's early motor skills relates directly to the reflexes present in infancy. Thus learning to crawl is an extension of the swimming reflex, just as learning to walk and learning to grasp are extensions of the stepping and the palmar grasp reflexes, respectively. Some of these motor accomplishments involve **gross motor development**. This refers to the development of skills related primarily to large body movements such as those involved in locomotion—like crawling, standing, and walking. Among other things, these skills require the development of control over major groups of muscles in order to direct their activity. **Fine motor development** refers to the development of control over smaller (*finer*) movements—hence using smaller muscle groups such as those involved in grasping and stroking.

Although the newborn's first movements appear to be largely uncoordinated and purposeless actions, they are marked by recurring patterns. To begin with, says Robertson (1993a), starting even in the prenatal period and continuing for about the first four months, the young infant's movements are **cyclic movements**. That is, the infant's spontaneous movements recur at relatively regular intervals, spaced within minutes, both during periods of sleep and wakefulness. At first these movements are typically irregular and rapid, as well as asymmetrical (Grattan, DeVos, & Levy, 1992). That is, they involve various parts of the body (arms and legs) as well as either side (right or left) at different times. Rapid cyclic movements are typically followed by brief

Elizabeth Crews

The normal sequence of motor development in infancy is highly predictable—although major developments occur at different ages for different children. At the age of about 8 months, this urchin can pull herself to a standing position. But it will be some time yet before she can crawl over the barricade.

periods of quiet. Later the movements become more coordinated and more symmetrical.

Some speculate that these cyclic movements are biologically important in that they provide a sort of built-in way of exercising muscle systems and of beginning to gain control over body movements. At the same time, periods of quiescence between those of action provide an opportunity for the infant to interact with the environment. Thus, notes Robertson (1993b), cyclic movements may regulate the infant's interactions. It is interesting that infant movements are typically suppressed during social interaction. In addition, the movement part of the

---

gross motor development The development of motor skills involving large (gross) bodily movements such as walking or throwing a ball.

fine motor development The development of motor skills involving relatively small (fine) body movements such as learning to grasp or to scribble with a pencil.

cyclic movements Expression used to describe the young infant's spontaneous, regularly recurring body movements.

cycle declines abruptly in strength at about 2 months as the infant begins to pay more attention to ongoing stimulation. By the age of 4 months, cyclic movements are much less frequent and are eventually replaced by more deliberate, controlled movements.

The order in which children acquire motor skills is highly predictable, although the ages at which these skills appear can vary considerably. Tables of developmental norms, such as that represented by the *Denver Developmental Screening Test*, are sometimes useful for assessing a child's progress. However, as always, there is no "average" child.

The normal sequence of motor development reflects the two developmental principles mentioned in Chapter 4. First, development is cephalocaudal in that it proceeds from the head toward the feet. For example, infants can control eye movements and raise the head before acquiring control over the extremities. Recall that fetal development proceeds in the same manner: The head, eyes, and internal organs develop in the embryo before the appearance of the limbs.

Second, development is proximodistal: It proceeds in an inward-outward direction. For example, internal organs mature and function before the (more external) limbs develop. Similarly, children acquire control over parts of the body closest to the center before they can control the extremities. Thus they can control gross motor movements before hand or finger movements.

An Example of Fine Motor Learning: Grasping

Learning to reach and grasp is a highly significant accomplishment for the young infant. Among other things, grasping permits chunks of the world to be touched and felt, to be looked at from different angles, to be brought to the mouth and sucked and tasted. Especially when combined with **locomotor abilities**, it provides an extraordinarily fruitful means of exploring and learning.

---

locomotor abilities Abilities involved in self-propelled motion; hence essential for moving oneself from one position or location to another (crawling or walking, for example, for those who—unlike kings, queens, and infants—don't have personal bearers).

At first, of course, the infant is incapable of reaching and grabbing. In fact, says Piaget, infants are probably incapable of forming the intention of doing so. Their movements are a wild-looking, apparently purposeless waving of hands and feet, uncoordinated with the act of looking. But clearly, successful reaching and grasping require looking, seeing, and intending. More than this, they require coordinating the reaching and closing of the hand with feedback from the visual system as well as from the physical system. Learning to reach and grasp, like learning to walk, is not a simple matter.

So, in the beginning, infants stare and wave and sometimes become almost uncontrollably excited. And then, perhaps accidentally, the hand closes on the object of interest, clumsily and temporarily. But with practice, the reach and the grab become more refined, more certain, so that by the age of 6 months or so, the infant has learned to reach and seize, and perhaps even to accommodate the reach and the closing of the hand to the characteristics of the object—its shape, size, and texture (Case-Smith, Bigsby, & Clutter, 1998).

Cultural Variations in Locomotor Learning While the sequence of early motor development reflects a genetically influenced timetable, the infant's context can dramatically influence both the ages at which different motor skills are acquired and their quality. Gerber (1958) reports an investigation of 300 Ugandan infants who, a mere two days after birth (all home deliveries without anesthetics), could sit upright, heads held high, with only slight support of the elbows—a feat that most American children cannot accomplish until close to the age of 2 months (Bayley, 1969). And all 300 Ugandan children were expert crawlers before they were 2 months old!

What accounts for these differences? A variety of factors, explains Adolph (1997). Thus, genetic factors, perhaps reflected in the infant's activity level as well as in distributions of muscle and fat, appear to be clearly important. For example, newborns with chubbier legs often learn to walk later than do those with more slender legs. At the same time, however, experience is clearly important. In one study, children with Down syndrome whose parents were trained to assist them in learning motor skills fared significantly better than those whose parents were relatively uninvolved (Torres & Buceta, 1998). Similarly, Ugandan infants, many of whom are typically held upright and carried around by their mothers, may learn much about locomotion both *visually* and through their bodily sensations of movements, as well as their sensations of the mother's movements.

Intellectual Development and Motor Learning
There is a close link between the development of control over physical actions and intellectual development. The infant's ability to manipulate and explore is what makes possible the discovery of the properties of physical objects, such as their permanence and their location in space. These discoveries, in turn, are related to the infant's growing ability to reason about objects, and to develop concepts (ideas) (Bushnell & Boudreau, 1993). Hence Piaget's (1954) term *sensorimotor* to describe development in the first two years of life.

PERCEPTUAL DEVELOPMENT IN INFANCY

The term *sensorimotor* underlines the fact that the infant's development involves the coordination of newly acquired and rapidly developing motor abilities (such as locomotion, reaching, and grasping) with sensory capabilities (such as those involved in seeing, touching, tasting, hearing, and smelling).

Sensation, Perception, and Conceptualization

Our existence as human beings depends largely on our ability to make sense of the world and of ourselves. The struggle to discover what things are and what they mean begins in infancy and depends on three closely related processes: sensation, perception, and conceptualization.

Sensation is the effect achieved when physical stimuli are translated into neural impulses (which

can then be transmitted to the brain and interpreted). Thus sensation depends on the activity of one or more of our specialized sense organs—eyes, ears, and taste buds, for example.

In its simplest sense, **perception** is the brain's interpretation of sensation. Thus wavelengths corresponding to the color red affect our retinas in specific ways, causing electrical activity in our optic nerve. When this activity reaches the part of our brain that deals with vision, we perceive the color in question. That we can now think about the color red, compare it to other colors, or make some decision based on it is a function of the third process, **conceptualization**.

To summarize, sensation is primarily a physiological process dependent on the senses (the effect of light waves on the retina of the eye), and perception is the effect of sensation (the recognition that this is a red light). Conceptualization (the realization that because this is a red light, I should stop) is a more cognitive, or intellectual, process. And these three processes, in combination, are the basis of our contact with, and understanding of, the world. Hence knowing about their functioning and their development in infancy is critical to understanding the world of the infant.

Vision in Infants

For years researchers assumed that newborns had poorly developed vision with little ability to detect form, patterns, or movements. One reason for this assumption relates to problems in doing research with infants, who can't communicate directly the effects of sensory experience. But with the development of increasingly sensitive instruments to detect subtle changes in an infant's behavior, earlier preconceptions are being replaced—although there still are difficulties with infants as research subjects (see *At a Glance:* "Research with Human Infants").

---

sensation The physical effect of stimulation; a physiological process dependent on activity of the senses.

perception Reaction to and interpretation of physical stimulation (sensation). A conceptual process dependent on activity of the brain.

conceptualization The forming of concepts (ideas or meanings); an intellectual process leading to thinking and understanding.

Research with Human Infants

Young infants, especially newborns, are not always very good research subjects. When Fantz (1963) wanted to see how newborns reacted to visual stimulation, one of the most important conditions for selecting subjects was whether they kept their eyes open long enough to be shown the stimuli. And when Meltzoff and Moore (1989) investigated newborns' ability to imitate, only 40 of 93 infants completed the 8-minute test session, even though the researchers chose only infants who showed no signs of hunger and remained alert for at least five minutes before the testing. The remaining 53 infants either fell asleep, cried, had spitting or choking fits, or had a bowel movement.

Young infants are not always very good research subjects. In Fantz's study, 53 of 90 infant participants did not complete an 8-minute test session. Of these, 19 started to cry, 17 had bouts of spitting, choking, or hiccuping, 5 were distracted by bowel movements, and like this little tyke, 12 simply fell asleep!

Jonathan Nourok/Photo Edit

Vision at Birth How well can an infant see? Is the world fuzzy and blurred, or is it crisp and clear? Is it 20/20, or better or worse?

Researchers' estimates of infant **visual acuity** vary, often because of the different methods used to assess vision. However, a number of important points are clear.

First, vision is probably the least well developed of the infant's senses. Researchers have determined that one of the reasons for this is that the newborn's retinal cells (which are responsible for vision) are very immature at birth, as are those parts of the brain involved in vision (Candy, Crowell, & Banks, 1998). Thus, visual acuity—that is, the sharpness of the infant's view—is estimated to be at about 20/400, or perhaps even 20/600 (Held, 1993; Slater & Johnson, 1998). This means that what infants see at a distance of 20 feet is no clearer than what a normal adult sees at a distance of 400 or even 600 feet.

Hence neonates' visual worlds are somewhat fuzzy and blurred, although they are far from blind.

Second, there is a four- or five-fold improvement in an infant's visual acuity by the age of 6 months—to about 20/100 (Aslin & Smith, 1988; Courage & Adams, 1990). Now the infant sees as clearly at 20 feet what the adult sees at 100 feet. And by the age of 1 year, infant visual acuity is close to that of a normal adult. Of interest, however, is that this improvement appears to be highly dependent on early experience. Remember that kittens raised with blindfolds during early critical periods of their lives never do learn to see properly. Similarly, Stroganova and Tsetlin (1998) report that infants born with **cataracts** in both eyes experienced significant developmental delays, even when the cataracts were surgically removed at around 8 months. In addition, these children with early visual deprivation displayed more intense and negative emotional reactions. These researchers speculate that those reactions may be related to the fact that poor vision in infancy is related to poor development of aspects of the nervous system. Related to this, Nevskaya, Leushina, & Bondarko (1998) report

visual acuity Sharpness and clarity of vision. Visual acuity is often expressed by Snellen ratings, in which 20/20 vision is considered average (the individual can see as well at 20 feet as individuals with normal vision). Vision can be poorer than 20/20 (for example, 20/40 when the individual sees as clearly at 20 feet as people with normal vision see at 40) or better (for example, 20/15, when the individual sees as well at 20 feet as average people do at 15).

cataracts Opaque coating over the lens of the eye, causing partial or sometimes total blindness.

that infants born with visual defects often manifest poorer intellectual functioning later in life.

Third, a newborn's visual accommodation is more limited than that of adults. It appears that newborns focus most accurately at a distance of approximately 12 inches (30 cm) (Banks, 1980). Significantly, that is about the distance of a mother's face when she is feeding her infant. This is but one of the ways in which neonates appear to be programmed to perceive important aspects of the environment.

Color and Movement No one has yet determined exactly when color vision is first present in the infant. In Knoblauch, Bieber, and Werner's words, "an efficient screening test for infant colour vision remains an elusive goal" (1996, p. 60.) There is some evidence that newborns (aged 1 to 7 days) can distinguish between lights that are pure white and those that are green, yellow, and red. But to do so, they require far more contrast—that is, far purer colors—than do adults (Adams & Courage, 1998). This, claim Adams and Courage, is again because of immaturities in the infant's visual system. Even by the age of two months, infants' color discrimination still requires higher levels of purity than is the case for adults (Teller, 1998). Infants are better able to discriminate among colors after the age of about 2 months. By the age of 4 months, infants can not only discriminate among colors, but even show a preference for certain colors like pure reds and blues (Burr, Morrone, & Fiorentini, 1996; Bornstein & Marks, 1982).

Pupillary reflexes—changes in the size of the pupil caused by changes in the brightness of visual stimulation—demonstrate that neonates are sensitive to light intensity. Also, eye movements indicate that an infant is capable of visually following a slowly moving object within a few days of birth and is sensitive to patterns and contours as early as 2 days after birth (Fantz, 1965). By the age of 5 months, the infant's reaching and grasping are largely controlled by visual cues (McCarty & Ashmead, 1999). So, too, is exploration of texture (Stack & Tsonis, 1999).

pupillary reflex An involuntary change in the size of the pupil as a function of brightness or darkness. The pupillary reflex is present in neonates.

Perception of Depth In the famous Gibson and Walk (1960) "visual cliff" studies, a heavy sheet of glass is positioned over a checkered surface, but only half this surface is flush with the glass; the other half is some 3 feet lower. Thus, an adult standing or sitting on the glass can plainly see a drop where the patterned surface falls away from the glass. So can goats which, at the age of only 1 day, avoid the deep side, either going around it or jumping over it when they can. So too can infants, who, when they are old enough to crawl, typically refuse to cross the deep part, even when their mothers call them from the other side. Thus perception of depth is present at least from the time that the infant can crawl.

For a number of years, a test for depth perception before an infant could crawl seemed impossible. Now, however, investigators can simply look at changes in the infant's heart rate when it is moved from the shallow to the deep side of the visual cliff

THOUGHT CHALLENGE: *A man, known to us only as S.B., was born blind and stayed that way for the first 52 years of his life. The psychologist Gregory (1973) reports that he adapted very well during those years, and that he could often be seen riding about his village on a bicycle with his hand on a friend's shoulder. He had also learned to build things with tools in his own workshop, and he spent much of his time trying to find out what the world looked like to sighted people.*

Then, at the age of 52, he underwent a successful cornea transplant. Now able to see for the first time in his life, he quickly learned to identify those things with which he was most familiar. But he never developed any sense of perspective, of depth, or of speed. He believed, for example, that he could easily lower himself to the ground from the ledge of his hospital window, even though it was more than 30 feet up. And he became terrified of crossing streets, although he had confidently done so all his life when blind. In the end, like many other individuals like him, he became depressed, choosing to spend more and more time sitting at home in the dark. Some three years after he was given his sight, he died.

What is the most likely explanation for S.B.'s visual problems after regaining his sight?

apparatus. And when this is done, it seems that infants who have not yet learned to crawl don't normally show much evidence of fear—that is, their heart rates do not accelerate significantly (Bertenthal & Campos, 1990). Hence either fear of falling is learned rather than innate, or these infants simply do not yet perceive depth. These authors argue that they do perceive depth but have not yet learned to fear it. Through self-locomotion, infants eventually develop the **visual-vestibular** sense essential to maintaining equilibrium (and related to fear of falling). In addition, locomotion requires them to develop skills of visual attention if they are to avoid colliding with objects; it allows them as well to learn about dangers

---

visual-vestibular sense Describes sensation relating to sensing and maintaining balance, involving both the inner ear and vision.

associated with height, perhaps from parental reactions as they approach stairs or stand on chairs.

Visual Preferences We know that young infants see, although somewhat fuzzily in the beginning. We know, too, that they have limited perception of color for the first few months, but that they are capable of detecting motion and of visually following moving objects very soon after birth. Do they also have preferences about what they look at?

Faces or Patterns The answer is yes, infants do have visual preferences. In one well-known study of infants' visual preference, 18 infants, ranging in age from 10 hours to 5 days, were shown six circular stimulus patterns of different complexity, the most complex being a human face (Fantz, 1963). In

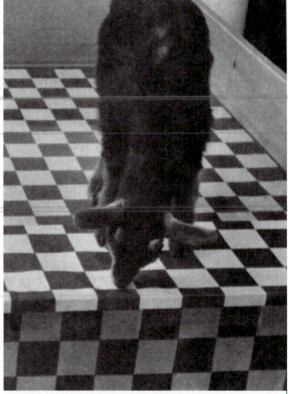

Use of the glass-covered visual cliff indicates that depth perception is developed at a very young age in humans and other animals. At left, an infant refuses to cross over even after receiving tactile assurance that the "cliff" is in fact a solid surface. At right, a goat exhibits a similar reaction—although, unlike a human infant, it can jump to the other side. Goats show this response at the tender age of 1 day.

diminishing order of complexity, the other stimuli included concentric circles, newsprint, and three circles of different solid colors. Figure 5.9 shows the percentage of total time spent by subjects looking at each of the figures. That the face was looked at for a significantly higher proportion of total time indicates not only that infants can discriminate among the various figures but also that they prefer faces—or perhaps that they prefer complexity.

It seems, argue de Haan and Nelson (1997), that infants are born with some innate knowledge about faces that allows them to recognize and be attracted to them. They suggest that this propensity is probably closely tied to the importance of recognizing primary caregivers if the infant is to form an attachment with them. There is evidence, for example, that by the second day of life infants already prefer their mothers' face to that of a stranger (Morton & Johnson, 1991). However, as Leon (1992) points out, studies of infant reactions to their mother's faces have generally provided the infant with the sound of the mother's voice and sometimes with her scent as well. So it isn't clear that infants actually prefer the sight of the mother rather than her scent or the sound of her voice.

How Infants Look

At the beginning of this chapter you were asked to consider the problem of taking something as primi-

tive and helpless as a newborn and engineering it so that in the end, it would be as sophisticated and elegant and graceful as a 2-year-old—and eventually a 12-year-old, a 42-year-old, a 92-year-old, and beyond. In designing this little organism, we considered that among other things, you would have to program it to become an extraordinarily capable information-processing system tuned to detect and respond to the most important features of the environment, and predisposed, as well, to make sense of these features.

Does what we know about an infant's visual system conform to our design requirements? Haith (1980) says yes. Infants, he informs us, do not respond to the visual world in a simple, reflexive manner, response following stimulus in predictable mechanical fashion. Instead, infants behave as though preprogrammed to follow specific rules that are clearly focused toward maximizing information. After all, acquiring information is the purpose of looking.

Infants Look to Acquire Information Haith's research, using infrared lights bounced off infants' corneas to show movements of their eyes, reveals the following.

First, contrary to what we might have expected, infants move their eyes even when there's no light, scanning the darkness in a highly controlled manner, using small movements appropriate for finding shadows, edges, spots. When viewing a uniformly lit but unpatterned field, their eye movements are

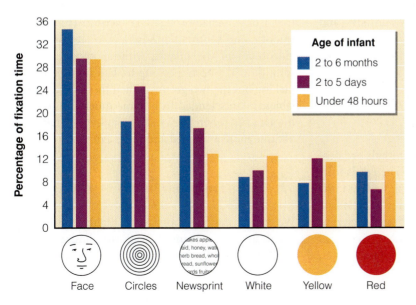

FIGURE 5.9 Relative percentage of time infants looked at six circular visual stimuli. The graph depicts infants' preference for the human face and for more complex stimuli. Source: Based on data in Robert L. Fantz (1963). Pattern vision in newborn infants. *Science* 40: 296–297. Copyright 1963 by the American Association for the Advancement of Science. Used by permission of the American Association for the Advancement of Science and the author.

broader sweeping movements suitable for discovering bolder contours. It seems clear that from birth, visual scanning patterns are not simply under the control of external stimuli (after all, scanning occurs in darkness as well as in light) but are internally controlled. It is as though infants, true to our speculative design, are preprogrammed to obtain information.

Second, newborns actually *look* at stimuli. They position their eyeballs so that a maximum amount of visual information falls on the *fovea*—the part of the retina that has the highest concentration of visual cells. It's as though the infant's scanning rules are designed to maximize stimulation—and, consequently, to maximize information.

Third, when a newborn looks at a simple stimulus (such as a vertical or horizontal line), the eyes cross back and forth repeatedly over the edges of the stimulus. The effect is to maintain a high level of neural firing in the visual cells.

Haith concludes that there appears to be a major principle governing a newborn's visual activity: Maximize neural firing. It is a built-in principle to assure that the newborn's visual activity will lead to the greatest possible amount of information—a vital feature for an organism that must be an outstanding information-processing system.

This view of an infant's visual perception as rule-governed and information-oriented, rather than as stimulus-bound, is a dramatic departure from psychology's traditional approach to these matters—a departure that is evident in many other areas of child study as well. Today's infant—and child—is no longer merely a passive recipient of external influences, but has become active, exploring, information-seeking.

Hearing

Dogs, bears, cats, and many other animals are deaf at birth; the human neonate is not. The ear is fully grown and potentially functional a few months before birth. Studies that use measures of electrical activity in the ear as an index of sensitivity to sounds indicate that newborns are responsive to all sorts of sounds (Schoonhoven et al., 1999). In fact,

most investigations indicate that neonates are only slightly less sensitive than adults to sound intensity.

Investigations of infants' responsiveness to frequency (high or low pitch) indicate that they appear to prefer higher frequencies and highly melodic, expressive voices. Parents must know this, suggest Aslin, Jusczyk, and Pisoni (1997), as is evident in the higher pitch and the rising inflections that are the main characteristics of "baby talk." Infants simply seem to attend more to this type of speech.

Sound Discriminations in Infants There appears to be little doubt that infants are extraordinarily attuned to hearing human speech sounds and to discriminating among them. It is amazing that an infant as young as 3 days is able to discriminate among different voices and seems to prefer the sound of its mother's voice. In a study in which systematic changes in an infant's sucking were reinforced with the sound of a woman reading a book, the infant responded strongly to its mother's voice (DeCasper & Fifer, 1980). DeCasper and Fifer suggest these findings are evidence that a fetus can hear sounds while in the uterus and can distinguish among them.

By the age of 6 months, infants have not only learned to discriminate among a wide variety of human sounds, but have also begun to assign meanings to many of them. This is also the case with music and songs. Rock, Trainor, and Addison (1999) played one of two versions of the same song recorded by mothers for their 6-month-old infants: a "play-song-style" version (more "brilliant, clipped, and rhythmic") or a "lullaby-song-style" version (more "airy, smooth, and soothing"). Adults who later looked at videotapes of the infants, without knowing which song they had been listening to, had no difficulty in picking out the two groups. When they heard the lullabies, infants tended to become quiet and to focus inward; but when they heard play-type songs, they became more animated and more externally focused.

Smell, Taste, and Touch

We know that newborns are highly sensitive to smells and tastes from birth. Within hours of birth, they turn their faces away when exposed to a strong and unpleasant smell like ammonia (Lipsitt, Engen, & Kaye, 1963). And their facial expressions are distinctly different when they are exposed to the smell of vanilla and to that of raw fish (Steiner, 1979). Like many adults, they like the smell of raw fish less than that of vanilla.

In much the same way, newborns smack their lips when sweet things are placed on their tongues; and they pucker their mouths in response to sour tastes. In fact, even premature infants respond differently to sweet than to nonsweet tastes (Bartoshuk & Beauchamp, 1994). As grandmothers have long suspected, and as science has now confirmed, giving crying newborns sucrose seems highly effective in quieting them. Giving them quinine, however, leads to an expression of "disgust." And giving them plain corn oil or water has little effect (Graillon et al., 1997).

Smell, explains Farbman (1994), is one of the most important senses for driving the behavior of most of Earth's animal species. Without a powerful sense of smell—and of taste—most animals would be in grave danger of not finding food or of poisoning themselves. It should hardly be surprising that newborns are highly sensitive to odors, as well as to tastes and touch. In fact, there is evidence of fetal sensitivity to odors as early as 28 weeks after conception (Bartoshuk & Beauchamp, 1994). Bartoshuk and Beauchamp speculate that it's possible that human infants begin to learn about the mother's diet and characteristic odors before they are born. Exposure to flavors in amniotic fluid, as well as in mother's milk, might have much to do with later food preferences (Mennella & Beauchamp, 1996; 1997).

Pain Sensitivity Earlier investigators had concluded that the neonate is remarkably insensitive to much of the stimulation that children and adults would find quite painful. Circumcision doesn't really hurt boy babies, they assured us. But they (whoever they are) were probably at least partly wrong: Boy babies do holler when circumcised! And more recent research indicates that neonates of both sexes are sensitive to pain. McLaughlin and colleagues' (1993) survey of 352 physicians found that the vast majority now agree that newborns feel pain.

Summary of the Newborn's Capacities

Neonates are remarkably alert and well suited to their environments. They can hear, see, and smell; they can turn in the direction of food, suck, swallow, digest, and eliminate; they can respond physically to a small range of stimuli; and they can cry and vomit. Still, they are singularly helpless creatures who would surely die if the environment did not include adults intimately concerned with their survival. There is much they need to learn, much with which they must become familiar before they can stand on their own two feet—not only physically, but cognitively as well. (See the following *Concept Summary.*)

MEMORY IN INFANTS

We know that infants are born with an impressive array of tools for cognition—tools that will eventually allow them to know and understand things they cannot yet even dream about. They can look and see; they can hear; they can smell and taste. And more impressive than anything else, they have an astonishing brain. In fact, everything we have learned about infants thus far reinforces the view that they are remarkably ready to become familiar with their world. "Babies are very competent," Bower (1989) informs us. "They are set to use whatever information we give them" (p. ix).

But, competent though they might be, they know so little; there is so much to learn and so little time to do it if they are to be as competent at the age of 2 as most of them will surely be. How do they learn? What do they learn? How do they remember? What do they know in the beginning, and what do they know at the end? Answers to these questions fill the remainder of this chapter.

Studying Infant Memory

If neonates, ignorant and helpless as they are at birth, are ever to reach the level of competence of the 2-year-old, there is much that must be organized

CONCEPT SUMMARY
Perceptual Development in Infancy

Sensation	• The physiological effect of stimulation on the sense organs; specifically, the translation of stimulation into neural impulses
Perception	• The brain's interpretation of sensation; the recognition of what is perceived
Conceptualization	• Conscious interpretation of the significance of perception; thinking; a more cognitive process
Characteristics of infant vision	• World somewhat fuzzy at birth; about 20/600 vision • Built-in accommodation for about 12 inches • Very limited color vision at birth; better by about 2 months • Ability to perceive depth present before infant can crawl • Infants look at reds and blues longer than at other colors • Recognize and prefer faces within days of birth • Prefer mother's face (hence recognize it) within 2 days • Prefer attractive to unattractive faces
Rules of visual perception	The objective is to maximize neural firing, hence maximize information by: • Keeping eyes open when awake • Maintaining searching eye movements even in darkness • Searching for edges using broad scans • When edge is found, changing to shorter eye movements to scan edge
Hearing	• Hearing present even prenatally • Recognize and prefer mother's voice within days of birth
Smell, taste, touch	• High sensitivity to odors • Preference for mother's smell • Possibility that some flavor preferences originate from prenatal learning • Preference for sweet tastes • Sensitivity to pain present in newborns

and stored in their **memory**. They must learn and remember what is edible and what isn't; how to get from here to there, or from there to here; how to ask for things; how to hold a cup; how to get people's interest and attention; and much more.

A neonate's memory does not appear to be nearly as efficient and powerful as yours or mine. Nor is it an easy thing to study, given that preverbal infants cannot easily tell the investigator what they remember.

The Orienting Response One way of investigating memory in very young infants is to look at the **orienting response**. Defined simply, the orienting response is our tendency (and that of other animals)

---

memory Relates to the storage of the effects of experience. May be evident in the ability to recognize or to recollect previous experiences, or in changes in behavior as a result of experience.

to respond to new stimulation by becoming more alert—that is, by attending or orienting to it. In animals such as dogs and cats, the orienting response is clear. On hearing a new sound, for example, a dog will pause and its ears may perk up and turn slightly toward the sound; its attitude says, in effect, "What the %$*#! was that?" The human infant may not respond so obviously, but distinct and measurable changes take place: alterations in pupil size, acceleration or deceleration of heart rate, changes in the conductivity of the skin to electricity (galvanic skin response [GSR], also termed electrodermal response), and other physiological changes that are observable by using sensitive instruments. These responses, in combination, define the human orienting response.

Habituation The value of the orienting response to child psychologists is that it can be used as an indication of attention, because it occurs only in response to a novel stimulation to which a child is then attending. It can also be used as an indication of learning because when an infant has learned a stimulus (when the stimulus has become familiar), the orienting reaction no longer takes place or at least decreases. This decrease in the orienting reaction is termed **habituation**. In a simple study of memory, for example, researchers might look at an infant's response to a single photograph (or other stimulus) presented on two different occasions. If the infant remembers something about the photograph, heart rate would not be expected to change in the same way as it might when the infant is presented with a completely new photograph.

When infants are older, of course, memory can often be studied by looking at behaviors that the infant can now control. For example, Rovee-Collier and her associates (1980) taught 3-month-old infants to make a mobile turn by moving their feet (each infant's foot was fastened to a lever that when

moved, caused the mobile to move). Infants remembered the procedure several weeks later.

With even older infants, studies of memory are often more similar to those conducted with children and adults. Many of these studies involve language. Researchers ask participants questions and make inferences about what they remember on the basis of their responses.

Characteristics of Infant Memory

Using these various approaches, investigators have found that even newborns have memories. True, they are not very elaborate memories, but they are a beginning. As we saw, for example, within days of birth, newborns are able to recognize their mothers' voice and smell. This seems to be clear evidence of memory, although it may be memory for prenatal learning rather than for new learning (Mennella & Beauchamp, 1997).

Evidence of retention of *new* learning has been found in neonates within the first 24 hours of birth. In one study, Swain, Zelazo, and Clifton (1993) had 1-day-old newborns listen to a word and then monitored them as they turned their heads toward the sound. Within a short period of time, these infants habituated to the word and stopped turning. One day later, half of these infants were again exposed to the same word; the other half heard a different word. Again, all infants initially oriented to the word, turning their heads toward it. But those who were exposed to the same word both days habituated significantly more rapidly than those who heard a new word—clear evidence that they remembered something of the word.

Still, evidence suggests that an infant's memory for most things appears to be of relatively short duration. For example, young infants who are conditioned to associate a puff of air with a tone, or a feeding schedule with a bell, may remember from one day to the next, or even perhaps for 6 or 10 days. But with no reminders in the interim, all evidence of memory is likely to be gone within a few days. However, various reminders, as Rovee-Collier (1987) showed, can reinstate apparently lost infant memories. In an intriguing series of studies, Rovee-Collier (1999) tied strings from a colorful mobile to the ankles of 3-month-old infants. The infants

---

orienting response The initial response of humans and other animals to novel stimulation. Also called the orienting reflex or orientation reaction. Components of the orienting response include changes in EEG patterns, respiration rate, heart rate, and galvanic skin response.

habituation To become accustomed to as a function of repetition. Habituation is evident when the organism no longer responds as it would to a novel stimulus.

quickly learned to kick their legs. And if the infants were put back in the cribs 1 week later and again attached to the mobiles, they quickly started to kick again: They had not forgotten what they had learned. But if they were put back in the cribs 2 weeks later, they kicked no more than infants who had never before been attached to a mobile: They appeared to remember nothing of an experience a mere 2 weeks old.

But in another series of experiments, Rovee-Collier and Hayne (1987) showed that the infants did in fact remember; they simply needed a reminder. In these experiments, they placed the infants back in the crib 2 weeks after training, but they didn't attach them to the mobile this time. Instead they had them lie there very briefly while the mobiles were jiggled. And when these infants were again attached to the mobile the next day, they kicked about as vigorously and determinedly as they had two weeks earlier.

Infantile Amnesia

It seems clear that memories of very young infants are far more fragile than adult memories; they are much more likely to be lost. Yet, by the age of 18 months to 2 years, infants' long-term memories are quite remarkable—as is evident because by that age most have learned, and will remember, hundreds of words. It's true, however, that they will be reminded of these words repeatedly. And it's also true that in the end, they will consciously remember virtually nothing of any of the specific experiences they have had as children. In fact, we all seem to be victims of this strange phenomenon labeled infantile amnesia: We recall nothing of the experiences of our infancies, and even of our early preschool periods. And there is as yet no agreed-upon explanation for this phenomenon, says Eacott (1999). One theory is that parts of the infant's brain associated with memory are insufficiently mature to permit long-term remembering; another is that the infant's memory strategies are too primitive to allow the organization and associations required; still another is that there can be no memory of personal events before the infant develops a strong sense of self with which to associate them (Howe & Courage, 1993). (See Chapter 7 for more information on infantile amnesia.)

Development of Infant Memory

Notwithstanding the fact that reminders can increase infant memory, the duration of infant memories are typically much shorter than that of adult memories. But, says Rovee-Collier (1999), they become progressively longer during the first $1^1/2$ years of life.

Perlmutter (1980) describes three sequential phases in the development of memory in infants. In the first phase, an infant's memory seems to be largely a matter of neurons firing when a new stimulus is presented and stopping with habituation. As the infant becomes more familiar with the stimulus (that is, learns and remembers), the period before habituation becomes shorter.

The second phase, which begins at around 3 months, is related to the infant's growing ability to accomplish intended actions. Infants now actively look and search; they begin to reach, even to grasp; they explore; and they recognize things and people. Recognition is a sure sign of memory.

In the third phase, by the age of 8 months or so, infant memories have become much more like our own in that they are more abstract and more symbolic. They remember classes of things like fuzzy objects and big people and pets and building blocks and beets.

Memory in adults and in older children is greatly facilitated by certain strategies, the most important of which are organization, rehearsal, and elaboration. Although infants do not systematically use any of these strategies, 2-year-olds already have some notions about what memory is and understand mental-event terms such as *remember*, *think*, *know*, and *pretend*. When asked to remember something, they pay attention and they try to remember. These actions, says Wellman (1988), are strategies in their own right.

There is a great gulf between the immature memory of the week-old child who can demonstrate a vague recollection of a familiar smell or sound, and that of the 1-year-old who mistakenly yells "Dada" when he sees a stranger's familiar-looking back in the supermarket. There is also a vast difference between this 1-year-old's memory and the memory of a 12-year-old, whose intellectual strategies permit mental feats of which the 1- year-old cannot yet even dream. (See Chapter 7 for more information about memory.)

SOME INTELLECTUAL ACHIEVEMENTS AND CHALLENGES OF INFANCY

The infant's rapidly developing memory makes possible a range of intellectual achievements—achievements that we, as adults, tend to take quite for granted. That I recognize my computer this morning, that I know it's the same computer that I left here last night, that I can anticipate the contents of this file before I open it, that I can intend to say to you what I am saying at this very moment—none of these things would be possible if I had no reliable memory of these matters, or if I did not know that I can control the actions that will turn my intentions into realities.

Matters are not exactly so for the infant, and not only because in the beginning, infants cannot control their own actions. Even if they could control their actions, they would also need to have some understanding of intention, of how means can be invented and bent and guided toward goals. And perhaps even more basic, they would need to know that objects are real and permanent, that they have an independent existence.

The Object Concept

But, says Piaget, infants act as if they don't know that the world is permanent and fixed, and that it continues to exist even when it isn't being looked at or touched or tasted. In his words, they haven't yet developed what he termed the **object concept**. An infant's world is a "blooming, buzzing mass of confusion," William James (1890) asserted more than a century ago. In those years, psychologists believed that a neonate's senses don't function at birth; or they function very poorly, so that colors, sounds, smells, and tastes are all indistinct and blurred. As we saw earlier, these psychologists were wrong: Children see movements and shapes almost from birth, they can detect and remember odors, and they can hear even before they are born.

---

object concept Piaget's expression for a child's understanding that the world is composed of objects that continue to exist quite apart from the child's immediate perception of them.

According to Piaget, an infant's world is a world of the *here* and *now*, a world without permanent objects. The nipple exists when the infant sees, touches, or sucks it; when it can't be sensed, it doesn't exist. Imagine what the world would be like, suggest Wellman and Gelman (1992), if we thought objects disappeared and reappeared—that is, if we had no concept of objective objects. This object concept, they explain, is absolutely fundamental to our reasoning about the world; our very conception of the world demands that objects be real, out there, substantive, and independent of us. There is no "out there" for infants; they must discover the permanence and objectivity of objects for themselves. This discovery is one of the truly great achievements of infancy.

Discovering Object Permanence Experiencing and exploring the real world are fundamental to learning that objects are permanent. In a series of investigations, Stambak et al. (1989) videotaped young infants' responses to different objects, such as nesting cups or hollow cubes or rods. Analysis of these videotapes reveals that even very young infants organize their behaviors in systematic ways, that their exploration is not simply the random exercising of behaviors. Thus, some infants typically banged different objects with a rod; some explored the insides of the hollow cubes with their fingers, or with their hands if the cubes were large enough. In a sense, it is as though infants have already begun to invent questions and problems and to devise little experiments to find the answers.

Not only does the exploration of objects by young infants become increasingly systematic with advancing age, but it also involves more varied activities. By the age of 3 or 4 months, most infants use both mouth and hands to explore. And, significantly, type of manipulation depends more and more on the objects being explored. Some things are more easily understood, more meaningful, when held in both hands, licked, drooled on, and gummed emphatically.

Piaget's Classic Object Concept Study To investigate infants' understanding of objects, Piaget (1954) showed children an attractive object and then hid it from view. If the object exists only when infants perceive it, reasoned Piaget, they will make no effort to look for it when they can't see it—even if they actually saw it being hidden. When children begin to look for an object they can no longer see, this is definite evidence that they can imagine it, and that they know the thing still exists.

Piaget noted that in the first few months of life, children did not continue to seek the object once it was removed. Then, by about 8 months, they may begin to search for the object if it has just been hidden. If a few seconds have passed, they are likely not to search at all. And if an object is hidden in one location—say under pillow A—and then moved to a second location *in full view of the child*—say pillow B—even a 12-month-old is likely to search only under pillow A and abandon the search when the object isn't found.

According to Piaget, this demonstration, replicated countless times, illustrates that until perhaps age 18 months, the infant has an incomplete and somewhat fragile understanding of the permanence of objects.

Another Interpretation Other investigators argue, however, that Piaget's test may not be entirely convincing, and that other approaches might lead to different observations. For example, Baillargeon (1987; Baillargeon & DeVos, 1991) conducted a series of investigations in which infants didn't have to reach or look for objects to demonstrate they understood something about their permanence. In one study, infants are habituated to a screen that rotates back and forth in front of them, through an arc of 180°. Then a box is placed behind the screen in full view of the infant, and in one test event (possible event), the screen rotates until it hits the hidden object, and then it reverses direction and goes back to its original position. In the other test event (impossible event), the screen rotates right through where the hidden box should be (it has been removed through a trapdoor). If infants don't have an understanding of the permanence of objects, argues Baillargeon, they

> **THOUGHT CHALLENGE:** *Does the fact that infants don't look for a hidden object prove that they don't realize that objects have an independent and objective existence?*

should be no more surprised at the impossible than at the possible event. But in fact, many of them spend more time looking at the impossible event. This, says Baillargeon (1987), suggests that infants understood that: "(a) the box continued to exist after it was occluded by the screen and (b) the screen could not rotate through the space occupied by the occluded box" (p. 656).

A second experiment makes much the same point (Baillargeon & DeVos, 1991). In this study, a short or a long carrot moves behind a windowless yellow screen on a track, so that they disappear from the infant's view. When the infant has habituated to these two events (that is, looks at them for about the same time), the windowless yellow screen is replaced with a blue one that has a window cut out of the top. The short carrot will still not be visible as it passes behind the screen, but the long one should be. That it isn't (due to the experimenters' surreptitious manipulations) would be surprising only if infants expected it to be (see Figure 5.10). Apparently many did, even at the age of 3.5 months, as is evident because they looked longer at the impossible event.

Do such findings mean that Piaget was wrong? Do infants have a notion of the permanence and independent identity of objects a long time before the age of 18 months? Perhaps. What these studies clearly indicate is that under the proper circumstances, infants appear to have a short-lived recollection of absent objects. In addition, infants as young as 3 or 4 months have begun to understand that objects are solid and stationary. In Baillargeon and De Vos's words, "Young infants are aware that objects (a) cannot exist at two successive points in time without having existed during the interval between them, (b) cannot appear at two separate points in space without having traveled the distance between them, and (c) cannot move through the space occupied by other objects" (p. 1245). Furthermore, infants appear to be able to use this knowledge to make predictions about objects and their probable and possible movements.

But, says Greenberg (1996), objects really aren't permanent at all. In fact, as the philosopher Hegel pointed out, nothing is truly permanent, and much of learning involves learning not about the permanence of objects, but about their impermanence.

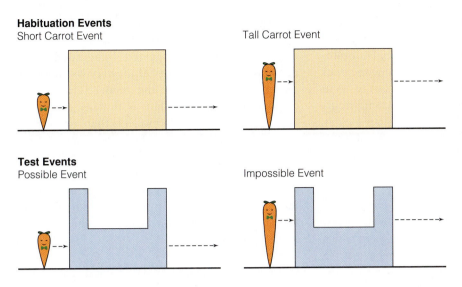

Habituation Events
Short Carrot Event

Tall Carrot Event

Test Events
Possible Event

Impossible Event

FIGURE 5.10 Representation of the *Tall and Short Carrot* demonstration. In this demonstration, infants as young as 3.5 months acted as though they were surprised when the tall carrot did not appear in the window (impossible event)—as though they understood something of the permanence and expected movements of the carrot. Source: Baillargeon, R., & J. DeVos (1991). Object permanence in young artists: Further evidence. *Child Development* 62: 1227–1246 (p. 1230). Reprinted with permission.

Impermanence, says Greenberg, has important cognitive and emotional implications. For one thing, the possibility of the destruction of an object (or a person, as happens when we die) is the basis of desiring or wanting. That we want some things so badly is evidence that we understand that they are potentially impermanent, that eventually we may lose them. That Piaget and his followers (and critics) have paid no attention to object impermanence, says Greenberg, is a weakness of these approaches.

Of course Piaget didn't mean to say that objects are always and irreversibly permanent. What he meant to say was that infants often act *as if* they weren't aware of the *relative* permanence of things, or that their occupation of space and movements therein follow certain rules of physics. And yes, it's probably true that he underestimated the ages at which infants might begin to achieve these understandings. But as Haith (1998) points out, researchers are often guilty of errors directly opposite to those of Piaget: They are guilty of too "rich" an interpretation of infant cognition. For example, on the basis of a few additional seconds of looking at a presumably impossible situation, we want to infer that infants understand things about objects that they probably don't. And the fact is that even though 4-month-old infants might seem surprised at the disappearance of expected objects, it will be a long time before they begin to look for these objects when someone has hidden them before their very eyes (Bower, 1989).

Intention and Imitation

Looking for a hidden object presupposes more than the realization that the object is permanent—that it does, in fact, exist under the pillow or in the hall closet. It assumes as well that the infant is capable of forming the **intention** of searching for it, and is also capable of acting out that intention.

In its ordinary sense, *intentional* means purposeful or deliberate. The difference between intentional and unintentional behaviors is captured by the distinction between *action* and *reaction* (Olson, Astington, & Zelazo, 1999). An action is a deliberate—hence intentional—act; a reaction is a response to a stimulus. Moral behavior (and immoral behavior as well) presupposes actions rather than reactions. That is, morality assumes the ability to form prior intentions.

The laws of many societies often assume that infants, and even much older children, are incapable of immoral acts simply because they are incapable either of forming prior intentions or of understanding the implications of their behaviors. One of the important questions for developmental psychologists is, when are infants capable of intentional behavior? At first glance it's a relatively difficult question, given

intention Relating to conscious, deliberate purposefulness. The ability to form intentions is central to guiding behavior, and is also the basis of morality.

that preverbal infants can hardly explain their intentions or their goals. Still, infants do many things that show at least the beginnings of intention. For example, they very quickly learn to follow someone else's gaze to see what they're looking at. This sort of "joint attention" says Flavell (1999), is an important precursor to intentional communication. Also, they look at, point to, or hold up objects apparently with the *intention* of having someone else react. Finally, infants' persistent attempts to imitate provide clear evidence of intention.

Imitation in Very Young Infants Imitation, as we saw in Chapter 2, is one of the important ways in which we learn new things or modify old behaviors. In some ways, it appears to be a natural, unlearned way of learning. But is it? Can newborns imitate?

Some researchers think yes; others don't agree (Wyrwicka, 1996). Some researchers report that at a mere 2 weeks of age, infants are already able to imitate simple actions like sticking out the tongue or opening the mouth wide (for example, Meltzoff & Moore, 1989; Ullstadius, 1998). Reissland (1988) claims to have detected imitation in the first hour after birth. His subjects were 12 awake and alert neonates; models bent over them, widening or pursing their lips as instructed. The results? Infants moved their lips in accordance with lip movements of the models significantly more often than at variance with them. Reissland concludes that the ability to imitate is already present at birth.

Other researchers don't agree that neonates are actually imitating when they stick out their tongue or purse their lips in apparent response to a model doing the same thing. Perhaps infants do not truly imitate these facial gestures, but instead simply manifest a generalized, almost reflexive response related mainly to feeding and released by the nearness of the model (Kaitz et al., 1988). It is possible, says Anisfeld (1991), that increased tongue protrusion following modeling occurs because tongue protrusion has been inhibited during modeling. Also, it's highly telling that the only behaviors that newborns seem to be able to imitate (and often very badly, or not at all) are opening the mouth, sticking out the tongue, or protruding the lips—all behaviors closely linked with the rooting, sucking, and swallowing reflexes.

Meltzoff and Moore (1989) concede that imitative behavior in the newborn is not completely automatic and easily triggered. In addition, many of the imitative behaviors of the very young infant do not continue when the model is no longer present. That is, the infant is initially capable of imitating only when the model is there or within a very short period of time thereafter. Piaget (1951) suggested that **deferred imitation**—the ability to imitate something or someone no longer present— is not likely to occur before the age of 9 to 12 months. The ability to imitate an action after the fact is strong evidence of the infant's ability to *represent mentally*.

Imitation in Older Infants The second year of life, claims Masur (1993), following a longitudinal study of 10 boys and 10 girls between 10 and 21 months of age, is a crucial period for the infant's burgeoning ability to represent mentally and to imitate. Although repetition of familiar behaviors like tongue protrusion might occur among very young infants, it isn't until the beginning of the second year that infants begin to imitate novel actions. In fact, some researchers point out that at about 9 months, there appears to be something of a revolution in the infant's understanding of others and of their intentions—a revolution evident in the development of what is labeled **theory of mind**. Theory of mind refers to the set of intuitive notions infants and children develop about their minds and those of others, as well as about things like beliefs and intentions (we discuss the development of theories of mind in Chapter 10). Evidence of this revolution, says Tomasello (1999), is found in the fact that infants between the ages of 9 and 12 months now begin to engage in triadic interactions. These are interactions involving not just the infant and another person, but also involving some outside entity such as another person or an object to which

deferred imitation Imitating people or events in their absence. Deferred imitation is assumed by Piaget to be critical to developing language abilities.

theory of mind The intuitive notions children have about the existence and characteristics of their own and others' minds. A theory of mind allows a child to predict and explain behavior by relating it to mental states such as beliefs and intentions.

both the infant and the adult direct their attention. Thus, at this age infants look where others are looking (**gaze following**), and they begin to look for the reactions of adults and other children to guide their own reactions (social referencing). Also, they now engage in persistent attempts to imitate.

Imitation provides a powerful tool for new learning—and especially for learning language. But the older infant's imitation is not limited to imitating and learning only from adults. Toddlers (older infants) imitating other toddlers is highly evident in child-care facilities. For example, Hanna and Meltzoff (1993) describe a series of experiments in which 14- to 18-month-old infants readily learned to imitate other "trained" toddlers.

Studies of infant imitation provide impressive evidence of the infant's growing ability to make inferences about other people's intentions. For example, Meltzoff (Meltzoff, Gopnik, & Repacholi, 1999) had 18-month-old infants watch while an adult performed an unsuccessful action. The reasoning is that if the infant later imitated what the model actually did, even though it didn't work, then all that might be involved is a simple, straightforward type of copying. But if the infant tried to imitate the "intended" act, then we might assume that a correct inference has been made about the actor's intentions. In one study, for example, the experimenter seems to be trying to pull apart a small dumbbell, but fails. In the testing phase, infants typically try to accomplish the inferred intention rather than imitate the model's actions literally. In fact, in a variation of this experiment, when the infants were presented with oversized plastic dumbbells that they couldn't possibly hold in the same way as the model, they made no attempt to mimic the model's surface behavior. Instead they tried novel solutions, like placing the dumbbell on a table and pulling on the other end with both hands (Meltzoff, Gopnik, & Repacholi, 1999).

Achievements of Imitation in Infancy There are at least three different kinds of learning that imitation

makes possible for infants, claim Hay, Stimson, and Castle (1991). First, they learn about places by following people around, in much the same way that young kittens and other animals learn about places by following their mothers and siblings. When given the opportunity, infants readily follow their mothers in unfamiliar surroundings; often, too, they will follow strangers or a moving toy. Significantly, once they have followed a leader, they are more likely to go back and explore on their own.

Second, imitation facilitates certain familiar social behaviors, like sharing toys. When experimenters (or parents, or siblings) play "give and take" games with infants, infants are subsequently more likely to want to give toys to others.

Third, infants learn new social behaviors by observing them in others. And among the most important of new behaviors that they learn, at least partly through imitation, are those that have to do with speaking and understanding a language. (See *Across Cultures*: "Saliswa, an African Child.")

BASIC PIAGETIAN IDEAS ON INFANCY

We saw earlier that Piaget may have underestimated the capacities of young infants. Still, his description of the development of the infant's intellect continues to be one of the richest sources of ideas for research, for debate, and for practical applications.

The Processes of Adaptation

In the beginning, Piaget tells us, the infant's world is a world of the here and now. He asserts because the infant has no *object concept*, the world makes sense only when the infant looks at it, hears it, touches it, smells it, or tastes it. Nor does the infant have concepts in the sense that we think of them—no store of memories or hopes or dreams, no fund of information with which to think. But what neonates have are the sensory systems and the cognitive inclinations that make them into a self-reinforcing, information-processing organism. When Piaget describes infants, he speaks of organisms that continually seek out and

gaze following The human tendency to look where others are looking, presumably based on the assumption that if someone else is looking or—even more—if many people are looking simultaneously, there must surely be something worth looking at. Gaze following is readily apparent in infants beginning around 9 to 12 months.

ACROSS CULTURES

Saliswa, an African Child

"In ethnographic literature about African peoples," writes Reynolds (1989), "reference is often made to 'the African child' as if such a composite creature exists" (p. 2). We make the same mistake in psychology. We insist "there is no average child," but then we keep talking about this nonexistent creature.

Saliswa is not just an average African child. She is one of many Xhosa children who, in 1980, lived in an urban squatter settlement about 20 miles (33 kilometers) from the center of Cape Town, South Africa. Saliswa, then 2, lived in a shack built of discarded panels of corrugated metal, framed with scraps of lumber, lined with bits of paper and plastic, and having a cardboard floor.

Major day-to-day problems in Saliswa's settlement involve getting water; staying warm in winter and cool enough in summer; getting access to schools, hospitals, shops, and "crèches" (child-care facilities); and managing to cook on paraffin stoves without burning the house down. "We sleep on our graves," said one of Saliswa's neighbors (Reynolds, 1989, p. 20).

There are other, perhaps even more serious, problems. For years, the Xhosas lived under the heel of South Africa's apartheid policies. The shacks they built in the sand were considered illegal; often they were torn down or burned before their eyes. Parents were imprisoned for being in "white man's territory." Children were beaten or sometimes killed; their lives were surrounded by violence. Yet, notes

Reynolds (1989), there was remarkably little violence in either their interactions with each other or their games. Educational opportunities were highly limited, future mobility and career opportunities almost nonexistent. (With the recent free elections in South Africa, these apartheid policies may now be history.)

Like Saliswa, more than 300 million of the world's children live in squatter's settlements, most of them in the poorest of Third World countries. And although more than 90% of all children in the developing world now start school, fewer than two-thirds reach fourth grade (Bellamy, 1999).

Military expenditures have increased by more than 5% over the past two decades in six of the poorest countries in Africa (Uganda, Burkina, Tanzania, Kenya, Liberia, and Malawi); however, during this same period, welfare expenditures have declined in each of these countries, sometimes by as much as 50%. In 1990, each spent about five times more on their militaries than on social programs (Grant, 1992).

To Think About: What impact do you suppose Saliswa's context might have on her fantasies? Her dreams? Her play? Her intellectual development?

Resources: R. O. Ohuche and B. Otaalam's (1981) *The African child and his environment* (Pergamon Press) summarizes a large number of studies that have looked at children's environments in 13 countries of sub-Saharan Africa.

---

respond to stimulation and that, by so doing, gradually build up a repertoire of behaviors and capabilities.

Adapting by Assimilating and Accommodating At first, infants' behaviors are limited mainly to the simple reflexes they are born with; but in time these behaviors become more elaborate and more coordinated with one another. The process by which this occurs is **adaptation**, and the complementary processes that make adaptation possible are assimilation and accommodation (see Chapter 2).

To review briefly, assimilation and accommodation are highly active processes whereby an individual searches out, selects, and responds to information, the end result of which is the actual construction of knowledge. Imagine, for example, a young child walking on a windblown beach, stooping now and again to pick up pebbles and toss them into the water. In Piaget's view, there is a schema involved here—a sort of mental or cognitive representation—that corresponds to the child's knowl-

---

adaptation The process whereby an organism changes in response to the environment. Such changes are assumed to facilitate interaction with that environment. Adaptation plays a central role in Piaget's theory.

edge of the suitability of pebbles as objects to be thrown upon the waves, as well as other schemata that concern the activities involved in bending, retrieving, and throwing. The pebbles are in a sense being *assimilated to* appropriate schemata; they are understood and used based on the child's previous knowledge.

Imagine, now, that the child bends to retrieve another pebble but finds instead that she has picked up a piece of driftwood. The wood is clearly not a pebble, and perhaps it should not be responded to in the same way. But still, why not? The "throwing things on the big waves" schema is readily available and momentarily preferred, and so the wood too is assimilated to the throwing schema. The child tries to hurl it toward the water, but the new object's heaviness is surprising, the child's throwing motion is inadequate, and the driftwood fails to reach the surf. Now, when she picks it up again, she doesn't hurl it in quite the same way. She holds it in two hands, grasps it tightly with her pudgy little fingers, and pushes hard with her little legs as she throws. In Piaget's terms, she has *accommodated* to the characteristics of this object that make it different from the pebbles she has been throwing.

Equilibration To simplify these sometimes difficult concepts, to assimilate is to respond in light of preexisting information. It often involves ignoring some aspects of the situation to make it conform to aspects of the mental system. In contrast, to accommodate is to respond to external characteristics and to make changes in the mental system as a result. And one of the governing principles that guides mental activity, says Piaget, is our sort of inborn tendency to find a balance between accommodation and assimilation. This tendency is labeled **equilibration**.

At one extreme, if an infant always assimilated but never accommodated, there would be no change in schemata (mental structure), no change in behavior, and, by definition, no learning. Everything would be assimilated to the sucking schema, the grasping schema, the looking schema (that is, everything would be sucked or grasped or simply looked

equilibration A Piagetian term for the process by which we maintain a balance between assimilation (using old learning) and accommodation (changing behavior; learning new things). Equilibration is essential for adaptation and cognitive growth.

at). Such a state of disequilibrium would result in little adaptation and little cognitive growth.

At the other extreme, if everything were accommodated to and not assimilated, schemata —and behavior—would be in a constant state of flux: First the nipple would be sucked, then it would be chewed, now pinched, then swatted. Again, such an extreme state of disequilibrium would result in little adaptation.

Factors That Shape Adaptation Equilibration, says Piaget, is an internal tendency that governs the balance between assimilation and accommodation and that accounts for the construction of knowledge; that is, it accounts for adaptation and cognitive growth throughout development. But equilibration is only one of the four forces that shape development (Piaget, 1961). Another is maturation, a sort of biologically determined unfolding of potential. Maturation—or biology—does not determine cognitive growth but is related to the unfolding of potential. A third factor is *active experience*, a child's interaction with the world. The fourth is *social interaction*, which helps a child develop ideas about things, about people, and about the self. These four factors—active experience, maturation, equilibration, and social interaction—are the cornerstones of Piaget's basic theory.

Sensorimotor Development

Piaget believed that children's understanding of the world throughout most of infancy is determined by the activities they can perform on it and by their perceptions of it—hence his label *sensorimotor*. He further simplifies infant development by describing six sequential substages, each marked by different predominant behaviors and different achievements. Although, as discussed earlier, recent studies have shown that infants do not necessarily move through clear stages in the time frame Piaget predicted. His descriptions of stages and substages remain a useful general guide. (See the following *Concept Summary*.)

1. **Ready-made reflexes (birth to 1 month)**
   According to Piaget, during the first stage, which lasts about a month, infants spend much of their waking time exercising the abilities they

Piaget's Stages of Cognitive Development

Stage	Approximate Age	Some Major Characteristics
Sensorimotor	0–2 years	Motoric intelligence World of the here and now No language, no thought in early stages No notion of objective reality
Preoperational (7)* Preconceptual Intuitive	2–7 years 2–4 years 4–7 years	Egocentric thought Reason dominated by perception Intuitive rather than logical solutions Inability to conserve
Concrete operations (9)	7–11 or 12 years	Ability to conserve Logic of classes and relations Understanding of number Thinking bound to concrete Development of reversibility in thought
Formal operations (11)	11 or 12–14 or 15 years	Complete generality of thought Propositional thinking Ability to deal with the hypothetical Development of strong idealism

*Numbers in parentheses refer to chapters containing detailed information.

are born with (sucking, looking, and crying, for example). In addition to their obvious survival functions, these activities have an important cognitive function. By repeatedly performing these activities, an infant eventually develops control over them and begins to gain control over aspects of the environment. By the end of the first month, infants are quite proficient at directing their gaze and at finding things to suck. But they still have trouble putting different actions together (coordinating their behavior) to obtain a single goal. For example, infants presented with a visually appealing object can look at it but cannot reach toward it. The ability to look at an object and to continue looking at it when it moves (or when the child moves) precedes the ability to direct the hand toward the object (Provine & Westerman, 1979). Deliberately reaching and grasping is a complex activity that depends on the purposeful coordi-

nation of looking schemes, reaching schemes, and grasping schemes. This coordination is not usually apparent until after 3 to 5 months.

2. **Primary circular reactions (1 to 4 months)** Many of the infant's first behaviors are highly repetitive (thumb-sucking, for example). Piaget labels these behaviors **primary circular reactions**. Essentially, these behaviors are initially reflexive, and they serve as stimuli for their own repetition. For example, if an infant accidentally gets a hand or a finger into its mouth, this triggers the sucking response, which results in the sensation of the hand in the mouth. That sensation leads to a repetition of the response, which

primary circular reaction An expression used by Piaget to describe a simple reflex activity (such as thumb-sucking) that serves as a stimulus for its own repetition.

leads to a repetition of the sensation, which leads to a repetition of the response. This circle of action is called primary because it involves the infant's own body.

Despite the infant's ability at this substage to acquire new behaviors (new adaptations through accommodation to different stimulation), these new behaviors come about accidentally and always involve the child's body. Interaction with the world is still highly one-sided; it is still a world of the here and now, a world that exists and has meaning when it is doing something to the child or when the child is doing something to it.

3. **Secondary circular reactions (4 to 8 months)** During the third substage, according to Piaget, **secondary circular reactions** appear. Like primary circular reactions, they are circular because the responses stimulate their own repetition; but because they deal with objects in the environment rather than only with the infant's body, they are called secondary. Six-month-old infants engage in many secondary circular reactions. They accidentally do something that is interesting or amusing and then repeat it again and again. By kicking, Piaget's infant son caused a row of dolls dangling above his bassinet to dance. The boy stopped and watched the dolls. Eventually, he repeated the kicking, perhaps not intending to make the dolls move, but probably because they had stopped moving and no longer attracted his attention. As he kicked, the dolls moved again, and again he paused to look at them. In a very short time he was repeating the behavior over and over—a circular reaction.

This behavior, which Piaget described as "behavior designed to make interesting sights and sounds last," is especially important because it signals the beginning of intention. In Frye's (1991) words, these are behaviors in which infants "knowingly employ means to goals" (p. 15). Recall that this is much the same sort of

behavior as that which Rovee-Collier (1999) later used in her investigations of infant memory.

4. **Purposeful coordinations (8 to 12 months)** The development of intention becomes even more apparent, says Piaget, when in the fourth substage, infants acquire the ability to coordinate previously unrelated behaviors to achieve some desired goal. They can now look at an object, reach for it, grasp it, and bring it to the mouth with the intention of sucking it.

During this substage infants also begin to recognize familiar objects and people—which explains why they may now become upset when a parent leaves or when a stranger appears (see Chapter 6).

At this time, too, an infant begins to use signs to anticipate events: Daddy putting on his jacket is a sign that he is leaving. Understanding that certain events are signs that some other event is likely to occur is closely related to the ability to understand causality. For the young infant, whose logic is not always as perfect as yours or mine, the sign itself is often interpreted as the cause. A child who realizes that daddy will be leaving when he puts on his jacket knows that the cause of leaving is putting on the jacket— just as the cause of going to bed is taking a bath or putting on pajamas.

5. **Tertiary circular reactions (12 to 18 months)** In the fifth substage, infants begin to modify their repetitive behaviors deliberately to see what the effects will be, according to Piaget. Rayna, Sinclair, and Stambak (1989) observed this so-called **tertiary circular reaction** in the behavior of a 15-month-old girl whose current preoccupation was with breaking objects. Breaking something often seemed to lead to a repetition of the behavior (hence a circular response), but with deliberate variation (hence tertiary; recall that primary and secondary reactions are repetitive, with only occasional accidental variations). For

---

secondary circular reaction Infant responses that are circular in the sense that the response serves as a stimulus for its own repetition and secondary because the responses do not center on the child's body, as do primary circular reactions.

tertiary circular reaction Infant responses that are circular in the sense that the response serves as the stimulus for its own repetition, but the repeated response is not identical to the first response. This last characteristic, the altered response, distinguishes a tertiary circular reaction from a secondary circular reaction.

example, in one session she picked up a ball of clay, scratched at it until a piece came off, examined the piece, and then repeated the procedure several times, each time examining the clay on her finger. Next she noticed a ball of cotton, picked it up, and pulled it into two halves; then she pulled one of the halves into two more pieces, and so on, again and again. Similarly, in another session a 15-month-old boy who had been tearing apart bits of clay happened across a piece of spaghetti, pressed it to the floor, broke it, picked up the largest piece, broke it again, and repeated the process a number of times. Once finished, he attempted to break a short plastic stick and then a pipe cleaner; finally, he tore a sheet of paper into tiny bits.

The most important feature of tertiary circular reactions is that they are repetitive behaviors deliberately undertaken to see what their effects will be; that is, they are explorations.

6. **Mental representation (18 months to 2 years)** Toward the end of the sensorimotor period, says Piaget, infants are well on their way to making a transition from what has been an *action-based* (hence *sensorimotor*) intelligence to a progressively more *cognitive* (symbolic or representational) intelligence. Toward the end of this stage, there is mounting evidence that infants represent objects and events mentally. They can even occasionally combine these representations to arrive at mental solutions for problems, and they are now able to anticipate the consequences of many of their activities before actually executing them. In Piaget's terms, it is as though the child can now begin to internalize (represent mentally) actions and their consequences without in fact having to carry them out. We do this all the time. We call it *thinking*. One of the advantages of Piaget's use of the expression **internalizing actions** is that it draws attention to how closely the infant's (and the child's) thinking is linked to actual physi-

cal action. It emphasizes how important early experiences are in the development of thought.

The process of internalizing actions is well illustrated by Piaget's account of his daughter's behavior when she was given a partly open matchbox containing a small thimble. Because the opening was too small for her to withdraw the thimble, she had to open the box first. A younger infant would simply grope at the box, attempting clumsily to remove the thimble. But Piaget's daughter, then 22 months, appeared instead to be considering the problem. She opened and closed her mouth repeatedly as if displaying internal thought processes—as if, in a sense, imaging (and unconsciously illustrating with her mouth) the opening and closing of the box. Finally, she placed her finger directly into the box's partial opening, opened it, and removed the thimble. (See *Concept Summary*.)

EARLY LANGUAGE DEVELOPMENT

Piaget's 22-month-old daughter could not only solve the opening-the-box problem: If she so wished, she could tell the world about her triumph! And she could now do so not only by jumping up and down and shrieking, but also by using actual words.

Language and Communication

Despite its tremendous power, **language** is not always essential for communication (the transmission of messages)—as Piaget's daughter, jumping up and down and shrieking, clearly demonstrates. Animals that don't have language can nevertheless communicate danger. For example, white-tailed deer wave their tails when alarmed, and pronghorn antelope bristle their rump patches. And while these signals communicate danger to other members of the same species, they sometimes communicate a

---

internalizing actions Piaget's expression for the mental representation of events, their characteristics, their relationships, and their consequences. The expression recognizes that the infant's early thinking is closely tied to real actions. Our thinking is potentially more abstract, more symbolic, more removed from the concrete.

language Spoken language consists of complex arrangements of sounds that have accepted referents and can therefore be used for communication among humans, and to represent and invent meanings. Some languages, such as American Sign Language (ASL), are based on gestures and signs rather than sounds. ASL also permits communication as well as the representation and invention of concepts.

CONCEPT SUMMARY

Piaget's Six Substages of Sensorimotor Development

Substage and Approximate Age in Months	Principal Characteristics	Object Concept and Imitation
1. Exercising reflexes (0–1)	Simple, unlearned behaviors (schemes) such as sucking and looking are practiced and become more deliberate.	• Preparation for development of object concept. • Some evidence of imitation of facial gestures like opening the mouth.
2. Primary circular reactions (1–4)	Activities that center on the infant's body and that give rise to pleasant sensations are repeated (thumb-sucking, for example).	• Fleeting recollection of objects hidden from view for only a few seconds. • "Sporadic imitation," in Piaget's terms.
3. Secondary circular reactions (4–8)	Activities that do not center on the child's body but that lead to interesting sights or sounds are repeated (repeatedly moving a mobile, for example).	• Search for objects where they were last seen. • Evidence of realization that objects are solid. • Beginning of systematic imitation (of sounds, for example).
4. Purposeful coordinations (8–12)	Separate schemes become coordinated (such as the ability to look at an object and reach for it); familiar people and objects are recognized; primitive understanding of causality begins, implicit in the use of signs to anticipate events.	• Beginning of imitation of new models. • Systematic search for desired objects.
5. Tertiary circular reactions (12–18)	Repetition with variation (repeating a sound with a number of deliberate changes, for example) is experimented with.	• Widespread imitation of models, including peers. • Search for objects in a variety of locations.
6. Mental representation (18–24)	Transition between sensorimotor intelligence and a more cognitive intelligence is made; activity is internalized so that its consequences can be anticipated before its actual performance; language becomes increasingly important in cognitive development.	• Deferred imitation, the imitation models and actions that aren't present. • Sophisticated notion of the permanence of objects.

different message to members of other species (Alcock, 1984). The tail-waving of the white-tailed deer, for example, may be highly meaningful to the wolf. It says, in effect, "I've seen you, so forget it." And the wolf, who is the deer's main predator in many areas, reads the signal. He knows he can't ordinarily catch a healthy deer in a prolonged chase, so he lies down and licks his chops, and dreams of other deer and other hunts. Thus his reading of signals—his literacy—allows him to save his energy.

A Definition of Language

But the wolf's literacy, its ability to derive meanings from signals, is a far cry from the kind of communication made possible by language.

Language is much more than just words. Even birds can use words. In fact, I once raised a magpie that learned to speak many words. It could say, impressively clearly, "Wacky wants a beetle." But, even before the neighbor shot it, it probably could never have said, "A beetle wants Wacky, heh, heh," with the intention of conveying a different meaning. The magpie merely mimicked; it spoke words but had no use of language.

Language is the use of arbitrary sounds—or, in some cases, gestures, as in American Sign Language (ASL)—with accepted referents, that can be arranged in different sequences to convey different meanings. This definition includes what Brown (1973) describes as the three essential characteristics of language: *displacement*, *meaning*, and *productiveness*. These characteristics apply to ASL as well as to spoken language.

Language involves displacement because it makes possible the representation of objects and events that are not immediate—that are displaced—in both time and space. "The moon was a ghostly galleon," we can say, "tossed upon cloudy seas." Yet neither ghosts nor galleons, nor even moons nor seas, need be where we can touch them or see them. Indeed, what you and I can speak of need not be more real than our dreams. There is no limit to how far words can be *displaced* from the things they represent.

One of the primary functions of language is the communication of meaning. Although **psycholinguists**—those who study the relationship between language and human functioning—do not always agree about the best definition for meaning, we in our ordinary conversations tend to agree much more than disagree. Indeed, it is because you and I have similar meanings for words and sentences that we can communicate as we are now doing.

The third characteristic of language, **productiveness**, means that given a handful of words, a set of mutually accepted rules about how they can be combined, and agreement about the significance of the various pauses, intonations, and other characteristics of speech, we can produce meanings forever. Language presents so many possibilities for meaningful combinations that almost every day of your life you will say something that no one else has ever said in exactly the same way. Language makes you creative.

Elements of Spoken Language

There are four basic components of spoken language: phonology, semantics, syntax, and pragmatics. Because it is not a spoken language, American Sign Language does not share those components that have to do with sounds.

Phonology refers to the **phonemes** or sounds of a language. A phoneme is the simplest unit of language and is nothing more complex than a single sound such as that represented by a consonant or word. There are 45 phonemes in the English language.

Phonemes can be combined to form **morphemes**, which are the units of meaning (**semantics**) in language. The study of semantics—of meanings—is a complex philosophical/psychological issue, says Miller (1999). Yet the learning of meaningful speech sounds, of morphemes, is easily done by most infants. Morphemes may be made up of sounds such as *ing* or *ed*—word endings that affect the meanings of words—or of whole words. Children cannot produce morphemes until they can first pronounce the phonemes. Simply making the sound is not enough;

---

psycholinguists People who study the relationship between language (linguistics) and development, thinking, learning, and behaving (psychology).

---

productiveness The quality of language that allows its users to *produce* an almost unlimited range of meanings simply by combining words and using pauses, intonations, and so on, in different ways.

phonology The phonemes or sounds of a language.

phoneme The simplest unit of language, consisting of a single sound such as a vowel.

morphemes Combinations of phonemes that make up the meaningful units of a language.

semantics The component of language that relates to meaning or significance of sounds.

they must be able to make it when they intend to do so, and they must also be able to combine morphemes into meaningful combinations.

Organizing words into meaningful sentence units requires an intuitive knowledge of **syntax**, or grammar, the set of rules governing the combinations of words that will be meaningful and correct for the speakers of that language.

As children practice and master sounds (phonemes), meanings (semantics), and grammatical rules (syntax), they must also learn a large number of unspoken rules and conventions governing conversation. Put another way, they must learn the **pragmatics** of language. An implicit knowledge of pragmatics is what tells children when and how they should speak. It includes countless rules and practices governing manners of expression, intonation, accents, and all the other subtle variations that give different meanings to the same morphemes and that might vary appreciably from one context to another. For example, that parents use shorter sentences, speak in higher-pitched voices, and use more concrete names and fewer abstractions when speaking with young children than with other adults is a function of their knowledge of pragmatics.

Phonology, semantics, syntax, and pragmatics are the elements of language. Most of us acquired these elements in an amazingly painless, effective, and efficient way without really being conscious of what we were doing.

Two Explanations for Language Learning

Language, some theorists insist, is a sort of special gift given only to humans and not other animals; its acquisition can be explained only by reference to things extraordinary and mysterious. Deacon (1997) describes such explanations as **hopeful monsters**; other theorists refer to them as a form of nativism (MacWhinney, 1998). The best known of the *hopeful monster* or *nativistic* theories of language development is that of the linguist, Noam Chomsky (1972). Chomsky argues that because children learn language—especially grammar—so rapidly, and because they make so few of the errors that one might expect them to make if they had to learn each rule and each exception individually, they must be born with a powerful biological predisposition to learn language. This predisposition, Chomsky speculates, takes the form of neurological prewiring in the brain, a sort of brain-organ whose wiring corresponds to language and to grammar. He labels this neurological prewiring the **language acquisition device (LAD)**.

Another explanation views language learning as the end result of a learning process highly dependent on interaction with other speakers. This explanation sees language as something that *emerges* gradually and is labeled **emergentism** (MacWhinney, 1998). Emergent explanations are often based on the principles of reinforcement in operant conditioning (described in Chapter 2). They might argue, for example, that while babbling, the infant emits wordlike sounds that tend to be reinforced by adults. In addition, parents or siblings may repeat the infant's vocalizations, thus serving as models. Eventually, through reinforcement, children learn to imitate the speech of those around them. (See Chapter 7 for more detail on these two theories of language development.)

---

hopeful monsters Deacon's label for explanations that resort to what is sometimes termed *Deus ex machina*—"God from a machine." Such explanations rely on an assumed but unprovable entity, organ, or feature to explain what cannot easily be explained otherwise.

nativism A hopeful monster type of explanation for language learning, like Chomsky's, which assumes that language learning depends on a preexisting neurological organ or pattern in the brain corresponding to a universal language grammar.

language acquisition device (LAD) Chomsky's label for the prewired neurological something in our brains that corresponds to grammar and explains how we can learn, understand, and use language.

emergentism An explanation that describes language learning as a gradual learning process involving social interaction, where understanding of grammar emerges step by step rather than being prewired.

---

syntax The grammar of a language, consisting of the set of implicit or explicit rules that govern the combinations of words composing a language.

pragmatics In reference to language development, implicit rules that tell children when and how to speak.

The Prespeech Stage of Language Development

For convenience, early language learning is often divided into two main stages: the prespeech stage and the speech stage. In the prespeech stage, infants learn important things like turn-taking, gesturing, discriminating sounds, and finally, producing controlled sounds. In the speech stage, infants progress from the first words to the complex combinations that mark adult language.

Turn-Taking: The Beginnings of Verbal Communication Researchers believe that the ability to use and to understand words grows out of the interactions that take place between infants and their caregivers, siblings, and other people. Bruner (1983) refers to these interactions as the language acquisition support system (LASS). One of the first things the infant learns through this support system is how to take turns.

Knowing when and how to take turns is basic to adult conversation. When we have conversations, we wait for the signals that tell us it's our turn, and we give others their signals—well, most of us do; there are some who simply shout a little louder. Most of us have learned the rules that govern turn-taking without really knowing that we have learned them, and without, in most cases, being able to verbalize them. These signals include an upward or downward change of pitch at the end of an utterance, the completion of a grammatical clause, a drawl on the last syllable, or the termination of a gesture. These are among the signals that children must learn if they are eventually to converse in socially acceptable ways.

It's amazing that children seem to have a relatively sophisticated awareness of turn-taking signals at very young ages (Haslett & Samter, 1997). In one investigation, Elias and Broerse (1996) looked at interactions between 48 mothers and their 3- to 24-month-old infants. They found a remarkable tendency for mother-infant pairs to interact in alternating fashion. Similarly, Mayer and Tronick (1985) found that even at the age of 2 months, infants and their mothers are already taking turns. They videotaped 10 mothers and their infants in face-to-face interaction when the infants were 2, 3, and 5 months old. Analyses of videotapes revealed that not only did infants rarely vocalize (other than

for occasional "fussy" vocalizations) when their mothers were speaking, but they seemed to understand the mother's turn-taking signals. They responded not only to head and hand movements, but also to changes in intonation at the ends of utterances, to terminal drawls, and to the completion of grammatical clauses. Accordingly, they cooed and smiled mostly during the mother's pauses. Mothers, for their part, modified the number of turn-taking signals they gave according to the child's responsiveness. This is very much what adults do in their own conversations.

Using Gestures Even before they have begun to use words, infants have typically developed a repertoire of gestures that are clearly meaningful for both infants and caregivers. Gestures, note Haslett and Samter (1997), are often associated with a gaze. Infants use gazing not only to indicate what they want, but to direct other people's attention. And they typically alternate the gaze between the desired object and the person whose attention they are trying to direct, as if to confirm that the message is being received. Also, very much like adults, they often follow another person's gaze, thus involving themselves in what we have described as a *triadic* interaction.

It is interesting that infants begin to associate their facial gestures and their vocalizations long before they can speak. Yale et al. (1999) looked at the vocal and facial actions of 12 infants, aged 3 to 6 months. They found a significant tendency for infants to coordinate these actions so that they tended to occur simultaneously.

During the first two years, infants develop a large number of different gestures. Interestingly, Pointing is one of the last to develop, at around ages 12 to 14 months (Masur, 1993). Other gestures, like offering objects and reaching for things, are relatively common by the age of 9 months. By the age of 15 months, infants can direct their gazing and their pointing or showing in different directions at the same time. This is evident, for example, when 16-month-old Zachary points to the plate he has just thrown on the floor and looks at his mother at the same time. Being able to refer to two objects at once is a remarkable new achievement, claim Haslett and Samter (1997).

Discriminating Sounds Communicating through language depends on sounds rather than gestures.

Specifically, it depends on the ability of infants to discriminate sounds as well as to produce them.

Auditory speech, Werker and Tees (1999) point out, is far more complex than written language. What you are reading at this moment consists of words that are separated by spaces and that are organized into sentence-sized chunks of meaning clearly identified with punctuation, capitalization, boldfacing, and italicizing. Furthermore, you can reread any part of it at your whim. Not so with speech. Examination of acoustic waves shows no regular breaks between words, and certainly no division between sentences or paragraphs. Yet infants are soon able to discriminate individual sounds. And before a year has passed, they have even begun to assign them meanings.

It seems that newborns begin life with a remarkable, built-in capacity to discriminate among sounds. For example, Moffitt (1971) monitored the heart rates of 5- and 6-month-old infants while they were exposed to taped recordings of sounds as similar as *bah* and *gah*. That their heart rate changed whenever the sound changed indicated that these infants could tell the difference between those sounds. In fact, research conducted by Patterson and Werker (reported in Werker & Tees, 1999) indicates that infants as young as 4 months can not only discriminate among such highly similar sounds, but can also match them to appropriate lip and mouth movements. Thus, infants seem to prefer "talking heads," whose mouth movements match what they hear, over talking heads that seem to be saying something different. But adults placed in this same situation often "hear" what they see rather than the actual sounds presented to them. For example, when adults hear the sound *ba* perfectly synchronized with a talking head that seems to be saying *va*, what they report hearing is *va*. The important point here is that even in early infancy, children have already begun to learn, and to rely upon, facial movements and gestures as important sources of language information.

There appears to be evidence that infants prefer the sounds of their own language rather than those of other languages. And within days of birth, they appear to be able to discriminate between their language and other languages that are substantially different (Nazzi, Bertoncini, & Mehler, 1998).

Some sounds may be more difficult to tell apart than others. For example, infants have trouble telling *sa* from *za*, but they can much more easily discriminate between *sa* and *fa* or *va* and *sa* (Eilers & Minifie, 1975). With language experience, however, children are eventually able to discriminate reliably among all these sounds. In some cases, however, if the sounds are not part of their language, they may experience difficulty discriminating among them even as adults—as is the case for the sounds *la* and *ra* for a native Japanese speaker, for example (Miyawaki et al., 1975). Werker and Tees (1999) report that this loss of ability to discriminate certain unused sounds seems to become evident by about age 4 years. But with training and experience, even adults can relearn to discriminate these sounds.

Sound Production Discriminating among sounds is one aspect of early language learning; producing intended sounds is the other. It starts with the crying, cooing, and eventual babbling of an infant. Eventually it progresses to a word, and then beyond.

It was long believed that all the sounds of every language in the world are uttered in the babbling of an infant—even in the babbling of deaf infants. This belief leads directly to the conclusion that the ability to produce speech sounds is innate, a conclusion that does not appear to be entirely true. For example, although the first sounds uttered by deaf infants are very similar to those of hearing children, their later vocalizations are typically quite different. These first sounds, say Eilers and Oller (1988), are precursors to the form of babbling in which infants finally utter well-formed syllables with clearly articulated consonants and vowels—a stage that does not occur until some time between 7 and 10 months. Before then, infants make unarticulated noises: They coo, squeal, growl, whisper, and yell. And although it might be possible to discern many sounds that resemble those found in the world's 5,000 or so languages in these early sounds, infants' utterances remain unsystematic and do not obey the laws of syllables (requiring clarity and a complete vowel of adequate duration).

Infants' first sounds are "soft sounds," notes Bijou (1989b), but eventually infants gain control over their sound-producing apparatus. Also, they discover that producing sounds is "fun," as is evident in the fact that contented infants may spend hours in solitary babbling with no prompting. As a result, by the age of 10 months, most hearing children babble clearly, systematically, and repetitively. Children who have hearing problems do not reach this stage until later (Robinshaw, 1996). If their hearing problems are serious enough, they do not progress through the normal stages of learning spoken language (Deal & Haas, 1996).

That babbling is highly dependent on learning is also evident in studies that have looked at the babbling of children from different language environments. By the age of 9 to 10 months, explain Werker and Tees (1999), infants' vocalizations reflect their language backgrounds. But prior to this, certain sounds typically appear in the babbling of almost all infants, while other sounds are almost never heard even though they are important parts of some languages. Not surprisingly, the most common sounds that infants babble are the easiest ones given the anatomical structure of their vocal apparatus: consonants such as *b*, *d*, *w*, and *m* (described by linguists as stop, glide, or nasal consonants). Thus words like *mama*, *papa*, and *dada* are among the simplest for virtually all infants. In fact, there are some who believe that *mama* and *papa* are common to an astounding number of the world's languages precisely because they are among the first systematic sounds infants babble. In many of these languages, says Ingram (1991), "'Mama'" emerges as a general request for the fulfillment of some need, while 'papa' is a more descriptive term for parents" (p. 711).

The First Word Not surprisingly, then, *mama* or *papa* is the first clearly recognizable word spoken by many infants. However, it is seldom easy to determine when infants say their first word. Many infants repeat a sound such as *bah* many times before it becomes associated with an object. The point at which sounds like *bah* cease to be babbles and become words (*ball*, for example) is unclear, but it has usually occurred by the age of 1 year. Infants' first words are often created by repeating two identical sounds, such as in *mama*, *dada*, or *bye bye*.

The appearance of the first word is rapidly followed by new words that the child practices incessantly. Most of an English-speaking child's first words are nouns—simple names for simple things, usually objects or people that are part of the here and now: *dog*, *mama*, *banket* (blanket), or *yefant* (elephant). Verbs, adjectives, adverbs, and prepositions are acquired primarily in the order listed here, with the greatest difficulty usually being the use of pronouns, especially the pronoun *I* (Boyd, 1976).

But before they learn words, infants have begun to show signs that they understand much more than they can say—words that are not yet part of their active vocabulary, even some entire sentences. "Stick out your tongue," she is told by a proud parent, and she sticks out her tongue. "Show Daddy your hand," and she shows it. "Can you wink?" Sure can (two eyes, though).

The Speech Stage

To simplify matters, the learning of language is described in this text in terms of six sequential stages (based on Wood, 1981; see *Concept Summary*). The first of these, the prespeech stage, lasts until approximately age 1. Its major achievements include learning to take turns, developing a repertoire of gestures, learning to discriminate and to produce sounds, and finally, arriving at the first deliberate, meaningful word. The next two stages—that of the sentencelike word and the two-word sentence—are described next. The remaining three stages are detailed in Chapter 7.

The Sentencelike Word (Holophrase) By the age of around 11.5 months, about half of all children have mastered their first meaningful word—although many have been making wordlike sounds like "dada" or "mama" for some time (Frankenburg & Dodds, 1992). About 25% will have arrived at their first word by the age of 10 months; 90% will normally have achieved it by age 15 months. This word's meaning is seldom limited to one event, action, or person but often means something that an adult would require an entire sentence to communicate; hence the term *holophrase*. Thus although most holophrases are nouns, they are not used simply for naming. When a child says "milk," he might mean, "There is the milk." He might also mean, "Give me some milk," "I'm thirsty," "I want you to hold me," "Go buy some milk," or "Are you going to do that to the cow again?"

Two-Word Sentences The progression of speech development is from one word to two (roughly by the age of 18 months), and later to more than two. There does not appear to be a three-word stage following this two-word stage, but rather a multiword stage in which sentences range in length from two to perhaps five or more words.

CONCEPT
SUMMARY

Stages in Children's Development of Language

Stage of Development	Nature of Development	Sample Utterances
1. Prespeech (before age 1)	Crying, cooing, babbling.	"Waaah," "dadadada"
2. Sentencelike word (holophrase) (by 12 months)	The word is combined with nonverbal cues (gestures and inflections).	"Mommy" (Meaning: "Would you please come here, mother.")
3. Two-word sentences (duos) (by 18 months)	Modifiers are joined to topic words to form declarative, question, negative, and imperative structures.	"Pretty baby." (declarative) "Where Daddy?" (question) "No play." (negative) "More milk!" (imperative)
4. Multiple-word sentences (by 2 to 2$\frac{1}{2}$ years)	Both a subject and predicate are included in the sentence types. Grammatical morphemes are used to change meanings (-*ing* or -*ed*, for example).	"She's a pretty baby." (declarative) "Where Daddy is?" (question) "I no can play." (negative) "I want more milk!" (imperative) "I running." "I runned."
5. More complex grammatical changes and word categories (between 2$\frac{1}{2}$ and 4 years)	Elements are added, embedded, and permuted within sentences. Word classes (nouns, verbs, and prepositions) are subdivided. Clauses are put together.	"Read it, my book." (conjunction) "Where is Daddy?" (embedding) "I can't play." (permutation) "I would like some milk." (use of "some" with mass noun) "Take me to the store." (use of preposition of place)
6. Adultlike structures (after 4 years)	Complex structural distinctions made, as with "ask-tell" and "promise."	"Ask what time it is." "He promised to help her."

Masur (1993) notes that there are three widely recognized general language-learning milestones in the first two years of life: The first is the acquisition of communicative gestures in the second half of year 1; the second is the appearance of the first words at about age 1; and the third is a dramatic vocabulary spurt at about 17 or 18 months. The appearance of two-word sentences coincides closely with this sudden acceleration in vocabulary growth (Goldfield & Reznick, 1996).

Baby Talk Children continue to acquire words during their second year, but the number of syllables they can use is limited. Many of their words are one- or two-syllable words, which often repeat the same syllable in different combinations ("mommy," "daddy," "baby," "seepy" [sleepy], "horsy," "doggy"). Even when it is incorrect to do so, a child may repeat the syllable in a one-syllable word, as in "car car" or "kiss kiss."

THOUGHT CHALLENGE: *Baby talk is found not only among caregivers talking to infants and young children, but also among male and female adults and among caregivers talking to elderly people—in which case it's termed* secondary baby talk. *What do you suppose the reasons might be for the use of secondary baby talk?*

Developmental norms indicate that this 5-month-old can laugh and squeal and may even have begun to imitate recognizable speech sounds. But she is still some distance from being able to say, "Hi mom. What big teeth you have!"

Stewart Cohen/Tony Stone Images

In an attempt to communicate with children on their level, parents sometimes exaggerate the errors committed by their infants in a type of speech labeled baby talk. The result is occasionally something like, "Wou my itsy bitsy witta baby come to momsy womsy?" But there is no evidence that parental (or grandparental) models of this type hamper the rapid and correct acquisition of language. And some developmentalists believe that baby talk might play an important role in parent-infant bonding.

Telegraphic Speech The transition from holophrases to two-word sentences generally occurs around 18 months and coincides with a period of extremely rapid vocabulary growth. Speech at this stage is sometimes described as being **telegraphic speech** because it eliminates many parts of speech while still managing to convey meanings—typically using only two words. "Dog allgone" is a two-word utterance "telegraphed" from the lengthier adult equivalent, "The dog is not here now."

telegraphic speech Speech of infants and young children that compresses meaning into short utterances, typically consisting of only two words.

Early Grammar Whether precise grammatical functions can be accurately assigned to these two-word utterances is a matter of some debate. The functions of the words *fish* and *eat* in the two-word utterance "fish eat" are, in fact, dependent on the intended meaning. But because children use neither number agreement (for example, "fish eats" to mean "the fish eats" and "fish eat" to mean "I eat fish") nor order ("eat fish" versus "fish eat") to signal meaning, psycholinguists can never be certain that children at this stage are aware of grammatical functions.

By the age of 2, infants have reached the point at which they can name all the familiar objects and people in their environment. Moreover, they can now combine words into meaningful sentencelike units. They can also use adjectives and adverbs, questions, and simple negatives and affirmatives; and they have begun to learn a variety of subtle and implicit rules governing intonation, inflection, and the conventions that guide conversations.

But there is much more yet to be learned; there remain three stages in our six-stage description of the sequence of language acquisition. The story of that sequence continues in Chapter 7.

By the age of 2, children can name all the familiar people and things they encounter: they can use adjectives and adverbs; and they can ask questions and answer simple questions. But there is still much learning and practicing to do, for which naming and counting things like teddy bears—and perhaps even feeding them—can be very useful.

Language and Infant Intelligence

Measuring the intelligence of infants is a difficult and uncertain thing. That's partly because intelligence is a highly verbal characteristic most often measured by looking at language and at verbal tasks involved in problem solving and concept formation. Still, there are a number of indicators of infant intelligence—such as, for example, the appearance of certain behaviors like walking, talking, smiling, and waving, at about the expected time. Scales of infant intelligence often use these indicators as crude measures of infant intelligence. Typically, however, these measures are considered indications of general development rather than specifically of intelligence. Hence we don't speak of infant IQ but of **developmental quotient (DQ)** (see Chapter 9 for information on the meaning and computation of IQ). Among well-known tests of infant development are the *Bayley Scales* (Bayley, 1993) and the *Fagan Test of Infant Intelligence* (Fagan, 1992). The *Bayley Scales* look at the average age at which children acquire a combination of motor and mental skills. The *Fagan Test*, which can be used with very young infants, is based on the concept of habituation described earlier. It presents infants with a picture on a screen,

followed by two pictures, one of which is different (the other remains identical). Normal infants typically spend more time looking at the new picture. Failure to do so is sometimes predictive of later developmental delays.

FROM SENSATION TO REPRESENTATION

The word *infant* derives from the Latin *infans*, meaning "without speech." And, in fact, throughout much of the period we call infancy, a child is without speech. As noted earlier, the world of the newborn is a world of the here and now, a world that cannot be represented symbolically but can only be acted on and felt—in short, a *sensorimotor* world.

But, although the term *sensorimotor* describes well the predominant relationship between infant and world, it doesn't describe the most important cognitive achievements of the first two years of life. By the time a child is 2, the world no longer exists only in the immediate, sensible present. Objects have long since achieved a permanence and an identity that no longer depend solely on the child's activities; there is a dawning understanding of cause-and-effect relationships; language is rapidly exercising a profound effect on cognitive development. These achievements, together with children's recognition of their own identities—their selves—represent a dramatic transition from a quasi-animalistic existence to the world of thought and emotions as we know it. But although it is a dramatic transition, at least in its import, it is neither sudden nor startling. Those who follow the lives of individual children closely (and daily) never see the transition from sensorimotor intelligence to preoperational thought. It happens suddenly and irrevocably on the second birthday only in textbooks. Real life is less well organized.

developmental quotient (DQ) Score reflecting infant development, based largely on infants' acquisition of expected motor and mental skills.

Bayley Scales Standardized scales used to measure infant development, reflecting extent to which infant has acquired motor and mental skills expected at specific ages.

Fagan Test of Infant Intelligence A nonverbal, individual intelligence test for use with infants, useful for screening infants at risk for mental retardation.

MAIN POINTS

The Design of a Newborn

Design specifications for an organism that begins as helpless as a newborn and that in two years ends up as sophisticated as a 2-year-old would stipulate mechanisms for biological change (geared to go from physical helplessness to controlled locomotion and astonishing manual dexterity); intellectual change (programmed to process and make sense of an extraordinary amount of information, culminating in the acquisition of advanced representational systems and language); and social change (designed to develop powerful emotional attachments, and perhaps a few fears as well so that it will later avoid metaphoric snakes).

Nutrition, Health, and Physical Growth in Infancy

Breast milk is among the most easily digested foods for infants, is useful in guarding against the possibility of childhood illness and disease (especially diarrhea in developing countries), may provide long-term protection against certain diseases, and contains nutrients essential for physical and neurological growth. The use of certain drugs by the mother, the presence of various diseases, and strong personal preference sometimes make formula feeding a better choice.

Optimal brain development in early infancy is influenced by nutrition (especially protein intake) and stimulation. Severe malnutrition may be manifested in *stunting* (retarded height) or *wasting* (severely below average weight).

Sudden Infant Death Syndrome

Sudden infant death syndrome (SIDS) accounts for the unexpected and largely unexplainable death of between 1 and 2 out of every 1,000 apparently healthy infants. It is slightly more common among males and among those who are placed to sleep facedown, whose mothers smoke or are drug addicted, who are aged 2 to 4 months, and who are born prematurely.

Brain and Behavior in Newborns

There is a spurt in brain growth at the end of the fetal period, continuing during infancy. The *fontanels* permit easier passage through the birth canal, as well as continued growth of the brain. The *cerebrum* is involved in higher mental functions, and develops very rapidly during infancy (brain proliferation, consisting largely of the mushrooming of neural connections and myelin sheaths). Experience is important for developing and maintaining neural connections. Degree of brain arousal is evident in infant states (conditions of sleep, alertness, or activity).

Motor Development in Infancy

The neonate's behaviors consist mainly of reflexes: the orienting response (an alerting response useful as a measure of attention and learning); the sucking reflex; the moro (startling) reflex; the Babinski reflex (fanning and curling the toes); the palmar (grasping) reflex; and the swimming, stepping, swallowing, and sneezing reflexes. Many of these disappear with brain development and the achievement of voluntary control over movements.

Motor development tends to be *cephalocaudal* (from head to foot) and *proximodistal* (from near to far). Although there is wide individual variation in the ages at which motor capabilities are attained, the sequence appears to be similar among most infants. Scales are sometimes used to detect extreme deviations that might indicate a developmental problem.

Perceptual Development in Infancy

Sensation is primarily a physiological process; perception is our interpretation of sensation. Depth perception, response to patterns, and the ability to detect movements are well developed in newborns; color vision develops later. Development of infant's sight seems to be based on a need to maximize information and is governed by certain visual rules.

Hearing is present before birth. Neonates are only slightly less sensitive than adults to sound intensity (loudness). Infants appear to recognize and prefer their mother's voice at ages as young as 3 days. Almost from birth, infants prefer pleasant odors and sweet tastes. They appear to be sensitive to touch (and to pain) within a few hours of birth.

Memory in Infants

A neonate's memory is not as efficient, as powerful, or as long-term as that of older children or adults. *Habituation* studies indicate that they have fleeting and fragile memories, at least during the first half-year—although *reminders* sometimes help them remember things longer. By the age of 8 months, neonates' memories have become more abstract, although they, like us, appear to be subject to the phenomenon of *infantile amnesia*—an inability to remember personal experiences of our infancies and young childhoods.

Some Intellectual Achievements and Challenges of Infancy

Infants behave as if they have no realization of the permanence of objects (theirs is a world of the here and now). Until about 8 months of age, infants fail to look for objects just hidden. Some research indicates that they do have a realization of some of the physical properties of objects before then.

Intention is evident in the very young infant's purposeful gaze, and later, in gestures such as pointing. It is also apparent in certain imitative behaviors when these become deliberate. Imitation among newborns is limited to facial reactions such as tongue protrusion and mouth opening, and does not persist when the model leaves. Older infants are capable of *deferred imitation*, an important indication of the ability to represent mentally.

Basic Piagetian Ideas on Infancy

In Piaget's theory, cognitive growth results from the interplay of assimilation (responding based on pre-existing information and well-practiced capabilities) and accommodation (adapting behavior to the demands of the situation). Equilibration is the gov-

erning force that strives to balance assimilation and accommodation. Other forces that shape development are maturation, active experience, and social interaction.

Piaget's six substages of the sensorimotor period are exercising reflexes (0–1 month), *primary circular reactions* (repetitive self-centered behaviors, 1–4 months), *secondary circular reactions* (repetitive environment-centered behaviors, 4–8 months), purposeful coordinations (the coordination of activities in goal-oriented behaviors, discovery of object concept, 8–12 months), *tertiary circular reactions* (exploration through deliberately modifying repetitive behaviors, 12–18 months), and mental representation (gradual transition to a more symbolic intelligence, 18–24 months).

Early Language Development

Language is characterized by displacement (allows remote events to be represented), meaningfulness (has significance), and productiveness (allows the generation of an unlimited number of meaningful combinations). Its four basic elements are *phonology* (sounds), *semantics* (meanings of words), *syntax* (grammar or rules that govern relationships among parts of speech), and *pragmatics* (rules and conventions concerning how and when to speak).

Infants as young as 2 months of age have a relatively sophisticated awareness of turn-taking signals ordinarily used in conversation. Gazing is among the earliest of their communicative gestures. Reaching for and giving are early gestures; pointing develops later. There is some evidence that infants have a built-in capacity to discriminate among certain sounds, and they are able to produce a large variety of sounds in their babbling.

The first word usually appears by the end of the first year and is often sentencelike in nature (a *holophrase*). Two-word sentences appear around the age of 18 months. These are telegraphic, condensing considerable information into two words. There is a dramatic spurt in vocabulary coinciding with the appearance of two-word sentences.

Focus Questions: Applications

1. How important is nutrition for a newborn?
   - As a class project, organize a breast-versus-bottle debate.
2. What are some important physical and intellectual characteristics of neonates?
   - Evolution, we are told, is a poor engineer. Try your hand at designing the human organism. Start with something as ignorant as a newborn. What kinds of capabilities and propensities would you design into a newborn? How do these compare with what is actually there?
3. What can a newborn see? Hear? Smell? Taste? Feel?
   - An infant's world is a blooming, buzzing mass of confusion, thought William James. Is it?
4. Can newborns think?
   - What sorts of thoughts, if any, do you suppose a newborn would have? What changes would you expect in the first year?
5. How can an infant manage to learn something as complicated as a language?
   - Why are theories based on imitation not entirely adequate explanations for language learning?

Possible Responses to Thought Challenges

Thought Challenge, page 190

Here are the bare bones of a possible answer. What you do is you program the organism for change, paying particular attention to change in three areas: biological, intellectual, and social. The section "What Is a Neonate?" on page 191 expands on this notion.

Thought Challenge, page 209

The development of the physiology of the visual system requires appropriate early experience. Recall, for example, that billions of unused neural connections present in the infant's brain atrophy and disappear.

Thought Challenge, page 218

Not necessarily. Perhaps even very young infants really do understand the permanence of objects, but aren't able to form the intention to search for an object. Or perhaps they're not especially motivated to do so. Or maybe they simply don't have the type of control over their physical movements that is required for an actual search.

Thought Challenge, page 233

1. The use of baby talk with elderly people may be due partly to their real—or presumed—problems related to hearing or comprehending. In a sense, they may be perceived as having become more childlike in these respects. A study of secondary baby talk in a nursing home in Germany reveals that it isn't necessarily bad for residents. Some elderly people report extremely positive reactions to baby talk (Sachweh, 1998).
2. Baby talk among adults may be an indicator of intimacy and attachment, and a means of achieving closeness, say Bombar and Littig (1996). After all, it mimics—and probably brings to mind—moments of great affection between caregivers and infants.

Key Terms

adaptation, 222
altricial, 203
apnea, 197
axon, 199
Bayley Scales, 235
brain proliferation, 200
brain stem, 199
cataracts, 208

cell body, 199
cerebellum, 199
cerebral cortex, 199
cerebrum, 199
conceptualization, 207
cyclic movements, 205
deferred imitation, 220
dendrites, 199

developmental quotient (DQ), 235
emergentism, 229
equilibration, 223
Fagan Test of Infant Intelligence, 235
fine motor development, 205
fontanels, 198
gaze following, 221
gross motor development, 205

Further Readings

The following is an excellent example of new directions in research and theorizing that have become increasingly popular in recent years. It deals with novel ways of thinking about and investigating the development of human mental phenomena such as intention and theories of mind:

Zelazo, P. D., J. W. Astington, & D. R. Olson, eds. (1999). *Developing theories of intention: Social understanding and self-control.* Mahwah, N.J.: Erlbaum.

For those who are breast-feeding and who are concerned about the potential effects of drugs on the infant, the following book provides useful information about many common and uncommon drugs:

Coustan, D. R., & T. K. Mochizuki (1998). *Handbook for prescribing medications during pregnancy,* 3rd ed. New York: Lippincott-Raven.

The following two books present readable and authoritative accounts of what is known about SIDS:

Guntheroth, W. G. (1995). *Crib death: The sudden infant death syndrome,* 3rd. ed. Armonk, N.Y.: Futura Publishing Co.

Sears, W. (1995). *SIDS: A parent's guide to understanding and preventing Sudden Infant Death Syndrome.* Boston: Little, Brown.

Here is a clear, useful account of Piaget's writings:

Wadsworth, B. J. (1995). *Piaget's theory of cognitive and affective development,* 5th ed. New York: Longman.

The environment, says Marian Diamond, has an enormous impact on the very anatomy of the brain. That there is much that parents, and educators, can do for cognitive growth of children is the theme of this provocative and stimulating book:

Diamond, M. C. (1998). *Magic trees of the mind: How to nurture your child's intelligence, creativity, and healthy emotions.* New York: Dutton.

Online Resources

For additional readings, explore *InfoTrac College Edition,* your online library. Go to http://infotrac-college.com/wadsworth and use the passcode that came on the card with your book. Try these search terms: infant brain, infant language, SIDS, stunting.

For breakfast and supper, milk, milk-pottage, water-gruel, flummery, and twenty other things, that we are wont to make in England, are very fit for children: only, in all these let care be taken, that they be plain, and without much mixture, and very sparingly seasoned with sugar, or rather none at all: especially all spice, and other things, that may heat the blood, are carefully to be avoided.

John Locke, *Essays Concerning Human Understanding*

Social and Emotional Development in Infancy

Jeffry W. Myers/Corbis

CHAPTER 6

John Locke doesn't ever spell out the "twenty other" bland English foods in his essay quoted on the opposite page. Not that it would have mattered to my mother.

Mother was not especially concerned about avoiding sugars, spices, and other seasonings that might have "heated" our young blood. Hot-blooded people, my grandmother explained, show their feelings; they're not cold and distant. They hug more and love more and feel happier. Being hot-blooded, she insisted, had nothing to do with how children were disciplined. If they occasionally had to be spanked, well, that was for their own good—which means that, by the age of 10, I should have been very good indeed.

In other cultures, attitudes toward child-rearing are sometimes vastly different. Mowat (1952) once asked an Eskimo father, Ootek, why he never spanked his children, even when they behaved in the most exasperating manner. Ootek was astounded at the question; he found it so difficult to understand that Mowat had to rephrase it several ways. And when he finally understood, he became quite angry.

"Who but a madman would raise his hand against blood of his blood?" he roared. "Who but a madman would, in his man's strength, stoop to strike against the weakness of a child?"

FOCUS QUESTIONS

1. How do infants influence caregivers?
2. Are all infants basically the same in terms of emotional reactions and personality?
3. Are mother-infant bonds "natural" and unlearned?
4. What are the consequences of separating infants from their caregivers?
5. How do the terms *average*, *normal*, and *exceptional* relate to each other?

⌐ SOCIAL AND EMOTIONAL DEVELOPMENT IN THE FAMILY CONTEXT

In many societies it is considered acceptable to occasionally strike one's own children—or almost certainly to raise our voices to them. Yet we are not mad, or at least not certifiably so. We—Ootek, you and I—are simply products of different cultures. So, too, are our children. A young Eskimo might expect to be treated with adultlike respect if he announces that he will now take up his small bow and arrow to hunt birds for dinner. But my neighbor's 4-year-old, Peter, hardly expects his parents to say, "Yeah, have a nice trip, then, Pete" when he informs them he's going to be a truck driver like his dad, and can he take the truck for a spin down the highway?

To understand what it's like to be a child, it's essential to know which child, when, and where. As Clitheroe, Stokols, and Zmuidzinas (1998) note, we have to be aware of children's contexts and of how these contexts have changed and continue to change, sometimes gradually and other times dramatically. That is, we need to know something of the child's changing ecology—something of the ethnic, cultural, social, political, and familial realities of that child. Perhaps most important, to understand the lives of infants, we need to ask about interactions in the family because, in most cases, the family defines the most important aspects of the child's physical and social context.

Child Development as an Interactional Process

Current approaches to the study of child development pay increasing attention to the reciprocal interactions that define relationships among individuals in the family. Interactions are *reciprocal* when they involve mutual influences—that is, where the behavior of each person interacting is affected by the other's behavior (Eddowes & Ralph, 1998). That is what Bronfenbrenner meant by microsystem (described in Chapter 2).

That parent-infant interaction is reciprocal—that is, that infants influence parents even as parents influence children—is easily illustrated. Consider, for example, the case of Louis, an especially difficult infant who cries a lot, refuses his mother's breast unpredictably, and soils his diaper at awkward times. His mother, in turn, is easily annoyed, impatient, highly emotional, and given to temper tantrums.

Sara, on the other hand, is a mother's dream. She sleeps regularly, seldom cries, loves her mother's breast, and soils her diaper only at regular intervals, always very politely. Sara's mother is a calm, enthusiastic, patient parent who is absolutely delighted with her infant. In Bronfenbrenner's terms, the ecology—the interactions—will be very different in each of these two *microsystems*. After all, since the characteristics of Louis, Sara, and their mothers are very different, the interactions between parent and child are not likely to be similar.

The Current Contextual Model

Traditionally, the emphasis has been on dyadic interactions—that is, on interactions involving two individuals. And the dyad considered most important in the study of infant development was most often that of mother and infant. Father-infant and infant-sibling interactions were taken into account as well. Now, however, many researchers look at more complex interactions. For example, contextual models of development, such as that described by Bronfenbrenner (see Chapter 2), look at how infants affect parents and change the family, which in turn affects the infant. Such models look, as well, at the social context in which the family functions, at the political and economic context, and the religious and philosophical context.

Complex Sociological Interactions This newer and more complex way of looking at influences in child development is more contextual and more family-based—hence it is more **sociological** in the sense that it is concerned not just with the individual but rather with the individual in social groups (Belsky, 1999). It is an approach that recognizes there are far more influences at work on an infant than just a mother on one hand and a father on the other. There is also a family, a social unit made up of husband and wife (as opposed to just father and mother) and characterized by a marital relationship—hence the triadic interactions (three-way interactions) of child-parent-family.

The model also suggests that many complex influences other than the obvious parent-infant links may come into play. Belsky (1981) refers to these as "second-order" effects. Some possible second-order effects include the influence that a father might have on a mother, which might then cause her to interact differently with their infant; the relationship that the mother has with the infant, which might influence the way the father interacts with the infant; the influence that the infant's arrival (or temperament) has on the marital relationship and the consequent effects on parenting; and the influence of economic changes. Note that these second-order effects are what Bronfenbrenner (1989) terms the *meso-*, *exo-*, and *macrosystems*.

Infant and Parent Characteristics That Affect Interactions Wide ranges of infant and parental characteristics are important in determining parent-infant interactions. For example, a variety of children's behaviors (or misbehaviors) such as truancy, delinquency, and defiance or superior academic achievement, outstanding musical or athletic achievement,

or astounding social skills, can affect how parents interact with their children. And, of course, how parents interact with their children depends partly on their own characteristics (such as patience or irritability). Physical appearance may also influence how parents interact with children—and perhaps how children interact with their parents. Recall how some fathers treated their attractive daughters more favorably than their less attractive daughters during the Great Depression (Elder et al., 1985). And, as we see later in this chapter, the infant's sex is also important—as is the parent's sex. It appears that in general, parents treat boys and girls differently. Also, infants' responses to parents differ according to the sex of the parent.

▐ INFANT TEMPERAMENT

Among infant characteristics that can clearly have an effect on many of the interactions that involve the infant are the infant's predominant emotional responses—as illustrated earlier, in the cases of Louis and Sara. Parents, siblings, perhaps even dogs, might interact differently with *difficult* as opposed to *easy* infants. These are among the broad characteristics that define **temperament**.

A Definition of Temperament

When psychologists speak of differences in the customary ways of reacting and behaving that differentiate adults from each other, they generally speak of **personality** differences. The term *personality* includes all the abilities, predispositions, habits, and other characteristics that make each of us different.

---

sociological Related to sociology, the study of the origin of and relationships among social groups and social phenomena.

temperament The biological basis of personality—its hereditary components. The expression *infant temperament* refers to infants' characteristic emotional responses.

personality The set of characteristics that we typically manifest in our interactions with others. It includes all the abilities, predispositions, habits, and other qualities that make each of us different.

Specific personality characteristics are called **traits**; a cluster of related characteristics is called a **type**.

When psychologists speak of differences among infants, they don't often use the term *personality*, because it implies a range of experiences and a degree of learning that have not yet had time to occur. Instead, they speak of infant temperament. Temperament is evident in the infant's characteristic emotional responses. One important difference between temperament and personality is that temperament is assumed to have a primarily genetic basis (Chess & Thomas, 1989a), whereas personality develops through interaction with the environment. Accordingly, Buss and Plomin (1985) define *temperament* as "inherited personality traits present in early childhood" (p. 84). Thus a child is born with a certain temperament rather than with a certain personality. We see this temperament in the prevailing moods or the states we discussed in Chapter 5 (crying, for example). The personality that later develops is an outgrowth of interaction between innate temperament and environmental influences (Carey, 1989).

Classifications of Infant Temperament

In the classical studies of infant temperament, known as the New York Longitudinal Study (NYLS), Thomas, Chess, and Birch (1968, 1970; Thomas and Chess, 1977, 1981) studied 141 children from 85 highly educated, professional families. They found at least nine different characteristics that are easily observed in infants (particularly after the infant is 2 or 3 months of age) and on which they can be rated as being high, medium, or low:

1. *Activity level*, evident in the extent to which infants are physically active.

2. *Rhythmicity*, defined as the infant's regularity in activities such as eating, sleeping, and toilet functions.

3. *Approach-withdrawal*, as seen in the infant's response to novel situations or strangers.

4. *Adaptability*, reflected in the infant's response to change.

5. *Sensitivity to stimuli* measured in terms of how much stimulation is required to elicit a response.

6. *Intensity of reaction*, seen in how strongly the infant responds to situations.

7. *General mood*, displayed in the infant's prevailing disposition (tendency to be cranky, friendly, happy, and so on).

8. *Distractibility*, reflected in how easily the baby can be distracted from ongoing activities.

9. *Attention span*, apparent in the infant's persistence in ongoing activities.

In addition to determining that infants could relatively easily be classified as being *high*, *medium*, or *low* on each of these dimensions of temperament, Chess and Birch also found that certain infants seem to have remarkably similar patterns of characteristics. These patterns fall into three distinct *types* of infant temperament that parents seem to recognize readily. Thus, **difficult infants** are characterized by irregularity (lack of rhythmicity) in such things as eating, sleeping, and toilet functions; withdrawal from unfamiliar situations; slow adaptation to change; and intense (as well as negative) moods. In contrast, **easy infants** are characterized by high rhythmicity (regularity in eating, sleeping, and so on), high approach tendencies in novel situations, high adaptability to change, and a preponderance of positive moods as well as low or moderate intensity of reaction. **Slow-to-warm-up** infants are characterized by low activity level, high initial withdrawal from the unfamiliar, slow adaptation to change, greater negativity in mood, and a moderate or low

---

trait Any distinct, consistent quality in which one person can be different from another.

types Any of several groupings of personality traits. *Extraversion* for example, is a personality type that includes traits such as boldness, outgoingness, assertiveness, sociability.

difficult infants A type of temperament characterized by irregularity with respect to things like eating, sleeping, and toilet functions; withdrawal from unfamiliar situations; slow adaptation to change; and intense as well as negative moods.

easy infants A temperament type marked by high regularity in eating, sleeping, and so on; high interest in novel situations; high adaptability to change; and a preponderance of positive moods, as well as low or moderate intensity of reaction.

intensity of reaction. Of the original 141 children in the NYLS, 65% could be classified as belonging to one of these three temperament types (40% easy; 15% difficult; 10% slow to warm up); the remaining 35% displayed varying mixtures of the nine temperament characteristics (Figure 6.1).

Assessing Infant Temperament

Although infant temperament is sometimes readily apparent in the behavior of infants, observing them in order to assess their temperaments can be a time-consuming and difficult task—and, if done too hastily, can also lead to faulty classifications. Even easy infants sometimes cry and fuss; and the most difficult of little urchins might occasionally laugh and seem approachable and adaptable. For these reasons, researchers often rely on parental observation reported in specially designed questionnaires. Many use the *Early Infancy Temperament Questionnaire (EITQ)* developed by Medoff-Cooper, Carey, and McDevitt (1993). It is designed for use with infants younger than 4 months of age, and is based on Thomas, Chess, and Birch's (1981) *Revised Infant Temperament Questionnaire*, which is more suitable for older infants. For example, Langkamp, Kim, and Pascoe (1998) used the *EITQ* with 4-month-old infants to determine if mothers' perceptions of their infants' temperament were affected by whether they were premature. Their findings? Yes, many mothers see their premature infants as being more difficult than more objective ratings would suggest. Hence reliance on mothers' perceptions alone may not always provide a very accurate picture of infant temperament.

---

slow-to-warm-up infants An infant temperament type marked by low activity level, high initial withdrawal from the unfamiliar; slow adaptation to change; and a somewhat negative mood, with moderate or low intensity of reaction.

Early Infancy Temperament Questionnaire (EITQ) A questionnaire, often used in research, designed to allow caregivers to systematize their perceptions of their infants in order to classify their infants' temperaments.

Temperament*	Description
Easy	Regularity in eating and sleeping (high rhythmicity); high approach tendencies in novel situations; high adaptability to change; preponderance of positive moods; low or moderate intensity of responses
Difficult	Irregularity in eating and sleeping (low rhythmicity); withdrawal in novel situations; slow adaptation to change; preponderance of negative moods; high intensity of reactions to stimulation
Slow to warm up	Low activity level; high initial withdrawal from unfamiliar; slow adaptation to change; somewhat negative mood; moderate or low intensity of reaction to stimulation
Varying mixtures; unclassified	

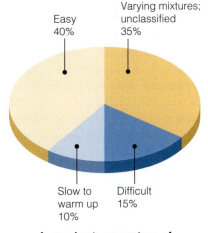

Approximate percentage of infants with each temperament

*Thomas and Chess (1981) caution that these temperaments do not exhaust all possibilities. Also, there are wide ranges of behaviors within each category. "Easy" children don't all react the same way to the same situations; nor do all "difficult" children. Note, too, that some 35% of all infants appear not to fit any of these categories.

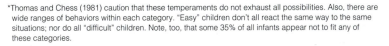

FIGURE 6.1 Infant temperaments. What sort of infant were you? Ask your mother, your father, a sibling, or someone else who can tell you. Do you see any relationship between who you are now and what you were like as an infant? Source: Based on classifications used by Thomas, Chess, and Birch (1968, 1970, 1981) in the New York Longitudinal Study (NYLS).

It might also be possible to eventually assess temperament by looking at physiological measures, perhaps even in the fetus (DiPietro et al., 1996). It may be, as Pavlov (1927) suggested, that some individuals have more *excited* nervous systems than others; their physiological reactions to stimulation are more intense. These infants, Kagan and Snidman (1991) speculate, may have more "difficult" temperaments.

Stability and Long-Term Implications of Infant Temperament

"An infant's temperament," say Kagan and Snidman (1991), "renders some outcomes very likely, some moderately likely, and some unlikely—although not impossible—depending on experience" (p. 856). As an example, Kagan (1997) found that 20% of a large sample (462 infants) of 4-month-olds were highly reactive (fearful of the unfamiliar; easily distressed); about 40% of this sample were nonreactive (relaxed in the face of the unfamiliar; not easily frightened). At the age of 14 to 21 months, about one-third of the highly reactives continued to be highly fearful in strange situations. In contrast, only 4% of the non-reactives were highly fearful, while the majority were calm, outgoing, confident. And these patterns, though less clear, were still evident at the age of $4^1/_2$ years. As Kagan and Snidman (1991) conclude, the temperament *uninhibited to the unfamiliar* (non-reactive), characterized by a tendency to approach in strange situations, is likely to lead to spontaneous, fearless, outgoing youngsters. In contrast, infants who are markedly inhibited in the face of the unfamiliar are likely to continue to be timid at the age of 8 years.

Several other studies have also found some long-term implications of infant temperament. For example, Teerikangas et al. (1998) found that children who had been rated as difficult at the age of 6 months were at greater risk of displaying psychiatric symptoms 14 years later. Note, however, that infant temperament is not always easy to classify accurately. Furthermore, for many infants, temperament may be quite variable, especially during the first two years of life; after age 2, it appears to be far more stable (Lemery et al., 1999).

Some Implications for Parenting

Significantly, however, Teerikangas et al. (1998) also found that an early home-based intervention program, which emphasized parent-child interaction, significantly reduced the risk of developmental problems for these "difficult" infants. Clearly, infant temperament may have some important implications for the type of parenting that is best for an infant.

We know that difficult temperaments are sometimes associated with later problems. And there is evidence that certain types of parenting may be associated with difficult temperaments, and may contribute to subsequent difficulties. For example, Papousek and von Hofacker (1998) found strained and disturbed patterns of mother-infant interaction for "difficult" infants characterized by persistent and extreme crying. Mothers of these infants tended to be less confident, more anxious, more frustrated and depressed, angrier, and more likely to be experiencing marital conflict. In addition, mothers of difficult infants are somewhat more likely to suffer from postpartum depression (Beck, 1996). Of course, studies such as this don't allow us to determine what causes what: Does difficult infant temperament impair caregiver-infant interactions? Or do maternal and contextual characteristics, reflected in how mothers interact with their infants, contribute to the development of the *difficult* temperament?

The best conclusion on the basis of available evidence is that infant temperaments affect caregiver-infant interactions *and* vice versa, a conclusion that underlines again the *reciprocal* nature of interactions in the family. This reciprocity, evident in the matching of caregiver and infant moods and behaviors, is termed **affect synchrony**. Affect synchrony is evident when Carla's mother smiles at her, says "kootchie kootchie koo" (which, in an ancient Inca language means . . . absolutely nothing), and Carla gurgles and coos. And then Carla suddenly becomes interested in the dog and grabs a fistful of dog hair, and now her mother, too, switches her attention to the dog, "You like Killer,"

---

affect synchrony Descriptive label for the matching of emotional states, a phenomenon often evident in mother-infant interactions. Sometimes described as a sort of dance: One moment, infant leads, mother follows; then perhaps mother leads, infant follows.

she says, placing Carla on the dog's back. Affect synchrony is illustrated here in the ebb and flow of matching emotions—a little like a dance where one partner leads for a moment, then the other, and in between, the movements overlap and match. Affect synchrony may be especially important in increasing the self-control of difficult infants, suggest Feldman, Greenbaum, and Yirmiya (1999). They found a positive relation between measures of affect synchrony between mothers and their difficult infants at the age of 3 and 9 months, and infants' self-control at age 2. Similarly, Wendland-Carro, Piccinini, and Millar (1999) argue that affect synchrony, in the form of *co-occurrences* of vocal exchanges, mutual looking, and physical contact, is very important to the healthy development of infants. They found that a simple intervention program using videotaped interactions could significantly enhance mother-infant interactions.

We should note, however, that predictions of later problem behaviors based solely on mothers classifying their infants as being of difficult temperament are often highly unreliable. For example, Oberklaid and associates (1993) found that maternal classifications predicted only 17.5% of children who had behavior problems in preschool. However, if socioeconomic status and sex are also used as predictors (males are far more likely than females to experience problems), accuracy of predictions is much higher. It is not surprising that predictions for the most difficult of the difficult group—for the "persistent and extreme criers," for example—may be the most valid. But here, as elsewhere, our generalizations and our predictions are subject to countless exceptions.

Cultural Context and Goodness of Fit

As Kagan (1992) emphasizes, behaviors influenced by temperament are not immutable. In his words, "Membership in a temperamental category implies only a slight, initial bias for certain emotions and actions" (p. 994)—which, of course, is one reason why developmental outcomes are hard to predict. The infant who is initially difficult may become an adolescent whose charm, grace, and other good qualities make a mother blush with pride; and the one who is initially easy may, it's true, become a thoroughly reprehensible, no-good #@%^^&. Or worse.

One factor that may be important in influencing developmental outcomes, deVries and Sameroff (1984) point out, is the goodness of fit between the infant's temperament and immediate context. For example, it is often an advantage for an infant to be easy in North American contexts, and a disadvantage to be difficult. However, in one study of the Masai in Africa, the opposite appeared to be the case, claims deVries (1989). There, six months after first being classified as easy or difficult, the difficult infants seemed to have fared much better. In fact, many of the easy infants had died. Why? One plausible explanation is that there had been a serious drought in the region, deVries explains, and many infants had died or suffered from malnutrition and disease. That the difficult infants had been least likely to die, speculates deVries, may have been because they yelled and hollered more when they were frustrated and hungry—and succeeded more often in being fed. Thus, their environmental context "fit" better with their difficult temperament.

In our contexts the easy temperament often has higher goodness of fit than the difficult temperament. As an example, consider Marlis, a resolutely difficult infant who reacts loudly and impatiently to frustration. Her father might well be distressed and annoyed at her behavior if he expects and wants Marlis to be more like Robert, who is a remarkably easy infant. But goodness of fit would be higher than expected if Marlis's father took pride in his daughter's lustiness, her independence, her aggressiveness. And if Robert's parents were concerned at how easy he is, afraid that he might not cope well in what they think is a dog-eat-dog world, goodness of fit between his temperament and his context might be unexpectedly poor. Here, as elsewhere, we need to consider the characteristics of the person in interaction with characteristics of the context. In Lerner and colleagues' (1986) terms, the most optimal situation, one where there is high goodness of fit between the infant and context, exists when external demands and expectations are compatible with the infant's basic temperament. Conversely, there is a poor fit when the infant's temperament is not in accord with environmental demands. (See *Concept Summary*.)

Annie Griffiths Belt/Corbis

Early experiences can play an important part in determining a child's temperament. Masai mothers are in close contact with their babies, often breast-feeding them until they are 2 or 3, which may help explain why their infants are good natured and have regular eating and sleeping habits.

CONCEPT SUMMARY   **Infant Temperament**

Temperament is a biologically based tendency for infants to react in predictable ways, a sort of cluster of characteristic emotional responses. Thus infants may be classified as easy (high regularity, high approach tendencies, preponderance of positive moods), difficult (low regularity, withdrawal tendencies, preponderance of negative moods), or slow to warm up (low activity, initial withdrawal from the unfamiliar, somewhat negative moods). Research suggests the following tentative generalizations about temperament:

- Many mothers can relatively easily recognize predominant temperament in their infants, but about 35% of infants cannot be classified.

- Because temperament has a biological basis, some aspects of it may be assessed through physiological measures; parent questionnaires are typically used in research.

- Temperament becomes progressively more stable after age 2.

- Very difficult infants (persistent criers, for example) are at higher risk of developmental problems.

- Parent-infant interactions are less positive with more difficult infants.

- Parent-infant affect synchrony may be especially important for the development of self-control among difficult infants.

- The ideal situation seems to be one where contextual emphases are compatible with the infant's temperament.

INFANT EMOTIONS

For the first three months of their infants' lives, Super and Harkness (1998) tell us, Kipsigis mothers in rural Kenya refer to their little ones as *monkeys*; after that, they call them *children*. And starting from about that time they, like most North American mothers, hold their infants more—on average—than they did before.

Why? One plausible answer is that at about this time, infants throughout the world show a remarkable increase in smiling. And the smile, the true social smile, is perhaps the first positive emotional signal that parents can begin to interpret.

Interpreting infant emotions is difficult, especially when they can express their feelings in nothing more sophisticated than gurgles, wails, grunts, sighs, sobs, and burps. Still, we can see infants smile and laugh and we can hear them cry. And from these behaviors, we can make inferences about what they might be feeling.

Some Theories of Emotions

Beginning with J. B. Watson's (1914) pioneering work, some psychologists have assumed that the infant is capable of reflexive emotional responses from birth. There are at least three such emotions, claimed Watson: *fear*, *rage*, and *love*. Because each of these is a reflex, each can be elicited by a specific stimulus. Thus rage results from being confined or from having movements restricted; fear, from a loud noise or from being dropped suddenly; and love, from being stroked and fondled. Unfortunately, it isn't possible for psychologists to know for certain that the infant's responses to these stimuli is, in fact, what we think of as fear, rage, or love. When we assume that infant Zahorny smiles because he is happy, we may be guilty of a **misattribution**—an inaccurate projection of what our own feelings would be were we to smile. Some of us might be guilty of this misattribution even though

misattribution An error of interpretation, relatively common in studies of infants and animals, in which the researcher makes incorrect assumptions about the meanings of certain reactions or behaviors, for example attributing them to motives characteristic of adult humans.

Shakespeare has made it clear that "one may smile, and smile, and be a villain."

Another approach to studying emotions in infants is that of theorists such as Izard and Malatesta (1987), who base their conclusions on examinations of human facial expressions. These, they claim, reveal a number of distinct emotions including interest (or general excitement), joy, surprise, distress, anger, disgust, contempt, fear, shame, and guilt. They suggest as well that the facial expressions of infants indicate they may be capable of most of these feelings (Termine & Izard, 1988).

In fact, however, it is extremely difficult to separate such closely related emotions as joy and surprise (or distress, anger, and disgust—or shame and guilt). Accordingly, much of the research on infant emotions has looked at actual behaviors such as crying, smiling, and trying to escape or approach—behaviors that we assume have some emotional significance.

Crying

Crying, explains Pinyerd (1994), is the infant's main way of communicating. We often assume that cries mean distress, discomfort, fear, hunger, or some other momentary crisis. But that isn't always the case, says Sroufe (1996). For example, 1-year-old infants are sometimes successful in fighting back their tears when their caregiver leaves them alone in a strange situation. And then they burst into tears when the caregiver returns—surely as much from relief as from distress.

Not all infants cry. Claire, my middle progeny, almost never cried as an infant. Her mother thought she might be saving it for when she became an adolescent and wanted a car. But she didn't cry then either.

Why Infants Cry

According to theorists John Bowlby and Margaret Ainsworth, whose theories are discussed in the section on attachment later in this chapter, crying is a biologically based behavior closely related to the development of mother-infant attachment. The infant's cry says, in effect, "Hey, I need a protective parent." Usually, infant crying elicits protective

THOUGHT CHALLENGE: *It seems likely that crying in infants has adaptive value. Lummaa et al. (1998) speculate that there might have been four distinct evolutionary benefits of intensive infant crying. Can you think what these might have been?*

emotions and behaviors in parents. And, explains Nelson (1998), throughout life, the urge to cry continues to be our natural reaction to real or threatened separation and loss (although many of us are socialized to suppress that urge). Like our infant cries, our adult cries express our grief, perhaps even our anger, at threatened or actual separation and loss. And throughout life, should we be so lucky as to be surrounded by people who care, crying elicits caring—and caretaking—responses in others.

A number of studies indicate that the peak period for infant crying is around the age of 6 weeks (for example, Lucas & St. James-Roberts, 1998). The reasons why this might be so are unclear. What does seem clear is that at least some infant cries are signs of real distress or of hunger. Persistent and excessive crying, sometimes termed **colic**, may be a sign of a serious problem. The causes of persistent crying (more than 3 hours per day) are sometimes linked to abdominal spasms following feeding; in many cases, however, causes cannot be determined (Barr, 1998). Continual and unexplained crying can occur in spite of very good maternal care and can be highly resistant to treatment (Lucas & St. James-Roberts, 1998). The good news, says Barr (1998), is that even among the most persistent of criers, the vast majority eventually stop crying—and there seem to be no lasting ill effects on the infant's development nor on infant-caregiver interactions. But for a few, excessive crying may evolve into more general problems, sometimes evident in mother-infant interactions.

Kinds of Cries If cries are important signals for caregivers, what do they mean? Is there more than one kind of cry? If so, can caregivers distinguish them?

To answer these questions, Wolff (1969) analyzed tape recordings of infants crying. He identified four distinct cries that he interprets as expressions of different emotions. The most frequent cry is called the *rhythmic cry*. It is the type of cry to which most infants eventually revert after initially engaging in another type of crying (Green, Gustafson, & McGhie, 1998). Most experienced parents apparently recognize their infant's rhythmic cries and typically interpret them as meaning that there is nothing seriously wrong.

A second kind of cry, the *angry cry*, is characterized by its protracted loudness and results from more air being forced through the vocal cords. It, too, does not fool an experienced caregiver.

A third distinguishable cry, says Wolff, is that of *pain*. An infant's pain cry is characterized by a long wail followed by a period of breath holding. Boero et al. (1998) compared the acoustic characteristics of infant cries recorded during routine blood withdrawal (associated with pain), just before feeding (associated with hunger), and when being manipulated during a medical examination. They found that each of these cries, and especially the cry of pain, was distinct. In particular, pain cries include wails, parts of which are often "voiceless." There is evidence that caregivers, especially mothers, recognize and respond quickly to infants' cries of pain (Boukydis & Lester, 1998).

Finally, there is the hunger cry, a cry to which caregivers also respond readily (Boykydis & Lester, 1998). In general, first-time parents tend to respond to infant crying sooner than parents who have more than one child. And mothers are more likely to be attentive than are fathers (Donate-Bartfield & Passman, 1985).

The meanings of an infant's cries are apparently not universal. Isabell and McKee (1980) observe that in many primitive cultures in which a child is carried about constantly by the mother, mother-infant communication can occur through physical contact. In these cultures, there appears to be little need for the vocal signals of distress that we have come to expect from our infants. For instance, among indigenous tribes in the northern Andes, infant crying is extremely rare and is invariably interpreted as a sign of illness. Why else would a warm, well-fed, and constantly embraced infant cry?

colic Infant disorder characterized by excessive crying, often following feeding. May occasionally, but not always, be due to intense abdominal pain resulting from muscular spasms.

Smiling and Laughing

We saw that Kipsigis mothers of rural Kenya call their infants *children* rather than *monkeys* after the age of about 3 months, and North American parents begin to hold their infants more at about the same age (Super & Harkness, 1998). Both of these behaviors may have a lot to do with a significant change in infants' apparent social responsiveness that occurs at about that time. And that change is probably very closely linked to the infant's smile.

Smiling is a universal phenomenon among human cultures. In the warm, well-fed infant, it occurs as a fleeting response even as early as 2 to 12 hours after delivery (Wolff, 1963). This early smile involves the lower part of the face, not the upper cheeks and eyes, and is labeled a **non-Duchenne** smile (Messinger, Fogel, & Dickson, 1999). Smiles that involve high cheek raising—*Duchenne smiles*—are more common among adults and older infants. The early smile of the infant is a type of reflex smile rather than a true social smile. It appears to be linked to the brain stem, the most primitive brain structure, because it's present even in children born with no cerebral cortex but with a functioning brain stem (termed **anencephalic**). These children sometimes survive for a few days, and seem to be able to smile. Thus the very first *reflexive* infant smiles have little to do with happiness or comfort, but are probably simply related to bursts of activity in the brain stem (Sroufe, 1996).

Developing the Ability to Smile and Laugh Gewirtz (1965) identified three stages in the development of smiling. The first phase, just described, is spontaneous or **reflex smiling**. It occurs in the absence of readily identifiable stimuli and is often, though perhaps incorrectly, attributed to "gas pains." **Social smiling**, the second phase, takes place initially in response to auditory and visual stimuli that are social in nature—that is, related to other humans. Finally, the child displays the **selective social smile**, common among children and adults. It occurs in response to social stimuli that the child can identify as familiar. With the appearance of the selective social smile, children smile less often in response to an unfamiliar voice or face and display more withdrawal behavior and other signs of anxiety in the presence of strangers. (Stranger anxiety is discussed in a later section of this chapter.)

Hodapp and Mueller (1982) note that the development of smiling in infants follows the same general pattern as the development of crying. Initially, infants smile and cry in response to internal states, primarily gastric disturbances. With the passage of time, however, infants become more responsive to external stimulation, and both crying and smiling begin to occur more in response to external stimuli. Thus, by the age of 4 or 5 weeks, many infants will interrupt their feeding to smile when they hear their mother's voice. Similarly, crying now occurs in response to external sources of frustration, such as having a pacifier presented and then taken away. In brief, the early development of these behaviors follows an internal to external progression.

The Baby's First Laughter At about 4 months, infants begin to laugh in addition to smiling. At first, laughter is most likely to occur in response to physical stimulation such as tickling; later, infants laugh in response to more social and eventually more cognitive situations—seeing other children laughing, for example (Sroufe & Wunsch, 1972). Although the function of laughter in infants has never been very clear, perhaps because it has not been investigated very much. Sroufe (1996) suggests that it probably serves to release tension. Fear, by contrast, signifies a continued buildup of tension.

---

non-Duchenne smile A smile, typical of a young infant, that involves the lower part of the face rather than the upper cheeks. Genuinely happy adults are more likely to manifest *Duchenne* smiles.

anencephalic A condition in which parts, or all, of the brain are missing.

reflex smiling Also termed *spontaneous smiling*, the earliest form of infant smile, reflecting bursts of cortical activity rather than contentment or social reactivity.

social smiling The second phase in the development of smiling, initially occurring in response to auditory and visual stimuli that are social in nature, like the caregiver's voice.

selective social smile Smiling in response to social stimuli that the infant can identify as familiar.

Wariness and Fear

Some years ago I went to a Halloween party. As part of my "costume," I attempted to grow a beard, and, after several months of effort, I had succeeded in covering most of my face with hair. Shortly after the party, I shaved off all my whiskers. And when I walked out of the bathroom clean-shaven, my 1-year-old daughter took one look at me and burst into tears. Why?

My daughter would not have cried to see me newly shaven when she was only 4 months old. At that age, argue Watson and Rayner (1920), infants *reflexively* fear loud noises and sudden loss of support. Only later do they learn to fear the unexpected. That's because fearing the unexpected first requires learning what to expect.

Some fears appear to be quite general: For example, fear of heights appears to be almost universal in infants by the age of 13 to 18 months and is present in more than 20% of all children by the age of 7 months (Scarr & Salapatek, 1970). Similarly, fear of snakes is quite often found even among people who have had no experience whatsoever with snakes (Gullone & King, 1997).

Following a detailed longitudinal investigation, Bronson (1972) found that fear of strangers—termed **stranger anxiety**—is not ordinarily seen before the age of 6 months. At the age of 3 or 4 months, the baby's most common response to a stranger is to smile. Fear reactions, which don't occur in all infants, peak between about 9 and 15 months (Bronson, 1972). (Fear of strangers is discussed in more detail in the next section.)

Most of the other situations that may evoke fear in infants have to do with the unexpected. For example, a jack-in-the-box may be frightening; so might an experimenter or parent wearing a mask—or a newly shaven parent. In addition, separation from the mother is frightening for some infants, as are sounds presented in irregular fashion. All these situations present something unexpected or novel. That the infant under the age of 6 months doesn't respond with fear to strangers is probably because

stranger anxiety *Fear reactions in the presence of unknown people; seldom seen in infants until the middle of their first year, after which some babies begin to "make strange."*

the ability to recognize familiar faces doesn't develop until about that age. A stranger is not a stranger until a familiar person is familiar.

That infants should have a tendency to be wary of the novel and unfamiliar—and of snakes and high cliffs and skinny branches—makes good evolutionary sense. After all, these are the things that might eat you or hurt you. Interestingly, at all ages objects are far less potent than strangers in bringing about reactions of wariness or fear. Objects are probably not going to eat you; strange people (and strange animals) well might.

Not all infants are fearful and wary—and some are far more fearful than others. There is considerable evidence that certain infant temperament traits—like high reactivity and negative moods—are more likely to be manifested in fears in later infancy and childhood. For example, Schmidt and Fox (1998) found that 4-month-old infants who were highly reactive *and* characterized by negative moods tended to be more wary and fearful as toddlers than other babies who were also highly active but who manifested more positive emotions.

Fear of Strangers

When he was 5 months old, Sam, my neighbor's little urchin, was a smiling, gurgling little guy; I loved to go over to his house and make him laugh. Then I went away on a trip. Eventually I came back. After a bit, I went over to Sam's house. There he was, sitting by himself on the floor, which was a trick I'd not seen before, playing with a pile of kitchen junk. And I said, "Hey, Sam old buddy, waddya' say?" and he looked at me and burst out crying. He was 9 months old now. Fortunately, I had brought a big yellow toy truck back with me, and after a while, we were friends again.

Fear of strangers is common to many infants. As we saw, it doesn't usually appear before the age of 6 to 9 months. It seems that once infants have become familiar with their environment, that is, once they have developed certain expectations of events that are most likely to occur, they may be uneasy and afraid when these events don't occur—or when different events happen. A common early reaction to the unexpected, Shreeve (1991) explains, is freezing (not doing anything) and mutism (not saying any-thing). These responses are, in fact, common fear responses in young infants and children.

Like all human characteristics and behaviors, emotional reactions are a product of the interaction between biological tendencies and environmental influences. The influence of experience in the devel-opment of stranger anxiety is evident in the obser-vation that fear arises in the face of the unexpected—labeled the **incongruity hypothesis** (Hebb, 1966). This hypothesis is bolstered by the observation that infants who are in contact with the largest number of people (strangers and siblings)—and for whom "unexpected" strangers are uncom-mon—are less likely to show fear, react with the least amount of fear, and stop being afraid of strangers at an earlier age (Gullone & King, 1997).

The influence of experience may also be evident in the finding that parental characteristics may influence reactions of their infants. We know that at a very early age, infants begin to use **social referenc-ing** as one way of determining what the emotional significance of a situation is. This may explain in part why it is that fearful and anxious mothers, as well as mothers who suffer from depression, are somewhat more likely to have children who fear strangers (Sugawara et al., 1999).

The influence of biology in the development of fear is apparent in the finding that infants whose temperament traits include high reactivity and nega-tive moods are more likely to react with fear (Kagan, Snidman, & Arcus, 1998; Schmidt & Fox, 1998).

Separation Protest

Closely related to fear of strangers is what is called separation protest—the fearful child's reaction to very short-term separations from a principal care-giver. Measures of separation protest are often used as an indication of degree and type of attachment that an infant has for a parent. These measures are typically obtained using Ainsworth's strange situa-tion, a setting designed to evaluate the infant's reac-tion at being separated from, and then later reunited with, a caregiver (most often the mother). The strange situation is used extensively in investiga-tions of infant attachment, and is described in the section on attachment later in this chapter.

Fear of strangers is sometimes quite extreme and may be perceived by parents as a serious prob-lem. In fact, it is sometimes one of the reasons why a parent—often the mother, but also sometimes the father—may choose to stay home after the birth of a child (Hertz & Ferguson, 1996).

One way of minimizing infant distress at being confronted by strangers or separated from a parent might be to ensure that the infant has frequent, short-term exposure to a variety of people (and siblings). In addition, the stranger's behavior may be important. For example, a study by Gunnar and colleagues (1992) looked at the effects of exposing infants to strangers for periods of 30 minutes. They measured infant fear through the infant's behavior, and also by looking at elevations of cortisol in the infant's saliva—a common measure of stress. They found that when caregivers were instructed to be warm and responsive and to interact with the infant, indications of anxiety were significantly lower than when caregivers were more distant (although not insensitive to the infant's distress). Not surprisingly, there is also evidence that moth-ers who are themselves attentive and interactive (rather than dismissing or preoccupied) are less likely to have highly fearful infants (Crowell & Feldman, 1991).

Shaffer (2000) provides a number of sugges-tions for reducing stranger anxiety and separation protest:

▲ Have familiar people and objects with the child at the time of separation or introduction of the stranger.

▲ Arrange for the physical setting to be familiar.

▲ Suggest that the "stranger" be sensitive and unobtrusive and perhaps take steps to appear less

incongruity hypothesis The supposition that infant fear reactions result from a discrepancy between reality and what the infant has learned to expect.

social referencing Using others' reactions as a norm or reference point to guide one's personal reactions. Thus a young child's response to a strange situation might be heavily influenced by the parent's apparent reaction.

strange (for example, a children's doctor or nurse may elicit less fear dressed casually and without instruments hanging around the neck).

▲ Choose sensitive substitute caregivers.

▲ Provide children with some reminder from home if they must be away from home.

Regulating Emotions and Emotional Expression in Infancy

Reminders from home—or people, animals, and things closely associated with safety and comfort—are among the ways in which infants try to control emotions that threaten to become too powerful (see *At a Glance:* "Old Pillows, Thumbs, and Other Security Blankets"). We, too, have our methods of controlling strong emotions, especially those associated with high stress. When you or I find ourselves in a frightening situation, when our hearts race and our knees turn to jelly, we do things to control or regulate our emotions. Perhaps we play cognitive games with ourselves: We tell ourselves that we have nothing to be afraid of, that we are such wonderful surgeons or public speakers or students that we will perform marvelously. Or we change the situation so that it isn't frightening anymore, perhaps by avoiding it.

There is a temptation to think that infants are not capable of this sort of control of emotions—that if they are frightened, all they can do is cry, and that if they are delighted, then, like little robots, they must smile. We sometimes think of them as responding almost blindly to the stimulation that the world provides willy-nilly for them. We are wrong; they are not nearly so helpless.

Beginning very early in life, infants are capable of what Gianino and Tronick (1988) label *self-directed regulatory behaviors* and *other-directed regulatory behaviors*. These behaviors are designed to monitor, to facilitate, or to inhibit emotional reactions, explain Buss and Goldsmith (1998).

As an example, Tronick (1989) describes a peek-a-boo game between a mother and her infant. In this little episode, the infant turns away from the mother just before the "peek" and begins to suck on his thumb, staring blankly into space. The mother

sits back. Within a few seconds the infant turns to the mother, pulls out his thumb, and contorts his body; his expression seems clearly interested. The mother smiles, moves closer, and says "Oh, now you're back!" The infant smiles and coos. Shortly, he goes back to sucking his thumb. But again, after a few seconds, he turns to the mother once more and smiles.

The infant in this instance *seems* to be attempting to control the mother's behavior. This other-directed regulatory behavior is evident in how he turns back to the mother, how he coos and smiles, how he tries to make her do things that he finds exciting. In effect, he is controlling her behavior and, by the same token, exercising control over his own emotions. And when things become too exciting, too emotional, he can regulate his emotions by turning away from his mother. Now he distracts himself by sucking his thumb and by staring into space—evidence of self-directed regulatory behavior.

Note the emphasis on the word *seems*, above. As Buss and Goldsmith (1998) point out, we should be cautious in assuming that these behaviors actually lead to a reduction (or intensification) of emotions in the infant. Nor do we know that the infant actually *intends* to regulate emotions in these ways. Assuming that this is the case may well be a *misattribution*. Perhaps all we have here is another example of mother-infant synchrony, a sort of dance of behaviors whose apparent effects are exciting or calming for the infant. Still, it is likely in the give and take of this synchrony that the infant begins to learn not only how to regulate emotions, but also how to communicate them. But, as we see in Chapter 8, there is still a great deal of socialization of emotional displays to be accomplished—that is, the infant still has a great deal to learn about when and how cultures expect emotions to be expressed.

◪ PARENT-INFANT ATTACHMENTS

Among the most important interactions in the early life of infants are those involving parent-infant attachments. Infants have two principal tasks, say Greenspan and Lieberman (1989). The first task is a biological one: to achieve a balance between what

| AT A GLANCE | **Old Pillows, Thumbs, and Other Security Blankets** |

One of my brothers developed an extraordinarily powerful attachment to his pillow when he was just a small person. So powerful was his devotion to this soft thing that for many months, he dragged it with him absolutely everywhere he went. Later some powerful social forces began to shape him—somewhat—and he stopped bringing the pillow out when there were other people around. But still, he would not give it up. And if we hid it or threw it in with the other dirty clothes, his reaction soon made us find it and give it back.

That my brother had a *security blanket*—often called a **transitional object**—made him no different from half of all middle-class North American children, report Passman and Halonen (1979), although his was not the most common of transitional objects, which are the blanket and the pacifier. A large number of children also suck their thumbs as a type of transitional object, most often to fall asleep, but also as a refuge against fear and stress (Lookabaugh & Fu, 1992). And a great many also use their pets as *transitional* objects (Triebenbacher, 1998). These objects are called transitional because they become the focus of children's affection and attention while they are in transition between a state of high dependence on the parent and the development of a more independent self (Winnicott, 1971). According to this psycho-analytic view, the development of self requires separation from the parent or **individuation**—the recognition of one's own individuality. The process of separating and becoming independent gives rise to anxiety; the blanket or the teddy bear or the dirty old pillow serves to comfort the child.

transitional objects Blankets, teddy bears, or other objects that children focus affection and attention on while in transition between a state of high parental dependency and the development of a more independent self.

individuation The recognition of one's own individuality.

Security blankets *are* effective. In fact, Passman and Weisberg (1975) found that in some situations, they were almost as effective as the presence of a mother in reducing a child's anxiety. Children who are attached to inanimate transitional objects, including their thumb, cope more effectively in stressful situations than children with no such attachment (Lookabaugh & Fu, 1992).

Still, some parents worry. Is the child who is attached to these inanimate, nonsocial objects perhaps more insecure, less well adjusted, than the child whose attachments are more social? The good news for my brother is that Passman's (1987) answer for these questions is, no; attachments of this nature do not predict future maladjustment.

As one of my professors used to say, "If you are anxious when you write my tests and cannot bring your mother with you, do bring your blanket . . . or whatever."

The presence of an "attachment object"—like a blanket, a mother, or even a teddy bear—can do a great deal to comfort a child in situations that are stressful and frightening.

Elizabeth Crews

the organism needs and what it assimilates, a balance termed **homeostasis**. In this context, homeostasis is maintained when the infant is not too hungry, thirsty, cold, or hot. Maintaining homeostasis is greatly facilitated by infants' increasing ability to regulate or control their behavior as they interact with their environment.

The second task, very closely related to maintaining homeostasis, involves forming an attachment—generally with a principal caregiver to begin with, later with other individuals in the immediate environment (the microsystem). "Neonates must form a bond with their mothers," explains Leon (1992), "if they are to receive the sustenance, protection, and comfort they require to grow and develop" (p. 377). Crying, as we saw, is one of the infant's powerful attachment-related tools (Nelson, 1998). The infant's cry says, "Pay attention, caregivers; I need you!" To need and to be needed present powerful motives for attachment.

Attachment and Biological Bonds

Attachment is a general term that includes the range of positive emotions that link parents, children, and other people; bonding is a more specific and more biological term. Thus, **mother-infant bonding** refers primarily to the very early, biologically based attachment that the mother develops for her infant.

Attachment between mother and infant is both biologically and psychologically important. From a psychological point of view, as we see later, the nature of attachments between parents and infants has important implications for the immediate and long-term psychological well-being of both parent and child. And biologically, the existence of a strong mother-infant bond serves to ensure that mother and

infant will stay close to each other—a condition that, for most animals, is essential to the infant's survival. Hence it seems reasonable to suppose that there would be powerful genetically based tendencies to establish such bonds.

Ethologists (those who study animal behavior in natural settings) inform us that yes, there are powerful preprogrammed attachment tendencies among many nonanimal species. They are evident in the fact that mothers and infants exposed to each other during a critical period—or in the case of humans, a sensitive period—generally shortly after birth, typically "bond." In the absence of appropriate experiences during this period, bonding may fail to occur. As we saw in Chapter 2, theorists such as Bowlby (1958) and Klaus and Kennell (1983) suggest that failure to establish a strong mother-infant bond is detrimental to the future adjustment and emotional health of the child, and may be related to such things as child abuse or "growth failure." Growth failure, or **failure to thrive (FTT)**—also called *maternal deprivation syndrome*—is a condition in which an apparently normal infant fails to gain weight, falling to the bottom 3% of normal standards. Coolbear and Benoit (1999) have since reported that infants characterized by FTT are also at greater risk of having disturbed patterns of attachment with their caregivers. This, of course, doesn't establish that FTT leads to insecure mother-infant attachments—or the opposite. But we do know that some cases of FTT may be marked not only by listlessness, loss of appetite, and illness, but also, in its more extreme manifestations, even death (Abramson, 1991). Such extreme manifestations are very rare, however. Still, as Drewet, Corbett, and Wright (1999) report, the lower weights of infants diagnosed with FTT are typically not overcome in later childhood. These children continue to show height and weight reductions and smaller head circumference at school age. It is reassuring to note, however, that they do not appear to be intellectually disadvantaged.

Biological Bonding Mechanisms It seems likely that no preexisting emotional bond links the infant to its

---

homeostasis A term used in theories that deal with organic, physiological, social, and other systems (hence *general systems theory*) to signify the apparent tendency of these systems to maintain a beneficial stability or balance among and within their functioning parts.

attachment A strong emotional bond that seems to have its roots in powerful biological tendencies. Parent-infant attachment is important for healthy infant development.

mother-infant bonding The emotional bond that exists between mother and infant.

failure to thrive (FTT) Infants' failure to gain weight at a normal rate (within the bottom 3% of the population) for no apparent organic reason. Also called *maternal deprivation syndrome* because maternal absence or neglect may be implicated.

mother at birth. A neonate taken from its mother and given to another will surely never know the difference unless, of course, the facts are disclosed later. But that a bond does form with the primary caregiver(s) is also clear.

Wellman and Gelman (1992) point out that the infant has certain biological preadaptations that facilitate the development of this bond. These include perceptual biases such as the infant's built-in visual accommodation for a distance of approximately 8 to 10 inches (about the distance to the caregiver's face during feeding), the young infant's apparent preference for the human face, and a sensitivity and responsiveness to the human voice. The authors also include some reflexive response tendencies that seem especially designed for social interaction. Like the young of most mammals, for example, the human infant clings and turns and roots and sucks. One of the functions of these vegetative reflexes is surely to ensure that the infant obtains nourishment and survives. But more than this, feeding is among the first important social interactions between caregiver and infant. Almost invariably, feeding leads to the mutual gaze, which is highly significant in the development of attachment and appears to be universal between mothers and infants in different cultures. In addition, as we saw earlier, the tendency for mothers and infants to develop *affect synchronies*—overlapping patterns of attention, activity, and emotion—may also be closely related to the development of attachment.

The Importance of Bonding The biological significance of bonding as a survival mechanism seems clear. From an evolutionary perspective, the survival benefits of a tight mother-infant bond would have been especially apparent at a time when physical survival was threatened by the "hissing serpents and dragons of Eden" (Sagan, 1977). One of the important functions of the infant's distress at being separated from the mother is that it serves to keep her close—and perhaps to protect the infant from wild beasts.

But now dragons and serpents no longer lurk so menacingly in our forests—or parking lots. Nevertheless, some early research with small groups of mothers indicated that there may be a critical period very early in our lives during which we must have contact with our mothers so that a bond may form.

Bonding failure, some claimed, can have serious negative consequences later (for example, Klaus & Kennell, 1976). We know now, however, that while *bonding failure* describes what sometimes happens with infant animals who are not exposed to their mothers during a *critical period*, the concept is not highly applicable to humans. For one thing, there doesn't appear to be a critical period—or even a sensitive period with clear time boundaries—for the formation of attachments between human mothers and their infants. Also, studies of attachment among human infants and their mothers reinforce the current view that attachment takes various forms, and that it is the *quality* of the attachment between infants and caregivers that is most important to their later well-being. As Klaus & Kennell (1983) phrase it, "The human being is highly adaptable, and there are many fail-safe routes to attachment" (p. 50).

Bowlby's Stages in Forming Infant Attachment

The why of infant attachment is clear: After all, the infant's very survival demands a solicitous caregiver. What better way to ensure that the caregiver will be there when needed than to program into the human gene pool powerful parent-infant attachment tendencies? However, nature does not program the attachment itself; it develops later. Nor do genes limit attachment to the biological mother or father, as is clear in cases involving adoption.

Bowlby, an important, psychoanalytically oriented clinician, describes four phases in the infant's development of attachment (Mitchell, 1999; Brennan, 1999). Through each phase, the infant's behavior seems to be guided by a single overriding principle: Keep the attachment object close. And in most cases, that attachment object is the mother.

Preattachment The *preattachment* phase spans the first few weeks of life, and is marked by the preadaptations that seem to predispose the infant for human

---

bonding failure A biologically oriented phrase to indicate the failure of a bond to form between a mother and infant, usually as a result of not being exposed to each other during a critical period. The concept has limited applicability to humans.

interaction: things like their preference for the human voice and face, their movements in synchrony with adult speech, and their built-in visual accommodation for about the distance of the mother's face.

Attachment in the Making During the second phase, *attachment in the making*, there is marked emphasis on behaviors that promote contact with important adults—for example, crying and smiling as well as sucking, rooting, clinging, looking at, and following with the eyes. The second phase culminates in clearly identifiable attachment during the second half of the first year of life. At this time, the infant manifests the "selective social smile"—the smile that occurs in recognition of familiar faces. At the same time, smiling in response to unfamiliar faces becomes less common.

Clear-Cut Attachment *Clear-cut attachment* becomes evident with the infant's development of locomotor abilities. Now infants are able to attract the mother or father's attention not only by smiling, crying, reaching, and so on; they can also crawl over and grab a leg; they can climb up and wrap themselves around a neck; they can cling to the strings that hang from the rear of old aprons. In brief, they can indicate very clearly what (and whom) the objects of their attachment are.

Goal-Corrected Attachment Sometime in the second year, Bowlby informs us, the infant enters a phase of *goal-corrected attachment*. The infant has now developed notions of self and has begun to understand something of the point of view of others. Gradually, infants learn to make inferences about the effects of their behaviors, as well as about their parents' behavior; and they learn to affect the behavior of parents in ways more subtle than crying, smiling, yelling, or toddling over and grabbing hold. (See *Concept Summary.*)

Assessing and Studying Attachment

Attachment is a powerful emotional bond, impossible for an infant to describe for us, and not easy to study because many of the experiments that might shed light on the area cannot be performed with humans. For this reason, infant monkeys have sometimes been used instead. (See *At a Glance:* "Monkeys without Mothers.")

Measurements of infant attachment to their caregivers are always indirect. Investigators look at behaviors that are directed toward the object of attachment (crying, smiling, vocalizing, following, clinging, holding, looking at, and so on); they focus on the infant's reaction to strange situations; and they look at the infant's reaction to being separated from a parent.

Measures of parents' attachments to their children can be more verbal as well as observational. That is, investigators can observe mothers interacting with their infants; they can also ask them to respond to a variety of probing questions. And in recent years, many studies have also looked at what parents remember of *their* relationships with their own parents. It seems that parents' perceptions of relationships they had with their parents are extraordinarily closely linked with the attachments their own children form with them (van Ijzendoorn & Bakermans-Kranenburg, 1997). In the next two sections we look first at attachment from the infant's point of view, and then at parents' perceptions of their attachments as children.

Infant Attachment: Ainsworth's Strange Situation

How do you determine whether, to whom, and how strongly an infant is attached? One way is Ainsworth and associates' (1978) *Strange Situation Procedure*, a procedure often sequenced as shown in Table 6.1.

What Ainsworth's *Strange Situation Procedure* provides is a way of assessing attachment under stress. It permits researchers to determine the infant's anxiety or security in these circumstances. A large number of studies using the Ainsworth procedure with infants reveals attachment behaviors that sort themselves into four broad categories.

Securely attached infants are those who use the mother as a base for exploration—who go out freely and play in the room, but who often reestablish contact, either by looking at the mother, interacting verbally, or returning to her physically. When the mother leaves, these infants are upset and often stop

---

securely attached Describes infants who are strongly and positively attached to a caregiver, who are distressed when that person leaves, and who quickly reestablish contact when the person returns.

CONCEPT SUMMARY

Bowlby's Sequential Phases in the Development of Infant Attachment

Phase	Approximate Age	Important Behaviors
Preattachment	First month	Crying, smiling, rooting, clinging, sucking, looking at; movements synchronized with adult speech; discrimination of mother's voice
Attachment in the making	Into second half of first year	Singling out objects of primary attachment; selective social smile—directed more toward attachment objects/persons than toward the unfamiliar
Clear-cut attachment	Second half of first year	Continued use of behaviors designed to draw attention—smiling, crying, squirming; use of newly developed locomotor skills to approach attachment object/person
Goal-corrected attachment	Second year	Begins to adopt mother's point of view and to make inferences about mother's behavior; manipulation of mother's behavior in more subtle ways following gradual recognition of cause-and-effect relationships

Source: Based on Bowlby (1969).

their exploration. Many also cry. During the reunion episodes, they greet the mother warmly and try to reestablish physical contact or some sort of interaction with her. Securely attached infants manifest few, if any, negative reactions toward their mothers during reunion. If upset, they are easily soothed by the mother and return readily to play or exploration.

In contrast, insecurely attached infants are those who display significant negative behavior toward the mother during reunion events. Some of these infants, the **insecure-avoidant** (also termed *anxious-avoidant*), either ignore the mother's reentrance or actively avoid contact with her—sometimes by looking away, sometimes by refusing to cuddle or cling. Interestingly, they rarely cry when the mother leaves.

A second group of insecurely attached infants, the **insecure-resistant**, are very upset when the mother leaves, their behavior being evidence of strong attachment. However, the mother's reappearance does not soothe their distress. Strangely, these infants sometimes display anger when the mother returns. The anger is sometimes very subtle; for example, they might push the mother away even when they appear to want to be held (hence the ambivalence).

A final group, originally termed unclassified by Ainsworth and associates (1978), is now often termed **disorganized/disoriented**. These infants typically display any of a range of disorganized or

insecure-resistant Describes infants who are profoundly upset when the principal caregiver leaves and who often display anger when that person returns.

insecure-avoidant Describes infants who are anxiously attached to a caregiver, who show little signs of distress when that person leaves, and who initially avoid reestablishing contact when the person returns.

disorganized/disoriented Describes infants whose attachment behaviors toward caregivers are confused, unclear, and sometimes contradictory.

| AT A GLANCE | **Monkeys without Mothers** |

Harlow (1958; 1959) found that infant monkeys seem to have a powerful need for their mothers—as well as for the company of other monkeys. Many of those who are raised without mothers and in isolation later experience serious developmental problems. Typically, they don't get along with other monkeys. For example, few of them are able to achieve sexual relations. Female monkeys raised under such conditions who then have infants of their own will often reject them. But when the mothers of infant monkeys are replaced with a substitute, infants typically form a strong attachment to the substitute and develop quite normally. Interestingly, however, not just any substitute will do. In fact, a wire model used as a substitute mother, even if it has a functional breast (that is, a bottle implanted where a breast should be), is not nearly as appealing as a soft, terry-cloth-covered mother, even if the soft mother doesn't have a working breast! This says something about the importance of physical contact. At least for infant monkeys.

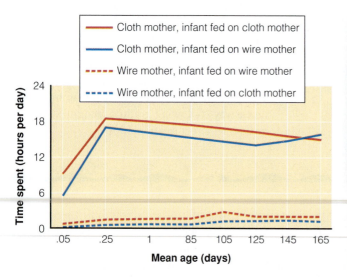

FIGURE 6.2 Amount of time spent by infant monkeys on cloth and wire surrogate mothers. Source: From Harry F. Harlow, Love in infant monkeys, *Scientific American*, 1959, 200, 68–74. Copyright 1959 by Scientific American, Inc. All rights reserved. Used by permission.

In the Harlow studies, infant monkeys developed a strong preference for the cloth mother regardless of whether the infant was fed on the wire model or on the cloth model.

disoriented behaviors, such as crying for a parent at the door and then moving quickly away when they hear the parent approaching; approaching the parent with the head turned away; or standing motionless with no clear reaction during the strange situation (see Figure 6.4).

Main's *Adult Attachment Interview* Does the quality of the attachment infants have with their parents have anything to do with the sorts of adults they will become? And do these early attachments have anything to do with the sorts of attachments their own infants will eventually have with them?

The answer to both questions seems to be yes. Part of the evidence for this answer lies in the results of a series of studies that have used *Main's Adult Attachment Interview (AAI)* (Main, 1995, 1996). This instrument is a semistructured interview that asks parents to recollect and tell stories about the relationships they had with principal caregivers as they were growing up. Interviewers then look at the consistency, the clarity, and the coherence of parents'

Adult Attachment Interview (AAI) A questionnaire developed by Main designed to uncover parents' recollections of their relationships with their own caregivers when they were children.

TABLE 6.1
Ainsworth's *Strange Situation Procedure*

(Each event lasts approximately 3 minutes.)

1. Mother and baby enter a room.

2. Mother puts baby down and stays while baby plays with toys.

3. Stranger enters and is silent (1 minute); speaks with mother (1 minute); approaches baby (3rd minute).

4. *Separation episode 1:* Mother leaves. If baby cries, stranger attempts to comfort; if baby is passive, stranger attempts to interest in a toy.

5. *Reunion episode 1:* Mother returns; stranger leaves. Mother greets/comforts baby.

6. *Separation episode 2:* Mother leaves; baby is alone.

7. Stranger comes back; adjusts behavior to reaction of infant.

8. *Reunion episode 2:* Mother returns; stranger leaves.

In first grade, George Leroy used to get such severe stomachaches that he often had to be taken home to his mother. "He's always been like that," claimed his mother. "Why, when he was little, he used to raise a stink every time I had to leave him. And one time, when I come back from bowling or something, he up and heaved his potty at me, he was still so mad, and the dang thing was about . . . as heavy as a brick." According to Ainsworth's classification, what sort of attachment did George display toward his mother?

Attachment classification	Common behavior when mother leaves or returns
Securely attached	Uses mother as a base from which to explore; upset when she leaves but quickly soothed when she returns; greets her positively on return
Insecure-avoidant	Rarely cries when mother leaves; ignores or actively avoids her when she returns, sometimes pointedly not looking at her or not clinging to her when picked up.
Insecure-resistant	Very upset when mother leaves; often angry when she returns, sometimes pushing her away
Disorganized/ disoriented	Contradictory, disorganized reactions to separation and reunion; may cry for mother but runs away when she returns, or approaches her while looking away

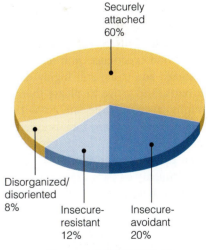

Securely attached 60%

Disorganized/ disoriented 8%

Insecure-resistant 12%

Insecure-avoidant 20%

Types and distribution of infant attachment

FIGURE 6.3 Types of infant attachment. Source: Based in part on Ainsworth et al. (1978). *Patterns of Attachment.* Hillsdale, N.J.: Erlbaum; and on M. Main & J. Solomon (1986). Discovery of an insecure, disorganized/disoriented attachment pattern: Procedures, findings, and implications for the classification of behavior. In M. Yogman & T. B. Brazelton, eds., *Affective development in infancy.* Norwood, N.J.: Ablex.

responses. That is, the emphasis is more on the *quality* of descriptions than on the content of what is said. Analysis of these descriptions permits classification of parents into four groups.

Autonomous adults provide highly coherent accounts of their childhood relationships with parents. Furthermore, they tend to be objective about these relationships, *whether they were negative or positive.* That is, they can discuss them relatively dispassionately. Typically, they describe one or both parents as having been very loving, and if they have had a more negative relationship with one parent, they have nevertheless forgiven that parent. Autonomous adults tend to value relationships highly. Interestingly, their infants are highly likely to be *securely attached* to them.

Dismissing adults are those whose recollections of their growing-up relationships are very poorly detailed. Thus, although they might seem to dwell on how positive or how negative their attachments were, they are hard pressed to provide specific illustrative examples (Hesse, 1999). *Dismissing* adults tend not to value relationships nearly as highly as do autonomous adults—that is, they *dismiss* their importance. Their infants have a higher probability of being insecurely attached to them.

Preoccupied describes a category of responses that are incoherent and confused even though these are adults who are highly preoccupied with their childhood experiences and relationships. Many *preoccupied* adults are still highly dependent on their parents, and strive to please them—although they might also still be angry with them. Unlike *autonomous* parents, preoccupied parents find it extremely difficult to discuss relationships with their parents objectively.

Unresolved parents may display features of any of the other three classifcations, but are unable to

---

autonomous A classification, based on the *Adult Attachment Interview*, marked by predominantly positive and highly consistent recollections of relationships with parents.

dismissing An *Adult Attachment Interview* classification reflected in fragmentary, poorly detailed adult recollections of childhood relationships with parents, often overidealized but devoid of specific memories.

preoccupied Parents who, on the *Adult Attachment Interview*, show evidence of being highly preoccupied with, and emotional about, their childhood relationships, but who cannot provide a very coherent description of these relationships.

---

present a coherent and integrated account of their childhood relationships. Typically, they have failed to come to terms with significant aspects of these relationships such as rejection, abuse, death of one or both parents, parental divorce or separation, and so on. Their infants, too, are likely to manifest a *disorganized-disoriented* attachment style (Steele et al., 1999). (See Table 6.2 for a summary of these categories and their relationships with infant patterns of attachment.)

Intergenerational Transmission of Attachment Patterns

That at least some aspects of parent-infant attachment patterns are transmitted across generations seems clear. For example, van Ijzendoorn (1995) summarized 18 different studies that had used Main's *Adult Attachment Interview (AAI)* to look at how closely parents' perceptions of their childhood relationships with parents predicted the attachment patterns of their own children. Amazingly, he reports that in about 75% of all cases, patterns are pretty much as would be predicted on the basis of Table 6.2. Similarly, Benoit and Parker (1994) report that the correspondence between parents' *AAI* ratings and their infants' *Strange Situation* ratings is between 66% and 82% in a variety of studies.

There is more evidence: Benoit and Parker (1994) used the *AAI* to rate a group of women whose daughters were pregnant. A year later, after the daughters had given birth to their infants, the daughters were rated with the *AAI*, and infant attachment patterns were classified using the *Strange Situation Procedure*. Results indicate that of the 51 grandmothers who were rated *autonomous*, 45 had daughters who were also autonomous. And of the 60 mothers who were autonomous, an impressive 56 had infants who were securely attached (see Figure 6.4).

Why might attachment patterns be transmitted from one generation to the next? There are a number of possibilities. One is that these patterns reflect

---

unresolved An *Adult Attachment Interview* category marked by incoherent and disintegrated recollections of childhood relationships, characterized as well by significant and unresolved emotional issues having to do with parents.

TABLE 6.2
Parental Recollections of Early Relationships and Infant Attachments

ADULT ATTACHMENT PATTERN (Main's *Adult Attachment Interview*)	MAIN CHARACTERISTICS	CORRESPONDING INFANT ATTACHMENT PATTERN* Ainsworth's *Strange Situation:*	MAIN CHARACTERISTICS
Autonomous	Value attachments; coherent, non-contradictory descriptions of loving relationships with parents	Secure	Preponderance of positive affect toward parents; uses mother as secure base; upset at her leaving; warm greeting at her return
Dismissing (insecure)	Minimize value of relationships; fragmented or idealized recollections of their relationships with parents, with few specific, detailed recollections	Insecure-avoidant	Rarely cries when mother leaves; ignores or even rejects her when she returns, despite high levels of distress
Preoccupied (insecure)	Still entangled in (preoccupied with) early, unresolved relationships; may still be dependent on, or angry at, parents; incoherent, inconsistent descriptions	Insecure-resistant	Highly upset when mother leaves; often angry when she returns
Unresolved (disorganized)	Overwhelmed by unresolved traumatic experiences like death or divorce of parents; incoherent and emotionally confused description of relationships	Disorganized/disoriented	Contradictory reactions to separation; sometimes initially rejecting her, then clinging excessively, or crying when she leaves and avoiding her when she returns

*Note that the correspondence is far from perfect. That is, not all *autonomous* parents will have securely attached infants; and not all the parents of *disorganized/disoriented* infants will be found to be *unresolved-disorganized*. Source: Based in part on van Ijzendoorn & Bakermans-Kranenburg (1997).

genetic tendencies, which are then passed on to infants. Another is that the environments provided by mothers reflect their recollections of early relationships, and affect their infants' attachment patterns. And yet another possibility is that mothers in different classifications share certain characteristics that influence their infants' attachment patterns. For example, Pederson et al. (1998) and Susman-Stillman et al. (1996) found that mothers who are autonomous tended to be more sensitive to their infants. **Sensitive parenting**, also sometimes referred to as *responsive*

parenting or *sensitive mothering*, is characterized by a high degree of mother-infant synchrony. In other words, the more sensitive mothers are better able to read their infants' emotions and to accommodate their behaviors to those of their infants. As we see in Chapter 8, sensitive mothering is most likely to be evident later in *authoritative* parenting—that is, in parenting that is based on reason, that permits independence and discussion, but that values obedience and sets expectations and regulations.

It's likely that all of these forces are involved in the transmission of attachment patterns. In addition, there is evidence that family-based interventions, using videotapes for example, can be effective in making nonautonomous mothers more sensitive to their infants. Juffer et al. (1997) report that this type of intervention can result in more secure infant attachments.

sensitive parenting   Phrase used to describe parenting characterized by a high degree of sensitivity to infant (and child) moods and emotions, and an ability to adjust parenting behaviors to these. Associated with *authoritative parenting*. Sensitive parenting is closely related to secure infant attachments and to positive developmental outcomes.

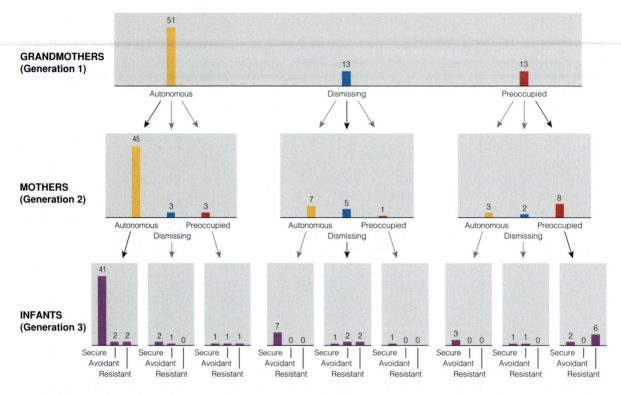

FIGURE 6.4   Transmission of attachment patterns across three generations. Note that of the 51 *autonomous* grandmothers, 45 had daughters who were autonomous, and 41 of these daughters had infants who were *securely attached*. Of the 13 *preoccupied* grandmothers, 8 had daughters who were also preoccupied, and 6 of these 8 had infants classified as *resistant*. Source: Adapted with permission from D. Benoit & K. C. Parker (1994). Stability and transmission of attachment across three generations. *Child Development:* 65, 1444–1456. (p. 1450.)

Some Implications of Patterns of Infant Attachment

Why should we want children to be more securely attached (rather than insecure or disorganized)? Are there any real advantages to being securely attached?

Both common sense and research evidence suggest a clear yes. Recall that among other things, securely attached infants are those who have achieved a good balance between the security of attachment and the ability to explore. Insecurely attached infants are more anxious, more timid, and less adaptable.

Here are a few research findings suggesting that, at least in North American cultures, securely attached infants fare better:

▲ Secure attachment in infancy is a strong predictor of social and emotional maturity at age 6 (Steele et al., 1999).

▲ In a number of investigations, securely attached infants have shown themselves to be more competent, better problem solvers, more independent, more curious, perhaps more resilient, and to fare better in kindergarten (Pianta & Ball, 1993).

▲ A review of nearly 80 studies that have looked at the implications of *disorganized* attachment (more than 6,000 parent-infant pairs) reveals a higher likelihood that infants so classified will grow up to be children who have difficulty managing stress and who present behavior problems (van Ijzendoorn, Schuengel, & Bakermans-Kranenburg, 1999).

▲ Insecurely attached infants are more likely to manifest anxiety disorders in later life (Warren et al., 1997; Sroufe et al., 1999).

▲ In one study, toddlers suffering from infantile **anorexia nervosa** (or simply *anorexia*) were more likely to be insecurely attached (Chatoor et al., 1998).

▲ In another study, infants classified as *disorganized* at the age of 12 months were significantly more likely to have problems involving disruptive behavior at age 5. Those who had been classified as disorganized and whose mothers perceived them as of difficult (as opposed to easy) temperament were also more likely to be excessively aggressive (Shaw et al., 1996).

Correlates of Infant Attachment Patterns

If being securely attached is good—and being insecurely attached or disorganized-disoriented is not—we need to ask what it is that determines how our infants will be attached.

As we saw earlier, parents' own childhood experiences—and those of their parents as well—are important factors. So, too, is maternal *sensitivity*—the extent to which mothers understand and respond well to infant emotions. Aber et al. (1999) report that mothers who enjoy their roles as mothers and who view these roles positively engage in more *positive* mothering. These mothers tend to be classified as *autonomous* on the *Adult Attachment Interview*, and as we saw, their children are more likely to be securely attached (Slade et al., 1999).

Clearly, attachments are a function of interactions. Furthermore, the nature of these interactions and their outcomes will be influenced by the characteristics of both infant and caregiver (or other significant people in the child's context). Hence the importance of the family—and of the culture in which the family is embedded, because it, too, influences child-rearing practices and attitudes toward children. Our North American macrosystem is relatively child centered: It emphasizes the rights

of children, and it encourages parents to provide physically and psychologically safe environments. It should not be surprising, then, that more than two-thirds of infants appear to be securely attached. (Perhaps it should be surprising that as many as one-third are not!)

Elsewhere in the world, cultures reflect different values, and sometimes child-rearing practices and attitudes toward children are quite different. In some of these cultures, insecurely attached infants are far more common than in North America (for example, West Germany, Japan, and Israel; see Sagi, van Ijzendoorn, & Koren-Karie, 1991; Wiley & Carlin, 1999).

Whether parents should attempt to change their infants' predominant patterns of attachment—and whether they would be very effective in doing so—are important issues. Unfortunately, they are also very complex issues. What does seem clear is that all infants must have the opportunity to develop attachments that will provide them with the security they need to engage in the exploration of a bewildering, exciting, and sometimes frightening world. As Belsky (1999; Belsky & Hsieh, 1998) emphasizes, those opportunities are not always related solely to the presence of the mother. Grandparents, siblings, uncles, and aunts can also be important—and so, too, can fathers.

Father-Infant Attachment: Changing Roles

Our traditional views of the family and of mother-father roles have typically focused on the importance of the mother in the early social development of the infant, and have often ignored the role of the father. Many of our developmental theorists (Freud, for example) have argued that the father becomes important after the child reaches the age of 2 or 3. Besides, the most common pattern throughout the world has typically been that of the mother as infant caregiver and the father as out-of-the-home breadwinner.

Some of these traditional values are still the norm in many of the world's cultures. For example, Jain and Belsky (1997) studied a group of Indian families that had emigrated to the United States. Prevailing norms in these families saw mothers caring for children and fathers relatively *disengaged*

anorexia nervosa A medical condition not due to any detectable illness, primarily affecting adolescent girls and involving a loss of 15% to 25% of ideal body weight. It usually begins with dieting and ends when the patient is unwilling or unable to eat normally.

from the entire infant-rearing process. Interestingly, however, with increasing acculturation, fathers became progressively more involved in all aspects of infant care.

In China, where about one-fifth of the entire world's population lives, looking after the young is also largely a female function; the father's role is more that of a disciplinarian. There, traditional values stress filial devotion and respect. Children, and especially sons, are taught to respect and obey their fathers (and grandfathers). In China too, however, there appears to have been a recent decline in some of these filial values. At the same time, fathers have begun to involve themselves more in child-rearing (Ho, 1987).

In North America, also, important changes are rapidly altering our conception of the father's role. These include an increasing number of "father-assisted" childbirths, in which the father has an opportunity to interact with the infant as early as the mother does. In addition, changing work patterns and changing male-female responsibilities in the home have done a great deal to change the role of the father with his infant (McBride & Darragh, 1995). As Lamb (1997) notes, mothers continue to be extremely important to the infant, but they are not unique. Fathers and other caregivers are also tremendously important.

Father-Infant Attachment Formation There is considerable evidence that the pattern of infant-father attachment formation is not very different from the infant-mother pattern (Lamb, 1997). In fact, considerable research indicates that newborns and young infants may form attachments almost as strong with fathers as with mothers (Geiger, 1996).

Nevertheless, it is still true that the most common family roles are those where the mother changes the diapers, feeds the infants, clothes them—in short, does the nurturing. Many studies find, for example, that fathers' interactions with their infants are still mostly in the form of playing rather than caregiving (Geiger, 1996).

Infants recognize—and appear to prefer—the sights, sounds, smells, and feel of their mothers at very young ages. In fact, they seem to recognize and manifest a preference for their mothers' voices almost from birth. Do they also recognize and prefer their fathers' voices?

The answer is no, claim Ward and Cooper (1999). These investigators found that even at the age of 4 months, infants still showed no preference for their fathers' voices over unfamiliar male voices. Yet they seemed to be able to discriminate among these voices. Ward and Cooper suggest that infants might well *recognize* their mothers simply by hearing their voices, but that in order to recognize their fathers they might need more cues (for example, visual or olfactory cues).

Fathers as Parents In summarizing the father-infant research, Lamb (1997) concludes that fathers are as competent and as important as mothers in a caregiving role. But there are some systematic differences between mother-infant and father-infant interactions. Typically fathers spend more time in play interactions with their infants; mothers spend more time in nurturant roles (feeding, bathing, changing). Furthermore, fathers play differently with their charges: They tend to be more aggressive, more boisterous, more physical. When mothers play with their infants, their games are more passive, quieter. Whereas the father is likely to throw the little one in the air or bounce her vigorously on his knee, the mother is more likely to play patty-cake or this-little-pig-went-to-market (Fagot, 1997). As a result, some infants—especially males—display more **affiliative behaviors** toward fathers than toward mothers (Lamb, 1980). Affiliative behaviors are defined as behaviors that demonstrate a social relationship that stops short of being attachment. Evidence of affiliation includes smiling, looking at, laughing, and giving; evidence of attachment might include seeking to be close, clinging, wanting to be picked up, putting the head in the lap, snuggling, and so on. It appears that infants (especially males) begin to affiliate with their fathers at a very young age when they are given the opportunity to do so (Phares, 1992).

What research has established is that the father is far from irrelevant in the early development of the infant. However, the mother typically has consider-

---

affiliative behaviors Behaviors that indicate wanting to interact with or do things with someone; for example, smiling, looking at, laughing, and giving things to. May be contrasted with attachment, which is a more powerful emotional bond evident in seeking to be close, clinging, wanting to be picked up, putting the head in the lap, snuggling, and so on.

ably more contact with young infants than does the father. And a study involving interviews of 63 fathers suggests that even today, many fathers whose wives work full-time outside the home view their increased infant-care roles with some negativity (Grych & Clark, 1999). Glass (1998) reports that even when parents attempt to adjust their working schedules so that both the mother and the father can share child-care responsibilities, father care seldom covers more than 60% of the mother's work hours. And by the end of the first year, few fathers in her sample of 324 dual-earner families were providing more than 20 hours per week of infant care. Still, that is a lot more care than my father—and his father—provided.

Long-Term Separation and Deprivation

As we saw, one way of studying the strength and nature of infant attachment is to look at the infant's reaction to short-term absence of the mother (or the father). Another way of studying the importance of parent-infant attachment is to look at the consequences of long-term separation from one or both parents—such as might happen, for example, in the case of parental death, separation, divorce, or child abandonment.

Spitz (1945, 1954) and Bowlby (1940, 1953) were among the first to describe the harmful consequences of parent-child separation. Spitz (1945), reporting the fate of institutionalized children, claimed that they had significantly higher mortality rates, that they were retarded in physical development, and that their emotional development was so severely thwarted by lack of mothering that they frequently withdrew, became depressed, and sometimes died as a result. In effect, what he described was FTT (failure to thrive, described earlier).

The infants that Spitz studied had, in fact, been abandoned. And perhaps there are some powerful built-in forces that lead us to fear abandonment and to react strongly against it. This, suggest Lummaa et al. (1998), is perhaps one of the reasons why infants sometimes cry. But most current studies of the effects of long-term parent-infant separation don't involve abandonment—although some psychoanalytically oriented therapists maintain that being given up for adoption always implies the possibility of feelings of abandonment (Jones, 1997). Thus, when parents separate or divorce, or even when a parent dies, the infant is not exactly abandoned. Nor is the infant abandoned when given up for adoption at birth.

Not surprisingly, the effects of parent-infant separation are highly dependent on the age at which infants are separated from parents. Separation before the age of 3 months usually does not have the same consequences as later separation, probably because the attachment bond between infant and parent doesn't seem to be as strong before then. Yarrow and Goodwin (1973) studied 70 adopted children between birth and 16 months of age. All these children were in foster homes before adoption, and all appeared to have had normal environments both before and after adoption. The aim of this study was to discover the effects on infants of separation from a parent figure. Because children were adopted at various ages, it was also possible to examine differences in their reactions as a function of age.

Not surprisingly, reactions were least apparent for children adopted while under 3 months of age. This finding is consistent with the observation that before this age children have not formed any strong attachments. Of those adopted later, however, only 15% were completely free of all disturbances; the remainder showed disturbances of varying severity (Figure 6.5). These disturbances were most obvious in infants' sleeping schedules and were also evident in feeding behaviors, social reactions (withdrawal, for example), and emotional behavior (crying). Disruptions in social reactions included decreased social responsiveness, increased stranger anxiety, and specific disturbances in interactions with the new mother evident in feeding difficulties, colic, digestive upsets, and most strikingly, physical rejection of the new mother or excessive clinging to her. In addition, developmental scores were lower in 56% of the cases following adoption.

Apparently, separation from the mother or mother-figure can have an adverse effect on many significant aspects of infants' development. In older children, it can lead to depression, disillusionment, and sometimes serious behavior problems (Urwin, 1998). And there is evidence, too, that childhood experiences such as divorce of parents increases the probability that the child will later be classified on the *Adult Attachment Interview* as *preoccupied*—still

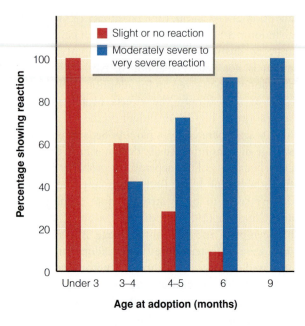

FIGURE 6.5 Severity of infant's reaction to separation from the mother according to age at adoption. Source: Based on data provided by Yarrow and Goodwin (1973).

preoccupied with early, unresolved relationships (Beckwith, Cohen, & Hamilton, 1999). As we saw earlier, such parents are more likely to have infants who are insecurely attached.

It's important to note that the effects of divorce are not always completely negative (as we see in Chapter 8). For example, Heinicke, Guthrie, and Ruth (1997) found that divorce of parents in conflict-ridden and highly unsatisfactory marriages often leads to *increased* sensitivity of the custodial parent to the infant. In their investigation, many of the 4-year-old children whose parents had divorced when they were infants fared better than children whose parents were also in conflict but had not divorced.

Note that the Yarrow study was undertaken in the early 1970s. The evidence suggests that divorce seems to have had a more negative impact then than it might have today. In fact, a review of a large number of studies that observed the effects of divorce on children found that these effects became progressively less negative with the passage of time (Rodgers, 1996). There are several possible reasons for this, including the greater social acceptability of divorce, as well as the fact that more social and eco-

nomic support is provided for single parents than was once the case.

Still, the permanent loss of a parent, as happens through death or sometimes through divorce, can have serious negative consequences for infants—and for older children as well (see Chapter 8). What about regular but temporary loss of parental contact, as happens in many forms of child care?

▂ INFANT CARE

In 1975, fewer than one-third of all U.S. women aged 18 to 44 were in the workforce within one year of having a child; now more than 60% are. As a result, about two of every three North American preschool children are now in child care (U.S. Bureau of the Census, 1998; see *At a Glance:* "Working Mothers and Child Care," and Figures 6.6 and 6.7). And, with increasing numbers of mothers going back to work within weeks of childbirth, the fastest-growing type of child-care facility is infant care. Given what we know about the importance of caregiver-infant interaction and attachment, questions relating to the effects of child care on the social, emotional, and intellectual development of infants become critically important. (See Chapter 8 for a discussion of the effects of child care on older children.)

An early concern of research on infant care was to determine whether nonparental care can prevent the formation of parent-infant attachments, can lead to insecure attachments, or can serve to redirect that attachment toward a different caregiver. Reassuringly, most of the evidence suggests that none of these is likely to be the case (Singer, 1997). Apparently, the infant's primary attachment to parents can be established in a wide variety of circumstances and is highly resistant to disruption. Konner (1982) reports that it occurs in societies as disparate as the !Kung, where infants are in immediate contact with their mothers 24 hours a day, and in the communal arrangements of some Israeli kibbutzim, where infants have contact with their mothers for only a short period each afternoon and on weekends.

Clarke-Stewart, Gruber, and Fitzgerald (1994), following a detailed investigation of the effects of child care, conclude that good-quality child care does not detract from parent-child relationships,

AT A GLANCE	**Working Mothers and Child Care**

Between 1960 and 1997, the percentage of married women in the U.S. workplace almost doubled (from 31.9 to 61.6). By 1997, more than half of women *with children under age 1 and a husband at home* worked outside the home (U.S. Bureau of the Census, 1998). In Canada, the percentage of women aged 25 to 44 who worked outside the home increased by almost 45% from 1976 to 1997 (from 54% to 78.2%; *Canada Yearbook, 1999*). As a result, the need for infant care has grown enormously.

Over half of all North American women who have children under age 6 now work outside the home.

Tony Freeman/PhotoEdit

FIGURE 6.6 Increase in percentage of mothers who live with husbands and work outside the home. Note by comparison that growth in employment is far more modest for wives without minor children at home. Source: Adapted from U.S. Bureau of the Census (1998), p. 409.

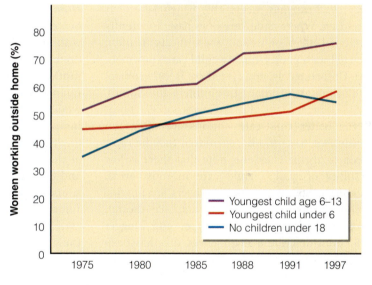

Women working outside home (%)

— Youngest child age 6–13
— Youngest child under 6
— No children under 18

1975   1980   1985   1988   1991   1997

FIGURE 6.7 Changes in percentages of women who enter the workforce within one year of giving birth. Source: From U.S. Bureau of the Census (1998), p. 85.

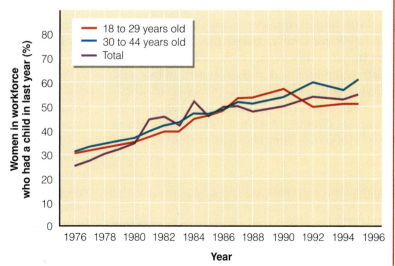

Women in workforce who had a child in last year (%)

— 18 to 29 years old
— 30 to 44 years old
— Total

1976 1978 1980 1982 1984 1986 1988 1990 1992 1994 1996
Year

nor does it decrease the influence of the family. In fact, it seems clear that good-quality day care has measurably positive effects on both cognitive and social development. In Clarke-Stewart, Gruber, and Fitzgerald's study, day-care-center children were consistently more advanced than children who stayed at home with their mothers. In their words, "This advance showed up on all our measures of development: cognitive development, social competence with unfamiliar adults, independence from the mother in an unfamiliar situation, general obedience and competence at dinnertime, compliance with requests made by a researcher, social interaction with a peer friend, and social competence with an unfamiliar peer" (1994, p. 233).

The point that needs to be underlined is that *quality child care* has measurably beneficial effects on children. Where child care does have apparently detrimental effects on infants, these effects are often associated with poorer-quality child care (Bowman, 1993). Unfortunately, however, there is little control of the standards of infant care centers and homes. And, as Pungello and Kurtz-Costes (1999) point out, the better child-care options are often too expensive for parents whose children may be most in need of them. They also note that there is low availability of quality child care in most areas. Increasingly, however, some employers are providing child-care options in the workplace (Secret, Sprang, & Bradford, 1998). Dugger and Dugger (1998) even describe a high school that has been highly successful in bringing back former dropouts and retaining them until graduation, partly because it provides in-school child care.

With respect to center infant care (as opposed to home-based care), characteristics of high-quality care include a low caregiver-to-child ratio, appropriate equipment and toys, adequate indoor and outdoor spaces, an organized, goal-directed schedule of age-appropriate activities, and qualified caregivers (See Chapter 8 for a more detailed discussion of the characteristics of high-quality child care.)

Parenting in Infancy

When O'Brien (1996) studied an ostensibly average sample of 413 parents of children aged 9 months to 3 years, she found high general agreement that raising children is a difficult and sometimes frustrating undertaking. Sadly, it's not a task for which all parents are highly suited—either by training or by temperament. In O'Brien's sample, for example, parents described a wide range of infant behaviors as irritating and difficult to deal with—behaviors such as whining, demanding attention, interrupting ongoing activities, and refusing to do as asked. Nor did parenting become easier with experience. In fact, parents who had more than one child typically reported more difficulties and more frustration than did those with a single child.

In the same way as quality of infant care can have measurable effects on children, so too can quality of parenting. As we saw earlier, *sensitive parenting* is closely related to positive developmental outcomes. Recall, for example, that it is associated with the development of secure attachments in children. In fact, McKim et al. (1999) found that among mothers who used out-of-home care for their infants, those who were least sensitive were the ones who were most likely to have insecurely attached infants.

Following a review of research that has looked at the effects of parents on infants, Belsky, Lerner, and Spanier (1984) describe six important dimensions of parenting: *attentiveness, physical contact, verbal stimulation, material stimulation, responsive care,* and *restrictiveness.* Strikingly, the first five of these, which all have positive effects on the infant's social, emotional, and intellectual well-being, are dimensions of *sensitive mothering.* The last, *restrictiveness,* is more negative. What this means, in effect, is that parents who are attentive to their children (for example, look at them more); who touch them, play with them, cradle and rock them; who speak to them and who provide them with objects to look at, to touch, to taste, to smell; and who are responsive to their cries and to their other signals of distress, amusement, interest, or amazement are more likely to have intellectually advanced and emotionally well-adjusted infants. Those who are restrictive by being insensitive to their infants' emotions and by verbally and physically limiting the infant's freedom to explore may, to some extent, influence their intellectual development negatively. (See Chapter 8 for further discussion of parenting styles.)

Cultural Similarities

In general, children rate their mothers and fathers differently with respect to important dimensions of parenting, such as warmth and control. In China, says Ho (1987), mothers look after children; fathers discipline them. Perhaps it isn't surprising that Berndt and associates (1993) found that Chinese children (as well as children from Taiwan and Hong Kong) see their mothers as warmer and less controlling than fathers.

Interestingly, children in Western societies express very similar views of their parents (Collins & Russell, 1991). No matter how involved fathers are in child-rearing, mothers are typically seen as more affectionate, warmer, and less strict. This is not surprising given that mothers are the ones who feed, wash, and clothe children—in other words, who nurture them. In contrast, fathers play with them—or discipline them. Thus, even in these earliest parent-infant interactions, gender has begun to make a difference.

⌐ EARLY GENDER-ROLE INFLUENCES

Children are not born knowing the difference between boys and girls. In fact, in the beginning, they don't even know that they're one or the other. But, says Kohlberg (1966), by the age of about 18 months, the infant can generally say, "I'm a girl," or "I'm a boy," with apparent understanding and conviction. Still, many at this age can't reliably identify others as being boy or girl. Nor do they realize that gender is permanent and unchangeable.

Nevertheless, the assigning of gender roles—and, very often, of the **stereotypes** associated with them—typically begins at the very beginning when parents wonder, "Hey, should we take a chance and paint the room blue? But, shoot, it might be a girl! Maybe we'd better stay with something neutral like desert tan, and we can add the blue or the pink later."

---

stereotype Denotes a fixed, firm, relatively unexamined belief typically generalized to a class of superficially similar situations or individuals.

When an infant is born, the attending physician or midwife doesn't say, "Holy jeepers, lady! It's a baby!" No. The key word is not *baby*; it's *boy* or *girl*. The simple anatomical fact of being a boy or a girl tells mother and father and all the significant others what to think and how to react. The knowledge that it's a "boy" or "girl" even colors the parents' perceptions. When Rubin, Provenzano, and Luria (1974) asked 30 parents to describe their day-old infants as they would to a relative or a close friend, without any hesitation they spoke of their alert, strong, well-coordinated, firm, and hardy sons—and of their fine-featured, soft, and delicate daughters. Yet these parents, especially the fathers (who were most guilty of exaggerating the sex-appropriate characteristics of their sons), had scarcely had any opportunity to interact with and get to know their infants. And hospital records clearly indicated that these male and female infants were indistinguishable in weight, muscle tone, activity, responsiveness, and so on.

But many parents waste little time making their new infants sexually distinct: They color the boy-infants blue, the girl-infants pink. Because of the connotations associated with these colors, they emphasize long-established sexual stereotypes. And in much the same way, the names parents give their infants reinforce their sometimes unconscious beliefs about male-female differences. Kasof (1993), for example, shows how male names (such as John or Michael) are seen as more attractive, more intellectually competent, and stronger. In contrast, many female names carry connotations of being less attractive, more old-fashioned, and less able. In some parts of the world, an infant's anatomy can even be a matter of life or death (see *Across Cultures: "Indira's Sister"*).

Early gender-typing influences also include how parents interact with their infants. We saw earlier that there is a tendency for fathers to interact more—and differently—with sons, even when they are infants. And Leaper, Anderson, and Sanders (1998), following a survey of a large number of studies that looked at how parents speak with their children, found that mothers talk more to their daughters than their sons. Also, they tend to use more supportive speech with them. Thus, even in these very early parent-infant interactions, the child's sex has begun to make a difference.

ACROSS CULTURES

Indira's Sister

Indira's sister was never named; her story is very short.

She was born in a little hut on a windswept and barren plain in northern India. When the midwife held her up, her mother felt a small twinge of sadness when she couldn't find the appendage between her legs; it would have saved her life. Her father shrugged and walked away; there was no need for words, no need to explain what everyone knew must be done. There was already one girl in the family: Indira. Indira had been allowed to live, but the cost of keeping her would be high. Boys run around or ride their ponies covered only in a short rag, or even naked, but girls must always be dressed in an expensive sari. And girls eat, too, though they don't need to be given as much as boys. And then there is the matter of the dowry. Such a price for having a girl!

There are different ways of killing an infant. The one Indira's mother chose is quite common: She stuffed rice into the newborn's mouth and nose and held a pillow tight against its face until the struggles stopped.

"Will you bury it," she asked Indira tiredly, "so the dogs don't find it?"

Although on average women survive longer than men in all of the world's developed countries, the opposite is occasionally the case in developing countries. In India, Pakistan, and Bangladesh, in parts of which infanticide is still practiced, more than a million female infants die each year simply because they are female. In certain provinces of northern China, thousands of fetuses are surgically aborted because they are female.

In most of the developing world, insists Grant (1992), there is an apartheid based on gender. In these countries, it is women who clean the house, cook the meals, care for the children, carry water and fuel, and look after the old and the sick. It is also women who grow most of the food in developing countries. In return, women get less food, less training, less income, and less protection.

"Employment rights, social security rights, legal rights, property rights, and even civil and political liberties," writes Grant (1992), "are all likely to depend upon the one, cruel chromosome" (p. 57). In the same way, access to education is far more limited for females than for males.

To Think About: What are the probable implications of granting equal educational opportunity to girls in developing countries? How might this affect their care of children? Are Indira's views of life and death, of what it means to be male or female, likely to resemble yours?

In some of the world's nations, being male or female can have tremendous implications not only for education, employment, and legal and social rights, but sometimes even for survival.

Brian Vikander/Corbis

Sex differences in attitudes and behaviors are evident in **gender roles** (or sex roles). Gender roles are the particular combinations of attitudes, behaviors, and personality characteristics that a culture considers appropriate for an individual's anatomical sex—in other words, those characteristics considered masculine or feminine. **Gender typing** describes the processes by which boys and girls learn masculine and feminine roles. Infants are only at the very beginning of their gender typing. Hence we consider these topics again, and in more detail, in Chapters 8 and 12, which deal with the socialization of preschool children and adolescents.

---

gender roles The particular combination of attitudes, behaviors, and personality characteristics that a culture considers appropriate for the individual's anatomical sex—what is considered masculine or feminine. Also termed *sex roles*.

gender typing Learning behavior according to the sex of the individual. The term refers specifically to the acquisition of masculine behavior for a boy and feminine behavior for a girl.

EXCEPTIONALITY IN INFANTS

This text deals mainly with the physical, intellectual, and social development of the "average" child from conception through adolescence. It is worth repeating, however, that there is no infant who is average in all ways, and that *average* is simply a useful mathematical invention. If we had no average child about whom to speak, we would have to speak instead of individuals. And there are so many different ones— more than 6 billion now—that the task would be absolutely overwhelming. (See *At a Glance:* "The Average, Socially Competent Infant.")

Still, we need to keep in mind that our average is a fiction and that the individual—Robert, Shannon, Jennifer, David—is our reality and our main concern. We need to keep in mind, too, that some children depart so dramatically from the average—are so exceptional—that they are worthy of study in their own right. Unfortunately, this brief section can provide you with only a glimpse into the many ways in which infants can be exceptional. The "Further Readings" section at the end of the chapter lists a number of resources with far more detail. (See *In the News and on the Web:* "A Looming Crisis?")

Exceptionality is a two-sided concept: On one hand are children who are exceptionally gifted; on the other are those who have an exceptional lack of normal abilities and competence. Furthermore, exceptionality is found in each of the three major areas of human development: physical, socioemotional, and intellectual (see Figure 6.8).

In this section we deal briefly with some of the most common manifestations of physical and socioemotional exceptionality in infancy. In Chapter 9 we look at physical and intellectual exceptionality in childhood, and in Chapter 10 we discuss socioemotional exceptionality in older children.

Motor Skill Disorders

Not all children learn to walk, tie their shoes, or dance as expected; some experience developmental delays in acquiring motor skills.

Cerebral Palsy Cerebral palsy, also labeled **significant developmental motor disability**, is a collection of symptoms (a syndrome) that includes motor problems and may also include psychological problems, convulsions, or behavior disorders (Abroms & Panagakos, 1980). It was originally known as Little's disease after the surgeon who first described it, but is in fact not a disease. It varies in severity from being so mild that it is virtually undetectable, to paralysis.

Cerebral palsy is most often congenital; that is, it is present at birth in more than two-thirds of all cases. It is generally associated with brain damage, although the damage is often mild and nonspecific. Sometimes it results from anoxia (lack of oxygen during the birth process, or before or after birth). It can also result from either maternal infection and disease or postnatal brain injury sometimes resulting from diseases such as meningitis or encephalitis (Deiner, 1999).

Estimates of the prevalence of cerebral palsy are imprecise because many of the milder cases are not reported, and because there is no "cure" for the condition. Kagan and Gall (1998) report there are about 2.5 cases for every 1,000 live births.

One of the most common signs of cerebral palsy is spasticity (inability to move voluntarily) in one or more limbs. Such motor impairments are sometimes so severe that it is difficult to assess a child's intellectual ability. As a result, it was often assumed that intellectual deficits were common among those suffering from cerebral palsy. However, more recent evidence suggests that fewer than half of cerebral palsy victims are mentally retarded (Deiner, 1999).

Physical therapy is sometimes effective in improving motor control and coordination of children with cerebral palsy (Pape et al., 1994).

Other Motor Skill Disorders and Physical Problems Some motor skills disorders are not associated with brain damage or cerebral palsy. These are often evident in delayed development among children, many of whom also have other developmental disorders, such as mental retardation, autism, or even attention-deficit disorders. These disorders may be apparent in difficulties in learning motor tasks such as walking,

---

exceptionality A category used to describe physical, social, or intellectual abilities and performance that are significantly above or below average.

significant developmental motor disability A collection of symptoms manifested early in life, evident primarily in motor problems, associated with brain damage, and commonly labeled "cerebral palsy." Can vary in severity from barely detectable to severe paralysis.

The Average, Socially Competent Infant

At birth, infants are not especially competent emotionally and socially. They recognize no one, have little if any control over their own emotions, know nothing of the emotions of others, and are largely incapable of any meaningful social interaction.

But by the age of 2, they will have learned to smile and laugh, to try to make others smile and laugh, to play pat-a-cake, to roll balls, and a hundred other things. Many will even be able to put on at least some of their clothing—and to take off even more of it.

Developmental norms, based on the Denver Developmental Screening Test (Frankenburg & Dodds, 1992), indicate that about 90% of all infants:

- can feed themselves by the age of 6¹/₂ months

- can play pat-a-cake by 14 months
- can drink from a cup by the age of 17 months
- can use a spoon and fork by the age of 20 months
- can undress by the age of 2 years.

The competent 18-month-old can even engage in little conversations.

Myrleen Ferguson Cate/PhotoEdit

IN THE NEWS AND ON THE WEB

A Looming Crisis?

Jimmy Moran was 34 years old when his parents died. He has had a developmental disability since birth and was highly dependent on them. They left $140,000 for his care. Now, 25 years later, the money is all gone, Jimmy is 59, and the state, with the help of his sister, must look after him.

Jimmy is only one of many similar examples. Medical advances have resulted in dramatic increases in the life expectancy of those with disabilities. For example, Felton (2000) reports that children with mental retardation could expect to live to about age 19 in the 1930s; those with Down syndrome might live to be about 30. Now both are expected to live into their 60s. At the same time, there has been an enormous reduction in institutionalization in the United States—from a high of about 200,000 individuals in the 1960s to fewer than 60,000 in 1998. As a result, about a half million U.S. adults with disabilities, *who are over the age of 60*, are known to be living with and cared for by their sometimes very aged parents; numbers might be twice as high if they included

cases that aren't officially counted. In a large percentage of cases, no provision has been made for their care after their parents die.

B. Felton, "Hard Choices as the Disabled Age." *New York Times,* 9 January 2000, section 3, pp. 1, 8, 9.

To Do: As a course project, track twentieth-century changes in incidence and treatment of disabilities, using Internet or library resources.

 Resources: Following is the website of the National Alliance of the Disabled, a U.S. organization dedicated to obtaining equal rights in all areas for persons with disabilities:

http://www.naotd.org/

 For additional readings, explore *InfoTrac College Edition,* your online library. Go to http://infotrac-college.com/wadsworth and use the passcode that came on the card with your book. Try these search terms: disabilities, developmental disabilities, learning disabilities.

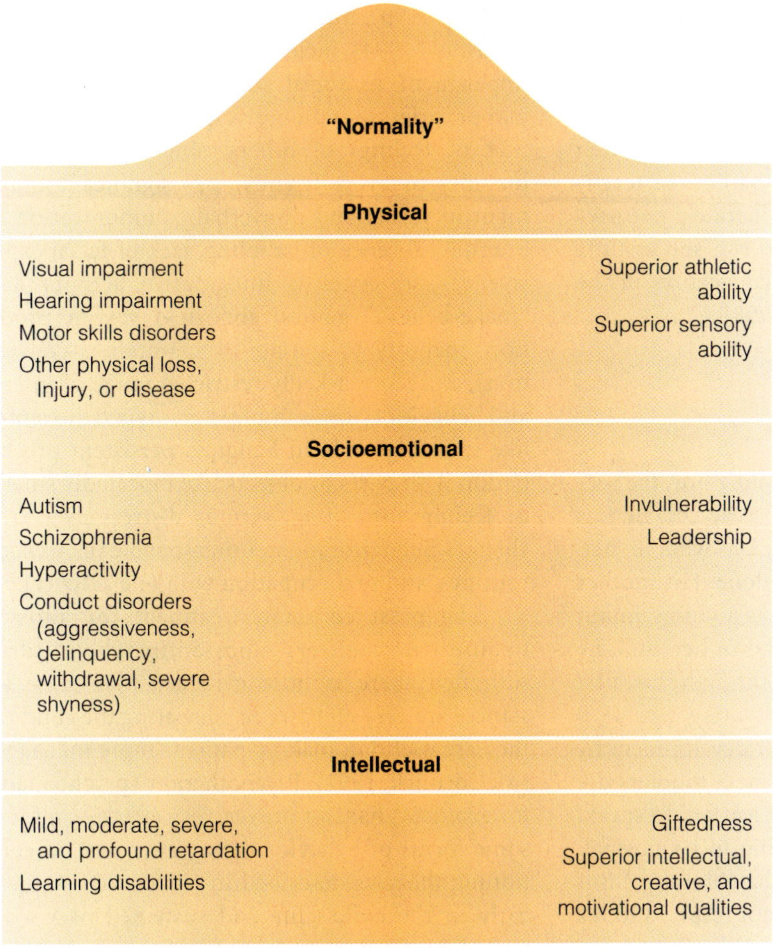

FIGURE 6.8 Some dimensions of exceptionality.

running, skipping, tying shoes, and so on; they may also be apparent in difficulties in carrying out motor activities. A common label for these problems is **developmental coordination disorder**.

According to the *Diagnostic and Statistical Manual of Mental Disorders (DSM-IV)* of the American Psychiatric Association (APA), a developmental coordination disorder exists when (1) a person's performance of activities requiring motor coordination (such as crawling, walking, sitting, handwriting, sports) is markedly below what would be expected for the person's age, (2) the disturbance interferes with academic achievement or activities of daily living, and (3) the disturbance is not due to a

known physical disorder (such as cerebral palsy) (American Psychiatric Association, 1994).

Epilepsy

Epilepsy is essentially a seizure disorder whose causes are sometimes genetic and sometimes unknown (Berkovic & Scheffer, 1997). Seizures involve abnormal electrical activity in the brain. The more serious forms of epilepsy (sometimes termed **grand mal**, as opposed to **petit mal**) can often be

---

developmental coordination disorder A childhood motor skills disorder not associated with brain damage or cerebral palsy, often evident in difficulties in learning or in carrying out motor tasks.

grand mal Label sometimes used for the more severe forms of epilepsy. Sometimes used to refer specifically to the seizures that accompany this form of epilepsy.

petit mal Label for the milder forms of epilepsy, not characterized by major seizures, and often controllable with drugs.

controlled with drugs. Petit mal seizures, which last only between 1 and 30 seconds, are seen in a "momentary absentness" of a child and are often accompanied by rhythmic, fluttering movements of both eyelids. These seizures may occur very often and are sometimes interpreted by parents or teachers as a sign that the student is deliberately not paying attention. Modern medication can successfully prevent the occurrence of petit mal seizures in the majority of cases (Kagan & Gall, 1998).

Autism

Tim was an apparently normal, healthy boy, the second child born to a couple in their early 20s. He was an easy infant who cried very little and who, in fact, appeared most content when left alone. His mother later recalled that he didn't smile as a young infant and that he didn't appear to recognize her. Still, he progressed apparently normally through his first year and learned to walk at the young age of 9 months, displaying advanced motor development by tripping or falling less often than most toddlers do. But at the age of 2, he still had not learned to speak. An examination showed his hearing to be normal. His parents hoped he would be a "late bloomer." But even at the age of 3, Tim still did not respond to his parents' speech. In addition, he had developed few social skills, and he engaged in unusual and repetitive behaviors, such as spinning the wheels of his toy car or sitting and rocking his body endlessly.

Tim's condition is very rare. It is what is labeled autism, a disorder described by the American Psychiatric Association (1994) as a **pervasive developmental disorder**. Autistic disorder is apparent mainly in infants' failure to develop normal communication skills. In fact, about half of all autistic children never learn to speak; and if they haven't learned by the age of 6, they are unlikely to learn later (Kagan & Gall, 1998). Other features of autistic disorder include a lack of normal responsiveness to other people, bizarre responses to aspects of the environment, and a pattern of developmental delays

pervasive developmental disorder A disorder first manifested in infancy or childhood, evident in delayed or abnormal development especially in social skills, communication, and emotional maturity. May take the form of autism or childhood schizophrenia.

(Deiner, 1999). Major symptoms of autism listed by the APA (1994) include (1) severe and consistent impairment in social relationships (for example, inappropriate emotional responses, lack of awareness of feelings of others, abnormal social play, inability to make friends), (2) significant impairment in verbal and nonverbal communication (for example, absence of babbling, lack of facial expressiveness, absence of imaginative activity as in "make-believe" games, abnormal speech production, inability to initiate or maintain a conversation), and (3) markedly restricted range of interests and behaviors (for example, stereotyped movements like spinning or head banging, persistent preoccupation with parts of objects like repeatedly smelling or feeling something, serious distress over trivial changes in environment, unreasonable insistence on routines, and preoccupation with one activity).

The most common treatment for autism is to use tranquilizers and antipsychotic drugs. Although there is little evidence that these substances are very effective in alleviating the condition, they are useful in making patients more manageable (McCormick, 1997). Psychotherapy (psychoanalysis, for example) has not proven very effective, although some forms of behavior therapies (based on conditioning theories described in Chapter 2) beginning early in the child's life and sustained over a long period of time are sometimes helpful (Hagopian, Fisher, & Legacy, 1994). In general, the long-term prognosis for autistic children is not good, with only a small percentage ever recovering enough to be classed as normal. (See *Concept Summary*.)

⌐ THE WHOLE INFANT

There is something frustrating about pigeonholing developing infants into such psychologically convenient descriptive categories as capabilities, physical development, motor development, socioemotional development, and intellectual development. We lose sight of the infant in our sometimes confused array of beliefs, findings, tentative conclusions, convincing arguments, and suggestions.

The average infant of which we speak is hypothetical. And although it's true that many infants are very close to the hypothetical average when they are 1 month old, fewer are still average at the age of

CONCEPT SUMMARY   Some Manifestations of Exceptionality in Infants

Exceptionality is a two-sided concept; it includes both ends of extreme deviations from average functioning and abilities. Here we look at only one end.

Exceptionality	Some Characteristics
Cerebral palsy (significant developmental motor disability)	
• Definition	• A congenital, nonprogressive motor disorder
• Causes	• Unknown in many cases; perinatal asphyxia in about 20% of all cases; often associated with prematurity
• Manifestations	• Symptoms range from nearly imperceptible to almost total paralysis; sometimes evident in spasticity (inability to move voluntarily) and dyskinesis (abnormal movements)
Developmental coordination disorder	
• Definition	• Difficulties in learning or carrying out motor activities, not associated with brain damage or cerebral palsy
• Symptoms	• Delayed or below-average performance of common motor activities; resulting impairment of normal activities
Epilepsy	
• Definition	• A seizure disorder of varying severity
• Types	• *Grand mal*—major seizures; *petit mal*—milder form of epilepsy
• Causes	• Sometimes genetic; often unknown
• Treatment	• Drugs can often be used to control seizures; in severe cases, brain surgery may be employed
Autism (pervasive developmental disorder)	
• Etiology	• Unclear; sometimes linked with a chromosomal abnormality
• Symptoms	• Impairment in social relations; impairment in communication; restricted range of interests, sometimes marked by repetitive and/or self-injurious behaviors
• Treatment	• One or more of drug therapy, behavior therapy, or psychotherapy; prognosis for long-term normalcy not good

2 months, even fewer at 6 months, and by the age of 1 year, almost none. By the time a child becomes as old as you or I, the average individual will no longer exist but will appear only in the overly simplified theories of the social scientist, or in the files of the market researcher who wants to know what the "average" person is wearing this spring.

Each person is an integrated whole whose intellect, emotions, and physical being all interact. Each part is linked with and dependent on every other part of the living organism. But if we try to describe a child in that way, the sheer complexity of the task might overwhelm us. So we continue to speak of the isolated forces that affect human development as though they existed apart from the integrated, whole child. But it bears repeating that our divisions, although necessary, are artificial and sometimes misleading.

MAIN POINTS

Social and Emotional Development in the Family Context

To understand infancy, it's necessary to ask about interactions within the family as well as in the larger context, keeping in mind that influences are reciprocal (infants affect parents too), involve a variety of individuals and relationships (dyadic and triadic interactions), and are strongly influenced by the characteristics of both parents and infants, as well as other aspects of the environment (contextual models).

Infant Temperament

Temperament is a biological predisposition to react in a given way. One classification of basic temperaments includes difficult infants (withdrawal from the unfamiliar, slow adaptation to change, negative moods), easy infants (high adaptability, high approach tendencies), and slow-to-warm-up infants (low activity level, high withdrawal, slow adaptation, more negative moods). Parent questionnaires are often used to assess infant temperament.

Temperament seems relatively stable and may have long-term implications for personality. "Goodness of fit" between infants' temperaments and environmental demands may affect developmental outcomes. In our culture, some difficult infants may run a higher risk of behavior and emotional problems than do easy infants.

Infant Emotions

Infants' facial expressions and other behaviors suggest that they feel various emotions. These behaviors include crying and smiling, both of which have important adaptive value, as well as laughing and being afraid. Cries are sometimes classified as rhythmic, angry, pain, or hunger cries.

The reflex smile is present within days of birth; the true social smile occurs by the age of 4 weeks (response to social stimuli); the selective social smile, often by about age 3.5 months, is a response to *recognized* social stimuli (such as a mother's face). Learned fears, and fear of strangers, are uncommon before 6 months, and may be evident in separation anxiety. Even infants have other-directed and self-directed strategies for controlling strong emotions.

Parent-Infant Attachments

Bonding refers to the biologically based processes by which mother and infant form attachment links. *Attachment* appears important to the healthy development and adjustment of infants (although there is no critical period during which this bonding must occur; nor must it occur only with the mother).

Bowlby identifies four attachment phases: *preattachment* (first month; crying, smiling, clinging, sucking, responding to caregiver's voice); *attachment in the making* (into second half of first year; selective social smile); *clear-cut attachment* (after 6 months; use of newly developing motor skills to approach attachment object); and *goal-corrected attachment* (second year; more subtle manipulation of attachment person's behavior).

Attachment is generally assessed by means of Ainsworth's *Strange Situation Procedure*, which looks at the infant's reaction to the mother's leaving, as well as response to the presence of a stranger. It permits classification of infants as securely attached (use mother as a base from which to explore; are upset when she leaves; react positively and attempt to reestablish contact when she returns) or insecurely attached (may be avoidant: rarely cry when mother leaves, ignore or avoid her when she returns; or resistant: are very upset when mother leaves, often angry when she returns; seek proximity while attempting to avoid mother, sometimes by pushing her away).

Main's *Adult Attachment Interview* looks at parents' verbalizations of their relationships with their own parents, and on that basis classifies them as *autonomous* (positive, value attachments, coherent descriptions of loving relationship with parents), *dismissing* (dismiss value of relationships; idealized, nondetailed recollections), *preoccupied* (obsessed with unresolved relationship issues; often angry with, though dependent on and anxious to please, parents), or *unresolved* (haven't come to grips with earlier traumatic experiences; incoherent, confused description of relationships).

There is a marked tendency for *autonomous* parents to have securely attached infants, and for insecure parents (dismissive or preoccupied) to have infants who are insecurely attached (resistant or avoidant). Sensitive mothering (highly responsive to infant behaviors and emotions) seems closely associated with secure attachments and autonomous parents. In North American cultures, being securely attached appears to present definite advantages.

Infants appear to become equally attached to their mothers and fathers when given the opportunity to do so, but display more affiliative (let's be friends) behaviors toward their fathers. Fear of strangers occurs in many infants (after age 6 months) but is less pronounced in those who have been exposed to more people. Transitional objects such as blankets and teddy bears are sometimes as effective as a parent in reducing anxiety in some stressful situations.

Infant Care

Long-term separation from parents may have harmful effects on infants, particularly after 6 months of age but seldom before 3 months. However, high-quality infant day care does not appear either to disrupt parent-infant bonds or to prevent their formation and has no consistent negative effects.

Important positive dimensions of parenting include attentiveness, physical contact, verbal stimulation, material stimulation, and responsive care; restrictiveness is more negative.

Early Gender-Role Influences

From the very beginning, parents often exert a subtle influence on the gender typing of their infants. However, young infants are not aware of gender differences. Most will not develop a notion of gender constancy until after infancy.

Exceptionality in Infants

Exceptionality has both positive and negative dimensions. Exceptional children are those who require special education and related services to realize their full human potential. Exceptionalities include physical and motor problems in infancy (for example, motor skill disorders such as cerebral palsy and developmental coordination disorder, epilepsy, various diseases, congenital physical problems, and physical problems resulting from accidents).

Autistic disorder is a rare but very serious early form of emotional disorder marked by failure to develop communication skills or normal social relationships, as well as by bizarre responses to aspects of the environment. It is seldom "cured" but is often treated with drugs.

Focus Questions: Applications

1. How do infants influence caregivers?
   - Write up a case illustration of reciprocal caregiver(s)-infant influence.
2. Are all infants basically the same in terms of emotional reactions and personality?
   - Arrange to observe two or three infants (perhaps in an infant day-care center) using one of the observation techniques described in Table 1.4. Look for evidence of temperamental differences. Write up your observations.
3. Are mother-infant bonds "natural" and unlearned?
   - In your opinion, what does the widespread attachment of children to inanimate objects such as blankets suggest about the source and importance of caregiver-infant bonds?
4. What are the consequences of separating infants from their caregivers?
   - Write a term paper on the effects of parental death on children of different ages.
5. How do the terms *average*, *normal*, and *exceptional* relate to each other?
   - Give examples of each term with respect to infants, referring to physical, socioemotional, and intellectual development.

Possible Responses to Thought Challenges

Thought Challenge, page 250

If intensive crying had evolutionary significance, it would have been because it promoted survival and chances of reproduction. Lummaa et al.'s (1998) four hypotheses about its importance are the following:

1. Crying indicates distress at separation from parents, probably because mothers would typically have carried their infants with them so that, more often than not, separation meant abandonment.

2. Intensive crying might have indicated to a parent that here was a lusty infant who should be spared from infanticide, a practice that might have been quite common.
3. Crying might have been one way of obtaining more parental care such as being fed and kept warm.
4. The infant who cried long and hard might have succeeded in lessening competition for parental resources (including food) by *reducing* the likelihood that parents would want to produce other offspring.

Key Terms

Adult Attachment Interview (AAI), 260
affect synchrony, 246
affiliative behaviors, 266
anencephalic, 251
anorexia nervosa, 265
attachment, 256
autonomous, 262
bonding failure, 257
colic, 250
developmental coordination disorder, 275
difficult infants, 244
dismissing, 262
disorganized/disoriented, 259
Early Infancy Temperament Questionnaire (EITQ), 245
easy infants, 244

exceptionality, 273
failure to thrive (FTT), 256
gender roles, 272
gender typing, 272
grand mal, 275
homeostasis, 256
incongruity hypothesis, 253
individuation, 255
insecure-avoidant, 259
insecure-resistant, 259
misattribution, 249
mother-infant bonding, 256
non-Duchenne smile, 251
personality, 243
pervasive developmental disorder, 276
petit mal, 275
preoccupied, 262

reflex smiling, 251
securely attached, 258
selective social smile, 251
sensitive parenting, 262
significant developmental motor disability, 273
slow-to-warm-up infants, 245
social referencing, 253
social smiling, 251
sociological, 243
stereotype, 271
stranger anxiety, 252
temperament, 243
trait, 244
transitional objects, 255
types, 244
unresolved, 262

Further Readings

The following book presents a clear and simple explanation of reciprocal interaction, and of some important contextual theories including that of Urie Bronfenbrenner. It also provides a highly practical description of many interactive activities that parents and teachers can arrange for children:

Eddowes, E. A., & K. S. Ralph (1998). *Interactions for development and learning: Birth through eight years.* Upper Saddle River, N.J.: Merrill.

Those interested in the impact of culture on infant development might consult this collection of articles. Many provide fascinating accounts of child-rearing in vastly different contexts:

Woodhead, M., D. Faulkner, & K. Littleton, eds. (1998). *Cultural worlds of early childhood.* New York: Routledge.

Shaffer's textbook is a straightforward, comprehensive account of social and emotional development beginning in infancy and continuing through childhood:

Shaffer, D. R. (2000). *Social and personality development* 4th ed. Belmont, Calif.: Wadsworth/Thomson Learning.

A comprehensive view of historical and current investigations of attachment and the various theories that have evolved in this area are presented in the following collection:

Cassidy, J., & P. R. Shaver, eds. (1999). *Handbook of attachment: Theory, research, and clinical applications.* New York: The Guilford Press.

Both of the following are clear and comprehensive discussions of exceptionalities. The first is especially informative with respect to infants (and young children), and is of particular value for teachers and parents:

Deiner, P. L. (1999). *Resources for educating children with diverse abilities: Birth through eight.* Fort Worth, Tex: Harcourt Brace.

Hallahan, D. P., & J. M. Kauffman (1997). *Exceptional learners: Introduction to special education*, 7th ed. Boston: Allyn and Bacon.

Online Resources

For additional readings, explore *InfoTrac College Edition*, your online library. Go to http://infotrac-college.com/wadsworth and use the passcode that came on the card with your book. Try these search terms: infants crying, autism, infant emotions, infant disabilities.

PART THREE

Bliss was it in that dawn to be alive,
But to be young was very heaven!

William Wordsworth, *The Prelude*

Early Childhood

Elizabeth Zuckerman/PhotoEdit

I f to be young is "very heaven," does it follow that to be old is hell? What is it that we lose as we age? Now that you are older, do you remember what you might have lost? Do you think it was innocence?

Perhaps, but it was surely ignorance, too, because there is a dramatic shedding of ignorance in the years from 2 to 6. As we see in the next two chapters, in those years there are astounding strides in the acquisition of language, and in the ability to think clearly and logically and to deal with complex things like numbers. There are stunning advances, as well, in the ability to interpret the emotions of others and to control one's own feelings and their expression.

And there are some wonderful developments in the ability to stretch the imagination, to see magical things, to play. . . .

Do you remember how you played?

Maybe it is what the old forget that makes life less like heaven.

I have to run real fast to keep up to my legs.

Five-year-old Jonathan, in Marie's kindergarten class

Physical and Cognitive Development in Early Childhood

CHAPTER 7

On Thanksgiving, we sat around a table laden with what surely would have passed for a grand feast in medieval times. And as we filled our plates, Harry tried to impress upon his 4- and 6-year-old sons the many things for which they should be thankful.

"If the pilgrims needed a loaf of bread or some meat, they couldn't just go and buy it," Harry explained.

"There were no stores?" the 4-year-old asked. "Not even for candy?"

No, they had to grow all their own food," said Harry.

"Gardens!" the 6-year-old shouted. "They had gardens."

"Good!" Harry beamed. "Now, if you were a pilgrim, what would you plant in your garden?"

"Corn!" the older boy said. "And peas!"

"And peas!"

Harry turned to his younger son. "And what would you plant?"

The boy eyed his plate. "Potatoes!" he answered.

"What else would you plant?"

The child studied his plate carefully. "I'd plant turkeys next," he announced solemnly.

Alan Oddie/Photo Edit

FOCUS QUESTIONS

1. What is magical thinking?
2. What parallels are there between motor and cognitive development?
3. How reliable are preschoolers' memories?
4. What is preconceptual thought?
5. How do biology and experience contribute to language learning?

CHILDREN AND MAGICAL THINKING

The mind of a 4-year-old is sometimes wonderfully inventive; it isn't limited by the rules that constrain our thoughts. The thinking of 4-year-olds, as Pearce (1977) put it, is **magical thinking**; it does not always need to be checked against reality. In these early years, thinking is wishful and fantastic. It somehow assumes that reality can be changed by a thought. Thus it is that a magic spell can produce a witch or a princess, a silver thread or a pot of gold; a dream can be real, and perhaps reality too can be a dream; and a wish can make a race car of a stone, a cave of a small corner, a giant sailing ship of a discarded matchbox.

But, Pearce tells us, we do not gladly accept—perhaps we do not even understand—the magical child. Our approach to children and our scientific research ask instead: "How can the child be made to attend to reality? Or how can we make the child abandon magical thinking?" (p. xv).

Perhaps we should try to understand more, and control and change less.

In this chapter we examine the early development of thinking and the growth of language. But first, we look at physical growth and motor development of children ages 2 to 6.

THE PRESCHOOLER'S PHYSICAL GROWTH

Just prior to birth, **growth velocity**—that is, gains in weight and height per unit of time—has been enormous. The fetus has been gaining about 24 centimeters and 10 kilograms (9.4 inches and 22 pounds) per year (Tanner, Whitehouse, & Takaishi, 1966).

THOUGHT CHALLENGE: *If growth velocity at birth remained unchanged, how tall and heavy would a 6-year-old be? How heavy and tall would you be?*

During infancy, however, there is a rapid reduction in rate of growth—a growth deceleration. As a result, between ages 2 and 6, the child gains 6 to 8 centimeters and about 2 kilograms (2 to 3 inches and 4.4 pounds) per year. As we see in Chapter 11, at adolescence there is a dramatic, but relatively brief, acceleration of growth; but by about age 16 for girls and 18 for boys, growth rates are almost zero.

Changes in Proportion and Appearance

Despite the deceleration in growth rates in infancy through the preschool period, phenomenal changes are taking place during this period, as a comparison of the 6-year-old with the 2-year-old shows (see Figures 7.1 and 7.2). Not only do preschoolers gain an average of an additional 30 centimeters and 9 kilograms (about 1 foot and 20 pounds), but there are also some marked differences in rates of change for various parts of the body. These differences are reflected in the very different, and far more adult, appearance of the 6-year-old compared with the 2-year-old. For example, the thick layers of fat that give 1-year-old infants their babyish appearance begin to disappear slowly during the second year of life and continue to recede gradually. Because these tissues grow much more slowly than other tissues, by the time children have reached age 6 their layers of fat are less than half as thick as they were at age 1.

Not only does the relative amount of fatty tissue change during the preschool years, but its distribution also changes as a result of the more rapid growth of bone and muscle. The squat appearance

magical thinking Phrase used to describe a type of thinking, often characteristic of preschoolers and young children, that is not entirely logical or scientifically valid, but rather inventive and surprising and sometimes bizarre—hence *magical*.

growth velocity A measure of how rapidly an individual gains height and weight—for example, kilograms per year.

of infants is explained by the fact that their waists are usually as large as their hips or chests. Six-year-old children, in contrast, have begun to develop waists that are smaller than their shoulders and hips. This becomes even more evident in early adolescence than at the end of the preschool period.

The relatively larger infant waists are due to layers of fat and also to the size of the internal organs, many of which grow at a much more rapid rate than other parts of the body. Given space limitations between the child's pelvis and diaphragm, their abdomens often protrude. This condition changes as they grow in height during the preschool years.

Growth Asymmetries

Not all aspects of the body grow at the same rate. Growth asymmetries are found, for example, in *genital* growth, *lymph tissue* growth, and *brain* and *head* growth. As shown in Figure 7.3, the rate of genital growth is very slow until **pubescence** (the changes

---

pubescence Changes of adolescence leading to sexual maturity.

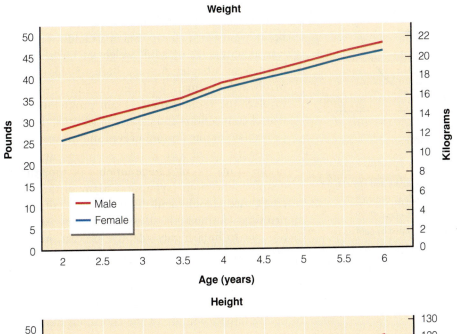

FIGURE 7.1 Weight at the 50th percentile for U.S. children ages 2 to 6. Source: Adapted from the Health Department, Milwaukee, Wisconsin; based on data by H. C. Stuart and H. V. Meredith, prepared for use in Children's Medical Center, Boston. Used by permission of the Milwaukee Health Department.

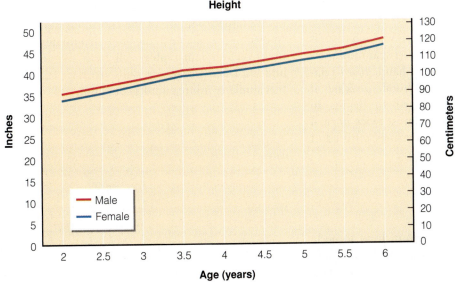

FIGURE 7.2 Height at the 50th percentile for U.S. children ages 2 to 6. Source: Adapted from the Health Department, Milwaukee, Wisconsin; based on data by H. C. Stuart and H. V. Meredith, prepared for use in Children's Medical Center, Boston. Used by permission of the Milwaukee Health Department.

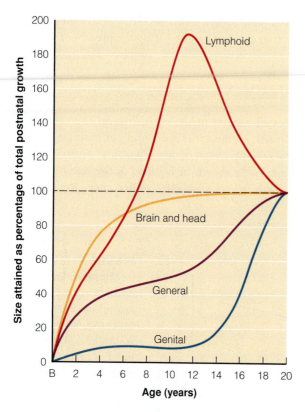

FIGURE 7.3 General growth curves in four areas of human development. As described in *Growth, Maturation, and Physical Activity* (p. 9), by Robert M. Malina and Claude Bouchard, Champaign, IL: Human Kinetics Publishers. Copyright © 1991 by Robert M. Malina and Claude Bouchard. Reprinted by permission. Also from *The Measurement of Man*, J. A. Harris et al., University of Minnesota Press, 1930 (p. 193). Copyright © 1930 by the University of Minnesota. Reprinted by permission.

leading to sexual maturity), following which there is a sudden and dramatic growth spurt spanning a few years. Lymph tissue, on the other hand, grows relatively rapidly throughout childhood, peaking at about the time that genital growth begins to increase. Note that it peaks at almost twice normal adult levels, and then actually declines until adult levels are reached at about age 20.

Brain and Head Growth

As we saw in Chapter 5, the ratio of head to body size (shown in Figure 7.4) decreases dramatically during the fetal period, and again during the first

years of life. Thus, the head of a 2-month-old fetus is approximately half the length of the entire body; at birth, it is closer to one-fourth the size of the rest of the body; and by the age of 6, it is close to one-eighth the size, which is a short step removed from the head-to-body relationship typical of the normal adult with a normal-sized head: one-tenth. From the age of 2 to 6, the head changes from approximately one-fifth to one-eighth of total body size—a significant enough change to be noticeable. Because of this, and because of changes in the distribution of fat and in the space that the child now has for internal organs, the 6-year-old looks remarkably like an adult; the 2-year-old looks more like a typical baby.

Part of the change in brain and head size after birth relates to the fact that by the age of two, the brain has reached about 75% of its adult weight (it was at only 25% of adult weight at birth). As we learned in Chapter 5, very little of this growth involves the formation of new neurons; instead, it involves the rapid growth (brain proliferation) of neural connections and of myelin sheaths, the fatty protective coating around **nerves** and neurons.

By the age of 3 or 4, brain proliferation has led to the formation of a huge number of superfluous neural connections (**synapses**). Many of those that aren't used atrophy and die in a process of **neural pruning** (Rumbaugh, 1998). Neural pruning is thought to be a highly adaptive process, not only because it, in a sense, streamlines brain activity, but also because it reduces the brain's energy requirements dramatically (Johnson, 1998). At the same time, neural pruning also reduces the brain's plasticity. It's largely because of the enormous number of connections available in the brain that infants sometimes recover remarkably well from serious brain injuries, often relearning skills (such as language) that similarly injured adults could not.

nerves Bundles of related neurons that function to relay messages (impulses) between the central nervous system and sensory and body systems. Some nerves can be very long; others, very short.

synapses Connections between neurons. A synapse is formed whenever the gap between neurons (the *synaptic cleft*) is bridged by an impulse.

neural pruning The process by which unused neural connections and brain cells atrophy and die.

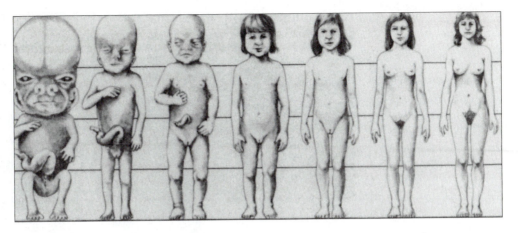

FIGURE 7.4 Changes in form and proportion of the human body during fetal and postnatal life.
Source: Reproduced with permission from Jensen et al., *Biology*. Belmont, Calif.: Wadsworth, 1979, p. 233.

Lateralization and Handedness

The brain consists of two halves, two **cerebral hemispheres**. These are mirror halves, but, at least in some respects, they have different functions—a phenomenon termed **lateralization**. For example, in the majority of individuals, the left hemisphere is somewhat more involved in language functions. Also, with respect to motor functions, each side of the body is controlled by the opposite hemisphere. Thus, in right-handed individuals (about 90% of the world's population), the left hemisphere is typically dominant (for language as well as for the *preferred* side of the body) (Lee et al., 1999). However, the right hemisphere does *not* appear to be the dominant hemisphere in as many as 80% of left-handed people (Kagan & Gall, 1998).

In the newborn, the hemispheres are not highly specialized, and handedness will not be firmly established before about age 1 (Leask & Crow, 1997). Still, beginning as early as 1 month, infants begin to reveal their hand preference in the positions they assume (Kagan & Gall, 1998). There is some speculation that handedness might be genetic, although recent evi-

> **THOUGHT CHALLENGE:** *How might it be possible to determine what percentage of our ancestral cave dwellers were right- and left-handed?*

dence that looked at handedness among adopted children and their biological as well as adoptive parents provides no evidence to support this hypothesis (Saudino & McManus, 1998). Nevertheless, it does appear to have some basis in the physiology of the brain as is evident in the fact that asymmetries corresponding to handedness are found between the two hemispheres even in the fetus prior to birth (Preis et al., 1999). Also, the proportion of left- to right-handers seems hardly to have changed since prehistoric times (Springer & Deutsch, 1993).

It was once considered important to be right-handed, and parents and educators sometimes went to great lengths to "correct" children's handedness—typically to no avail. Although there are clearly some disadvantages to being left-handed in a world built primarily by and for right-handed people, for most children, there are no psychological disadvantages. In fact, some researchers suggest that the hemispheres in some left-handed individuals may share dominance more equally, presenting certain advantages for learning mathematics and perhaps languages (Flannery & Liederman, 1995). (See *At a Glance*: "Preschoolers' Health Problems," and Figure 7.5.)

cerebral hemispheres The two opposite halves of the cerebrum. In adults, their functions overlap but are not exactly duplicated.

lateralization The specialization of brain functions so that one hemisphere becomes more involved than the other in certain functions. Lateralization occurs in infancy and early childhood.

| AT A GLANCE | **Preschoolers' Health Problems** |

Most preschoolers occasionally suffer from illness or injury serious enough to require medical attention or to keep them home at least one day (Figure 7.5). About half will have an upper-respiratory infection at least once (a cold, for example), and about 3 out of 10 will suffer some physical injury. Between ages 5 and 17, the rates for most common health problems decline—except for injuries and influenza. Males have higher injury rates than do females.

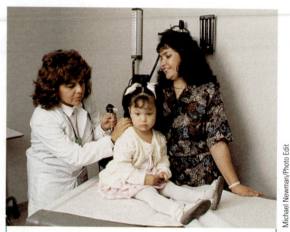

Most preschoolers occasionally require medical attention.

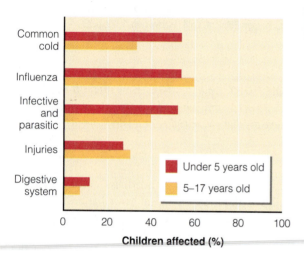

FIGURE 7.5 Preschoolers' and older children's susceptibility to injury and illness. The graph shows the percentage of children who will be affected at least once by the indicated condition. Source: Adapted from U.S. Bureau of the Census (1998), p. 148.

MOTOR DEVELOPMENT

Learning the tricks of self-propulsion—especially learning to walk—are among the infant's most significant motor achievements. Locomotion has extremely important social and cognitive implications. Infants who can walk (or at least crawl) can approach those to whom they are attached, and can also leave them to explore places they would otherwise see only from somebody's arms—or looking over the edge of some wheeled baby-thing. Self-locomotion greatly facilitates the process of becoming familiar with the world.

By the age of 2, infants have not only learned to walk, but they have also practiced and learned a wide range of other motor activities. Most have become remarkably adept at picking up objects,

stacking blocks, unlacing shoes, and dropping messy things on the floor.

Throughout early childhood, children continue to progress in motor development, their locomotion becoming more certain as they lose the characteristic wide-footed stance of the **toddler**. As their equilibrium stabilizes and their feet move closer together, their arms and hands also move closer to their bodies. They no longer need as wide a stance to maintain their balance—nor do they always need to keep their arms out as if they were perpetually walking a rail. Still, they fall far more often than you or I.

But it doesn't hurt so much.

toddler General term with imprecise age boundaries. Often used to encompass the end of infancy and beginning of the preschool period—about ages 18 to 30 months.

Developmental Timetables

Most parents are keenly interested in the developmental progress of their infants and children. They feel proud of their offsprings' accomplishments and are sometimes distressed and worried when their children do not develop as rapidly as they expect— or as rapidly as someone else's children.

Here, as in all areas of human development, there are no absolute norms, no definite, preestablished levels of performance that must be reached by certain ages. Our definitions of what is normal are vague and inexact. Still, psychology and medicine provide us with indications of what we might expect—that is, with **developmental timetables**; and these timetables may be used as benchmarks against which to evaluate our children—if we must.

Many different scales of infant and child development might be used for these purposes. As we saw, there are neonatal scales with which to assess the physiological and neurological condition of the newborn (for example, the *Brazelton Neonatal Behavioral Assessment Scale* or the Apgar score). There are also scales to assess motor and mental development in infancy (for example, the *Bayley Scales of Infant Development*). And there are developmental scales that span infancy and childhood (for example, the *Denver II* or the *Gesell Developmental Schedules*). Each of these instruments typically provides simple tasks that can be presented to the infant or child, or describes observations that can be made. Each also provides specific tables of norms describing what sorts of infant or child behaviors can be expected at different ages.

The *Denver Developmental Screening Test*, for example, was initially designed primarily to permit identification of infants and children suffering from developmental delays (Frankenburg et al., 1981). It has subsequently been revised and restandardized with various ethnic groups, and is now known as the *Denver II* (Frankenburg & Dodds, 1992). It provides age norms corresponding to the levels at which 25%, 50%, 75%, and 90% of

children are expected to demonstrate a given capability. Four different areas are examined by the test: language, personal-social, fine motor, and gross motor. A child is considered developmentally delayed when incapable of performing a task of which 90% of children of the same age are capable. Isolated developmental delays are not considered serious. But when a child is delayed on two or more tasks and in more than one area, further assessment may be required.

Motor Development and the Growth of Intellect

It is not surprising that there is a very close relationship between motor development and other aspects of development—a relationship well expressed in Piaget's label *sensorimotor*. It is as a result of *sensing* the world and *acting* upon it that the child begins to build up a representation of the world, and begins to learn to think, insisted Piaget. Evidence suggests this idea is correct.

In infancy, for example, learning to crawl, and eventually to walk, is important for developing notions of depth (Bushnell & Boudreau, 1993). Similarly, the development of a variety of other motor skills in the preschool period appears to be closely related to the maturation of the brain and nervous system, as well as to increasing motor control and coordination, and is reflected in the child's growing intelligence. In fact, different motor tasks are often used as items on measures of intelligence. Among these are the skills required for tracing geometric figures or for copying them freehand. Gesell (1925), whose work maps out in detail the sequential progression of children's motor development, reports that before age 2, the child is usually incapable of copying a circle or a horizontal line, although the 2- to 3-year-old can do so quite easily. By the age of 4, children can also copy a cross but are unable to copy a diamond (see Figure 7.6).

The increasing detail and sense of proportion with which children draw the human figure also seems to reflect their growing intellectual sophistication. As far back as 1926, Goodenough devised a simple intelligence test for children, the *Goodenough Draw-a-Man Test*. It required only that children draw a man—the *very best* man they could. Later,

---

developmental timetables Lists of observable developmental achievements with information concerning the average ages at which children normally attain these achievements. Such timetables are often used as instruments to assess the relative development of individual children.

FIGURE 7.6 Usual order of difficulty, with very approximate ages, for copying simple geometric designs reasonably well. Because of the close relationship between motor and intellectual development in early childhood, many intelligence tests for young children include tasks such as these.

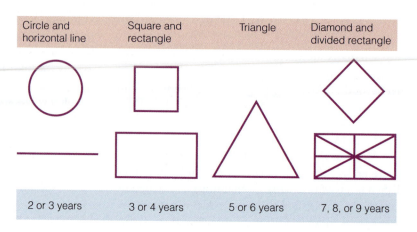

Circle and horizontal line	Square and rectangle	Triangle	Diamond and divided rectangle
2 or 3 years	3 or 4 years	5 or 6 years	7, 8, or 9 years

more politically correct revisions titled it the *Goodenough-Harris Drawing Test* (Harris, 1963) or the *Draw-a-Person Test* (Naglieri, 1988) (see Figure 7.7). Amazingly, this very simple little test correlates quite highly with far more detailed and expensive measures of intelligence (Abell, Horkheimer, & Nguyen, 1998).

Motor and Social Development

It makes sense that motor development, insofar as it reflects maturation of the brain and body, should be related to intellectual development; it also makes sense that motor development should be related to social development. Why? Because normal motor development allows the child to interact with parents, siblings, and peers in age- and sex-appropriate ways. For example, a child's play, particularly with peers, is often influenced by motor skills. Gerry, who is still incapable of jumping with both feet, is not likely to be invited by older children to join in a game of jump rope; Sally, who can't hold her marbles very well yet, will probably be left out of the traditional springtime marble games. Conversely, Robert, who is precocious in physical and motor development, is likely to be the first one asked to participate in games—indeed, may be the one to

FIGURE 7.7 Two examples of the *Goodenough-Harris Drawing Test*. Both artists were boys aged 10½ years. The raw scores and IQ equivalents, respectively, for the drawings are (a) 41 and 110, (b) 4 and 54. The child who drew (b) also had a low *Stanford-Binet* IQ score. Source: From the *Goodenough-Harris Drawing Test*, as reprinted in *Children's Drawings as Measures of Intellectual Property*. Copyright © 1963 by The Psychological Corporation. Reproduced by permission. All rights reserved.

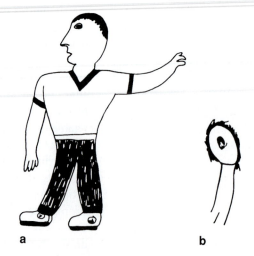

a   b

initiate them. Clearly, then, physical and motor development have an important influence on the child's social development; game playing is one important means of socialization (more about this in Chapter 8).

From Doing to Thinking

The relationship between doing and thinking in these early years is very close. Thinking is born from action; it is *sensorimotor*, to use Piaget's descriptive term. The capacity to remember and the ability to think don't just simply appear one day, fully formed. They develop gradually, and their genesis is a fascinating and complex subject.

Infants, notes Rovee-Collier (1996), are not simply incompetent adults who get better and better as they age and grow and develop. Rather, they are highly competent organisms within their own particular niches, displaying remarkable adaptations in their responses to the immediate demands of their environments. What we should ask, she insists, is not so much "what do children do?" but "why do they do it?"

Still, the infant's responses are often startlingly different from those you or I would make in the same situation. And that difference may serve to inform us about "why" children do what they do. For example, Fabricius and Wellman (1993) had children aged 4 to 6 judge the distances covered by different routes to the same location. Sometimes the routes were direct; at other times they were indirect; and still other times, some object placed along the route served to segment it. Many of these children insisted that the indirect and the segmented routes were shorter. Why? Perhaps, as Piaget thought, because these children focused only on one aspect of the route; or perhaps because they have difficulty representing the routes mentally.

Even if we don't always understand them, we are never totally surprised at the errors our preschoolers make. We don't expect preschool children, much less infants, to be completely logical. We are seldom dismayed when 3-year-olds insist loudly that a small cat, identical in appearance to their small cat, must surely be theirs; we are not shocked when a 4-year-old fails to realize that there really aren't more candies in his sister's dish just because

they're all spread out; we express little dismay when a 2-year-old calls a duck a chicken. For some reason, these instances of prelogical thinking and inexact memories simply amuse us; they are what we expect of young children.

But we would be surprised and perhaps alarmed if our 7-year-olds persisted in calling all shaggy-looking pigs "doggie"; if they refused to believe that 6 ounces of soft drink in a glass is the same amount as 6 ounces in a bottle; or if they thought they could increase the mass of a wad of gum simply by stringing it out and wrapping it around their ears. We expect some intellectual (cognitive) differences between preschoolers and older children. And among these cognitive differences will be some important developments having to do with memory.

◤ COGNITIVE DEVELOPMENT: THE PRESCHOOLER'S MEMORY

Between birth and the end of the early childhood period (around age 6), children learn and remember an overwhelming assortment of things: the identities of people and animals; the locations of things; numbers, letters, and songs; and thousands of words and all sorts of complex rules for putting them together.

From the very beginning children clearly have some ability to learn and to remember. But, as we saw in Chapter 5, neonates' memories are very brief. The effects of simple conditioning procedures sometimes last only hours, or perhaps a day. Still, an infant is not long confused about whether this is her mother's voice, or her face. Recognition of things like voices and faces is a certain sign of memory. But there are some important differences between the memories of infants and those of adults.

Preschool Memory Strategies

For one thing, infants don't deliberately and systematically organize, group, or elaborate material to remember it—and these three activities are the most important **memory strategies** of adults and older

---

memory strategies Systematic plans or procedures designed to improve the likelihood of remembering. The most common adult memory strategies are *organization, grouping, rehearsing,* and *elaboration.*

children. Most of what preschoolers remember is the result of what Wellman (1988) calls incidental mnemonics. **Incidental mnemonics** are not deliberate; hence they are not really strategies. They are what happens when someone pays attention, for whatever reason, and later remembers, or what happens when someone is exposed to the same thing often enough that it becomes familiar and known. Remembering, in these cases, is not the result of a deliberate and systematic attempt to elaborate or to rehearse; it is, in a sense, involuntary (or incidental).

We know that incidental mnemonics underlie much of preschoolers' learning. We also know that if preschoolers are *reminded* often enough, they can easily remember some of their personal experiences right through the normal period of infantile amnesia (Rovee-Collier, 1999). Because these are incidental and involuntary processes, and because there is little evidence of adultlike strategies such as deliberately rehearsing or organizing, researchers have sometimes assumed that memory strategies develop only in later childhood. But, says Wellman (1988), there is evidence of some memory strategies beginning in the preschool period. For example, Wellman (1988) asked 3-year-olds to bury a toy in a sandbox before leaving the room with the experimenter. Some of the children were asked to remember where they had buried the toy; others were asked if there was anything they would like to do before leaving, but were given no instructions about remembering the toy's location. Strikingly, half the children who

had been instructed to remember the toy's location marked it by placing a mound over the object, by marking the sand, or sometimes by placing another toy on top of it; only 20% of the no-instructions group did likewise (Figure 7.8).

Marking the toy's location is an intelligent and effective strategy. As we noted, however, many of the preschoolers' memory strategies are not so effective. Heisel and Retter (1981) asked 3- and 5-year-old youngsters to hide an object in one of 196 separate containers arranged in a large 14-by-14 matrix and instructed some of them to remember where they had hidden the object. Many of the children in both age groups used memory strategies when they had been instructed to remember. The strategies used by the 5-year-olds were often very effective—namely, hiding the object in one of the corner locations because they could be remembered and relocated very easily. But what is perhaps most striking is that the 3-year-olds' strategies, while every bit as consistent as those of the older children, were often very ineffective. Almost half of these 3-year-olds tried to hide the object in the same location on every trial, thus demonstrating that they were using a systematic strategy; but the location was typically somewhere near the center of the array. As a result, when they were later asked to find the object, these children fared almost as poorly as those who had not used any strategy.

Overusing an inappropriate memory strategy is one of the most common mistakes made by young children trying to remember, says Wellman (1988). An important developmental change in memory strategies is a gradual reduction in the use of faulty strategies and an increase in more effective strate-

incidental mnemonics Nonsystematic, *incidental* approaches to remembering sometimes used by young children, such as paying attention.

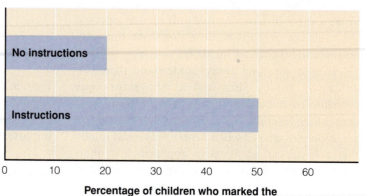

FIGURE 7.8 Of 3-year-olds asked to hide a toy in a sandbox, half who were asked to try to remember where the toy was hidden (the instructions group) marked its location; only 20% of the no-instructions group did likewise. Preschoolers may be capable of using simple memory strategies, but often do not do so spontaneously.

No instructions

Instructions

0   10   20   30   40   50   60

Percentage of children who marked the hidden toy's location in the sandbox

gies. Effective strategies increase dramatically in elementary school.

It is also noteworthy that a variety of studies have shown that preschoolers' memories are *better* in more natural settings (like their homes or kindergartens) than they are in laboratory settings. In these natural settings, they not only remember more, but they are also more likely to make use of *incidental mnemonics* (like trying to pay attention)—sometimes termed *prestrategies* (Jagodzinska, 1997).

Development of Memory Strategies

A preschooler's increasing ability to remember results in part from increasing familiarity with things and events. For example, Saarnio (1993) showed that the more familiar preschoolers were with certain scenes, the better they were able to remember objects in the scenes.

The development of memory skills may also depend on social interaction. Recall from Chapter 2 that Vygotsky (1977) argues that a child's learning process is guided by interaction with adults or more advanced peers. When Harris and Hamidullah (1993) asked mothers to teach their 4-year-olds to remember different things (like the names of four cartoon characters or the location of animals in a zoo), the mothers spontaneously used strategies. The most common strategy used was rehearsal (repeating and having children repeat). In addition, many mothers combined these verbal rehearsal strategies with nonverbal strategies such as pointing out cues (like spots on the cartoon dog, whose name was Spotty the Dog).

In summary, preschoolers are clearly able to remember. But in most cases, memory results not from the deliberate use of memory strategies, but from incidental mnemonics—for example, paying attention to something or being exposed to something more than once. In contrast, elementary-school children often deliberately use memory strategies.

One of the important differences between older memorizers and preschoolers is that older children have acquired some understanding of the processes involved in learning and remembering. They have developed intuitive notions of themselves as information processors capable of applying strategies and of monitoring and changing them as required. In the current jargon, they have developed some of the skills involved in **metamemory** (defined as the knowledge children have about the processes involved in remembering). (More about the memories of older children in Chapter 9).

Infantile Amnesia

The immaturity of brain structures, together with the eventual *pruning* of a large number of neural connections, is sometimes used as one possible explanation for the curious phenomenon of **infantile amnesia** (Nelson, 1998). As we saw in Chapter 5, this is a phenomenon to which we all appear to be subject: We remember virtually nothing about our infancies or even about the earliest of our preschool years. So powerful is infantile amnesia that when Newcombe and Fox (1994) showed 9- and 10-year-olds photographs of their preschool classmates, they were typically unable to recognize them. But studies indicate that if you, as an adult, were shown photographs of your elementary-school classmates, you would recognize more than 90% of them even if you had not seen any of the individuals for as long as 50 years (Babrick, Babrick, & Wittlinger, 1975).

Researchers don't agree about the best explanations for infantile amnesia (Eacott, 1999). As we saw, one theory relates to the immaturity of the young child's brain. Another refers to the possibility that the infant has not developed the sorts of memory strategies that are most useful for long-term recall.

Reliability of Preschooler's Memories

Say you had a group of 3- to 5-year-olds playing in a room, and along came a distinct-looking stranger

---

metamemory The knowledge that we develop about our own memory processes—knowledge about how to remember rather than simply about our memories.

infantile amnesia A mysterious but apparently universal human phenomenon evident in the fact that most people do not remember events of infancy or of the early preschool period.

who happened to be a thief—not a thief who sneaked quickly in and out of the room, but one who came in boldly and, right before the children's eyes, stole a big box full of Mrs. Quigley's very personal things.

Now suppose you do the same thing with a room full of older children, and also with adolescents and adults. Later you drag all these people, all these witnesses to this heinous crime, to view a lineup that includes the culprit, and you ask your witnesses to pick out the guilty person. How well do you suppose your preschool witnesses will fare compared with older children? Adolescents? Adults?

Now, let's imagine you throw a twist in the proceedings, and you expose your witnesses to a lineup that doesn't include the crook. Will your witnesses say, "Hey, the thief isn't here"? Or will they point the finger at the wrong person?

These are especially important questions in courts of law, because children (and, of course, adults) are sometimes witnesses to serious crimes. And sometimes, unfortunately, they are victims too. Especially recently, children have often been asked to recollect things that might have been done to them— for example, instances of physical or sexual abuse. Many of these child witnesses have seemed remarkably informative; some have been able to provide very damning evidence. How reliable is this evidence?

Literally hundreds of studies have been conducted to answer this question. Quite a number of them have involved procedures very much like that just described, where people witness an apparent crime and are then asked questions about it. When Pozzulo and Lindsay (1998) summarized a large number of these studies in a **meta-analysis**, they reached two clear conclusions: Preschoolers are significantly less likely than adults to make correct identifications in the first place; and preschoolers are also more *unlikely* to reject all individuals in the lineup of false suspects. Even if the culprit is clearly not in the lineup, they will very often point their little fingers anyway.

Many studies in this area have looked at the accuracy of preschoolers' memories for events they experience as well as for events they witness. They attempt to answer questions such as: Can children be made to remember things that didn't happen? Do children remember more accurately immediately after the event or some time later? Does repeated questioning help children dredge up details they might have forgotten? Are children more predisposed than adults to acquiesce to grownups, and to say "yes" when they should say "I don't know"? As answers to these questions, research reveals the following:

▲ Preschoolers (as we just saw) are less likely to recognize a suspect and are more likely to make false identifications. They are also less likely to remember the details of a crime (Ricci & Beal, 1998).

▲ Preschoolers can be made to remember medical procedures they never had (Quas et al., 1999). For example, with appropriate questioning, some falsely alleged that their pediatrician had stuck a stick or a finger in their genitals (Bruck et al., 1995).

▲ In a number of studies, preschoolers have been influenced to falsely recall that some man had touched their genitals, kissed them, or done these things to one of their friends (for example, Lepore & Sesco, 1994).

▲ When children are asked to imagine that something happened and to create visual imagery for the event, many will later report the imagined event as though it actually happened (McBrien & Dagenbach, 1998).

▲ There is some doubt as to the reliability of any memory of events that allegedly occurred during the period normally covered by infantile amnesia—that is, during the early preschool years (West & Bauer, 1999).

▲ Young children (3 to 4 years old) appear to have a "yes" response bias. They are more likely to say that something happened than that it didn't or that they don't know (McBrien & Dagenbach, 1998).

▲ When preschoolers are made to guess, to provide answers they are uncertain of, if the questions leading to these guesses are repeated often enough, they become progressively more certain,

meta-analysis A research technique involving careful, systematic analysis of all or most of the relevant studies that have looked at a research question in an attempt to arrive at conclusions far more general and reliable than those based on the results of a single study.

eventually sounding totally confident of their responses (Poole & White, 1991).

In interpreting these and related studies, Bruck and Ceci (1999) conclude that young children—especially preschoolers—do not remember as accurately and in as much detail as older children and adults; perhaps even more important, they are highly suggestible as well. Young children are cooperative; they trust interviewers, lawyers, judges, and politicians. They think people are honest rather than deceptive. They try to please. They try to follow wherever leading questions take them (Bruck & Ceci, 1999). And, clearly, they can be made to remember things that never happened (as can older children and adults, although to a lesser extent).

Interviewers, sometimes deliberately and sometimes inadvertently, plant false memories or distort existing memories using any of a number of techniques: They ask leading rather than open-ended questions. That is, they don't say to the child, "Tell me what happened." Instead they ask questions such as, "Was the man wearing a blue cap?" They ask the same question repeatedly. They suggest desired answers, repeating the questions that lead to these answers. They use emotional inducements to entice interviewees to respond as desired (or as expected), saying things such as, "If you tell me about when he touched you, you'll feel so much better." They present children with stereotypes of the alleged perpetrator of bad deeds—for example, "That man has done bad things to other little children." Any of these approaches can be highly effective in planting false memories in preschoolers, say Bruck and Ceci (1999); used in combination, they are even more effective.

Notwithstanding the conclusion that preschoolers appear to be the most suggestible age group, it is nevertheless true that some young preschoolers are remarkably resistant to suggestion. It is also true that many *are* victims—or witnesses—of crimes that have no other witnesses. And many, note Bruck and Ceci (1999), when questioned by a sensitive and *neutral* interviewer, show impressively good recall for significant events. Unfortunately, it isn't always possible for courts of law to determine how reliable child witnesses actually are (see *In the News and on the Web*: "The Devil's Church").

▢ COGNITIVE DEVELOPMENT: PIAGET'S VIEW

In the beginning, says Piaget, the infant's understanding of the world is *sensorimotor*. That is, things are represented in sensation and in action. Later, things come to be represented more abstractly. At the most sophisticated level, they will be represented in symbol systems, the most powerful of which is language.

Preoperational Thought

But the preschooler is not yet an *operational* thinker, according to Piaget. In some ways, he argues, preschoolers are still somewhere between sensorimotor representation and a complete understanding and use of the rules of logic: They use **preoperations**.

In Piaget's theory, an **operation** is a thought characterized by some specific logical properties; it is a logical thought. When Robert believes he has more gum when he rolls it into a fat ball and less when he spreads it out like a thin pancake on his sister's pillow, he is demonstrating preoperational (or prelogical) thinking. His thinking is not yet characterized by **reversibility**; that is, he doesn't yet understand either the possibility or the implications of undoing an action mentally.

The preoperational period (ages 2 to about 7 years) includes two subperiods, according to Piaget. The **preconceptual** lasts from 2 to 4; the intuitive

---

preoperation Piaget's label for a thought that is not limited by ordinary rules of logic. Preoperations tend to be unstable, idiosyncratic, perception dominated, and egocentric.

operation Piaget's term for mental activity. An operation is a thought process characterized by certain rules of logic. Preoperations are more intuitive and egocentric, and less logical.

reversibility A logical property manifested in the ability to reverse or undo activity either empirically or conceptually. An idea is said to be reversible when a child can imagine its opposite, and realize that certain logical consequences follow from doing so.

preconceptual thought In Piaget's system, a substage of preoperational thought, beginning around 2 and lasting until 4. It is so called because children have not yet developed the ability to classify and therefore have an incomplete understanding of concepts.

The Devil's Church

When a mother in the little town of Martensville, Saskatchewan, noticed a diaper rash on her 30-month-old child, she became alarmed and suspicious. She talked to other mothers; they too had heard or noticed things. And all their children were cared for by the same baby-sitting service. They spoke with the police; expert interviewers were brought in; the children told their increasingly horrifying stories. Subsequently charged were Ron Sterling; Linda Sterling; their 25-year-old son, Travis; five other males; and one minor female—with a total of 190 counts of physical and sexual abuse against 2 dozen children. Children were later to testify that they had been driven to a "devil's church" and made to drink urine and eat feces. One child swore he'd had an axe handle driven into his penis. Others said they had been victimized with penis-shaped vibrators. And after photographs of a building thought to be the devil's church were circulated, some children remembered being locked up in the wire cages that were evident in the photographs. Public hysteria ran high.

But there were no scars on any of the children, no physical evidence of abuse, and the wire cages were too small to have held any of the children. Interviews of the children were repeated numerous times. After a sensational 3-month trial, the Sterling parents were acquitted, although the son was found guilty of some charges. But these convictions, too, were later overturned.

Eisler, D. (1997). A cautionary tale. *Maclean's*, Feb. 10.

To Think About: As a major paper, research the proposition that young children make unreliable witnesses in criminal trials. Consider both sides of the argument.

 Resources: Most sexual and physical abuse cases are not "witch hunts," but links to websites dedicated to exposing what some people consider to be modern-day witch hunts, primarily involving child sex abuse or satanic rituals, can be seen at:

http://www.ags.uci.edu/~dehill/witchhunt/cases.htm

For additional readings, explore *InfoTrac College Edition*, your online library. Go to http://infotrac-college.com/wadsworth and use the passcode that came on the card with your book. Try these search terms: child sexual abuse, child sexual abuse victims.

---

spans ages 4 to 7 (see the *Concept Summary* in Chapter 5, p. 224).

Preconceptual Thinking

As we saw, toward the end of the second year, and especially with the advent of language, infants begin to symbolize. Now they can represent their actions mentally and anticipate consequences before the action actually occurs. Also, they have begun to develop some understanding of causes—of actions as means to ends.

Preconcepts Being able to symbolize, says Piaget, allows preschoolers to *internalize* objects and events

in the environment—that is, to represent them internally. In fact, in Piaget's system, thinking is *internal representation* (as opposed to the representation-in-action of sensorimotor thought). Internalizing by means of symbols is what allows preschoolers to begin to relate objects and events in terms of their common properties. That is, it allows them to form **concepts**. But these concepts are not as complete and logical as adults' and are therefore referred to as **preconcepts**. Thus children recognize an adult because they have a budding concept—a preconcept—that tells them an adult is whatever

---

concept A collection of perceptual experiences or ideas related by virtue of their possessing common properties.

walks on two legs, is very tall, and speaks in a gruff voice. Preconcepts such as these allow children to identify burros, birds, bats, and beetles. But one of the limitations of these preconcepts is that they often don't allow the child to distinguish among different individuals belonging to the same species. Piaget (1951) illustrates this with his son, Laurent, who one day pointed out a snail to his father as they were walking. Several minutes later they came upon another snail, and the child exclaimed that here again was the snail. The child's failure to recognize that similar objects can belong to the same class and still be different objects—that is, that they can retain an identity of their own—is an example of a preconcept. The preschooler who steadfastly continues to believe in Santa Claus, even after seeing 10 different Santas on the same day, is demonstrating preconceptual thinking. For the child the Santas are all identical; they are one.

There are three other striking features of preschoolers' thinking during the preconceptual period, according to Piaget. These are apparent in transductive reasoning, syncretic reasoning, and animism.

Transductive Reasoning There are two main types of logical reasoning: *deduction* and *induction*. To deduce is to go from the general to the particular. For example, if you know that birds have feathers, you can deduce that the pileated woodpecker, which is a bird, has feathers. In contrast, to induce is to go from specific examples to a broader generalization. From the observation that the birds you see have feathers, you might induce that all birds have feathers—until you meet the hairless waganape.

Transductive reasoning makes inferences not from general to particular or from particular to general, but rather from one particular to another—that is, from one instance to another—often because

THOUGHT CHALLENGE: *Invent an example of transductive reasoning that leads to a correct conclusion. Invent another that leads to an incorrect conclusion.*

of superficial similarities. It is like one-case inductive reasoning. If I find that a redheaded person has a particularly charming personality, I might transduce that all redheaded people will also be charming. Transductive reasoning can occasionally—and somewhat accidentally—lead to a correct inference. It can also lead to totally incorrect conclusions (as would be the case in the preceding illustration if, in fact, not all redheaded people are charming—which, I suppose, is possible).

Syncretic Reasoning Preschoolers are far better than infants at classifying objects in terms of their common characteristics. As we saw, they have *preconcepts* that allow them to recognize objects and events on the basis of their common properties. Still, their classification behavior is not always very objective or very logical. In Piaget's words, preconceptual thinkers often make use of **syncretic reasoning** when they classify. To reason syncretically is to group objects according to personal and highly unstable rules. For example, if you place a 2-year-old child in front of a table on which there are many objects of different kinds and colors, and you ask this child to put the objects together that belong together, the child might reason something like this: The blue truck goes with the red truck because they're both trucks, and this thing goes with them because it's blue and that truck is blue. Here's a ball and here's a marble and they go together, and here's a crayon that's yellow like the ball, so it goes with them too.

The important point is that preschoolers' classification rules change constantly; they see little reason to use the same rule consistently. We adults, whose thinking is not so magical, do not have the same luxury.

---

preconcept The label given to a preconceptual child's incomplete understanding of concepts, resulting from an inability to reason correctly about related classes.

transductive reasoning The type of semilogical reasoning that proceeds from particular to particular, rather than from particular to general or from general to particular. One example of transductive reasoning is the following: (1) Cows give milk. (2) Goats give milk. (3) Therefore, goats are cows.

---

syncretic reasoning A type of semilogical reasoning characteristic of the classification behavior of very young preschoolers. In syncretic reasoning, objects are grouped according to egocentric criteria, which are subject to change from one object to the next. In other words, children do not classify on the basis of a single dimension but change dimensions as they classify.

Between the ages of 2 and 4, children begin to classify objects they encounter by noting their characteristics. At first, through what Piaget labels transductive reasoning, this girl might conclude that here are a whole bunch of dogs—a sort of preconcept. Eventually, however, long tails, hooves, and snorting noises will help her identify these as horses.

Amy Etra/PhotoEdit

Animism We tolerate, perhaps even expect, magical thinking in preschoolers. But, says Pearce (1977), magical thinking in older children makes us uneasy, and we try to "teach" them to be more logical— more like us.

Magical thinking is especially evident in the **animistic thinking** of the preschooler. "Does the sun move?" Piaget (1960) asked his young companion as they walked (p. 215). "Yes," the child answered, going on to explain to Piaget that the sun followed him wherever he went, that it turned when he turned, and that it must surely be alive because otherwise it couldn't follow the way it does.

This, the belief that inanimate objects are alive, describes the *animism* of the preschooler. Animistic thinking is what leads 2- or 3-year-olds to argue that the moon and the wind are alive. And if pressed to substantiate their beliefs, to explain how they know these things are alive, sometimes they argue that it is because they move that one knows they're alive.

"Ah! But cars move too," the clever psychologist interrupts. "Are they alive?" But animism has its limits, and most children at this stage don't think cars are alive. In fact, suggests Bullock (1985), while animistic thinking is sometimes characteristic of very young preschoolers, it is far less common among 4- and 5-year-olds. Also, the child's animism applies

mainly to natural rather than to artificial things. Four- and five-year-olds have little difficulty differentiating between these two classes, reports Petrovich (1999). Furthermore, the natural phenomena to which animism seems to apply include mainly things such as the sun, moon, wind, and clouds, about which even adults don't always know a great deal. The preschooler doesn't normally apply animism—the belief that things are alive—to things like rocks and trees and water and dead cats.

Intuitive Thinking

During the period of **intuitive thinking**, which begins at about age 4 and ends at approximately 7, according to Piaget, children have learned to solve many problems correctly. But they don't always do so using logic. During this period their thinking is often intuitive, egocentric, perception-dominated, and characterized by classification errors.

An Illustration of Intuitive Thinking One of Piaget's demonstrations goes something like this: Take three balls, say a blue one, a red one, and a yellow one, and insert them one at a time into an upright cardboard

---

animistic thinking Attributing lifelike qualities to inanimate objects. In Piaget's theory, young preschoolers are sometimes described as using animistic thinking.

intuitive thinking A Piagetian stage (ages 4 to 7) in which thought is based on immediate comprehension rather than logical processes. Also characterized by difficulties in class inclusion, egocentricity, and marked reliance on perception.

tube so that the preschooler in front of you can no longer see them. This is a bright preschooler who knows that the red ball is on top, the yellow in the middle, and the blue at the bottom. Now turn the tube a half rotation (180 degrees). The preschooler now knows that the blue ball is on top. Turn it another half turn; the preschooler still knows which is on top. But if you make the problem much more complicated, say by rotating the tube 3 turns or $2^1/_2$ turns, the child can become quite confused. What Piaget found was that as long as preschoolers could continue to "imagine" (keep track of) the position of the balls inside the tube, they could answer correctly, but they could not generate a rule about the relationship between odd and even numbers of turns or half turns and the location of the balls. They solved the problem through intuitive mental images rather than logical reasoning.

Problems of Class Inclusion Piaget asserted that preschoolers' difficulties with class inclusion are easily demonstrated in experiments in which children are shown a collection of objects made up of two subclasses—for example, a handful of wooden beads of which 15 are brown and 5 are blue. The subject is asked what the objects are. "Wooden beads," says the child. The experimenter then divides the beads into subclasses, brown and blue, and asks whether there are more brown beads or more wooden beads. The trick is obvious, you say? Not to a child at this stage of development. "There's more brown beads," the child replies, as though breaking down a class into its subparts destroys the parent class.

Preschooler Egocentricity Piaget also argued that preschoolers exhibit egocentric thought. In one Piaget study, a girl doll and a boy doll are suspended side by side on a string in plain view of a child. The experimenter, holding one end of the string in each hand, steps behind a screen so that the dolls are hidden from the child's view. The child is asked to predict which of the dolls will appear first if the experimenter moves the string toward the right. The experimenter then hides the dolls again and repeats the same question: "Which of the dolls will come out first if they are moved to the same side again?" The procedure is repeated several times. Typically, the child will answer correctly for every early trial. What happens in later trials is striking: The child eventually makes the

opposite and clearly incorrect prediction! If asked why, one of the more common answers is that it isn't fair for the same doll to come out first every time; now it's the other doll's turn. Children inject their own values, their own sense of justice, into the experimental situation, demonstrating their egocentric thought processes. The term **egocentric** is not derogatory but simply points out an excessive reliance on the thinker's individual point of view coupled with a corresponding inability to be objective.

Piaget further identified what he called *egocentric speech*, the characteristic self-talk of budding young linguists who repeat words and sounds to themselves—much as young prelingual infants might babble, but using real words. He also asserted that egocentricity abounds in the conversations of young children in which speakers pay little attention to their listeners or to other speakers, except that they sometimes take turns in delivering their little pronouncements:

> Geoff: It's a black one.
> Jason: I have to go home soon.
> Geoff: I'm going to find a red one.
> Jason: I'm thirsty.
> Geoff: I don't like black ones.

A conversation? No: More a *collective monologue*, says Piaget. But real conversations, which require the nonegocentric ability to adopt another's point of view, are not far behind (and are discussed later in this chapter).

Reliance on Perception Preschoolers' perceptions also dominate thinking, according to Piaget, as he demonstrated in his **conservation** problems (see Chapter 9). In a typical Piagetian conservation-of-mass problem, for example, a child is shown two

---

egocentric Adjective based on Latin words for *self* (ego) and *center*. Literally, it describes a self-centered behavior, attitude, or personality characteristic. Although egocentrism often has negative connotations of selfishness, it is simply descriptive rather than evaluative when applied to children's perception of the world. For example, egocentric perception is characterized by an inability to assume an objective point of view.

conservation A Piagetian term implying that certain quantitative attributes of objects remain unchanged unless something is added to or taken away from them. Such characteristics of objects as mass, number, area, and volume are capable of being conserved.

identical balls of modeling clay (or similar substance) and acknowledges that there is the same amount of clay in each. One of the balls is then either flattened into a thin pancake, broken into small pieces, rolled into a long snake, or otherwise deformed. The child now believes that the altered shape(s) contains either more or less clay, depending on its appearance. Preschoolers rely on actual perception of the object rather than on any of the logical rules that will later govern thinking (for example, nothing has been added to or taken away from the clay, and so it must still contain an identical amount). Figure 7.9 illustrates simple tasks that can be used to demonstrate some of the important prelogical characteristics of preschoolers' thought processes.

Some Replications of Piaget's Work

An increasing number of researchers, sometimes referred to as neo-Piagetians, no longer consider it appropriate to refer to preschool children as "pre-logical" (or preconceptual). Preschoolers' logic may not be as advanced as yours or mine, and there may be something to be learned by contrasting it with a more advanced logic, but it is, nevertheless, a logic that is worthy of study in its own right.

The term *neo-Piagetian* is a collective word for developmental theorists whose research stems from a Piagetian tradition, but who have gone beyond where Piaget stopped. It includes all those who continue to replicate his work, and in a loose sense, those who ponder his questions and his answers.

Literally hundreds of studies have been conducted to investigate Piaget's view of children's progression through stages of cognitive development. Many researchers continue to feel that the sequence described by Piaget is valid, not only in European and North American countries, but in many other parts of the world as well. However, some have found that Piaget's estimates of the ages of attainment are underestimates for some North American and European children on specific tasks. This evidence typically comes from experiments that attempt to make it simpler for children to demonstrate knowledge of the concept or ability in question. One type of study that illustrates this point concerns Piaget's "mountains" problem, which illustrates preschool-

ers' egocentricity (inability to adopt someone else's point of view).

In the original study, children observed three mountains of unequal height set on top of a table. They were allowed to walk around the display to become familiar with all sides of the mountains. Later they sat on one side of the table, a doll was placed on the other side, and they were asked to select photographs representing the doll's view of the mountains. Piaget found that children in the preoperational period usually indicated that the doll would see the same things they themselves saw, a finding that he interpreted as evidence of egocentricity.

However, when Piaget's mountain task is made simpler, children sometimes respond quite differently. Liben (1975) asked preschoolers to describe what a white card would look like from both their and the experimenter's point of view under a number of different conditions in which colored glasses would be worn. In one condition, for example, the experimenter would wear green-tinted glasses and the children, no glasses. A correct, nonegocentric response in this case would be that the card would look green to the experimenter. Liben found that almost half the 3-year-olds answered correctly, and most of the older children had no difficulty with the questions. Similarly, when Hughes (reported in Donaldson, 1978) presented preschoolers with a situation in which they had to determine whether a "police officer" could see a doll from a vantage point quite different from the child's, subjects had little difficulty determining what the officer's point of view would actually be (see Figure 7.10).

Was Piaget Wrong?

What these and related studies most clearly point out is that egocentricity and other characteristics of children's thinking are far more complex than had been suspected. Indeed, they are far more complex than Piaget himself had suspected. As Lourenco and Machado (1996) point out in their defense of Piaget against his critics, there have been widespread misinterpretations of Piaget's theory. Many have assumed, for example, that the most important aspects of the theory have to do with discovering the ages at which

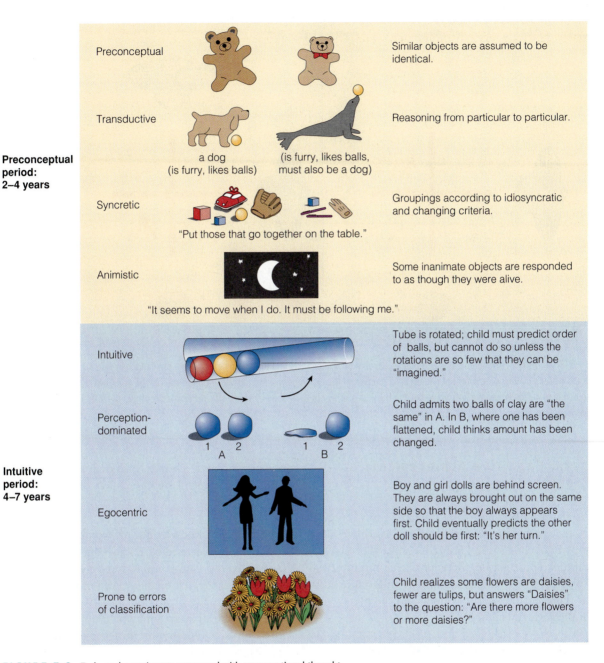

Preconceptual period: 2–4 years

Preconceptual — Similar objects are assumed to be identical.

Transductive — Reasoning from particular to particular.

a dog (is furry, likes balls) (is furry, likes balls, must also be a dog)

Syncretic — Groupings according to idiosyncratic and changing criteria.

"Put those that go together on the table."

Animistic — Some inanimate objects are responded to as though they were alive.

"It seems to move when I do. It must be following me."

Intuitive period: 4–7 years

Intuitive — Tube is rotated; child must predict order of balls, but cannot do so unless the rotations are so few that they can be "imagined."

Perception-dominated — Child admits two balls of clay are "the same" in A. In B, where one has been flattened, child thinks amount has been changed.

1 2   1 2
   A   B

Egocentric — Boy and girl dolls are behind screen. They are always brought out on the same side so that the boy always appears first. Child eventually predicts the other doll should be first: "It's her turn."

Prone to errors of classification — Child realizes some flowers are daisies, fewer are tulips, but answers "Daisies" to the question: "Are there more flowers or more daisies?"

FIGURE 7.9 Tasks and experiments concerned with preoperational thought.

children achieve certain understandings and capabilities. In fact, the central aspects of the theory have more to do with the processes by which children interact with the world, how they develop ideas, and how conflict among ideas leads to cognitive change and to the construction of progressively more logical representations of reality (Siegler & Ellis, 1996).

Some of Piaget's critics have been concerned that Piaget's emphasis, especially when dealing with the preschooler, has been on what children cannot do, on their mistakes and their incomplete and sometimes laughable logic. More recent emphases have done better justice to what young children can rather than what they cannot do.

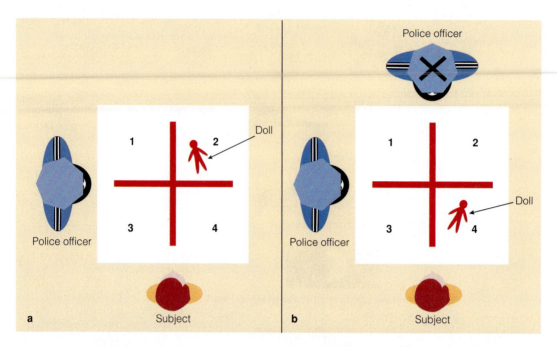

FIGURE 7.10 Arrangement for the Hughes experiment. (a) Subjects had to determine whether a doll hidden in 1, 2, 3, or 4 could be seen by the police officer at left. (b) In a later part of the experiment, a second police officer was placed at X. The child then had to decide where the doll would have to be hidden so as not to be seen by either officer. Preschoolers had little trouble answering correctly.

Some Cognitive Achievements of Preschoolers

As Flavell (1985) notes, given what we now know, it is inappropriate and misleading to think of a preschool child's mind as preoperational or preconceptual. For example, there have been monumental advances in our understanding of children's ability to represent the world symbolically, highly evident in their use of language.

Preschoolers' Knowledge of Relationships Researchers now know a great deal more about children's ability to solve problems that require understanding relationships among different ideas. For example, when Smith (1979) asked 4-year-olds questions of the type, "A basenji is a kind of dog but not a poodle. Is a basenji an animal?" many answered correctly. Similarly, many had no difficulty with questions of the form, "An abalone is a kind of food but not a plant. Is an abalone a vegetable?" These are class-inclusion questions; they require at least some knowledge of class membership (animals include

dogs; nonplants are not included among vegetables). They depend on the child's ability to relate concepts.

Preschoolers' Knowledge of Numbers The first number word learned by English-speaking children is usually *two*—not *one*. It typically appears very shortly after the first birthday. And in its early incarnation, it usually means not just two, but a whole bunch, more or less (Sophian, 1996). For the next little while, children may practice many number names, often in correct sequence, as in "one, two, three, giddyup!" By the time they are a little older, there are very few preschoolers who cannot count objects and who do not understand that six jellybeans are more than four. Indeed, most will tell you without prompting that six is exactly two more than four, or that if you had seven jellybeans to begin with and your little brother ate five of them, you would have only two left. Children invent their own solutions for problems of this kind, claim Louden and Hunter (1999). As a result, they come to school with a wide range of competencies, not all of which

Not all preschoolers can copy numbers as elegantly and precisely as this little 4-year-old. But most can tell you without hesitation that if you had seven jellybeans to begin with and your little brother ate five of them, you would have only two left. Many would even be able to name the mathematical operation involved. Piaget is sometimes criticized for having focused too much on what preschoolers cannot do—and too little on the remarkable cognitive achievements of children during this period.

By the time children begin school, they have developed a wide range of abilities related to understanding number—abilities having to do with classifying, setting up correspondences, seriating, and counting (Van de Rijt & Van Luit, 1999). These abilities relate to two kinds of knowledge about numbers that appear during the preschool period (Gelman, 1982; Gelman & Gallistel, 1978). First there are number abstraction skills that give children an understanding of numerosity—of how many things there are in a collection of, say, snails in one's pockets. Second, there are numerical reasoning principles that allow children to reason about or predict the outcome of certain simple numerical operations, such as adding to or taking from. Finally, there are the principles that allow us to count. We take them completely for granted even though they are remarkably complex and wonderfully logical. And amazingly, preschoolers discover these principles and actually use them in ways far more logical than we had expected.

As Gelman (1978) notes, our preoccupation with what preschool children cannot do may have blinded us to some of their achievements. Number abstraction and numerical reasoning skills are important and complex cognitive abilities that illustrate dramatically some of these achievements—as do their enormous language skills. In short, preschoolers (ages 3 to 5) are a tremendous cognitive distance from infants. (See *Concept Summary.*)

PRESCHOOL EDUCATION

Can preschoolers' capabilities be influenced through preschool education? Should they be? These questions concerning preschool education are a source of considerable debate. On one side of the debate are people such as Elkind (1987a, b), who fears that so relentlessly do we push our children toward competence that the **hurried child** misses much of childhood, and Sigel (1987), who deplores the hothouse atmosphere of many early childhood programs. There are a number of misconceptions about

hurried child Expression coined by Elkind for children whose parents are so eager for them to learn and to accomplish that they "rush" them through childhood, dragging them from one lesson or school to another, scarcely giving them time to pause and play and just be children.

are always taken into account by the school curriculum. For example, their understanding of fractions, and their apparently intuitive ability to reason about them, are far more advanced than has generally been thought (Mix, Levine, & Huttenlocher, 1998). The development of these competencies, notes Naka (1999), appears to be greatly aided by the fact that caretakers typically adjust their language and their use of number concepts according to the level of understanding of their preschoolers. And, as Piaget makes clear, it depends greatly on children's experience with real objects.

CONCEPT SUMMARY **Some Characteristics of Preoperational Thought According to Piaget**

As Piaget defines it, an *operation* is a thought subject to certain rules of logic—hence a *logical* thought. A *preoperation* is a thought that stops somewhat short of being completely logical. In spite of their remarkable achievements in language learning and number competence, Piaget describes preschoolers as *preoperational*. Instead of being completely logical, their thinking may show signs of being in one of the following periods.

Preconceptual Period (2–4 years)

• **Preconceptual**	Similar objects (like the toy at home and the one at the neighbor's) are considered identical
• **Transductive**	Reasoning from particular to particular; conclusions on the basis of a single example
• **Syncretic**	Changing criteria when grouping objects
• **Animistic**	Believing inanimate objects are alive, have a will, intend to do things

Intuitive Period (4–7 years)

• **Intuitive**	Reasoning based on mental images, on feelings, rather than on logic where appearances contradict logic, go with appearances
• **Egocentric**	Inject personal point of view into equation; inability to adopt another's point of view
• **Prone to classification errors**	Confusion among classes and their subclasses, as though dividing a class into its components destroys the parent class

preschool education, say Canning and Lyon (1991). One is the assumption that children need to be given experiences not provided in most homes; another is the belief that structured experiences (such as learning to play the violin as a toddler, or being taught a second language) will inevitably have a beneficial effect on a child's development in general. This "myth of early experience," write Canning and Lyon (1991), has led us to forget that "the adult's role in preschool environments should be to provide appropriate play opportunities and be available to children" (p. 2).

On the other side of the debate are people who reason that preschool children can benefit tremendously from formal academic instruction. Even infants can be—and, according to Doman (1984), should be—taught basic reading skills. Accordingly, there has been a strong trend toward providing progressively more structured educational programs at the preschool level. This trend, says Rescorla (1991),

stems from psychology's emphasis on the importance of early experience, a perception of decline in achievement of North American students relative to other groups (for example, the Japanese), and parents' desire for their children to be the best.

There is no simple and clear resolution for this debate, which may be one reason why there are so many different forms of preschool education programs. Some are distinct; they are based on specific principles and procedures. Most, however, are highly eclectic. They include kindergartens, nurseries, preschools, playschools, intervention programs, compensatory education programs, and day-care centers (day care is discussed in Chapter 8). They are found in schools and homes, in church basements and community centers, in parks and shopping malls, in universities and technical schools, even in office buildings. Their offerings are a varied mixture dictated in part by the ages of their charges, the resources available, the wishes of par-

There is considerable debate concerning methods and goals in preschool education. Some argue that its main purpose should be academic preparation; others insist that it should focus on social development, and that teachers should therefore facilitate play.

Myrleen Ferguson Cate/PhotoEdit

ents, the restrictions and mandates of local laws and regulations, and the inclinations and capabilities of instructors and caregivers.

Preschools in the Developing World

As in many other poor cities throughout the world, when cars stop at busy intersections in Manila and Quezon City in the Philippines, says Tsuchiyama (1992), children rush out to sell things or to beg for money. "They are called 'street children,'" he writes. "They have dropped out of school. . . . They sleep on the roadside" (p. 56).

In the Philippines, almost 20% of children ages 6 to 11 are not enrolled in school; one-third of all children don't graduate from fourth grade. Similarly, in Africa and in most other developing countries, only about 60% of males and 51% of females attend primary schools; about one-third of these drop out before they finish fifth grade (Bellamy, 1999a). In contrast, about 98% of all children in industrialized countries attend primary schools, and an impressive 99% of these reach fifth grade.

Access to primary schools is clearly still a problem in many of the world's least-developed countries; access to preschools is even rarer. In most of these countries, only a tiny percentage—those from rich families—have access to nurseries and kindergartens. But in North America and much of Europe, children have free (even compulsory) access not only to elementary and high schools but also to a tremendous

assortment of preschools, including nursery schools, compensatory preschool programs, and kindergartens. (See *At a Glance*: "Preschool Enrollment" and Figure 7.11.)

Nursery Schools

The metaphors for the two most common forms of preschool education are of German origin. Thus we have kindergartens—literally gardens (*garten*) for children (*kinder*). These are intended as places where children can grow like celery and tomatoes and potatoes, and, perhaps, even weeds. But, says the metaphor, before our *kinder* are robust enough, strong enough, to be planted in the garden—where they might have to weather storms and voracious insects and birds and small boys chasing cats—they must be sheltered and nurtured in the *nursery* school.

For many years nursery schools were among the most prevalent forms of preschool education. They typically take in very young preschoolers and emphasize social and emotional development. Their principal activities consist of games, dancing, singing, listening to stories, and so on—many of the same functions performed by good day-care facilities. In fact, as Caldwell (1991) points out, so close are the functions of nurseries and day-care facilities that many of today's day-care centers are essentially the same as what were once called nursery schools (see Chapter 8 for a discussion of day care). Caldwell coins a new term for the function of these facilities: educare.

Preschool Enrollment

In 1995, 55% of all new mothers went back to work within one year of giving birth (U.S. Bureau of the Census, 1998). The number one reason for going back to work is financial need; career development and personal enjoyment are also important reasons (Volling & Belsky, 1993). Of the more than 12 million U.S. children ages 3 to 5 in day care in 1995, about 8 million were in nursery schools and kindergartens. Only 6% of the 5- and 6-year-olds were not enrolled in preprimary or primary schools.

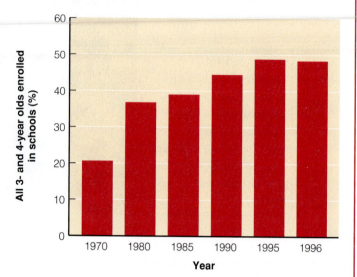

FIGURE 7.11 Increase in U.S. preprimary school enrollment, 3- and 4-year-olds, 1970 to 1996. Source: Adapted from U.S. Bureau of the Census, 1998, p. 165.

The long-term effects of nursery schools—and of high-quality day care—have proven to be very positive. Clarke-Stewart (1984; Clarke-Stewart, Gruber, & Fizgerald, 1994) reports that children who attend nursery schools are, on the average, more self-reliant, more outgoing, more spontaneous, and more confident than comparable children who do not attend nursery school.

Kindergartens

Not long ago, kindergartens were mainly an optional preschool program, typically limited to the more affluent families in the most affluent nations. Now, a majority of preschoolers in the world's industrialized countries attend kindergartens. For example, in Canada and the United States, about 98% of children in primary schools have attended kindergartens (National Center for Education Statistics, 1995).

Most kindergarten facilities are housed in regular schools, funded in the same manner as schools, and staffed by teachers whose certification requirements are the same as those who teach at more advanced levels. In many ways, kindergartens are part of regular school. Many no longer simply pre-

pare children for the first-grade tasks of learning to read and write and count; they actually engage in the business of teaching these things (if the children don't already know them). One of the big differences between kindergarten and regular schools, in most (but no longer all) jurisdictions, is that kindergartners can go home at lunchtime and stay there the rest of the afternoon, or they can stay home all morning and go to school only in the afternoon.

But perhaps we are hurrying our children too much, Elkind (1981a) warns. Maybe we should let them slow down and be children, let them play and dream and do magical things that don't require knowing how to read and write and count things in perfect sequence.

Not only are we hurrying our children, says Elkind (1987), but many parents are also miseducating them. These are "Gold Medal" parents whose burning ambition is to produce a star basketball or hockey player, a world-class gymnast, a violin prodigy. Or they are "College Degree" parents whose babies are destined for Harvard or MIT or the University of Alberta. For these parents, children have become symbols of parental ambitions and proof of parental success.

We must strike a balance, Elkind (1981a) urges, between the spoiled child, who remains a child too long, and the hurried child, who does not remain a child long enough and whose life might be plagued by "a fear of failure—of not achieving fast enough or high enough" (p. xii). The description of a kindergarten in China in *Across Cultures:* "Wai Wong's Kindergarten" provides some perspective in this matter.

Compensatory Preschool Programs

Compensatory preschool programs are designed to make up for initial deficits in children. The best-known and most massive compensatory education program ever undertaken in the United States is **Project Head Start**, which began in 1965 and was conceived as part of that country's "war on poverty." The program allocated large amounts of funds to the creation of 8-week summer programs for children from disadvantaged backgrounds. More than 700,000 preschoolers are now enrolled in the program (Kagan & Gall, 1998).

Project Head Start is available only to children below the poverty line—of whom there were more than 14 million below age 18 in the United States in 1996. This is an amazing 20% of all races; and a shocking 40% of Hispanic children aged 17 and younger (U.S. Bureau of the Census, 1998; see Figure 7.12). Project Head Start aims to provide health and nutritional services, as well as educational services, to disadvantaged preschoolers. Classes are typically limited to 20 or fewer children, and are often serviced by two teachers in addition to parent aides.

Because of the variety of approaches used in these projects, it has been difficult to assess their effectiveness. Many early studies indicated that chil-

dren enrolled in Head Start programs continued to be inferior to more advantaged children who had not been exposed to such programs, and critics were quick to conclude that huge amounts of money had been squandered in poorly planned, poorly executed, and basically ineffective programs. However, research conducted in the last decade or so has found more consistent improvements resulting from Head Start programs (McDill & Natriello, 1998; Reynolds & Temple, 1998). Some of these improvements are found in better performance in school; others are more long-term and more difficult to assess. For example, Barnett (1992, 1993) concludes that the best forms of preschool compensatory education may produce detectable long-term benefits in "life success measures"—such as, for example, reductions in teenage pregnancy, delinquency, unemployment, and reliance on welfare assistance. Kagan and Gall (1998) report that some government statements have claimed that for every dollar invested in Head Start, another six will be saved later in reduced social costs.

"Good" Compensatory Programs It is now generally accepted that the better compensatory programs can be highly effective. The important question, say

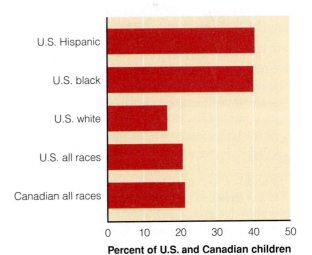

Percent of U.S. and Canadian children under age 18 living below poverty level in 1996

FIGURE 7.12 Percentage of U.S. and Canadian children aged 17 and under living below poverty level, 1996, by racial origin. Based on U.S. Bureau of the Census, (1998), p. 478, and *Canada Yearbook 1999*, p. 207.

compensatory preschool programs Preschool education programs that attempt to make up for early disadvantages in the lives of some children. The best known of these programs in the United States is Project Head Start.

Project Head Start A large-scale, federally funded preschool program in the United States, conceived as part of the war on poverty. It is designed to overcome some of the disadvantages associated with economic and social deprivation in early life and, in a sense, to give children a head start.

Wai Wong's Kindergarten

Wai Wong attends East-is-Red Kindergarten in Guanzhou, China. Today the children have been told there will be visitors. Lei has been given the honor of watching the door.

"They're coming," shouts Lei, and everyone stops work and applauds loudly, calling out several times in unison, *Ni hao anti*, the traditional greeting meaning "Hello uncles and aunts."

The visitors, a delegation of American and Canadian early childhood educators, enter amid smiles of welcome. But almost immediately, everyone in the class turns back to the work at hand. During the next hour, the teacher directs the students in a series of lessons, demonstrations, games, and songs not dramatically different from what might be seen in a North American kindergarten. Nevertheless, delegation members notice some differences. First, the room seems stark—lit with two naked lightbulbs, the walls painted white, the floor made of stone. The simplicity of the physical plant, the visitors later discover, is common in much of China—although many preschools are brighter, more cheerfully decorated, and better equipped (Kessen, 1975). In contrast, unlike the adults in the community, who all seem to be dressed in the same drab, colorless clothes, the children are dressed in brightly colored clothing, and the girls, like Wai Wong, have bright ribbons in their hair.

But what strikes the delegation most is the eagerness of the children, their willingness to learn, their attentiveness, their laughter, their apparent happiness. "Not once during the whole morning," writes Sparkes (1990) of a visit to a similar preschool, "was there a tearful eye, a noncompliant behavior, or an aggressive interaction" (p. 21). The delegation wonders and asks why things are thus. Sometimes people are puzzled at their questions. Physical punishment is extremely rare in modern China; child abuse is almost unheard of (Korbin, 1981). "See the tree," says one teacher, pointing to a picture on the wall of a tree in glorious bloom. Such pictures are found in most preschools in China. The rows of blossoms indicate how well the children live up to the school's demands for four expressions of "beauty": beauty of the mind, beauty of language, beauty of behavior, and beauty of the environment (Noren Bjorn, 1982). To quarrel, to disobey, to refuse to cooperate—these would not be "beauty."

Another teacher emphasizes the unity, the cooperativeness, the socialism upon which Chinese society today is based. The rules are clear: The individual is subordinate to the organization; the minority is subordinate to the majority; the lower level is subordinate to the higher; and all are subordinate to the Central Committee (Liljestrom, 1982). The rules are seen not as a form of oppression, but as a rational and sensible social system.

China, the delegation is repeatedly told, is not what it used to be. You would look in vain, now, for the children you would have seen at the turn of the twentieth century, "lice-ridden children . . . children with distended stomachs and spindly arms and legs . . . children who had been purposely deformed by beggars . . . children covered with horrible sores . . . children cast into the streets to beg and forage in the garbage bins for subsistence" (Korbin, 1981, p. 167).

Children are our most prized possession, the Chinese insist. They treat them accordingly.

British Library, London, UK/Bridgeman Art Library

A picture of a tree such as this might be found in a Chinese kindergarten. The blossoms are symbols of four kinds of "beauty"— of the mind, of language, of behavior, and of the environment.

To Think About: Quick sketches such as these *Across Cultures* inserts often mislead: They cannot deal with exceptions, nor can they provide the detail that is necessary for a more complete and accurate understanding. How would your quick sketch of a North American preschool compare with that of Wai Wong's school? What do the apparent differences and similarities tell us about cultures?

Zigler and Styfco (1996), is: What are the characteristics of good compensatory programs?

Answers to this question depend, of course, on what the goals of the programs are. These goals, in turn, often determine the types of programs that are developed. Thus, there are *child-centered* programs that focus on educational programs and on preparation for academic tasks. And there are more *family-focused* programs that provide family support and try to educate and assist parents in providing more stimulating environments for their children. Many programs attempt to combine these two emphases so as to provide at-risk infants and preschoolers with family involvement as well as with intellectual stimulation.

The Abecedarian Project: A Combined Focus The Carolina Abecedarian Project is a good example of a well thought out and highly researched longitudinal compensatory education program involving multiple interventions—that is, combining aspects of both family-focused and child-centered programs (Ramey & Campbell, 1994). It involved children beginning in infancy, who were enrolled in the program between 1972 and 1977 and who were then followed into adolescence and early adulthood (Campbell et al., 1998). The Abecedarian Project provided intensive early childhood education and family support for children from low-income families (primarily African American). A large variety of social, emotional, cognitive, and academic measures are available for these participants beginning in infancy and continuing to early adulthood. Much of this information was collected and evaluated by examiners who didn't know that these children were part of an intensive, compensatory education program. Recall from Chapter 1 that this defines a *blind* experimental procedure, designed to minimize the effects of experimenter expectations and biases.

Results of the various longitudinal examinations of participants in the Abecedarian project provide strong evidence of significant gains in measured intelligence and in academic performance. These gains are apparent beginning in the preschool period as early as 18 months (Ramey & Landesman, 1998; Spitz, 1997), and they persist even into adolescence (Ramey & Blair, 1996).

The Montessori Method: An Academic Focus The Montessori method, which dates back to the turn of the twentieth century, is an example of a highly structured approach sometimes used in compensatory education programs (Montessori, 1912). Its focus is mainly on the child rather than on the family. It was initially developed for use with mentally retarded children but has proven to be effective and popular as a general program. Unlike most preschool programs, it is designed for use in elementary and high schools as well (Wentworth, 1999). It has even been used with elderly people with cognitive impairments such as Alzheimer's (Dreher, 1997).

The most distinctive feature of the Montessori method is the use of specially developed materials and elaborate, detailed procedures for teaching sense discriminations (how to differentiate among related stimuli such as sounds or colors). Montessori believed that all learning stems from sense perception and can therefore be improved by training the senses. Perhaps the best known of her materials are large letters of the alphabet, covered with sandpaper, that are used to teach children to read. The prescribed teaching method requires not only that children look at the letters, but that they also trace letter shapes with their fingertips, saying the sound of the letter and getting a tactile sensation of it at the same time.

Evaluations of Montessori programs have generally been quite positive, in spite of the criticism that such programs, given their highly structured nature, might stifle a child's creativity. For example, a study of the long-term effects of preschool programs found that the highest achievers in grades six, seven, and eight were males who had been exposed to a preschool Montessori program (Miller & Bizzell, 1983).

Bronfenbrenner's Suggestions: A Family Focus Some researchers insist that the essential requirement for an effective intervention program is to take into account the family as a child-rearing unit and to provide conditions that will ameliorate a negative home environment. Accordingly, health, nutrition, housing, and employment must be raised to adequate levels if intervention programs are be effective. And parents need to be involved directly in the program, although how they are involved is also critical.

Bronfenbrenner (1977b) describes a sequential, five-stage strategy for family-focused intervention:

Stage 1, *Preparation for Parenthood*, begins before parenthood. Its goal is to give schoolchildren information about the care of children and the nutritional and health requirements of pregnant women.

Stage 2, *Before Children Come*, involves taking steps to ensure that the family into which a child will be born will provide adequate shelter, food, and economic security.

Stage 3, *The First Three Years of Life*, is concerned with establishing emotional bonds between parents and children through care-giving activities and other interactions.

Stage 4, *Ages 4 through 6*, involves intervention in the form of a preschool program. Bronfenbrenner suggests that this program be cognitively oriented and that it involve parents directly. Nor does intervention cease when children enter first grade.

Stage 5, *Ages 6 through 12*, is a continuation of intervention geared mainly at involving parents in school activities. However, for many parents who work outside the home, becoming involved in school activities may be very difficult.

LANGUAGE AND THE PRESCHOOLER

When psychologist Hayes and his wife tried to teach a chimpanzee to speak—that is, to actually say words the way humans do—they failed completely (Hayes & Hayes, 1951). Apparently the chimpanzee's vocal apparatus simply does not lend itself to speaking a language.

About four decades later, Savage-Rumbaugh and associates (1993) raised a child and an ape together, exposing both to the same language environment. When the child was 2 and the ape 8, both were asked to respond to 660 novel sentences. And both did about equally well, indicating that although the ape had not learned to speak English, it had learned to comprehend it. In fact, it appears that apes, chimpanzees, and bonobos (and perhaps other primates as well) share some language and communication abilities with us, claim Langs, Badalamenti, and Savage-Rumbaugh (1996)—at least when it comes to comprehension.

Comprehension, most linguists agree, precedes the ability to speak. One of the major differences between apes and humans, in an evolutionary sense, Rumbaugh and Savage-Rumbaugh (1996) speculate, may be that when humans raised themselves up on their hind legs to become bipedal, there followed adjustments in their vocal tract and in the soft palate. These adjustments made possible the production of speech sounds. Thus the capacity to comprehend speech might have existed some millions of years before the capacity to produce it; apes are still at that first stage.

Since the Hayes's attempt to teach a chimpanzee to speak, a succession of researchers have undertaken to teach chimpanzees American Sign Language (ASL). Its big advantage is that it does not require chimpanzees (or gorillas) to make sounds, but simply to make gestures. A number of these individuals report what seemed like remarkable success (for example, Fouts, 1987). However, critics insist that none of the chimpanzees in question have actually learned a language. Detailed examinations of videotapes of "sign-speaking" chimpanzees indicated that what they had learned was simply to imitate—to associate a symbol or gesture with food, or to use some movement or gesture to make some demand associated with reinforcement (Terrace, 1985). But the debate is by no means over, and researchers continue to report the development of "communicative" or "conversational" competence among various nonhuman primates (for example, Greenfield & Savage-Rumbaugh, 1993; Miles, 1997).

Language Development in Infants

The human brain, notes Gibson (1996), equips infants remarkably well to learn language. As we saw in the Chapter 5 discussion of the first stages of language development (see Table 7.1), even before speech (in the *prespeech* stage), there are remarkable language-related adaptations. Thus, early in the first year of life, children have begun to learn turn-taking, the use of gestures, how to discriminate sounds, and even how to produce them—all essential aspects of communicating with spoken language. These adaptations culminate in the first word by about age 1, followed quickly by the *holophrase*,

TABLE 7.1
Stages in Children's Development of Grammar

STAGE OF DEVELOPMENT	NATURE OF DEVELOPMENT	SAMPLE UTTERANCES
1. Prespeech (before age 1)	Crying, cooing, babbling. Learning turn-taking, the use of gestures, babbling, and sound discrimination.	"Waaah," "dadadada."
2. Sentencelike word (holophrase) (by 12 months)	The word is combined with nonverbal cues (gestures and inflections). Complex meanings are compressed into short utterances (*telegraphic*)	"Mommy." (meaning: "Would you please come here, mother.")
3. Two-word sentences (duos) (by 18 months)	Modifiers are joined to topic words to form declarative, question, negative, and imperative structures.	"Pretty baby." (declarative) "Where Daddy?" (question) "No play." (negative) "More milk!" (imperative)
4. Multiple-word sentences (by 2 to 2½ years)	Both a subject and predicate are included in the sentence types. Morphemes and grammatical inflections are used to change meanings (-*ing* or -*ed* or -*s*, for example).	"She's a pretty baby." (declarative) "Where Daddy is?" (question) "I no can play." (negative) "I want more milk!" (imperative) "I running." "I runned."
5. More complex grammatical changes and word categories (between 2½ and 4 years)	Elements are added, embedded, and permuted within sentences. Word classes (nouns, verbs, and prepositions) are subdivided. Clauses are put together.	"Read it, my book." (conjunction) "Where is Daddy?" (embedding) "I can't play." (permutation) "I would like some milk." (use of *some* with mass noun) "Take me to the store." (use of preposition of place)
6. Adultlike structures (after 4 years)	Complex structural distinctions made, as with "ask-tell" and "promise."	"Ask what time it is." "He promised to help her."

Source: Based on Barbara S. Wood (1981). *Children and communication: Verbal and nonverbal language development*, 2nd ed. Englewood Cliffs, N.J.: Prentice-Hall, Inc., p. 142. © 1981. Reprinted by permission of Prentice-Hall, Inc., Englewood Cliffs, New Jersey.

the sentencelike word. And by the age of 18 months, the infant readily uses two-word sentences.

Children with hearing difficulties who learn ASL rather than a spoken language also develop much the same sorts of language communicative skills as do children who learn spoken language, although often more slowly. That is, they learn to represent meanings, to produce them, and to represent concepts and actions that are displaced in time and space. These three characteristics, *meaningfulness*, *productivity*, and *displacement*, as we saw in Chapter 5, are the defining characteristics of language.

Increasing language sophistication in the second year of life makes it possible for the infant to combine words with different modifiers in order to ask questions, make declarations, express denial, or issue commands. And through the last 6 months of the infant's second year, there is an astonishing vocabulary spurt. As Smith (1995) notes, the 2-year-old is so good at learning words that if you show her a new object like, say, a tractor, and you tell her, "Hey, this is a tractor," from that day on, she will likely be able to recognize and correctly name every tractor she encounters for the rest of her life! This remarkable ability to learn the meaning of a word after just a few incidental exposures is termed **fast mapping**. Some psychologists believe that fast mapping is possible

fast mapping Describes learning that occurs extraordinarily rapidly—typically after only one or two exposures. Often used to describe the process by which young children learn the meanings of words.

because of some dedicated language mechanism in the brain (Chomsky's *Language Acquisition Device*, or LAD, for example). Others, such as Markson and Bloom (1997), argue that fast mapping occurs not only among children learning a language but also among adults learning other matters, and that this phenomenon is therefore not evidence of a dedicated language mechanism in the brain.

This startlingly rapid acquisition of words—or *fast mapping*—that occurs toward the end of infancy is greatly helped by a number of specific language-learning strategies. These include the use of questions ("what dis?"), the testing of hypotheses or guesses ("book?"), and other utterances used mainly to uncover the names of things (Domingo and Goldstein-Alpern, (1999).

Multiple-Word Sentences

By the end of infancy, children move from 2-word combinations to multiple-word sentences. This typically occurs around the age of $2^1/_2$. "Allgone dog" becomes "dog is gone" and eventually "the dog is gone" or "my dog is gone." Two-word combinations, as Kagan and Gall (1998) point out, are necessarily more telegraphic, and also much less precise than multiple-word sentences.

Note that the transition to multiple-word sentences does not mean that all expressions before this stage are limited to two or fewer words. In fact, many children use 3- and 4-word utterances very early in their development of language. A widely used measure of language development among preschoolers looks at their **mean length of utterance (MLU)**—arrived at by counting and averaging the number of morphemes, including **inflections**, a child uses. Recall that morphemes are the simplest meaningful sounds of a language; inflections are morphemes such as -*s*, -*ed*, -*ing*, and other endings that change the meanings of words. Thus, when cal-

culating MLU, the utterance "dog is bad" would be counted as 3 morphemes; the utterance "dogs isn't bad" would be counted as 5 (dog-s-is-not-bad).

The earliest multiple-word combinations seldom use complete subjects and predicates and are less complete grammatically. In other words, even after children have begun to use relatively lengthy multiple-word sentences, there are fewer MLUs, primarily because of a more limited use of inflections. Very soon, however, children begin to make increasing use of inflections to express meaning (Brown, 1973). The use of grammatical inflections is what allows the child to transform the verbs *go* to *going*, *jump* to *jumped*, *eat* to *eated*, and *do* to *dood*. These types of errors are referred to as **overregularization**. They result when the budding linguist has begun to learn a rule but, not yet having learned all its exceptions, applies it incorrectly.

Speech at this stage is also often highly inventive. When our daughter Claire was about 3, she had learned that "pitch black" was very, very, very black—and she insisted for a long time that other things can be "pitch clean," "pitch empty," or "pitch big." And Rémi, our youngest linguist, once insisted, "Daddy unpickmeup," as he squirmed to be put down. "You already feeded me."

More Complex Changes

Between the ages of 2 and 3 or 4, children begin to acquire some of the more complex aspects of syntax (grammar). Among other things, they begin to use auxiliaries (the verb *to be* for example) and tenses, and to learn that word order can alter meanings (Kagan & Gall, 1998). As a result, they develop the ability to make meaningful changes in sentences. These typically take one of three forms: *conjunction*, *embedding*, and *permutation* (Wood, 1981). Simple conjunction is illustrated by the addition or combination of the two sentences "Where?" and "We go" to form a third sentence, "Where we go?" Embedding is inserting. For example, the word *no* may be embed-

---

mean length of utterance (MLU) Average number of morphemes per utterance.

inflections Morphemes that alter the meanings of words. Thus *dog* consists of a single morpheme, whereas *dogs* consists of two morphemes: DOG and the inflection S.

overregularization The misuse of grammatical rules, often because they are applied to irregular forms. (Saying "I eated," or "I broked it," for example.)

ded in the sentence "I eat" to form a sentence with quite a different meaning: "I no eat." Permutation is altering the order of words in sentences to change their meaning. Initially, children make use of intonation rather than permutation. For example, the sentence "I can go" may be a simple declaration when the *I* or the *can* is emphasized but becomes a question when *go* is uttered with rising intonation. A simple permutation from "I can go" to "Can I go?" achieves the same meaning with much less ambiguity.

As children begin to show an understanding of various adult-accepted rules for transforming sentences, they also behave as though they had an implicit understanding of the grammatical function of various words and phrases. They use nouns as nouns and not as verbs, adjectives are no longer treated as verbs, and nouns are further categorized as plural or singular. Evidence of children's understanding of this type of categorization is evident in their appropriate use of both verbs and such determiners as *that, the, those,* and *these.* For example, the child will now say, "That box is empty"; an earlier error might have taken the form of "This boxes is empty." (See *At a Glance:* "Speech at Age 4 Years, 6 Months" for an example of the use of invented sounds in one preschooler's language.)

Speech at Age 4 Years, 6 Months

Language development in the preschool period is almost explosive, so rapidly do children's vocabularies grow and the sophistication of their grammar improve. Rémi's story at 4½— with accompanying art—displays imagination and verbal skills far in advance of a 2-year-old's.

> **The Story of the Gas Station**
> (as told by Rémi—
> 4 years, 6 months—with his Legos)
>
> I'm going to fill up with regular. *Vrooooom.*
>
> Thanks. *Vrr-rrr-rrr.*
>
> I'm coming to fill it with regular. *Whtttt-taah.*
>
> *SMASH!!*
>
> Broken car now. They crashed into each other.
>
> I want to oil my car.
>
> Oh. Oh. I have a flat tire. I need some air.
>
> *Phhh. Phhh. Phhh.*
>
> *Tchuuu.*
>
> I'm stuck. He broke the house down. He needs a new tire.
>
> *Neeowrr. Neeowrr.*
>
> *WOWEE!* He got a flat tire.
>
> I need unleaded gas.
>
> *Tchuu. Schewww.*
>
> The end

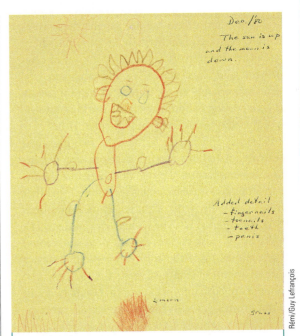

Rémi's drawing at the age of 4½ of a man—including such remarkable details as fingernails, knees and elbows, toes, a navel, and even a penis.

Adultlike Structures

The further refinement and elaboration of speech requires mastery of countless subtle and intricate grammatical rules that we all use unconsciously. Some of these rules govern the arrangement of words in meaningful expressions; they specify what is (and is not) grammatically acceptable and meaningful. They tell us that "the fat mosquito" is a correctly structured phrase, but "Fat the mosquito" is not (although "fat, the mosquito" might be). Other rules permit us to transform phrases or to combine them to create a variety of meaningful statements. Thus there are rules that allow us to transform a passive sentence into an active one ("The dog was bitten by the man" to "The man bit the dog") or a negative to a positive ("I did not go" to "I went"). Much of this learning occurs in the first elementary grades.

EXPLANATIONS OF LANGUAGE DEVELOPMENT

Each of us uses language as if we had a relatively complete understanding of a tremendous range of grammatical rules. Yet, unless we are taught these rules formally, we can't explain them. In fact, linguists have not yet been able to work out a complete set of consistent and valid rules even for a single language.

The remarkable thing is that in an amazingly short time, young children acquire a working knowledge of this very complex system of rules. How?

As we saw in Chapter 5, there are two principal classes of explanations for the development of language. One emphasizes the role of experience (learning) and, because it views language as something that emerges gradually with experience, is sometimes labeled emergentism. The other emphasizes the importance of biology (hereditary predispositions) and sometimes takes the form of hopeful monster theories. Current evidence suggests that biology and experience are both important but that each, by itself, does not present an entirely adequate explanation.

Hopeful Monster Theories: The Role of Biology

As we saw earlier, *fast mapping*, the astonishing ease and rapidity with which infants and preschoolers learn words, has been taken by some theorists as evidence that the human brain is specially prewired for language. Some, like Chomsky, believe that our brains have evolved in such a way as to make language development not only possible but almost inevitable. Rymer (1993) quotes Chomsky in an interview: "If you were to put prelinguistic children on an island, the chances are good that their language facility would soon produce a language. Maybe not in the first generation. And that when they did so, it would resemble the languages we know. You can't do the experiment because you can't subject a child to that experience" (p. 38). (However, Genie's experience is that experiment—a natural experiment—as we see later in this section.)

Chomsky's theory of language development—and that of others such as Lenneberg (1969) and Nelson (1989)—is a *hopeful monster theory*. Its monster is the biological metaphor of a language acquisition device (LAD). Furthermore, Chomsky's theory of language development is critical-period based. It argues that the critical period for learning language is before age 5 and that almost invariably, language learning is pretty well complete by puberty.

The Evidence for Biology Several observations support the hypothesis of a strong biological influence on language learning. For example, there is the fact that the earliest speech sounds of infants from very different backgrounds—even those of children whose parents are deaf—are highly similar. There is *fast mapping*, the enormous rapidity with which languages are learned in early childhood. And there is also the observation that many of the mistakes children make when they learn a language are not imitative—as one would expect if they were learning language primarily through imitation. Instead, as we saw, many of these are errors of *overregularization*; they result from the overapplication of rules that are themselves correct.

Genie's Story Another line of evidence for the role of biology is Genie's story, described briefly in Chapter 3. Recall that Genie was abandoned from the age of 20 months until almost 14 years. When she surfaced, she made few sounds other than a peculiar laugh. For example, when angry, she wouldn't yell or scream; instead, she would scratch or gouge her face, urinate, smear mucus on herself, or blow her nose loudly into her clothes—or all of these. Rymer speculates that because her father had prevented her from making noise, she had learned to turn her emotions inward. When she really needed to make a noise, she would use other things to do so like dragging a chair, banging objects, or scratching her nails on a balloon.

At first, Genie's vocabulary seemed to be increasing relatively rapidly. She would often drag people around pointing at things and asking that they be named, much as young children sometimes do. But, at least for the first year, her expressions remained limited to short, largely incoherent one-word utterances. Even a year and a half after being "found," Genie would only rarely put two words together, and almost never three. And, unlike normal children, who, after they reach the 2-word-sentence stage, typically experience an explosion in MLU (mean length of utterance), Genie continued to plod along. Even four years later, the kinds of sentences she would build when pushed to do so included confused combinations such as "Where is may I have a penny?" or "I where is graham cracker on top shelf?" She continued to have no understanding of personal pronouns, totally confusing *I*, *me*, and *you*, never quite able to figure out who she was and who was somebody else. Nor did she ever learn to respond to "hello" with "hello," or even to understand the meaning of "thank you."

Scans of activity in Genie's brain subsequently showed that her left hemisphere remained virtually unresponsive to language (recall that it's normally centrally involved in language functions). This is additional evidence that early experience may be essential for organizing the brain in the first place.

At the time of Rymer's writing, Genie had apparently regressed to a largely nonverbal existence and lived in a home for retarded adults. In the last photos Rymer saw of her, Genie was 29, a large, bumbling person with an expression of "cowlike incomprehension" on her face, an inmate of an asylum, totally withdrawn from the world.

In support of Chomsky's theory, Curtiss (1977) writes, "Language grows like an organ. When it comes to physical growth, no one asks why—why do arms grow? Learning a language is like learning to walk, a biological imperative timed to a certain point in development. It's not an emotional process" (p. 205).

Still, hopeful monsters such as LAD are metaphors rather than explanations. As a metaphor, LAD says that infants behave as if they already have at their command a range of cognitive skills, of language-related predispositions. And from this observation, we might infer that there must be some innate neurological prewiring at birth. But as Rice (1989) observes, this is not a completely satisfactory explanation of how these things work. Metaphors are not machines; they are simply comparisons.

Emergentism: The Role of Experience

We know that there is an overwhelming amount of learning involved in making the transition from the first meaningful sound to the fluent conversations of the 6-year-old. Yet most children accomplish this learning apparently effortlessly and in much the same sequence across different cultures. Strangely, however, adults who were initially without language (because of isolation, for example) do not fare as well, as Genie's story illustrates. Similarly, adults who try to acquire a second language usually experience more difficulty doing so than do young children; and even if they are successful, their pronunciation will often be characterized by a variety of errors that would not be found among those who learned the language at a younger age. In support of biological theories, there does appear to be a sensitive period early in life when learning one or more languages is easiest.

The Role of Parents That children acquire the speech patterns, idioms, accents, and other language characteristics of the people around them makes it clear that learning is centrally involved in language acquisition. Parents and other caregivers play an important role as language models: They provide children with verbal and nonverbal models of correct language and of the subtle rules governing conversations and the communication of messages. In addition, parents also serve as important dispensers of reinforcement for the child's verbalizations.

The role of parents is apparent as well in studies that have looked at intervention programs with children who have language development problems. In a study of a parent-implemented intervention program with children with Down syndrome, for example, Iacono, Chan, & Waring (1998) found that parents could be effective in improving children's language skills.

In Chapter 5 we spoke of the bidirectionality of parent-child influence, noting that what a caregiver does influences the infant—and no less true, what the infant does influences the caregiver. We see evidence of bidirectionality of influence in the development of language as well. Throughout the world, infants' level of language sophistication appears to have marked effects on the behavior of parents. For example, Naka (1999) analyzed conversations between mothers and 2-year-olds over a period of one year, and reports that there were remarkable changes in the speech of both infant and mother during this period. Mothers' conversations changed as they adapted to the speech and understanding of their infants. There is a *fine tuning* of the caretaker's speech, says Bruner (1978), so that the mother becomes a teacher—not because she consciously intends to teach, but because she unconsciously "fine-tunes" her responses and behaviors to the immediate demands of her child.

Parentese In later stages of language development, the role of parents as sensitive, fine-tuned teacher becomes even more apparent. Boyd (1976) notes that the language mothers use when talking to their children—sometimes called **parentese** (or *child-directed language*, or *motherese* in a less politically sensitive age)—is quite different from what they would normally use when speaking with adults. Parentese is a good example of *pragmatics* in language; the mother adjusts her speech to the requirements of the situation. Thus, mothers tend to use simpler, shorter, and more repetitive utterances. In other words, they reduce (by simplifying and repeating). On other occasions, mothers expand the child's expressions. A child might say, "Daddy gone," to which the mother might reply, "Yes, Daddy is gone." Moerk (1991) points out that most expansions are corrections, and that corrections of this kind are especially important in early language learning.

There are other, perhaps more subtle, ways in which the speech of a mother (or other caregivers, and even siblings) is influenced by the presence of infants. Moskowitz (1978) describes the typical speech of caregivers as simpler, higher pitched, char-acterized by exaggerated intonation, made up of shorter sentences, and consisting of a higher than normal percentage of questions. In addition, the speech of caregivers vis-a-vis their infants is almost always centered on the present and only seldom on the past or future, almost as though they knew, as did Piaget, that the young infant's world is a world of the here and now. Not surprisingly, most of the child's first words deal with things that are immediate, directly perceivable, and important to the child (Rice, 1989).

Studies of parentese in different languages have typically found that the most important features of mother-to-infant speech appear to be universal. For example, Grieser and Kuhl (1988) found this to be true even in Mandarin Chinese, which is very different from English in that it is tonal (inflection and intonation are far more meaningful). Mothers' speech in Mandarin Chinese also tends to be grammatically and semantically simpler and pitched at a higher frequency.

The importance of child-directed speech may also be apparent in differences that are sometimes found in the language development of children from different socioeconomic backgrounds. For example, Hoff-Ginsberg (1998) found that children from higher socioeconomic levels—as well as those who were first born—were more advanced in grammar and conversational skills than comparable children who were later born or from lower socioeconomic levels. An analysis of mothers' child-directed speech found measurable differences according to socioeconomic level. The authors also found that first-born children are, on average, exposed to more child-directed speech than later-born children. Related to this is evidence that one of the differences between the fastest and the slowest language learners may be the extent and quality of the parentese to which they are exposed. Hampson and Nelson (1993) videotaped a sample of 45 toddlers and analyzed their speech and that of their mothers. They found that the mothers of the most linguistically advanced children used a higher percentage of object names in their speech, and fewer commands.

In summary, it seems clear that the shorter sentences, uncomplicated grammars, and absence of pronouns and complex verb tenses of parentese contribute positively to language development. It's as though the level of parents' language usage

---

parentese (Also called *child-directed speech* or *motherese*) Describes the characteristics of parental speech when interacting with language-learning infants and preschoolers. Characterized by simpler, shorter, more repetitive utterances, often with exaggerated intonations, and by a preponderance of nouns.

remains relatively constant at about 6 months in advance of their children's, says Moskowitz (1978). This presents another example of the remarkable *synchrony* that often marks interactions between parents and their infants and children. Research has scarcely begun to explore the nature and dimensions of this synchrony. (See *Concept Summary.*)

LANGUAGE PROBLEMS, THINKING, AND COMMUNICATING

Language, this absolutely awesome human invention without which you and I would not, at this moment, be communicating, is clearly involved in the very fact of being human, of thinking, of consciousness. Those things for which we have no words, says Bruner, are "doomed to be a gem serene, locked in the silence of private experience" (1957, p. 125).

Language Problems

If we have imperfect languages or difficulty in understanding or speaking words and sentences, will our thinking be affected? Will our school experiences suffer?

Nonstandard Language Forms The answer is, in many cases, yes. For example, research indicates that students whose language is not the standard language often have problems in school (Garcia, 1993). The standard language is that which most speakers of a language in a given culture or area understand, read, and speak. Within multicultural societies, there are often many who speak nonstandard languages, which are variations (different dialects) of the dominant language. For example, the most common nonstandard dialect in the United States is Black English, which is spoken by an estimated 60% to 70% of African Americans (Garcia, 1993). Other common

---

CONCEPT SUMMARY

Influences in Language Learning

Source of Influence	Theorists and Some Supporting Evidence
Biology: Hopeful monster theories	• Chomsky (LAD) and Lenneberg • Earliest sounds made by all infants (even those who are deaf) are highly similar • Fast mapping—the ease and rapidity with which children learn word meanings and complex grammars • The difficulties people experience when trying to learn a language later in life • The observation that many errors children make are not learned through imitation but appear to result instead because the grammars they have invented don't yet admit exceptions • The case of Genie; little language exposure for first 14 years of her life; relatively little language recovery later
Experience: Emergentism	• Bruner and Piaget • Children not exposed to language don't naturally invent it (Genie's case) • The enormous difficulties deaf children experience in learning language • The specifics of language reflect the child's language environment • Parentese (child-directed language) appears important for the child's language learning

dialects include the English sometimes spoken by Hispanic Americans or by French Canadians.

Bernstein (1958, 1961) argues that the reason for often poorer school performance of children who speak nonstandard forms of English is that forms are usually overly simple, grammatically incorrect, and limited in vocabulary; and the children are apt to use gestures rather than words to make a point (accordingly, his label for nonstandard language forms is **restricted language code**). Standard forms of the language tend to be more elaborated, grammatically correct, complex, and precise (hence Bernstein's phrase: **elaborated language code**).

Bernstein suggests the reason that children whose homes are characterized by nonstandard language forms are often at a disadvantage in school is that for the first time in their lives, they are required to use increasingly precise and grammatically correct language. As a result, they almost invariably begin by performing less well than those who have had more standard early language experiences. Before they can catch up, they find themselves so far behind that they may feel it is hardly worth trying. Others point out that it may not be the impoverishment of nonstandard languages that presents a disadvantage so much as the simple fact that this language is *different*. Because instruction in school occurs in the standard language, and because achievement is measured in that language, these children are clearly at a disadvantage—no matter how sophisticated their nonstandard language skills may be (Harrison, 1985). In addition, notes Garcia (1993), children whose dialect is noticeably different tend to be judged inferior by teachers and other students. Their poorer performance may then be partly a result of a negative self-fulfilling prophecy.

Speech and Language Problems in Early Childhood

We assume that by the time children reach school age, their language skills will be sufficient for them to understand and follow instructions, express interests and wants, tell stories, ask questions, carry on conversations—in short, communicate. Unfortunately, that is not always the case.

There are a number of different language and speech problems; they can vary tremendously in seriousness. At one extreme are children who are essentially nonverbal because of severe mental retardation, neurological damage or disease, deafness, or mental disorders such as autism. There are other children whose speech is largely incomprehensible, sometimes because conceptual development is so poor that thought sequences seem illogical and speech becomes largely nonsensical, and sometimes because of speech production problems like those reflected in poor articulation, voice control problems, and stuttering. And there are children whose language development is less advanced than normal, perhaps because of mild mental retardation or because of a learning disability reflected in specific language impairments. The predominant view is that these children don't learn different language forms or acquire language differently; their skills simply develop more slowly. Often, for example, they continue to use a preponderance of nouns in their speech, long after other children have begun to use more verbs and other parts of speech (Conti-Ramsden & Jones, 1997).

Speech problems and delayed language development are most common among children who have some other handicap—that is, children with learning handicaps or motor, neurological, or mental disorders. Nevertheless, some children with speech problems are of normal or above-normal intelligence and have no deficits other than their problems with language. However, because our schools use predominantly verbal teaching and testing methods, many of these children are viewed as having intellectual handicaps, and their language problems may be interpreted as the result of inferior ability rather than as the cause of poor achievement.

Programs designed by speech pathologists, often involving parents and teachers, are sometimes quite successful in improving children's language skills (for example, Tallal et al., 1998). Fortunately, serious language problems are relatively uncommon among the majority of children.

Bilingualism and Multiculturalism

In 1900, almost 90% of the U.S. population was white; most of the remainder was black. And there

---

restricted language code A term used by Bernstein to describe the language typical of the lower-class child. Restricted language codes are characterized by short and simple sentences, general and relatively imprecise terms, idiom and colloquialism, and incorrect grammar.

elaborated language code A phrase used by Bernstein to describe the language of middle- and upper-class children. Elaborated language codes are grammatically correct, complex, and precise.

FIGURE 7.13 Rate of annual population growth per 1,000 population for five U.S. groups (1997). Source: Based on U.S. Bureau of the Census (1998), p. 20.

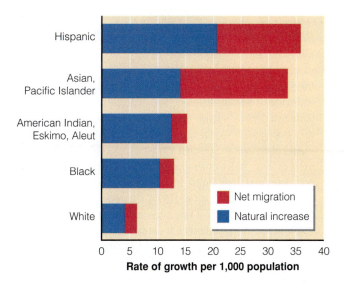

Rate of growth per 1,000 population

were so few Hispanics that they weren't even included as a category in official census tables (U.S. Bureau of the Census, 1998).

By 1997, there were more than 33 million blacks in the United States, and almost 30 million people of Hispanic origin; about 72% were non-Hispanic whites. And, as shown in Figure 7.13, the fastest growing group in the United States is Hispanic; the second fastest growing is Asian. Population growth of the white group is considerably slower.

Eighty-six percent of United States residents over the age of 5 speak only English. Of the 14% who speak another language, over half (54%) speak Spanish. In Canada, about 60% of residents claim English as their mother tongue; nearly 25% claim French as their maternal language (see Figure 7.14).

The impact of these demographic realities and changes is considerable. In Canada, two official languages are recognized, and the expression **distinct societies** is sometimes used to describe the country's multicultural nature. **Multiculturalism** in the United States is sometimes described using labels such as **melting pot societies**.

One of the clear implications of these changing conditions is an increasing need for **multicultural education**—that is, education that reflects an

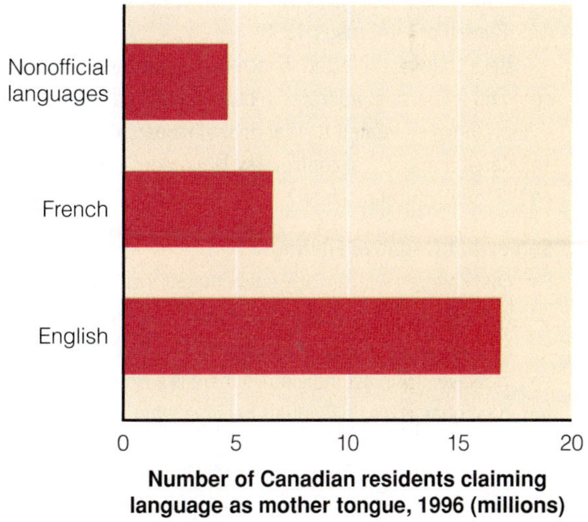

Number of Canadian residents claiming language as mother tongue, 1996 (millions)

FIGURE 7.14 Mother tongue of Canadian residents, 1996. The most common nonofficial language is Chinese (715,640 residents), followed by Italian, German, Polish, and Spanish, in that order. Source: Based on *Canada Yearbook, 1999*, p. 99.

multiculturalism Having to do with many cultures.

melting pot societies Geographical or political entities composed of a variety of cultures that are gradually assimilated to the dominant culture. The result is that individual cultures are no longer identifiable, and the dominant culture becomes a *macroculture*.

multicultural education Educational procedures and curricula that are responsive to the different cultures and languages of students, with the goal of assuring that all children experience high-quality education.

distinct society A metaphor used to describe the Canadian cultural scene where, theoretically, two distinct cultures coexist with neither being assimilated to the other as would be the case in a melting pot society.

ACROSS CULTURES

Bilingual Education

The preschooler who is exposed to two, or more, language environments typically experiences no difficulty in learning those two or more tongues. Nor is there confusion or interference among them—as Stefanik (1999) found following case studies of his own two children. While he spoke only English to his children, their mother spoke to them only in Slovak. Both developed fluent Slovak-English bilingualism.

Today, note Kagan and Gall (1998), classroom instruction takes place in 115 different languages in the schools of New York City. And in Massachusetts, it's possible to take a driver's test in any of 24 different languages. In California, the "minority" is now the majority: By 1990, 52% of students belonged to "minority" categories (Garcia, 1993), and projections are that by 2020, more than 70% of beginning first-grade students in California will belong to nonwhite groups (U.S. Bureau of the Census, 1998).

These changes, reflected in increasing numbers of bilingual and immersion programs in both public and private schools, have generated a great deal of research, and much emotional and political controversy. What does the research on bilingual education show?

Somewhat Negative Findings

For most children whose early environment includes two languages, learning a second language does not appear to be much more complicated than learning to ride a bicycle. In the end, however, for most individuals there is a dominant or preferred language. Few individuals become what Diaz (1983)

calls *balanced bilinguals*—people who are equally fluent and comfortable in both languages.

One of the possibilities when learning a second language is that a child's skills in the less valued language will deteriorate over time. This happens not because learning the second language interferes with learning or remembering the first, but because of one or all of the following reasons:

- The majority language tends to be more heavily reinforced by society and in the media, whereas the minority language often receives little support or reinforcement outside the home. Minority languages are often used in less valued roles and situations.
- Many parents actively discourage the use of a minority language in the home, believing that doing so will help their children fare better in the dominant language.
- The minority language employed in the home and on the street is sometimes a grammatically poor and impoverished model of the language.
- When a minority language is not part of the school curriculum, children are unlikely to learn to read and write it. Thus, although they might develop relatively advanced oral proficiency in the language, they are not likely to develop competency in reading and writing it.

(continued on next page)

---

understanding and appreciation of different cultures and languages, and that accommodates the needs of children from different backgrounds. But these issues are not without controversy. In particular, **bilingual education** has met strong, organized opposition, often from powerful, well-funded groups, such as U.S. English, which advocate that English should be designated the official U.S. language—as it was in California in 1986, and now has been in many other states (Kagan & Gall, 1998).

But these are political—and often emotionally charged—issues; our concerns are with more psychological questions. (See *Across Cultures:* "Bilingual Education.")

Language and Thought

The significance of language acquisition for children is in many ways obvious. Not only does language allow children to direct the behavior of others (as when they ask for something), but it also provides a means for acquiring and understanding information that would otherwise be inaccessible (as when

bilingual education Use of more than one language in a classroom. In North America, typically means instructing in English part of the time and using a language other than English the rest of the time.

ACROSS CULTURES

Bilingual Education (continued)

More Positive Findings

The research indicates clearly that bilingual programs designed to teach a second language can be very successful in developing high levels of linguistic skills in children whose first language is the majority language. Following a review of the relevant research, Cummins (1999) and Winsler et al. (1999) summarize several important conclusions:

- Well-implemented bilingual programs have been successful throughout the world, and do not impair students' performance in the majority language even when they spend vast amounts of time being instructed in a second language.
- Spending more time in English instruction in bilingual programs does not, in and of itself, lead to better student achievement in English.
- There is a tendency for students in bilingual programs to do better than unilingual students on a range of cognitive and academic tasks.

Bilingualism in Today's Schools

North American societies have been multilingual and multicultural from the very beginning—although education has more often been unilingual. This has often posed problems for students and teachers—problems that were traditionally viewed as those with students rather than with the educational system. In most cases schools accepted no responsibility for any trouble a minority-language child might experience. Teachers simply assumed that the problems would rectify themselves with exposure to traditional schooling. If they didn't . . . well, too bad, students would simply have to fail.

The current emphasis in education is for schools to accept responsibility for problems related to minority languages. A common educational response is to establish a bilingual or **English as a second language (ESL)** program. The main purpose of these programs has been to prepare students to fit into the traditional, English-only school curriculum (Brisk, 1991). There are different opinions about the best way of doing this. Some argue that it is better to teach and strengthen the native language first to develop a high level of proficiency in it before teaching English. Others recommend immersing students in an English environment from the very beginning with as little use as possible of the native language. These recommendations have given rise to a variety of bilingual programs in schools (Lam, 1992)—and to some controversy as well. Some people are concerned about spending public funds for these programs; others fear the possible erosion of English programs. Some advocate that there should be no bilingual programs at all.

Others, like Cummins (1999), argue that as our societies become increasingly multilingual and multicultural, schools must become more responsive to the needs of students. What schools should be focused on, say Artiles et al. (1998), is becoming truly inclusive—that is, truly multicultural. Schools should not simply admit students from different backgrounds and then try to make them all the same.

---

they ask questions, listen to stories, or watch television). In addition, it seems clear that language is closely involved in thinking and imagining, although the exact relationship between thinking and language remains unclear.

One position, the **Whorfian hypothesis**, holds that all thinking is verbal. The extreme form of this hypothesis maintains that language is essential for thinking and will therefore not occur in the absence of language. A modified version of the Whorfian hypothesis maintains that while language is not absolutely essential for thought, it influences it greatly.

The extreme form of the Whorfian hypothesis (language is essential for thought) is no longer widely accepted. To accept it would be to deny that there is thought among those who are prelinguistically deaf and who have not acquired another form

---

Whorfian hypothesis In its extreme form, the belief that language is essential for thinking, that thinking does not occur in its absence. In its more moderate form, the belief that language *influences* thinking.

English as a second language (ESL) Common phrase to describe educational programs designed to develop English proficiency among those whose first language is not English.

of language—as well as among preverbal infants. It would also mean denying the existence of thought among cows, which some theorists and street philosophers are not willing to do.

Agreeing with psychologists such as Piaget and Vygotsky, most linguists now accept that thought often precedes language. Piaget (1923), for example, points out that the development of certain logical concepts often precedes the learning of words and phrases corresponding to those concepts. Words such as *bigger*, *smaller*, *farther*, and so on do not appear to be understood until the concepts they represent are themselves understood. Both Vygotsky and Piaget argue that language and thought first develop independently. Thus, there is considerable evidence of what we consider to be thought among preverbal children and nonhuman animals. But after the age of 2, language and thought become more closely related. After that age, thought becomes increasingly verbal, and the use of language allows children to control behavior.

In brief, both research and good sense inform us that our sophisticated thought processes are inextricably bound with language—as are our belief systems, our values, our world views (Hunt & Agnoli, 1991). So convinced are we of this that attempts to bring about difficult social changes often begin with attempts to change language. Antiracist and antisexist movements are a case in point. In the first edition of this text, it was acceptable to use masculine pronouns as though all children, all psychologists, and indeed, all significant people were male. Speaking of one of Blaise Pascal's Pensées, for example, I wrote: "One of the paradoxes of human existence is that despite man's great intelligence it is impossible for him to know where he came from or where he is going" (Lefrançois, 1973, p. 351). That this type of chauvinistic sexism is no longer acceptable in our language may eventually be reflected in its eradication from our thoughts and from those of our children.

Communication

Language is more than a collection of sounds that refer to objects and actions that convey our meanings. And it is more than a way of thinking and expressing our thoughts. Language is the means by which we draw information from past generations, record our own small contributions, and pass them on to generations that will come later. Language creates tribes and cultures, it binds people, it allows the sharing of consciousness.

But infants, newly learning language, aren't concerned with its contributions to the tribe or the culture. Their first interest is in communicating, and the first communications are simple assertions ("dog"; "daddy"; "ball") or requests ("milk!"; "more candy"). Their second concern is with conversation.

A conversation is an exchange typically involving two or more people (although some people do talk to themselves—and answer themselves as well). It is generally verbal, although it can consist of a combination of gestures and verbalization, or it can consist entirely of gestures, as in the case of ASL (American Sign Language). Genuine conversational exchanges begin around age 2. Initially, they are highly telegraphic, as is the child's speech; there aren't many variations possible when your sentences are limited to a single word. A short excerpt from an intelligent conversation with one of my children illustrates this:

> Child: "Fish."
> Me: "Fish?"
> Child: "Fish!"
> Me: "Fish? Fish swim."
> Child: "Fish! Fish!" (The conversation becomes more complex.)
> Me: "There are fish in the lake." (An original thought, meant to provide cognitive enrichment and stimulate creativity.)
> Him: "Fish." (Pointing, this time, in the general direction of the lake, I think.)

From such primitive, repetitive conversation, children progress to more complex expressions and begin to learn the importance of subtle cues of intonation, accentuation of words, rhythm of sentences, tone, and accompanying gestures. They learn, as well, about the implicit agreements that govern our conversations—the well-accepted rules that determine who shall speak and when, whether interruptions are permissible and how they should occur, what information must be included if we are to be understood, and what we can assume is already known. Thus, more or less, do infants progress from a sound to a word, from one word to two, from an expression to a conversation, from a conversation to a book.

MAIN POINTS

Children and Magical Thinking

Children's thinking is more *magical* than ours: It has more powers to transform reality; and it need not conform quite so rigidly to the real world.

The Preschooler's Physical Growth

Growth velocity declines rapidly (growth deceleration) during infancy. Also, parts of the body grow at different rates. Growth asymmetries are seen in brain and head growth, genital growth, and lymph tissue growth. With respect to brain growth, head size changes from one-fifth to one-eighth adult size between ages 2 and 6 (75% of adult weight), mostly as a result of brain proliferation (increased synaptic connections and myelin sheaths) followed by significant pruning during the preschool period. Lateralization is poorly defined at birth but quite well established by age 1.

Motor Development

Learning to walk and to coordinate motor activities (such as those involved in tracing geometric designs) are important motor achievements of the preschool period. Physical and motor development may be assessed using measures such as the *Denver Developmental Screening Test*. Motor development is closely linked with cognitive development.

Cognitive Development: The Preschooler's Memory

Infantile amnesia may be due to the immaturity of the infant brain, and eventual pruning of many synapses. The younger preschooler's memory often makes use of incidental mnemonics (paying attention) rather than of deliberate strategies such as organizing. Older preschoolers may use more deliberate strategies, many of them learned through social interaction with mothers or peers.

Preschoolers don't remember as well or in as much detail as older children and adults. They are also far more suggestible in the hands of biased interviewers. But with sensitive, neutral interviewers, their memory for autobiographical events may be quite reliable.

Cognitive Development: Piaget's View

Piaget's preschooler is in the preoperational period (ages 2 to about 7), which includes the preconceptual stage (ages 2 to 4; marked by errors of classification, transductive reasoning, animistic thinking, and syncretic reasoning) and the intuitive stage (ages 4 to 7; marked by egocentricity, class-inclusion problems, and reliance on perception). Replications of Piaget's work have often confirmed the sequence he describes but sometimes find specific competencies at younger ages.

Preschool Education

Preschool education programs include nursery schools, kindergartens, and compensatory programs such as Head Start and the Montessori method. High-quality programs have positive effects. Kindergartens are often compulsory in North America but are rare and elitist in developing countries. Some critics fear that emphasis on formal instruction at the preschool level hurries children needlessly and robs them of their childhood.

Language and the Preschooler

Language is the use of arbitrary sounds with established referents that can be arranged in sequence to convey meaning. During the preschool period, the child goes from two-word expressions to multiple-word sentences that make extensive use of grammatical morphemes such as the inflections *-ing*, *-ed*, and *-s* to convey meaning. More complex sentences and adultlike grammatical structures are usually present by age 4.

Explanations of Language Development

Hopeful monster theories in language learning (Chomsky's LAD, for example) emphasize the role of biology. Their supporting evidence includes *fast mapping*, the fact that the earliest speech sounds of all infants are highly similar, the observation that children make relatively few imitative errors in learning a language, and the finding that languages are more easily learned during an early sensitive period.

Emergentism emphasizes the role of experience—especially interactions with a caregiver. Caregivers typically adjust their speech (use parentese, with its higher intonations, shorter sentences, more repetition, and simpler concepts), fine-tuning it to a level about 6 months in advance of their infants.

Language Problems, Thinking, and Communicating

Children who speak nonstandard dialects are often at a disadvantage because schoolwork and commerce in the community are generally in the standard dialect. Some children experience language problems ranging from complete absence of speech and comprehension to minor articulation and voice problems (often related to mental retardation, neurological damage or disease, mental disorders such as autism, or deafness).

A strong version of the Whorfian hypothesis maintains that language is necessary for thought; a weaker version holds that language influences thinking. Piaget and Vygotsky maintain that thought and language are initially separate (prelinguistic children can think) but become progressively more closely related. The existence and development of cultures is highly dependent on language.

Focus Questions: Applications

1. What is magical thinking?
   - Arrange to observe one or more preschoolers, using specimen sampling or some other appropriate observational approach (see Chapter 1) to find evidence of magical thinking.
2. What parallels are there between motor and cognitive development?
   - What sorts of motor skills might be used as indicators of developmental progress in early childhood? How would you devise a developmental test based on these motor skills?
3. How reliable are preschoolers' memories?
   - As a major term assignment, research the literature to answer the following question, posed

to you by a court of law in your capacity as expert witness: Under what circumstances should we rely on the eyewitness testimony of a 4-year-old?
4. What is preconceptual thought?
   - Arrange to conduct a demonstration of some aspect of preconceptual or intuitive thinking (refer to Figure 7.9).
5. How do biology and experience contribute to language learning?
   - Explain what a *hopeful monster* theory is.

Possible Responses to Thought Challenges

Thought Challenge, page 286

At 24 centimeters per year, the 6-year-old would stretch another 144 centimeters (4.69 feet); and at 10 kilograms per year, weight would have increased by an additional 60 kilograms (132 pounds). At this growth velocity, the 20-year-old, born at an average 88 centimeters (20 inches) and 3.2 kilograms (7 pounds), would be an impressive 18.5 feet tall (568 centimeters) and weigh a gargantuan 203 kilograms (447 pounds)—which, come to think of it, might look strangely skinny.

Thought Challenge, page 289

If you haven't figured it out, here's a hint: These ancestral cave dwellers drew many pictures—often simple, sticklike figures such as a child might draw. Sometimes

all they did was trace things as they held them up against a cave wall, things like sticks and leaves and stones and even their own hands.

So there's the answer: Left-handed artists tracing their own hands will most likely trace their right hands—and vice versa.

Thought Challenge, page 299

A flies; B flies; therefore B is A. Clearly, if A is a bird and B is also a bird, then A is a B and vice versa. (Transductive reasoning leading to a correct conclusion.) But if A is a plane and B is a bird, then B is not an A. (Transductive reasoning leading to an incorrect conclusion.)

Key Terms

animistic thinking, 300
bilingual education, 322
cerebral hemispheres, 289
compensatory preschool
    programs, 309
concept, 298
conservation, 301
developmental timetables, 291
distinct society, 321
egocentric, 301
elaborated language code, 320
English as a second language (ESL),
    323
fast mapping, 313
growth velocity, 286
hurried child, 305

incidental mnemonics, 294
infantile amnesia, 295
inflections, 314
intuitive thinking, 300
lateralization, 289
magical thinking, 286
mean length of utterance (MLU),
    314
melting pot societies, 321
memory strategies, 293
meta-analysis, 296
metamemory, 295
multicultural education, 321
multiculturalism, 321
nerves, 288
neural pruning, 288

operation, 297
overregularization, 314
parentese, 318
preconcept, 299
preconceptual thought, 297
preoperation, 297
Project Head Start, 309
pubescence, 287
restricted language code, 320
reversibility, 297
synapses, 288
syncretic reasoning, 299
toddler, 290
transductive reasoning, 299
Whorfian hypothesis, 323

Further Readings

Wadsworth provides a clear summary of Piaget's theory in:

Wadsworth, B. J. (1996). *Piaget's theory of cognitive and affective development,* 5th ed. New York: Longman.

The first of the following two references presents a detailed view of North American preschoolers' mastery of the skills and signs of literacy that define *readiness to learn.* The second is a compilation of information about the dozens of different tests, surveys, and procedures that might be used to assess a preschooler's readiness to learn.

National Center for Education Statistics (1995). *Approaching kindergarten: A look at preschoolers in the United States.* Washington, D.C.: U.S. Department of Education, Office of Educational Research and Improvement.

Human Resources Development Canada (1999). *Readiness to learn, child development and learning outcomes: Potential measures of readiness to learn.* Hull, Quebec, Canada: Applied Research Branch.

Morgan's book provides an intriguing look at the history of preschool education; the book by Jalongo and Isenberg is a comprehensive and practical look at early childhood education programs:

Morgan, H. (1999). *The imagination of early childhood education.* Westport, Conn.: Bergin & Garvey.

Jalongo, M. R., & Isenberg, J. P. (2000). *Exploring your role: A practitioner's introduction to early childhood education.* Upper Saddle River, N.J.: Merrill.

Language development is described in more detail in:

Berko-Gleason, J., ed. (1997). *The development of language,* 4th ed. Columbus, Ohio: Merrill.

Online Resources

For additional readings, explore *InfoTrac College Edition,* your online library. Go to http://infotrac-college.com/wadsworth and use the passcode that came on the card with your book. Try these search terms: bilingual education, preschool education, children physical growth, preschool memory, multicultural education.

The face of a child can say it all, especially the mouth part of the face.

Jack Handy, *Deep Thoughts*

Social and Emotional Development in Early Childhood

Richard Hutchings/PhotoEdit

CHAPTER 8

When my children were still very young, my mother, their grandmother, used to take perverse pleasure in telling them stories about the various humiliations I suffered as a child. And because most of these episodes occurred during the period of my infantile amnesia (which, if the stories are all correct, covered an impressive number of years), I could never say for certain whether they were true.

For example, when my son Laurier hurt his knee one day chasing the cat through the garden, his grandmother consoled him with, "It's okay, your dad used to cry lots too." And then she told him the old story of when Aunt Lucy brought over a nicely wrapped present for my third birthday. I got all excited because I was sure it was going to be one of those exquisitely engineered, sealer-ring-shooting, homemade toy pistols like the one that Uncle Réné had made for my cousin Luc. But when I tore off the wrapping, what I found was a nice little pair of blue serge short pants that Aunt Lucy had sewed on her new Singer—and I burst into tears. "And his poor aunt," explained my mother, "She felt so bad."

FOCUS QUESTIONS

1. What do preschoolers understand of what others feel?
2. Of what importance is play in childhood?
3. To what extent are masculinity and femininity determined by our genes?
4. What difference does parenting make? Family size? Position in the family? Age differences among siblings?
5. How significant is the loss of a parent?
6. Is nonparental child care as good as parental care?

EMOTIONAL DEVELOPMENT AND EMOTIONAL INTELLIGENCE

What the opening story illustrates is that I was not yet as socially competent as I later became. I didn't yet have as fine a control over my emotions or over their expression as adults and older children do over theirs. I was more easily moved to tears—and, I would hope, to laughter. I was not as keenly aware that others, too—even my Aunt Lucy—have feelings, and that my behaviors might affect those feelings. I had not yet learned that there are occasions when one should stiffen the upper lip and hide the way one truly feels.

Emotions are generally defined as the feeling or affective component of human behavior. As Oatley (1992) puts it, our emotions are really communications, to ourselves and to others, that relate to the occurrence of events concerning important goals. Thus, my expressions of sorrow communicate that a specific event (receiving a nice pair of blue short pants) signals failure to achieve an important goal (getting a wonderful wooden sealer-ring launcher). In much the same way, our expressions of joy signal events relating to reaching (or anticipating reaching) our goals.

The socialization of emotions in childhood involves at least three things: learning to interpret emotions; achieving some control over them; and

---

emotions The *feeling* or *affective* component of human behavior; an individual's responses to the occurrence of events relating to important goals.

learning when, where, and how displaying them is appropriate and expected.

Interpreting Emotions

An important thing that happens relatively early in infancy is that infants begin to realize that they, and others, are capable of feelings. Initially infants don't know how to interpret the feelings of others. Facial expressions of joy or sadness, for example, are meaningless for a 1-month-old infant. But as we saw in Chapter 6, even before the age of 1, infants begin to use social referencing. Especially in cases of uncertainty, infants attempt to interpret the emotional significance of events. That is, they look at the reactions of others to glean information about how they should react, to find out whether they should be afraid or excited, happy or sad (Dunn, 1998).

Evidence of increasing sophistication in interpreting emotions can also be seen in older preschoolers, who have little difficulty determining the most likely parental reaction to their own emotions and behaviors (Denham, 1997). As an example, Dunn (1998) reports the following conversation. The child, who is nearly 3, is talking to her mother after her brother has bitten her on the forehead.

Child: Look what Philip did! He bited me! (crying)
Mother: He bit you on the head?
Child: Yes.
Mother to brother: Philip, is that true?
Brother: No.
Child: Yes! On purpose!
Mother to child: He did it on purpose?
Child: Yes.
Mother to sibling: Come on over, Philip.
Brother to mother: I didn't do it on purpose, Mom.
Child to mother: Yes he did. (p. 105)

Notice how each child clearly understands that the mother will be upset. But notice, too, how each also realizes that the mother's reaction will reflect her belief about whether the act was intentional. Common reactions of preschoolers to sibling conflict, explains Dunn (1998), are to blame the other sibling—or, when the child is clearly to blame, to plead that the misdeed was unintentional. And sometimes, too, children cleverly plead that their intentions were irreproachable. "But Mom, I didn't mean to break the fishbowl. I was trying to clean it for you. Honest, I was trying to clean it so you would be happy."

Teasing: Knowing How Others Will React By the second year, infants engage in various behaviors that indicate they have some understanding of others' feelings, and some awareness that their behaviors can affect these feelings. For example, 2-year-olds often engage in simple forms of teasing—as when Liam, my grandson, repeatedly knocks over his older sister's block tower, apparently intrigued by her displays of childish anger. She retaliates by calling him "Liam-baby." She, too, is intrigued by his reactions.

Later in the preschool period, the child's ability to interpret others' emotions becomes increasingly accurate. For example, many preschoolers respond with obvious distress when they hear someone crying. Still, they are not always clear about why others feel certain emotions. Children at age 3½ have little difficulty picking out the photograph that accurately reflects the emotion of the character in a story that has just been read to them (Boyatzis, Chazan, & Ting, 1993). But when they are asked why the person in the story is happy or sad, they often respond by saying things like, "He's happy 'cause he's laughing," or "She's sad 'cause she's crying."

Deception: Understanding Real Emotions and Pretense During the early preschool years, children's ability to make inferences about other people's emotions, and to interpret their own emotions, appears to be global and relatively imprecise. For example, they can't readily tell the difference between emotions that are real and those that are a pretense. If someone falls down but jumps up and "laughs it off," the 2-year-old is likely to conclude that the person is happy. In contrast, 3- to 5-year-olds have little trouble spotting the pretense (Banerjee, 1997). Harris and Gross (1988) speculate that children probably discover that some expressions of emotion are false when they begin to realize that they themselves are able to mislead others about their own emotions. When 3-year-old Eddie plays hide-and-seek with his sister, she always finds

him. All she has to do is say, "Where are you, Eddie? Are you in the bedroom?" and Eddie yells from behind the couch, "No way, I'm not in the bedroom." He can't deceive his sister any more than could the 3-year-olds, in a study by Sodian (1991), who were asked to mislead a competitor in a game by pointing to the container that did not hold an object. Invariably, these 3-year-olds were unable to conceal the information; they insisted on pointing to the correct container.

It isn't until about age 4, claim Ruffman et al. (1993), that children begin to understand that deceiving others involves getting them to believe things that are false. In one experiment, for example, the researchers had a story character, John, put on another character's (Katy's) much-too-large shoes to steal a piece of chocolate. The shoes left huge footprints in flour leading to the chocolate. Although the 3-year-olds understood clearly that the huge footprints were associated with Katy, they nevertheless predicted that a third character, Mr. Bubbly, would believe that John—not Katy—had stolen the chocolate. After all, John *was* the thief.

Regulating Emotions

We saw in Chapter 6 that even very young infants can do things to control the emotions they feel. For example, when Leila is frightened, she might close her eyes, suck her thumb, or bury her face in her mother's lap—examples of what Gianino and Tronick (1988) call self-directed regulatory behaviors. Or she might push away the frightening thing—an example of other-directed regulatory behaviors.

Preschoolers, with their expanding mobility and rapidly developing cognitive and social skills, become increasingly adept both at avoiding situations that lead to negative emotions and at seeking out and maintaining emotions associated with good feelings. But, somewhat like infants, their control of emotions is situational and behavioral rather than cognitive. When they hear the ice-cream man's bell, they run excitedly to get mother—or money; when the frightening part of a story comes, they close their eyes and cover their ears. In Brown et al.'s (1991) investigation in which children were questioned following emotion-related events in stories, the younger children saw emotions as being situation-specific: To change a feeling, one need only change the situation. Monica is sad because she has lost a toy. "But," she predicts, "I will be happy when I go to bed." Why? "Because I won't have to look for it."

In contrast, older children's control of emotions is more cognitive. One way of not feeling sad about a lost toy, the older child insists, is not to think about it, or to think a happy thought. Most of us are more like older than younger children. We can't just go to bed.

Among the strategies of emotional control available to preschoolers and older children, Saarni (1997a) discusses the following:

- ▲ problem-solving (if having untied shoelaces is frustrating, learning to tie them effectively regulates that emotion)

- ▲ externalizing (if our loneliness threatens to overwhelm us, frustrates us and makes us mad, then perhaps we can hit somebody or smash the Christmas tree light bulbs when nobody is watching)

- ▲ support-seeking (if the witch that lurks under our beds threatens our sleep, we might sleep better if we seek the help of our older brother who has a big stick and fiercely protective instincts)

- ▲ distancing (on second thought, the witch-fear that keeps us awake might be better eased by dragging our favorite pillow and blanket into our parents' room)

- ▲ internalizing (or perhaps we can, in a sense, swallow our fear, hide it, deny its existence, distract ourselves with thoughts of magic fairies and wild white horses)

Displaying Emotions

Had I been 4 or 5 when Aunt Lucy gave me those sweet little pants, it would have embarrassed me terribly to cry in front of her. But it wouldn't have bothered me so much to cry in front of my mother or my mean older brother. By then, I would have

begun to learn what researchers refer to as **emotional display rules**. One aspect of display rules has to do with learning when and how it's appropriate to display certain emotions; another deals with understanding the emotional expressions (emotional displays) of others.

Young children use two principal sorts of display rules, says Saarni (1999): **prosocial display rules** and **self-protective display rules**. Behaviors that reflect *prosocial* rules are those designed to get along with others. The rule that says you shouldn't cry when you receive a gift is a prosocial rule. Behaviors that reflect self-protective rules are motivated more by the actor's desire not to suffer. The rule that says "Don't cry little guy when you knock your silly head on the swing" has the effect of saving the little guy from embarrassment and perhaps from teasing as well.

Part of display-rule learning involves discovering that expressed emotion does not always correspond to underlying emotion. Even young children are able to smile when they lie, or pretend it doesn't hurt when it would be embarrassing to cry. But they are less skilled than older children at judging the intensity of another's emotion when that person's emotional display contradicts the emotion. If I hurt myself and laugh, the preschooler is likely to judge that it hurts much less than if I wince and use bad words (Rotenberg & Eisenberg, 1997). That, suggests Banerjee (1997), is because their theory of mind—their realization that other people, too, have *minds*, and their intuitive notions about what others think and feel—are not as well developed as they will later be. (There's more about the development of *theory of mind* in Chapter 9, and in a later section on *pretend play* in this chapter.)

---

emotional display rules Implicit, socially accepted rules that tell us when it is appropriate to display emotion, how it should be displayed, and what other people's emotional displays mean.

prosocial display rules A rule of emotional expression implying that there are certain things one should and should not say and do to please others, and not hurt their feelings—for instance, profusely expressing thanks for unattractive and useless gifts.

self-protective display rules An emotional expression rule motivated by the desire to save face, not to suffer, to project a desired image—such as not crying even when it really hurts.

Preschoolers do not control their expression of emotions as well as or as carefully as do adults. When it hurts, it embarrasses them little to cry. And when it's funny, it is simple to laugh without restraint.

It's not clear how preschoolers learn simple display rules, such as the rule that says that if you don't like a gift, you should hide your disappointment. When Cole (1986) filmed 3- to 4-year-old girls opening a disappointing gift either alone or in front of the giver, she found highly noticeable differences between the facial displays in the two situations. Although the girls' disappointment was clear when they opened the gift alone, most of them covered their feelings with smiles when the giver was present. What is interesting, however, was that these girls were unaware of their deception.

It seems that preschoolers begin learning to control their emotional expression before they realize the effects of their behavior on others. As we saw in Chapter 6, learning emotional control may begin early in infancy, perhaps with the first manifestations of mother-infant affect synchrony—the give and take of mother-infant emotional reactions, the emotional dance where infant and mother alternately lead and follow each other in sequences of emotional responses. Feldman, Greenbaum, and Yirmiya's

(1999) research suggests that higher levels of mother-infant synchrony seem to be associated with higher levels of emotional control at the age of 2.

Although older preschoolers attempt to control their emotional displays, they aren't always completely successful. They continue to cry and laugh more easily than adults do. And even as adults, we're not always able to hide our feelings. If someone gives us a dollar when we fully expected a hundred, we might find it very difficult to smile, even though our socialization is far more advanced than that of children. Crying on occasion doesn't mean we're emotionally stupid; in fact, under some circumstances, it might mean just the opposite.

Emotional Intelligence

Research indicates very strongly that learning to regulate emotions and their expression may be very important for young children. There is overwhelming evidence, report Fabes et al. (1999), that social competence is very closely tied to the child's ability to identify emotions in both self and others, to regulate these emotions, and to control their expression. For example, Walden, Lemerise, and Smith (1999) found that those preschoolers best able to regulate their emotions were also those most likely to have the greatest number of friendships. Similarly, Raver et al. (1999) found that preschoolers who were most successful in regulating their emotions—in this case, by using self-distracting strategies—were judged by both peers and teachers to be the most competent in peer interactions.

Emotional intelligence, explains Saarni (1997b), involves understanding and controlling our own emotions, as well as understanding the emotional reactions of others. Some skills and abilities that are most characteristic of emotional intelligence among older children and adults are listed in Table 8.1 (Saarni, 1999). All of these capacities begin to develop in infancy and are present, to a greater or lesser extent, in the preschooler. They are learned through the process of **socialization.**

PROCESSES OF SOCIALIZATION

Simply defined, socialization is the process by which children learn behaviors that are appropriate for people of their sex and age. As children are socialized, they acquire the traditions, beliefs, values, and customs of their groups. It is the way they learn the rules of membership in a society—rules like how and when to display emotion, and what people

mean when they smile or laugh, or say this or that about their feelings.

What is learned through socialization is determined by cultural context. In some cultures, children might learn to cry openly when they have been hurt or shamed; in other cultures they might learn to smile instead, or hide their faces in their hands. This makes the "average child" even more of a myth. But the processes by which socialization occurs are highly similar among different cultural groups.

Erikson's Psychosocial Stages

As we saw in Chapter 2, an important theory of social development is Erik Erikson's. It describes children's development as a series of stages, each characterized by conflicting tendencies or desires, and each requiring the attainment of some new competence. The theory clearly emphasizes social development (hence the label psychosocial development). The first three of Erikson's psychosocial stages span the years from birth to around the end of the preschool period.

emotional intelligence A type of emotional competence reflected in high levels of emotional self-knowledge and self-control, as well as the ability to discern and empathize with others' emotional states.

socialization The complex process of learning those behaviors that are appropriate within a given culture as well as those that are less appropriate. The primary agents of socialization are home, school, and peer groups.

Table 8.1
Dimensions of Emotional Intelligence

High emotional competence is marked by:

- Awareness of one's own emotions
- The ability to read and understand the emotions of others
- Command of the language and expression of emotions
- The capacity to empathize
- The ability to separate internal emotions from external emotional displays
- The capacity to cope with negative emotions
- The ability to communicate emotion in relationships
- Feelings of emotional competence and strength

The first stage, trust versus mistrust, lasts through most of infancy. The important task in this stage is to develop sufficient trust in the world to be able to go out and begin exploring it actively. Throughout this period, the most important influence in an infant's life is clearly the principal caregiver(s)—often, though not always, the mother. As noted in Chapter 6, secure attachment to the principal caregiver is closely tied to the infant's willingness to go out and explore; it provides a secure base, a place of trust, to return to.

The second stage, autonomy versus shame and doubt, spans the first year or so of the preschool period. At this time, children begin to discover they are responsible for their own actions. This discovery is closely linked with the development of intentionality, and with the recognition of intention in others. The child's developing autonomy depends on opportunities to explore and to be independent, says Erikson (1959), hence the need for a balance in parental control. Overprotection can lead to doubt and uncertainty. Yet there is clearly a need for continued protection; the young preschooler cannot be permitted unsupervised and unlimited freedom to explore. Although few saber-toothed tigers or meat-eating dinosaurs are lurking out there, cars, trucks, and other things can be just as deadly.

The third stage, initiative versus guilt, spans the remaining preschool years. The new sense of competence required of the child involves a sense of initiative, a sense of personal agency. But there still lingers a desire to retain the comfort and security that come from allowing other people—especially parents—to maintain control and responsibility.

According to Erikson's theory, then, much of "growing up" during the preschool period involves developing a sense of an autonomous self—a self that is capable of forming intentions and of behaving in ways that are effective. The underlying competencies are greatly facilitated by infants' physical exploration of the environment, as well as by mushrooming language skills that make it possible to explore in other ways—as, for example, when the 4-year-old bombards caregivers with questions. And, as we saw, the development of social competence through the preschool period requires learning about interpreting and controlling emotions, and learning the emotional display rules that will make us emotionally competent—emotionally

To become autonomous, says Erikson, children must explore and be independent—and parents must provide children with opportunities to do so. Overprotection can lead to doubt and uncertainty. Yet there is clearly a need to continue to protect; not all trees are for climbing.

Elizabeth Crews

intelligent. (See Chapter 2 for more details on Erikson's theory; see also Table 8.2.)

Socialization through Imitation

Erikson (1968) believed that imitation is an important means by which preschool children become socialized, especially in the first two or three years of life. Later, identification (a process whereby children do not merely imitate models, but adopt their values and beliefs—in a sense, become like them) gains importance.

As we saw in Chapter 2, an important theory of social learning based on imitation has been proposed by Albert Bandura. To summarize briefly, Bandura's theory explains the complex effects of modeling,

Table 8.2
Erikson's Psychosocial Stages of Preschool Development

STAGE	APPROXIMATE AGE	PRINCIPAL DEVELOPMENT TASK
Autonomy vs. shame and doubt	18 months to 2 or 3 years	Developing a sense of control and mastery over actions; learning that one is autonomous, that intentions can be realized; overcoming the urge to return to the comfort of trusting parents, and especially the mother, to do all important things
Initiative vs. guilt	2 or 3 to 6 years	Developing a sense of self, largely through identifying with parents; developing a greater sense of responsibility for own actions; achieving progressive independence from parents

partly in terms of rewards and punishments. But it is also a cognitive theory: It gives a crucial role to the informative function of models and to observers' understanding and interpretation of that information. In learning through imitation, it is what the observer imagines and expects that is important.

Bandura describes three separate effects of imitation: the modeling effect, evident in learning new behavior; the inhibitory effect and disinhibitory effect, in which the reward or punishment a model receives serves to disinhibit (bring about) some previously suppressed behavior or, alternatively, to inhibit current deviant behavior; and the eliciting effect, in which the model's behavior serves to evoke a related behavior in the observer.

Imitation-based theories of social learning are especially useful for explaining how children in non-technological societies learn to do things like set snares and traps, or wield brooms, or use corn-grinding stones. But most of us no longer need to learn how to operate a corn-grinding stone or lay out a trap. So what do we learn by social imitation? Among other things, perhaps we learn important social tendencies such as cooperation and competition. (And, in Chapter 10, we also see how we might learn to be violent and aggressive through imitation.)

Learning Cooperation and Competition

Considerable research supports the belief that children are socialized to be cooperative or competitive by the predominant way of life—the mores and traditions—of their immediate social environment. Children from different ethnic groups can be remarkably different in terms of cooperation and competition.

Studying Cooperation In one study, Brownell and Carriger (1998) gave toddlers 7 minutes to retrieve a stuffed toy from a Plexiglas case. The problem required that one child manipulate a lever (or in some cases a piston or rotating handle) to access the toy. But the apparatus was so designed that the child operating the lever couldn't reach the toy without letting go—in which case the lever returned to its original position, rendering the toy inaccessible. The solution thus requires the cooperation of the second child, who can easily retrieve the toy while the first manipulates the lever. What is most interesting about these studies is that they involve only toddlers and not parents. While collaboration between parents and young children is common, it most often involves the guidance and direction of the parent. Can young preschoolers establish mutual goals and cooperate to achieve them?

Collaboration among Preschoolers Brownell and Carriger (1998) found that none of the 1-year-olds in their study collaborated and solved the problem. By 18 months, half of the children were successful. It is interesting, however, that successful solution of the problem didn't always indicate a high level of cooperation. Often, for example, the child not manipulating the lever would soon become distracted and do something else while the first child pulled and pushed and twisted and fiddled in vain. But if the second child then happened to glance at the apparatus and noticed that the toy was momentarily accessible, she might retrieve it and perhaps even share it with the other.

By the age of 30 months, all of the children in the investigation managed to solve the problem. By the age of 3, say Brownell and Carriger, children have developed the social skills necessary for establishing joint goals and for collaborating to achieve them.

In another investigation of cooperation among preschoolers, Wiegel (1998) taught mathematics concepts to 5 pairs of students, supplying each pair only one set of counting materials. Over a 4-month period, without instruction or direction, pairs of students generated several different strategies to organize their use of the counting materials, such as counting side by side, taking turns with the materials, or counting cooperatively. All of these kindergarten children were clearly able to establish mutual goals and cooperate to reach them. Many of them, however, seemed to want to achieve their own solutions. This, as Johnson and Johnson (1994) point out, may be a reflection of the competitive nature of North American societies. According to these authors, this competitiveness is clearly reflected in the schools:

In every classroom, no matter what the subject area, teachers may structure lessons so that students:

1. engage in a win-lose struggle to see who is best (competitive)

2. work independently on their own learning goals at their own pace and in their own space to achieve a preset criterion of excellence (individualistic)

3. work cooperatively in small groups, ensuring that all members master the assigned material (cooperative). (p. 3)

They strongly advocate increased use of cooperative teaching approaches in schools. Such approaches, they argue, would not only improve academic performance. It might also do much to reduce feelings of alienation, of purposelessness, of isolation, and of social unease among students.

Cooperation and Competition in Other Cultures

Madsen and Lancy (1981) used a cooperation board (shown in Figure 8.1) to look at competition and cooperation among children from two Papua New Guinea groups. One group of children were Imbonggu, a highly intact tribal group whose traditional way of life is based on cooperation; the other children were Kila-Kila, a more heterogeneous group, heavily influenced by rapid modernization and living in an urbanized setting characterized by violence and crime.

First, groups of four children from each tribe were simply instructed to draw a line through each of the numbered circles, in order. They were rewarded as a group for being successful (each child was given a coin). The researchers' objective was simply to determine whether children from both tribes were able to cooperate when so instructed and when rewarded for doing so.

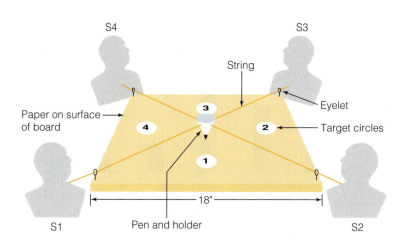

FIGURE 8.1 The competition board is used to study cooperation and competition. When target circles are placed as shown, subjects will succeed in drawing a line through a given target only if they cooperate. Source: Madsen & Lancy (1981), p. 397.

After three 1-minute trials under this "group reward" condition, participants were then asked to write their names next to one of the target circles (either to their right or left). They were also told they would receive a coin each time a line was drawn through their circle. Again, in order to be successful, subjects had to cooperate. If they did not, the most competitive and aggressive subject would succeed in pulling the pen over to his or her corner, and nobody would win.

The results of the study are striking. There were no differences between the Imbonggu and Kila-Kila on the first three trials. Each of the groups improved on every trial; and by the third trial, each succeeded in crossing an average of slightly more than 12 circles. But the results on the fourth, fifth, and sixth trials, when subjects were being rewarded individually rather than as a group, are intriguing. Whereas the Imbonggu continued to improve on each of the trials—a clear sign that they continued to cooperate—the performance of the Kila-Kila foursomes deteriorated dramatically. In fact, two-thirds of the Kila-Kila groups did not cross a single circle on the fourth trial. In contrast, the Imbonggu group that cooperated the least still managed to cross six circles (see Figure 8.2).

These marked differences in competitive and cooperative tendencies, claim Madsen and Lancy (1981), are due to differences in immediate cultural contexts. Thus there are societies whose world view is predominantly peaceful, and who socialize their children to be nurturant and helpful to others rather than fiercely competitive. These societies, explains Bonta (1997), tend to devalue achievement because it often results in competition. At the same time, they are more likely to exemplify and to reward cooperative behavior. Hence it's not surprising when research reveals that rural people—for whom cooperation has often been linked with comfort, if not survival—tend to be more cooperative than city dwellers. Thus rural Mexican children have been found to be more cooperative (less competitive) than urban Mexican children, as have kibbutz Israeli children compared with urban Israeli children; Blackfoot Indians compared with urban Caucasians in Canada; urban and rural Colombians; urban and rural Maoris in New Zealand, and various other groups (Madsen & Lancy, 1981).

Competition and Cooperation In North America
Among the most important social skills that the preschooler must learn are the skills of social cooperation. These skills are often lacking among less mature children or among those with attention and hyperactivity disorders (Merrell & Wolfe, 1998). Sometimes they're lacking among adults as well.

In fact, North American societies are often contrasted with highly cooperative societies of the kind described by Bonta (1997). We socialize our children to compete, explain Johnson and Johnson (1994). We have structured our most powerful socializing agency, our schools, in such a way that competition is usually the best way to succeed. Thus, in schools, students are engaged in a fierce struggle to see who is best; and only one, or a few, can be best. This ensures that students work primarily on their own, *competi-*

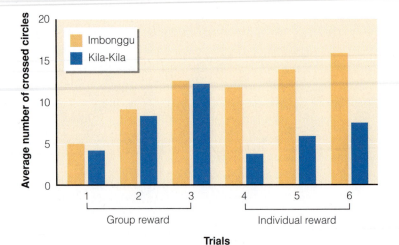

FIGURE 8.2 Differences in cooperation and competition between Imbonggu and Kila-Kila children. While both groups performed equally well when each member was rewarded for the entire group's performance, the highly competitive Kila-Kila found it difficult to cooperate under conditions of individual reward. Source: Adapted from Madsen & Lancy (1981), p. 399.

tively rather than *cooperatively*. Not surprisingly, many are highly competitive; but, too, many are not. And, in general, females are often found to be more cooperative than males (for example, Segal, Connelly, & Topoloski, 1996).

Most people tend to think of competition and cooperation as opposites. In fact, explains Charlesworth (1996), they might be more closely related than we think. That is, most individuals are not one or the other in all circumstances; our behavior changes depending on our immediate goals, the people with whom we're interacting, our mood, and a host of other factors. Thus schools can be structured so that some activities are intensely competitive and others cooperative. And the same children may do very well (or very badly) in either case.

One characteristic of highly heterogeneous societies such as ours is that the models they present are highly varied. In advanced societies, many of these are symbolic models, which need not be real, immediately present people. Symbolic models may include characters in literature; movies; verbal and written instructions; religious beliefs; or folk heroes (such as musicians or athletes). One of the most powerful of these symbolic models may well be television (about which we say more in Chapter 10). Another very powerful source of social influence is young children's playmates.

PLAY

Play is activity that has no long-range goal, although it might have some immediate objectives (to hop from here to there; to make a sand hill; to fly a kite). Play is what children (and grown-ups) do for the fun of it. But that play has no ultimate purpose does not mean it is unimportant and useless. In fact, it is important for all aspects of children's development: social, physical, and intellectual.

Purposes of Play

Play appears to be nearly universal. It is even found among animals, as anyone who has raised cats and dogs can attest. Ethologists argue that animal play is useful in developing and exercising physical skills that might be important in hunting or escaping

from predators—such as from small boys with big sticks. Play also serves to establish social position and to teach acceptable behaviors, as in the mock-fighting, rough-and-tumble play of lion cubs or chimpanzees.

Some of the functions of play among children are not very different from those among animals. Some forms of physical and motor play are useful in developing and exercising physical skills and might also contribute to social adaptation. In addition, as Piaget points out, physical manipulation of real objects is closely linked with the development of *ideas* about things.

The functions and contributions of more imaginative play are even more clearly intellectual. Imagining involves important cognitive abilities related to symbolizing, imitating, anticipating, and problem solving. Children's growing awareness of self and of others, and their gradual realization that we are all thinking beings, has its roots in play, claims Hughes (1999). In the make-believe games of the preschooler, emotions, intellect, and social life are all joined.

Categories of Play

There are two main types of play: practice play (also called **sensorimotor play** or sometimes *exploratory play*) and pretend play (sometimes called **imaginative play**).

Practice Play Practice play is mainly physical activity. It is the kind of play evident among the young of many animals (for example, a kitten chasing a ball). Practice play involves manipulating objects or performing activities simply for the sensations that result. It is evident in activities such as skipping, hopping, jumping, waving, and countless solitary games of young children. It is often the only type of play infants are capable of during the early stages of development.

---

sensorimotor play (also called *practice play*) Activity involving the manipulation of objects or execution of activities simply for the sensations that are produced.

imaginative play (also called *pretend play*) Activities that include make-believe games, daydreaming, imaginary playmates, and other forms of pretending; highly prevalent during the preschool years.

Pretend Play Many of the preschooler's solitary games are not simply practice play but also *pretend* play. Even infants as young as 1 can pretend, although their pretending usually takes the form of simulating common activities—for example, pretending to eat or pretending to sleep. By age 2, however, a wide range of make-believe games becomes possible as children learn to transform objects, people, and activities into whatever they wish. In pretend play, boys are often superheroes such as Superman (or super antiheroes such as dragons or monsters); girls are often mothers or nurses (Paley, 1984). Many of these pretend games are suggested by the immediate environment, notes Jaffke (1996). Thus, a picture, a crooked stick, a broken teacup, a squished worm . . . each can inspire a new game.

The Real and the Fantastic When they make their first forays into purely imaginative play, preschoolers have not always learned the distinctions between reality and fantasy. Three-year-old Mollie wants to play a pretend game with the other nursery school children, and she knows some pretend bad thing is going to happen. But, as we see in the following exchange among Paley's kindergarten children, even pretend things can be frightening, especially if someone else has invented them. As Paley puts it, "What if the bad thing doesn't know it's pretend?"

Pretend play feeds children's imagination and contributes a great deal to the development of the mind. It also allows them to practice important language and social skills, even if only with hungry stuffed bears.

> "Go to sleep, Mollie," Libbie orders. "There might be something dangerous. You won't like it."
> "I know it," Mollie says. "But I got a bunk bed at home and I sleep there."
> "Bunk beds are too scary," Amelia says.
> "Why are they?" Mollie looks worried.
> "It's a monster, Mollie. Hide!"
> But Mollie protests that there are no monsters in her house today. Still, she is unwilling to take any chances:
> "I'm going to be a statue," Mollie whispers. "So he won't see me."
> Now Frederick comes roaring in on all fours.
> "I'm a lion. I'm roaring," he says.
> "Is he scaring you, Mollie?"
> "No."
> "Is anyone scaring you?"
> "The bunk bed," she answers solemnly (Paley, 1986, p. 45).

Mollie, like many other 3-year-olds, can create her own ghosts and monsters, and she has developed her own ways of dealing with them. If they threaten too frighteningly, she can become a statue so they won't see her, or she can hide by the teacher. Or she can, ultimately, resort to her knowledge that the monsters are pretend monsters.

But when others create monsters, Mollie can never be quite certain that they are truly *pretend* pretend. Perhaps, just perhaps, one of them might be *real* pretend. As Wooley et al. (1999) found during a study of 92 children from 3 to 6 years old, although most older preschoolers understand that *wishing* things to happen (or to go away) is not usually sufficient to alter reality, about one fourth of them still think that maybe, just maybe, wishing might work. For these children, wishing is still somewhere beyond the realm of ordinary processes; it is still a magical thing.

As adults, of course, we don't suffer from the same limitations as does Mollie (nor do most of us enjoy quite as boundless an imagination). We have somehow learned to tell the difference between fantasy and reality; we can dismiss our monsters if they frighten us. Can't we?

Daydreams and Imaginary Playmates One type of imaginative play that becomes increasingly prevalent as preschoolers age is daydreaming. Unlike other types of imaginative play in which children actively engage in fantasy, daydreaming is the imagining without the activity. Daydreaming is a normal and healthy activity (one in which I—and, I suspect, you—engage quite often.) And although daydreaming is a form of play, it can also be a coping strategy, a way of dealing with disappointments and with emotional upset and turmoil. In fact, when looking at the coping strategies of Iranian refugee preschoolers and their parents, Almqvist and Hwang (1999) found that daydreaming was one of the most common strategies used by the preschoolers.

Daydreaming, which is a solitary type of imaginative play, sometimes gives rise to the imaginary playmate, a constant companion and friend to approximately half of all preschool children (Pines, 1978). These imaginary friends, complete with names and relatively stable personality characteristics, are spoken to, played with, teased, and loved by their creators. They are given names, forms, and places—and young preschoolers will seldom admit their imaginary nature. In one study, Taylor, Cartwright, and Carlson (1993) interviewed a dozen 4-year-olds who had imaginary playmates, asking them to describe their imaginary friends, which they did quite readily. The remarkable thing is that when these children were interviewed again seven months later, their descriptions of their imaginary playmates had scarcely changed; they were every bit as stable as descriptions of real friends.

There is little information about the role imaginary companions might play in preschoolers' development. However, it seems clear that although most children who have imaginary companions act as though they are real, most realize they are imaginary. There is some evidence that the creation of an imaginary playmate may be associated with more advanced language and social development, and may predict later creativity (Singer & Singer, 1990).

Pretend Play and Theory of Mind

Pretend play, says Leslie (1988), contributes to one of the cognitive capacities that set us apart from other species. Specifically, it eventually enables us to think about ourselves and about others as thinkers, as organisms capable of having different states of mind. When mother puts a banana to her ear and says "Hello," 4-year-old Nancy recognizes at once that the banana is a pretend telephone. But there is no confusion here between reality and fantasy; she still knows very clearly that it is a banana. What is also clear to Nancy, however, is that mother can have different states of mind, and that Nancy can too. She has begun to develop a theory of mind, says Leslie (1988). And one important aspect of this theory is the recognition of others and of self as thinkers capable of deliberately selecting and manipulating ideas—even pretend ideas. Here, in the preschool period, is the dawning of what psychologists label **metacognition**—knowing about knowing.

If preschoolers have a well-developed theory of mind, the argument goes, they should realize that others can know things they don't know—and also that *they* can know things others don't know. In an ingenious series of experiments designed to test these notions, a child sees a video of a doll, "Maxi," hiding candy in a blue cupboard. But as soon as Maxi leaves the room, his "mommy" comes in and moves the candy to the adjacent white cupboard. Then mommy leaves and Maxi returns. "Where will Maxi look for the candy?" asks the investigator. "In the white cupboard," say typical 3-year-olds. They fail to make a distinction between what they know and what others know. But 4-year-olds are not so easily fooled; they know that Maxi doesn't share the information they have—that they and Maxi have different *states of mind*.

It is interesting that those children who engage in the greatest amount of pretend play are those who are least likely to be deceived by this problem, according to a number of investigations (for example, Youngblade and Dunn, 1995; Lillard, 1998).

metacognition Knowledge about knowing. As we grow and learn, we develop notions of ourselves as learners. Accordingly, we develop strategies that recognize our limitations and allow us to monitor our progress and take advantage of our efforts.

Social Play

Recall that both practice and pretend play can be solitary or social. Social play has tremendous implications for the development of the child's social skills and emotional intelligence.

Social play is any type of play that involves interaction among two or more children. Accordingly, either practice or pretend play is social when it involves more than one child. Skipping rope alone in the darkness of your basement is a solitary sensorimotor activity; skipping rope out on the playground with others turning the rope and chanting, "pepper, pepper, salt and . . ." is a cooperative or social activity. Similarly, creating daydreams in the solitude of your bedroom is private imaginative play, but playing "let's pretend—you be the veterinarian and I'll be the dog" is social imaginative play.

Parten (1932) observed the play behavior of groups of nursery school children and identified five different kinds of social play, distinguishable by of the type and amount of peer interaction involved. Although these develop sequentially, they also overlap (see *Concept Summary:* "Classifications and Examples of Children's Social Play").

Solitary Play As the label implies, in **solitary play**, the child plays alone—sometimes with toys, often simply engaging in some solitary motor activity. Much of the child's play before age 2 is solitary. And even later, when children engage in many forms of social play, most also continue to play in solitary ways.

Primitive Social Play Some forms of **primitive social play** can occur even before the age of 6 months. Many of these, such as "peek-a-boo" games, as well as games that include tickling, tossing, and related activities, typically occur with parents or older children, rather than with peers. Others, such as the "chase" games of toddlers, or the "touch me and I'll touch you" game, are a primitive type of social play. These are games that share meaning rather than rules, as Brenner & Mueller (1982) explain.

Onlooker Play As the label implies, **onlooker play** consists of a child watching others play, but not participating actively. Onlooker play occurs throughout childhood. Often, the onlooker talks with the players, perhaps even giving them advice or asking questions.

Parallel Play In **parallel play**, children play side by side, often with similar toys. But they do not interact, do not share the activities involved in the game, and do not use any mutually accepted rules. Parallel play is nevertheless social play of a primitive sort because it involves two or more children who apparently prefer to play together, even if they don't interact. Some research indicates that the presence of toys often detracts from social interaction and leads to parallel or perhaps solitary play, particularly among very young children (Vandell, Wilson, & Buchanan, 1980). In the absence of toys, of course, children are more likely to interact with each other.

Associative Play With advancing age, children become more interested in interacting with peers and are more likely to include toys in what is termed **associative play**. This type of play involves interaction among children, even though they continue to play separately. In associative play, children sometimes share toys, but each child plays independently without mutually accepted goals or rules.

Cooperative Play Children who play cooperatively help one another in activities that require shared goals and perhaps even a division of roles. Most research on preschoolers' play behavior indicates

---

social play Activity that involves interaction between two or more children and that frequently takes the form of games with somewhat defined rules.

solitary play Nonsocial child play that a child undertakes alone. It is the most common form of play before age 2.

primitive social play An early form of social play involving "shared meaning" rather than shared rules; for example, infant "peek-a-boo" games or toddler "chase" games.

---

onlooker play Consists of child watching others play but not actively participating.

parallel play A form of play in which children play side by side but individually, sharing neither activities nor rules.

associative play A form of social play in which children sometimes share toys, but each child plays independently without mutually accepted goals or rules.

Social play provides important opportunities for acquiring and practicing behaviors involved in social interaction, for developing cooperative behaviors, for learning how to resolve conflict, for making friends, and for fostering imagination and creativity.

Mary Kate Denny/PhotoEdit

that associative and cooperative play are not common before the age of 4 or 5. But sometimes there is evidence of cooperation in the play of much younger children, especially if they have had experience with siblings or similar-aged peers (Dunn, 1998). Among older children, as is shown in Figure 8.3, play occurs in a wide variety of places.

It is largely through cooperative social play that preschoolers form friendships. Not surprisingly, the best-liked children appear to be those who are most cooperative (as well as least aggressive and least difficult) (Denham & Holt, 1993).

Cultural Differences in Play

Play appears to be universal. It is seen in virtually all human cultures (Hoorn et al., 1999). And in most cultures, as Johnson, Christie and Yawkey (1999) explain, very young children typically begin by playing physical, sensorimotor games; later they progress to more symbolic and imaginative play. However, the extent of play and the form it takes may be quite different in different cultures. For example, Bornstein et al. (1999) found that Argentinian children and their mothers engaged in more exploratory and less symbolic play than did comparable U.S. mothers. And Gaskins (1999) reports that Mayan children play less than U.S. children; that their mothers seldom, if ever, play with them; and that their play is more likely to involve large motor activities (like twirling or climbing trees) than make-believe games.

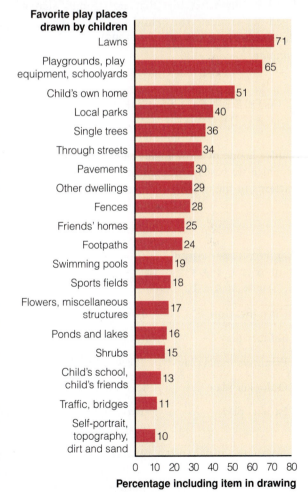

Favorite play places drawn by children

Play place	Percentage
Lawns	71
Playgrounds, play equipment, schoolyards	65
Child's own home	51
Local parks	40
Single trees	36
Through streets	34
Pavements	30
Other dwellings	29
Fences	28
Friends' homes	25
Footpaths	24
Swimming pools	19
Sports fields	18
Flowers, miscellaneous structures	17
Ponds and lakes	16
Shrubs	15
Child's school, child's friends	13
Traffic, bridges	11
Self-portrait, topography, dirt and sand	10

Percentage including item in drawing

FIGURE 8.3 Children's favorite places. When 48 boys and 48 girls were asked to draw their favorite places, these are the items they drew most often. Numbers indicate the percentage of children who included each item in their drawings. Source: Based on Moore (1986).

There is evidence, as well, that in societies in which children must assume work responsibilities at very early ages, there is less childhood play. Often, this observation is also true of children who are economically and socially disadvantaged. O'Reilly and Bornstein (1993) suggest this is probably because children learn many of their first play behaviors in interaction with principal caregivers. If caregivers are too busy or preoccupied, they devote less time to interacting with infants.

Not only are there cultural and social group differences in play, but there are also gender differences. It is not surprising that when college students are asked to select toys for children who are described as masculine, feminine, or gender neutral, they typically select toys that are strongly stereotyped to reflect the child's gender (Fisher-Thompson, Sausa, & Wright, 1995). (See *Concept Summary*.)

GENDER ROLES IN EARLY CHILDHOOD

Gender is one of those highly salient characteristics on which we base our judgments of people and our reactions to them; others are age, race, and physical appearance. Gender is evident in the characteristics and behaviors that define masculinity and femininity. Accordingly, gender is a *social construct:* That is, it is defined by social groups, and it typically develops according to accepted social norms. Gender normally corresponds to sex, which is a biological category.

In most cultures, including ours, there are usually marked differences between the ways in which males and females are expected to think, act, and feel. The range of behaviors considered appropriate for males and females—those that are considered masculine or feminine, together with the attitudes and personality characteristics associated with each—define gender roles. The learning of sex-appropriate behavior is gender typing.

In Chapter 6 we saw that gender typing begins from the very earliest moment, when the mere fact that a child is male or female determines much of what a parent's reactions to the infant will be. When Grieshaber (1998) interviewed 20 expectant parents, she found that almost half wanted to know the sex of the child before birth. Why? So that they could paint

gender A social construct defined in terms of the characteristics generally associated with biological sex in a given culture. Thus there is a *masculine* and a *feminine* gender.

CONCEPT SUMMARY

Classifications and Examples of Children's Social Play

Classification	Possible Activity
Solitary play	Child plays alone with blocks.
Primitive social play	"Peek-a-boo."
Onlooker play	Child watches others play tag, but does not join in.
Parallel play	Two children play with trucks in sandbox, but do not interact. They play beside each other, but not together.
Associative play	Two children play with dolls, talk with each other about their dolls, and lend each other diapers and dishes; but they play independently, sharing neither purpose nor rules.
Cooperative play	"Let's pretend. You be a monster and I'll be the guy with the magic sword and . . ."

the room the right color, buy the right toys, choose the right name. And what would they prefer—girl or boy? The answer is that where a preference is expressed, it's more often for a male than a female. This reflects a bias that has been pervasive in much of the world, and that—as we saw in Chapter 1—sometimes leads to the abortion of female fetuses and even to the killing of female babies. (See *In the News and on the Web:* "Male-Making Recipes.")

> **THOUGHT CHALLENGE:** *Many parents, if given a choice, would apparently prefer a male child—often for cultural reasons. Can you think of at least one good reason (other than personal preference) why some parents might prefer to have a female child?*

Developing Notions of Gender: Earlier Theories

Children aren't born knowing that they're male or female—or knowing which gender-linked behaviors are expected of them. But it's very important that they discover these things, to "get it right," as Yelland and Grieshaber (1998) put it. Those who "haven't got their gender quite right . . . are often treated with suspicion by peers, teachers, family, and society" (p. 3).

How do children "get it right"? Psychologists have proposed a number of theories to explain gender typing, the learning of sexual identity, and the modeling of sex-appropriate behavior.

Freudian Theory One long-held theory is based on Freud's suggestion that boys learn to behave like "boys" and girls like "girls" at least partly through

IN THE NEWS AND ON THE WEB

Male-Making Recipes

Pogrebin (1980) lists these folk beliefs about procedures for increasing the probability of conceiving a male child:

- The couple should have intercourse in dry weather, on a night with a full moon, after a good nut harvest, and/or when there is a north wind.
- The man should wear boots to bed, get drunk, tie a string around his right testicle, cut off his left testicle, take an ax to bed, hang his pants on the right bedpost, and/or bite his wife's right ear.
- The woman should lie on her right side during intercourse, eat red meat or sour foods, let a small boy step on her hands or sit in her lap on her wedding day, sleep with a small boy on her wedding eve, wear male clothing to bed on her wedding night, and/or pinch her husband's right testicle before intercourse. (p. 82)

Those of you who are exquisitely well educated and highly cynical about these old beliefs can always resort to science. You see, science can now separate Y- and non-Y-bearing sperm. This, coupled with artificial insemi-nation, provides an almost certain method of selecting the sex of your offspring.

To Think About: But if you are so well educated, and so *today*, why would you want a male child more than a female child?

Resources: The following *Parenthoodweb* site offers a wide variety of articles and resources for parents, including some that discuss current, and less current, methods of gender selection, as well as the ethics of gender selection.

http://www.parenthoodweb.com

For additional readings, explore *InfoTrac College Edition*, your online library. Go to http://infotrac-college.com/wadsworth and use the passcode that came on the card with your book. Try these search terms: sex preselection, sex determination, diagnostic, germ cells, sexism.

identifying with their parents and with other males and females. In Freud's terms, the values, the behaviors, the beliefs, and the attitudes of each sex become the child's through **introjection**. In this context, introjection is something like borrowing. It involves the unconscious process of taking someone else's inferred attitudes, beliefs, desires, and so on, and making them part of one's own belief system.

Freud's theory, as we saw in Chapter 2, describes development as a continuing struggle between sexually based instincts and reality. During the preschool period, said Freud, children (especially males) become increasingly aware of the sexual significance of their genitals. It is during this period, according to Freud, that boys find themselves in the throes of the Oedipus complex—subconsciously in love with their mothers and guilt-ridden at their wish to replace their father. And girls, confounded by their Electra complex, experience the same sort of crisis, but reversed.

Most contemporary theorists no longer agree with Freud's description of how children develop notions of masculinity and femininity. For one thing, most don't accept the notion that children suffer these complexes and need to resolve them. For another, most reject Freud's emphasis on the importance of male development, and his relative neglect of female development. Finally, there is convincing evidence that children are well on their way to developing clear notions of sexual identity before age 6 or 7, which is when Freud assumed it occurred (Martin, 1993).

Social Learning Theory A second important explanation of gender typing is social learning theory. As we saw in Chapter 2, this theory holds that parents, siblings and other children, and powerful symbolic models such as television and story characters suggest sex-appropriate behaviors for children. And as these behaviors occur, they are in turn reinforced by the models and by society. Thus do boys learn to be masculine, and girls feminine.

That parental and cultural models are involved in gender typing seems clear. If that were not the case, our masculine and feminine behaviors would probably be far more universal than they now are.

Kohlberg's Gender Constancy Theory A more cognitive explanation suggests that gender typing results from the preschooler's growing understanding of the *meaning* of gender. Kohlberg (1966) describes two broad stages—two levels of understanding—that reflect the child's increasing awareness of gender.

▲ Stage 1. **Basic gender understanding** describes the initial stage where the infant recognizes that there are two different genders, and that he is a boy or she is a girl. Although many 18-month-old infants can identify themselves as being a boy or girl, many at this age still cannot readily determine whether other children are boys or girls.

▲ Stage 2. **Gender constancy** refers to the realization that gender is permanent and unchangeable. It reflects the child's eventual understanding that superficial changes (in ways of behaving or dressing, for example) are irrelevant to basic gender. Gender constancy is generally achieved by most children by the end of the preschool period.

Kohlberg argues that once children become aware of their **gender identity** and its meaning, they actively participate in organizing their behaviors as well as their environments to conform to sex-appropriate patterns. Thus, having decided that she is a female, a girl selects feminine toys and behaviors. And having decided that he is a male, the boy leaves the doll corner except when he raids it with his phasers and missiles or haunts it as a pretend monster. The most widely used indicators of gender typing at the preschool level are based on selection of toys and activities. In the elementary school years, more abstract measures of self-perception are possible (Boldizar, 1991).

---

basic gender understanding An early stage in the development of gender awareness in which the infant recognizes that there are two different genders and that he is a boy or she is a girl.

gender constancy Refers to the developing child's realization that gender is permanent and unchangeable.

---

introjection Freudian term for the unconscious process of adopting as part of one's own belief system the inferred attitudes, beliefs, desires, and so on, of significant other persons—especially of parents.

gender identity The recognition, which begins in early childhood, that one is male or female, coupled with an understanding of the meaning and permanence of maleness and femaleness.

Developing Notions of Gender: Gender Schema Theory

Kohlberg's notions about gender constancy have led to the development of what researchers label **gender schema theory** (Bem, 1981; 1989). **Gender schemas** (also sometimes labeled *gender scripts*) are children's knowledge about characteristics associated with being male and female. Much of this knowledge consists of stereotypes such as those associated with common occupations or with predominant personality characteristics. Children use their gender schemas both as guides for interpreting and understanding the behavior of others and for directing their own behavior.

According to gender schema theory, the child begins with no understanding of the nature of gender—that is, without what Kohlberg labels *basic gender identity*, the recognition that one is male or female. With the development of notions of gender identity, the child begins to acquire notions of what it means to be a boy or a girl. These notions come largely from the information implicit in the models that the child's culture provides, and from the ways in which parents and others tend to reinforce sex-appropriate behaviors—and perhaps to punish, in subtle ways, those that are less appropriate.

Children's gender schemas—that is, their notions of what males and females are and *should be*—are already quite well established in the late preschool period. These schemas color children's perception of the world and serve to organize their understanding of the behavior of others, as well as to guide their own behavior. Most often, children's gender schemas reflect the predominant values and beliefs of their cultures and their families. As a result, there are sometimes important differences in the beliefs and attitudes of different children about appropriate gender roles. These differences, as Crouter, McHale and Bartko (1993) have shown, are often related to the gender roles that parents display in the home. Thus, children of working mothers, and especially those whose mothers occupy nontraditional roles, tend to be more **androgynous** in their gender role stereotypes. That is, they display a greater balance, a greater acceptance of both masculine and feminine characteristics, interests, and activities as appropriate for either gender.

In summary, although children begin to discriminate between male and female very early in life—that is, they begin to develop gender schemas early—it isn't until later in the preschool period that they finally understand that gender is a permanent category that can't easily be changed. At the same time, children begin to assume the roles they associate with their sex. And their understanding of these roles determines and constrains much of their behavior. Because boys aren't supposed to cry, Johnny tries hard not to. And because girls aren't supposed to be truck drivers, Sarah ignores the dump truck in the sandbox.

Gender Identity Disorder

All normally socialized children develop similar gender schemas—similar notions of differences between male and female genders. In rare cases, however, some children experience significant difficulty in developing a strong and clear notion of personal gender identity and in being comfortable with that identity—a problem technically labeled **gender identity disorder.** Kagan and Gall (1998) report that gender identity disorder affects about 1 in 20,000 males and only about 1 in 50,000 females. Gender identity disorder is evident in situations where boys feel themselves to be girls or wish desperately that they were, and in cases where girls wish themselves male (Soutter, 1996).

The causes of gender identity disorders are not clear. Such disorders are far more common among

---

gender schema theory A cognitive gender-typing theory that recognizes that elements of both cognitive explanations (the child's growing understanding of the nature and meaning of gender) and social learning explanations (the influence of models and reinforcements) are useful to account for the shaping of gender roles.

gender schemas Knowledge about the characteristics associated with being male and female.

---

androgynous Characterized by a balance of masculine and feminine characteristics.

gender identity disorder Label for the relatively rare condition in which individuals don't feel comfortable with their anatomical sex—where they feel themselves to *be* the other sex, and have strong preferences for that alternative.

children born as **hermaphrodites** or partial hermaphrodites (Slijper et al., 1998). Gender identity disorders also appear to be more common among some adoptees, although the reasons for this are not at all clear (Zucker & Bradley, 1998). And a study by Fridell and associates (1996) found that girls with gender identity disorder were rated as significantly less attractive than other girls. Again, it's not clear whether this might have been a contributing factor in the disorder.

In some cases gender identity disorder is pervasive, leading affected individuals to undergo sex-change procedures. In some cases the disorder can apparently be corrected. Soutter (1996) reports the case of three boys, all suffering from gender identity disorder, of whom two had gone so far as to give themselves girls' names. Following longitudinal therapy involving acceptance by teachers and protection from ridicule and teasing, all three had developed clear masculine gender identities in adolescence. Kagan and Gall (1998) report that most children with gender identity disorder "outgrow" it, but that 75% of the boys later adopt homosexual or bisexual lifestyles. (See Chapter 11 for more information.)

Gender Differences and Stereotypes

There are obvious biological differences between the sexes; that there are also psychological differences is less obvious, and certainly far more controversial. Nevertheless, as is shown in Chapter 12, there are some small (and declining) differences between males and females in some areas—perhaps most notably in aggressiveness, where males have the doubtful distinction of being considerably more aggressive.

That our common stereotypes of masculinity and femininity are still clearly different is apparent even at very young ages. For example, Henshaw, Kelly, and Gratton (1992) asked 15 boys and 15 girls, age 8 to 9, to give an experimenter advice about whether a boy (John) and a girl (Sally) would like

masculine toys (cricket bat, train set, skateboard), feminine toys (doll, skipping rope, baby carriage), or neutral toys as a present. Only 7% of the children thought John would like girls' toys; in contrast, almost half thought Sally would like boys' toys.

In the same study, children were also asked whether John and Sally would like activities such as karate, football, and climbing trees (masculine activities); or activities such as dancing, gymnastics, and skipping rope (feminine activities); or more neutral activities. They were also asked similar questions relating to traditionally male occupations (farmer, bus driver, judge) and to those that have traditionally been female (cook, secretary, librarian). Finally, they were asked whether a stylized drawing of a cat with either a pink bow, a blue bow, or a yellow bow would be a boy or a girl cat. Results, summarized in Figure 8.4, indicate that the children clearly differentiated between masculine and feminine interests and activities. Perhaps more striking, they also reveal that boys' roles are more constrained than those of girls. That is, it is considered less likely and less appropriate for a boy to be interested in girls' toys or activities than for a girl to show interest in boys' things. As Henshaw and associates (1992) put it, boy sissies are more strongly sanctioned than girl tomboys: "Girls in trousers are acceptable in a way that boys in dresses will probably never be" (p. 230). Or, in the words of one of the children who participated: "Skipping's for girls—I wouldn't skip rope and my friends wouldn't skip" (p. 234). In much the same way, pink is for girls and blue is for boys, even for cats. Not a single child thought the cat wearing pink would be a boy cat—or vice versa. Ten percent thought the cat wearing yellow might be male; 27% thought it might be female.

Gender Differences in Play

When they are only 3, Paley (1984) informs us, boys will gladly pretend to be babies, mothers, fathers, or monsters. Most are as comfortable wearing the discarded apron and the nursery school teacher's high-heeled shoes as the firefighter's hat or the ranch hand's boots. They play in the "doll corner" as easily as do the girls.

But when preschoolers reach age 5, the atmosphere in the doll corner changes dramatically. Now

hermaphrodite Individual having both male and female reproductive organs, often with ambiguous external genitalia. The condition is sometimes corrected anatomically shortly after birth, but is nevertheless frequently associated with gender identity problems later.

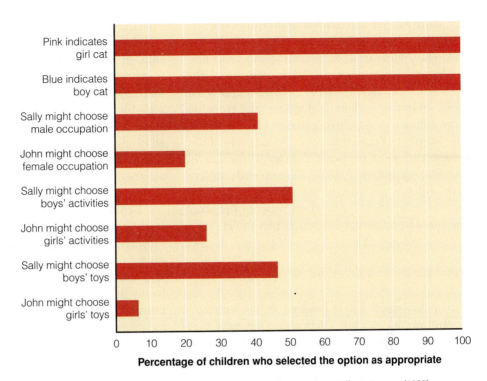

FIGURE 8.4 Children's gender stereotypes. Source: Based on Henshaw, Kelly, & Gratton, (1992).

when there are pretend games, the boys are monsters and superheroes; and in the pretend games of the girls, there are princesses and sisters. But these are not the only changes that come with age. In Paley's (1984) words:

> In the class described in this book, for example [a kindergarten class], you hop to get your milk if you are a boy and skip to the paper shelf if you are a girl. Boys clap out the rhythm of certain songs; girls sing louder. Boys draw furniture inside four-story haunted houses; girls put flowers in the doorways of cottages. Boys get tired of drawing pictures and begin to poke and shove; girls continue to draw. (p. xi)

Several consistent findings have emerged from studies that have examined sex differences in play behavior. To begin with, after the age of 4, boys' play tends to be more active, more physical, and more boisterous than girls' play (Johnson, Christie, & Yawkey, 1999). On the other hand, there is little evidence of any greater predisposition toward fantasy (imaginative play) or social play in either girls or boys, but there is repeated evidence of sex typing, not only in the toys that boys and girls are given but also in the toys they choose.

Another consistent finding about the play behavior of young children is that beginning early in the preschool period, but especially after age 4, both boys and girls show a marked preference for playing with members of their own sex (Albers, 1998). This situation doesn't change much until adolescence. Hughes (1999) suggests that this preference may have much to do with the fact that members of the same sex have similar abilities and interests, and also share the same sex-role stereotypes.

Among additional sex differences in play behavior are that boys use more physical space in their play, play outdoors more, and are more interested in "rough and tumble," noisy play. Girls are more interested in "nurturant" play (helping, caring for). Boys tease, wrestle, push, run, and engage in sex-typed role-playing games in which they are firefighters, builders, warriors, and so on; girls often play house, cooking, cleaning, looking after children, and helping each other with aprons, hats, and other items of clothing.

Many parents have tended to maximize sex differences in the play (and other interests) of young children, sometimes even punishing and ridiculing children whose games seemed less appropriate for their sex. More recently, there have been concerted social efforts toward understanding and reducing these differences. As Christopherson (1988) puts it, "the learning of gender roles . . . reflects one of the earliest and most profound focuses in the family socialization process" (p. 129). But are gender differences entirely a matter of social learning? Or are there basic biological differences between the sexes that make some gender differences inevitable?

Genetic Influences on Gender Roles

Clearly, biological sex is involved in the development of gender identity. There is also evidence that biology may influence some gender-role differences. If a difference is genetically based, argues Lynn (1974), it would (1) be displayed at a very young age, before other environmental forces could have influenced it; (2) be evident in a wide variety of cultures; (3) be seen among nonhuman primates; and (4) be related to the effects of hormones on masculinity and femininity.

All these criteria hold with respect to the greater aggressiveness of males than females. Males are more aggressive than females at an early age, a finding that is consistent in most cultures and also for nonhuman primates; and the injection of male hormones into pregnant mothers affects the subsequent aggressiveness of female children who were in utero at the time (Maccoby & Jacklin, 1980; Jacklin, 1989).

Cultural Models

Do not conclude, however, that the greater aggressiveness of males in our culture is inevitable given probable genetic differences in aggression. The influence of cultural factors cannot be discounted. For example, many occupations requiring physical aggression and strength have traditionally been restricted to males, whereas those requiring nonaggressive, passive, nurturant behavior have been considered more appropriate for women. The models society provides for children are clear. Children encounter them everywhere: on television, in books, in schools, on the playground. The message clearly is that certain behaviors, attitudes, and interests are appropriate—and inappropriate—for one's sex. And, as Connell (1985) notes, almost all the soldiers, police officers, wardens, admirals, bureaucrats, and politicians who control the machinery of collective violence are men—as are most murderers, rapists, muggers, and scoundrels.

Gender role messages are also highly apparent in the way parents treat their children—how they dress them, what toys they buy for them, what they expect of them, how they react to their displays of aggression and nurturance (Witt, 1997). In fact, the family is probably the greatest single socializing influence in the life of the preschooler (see *Concept Summary*).

THE FAMILY

"It takes a village to raise a child," goes the old African proverb, reflecting that in tribal Africa, the use of multiple caregivers is common (Corsaro, 1997). Among the Efe (pygmies) of Zaire, for example, infants are commonly cared for by most of the adult women of the community, many of whom nurse the child or try to soothe it when it needs comforting (Tronick, Morelli, & Winn, 1987).

Not so in North America. Here, we believe it takes a family to raise a child properly—or, at least, a loving caregiver or two. Our theories, and the conclusions of our research (which are, of course, based on our theories) convince us that it is very important for children and infants to have an opportunity to form a warm, loving, *secure* attachment to a principal caregiver.

But in North America, as in most of the world's societies, the family and the cultures in which families operate have changed enormously, and continue to do so. For example, not long ago, the "typical" North American family was the **nuclear family**— mother, father, and children (as opposed to the **extended family**, far more common throughout the world, which includes grandparents and assorted other relatives). Even as recently as 1980, for example, nearly 80% of all children under 18 in the United

CONCEPT
SUMMARY

Important Theories and Concepts in the Development of Gender Roles

Concept/Theory	Explanations/Comments
Gender Schema	Personal knowledge about the characteristics, behaviors, interests, and so on that define masculine and feminine
Freudian Gender Attainment Theory	The belief that gender schemas develop as a function of identifying with parents and resolving the Oedipus and Electra complexes
Social Learning Gender Attainment Theory	The belief that gender schemas result from the influence of models and the reinforcements that cultures provide regarding sex-appropriate behaviors
Kohlberg's Cognitive Gender Attainment Theory	The belief that gender schemas arise from the cognitive understanding of the meaning of gender identity, the development of gender constancy (the notion that gender is permanent, unchangeable), and the subsequent organization of interests and activities to conform with the appropriate gender roles
Gender Schema Theory	Recognizes that elements of both cognitive explanations (the child's growing understanding of the meaning of gender) and social learning explanations (the influence of models and reinforcements) shape gender roles
Gender Identity Disorder	Profound discomfort with one's anatomical sex
Gender Stereotypes	Fixed beliefs about behaviors and interests that are masculine or feminine
Gender Differences in Play	• Reflect basic cultural stereotypes; recognized by preschoolers at very young ages • Evident in the more physical, boisterous play of boys
Influences on Gender Roles	• Some evidence of genetic influences, especially in greater overt aggressiveness of males • Considerable evidence of strong cultural and familial influences

States lived in a two-parent family. By 1997, only about two-thirds were still in two-parent families. Among blacks, 64% lived in one-parent families in 1997 (U.S. Bureau of the Census, 1998). In Canada in 1997, about 13% of all families were one-parent families (*Canada Yearbook, 1999*). Hence the traditional two-parent definition of the North American family is no longer entirely general (Figure 8.5). Now families might be one- or two-parent; they might be intact or blended; they might be white, African American, Hispanic, or some other mix; they might be a gay or a lesbian family. But what we do know is that on average today's North American family is a less stable and a smaller family. Average family size has decreased from 3.67 in 1960 to 3.19 in 1997.

Not only is the family difficult to define, it is also very private and highly dynamic rather than static. The family is dynamic in that it changes with the addition of new members (and sometimes the loss of old ones), as well as in response to both external and internal pressures.

nuclear family A family consisting of a mother, a father, and their offspring.

extended family A large family group consisting of parents, children, grandparents, and occasionally uncles, aunts, cousins, and so on.

Given the family's privacy, researchers seldom have access to the most intimate aspects of its functioning. And given its dynamic nature, the relationships and influences within it do not expose themselves clearly and simply to the scrutiny of social scientists. Hence the family is difficult to research; there is much about which we can only speculate. (See *Across Cultures*: "Baruch, a Kibbutz Child.")

Parenting Styles

The family serves three principal functions in North American societies, says Westman (1991a): It has a sustenance function (to provide food, shelter, and clothing); it has developmental functions (through caregiving and parenting); and it has advocacy functions (through ensuring children's access to education, health care, a safe environment, and so on).

In Chapter 6 we saw that for infants the most important features of caregiving are attentiveness, physical contact, verbal stimulation, material stimulation, responsive care, and absence of restrictiveness. Recall that these are dimensions of sensitive parenting—parenting characterized by a high level of sensitivity to the child's emotions, and the constant adjustment of parental behaviors in response to these emotions (termed *affect synchrony*). Sensitive parenting is closely associated with what Baumrind (1967) describes as *authoritative parenting*—as opposed to parenting that can be described as *permissive* or *authoritarian*.

Permissive Parenting **Permissive parenting**, explains Baumrind, is a laissez-faire approach to parenting. Permissive parents allow children to make their own decisions and to govern their own activities. Such parents don't try to control through the exercise of the power that comes from authority, physical strength, status, or the ability to grant or withhold rewards; but they might, on occasion, try to appeal to children's reason.

There appear to be two different kinds of permissive parents (Maccoby & Martin, 1983). On one hand, there is *permissive indulgent parenting*; on the other, *permissive indifferent parenting*—also referred to as *neglectful parenting*. Permissive indulgent parents typically care a great deal about their children, but don't often attempt to exercise control over their behavior. Instead, they rely on their children to do the right things, to set their own limits. When their children make unwise decisions, they find it difficult to intervene, but are more likely to simply allow their children to behave as they please.

Permissive indifferent parents tend to be emotionally detached from their children—in contrast with permissive indulgent parents. They are permissive not because they expect—or particularly want—their children to do the right things, but more because they neglect them. As a result, they set few expectations or standards for their children.

Authoritarian Parenting In sharp contrast with permissive parenting, **authoritarian parenting** is grounded on firm and usually clearly identified standards of conduct, often based on religious or political beliefs. Authoritarian parents value obedience above all and exercise whatever power is necessary to make children conform. Children in authoritarian homes are neither given responsibility for personal decisions nor involved in rational discussion of the family's standards.

Authoritative Parenting Authoritative parenting falls somewhere between permissive and authoritarian control. It uses firm control but allows discussion of standards and expectations; it values obedience but tries to promote independence. Authoritative parenting sets clear standards and expectations for children, but in contrast with authoritarian parenting, the standards are derived more from reason than from religious or political beliefs (see Table 8.3).

---

permissive parenting A parenting style that may be characterized as "laissez-faire." Permissive parents are nonpunitive and undemanding. Their children are autonomous rather than obedient and, as such, are responsible for their own decisions and actions.

authoritarian parenting A highly controlling, dogmatic, obedience-oriented parenting style in which there is little recourse to reasoning and no acceptance of children's autonomy.

authoritative parenting A moderately controlling parenting style in which value is placed on independence and reasoning, but in which parents impose some regulations and controls.

Baruch, a Kibbutz Child*

Two days after he was born, Baruch and his mother returned from the hospital to the kibbutz. His mother went to the quarters she shared with her husband; little Baruch was put into the "infant house." For the first 6 weeks, Baruch's mother was available to nurse him "on demand." After that, he was put on a 4-hour schedule, although his mother continued to look after him at intervals during the day, with the help of his *metapelet*, an unrelated woman assigned to look after him.

At the age of 9 months, Baruch, like all other like-aged kibbutz infants, was given over almost entirely to the care of his metapelet. With the help of an assistant, Baruch's metapelet looked after five other children as well, playing with, washing, dressing, feeding, and talking to them. In short, these women, and often other children's metaplot (which is the plural of metapelet), did all the things a mother might do.

At the age of 15 months, Baruch was moved to the "toddler's house." A metapelet and her assistants continued to be responsible for all aspects of his care, interrupted only by short daily visits to his parents' home and by somewhat longer visits on Saturdays and Sundays.

At age 4, Baruch became a member of the kindergarten group. A teacher, along with two assistants, began to familiarize him and some 15 other students with the activities and chores of the kibbutz. The emphasis was on cooperation, group activities, and discipline.

For elementary school, Baruch was moved to a combined school/dormitory serving about 20 students. With three others he moved into a bedroom, acquired a new metapelet (responsible primarily for his physical care), and began to study in a clearly cooperative, noncompetitive setting.

Through all of this, Baruch was always a member of a group, although its composition changed from time to time. Until puberty, groups remained completely coeducational, with boys and girls sharing classrooms, bedrooms, even showers (although taboos prohibiting sexual exploration were always clear and strict).

Had Baruch been born more recently, his upbringing in the kibbutz might have been very different. There have been dramatic changes, note Rabin and Beit-Hallahmi (1982), in communal child-rearing in the kibbutz. There is now much closer contact between parents and children; in fact, they often sleep in the same quarters (this arrangement sometimes lasts until adolescence). In some cases, parents have become principal caregivers and socializers. Under these cir-

cumstances, "children's houses" serve more as day-care facilities than as the "multiple mothering" and socializing centers they traditionally were. In addition, many families have television sets, their own dining areas, even their own kitchens and refrigerators. Thus, the family is taking over many of the roles once given over to the commune.

*Based in part on Lieblich (1982), and Rabin & Beit-Hallahmi (1982).

To Think About: Historically, kibbutzim deemphasized the nuclear family at a time when most Western societies held it up as the child-rearing ideal. Now children in Western societies are increasingly exposed to aspects of "multiple caregiving" (through nonparental child care and through changing family structures); at the same time kibbutzim appear to be reemphasizing the role of the nuclear family. What do you think are the best features of each of these systems? Can they be combined? How do you suppose Baruch might turn out in a traditional kibbutz system? In one less traditional?

Resources:

Rabin, A. I., & Beit-Hallahmi, B. (1982). *Twenty years later: Kibbutz children grown up.* New York: Springer.

Lieblich, A. (1982). *Kibbutz Makom: Report from an Israeli kibbutz.* London: Andre Deutsch.

David Young-Wolff/PhotoEdit

In Kibbutzim, the nuclear family has historically played a relatively minor role in childrearing.

Table 8.3
Baumrind's Parenting Styles

STYLE	CHARACTERISTICS	EXAMPLES
Permissive	Laissez-faire; nonpunitive; child responsible for own actions and decisions; autonomy more important than obedience; nondemanding.	"Okay. I mean, sure. Whatever you want. You decide."
Indulgent	Care for children, but rely on them to do the right things; find it difficult to set limits.	"We love you, Ethan, and, well, if that's what you think you should do. . ."
Indifferent	Neglectful parenting; emotionally detached, uncaring.	"No, I don't have time to look at your report. And don't call me at work."
Authoritarian	Dogmatic; very controlling; obedience highly valued; self-control and autonomy limited; little recourse to reasoning.	"You're going to darn well study for 40 minutes right now. Then you say your prayers and go right to bed. Or else!"
Authoritative	Based on reason; permits independence but values obedience; imposes regulations, but allows discussion.	"Don't you think you should study for a while before you go to bed? We'd like you to get good grades. But you know we can't let you stay up that late. It isn't good for you."

Effects of Parenting Styles

Do parents really matter? And if so, which of these parenting styles is best?

The Freudian model says yes, parents matter a great deal because children are extremely sensitive to the emotional experiences of their early lives and especially to their relationships with their parents. The behavioristic model says yes, too, because children are highly responsive to the rewards and punishments of their environments. And science, insofar as research speaks for it, also says yes.

For example, Baumrind (1989) looked at the kinds of parenting associated with three distinct groups of children. One group consisted of buoyant, friendly, self-controlled, and self-reliant children; another, of discontented and withdrawn children; and a third, of children who lacked self-reliance and self-control. She found some consistent and striking differences among the parenting styles of the mothers and fathers of these children. Parents of the friendly, self-controlled, self-reliant children were significantly more controlling, demanding, and loving than parents of either of the other groups; in other words, their parenting styles tended to be *authoritative*. Parents of the discontented and withdrawn children also exercised much control but

were more detached and more autocratic; their parenting styles were *authoritarian*. And parents of the children low in self-esteem were sometimes warm, but also highly permissive.

Other research is in general agreement. For example, Lamb, Keterlinus, and Fracasso (1992) report that as adolescents, children raised by permissive indulgent parents tend to lack self-reliance and to have lower self-esteem. And Martin and Waite (1994) found that children prone to depression and to suicidal thoughts were highly likely to have been raised by indifferent and neglectful parents. Similarly, Allison et al. (1995) also found that among a sample of 156 Australian high school students, those most likely to be characterized by feelings of hopelessness and despair were also most likely to have perceived their parents as less caring (and often more critical, as well). Faulty parenting, insists Imbesi (1999) following experience with more than 100 cases of children in psychoanalytic treatment, lies at the root of most psychological disturbances.

In conclusion, says Baumrind (1993), much of the research suggests that in North America, authoritative parenting is associated with more positive outcomes; permissive (especially neglectful) parenting is associated with more negative outcomes.

A Caution

The foregoing conclusion should not be interpreted to mean that *authoritative* parenting is always preferable—or that neglectful parenting inevitably results in a significant increase in children's chances of maladjustment and unhappiness. It's true that retrospective studies (looking backward in time, often using interviews or questionnaires) with delinquent and otherwise disturbed adolescents and adults have generally found that their childhoods were marked by a variety of traumas—sometimes associated with alcoholic or abusive parents, poverty, rejection, and various other factors—and often included authoritarian and neglectful parenting. But when researchers try to predict which of a group of children will be maladjusted and which will be happy and well adjusted, they are often unsuccessful. Indeed, there are many very successful, well-adjusted individuals who were reared in home environments that should have placed them at high risk. Some children appear to be far more susceptible than others to environmental influences—perhaps for genetic reasons, says Belsky (1997).

Scarr (1997) argues that what matters most in determining child outcomes is the combined effect of parental characteristics and the sorts of environments parents provide for their children—rather than things such as quality of out-of-home child care or specific parenting styles. By early childhood, she reports, the effects of quality of child care are often no longer apparent—but the effects of parental characteristics continue to be (Scarr, 1998). By the *effects of parents*, however, Scarr doesn't mean *parenting* alone, but the combined influence of the environments parents provide and their genetic characteristics. Scarr's (1993) somewhat controversial view is that parents don't have to be "super parents"; they simply have to be "good enough." Her point is that as long as family and child relations are within a relatively normal range, *ordinary* differ-

ences in parenting practices won't have a measurable effect on eventual outcomes.

The emphasis, however, should be on the phrase *ordinary differences*. More extreme differences in parenting definitely can make a significant difference, as Scarr readily admits (1993). There is little doubt that neglectful parenting, for example, rather than concerned parenting, is more often associated with behavior problems and psychological disturbance. Thus, research has not clearly demonstrated that there is always only one best way of rearing children. But it does indicate that there are some general characteristics of parents, reflected in their behaviors and attitudes toward their children, that clearly have highly positive effects—and others that have negative effects, too.

Learning How to Parent

Some parents are probably better at parenting than others. In Cooke's (1991) terms, some are *novices* and some are *experts*. Experts are better at sensing children's needs and goals, especially in problem-solving situations. They have better general knowledge of child development and child-rearing; they have consciously thought about their roles and their goals; and they foster activity that provides their children with opportunities to be self-directive. How have they learned these things?

In many close-knit, nonindustrialized societies, the old ones show the young ones how to parent. There is evidence that at least to some extent, the same thing happens in our more complex, industrialized societies. Ijzendoorn (1993) surveyed a large number of parenting studies and found a significant amount of *intergenerational transmission* of parenting styles. It seems that we have a tendency to parent as did our own parents.

Sources of Child-Care Advice But not all parents simply rely on their own intuition, common sense, and intelligence, or on the transmitted wisdom of their parents and grandparents. Many others turn to one or more of the major groups of commercial child-care advisors: the medical profession, whose doctors and nurses readily provide advice relating to psychological as well as physical health; books; the World Wide Web; and parenting courses.

THOUGHT CHALLENGE: *How might the Scarr-McCartney model of gene environment interaction, described in Chapter 3, account for Scarr's view that good enough parenting need not be super parenting?*

Parenting Courses There are many widely established parent-education courses, most of which require relatively lengthy training and practice sessions. Some of these have proven especially valuable for children with learning and behavior problems (Thompson, Grow, & Ruma, 1993).

Parenting courses are almost invariably based on recognizing the rights of children and taking into consideration their needs and desires. They advocate treating children as important human beings and discourage punitive approaches to parental control (such as shouting, threatening, physical punishment, and anger-based behaviors), instead encouraging reasoning. The ultimate aim of most of these courses is to foster a warm, loving, and nurturant relationship between parent and child. And the principal method by which each of the various techniques operates involves communication.

In short, most parent education programs encourage parents to be authoritative (firm, democratic, reasonable, respectful) rather than authoritarian (harsh, controlling, demanding, dogmatic, powerful) or permissive (indulgent or neglectful; laissez-faire, noncontrolling, weak). In addition, they teach specific techniques to help parents become authoritative. The major weaknesses of these programs are often that the solutions they provide are too simple for the complexity of the problems that parents must occasionally deal with. The programs typically do not take into account important differences among children of different ages and of different sex; and they sometimes mislead parents into thinking that all answers are to be found in a single method (Brooks, 1981).

THOUGHT CHALLENGE: *William Cadogan, writing in 1748, declared:* It is with great Pleasure I see the preservation of Children become the Care of men of Sense. In my opinion this Business has been too long fatally left to the management of Women, who cannot be supposed to have a proper knowledge to fit them for the Task. *(Cited in Hardyment, 1983, p. 10). If Cadogan's view now seems to reflect a time of shocking ignorance and baseless sexism, what do you suppose science will be writing about us in another three centuries?*

◰ FAMILY COMPOSITION

The family, says Hoffman (1991), is a dynamic (changing) and interactive social unit. The experiences of siblings in the same family can be very different, depending not only on characteristics of the parents and the siblings but also on factors such as birth order, family size, and spacing of siblings.

Birth Order

About a century ago, Galton (1896) noticed that there was a preponderance of firstborn children among great British scientists. Since then, research has attributed many advantages to being the firstborn (or an only child). Among them are more rapid and more articulate language development, higher scores on measures of intellectual performance, higher scores on measures of achievement motivation, better academic performance, better peer relations, fewer symptoms of stress, more curiosity, a higher probability of going to college, and a higher probability of being a president—and, of course, a king or queen (see, for example, Gaynor & Runco, 1992; Pilkington, White, & Matheny, 1997).

There are several plausible explanations for the observed effects of birth order. Certainly, these effects are not due simply to being a firstborn, a middle, or a lastborn child. In White and associates' words, they result, instead, from "the pattern of behaviors and attitudes that emerge from family experiences" (1997, p. 89). What being firstborn means, says Marjoribanks (1997), is that the child is initially exposed to a family environment with "undiluted" resources. Siblings who come later are born into a family where the attentions of the parents are less focused on the only (and first) child, and their interactions with each child are different in subtle but highly important ways.

Family Size

In general, although things may be "cheaper by the dozen," the larger the family, the more limited the advantages to the children. In fact, many investigators report lower intelligence test scores among members of larger families (for example, Zajonc &

Mullally, 1997; Morand, 1999). Many of these same investigations also report distinct birth order effects. Thus the most advantaged individuals, *taken as a group*, are firstborn children in very small families (or, of course, *only* children who, by definition, are firstborn in the smallest of possible families). And the least advantaged are those born later, those born in very large families, and, as we see in a moment, those born in families where there is little spacing among siblings.

Zajonc's explanation of these findings takes the form of what he labels the **confluence model**. According to this model, homes are characterized by a measurable quality termed "intellectual climate." Intellectual climate is measured as follows: Each person in the family is assigned a value relating to age. Parents, for example, are given 30 points each, a newborn, 0, and other children, values ranging from 0 to 30 according to their ages. The average intellectual climate of the home is computed very simply by summing these values and dividing by the number of individuals in the family. Thus, a newborn child born into a two-parent family is born into a family with an intellectual climate of $(30 + 30 + 0)/3 = 20$. But had the child been a twin, the intellectual climate would have been five points lower $[(30 + 30 + 0 + 0)/4 = 15]$.

Put another way, a measure of intellectual climate reflects the many different home-based environmental factors that might contribute in important ways to the development of a child's intellect. Some examples are the nature and frequency of conversation with intelligent adults and older siblings; opportunity to interact with appropriate play and learning materials; guidance and assistance from more competent adults and older siblings, and so on. It follows from this model that the best home environment is the one with the greatest number of adults who interact with the child. The environment least conducive to intellectual development is one in which the family's resources are shared among a large number of siblings, causing what Marjoribanks (1997) refers to as *resource dilution*. Thus, Zajonc's *confluence model*

---

confluence model Zajonc's term for the hypothesis that various factors such as family size, birth order, and family spacing interact to determine the intellectual climate of the home, and have a profound influence on the intellectual development of children.

> **THOUGHT CHALLENGE:** *Many studies report higher average intelligence test scores for children from small families relative to those from larger families, especially with respect to measures of* verbal *intelligence. Should you also expect the same sorts of differences for measures of* emotional *intelligence? Why?*

takes into account not only birth order and family size, but also family spacing—that is, length of intervals between siblings.

Age Intervals

Family size and birth order, taken together, are important predictors of academic success, achievement, and even creativity; and the prediction becomes even more powerful if a third variable is introduced into the equation: that of *family spacing*, or age intervals. Simply put, children whose siblings are significantly younger or older seem to be at an advantage. Close spacing among siblings has repeatedly been found to be associated with intellectual disadvantages, and, occasionally, with peer adjustment and parent-child relation problems as well (Pilkington, White, & Matheny, 1997).

The influence of age intervals, like that of birth order and family size, is probably best explained by the sorts of family relationships and interactions that are most likely to result. A child whose siblings are much older or much younger is more likely than other children to be perceived by parents as special. Furthermore, on average, there may well be less dilution of resources in families where children are widely spaced. And, by definition, the measured intellectual climate in a home with closely spaced children becomes progressively lower with each new child. With multiple births, of course, the spacing is zero, and the index of intellectual climate is accordingly lower.

Some Cautions

Before we go running off bragging that we're firstborns or only children—or complaining that we're not—we should note that the contribution of birth order, family spacing, and family size to intelligence and academic achievement are not overwhelmingly high. Furthermore, there are many other crucial factors that a simple model like the *confluence model* doesn't take into account—not the least of which is the influence of genes. In addition, it's difficult to separate the effect of family size from the effects of social class, religion, or rural versus urban environment. Larger families are far more common among the poor, the culturally deprived, and certain ethnic minorities. When these factors are taken into account, socioeconomic status often emerges as a more important predictor of developmental outcomes than does family size or birth order (Freese, Powell, & Steelman, 1999).

Also, always bear in mind that the conclusions of our social sciences are usually based on the average performance of large groups of individuals. Within these groups, there are those whose behavior does not come close to matching the predictions that social science might make based on its conclusions. Thus there are saints and geniuses whose siblings numbered in the tens and twenties, all closely spaced; and there are poltroons and oafs who were born first into tiny little families.

DIVORCE, ONE-PARENT FAMILIES, AND STEPFAMILIES

Close to half of all American children are spending (or will spend) an average of six years in a family with only one parent. Most of these one-parent families are the result of separation or divorce, and most of them are headed by mothers rather than fathers (see *At a Glance:* "Family Living Arrangements of U.S. and Canadian Children" and Figure 8.5).

Effects of Loss of a Parent

There is considerable evidence that separation and divorce, or the death of one or both parents, is a difficult—sometimes traumatic—experience for most children. At the same time, in some cases divorce *is* the best outcome for children. Also, as we see later, there are indications that the effects of

divorce may be less negative now than they were some decades ago.

Research Findings Rodgers (1996) did a meta-analysis of a large number of studies that had looked at the effects of divorce. (A meta-analysis combines and analyzes the results of separate but related studies in an attempt to arrive at a single, valid conclusion.) He concludes that the negative effects of divorce have often been *understated*, and that they present as great a risk for children's mental health and happiness as other important early life factors. Others, such as Burns, Dunlop, & Taylor (1997), disagree with Rodger's conclusions. They suggest that the effects of divorce on child outcomes are very weak—that in fact the child's gender, father-child and mother-child relations, and father's occupation are by themselves better predictors of important child characteristics such as anxiety, depression, and self-concept.

That the effects of divorce might be relatively weak compared with those of other variables in the child's life does not make them unimportant (Rodgers, 1997). In fact, in a range of investigations dealing primarily with the effects of parental divorce on preschoolers, researchers concur that divorce has at least some negative effects on most children. Here are specific findings from some of this research:

▲ Much of the negative impact of divorce can be attributed to conditions that exist well before the divorce, rather than just to the divorce itself (Booth, 1999). Hence similar problems are often evident in to-be-divorced families as in just-divorced families (Shaw, Winslow, & Flanagan, 1999).

▲ The negative effects of divorce are sometimes evident in infants who display emotional distress by erratic feeding and sleeping routines, loss of toilet habits, bewilderment, and clinging behavior; in preschoolers as the loss of confidence and self-esteem and increased self-blame; and in older children as lingering sadness, truancy, and behavior problems (Wallerstein/Kelly, 1976, 1980; Oppawsky, 1999).

▲ Divorces characterized by a high level of conflict between parents, by disputes over custody rights, by interspousal violence, or by violence toward

AT A GLANCE **Family Living Arrangements of U.S. and Canadian Children**

As recently as 1970, more than 85% of U.S. children lived in a family with both parents present, and 11% lived with only their mothers. Now, only about two-thirds live with both parents. Among African-Americans, two-thirds live with only one parent—90% of them with their mother. The proportion of children living with neither parent has remained constant at about 3%. In Canada in 1997, about 13% of all families were one-parent families (U.S. Bureau of the Census, 1998; *Canada Yearbook, 1999*).

Laura Dwight/Photo Edit

Of children raised by only one parent, only about 1 in 20 is raised by the father.

FIGURE 8.5 Percent distribution in 1997 of family groups with children under 18 in the United States, by race, and in Canada. Source: Based on U.S. Bureau of the Census, 1998, p. 66 and *Canada Yearbook, 1999*, p. 201.

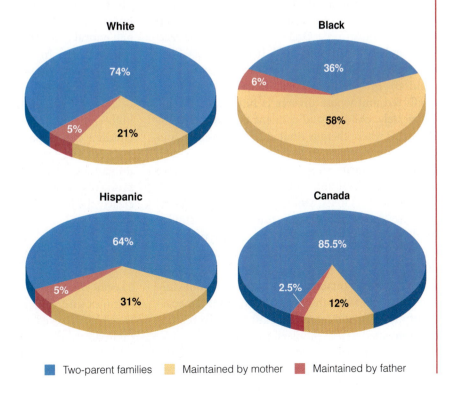

children lead to more immediate emotional distress in children and more adjustment problems later (Johnston, 1994; Ayoub et al., 1999).

▲ Even in adulthood, some negative effects of earlier parental divorce are often discernible in adjustment problems (Acock & Kiecolt, 1989).

▲ Long-range effects of parental divorce are also evident in a higher risk of early death among grown children of divorced parents (Tucker et al., 1997).

Why Might Divorce or Separation Have Negative Effects? Why should adults whose parents divorced when they were young be at higher risk of early mortality? Following an analysis of data involving more than 1,200 adults (from the Terman study of giftedness), Tucker and associates (1997) found that several factors contributed significantly to the earlier average mortality of adults whose parents had divorced: a higher probability of eventual divorce among both men and women, lower educational levels among men, and more smoking among the women. Each of these factors appears to be associated with earlier mortality.

Other research suggests that there are two strong predictors of negative effects on children whose parents divorce. One is the nature of the relationship between parents, both before and after the divorce. As we saw, negative outcomes are worse for children of parents whose marriage is highly conflicted and whose divorce is bitter and hostile. Conversely, children's adjustment to divorce seems far better where there is limited family conflict; and where parents continue to communicate with each other, both during and after the divorce, and are able to make amicable child custody and support arrangements (Linker, Stolberg, & Green, 1999).

The second important predictor of adjustment to divorce is the nature of the interaction that occurs between the child and the caretaking parent after the divorce. Following a comparison of 99 divorced and 99 intact families with preschool children, Pett and associates (1999) found that the quality of mother-child interaction after the divorce was closely related to preschoolers' adjustment.

Also potentially important in determining the impact of divorce on children are its economic implications. We know that the economic circum-
stances of one-parent families are, on average, considerably less advantageous than those of two-parent families. In both Canada and the United States, the average income in mother-headed homes is only about 60% that of father-headed homes—and only 40% that of two-parent homes. More telling, almost half of single-mother families are below the poverty level, compared with only 7% of married couples with children (U.S. Bureau of the Census, 1998; *Canada Yearbook, 1999*). The change from relative affluence to poverty can be enormously difficult for children, many of whose peers now become significantly more advantaged. Poverty also increases the risk of trouble with the law and reduces the probability of finishing school and obtaining good employment.

Family Conflict

As we saw earlier, children whose parents go through a conflict-filled divorce, and whose battles continue after divorce, are more likely to suffer negative consequences. Smith, Berthelsen, and O'Connor (1997) report that 42% of the 54 preschoolers in their study of children living in homes characterized by spousal violence exhibited behavioral problems serious enough to require intervention. In fact, one of the most striking findings was revealed in Amato and Keith's (1991) summary of a large body of research on the effects of divorce. The authors found that children living in high-conflict but intact families fared *less well* than children whose parents had divorced. Children in high-conflict families manifested more adjustment difficulties, lower self-esteem, and more behavior problems. For some children, parental divorce is clearly the best solution.

Parental Disengagement

Marital disruption and its effect on children is a complex and difficult subject. There are too many variables involved for us to identify them easily, lay them flat on the tables of our reason, see their interrelatedness, and understand them clearly. Even our simplest summaries remain in need of further summarizing and simplification.

Peterson, Leigh, and Day (1984) provide an approach that separates the variables involved and examines their interaction. It's an approach that looks at the relationship between degree of parental disengagement and children's social competence. Degree of parental disengagement ranges from varying levels of marital discord through temporary separation, long-term separation, divorce, and death; children's social competence is defined by their ability "to engage in social relationships and possess adaptive psychological qualities" (Peterson, Leigh, & Day, 1984, p. 4).

In examining the relationship of these two variables—parental disengagement and children's social competence—Peterson and colleagues (1984) take into account much of the wealth of research in this area and reduce it to a handful of conclusions:

▲ The higher the degree of disengagement, the greater the impact on children. In other words, divorce is generally more stressful than temporary separation. Similarly, a situation in which one of the parents breaks all ties with the child is more stressful than one where both parents continue to maintain close ties with the child.

▲ The severity of the immediate crisis brought about by the divorce is closely related to the negative impact of divorce. Children who have been abused or neglected by a parent are less likely to view the divorce as a very serious calamity and are likely to experience a lower degree of stress.

▲ The more accurate the child's perception of the parents' relationship before marital breakup, the less negative the consequences. Children who incorrectly view their parents' relationship as "happy" immediately before separation or divorce suffer the greatest stress.

▲ The more positive and amicable the parents' relationship following the marriage breakup, the less negative the effect on the child.

▲ The closer the relationship between the leaving parent and the child before marital breakup, the more serious the effect on the child.

▲ Age is related to the severity of consequences in a curvilinear fashion, with the most serious consequences occurring for children between the ages of 3 and 9 and the least severe occurring before and after those ages.

The Changing Impact of Divorce

Note that the Terman studies, which reveal a rather frightening relationship between divorce and longevity, began about 7 decades ago. For a variety of reasons, divorce appears to have been a far more negative event in the days of our parents and grandparents than it is today. In fact, in Rodgers's (1996) meta-analysis of divorce effects, the oldest studies consistently reported greater negative effects. More recent studies, as we have noted, often report much weaker effects. In Burns, Dunlop, and Taylor's (1997) words, "Our data suggest that not all children of divorced families suffer adverse consequences." Their point is that the emphasis should be on identifying children who are most likely to experience negative effects, and on preventing or lessening these effects.

Why would divorce have had more negative effects some decades ago than it does now? One possible reason is that some of the earlier research may have been flawed. Demo (1993), for example, argues that much of the research failed to take into consideration the predivorce status of the children involved.

A second reason for the less negative conclusions of more recent research, suggests Kurdek (1993), is that these conclusions have often reflected an unacknowledged bias toward the traditional family structure, and a pervasive negative attitude toward divorce.

A third reason may be because divorces in the 1950s and 1960s were less common, less culturally acceptable, and more difficult to arrange. Consequently, both children and parents had to cope with more disapproval, and were provided with less support. Mothers found it more difficult to arrange for satisfactory child care, and to obtain the kind of employment that gave them both the time and money for their child-caring commitments.

Interpreting the Research

Several dangers are implicit in interpreting studies such as those just described. One is that our conclusions might inadvertently stress either the negative or the positive aspects of divorce. Although divorce is often a trying time for children, living in conflict (and sometimes with physical and mental abuse) can also be very trying. At a certain point, family conflict in the intact home may have negative effects on children far greater than the potentially negative effects of divorce. Before that point is reached, divorce often is the best solution for parents as well as their children. It bears repeating that some loving single parents can effectively overcome whatever trauma might be associated with the loss of one parent; and there are countless two-parent families in which parenting is inadequate and love is seldom if ever shown.

Much of the current emphasis in this area is no longer on establishing whether divorce and separation have negative effects, and how pervasive and serious these might be. Rather, an increasing number of researchers are trying to uncover the characteristics of postdivorce parenting, and of child and family support, that are most likely to prevent or lessen negative consequences of marital dissolution. For example, Baris and Garrity (1997) suggest that parents who plan their divorce in order to lessen conflict and stress and to provide for continued co-parenting are least likely to have children who are negatively affected.

Most children (and parents) adapt to life in a single-parent home within two or three years of the initial disruption. Richards and Schmiege (1993) interviewed 71 single parents. They found that money was the number-one problem for mothers; conflict with the ex-spouse was a greater problem for men. Both men and women reported that parenting became easier over time. However, at about the time that adjustment to life in the one-parent family seems almost complete, remarriage often occurs. And that, too, can require major readjustments.

Children in Stepfamilies

About half of all first marriages in the United States now end in divorce. For example, in 1996 there were 8.8 marriages and 4.3 divorces per 1,000 population (U.S. Bureau of the Census, 1998). And about half of those who divorce remarry within 5 years. As a result, about half of all American children spend at least some time in a one-parent family. And about one fourth of all children will live with at least one stepparent before adulthood (Mason & Mauldon, 1996).

A stepfamily is the family grouping that results from the remarriage of a widowed or divorced parent. Consequently, only one of the two married adults in the new family is the child's biological parent. Stepfamilies are no more enduring than first marriages; about 60% end in divorce (Pill, 1990). In addition, remarriages in which there are stepchildren are more likely to dissolve than if there are no children, especially if the children are older—above 9 (Visher & Visher, 1996).

Problems in Stepfamilies

There is little doubt that parenting can be considerably more difficult in stepfamilies. For one thing, the roles of stepparents and stepchildren are not nearly as clear as they are in intact families. And as Fine, Coleman, and Ganong (1998) discovered, children and their stepparents sometimes have very different perceptions of what these roles should be. In their investigation of 40 stepfamilies, Fine and colleagues found that both the stepparent and the biological parent tended to view the stepparent's role as an active, parenting role. In contrast, stepchildren saw the stepparent's role as more of a "friend" role. Of course, there was the least conflict within these families when there was the greatest agreement about stepparents' roles.

Another factor that complicates stepparenting concerns the enormous number of complex relationships that can result from remarriage. For example, the marriage of a man and woman who have both been married previously, and who both have children, can create a staggering number of new relationships. These include the biological relatives of each of the stepparents, not to mention previous spouses and their parents, siblings, uncles, aunts, and cousins. In addition, considerable legal ambiguity surrounds the rights and obligations of stepparents and stepchildren, especially in cases where the stepfamily breaks up (Mason & Mauldon, 1996).

The remarriage of the parent in a one-parent family sometimes brings new problems for a child who has already had to cope with the initial disruption of the family through death or divorce and must now cope with another reorganization of the family. The parent almost invariably sees remarriage as a highly positive event because it reestablishes an important relationship. But the child often sees it as a loss because it implies a change in the relationship between the child and the natural parent. Many children experience feelings of abandonment following the remarriage of a parent (Kaiser, 1996).

In addition to the loss, real or imagined, of some of the biological parent's attention and perhaps affection, the stepchild must now also deal with establishing new relationships with the stepparent, with stepsiblings if there are any, and perhaps with a new set of grandparents and other relatives. Furthermore, the stepchild's role in the family often changes. This can be particularly difficult for adolescent children. Their newly developed adult roles, sometimes accelerated by the absence of the parent, can be severely disrupted by the appearance of a new stepparent (for example, the boy has become "man of the house" following his biological father's departure). Similarly, the creation of a new stepfamily can disrupt established patterns of control and discipline and sometimes lead to serious problems ("You're not my dad! I don't have to listen to you!").

Other possible problems sometimes associated with the stepfamily include sexual fantasies and inclinations between stepsiblings as well as between children and their stepparents (and resulting feelings of guilt and confusion); stepsibling rivalry and competition; ambivalence about the stepchild's role in the family; confusion over whether and how the departed parent should continue to fit into the child's life; and the need for the child to abandon the fantasy or wish that the natural parents might one day be reunited. These problems, report Ganong et al. (1999), tend to be aggravated in situations where the noncustodial parent competes for the attention and affection of the child.

The Positive Side

On the other hand, Ganong and associates found that the problems of stepparenting tend to be lessened where stepparents adopt what they label affinity-seeking strategies—that is, strategies designed to establish friendship and closeness with the stepchild. In their study of stepfamilies, they found that stepparents were most likely to be successful in establishing warm relations with the stepchild if they began using these strategies before the marriage, and continued afterward. Also, say Wark and Jobalia (1998), the most successful stepparents are those who understand that they can't have "instant closeness" with their stepchildren, that developing close relationships takes time and effort.

Fortunately, the effects of stepfamilies on children are often highly positive. The fairy-tale stereotype of the stepfather or stepmother as the wicked wielder of terrible powers is, in fact, a fairy tale. Clearly, many stepparents are kind and considerate people who want to love and be loved by their stepchildren. When the initial adjustments have been made, the stepchild might, in many cases, be as fortunate as many in intact nuclear families.

NONPARENTAL CAREGIVERS

In the old days, most North American children spent their preschool years with their mothers. Today an increasing number of children are cared for during the day by others. In fact, child care by someone other than a parent is now the norm for more than 50% of all American preschool children—a percentage that is climbing (Clarke-Stewart, Gruber, & Fitzgerald, 1994).

Nonparental child care takes various forms, ranging from situations in which families can afford to hire a private, in-the-child's-home caregiver to substitute for the mother during her absence, to institutionalized centers for large numbers of children with many caregivers. Most common, however, are private homes that look after perhaps a half-dozen youngsters—referred to as family child care. About half of all children are cared for by grandparents or other relatives (Hofferth, 1992).

In addition to arranged care for children, there are self-supervised or **latchkey children**, so called because their parents sometimes hang keys around the children's necks so they can let themselves into their homes after school. Some studies report that self-supervision is sometimes associated with more behavior problems (Vandell & Ramanan, 1991).

---

latchkey children Label for children who return (from schools, playground, gym, or wherever) to caretakerless homes. So called because parents sometimes hang their home keys around children's necks so that they are less likely to lose them.

Many find no measurable difference between self-supervised children and those who are looked after by their parents.

General Effects of Child Care

Given the proliferation of nonparental child care, it's important to ask whether it is as good for infants and preschoolers as parental care, and what the characteristics of good child care are. There is no lack of research. The early emphasis in much of this research was to determine whether infants and preschoolers cared for by someone other than their mother might suffer harmful consequences relating to difficulties in forming secure attachments with their mother. In spite of this largely negative orientation, a review of several dozen early studies found few significant differences in social, intellectual, and motor development between child-care and home-care children (Bronfenbrenner, Belsky, & Steinberg, 1977). More recent research has generally corroborated these findings. As Bowman (1993) puts it, "In general, nonfamily care and education have not been found to jeopardize the development of young children" (p. 109). In fact, the opposite may well be true. For example, in several investigations where child-care providers have been trained to be more sensitive to preschoolers, measures of the security of infant attachments to their mothers have actually increased (Howes, Galinsky, & Kontos, 1998).

The research also indicates that although family-based child care and center-based care are often quite different, neither appears to be superior (Shpancer, 1998). It also indicates that parents tend to have biases about which is preferable for children: home care or nonparental child care. And their biases, report Shpancer and Britner (1995), are often in the direction of parental home care. In one investigation, Erwin and Kontos (1998) found that most mothers tend to favor whatever they have themselves experienced with their children. Thus, when mothers were asked to rate two hypothetical children, one cared for at home and the other out of the home, those who had used child care rated the out-of-home child higher. Those who had kept their own children at home rated the home child higher.

Characteristics of High-quality Child Care

Child-care research now often focuses on the characteristics of programs that seem to have the most positive effects on children (for example, Shpancer, 1998). It is no surprise that this research reveals that children who are most in need are most likely to benefit from high-quality child care. For example, Caughy, DiPietro, and Strobino (1994) looked at the effects of nonparent child care among 867 5- and 6-year-old children. Children from the more impoverished homes in the sample typically fared better on later tests of reading and arithmetic, especially if they had been placed in child care before the age of 1, and also when the child care occurred in a center rather than in a private home.

How can parents determine what is likely to be good or bad child care? Clarke-Stewart, Gruber, & Fitzgerald (1994) suggest that these are some characteristics of high-quality child care:

▲ Qualified caregivers. That is, caregivers who have the training and the inclination to provide children with the sorts of experiences that are conducive to intellectual and social growth.

▲ A well-designed program that offers educational and social experiences not readily available in the home.

▲ Low caregiver-child ratio, so that there is a high degree of interaction between each child and caregivers.

▲ An environment that is not highly discipline oriented. In the Clarke-Stewart, Gruber, & Fitzgerald (1994) study, children who received less discipline (in the sense of fewer demands, less control, less punishment, more choices, and more responsibility for responses) were more advanced cognitively, more obedient, and more likely to get along with peers.

▲ Ample opportunity for interaction with peers. An advantage of care centers that cater to mixed-age groups is that they provide opportunities for younger children to interact with older children (Dunn, Kontos, & Potter, 1996).

▲ A stimulating physical setting.

▲ A high degree of agreement between parents' and caregivers' goals and beliefs about children and child care.

Poorer quality child-care programs are easily recognized, note Endsley and Bradbard (1981), by the characteristics they have in common. These might include unsanitary and unhealthful physical surroundings, obvious physical hazards, excessive overcrowding, high adult-child ratios (exceeding 1 to 20 or, in the case of infants, 1 to 10), lack of activities and materials that are interesting and challenging to young children, untrained staff who are at best thoughtless and insensitive and at worst reject and abuse young children, and disregard for parents' feelings about child rearing (p. 32). Interestingly, parents who are most satisfied with their child-care arrangements are those whose child rearing practices and beliefs are reflected in the child-care facility (Britner & Phillips, 1995).

Licensing requirements for establishing child-care facilities vary tremendously throughout North America, and are usually nonexistent for smaller, family-based centers (Hernandez & Myers, 1993). As a result, although many high-quality facilities are available, there are others whose environments are of far lower quality. To evaluate these facilities, Endsley and Bradbard (1981) suggest that parents should obtain personal references, and perhaps most important, visit the centers, observe them in operation, and talk with the people in charge. Unfortunately, however, some of us are likely to spend more time looking, comparing, and obtaining references when buying a car than when finding someone to care for our children.

MAIN POINTS

Emotional Development and Emotional Intelligence
By the age of 9 months, infants can interpret emotions in others and are capable of self- and other-directed regulatory behaviors. Later in the preschool period they begin to learn emotional display rules, but are not always successful in controlling their expressions of emotion. In their teasing, their use of intention (or lack thereof) as excuses for misbehaviors, and their growing ability to distinguish between the real and the pretend, young children begin to show evidence of an understanding of others' states of mind (theory of mind).

Emotional intelligence is a fundamental aspect of social competence, highly dependent on age-appropriate abilities relating to interpreting, controlling, and expressing emotions.

Processes of Socialization
Erikson's stage theory of social development describes the resolution of psychosocial conflicts through the development of competence. In the preschool stage, initiative versus guilt, children develop a sense of control and responsibility for their actions. Bandura explains social learning through imitation of models, many of which are symbolic. Imitation may account for people's tendency to cooperate or to compete, which is highly influenced by our immediate culture.

Play
The two broad categories of children's play are practice (or sensorimotor) play (mainly physical activity, useful in developing and exercising important physical skills) and pretend play (or imaginative play, such as daydreaming or imaginary playmates, importantly related to cognitive development). These can be social, in which two or more children interact, or solitary. Social play underlies personality development and the development of social skills. It may be onlooker play (watching without joining in), parallel play (play side by side but not together), associative play (children play together physically but do not share rules or goals), or cooperative play (children share rules and roles).

Gender Roles in Early Childhood
Gender roles are the range of behaviors considered appropriate for males and females and the personality characteristics that define masculinity and femininity. Gender schemas are children's knowledge

about gender roles. Gender typing is the learning of sex-appropriate behavior. A three-stage cognitive explanation for gender typing involves (1) recognizing basic gender identity (maleness or femaleness); (2) realizing that gender is stable, permanent, and unchangeable; and (3) realizing that superficial changes (such as in dress or behavior) do not change gender.

Gender identity disorders are sometimes evident in situations where children are uncomfortable with their anatomical sex. Genetic influences on gender differences are especially evident in the greater aggressiveness of males. Family-based influences are reflected in the fact that most parents treat boys and girls differently, reflecting prevailing cultural stereotypes. Thus they encourage aggression, independence, and boisterousness in boys and reward nurturant, affective, compliant behavior in girls.

The Family

A nuclear family consists of mother, father, and children; extended families also include a variety of other blood relatives. The family has sustenance, developmental, and advocacy functions. Baumrind's parenting styles are permissive indulgent (caring but nonpunitive, noncontrolling, nondemanding), permissive indifferent (neglectful, uncaring, detached, and uncontrolling), authoritarian (dogmatic, controlling, obedience oriented), and authoritative (firm but based on reason, nondogmatic, geared toward promoting independence but encouraging adherence to standards).

It is difficult to predict future adjustment and personality characteristics of children on the basis of what might be known about the child-rearing practices of their parents. However, in North American societies, authoritative parenting style may be preferable to either a permissive or authoritarian style. Neglectful parenting may be linked with behavioral and psychological problems. Important sources of child-care advice are the medical profession, books, the Web, and parenting courses.

Family Composition

There is a tendency for firstborn and only children to achieve better in school, score higher on tests of intellectual performance, and develop language facility sooner. Children from larger families do less well on average than children from smaller families on measures of intellectual performance. Other things being equal, the more closely spaced the family, the greater the disadvantage to children. These effects are largely attributable to the most likely interactions and relationships in the family and to related socioeconomic factors.

Divorce, One-Parent Families, and Stepfamilies

Some negative effects of divorce may be related to conditions that existed before the divorce. These negative effects are sometimes evident in emotional distress, disruption in feeding and sleeping routines among infants, loss of self-esteem and increased self-blame in preschoolers, and in lingering sadness and behavior or emotional problems at all ages. High-conflict divorces (before, during, and following separation) tend to have more negative outcomes.

Some effects of one-parent families on children may be due to the lack of a parent. They may also be due to altered economic conditions, changed interaction with the remaining parent, the degree of parental disengagement with the child, and other factors. Recent research finds less negative effect than did earlier research.

Divorce sometimes affects children's social competence (adjustment and relationships). The severity of the effect relates to children's sex (more severe for males), children's age (more severe between ages 3 and 9 than before and after that period), the accuracy of children's perception of the parents' previous relationship, the severity of the immediate crisis, and the parents' relationship following marital breakup (the more positive the relationship, the less serious the consequences).

Stepchildren sometimes face problems relating to loss (real or imagined) of some of the biological parent's time and affection; establishing new relationships with the stepparent, stepsiblings, and others; coping with stepsibling rivalry; dealing with new sexual inclinations and fantasies; and abandoning the fantasy that the biological parents might one day be reunited.

Nonparental Caregivers

About 50% of North American preschoolers spend time in child-care facilities. In general, child care does not have detrimental effects on the social, emotional, and intellectual development of children, especially with high-quality child care (characterized by high staff-children ratios, adequate equipment and materials, trained and caring staff, and adequate financial resources).

Focus Questions: Applications

1. What do preschoolers understand of what others feel? Can you explain why it is that young children are so easily moved to tears? And to laughter?
2. Of what importance is play in childhood?
   - Observe children playing in a park or playground. Categorize the play you observe as practice or pretend, solitary or social. Can you make even more detailed analyses of the types of imaginary or social play you observed?
3. To what extent are masculinity and femininity determined by our genes?
   - Identify two or three arguments for and against the proposition that gender is largely biologically determined.

4. What differences does parenting make? Family size? Position in the family? Age differences among siblings?
   - What is your position in your family? Was that important to who you are? Why?
5. How significant is the loss of a parent?
   - Using library resources, write a paper on the effects of parental death on children of different ages.
6. Is nonparental child care as good as parental care?
   - Develop a checklist of the most important dimensions of quality child care—the sorts of things a parent might find useful when choosing a child-care facility.

Possible Responses to Thought Challenges

Thought Challenge, page 345

As we saw in Chapter 3, a large number of sex-linked genetic defects are manifested in male but not female offspring. The known presence of one or more of these defects in the mother's family might be a good reason to wish for a female child.

Thought Challenge, page 355

Recall that the Scarr-McCartney model describes how the genotypes of both parents and child interact and affect the environment. Accordingly, Scarr's focus is more on the larger, evolutionary picture—on questions having to do with how children adapt to function in society, rather than on questions having to do with differences among individuals. Her argument is that the effects of genotypes on environments are strong enough that a wide range of variations in parenting—and in nonparental child care—are not likely to have very noticeable effects.

Thought Challenge, page 356

Imagine, at the turn of the last millennium, anyone who wanted to was actually permitted to produce offspring (using the Old Method, no less) *no matter what their genetic or psychological profile*!!! And, amazing and horrifying as it sounds, biological parents were permitted—no, they were *expected*—to crèche these humanoids in their very domiciles *without* Motherworld's supervision! . . .

Thought Challenge, page 357

The answer is no, says Morand (1999). Following an investigation of 41 participants, he reports exactly the opposite: There is a tendency for measures of emotional intelligence to be *higher* in larger families. This, given the nature of emotional intelligence, makes sense because in large families, siblings have many opportunities to interact with others and to develop the skills of emotional intelligence (defined as a type of social competence reflected in high levels of emotional self-knowledge and self-control, as well as the ability to discern and empathize with others' emotional states).

Key Terms

androgynous, 347	gender constancy, 346	onlooker play, 342
associative play, 342	gender identity, 346	parallel play, 342
authoritatian parenting, 352	gender identity disorder, 347	permissive parenting, 352
authoritative parenting, 352	gender schema theory, 347	primitive social play, 342
basic gender understanding, 346	gender schemas, 347	prosocial display rules, 332
confluence model, 357	hermaphrodite, 348	self-protective display rules, 332
emotional display rules, 332	imaginative play, 339	sensorimotor play, 339
emotional intelligence, 334	introjection, 346	social play, 342
emotions, 330	latchkey children, 363	socialization, 334
extended family, 351	metacognotion, 341	solitary play, 342
gender, 344	nuclear family, 351	

Further Readings

In the first of the following two books, the Wolfgangs present a large number of highly practical suggestions for educational and play activities geared specifically to the capabilities and interests of preschoolers. Of special relevance to this chapter are the three chapters (2, 3, and 4) that deal with play. The second book also presents many useful ideas for organizing preschoolers' play:

Wolfgang, C. H., & Wolfgang, M. E. (1999). *School for young children: Developmentally appropriate practices* (2nd ed.). Boston: Allyn & Bacon.

Hoorn, J. V., Scales, B., Nourot, P. M., & Alward, K. R. (1999). *Play at the center of the curriculum* (2nd ed.). Upper Saddle River, NJ: Prentice Hall.

A fascinating historical account of the nature of toys through history, and of twentieth-century changes in the production and marketing of toys, as well as their importance in the lives of children, is presented in:

Cross, G. (1997.) *Kids' stuff: Toys and the changing world of American childhood.* Cambridge, Mass.: Harvard University Press.

Paley's books offer fascinating, often delightful descriptions of life in the preschool period. The first of these short books follows 3-year-old Mollie through a year of nursery school, revealing her excitement and her fears in the little dramas that are an intrinsic part of Paley's classes. The second follows the lives of a kindergarten class, providing insights into how children struggle to arrive at their own understanding of what it means to be a boy or a girl. And the third is a sensitive and exceptionally well-written account of observations of young children at play:

Paley, V. G. (1984). *Boys and girls: Superheroes in the doll corner.* Chicago: University of Chicago Press.

Paley, V. G. (1986). *Mollie is three: Growing up in school.* Chicago: University of Chicago Press.

Paley, V. G. (1997). *The girl with the brown crayon.* Cambridge, Mass.: Harvard University Press.

The following is a collection of articles that explore the many ways in which parents, communities, and schools interpret and shape gender:

Yelland, N. (Ed.) (1998). *Gender in early childhood.* New York: Routledge.

Corsaro's book is a useful look at the history of childhood, and at how childhood is defined and shaped by the cultures in which children find themselves:

Corsaro, W. A. (1997). *The sociology of childhood.* Thousand Oaks, Calif.: Pine Forge Press.

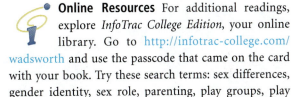 **Online Resources** For additional readings, explore *InfoTrac College Edition,* your online library. Go to http://infotrac-college.com/wadsworth and use the passcode that came on the card with your book. Try these search terms: sex differences, gender identity, sex role, parenting, play groups, play behavior in animals.

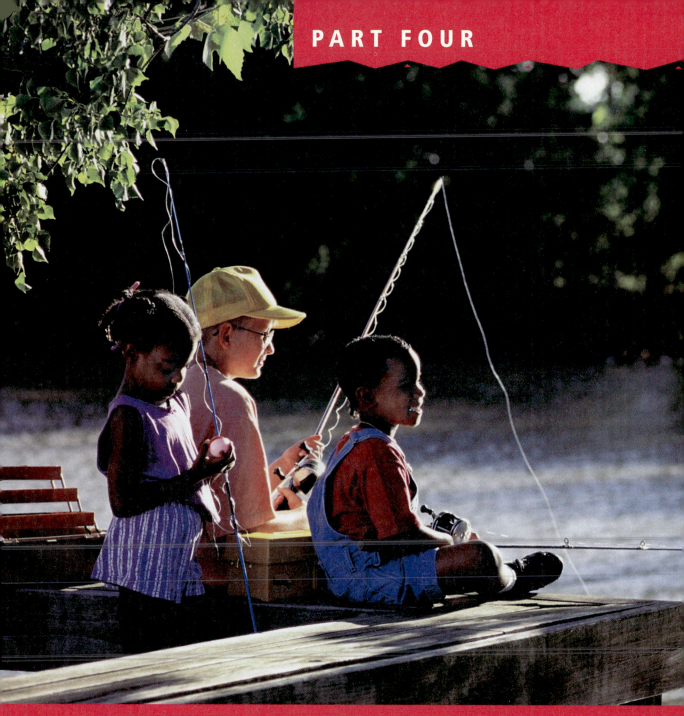

PART FOUR

Sweet childish days, that were as long
As twenty days are now.
William Wordsworth, "To a Butterfly"

Middle Childhood

Do you recollect some "sweet childish days"? For example, do you remember the long days of summer with pleasure? Do you remember childhood fantasies where trees were giants, butterflies wore shimmering coats of dazzling colors, and birds warbled startling songs you can no longer hear?

It is a sadness to see the days shrink so, to find the seasons whirling mindlessly on each other's heels, to sense the years slip away. To think there was once time to kill.

> "What are you doing here?" growled the watchdog.
> "Just killing time," replied Milo apologetically. "You see. . ."
> "Killing time!" roared the dog—so furiously that his alarm went off. "It's bad enough wasting time without killing it." And he shuddered at the thought.
>
> Norton Juster, *The Phantom Tollbooth*

"Time to kill"—such a senseless phrase. Even children have better things to do with time than trying to kill it—things like learning about the fine, concrete logic that explains the world; about elegant strategies for remembering important things, and trivial ones too; about how valuable the self is, and how important friends are. These are the subjects of the next two chapters. As you read them, it might be worthwhile to stop and wonder whether the trees that crowd the forest are as tall to a 12-year-old as to a 6-year-old, whether the butterflies are as brilliant, and the birds' songs as stunning.

Do you think there might be some way that we, like children, can put more than 24 hours of living between each rising sun?

"Well," said the boy, "in my family everyone is born in the air, with his head at exactly the height it's going to be when he's an adult, and then we all grow toward the ground."

Norton Juster, *The Phantom Tollbooth*

Physical and Cognitive Development in Middle Childhood

Robert Brenner/PhotoEdit

CHAPTER 9

Because of where I lived, I was young before television, even before electricity, in the days of long, long nights of winter darkness. During those nights, I read all the books I could find. Some of them, like Juster's *Phantom Tollbooth* or Lewis Carroll's *Alice in Wonderland* and *Through the Looking Glass*, drew me back over and over again. These books, and others like Antoine de Saint-Exupéry's *The Little Prince*, are so exquisitely imaginative and insightful that even as a cynical old grown-up, I still go back and read them now and again.

Which I did again last night, in the middle of an early winter storm when the icy wind hurried me indoors and made me nostalgic. And I stumbled across the passage quoted on the opposite page, where Milo, the boy whose phantom tollbooth has transported him into a wonderful magic world, has just met Alec, a boy whose feet are 3 feet above the ground.

"There are a few of us," says Alec, "whose feet never reach the ground, no matter how old we get."

Then he adds, "You certainly must be very old to have reached the ground already."

"Oh no," says Milo seriously. "In my family, everybody starts on the ground and grows up and nobody knows how far until they actually get there."

"What a silly system," the boy laughs. "Then your head keeps changing its height and you always see things in a different way? Why, when you're fifteen things won't look at all the way they did when you were ten, and at twenty everything will change again.

"We always see things from the same angle," the boy continues. "It's much less trouble that way."

1. Are North American children in good physical condition?
2. How does Piaget describe development through middle childhood?
3. What memory model underlies current views of information processing?
4. What is intelligence? How do we measure it? How important is it?
5. What are the dimensions of intellectual exceptionality?

PHYSICAL AND MOTOR DEVELOPMENT

The fact is, as Alec so cleverly deduced, we don't always see things from the same angle. "When you're fifteen," he says, "things won't look at all the way they did when you were ten."

It might be wise to keep this thought in mind as you read this chapter—that is, keep in mind that the schoolchild's head is not where yours is. It's not just a matter of physical growth—it's perhaps more a matter of intellectual change—the fact that their intellectual feet are still not firmly grounded. Too, their heads may be closer to the clouds. And perhaps that's why they see magic more clearly than we adults do.

Those of us whose feet have long since reached the ground might not always see everything there is to see.

Physical Growth

For example, we easily assume that, with few exceptions, physical growth is much the same among all children throughout the world. But the fact is that the physical development of many of the world's children is neither normal nor optimal. This may occur because of inadequate diet or sometimes simply because of lack of exercise, bad nutrition, overeating, or undereating. As we saw in Chapter 5, some 40% of children in the world's most undeveloped countries are significantly underweight, 10% suffer from wasting (abnormally low weight for their height), and an alarming 47% suffer from moderate to severe stunting (abnormally short

stature). In North America, as we see shortly, the most serious problem of physical development is far more likely to be obesity than stunting or wasting.

Normal Growth Curves Although girls tend to be slightly shorter and lighter than boys from birth until the end of the preschool period, the shapes of the growth curves for each are almost identical; that is, both sexes gain at approximately the same rate. But this pattern begins to change in middle childhood, so that the average girl—who is ¾ inch (2 cm) shorter at age 6—has caught up with and surpassed the average boy by the age of 11 and is still slightly taller at the age of 12 (see Figure 9.1).

In weight, girls are close to 2 pounds (1 kg) lighter at age 6; but again, they catch up with boys at about age 11 (see Figure 9.2). And between ages 11 and 12, they experience a sudden spurt in weight gain that puts them 3 pounds (1.4 kg) ahead of boys in the course of a single year. As we see in Chapter 11, it isn't until about age 14.5 that boys overtake girls in weight, and not until age 13.5 that they exceed girls in height. From then on, the weight and height of average men exceed those of women—until death renders us all equally short and light.

The growth spurt that heralds sexual maturation occurs about 2 years earlier for girls than for boys. But in specific instances, it can occur much earlier or much later than normal. This, as we see in Chapter 11, can have important implications for the adolescent's well-being and happiness. Being an early or late bloomer can be very good; it can also be very bad—although nature often compensates for initial discrepancies. When Doris Doré was 9 or 10, we called her "chimney" (or another less kind name), so tall was she—and so cruel were we. But when she was 15, most were as tall as she was. But I wasn't. In fact, when I was 14 or 15, there were some who dared call me *bûche*—which means "stump"—so late was I in starting to grow. But now, as one of my grandmother's French sayings goes, "Je mange de la tarte sur leurs têtes"—meaning, "I eat pie off their heads."

However, nature doesn't always make up for early differences. The early bloomer doesn't invariably stop growing while later developers catch up. Clearly, we're not all destined to reach the same end. Some end up short and others tall; some are light and others heavy. Our hypothetical average child hides these individual differences.

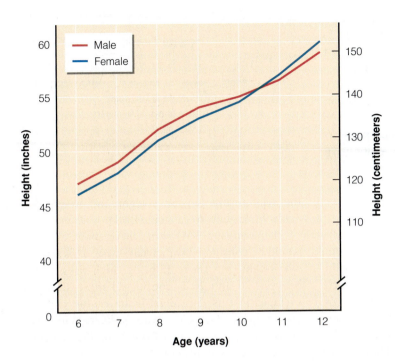

FIGURE 9.1 Height at 50th percentile for U.S. children. Source: Health Department, Milwaukee, Wisconsin; based on data by H. C. Stuart and H. V. Meredith, prepared for use in Children's Medical Center, Boston. Used by permission of the Milwaukee Health Department.

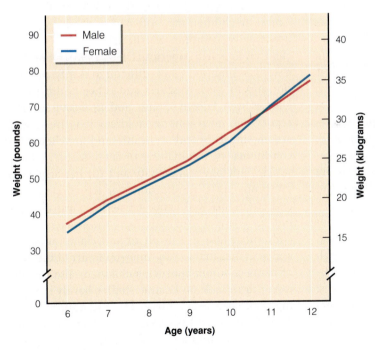

FIGURE 9.2 Weight at 50th percentile for U.S. children. Source: Health Department, Milwaukee, Wisconsin; based on data by H. C. Stuart and H. V. Meredith, prepared for use in Children's Medical Center, Boston. Used by permission of the Milwaukee Health Department.

Fat and Fat-Free Mass Another trend of physical growth that continues throughout middle childhood is a gradual decrease in the growth of fatty tissue (termed **fat mass**), coupled with increased bone and muscle development (part of **fat-free mass**). Fat mass, consisting mainly of white adipose tissue, is most susceptible to the effects of diet and exercise.

fat mass Made up mostly of white adipose tissue (fat cells). Accounts for an average of about 30% of body weight in adult females and about 15% in adult males.

fat-free mass The major constituent of the human body, consisting largely of organs, muscles, and bone (which in turn consist primarily of water).

In middle childhood, proportion of fat mass is relatively equal in boys and girls at about 25%. But following the growth spurt of adolescence, there is a reduction of fat mass for the average boy, and a slight increase in fat mass among girls. As a result, in the average adult male, about 85% of weight is accounted for by fat-free mass; in females, percentage of fat-free mass is somewhat lower at about 70 (Malina & Bouchard, 1991).

Nutrition and Health

If they are well nourished, between the ages of 6 and 12, children grow 2 to 3 inches (4.4–6.6 cm) and gain about 5 to 7 pounds (approximately 2–2.75 kg) each year. Normal gains in height are a better indicator of the long-term adequacy of the child's nutrition than are weight gains; gains in weight often reflect the shorter-term effects of nutrition. Hence the significance of the observation that 38% of children in developing countries and 47% of those in the least-developed countries are stunted (Bellamy, 1999a).

Nutrients are found in various classes of food and drink, among the most important of which is water. It makes up slightly more than 60% of the body weight of children (and of adults). Also critical are carbohydrates, fats, proteins, and various minerals and vitamins. In fact, during middle childhood, the recommended daily allowances of substances like calcium and most vitamins and minerals are almost as high for children as for adults (Food and Nutrition Board, 1989).

Unfortunately, as we saw in Chapter 1, many of the world's children are not well nourished, and many millions die of starvation each year. Although starvation is uncommon in North America, malnutrition is not. Malnutrition takes one of two forms: overnutrition, often leading to obesity; and undernutrition, often reflected in the intake of foods low in protein and essential vitamins and minerals.

Obesity

As we saw in Chapter 4, the concept of body mass index (BMI), rather than weight alone, is currently used to determine whether an individual is obese, excessively thin, or ideal. Body mass index reflects

TABLE 9.1
Calculating Body Mass Index

$$BMI = \frac{\text{weight in kilograms}}{\text{square of height in meters}}$$

$$\text{Or } BMI = \frac{\text{weight in pounds} \times 703}{\text{square of height in inches}}$$

the relationship between height and weight (see Table 9.1 for how to calculate BMI).

For adults, a BMI somewhere above 27 or 28 would be considered somewhat obese; 32 is severely overweight, and above 45 brings high risks. A BMI between 20 and 26 is considered most ideal. But average BMI is considerably lower for children. Hence much lower BMI scores indicate being overweight—between about 18 and 21 or 22, depending on age (Sizer & Whitney, 1997).

Estimates are that as many as 30% of all North American children may suffer from obesity, making it the most common nutritional problem among children in North America (Dietz, 1995). Obesity is a serious condition that is difficult to rectify. Its relationship to cardiovascular and other health problems is well known. Smith and associates (1999) report that even among children, it is frequently accompanied by other health and psychological conditions (such as diabetes or depression), many of which limit physical activity and further aggravate the problem. Its implications for the child's social and emotional well-being are perhaps less obvious but no less real. Not only does the severely obese child often find it difficult to participate in games and activities that are an important part of the lives of many children, but such a child may also be subjected to ridicule and ostracism. It's hardly surprising that when Braet, Mervielde, and Vandereycken (1997) compared 139 obese 9- to 12-year-olds with 150 normal children, they found that the obese group reported far more negative self-perceptions and feelings of self-worth. Moreover, their parents reported more behavioral and emotional problems for them than did parents of normal children.

Contributing Factors Overeating of both fat and energy (calories) is one of the most important contributing factors in obesity: Children simply take in more than they expend in growth and activity. This, of course, does not mean that the obese child eats excessively all the time. In fact, many obese children might eat only slightly more than they require each day, but the cumulative long-term effect is obesity.

Also important is the child's genetic background. Some children are clearly more susceptible to obesity than others. Those whose parents are themselves obese are more likely to also become obese than are children of slim parents (Malina & Bouchard, 1991). Similarly, when one member of an identical twin pair is obese, the other is also more likely to be. However, studies of identical twins indicate that those who are genetically predisposed to being thin are much less likely to show the consequences of overeating. It's as if their bodies are programmed to burn more calories (Bouchard et al., 1990).

Another possible factor in childhood obesity, often overlooked partly because it may be confounded with heredity, is the influence of parents who themselves have eating and nutrition problems. Franzen and Gerlinghoff (1997), for example, report a number of **case studies** where mothers with eating disorders also have children with similar eating disorders. In these cases, the influence of the mother may be partly a function of modeling and a function of the nutritional opportunities provided for the children.

A fourth important factor in childhood obesity is inactivity. Children who lead sedentary lives, who spend much of their day watching television, are more likely to gain excess weight. Watching television is especially important in contributing to weight gain, not only because it is physically passive but also because it encourages high-calorie snack and drink consumption. In fact, one treatment for obesity involves efforts to make children more knowledgeable about the media, and especially about the nature and purposes of advertising. Unfortunately, media advertising is not only highly pervasive but extremely effective with children. Thus, when Levine, Smolak, & Schermer (1996) undertook a 10-week media resistance program with 386 fourth- and fifth-grade students, they were not highly successful in bringing about more critical evaluation of mass media.

A fifth factor in obesity is the use of food as a reward—or a punishment. Children who are given "treats" for good behavior may learn to reward themselves with junk food—or to console themselves in the same way. Striegel-Moore and associates (1999), who investigated more than 2,000 U.S. schoolgirls, found that what they term emotion-induced eating—that is, eating in response to emotional states—is relatively common, and is often associated with increased intakes of sugar.

Control of Obesity Obesity in children, as in adults, is not easily controlled or reversed. And obese children stand a higher chance of being obese in later life. Power, Lake, and Cole (1997) found in their study of 17,733 British participants that more than $\frac{1}{3}$ of children who were obese at age 7 were obese at age 33. And with increasing age, the relationship becomes stronger. Thus, about $\frac{2}{3}$ of children who were very obese at age 16 were also obese at age 33. (See *In the News and on the Web:* "Apples and Pears," and Figure 9.3)

Although obesity is difficult to reverse, it can be prevented in most children even where genetic background predisposes the child to gaining excess weight. Two factors, exercise and diet, need to be controlled. But to control these, the child's motivation also needs to be brought into play. Children who aren't overly concerned, or for whom the attraction of food and of a sedentary lifestyle are too strong, will not so easily alter their patterns of eating and exercise. As Felton and associates (1998) found when they investigated a sample of 352 rural, predominantly black U.S. sixth-graders, many children appeared highly unconcerned about the risk factors they exposed themselves to—risks such as obesity, physical inactivity, alcohol use, and smoking. In this sample, 25% of the children were characterized by two or more of these risk factors, 44% had one, and only 32% had none.

Care needs to be taken to ensure that children consume adequate amounts of proteins, vitamins, minerals, and fibers—and also that they resist the ever-present temptation of junk foods. Unfortunately, this presupposes that children (and their parents) have a high level of knowledge about nutrition and about the relationships among exercise,

---

case studies A research technique in the social sciences in which investigators do an in-depth analysis of only one case (or individual), or a small number of them.

Apples and Pears

In the early 1980s, Britain's John Garrow invented the concept of body mass index (BMI), now widely used as a quick indication of obesity in adults.

Now Britain's Margaret Ashwell, former scientific director of the British Nutrition Foundation, has invented the Ashwell Shape Chart. Unlike the BMI, it doesn't compare weight to height, but rather waist size to height. The advantage, says Ashwell, is that science has shown that *where* fatty tissues are deposited may be a very important clue to their implications for health. Fatty tissues deposited around the waist (as they typically are in men) tend to be stored around internal organs and break down easily, find their way into the bloodstream, and cause heart and circulatory problems, diabetes, and some forms of cancer. Fatty tissues deposited around the hips and thighs (as they typically are in women) are far less likely to be mobilized into the bloodstream. Hence "weighty women," with their typical *pear* shape, may be healthier than weighty men, with their typical apple shape. "For women, this makes a huge difference," says Ashwell. "In particular, I think it is important for young women, who may see themselves as overweight on a BMI chart and get very worried about their size, even developing eating disorders. Indeed, they should get the message that it is perfectly normal for women to be pear-shaped."

 Resources: Margaret Ashwell's Web page, including her shape chart, is found at the first of the following two sites. The second provides information regarding the U.S. Food Guide Pyramid, a widely recommended guide to good nutrition:

http://www.ashwell.uk.com
http://www.nal.usda.gov/fnic/Fpyr/pyramid.html

Rumbelow, H. (1999, Dec. 6). Weighty women are in better shape than men. *The London Times*, P. News 7.

 For additional readings, explore *InfoTrac College Edition*, your online library. Go to http://infotrac-college.com/wadsworth and use the passcode that came on the card with your book. Try these search terms: obesity gene; obesity in children; weight loss; and weight-reducing preparations.

FIGURE 9.3 Margaret Ashwell's shape chart from http://www.ashwell.uk.com/shape.htm

© Dr. Margaret Ashwell. Reprinted by permission.

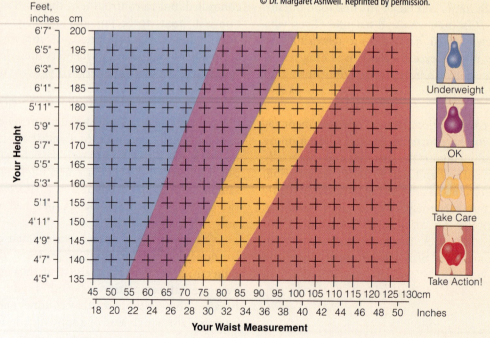

nutrition, and health—and that they have access to nutritious food in adequate amounts. As Mobley (1996) found out when she tested 3- to 6-year-olds' health knowledge, young children don't know very much about nutrition. Preschoolers tend to learn safety items first (for example, how and when to cross a street), and nutrition and health promotion items much later. And contrary to popular wisdom, the body does not automatically hunger for the specific minerals, vitamins, or other nutrients it might lack. Nor does it drive us to exercise when television beckons. Even animals do not select the most nutritious meal when there are other more appealing alternatives (Galef, 1991). Evolution, which saw us through some lean times, has prepared us poorly for refrigerators full of wonderful food-stuffs. There must have been many times when, had our forebears not eaten everything in sight, we would probably not be here today. Which is why Sagan's (1977) dragons of Eden continue to whisper in our ears, "Eat, you fool! There might be none tomorrow." At least, that's what I've been hearing.

Physical Fitness

There is a widespread belief that schoolchildren today are not as fit as schoolchildren were several decades ago. The belief is based partly on the obser-vation that as many as 20 or 30% of school-age chil-dren are obese. It also stems from the fact that many children spend much of their time watching televi-sion, playing on and working with computers, or engaged in other relatively nonactive endeavors. And in fact, a study of California fourth-graders found that the amount of time spent watching tele-vision is related to lower cardiovascular fitness as well as to higher body mass index (Armstrong et al., 1998). There is evidence, as well, that teenagers are not as active now as they were a decade ago (Center for Disease Control, 1992).

But, claim Pangrazi and Corbin (1993), this doesn't mean that youngsters are less fit now than they were. "Recent research suggests that they are more fit than previously reported," they explain (p. 14). Part of the confusion stems from the fact that definitions of physical fitness have changed from a concern with performance on various tests of speed, skill, strength, and flexibility, to a concern

with more health-related criteria like stamina and body fat percentage. Children are only slightly fatter now than they were 20 years ago, claim Looney and Plowman (1990); more than 80% meet high stan-dards of physical fitness. And when they are exposed to health-education programs designed to increase their activity level and health knowledge, they typi-cally become not only more fit but also develop increased interest in maintaining high levels of physical activity outside of school (Manios, Kafatos, & Mamalakis, 1998).

Childhood Diseases

Although the development of vaccines has drasti-cally reduced the incidence of many infectious dis-eases among children, most nevertheless suffer occasionally from a variety of problems. Most com-mon are respiratory infections such as colds, although these are less common after age 5 than they were before age 5 (U.S. Bureau of the Census, 1998). Far less common than respiratory infections are communicable diseases such as chicken pox, mumps, mononucleosis, and measles. Very uncom-mon in the industrialized world are vaccine-preventable diseases such as tetanus, poliomyelitis, pertussis (whooping cough), and smallpox. Rabies, too, is uncommon.

Motor Development

Children's muscular control continues to develop through middle childhood. Early in this period, their control of large muscles is considerably better than their control over smaller muscles. By the end of middle childhood, control of the large muscles has become nearly perfect, and control over the small muscles is much improved.

Children's less well developed control over small-muscle movements explains in part the some-times labored writing of first- and second-grade children. It also explains why Sakihara (1998) found that Japanese children's copies of complex Kana (Japanese) were largely unintelligible when the chil-dren were 3 or 4 years old. In contrast, copies made by older children (6 years) were generally correctly constructed.

Sex Differences in Motor Skills Changes in locomotor skills, agility, coordination, and physical strength reflect the effects of age; they also demonstrate consistent differences between sexes. These differences may be important in explaining some of children's interests; they may also be partly a result of different interests in the first place. As Wegman (1999) showed in a study of motor-skill learning among fourth-grade students, practice can be very effective in increasing motor skills.

We know that throughout middle childhood, physical strength of boys (measured in grip strength) is superior to that of girls, even though the average girl is taller and heavier than the average boy (Corbin, 1980). Similarly, boys consistently out-jump girls after the age of 7, presumably because boys have greater leg power and arm-leg coordination for jumping than girls do. Malina and Bouchard (1991) also cite evidence that boys do better than girls in tests of kicking, throwing, catching, running, broad jumping, and batting.

Girls surpass boys in motor skills that are more dependent on muscular flexibility, balance, or rhythmic movements—such as those in hopscotch and jumping rope and some forms of gymnastics—as well as in the ability to balance on one foot (Morris et al., 1982).

These differences are consistent with the gender typing of these activities, as one would expect. That is, jumping rope and hopscotch have traditionally been more feminine than masculine; and throwing balls, catching, running, and jumping are considered more masculine. In addition, the differences between boys and girls—when there are differences—are seldom very great. There is typically much overlap, so that in activities in which boys are better than girls, some girls are better than some boys; conversely, when girls are, on the average, better than boys, some boys are better than some girls (Lockhart, 1980). After adolescence, however, most of these sex differences increase dramatically, generally in favor of males (Smoll & Schutz, 1990).

Elizabeth Crews

Through middle childhood, children's muscular control continues to develop, manifesting remarkable increases in locomotor skills, agility, coordination, and physical strength. Some of these skills are especially important for participation in games, and relate in important ways to the child's acceptance and happiness.

Explanations for Sex Differences What is not clear is the extent to which sex-related differences in motor skills, both in childhood and later in adolescence, result from innate biological differences between the sexes, and the extent to which cultural norms, expectations, and experience are involved. We do know, however, that at least for some activities, proportion of adipose (fatty) tissue is closely related to performance for both boys and girls. In a comparison of the motor performance of more than 2,000 children ages 9 to 17, Smoll and Schutz (1990) found that fatness alone accounted for as much as 50% of the variance between males and females. Because females on average retain significantly more adipose tissue than boys from early childhood on, some of the observed male-female differences in motor performance are probably related to this biological difference.

With advancing age, note Smoll and Schutz (1990), sex differences in motor activity and skills are increasingly influenced by environmental factors reflected in social expectations and opportunities. For example, there are far more opportunities for boys to participate in a variety of sports considered "masculine" (hockey, basketball, and baseball, to name a few), which explains in part why they become more proficient at them. Also, as we saw in Chapter 8, boys engage in far more rough-and-tumble play than girls. They chase each other, fight and wrestle, tug, push, pull, hit and smash (Boulton, 1996). All of these activities provide experience with those skills where sex differences are most consistently found.

Some Physical and Sensory Problems

Not all children are born with normal sensory abilities or physical skills; nor do all have the same potential to develop these capabilities. Those who differ markedly from the average are termed *exceptional.*

Exceptionality is seen in all areas of human development: physical and motor, intellectual, and socioemotional. It might be manifested in extraordinary talents and skills, or it may be apparent in deficits and disorders. Later in this chapter we look at intellectual exceptionality in middle childhood. Here we look briefly at physical and sensory problems.

Visual Impairment People who can see at 20 feet what a "normal" person can see at 20 feet are said to have 20/20 vision (or normal vision); those who see at 20 feet what normal people can see at 200 feet are said to have 20/200 vision, and are classified as legally blind (providing their corrected vision in their better eye is no better than 20/200). Accordingly, most individuals who are classified as legally blind can in fact see, which is one reason why the term **visually impaired** is highly preferable to the term *blind.* About half of all children with visual impairment can read large type or print with the help of magnification. For the **special needs** teacher, it's especially important to determine whether a child is capable of learning to read by sight or will have to learn to read by touch. For those who can read visually, the "special" qualities of education might not need to go beyond providing magnifying equipment or material with large print—sometimes presented using a computer—unless other problems are involved.

Although it's true that children with severe mental handicaps also have an unusually high rate of visual disorders (as many as 25% are severely visually handicapped (Kwok et al., 1996), most children with visual impairment are not intellectually challenged. With appropriate education, they often do as well on measures of **intelligence** and of creativity (for example, Wyver & Markham, 1999) .

Special classrooms and special teachers for children with visual impairments are much less common today than they once were. Many of these children are now educated in regular classrooms, a practice termed **mainstreaming** (or *inclusive education*),

---

visually impaired Technically, those who, with corrected vision in their best eye, can see at 20 feet what normal people see at 200 feet. An expression for *legal blindness.*

special needs Global term that includes all who need special training, equipment, or services to reach their full human potential. What is often termed *special education* is also *special needs education* or education for those with *special needs.*

intelligence A property measured by intelligence tests. Seems to refer primarily to the capacity of individuals to adjust to their environment.

mainstreaming The practice of placing students in need of special services in regular classrooms rather than segregating them. Also called *inclusive education.*

about which more is said in a later section of this chapter. Those who must learn to read Braille, however, require special equipment and teachers.

Hearing Impairment Deafness is the inability to hear sounds clearly enough for the ordinary purposes of life. The hard of hearing are those who suffer from some hearing loss, but can function with a hearing aid—and sometimes without.

A useful way of describing deafness is to distinguish between *prelinguistic* and *postlinguistic* deafness—in other words, between loss of hearing that occurs before learning a language and that which occurs later. Unfortunately, in 9 out of 10 deaf children, loss of hearing was congenital (present at birth) or occurred within the first two years, often resulting from infections such as **otitis media** (Maeki-Torkko et al., 1998).

Otitis media is the second most common reason parents bring their children to doctors (the first involves upper respiratory infections). It's a middle-ear disease that may be accompanied by mild to severe loss of hearing that sometimes lasts for months. Because it's highly common in infancy, when the child is acquiring language, otitis media can be associated with retarded language growth and related cognitive problems. The milder forms of otitis media, lasting only a few weeks, are often treated effectively with antibiotics. More severe, recurring (chronic) cases lead to buildup of fluid in the middle ear, which causes deafness. In these cases, treatment often involves surgically inserting tubes in the ear to allow the fluid to drain (Feagans & Proctor, 1994).

For children's cognitive development, prelinguistic hearing impairment generally presents a more serious handicap than does visual impairment. This is largely because of the severe difficulties it presents for learning to understand and to speak—hence the historical, but no longer popular expression, "deaf and dumb" or "deaf mute." For children with prelinguistic hearing impairments who have learned American Sign Language (ASL), being forced to also learn to read and write in English (or some other language) is not very different from asking children who are not deaf to speak their first language but to do all their reading, writing, and studying in a second language. The intellectual challenges are considerable, especially given that many children with hearing impairments don't learn ASL until later in life.

The academic achievement of children with hearing impairments, and their scores on measures of intelligence, often lag behind—a problem that can be attributed largely to language deficiencies. In fact, on measures of creativity, which are not so language-dependent, children with hearing impairments can perform as well as children who can hear (Moorjhani, Jacob, & Nathawat, 1998).

In addition to the academic problems associated with deafness, there can also be emotional and social problems. These problems probably result from lack of social interaction, in turn resulting from impaired ability to communicate through language.

The education of children with hearing impairments generally requires specially trained teachers and often occurs in special schools. Understandably, the principal emphasis is on acquiring language—usually a combination of American Sign Language, finger spelling, and speech reading (lipreading).

The education of children with only a partial hearing loss may also require special instruction, particularly if the loss is manifested in speech disorders. Although many children with partial hearing are capable of following conversations if the conversations are at close range or sufficiently loud, they often experience difficulty in distinguishing among consonants for which there are no visual clues (for example, p–b, t–d, and f–v). Their own speech may consequently be affected. Special education for these children can often be implemented without removing them from regular classrooms, simply by providing special instructional sessions for them. Itinerant teachers (who travel from class to class) are often used for this purpose.

otitis media A highly common childhood disease of the middle ear, sometimes accompanied by prolonged hearing loss, the main medical symptom of which is fluid in the middle ear. May be associated with language problems.

Other Physical Problems Some other physical problems in middle childhood require special education or services. These include diseases and conditions such as muscular dystrophy, cancer, asthma, diabetes, the absence of one or more limbs, and paralysis. Some are congenital, some are caused by infections, and others result from accidents of various kinds. In many cases, serious emotional and social problems are associated with the physical problems. Many of these emotional problems are related to difficulties the child experiences in being accepted by others and in developing a positive self-concept. Hence, a great deal of what special-needs programs, parents, and therapists can do for physically exceptional children relates to their emotional and social well-being.

COGNITIVE DEVELOPMENT: PIAGET'S VIEW

When we left our discussion of children's minds in Chapter 7, it was not because their minds had stopped growing while they continued to advance physically and socially. Rather, it was because considering all aspects of development at once is too complex and confusing. So now we pick up the thread of intellectual development once more, keeping in mind that as their intellect is developing, children are also growing in other ways. We will start again with the views of Jean Piaget, and the period we're exploring is the one he termed *concrete operations*. Recall that he postulated that children reached this stage by way of the sensorimotor period (birth to 2 years) and two preoperational subperiods: preconceptual thought (2–4 years) and intuitive thinking (4–7 years); see *Concept Summary*. Later in the chapter, we will explore the views of those who believe that children show the gains of operational thinking due to a gradual increase in their information-processing capacity, rather than because of a transition to a new, discrete stage. However, Piaget's descriptions of this changing cognitive ability are extremely useful.

Toward the end of the intuitive stage, says Piaget, the child's thinking is egocentric, perception-dominated, and intuitive. Despite the remarkable strides that children have made in their ability to deal with language, with number, with logic, and

even with emotion, their thinking still abounds in contradictions and errors of logic. So when I show 4-year-old Lena a chunk of cookie dough, and then roll out the dough long and thin on the table in front of her, she confidently insists that there is now more dough. But when I restore the dough to its original shape, she quickly changes her mind. "It's the same again," she says. "So can I eat it?"

The Conservations

But when Lena is 7, she scoffs at the ridiculous simplicity of my question. "Of course it's the same," she says, "You didn't add any more dough, did you?" Lena has now acquired concepts of conservation of solid matter—and that, in Piaget's system, is the surest sign that she has made the transition from preoperational thought to **operational thought**—albeit, *concrete* operational thought.

Constructing Knowledge The significance of acquiring conservation—the realization that amount doesn't change if only appearance has been altered—is not so much that children are no longer deceived by the problem, but rather that they have now learned some basic logical rules that become evident in much of their thinking. These rules make it possible for children to overcome many of the errors that characterized their thinking during the preoperational period. They can now rely on operations (thought processes governed by rules of logic) rather than on preoperations (thinking based on perception and intuition).

That children attempt to use logic does not mean that they will always respond correctly. For example, one of the most dramatic illustrations of incomplete or misapplied logic occurs when 4-year-old Roberto is asked to draw the water level in a tilted jar. He draws something like illustration (A) in Figure 9.4, rather than the correct response, (B). Yet Roberto has never actually seen anything like (A) in real life. None of us has. Therefore, his drawing doesn't reflect actual experience, but rather his attempt to make sense of experience.

operational thought A Piagetian developmental stage beginning around the age of 7 or 8. Specifically, an operation is a thought that is governed by certain rules of logic.

Piaget's Stages of Cognitive Development

Stage	Approximate Age	Some Major Characteristics
Sensorimotor (discussed in Chapter 5)	0–2 years	Intelligence in action World of the here and now No language, no thought, no notion of objective reality at beginning of stage
Preoperational (discussed in Chapter 7)	2–7 years	
Preconceptual	2–4 years	Egocentric thought Reason dominated by perception Animistic thinking
Intuitive	4–7 years	Intuitive rather than logical solutions Inability to conserve
Concrete operations (discussed in this chapter)	7–11 or 12 years	Ability to conserve Logic of classes and relations Understanding of numbers Thinking bound to concrete Development of reversibility in thought
Formal operations (discussed in Chapter 11)	11 or 12 to 14 or 15 years	Complete generality of thought Propositional thinking Ability to deal with the hypothetical development of strong idealism

Roberto has begun to use (and to misuse) some rules of logic—for example, the rule that the level of

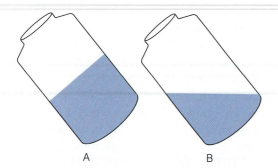

FIGURE 9.4 When asked to draw the fluid level in a tilted jar, young children typically draw the figure shown in (A) rather than (B)—not because they have ever seen anything like (A) in the real world, but because the logic they use in their attempts to make meaning out of their experiences is not always appropriate.

things like water is ordinarily parallel to the bottom of the container in which these things find themselves. He has begun to recognize some of the logic that governs things. It is interesting, however, as many researchers have demonstrated with the Piaget *water-level test*, that even adults often make mistakes with these sorts of problems. This occurs although Piaget had thought that by the age of 9, most children should respond correctly. Li, Nuttall, and Zhao (1999) presented 486 Chinese students in grades 4, 5, 6, 8, and 11 with drawings of eight bottles, each at a different angle above a flat surface that represented a table. Participants were told to imagine that each bottle was sealed and about half full of water, and were asked to draw a line representing the level of the water in each bottle. Responses were scored correct if they were within 5 degrees of horizontal. Results indicate that it isn't until between ages 14 and 17, well into the period of formal operations, that most participants responded correctly. And the performance of these Chinese students, note Li, Nuttall, and Zhao, is better than the typical performance of North American students. They suggest this is probably because learning how to construct Chinese language characters helps develop some of the spatial skills involved in the water-level test.

Rules of Logic The advent of concrete operations brings with it the eventual discovery of three important rules of logic that are especially important for the acquisition of conservation: identity, reversibility, and compensation. Each can be illustrated by Lena's response to the question, "Is there as much dough in the long piece as there was to begin with?" When she answers correctly, she may be reasoning in one of three ways: Nothing has been added or taken away, so the deformed object must be identical to what it was (identity); the deformed object can be reformed into what it was and so must contain the same amount (reversibility); or the deformed object appears to have more material because it is longer, but its thinness makes up for its length (**compensation**).

Once a child has learned about identity, reversibility, and compensation, do these rules apply to all thinking? The answer is no. There is, says Piaget using his elegant Swiss French, a sort of **horizontal décalage**—a horizontal displacement—that occurs in the thinking of most children. That is, accomplishments in one area aren't always generalized to other similar areas. And, there are as many different kinds of conservation as there are characteristics of objects that can vary in quantity

(for example, mass, number, weight, area, volume, and so on). If the rules of logic that make these conservations possible were completely general, they would all be acquired at the same time. When children realize that the amount of dough doesn't change when a chunk is flattened, they should also realize that the amount of water doesn't change when it is poured from a tall, thin vase into a shallow, wide bowl. But, as Figure 9.5 shows, the approximate ages at which the various conservations are acquired span a number of years. *Voilà! Décalage.*

The so-called *extinction studies* provide additional evidence of décalage—of the lack of generality of the child's newly discovered rules of logic. In these studies, children who have already acquired a specific kind of conservation are given evidence that their reasoning is incorrect. The argument is that if a conserver (in this case, a child) truly believes that conservation is a logical and necessary consequence, there should be strong resistance to extinction of that logic.

In a typical extinction experiment in conservation of weight, subjects agree that two balls of modeling clay weigh the same, and they continue to maintain that this is the case even after one or both of the balls have been deformed or broken into little pieces. At this point, however, the experimenter asks subjects to verify their conservation response by using a balance scale. But it's a trick! The scale is rigged so that one of the balls now seems to weigh more than the other!

Miller (1981) reviewed more than 25 extinction experiments. In most of them, subjects believed evidence that contradicted their original conservation response and, by the same token, contradicted the logical rules leading the subjects to that response. Young conservers (and sometimes older ones) do not always behave as though they believe these rules of logic to be necessarily true in all relevant cases. However, further questioning of subjects in extinction studies often reveals that they don't doubt the certainty of the logical rule. Rather, they are simply not always clear about when to apply the rule. Even young children realize that social rules are arbitrary and uncertain, says Miller (1981); but they also know that Piagetian rules of logic are more universal. However, the rigged balance scale presents a real-life problem rather than a problem in logic. In

---

compensation A logical rule relating to the fact that certain changes can compensate for opposing changes, thereby negating their effect. For example, as a square object becomes longer, it also becomes thinner. Increases in length compensate for decreases in width. These changes combine to negate any actual changes in mass.

horizontal décalage Literally, a displacement or gap. Piaget's term for the observation that certain skills or understandings that clearly apply to a variety of situations are sometimes treated as though they apply in only a few specific instances. Horizontal décalage is a gap *within* a stage (hence *horizontal* rather than *vertical*). It is evident in the wide range of ages between the acquisition of the first conservation (conservation of mass, for example) and the last (conservation of area or volume).

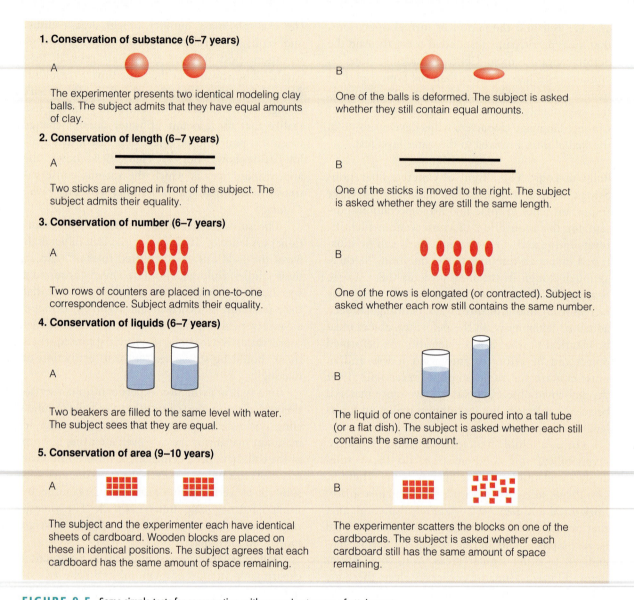

1. Conservation of substance (6–7 years)

A

The experimenter presents two identical modeling clay balls. The subject admits that they have equal amounts of clay.

B

One of the balls is deformed. The subject is asked whether they still contain equal amounts.

2. Conservation of length (6–7 years)

A

Two sticks are aligned in front of the subject. The subject admits their equality.

B

One of the sticks is moved to the right. The subject is asked whether they are still the same length.

3. Conservation of number (6–7 years)

A

Two rows of counters are placed in one-to-one correspondence. Subject admits their equality.

B

One of the rows is elongated (or contracted). Subject is asked whether each row still contains the same number.

4. Conservation of liquids (6–7 years)

A

Two beakers are filled to the same level with water. The subject sees that they are equal.

B

The liquid of one container is poured into a tall tube (or a flat dish). The subject is asked whether each still contains the same amount.

5. Conservation of area (9–10 years)

A

The subject and the experimenter each have identical sheets of cardboard. Wooden blocks are placed on these in identical positions. The subject agrees that each cardboard has the same amount of space remaining.

B

The experimenter scatters the blocks on one of the cardboards. The subject is asked whether each cardboard still has the same amount of space remaining.

FIGURE 9.5   Some simple tests for conservation, with approximate ages of attainment.

this situation, children are not deciding whether the logical rule is correct (they know it is), but whether the scale is correct.

In a similar series of experiments, Winer and McGlone (1993) asked children and college students misleading conservation questions such as: "When do you weigh more, when you are walking or running?" Or, after presenting two equal rows of checkers in a conservation of number problem and then spreading one row out, they asked, "Who has more, you or I?" Strikingly, some college students

show lack of conservation in these circumstances—as do even more third- and sixth-grade students. Why? Perhaps, though not likely, because we are acquiescent, suggest Winer and McGlone. Or maybe because subjects are responding to what they think the experimenter means rather than says ("She probably means, 'Who looks like they have more?' rather than 'Who actually has more?'"). Or, most likely, these experiments simply illustrate that both children and adults are capable of thinking at various levels of sophistica-

Piaget describes the preschooler's thinking as abounding in contradictions and errors of logic. During middle childhood, a new logic begins to guide thinking. But there are major cognitive achievements yet to come; and tremendous individual differences in the ease with which they will be mastered.

tion, and that even after we have learned a dozen elegant rules of logic, we don't always behave as though we had.

Can Conservation Be Accelerated?

Many researchers and educators were fond of asking Piaget questions like: "If we can accurately describe some of the important capabilities that children develop and the sequence in which these appear, might it not also be possible to accelerate their appearance by providing children with appropriate experiences? And could we not, by so doing, speed up the developmental process, increase children's cognitive capabilities, and perhaps even make them more intelligent?" But Piaget did not answer such questions directly. He had always been more concerned with describing and explaining cognitive development than with trying to change its course. However, an impressive number of other researchers have attempted an answer. Many have looked at the possibility of accelerating the development of con-

cepts of conservation—concepts that are simply defined, easy to measure, and important in cognitive development. But the results have generally been mixed, with many researchers failing to bring about significant change, while others have reported some success, especially with children with delayed development (see, for example, Campbell & Ramey, 1990; Perry, Pasnak, & Holt, 1992).

The evidence does not support the conclusion that development can be altered easily and significantly through short-term training programs. Conservation can be accelerated, but training programs need to be detailed and systematic, especially if the children are still some distance from acquiring conservation naturally (Furth, 1980). Whether such efforts, when successful, contribute significantly to intellectual development—or to happiness and self-esteem—remains unclear.

Classes, Series, and Numbers

In addition to acquiring various conservations, children gain or improve three other abilities as they enter concrete operations.

Classes For example, children increase their ability to understand **class** inclusion and to reason about the combination and the decomposition of classes. Ten-year-old Felicia snorts in derision that I should ask her whether there are more roses or more flowers in a bouquet consisting of 15 roses and 5 tulips. She understands with unshakeable certainty that roses make up a subclass of the larger class of flowers. Similarly, she has little difficulty answering the question, "If there are red balls and green balls, and some are large whereas others are small, how many different kinds of balls are there?" Felicia knows that by multiplying the number of colors by the number of sizes (see Figure 9.6), she can answer the question. In contrast, 5-year-old Samuel does not easily understand this problem. And when asked the flowers question, he says, "Yeah, well, there's more roses." But he, too, has some ability to deal

class In logic, an abstraction signifying a collection of items (for example, people, ideas, things) that share one or more identifiable characteristics (for example, the class of blue things; or the class of blue things that are also hairy).

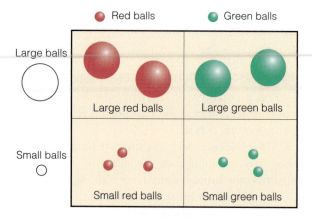

● Red balls   ● Green balls

Large balls

| Large red balls | Large green balls |
| Small red balls | Small green balls |

Small balls

FIGURE 9.6   Suppose X comes in exactly two shapes, each of which can be either black of white. How many different X's are there? Right. There are four. The concrete-operations child may have some difficulty with this simple classification problem because it's too abstract. X is not concrete enough. The problem is simpler if we ask, instead, "How many kinds of balls do we have if we have big and small red ones, and big and small green ones?" Such a problem can be used to test a child's ability to classify objects.

with class-inclusion problems, as is evident when he answers this question correctly: "A charolais is an animal, but it's not a horse. Is a horse an animal?"

Series   A second achievement of the period of concrete operations is an increased understanding of

seriation (ordering in sequence). Piaget's seriation task presents children with a series of objects (for example, dolls), each a different height so they can easily be arranged from tallest to shortest. The bottom row of Figure 9.7 illustrates the correct arrangement, quickly produced by concrete-operations children. However, intuitive-stage children are ordinarily incapable of responding correctly. A typical response is to place several of the dolls in order, while ignoring the others that may fit in between those already positioned (top row). If the next doll the child selects is too short to be placed where the child intended it to be (at the upper end), it is placed without hesitation at the other end, even though it might be taller or shorter than the adjacent doll. The child does not yet understand that if A is greater than B, and B is greater than C, then A must also be greater than C. Understanding this concept eliminates the necessity of making all the comparisons that would otherwise be necessary.

Numbers   Understanding seriation also makes it possible to understand the concept of numbers more completely, because the ordinal properties of numbers (their ordered sequence: first, second, third, . . .) depend on a knowledge of seriation. Similarly, their cardinal properties (their quantitative properties, the fact that they represent collections of different magnitude) depend on

FIGURE 9.7   A test of a child's understanding of seriation. The elements of the series are presented in random order, and the child is asked to arrange them in sequence by height. The top row was arranged by a 3½-year-old; the bottom, by an 8-year-old.

classification. As we saw in Chapter 7, however, many preschool children already have an impressive knowledge of number, a fact that Piaget largely overlooked as he searched for the limitations of pre-operational versus operational thought.

What Are *Concrete* Operations?

An operation is a thought that is characterized by rules of logic. Because children acquire conservations early in this period and because these concepts are manifestations of operational thinking, the period is called operational. It is termed *concrete* because children's thinking deals with real—or concrete—objects, or at least those that they can easily imagine, rather than more abstract, hypothetical ideas. As a result, children in the concrete operations stage are bound to the real world. They do not yet have the freedom made possible by the more advanced logic of formal operations—freedom to contemplate the hypothetical, to compare the ideal with the actual, to be profoundly unhappy and concerned about the discrepancy between this world and the one they imagine is possible.

COGNITIVE DEVELOPMENT: INFORMATION PROCESSING

In Piaget's view of cognitive development, the emphasis is on how children discover (*construct*) notions of reality and of logic. A somewhat different emphasis in the study of cognitive development looks at the intellectual processes by which children learn and remember. This emphasis defines the information-processing approach.

The Information-Processing Approach

The information-processing approach begins, as all views of developing children must, with the observation that a newborn infant is, as my grandmother so poetically put it, "pretty doggoned ignorant." The expression is not at all derogatory when applied to an infant, although it was when she applied it to 15-year-old Frank. The difference, you see, is that infants are supposed to be ignorant. They are not expected to know that day follows night, which itself follows day; that butterflies whisper to each other when they perch on buttercups in the sunshine; or that tigers have tails. In fact, they are strangers to their very own hands and feet, strangers to the world. And, as Rheingold (1985) points out, the process of development is a process of becoming familiar with the world.

The difference between newborns—who are almost totally unfamiliar with everything around them—and older children—who have learned about tigers, tautologies, and tarantulas—can be described in a number of ways. We can say, with Piaget, that the developing child, through the processes of assimilation and accommodation, has constructed a picture of reality that conforms, more or less, to certain logical rules that in turn define a sequence of orderly stages. Or we can say that the developing child begins with no **knowledge base**, few strategies for dealing with cognitive material, and no awareness of the self as a knower or as a processor of information. This approach permits us to view development as the business of acquiring a knowledge base, developing cognitive strategies, and gradually gaining an awareness of self as a knower. This is an information-processing approach to cognitive development.

Ways of Classifying Memory

The information-processing model views children as consumers and processors of information, little organisms that shed their ignorance as they build up a store of memories. The most common description of this model is based on the work of Atkinson and Shiffrin (1971), which describes three types of information storage: sensory memory, short-term memory (also called *working memory*), and long-term memory. Each is distinguished mainly by the amount and nature of processing it involves. By *processing* is

---

knowledge base All that is in memory. Information-processing approaches to learning and development look at the nature and construction of the knowledge base, at strategies for adding material to, or retrieving from, the knowledge base, and at the knower's awareness of self as knower.

Danny Lehman/Corbis

The knowledge base that the teacher brings to her embroidery consists of skills and information of which her young charges have not yet dreamed—although with the right experiences and a little help, they too will get there. Information processing theorists look not only at the content of the knowledge base but also at the processes and strategies that allow it to grow and to be used, as well as at the emergence of the child's awareness of the self as a knower and processor of information.

meant activities such as **rehearsing**, analyzing, sorting, elaborating, and summarizing.

Sensory memory refers mainly to sensation—the momentary impressions associated with sensory stimulation. It requires no cognitive processing, and has a fleeting (less than one second) and unconscious effect on memory.

Short-term memory is what is involved when you look up a phone number, pick up your phone, dial the number, and immediately forget it. Short-term memory lasts only seconds, is highly limited in capacity, is easily disrupted, and typically depends on a single cognitive process: rehearsing.

Continued rehearsing, and the use of other cognitive strategies such as organizing and analyzing for meaningfulness, is what allows us to remember things for a long time. These are some of the strategies contributing to **long-term memory**. Long-term memory includes all our stable information about the world—everything we know. Its capacity is relatively unlimited, and it is not easily disrupted by external events. Many of the things that we know—like the names of popes and kings and what happened to us on our last birthday—can be put into words. They make up our **explicit memory** (or *declarative memory*). But we also know many things that we can't put into words: These things define **implicit memory** (or *nondeclarative memory*).

rehearsing A memory process involving repetition, important in maintaining information in short-term memory and transferring it to long-term memory.

sensory memory The simple sensory recognition of stimuli (also called *short-term sensory memory*). Sensory memory requires no cognitive processing and does not involve conscious awareness.

short-term memory Information that lasts from a few seconds to a minute, requiring limited cognitive processing. It defines our immediate consciousness. Also termed *primary memory* or *working memory*.

long-term memory Memory that lasts from minutes to years and that involves rehearsal and organization.

The complex skills involved in learning to ride a horse cannot easily be put into words and retrieved from long-term memory so that they can be analyzed and discussed. They are part of implicit memory. But the details of putting halter and bridle even on a reluctant horse might be made more explicit. All complex activities require a stable knowledge base—which is, in effect, long-term memory.

Implicit memory is well illustrated by the unfortunate centipede when it was asked by a meddling scientist how it managed to walk with its many legs, which leg went where, which one went next, or did some move simultaneously—all important scientific questions the centipede had never thought about. All its life, it had simply walked when it felt like it. But while thinking about this extraordinarily complex problem, it became completely confused and wound up tying its legs in a nightmare of little knots. The centipede knew implicitly how to walk, in the same way that we know various motor skills that can't easily be made explicit—like how to do a somersault or throw a Frisbee.

There are basically two kinds of explicit memories: those consisting of all the stable, abstract knowledge we possess, and all the objective things we have learned (or think we remember) from reading or going to school or listening to people. This first type of knowledge is called **semantic memory** to distinguish it from explicit memories that are more personal—that, in effect, make up the second kind of knowledge, called **autobiographical memory** (also termed *episodic memory*; see Figure 9.8). Our autobiographical memories consist of our recollection of all the things we have experienced personally. Significantly, our autobiographical memories are often far more accurate than our semantic memories. When Wynn and Logie (1998) questioned 63 adults about trivial incidents that had happened in their lives, they found remarkable consistency in recollections over a long period of time.

Memory and the Brain

Research with people who have suffered brain injuries suggests that different parts of the brain are involved in semantic and autobiographical memories. For example, there is the case of K. C., a 30-year-old motorcyclist who missed a curve and suffered severe brain damage. He appears to remember everything he has learned (for example, how to play chess, who his parents are, where he lives, what he and they own), but recalls absolutely nothing that has ever occurred to him personally. "K. C.," writes Tulving (1989), "knows that his family owns a summer cottage, knows where it is located, and can

explicit memory *Declarative*, conscious, long-term memory, in contrast with implicit (or nondeclarative) memory. May be either semantic or episodic.

implicit memory Refers to unconscious, nonverbalizable effects of experience such as might be manifested in acquired motor skills or in classical conditioning. Also termed *nondeclarative memory*.

semantic memory A type of declarative (conscious, long-term) memory consisting of stable knowledge about the world, principles, rules, and procedures, and other verbalizable aspects of knowledge, including language.

autobiographical memory A type of declarative (conscious, long-term) memory consisting of knowledge about personal experiences, tied to specific times and places—hence personal *episodes*; also called *episodic memory*.

point out the location on a map of Ontario, and he knows that he has spent summers and weekends there. But he does not remember a single occasion when he was at the cottage or a single event that happened there" (p. 363). Thus, his *semantic* memory appears to be intact, but his *autobiographical* memory is not.

The case of K. C., together with studies of brain functioning using **positron emission tomography** or **magnetic resonance imaging** (imaging techniques that can reveal location and patterns of neural activity in the brain) suggest that different parts of the brain may be involved in different kinds of memories. They also indicate that there isn't just one single memory trace for each item that we remember (Gabrieli, 1998). As a result, remembering may often involve gathering from different brain locations isolated features of an experience and then putting them together. Several problems can, and *do*, result, note Schacter, Norman, and Koutstaal (1998). Often it's as though elements of an experience aren't bound together well enough to be recalled in their entirety, so that only fragments are remembered. Or we remember fragments from *different* experiences and think they belong together. Or we remember experiences that we have read or heard about and think they are ours when they actually happened to someone else. We, like children, sometimes make very poor witnesses even when we don't intend to lie.

Main Processes in Long-Term Memory

Three basic processes are involved in long-term remembering: rehearsing, elaborating, and organizing.

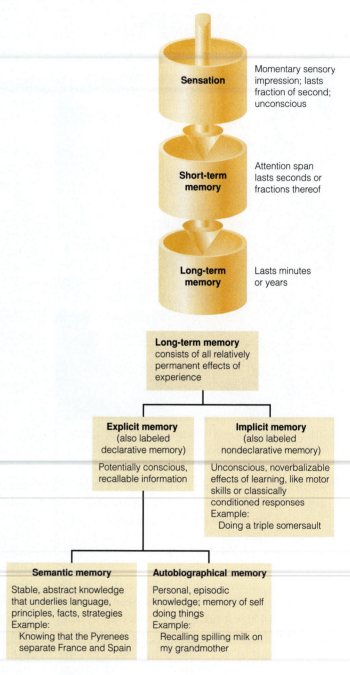

FIGURE 9.8 A model of memory.

---

positron emission tomography Also referred to as *PET scan*, a medical diagnostic technique, as well as a research tool, which can be used to provide computer-enhanced images of body structures and also of neurological functioning. A powerful tool in brain and memory research.

magnetic resonance imaging Popularly referred to as an MRI, a powerful medical diagnostic tool that makes use of computer-enhanced images of magnetic fields in the body to reveal details about physical and neurological structure and functioning. Highly useful in brain and memory research.

Rehearsing Rehearsing involves repetition and has an important role both in maintaining information in short-term memory and in transferring material from short- to long-term storage. The simplest rehearsal strategy is to name the material (five, five, five, one, two, one, two) over and over until it seems unlikely that it will escape. Most children younger than 5 do not spontaneously rehearse and cannot easily be taught to do so (Wellman, 1988).

Elaborating To elaborate is to extend material or add something to it in order to make it more memorable. For example, **elaborating** might consist of forming associations between new material and existing knowledge, or of creating mental images that go beyond (elaborate on) the actual material. Elaboration that relates to the meaning of what is being learned seems most effective. Bradshaw and Anderson (1982) had subjects try to recall sentences such as "The fat man read the sign." Those who elaborated this sentence to something like "The fat man read the sign warning of thin ice" significantly improved their ability to remember that the man in question was fat. Younger children do not spontaneously elaborate to improve recall.

Organizing Organizing involves arranging items or concepts by their relationships. Assume, for example, that you have been asked to memorize this list: pencil, horse, pen, house, barn, cat, apartment, bear, typewriter. You might have noticed that the list can easily be organized into three groups of related items (animals, dwellings, writing instruments), and you can use this organization to help remember the items. Young children will not usually notice these relationships and will not organize material the way you would. Their use of strategies is more limited than yours; they know less about knowing.

Some Characteristics of Long-Term Memory

Long-term memory has three important characteristics. First, it is highly stable. What you can remember today of what you learned in high school, you are relatively likely to remember tomorrow or next week, or next year.

Second, long-term memory appears to be generative rather than simply reproductive. That is, we remember main ideas, termed **gist memory**, and tend to "generate" (make up) details on the basis of our knowledge of **scripts**—that is, our knowledge of what goes with what, of what ordinarily follows what. Research on children's memories indicates that they, too, tend to fill in gaps according to their personal scripts. In one study, Johnson, Bransford, and Solomon (1973) presented subjects with the following short passage:

> John was trying to fix the birdhouse. He was pounding the nail when his father came out to watch him and to help him do the work.

Subjects were later shown the preceding sentence along with others, including this one:

> John was using the hammer to fix the birdhouse when his father came out to watch and to help him do the work.

When questioned, the subjects overwhelmingly agreed they had seen the last sentence rather than the two they had actually seen. Note that the hammer was not even mentioned in the original text. It seems that participants recalled the central ideas of the two sentences and generated the hammer, because hammers are what we use to pound nails. Their birdhouse-building scripts, like yours and mine, use hammers.

The third characteristic of long-term memory is that understanding facilitates remembering—as would be expected, given that we tend to generate on the basis of our understanding. Paris and Lindauer (1976) asked children to remember the simple sentence "The workman dug a hole in the ground," adding "with a shovel" for half their subjects. One of the recall procedures was to present subjects with cue words (in this case, *shovel*). Significantly, the word *shovel* served equally well as a

---

elaborating A long-term memory process involving changing or adding to material or making associations to make remembering easier.

organizing A memory strategy involving grouping and relating material to maintain it in long-term memory.

gist memory Describes the remembering of main ideas and central themes, rather than details. Much of our memory appears to be *gist memory*. We remember the gist of something and generate the details.

scripts Our knowledge of what goes with what and in what sequence. Scripts are a part of cognitive structure that deals with the routine and the predictable.

TABLE 9.2
Three Levels of Memory

	SENSORY	SHORT-TERM	LONG-TERM
ALTERNATE LABELS	Echoic or iconic	Primary or working	Secondary
DURATION	Less than 1 second	Less than 20 seconds	Indefinite
STABILITY	Fleeting	Easily disrupted	Not easily disrupted
CAPACITY	Limited	Limited (7 ± 2 items)	Unlimited
GENERAL CHARACTERISTICS	Momentary, unconscious impression	Working memory; immediate consciousness; active, maintained by rehearsal	Knowledge base; associationistic; passive; the result of **encoding**

Source: From G. R. Lefrançois (2000), *Psychology for Teaching*, 10th ed. Belmont, Calif.: Wadsworth Publishing, p. 175.

cue for children who had not seen the word in the original sentence. Clearly, the cue word would have been totally meaningless for children who did not initially understand that holes can be dug with shovels. (Some characteristics of these three components of memory are summarized in Table 9.2).

Developmental Changes in Memory

An information-processing model of memory leads to some predictions about infants' and children's memory that can be tested directly. For example, we would expect that for stages of memory that involve little cognitive processing, young children might not perform very differently from older children or adults, but that when processing strategies are necessary, there should be greater differences between younger and older children.

Sensory and Short-term Memory In general, these predictions have been supported by research. Recall that does not depend on processing strategies does not appear to change very much as children develop. For example, recognition memory, a task that does not ordinarily involve complex strategies, is highly accurate from early childhood on (Nelson, 1993). Similarly, comparisons between adults and children regarding sensory and short-term memories—neither of them requiring any strategy more elaborate than simple repetition—have found few significant differences. It appears that short-term memory and

sensory memory change little from childhood to adulthood, because they do not require the use of elaborate or cognitively demanding strategies.

Longer-term Memory Memory that is highly dependent on the use of processing strategies should improve as children's recognition and understanding of strategies improve. This prediction is also supported by the evidence. It appears that very young children do not rehearse and organize as systematically as older children. Preschoolers apparently seldom use these strategies to learn and remember. Appel et al. (1972) showed pictures to children ages 4, 7, and 11 under one of two sets of instructions: "Look at these pictures" or "Remember these pictures." When the 7- and 11-year-olds were asked to remember, they deliberately used strategies to aid their recall. In contrast, 4-year-olds behaved exactly the same way under both sets of instructions.

Gathercole (1998), following a review of memory research, concludes that children's memory seems to improve significantly from infancy, through the preschool period, and until about age 7. After that, changes are more gradual. Not surprisingly, research indicates that children become progressively better at remembering as they get older, although longitudinal studies find that there are marked individual variations in memories. Some 8-year-olds remember remarkably well; others don't

encoding Change into a form that can be represented in memory.

(Schneider & Sodian, 1997). Needless to say, those with learning disabilities are more likely to experience memory problems (Davydova et al., 1999).

It isn't clear that children become better memorizers as they age solely because they develop better memory strategies. There is at least one other possibility, argues Reyna (1996): They *know* more. We have known for some time, for example, that experts in specific fields are far better at remembering things that relate to those fields. For example, chess masters can recall chess positions with an accuracy that amateur chess players find amazing (Chi, 1978). In much the same way, as children learn more about certain domains, their memories in those domains increase dramatically. In fact, when younger children know significantly more than older children in a specific area, they can outperform them on memory tests for newly presented material relating to that area. Thus, when Schneider, Schlagmueller, and Vise (1998) presented two different lists of pictures to 8- and 9-year-old boys, one of which consisted of soccer pictures, boys who were themselves soccer players (hence "experts" in that area) consistently outperformed the other boys who were not so expert.

Metacognition and Metamemory

In general, younger children are less capable of organizing material to facilitate their recall; they also seem to be less aware of the importance of doing so. They still lack many of the skills of metacognition. It is our metacognition skills that tell us there are ways to organize material so that it will be easier to learn and remember, there are rehearsal and review strategies that are more effective for one kind of learning than another, and there are some kinds of learning that require the deliberate application of cognitive strategies. Because memory is inseparably linked with cognition, metacognition includes what is sometimes termed metamemory—knowing about remembering.

Metacognitive skills seem to be largely absent in preschoolers. This does not mean that they use no memory or learning strategies; it simply means that they are not aware of them—that they do not consciously apply them. When Moynahan (1973) asked young children whether it would be easier to learn a categorized list of words or a random list, children below the third grade selected either list; children in the third grade were more likely to select the categorized list.

Hall, Bowman, & Myers (1999) found that by the age of 9, most children have relatively high metacognitive awareness. The authors assessed metacognitive awareness among 59 nine-year-olds by asking them whether they were good readers. The ability to monitor and evaluate one's own cognitive processes is one of the clearest indicators of metacognition. Most of these 9-year-olds were confident they knew what sorts of readers they were; and for most of them, teacher judgments agreed with their self-evaluations. The vast majority considered themselves good readers (83%)! It may be, as Juliebo, Malicky, and Norman (1998) suggest, that metacognitive skills are closely related to the development of reading skills. Can these be taught? Should they be?

Teaching Cognitive Strategies

Teachers have traditionally not taught cognitive strategies systematically in schools. Instead, they simply assume that students will learn them incidentally. However, some researchers argue that these strategies should be deliberately taught and encouraged, and many programs have been designed for this purpose (see Royer, Cisero, & Carlo, 1993). For example, Mulcahy (1991) uses a Socratic dialogue question-and-answer teaching method to lead students to a recognition of their own cognitive strategies. Similarly, Collins, Brown, and Newman (1989) suggest a *cognitive apprenticeship* approach where **mentors** (parents, teachers, peers, siblings) serve as both models and teachers. The object is to provide learners with cognitive strategies so that they are equipped to explore, organize, discover, and learn on their own. Research makes it plain, claim Perkins, Jay, and Tishman (1993), that instruction in the skills that define metacognition can significantly improve learning and memory.

mentors Individuals engaged in a one-to-one teaching/learning relationship in which teachers serve not only as a source of information, but also as important models with respect to values, beliefs, philosophies and attitudes.

The Game of Cognition

Metacognition and metamemory deal with our knowledge about how we know—our awareness of ourselves as players of what Flavell calls the game of cognition. The object of the game of cognition is to pay attention, to learn, to remember, to retrieve from memory, and to do a variety of things such as sorting, analyzing, synthesizing, evaluating, and creating.

There is more than one way to play the game of cognition. Some people play it very badly. They learn slowly, remember inaccurately, and seem lost and clumsy when faced with tasks requiring evaluation, synthesis, or creation. Others play the game very well. Their responses are quick and accurate, their syntheses elegant, their creations startling.

Children do not play the game of cognition as well as adults. Why? Research reviewed in this section suggests at least four reasons: Children do not have (or do not use) strategies that are as effective; they lack basic knowledge about the world; their metamemory skills (their awareness of the need to monitor, to evaluate, to use strategies) are absent or less well developed; and their short-term memory capacity is more limited. These four factors, says Peverly (1991), are basic to the development of memory; they are the tools of intelligence.

⬕ INTELLIGENCE

"Intelligence is what the tests test," Boring (1923, p. 35) informs us. This simple definition of what is not a simple concept is a useful and not entirely tongue-in-cheek definition. Weight is not a simple concept either, yet to say that weight is what a scale measures is both useful and accurate. A butcher doesn't have to understand the scientific notion of weight—the interaction of gravity and mass and altitude—to use a scale in order to slap a price on a rump roast. Perhaps a psychologist or a teacher need not know what intelligence is to make use of the results of intelligence tests.

Then again, maybe we do need to know, because there is an important difference between weighing and pricing a roast and tagging a child with an intelligence test score. We agree about what weight is; we define it precisely and objectively. Our scales measure weight with marvelous accuracy. They measure exactly what they're supposed to measure, and nothing else—that is, they are **valid**. And they measure consistently, yielding the same weights for the same objects over and over again—that is, they are **reliable**.

Different Ways of Describing Intelligence

But we don't know exactly what intelligence is. Some theorists, beginning with Spearman (1927), have assumed that it is a quality of human functioning that depends on some basic, general capacity or trait in a person—that if you have a lot of this general something (which Spearman labeled *g* for *general intelligence*), then your behavior will be intelligent in all areas. If this supposition is correct, then those who are highly intelligent (have high *g*) should do well in all tasks: mathematical, verbal, spatial, reasoning, memory, and so on. This **general factor theory**, as it is known, is reflected in the two most widely used and highly respected intelligence tests in current use, the Stanford Binet and the Wechsler. Both yield a single IQ score, even though the Wechsler also provides separate *verbal* and *performance* measures.

General factor theory stands in contrast to **special abilities theory**, which assumes that rather than depending on a common underlying factor, intelligence consists of separate abilities. Special abilities theory is evident, for example, in Gardner's theory of multiple intelligences, which is discussed later.

valid A measure is said to be valid to the extent that it measures what it is intended to measure.

reliable A measure is reliable to the extent that it measures accurately whatever it measures.

g Spearman's abbreviation for general intelligence, a notion based on his observation that people who do well on one kind of intelligence test also tend to do well on others, as though there is some general mental ability that affects performance in all areas.

general factor theory A theory of intelligence based on the assumption that there is a basic, underlying quality of intellectual functioning that determines *intelligence* in all areas. This quality is sometimes labeled *g*.

special abilities theory A theory of intelligence based on the assumption that intelligence consists of several separate factors (for example, numerical, verbal, memory) rather than a single underlying factor common to performance in all areas.

Fluid and Crystallized Intelligence

One approach that combines concepts of both general factor and special abilities theory is Cattell's (1971) theory of two main kinds of intellectual abilities. On one hand, he explains, there are certain abilities, labeled **fluid abilities** (or sometimes fluid intelligence), that seem to underlie much of our intelligent behavior. These abilities are not learned and are therefore relatively unaffected by cultural and environmental influences. These abilities represent something like Spearman's *g*. Fluid abilities are manifested in individuals' ability to solve abstract problems and are evident in measures of general reasoning and analysis of figures. They are also very closely related to those aspects of memory involved in attention span (Engle et al., 1999).

In contrast to these basic fluid abilities is a grouping of intellectual abilities that are mainly verbal and that are therefore highly influenced by culture, experience, and education. These abilities, labeled **crystallized abilities** (or crystallized intelligence), are reflected in measures of vocabulary, general information, and arithmetic skills.

Several developmental predictions can be based on the distinctions between fluid and crystallized intelligence. First, because fluid intelligence is independent of experience, it should remain constant throughout most of development, perhaps increasing slightly as the nervous system matures through childhood and adolescence, and maybe decreasing somewhat in old age as the nervous system ages. Second, because crystallized intelligence is highly dependent on experience, it should grow with increasing age, maybe right through old age.

These predictions have received some support: Crystallized abilities appear to increase with age and experience (Kaufman et al., 1996). Thus, measures of intelligence that reflect these abilities often continue to increase in adulthood (Horn, 1976; Horn & Donaldson, 1980). In contrast, fluid abilities are more likely to deteriorate as neurological functioning deteriorates (Boone, 1995).

Sternberg's Successful Intelligence

Maybe we've been paying too much attention to measured intelligence, says Sternberg (1996a; 1998). Maybe we should focus instead on the people who are most successful in adapting to the world. It seems, argues Sternberg, that these people are successful not just because they learn well, but also because they're good at selecting and shaping their environments. What they have is **successful intelligence**—as opposed to measured or **psychometric intelligence**. In Sternberg's (1984) words, intelligence is the "purposive selection and shaping of and adaptation to real-world environments relevant to one's life" (p. 312).

A Closer Look This definition has two very important features: First, it emphasizes the individual's control over the environment. It says, in effect, that intelligent people choose their environments and also try to change them. Thus, it would have been more than a little stupid of me, whose voice used to send my grandmother to the outhouse even when she didn't really need to go, to choose to sing for a living. In retrospect, however, I might have been smart to have taken singing lessons—or even to have changed my audience. (Céline Tremblay said she liked the way I sang, and her father was quite well off.)

Second, Sternberg's view emphasizes the *contextual* nature of intelligence. It says that successful intelligence is adaptation to real worlds, to real

---

fluid abilities Cattell's term for intellectual abilities that seem to underlie much of our intelligent behavior and are not highly affected by experience (general reasoning, attention span, memory for numbers). Fluid abilities are more likely to decline in old age than are crystallized abilities.

crystallized abilities Cattell's term for intellectual abilities that are highly dependent on experience (verbal and computational skills and general information, for example). These abilities may continue to improve well into old age.

successful intelligence Sternberg's view that intelligence involves a balance between selecting and shaping environments and adaptation to achieve personal goals.

psychometric intelligence Psychometrics has to do with measuring psychological functioning. Hence psychometric intelligence is a label for approaches that describe or define intelligence in terms of its measurement.

contexts. This, argues Sternberg (1999), makes it a multicultural model of intelligence. It recognizes that certain behaviors may be highly intelligent in one cultural context but quite unintelligent in another. In North American cultures, for example, we consider intelligent those people who can solve practical problems, who have high verbal ability, and who are socially competent. Elsewhere, highly developed spatial skills, such as might be required for finding one's way through a sunless jungle, coupled with a tendency to keep one's mouth shut, might be a mark of successful intelligence.

A TRIARCHIC THEORY OF SUCCESSFUL INTELLIGENCE

Successful intelligence, Sternberg (1996a) explains, requires three different sorts of abilities. First, *analytical* abilities are essential for understanding real-life situations—that is, for analyzing, evaluating, comparing, and contrasting them. Analysis is essential for determining and evaluating options, for monitoring successes and failures, and for organizing and selecting strategies. Put another way, analytical abilities are basic to understanding situations, to understanding one's abilities and goals, and to understanding what sorts of options are available.

Second, successful intelligence requires *creative* abilities—the sorts of abilities that are involved in creating, inventing, or discovering. They allow the intelligent individual to generate options, to try new ways of selecting and shaping the environment and adapting to it.

Third, successful intelligence requires *practical* abilities. These are the skills involved in actually putting options into practice—in carrying out the behaviors involved in selecting, shaping, and adapting to environments.

These three components of successful intelligence make up what Sternberg labels the **triarchic theory of successful intelligence** (Figure 9.9). It's a theory that has important implications for measuring intelligence. It suggests that conventional mea-

triarchic theory of successful intelligence Sternberg's model of successful intelligence as involving analytical, creative, and practical abilities.

Successful Intelligence: a balance among selecting and shaping the environment and adapting to it to achieve social and personal goals requires three sorts of abilities:

| **Analytical Abilities** (analyzing, evaluating, comparing, contrasting . . .) | **Creative Abilities** (inventing, discovering, imagining . . .) | **Practical Abilities** (putting into practice, using, doing . . .) |

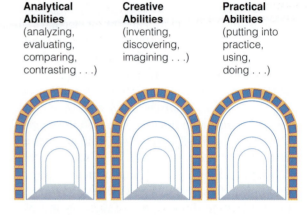

FIGURE 9.9 A representation of the three arches of Sternberg's triarchic model of successful intelligence.

sures of intelligence are inadequate because, as we see later in this chapter, they seldom measure either creative or practical abilities. Their emphasis is on verbal and analytical skills.

One advantage of this model is that it removes intelligence from the realm of the abstract and theoretical, emphasizing instead the individual's success in adapting to the demands of the real world. It makes intelligence more concrete, more practical, perhaps more understandable. But it also has the disadvantage of not being specific enough. It says, in effect, that all behaviors that are successful—that lead to apparent adaptation—are intelligent, at least in that context (although they might be quite stupid in another).

Gardner's Multiple Intelligences

But, says Gardner (1983), how well we adapt, the *success* of our intelligent behavior, may well reflect our basic talents and capabilities. Simply to say that successful intelligence involves a high level of adaptation is not to say very much about the underlying characteristics of the individual.

A Closer Look Gardner's **theory of multiple intelligences** speaks directly about underlying characteris-

Howard Gardner's Seven—or More—Intelligences

Intelligence	Possible Occupation	Core Components
Logical-mathematical	Scientist Mathematician	Sensitivity and capacity to discern logical or numerical patterns; ability to handle long chains of reasoning
Linguistic	Poet Journalist	Sensitivity to the sounds, rhythms, and meanings of words; sensitivity to the different functions of language
Musical	Composer Violinist	Abilities to produce and appreciate rhythm, pitch, and timbre; appreciation of the forms of musical expressiveness
Spatial	Navigator Sculptor	Capacities to perceive the visual-spatial world accurately and to manipulate the mental representations that result
Bodily-kinesthetic	Dancer Athlete	Abilities to control one's body movements and to handle objects skillfully
Interpersonal	Therapist Salesperson	Capacities to discern and respond appropriately to the moods, temperaments, motivations, and desires of other people
Intrapersonal	Poet Writer	Access to one's own feelings and the ability to discriminate among them and draw upon them to guide behavior; knowledge of one's own strengths, weaknesses, desires, and intelligences
Naturalist	Biologist Evolutionary-theorist	Ability to detect patterns and organization in nature
Spiritual	Preacher Monk	A concern with the spiritual, with origins, and with the afterlife
Existential	Philosopher Theologian	Interest in the purpose and meaning of existence

Note: The last three intelligences are recent additions, based on incomplete and uncertain evidence, and not yet clearly distinguishable.

Source: From H. Gardner & T. Hatch (1989). Multiple intelligences go to school: Educational implications of the theory of multiple intelligences. *Educational Researcher* 18(8): 4–10; and H. Gardner (1998). Are there additional intelligences? The case for naturalist, spiritual, and existential intelligences, in J. Kane (ed.), *Education, information, and transformation*. Englewood Cliffs, N.J.: Prentice Hall.

tics. In effect, it says that we don't have one single underlying *general* type of intelligence; we have at least seven separate and distinct intelligences—and we may have as many as 10 (see *Concept Summary*). In Gardner's words, we have *multiple intelligences*:

theory of multiple intelligences Howard Gardner's belief that human intelligence consists of 7—or perhaps 8 or even 10—distinct and largely unrelated areas of talent or capability: logical-mathematical, linguistic, musical, spatial, bodily-kinesthetic, interpersonal, and intrapersonal—and perhaps naturalist, spiritual, and existential.

linguistic, musical, logical-mathematical, spatial, bodily-kinesthetic, and personal (including *inter* and *intra* personal)—and, just maybe, naturalist, spiritual, and existential (Gardner, 1998).

In any given society, some of these intelligences will be considered more important than others. In North American societies, for example, linguistic and logical-mathematical skills are clearly most important. Accordingly, these are the skills taught in our schools, and they are also the skills most often measured by our intelligence tests (Gardner & Hatch, 1989).

The theory of multiple intelligences has been of considerable interest to educators. It suggests that our emphasis on logical-mathematical and linguistic skills overlooks the development of at least five other important human dimensions. This theory has resulted in the creation of various programs designed to develop intelligences that traditionally have not been of much interest to schools (Linich, 1999). It has also stimulated new approaches to measuring intelligence. As Lowenthal (1997) points out, assessing individual intelligences can serve as a basis for identifying and building on the strengths of individual students, as well as for improving their functioning in their weaker areas.

Emotional Intelligence in Gardner's Theory As we saw in Chapter 8, of special recent interest is a dimension often labeled emotional intelligence. Emotional intelligence is defined by Gardner's *interpersonal* and *intrapersonal* intelligences. It is reflected in people's ability to interpret others' moods and emotions, and to control and express their own emotions in socially appropriate ways. Clearly, emotional intelligence is closely tied to social competence. As we saw, preschoolers best able to regulate their emotions tend to have the most friends (Walden, Lemerise, & Smith, 1999).

There has been considerable research on emotional intelligence, even though it is difficult to measure. Self-ratings tend to be highly unreliable, and evaluators such as parents and teachers often don't agree with each other (Davies, Stankov, & Roberts, 1998). Nevertheless, various questionnaire-type measures have been developed (for example, Schutte et al., 1998). Research using some of these measures indicates, not surprisingly, that high levels of emotional intelligence are correlated with success in the workplace (Abraham, 1999) as well as with realistic

and adaptive goals, higher levels of satisfaction with life, and lower incidence of emotional disturbances (Martinez-Pons, 1997). In fact, many educators advocate including the development of emotional intelligence as an important focus of schools (for example, Lang, 1999).

Measuring Intelligence

One important emphasis common to Sternberg's, Gardner's, and Cattell's theories is that intelligence is an activity—an information-processing activity. These authors tend to see intelligence as more than a mysterious quality that some people have a great deal of—and others, unfortunately, much less. In this view, intelligence is like a box of tools that we use to play the game of cognition or, if you will, the game of adapting to the real world. We may not all have the same tools in our little kits, but we can certainly learn to use them better. And maybe we can learn a great deal from watching how others use their tools.

In the same sense, measuring intelligence is like trying to find out both the sorts of tools there are in the tool kit and how well these tools are being used—although most of our measures don't allow us to make so fine a distinction.

The Meaning of IQ The principal use of intelligence tests is for prediction. An intelligence test score is, in effect, a prediction that an individual will do well (or not do well) on tasks that require intelligence, like passing a grade or succeeding in college. But what most intelligence tests yield is referred to as an **intelligence quotient** (IQ)—about which there is a great deal of confusion and mythical beliefs, as we see shortly.

The concept of IQ, invented by William Stern (1914), is quite simple. A given 8-year-old, he explained, should be able to do about the same sorts of things as all other 8-year-olds. The **mental age** of an average group of 8-year-olds is, in fact, 8. That also happens to be their *chronological* age. So the

---

intelligence quotient (IQ) A way of describing intelligence by assigning it a number. May be arrived at by giving tests to estimate mental age, and then multiplying the ratio of mental to chronological age by 100. Average IQ is therefore 100.

ratio of mental age to chronological age for an average child is 8 ÷ 8, which is 1. Multiply that by 100 so that there will never be any decimals, and there you have it, an average IQ of 100!

But some 8-year-olds can do more than the average 8-year-old. In fact, some can answer questions and solve problems at about the same level as a 10-year-old. The ratio of their mental to chronological age would be 10 ÷ 8. Multiply that by 100, and the IQ becomes 125 (see Figure 9.10).

Nowadays mental age is seldom computed in this way. Instead, tests provide users with tables that allow scores to be converted directly into an IQ. These tables are constructed so that the average IQ for a large, unselected population is around 100. Scores are distributed roughly as shown in Figure 9.11.

Intelligence Tests Some intelligence tests can be administered to only one child at a time. These are individual intelligence tests. Administering, scoring, and interpreting them typically requires extensive training and time. Hence they are quite expensive, but they yield a richer picture of intellectual functioning than do group intelligence tests—tests that can be administered to a large group at one time and that are commonly of a paper-and-pencil variety.

Most group tests tend to be highly verbal, given that they are mainly paper-and-pencil tests. One example of an individual test that isn't verbal is the *Goodenough-Harris Drawing Test* described in Chapter 7. Recall that it asks participants to draw the best person they can, and then scores drawings according to detail and style. Other widely used group tests include the *Cognitive Abilities Test (CogAT)* for grades 3 through 13 and the *Otis-Lennon School Ability Test* for grades 1 through 12.

Measures of intelligence tend to become progressively more reliable with advancing age. That is, for older children and adults, scores obtained from tests given at different times tend to be similar. Measures of intelligence during the preschool period are less reliable; those given in infancy, even less so. Still, as we saw in Chapter 5, there are several

IQ was originally defined as the ratio of mental age to chronological age multiplied by 100 (multiplying by 100 gets rid of the decimal point and makes the average IQ exactly 100).

That is, $IQ = \dfrac{MA}{CA} \times 100$

For example: If 10-year-old Len performs at the level of average 8-year-olds, his IQ is:

$$\frac{8}{10} \times 100 = 80$$

If 10-year-old Lena performs at the level of average 12-year-olds, her IQ is:

$$\frac{12}{10} \times 100 = 120$$

FIGURE 9.10 The original meaning of the IQ. In current practice, mental age is seldom computed. Instead, tests come with tables of norms based on the average performance of large samples. These permit the tester to convert actual test scores directly into IQs.

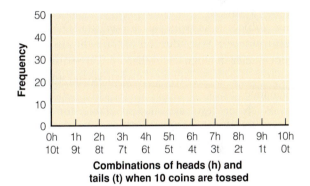

Combinations of heads (h) and tails (t) when 10 coins are tossed

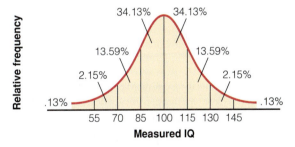

Measured IQ

FIGURE 9.11 On a sheet of paper, draw two axes as shown at top. Now shake 10 coins in a cup, roll them out, count the heads and tails, and record them. Do this at least 50 times, although 500 would be better. When you are finished, plot your results. The resulting graph should be a close approximation of the figure above, which is a *normal curve* depicting the theoretical distribution of IQ scores. Note that average events (an average IQ of 100, an equal number of heads and tails) are most frequent, and more unusual events (10 heads or 10 tails, IQs above 130 or below 70) are least frequent. Only 2.28% of the population scores above IQ 130 or below 70. Two-thirds of the entire population scores between IQ 85 and 115.

---

mental age A measure or estimate of intellectual functioning expressed in terms of age. Thus an average 7-year-old has a mental age of 7.

infant tests of development, like the *Bayley Scales* and the *Fagan Test of Infant Intelligence*. Infant measures of development are not especially good predictors of later intelligence, although they can be useful for screening children at risk of developmental problems.

Among the most widely used individual intelligence tests are the *Stanford-Binet* and the *Wechsler*. The *Stanford-Binet* yields scores in four areas: verbal reasoning, quantitative reasoning, abstract/visual reasoning, and short-term memory. It also provides a composite score that is described as a measure of "adaptive ability" and that can be interpreted as an IQ score.

The *Wechsler Intelligence Scale for Children* (3rd ed., 1991), also called the *WISC-III*, yields a composite IQ score comparable to that obtained with the *Stanford-Binet*. The tests differ in several important ways, however. Most notably, the *WISC-III* also yields separate standardized scores for various subjects, as well as a verbal IQ and a performance IQ (in addition to the composite IQ). Deficiencies in language background are sometimes apparent in discrepancies between verbal and performance scores.

Wechsler tests are also available for adults (*WAIS-R: Wechsler Adult Intelligence Scale Revised*, ages 16 to 75), and for preschool children (*WPPSI:*

Wechsler Preschool and Primary Scale of Intelligence, ages 4 to 6½). The various subtests of the *WISC-III* are described in Table 9.3.

Developmental Changes in IQ

A normal 6-year-old child can correctly repeat two or three digits if they are presented clearly and distinctly at a rate of approximately one per second, but would not be expected to repeat four digits in reverse order. An average 3-year-old can quickly identify legs, arms, hands, nose, and mouth on a doll, but might hesitate if asked to point to the infranasal depression. Clearly, there is a marked improvement in children's problem solving, remembering, language, reasoning, and so on. Does that mean that intelligence improves?

The answer, of course, depends on how intelligence is defined. If it's defined simply as being able to do those things we consider to be examples of intelligent behavior (such as remembering, reasoning accurately, and expressing oneself clearly), then the answer is yes—children become more intelligent with age. But if intelligence is defined psychometrically (that is, by how we measure it) the answer is no, because measured IQ is not an absolute indicator of what or how much a child can do. Instead, it is

---

TABLE 9.3
The Wechsler Intelligence Scale for Children Revised (*WISC-III*)

VERBAL SCALE	PERFORMANCE SCALE
1. *General information.* Questions relating to information most children have the opportunity to acquire. (M)*	1. *Picture completion.* Child indicates what is missing in pictures. (M)
2. *General comprehension.* Questions designed to assess child's understanding of why certain things are done as they are. (M)	2. *Picture arrangement.* Series of pictures must be arranged to tell a story. (M)
3. *Arithmetic.* Oral arithmetic problems. (M)	3. *Block design.* Child is required to copy exactly a design with colored blocks. (M)
4. *Similarities.* Child indicates how certain things are alike. (M)	4. *Object assembly.* Puzzles to be assembled by subjects. (M)
5. *Vocabulary.* Child gives meanings of words of increasing difficulty. (M)	5. *Coding.* Child pairs symbols with digits following a key. (M)
6. *Digit span.* Child repeats orally presented sequence of numbers, in order and reversed. (S)	6. *Mazes.* Child traces way out of mazes with pencil. (S)
	7. *Symbol Search.* Child performs symbol location task that measures mental processing speed and visual search skills. (S)

*(M) Mandatory; (S) Supplementary

a measure of what a child can do compared with other children of similar ages and experience. And because children improve at similar rates and in similar ways, the average child's measured intelligence does not change from year to year. By definition, it stays right around 100.

But, as we have said more than once, there is no average child; the average is merely a mathematical invention. What about the individual?

The individual, research informs us, may display a great variety of intellectual developmental patterns. As a result, measured differences between two individuals do not necessarily remain constant. For some children, measured IQ may increase over a period of years, or it may decrease, or it might go up and down like a bouncing ball. For most children, however, measured IQ is relatively stable; it fluctuates within a range that would be expected given the imprecision of the tests. This indicates, claim Gustafsson and Undheim (1992), that the factors underlying intelligence are relatively stable.

The Influence of the School

Outside of the family, the school is the most pervasive socializing influence in a child's life. In fact, notes Stevenson and colleagues (1991), the influence of the school is so pervasive in our societies that much of what developmental psychologists view as "normal" development is a reflection of what children learn in schools.

How Schools Affect Measured Intelligence Schools do more than socialize children and teach them important information and skills. There is evidence that schools also increase measured intelligence. Thus, for several of decades now, measured intelligence has been increasing in most of the world's industrialized countries. This increase, labeled the Flynn effect, has been quite dramatic in some instances. Flynn (1987) reports increases of about 24 points in the United States since 1918, and of 27 points in Britain since 1942.

Additional evidence that formal schooling is closely tied to measured intelligence is found in studies that show a relationship between level of schooling (grade attained) and IQ; between missing school and declines in IQ; between delayed school

entrance and lower IQ; and between increasing school attendance in an area and general increases in measured IQ (Ceci, 1991). And Stevenson and associates (1991) found significant differences in cognitive development between Peruvian children who attended school and those who didn't. Perhaps more striking, the authors found remarkable similarities in the cognitive functioning of first-graders from such diverse cultural backgrounds as Peru, Taiwan, Japan, and the United States—almost as though the experiences of first grade had already begun to wipe out what would otherwise have been highly noticeable differences.

Mastery-Oriented versus Helpless Children Schools don't affect all children the same way. And while they might increase measured intelligence in some, they may have little or no effect on others. Part of the reason for this may be that some children typically have many success experiences in schools, while others experience more failure. But perhaps even more important than whether the student succeeds or fails is how children typically view their successes and failures—what they *attribute* them to.

An *attribution* is an assignment of cause or blame for the outcomes of our behaviors. If I think my stupidity is due to my having hit my head on a low branch when I was 10, then I attribute my stupidity to that event. Attribution theories look for regularities in how we assign causes to the things that happen to us (Weiner, 1980; 1994).

Some people accept personal responsibility for the consequences of their behavior. They are said to have an **internal orientation** (or to be persistent; Dweck, 1986). Others are more likely to attribute successes and failures to circumstances or events over which they have no control, and are described as having an **external orientation** (in Dweck's terms, they are characterized by **learned helplessness** rather

---

internal orientation A tendency to attribute the outcomes of behavior to factors within the individual's control (such as effort or ability).

external orientation A tendency to attribute the outcomes of behavior to factors outside the individual, hence not under the individual's control (such as luck or the difficulty of a task).

learned helplessness Personality characteristic evident in a tendency to attribute outcomes to causes over which the person has no control.

TABLE 9.4
Why did you fail or succeed?
Internally oriented versus externally oriented attributions

In Chapter 3, you were asked to figure out what Henry VIII didn't know that might have influenced his habit of beheading various wives who failed to give him sons. Did you succeed or fail? Why? Are you one of those who characteristically accept personal responsibility for successes and failures? Or are you more likely to invoke luck, the difficulty (or easiness) of the task, or other factors over which you have no control? How do you explain your high (or low) grades to yourself? Your reasons reveal important things about your personality and achievement motivation.

EXTERNAL	INTERNAL
Difficulty (task easy or too difficult)	Ability (intelligence, skill, or the lack thereof)
Luck (bad or good)	Effort (hard work, industriousness, and self-discipline; or laziness, distractions, lack of time)

than by persistence). Thus, **mastery-oriented** children are most likely to attribute their successes to ability or effort (factors that are personal, or factors over which they at least have personal control). In contrast, helpless children are more likely to attribute their successes or failures to luck or the difficulty of the task (factors over which they have no personal control; (see Table 9.4).

There is a tendency, says Dweck, for children who are internally oriented to believe that intelligence is malleable. They subscribe to what she labels the **incremental theory of intelligence**. These students are mastery oriented; they work hard, they seek challenges, and they are persistent (Mueller and Dweck, 1998). In contrast, many externally oriented students seem to subscribe to the **entity theory of intelligence**. They believe that intelligence is fixed. If they don't have enough, well, working hard isn't going to pay off that much, especially if they aren't lucky or if schoolwork is too hard. These students are more likely to be characterized by pessimism and by external motivation, explain Harju and Eppler (1997).

---

mastery-oriented Personality characteristic marked by a tendency to attribute the outcomes of behavior to factors under personal control.

incremental theory of intelligence Dweck's label for the belief that ability is malleable through work and effort. Associated with mastery goals—that is, with increasing personal competence.

entity theory of intelligence Dweck's label for the belief that ability is a fixed, unchanging entity. Associated with performance goals—that is, with doing well in order to be judged positively by others.

There appear to be some clear advantages to being mastery oriented, especially in school. For this reason, some programs have been developed to change attributions. These are based on the assumption that the tendency to attribute outcomes to internal or external factors is at least partly learned, and can therefore be changed (Ames, 1992).

Misconceptions and Facts about IQ

The IQ is not always clearly understood, nor is it always used intelligently. The following misconceptions are still common.

Misconception 1 *IQ is a mysterious something, synonymous with intelligence, that everybody has in different quantities.* In fact, measured IQ is simply a number based on a person's ability to perform in prescribed circumstances. It reflects performance on a test that typically has limited reliability (consistency) and validity—that is, it doesn't always measure what it intends to. In fact, it often measures other things, such as fatigue or motivation. The terms *IQ* and *intelligence* are not synonymous at all. IQ is a score (we don't always know exactly what that score means); intelligence, on the other hand, is made up of various mental abilities. Thus IQ tests don't reveal mystical, hidden qualities that would otherwise be known only by clever psychologists who have dedicated their lives to the pursuit of the hidden truth.

Misconception 2 *IQ is a constant. I have* x *amount, you have* y, *and that's that.* Not so. Research increasingly points to the conclusion that measured IQ has, in fact, been increasing in recent decades. This is the Flynn effect, described earlier. As we saw, schooling and interaction with new technologies have much to do with the Flynn effect. The Flynn effect, as Capron et al. (1999) point out, underlines the fact that intelligence is not a genetically fixed quality. Increases in measured IQ have been too large and have occurred too rapidly to be explained on the basis of evolutionary changes.

Misconception 3 *IQ tests measure all the important things.* Not so. In fact, most IQ tests measure relatively limited sorts of things, like how well and how rapidly we can work with abstract ideas and symbols. As Sternberg (1996b) notes, IQ tests often don't provide information about the components of *practical* intelligence. They tell us nothing about emotional intelligence, motivation, or adaptive skills. Nor do they reveal anything about athletic ability, creativity, self-concept, or a host of other important personality variables.

Misconception 4 *IQ tests are fair.* Many IQ tests are culturally biased; they penalize children whose backgrounds are different from the groups on which they were normed (typically, the white, middle-class majority). It is not surprising that children from minority groups often do less well on these tests than their like-aged, middle-class, white counterparts. However, the most recent revisions of the *Wechsler* and the *Stanford-Binet* have taken this weakness into account and have used more representative norming samples. Accordingly, they are much fairer to minorities.

Fact *IQ is related to success, particularly in school, but also in later life.* Although intelligence tests have weaknesses and limitations, they can be useful predictors of successful adaptation to school and life. Unfortunately, although they are widely used, they are not always widely understood—hence the need to urge that information derived from tests be used in a restrained and intelligent way. This means that no important decisions should be based on a single test and without considering information from all other important sources. And perhaps nowhere is

Wayne Eastep/Tony Stone Images

It is a misconception that intelligence tests measure all the important things. Among other things, they don't measure a large number of personality characteristics such as motivation, persistence, creativity, and the ability to influence others. Nor do they measure adjustment—or physical strength.

this admonition truer than when we are dealing with exceptional children.

INTELLECTUAL EXCEPTIONALITY

Exceptionality refers to mental, physical, or social-emotional functioning that is significantly better or poorer than average. At one extreme are those who are exceptionally gifted, who possess extraordinary talents. At the other extreme are those to whom nature and nurture have been less kind—those who experience difficulty in learning some, or most, of the things that others learn easily. This manifestation of exceptionality includes two broad categories: those with mental retardation, and those with learning disabilities.

Mental Retardation

The most obvious feature of **mental retardation** is a depression in the ability to learn; a second important feature involves problems with adaptation. Both of

mental retardation A global term referring to the mental state of individuals whose intellectual development is significantly slower than that of normal children and whose ability to adapt to their environment is consequently limited.

these features are reflected in the widely accepted definition presented by the American Association on Mental Retardation (AAMR, 1992):

> Mental retardation refers to substantial limitations in present intellectual functioning. It is characterized by significantly subaverage intellectual functioning existing concurrently with related limitations in two or more of the following applicable adaptive skill areas: communication, self-care, home living, social skills, community use, self-direction, health and safety, functional academics, leisure, and work. Mental retardation manifests before age 18.

The meaning of this definition may be clarifed by looking at each of the key terms involved. First, *significantly subaverage intellectual functioning* is defined by test scores on one or more of the well-known individual intelligence tests—for example, the *Stanford-Binet* or the *Wechsler*. An IQ of about 70 is the accepted (and admittedly inexact) cutoff between normality and mental retardation.

Second, *limitations in . . . adaptive skill areas* are significant maturational deficits that are most often manifested as inability to learn or inability to reach the levels of independence, social responsibility, and social effectiveness that would normally be expected of others of similar age and experience. Failure to learn to dress oneself during the preschool period might be one indication of an impairment in adaptive behavior; failure to toilet train would be another (Reschly, 1990).

Developmental Delays The definition of mental retardation specifies that the deficits must be manifested during the developmental period—a period that extends from conception to age 18. However, a 1997 amendment of the Individuals with Disabilities Education Act (IDEA) recommends that for younger children, the phrase **developmentally delayed** should be used instead of *mentally retarded*. That's because some young children experience apparent retardation in development, or uneven patterns of

developmentally delayed Term used to describe apparent cognitive or adaptive deficits in children below age 3 or sometimes 5, or even as old as 9. Recommended term because of problems in identifying both the existence and the causes of apparent deficits at very young ages.

development not because of mental retardation, but because of language problems, hearing problems, or other conditions. It is often difficult to determine the very early causes of developmental delays.

Identifying Children with Mental Retardation In practice, mental retardation is most often identified and defined by performance on intelligence tests. More limited attention is given to adaptive behavior, a characteristic that is difficult to measure or define. This excessive reliance on measured intelligence is sometimes unfortunate, for at least two reasons. First, measures at the lower levels of mental retardation are extremely unreliable because almost nobody in the norming samples ever scores below 50 (Reschly, 1992); and second, intelligence may be reflected more accurately—and more usefully—in the individual's level of adaptation than in more abstract measures of IQ, especially for those from different cultural or language backgrounds.

The AAMR provides a detailed discussion of what is meant by "adaptive behavior" and how it might be assessed. For example, adaptation during infancy and early childhood is evident in the child's development of sensory motor skills, the ability to communicate, the appearance of self-help skills, and progressive socialization. During later childhood, children would also be expected to learn and apply basic academic skills, develop age-appropriate reasoning and judgment, and develop social skills evident in participation in group activities. During adolescence, in addition to the continued age-appropriate development in all these areas, the individual would also be expected to assume more adult roles as reflected in work and social responsibilities. Various standardized inventories are available for assessing the level of adaptive behaviors. One developed by the AAMR provides a relatively good indication of the child's independence and social behavior (Stinnet, Fuqua, & Coombs, 1999).

Prevalence of Mental Retardation Estimates of the prevalence of mental retardation vary. The normal distribution of intelligence in the general population suggests that 2.68% of the population should score below IQ 70. But if level of adaptation is taken into account, the figure is closer to 1% (Deiner, 1999).

As we noted in Chapter 6, the existence of multiple developmental problems is not uncommon

(Kagan and Gall, 1998). Thus many children who are mentally retarded also manifest other developmental disorders.

Causes of Mental Retardation The causes of mental retardation are so varied that it is almost always classified by severity rather than cause. Still, researchers identify two main groups of causes: biological and environmental. Biological causes, sometimes termed **organic causes**, can be either prenatal or postnatal and include chromosomal aberrations such as Down syndrome and fragile X syndrome (see Chapter 3); maternal conditions such as rubella, malnutrition, or diabetes; drugs or chemicals; and radiation. Environmental causes, sometimes termed **familial causes**, include unstimulating environments, malnutrition, and perhaps abuse or other traumas. As Deiner (1999) points out, in as many as 40% of all cases, the causes of mental retardation are unknown.

Categories of Mental Retardation The American Association on Mental Retardation distinguishes among four categories of retardation: mild, moder-

ate, severe, and profound (Figure 9.12). The American Psychiatric Association makes exactly the same distinctions but allows for more overlap between categories. The categories are defined through scores on intelligence tests. Overlapping categories that are of more practical use for special-needs educators distinguish among educable, trainable, and custodial retardation.

The largest proportion of intellectually handicapped children (about 85%) has **mild retardation**. Most of these children are not identified as being retarded until they have been in school for some time. They ordinarily develop social and language skills and experience relatively normal motor development. Most mildly retarded children are capable of acceptable academic achievement in elementary school. This group roughly corresponds to the group described as educable mentally retarded (EMR).

Children classified as having **moderate retardation** compose about 10% of the retarded group and, along with some of the severely retarded, are often described as trainable (Deiner, 1999). These children can learn to talk during the preschool period;

organic causes With respect to mental retardation, physiological or biological causes including genetic conditions or maternal diseases, drugs, and radiation.

familial causes Relating to mental retardation, environmental causes often associated with lower socioeconomic levels, including unstimulating environments and malnutrition.

mild retardation Mild cognitive deficits, usually defined in terms of an IQ range between 50 and about 70. Also termed *educable*, children with mild retardation are capable of achievement at about the sixth-grade level, and of adequate social adaptation.

moderate retardation A degree of mental retardation defined in terms of an IQ range between 35 or 40 and 50 or 55. Can achieve at about the second-grade level, and can profit from training in social and occupational skills.

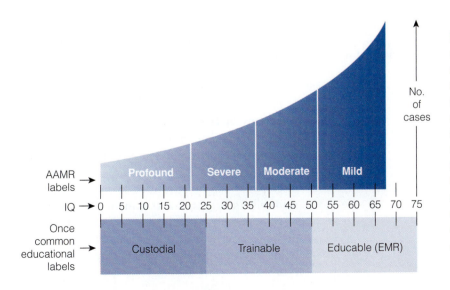

FIGURE 9.12 Two common classification schemes for mental retardation, both based entirely on measured IQ; in practice, adaptive skills would also be taken into account. The American Association on Mental Retardation classifications shown here are based on the Stanford-Binet or Cattell tests. The Wechsler Scales (not shown) have a different distribution and therefore different IQ ranges: 55–69 (mild), 40–54 (moderate), 25–39 (severe), and 0–24 (profound).

THOUGHT CHALLENGE: *Frederick is a child with profound mental retardation, who also has severe visual and hearing impairments. Are the causes of his retardation most likely to be familial or organic?*

most will also learn to walk, although their verbal and motor skills may be inferior to those of normal children. Many moderately retarded children are educated in regular schools, though often with special teachers and equipment.

Severe mental retardation is usually associated with poor motor development, few communication skills (although these skills sometimes develop slightly later in life), and a high degree of dependence throughout life. Children with **profound mental retardation** may not learn toilet or dressing habits; in addition, many do not learn to walk.

Learning Disabilities

A significant number of schoolchildren in the absence of apparent emotional or physical disturbances and without being mentally retarded, experience serious learning difficulties in one or more areas. Such children are described as having a **learning disability**. Unfortunately, however, the term *learning disabilities* includes a wide variety of conditions, and is not always clearly defined. IDEA, the U.S. act that provides funding programs for children with special needs, includes a definition of learning disabilities that serves as a guideline for the allocation of funds:

> The term means a disorder in one or more of the basic psychological processes involved in under-

standing or using language, spoken or written, that may manifest itself in an imperfect ability to listen, think, speak, read, write, spell, or do mathematical calculations including such conditions as perceptual handicaps, brain injury, minimal brain dysfunction, dyslexia, and developmental aphasia. (Individuals with Disabilities, 1997).

The definition goes on to specify that learning problems due to other causes, such as mental retardation or environmental disadvantage, are not learning disabilities.

Because the IDEA definition is open to various interpretations, many jurisdictions have developed their own criteria for identifying children with learning disabilities. In general, these definitions emphasize four groups of characteristics:

1. There is a marked disparity between expected and actual behavior. This disparity is often evident in general academic achievement well below what would be expected on the basis of measured IQ.

2. There is an uneven pattern of achievement. While learning-disabled children do reasonably well in many subjects, there are specific subjects and areas in which they are unable to do certain things that other children do quite easily.

3. Children with a learning disability typically experience problems in one of the basic psychological processes involved in language or in arithmetic. Hence, the condition is often evident in disorders of listening, thinking, talking, reading, writing, spelling, or arithmetic.

4. The problems associated with learning disabilities are not the result of other problems relating to hearing, vision, or general mental retardation.

severe mental retardation A level of mental retardation defined in terms of an IQ range between 20 or 25 and 35 or 40. The individual can learn to communicate and, with systematic training, take care of simple hygiene.

profound mental retardation A degree of mental retardation defined in terms of a measured IQ below 20 or 25 and marked by limited motor development and a need for nursing care.

learning disability Significant impairment in a specific skill or ability in the absence of a general depression in ability to learn (mental retardation).

Symptoms of Learning Disabilities In practice, the most often used characteristic for identifying learning disabilities is the presence of a significant discrepancy between IQ and achievement, when that discrepancy can be attributed to specific problems primarily in language or arithmetic. Educators have to be especially careful, however, when using this discrepancy criterion. As Tomasi & Weinberg (1999) point out, one problem with this approach is that measures of IQ for children with serious learning disabilities are sometimes significantly lower *because* of the disability. This is especially true of tests that are highly verbal, given that the vast majority of learning disabilities involve language (as many as 80% of all disabilities; Deiner, 1999).

Other general symptoms sometimes associated with learning disability include inattentiveness, mood shifts, hyperactivity, and impulsiveness (see Table 9.5). Various tests are typically used in identifying the learning disabled. Some provide information about general intelligence; others look more specifically at basic psychological processes involved in learning and remembering, and especially at processes involved in written and oral language. It's also important to consider the possibility that other factors, such as visual problems, hearing deficits, and physical or health handicaps might be involved. In fact, there is evidence that between 14% and 65% of children with visual disabilities also have learning disabilities (Erin & Koenig, 1997). There is evidence, too, that some gifted children have learning disabilities, although these are seldom identified (Brody & Mills, 1997).

Main Categories of Learning Disabilities Relatively little is known about the origins and causes of specific learning disabilities, although brain damage or some other neurological impairment is suspected in many cases (Castles et al., 1999; Rumsey, 1998). Various diseases and infections, malnutrition, and other environmental or genetic factors might also be involved (Umansky & Hooper, 1998). The vast majority of those diagnosed with learning disabilities are boys.

By far the most frequently diagnosed learning disabilities are those having to do with language, and more specifically with reading. Thus the most common learning disability is **developmental reading disorder**—also called **dyslexia** or *specific reading disorder*. The main feature of developmental reading disorder, according to the American Psychiatric Association, is impairment in recognizing words and in understanding what is read (American Psychiatric Association, 1987). Developmental reading disorder is usually first manifested in problems associated with learning to read and may later be evident in spelling difficulties (erratic rather than consistent errors). Remedial teaching can sometimes be highly effective in overcoming some of the effects of dyslexia.

Another specific learning disability is **developmental arithmetic disorder** (American Psychiatric Association, 1994). Its essential feature is significant impairment in developing arithmetic skills. It is usually most apparent in computational problems (difficulties in adding, subtracting, multiplying, or dividing), and is sometimes labeled *dyscalculia*.

In addition to reading and arithmetic disorders, learning disabilities also include what are referred to as **process disorders**. These have to do with deficits in a basic psychological process such as perception

---

TABLE 9.5
Some Symptoms That May Be Associated with Learning Disabilities

Inattentiveness (short attention span)

Impulsiveness

Hyperactivity

Frequent shifts in emotional mood

Impaired visual memory (difficulty in recalling shapes or words)

Motor problems (difficulty in running, hitting a ball, cutting, writing)

Disorders of speech and hearing

Specific academic difficulties (reading, writing, spelling, arithmetic)

---

developmental reading disorder A learning disability manifested in reading problems of varying severity; sometimes evident in spelling difficulties. Also labeled *dyslexia* or *specific reading disability*.

dyslexia A form of learning disability manifested in reading problems of varying severity. Dyslexia may be evident in spelling errors that are erratic rather than consistent.

developmental arithmetic disorder A learning disability evident in specific problems in developing arithmetic skills in the absence of other problems such as mental retardation. Sometimes labeled *dyscalculia*.

process disorders A type of learning disability that involves a deficit in a basic psychological process such as perceiving, remembering, or paying attention. In practice, process disorders are difficult to separate from other specific learning disabilities such as developmental reading or arithmetic disorder.

(some students are confused by words that sound or look alike), memory (sometimes evident in problems associated with remembering and generalizing what has been learned), and attention (a condition labeled "attention deficit disorder" is sometimes associated with restlessness, hyperactivity, low frustration tolerance, and distractibility. We deal with this disorder in Chapter 10). In practice, however, it is often difficult to separate a basic process disorder from a disorder that is manifested in a specific subject area.

Learning disabilities, as they are currently defined, are usually treated in the regular classroom—a practice termed **inclusion** (or *inclusive education* or *mainstreaming*—discussed in more detail toward the end of this chapter). Sometimes learning disability specialists, many of whom specialize in reading or writing skills, work with learning-disabled children in the regular classroom.

Intellectual Giftedness

Learning problems represent one extreme of exceptionality. The other extreme is intellectual giftedness, which may be evident in one or a combination of factors including high intelligence, high creativity, motivation, and personality (Robinson & Clinkenbeard, 1998).

U.S. Public Law 91-230 defines giftedness as follows:

> Gifted and talented children are those identified by professionally qualified persons, who by virtue of outstanding abilities, are capable of high performance. These are children who require differentiated educational programs and/or services beyond those normally provided by the regular school programs in order to realize their contribution to society.

The law goes on to state that capacity for high performance may involve demonstrated achievement, or the potential for high achievement, in one or more of the following areas: general intellectual ability, specific academic aptitude, creative thinking, leadership ability, visual and performing arts, or psychomotor ability.

Estimates of the incidence of giftedness vary considerably. Conservative estimates, note Robinson and Clinkenbeard (1998), are at about 1% of the general population. However, special education programs are provided for nowhere near that number. This is especially true of the gifted who are culturally disadvantaged and who, as a result, are often not identified as gifted (Stephens et al., 1999). In fact, argues Babaeva (1999), not only do we fail to identify many gifted children, but we also fail to develop a great deal of potential among more ordinary children.

Identifying the Gifted and Creativity

One of the reasons it's difficult to identify gifted children has to do with defining and measuring the qualities in question, says Porath (1996). In practice, these qualities have most often been defined by test scores: Intellectual giftedness is defined as very high measured IQ, and high **creativity** is defined as an extraordinarily high score on a test designed to measure creativity. And the school administrator who must decide who will be labeled "gifted" (and who, at least by implication, will be labeled "not gifted") also looks at school achievement and perhaps asks teachers for their nominations.

Grossman (1995) notes some serious problems with this approach. First, there is considerable ambiguity about the meaning of high IQ or high creativity scores; second, what is measured by these tests often does not reflect the definitions that government agencies or school jurisdictions have adopted; and third, identifying a group of students as gifted and talented also means, by implication, identifying an even larger group that does not qualify. There are serious ethical and equity issues here.

Some researchers have attempted to develop procedures for identifying gifted learners. For example, Renzulli, Reis, and Smith (1981) suggest that teachers can begin to recognize gifted students in their classrooms by looking for a combination of three things:

---

inclusion The practice of placing students in need of special services in the regular classroom rather than segregating them. Also termed *inclusive education,* or *mainstreaming.*

creativity Generally refers to the capacity of individuals to produce novel or original answers or products. The term *creative* is an adjective that can be used to describe people, products, or processes.

▲ High ability (perhaps evident in high achievement or high measured intelligence)

▲ High creativity (sometimes apparent in problem-solving ability or in the production of novel ideas)

▲ High commitment (evident in a high level of persistence and task completion)

Unfortunately, however, an observation made by Terman (1925) more than half a century ago might still be true today: When comparing potential and achievement, we find that the most "retarded" group in our schools is that of the highly gifted.

Among these highly gifted are the highly creative.

Measuring Creativity

Stephen Winsten (1949), George Bernard Shaw's biographer, in alluding to the "hair's breadth" separating genius and madness, said to Shaw one day: "The matter-of-fact man prefers to think of the creative man as defective, or at least akin to madness." And Shaw quickly replied, "Most of them are, most of them are. I am probably the only sane exception" (p. 103).

Not so; there are other exceptions. Although some research indicates that the highly creative might share some personality characteristics with schizophrenics, this would hardly make them "mad" (Cox & Leon, 1999). In fact, we have little evidence that very many of the highly creative are mad—or that many of the mad are creative. (See *Across Cultures:* "Ruth Duskin and Other Quiz Kids.")

Some Tests of Creativity Before measuring creativity, it might be useful to know what it is. Unfortunately, psychology offers us a creative assortment of definitions for creativity. But in the end, teachers who are charged with identifying gifted and creative students, or parents who want to foster gifts in their children, have to rely on the more practical advice and measuring instruments that psychology provides.

In the same way intelligence is typically assessed with tests, creativity, too, can be appraised with tests. But there is considerable disagreement about their validity, their reliability, and their meaningfulness. As a result, researchers often use a combination

of measures including personality inventories, biographical and activity inventories, and behavioral measures (Heinzen, 1991). Personality inventories focus on what are considered to be the characteristics of creative people (for example, openness, flexibility). Biographical and activity inventories are based on the assumption that past creative activity is the best predictor of future creativity. They look at the extent to which individuals have already been creative. And behavioral measures try to predict future creativity by looking at specific behaviors such as performance in school. With all of these approaches, there is, in Heinzen's (1991) words, tremendous "diversity and lack of coherence" (p. 8).

Production Measures In studies of creativity, the most frequently used measures are open-ended tests requiring participants to produce a variety of responses—hence the term **production measures**. These are sometimes called **tests of divergent thinking**. Individuals think divergently when they produce several different solutions for a single problem. In contrast, measures of intelligence typically present items that require **convergent thinking**—the production of a single correct response.

Most production measures of creativity are based on Guilford's (1950) assumption that the most important factors involved in creative ability are **fluency**, **flexibility**, and **originality**. Accordingly,

---

production measures Tests that require testees to *produce* or *invent* responses rather than being allowed to select or calculate them. Commonly used as measures of creativity.

tests of divergent thinking Creativity tests. Usually open-ended, *production* tests designed to measure factors such as fluency, flexibility, and originality.

convergent thinking Guilford's expression for thinking that leads to a unique, correct solution, in contrast with *divergent thinking,* which leads to the production of a wide variety of solutions.

fluency A factor thought to be involved in creativity, evident in the production of a large number of responses or solutions in a problem situation.

flexibility A factor tapped by production measures of divergent thinking (of creativity). Evident in the ability or propensity to switch from one class of responses or solutions to another.

originality A measure of creativity evident in the production of novel (unexpected or statistically rare) responses or solutions in a problem situation.

Ruth Duskin and Other Quiz Kids

© Corbis/Bettmann

While some of the "quiz kids" had unexpectedly unhappy lives, many fared far better than average.

Beginning in 1939 and lasting for more than a dozen years, *The Quiz Kids* radio (and, later, television) program captivated Sunday afternoon audiences. On this show, children as young as 7 competed against each other, answering mind-boggling questions. "Kids can't be that smart," some complained. "The show's fixed."

Not so, declares Ruth Duskin Feldman (1982), one of the dozen or so Quiz Kids who served as regulars on the show from age 7 to 16 (there were more than 600 occasional Quiz Kids who didn't earn enough points to continue). These were normal, bright children, she says. Terman (1925), a leading authority on giftedness, predicted tremendous future success for these children.

Not all share Terman's optimism. Some see the gifted child as a social misfit doomed to misery and failure. One example to support this view is the case of William Siddis, whose father had deliberately raised him to be a genius. At 2, the boy could read; at 3, he knew four languages; at 11, he entered Harvard; and at 16 he graduated *cum laude* and began teaching at Rice University. But at 19, he had become a recluse, drifting from one job to another, finally dying in poverty and obscurity at age 46.

It wasn't until Ruth Duskin had married, had children, and lived a normal, productive life that she finally asked the question, What happened to the Quiz Kids? Here, briefly, are the stories of five of them.

Gerald Darrow: The youngest of the original Quiz Kids, Gerald Darrow was on the cover of *Life* magazine at age 9. His knowledge of birds, his precise memory for everything he read, and his ability to recite entire Greek myths were astounding. But at 47 he died almost unnoticed, having spent many of the last years of his life on social assistance. He had never married. When he died, he had been living with a 91-year-old aunt.

Claude Brenner: A Quiz Kid at age 12, Claude Brenner reportedly already knew four languages and tons of facts. When Ruth Duskin tracked him down 40 years later, he had just lost both his job and his wife. When asked about his Quiz Kids experience, he confessed, "I think, on the whole, it was an exceedingly damaging experience" (Duskin Feldman, 1982, p. 126). He feels that in many ways he is still a Quiz Kid, almost desperately needing to compete and to win.

Jack Lucal: Jack Lucal holds the record for the greatest number of consecutive wins on *The Quiz Kids*. He was an extremely popular boy who studied his school subjects only if they were exceptionally interesting, and who didn't get the highest marks in his class. High grades, said Jack, are not the point of studying. Jack had wanted to become an ambassador to China when he was 14; in the end he became a Jesuit priest.

Margaret Merrick: A childhood polio victim (she walked with crutches), Margaret Merrick became a Quiz Kid at age 14. At 52, she had a Ph.D. and worked as an educational consultant. Happily married, she was a mother of four and grandmother of eight.

Smylla Brind: Smylla Brind's IQ of 169 propelled her onto *The Quiz Kids* for a handful of appearances before her good looks moved her to Hollywood and a new name: Vanessa Brown. Vanessa Brown starred in some 20 movies, made the cover of *Look* magazine at 16, and modeled for *Life*. At 53 she was a contented ex-actress, married for the second time, raising a 17-year-old daughter.

A Conclusion: The Quiz Kids have done better than average. One-third have Ph.D.s or M.D.s; one (James D. Watson) won a Nobel Prize; many of the women have successfully managed both child-rearing and other careers.

To Think About: "Exceptional intelligence does not preclude ordinary happiness or worldly success," writes Duskin Feldman (1982). "But neither does it guarantee extraordinary accomplishment" (p. 348). How important do you think intelligence is for happiness? Why?

the open-ended tasks require the production of a variety of responses that can then be scored according to these three factors. For example, one item asks subjects to think of as many uses as they can for a brick. Counting the total number of responses gives a measure of fluency. Flexibility is revealed in the number of shifts from one class of uses to another (for example, shifting from responses where bricks are used for building purposes to responses where they are used for holding objects down). Originality is revealed in the number of unusual or rare responses. Table 9.6 gives one example of a creativity item and how it might be scored.

Some Characteristics of Creative and Gifted Children

Runco (1986b) makes the important point that while measures of creativity reflect creative potential, they do not reflect creative performance. The greatest achievers—those who eventually attain eminence in the world—are characterized by more than just high scores on measures of intelligence and creativity. Because of this, and because creativity tests have relatively low reliability and validity, some researchers suggest that it might be useful to look at how creative people think, rather than simply looking at their responses on production tests. Accordingly, some recently developed questionnaires and tests are attempting to look at the *cognitive styles* of creative people—for example, the *Creativity Styles Questionnaire* (Kumar, Kemmler, & Holman, 1997). These questionnaires look at how participants value ideas, their attitudes toward originality, their approaches to problems, their persistence, their abilities, and various aspects of their personalities (Martinsen, 1997).

Analysis of responses to creative styles questionnaires indicates that most creative people tend to value new ideas, are less likely to see themselves as too busy to think of new ideas, and hold fewer stereotypes about creativity (Basadur & Hausdorf, 1996). Similarly, when compared with less creative people, creative people are less concerned about developing a final product, have a stronger belief in unconscious processes, and tend to use a larger vari-

TABLE 9.6
Sample Answers and Scoring Procedure for One Item from a Creativity Test

ITEM: HOW MANY USES CAN YOU THINK OF FOR A NYLON STOCKING?

Answers:

*	Wear on feet
§*	Wear over face
*	Wear on hands when it's cold
†*	Make rugs
*	Make clothes
§†*	Make upholstery
†*	Hang flower pots
*	Hang mobiles
§†*	Make Christmas decorations
§*	Use as a sling
†*	Tie up robbers
§†*	Cover broken window panes
§†*	Use as ballast in a dirigible
†*	Make a fishing net

SCORING:

* Fluency:	(total number of different responses)
† Flexibility:	(number of shifts from one class to another)
§ Originality:	(number of unusual responses—responses that occurred less than 5% of the time in the entire sample)

ety of techniques and approaches in an effort to be creative (Kumar, Kemmler, & Holman, 1997).

Other research that has looked at the characteristics of creative children has not painted a simple picture of what these children are like—probably because each is unique, very different from the others. Hoge and Renzulli (1993), for example, looked at the self-concepts (the self-esteem) of gifted students in an effort to discover whether the gifted have higher evaluations of themselves. It might be reasonable to expect that they would have, argue Hoge and Renzulli, given that their accomplishments should be superior to those of more ordinary individuals. Also, if they are labeled as gifted, that too

THOUGHT CHALLENGE:

1. *Suppose that one day you walk from Pascal to Shell River. You leave at 8:00 A.M., stop five times to rest, each time for one minute, fish off the bridge for one hour at lunchtime, and finally arrive at Shell River at 4:00 P.M. You spend the night in Shell River and return to Pascal the next day, following exactly the same route. Again you leave at 8:00 A.M., but this time you don't stop and you reach Pascal by noon. Is it true that at some point on your return trip you will be at a place at exactly the same time you were at that place the day before?*

2. *Using only six matches of equal length, make four equal-sized triangles in which the length of each side is equal to the length of one match.*

might have a positive effect on their self-concepts. But there is the possibility, they also caution, that the high expectations sometimes placed on the gifted might lead them to greater feelings of frustration and dissatisfaction, and might be evident in lower rather than higher self-concepts.

Hoge and Renzulli looked at 15 different studies that compared the self-concepts of gifted and nongifted children. Their conclusions? "In general, gifted children displayed slightly higher self-concept scores than more average children" (p. 458). This finding was most evident in measures of what is termed academic self-concept—the children's evaluations of their academic abilities. However, a review of seven studies that had looked at the possibility that labeling a child as gifted might increase self-esteem found no relationship between labels and self-concept.

In general, research on the personality characteristics of gifted children indicates that they are different from the nongifted in a number of dimensions. For example, they are generally more highly motivated to learn and to achieve (Porath, 1996); they have been found to be more playful or, as Runco (1996) puts it, more "childlike in their behavior and thinking" (p. 3); and indications are that they are more open to emotion in their fantasy and in their play (Russ, 1996).

Other research indicates that the gifted are, in fact, probably better players of what is sometimes called the game of cognition. Both Swanson (1992) and Cheng (1993) found that the gifted children manifest higher metacognitive skills. That is, they are more aware of their cognitive processes, and better at selecting and applying cognitive strategies and at evaluating their effectiveness.

The Origins of Eminence

For practical purposes, there is seldom a need to separate high intelligence and high creativity. The two are closely related, and programs for gifted and talented children are not tailored for one or the other. Studies of eminent individuals—that is, those who have achieved fame and recognition on the basis of outstanding performance in any area—typically find that these individuals are both highly intelligent and specially gifted in a creative sense (Runco, 1996).

But truly eminent individuals are not just highly intelligent and specially gifted. Countless individuals have scored extremely high on all our measures of giftedness and intelligence and never approached eminence. A follow-up of the Terman studies of genius, for example, found that very few of the original sample ever attained eminence (Oden, 1968). Nevertheless, a relatively high proportion of the men—but significantly fewer of the women—achieved at high levels academically and in their careers. For the women, suggests Holahan (1996), the single greatest obstacle to their success was the perceived incompatibility between a homemaking and a working career. Note, however, that these women were born around 1911, and would have been young adults prior to the enormous social changes that have made out-of-home careers far more accessible to women.

What is special about the few gifted individuals who achieve eminence? Perhaps a number of personality characteristics, qualities such as high motivation and persistence—and, perhaps most important, the right family context. Family background seems to have been an important factor in the lives of most of those who have achieved eminence. In fact, report Kagan and Gall (1998), even

> **THOUGHT CHALLENGE:** *In the history of the world, a large number of very eminent and highly creative people have been thrown in jail. Do you suppose this is evidence that such people have a tendency toward criminality?*

the achievements and eminence of grandparents are often closely related to the eventual accomplishments of grandchildren.

Albert and Runco (1986) warn that perhaps we have taken too simple and too cognitive a view of giftedness and have thus been guilty of neglecting important personality and family variables. These authors identify seven factors related to the development of eminence. If children are to become eminent in later life, say Albert and Runco, it is best that they:

▲ Be both intelligent and creative

▲ Develop the values, motivation, and abilities that allow them to undertake important or highly unusual work

▲ Live in families that encourage the development of these values and drives

▲ Choose careers that "fit" with their talents, and present demands that are sufficiently challenging to lead to eminence

▲ Be born in a family that provides the right combination of experiences (that is, musical, athletic, academic, and so on)

▲ Be part of a family whose history is consistent with appropriate experiences and values (that is, grandparents, who were influenced by their parents, also influenced their children, who now influence the children of whom we speak)

▲ Be subject to family direction consistent with the development of the gifted child's talents (rather than unrealistic, overly demanding, or uncaring)

Notice how important the family is among these suggestions. In much the same way, Winner (1996) offers numerous suggestions for parents of gifted children, identifying many of the myths and misconceptions that surround our understanding of them.

Trends in Special-Needs Education

Unfortunately, misunderstanding often leads to mistreatment in the sense that not everything is done that could be done to foster the development of the full potential of these children—or, for that matter, of *all* children. But clearly, a great deal more is now being done than was the case a few decades ago. Deiner (1999) summarizes some of the ideas underlying what are generally recognized as the *best practices* in special-needs education today:

▲ *Inclusion.* All special-needs children are placed in regular classrooms.

▲ *Normalization.* "Normal" experiences are provided for these children, meaning that they are cared for at home, play with other children, attend day-care facilities, and so on.

▲ *Zero reject.* All children are included, no matter the nature or level of their disability.

▲ *Same range of program options.* All schools and programs available to children without disabilities should also be available to those with disabilities.

These ideas reflect a gradual shifting of the responsibility for the care of children with special needs from organizations and institutions to the family and the public school system. In part, this shift reflects a growing recognition that disadvantaged children should have an opportunity to lead lives as nearly normal as possible. Deinstitutionalization and nonsegregation are the natural consequences of this trend, and perhaps nowhere is this more obvious than in inclusion (or *inclusive education*, or *mainstreaming*—placing in regular classrooms children who might once have been placed in "special" classrooms or even in institutions). Inclusive education remains controversial, however, for several reasons: It is expensive; caring for special-needs students sometimes presents a burden for teachers who have many other responsibilities, and who are not always trained for their new tasks; and some argue that some special-needs children (like those who are excessively aggressive or disruptive) might fare better in segregated classrooms (Chester, 1992). However, other researchers dispute the notion that some children don't fare as well in integrated classes. As Sobsey (1993) puts it, "The majority of the research to date shows both educational and social advantages for integrated settings over segregated alternatives" (p. 1). However, he advises that in many cases, the needs of exceptional children can best be served through adaptive education; that is, by providing intensive, individualized, "special" programs for these children within the regular classroom.

One alternative to the inclusive classroom is the **pull-out program**, in which students with special needs are taken out of the regular classroom for special programs. Pull-out programs are sometimes used with gifted children as well as with those with learning disabilities.

THE MAGICAL CHILD

"The parents of the magical child lead him into the world by example," Pearce (1977, p. 213) tells us. "At seven, he is open to suggestion, able to construct the abstractions needed for moving into the world. . . .

---

pull-out program A school program, sometimes used in language immersion classes or for children with special needs, in which the child is removed from the regular classroom for special instruction and experiences.

He is fascinated with the world and becomes analytic. He wants to take the world apart and see what makes it tick."

In Piaget's terms, the children we have spoken about in this chapter have begun to construct a knowledge system that will lead to a sometimes startling understanding of the world.

Or, in the language of information-processing theory, the children of these early school years have been gathering information to build their knowledge bases, they have been discovering and inventing processes and strategies to be used in their constructions, and they have begun to imagine and know themselves as perceivers, knowers, and rememberers.

As we noted, infants are not expected to know that day follows night; that butterflies whisper to each other when they perch on buttercups in the sunshine; and that there is a smooth, cold logic that can be invented to explain the mysteries of numbers and classes and series, though perhaps not the whispers of butterflies. Those are among the discoveries of later childhood.

But happily, the grand mysteries of cognition are not all solved in middle childhood. There is yet concreteness to the child's logic, a limit to the reaches of imagination. We continue the story of cognitive development in Chapter 11.

MAIN POINTS

Physical and Motor Development

Boys are heavier and taller than girls throughout their lives, except for a brief period late in middle childhood. (Girls undergo their adolescent growth spurt about two years earlier than boys.) Height is a good indicator of the long-term effects of nutrition; weight sometimes reflects more short-term effects.

Obesity (linked to overeating and underexercising, as well as to genetic background and parental influence) is the most common childhood nutritional problem. Although children are slightly more obese now than they were a few decades ago, most

have a relatively high level of physical fitness. Sex differences in motor abilities are usually very small during childhood and are consistent with the gender typing of the skills measured.

Physical and motor problems that sometimes cause children to require special services include cerebral palsy, epilepsy, various diseases, congenital physical problems, physical problems resulting from accidents, and deafness and blindness. Hearing impairments often have more socioemotional and academic problems associated with them than do visual impairments, because of the crucial role that hearing plays in the acquisition of language.

Cognitive Development: Piaget's View

Piaget describes middle childhood in terms of concrete operations, which is well illustrated by conservation—the realization that certain transformations do not change the quantitative features of objects. In addition to the conservations, children acquire abilities relating to classification, seriation, and number during this period.

Cognitive Development: Information Processing

The information-processing model looks at how children develop a knowledge base, strategies for dealing with cognitive material, and awareness of the self as a processor of information. A basic information-processing model describes memory in terms of three components: sensory memory (momentary effect of sense impressions; no cognitive processing); short-term memory (attention span lasts a few seconds; involves rehearsing; limited to 7 plus or minus 2 items); and long-term memory (longer-term retention involving cognitive processing—rehearsal, elaboration, and organizing).

Long-term memory may be implicit (cannot be put into words) or explicit (verbalizable); explicit memory may be semantic (objective, abstract, what we know about things) or autobiographical (episodic, personal memories). Sensory and short-term memory do not appear to be substantially different in younger children and adults, but long-term memory improves.

Metacognition refers in part to our awareness of ourselves as players of the game of cognition. We play this game with rules called cognitive strategies and are influenced by our estimates of how good we are (how optimistic our estimates of self-efficacy).

Intelligence

Spearman is associated with the general factor theory (*g*) of intelligence. Special abilities theory describes intelligence as a collection of separate abilities. Cattell describes two classes of abilities: fluid (abstract, unaffected by culture) and crystallized (learned, highly influenced by culture). Sternberg describes a *triarchic theory of successful intelligence* in which the three arches are analytical abilities, creative abilities, and practical abilities. Gardner suggests we have multiple intelligences (linguistic, musical, logical-mathematical, spatial, bodily knowledge, and intra- and interpersonal)—and maybe naturalist, spiritual, and existential.

Two widely used individual (one person at a time) intelligence tests are the *Stanford-Binet* (ages 2 to adulthood; widely used with young children; highly verbal) and the *Wechsler Scales* (ages 4 to adult; yield separate performance and verbal scores, as well as a composite IQ). Group tests (given to many at once) include the *Otis-Lennon Test* and the *Cognitive Abilities Test*. Schooling can increase measured intelligence (the Flynn effect). Measured IQ is not a mystical, fixed, unchanging, and unmodifiable something. Intelligence tests often do not measure a variety of important things (interpersonal skills, motivation, creativity, athletic and musical ability) and are sometimes culturally biased. Measured IQ is related to success, especially in school.

Intellectual Exceptionality

Mental retardation is characterized by a general depression in ability to learn and is defined as subnormal performance on measures of intelligence and impairments in adaptive behavior. Classified by its severity, retardation may be mild, moderate, severe, or profound. (Educationally relevant labels are educable, trainable, and custodial.) Those who are mildly retarded are typically capable of acceptable achievement in ordinary elementary school classrooms.

Learning disability includes specific learning problems not associated with mental retardation or other physical or emotional disturbance, the most common of which is developmental reading disorder (dyslexia).

Intellectual giftedness is manifested in exceptional intelligence, exceptional creativity, and high motivation. Creativity is often defined by innovation or originality and appears to be a relatively stable personality characteristic closely related to intelligence.

Ideas underlying recent trends in special education are inclusion (placing children with special needs in regular classrooms), zero rejection (accepting all children in all programs), normalization (providing normal growing-up experiences for children with special needs), and a full range of program options (providing these children with all the options available to children without disabilities).

Focus Questions: Applications

1. *Are North American children in good physical condition?*
   - Plan the sort of physical activity program you think would be ideal in an elementary classroom.
   - How does Piaget describe development through middle childhood?
2. Replicate one or more of Piaget's conservation problems (Figure 9.5) with children several years below and above the approximate normal age of attainment.
   - What memory model underlies current views of information processing?

3. Provide your own examples of sensory, short-term, and long-term memory.
   - What is intelligence? How do we measure it? How important is it?
4. If intelligence is the capacity to adapt, how might children's intelligence be measured?
   - What are the dimensions of intellectual exceptionality?
5. Using library resources, write a reasoned and well-documented argument against (or for) inclusive education for exceptional children.

Possible Responses to Thought Challenges

Thought Challenge, page 382

There are likely several contributing factors, explain Stores and Ramchandani (1999). One of the most intriguing is that it might be a *chronobiological* problem, especially among children who do not see any light. As a result, their biological clocks are less easily adjusted to night and day. Other contributing factors might include physical problems and parenting problems.

Thought Challenge, page 408

In all probability, the causes are organic (biological). First, multiple handicaps of this nature are typically biological (organic) rather than environmental (familial); second, when a cause for severe or profound retardation is identified, it is most often biological; when a cause for mild or moderate retardation is identified, it is most often environmental.

Thought Challenge, page 413

Some people run out of ideas very quickly; others continue to generate them for a long time. Some people's ideas are very common; others are highly unusual. Open-ended questions such as these can be used to measure creativity (See Table 9.6).

Thought Challenge, page 414

1. Yes, you will be at exactly the same place and time once on your way back from Shell River. This is easy to explain (and understand) if you consider what

would happen if one person left Shell River and the other, Pascal, at the same time and on the same day. It makes no difference how fast each goes; providing they follow the same route, they must meet (that is, they must be at the same place and time on one occasion). The problem is identical to this situation; you are simply "meeting" yourself on a different day.

2. If you had trouble with this one, it is probably because of "set"—the predisposition to respond in certain ways. You likely tried to lay the matches flat on some horizontal surface. The solution (below) requires a shift from horizontal to vertical.

Thought Challenge, page 415

Brower (1999) says no, it doesn't mean that at all. What it means is that highly creative people often produce ideas that run counter to established beliefs. And, especially in societies characterized by rigid doctrines, those in power have developed methods of discouraging what are often interpreted as *dangerous* ideas. Prisons are among these methods.

Key Terms

autobiographical memory, 391

case studies, 377

class, 387

compensation, 385

convergent thinking, 411

creativity, 410

crystallized abilities, 397

developmental arithmetic
disorder, **409**

developmental reading disorder,
409

developmentally delayed, 406

dyslexia, 409

elaborating, 393

encoding, 394

entity theory of intelligence, 404

explicit memory, 391

external orientation, 403

familial causes, 407

fat mass, 375

fat-free mass, 375

flexibility, 411

fluency, 411

fluid abilities, 397

g, 396

general factor theory, 396

gist memory, 393

horizontal décalage, 385

implicit memory, 391

inclusion, 410

incremental theory of
intelligence, **404**

intelligence, 381

intelligence quotient (IQ), **400**

internal orientation, 403

knowledge base, 389

learned helplessness, 403

learning disability, 408

long-term memory, 390

magnetic resonance imaging, 392

mainstreaming, 381

mastery-oriented, 404

mental age, **400**

mental retardation, 405

mentors, 395

mild retardation, 407

moderate retardation, 407

operational thought, 383

organic causes, 407

organizing, 393

originality, 411

otitis media, 382

positron emission tomography, 392

process disorders, 409

production measures, 411

profound mental retardation, 408

psychometric intelligence, 397

pull-out program, 416

rehearsing, 390

reliable, 396

scripts, 393

semantic memory, 391

sensory memory, 390

severe mental retardation, 408

short-term memory, 390

special abilities theory, 396

special needs, 381

successful intelligence, 397

tests of divergent thinking, 411

theory of multiple intelligences,
399

triarchic theory of successful
intelligence, 398

valid, 396

visually impaired, 381

Further Readings

The following book is a highly readable and excellent analysis of cognitive development. It looks in detail both at Piaget's theory and other work in information processing and metacognition. The second is an in-depth but understandable look at Piaget's theory:

Flavell, J. H. (1985). *Cognitive development.* Englewood Cliffs, N.J.: Prentice-Hall.

Wadsworth, B. J. (1996). *Piaget's theory of cognitive and affective development* (5th ed.). New York: Longman.

In the following two textbooks, Hallahan and Kaufman present a clear and comprehensive look at children with exceptionalities, and especially at educational approaches for these children:

Hallahan, D. P. & J. W. Kauffman (1999). *Introduction to learning disabilities* (2nd ed.). Boston: Allyn and Bacon.

Hallahan, D. P., & J. M. Kauffman (1997). *Exceptional learners: Introduction to special education* (7th ed.). Boston: Allyn and Bacon.

A vivid and complex picture of the gifted child is presented in the following book, which also looks at common misconceptions about gifted children:

Winner, E. (1996). *Gifted children: Myths and realities.* New York: Basic Books.

 Online Resources For additional readings, explore *InfoTrac College Edition,* your online library. Go to http://infotrac-college.com/wadsworth and use the passcode that came on the card with your book. Try these search terms: constructivism education, memory children, autobiographical memory, cognitive strategies, intelligence tests, intelligence levels.

For this curious child was very fond
of pretending to be two people.
"But it's no use now," thought poor
Alice, "to pretend to be two
people! Why, there's hardly
enough of me left to make one
respectable person."

Lewis Carroll, *Alice in Wonderland*

Social and Emotional Development in Middle Childhood

David Stewart/Tony Stone Images

CHAPTER 10

Alice's complaint quoted on the opposite page comes after she drinks from a magic bottle and finds herself shrunken to a mere 10 inches. She's too small to reach the golden key that unlocks the door to Wonderland, so she starts to cry. Then she sharply tells herself not to weep. Alice often pretended to be two people so she could talk to herself or play games. Once, she even caught herself cheating at croquet and tried to box her own ears.

I don't know whether our daughter, Claire, ever pretended to be two people. But if she did, that would have made three, since she was never without her imaginary playmate, Horton.

Horton moved in with us when Claire was 4. We paid little attention at first; he didn't take up much room at the dinner table, usually just wanting to sit on her lap and eat small tidbits from her plate. Later he sometimes insisted on having his own chair.

But generally Horton was no bother. He spent most of his time sitting in a chair where Claire could talk to him, which she did at great length and sometimes with breathless intimacy. And whenever we went anywhere, he always came along. Often we had to wait for him; he had the annoying habit of not being ready on time. Whenever this happened, Claire would drag him out, complaining and scolding so severely that I sometimes felt sorry to see him so humiliated in front of the family.

Near her seventh birthday, when we hadn't seen Horton for some time, I asked Claire about him. "He likes chocolate and he wears different clothes," she answered. "Is he real?" I inquired. She looked up rather sadly. "No, he isn't. He's imaginary."

FOCUS QUESTIONS

1. Are children as sensitive as adults to others' emotional states?

2. How many friends does a typical child have? How important are they?

3. How common is child victimization? What forms can it take?

4. Does violence on television translate into violence on the street and in the home?

5. What are some of the most common forms of socioemotional exceptionality in elementary schools?

SOCIAL COGNITION

Claire's 7-year-old sense of reality had begun to change. Still, at age 6 or 7—the beginning of the period we deal with in this chapter—life has not yet drawn that thick, black line between the real and the unreal. Most of us see it very clearly, that line; our frames of reference are quite different from those of childhood. Our worldviews are more scientific, more reasonable. And our cognitions do not so readily admit magic.

The Early Development of Social Cognition

But the magic of Claire's creation of, and interaction with, her imaginary friend reveals more than the fact that she didn't yet see clearly the line that we adults are always so careful to keep in sight. (We do it for fear that we should one day mistake the fanciful for the real; our society has built unpleasant places for those so afflicted). It reveals, too, that she was well on her way to developing **social cognition**—an awareness of the self and of others as social beings capable of feelings, motives, intentions, and so on. In Claire's mind, Horton, too, was a social being; he could feel pain and joy; he could laugh and cry; sometimes he could even lie and play tricks and know very big secrets.

---

social cognition The realization that others have feelings, motives, intentions, and so on; knowledge of the emotions of others.

The purpose of social cognitions, says Fiske (1993), is for people to make sense of others. In the preschool period, social cognitions take the form of a theory of mind. As we saw in Chapters 6 and 8, social cognitions start to develop in early infancy. Infants begin to differentiate between the self and others and begin to recognize that some things out there are persons, and others are nonpersons (Wellman & Gelman, 1992). At about the same time, infants begin to form strong attachments, usually to their caregivers. Thus begins the process of socialization.

But infants' social cognitions unfold slowly and reflect many of the limitations that characterize nonsocial cognitions. Still, research suggests that preschoolers may be far better social thinkers than had been thought.

Theory of Mind in the Preschool Period

"It is now widely accepted," write Cutting and Dunn (1999), that by 4 years of age most normally developing children have acquired an understanding of mind" (p. 853). As we saw in Chapter 8, one important aspect of this theory of mind is the recognition of some of the differences between wishes, thoughts, and beliefs. Understanding these notions makes it possible for children to realize that others can know things they don't know, that beliefs aren't the same as wishes, and that thoughts without action can't do much to change reality.

Investigators have devised a series of intriguing experiments to investigate what children know about these matters. Recall from Chapter 8, for example, the *unexpected-location* experiment in which a doll, "Maxi," hides a candy in one cupboard, someone later moves the candy to another cupboard while Maxi is away, and the child, who has witnessed all this, is asked where Maxi will look for the candy when he returns. By age 4, most children realize that Maxi doesn't know what they know, and that the poor sap will look in the wrong place.

In the *unexpected-identity* procedure, children are read a story from a book on which each page has a hole with a drawing of an eye peeking through, but the very last page reveals that it isn't an eye at all, but a spot on the tail of a snake. Now they are asked to predict what a puppet will think the picture is before getting to the last page (Hughes, Dunn, & White, 1988). Again, younger children confuse their own more advanced knowledge with that of the naïve puppet, but 4-year-olds are not so easily swayed.

We saw in Chapter 8, too, that preschoolers' understanding of the thoughts and emotions of others is evident in their use of intention as a way of manipulating a parent's reaction. ("Hey, Dad, I was cleaning your fishing reel when it broked by itself on accident not on purpose. I was cleaning it real good for you," said Laurier, somewhat tearfully, holding many small inner parts of a dead reel.)

Theory of mind is also evident in lies and deceptions. If 4-year-old Sammy does not have a theory of mind—that is, does not understand that his mother has her own thoughts and beliefs—then it might not occur to him to lie to her when she asks, "Did you poke that hole in your bed sheet, Sammy?" Intentional deception, claim Ruffman et al. (1993), requires that children understand not only that people can believe different things, but also that it is possible to make people believe things that are false.

As Wooley et al. (1999) found, following interviews with preschoolers in which they probed their understanding of beliefs, wishes, reality, and magic, by the age of 4—and even 3—children, in their words, "have a rich set of adult-like beliefs about the mind, and mental-physical causality" (p. 583). It is strange, however, that even after children know clearly that simply wishing doesn't make things happen, they continue to believe in wishes. Consider, for example, this exchange in Paley's (1986) kindergarten class:

Lisa: Do plants wish for baby plants?
Deanna: I think only people can make wishes. But God could put a wish inside a plant.
Teacher: What would the wish be?
Deanna: What if it's a pretty flower? Then God puts an idea inside to make this plant into a pretty red flower—if it's supposed to be red.
Teacher: I always think of people as having ideas.
Deanna: It's just the same. God puts a little idea in the plant to tell it what to be.
Lisa: My mother wished for me and I came when it was my birthday. (pp. 79–80)

Role Taking and Empathy

It's absolutely essential that children—and grownups too—have a theory of mind if they are to understand others and interact intelligently with them. We must not only understand that others are capable of thoughts, feelings, wishes, and other mental states but also be able to anticipate what these are most likely to be. Put another way, we have to be able to put ourselves, figuratively, in the shoes—or minds—of others. This defines **role taking**. And we have to be able to recognize and share the feelings of others. This defines **empathy**.

Early investigations of the development of empathy (the ability to recognize and share the feelings of others) often asked children to recognize the

---

role taking A role is a part or a character played by an actor. In psychology, role taking implies assuming the character of others in the sense of being able to understand and empathize with their emotions.

empathy The mental apprehension of another's feelings and state of mind.

Eight year olds have no difficulty interpreting the pain that a hurt child might feel. Their understanding of others' minds and feelings, what psychologists refer to as their theories of mind, allows them to recognize feelings in others, and to feel empathy—as is clear from their expressions in this scene.

Elizabeth Crews

emotion that would accurately reflect the reaction of a person in a story. Many of these investigations relied heavily on Piaget's interviewing techniques (the *méthode clinique*). In one of the best-known of these studies, for example, Selman (1980) told children the following story:

> Holly is an 8-year-old girl who likes to climb trees. She is the best tree climber in the neighborhood. One day while climbing down from a tall tree, she falls off the bottom branch but does not hurt herself. Her father sees her fall. He is upset and asks her to promise not to climb trees anymore. Holly promises.
>
> Later that day, Holly and her friends meet Shawn. Shawn's kitten is caught up in a tree and can't get down. Something has to be done right away, or the kitten may fall. Holly is the only one who climbs trees well enough to reach the kitten and get it down, but she remembers her promise to her father. (p. 36)

Children were then asked whether Holly knows how Shawn feels about the kitten; what Holly thinks her father will do if she climbs the tree; how Holly's father will feel if he knows she has climbed the tree; and what the child being questioned would do in the same situation.

Selman (1980) describes the development of children's ability to understand and verbalize another person's point of view in five stages, labeled 0 to 4 (see *Concept Summary*). In general, these stages describe the preschooler as largely unaware of others' states of mind and as developing a gradually more sophisticated and abstract understanding of the thinking of others through middle childhood. Even after the child has a relatively well developed theory of mind—that is, an understanding that others can have different thoughts and feelings, and that these can be affected by external events, and can affect their

---

CONCEPT SUMMARY

Selman's Developmental Progression in Social Cognition.*

Perspective-taking stage	Description	Typical responses to cat story (see text)
Egocentric (3 to 7 years)	There is no perspective but mine. People feel the way I would in that situation.	"Her daddy will be happy 'cause he likes the kitten."
Social-informational (4 to 9)	Okay, so others have a point of view too, but they would feel the way I do if they had the same information.	"He'd let her climb if he understood how she felt."
Self-reflective (6 to 12)	Actually, we can have different points of view. There's hers and there's mine. I can see mine; she can see hers.	"He'll be mad 'cause he doesn't want her to climb trees."
Mutual (9 to 15)	Well, maybe I can see hers and she can see mine. We can even talk about our different points of view.	"Holly and her father can talk to each other. They will understand each other. They can work it out."
Social and conventional (12 to adulthood)	"Actually, within the context of discombobulism, and taking into consideration the teachings of MUMU and the charter of personal delimitations, her point of view is totally philanthropic. On the other hand . . ."	"It depends on whether her father thinks the cat's life or Shawn's feelings are more important than obedience. Besides . . ."

*Note that this progression of stages reflects children's ability to verbalize their perspectives and their understanding of other perspectives. However, their actual behavior reflects more advanced understanding of other people's thoughts, beliefs, and feelings during the preschool period. Note, too, that the ages given are approximate, and overlap considerably.

behavior—their ability to adopt another's point of view remains limited.

We also know that the ability, or the tendency, to empathize are not the same in all children—as is easily revealed using measures of empathy or of role-taking skills (for example, Vernberg et al., 1994). Research also reveals that empathy can be increased in children. For example, in one school, children who were trained to be **mediators** (to find solutions for conflicts among children in the school) experienced significant improvements in measures of empathy and social cognition over the course of one year (Lane-Garon, 1998).

Why might it be a good idea to develop empathy in children? There are several reasons. For one thing, it seems reasonable to suppose that children who have a tendency and ability to empathize with others may be less likely to do them harm. In fact, research indicates that high empathy correlates *negatively* with all sorts of **aggression**, including sexual aggression (Kaukiainen et al., 1999). And further, high empathy is one of the hallmarks of high social competence; it is part of being *emotionally intelligent*. It is understandable that there is a close relationship between the development of friendships in childhood and the development of social cognition.

SELF-ESTEEM

The child's theory of mind, says Astington (1991), "is the understanding children have of their own and others' minds. . . . This understanding enables children to predict and explain actions by ascribing mental states . . . to themselves and to other people" (p. 158). Thus theory of mind implies an awareness of self and of others as distinct selves. Put another way, it implies a concept of the **self**, a self-concept. Concepts such as self-worth, self-esteem, or self-

concept are all aspects of what we refer to in Chapter 2 as self-referent thought—thought that has to do with our selves.

Self-concept is a general term that is reflected in the description we would provide if we were asked to describe our roles and our personality characteristics for some stranger (Kahne, 1996). Montemayor and Eisen (1977) report that through childhood, self concept changes from initially very simple, highly tangible descriptions to progressively more abstract and more psychological descriptions. Thus, when asked to describe herself, 6-year-old Laura says, "I'm Laura. My Mom's name is Jennifer. I'm a girl. I have two cats and my dad threw one in the lake . . ." In contrast, 12-year-old Evelyn responds, "I'm a bit shy, but I'm honest and quite smart and I work very hard. I'm very religious, which is important to me, and . . ."

One of the most important aspects of self-concept is evaluative: It refers to what we think of ourselves, to our **self-esteem** (also termed *self-worth*). If we have a high opinion of ourselves—that is, of our different qualities as we understand them—we are said to have high self-esteem (or positive self-concepts). If we think we're not worth very much, then we have more negative self-concepts (low self-esteem).

Two Approaches to Self-Esteem

How do we develop notions of our self-worth? How do we decide whether our selves are good, bad, or so-so? Historically, there have been two major approaches to these questions.

James's Approach William James's approach to self-worth says: My self-worth is a direct function of

---

mediators Those whose function it is to act as peacemakers, to intervene between disputing parties. In schools, teachers often act as mediators. In some cases, older children and adolescents are trained to serve as mediators.

aggression Forceful action intended to dominate or intimidate, including actions such as insisting, asserting, intruding, or being angry or even violent.

self The *I*. Also the *me* and the *myself*. Notions of our *self*. The subject of our own consciousness.

self-concept The ideas an individual has of him- or herself. Notions of the self reflect what we think others think of us; our own estimates of what we are, relative to what we would like to be; and our estimates of our competence and "goodness" in various important areas.

self-esteem The evaluative aspect of our concepts of self. What we think of ourselves. Our *self-image*. Our opinions about the relative worth of our different characteristics.

James's approach to self-worth The belief that notions of self-esteem are a direct function of the difference between perceived self and self-ideal.

the difference between what I would like to be and what I think I am. The closer my actual self (as I perceive myself) to my ideal self (the way I would like to be), the more I will like myself, and hence, the higher my self-esteem (James, 1892).

Cooley's Approach Cooley's approach to self-worth says: My self-worth is a direct function of what I think others think of me; my worth is reflected in their behavior toward me (Cooley, 1902). (Hence Cooley's phrase "looking-glass self.") If people avoid me, that is evidence that I am not very worthy; if they seek me out, the evidence is more positive. Those who are most important in serving as mirrors in whose behavior I can view my self are people who are important to me—part of the microsystem, in Bronfenbrenner's terms. So for preschoolers, parents and siblings are most important; for elementary school children, peers and teachers also become important—and perhaps also coaches, mentors, tutors, religious leaders, and so on. (See Table 10.1.)

Investigating Self-Esteem

There are different instruments for measuring self-esteem, among them the Rosenberg Self-Esteem Scale and the Harter Self-Perception Profile for children (SPPC). These instruments typically ask children questions about how well they think they perform in various areas considered important for self-esteem. For example, Harter's SPPC asks children questions relating to five areas: athletic, scholastic, social, physical, and moral.

In some of Harter's (1987, 1988) studies, children were asked how important they thought it was to do well in these areas. Thus investigators could look at the difference between actual performance and the child's wishes, and arrive at a measure relating to James's approach to self-esteem.

Children were also asked to what extent they felt their importance was recognized by others, how well others treated them, and whether they thought they were liked, admired, and respected. This line of questioning provides information relating to how others regard the child (Cooley's approach).

Finally, children were asked questions relating to a more global concept of self-worth—questions relating to how well they like themselves as people.

Use of questions such as these permits investigators to answer some important questions: Are competence/aspiration-based estimates of self-worth (James's theory) or looking-glass estimates (Cooley's theory) actually related to general concepts of self-worth? Are discrepancies between competence and the ideal more important in one area than another (for example, are athletics more important than scholastics)? Are there developmental changes in areas of importance? Is the source of approval and social regard important?

Some Research Findings Harter (1987) provides answers for several of these questions about self-esteem, based on her investigations of children in grades three through eight (approximately 8 to 13 years of age). Before the age of 8, children don't

---

Cooley's approach to self-worth The belief that evaluation of our self reflects what we think others think of us.

TABLE 10.1	
Two Theories of the Basis of Self-Esteem	
THEORY	EXAMPLE OF REASONING PROCESS
James: Discrepancy between actual and ideal self (What I would like to be versus what I think I am)	"I'm a blond, which is what I would want to be if I had a choice. And I know I have nice eyes. So physically, I know I'm well, pretty attractive. I've just been pulling off C's in school, but I know I'd do better if I worked like Reggie. So, overall, I'm pretty happy with myself.
Cooley: Looking-glass self (What I think important others think of me)	"Sam asked me to the movies. And Robert wanted me to go to his family's cabin. And I know darn well that Sam wants to ask me out. I must be pretty attractive. And I have lots of girlfriends too, for sure. So, yeah, people like me. I think I must be pretty OK. "

seem to have a single, clearly defined, and measurable notion of self-worth; accordingly, younger children are not included in Harter's samples. Following are some findings by Harter and other researchers.

1. Although children have a general estimate of personal worth, they also make individual estimates of self-worth in at least five separate areas: scholastic competence, athletic competence, social acceptance, behavioral conduct, and physical appearance (Table 10.2). In other words, even though some children may see themselves as athletically competent (good and worthwhile), these same children may have decided that they are not "good" in a moral sense, or that they are not as worthwhile scholastically.

2. Harter's studies indicate that children's judgments of self-worth reflect both major sources described by James and Cooley; that is, the difference between competencies (in each of the five important areas) and the child's aspirations and desires is reflected in estimates of self-worth. At the same time, how others regard the child also has an important influence on self-esteem.

3. Not all five areas are equally important to every child. High or low competence in important areas will have a more powerful influence than competence or incompetence in less important areas. If athletics are more important than being good (behavior conduct), not being a good athlete will be more damaging to self-esteem than

David Young-Wolff/PhotoEdit

Strong positive feelings that we are worthwhile contribute to mental health, happiness, confidence, and high achievement. What we think of ourselves is related to two things: how competent we think we are in important areas (James's competence/aspiration theory) and what we think important others think of us (Cooley's looking-glass theory). Having the very best apple pie is this girl's proof that she is competent and that others think so too. It's almost enough to make her smile.

TABLE 10.2
Areas in Which Children Evaluate Their Self-Worth

AREA	DESCRIPTION
1. Scholastic competence	How competent and smart the child feels about schoolwork
2. Athletic competence	How competent the child feels at sports and games requiring physical skill, athletic ability
3. Social acceptance	How popular or socially accepted the child feels with peers
4. Behavioral conduct	How adequate the child feels about behaving in the way one is supposed to behave
5. Physical appearance	How good-looking the child feels, how much the child likes such characteristics as their height, weight, face, and hair

Note: Children's estimates of self-worth are based on (1) what significant other people think of the child's capabilities and worth (Cooley's looking-glass theory) and (2) the extent to which the child lives up to personal ideals and aspirations (James's discrepancy between aspirations and competence theory). Both kinds of evaluations occur in the five areas described here.
Source: From S. Harter (1987). The determinants and mediational role of global self-worth in children; in N. Eisenberg (ed.), *Contemporary topics in developmental psychology*, p. 229. New York: John Wiley.

behaving immorally. In Harter's studies, physical appearance is the most important area in determining self-worth, both for younger (grades three to six) and older (grades six to eight) children. Children who see themselves as attractive are most likely to like themselves. Similarly, in a study of 760 Dutch-speaking Belgian children in grades 4, 5, and 6 (using a Dutch version of Harter's scale), physical appearance was also the best predictor of global self-esteem (Van den Bergh & Marcoen, 1999). In Harter's studies, behavioral conduct (goodness of behavior in a moral sense) was least important for both age groups (see Figure 10.1).

4. As we noted, some sources of social regard and support are more important than others. For example, it might not matter very much that some nameless fan yells disparaging remarks while 10-year-old Willie stands, stunned, at the plate and lets all the strikes go by. But it might matter a great deal if his father or his coach, or even his friends, later make the same remarks. Not surprisingly, parents and friends are among the most important sources of support for determining self-worth (Fordham & Stevenson-Hinde, 1999).

5. Estimates of self-worth are closely linked with affect (emotion or mood), which in turn has much to do with motivation. As Harter (1988) comments, elementary schoolchildren who like themselves (who have high self-esteem) are the happiest; in contrast, those who don't think very highly of themselves are more likely to feel sad or even depressed. Also, children who are happy are most likely to feel motivated to do things; those who are sad are least likely to want to do things. Their coping strategies, as Chapman & Mullis (1999) found, are often *avoidance* strategies. That is, they find themselves avoiding potentially stressful or socially embarrassing situations rather than finding ways of coping with them. Figure 10.2 depicts the relationship between mood and self-worth scores for three groups of children from grades three through eight. Note that for all three groups, very low affect scores (sadness bordering on depression) are associated with very low self-worth scores; conversely, high affect is associated with high measures of self-worth.

Some Implications Some of the practical implications of self-worth are clear. To the extent that positive self-esteem is closely related to happiness and to high motivation—and, by the same token, to social adjustment and general well-being—parents, teachers, and others who share responsibility for rearing youngsters must be concerned with far more than their cognitive development or their physical well-being. They must do what they can to ensure that the evaluation that every child places on the self is a positive judgment.

Unfortunately, the causes of self-worth are not simple. They include factors over which we have limited control, such as scholastic competence or physical appearance. But they also include things over which we have more control, such as our personal estimates of children and our communication of love and support. But perhaps, suggest a number of experts, we overuse some of the factors under our control, rendering them far less useful than they might be (see *In the News and on the Web:* "Mommy's Soooo Very Glad That You . . .").

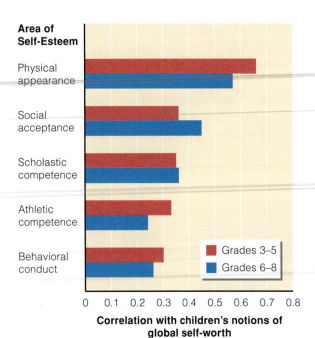

FIGURE 10.1 Correlations between children's self-worth and perceived inadequacies in specific areas. Source: S. Harter, 1987. "The Determinants and Mediational Role of Global Self-Worth in Children." In Contemporary Topics in Developmental Psychology (p. 229), N. Eisenberg (ed.), New York: John Wiley. 1987 John Wiley & Sons, Inc. Used by permission of the publisher.

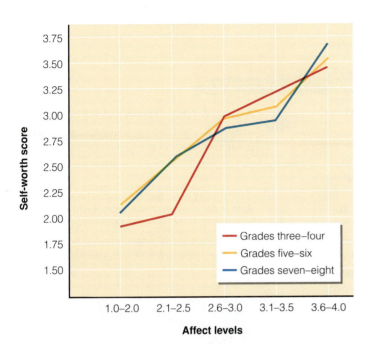

FIGURE 10.2 The relationship between mood and self-concept. In Harter's study, children who were sad (low affect level) had the lowest opinions of themselves. Lowest scores indicate lowest estimates of self-worth and least positive moods.

FRIENDS, PARENTS, AND PEERS

"Friendships of children," writes Berndt (1989), "appear to exist in a kind of never-never-land, a world of fun and adventure that adults rarely if ever enter and cannot fully understand" (p. 332). But science, in its careful and analytic way, pokes and probes so that we might understand better, asking pointed questions in suitably oblique ways—questions like, "How do children view friendship?"

Children's Views of Friendship

For the 3- to 5-year-old, claims Selman (1980, 1981), a friend is merely someone who happens to be available to play with; and friendship is nothing more complex than "playing together." At this stage, children have no concept of friendship as an enduring kind of relationship. When asked how friendships are formed, they are likely to say, "By playing together." When asked to describe a friend, they will speak of activities, but not of traits or characteristics ("He plays with me" or "He doesn't hit me").

Later in the preschool period, children describe their friends as those who do what they want, those who share their likes and dislikes. Friends are a little like assistants or helpers. Later, friends are seen more as *cooperators* than as assistants. And eventually (perhaps by age 11 or 12) children understand that friendships develop over time, and that they involve a reciprocal sharing of thoughts and feelings and a high degree of mutual trust and intimacy. Now, when asked to describe their friends, they are likely to speak of qualities ("She understands people; she's so sincere") and of mutual interests ("We like a lot of the same things"). Whereas earlier, parents were largely responsible for determining their children's peers (hence their playmates and friends), largely by virtue of where they lived and what schools they put them in, now children actively select their own friends, says Corsaro (1997). They no longer simply play or cooperate; instead, their relationships have become more verbal and more abstract (see Table 10.3).

Dimensions of Childhood Friendships

"Not having friends," writes Bullock (1994), "contributes to loneliness, low self-esteem and inability to develop social skills" (p. 95). As we see later, it is also associated with being victimized (bullied), with depression, and with other negative developmental outcomes.

Mommy's Soooo Very Glad That You ...

In the seventies and eighties, says Kropp (1998), parents were told to praise their children regardless of what they did. Unconditional love and unrestrained praise, parents were assured, will go a long way toward ensuring that children have positive self-esteem.

And now, say many experts, parents have learned to praise too much, too indiscriminately, too lavishly (for example, Kropp, 1998; Seligman, 1995; Coloroso, 1994). Children are praised for watching television, for sleeping, for eating, for dressing themselves. Praise is no longer reserved for important accomplishments; as a result, it's not always very meaningful. "After years of diligently complimenting our children to bolster self-esteem, experts suggest we've become a generation of parent cheerleaders raising praise-junkie kids," writes Moyle (1999, p. 46).

E. Moyle, "Cheerleading parents may be hurting kids: Damned with praise?" *Edmonton (Alberta) Sun, Express*, 9 December 1999, p. 46.

To Think About: Coloroso warns that excessive praise can lead children to become highly dependent on the approval of their parents—and later highly anxious to seek the approval of their peers. Do you think this likely? Why might it be dangerous? What would you suggest regarding the use of praise?

Resources: Extensive WWW resources are available for parenting. The following site points to hundreds of them: http://directory.netscape.com/Home/Family/Parenting/Resources

For additional readings, explore *InfoTrac College Edition*, your online library. Go to http://infotrac-college.com/wadsworth and use the passcode that came on the card with your book. Try these search terms: parenting praise; discipline and praise.

Spencer Grant/Photo Edit

It seems clear that some parents praise their children too little. Do some praise too much?

TABLE 10.3
Selman's Developmental Progression of Friendships

STAGE AND APPROXIMATE AGES	MAIN CHARACTERISTICS
Playmates (3–7)	Friends are those who play together.
Assistants (4–9)	Friends are those who help, who do each other's bidding.
Cooperators (6–12)	Friends have to cooperate, share goals and procedures, and make compromises.
Intimates and mutual supporters (9–15)	Friends share goals and values, and provide intimacy and support; strong friendships can survive occasional disagreements.
Dependent but autonomous (12 and up)	Adult-like understanding of the mutual dependence of friends on each other, paired with the need to maintain individuality and independence and to cultivate other relationships.

Source: Based on Selman, 1981. Note that the age ranges given are very broad and overlap considerably.

Best Friends Strictly speaking, only one of our friends can be our best friend; none of the others can be more than second best. However, in common usage, *best friend* refers to a close type of friendship in which several people can be best friends all at the same time.

Most 6- to 12-year-old youngsters have more than one best friend, although that is not always apparent in the research. Berndt (1988) points out that if children are asked to name their best *friend*, they will obligingly name only one person. But if they are asked to name their best *friends*, they gladly name several people. And if the question is changed only slightly, and they are asked instead to indicate whether each child in their class is a best friend, a friend, or not a friend, some children will name most of the class as best friends.

Sex Differentiation Most children have a number of close friends who are most often of the same race and school grade, and who share common interests. And by the later preadolescent period, friends are almost invariably of the same age and sex. Sex differentiation begins at about 5 or 6, reports Corsaro (1997). Before then, boys and girls often play together. But as we saw, preschoolers' notions of friendships are quite different and tend to revolve around playing rather than around sharing and intimacy.

In a study of friendship patterns among 4- to 19-year-olds of both sexes attending an ungraded school where children of all ages interacted with others of different ages, Gray and Feldman (1997) found that gender mixing was rare except for the youngest children (below age 7) and, of course, for the older ones. Similarly, there were very few instances of age-mixing (where *age-mixing* was defined as involving children separated by at least 24 months). And where age-mixing did occur, it almost invariably involved athletic activities and games rather than conversation.

Both boys and girls usually have two or three close friends rather than just one best friend. In fact, **triadic friendships** (three "best" friends), as opposed to dyadic friendships, are quite common. And for both sexes, friendships tend to be highly mutual: If one child indicates that another is a best friend, that child will very likely also have chosen the other as a best friend.

One of the main differences between girls' and boys' friendships is that girls' relationships tend to involve more kindness, empathy, and self-revelation. In contrast, boys' friendships tend to be more aggressive. Lansford and Parker (1999) found that this is generally true among triads as well. In their investigation of 56 third-, fourth- and fifth-grade same-sex triads of close friends, girls tended to be more intimate, to share more information, and to engage in far more verbal interaction than did the boys. In general, elementary-school boys tend to have more friends than girls of that age, although they are less intimate with them. Also, as we saw in Chapter 8, boys play more aggressively and more competitively at all ages.

Who Are Friends? Close friends, as noted, tend to be of the same sex, age, and grade; and they share interests. In general, they also tend to share personality characteristics. As Haselager et al. (1998) found, this is even truer for antisocial than for more prosocial characteristics. Research is clear, for example, that highly aggressive children seek out the friendship of other highly aggressive children—even though these friendships tend to be characterized by "frequent, lengthy, and intense conflicts" (Snyder, Horsch, & Childs, 1997, p. 145). This tendency continues right through adolescence, the authors claim: "Aggressive adolescents seek out peers with similar antisocial characteristics who provide further modeling, opportunity, and reinforcement for antisocial behavior" (p. 145). By the same token, the least aggressive children among the 72 boys and girls in the Snyder, Horsch, and Childs study were most likely to form friendships with others like themselves. And, as Berndt (1999) points out, friends not only select each other on the basis of similarities but also influence each other's characteristics.

Importance of Friends

Among other things, explains Erwin (1998), friendships contribute significantly to the development of social skills (such as being sensitive to other people's points of view; learning the rules of conversation, learning sex- and age-appropriate behaviors, and learning how to be intimate). In addition, interactions with friends are involved in developing notions of self and self-worth. Friendships may also

---

triadic friendships A grouping of three very close friends. More common among girls than boys.

be important in developing feelings of belonging to a group, and may therefore play a crucial role in the development of notions of cultural identity.

Sadly, Bullock (1994) reports that between 6% and 11% of elementary school-age children have no friends. Researchers have found that these children are more likely to suffer from depression (Hecht, Inderbitzen, & Bukowski, 1998), to manifest behavioral problems including excessive aggression and "acting out" (Ialongo, Vaden-Kiernan, & Kellam, 1998), to be maladjusted (Schwartz et al., 1998), and to be victimized (bullied) (Hodges & Perry, 1999). In fact, more than half the children referred for emotional or behavioral problems have no friends or have difficulty in peer interactions (Bullock, 1994).

Close friends are one source of influence on the developing child; peers are another.

Peer Groups

A **peer group** is a group of equals. Most individuals have a peer group, including hermits, whose peers, by definition, are also isolated and therefore of little consequence to their development. Possible exceptions are saints and other luminaries, who are peerless. The peer group is one of the major transmitters of cultural expectations and values, particularly during middle childhood. So, of course, is the family.

Parents and Peers in Early Childhood In infancy and early childhood, parents have traditionally been the center of the child's life. However, with increasing numbers of children in day-care facilities, the importance of peer groups during the preschool period has increased significantly in recent decades. By the beginning of middle childhood, peers have assumed tremendous significance. And as children's interests and allegiance shift gradually toward peers, there are important changes in the ways they interact with and conform to their parents.

In early childhood, parental authority is largely unquestioned. This doesn't mean that all children always obey their parents. Sometimes temptation or

---

peer group A group of equals. Peer groups may be social groups, age groups, intellectual groups, or work groups. Young children's peer groups are usually age and grade mates.

> **THOUGHT CHALLENGE:** *Robert is a relatively bright, attractive, athletic 10-year-old who has two older siblings (a brother and a sister) and one younger brother. For reasons that aren't clear to anyone, his parents don't treat him nearly as well as they do his siblings. Robert has now been referred to the school counselor, the referral being precipitated by the latest of a series of beatings he receives quite regularly from his schoolmates. The counselor determines quickly that Robert is a victim of bullying, and also uncovers that he feels considerable anger toward his siblings, although he loves his parents. How might these observations be explained?*

impulse is just too overwhelming. And sometimes, too, parents overstep the unwritten but clearly understood boundaries of authority. As Braine and colleagues (1991) note, parental authority does not extend to immoral acts; and it is likely to be resisted if it infringes on important areas of personal jurisdiction, such as choice of friends.

Parents and Peers in Later Childhood In later childhood and adolescence, parental authority is subjected to more constraints, and the child's area of control increases. It is interesting to note that although dependence on parents decreases with age, relationships with parents appear to be important to peer acceptance and the development of close friendships. As we saw in Chapter 6, securely attached infants tend to have better peer relations in elementary school. For example, in a study of 541 children aged 9 to 14, Lieberman, Doyle, & Markiewicz (1999) found that the quality of parent-child attachments (secure, loving) was closely reflected in the quality of their children's close peer relationships. In this study, continued *availability* of parents was highly predictive of good peer relations. Similarly, authoritative as opposed to authoritarian parenting is associated with the most positive peer relationships.

The relative influence of parents and peers on children's behavior is illustrated in a study by Berndt (1979) that included 251 children in grades 3, 6, 9, and 11–12. The children were asked to respond to hypothetical situations in which parents or peers urged them to do something antisocial, something prosocial, or something neutral. As expected, Berndt found that conformity to parents decreased steadily with age; and so did conformity to peers, except with regard to antisocial influences, which increased until about grade 9 (age 14) before beginning to decline again.

Peer Acceptance

Peer acceptance or rejection (sociometric status) is typically assessed using one of two methods: *peer ratings* or *peer nominations*. In a peer-rating study, each member of a group (for example, a classroom) might be asked to rate all other members of the group by how well they like them, whether they would like to play with them, how smart they are, how popular, and so on. A study using peer nominations might ask participants to name the three individuals they like best, the three they like least, the three smartest kids, and so on. Data gathered in this way can then be analyzed to provide an index of sociometric acceptance or rejection, and can sometimes be depicted pictorially in a **sociogram** (Figure 10.3). Information of this kind is sometimes useful in research that looks at the qualities associated with popularity or social isolation. Gottman et al. (1997) caution, however, that

sociogram A pictorial or graphic representation of the social structure of a group.

sociograms focus too much on the child as the source of social and emotional competence that determines status within the group. They suggest that a better understanding of sociometric status might result from looking at the dynamics of the interaction between peers and the child.

Sociometric Status

We are not all equally loved and sought after by our friends. Indeed, not all of us have friends. Some of us are social isolates (see the lone, disconnected, floating circle in Figure 10.3). Social isolates are those who do not often interact with peers, or those who are seldom selected as "best friend" by anyone. These two categories are different, says Gottman (1977). Some children are liked and accepted but do not interact much with their peers; on the other hand, some children are very low on everybody's list of "my best friends" or "who I would most like to be with" or "who I would most like to be like," but they nevertheless interact frequently with peers.

Five Levels of Social Status

In an attempt to investigate definitions of social status and clarify the nature of social isolation, Gottman studied 113 children in depth. His

Through middle childhood, the approval of parents is at least as important as that of peers in determining feelings of self-worth. In addition, it is misleading to compare and contrast parents and peers because relationships with each are so closely related.

Cleo Photography/PhotoEdit

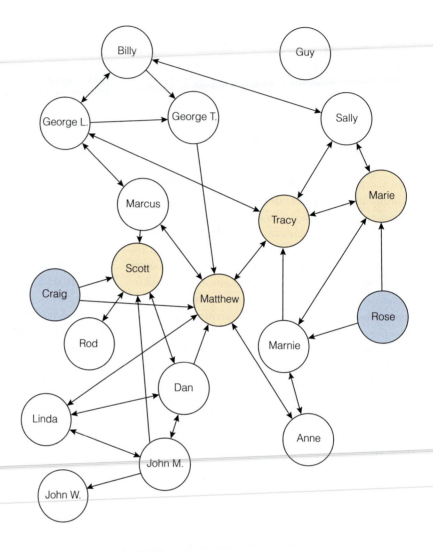

observations suggest five distinct categories of children (see Table 10.4). *Sociometric stars* are those who are consistently "especially liked." *Teacher negatives* are usually in conflict with teachers, and might be either high or low on measures of peer acceptance. *Mixers* are those who interact often with peers; they too might be high or low on measures of acceptance. The *tuned out* are those who are usually not involved with what is going on—they are tuned "out" rather than "in." The tuned out, rather than being strongly rejected, are simply ignored. And finally, *sociometric rejectees* are those who are not only disliked by their peers but also actively rejected by everyone. These are the children who, in childhood, are the butts of all the cruel jokes and taunts. In bullying situations they are the victims, especially if they are among the **withdrawn-rejected**. These children are rejected because they are withdrawn or otherwise socially incompetent. Children who are rejected primarily because they behave overly aggressively are termed **aggressive-rejected**.

Characteristics Related to Peer Acceptance

The characteristics related to peer acceptance and rejection are similar to those involved in forming

withdrawn-rejected Category of children who are rejected mainly because they are timid, withdrawn, socially awkward.

aggressive-rejected Category of children who are rejected primarily because of their high aggression.

TABLE 10.4
Five Categories of Social Status

CATEGORY	CHARACTERISTICS
Sociometric stars	Especially well liked by most.
Mixers	High peer interaction. Some well liked; others not.
Teacher negatives	Typically in conflict with teachers. Some are liked; others not.
Tuned out	Not involved; ignored rather than rejected.
Sociometric rejectees	Not liked very much. Actively rejected rather than simply ignored, often for being overly aggressive (aggressive-rejected) or withdrawn and socially inept (withdrawn-rejected).

Source: Based on Gottman, 1977.

friendships. Thus, in general, children who are friendly, sociable, and evaluate others positively are more easily accepted than those who are hostile, unsociable, withdrawn, or indifferent. The former children are high in social competence, explains Rose-Krasnor (1997).

Children who are intelligent and creative are also more accepted than those who are slow learners or retarded. Size, strength, athletic prowess, and daring are particularly important characteristics for membership in boys' peer groups; maturity and social skills are more important for girls, especially as they approach adolescence. Physical attractiveness is very important for both (Van den Bergh & Marcoen, 1999).

The observation that friendly, socially competent children have more friends (have higher status, as the sociologists put it) raises an interesting and important question: Are the characteristics of high-status (accepted) and low-status (rejected) children the cause or the result of their status? Does a friendly child have many friends because she is friendly, or is she friendly because she has many friends? Similarly, does social rejection lead to socially incompetent behavior, or is the socially incompetent behavior present to begin with, and lead to social rejection?

A review of numerous studies strongly suggests that popular children are popular because they are more competent socially, and that unpopular children lack social skills (Newcomb, Bukowski, & Pattee, 1993). In other words, how a child interacts with oth-

ers is a primary cause of social status. The most socially competent children quickly sense what is happening in an unfamiliar social situation and are able to modify their behaviors accordingly. Thus they are less likely to engage in inappropriate or unexpected behaviors than are socially incompetent children. Their social strategies are more competent, and their reactions more appropriate, say Eronen and Nurmi (1999). The most socially preferred children are those most likely to use calm approaches to resolve conflicts.

Characteristics Related to Peer Rejection

In contrast, children who react to conflict either with anger, retaliation, or aggression are most likely to be rejected by peers (Henington et al., 1998). These are the aggressive-rejected. Also, those who are highly anxious and socially withdrawn are more likely to be rejected (the withdrawn-rejected).

Other characteristics sometimes associated with peer rejection are those that make the child different or are perceived as undesirable. Thus, children who are learning disabled are sometimes more likely to be rejected (Frederickson & Furnham, 1998). Similarly, in a study of tolerance and rejection, Crystal, Watanabe, & Chin (1997) found that children who were different from their peers were most likely to be rejected. In that study, the nontypical children were either highly aggressive, withdrawn, learning disabled, unathletic, or poor.

Consequences of Peer Acceptance and Rejection

As we saw, the quality of children's relationships with their peers is very important for their happiness and adjustment. Withdrawn-rejected children, Ladd (1999) reports, are more lonely, more socially anxious, more likely to avoid social situations, and more likely to manifest deviant behavior later. They are also more likely to drop out of school (Garnier, Stein, & Jacobs, 1997). In contrast, aggressive-rejected children are often not aware of their social isolation. In fact, they're likely to overestimate their popularity and misinterpret other people's reactions to them, for example, taking teasing seriously and reacting aggressively.

Note that although peer rejection may be associated with poorer adjustment, that is certainly not always the case. In a study of 881 children in grades three through five, Parker and Asher (1993) found that many children who are not very popular nevertheless have some close and satisfying friendships. There are wide individual differences in the sociability of different children. Not all are outgoing, talkative, expansive; many appear withdrawn and shy. We should not make the mistake of assuming that children who appear shy are also lonely and friendless. Nor should we assume that they are likely to be rejected by their peers or socially tuned out. Some of these children are extraordinarily socially competent. Many have a large number of close friendships. Some might, in fact, be among Gottman's sociometric stars.

Bullying and Victimization

Others, sadly, might be victims—or bullies. **Bullying** is repeated infliction of pain, fear, and intimidation. A bully is an aggressive, quarrelsome person who appears to take pleasure in inflicting pain or harm, or in terrorizing people who are weaker. Victims are those who are repeatedly the target of bullying. Bullying, as Bosworth, Espelage, & Simon (1999) explain, includes a wide range of behaviors from very mild (verbal taunts, for instance) to extreme (aggressive behaviors leading to physical injury and even death).

---

bullying Repeatedly and habitually attempting to inflict pain, to terrorize, or to intimidate. Can be verbal or physical.

Who Bullies? Contrary to the popular belief that there are only a few bullies here and there—mostly highly aggressive boys—and that there are correspondingly few victims—mostly the weak and socially incompetent—research indicates that bullying is very often a group phenomenon. In fact, the larger the group in which a child hangs out, the higher the "bullying score," reports Boulton (1999). Often a ringleader initiates the bullying behavior, and others join in or remain engaged as passive observers (Sutton & Smith, 1999). Almost all the most horrifying instances of bullying that result in media attention involve group bullying (see *In the News and on the Web:* "Two Victims").

Frequency of Bullying Unfortunately, bullying is not a rare occurrence. Surveys indicate that there are astonishingly high numbers of bullies and victims in schools throughout much of the world. For example, a survey of more than 6,000 students in Malta (ages 9 to 14) found that serious bullying (more than once a week) involved no fewer than a third of all students—either as victims, bullies, or both (Borg, 1999). An investigation of 238 students in Rome found that over half of all students (from 11- to 14-years old) had bullied someone in the preceding three months (Baldry & Farrington, 1998). Examination of a videotape of classroom interaction in a Canadian school found an average of two bullying episodes per hour (Atlas & Pepler, 1998). And Bosworth, Espelage, & Simon (1999) report that in their study of 558 sixth- to eighth-graders in U.S. schools, only 20% reported that they had not been involved as either victims or bullies.

Who Is Bullied? Who are the children most likely to be victims of bullying? The simplest answer is those who are also socially rejected, particularly if they are withdrawn-rejected (rather than aggressive-rejected). Those who have friends, explain Pellegrini et al. (1999), are far less likely to be victimized. Also, children who have behavior problems as preschoolers are more likely to be victims of bullying later (Gregory & Bates, 1999). Gregory and Bates suggest this may be at least partly because these children, many of whom are impulsive, immature, and prone to acting out, end up having fewer friends and perhaps even being rejected. But as Hodges and Perry (1999) explain, many of these problems of social

Two Victims

Nisho City, Japan: They began to bully Koyoteru Okouchi of Tobu Junior High School in Nisho City when he was only 10. First they teased him; then they beat him up; finally, they asked for money, and they dunked him in the river to make sure he wouldn't forget. Over the next three years, they extorted more than $10,000 from Koyoteru, much of which he stole from his parents and grandparents after he had sold all he had of value. "If only I'd had the courage to say no," he wrote just before he hanged himself. He was only 13. ("Bullies drive teen to suicide," 1994).

New York, U.S.: Lewis Santiago Pagan stands accused of murder. Lewis is a shy, awkward boy, already 6 feet tall and more than 200 pounds at the age of 13. For a long time, he was a victim of bullying. One day, one of his attackers included David Harris, age 12. David was a puny 4 feet 5 inches, and weighed only about 80 pounds. But emboldened by the group, he joined Lewis's attackers, taunting him, pulling his feet out from under him. In the end, Lewis pulled out a knife and allegedly

stabbed David three times in the chest, killing him. "It seems that Lewis had finally had enough," said Detective Kim Royster ("'Gentle Giant' Stabs Boy for Taunts," 1994).

To Do: Media reports might lead us to believe that bullying and gang violence are becoming increasingly common. What evidence can you find that this is true? (Not true?) Why do you suppose it is true? (Not true?)

Resources: For practical information on crime prevention, see the U.S. Department of Justice's Justice for Kids and Youth site:

http://www.usdoj.gov./kidspage/

For additional readings, explore *InfoTrac College Edition*, your online library. Go to http://infotrac-college.com/wadsworth and use the passcode that came on the card with your book. Try these search terms: bullying, crimes against students.

---

incompetence that characterize children who are victims are also exacerbated by the act of being victimized. Thus the rejected child who is a habitual victim in school becomes even less likely to be accepted, and then becomes even more likely to be victimized, thus becoming part of a vicious cycle that maintains the victim's status over a long period of time.

Some Consequences of Bullying That bullying is so common doesn't lessen the potentially devastating impact it can have on the lives of victims. At the very least, most victims feel self-pity and unhappiness, reports Borg (1998). At the same time, others—especially in secondary school rather than in the earlier grades—feel anger and vengefulness. Sometimes the vengefulness has chilling consequences, as several recent mass killings testify.

Although some verbal bullying behaviors might appear less extreme than physical aggression, their

effects can be even more devastating. For example, Solhkhah, Olds, and Englund (1999) report the case of a 12-year-old girl who, following several years of constant teasing and taunting, had developed *enuresis* (bed-wetting) and had contemplated suicide prior to being referred for therapy. It is no surprise that female victims of bullying are most likely to suffer from verbal bullying; males are more likely to experience overt physical aggression (Crick & Bigbee, 1998).

What Can Be Done? There are various approaches to reducing incidence of bullying in schools and in society. Some of these attempt to teach children conflict resolution skills; others are directed toward increasing tolerance of differences and trying to make children understand the consequences of their behaviors and accept responsibility for them. Still other approaches are geared toward raising victims' self-esteem and social competence. Young (1998) describes a group approach in which bullies and bystanders are asked to examine specific bully-victim episodes in which they are involved, and are urged to come up with solutions for these situations.

Here, as in most areas involving complex human interactions, there are no simple solutions. But clearly, the kind of parenting to which children are exposed, as well as the examples the media and other representations of culture provide for them, share much of the responsibility for this particular manifestation of human cruelty.

CHILD VICTIMIZATION

Some children, as we have seen, are victims of bullying; many others are victims of other forms of maltreatment.

In the United States each year, there are a frightening number of crimes against persons—crimes like rape, robbery, assault and homicide. And in an astounding 50% of cases, the offenders are friends, relatives, or at least acquaintances of the victims; that percentage rises to an astonishing 64% in cases of rape or sexual assault. In 1996, more than 3 million cases of alleged child abuse or neglect were investigated in the United States, and almost one million were substantiated (U.S. Bureau of the Census, 1998).

But neglect and abuse are not the only types of child victimization, explain Finkelhor and Dziuba-Leatherman (1994); there are others.

▲ *Pandemic victimization* refers to instances of victimization that most children are at least occasionally exposed to while growing up—things like sibling assault, physical punishment by parents, peer assault (like bullying, for example), and various crimes. As an example of pandemic victimization, Boulton (1993) surveyed more than 100 elementary-school boys and girls and found that half had engaged in at least one physical fight during the preceding year. Typically, boys engaged in more fights than girls.

▲ *Extraordinary victimization* refers to more extreme, and far rarer, instances of victimization such as homicide, rape, or nonfamily abduction. Extraordinary victimization commonly receives a great deal of media attention, but is too rare to

have attracted much research attention. The recent discovery of various parts of a child's body in garbage bags in a park in a Canadian city is an example of extraordinary victimization. Several bags, and many parts, have now been found, but the head and torso are still missing and, as of this writing, the child and her assailants remain unidentified ("Suspects released: Child's head and torso still not found," 1999). (For an example of extraordinary victimization, see *In the News and on the Web:* "Children in Cages.")

▲ *Acute victimization* is the type of victimization that has been researched most. It includes child abuse and neglect, and—as we just saw—it occurs to a relatively large number of children. Some argue that the prevalence of acute victimization reflects a society whose models reek of violence. Not only is there violence in school and on television, but there is a shocking amount in the home. (See *At a Glance:* "Violence and Punishment in the Home.")

Prevalence of Child Maltreatment

Reported cases of child maltreatment increased dramatically through the eighties—from 3.5 per 1,000 population (or about three times that many per 1,000 *children*) in 1980 to more than 10 per 1,000 in the nineties (U.S. Bureau of the Census, 1998). (See *At a Glance:* "Acute Child Victimization," and Figures 10.4 and 10.5). However, it isn't clear whether this means that child maltreatment is actually increasing or whether reporting and detection are more thorough. Still, given the difficulty of obtaining information from parents and even from doctors in cases of child abuse, this figure may represent a very conservative estimate.

In a survey of child abuse in the United States, Straus and Gelles (1986) found that 43% of a sample of 1,428 parents had used some form of physical violence on a child at least once during the past year. An astounding 2.9% admitted to having used a knife or a gun on one of their children at least once in their lifetimes—small wonder that one out of every five murders in the United States is committed among immediate family members in their own home.

Children in Cages

A 7-year-old girl was found in a dog cage in a cold, dark, basement after her 11-year-old brother walked into a nearby police station in Brillion, Wisconsin. Despite below-freezing temperatures, the boy was barefoot and wore no coat. The girl had apparently been in the dog cage, a tiny, two-foot-square cage, for most of the past two weeks, with nothing but a single blanket—evidently as punishment. She and her four other siblings (aged 16 months to 11 years) have been placed in foster care. Their 28-year-old parents face charges of felony child abuse.

Meanwhile, in Auburn, Washington, a 14-month-old boy, who was discovered when police were evacuating a burning building, is believed to have been left alone in his crib for five days with little food or water—although his mother, LaDawn Jump, reportedly brought him peanut butter and jelly sandwiches or cheese on occasion. The boy's thumb was covered with raw sores. Doctors believe this was probably because most of the time, the toddler had nothing else to eat. The mother apparently had a new boyfriend and was afraid the boy's presence might chase him away. She had previously been arrested for suspected child abandonment, and now faces new charges.

"U.S. parents kept girl, 7, in dog cage, say police," *Edmonton (Alberta) Sun*, 20 November 1997, p. 43.

"Tot gnawed on his thumb during five days alone: Cops," *Edmonton Sun*, 20 November 1997, p. 43.

To Debate, Research, or Write up: Examine the proposition that in the same way people are not permitted to drive cars until they have demonstrated some minimum level of car-handling competence and knowledge of traffic rules, so too should prospective parents be required to demonstrate their ability and willingness to care for children.

Resources: The National Child Protection Clearing House is dedicated to providing a forum for ideas related to the prevention of child maltreatment. Its website:
http://www.aifs.org.au/external/nch/pubs.html

For additional readings, explore *InfoTrac College Edition*, your online library. Go to http://infotrac-college.com/wadsworth and use the passcode that came on the card with your book. Try these search terms: abuse against children; and child crime victims.

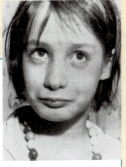

© UPI/Corbis Bettmann

This is Genie, the girl whose story is told on pages 107–8 in Chapter 3 and on pages 316–17 in Chapter 7. From the age of 22 months until 13 years, Genie was kept imprisoned and malnourished in her tiny, barren room, almost completely deprived of human contact. Later attempts to "socialize" her and teach her to speak were largely unsuccessful.

Classes of Acute Child Victimization

Current research makes distinctions among five classes of child maltreatment: physical abuse, neglect, emotional maltreatment, medical neglect, and sexual abuse. A sixth, very serious form of child maltreatment, *shaken baby syndrome*, is actually a variety of physical abuse.

Physical Abuse Physical injury to the child is the main criterion of **physical abuse.** However, the distinction between what is abuse and what is permissible punishment (or attempted control) by a parent is

physical abuse Child victimization defined mainly in terms of actual physical injury, as might result from excessive beating or "shaken baby syndrome."

Violence and Punishment in the Home

Even very conservative estimates of violence in the North American family are shocking. There were more than 15,000 murders in the United States in 1996; the perpetrators in about 20% of these were members of the victim's family. And of the almost 100,000 forcible rapes that year, about 33% were committed by relatives; only 33% were committed by total strangers. Also in 1996, more than 3 million children were reportedly victims of maltreatment, most often suffered at the hands of parents, other caregivers, or siblings (U.S. Bureau of the Census, 1998).

Some argue that much of the violence in our society begins with violence in the home, and that much of the violence in the home begins with cultural values that, at least implicitly, have maintained that it is acceptable for parents to use physical force to control and punish their children (de Jonge, 1995).

The case against physical punishment

There is a fine line, claims Sabatino (1991), between physical punishment and child abuse. But that is only one reason for discouraging the use of physical punishment. The following are other reasons:

- Punishment does not ordinarily illustrate desirable behavior; rather, it draws attention to undesirable behavior thus contributing little (if anything) to the learning of socially acceptable behavior.

- The use of violence against children is objectionable on moral and humanitarian grounds.

- Punishment is often accompanied by negative emotional side effects that can become associated with the punisher

perhaps as easily as with the behavior for which the child is being punished

- Punishment sometimes has effects opposite those intended. Children whose parents punish them for aggressive behavior are more likely to be aggressive; those who are punished for "bad conduct" are more likely to suffer from conduct disor-

(continued on next page)

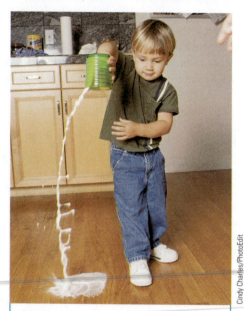

Cindy Charles/PhotoEdit

That the spilling of the milk seems deliberate may influence how a parent reacts. So too might the parent's beliefs about praise and punishment.

not at all clear and may vary dramatically from one situation to another. In some cultures, for example, parenting may involve levels of violence that would be viewed as abusive in other contexts. Segal (1995) reports a survey of 319 middle-class professionals in India, of whom more than 90% reported that during the past year they had used violence as a means of conflict resolution with their children. A frightening 41% of these revealed that their use of violence might have been more "abusive" than "acceptable." (See *At a Glance:* "Shaken Baby Syndrome.")

In many North American societies, some forms of violence are widely accepted as a parenting tool. This is reflected in the observation that many insti-

tutions charged with the care of children resort to physical punishment and sometimes other forms of abuse as a means of control (Jones, 1995).

Physical Neglect **Physical neglect** involves acts of omission rather than commission and is usually evident in parents' failure to ensure that children have adequate nourishment, shelter, clothing, and the other important things of contemporary life.

---

physical neglect Most common form of child maltreatment. Involves failure to provide for children's needs (failure to provide nourishment, shelter, clothing).

| AT A GLANCE | **Violence and Punishment in the Home** (continued) |

ders (Frick, Christian, & Wooton, 1999). And, research shows, they're also more likely to punish their own children later. Murphy-Cowan and Stringer (1999) found that the severity of the punishment grandparents had administered to their children correlated very highly with the severity of punishment their children used on the grandchildren a generation later—an *intergenerational transfer* effect. In this study, an alarming 91% of parents reported using physical punishment on their children.

The case for nonphysical punishment

There are occasions, some argue, when a child's behavior is dangerous to the child or to others—behaviors such as touching matches to the family drapes or shooting neighborhood cats with big brother's air rifle. Some argue that under certain circumstances, physical punishment can be effective in suppressing undesirable behavior. Others caution that if physical punishment seems effective, any desirable changes that occur in children's behavior as a result reinforce the parents' punitive behavior and may lead to child abuse (Whipple & Richey, 1997).

Many experts insist that physical punishment should *never* be used with children under any circumstance. There are at least three other kinds of punishment that parents and teachers often use and for which common objections are not as relevant:

Reprimands are verbal or nonverbal indications of disapproval. They can be mild (a gentle headshake) or harsh (a shout). They are, in a sense, the opposite of praise. Praise says "I like . . . "; reprimands say "I do not like . . . " Research clearly indicates that reprimands can be very effective in sup-

pressing undesirable behavior and in bringing about more desirable responses. The most effective reprimands:

- Not only identify the undesirable behavior but also provide specific rationales for doing something (or for not doing the opposite) (Van Houten & Doleys, 1983).

- Are consistent (Acker and O'Leary, 1996).

- Are given at a close distance (Van Houten et al., 1982).

- Are given softly—whereas praise is louder, more public (O'Leary et al., 1974).

- Are simple and unobtrusive, so as to minimize disruptions.

Time-out procedures involve removing children from a situation they enjoy, such as watching television. Brantner and Doherty (1983) describe several time-out procedures that can be used in a classroom. *Isolation* involves removing a student from the classroom. A less severe time-out procedure, *exclusion*, does not remove students from the classroom but simply prevents them from participating in ongoing activities.

Response-cost procedures are a form of punishment in which the penalty for bad behavior is the loss of rewards that have been awarded for good behavior. For example, in a school-based response-cost system, children earn tokens for certain behaviors but also run the risk of losing them for misbehaviors (Munson & Crosbie, 1998). One advantage they have over time-out procedures is that they do not remove the child from ongoing activities. In addition, they are usually combined with reinforcement programs, making it easier for parents and teachers to use them to bring about desirable behavior as well as to eliminate less desirable behavior.

Physical neglect is somewhat more difficult to detect than physical abuse, but nevertheless makes up more than half of reported abuse cases (U.S. Bureau of the Census, 1998).

Medical Neglect More than 25,000 cases of **medical neglect** were substantiated in the United States in

1996 (U.S. Bureau of the Census, 1998). Many of these involve parents lacking in the knowledge or financial resources required to provide their children with adequate medical treatment. Others are cases where medical help is denied children for religious reasons (Bottoms and associates, 1995).

Emotional Abuse Emotional abuse, sometimes referred to as *psychological abuse*, consists of parental behaviors that cause emotional and psychological harm to the child, but that are not instances of physical abuse or neglect—for example, continually shaming or ridiculing children (especially in public), isolating them, confining them in

medical neglect Child maltreatment where caregivers fail to provide adequate medical care to children in need—sometimes through carelessness, ignorance, or poverty; sometimes for religious reasons.

reprimands Expressions of disapproval commonly used as a form of mild punishment. Often verbal ("You're not supposed to. . ."), but also nonverbal (an admonishing finger, for example).

AT A GLANCE   **Acute Child Victimization**

Reported instances of child abuse and neglect have risen dramatically in recent decades—from 10.1 cases per 1,000 children in 1976 to 32.8 cases in 1986. (The numbers in Figure 10.4 are per 1,000 *population* and are therefore lower). More than 3 million children were subjects of reported acute child victimization in 1996. Of these, 48% were male and 52 were female. It's unclear to what extent rising rates represent an actual increase in maltreatment and to what extent they reflect increased awareness and reporting by teachers, physicians, relatives, and family acquaintances.

FIGURE 10.4 Reported cases of child neglect and abuse per 1,000 population, 1980 to 1996. (Note that these figures would be much higher per 1,000 children. Note, too, that these are numbers of reports, rather than numbers of children involved. Many reports involve more than one child, so that for every two reports, three children are involved. Source: Adapted from U.S. Bureau of the Census (1992), p. 176; 1993, p. 209; and 1998, p. 227.

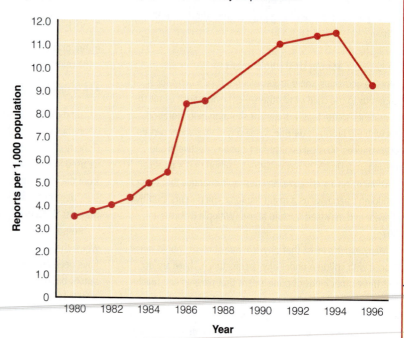

FIGURE 10.5 Child maltreatment cases, with type of maltreatment as a percentage of the nearly 1 million cases reported and substantiated in the United States in 1996. (Note that some children are classified more than one way; hence percentages total more than 100.) Source: Adapted from U.S. Bureau of the Census (1998), p. 227.

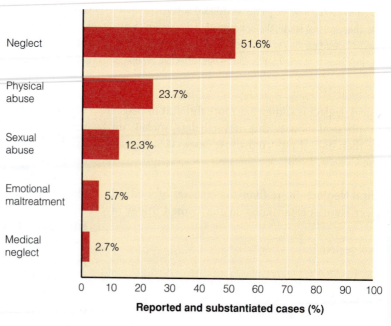

AT A GLANCE	**Shaken Baby Syndrome**

An especially horrifying kind of physical abuse is called **shaken baby syndrome**. Essentially, shaken baby syndrome is infant abuse by whiplash-shaking of the infant. This results in the brain being battered against the inside of the skull. Effects can include severe brain injury and neurological damage; it is frequently fatal. Death often occurs relatively soon after the traumatic infant-shaking episode (Nashelsky & Dix, 1995). Many who survive, explains Dr. Lloyd Denmark, Alberta's deputy chief medical examiner, become quadriplegic, lose their sight or speech, or suffer from cerebral palsy or mental retardation ("Baby shakers are rarely prosecuted," 1999). Loss of sight is typically caused by retinal hemorrhages, which are sufficiently different from other kinds of hemorrhages that they can often be used as evidence that the infant has been shaken (Betz and associates, 1996). Pathologists also look for damage under the dura, the lining of the skull, which is designed to protect the brain from these sorts of assaults.

It is not surprising that difficult, colicky, crying infants are more likely to be abused than are happy, easy infants (Wong, Wong, & Yech, 1995). Twins, too, are more likely to be abused, presumably because of the added stress of caring for two infants (Becker et al., 1998). Slightly more of the victims are male than female, and fathers appear to be about three times as likely as mothers to be guilty of shaking their infants (Starling, Holden, & Jenny, 1995). In fact, say D'Lugoff and Baker (1998), the nonoffending parent (typically the mother) is also a victim; she may suffer the consequences for years.

Relatively few cases of shaken baby syndrome are ever prosecuted, and convictions are difficult to obtain. Not only are there ambiguities in medical diagnoses of the syndrome, but there are also seldom any witnesses. Cases based solely on medical evidence are rarely upheld. "We don't have blood stains on somebody's shoes," explains medical examiner Dr. Denmark ("Baby shakers are . . .," 1999, p. B1).

To Think About: "I've changed my viewpoint over the last couple of years," says medical examiner Denmark. "If we're going to protect children, prosecution shouldn't be our main thrust, partly because it's not working."

Do you agree? What do you think can and should be done?

small spaces, severely verbally abusing them, depriving them of emotional contact and comfort, blaming, yelling, and other behaviors that might be classified as involving mental cruelty (Burnett, 1993). The effects of emotional abuse, unlike those of physical abuse or neglect, are often invisible. Consequently, instances of emotional abuse are seldom reported—and substantiated even less often (only 6% of all substantiated cases in 1996). However, the long-term effects of emotional abuse and neglect are sometimes more serious than those of physical abuse. They may come to light years later and may involve serious adjustment and emotional problems (Rowan, Foy, & Rodriguez, 1994).

Sexual Abuse Sexual abuse is a form of child maltreatment in which sexual behaviors are forced upon a child. Victims of sexual abuse are primarily female and are often very young—in fact, they are sometimes still infants. Incest is often but not always involved in the sexual abuse of children.

Estimates of the prevalence of sexual abuse vary considerably. There are several reasons for this. One is the problem of definition. Sexual abuse may be defined as an unwanted sexual act involving physical contact; it may also be defined as any of a number of actions that do not involve physical contact (for example, a proposition or suggestion, verbal enticements, exhibitionism). Estimates vary depending on the researcher's definition.

A second problem in arriving at accurate estimates has to do with the extreme social taboos surrounding all forms of incest, especially father-daughter incest (Schmidt, 1995). Estimates of these acts have typically been based on cases reported to courts or other legal jurisdictions, or cases that

shaken baby syndrome The effects of violent shaking of an infant. Essentially a whiplash-related brain injury, typically with retinal damage sometimes leading to blindness or other physical disability, or death.

emotional abuse Child maltreatment that causes emotional and psychological rather than physical harm (for example, shaming, ridiculing, ignoring, or humiliating children). A form of "mental cruelty" to children.

sexual abuse A form of maltreatment in which the victim is forced—physically or by virtue of the abuser's status and power—to submit to sexual behaviors.

come to light in the course of mental health treatment, and are probably gross underestimates.

A third problem is that many victims are too young to understand or clearly describe what is happening. Researchers sometimes rely on relatively vague methods, such as reenactment with dolls or children's drawings, to detect possible victims of sexual abuse. However, as we saw in Chapter 6, children often make unreliable witnesses, especially in cases of physical and sexual abuse (Hershkowitz & Elul, 1999). For example, in one investigation involving 68 separate interviews, researchers found that when interviewers distorted or misinterpreted what children said, children didn't correct them fully two-thirds of the time (Roberts & Lamb, 1999).

Because of these problems, estimates of sexual abuse are largely meaningless. We do know, however, that over 12% of all substantiated cases of child maltreatment in the United States in 1996 involved sexual abuse—a total of 119,397 cases (U.S. Bureau of the Census, 1998).

Physical Consequences of Victimization

The most serious possible physical consequence of child abuse—child death—is substantially underdiagnosed. Kotch (1993) made this claim after analyzing 92 cases of fatally injured children in New Zealand and another 393 cases of children who were intentionally injured. Shaken baby syndrome, as we saw, is another form of victimization where death is often misattributed.

In addition to child death, some possible physical consequences of victimization include blindness, deafness, disfiguration, and other atrocities. These are visible consequences. There are other serious— but far less visible—emotional and psychological consequences. (See *Across Cultures:* "Mash, an Ixil Indian.")

Some Psychological Consequences of Victimization

Abused children are often frightened, confused, and unhappy. Some withdraw completely; others become excessively aggressive; others regress to behaviors characteristic of younger children. Many become truant and delinquent, and both their school achievement and their social relationships suffer (Leiter and Johnsen, 1997).

Among adolescents who have been victims of sexual abuse, there is a higher than normal incidence of running away, attempted suicides, emotional disorder, and adolescent pregnancies— particularly if the father was the abuser. One investigation of 73 adolescents who had imagined or attempted suicide, or who had mutilated themselves, found that an astounding 44% of them had been physically abused and 38% reported having been sexually abused (Lipschitz et al., 1999).

Children who are sexually abused are especially prone to emotional disorders. For example, Johnson and associates (1999) looked at the psychiatric health of 639 adults. Their most striking finding was that those who had been abused as children were four times more likely to be diagnosed with personality disorders in adulthood. And many other researchers have been reporting an extraordinarily high rate of **posttraumatic stress disorder** (PTSD) among adults who were victimized as children (for example, Widom, 1999; Dubner & Motta, 1999).

The Abusive Family Context

Child abuse is clearly a symptom of a dysfunctional family. When Madonna, Van Scoyk, and Jones (1991) compared 30 families in which there had been reported incest with comparable but nonincest families, they found clear patterns of dysfunction in the incest families. Not only were these families typically characterized by very rigid belief systems, but one parent was usually highly dominant. In addition, these families were characterized by parental neglect and emotional unavailability of parents, and by lack of autonomy among children. There is evidence, as well, that in families where children are abused, spouse abuse is also common (McKay, 1994).

Membership in an abusive family system would be expected to have negative effects not only on the victims of abuse, but on other family members as well. Accordingly, it is perhaps not surprising that

---

posttraumatic stress disorder (PTSD) A serious emotional disorder that is attributed to a stressful event (or a series of such events), but that doesn't appear until after the event. A possible consequence of armed conflict, for example, or of early sexual abuse. Possible symptoms include fatigue, depression, loss of appetite, and obsessive thoughts.

Mash, an Ixil Indian

The reporter found Mash polishing the major's boots in an army camp in Guatemala. He is an Ixil boy, perhaps 7 or 8; no one knows for sure. Nor does anyone know his full name. He speaks to no one.

Mash has already been a guerilla. He can load and fire a rifle faster than most of the major's soldiers; he can hide like a snake in the jungle and strike like a panther.

But that was before the soldiers came. Before his very eyes, they shot his mother and father. Then they dragged him away, kicking and screaming. Now that Mash has gotten used to the soldiers, they keep him around like a little mascot, strangely proud of their 7- or 8-year-old little ex-guerilla. But still he refuses to speak, or smile, or laugh, or even cry; he only stares with his black eyes.

The reporter, Alison Acker (1986), arranges to take Mash away to a children's home. The boy fights his would-be rescuers and tries to bite them. For a long time they hold him tightly in the back of the station wagon as they bounce through the jungle and over the dry river beds. After seven hours, they finally reach the children's home. Mash has refused to eat. He would take neither peanuts nor Coca Cola and still will not speak. The children's home accepts him; but when they try to fill out the identification form, all they know to write is *Tomas*, the Spanish form of Mash. Every other blank is filled with the word *desconocido*—unknown.

"Will Mash eventually start to talk?" Acker asks the doctor who runs the home (Acker, 1986, p. 23).

"Sure," the doctor answers, pointing as an example to a 5-year-old girl in the next room. "She was raped so many times her vagina and anus are now fused into one passage. She'll recover. So will he" (p. 24).

When Acker returns to see Mash three weeks later, the boy still trusts no one. But there is now hope, reports his housemother. When she heard him crying one night and asked him why, at first he would say nothing; but when she asked whether it was because of his mum and dad, he said, "Yes."

And the next day, when he again climbed the big tree he climbs every day, he finally explained to the housemother why he does so.

"They're coming for me," he said. "My mum and dad" (p. 25).

More Facts: The under-5 mortality rate in Guatemala is 55 for every 1,000 children; in Canada and the United States, it is 8. In some countries, like Malawi and Angola, it is over 200 (Bellamy, 1999a). Under-5 mortality rate is a widely accepted index of how a nation treats its children. Other important differences among nations are evident in literacy rate, primary-school enrollment, life expectancy, and poverty level. In all these, Guatemala fares less well than North America.

To Think About: What do you think Mash's chances for a normal life are? Why?

David Hiser/Tony Stone Images

The under-5 mortality rate in Guatemala is almost seven times higher than in Canada or the United States.

when Jean-Gilles and Crittenden (1990) made a comparison of reported abuse victims and their siblings, they found remarkable similarities between the two. Siblings were also frequently subjected to abuse (often not reported) and manifested similar behavior problems. The common view that one child in a family serves as a scapegoat and the others are spared is largely inaccurate and misleading, claim Jean-Gilles and Crittenden. Thus, our attempts to understand, prevent, and treat child abuse and neglect need to take into consideration the entire family as a dynamic, functioning system.

Some Characteristics of Abusive Parents and of Victims Finkelhor and Dziuba-Leatherman (1994) report that there are some broad characteristics that might serve to identify situations where the risk of sexual and other forms of victimization is higher than normal. For example, research suggests that children who are abused are themselves more likely to be abusive as parents. When New, Stevenson, and Skuse (1999) studied 80 mothers whose sons had been referred for abuse, they found that 30% of these mothers had been sexually abused as children. Equally significant, 55% of the mothers of the perpetrators of abuse in this sample had also been sexually abused.

Research further suggests that parents of abused children tend to be from lower socioeconomic levels and have lower educational achievement. They are also more likely to be unemployed and on social assistance (Trickett et al., 1991). However, it is also possible that higher-class parents are better at hiding child maltreatment. When the poor and uneducated need help, they go to the police; when the well-to-do need help, they hire professional counselors.

Among the factors contributing to the likelihood of an infant's being abused are prematurity, the presence of deformities, being a twin, being born to a mother who has often been pregnant, and being born to a very busy or depressed mother. In addition, there is some evidence that infants of difficult temperament (who adjust to change less easily, who cry more, whose routines are less predictable) are more often victims of abuse. Thus, children who are abused are sometimes characterized by extreme irritability, feeding problems, excessive crying, and other behaviors that are annoying to parents (Ammerman, 1990).

Girls are at higher risk of sexual abuse than are boys, although boys too are at risk. Teenage girls are at especially high risk, although 40% of sexual abuse victims are under age 12. Those who live alone with their fathers or who live with stepfathers are at higher risk, as are those whose mothers are employed outside the home or who are ill, disabled, battered, or alcoholics. Other research indicates that marital dissatisfaction, poor mother-daughter relationship,

social isolation of the family, a history of child abuse in the family, and violence in the home all increase the likelihood that a daughter will be sexually abused (New, Stevenson, & Skuse, 1999; Finkelhor et al., 1986). Note, however, that these are extremely broad categories, including so many individual exceptions that their predictive value is severely limited.

What Can Be Done? Although it is unlikely that child abuse can be completely eliminated—particularly because physical force is a widely accepted child-rearing technique in contemporary societies and also because of the privacy of the family—a number of things can be done. These include direct interventions to remedy neglect and abuse, family-focused interventions to prevent recurrence, efforts to strengthen and preserve functional families, group approaches involving both victims and perpetrators, and legal intervention where necessary.

Some prevention strategies have tried to discover ways of predicting which parents or children are most likely to be involved in child abuse, so that something can be done before the problem occurs. Unfortunately, although abused children have several characteristics in common, many of these characteristics are also found among nonabused children. Similarly, although we know that certain racial, economic, and social factors are involved in child abuse, we cannot reliably predict who is most likely to be abused (or abusive). Prevention based on prediction remains difficult, costly, and susceptible to the error of false identification.

Other preventive strategies that might be highly effective in the long term include Jordan's (1993) suggestion that parents and communities be more closely involved in both prevention and remediation. Specific programs, such as the "Talking about Touching" program for use with young children, can increase children's knowledge about abuse and also can suggest ways of avoiding it (Madak & Berg, 1992).

Neither the problem nor its solution is simple. But perhaps a look at the role of television, which is much like a window on at least some aspects of our cultures, can contribute something to our understanding of child victimization. And ultimately, greater understanding might suggest the beginning of a solution (see *Concept Summary*).

CONCEPT SUMMARY

Concepts and Findings in the Study of Child Victimization

Concept	Explanations/Comments
Forms of child victimization	• Pandemic victimization (suffered by most children) • Acute victimization (serious, but less common, forms of maltreatment including physical and sexual abuse and neglect) • Extraordinary victimization (extreme maltreatment, including child abduction, rape, and homicide)
Classes of acute victimization	• Physical abuse (involves physical harm; includes shaken baby syndrome) • Physical neglect (failure to provide for child's physical needs) • Medical neglect (failure to provide for proper medical care of child) • Emotional abuse (psychological abuse, a type of mental cruelty including humiliation) • Sexual abuse (involving behaviors of a sexual nature)
Possible consequences of child victimization	• Physical consequences can include blindness, deafness, disfigurement, loss of limbs, paralysis, death. • Emotional consequences can include depression, aggression, sexual maladjustment, school failure, profound unhappiness, suicide, posttraumatic stress disorder.
Who abuses, who is abused, and what can be done	• Abuse is often a symptom of a dysfunctional family. • Abusive parents may themselves have been abused as children, and manifest low tolerance for "annoying" child behaviors. • Slightly more girls than boys are abused; more irritable infants are somewhat more susceptible to abuse. • Abusers are more often male than female. • Two types of possible intervention include apprehension and punishment of abusers, and social as well as therapeutic programs.

THE POWER OF TELEVISION

We're still not sure what to make of television. On the one hand, we've invented all sorts of pejorative labels for it: idiot box, vidiot, one-eyed monster, rug-rat babysitter, plug-in drug, boob tube. Yet we must surely like it; most of our homes have at least one set.

But deep down, many fear it—or at least fear what it might do to our children. For some time now, our prophets of doom and gloom have been spreading the alarm. Television, they croak as they lurch about our villages wagging their fingers, will destroy our children. Some of these prophets claim that television is producing a generation of passive people, inactive, lethargic, apathetic, fat, and out of shape—but responsive, and well-informed, consumers. Some prophets mutter—while double-bolting their doors, barring their windows, and checking their weapons—that the violence that saturates television is creating a world of violent people. Still other doomsayers, bent in prayer, shudder with the certainty that television corrupts as surely as does money and other Great Evils. Alarmists also warn against the possibility that given the amount of the child's time it consumes, television may have a harmful effect on family relationships, on the social development of children, and on badminton, bicycling, bird-watching, and bingo.

Although the research evidence is incomplete, we have enough answers to respond to these concerns and to present a more balanced impression of the actual influence of television on the lives of children.

Children's Viewing Patterns

In 1950, there were about 100,000 television sets in North American homes; one year later, there were more than 1 million. Now it is no easy thing to find any home without at least one set. A conservative estimate is that preschoolers spend more than a third of their waking time watching television. Even 9-month-olds watch about 90 minutes of television a day (Cohen, 1993–1994). Many young children spend more time watching television than they spend in conversation with adults or siblings. In one survey, more than 25% of 4,000 U.S. children aged 8 to 16 watched television for more than four hours per day (Andersen et al., 1998). In fact, by age 18, many children will have spent about 50% more time watching television than going to school and doing schoolwork combined. Only sleeping will have taken more time than watching television (Huston et al., 1990).

Young Children's Comprehension of Television

What children see and understand from television might be quite different from what you or I might see. They lack the experiences that we have, and their conceptual bases are more fragmented, less complete. Researchers now recognize that children don't understand everything they watch. For example, Hayes and Casey (1992) report that preschoolers understand very little of the emotions and motives of characters—hardly surprising given their social cognitions. What they don't understand, says Evra (1998), they simply ignore.

But even at the age of 5 or 6, children use fairly sophisticated cognitive skills to understand television's messages. With advancing age, they become more sensitive to motives and more attentive to implications of actions for the characters involved. And research indicates that children's memory for what they see on television may be far better than for what they read. Walma van der Molen & van der Voort (1997) presented 152 fourth- and sixth-graders with brief sequences of children's news items, either televised or in written form. When these children were subsequently tested for their recollections of what they had read or seen, the television-presented material proved significantly more memorable than the printed material. But what is it that children see on television?

The Content of Television

If children watch the typical Saturday morning avalanche of animated, child-oriented programs, they will certainly see less sex, though perhaps no less violence, than if they watch prime time, adult-oriented television. And they will also see some community-oriented, public service messages relating (for example) to school, nutrition, drugs, safety, and the environment, reports Swan (1998) in a detailed analysis of U.S. television programming. What Saturday morning television teaches our children, says Swan, is "that White men are the most important and powerful people in that society, that women are underrepresented everywhere, that minorities are excluded in some places, that old people are incompetent and evil and best left alone" (p. 109). Furthermore, he adds, television teaches children to be active consumers; to be concerned about the environment; to be courageous, kind, and persistent; always to cooperate with the group; and never to be an individual. "The messages of Saturday morning," Swan writes, "are not really very different from the messages of American society. But," he adds, "are they really the messages we want our children to hear?" (p. 109)

If they watch prime time television, children are almost certain to see a lot of both sex and violence. A recent survey indicates that across four major networks, viewers would have seen an average of 28.2 instances of sexual activity per hour, including kissing, hugging, touching, sexual innuendo, and actual intercourse (Truglio, 1998). Truglio suggests that this might serve as a source of sex education—presumably a worthy undertaking, since most school jurisdictions advocate teaching children about sex at some point. But, says Truglio, the values and messages that television conveys may not be those we want to teach. Simply put, television's portrayal of sex is idealized and distorted, it rarely involves people who are committed to each other, safe sex is almost never practiced, and sexual activity almost never has negative consequences (such as a sexually transmitted disease or an unwanted pregnancy).

Violence is hot on the heels of sex. In prime time, says Lamson (1995), viewers see somewhere between 8 and 12 violent acts per hour—and some studies have reported as many as 100 acts of violence in a single hour. Despite increasing numbers of channels dedicated to commercial-free, nonviolent children's programming, much of this violence is embedded in rapid action, constant change, high noise levels, and slapstick acting. Much of the violence is unrealistic, excessive, and carried out by characters clearly identified with some of our culture's negative stereotypes. For example, following a detailed analysis of the content of television programming, Diefenbach (1997) reports that one recurring stereotype links mental disorders with violence. The mentally ill, he notes, account for 10 times more violence than other television characters (and close to *20 times* more violence than people in the real world). One very important question concerns the effects of television violence on children.

Overt and Social Aggression

Violence is an extreme form of what is termed **overt aggression**. Violence implies overt physical action and the possibility of real harm or injury to people or objects. Overt aggression is not always violent. It includes a range of forceful human actions intended to dominate, to frighten, and perhaps even to hurt physically.

Our psychological research, if not our powers of observation, makes it clear that overt aggressiveness is predominantly a male characteristic. This information has led many to mistakenly assume that *aggressiveness* is a male, but not a female, trait. In fact, although *overt* aggressiveness is primarily a male propensity, there are less obvious—but at least in some ways, no less harmful—forms of aggression that girls engage in more than boys. These forms of aggression are labeled **relational aggression** (or sometimes *social aggression*). Overt aggression seeks to do harm through physical damage, note Crick, Casas, and Mosher (1997); in contrast, relational aggression seeks to do harm by damaging peer relationships. Thus the methods of overt aggression are kicking, punching, pushing, and gouging eyes; the methods of relational aggression are ridicule, social exclusion, rumor mongering, malicious teasing, contempt, and disdain.

Relational aggression, report Galen and Underwood (1997), is recognized by children, and especially by girls, as highly hurtful—in fact, often more hurtful than overt aggression. Evidence suggests that children who are victims of social aggression frequently suffer from adjustment problems and unhappiness. At the same time, in the same way as overtly aggressive children are most likely to be rejected by peers, so too, children who engage in high levels of relational aggression are also more likely to suffer peer rejection (Grotpeter& Crick, 1996). Recall that these children are termed the aggressive-rejected (in contrast with the withdrawn-rejected).

Unfortunately, those concerned with the effects of television violence on children's aggressiveness have not usually distinguished between overt and social aggression. The research predominantly looks at the effects of extreme overt aggression (violence, in other words) on manifested aggressive behavior. There is much that we don't yet know about the extent of relational aggression in television programs, or about the effects that television's portrayal of social aggression might have on child viewers.

---

violence An extreme form of aggressiveness, implying physical action and real or possible physical harm to people or objects.

overt aggression Visible, outwardly manifested form of aggression that includes a range of possible forceful human actions intended to dominate, to frighten, perhaps even to hurt physically. One extreme form of overt aggression is violence.

relational aggression A form of aggression that seeks to harm people by disrupting their social relations (also called *social aggression*). The methods of relational aggression are ridicule, social exclusion, rumor mongering, malicious teasing, contempt, and disdain.

Laboratory Research on Television Violence

We do know that television programming for children (and for adults) is marked by a great number of violent images. Many of these, note Kalamas and Gruber (1998) involve *implied* rather than actual violence. It is interesting that the effects of implied violence on children, measured by their physiological reactions—in this case, **electrodermal response (EDR)**—appear to be even greater than the effects of actual violence. Thus the appearance of the villain, or the threat of his appearance, is more frightening than the actual stabbing with the knife! But if violence on television is sometimes frightening for children, does it also affect their behavior?

In an early series of laboratory studies, Bandura and his associates (Bandura, 1969; Bandura, Ross, & Ross, 1963) exposed children to violent models that were either live actors, films of real people, or films of cartoon characters. Following exposure to a violent model (typically, the model was aggressive toward an inflated rubber clown), children were given objects similar to those the model had been aggressive toward. The children were then observed at play through a one-way mirror. In most studies of this kind, most of the children who were previously exposed to models of violence behave aggressively; in contrast, those who were not exposed to violent models most often respond nonaggressively.

Naturalistic Research on Television Violence

Studies that look at children's behavior toward inflated dolls in laboratory situations may not tell us a great deal about aggressiveness in real life. Investigations in more natural circumstances may provide clearer information. Unfortunately, because it's difficult to find children who have not been exposed to television and can therefore serve as control groups for these studies, there are few studies.

---

electrodermal response (EDR) A measure of changes in the skin's electrical conductivity. With increasing arousal (emotion), minute increases in perspiration result in increased skin conductivity. Hence EDR (also termed *galvanic skin response* or *GSR*) is a physiological measure of arousal (emotion).

THOUGHT CHALLENGE: *The Bandura studies, in which children exposed to filmed violence toward "Bobo" clowns later attempt to beat up similar clowns, have been widely interpreted as evidence that violence on television leads to violence in real life. Can you think of any reasons why this conclusion might not be very convincing?*

A study conducted by Joy, Kimball, and Zabrack (1977), which involved children in a town where television was just being introduced, found a measurable increase in aggressive behavior two years later. Similar results were also reported in Sweden, where researchers found high positive correlations between television viewing and aggressiveness (Rosengren & Windahl, 1989). Further evidence also comes from a series of studies that looked at the effects of television violence on aggressiveness in children from five countries: the United States, Finland, Israel, Poland, and Australia (Huesmann & Eron, 1986b). Not only are these cultures very different, but television accessibility and the nature of television programming varied tremendously. For example, in the Israeli kibbutz, children watched TV for only one or two hours a week and were almost never exposed to television violence. In contrast, American children watched 20 or more hours of television, most of it characterized by violent themes and violent acts.

The main conclusion of the Huesmann and Eron study is essentially the same conclusion advanced by Singer et al. (1998) following a survey of 2,245 children in grades three to eight (in Ohio). Television violence does have an adverse effect on *some* children. That is, the most aggressive children tend to select the more violent television programs and to view more of them; at the same time, those who watch more violent programs tend to be more aggressive.

Other Possible Negative Effects of Television

Television may be linked with various other negative outcomes, such as the following:

▲ *Instilling fear in some children.* This effect, for some, may be more serious than increased aggressiveness. A survey conducted by Ridley-Johnson, Surdy, and O'Laughlin (1991) found that many parents are as concerned about fear-related influences of television as about aggression-related effects.

▲ *Changes in levels of physical activity.* Andersen et al. (1998) surveyed 4,063 children (ages 8 to 16) and found that the more television children watched, the less they engaged in vigorous physical activity.

▲ *Changes in levels of fitness.* Because children who watch more television engage less in physical activity, we might expect them to be less fit and more obese. However, research has generally not provided strong support for this belief. Stafford, Wells, and Fewtrell (1998) found that while physical activity is closely linked with fitness, television viewing is not. Similarly, Katzmarzyk et al. (1998) found little relationship between time spent watching television and measures of fitness in a sample of Canadian children.

▲ *Changes in the nature of social interaction.* Cohen (1993–1994) notes that the influence of parents and peers seems to have declined with the television generation. Television is now a primary source of information and influence, he argues. It not only reinforces models of social behavior but also creates them. It is so important that children and even families often arrange their schedules (and their furniture) around television.

Possible Positive Effects of Television

However, the potential effects of television are not all negative. For example, children who watch the news show *Channel One* in the classroom learn more news than those who don't (Greenberg & Brand, 1993). And evidence shows that the language development of preschoolers can be significantly improved with educational television (Koutsouvanou, 1993). In fact, children are able to learn some aspects of a second language by watching foreign language television (d'Ydewalle & Van de Poel, 1999).

As Meskill (1998) notes, television is not only a model of correct language forms, which can be exceptionally informative for young minority-group children, but also a window into our culture. In the same way that television might be instrumental in undermining values such as nonviolence, family stability, cooperation, altruism, and gender equality, so too might it serve to bring about and strengthen these values. Rosenkoetter (1999) found that many first-graders are able to identify and understand moral lessons even in adult sitcoms. And Potts and Swisher (1998) found that children (ages 5 to 8) who were shown safety-oriented educational programs were subsequently more safety conscious. Not only were they more likely to identify potential dangers, but they were also less likely to take risks. Similarly, research with episodes from *Mister Rogers' Neighborhood* and with several other deliberately prosocial programs found clear evidence of improvement in prosocial behaviors such as friendliness, generosity, cooperation, creativity, empathy, racial tolerance, and others (Rosenkoetter et al., 1990). Unfortunately, however, as Cohen (1993–1994) points out, only rarely does commercial television teach these messages.

Some Newer Technologies

What messages does the new television-related technology provide, and what is their potential influence on children?

Rock Videos Close to the cutting edge of television technology, and sometimes very close as well to the edge of what society's evolving tastes and morals find acceptable, are rock videos. They are very simple: Take a popular, avant-garde, rock-type song; create images to accompany the lyrics; and combine the two in a frenetic, jarring, surprising, evocative, and sometimes bizarre way. The result? A dazzling, seductive, intriguing, audiovisual experience that has transformed the music industry—and that has alarmed some parents and educators as well. Why? Because, as one commentator put it, "Some of them are sending messages that are questionable, to say the least: anti-work, anti-marriage, anti-family, pro-violence, pro-casual sex, pro-woman-as-victim" (Television & Your Children, 1985, p. 52).

Rock videos, says Luke (1988), have much the same faults that are found in commercial television: They are racist, sexist, violent, and highly commercialized. Although research on their effects is rare, it is likely that they will be at least as influential as more ordinary television programs. Indeed, they might even be more influential given their technological slickness, the addictive quality of their lyrics and their rhythms, and their popularity with the teen and preteen generation. At the same time, their popularity might also be used to advantage in some circumstances, perhaps as a motivational tool in the classroom.

Videocassette Recorders VCRs About 70% of American homes now have VCRs (Clifford, Gunter, & McAleer, 1995). Their rapid proliferation brings an additional worry for those concerned with the potentially harmful effects of television. Attempts are being made to control television programming for children. For example, the **V-chip**, an electronic device available on some television sets, allows parents to block reception of programs considered unsuitable for children. But parents and society either do not have, or often don't exercise, significant control over children's selections of the video recordings that they rent for home viewing. In most areas, it is possible for children to rent videos that depict aggression and standards of morality that would not be considered acceptable on public television. Similarly, the increasing availability of quasiprivate channels through home satellite systems means that increasing numbers of children may be exposed to extreme forms of violence and pornography at very young ages. Buckingham (1998), for example, reports the speculation that the child perpetrators of the sensational murder of 2-year-old Jamie Bulger in England might have been influenced by their viewing of violent videotapes. There is clearly a need for more research to ascertain the probable effects of this medium, and to identify the parameters that might interact to make some children more vulnerable than others.

Computers and the Internet The Internet (or World Wide Web), too, presents some reason for fear. It has the potential of exposing children to levels of violence and pornography that would be unimaginable on commercial television—not to mention recipes for chocolate chip cookies and plans for birdhouses and nuclear weapons. And about 90% of all U.S. schools are now linked to the Web (U.S. Bureau of the Census, 1999; see Figure 10.6).

In addition to the possible effects of the content available on the Internet, there is also the question of the amount of time some children spend with computers, and the possible effects of involvement in **chat groups** and **bulletin boards.**

Children use the Internet for various reasons, explain Izenberg and Lieberman (1998), including entertainment, obtaining information, and establishing personal connections. Each of these uses gives rise to separate concerns. For some children, the entertainment functions of the Internet are almost addictive. The effect, says Evra (1998), is that children may spend far more hours isolated from other family members; and of course, other family members might spend their own big chunks of time isolated from the children.

The use of the Internet for information gives rise to concerns about the sorts of information the child is likely to get from the Internet. Although several programs are readily available that allow parents to block access to sites where certain key subjects appear (typically dealing with sex, pornography, violence, hatred, and other related topics), these aren't widely used. Most children, therefore, can access whatever adults can access. And as Durkin and Bryant (1999) found, it isn't particularly difficult to find **pedophiles** on the Internet.

Dangers arising from using the Internet to establish personal connections relate directly to the

---

V-chip A Canadian-designed technological device which, when installed in a television set, blocks reception of programs that have specific codes. The codes are ratings that reflect whether programs are designed specifically for children, whether they contain violence, sex, fear-inducing elements, and so on.

chat groups An Internet phenomenon whereby pairs or groups of individuals, typically unidentified or using pseudonyms, can communicate with one another in real time by computers.

bulletin boards An Internet phenomenon whereby groups who share specific interests can *post* and read information, advice, and propaganda relevant to their interests, typically anonymously.

pedophiles Literally, lovers of children. Describes a category of sexual deviance where sexual gratification is tied to activities involving children.

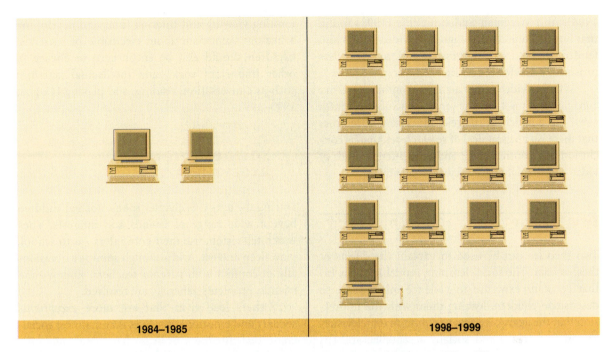

FIGURE 10.6   Computers per 100 students, 1984–85, 1998–99. Source: U.S. Bureau of the Census, 1999, p. 183.

anonymity that cloaks people in chat rooms and on bulletin boards. Children, who are inexperienced and unfamiliar with so much, can be easily misled. What Griffiths (1997) calls "electronic friendships" are highly common among children and adolescents. These are friendships not only with anonymous people but also with an electronic machine. The machine has the advantage of being solid, substantial, knowable. The chat-room friend is only an idea painted on the child's mind with words, and maybe pictures, drawn in cyberspace. There is seldom any proof that the "friend" is male or female, old or young, green or purple.

So what are the effects, the risks, the benefits of Internet access and use? The research is still young. One longitudinal study reports that use of the Internet is linked with declines in social interaction among family members, and with increasing depression and loneliness among users (Kraut et al., 1998). Others have been skeptical of these findings and their interpretation, however, arguing that the observed effects are very small (for example, Shapiro, 1999; Rierdan, 1999). As Kiesler and Kraut (1999) point out, the significance of these findings is not their magnitude but their direction.

Despite these risks, argue Bremer and Rauch (1998), the Internet has some significant potential benefits. These include access to information that might be important for school assignments and other purposes, entertainment, and an opportunity to practice social interaction skills. Silverman (1999) points out that the Internet gives all children a voice and a listener, or a group of listeners, no matter how withdrawn the child might be.

Video Games Video games have been a source of concern for some parents as well, particularly in light of their quasiaddictive qualities and their overwhelmingly violent themes. In many of these violent games, users are wiped out if they make the wrong moves. And if they make the right moves, hey, they blow up, tear apart, explode, and annihilate . . . something or someone.

Research on the effects of video games has reached much the same conclusions as those about the effects of television. For example, research on the short-term effects of playing a violent as opposed to a nonviolent game found a marked tendency for violent players to interpret neutral situations in more violent and negative terms (Kirsh,

1998). And Wiegman and van Schie (1998) found that boys who preferred aggressive video games also tended to be more aggressive and to show less prosocial behavior in real life.

Whether video games actually promote aggressive behavior can't yet be answered, concludes Griffiths (1997) in a review of the relevant research. He notes that there isn't a great deal of research yet, that its conclusions are contradictory, and that different kinds of video games might have very different effects.

Two Sides of the Media Controversy

Two theories can be used to explain the effects of these media. The social learning model suggests (a) that constant exposure to violence might serve to desensitize children, leaving them with the impression that the aggressive acts so common on television are, in fact, trivial and socially acceptable; and (b) precisely what to do in order to be aggressive, to succeed, to win. That is, it provides models of violence. The social learning model predicts that violence in the media, in games, in books, and elsewhere in the culture will serve to *increase* aggression in children.

The Freudian **cathartic model** claims that television might serve as a catharsis (release) for pent-up emotions. For some individuals, painting might be a catharsis for aggressive impulses that cannot be acted on for moral reasons; others might try to kick their cats, except they don't usually sit still. In the same way, exposure to television violence may be a release for pent-up hostility, aggressive urges, and other antisocial tendencies. The cathartic model predicts that television violence should result in a decrease in violent behavior.

There is more evidence to support the social learning than the cathartic model, Griffiths (1997a) concludes after reviewing the research. But most of the evidence is still weak.

An increasing number of researchers are now arguing that schools should teach children the basic skills of television and Internet literacy—skills relating to distinguishing between reality and fantasy, making wise choices among available programming,

limiting viewing and Internet time, and developing a healthy skepticism about electronic pen-friends. Children should also be encouraged to engage in other important social and intellectual activities such as conversation, reading, and playing (Cohen, 1993–1994).

SOCIOEMOTIONAL EXCEPTIONALITY

During the ages this chapter spans, normal children have a wide range of friends and interests. They watch television, use their computers, go to school, play, sleep and eat. And although some are occasionally in conflict with parents, teachers, siblings, and friends, problems generally are resolved.

Others lead lives that are more *exceptional* socially and emotionally—lives that manifest social-emotional giftedness, or lives where nature and nurture have been less kind. For instance, there are children who manifest a variety of adjustment problems and **emotional disorders**. These problems tend to be both varied and highly individualistic; they are not easily classified or even defined. They include a wide variety of nonphysical exceptionalities ranging from relatively minor behavior problems to serious mental disorders such as autism or schizophrenia. Other terms that are sometimes used to refer to children with problems in this area are *behavior disordered*, *emotionally disturbed*, and *socially maladjusted*. Each of these terms describes children who are troubled and who may also cause trouble for parents, teachers, peers, and others. However, these terms are not explanations or even very good descriptions; they are simply labels for children who share common characteristics.

Defining and identifying social-emotional maladjustment is more difficult than describing physical exceptionality. Whereas reasonably competent individuals can usually agree on a diagnosis of visual or hearing impairments, the same doesn't hold for the common social-emotional problems of middle childhood.

---

cathartic model Expression of the Freudian notion that certain experiences or events can serve to release pent-up negative tendencies, serving a purifying or purging function.

emotional disorder Also termed *behavior disorder*, a classification used to include a wide range of nonphysical exceptionalities ranging from relatively minor behavior problems to serious mental disorders such as autism or schizophrenia (including ADHD).

Prevalence and Classifications

Estimates of the prevalence of emotional disorders vary considerably depending on the criteria used for identification and on whether estimates include mild as well as severe instances of disturbance. The APA (1994) estimates that somewhere between 3% and 5% of schoolchildren manifest the most common form of emotional disorder for this age group: attention deficit hyperactivity disorder (ADHD).

Problems in Classification Classifying emotional disturbances in childhood presents special difficulties. First, because many childhood disorders are characteristically different from adult behaviors, models of adult affective disorders are not always appropriate. For example, some behaviors that might be symptoms of underlying disorders in adults are relatively common in younger children: If I walked around here giggling like 4-year-old Elizabeth—or having temper tantrums like 2-year-old Liam sometimes does—my behavior might seem more than a little bizarre and might be interpreted as a symptom of some new underlying disorder. But in Liam and Elizabeth, these behaviors alarm no one.

When looking at the appropriateness of young children's behavior, we also have to take developmental changes into account. Thus, excessive aggression may be manifested in different behaviors depending on the child's age. A very aggressive 5-year-old may simply shove other children out of the way; later, he may threaten instead, or he may fight, or he may even use weapons.

Further, some disorders are primarily childhood problems; others are more common in adulthood. For example, *hyperactivity* (discussed in the next section) appears to be primarily a childhood disorder, although there is now evidence that many children do not "outgrow" it (Faraone et al., 1999). In contrast, serious affective (emotional) disorders such as depression and mania were long thought to be adult rather than childhood disorders. We now know, however, that although children rarely suffer the manic disorders, they do suffer depression (Deiner, 1999).

Classifications Three of the most common manifestations of emotional disorders in childhood are conduct disorder, oppositional defiant disorder, and attention deficit disorders.

The main characteristic of **conduct disorder**, according to the American Psychiatric Association (APA, 1994), is persistent violation of the basic rights of others or violation of society's norms and rules. Conduct disorders may be evident in behaviors such as aggression toward people and animals, destruction of property, deceitfulness and theft, and other serious violations of rules. They are also often accompanied by other disorders such as ADHD (Stahl & Clarizio, 1999). The APA lists specific criteria of seriousness and frequency of these behaviors before the child can be classified as having a conduct disorder.

Oppositional defiant disorder is evident in habitually hostile, negative, defiant behaviors. It may be evident in frequent loss of temper, arguments with adults, and outright refusal to obey rules of conduct. The APA specifies that both conduct disorder and oppositional defiant disorder have to cause significant impairment in academic, social, or occupational functioning to be so classified.

Attention Deficit Hyperactivity Disorder

Attention deficit hyperactivity disorder is marked by excessive general activity for the child's age (often taking the form of incessant and haphazard climbing, crawling, or running); difficulty in sustaining attention and apparent forgetfulness; and impulsivity (tendency to react quickly, difficulty taking turns, low **frustration** tolerance). The criteria

---

conduct disorder An emotional disorder evident in persistent and significant violation of rules and laws, and of others' basic rights, often manifested in excessive aggression, vandalism, theft, and deceitfulness.

oppositional defiant disorder An emotional disorder evident in open defiance of authority and serious displays of anger and hostility that cause the individual significant social, academic, or occupational problems.

attention deficit hyperactivity disorder (ADHD) A disorder marked by excessive general activity for the child's age, attention problems, high impulsivity, and low frustration tolerance.

frustration An affective (emotional) reaction to the inability to gratify one's desires.

described by the APA also stipulate that the duration of the child's hyperactivity be at least six months.

Attention problems can also exist without hyperactivity (attention deficit disorder, or ADD). Many ADHD children experience considerable difficulty adjusting to school and home and are considered to have relatively serious problems.

Causes The factors contributing to the development of ADHD are varied. There is evidence that in many cases, genetic factors may be involved. Thus ADHD is more common in some families than in others. Also, it is between four and nine times more common among males than females (APA, 1994). Faraone and associates (1999) report a recently discovered link between a specific gene and ADHD.

There is evidence, too, regarding the contribution of certain environmental factors such as neglect, maltreatment, malnutrition, head injuries, and diseases and illnesses, as well as conditions within the family such as stress associated with conflict. In addition, poverty, parental abuse, parental rejection, physical handicaps, age, sex, and racial and religious discrimination have been implicated (Kazdin, 1989).

Considerable evidence also exists regarding what is termed **comorbidity** in ADHD—the joint presence of several other disorders accompanying the disorder. For example, Nolan et al. (1999) found that many of the ADHD children in their sample of 3- to 18-year-olds also met the criteria for oppositional and conduct disorder. And Biederman et al. (1999), who studied girls with ADHD, found that they were also more likely to have mood, conduct, and anxiety disorders. This is not especially surprising given the problems such children often experience in adjusting to home and school.

Diagnosis Diagnoses of ADHD, or simply of hyperactivity, are sometimes—perhaps even often—made inappropriately by parents and teachers when confronted by children who are restless and find it difficult to do the quiet things that adults sometimes demand. Unfortunately, the diagnosis is perhaps inappropriately made by professionals as well.

Robison et al. (1999) report that doctors diagnosed well over 2 million cases of ADHD in 1995; five years earlier, they had diagnosed fewer than 1 million cases.

Strictly speaking, attention deficit hyperactivity disorder as defined by the American Psychiatric Association (1994) needs to begin before the age of 7 to differentiate it from disorders that might arise as reactions to stressful events or illness. In addition, children must manifest a combination of six or more symptoms of inattention, and six or more specific signs of hyperactivity or impulsivity. These symptoms must have persisted for a period of at least 6 months, and must be serious enough to be maladaptive and inconsistent with the child's age. Some symptoms of hyperactivity and inattention/impulsivity listed by the APA are shown in Table 10.5.

Clearly, not all children suffering from this disorder will display the same combination and seriousness of symptoms. However, given that the condition appears easy to diagnose (it is defined largely by observable behaviors) and that it can therefore easily be overdiagnosed, extreme caution should be exercised before applying the label to any child.

Treatment The most common treatment for a child diagnosed as having an attention deficit disorder with hyperactivity involves the use of stimulant drugs such as dextroamphetamine (Dexadrine) and methylphenidate (**Ritalin**). This might seem strange since stimulants ordinarily increase activity, and the ADHD child already suffers from excessive activity. However, these drugs appear to sedate rather than stimulate ADHD children (Swanson et al., 1991). Their use is sometimes highly effective in preventing continued achievement declines in school (Berman, Douglas, & Barr, 1999), as well as in increasing the manageability of the children in question. Use of methylphenidate is associated with detectable changes in the brain activity of ADHD children (Loo, Teale, & Reite, 1999). Nevertheless, drug therapy with ADHD children remains a controversial

---

comorbidity A medical term for the frequent co-occurrence of a number of conditions. For example, profound mental retardation often includes visual or other sensory problems as comorbidities.

ritalin A stimulant drug of the amphetamine family designed to sedate rather than stimulate children diagnosed with hyperactivity. Also a relatively common street drug that is combined with the drug *talwin* to produce what is sometimes known as "poor man's heroin," with the street name *R and T's*.

TABLE 10.5
Some DSM-IV Diagnostic Criteria for ADD and ADHD

Attention Deficit Disorder (ADD) requires the presence of at least six criteria of inattention (of nine listed, only four are included here); Attention Deficit Hyperactivity Disorder (ADHD) requires, in addition, the presence of six or more symptoms of hyperactivity or impulsivity (of nine listed, five are shown here). Symptoms need to be maladaptive as evident in school or home adjustment, of at least 6 months duration, and present before age 7.

INATTENTION

- Often doesn't pay attention to details or makes careless mistakes in schoolwork or other activities
- Is often forgetful in daily activities
- Is often easily distracted by outside stimuli
- Often seems not to be listening when spoken to directly

HYPERACTIVITY AND IMPULSIVITY

- Often fidgets with hands or feet or squirms
- Often leaves seat in classroom, or other situation when remaining seated is expected
- Often talks excessively
- Finds it difficult to wait to take turn in group situations; often blurts out answers to questions before they have been completed
- Often interrupts or intrudes

treatment. Some are alarmed at the tremendous increase in the use of these drugs in North America. Diller reports that there has been an eight-fold increase in use of stimulant drugs for ADHD in the past decade, and that the United States accounts for use of 90% of all the methylphenidate (Ritalin) used in the world. These drugs can also have some negative side effects such as weight loss, growth retardation, and mood changes (Henker & Whalen, 1989).

As McClure and Teyber (1996) point out, ADHD children are often greatly in need of teacher and family support. These children have considerable difficulty completing tasks and may have relatively few success experiences to help them overcome the growing suspicion that they might be "dumb" or in other ways inferior. Such children are highly vulnerable, argue McClure and Teyber, and require firm but affectionate discipline.

Stress in Childhood

Many of the emotional and behavioral problems of childhood, and perhaps some physical problems as well, are related to something we call **stress**—a difficult concept that everybody understands at least intuitively.

Stress Defined In the physical sciences, stress is a force that is exerted on a body, sometimes causing deformation or breakage. In psychology, stress is a nonphysical force that is exerted on an individual, sometimes causing negative change. Skinner and Wellborn (1994) suggest that there are two approaches to defining stress. One is concerned with stimuli; the other with responses. Stimuli are said to be stressful when they make excessive demands on the individual; responses are stressful when they are accompanied by the physiological changes of high arousal such as increased heart rate, perspiration, trembling, and so on.

The Effects of Stress Lazarus (1993) classifies stress by the severity of its effects. Thus, there is *harm*, which implies actual damage; *threat*, which implies the possibility of damage; and *challenge*, which implies demands that can be met.

stress A force exerted on an individual, often related to change or to high environmental demands; sometimes associated with high arousal.

This classification recognizes that stress is clearly not always negative. Challenge, and even threat, may lead to what are essentially adaptive physiological responses. In such cases, stress prepares the individual for action. The sudden shot of adrenaline and the acceleration of heart rate when we are threatened or challenged increase the effectiveness of our running, our fighting, or our speechmaking.

But under other circumstances, we may have an overload of stress and suffer harm. The implications of this overload vary from one individual to another, but are clearly not limited to adults. As we saw in Chapter 6, infants and preschoolers can suffer profound distress at the loss of a parent or sometimes even as a result of temporary separation from a parent. The effects may be apparent in sleeping or eating disturbances, as well as in a general listlessness that may border on depression.

Among children, the effects of stress might include physical complaints (such as stomach pains, sometimes caused by ulcers, or asthma), emotional problems (such as persistent fears, high anxiety, or other signs of posttraumatic stress disorder), or behavior problems (such as truancy, defiance, or high aggression) (Holmes, Yu & Frentz, 1999).

Child Stressors

Many of the things that children fear, notes Kupetz (1993), are a source of considerable stress for them. She warns that parents often trivialize these fears because they judge them by adult standards ("Don't be silly, Guy, there's nothing in the closet. Hey, you guys, did you hear what Guy's scared of now?"). Parents need to realize that children's fears are real, and they need to help their children reduce the stressors in their lives.

Fears are just one source of childhood stress; Elkind (1981a; 1987) describes several other stressors, many of which are more common to this generation of children than they were to earlier generations. They relate to *stimulus* or *demand overloads*. There is, for example, *responsibility overload*, in which young children whose parents work are made responsible for tasks like looking after younger siblings, buying groceries, preparing meals, cleaning the house, and so on. There is

change overload, in which children from mobile families are shunted rapidly from one community to another, transferred from school to school, and left with a sequence of caregivers. *Emotional overload* may result when children are exposed to emotion-laden situations that directly affect their lives, but over which they have little control (parents quarreling, for example). Finally, there is *information overload*, resulting largely from the tremendous amount of information to which television exposes the child. Add to all these potential sources of stress the sometimes exorbitant achievement demands that are placed on the child by school, parents, and society. "Hurry," they all say to Elkind's (1981a) *hurried child*. "Hurry! Grow up! There isn't much time!"

Other sources of high stress are perhaps rarer, although their effects might be far more apparent. Physical and sexual abuse, for example, are highly stressful and are often associated with *posttraumatic stress disorder (PTSD)* (Dubner & Motta, 1999). Also associated with posttraumatic stress disorder, not surprisingly, is war. In one sample of 239 Palestinian children (6 to 11 years old) exposed to war, almost 75% manifested at least mild symptoms of PTSD; 41% had moderate to severe symptoms (Thabet & Vostanis, 1999). Similarly, physical trauma, such as might result from an automobile accident, quite frequently results in symptoms of PTSD (Aaron, Zaglul, & Emery, 1999).

Clearly, not all children are exposed to the same stressful situations; nor will all react the same way. Some children remain unperturbed in the face of events that might prove disastrous for others. Nevertheless, psychology provides several approaches to assessing stress in the lives of children, or at least determining the likelihood of stress. Many of these approaches are based on the assumption that all major changes in a person's life are potentially stressful and that, although most individuals can cope with a limited number of changes, eventually there is a breaking point. Accordingly, these stress scales simply ask individuals to identify all major changes they have recently experienced. Some changes are clearly more important than others (the death of a parent compared with changing schools, for example). Values are assigned accordingly. Table 10.6 is one example of this approach for children.

TABLE 10.6
Stressful Events in Children's Lives

LIFE-CHANGE EVENT	POINTS	LIFE-CHANGE EVENT	POINTS
Parent dies	100	Older brother or sister leaves home	29
Parents divorce	73	Trouble with grandparents	29
Parents separate	65	Outstanding personal achievement	28
Parent travels as part of job	63	Move to another city	26
Close family member dies	63	Move to another part of town	26
Personal illness or injury	53	Receives or loses a pet	25
Parent remarries	50	Changes personal habits	24
Parent fired from job	47	Trouble with teacher	24
Parents reconcile	45	Change in hours with baby-sitter or at day-care center	20
Mother goes to work	45	Moves to a new house	20
Change in health of a family member	44	Changes to a new school	20
Mother becomes pregnant	40	Changes play habits	19
School difficulties	39	Vacations with family	19
Birth of a sibling	39	Changes friends	18
School readjustment (new teacher or class)	39	Attends summer camp	17
Change in family's financial condition	38	Changes sleeping habits	16
Injury or illness of a close friend	37	Change in number of family get-togethers	15
Starts a new (or changes) an extracurricular activity (music lessons, Brownies, and so forth)	36	Changes eating habits	15
Change in number of fights with siblings	35	Changes amount of TV viewing	13
Threatened by violence at school	31	Birthday party	12
Theft of personal possessions	30	Punished for not "telling the truth"	11
Changes responsibilities at home	29		

If scores for a 1-year period total 150, stress exposure is average; if between 150 and 300, there is a higher probability of stress-related symptoms; above 300, serious consequences are even more probable.

Source: From David Elkind (1988). *The hurried child*, pp. 162–163. Reading, Mass.: Addison-Wesley Publishing Co., Inc. Adapted with permission of Perseus Books.

Social-Emotional Giftedness

In the socioemotional sphere, as elsewhere, exceptionality has two dimensions: the disadvantaged, among them the autistic, the depressed, the hyperactive, and those exhibiting personality and conduct disorders; and the advantaged, to whom we have paid little special attention.

Among the advantaged are the highly resilient, sometimes labeled invulnerables or "superkids." Invulnerables are children who, because of their bio-logical history and environment, are at greater psychiatric risk than others. Werner (1993) describes several risk factors: birth problems, poverty, and family environments marked by alcoholism, mental illness, or conflict. And we could add to these wars, abuse, physical trauma, and other fearsome things. All of these risk factors have been linked with subsequent emotional and behavior problems in children.

Significantly, many children whose backgrounds include one or even all of these risks nevertheless grow up to be well-adjusted, socially competent individuals. In Werner's (1993) study of at-risk children, for example, about a third of the at-risk children grew up to be apparently strong, well-adjusted individuals. (It is also significant that 129 children, fully two thirds of the original sample, developed serious learning or behavior problems in elementary school, manifested delinquent behavior in adolescence, or experienced mental health problems at some point in their development.)

Research on high-risk children who turn out well suggests that they share some common characteristics. For example, as infants, most seem to be characterized by easy temperaments. They are outgoing, adjust quickly to change, cry little, establish eating and sleeping routines, and are alert and responsive (Werner, 1993). As elementary school students, they concentrate well and are active and sociable. Also important, their environments typically include some clear source of social support that helps them withstand stress (Landow & Glenwick, 1999). Support often takes the form of substitute parents (perhaps grandparents or older siblings), as well as close friends. And, perhaps most significant, argue Magnus et al. (1999), stress-resilient children tend to manifest a much stronger sense of personal competence and more positive self-concepts.

The importance of understanding why some children survive and even thrive in high-risk situations and why others do not is related directly to the possibility of "inoculating" children against risk or of ameliorating risk for those who are most vulnerable. Anthony (1987) suggests that perhaps exposure to a certain amount of adversity may be crucial in developing resistance to disturbance. At the same time, exposure to too many stresses may have just the opposite effect. It may be that a particular combination of personality characteristics or genetic predispositions—interacting with a stressful environment—produces a highly adjusted, healthy person. The critical problem is to identify this combination of characteristics and environment in an effort to maximize the development of human potential. The emphasis is dramatically different from approaches used in identifying and treating disorders.

Exceptional social and emotional competence may be seen not only in those who survive high risk but also in exceptional individuals whose early lives and biological history present no unusual psychological threats. Among these socially gifted children may well be found the leaders of tomorrow. Perhaps we should provide "special" education not only for those with disabilities, but for the socially gifted as well.

MAIN POINTS

Social Cognition

Social cognition refers to an awareness of ourselves and of others as being capable of feelings, motives, and intentions. Even in infancy, children begin to develop this awareness, manifested in their intuitive theories of mind. Selman describes five stages in children's ability to adopt the point of view of others (perspective-taking): egocentric (to age 6; don't realize there might be other views); social-informational (6–8; are aware of but don't understand other views); self-reflective (8–10; begin to infer other views); mutual (10–12; can switch perspectives); social and conventional (12–15; can analyze perspectives in abstract terms).

Self-Esteem

Self-esteem (or self-worth) refers to self-appraisal. Self-esteem, said James, reflects the discrepancy between the individual's actual performance and ideal competence. Cooley believed we evaluate ourselves on the basis of how we think others evaluate us (the looking-glass self). School-age children can assess their worth in general terms as well as in five areas: scholastic, athletic, physical appearance (most important in elementary grades), social acceptance, and morality. High self-worth is associated with happiness; low self-worth, with sadness and depression.

Friends, Parents, and Peers

During the preschool period, children see friendship as simply a matter of playing together; later of helping each other; and later still, of cooperating. And finally, during adolescence, they realize friendships are enduring and reciprocal relationships based more on similarity, trust, and affection. Most children tend to have more than one "best friend," typically of the same sex and similar age and interests. Girls have fewer but more intimate best friends.

A *peer group* is a group of equals. Social competence—reflected in children's ability to sense what is happening in social groups, in a high degree of responsiveness to others, and in an understanding that relationships develop slowly over time—is important for peer acceptance. Gottman's five categories of social status are sociometric stars (especially well liked); mixers (high interaction); teacher negatives (conflict with teachers; some high status, others not); tuned out (uninvolved; ignored rather than rejected); and sociometric rejectees (not liked; rejected).

Socially competent children tend to have more friends and be rejected less. Among rejected children are the *aggressive-rejected* (rejected because of excessive aggressiveness, often not aware of their rejection) and the *withdrawn-rejected* (rejected because of their anxiety and social withdrawal, often sadly aware of their rejection). Being accepted, and especially having friends, is important for happiness and adjustment.

Bullying, the deliberate infliction of pain, fear, and intimidation, is relatively common (many stand by and let it happen, tacitly encouraging it). Victims are often among the withdrawn-rejected. Possible consequences include emotional problems, depression, suicide, and revenge.

Child Victimization

Maltreatment of children may be *pandemic* (widespread, almost universal, including physical punishment, sibling assault, theft); *acute* (sexual, physical, medical, and emotional abuse); or *extraordinary* (extreme, like murder, rape, and abduction). There are both pros and cons for punishment, but far more cons for *physical punishment* as opposed to procedures such as time-outs, reprimands, and response-cost.

Acute child victimization includes physical abuse (punching, kicking, beating, shaken baby syndrome), physical neglect (failure to provide food, clothing, shelter), medical neglect (failure to provide health care), emotional abuse (habitual ridicule, scolding, ostracism, humiliation), or sexual abuse (sexual behaviors forced upon the child). Any of these forms of abuse can have serious and long-lasting physical and psychological consequences, including posttraumatic stress disorder or similar symptoms.

Infants are more often abused than older children (more probable if the infant is premature, deformed, or irritable; or if the mother is overworked, often pregnant, or depressed). Many abusive parents have also been abused as children. Males are more often abusers than females.

The Power of Television

Young children watch TV, much of which contains violence and unrealistic sex, about one-third of their waking hours. Older children are more sensitive to motives, more attuned to why things happen and to the consequences of program events. Aggressive children prefer violent television programs; children who prefer violent television programming tend to be more aggressive. Overt aggression (physical aggression and violence) are more masculine traits; girls are more likely to engage in relational (social) aggression (designed to disrupt social relations).

Some possible negative effects of television are that it may contribute to violence and aggression, instill fears in some children, cause changes in physical activity (and perhaps in fitness), and disrupt normal social interactions. Possible positive effects include enhanced language development, acquisition of knowledge, and the inculcation of desirable social and environmental values.

Some people also fear that the antiwork, antifamily, proviolence, procasual sex, antiestablishment messages of rock videos may have negative influences on children. The Internet brings related risks of increased social isolation, exposure to objectionable content, and exposure to potentially damaging relationships. It also has significant potential benefits.

Socioemotional Exceptionality

Emotional disturbances in childhood include *conduct disorder* (persistent violation of others' rights), *oppositional defiant behavior* (extreme noncompliance, persistent hostility and negativity), *attention deficits* (frequent, persistent, and maladaptive inability to maintain attention), *hyperactivity* (frequent, persistent, unexpected, and maladaptive inability to sit still or remain inactive), and, most common, *attention deficit hyperactivity disorder* (symptoms of both hyperactivity and attention deficits present before age 7 and meeting various DSM-IV criteria).

Stress can cause harm, or might simply pose a threat or a challenge. Among children, it can result from responsibility overload, change overload, emotional overload, school-related stress, and information overload—not to mention abuse, wars, and physical trauma. Scales that look at major life-change events sometimes identify the possibility of stress-related problems. A common consequence of *severe* stress is *posttraumatic stress disorder.* Some children are more "invulnerable" than others to risk of emotional disorder. They tend to be more socially competent and to have good social supports.

Focus Questions: Applications

1. *Are children as sensitive as adults to others' emotional states?*
   - Pretend you're a 7-year-old, and write down the most important details of your middle-childhood "theory of mind." Include in it your beliefs about how others think, imagine, feel, and so on.
2. *How many friends does a typical child have? How important are they?*
   - Write a short essay recalling the role your "best" friend played in your life at some point in middle childhood.
3. *How common is child victimization? What forms can it take?*
   - Outline what you think should be done about child abuse.

4. *Does violence on television translate into violence on the street and in the home?*
   - Using library or Internet resources, support what you think is the best conclusion to the following question: Does television violence cause violence in society?
5. *What are some of the most common forms of socioemotional exceptionality in elementary schools?*
   - Consult the latest revision of the *Diagnostic and Statistical Manual of the American Psychological Association* and review operational definitions for one or two childhood disorders, including ADHD.

Possible Responses to Thought Challenges

Thought Challenge, page 432

Family and peer dynamics are highly complex and don't lend themselves easily to simple analyses. However, Freudian theory, and specifically the defense mechanism labeled *displacement* (see Chapter 2) suggests one explanation. Brody (1998) hypothesizes that children who become aware of a significant discrepancy between the quality of emotional interaction their parents afford their siblings and that which *they* experience frequently *displace* their anger toward their siblings. Furthermore, parental rejection and emotional unavailability appear to be related to the development of low self-esteem and to behavioral and emotional problems, which are themselves related to peer rejection. Peer rejection is, in turn, associated with an increased probability of being victimized.

Thought Challenge, page 450

There are at least three reasons why this kind of generalization may be unrealistic: (1) Violence in these studies is typically directed toward inanimate objects rather than people. Children learn early in life, through socialization, that aggression against people is normally punished. (2) The experimental situation generally exposes the child to objects identical to those aggressed upon by the model, and usually immediately afterward. But a child who watches a violent scene on television is rarely presented immediately with a situation similar to the one just viewed. (3) Striking a rubber clown with a mallet, or kicking or punching it after seeing a model do it, may not represent very aggressive behaviors. The child has simply learned that these are appropriate and expected play behaviors with this inanimate object.

Key Terms

aggression, 425

aggressive-rejected, 434

attention deficit hyperactivity disorder (ADHD), 455

bulletin boards, 452

bullying, 436

cathartic model, 454

chat groups, 452

comorbidity, 456

conduct disorder, 455

Cooley's approach to self-worth, 426

electrodermal response (EDR), 450

emotional abuse, 443

emotional disorder, 454

empathy, 423

frustration, 455

James's approach to self-worth, 425

mediators, 425

medical neglect, 441

oppositional defiant disorder, 455

overt aggression, 449

pedophiles, 452

peer group, 432

physical abuse, 439

physical neglect, 440

posttraumatic stress disorder (PTSD), 444

relational aggression, 449

reprimands, 441

ritalin, 456

role taking, 423

self, 425

self-concept, 425

self-esteem, 425

sexual abuse, 443

shaken baby syndrome, 443

social cognition, 422

sociogram, 433

stress, 457

triadic friendships, 431

V-chip, 452

violence, 449

withdrawn-rejected, 434

Further Readings

The following collection provides a detailed look at one important aspect of the development of the child's theory of mind: the development of intention.

Zelazo, P. D., J. W. Astington, & D. R. Olson, (eds.) (1999). *Developing theories of intention: Social understanding and self-control.* Mahwah, N.J.: Lawrence Erlbaum.

Friendships are close to the very center of the lives of most children and adolescents. The following two books present detailed and fascinating accounts of the development and functions of friendship:

Erwin, P. (1998). Friendship in childhood and adolescence. New York: Routledge.

Adler, P. A., & P. Adler. (1998). *Peer power: Preadolescent culture and identity.* New Brunswick, N.J.: Rutgers University Press.

The following two books look at the nature of television programming and its effects on children. The Evra book also presents an intriguing look at the new technologies, including the Internet and video games.

Evra, J. V. (1998). *Television and child development* (2nd ed.). Mahwah, N.J.: Erlbaum.

Swan, K., C. Meskill, & S. DeMaio (eds.) (1998). *Social learning from broadcast television.* Creskill, N.J.: Hampton.

Online Resources

For additional readings, explore *InfoTrac College Edition*, your online library. Go to http://infotrac-college.com/wadsworth and use the passcode that came on the card with your book. Try these search terms: social cognition children, acute victimization, adhd, overt aggression, child neglect.

. . . the next question is, Who in the
world am I? Ah that's the great
puzzle!

Lewis Carroll, *Alice in Wonderland*

Adolescence

Stewart Cohen/Tony Stone Images

Very much like the adolescent who is jolted by the enormous changes of pubescence, when Alice awakens to find that she has grown to be more than 9 feet tall, everything seems strange and bewildering.

Let me think, says Alice. Was I the same when I got up this morning?

How can she find out? First, trying to prove that she hasn't changed, she asks herself whether she still knows all the things she used to know—multiplication tables, geography, and rhymes. But Alice's voice sounds strange and hoarse as she recites her little lessons, and she begins to think she might be somebody else, perhaps even Mabel, who lives in a poky little house and has no friends.

If I'm Mabel, she says, I'll stay down here.

And so now she plans to poke her head up into the world and say

Who am I, then? Tell me that first and then, if I like being that person, I'll come up; if not, I'll stay down here till I'm somebody else.

As we see in the next two chapters, adolescents, too, when their voices turn strange and hoarse, often struggle with the question of who they are—or perhaps who they *should* be.

And maybe some of those who don't like the answers they hear simply don't come out.

"Then you shall judge yourself," the king answered. "That is the most difficult thing of all. It is much more difficult to judge yourself than to judge others. If you succeed in judging yourself rightly then you are indeed a man of true wisdom."

Antoine de Saint-Exupéry, *The Little Prince*

Physical and Cognitive Development in Adolescence

CHAPTER 11

Lori Adamski Peek/Tony Stone Images

I was about 15. Uncle Gerard had hired me that summer to work on his farm. I loved it enough that I thought maybe I would never quit, never go back to school, never even bother growing up more than I already was.

But one day my father and the priest, Father Paradis, came shuffling toward me across my newly plowed dirt field. When I saw them, I shut off the tractor.

Father Paradis came up close enough that I could smell the garlic on his breath. He scuffed one foot in the dust as if uncertain where to begin. My dad beat him to it.

"You know why we're here?" he said. I shook my head no. "What is your . . . how . . . what kind of explanation . . ?" My dad sputtered.

"Let me . . . ," the priest offered. "Maybe he can just confess quietly and you can take him away."

"Confess?" I blurted.

"Did his uncle tell him?" the priest asked, speaking to my dad as if I weren't there. "Maybe he doesn't know."

"Know what?"

"Why your uncle's fired you?" my dad said.

"Fired?" I said. My uncle wouldn't fire me!

"Yes, you're fired," said my father. "You know why . . . Sylvia."

"Huh?"

"Maybe a short confession," Father Paradis said, as he clasped his hands and looked at me with sad eyes.

"There's nothing to confess," I protested.

"Your uncle saw you with Sylvia—always sitting together talking." My father sighed. "And she's your cousin!"

"Your cousin," Father Paradis repeated. "A mortal sin."

"You don't want to go to hell, now do you?" said Father Paradis. "A confession will just take a minute. Right here. Get it over with right now."

"We never did anything," I insisted.

"But were you tempted? That's where it starts."

"And neither of you is even grown up yet!" my father added.

FOCUS QUESTIONS

1. Is adolescence a universal phenomenon, or is it largely cultural?

2. What are the most important biological changes of adolescence?

3. What are the defining characteristics of anorexia nervosa? Of bulimia nervosa?

4. How does adolescent thinking change?

5. How are adolescents egocentric?

6. Is being good or bad an inescapable part of our personalities?

⌐ A PERIOD OF TRANSITIONS

Would it have been different if I had been grown up? Would they then have let me judge myself? Would they have cared if I went to hell? Should I have made up a confession? Maybe I was grown up and my dad and the priest didn't know it yet. Or was I still in transition—in adolescence?

Simply defined, **adolescence** is the transition between childhood and adulthood, the period during which children have achieved sexual maturity but have not yet taken on the roles and responsibilities—or the rights—that accompany full adult status. In contemporary industrialized countries, adolescence is easily defined, say Schlegel and Barry (1991): It spans the period of the teen years. But in preindustrial societies, it is not always clear that the period even exists.

Rites of Passage

In many societies, passage from childhood to adulthood is clearly marked by ritual and ceremony, collectively termed **rites of passage** (or puberty rites). These rites are astonishingly common, especially in preindustrial societies: Schlegel and Barry (1980) report that they are found in more than half of all of the world's preindustrial societies.

---

adolescence A general term signifying the period from the onset of puberty to adulthood, typically including the teen years (13 to 19).

rites of passage Ritualistic ceremony marking the passage from childhood to adulthood in many societies.

Puberty rites, explains Weisfeld (1999), are a sort of crash course in adulthood. That is, one of their main functions is to prepare adolescents for full adult roles—and at the same time, to prepare them for abandoning the games and the irresponsibility of childhood. Thus, among the !Ko Bushmen, when girls reach puberty they are taken to a hut outside the village. There, a grandmother or some other elder woman instructs the girl in important social and cultural matters like not touching the husband's hunting gear, not sitting at the fires of strangers, and how to give birth to and care for infants. And all of this occurs in just six days (Eibl-Eibesfeldt, 1989).

During the !Ko Bushmen girl's rites of passage, the *antelope fertility dance* is performed every day outside her hut. Fertility is almost always an important feature of girls' puberty rites. This is but one of several common features found in the puberty rites of even totally unrelated societies. In the prototypical puberty rite, for example, there are four highly common steps. First comes separation, a period during which the children are separated from the group. Among some tribes (the Navaho and Pueblo, for instance), young boys are sent to live in buildings constructed specially for this purpose (Cohen, 1964). A common **taboo** (socially forbidden behavior) during this period is that of brother-sister or mother-son contact.

Second is *training*, the teaching (or review and reinforcement) of behaviors expected of adults—and the sorts of childish behaviors adults are expected to leave behind. Typically, same-sex elders of the group are charged with these instructional roles.

The third step is that of the *initiation*: the actual rituals that mark passage from childhood to adulthood. Often, these are a time of celebration; they are also usually a time of pain and suffering. Many initiation ceremonies include one or more of the following: fasting, scarification (the inflicting of wounds with resulting scars), and circumcision. In fact, Barry and Schlegel (1980) report that circumcision is performed in one third of the more than 200 cultures they studied.

---

taboo A prohibition imposed by social custom; a behavior widely accepted as forbidden and inappropriate by a culture.

The final step of the passage rite is *induction*, actual absorption into the tribe. Inductees now know without any doubt that they are full-fledged, adult members of their social group.

Rites of passage serve at least three important functions, explains Weisfeld (1997). They provide instruction in adult sex roles (often through direct teaching); they increase the value of the adolescent as a potential mate (perhaps by increasing cultural attractiveness through scarification; perhaps by emphasizing the adolescent's fertility); and they instill a sense of loyalty to the group (partly by subjecting all adolescents to the same hardships and trials, and by allowing them to share the same cultural information and even secrets). These functions, notes Weisfeld (1999), are highly compatible with an evolutionary interpretation; they conform with evolutionary pressures toward reproduction and survival. (See *Across Cultures:* "Byoto's Superincision.")

ACROSS CULTURES

Byoto's Superincision

© Jen and Des Bartlett/Photo Researchers

As the elder explains the meaning of the strange sticks, Byoto prays that he will not cry out like a boy, or a child, when they make him a man.

Byoto struggled not to cry out; it would have embarrassed him.* He knew that in the olden days—even in the days of the uncle, the *tuatina* who was about to cut into his penis—it had been common for boys to cry out when it happened to them. In those days, the tuatina used shells and often they had to slash many times before the cutting was done. Now the uncle had a razor and, unless he were terribly unlucky, there would be only a single slash.

Preparations had begun many days earlier. The first indication that he would be made a man had come the night the men took him on the *mataki ramanga*, the torch-fishing expedition, even though all he had been allowed to do was to paddle.

In the days that followed, he had been invited to visit all the houses and villages of his relatives. And in each, his body had been smeared with turmeric mixed with coconut oil. All the other boys his age, those who were to become men with him, had also walked about the village smeared with turmeric, as though covered with the fresh blood of many wounds—a sign of the bloodletting yet to come. Meanwhile, huge mounds of coconuts, bananas, taro, and breadfruit had been piled in front of his parents' house in preparation for the feasting, and his relatives had written new songs and rehearsed old ones that would be sung in his honor. And yesterday both the men and women had taken nets out in the boats and filled many baskets with fish. All the mats had been made, the gifts prepared.

But first the razor. Byoto stood rigid with fear, held tightly by the *tangata me*, the man who would cover his eyes just before the superincision. The entire village, all his relatives and all the other boys' relatives, had assembled. Throughout the morning, each group had taken turns moaning and scratching at their faces or even nicking them with knives so that, as Byoto stared wildly around, he saw nothing but bloodied faces and saddened eyes. Suddenly, the *tangata me* covered Byoto's eyes, as Byoto knew he would. He felt his foreskin being drawn forward by the *tuatina*; involuntarily, his penis withdrew, but the *tuatina* pulled it firmly, laid the razor on the top of the foreskin, about two inches from the top, and slashed straight through to the end . . . . "Aaaaayayaya! . . ."

*This depiction is based in part on an account of rituals among the Tikopian, a Polynesian culture living on islands southeast of Taiwan. Fried, M. N., & Fried, M. H. (1980). *Four rituals in eight cultures*. New York: W. W. Norton.

To Think About: What purposes might be served by a ritual such as that among Byoto's people? How universally valid do you think our conceptions of adolescence are?

Today's Rites of Passage

Preindustrial societies have no adolescence as we citizens of industrialized societies commonly know it. There is only childhood, the rite of passage, and then suddenly adulthood. In contrast, most developed nations recognize a distinct period labeled adolescence, a period of life sometimes described as the most troubled, the most stressful, and the most difficult of all stages of development. The individual most responsible for this description of adolescence is G. Stanley Hall (1916), who believed that all adolescents go through a period marked primarily by **Sturm und Drang** (storm and stress). He believed that because this period of upheaval and turmoil is biologically based, it is therefore largely inevitable, and that it must also be common to all cultures. We now know that this view is fundamentally incorrect and misleading, that adolescence is not tumultuous for the majority of adolescents—although it is for some (Lerner & Galambos, 1998).

In contemporary Western cultures there are only a few formal ceremonies that act as rites of passage, such as the bar mitzvah or bat mitzvah, in which Jewish boys or girls symbolically become "adults" at the age of 13 through a religious ceremony, and the "coming-out" or debutante party in certain social groups. However, no one tells the child, "Today you are an adult, although yesterday you were a child." In general, the "rites" of passage are less definite in industrialized Western societies, more confusing. They vary from one place to another and from one decade to the next. They might include, among other things, getting a driver's license, being old enough to vote or to drink, losing virginity, beginning work, growing (or trying to grow) a mustache, starting to date, graduating from high school, and so on. These events can span a wide range of ages, and none of them alone is certain evidence that adulthood has been reached.

Some writers claim that secondary schools are now the setting for rites of passage very similar to the traditional rites of many nonindustrialized soci-

eties. Going through secondary school has all the same characteristics as a traditional rite, Fasick (1988) claims. It exemplifies separation (children are segregated into schools) and training (adolescents are formally socialized for the responsibilities of adult life); and there is something like initiation and induction in the high school graduation ceremony. Fasick suggests that this ceremony is almost universal for much of the middle and working class; for many adolescents it clearly marks passage from the world of childhood to a world of adult responsibilities.

In general, however, the industrialized West can be described as a **continuous society** rather than a **discontinuous society**; passages from one stage to the next are not clearly demarcated. Accordingly, there is no easy way to determine the end of adolescence and the beginning of adulthood. But there are a relatively large number of writers who now suggest that there is much we might learn from studying classic rites of passage. Explains Scott (1998), formal rites of passage might serve important psychological and social functions. The lack of such rites may be one of the reasons many adolescent college students use alcohol; it becomes part of their informal rite of passage.

In the United States, there are now an increasing number of African American rites of passage programs, many of them linked to specific schools and communities. Warfield-Coppock (1992) describes 20 such programs. These are typically organized and supervised programs that include training in life skills and social skills, as well as social events. Some also include opportunities for volunteer community service. Their goals are primarily to foster greater cultural awareness, to enhance the development of self-esteem, and to ease the transition from childhood to adulthood. These programs are often used with African American males living in high-risk environments (see, for example, Harvey & Rauch, 1997; Gavazzi, Alford, & Mckenry, 1996).

Sturm und Drang Literally, storm and stress (German). G. Stanley Hall's expression to describe what he thought was the confusion, the turmoil, the stresses, the difficulties of the adolescent period.

continuous society A society that doesn't clearly demarcate passage from one major life stage to the next.

discontinuous society A society, typically *traditional* or *preindustrial*, that clearly marks passage from one major life stage to the next. Puberty rites are the hallmark of discontinuous societies.

BIOLOGICAL AND PHYSICAL CHANGES OF ADOLESCENCE

"The transition from childhood to adulthood is an uneven, often disharmonious process of *biological maturation*, complicated by sociocultural factors," writes Wolman (1998, p. 5). The disharmony is found in the gap that exists between biological maturity and psychosocial maturity, he explains. Thus, although biological maturation readies the adolescent for the adult roles of mating and procreation, both psychological and social constraints often delay the adoption of these roles.

Clearly, the sociological and psychological phenomenon of adolescence is not the same in all cultures—nor even for all individuals within the same culture—but the biological changes of this period are universal. Biologically, adolescence is the period from the onset of puberty to adulthood. Puberty signifies sexual maturity; pubescence refers to the changes that result in sexual maturity. These changes occur in late childhood or early adolescence. Although adulthood is not easily defined, age 20 is a convenient, although arbitrary, beginning point. The beginning of adolescence is highly variable, but age 12 is often used as an approximation.

Physical Changes

Only during infancy do humans experience a more rapid period of postnatal growth—that is, higher growth velocity—than they do at adolescence.

Height and Weight After infancy, everything slows down to a weight gain of maybe 2 or so kilograms per year (as opposed to about 10 at birth). But the growth spurt that signals impending sexual maturation sees weight velocity abruptly climb back up to almost 10 kilograms per year. Then there is a very rapid decline again, so that about five years after the onset of the growth spurt (by age 16 for girls and about 18 for boys), weight and height velocity approximate zero. (See Figure 7.1, Chapter 7, for a depiction of male and female weight velocity curves between birth and age 18.)

The rapid changes in height and weight characteristic of pubescence begin before the age of 12 and are shown in Chapter 9 (Figures 9.1 and 9.2).

Figures 11.1 and 11.2 in this chapter show average height and weight changes for boys and girls from 12 to 18. On average, by the age of 11½, girls surpass boys in height and maintain a slight advantage until 13½. Girls outweigh boys at approximately 11, but by 14½, boys catch up to and surpass girls.

An additional physical change, of particular significance to boys, is a rapid increase in the length of limbs. As Kagan and Gall (1998) note, there is an unevenness to physical growth during this period. For example, hands and feet grow faster than arms and legs; and to complicate matters, the torso grows more slowly than any of these. As a result, many boys acquire the gangling appearance often associated with early adolescence, exaggerated because their rate of purchasing clothes is often considerably behind the rate at which they outgrow them. Many also develop a certain awkwardness as they move themselves around in these strange new bodies— bodies that continue to change at an unexpected rate. It's hardly surprising that Visser, Geuze, and Kalverboer (1998) found a negative relationship between measures of motor competence and growth velocity. The higher the growth velocity, the lower the adolescent's motor coordination.

Body Composition As we saw in Chapter 9, the body composition of boys and girls is different throughout childhood, with boys having relatively more fat-free mass and less fat mass; the two, taken together, determine body weight. During the adolescent growth spurt, boys' proportion of fat decreases even more because fat-free mass grows at a faster rate than does fat mass. This is not the case for girls, however, so that average sex differences in proportion of body weight due to fat mass are magnified (see Figure 11.3).

THOUGHT CHALLENGE: *During adolescence, the sebaceous (oil-producing) glands experience a sudden increase in their secretions. And certain aspects of the adolescent's facial features manifest different growth rates. Thus the lips, the nose, the mouth, and even the ears grow at different rates, and often somewhat more rapidly than the rest of the head. But eventually, all the slow parts catch up. So are these observations of any consequence?*

FIGURE 11.1 Height at 50th percentile for U.S. children. Source: Health Department, Milwaukee, Wisconsin; based on data by H. C. Stuart and H. V. Meredith, prepared for use in Children's Medical Center, Boston. Used by permission of the Milwaukee Health Department.

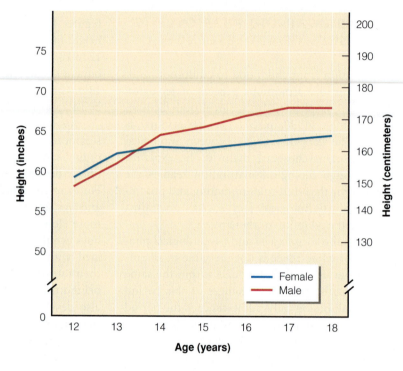

FIGURE 11.2 Weight at 50th percentile for U.S. children. Source: Health Department, Milwaukee, Wisconsin; based on data by H. C. Stuart and H. V. Meredith, prepared for use in Children's Medical Center, Boston. Used by permission of the Milwaukee Health Department.

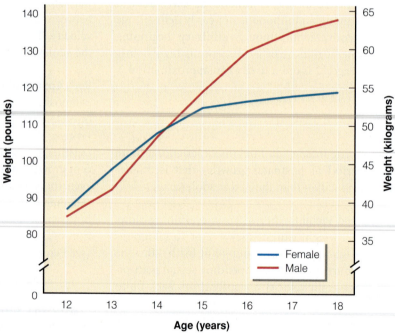

Strength and Motor Performance The internal organs also experience a growth spurt during adolescence. In fact, the heart doubles in size during puberty (Kagan & Gall, 1998). This, coupled with dramatic increases in lung capacity, results in important increases in muscular strength, aerobic performance, and motor capacity—especially in boys, but much less in girls. Despite the occasional awkwardness of some adolescent males, their performance in running, jumping, and throwing, as well as their physical strength, increase enormously through puberty. Thus, boys who mature earlier tend to be

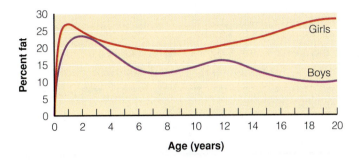

FIGURE 11.3 Growth curve for fat mass in boys and girls. Distinct *average* sex differences in ratio of fat-free to fat mass may account for many of the observed sex differences in motor performance. Source: Adapted from Malina & Bouchard, 1991.

stronger and faster, and to perform better in sports. In contrast, girls' motor performance does not appear to be closely related to maturity status; younger, less mature girls frequently outperform more mature girls (Malina and Bouchard, 1991). One explanation is that with increasing maturity, the girl develops a higher proportion of fat relative to fat-free mass. As a result, sex differences in many areas of motor performance increase in favor of males. This is especially evident in competitive athletics, where boys' records almost invariably surpass those of girls.

Pubescence: Sexual Changes

Pubescence refers to all the changes that lead to sexual maturity. These changes, which are universal, are precipitated by a dramatic increase in **hormones** produced by **endocrine glands** such as the **gonads** (*testes* in boys and *ovaries* in females). Most signs of pubescence are well known. Among the first in both boys and girls is the appearance of pigmented pubic hair, which is straight initially but becomes characteristically kinky during the later stages of pubescence. At about the same time as pubic hair begins to appear, the boy's testes begin to enlarge, as do the girl's breasts. The girl then experiences rapid physi-

cal growth, her first menstrual period (**menarche**, a relatively late event in pubescence), the growth of axillary hair (armpit hair), the continued enlargement of her breasts, and a slight lowering of her voice. The boy's voice changes much more dramatically than the girl's; and he also grows rapidly, particularly in height and length of limbs. In addition, boys acquire the capacity to ejaculate semen, grow axillary hair, and eventually develop a beard.

The changes of pubescence relating directly to the production of offspring involve **primary sexual characteristics**. These include changes in the ovaries (organs that produce ova in the girl) and the testes (organs that produce sperm in the boy) so that these organs are now capable of producing mature ova and sperm.

Changes accompanying the maturation of the sex organs but not directly related to reproduction are said to involve **secondary sexual characteristics**. The appearance of facial hair in the boy and the development of breasts in the girl, voice changes, and the growth of axillary and pubic hair are all secondary sexual characteristics.

The ages at which primary and secondary sexual characteristics develop vary greatly, but the sequence of their appearance is more predictable—although not entirely fixed. Table 11.1 summarizes that sequence.

---

hormone Substance secreted by an endocrine gland (such as testosterone or estrogen) into the bloodstream and carried to some part of the body where it has a specific effect.

endocrine glands Ductless glands, such as the pituitary, the adrenals, and the gonads, that secrete hormones directly into the bloodstream. Centrally involved in regulating growth as well as sexual maturation and sexual behavior.

gonads Sexual endocrine glands. Testes in the male; ovaries in the female.

---

menarche A girl's first menstrual period, an event that transpires during pubescence.

primary sexual characteristics Changes of sexual maturation involved in the production of offspring (for example, the ability of the testes to produce sperm and of the ovaries to produce ova).

secondary sexual characteristics Changes of pubescence that accompany maturation of the sexual organs (for example, growth of facial hair, development of breasts, voice changes).

TABLE 11.1
Normal Sequence of Sexual Maturation
for North American Girls and Boys

GIRLS' SEQUENCE	PHYSIOLOGICAL EVENT
1	Beginning of adolescent growth spurt
2	Appearance of unpigmented pubic down
3	Breast elevation ("bud" stage)
4	Appearance of pigmented, kinky pubic hair
5	Increase in size of vagina, clitoris, and uterus
6	Decline in rate of physical growth
7	Menarche
8	Development of axillary (armpit) hair; continued enlargement of breasts; slight lowering of the voice
9	Increase in production of oil; increased perspiration; possible acne

Note: The first of these changes in girls may occur as young as age 7¼; the last may not be completed before age 16. Average age of menarche in North America is about 12.8 years.

BOYS' SEQUENCE	PHYSIOLOGICAL EVENT
1	Appearance of unpigmented pubic down; growth of testes and scrotum (sac containing testes)
2	Beginning of adolescent growth spurt
3	Enlargement of penis
4	Appearance of pigmented, kinky pubic hair
5	Lowering of voice; appearance of "down" on upper lip
6	First ejaculations occur
7	Decline in rate of physical growth
8	Development of axillary (armpit) hair; growth of facial hair
9	Increase in production of oil; increased perspiration; possible acne
10	Growth of chest hair

Note: The first of these changes in boys may occur as young as age 9½; the last may not be completed before age 18. Average age of first ejaculation in North American boys is about 12 to 14.

Puberty: Sexual Maturity

Puberty is sexual maturity—the ability to make babies. However, it is very difficult to determine exactly when a person becomes fertile. Although research has often used the girl's first menstrual period (*menarche*) as an indicator, a girl is frequently infertile for about a year after her first menstruation. That is, menstruation is typically **anovulatory** for most of the first year. As a result, the menarche is not an accurate index of puberty although it does indicate impending sexual maturity.

It is almost impossible to arrive at a clear index of sexual maturity for boys, although first ejaculation (**spermarche**) is sometimes taken as a sign comparable to menarche. However, the probability that a boy can become a father immediately after first ejaculation is low—although not zero—as the concentration of sperm in the semen remains very low for as long as one to three years (Kagan & Gall, 1998).

anovulatory Literally, occurring without ovulation. Characteristic of a girl's first menstrual periods.

spermarche A boy's first ejaculation, often a nocturnal event.

Age of Puberty The average age for puberty in North America is about 12.8 for girls and 14 for boys, immediately following the period of most rapid growth (the adolescent growth spurt). Consequently, the age of puberty may be established by determining the period during which the person grew rapidly. The period of rapid growth may begin as young as 8.7 for girls compared with 10.3 for boys (Malina, 1990). However, there is a wide age range. Some girls may not reach sexual maturity until age 16; some boys, not until age 18 (Dubas & Petersen, 1993). And in other parts of the world, sexual maturity may occur much earlier or much later. For example, in New Guinea, menarche occurs at ages ranging from an average of 15.5 to 18.4. Similarly, among a large sample of Nigerian boys, spermarche occurred at an average age of 14.3 (Adegoke, 1993).

The Secular Trend Age of menarche in Western cultures, claims Tanner (1998), has dropped from an average close to 17 to an average closer to 12 in the past 100 or so years. That is a drop of as much as 4 months to 6 months per decade since 1850. In addition, adolescents are often taller and heavier than they were several generations ago. This trend is labeled the **secular trend**. There is evidence that the secular trend has slowed or stopped in most developed countries (Frisch & Revelle, 1970). But it continues in some parts of Africa, such as in Cameroon, where Pasquet et al. (1999) found a reduction in menarche age of between 2.5 and 3.2 months per decade. Similarly, Graham, Larsen, and Xu (1999) found a clear secular trend in a survey of 12,727 females in Anhui Province in China. Over a 40-year period, average age of menarche had dropped a full 2.8 years.

The fact that average age of menarche remains relatively stable in industrialized countries, while it continues to drop in less-developed countries, suggests that improved health care, nutrition, and living conditions may be part of the explanation for this secular trend. In fact, in the Pasquet et al. (1999) investigation of Cameroonian girls, menarche occurred about 1.5 years earlier among girls attending "privileged schools" than among poorer, rural girls.

secular trend The trend toward earlier maturation.

THOUGHT CHALLENGE: *Can you think of a reason that the secular trend makes evolutionary sense?*

The Implications of Early and Late Maturation

Like the average child, the average adolescent whose growth is depicted in Figures 11.1 and 11.2 is an abstraction, an invention designed to simplify a complex subject. Hence, although the average adolescent matures at about 12 or 14 depending on sex, some mature considerably earlier and some considerably later. The timing of this event may be very important to the child.

In Western cultures, the age of menarche dropped from around 17 one hundred or so years ago, to about 12 today. It remains much higher in most less-developed countries, which suggests that improved health care, nutrition, and living conditions may be part of the explanation for this secular trend. One of the results of delayed sexual maturation is that childrearing begins somewhat later than it otherwise might.

Effects for Boys Relevant research indicates quite consistently that early maturation may be a definite advantage for boys. Early-maturing boys are typically better adjusted, more popular, more confident, more aggressive, and more successful in heterosexual relationships. They are also likely to begin dating earlier and to have first sexual intercourse earlier (Kim & Smith, 1999). In addition, they appear to have more positive self-concepts (about which more is said in the next chapter). In contrast, adolescent boys who mature later than average are, as a group, more restless, more attention-seeking, less confident, and have less positive self-concepts (Crockett & Petersen, 1987).

Effects for Girls Findings are quite different for girls. Most studies indicate that on measures of adjustment, early-maturing girls are initially at a disadvantage in contrast to early-maturing boys. The main findings are that early-maturing girls are more likely to have poorer self-concepts, to feel depressed, to date earlier, to engage in more disapproved behavior such as getting drunk, taking drugs, and skipping school, and to be overly concerned about their body weight (Slovak Academy of Sciences, 1998; Laitinen-Krispijn et al., 1999). Ruiselova (1998) also reports more problem behaviors among early-maturing Slovak girls.

There is evidence, however, that the initial disadvantages of early maturation for girls may disappear later. It appears, claim Simmons and Blyth (1987), that the effects of early and late maturation in girls depend on their ages. Early maturation is a disadvantage in the very early grades (fifth or sixth), when most girls have not yet begun to mature and when the early-maturing girl is likely to find herself excluded from peer group activities. At a later age, however, when most of her age-grade mates have also begun to mature, the early-maturing girl may suddenly find herself in a more advantageous position. Her greater maturity is now something to be admired.

A Contextual Explanation As Petersen (1988) notes, pubertal change is most stressful when it puts the adolescent out of step with peers, especially if the change is not interpreted as desirable. And the consequences of maturational timing are most clearly understood by their effects on relationships and interactions that are important to the adolescent.

Thus, early maturation may enhance peer relations for boys largely because early-maturing boys often excel in activities and abilities that are highly prized in the adolescent peer culture. Not only are boys larger and stronger and therefore more likely to be better athletes, but they are also more socially mature and hence more likely to lead in heterosexual activities. Furthermore, evidence suggests that relations with parents are better for early-maturing boys—and for late-maturing girls (Laitinen-Krispijn, 1999).

Early-maturing girls, on the other hand, are more likely to be out of step with their peers. Given that girls are on the average 2 years in advance of boys in physical maturation, the early-maturing girl may well be 4 or more years in advance of like-aged boys—which might not contribute positively to her social life. Nor is her sexual precocity as likely to be admired by her immature-age peers as is the sexual precocity of early-maturing boys.

From an ecological perspective, what we know of the implications of maturational timetables presents an excellent example of child characteristics interacting with each other (specifically, degree of sexual maturity interacting with age) to determine important elements of the child's ecology (namely, the nature of interaction with parents and peers). But we should note that the child's ecology is unique to that child. So although there may be some general advantages or disadvantages associated with the timing of pubescence, there are many individual exceptions to our generalizations. Not all early-maturing boys and girls are characterized by the same advantages or disadvantages of early maturation; nor are all those who mature later affected in the same way.

Some Concerns of Adolescents

In Harter's (1990) studies of the self, physical appearance is one of the most important factors in determining self-worth. Hence, it is not surprising to find that in a major survey, almost half of all teenagers list their appearance as one of their major concerns—and the presence of blackheads or pimples ("zits") as a serious worry. Acne is a pervasive problem for many teenagers, many of whom consult physicians in search of relief. Treatments sometimes involve dietary change (to diets lower in fat content), the use of special soaps and lotions, abrasive cleaners, drugs, and even abrasion of the skin to stimulate new skin growth.

But physical appearance is *not* teenagers' most persistent or universal worry. A 13-nation survey of adolescent concerns reveals that the most-often mentioned cause of adolescent worry concerns schooling issues—most specifically fear of academic failure (Gibson-Cline, 1996). And a survey of 585 adolescents in Hong Kong found much the same thing: School grades, career plans, and future schooling were their main concerns (Violato & Kwok, 1995). Second as a source of concern in the Gibson-Cline survey were family issues; and third, personal identity and self-concept problems. Not only is this pattern of adolescent concerns common to adolescents in all 13 countries, but it is common to both the advantaged and the nonadvantaged in these countries. It is both interesting and significant, however, that patterns of concerns are different for a third group from these nations: those in the *poverty* group. For the poorest children, of course, family matters—specifically those having to do with money and extreme poverty, are more pressing con-

cerns than academic failure (Ondis et al. 1996). (See Figure 11.4.)

In a survey of 3,600 Canadian adolescents from 150 different schools, the adolescent's greatest worry concerned life beyond graduation—"What am I going to do after high school?"—a problem that affected almost 70% of all respondents. Other important concerns had to do with money, achievement in school, boredom, loneliness, and the parents' marriage (see Table 11.2). Almost half indicated that their physical appearance was a matter of considerable concern, and about the same number were worried about their height or weight (Bibby & Posterski, 1985). Unfortunately, these concerns are sometimes evident in some serious eating disorders.

NUTRITION AND EATING DISORDERS

Most adolescents, especially if they are very active physically, expend a large number of calories each day. Some, however, take in more than they need; others take in fewer.

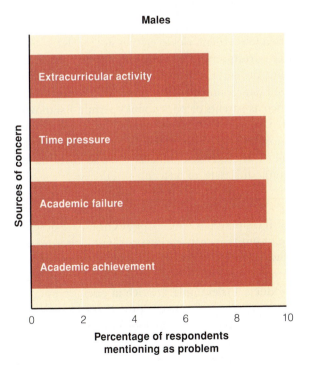

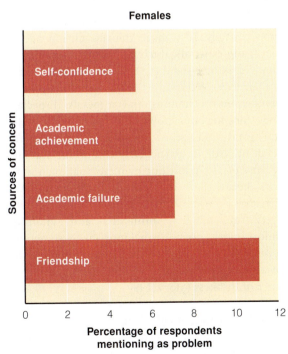

FIGURE 11.4 Four sources of concern most often mentioned by middle-class U.S. male and female adolescents. Source: Based on Gibson-Cline (1996), p. 217.

TABLE 11.2
Personal Concerns of Adolescents

CONCERN	PERCENTAGE INDICATING "A GREAT DEAL" OR "QUITE A BIT" OF CONCERN
What am I going to do when I finish school?	68
Finances (40% of respondents worked part-time)	54
School concerns	50
Time (not enough time to do the things they want)	48
Appearance	44
What is the purpose of life?	44
Boredom	43
Height or weight	43
Loneliness	35
Feelings of inferiority (poor self-image)	29
Sex	28
Parents' marriage	20

Source: Adapted from R. W. Bibby & D. C. Posterski (1985). *The emerging generation: An inside look at Canada's teenagers,* Toronto: Irwin Publishing, Table 4.1, p. 60. Reprinted with permission of Stoddart Publishing Co., Ltd.

Nutritional Requirements

Estimates are that normal, active adolescents require approximately 50% more calories during adolescence, and especially during the growth spurt, than they did earlier—or that they will through the rest of their lives. At the same time, they require proportionally more vitamins and minerals. Especially important for bone growth is calcium, which many adolescents don't get enough of. Many are also iron deficient. Iron is particularly important for girls because of blood loss during menstruation, and for boys because of increased muscle mass. And teenagers who are pregnant have an even greater need for calories, minerals, and vitamins. Unfortunately, many are malnourished—sometimes because of lack of information, but more often because of cultural models that stress the importance of thinness (Story, 1997).

Adolescent Eating Habits Parents are often alarmed not only at how much their teenagers eat, but also at what they eat. Many parents fear either that the refrigerator will always be empty, or that the fast foods their offspring gorge on will be detrimental to their health. But Baranowski and associates (1997) found that when given access to fruits and vegetables during school lunches, for example, adolescents often select them. However, they are much less likely to eat fruits and vegetables at home or when they eat out. And given the social functions served by fast-food establishments, teenagers are likely to eat out as often as parents or pocketbooks permit. Baranowski et al. suggest that it isn't so much lack of nutritional information as the availability of food and the eating habits of peers and models—not to mention the wonderful taste of ketchup-smothered fries—that may determine the adolescent's eating habits.

Nutritionists, whose concern is less with empty refrigerators than with empty calories, are quick to point out that certain classes of "fast" foods are not always "junk" foods. That is, some fast foods are in fact nutritious. Milk shakes and other ice-cream products, for example, are rich in calcium; potatoes contain vitamin C; there is protein in cheese and in meats. But there is a need, too, for fruits and vegetables, and for balance.

Clearly, not all adolescents have bad eating habits. But for the many who do, two different sorts of problems other than those of malnutrition may result: problems of obesity resulting largely from overconsumption and underexercise; and problems more closely related to "dieting" in its various forms, including "yo-yo" dieting, binge eating followed by fasting, and so on.

Obesity

As we saw in Chapters 4 and 9, the ratio of weight to height—expressed as body mass index (BMI), rather than weight alone is now used to determine whether an individual is obese, excessively thin, or ideal. (See Table 9.1 for how to calculate BMI.)

Obesity is generally defined as being more than 20% above average. For adults, a BMI somewhere above 27 or 28 would be considered somewhat obese; 32 is severely overweight, and above 45 brings high risks. A BMI between 20 and 26 is considered ideal.

Average BMI is considerably lower for children than adults. A 33-year-old female has an average BMI of about 24 or 25, whereas an average 16-year-old female has a BMI closer to 20 (Power, Lake, & Cole, 1997). Hence, for adolescents considerably lower BMI scores indicate being overweight.

Obesity is the most common nutritional problem among both children and adolescents, affecting up to 25% of all North American teenagers (Whitney & Hamilton, 1984). And obesity in adolescence is a strong predictor of obesity in adulthood (Kagan & Gall, 1998).

The increased medical risks for cardiovascular disease that obesity poses are serious and well known; its psychological risks are less apparent. However, there is little doubt that obesity can contribute to peer rejection, negative peer interactions, low self-esteem, and unhappiness (Smith et al. 1999). Obesity is also associated with poorer performance in school, although it isn't clear whether this is because obese adolescents are subject to discrimination, because they are expected to do less well, because they avoid participation, because teachers involve them less, because they lack self-esteem or independence, or for other reasons.

Obesity, as we saw in Chapter 9, is linked to overeating, genetics, parental influence, inactivity, and the use of food as a reward. However, there is little evidence that overweight adolescents have a marked preference for sweets. In fact, say Perl and associates (1998), the opposite seems to be the case, with normal-weight adolescents showing a preference for sweet foods. This, they reason, may be partly due to the social stigma attached to obesity, resulting in the obese person's rejection of sweets because they are associated with obesity.

We saw, too, that obesity is a stubborn problem, not easily controlled. Its alleviation requires nutritional information that not all adolescents have or are interested in acquiring. It requires changing habits that are not only self-rewarding but also encouraged by the media, and that are consequently extraordinarily persistent. And the problem is compounded because weight levels that Western societies consider "ideal," both esthetically and for health reasons, may not be reasonable weight levels for those who are severely obese—or even for many of the nonobese. Because these so-called ideal weights seem unattainable, they discourage rather than encourage weight loss. As a result, obesity continues to be a significant North American problem—and its alleviation, a major industry. In fact, approximately 33% of all adult U.S. males are considered overweight (BMI greater than 27.8); the percentage for females is 35.9 (U.S. Bureau of the Census, 1998). The paradox, however, is that about 25% of all males and an astonishing 44% of all adult females *who aren't overweight* think they are (Figure 11.5). This preoccupation with an *ideal* body size that is typically skinnier than our own is sometimes apparent in one or more serious **eating disorders**.

Anorexia Nervosa

Hey, you can never be too rich or too skinny, says at least one North American ideal. Wrong. I don't know about rich, but you *can* be too skinny—witness anorexia nervosa (or simply anorexia). Indirectly, anorexia is what killed Karen Carpenter, a well-known pop singer of the 1970s. She died at the age of 32. Cause of death: heart failure due to a chemical imbalance assumed to be related to the

eating disorder A clinical disorder, as defined by the American Psychiatric Association, involving a serious disturbance in eating habits. The two principal eating disorders are anorexia nervosa and bulimia nervosa.

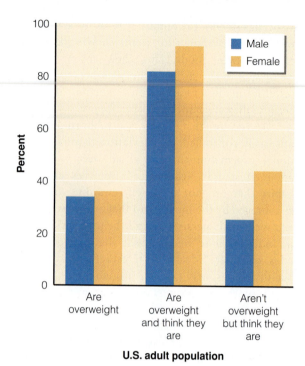

FIGURE 11.5 Adults who are overweight (BMI > 27.8 kg/m² for men and > 27.3 for women), and their perceptions/misperceptions about weight. Source: U.S. Bureau of the Census, 1998, p. 154.

medical condition she had been undergoing treatment for—anorexia nervosa.

Translated literally, *anorexia nervosa* means "loss of appetite as a result of nerves." Anorexia is defined medically as involving a loss of at least 15% to 25% of "ideal" body weight, this loss not being due to any detectable illness. The American Psychiatric Association (1994) definition includes as important criteria intense fear of gaining weight, disturbance in body image, and significant weight loss. In the absence of medical intervention, anorexia nervosa can be fatal.

Anorexia nervosa almost always begins with a deliberate desire to be thin, accompanied with consequent dieting, and ends in a condition in which the patient seems unwilling or unable to eat normally. Many affected females cease menstruating relatively early following initial dieting, and many become excessively active and continue to engage in strenuous exercise programs even after their physical conditions have deteriorated significantly. Compulsive physical activity among individuals suffering from anorexia is sometimes a sign of obsessive-compulsive

personality disorder or addictive personality (Davis, Katzman, & Kirsh, 1999).

In this connection, it is interesting to note that mice and rats who are exposed to restricted feeding (unlimited food, but only for 60 minutes per day) and unlimited exercise (free access to a "running wheel") will sometimes starve themselves to death (Epling, Pierce, & Stefan, 1983). It seems that it is possible to develop something like anorexia among these animals through exercise and dieting. However, when rats and mice are exposed only to the diet (60 minutes per day of food access) but not to the exercise wheel, their body weight stabilizes and is maintained.

Are some people with anorexia in a spiral similar to that shown by the experiment with these rats? Epling and associates suggest that yes, at least part of the time anorexia is related to activity. They cite evidence indicating that under some circumstances humans, like the test rats, will eat less when they exercise.

Prevalence Anorexia nervosa is a complex and only partially understood condition that may be increasing in frequency. Apparently, in some European cultures where body ideals have been somewhat more generous than North American ideals, anorexia was not a serious problem until recently. Now, report Morande, Celada, and Casas (1999), eating disorders are on the rise in Madrid, and are fast approaching levels of other developed countries. The authors found that among a sample of 1,281 adolescents, 4.7% of the girls and 0.9% of the boys had eating disorders. Similarly, Ampollini and associates (1999) report that in Italy, eating disorders have increased dramatically among adolescents. And there, also, eating disorders are about 10 times more common among girls.

Estimates of the prevalence of anorexia vary considerably depending on the criteria used. Although surveys often find that only about 1% of the population is severely anorexic, when estimates of anorexia are based on eating attitudes and habits, estimates are often as high as about 10% of females (Stoutjesdyk & Jevne, 1993). Following a detailed review of 33 years of literature on eating disturbances, Shisslak, Crago, and Estes (1995) identified at least twice as many people with partial-syndrome eating disorders as those with fully defined disorders. Many of those with partial eating disorders are binge eaters with periods of normal eating interspersed among binges; or they are individuals who subject themselves to severe fasts between normal eating periods.

Bulimia Nervosa

Whereas anorexia nervosa is characterized by not eating (even though some individuals with anorexia occasionally do go on eating binges), bulimia nervosa (or simply bulimia) involves recurrent episodes of binge eating. It is, in fact, a more common eating disorder than anorexia, with a higher than expected proportion of males (Lachenmeyer & Muni-Brander, 1988). It is interesting to note that bulimia often develops after a period of dieting and weight loss (Santonastaso, Ferrara, & Favaro, 1999).

The American Psychiatric Association (1994) describes bulimia nervosa as recurrent episodes of binge eating (rapid consumption of large amounts of food in a short time). Other criteria for a diagnosis of bulimia nervosa include a feeling of lack of control over eating behavior; regular episodes of self-induced vomiting, use of laxatives or diuretics, strict dieting or fasting, or vigorous exercise; a minimum average of two binge-eating episodes per week; and persistent concern with body shape and weight.

Typically, foods consumed during a binge are high calorie and are eaten inconspicuously. Abdominal pain is a common result, as are frequent weight fluctuations. Other possible medical consequences of bulimia nervosa are listed in Table 11.3. Unlike anorexia, bulimia does not usually present an immediate threat to life—although its eventual medical consequences can be quite serious, as can its psychological consequences. Unlike people suffering from anorexia, who often don't realize or admit that they have a problem, people with bulimia are generally fully aware of their eating disorder. Many experience strong feelings of guilt and shame at their inability to control binges or purges.

Causes of Eating Disorders

The causes of eating disorders are neither simple nor well understood, probably because of the variety of possible contributing factors that can interact

TABLE 11.3
Possible Medical Consequences of Bulimia Nervosa

- Dehydration
- Constipation
- Abnormal heartbeat, atrial flutter, fibrillation
- Increased susceptibility to cold
- Menstrual irregularities
- Abdominal distention
- Excessive weight fluctuations
- Dehydration and fluid shifts, sometimes resulting in headaches and fainting. Problem more serious if diuretics are used or if bulimia follows prolonged fasting.
- Electrolyte imbalance, aggravated by laxative or diuretic use as well as by repeated vomiting
- Hypoglycemic symptoms
- Malnutrition-related problems (might include cardio-vascular, kidney, gastrointestinal, or blood problems as well as insomnia)
- Dental/oral problems sometimes associated with loss of enamel as a result of frequent exposure to stomach acidity during vomiting episodes. Other possible gum, salivary duct, and tongue problems associated with emesis (vomiting)
- Specific gastrointestinal difficulties, sometimes associated with Ipecac abuse. Prolonged use can lead to cardiac problems and death.
- Laxative-related problems, which vary depending on the nature of the laxative abused
- Insomnia resulting from malnutrition, nocturnal binges, or underlying depression
- Various neurological and endocrine problems

Source: Based on Goode (1985), Brown (1991), and Kagan and Gall (1998).

in complex ways. Although endocrine imbalances are sometimes (although infrequently) involved, they are thought to result primarily from the interaction of at least three overlapping classes of factors: psychological, sociocultural, and family based.

Psychological factors include the adolescent's excessive concerns about body shape—a concern which, given current cultural emphases on thinness, may not be entirely misplaced. Halpern et al. (1999) found, to no surprise of the girls they were studying, that body fat has real implications for dating (and consequently for sexual activity). Specifically, in a longitudinal investigation of 200 white and black girls, aged 13 and 14 at the beginning of the study, the authors found a significant negative correlation between body fat and number of dates for girls. Increasing weight was linked to fewer dates—even for girls who were not obese (in this sample, 10% of the white girls and 30% of the black girls were obese).

Eating disorders have also been associated with low self-esteem, coupled with disorderly eating habits and chronic dieting (Shisslak, Crago, & Estes, 1997). Anorexia has sometimes been linked with depression, as well as with feelings of personal ineffectiveness (Lyon and associates, 1997). Some speculate that individuals with anorexia typically do not feel in control of their lives, but discover that they *can* control their body weight; in the end, control becomes an obsession. Others suggest that lack of positive self-image coupled with the emphasis society places on thinness (particularly among females) may be manifested in eating disorders. Many adolescents with anorexia have highly distorted body images; they see themselves as being overweight when they're not (Keel, Fulkerson, & Leon, 1997). This perception is much like that of the 44% of adult females who aren't overweight but think they are.

Sociocultural factors are evident in the body shapes and sizes that society presents as ideal. Dorian and Garfinkel (1999) argue that if we were to succeed in changing these sociocultural factors, we would also change the nature of these eating disorders. Consider, for example, that eating disorders such as anorexia are far less common among African American females, for whom cultural body ideals have traditionally been fuller than those of white North American cultures. As a result, African American girls are often far happier with their bodies, less likely to have distorted body images, and less likely to suffer from eating disorders (Abood & Chandler, 1997).

Family-based factors are evident in the finding that parental conflict, sibling delinquency, and abuse can all contribute to eating disorders (Gowers and North, 1999). In fact, a considerable body of research indicates that adolescent girls with eating disorders are far more likely to have been sexually abused as children than girls without eating disorders (see *At a Glance:* "Sexual Abuse and Eating Disorders").

Some Treatments

Anorexia nervosa and bulimia are frightening and baffling conditions for parents. Anorexia is especially frightening because it can be fatal. It is baffling and frustrating because it may seem to parents that the adolescent suffering from anorexia deliberately and totally unreasonably refuses to eat. And neither pleas nor threats are likely to work. What is?

Because anorexia and bulimia are not, in most instances, primarily biological or organic disorders, their treatment is often complex and difficult. Becker and colleagues (1999) point out that these disorders are often associated with serious medical complications. They argue that treatment needs to consider these complications, as well as the underlying causes of the disorder. Also, Halpern and colleagues (1999) suggest that because obesity has important social implications (in dating and popularity, for example) as well as health consequences, attempts to change eating habits need to take these factors into account.

There are no drugs or simple surgical procedures that can easily cure anorexia or bulimia. In some instances, patients respond favorably to antidepressant drugs; at other times, it is necessary to force-feed dangerously thin patients to save their lives. Successful treatments have often involved one of several forms of psychotherapy. Among these, what is termed cognitive-behavior therapy—the use of reinforcement and/or punishment combined with the use of reasoning—has sometimes been effective). For example, Bulik and associates (1998) reduced binge eating among 101 bulimic women by using group cognitive-behavioral therapy. But when they looked at these women again 1 year later, they found that many had relapsed. Those most likely to have maintained the beneficial effects of therapy were those who were most independent and self-directed. Those who had a history of obesity and depression were most likely to relapse.

Herzog and associates (1999) also reexamined a group of women with eating disorders—in this case, 246 women with anorexia or bulimia who were reassessed an average of 7.5 years after treatment. Recovery rates for anorexia nervosa were substantially higher (74%) than were recovery rates for bulimia (33%). The vast majority of women had made at least a partial recovery over this period of time. Unfortunately, about one-third of both the

Sexual Abuse and Eating Disorders

Girls for whom puberty is too overwhelming, some speculate, might unconsciously take steps to minimize their sexuality. Overeating with resulting obesity might be one outcome; anorexia (or bulimia) with resulting emaciation, loss of figure, and cessation of menstruation might be another.

This speculation may partly explain the findings of studies reporting that somewhere between 30% and 65% of women with eating disorders have been sexually abused, compared with between 10% and 30% of the general population. For example, among a group of women with eating disorders studied by Deep and associates (1999), a shocking 40% had been sexually abused *before* the onset of their disorder. But, these researchers caution, this doesn't prove that sexual abuse *causes* eating disorders. Consider that 60% of the women with eating disorders had *not* been sexually abused. Also, it may be that eating disorders are related to poor impulse control and failure to appreciate the risks of certain behaviors—factors that might themselves increase the likelihood of sexual abuse. Note that women with bulimia *and* a history of substance dependency are almost twice as likely to have been sexually abused as bulimic women without substance dependency.

Among the American Psychiatric Association's criteria for anorexia nervosa are significant weight loss, an intense fear of gaining weight, and distortion of body image. Many very thin anorexic women consistently overestimate their body size.

bulimic and the anorexic women relapsed after full recovery.

INTELLECTUAL DEVELOPMENT IN ADOLESCENCE

In earlier chapters, we traced the development of the child's mind from birth to the beginning of adolescence, using as our guides both Jean Piaget's work and notions from more recent studies of information processing.

Through Piaget's eyes we saw how infants interact with the world, using previously learned behaviors when they can (assimilating), changing these behaviors when they must (accommodating), and balancing these twin processes of adaptation (equilibration). Thus do they succeed in constructing ever more advanced views of reality and in understanding and reasoning about the world in increasingly sophisticated ways. By the end of concrete operations, children understand the logical necessity of conservation, can solve a variety of problems, and can classify, seriate, and deal with numbers at a surprisingly sophisticated level (see Table 11.4).

The picture drawn by the information-processing approaches complements that of Jean Piaget. It describes how, in time, infants succeed in separating

TABLE 11.4
Piaget's Stages of Cognitive Development

STAGE	APPROXIMATE AGE	SOME MAJOR CHARACTERISTICS
Sensorimotor (5)*	0–2 years	Intelligence in action
		World of the here and now
		No language, no thought, no notion of objective reality at beginning of stage
Preoperational (7)	2–7 years	
		Egocentric thought
Preconceptual	2–4 years	Reason dominated by perception
		Animistic thinking
Intuitive	4–7 years	Intuitive rather than logical solutions
		Inability to conserve
Concrete operations (9)	7–11 or 12 years	Ability to conserve
		Logic of classes and relations
		Understanding of numbers
		Thinking bound to concrete
		Development of reversibility in thought
Formal operations (11)	11 or 12 to 14 or 15 years	Complete generality of thought
		Propositional thinking
		Ability to deal with the hypothetical development of strong idealism

*Numbers in parenthesis refer to chapters containing detailed information.

the self from the world, in representing aspects of the world symbolically, and in developing cognitive strategies to process information. Further, the developing child learns to store information in the vaults of memory (creating a knowledge base), as well as strategies to retrieve and manipulate information (remembering)—even strategies to think about and contemplate the very processes involved in doing these things (metacognition).

Piaget's View of Adolescent Thought

There is little doubt that adolescents are better thinkers than are preadolescents—that formal operations present an advance over concrete operations. As Brainerd (1978) put it, "Concrete operations consist of thought thinking about the environment, but formal operations consist of thought thinking about itself" (p. 215). Which, in the words of the information-processing theorists, amounts to saying that during concrete operations, the child's

metacognitive skills are less advanced and less abstract.

As a case in point, consider the following problem: I present two children, 7-year-old Angela and 13-year-old Angel, with four test tubes that contain different, colorless and odorless unidentified liquids, numbered 1 to 4 (diluted sulfuric acid, water, oxygenated water, and thiosulphate), and a fifth tube, labeled X, containing potassium iodide. "If you combine a little bit of liquid from the right tubes," I tell them, "with this fifth tube, the result will be a yellow liquid." I prove this by pouring a little potassium iodide into a mixture of diluted sulfuric acid and oxygenated water, without letting them see which tubes have been combined. "So, can you find which tubes you have to combine to make this yellow liquid?" I ask. (See Figure 11.6.)

Angela, the 7-year-old, grabs tube 4, mixes a little of it with some X, and then tries 2 and X, then 3 and X. "I think I did everything. . . I tried them all," she says, exactly parroting one of Inhelder and Piaget's (1958, p. 111) subjects. "What else could you

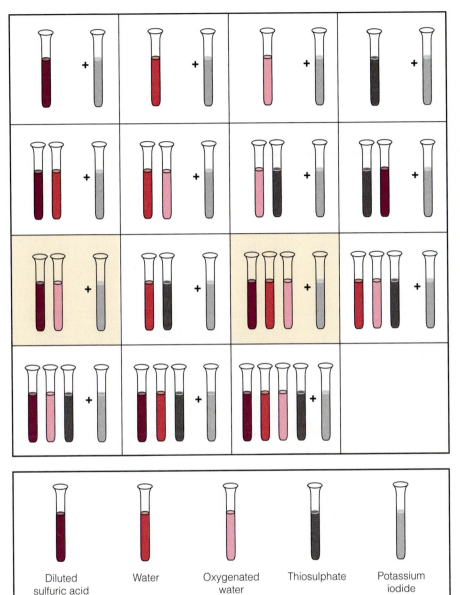

FIGURE 11.6 All possible combinations of the four test tubes to which the fifth can be added. The experiment requires the subject to discover the combination(s) that yields a yellow liquid when potassium iodide is added. The correct solutions have a yellow background.

try?" I ask, trying to be helpful. "I don't know," she says. "You took each tube separately. What else could you do?" I prompt. "I know," she says, "I could try two." And now she mixes a few pairs, doesn't find the correct answer, and gives up. I urge her to try again. She tries a few more combinations, some of which she has tried before. Then she wants to go and watch television.

Angel, the 13-year-old, talks to himself as he works—also parroting one of Piaget and Inhelder's 13-year-old subjects: "You have to try with all the bottles. I'll begin with the one at the end. [Combines 1 through 4 with X.] It doesn't work any more. Maybe you have to mix them. [Combines 1 + 2 with X, 1 + 3 with X. . . and bingo! A yellow precipitate.] It turned yellow. But are there other solutions? I'll try." [Continues to combine 1 + 2 + 3 and X, 1 + 2 + 4 and X, etc.] (p. 117).

Major Changes in Thought There are five major changes in the thinking of the adolescent, explain Kagan and Gall (1998) (see also, Keating, 1990).

Most of them are illustrated by the test tubes problem.

First, adolescents are better able to deal with the possible rather than simply what is real. In Piaget's terms, their thinking is less *concrete*. Thus, 7-year-old Angela's approach is to attempt actual combinations. Her hypotheses are real behaviors. In contrast, 13-year-old Angel begins by imagining the possibilities. He sees very quickly the possibility of combining the tubes by twos, and when that doesn't work, he scarcely hesitates before *systematically* combining them by threes.

Second, adolescents are better at thinking about abstract things. Even after discovering a correct solution, Angel sees the possibility that there might be another. Had Angela accidentally solved the problem, she would probably not have continued trying new combinations, unless asked to do so.

The potentially abstract nature of adolescent thinking is also evident in their more sophisticated understanding of humor. The idea of naming a cat *Cochon* (Pig) because he kept tripping and falling and getting dirty was very funny to my 7-year-old cousin, Robert. But for me—age 14 at the time—it was just another stupid cat (or stupid cat joke). In contrast, the idea of naming a cat *Demain* (Tomorrow) because the good nuns had arranged to have the poor thing neutered was side-splittingly funny to me. Still is, come to think of it. Understanding why requires a level of abstraction that was well beyond cousin Robert. Still is.

Third, adolescents think more about the process of thinking itself. They have better metacognitive skills; they're more aware of their own cognitive processes. Metacognitive skills, as we see in a later section, are closely related to school achievement.

Fourth, the thinking of the adolescent has become more multidimensional. This is especially apparent in the complexity with which adolescents answer questions that might earlier have been answered very directly and very concretely. Ask a class of 8-year-olds, "Is Orville Beanhead a good person?" and receive a chorus of yes's and no's in answer. Now ask, "Why?" and receive a chorus of one-dimensional (and typically, one-sentence) answers. Ask a class of 15-year-olds the same question. "Depends on your point of view," answers Samantha. "In a way, he was a good boxer, yes. But, well, the way he treated his kids, I'm not so sure. . ."

Multidimensional thinking allows adolescents to interpret events in richer ways, and to understand people in greater depth. It grants them a degree of social intelligence, of social competence, still not accessible to the preadolescent.

Finally, adolescent thinking is more relative—and, in that sense, more adult-like. That is, adolescents are able to look at a question from more than one angle, to consider more than one possible correct answer. Things have become progressively less black and white—and increasingly uncertain. As many high school teachers have discovered, adolescents don't accept "fact" as readily as do younger children. They question more. And sometimes they make life more difficult for teachers and parents.

But one day, they, too, will be parents and teachers.

Some Implications of Adolescents' Formal Thinking
To summarize, adolescent thought is more hypothetical, more abstract, more metacognitive, more multidimensional, and more relativistic. These are the characteristics of *formal operations thinking*.

These characteristics of new and improved thinking might not be very obvious, or perhaps even very important, if they were apparent only in problems of chemistry and physics and Boolean logic. But formal operations extend well beyond the realms of science. They are apparent in new preoccupations with understanding the self as an abstraction (Harter, 1990), in an egocentric reliance on logic (Lapsley, 1990), and in an intense new idealism. Children can now contemplate states of affairs that don't exist; they can compare the ideal to the actual; they can become profoundly distressed at the failure of preceding generations to avoid the confusion that they now observe around them; and they can be perplexed by some of the profound questions that have always puzzled philosophers. It is precisely adolescents' ability to deal with the hypothetical that made it possible for 44% of the subjects in Bibby and Posterski's (1985) study to claim that they were very concerned about the purpose and meaning of life. Such questions do not often suggest themselves to 10-year-olds.

With the idealism of formal operations there also comes a belief in the omnipotence of thought. Despite the adolescent's increasingly relativistic view of the world, there is a profound egocentrism during this period (which we discuss later in this chapter)—an egocentrism that is apparent in the belief that reason and logic can provide all the answers. It is an egocentrism evident in an apparent inability to adopt the point of view that even if reason and good sense do provide all the answers we need, social, political, and other human realities sometimes oppose their implementation. It is this unshakable belief in the power of thought that may underlie adolescents' absolutely insistent political, social, and religious arguments with parents and others.

An Information-Processing View

Piaget's stage-bound description of intellectual development, although it provides many important insights into cognitive functioning, is not always an accurate description of children's capabilities. The irony is that whereas Piaget seems to have underestimated the cognitive achievements of infants and preschoolers, he may have overestimated those of adolescents. There is evidence, for example, that the abstract and logical thinking defined by formal operations, which is not ordinarily present at the beginning of formal operations (at age 11 or 12), is often absent even among adults.

The **information-processing approach** to understanding intellectual development provides new directions and emphases. As we saw in Chapter 9, information-processing theories are concerned with three important aspects of cognition: the acquisition of a knowledge base, the development of information-processing strategies, and the development of metacognitive skills.

To review briefly, the knowledge base consists of concepts, ideas, information, and so on. Infants begin life with very little knowledge base. It builds with experience, as the infant, later the child, then the adolescent, and finally the adult, acquires experiences and learning. In the end, our knowledge base consists of everything we have learned—the entire contents of our memory. Schools do a great deal to expand and organize the knowledge base.

Information-processing strategies are the procedures involved in learning and remembering. In a sense, they are the tools for building a knowledge base. They include strategies, such as organizing and rehearsing, which allow the effects of experience to be encoded for long-term storage. And they include strategies involved in remembering.

Metacognition relates to information the knower has about knowing and remembering, and to awareness of the self as an information processor and, consequently, as a player of Flavell's (1985) game of cognition. As metacognitive skills increase, so too do children's abilities to analyze performance, to predict the likelihood of success, to change strategies, and to evaluate and monitor.

An information-processing view of development describes how each of these three aspects of information processing (knowledge base, processing skills, and metacognitive skills) changes with age and experience.

Changes in Knowledge Base Clearly, the knowledge base grows with increasing experience and exposure to schooling: Adolescents know enormously more than young children (and far less than some of you). Indeed, as long as you have an intact neurological system and a good set of cognitive strategies at your disposal, and you continue to have experiences, your knowledge base is likely to continue growing. (And if it's large enough one day, and someone asks you the right question—and your final, final answer is correct—you might win a million dollars. Which might not be worth beans by that time.)

Anderson (1980) describes how children progress from being novices in all areas to being experts in at least some areas—most especially in certain games, in aspects of social interaction, in certain levels and classes of school subjects, and perhaps in hobby-related or cultural pursuits. One important difference between experts and novices has to do with knowledge base. But the difference is not simply that experts know more (have more content in their knowledge structures), but also that they have formed more associations among the things they know. Their knowledge is richer in

---

information-processing approach A psychological orientation that attempts to explain cognitive processes such as remembering, decision making, or problem solving. This orientation is primarily concerned with how information is acquired and stored (acquisition of a knowledge base), as well as the development of cognitive strategies and notions of the self as a processor of information (metacognition).

the sense that it suggests more relationships. The artist who is an expert in color does not understand the color blue in the same way as a novice such as I might. My pitiful understanding permits me to relate blue to robin eggs and morning skies; the expert might relate it to these as well but might also break it down into a dozen hues whose subtlety and associations have no meaning for me. More than this, the expert might well understand blue as a wavelength, might understand its relationships to other waves of different lengths, and might have a sense of its crispness or fragility that totally escapes me.

Changes in Processing Development, then, is a process of shedding some of the novice's ignorance and acquiring increasing expertise. But expertise involves more than just changes in knowledge base; it also involves changes in information-processing capacity.

Among other things, information-processing capacity depends on the availability of appropriate strategies; and it depends on **attention span**. That attention span increases with age is clear. Intelligence tests such as the *Stanford-Binet*, for example, require that subjects try to recall sequences of digits presented at 1-second intervals. Whereas a preschool child might correctly recall a string of two or three digits, an adolescent might easily recall six or seven.

Changes in the availability of appropriate strategies are not as readily investigated, partly because it isn't always easy to identify a strategy and determine whether it is present. However, Piaget's investigations of concrete and formal operations suggest that the strategies available to older adolescents are substantially different and considerably more powerful than those available to younger children. First, the adolescent is more systematic, plans more carefully, and considers more options. Second, the adolescent has more ready-made solutions. For example, many Piagetian tasks that present real problems for a younger child can be solved almost from memory by an older child. A 6-year-old might

need to "figure out" whether there is still the same amount of material in a deformed object; the adolescent need not figure.

Training programs designed to improve cognitive strategies and to encourage their use are often highly successful in increasing learning (for example, Hoek, van den Eeden, & Terwel, 1999).

Metacognitive Changes Clearly, adolescents have more advanced metacognitive skills. They have a better understanding of the self as a processor of information and an increasing understanding of the processes of cognition. As we saw in Chapter 9, metacognitive skills seem to be largely absent in young children, but are clearly present in older children and adolescents.

The importance of metacognitive skills is especially evident in learning from textual material, explain Britton and associates (1998). As you read (and learn) from this text, for example, your learning depends on the connections you make among ideas—not simply ideas that are hidden here in these words, but ideas that you have in your own mental representations. How well you make these connections depends greatly on your metacognitive skills. It reflects your awareness of how well you're learning, your ability to determine whether you need additional connections, and your decision whether you need to reread, to look for additional information, to ask questions, to start over again, to concentrate more, or simply to give up. Measures of metacognition correlate very highly with school achievement (Landine & Stewart, 1998).

In summary, information-processing views of cognitive development describe changes in three areas: content (knowledge base increases in specific knowledge as well as in relations and associations among items of information); processing capacities (increases in memory and attention capacities and increases in the availability of more sophisticated strategies); and metacognitive changes (increasing awareness of self as information processor and increasing ability to monitor, evaluate, and control ongoing cognitive activities). These changes make more of an expert of the adolescent. But they do not eliminate adolescents' egocentrism (see *Concept Summary*).

---

attention span A measure of the capacity to hold more than one item in consciousness at one time.

CONCEPT SUMMARY

Approaches to Describing Adolescent Intellectual Development

Approach	Explanations/Comments
Piaget's Formal Operations	• age 11–12 on
	• ability to deal with abstractions, with the hypothetical (logic of propositions)
	• apparent in new preoccupations with understanding self as an abstraction, in an egocentric reliance on logic, and in a new sense of abstract idealism
	• reflect five major changes in thinking: Adolescent's thought is now more hypothetical, more abstract, more metacognitive, more multidimensional, and more relativistic.
Information Processing	Describes changes in three areas:
	• knowledge base (increases in specific knowledge; more relations and associations among items of information)
	• processing capacities (increases in memory and attention capacities; more sophisticated cognitive strategies)
	• metacognition (increasing awareness of self as information processor; increasing ability to monitor, evaluate, and control cognitive activities)

THOUGHT CHALLENGE: *Bill and Laura are shown a series of cards, each of which contains six nearly identical figures at the top and a single figure at the bottom that exactly matches only one of the six figures. Each is required to find correct matches. When they answer correctly, they go on to the next card; if they answer incorrectly, they are asked to try again. The time required for each response is noted, and errors are counted. Laura takes much longer than Bill on this task, but she makes fewer errors. He answers very quickly, but often makes errors, which he can then easily correct. It's clear that both would almost always answer correctly if they took long enough. Do you have enough information to make an intelligent guess about which of these two would score highest on measures of metacognition?*

◰ ADOLESCENT EGOCENTRISM

In Piagetian theory, egocentrism is not the derogatory term it might be in ordinary usage. It refers less to a selfishness than to a cognitive and emotional self-centeredness. Egocentrism is apparent in children's inability to be completely objective in their understanding of the world and in their interactions with others. Recall, for example, that in early infancy (early in the sensorimotor period), infants don't readily separate the self from the physical world: Objects exist only when they are being looked at, tasted, felt, or smelled—a rather extreme egocentrism. And in the preschool period there is evidence of egocentrism, says Piaget, when children focus on the perceptual features of objects and respond incorrectly to conservation problems.

The egocentrism of adolescents is not as extreme or naive as that of infants. Unlike the

Marc Dolphin/Tony Stone Images

Adolescents' great concern with hair and dress may have much to do with the imaginary audience that constantly judges them. At least one of these adolescents has an imaginary audience that loves wild hair action.

egocentrism of earlier childhood, it has more to do with the social than with the physical world. Adolescent egocentrism is characterized by an inability to differentiate between objects and events of concern to others and those of concern to the adolescent. This egocentrism is sometimes apparent in behaviors that seem to be influenced by the adolescent's belief that everybody is watching and is terribly concerned. In a sense, it's as though every adolescent has an *imaginary audience*, explains Elkind (1967)—a group of people watching how the adolescent dresses, moves, talks. And, too, it's as though the adolescent is really special, unique, important. That, says Elkind, is part of the adolescent's *personal fable*. These two concepts—the imaginary audience and the personal fable—are the two main dimensions of adolescent egocentrism.

The Imaginary Audience

When my 17-year-old nephew, Jonathan, was getting ready to go to the U-2 concert last June, he agonized over the fit of his jeans. Apparently his legs had stretched overnight, so now he was desperately trying to find a way to wear his jeans low enough to meet the pant-bottom-must-scrape-the-dirt rule, but not so low as to violate the cover-the-navel rule. He was going to have to sacrifice one or the other.

"Nobody'll notice, they look fine," said his ma.

"Everybody'll see..." he retorted. His **imaginary audience** that night would consist of about 50,000 people! And he's not exceptionally egocentric.

What Is the Imaginary Audience? The adolescent's imaginary audience is an imagined collection of all who might be concerned with the adolescent's self

THOUGHT CHALLENGE: *There are at least three ways in which adolescents are a little like, say, 2-year-olds. How many can you think of?*

---

imaginary audience An expression of adolescent egocentrism; an imagined collection of all who might be concerned with the adolescent's self and behavior.

and behavior. It is the "they" in expressions such as "they say . . ." or "they predict . . ." Social psychologists inform us that each of us behaves as though "they" are watching and care. Each of us has an imaginary audience—except perhaps some of those who suffer from mental disorders and who sometimes lose both their *real* and their imaginary audiences (Leferink, 1998). But our imaginary audiences (at least, those of us who are adults) are much smaller, much less pervasive, and far less important than those of adolescents.

According to Elkind (1967), it's because of this imaginary audience to which adolescents are continually reacting that young adolescents are often very self-conscious. It's also because of this same audience that many become so concerned with their hair, clothing, and other aspects of their physical appearance. It's as though adolescents believe that others are as deeply concerned about them as they themselves are, and that these others constantly judge them.

Measuring the Imaginary Audience In fact, the adolescent's self-consciousness gives researchers an interesting, and potentially highly useful, measure of the imaginary audience and, indirectly, of adolescent egocentrism. The argument is that the imaginary audience will be reflected in the adolescent's self-consciousness. Thus, instruments such as the *Imaginary Audience Scale (IAS)*, developed by Elkind and Bowen (1979), asks respondents how they would feel and what they would do in various potentially embarrassing situations—such as might occur, for example, if their pant legs are too stupidly short. Accordingly, the scale is really a measure of self-consciousness. Items for the *IAS* were selected from a pool of suggestions given by students who were asked to describe situations they might find embarrassing. The final scale consists of 12 items, the first 4 of which are reproduced in Table 11.5.

Elkind and Bowen administered the *IAS* to 697 students in grades 4, 6, 8, and 12. They found that young adolescents (eighth-grade students) were more reluctant to reveal themselves to an audience than were younger children or older adolescents, and that girls were more self-conscious than boys on the test. Using the *IAS*, Rycek and associates (1998) also found higher self-consciousness in late-adolescent

girls than in boys. But, as Enright and associates (1980) point out, there is considerable variability not only in the extent to which children appear egocentric, but also in the ages at which they appear most self-conscious.

The adolescent's imaginary audience has at least two identifying characteristics, reports Vartanian (1998) following an investigation of 264 fourth- and seventh-graders: It is made up of an imagined group that is *attentive* to the adolescent; and it's made up of individuals who are focused *uniquely* on the adolescent. But contrary to what we might have expected, it is not a critical, but a highly supportive, even admiring, audience.

The Personal Fable

It makes sense that the adolescent's **personal fables** would not allow them to create critical imaginary audiences. Personal fables are stories adolescents tell themselves, fantasies they elaborate on and in which, not surprisingly, they are the heroes. These fantasies have a number of identifying themes, the most common of which are "I am special," "I will not get pregnant," "I will not become addicted to these drugs I take only for recreation," "Mom, you just don't understand what real love is," and "Neither do you, Dad!" Thus, the personal fable is characterized by a feeling of being special and unique, as well as by a sense of power and of invulnerability. Unfortunately, this feeling of invulnerability is often sadly inappropriate, as is evident in the fact that adolescents—especially males—have the highest accident rate of all age groups except those over 65 (U.S. Bureau of the Census, 1998).

Elements of the personal fable run through the lives of most of us. Most of us believe that we are somewhat unique, just a little special. But these beliefs appear to be greatly exaggerated in adolescence and may account in part for the casualness with which adolescents will take risks that they know cognitively to be horrendous.

---

personal fable An expression of adolescent egocentrism marked by the elaboration of fantasies, the hero of which is the adolescent.

TABLE 11.5
The Imaginary Audience Scale (IAS)

Instructions: Please read the following stories carefully and assume that the events actually happened to you. Place a check next to the answer that best describes what you would do or feel in the real situation.

1. You have looked forward to the most exciting dress-up party of the year. You arrive after an hour's drive from home. Just as the party is beginning, you notice a grease spot on your trousers or skirt. (There is no way to borrow clothes from anyone.) Would you stay or go home?
   ___ Go home.
   ___ Stay, even though I'd feel uncomfortable.
   ___ Stay, because the grease spot wouldn't bother me.

2. Let's say some adult visitors came to your school and you were asked to tell them a little bit about yourself.
   ___ I would like that.
   ___ I would not like that.
   ___ I wouldn't care.

3. It is Friday afternoon and you have just had your hair cut in preparation for the wedding of a relative that weekend. The barber or hairdresser did a terrible job and your hair looks awful. To make it worse, that night is the most important basketball game of the season and you really want to see it, but there is no way you can keep your head covered without people asking questions. Would you stay home or go to the game anyway?
   ___ Go to the game and not worry about my hair.
   ___ Go to the game and sit where people won't notice me very much.
   ___ Stay home.

4. If you went to a party where you did not know most of the kids, would you wonder what they were thinking about you?
   ___ I wouldn't think about it.
   ___ I would wonder about that a lot.
   ___ I would wonder about that a little.

Source: From D. Elkind & R. Bowen (1979). Imaginary audience behavior in children and adolescents. *Developmental Psychology* 15(1): 38–44, p. 40. Copyright 1979 by the American Psychological Association. Reprinted by permission of the author.

Implications of Adolescent Egocentrism

We don't yet understand very much about adolescent egocentrism, and our instruments for measuring it need improvement. Simple questionnaires may not always be the most accurate way to assess such a complex set of characteristics.

Understanding adolescent egocentrism might do a great deal to clarify the adolescent experience for us; it might also have some practical implications. For example, Elkind (1981b) suggests that it might contribute in important ways to our understanding of vandalism, teenage pregnancy, drug abuse, and other related behaviors. Measures of the imaginary audience and the personal fable have been found to be among the best predictors of whether sexually active, unmarried adolescent girls use contraception (Greene et al., 1996) And

Montgomery, Haemmerlie, and Zoellner (1996) report that among a college sample of 80 students, high scores on an *Imaginary Audience Scale* were significantly related to risk taking as it relates to excessive drinking of alcohol.

Reckless Adolescent Behavior

Adolescents—especially males—engage in a variety of reckless behaviors, many of which have potentially devastating consequences (see Table 11.6 in *At a Glance:* "Adolescents' Risks and Violent Death").

Examples of High-Risk Adolescent Behaviors Where I live, automobile insurance rates for 16-year-old male drivers are about four times higher than they are for me. Why? Not because I am a technically better driver than they are, but simply because more of

AT A GLANCE	**Adolescent Risks and Violent Deaths**

Adolescents are at high risk for accidental injury or death, or for the initiation of addictive habits with long-term negative consequences. A hunger for risk taking and sensation seeking, feelings of invulnerability tied in with the personal fable, peer pressure—all of these factors (and others) may be involved in the adolescent's willingness to take risks. Risk-taking behavior is especially evident in the incidence of violent death among white and black adolescent males, and in the very high rates of homicide deaths among black youth. Also, suicide rates among males aged 15 to 24 are enormously higher than among females (24.1 compared with 3.8 per 100,000 for whites; 20.6 versus 2.7 for blacks).

Many adolescents not only feel invulnerable, but also underestimate the risks associated with their behaviors.

David Stewart/Tony Stone Images

TABLE 11.6
1995 U.S. death rates (per 100,000 population)
by age for accidents and homicides

| AGE | WHITE | | | | BLACK | | | |
| | MALE | | FEMALE | | MALE | | FEMALE | |
	Accidents	Homicide	Accidents	Homicide	Accidents	Homicide	Accidents	Homicide
15–24	58.3	17.4	21.0	3.9	52.6	157.6	15.0	18.7
25–44	48.8	12.3	14.3	3.7	65.3	90.9	9.7	19.5
45–64	40.4	NA	15.9	NA	78.4	33.4	23.3	NA
65 and older	103.4	NA	73.1	NA	126.4	NA	65.5	NA

Source: U.S. Bureau of the Census (1998), p. 104.

them drive at high speed when sober—and even more of them drive at high speed when drunk. Over one-third of all drunk drivers involved in fatal accidents are ages 16 to 24, even though this age group represents fewer than one-fifth of all licensed drivers (U.S. Bureau of the Census, 1998). Compared to sexually active women ages 25 to 44, about 50% more sexually active teenage girls do not use contraception. And over one million unmarried teenagers become pregnant in the United States each year (U.S. Bureau of the Census, 1998).

Adolescents have the highest rate of illegal drug use of any age group (Arnett, 1992). In 1996, nearly 20% of all arrests in the United States were of those under 18 (U.S. Bureau of the Census, 1998).

Adolescent recklessness is seldom manifested in only one form of high-risk behavior. Teenagers who drink are also more likely to take illegal drugs, to be involved in automobile accidents, or to commit crimes. For example, Wells and Macdonald (1999) surveyed accident data for more than 10,000 Canadians. They found that alcohol consumption was highly related to accidents for the younger groups, but this wasn't the case for the older groups. Perhaps, suggest Wells and Macdonald, younger drinkers have less tolerance for alcohol; or perhaps it's their greater willingness to take risks that interacts with alcohol and leads to more accidents.

Why Adolescents Take Risks Adolescents' personal fable of invulnerability may be one reason why they take risks. It seems that even when they clearly recognize certain activities as dangerous, they often underestimate the dangers to themselves and ignore precautions that might be taken. When Beyth-Marom et al. (1993) asked adult and adolescent subjects to describe the possible consequences of high-risk behaviors such as drinking and driving, their responses were remarkably similar. Adolescents know the risks involved in their behaviors; they can anticipate their possible outcomes as clearly as adults can. But they consistently underestimate risks associated with activities in which they themselves engage. Benthin, Slovic, and Severson (1993) had adolescents rate perceived risks and benefits of 30 high-risk activities such as smoking, drug use, drinking, and sex. Not only did participants perceive lower risks for their own high-risk behaviors, but they also perceived greater benefits. And they consistently overestimated the extent to which their peers engaged in the same activities!

Adolescents' tendency to underestimate the probability of bad outcomes for themselves—their personal fable of invulnerability, expressed in the belief that "It won't happen to me"—is one reason they take risks (Arnett, 1992). Another reason relates to a personality trait labeled **sensation seeking**. Sensation seeking implies a desire to take risks for the sensations involved. Driving motorcycles, water skiing, and using drugs have all been shown to be related to high scores on the *Sensation-Seeking Scale* (Zuckerman, Eysenck, & Eysenck, 1978). Watching violent television is also positively correlated with high sensation-seeking scores (Krcmar & Greene, 1999).

A wealth of research also suggests that peer influences contribute to the likelihood of reckless behavior. For example, smoking and use of alcohol are both strongly predicted by peer associations (Simons-Morton et al., 1999).

---

sensation seeking A personality trait reflected in an eagerness to take risks for the sensations involved. A high sensation-seeking drive might be evident in activities such as driving motorcycles, automobile racing, ice climbing, or using drugs.

The Cautious Adolescent Not all adolescents are high risk takers. Many, when they do take risks, take well-calculated risks. In fact, explains Neihart (1999), risk taking is an important aspect of development, closely related to the development of self-confidence, self-esteem, and even courage. She suggests that some children might benefit from being taught systematic strategies for risk taking—strategies that encourage them to look at all possible outcomes and to evaluate their implications.

Although adolescence is a period of greater apparent recklessness than any other period of life, it would be misleading not to emphasize that the majority of adolescents are not reckless. In 1997, more than 7.9 million Americans age 16 to 19 worked, and more than 12 million were in school—and that, too, for a lot of them, is serious, nonreckless work. In fact, more than 4.4 million of the 12.6 million adolescents in school also worked (U.S. Bureau of the Census, 1998). In Canada, almost half of all 15- to 19-year-olds were employed (*Canada Yearbook, 1999*). It is also worth noting that in a 1996 survey, 92.9% of all adolescents age 12 to 17 had never used marijuana and more than half had never used alcohol (U.S. Bureau of the Census, 1998).

Clearly, not all adolescents are totally unrestrained, reckless, and immoral.

MORAL DEVELOPMENT IN ADOLESCENCE

"I don't think it's right," said my 16-year-old niece, Janis. "How can they force her to leave?" We were talking about a current news story describing how a Philippine woman had come into the country legally, as an *au pair*, looking after a family's children. But then she had taken another job during the evenings in an effort to save enough money to bring one of her sisters over. Working at a second, "unapproved" job was in violation of her entry permit; someone had reported her, and the authorities had decided she would have to be deported. "It's not right. Imagine how she feels," Janis argued.

"Hey," said her brother, Jonathan, "She broke the law. She knew she broke it. I mean, I feel for her, but what do you think would happen if they just let everybody do what they want? There's a reason for the law."

The reactions of these two adolescents, as we see later, reflect an important difference that is often found in the moral judgments of males and females. It reflects, as well, the adolescent's concern over moral issues. This is a development made possible, at least in part, by the changes in adolescents' thinking that we described earlier—specifically, that their thinking is now more abstract, more able to deal with the possible and the ideal, more multidimensional, and more relative.

Morality involves human interactions in which questions of trust, ethics, values, and rights are involved. In this sense, human morality has a universal aspect: Moral goodness is judged in similar ways through most of the world (de Mey, Baartman, & Schulze, 1999). Clearly, learning to be "morally good" is quite different from learning social conventions (Nucci and Turiel, 1978). Learning social conventions involves learning behaviors that are accepted or not accepted but that are essentially arbitrary. Thus in Western cultures, conventions relating to eating tell us we should use knives and forks, sit at tables, eat off plates and out of bowls, and try to refrain from belching and doing other things unmentionable in polite textbooks. Elsewhere, we might learn to eat while squatting on the ground, lapping our food off rocks, belching, and making other fine noises with great gusto. These behaviors are arbitrary; if different behaviors were substituted for them, we would not likely be judged evil—foolish and disgusting, perhaps, but not truly evil. Morality, in contrast, is far less arbitrary. It refers to behaviors and judgments relating to broad issues of human justice, such as the value of human life, the ethics of causing harm to others or to their property, and the importance of trust and responsibility.

Most of us believe implicitly that some people are good and others less good—that goodness or evil is an intrinsic part of what we are—of ourselves. When we judge people morally "good" or "bad," says Kohlberg (1964), we might be referring to any one of three things: their ability to resist temptation, the amount of guilt that accompanies failure to resist temptation, or the individual's evaluation of the morality of a given act based on some personal standard of good or evil. These dimensions of morality are not necessarily very closely related. A person may repeatedly violate some accepted code of conduct—behave immorally, in other words—and yet feel a great deal of guilt. A second may engage in exactly the same behavior and feel no guilt. Yet both may judge the act equally evil. Who is most moral?

Morality as a Cognitive Phenomenon

Carroll and Rest (1982) present a highly cognitive view of moral behavior. They suggest that there are four steps involved in behaving morally:

1. Recognizing a moral problem (termed *moral sensitivity*)

2. Judging what is right and wrong (*moral judgment:* deciding what the situation *ought* to be)

3. Making a plan of action (*moral motivation:* taking into account relevant ideals and values)

4. Putting the plan into action (*moral action*)

It is entirely possible, Narváez and Rest (1995) argue, to fail to act morally because of a deficiency in only one of these components. Research on **bystander apathy**, stimulated by the now-famous murder of Kitty Genovese, is a case in point (Latané & Darley, 1970). Kitty was a New Yorker who, returning home from work at 3 o'clock one morning, was set upon by a maniac and murdered. The murder took an entire half hour to complete and was watched by at least 38 of Kitty's upper middle-class neighbors peering out of their windows. No one tried to help her; no one yelled at the murderer; no one even called the police. Table 11.7 shows how the behavior of the bystanders might be interpreted in light of Carroll and Rest's analysis of what is required for moral behavior.

---

morality The ethical aspect of human behavior. Morality is intimately bound to the development of an awareness of acceptable and unacceptable behaviors. It is therefore linked to what is often called conscience.

bystander apathy The well-researched tendency of many people not to intervene even when they witness perpetration of some horrendous act.

TABLE 11.7
Carroll and Rest's Four Components of Moral Behavior as Illustrated by the Kitty Genovese Murder

REQUIREMENTS OF MORAL BEHAVIOR	POSSIBLE REASONS FOR NOT INTERVENING IN THE MURDER
Moral sensitivity (recognition of a moral problem)	Failure to recognize seriousness of situation ("It's only a lover's quarrel.")
Moral judgment (deciding what ought to be done)	Individual's values run counter to helping someone in this situation ("If he wants to kill her, hey, it's up to him.")
Moral motivation (devising a plan of action compatible with values and ideals)	Inability to devise a plan that doesn't conflict with important values ("How can I save her life without endangering mine?")
Moral action (implementing moral or immoral behavior)	Inability to implement the plan ("I should restrain the attacker physically, but I'm not strong enough.")

Piaget's Two-Stage Approach

Carroll and Rest's view of morality is clearly based on the individual's understanding of the situation, as well as on that person's values. Hence it is primarily a *cognitive* interpretation. So, too, is Piaget's description of moral development. Piaget investigated children's morality by telling them stories and asking them to judge how good or bad the characters were. Judging is mainly a cognitive activity.

In one story, for example, child X accidentally breaks 15 cups; child Y deliberately breaks a single cup. We, whose morality is adult-like, know very clearly that child Y is a bit of a scoundrel. About child X, we can make no moral judgment. We know her to be clumsy, but we can say little about her moral goodness (unless she later lies to us about her deed).

Younger children, notes Piaget, judge this situation quite differently. They know very clearly that X is *bad, bad, bad*. In the reality-oriented perception of the preschooler, the apparent consequences of the act are all-important.

Based on children's responses to these stories, Piaget identified two broad stages in the evolution of morality. In the first stage, lasting until about age 8 or 10, children respond to the immediate consequences of behavior, manifesting a morality that is governed by the principles of pain and pleasure. Thus, good behaviors are those that have pleasant consequences; bad actions have unpleasant consequences. Accordingly, the child responds primarily to outside authority, because authority is the main source of reinforcement and punishment. Piaget labels this first stage of moral development **heteronomy**. The morality of this stage is a morality of *obedience*, notes DeVries (1997). It reflects what Piaget thought to be a predominantly authoritarian relationship that typically exists between young children and their parents.

In the second stage, beginning at around 11 or so, morality comes to be governed more and more by the individual's own principles and ideals. Moral judgments thus become less obedience-bound, more autonomous; hence Piaget's label, **autonomy**, for the second stage. Autonomous morality, suggests Piaget, reflects a change from the authoritarian, obedience-oriented parent-child relationship of earlier years to a more cooperative and more mutually respectful relationship (DeVries, 1997).

Kohlberg's Morality of Justice and Reason

Kohlberg studied moral development by posing moral dilemmas to groups of children, as well as to

---

heteronomy Piaget's label for the first stage of moral development, marked by reliance on outside authority.

autonomy Piaget's label for the second stage of moral development, marked by a reliance on internal standards as guides for behaving and for judging morality.

adolescents and adults. These dilemmas take the form of stories, one of which is paraphrased and illustrated in Table 11.8. Moral dilemmas have subsequently been widely used in investigations of morality in a form labeled the *Moral Judgment Interview.*

Children's responses to moral dilemmas suggest three levels in the development of moral judgments,

Moral Judgment Interview A procedure for determining stage and level of moral reasoning. Uses stories illustrating moral dilemmas developed by Lawrence Kohlberg.

each consisting of two stages of moral orientation (shown in Table 11.8). The three levels are sequential, although succeeding levels never entirely replace preceding ones, making it almost impossible to assign ages to them.

Similarity to Piaget's Theory Note that Kohlberg's (1969; 1980) theory of morality, strongly influenced by Piaget's work, describes a very similar progression. Both of these theories, explains Langford (1997), describe how moral development begins with the self (egocentric), eventually takes into

TABLE 11.8
Kohlberg's Levels of Morality

Kohlberg identified levels of moral judgment in children by describing to them situations involving a moral dilemma. One example is the story of Heinz, which can be paraphrased as follows:

Heinz's wife was dying of cancer. One special drug might save her, a drug recently discovered by a local druggist. The druggist could make the drug for about $200 but was selling it for 10 times that amount. So Heinz went to everyone he knew to try to borrow the $2,000 he needed, but he could only scrape together $1,000. "My wife's dying," he told the druggist, asking him to sell the drug at a lower price or let him pay later. But the druggist refused. Desperate, Heinz broke into the drugstore to steal the drug for his wife. Should Heinz have done that? Why? (Kohlberg, 1969, p. 379)

Interaction: As a crude assessment of your moral development, write out your responses to these questions, and then compare them with the following illustrative responses.

LEVEL I PRECONVENTIONAL	Stage 1: Punishment and obedience orientation	"If he steals the drug, he might go to jail." (Punishment.)
	Stage 2: Naive instrumental hedonism	"He can steal the drug and save his wife, and he'll be with her when he gets out of jail." (Act motivated by its hedonistic consequences for the actor.)
LEVEL II CONVENTIONAL	Stage 3: "Good-boy, nice-girl" morality	"People will understand if you steal the drug to save your wife, but they'll think you're cruel and a coward if you don't." (Reactions of others and the effects of the act on social relationships become important.)
	Stage 4: Law-and-order orientation	"It is the husband's duty to save his wife even if he feels guilty afterward for stealing the drug." (Institutions, law, duty, honor, and guilt motivate behavior.)
LEVEL III POSTCONVENTIONAL	Stage 5: Morality of social contract	"The husband has a right to the drug even if he can't pay now. If the druggist won't charge it, the government should look after it." (Democratic laws guarantee individual rights; contracts are mutually beneficial.)
	Stage 6: Universal ethical*	"Although it is legally wrong to steal, the husband would be morally wrong not to steal to save his wife. A life is more precious than financial gain." (Conscience is individual. Laws are socially useful but not sacrosanct.)

Source: Based on Kohlberg (1969, 1980).
*None of Kohlberg's subjects ever reached Stage 6. However, it is still described as a "potential" stage. Kohlberg suggests that moral martyrs like Jesus or Martin Luther King exemplify this level.

account others in the immediate context (parents, teachers), and finally becomes more universal and more independent. These changes can be described in three very broad stages:

1. A stage of *heteronomy* or *egocentricity* where moral judgments reflect the child's highly egocentric point of view. Kohlberg labels this the **preconventional level**. At this level, the child believes that evil behavior is that which is likely to be punished, and good behavior is based on obedience or the avoidance of the evil of disobedience (Stage 1). Similarly, the child's judgments tend to be **hedonistic**: Good is that which is pleasant, and evil is that which has undesirable consequences (Stage 2).

2. A transitional stage where the child is highly concerned with maintaining peace and harmony in important social relationships (peers, parents, and schools). Kohlberg calls this the **conventional level**. Here is a morality of conformity and obedience that reflects the increasing importance of peer and social relations. The child judges behavior moral if it receives wide approval from significant people—parents, teachers, peers, and society at large (Stage 3). Similarly, conforming to law becomes important for maintaining adults' approval (Stage 4).

3. A final stage where moral judgments reflect wider, more universal, and more independent values. At the highest level, the **postconventional**, the individual begins to view morality in terms of individual rights and as ideals and principles that have value as rules or laws, apart from their influence on approval (Stage 5). Stage 5 moral judgments are rare even among adults; and Stage

6 judgments, based on fundamental ethical principles, even rarer. Colby and Kohlberg (1984) suggest that there is some doubt as to whether Stage 6 should even be included as a stage in moral development.

A Seventh Stage? But Kohlberg (Kohlberg & Ryncarz, 1990) also spoke of the possibility of a seventh stage—a mystical, contemplative, religious stage—a metaphorical stage in which, through the "logic of contemplation and mystical logic . . . we all know that the deepest feeling is love and the ultimate reality is life" (Hague, 1991, p. 283).

Research on Kohlberg's View of Morality

There is little doubt that Kohlberg's contribution to the understanding of morality is enormous. At the same time, many researchers have found reason to criticize his approach and his conclusions. Among other things, these researchers point out that Kohlberg's view of morality is overly narrow; that the dilemmas he used to study morality might not have been especially meaningful for most of his subjects; and that by restricting his samples to males, he overlooked a dramatically different form of female moral reasoning. We look at each of these criticisms briefly.

Too Narrow a View of Morality Kohlberg's emphasis is clearly on morality as a question of justice and rational decision making, notes Burman (1999). It assumes that the most moral individuals are those who make the most ethical *abstract* judgments, the ones who weigh the far-reaching consequences of their judgments and actions using individually determined principles of morality. But when you ask people to describe *real* moral dilemmas they have faced, and you get them to discuss what they did and why, you quickly discover that there are at least three fundamentally important aspects of actual day-to-day moral behavior that Kohlberg's dilemmas do not take into account (Walker et al., 1995).

First, adult moral decisions typically reflect real, practical considerations—that is, they take into account the actual implications of a moral action. They weigh responses to questions such as "Will I lose my job?" "Will he be arrested?" "What's in it for me?"

---

preconventional level The first of Kohlberg's three levels of moral development, based on hedonistic or obedience-oriented judgments.

hedonistic Relating to the pain-pleasure principle, to the tendency to seek pleasure and avoid pain.

conventional level Kohlberg's second level of morality, reflecting a desire to establish and maintain good relations with others (law and order; obedience).

postconventional level Kohlberg's third level of morality, reflecting an understanding of social contract and more individualistic principles of morality.

Second, individuals' responses in situations requiring moral decisions and actions reflect their cultural background. Kohlberg had argued that the development of his moral stages is universal. In fact, Walker and associates point out, the dominant values of a culture often determine how a person will respond to a moral dilemma—and will determine, as well, what that culture defines as moral. In China, for example, **filial piety** is one of the highest virtues.

---

filial piety A fundamental virtue in many oriental cultures. In effect, the premise that people should always, under all circumstances and at all ages, display the highest devotion and complete obedience to their parents, and that the welfare of parents always comes first. My kids are occidental.

The notion of filial piety says, in effect, that not only in their childhood, but also throughout their lives, people should display the highest devotion to their parents, that the welfare of parents always comes first, and that parents should always be obeyed, and at all ages (Wu, 1981). Not surprisingly, when Walker and associates included Chinese participants in their study of morality, they found that the judgments of even the adult respondents often reflected Kohlberg's lowest, obedience-oriented levels of morality. At the same time, however, other studies report displays of altruism among adolescents in China similar to those in North America (Chou, 1998). Chou's study also found a similar progression through Kohlberg's stages. (See *Across Cultures:* "Yeo-hsien Han, a Pious Child.")

Yeo-hsien Han, a Pious Child

Yeo-hsien Han, a Chinese boy, desperately wanted to be a good son, so he read the ancient stories of children who serve as the best examples of filial piety. These stories are found in dozens of official historical books, in biographies, in local papers, throughout China (see Wu, 1981). Han read, for example, of a son who mourned, in costume, the death of his father for 30 years and then dedicated the rest of his years to being a vegetarian bachelor. He studied the life of Wu Meng who, at the age of 8, so loved his parents that when the mosquitoes were especially bad at night, he would remove his clothes and lie naked next to them to attract the insects. He heard of Wang Xiang, who lay on the frozen river to melt the ice with his body so that his stepmother might have fresh fish. This same Wang Xiang, when asked to guard the fruit on his stepmother's tree, spent an entire windy night sleeplessly holding the trunk so that the branches would not sway and the fruit fall to the ground. But the story that moved Yeo-hsien Han most was that of the son who, when his father had committed a capital crime, offered to die in his place, so impressing the emperor that he forgave the father.

To Think About: Among important cultural values reflected in stories of filial devotion, says Wu (1981), are the beliefs that (1) from the earliest age, children should show great devotion to their parents; (2) parents' welfare comes before that of children; and (3) children should be obedient and try to make their parents' lives pleasant and comfortable no matter what.

Are there similar values in your culture? Are cultural values important? How? Why?

Private Collection/Bridgeman Art Library, London/SuperStock

Stories, and images such as this, have traditionally been used in China to emphasize for children the virtues of unquestioning obedience and devotion not only to parents but to all elders.

Third, Kohlberg's approach fails to consider the importance of religion or faith or spirituality in morality. In real life, actions are often judged moral or immoral based on the extent to which they promote or violate explicit rules of faith—or, very often, explicit rules of law (Hommers, 1997; Okonkwo, 1997).

Dilemmas Not Meaningful Enough For these reasons, some critics argue that Kohlberg's Moral Judgment Interview procedure might not always be very meaningful—that it presents a view that is too rational, too abstract. When you ask people to define "moral excellence," claim Walker and Pitts (1998), you get much more than a description of a Kohlberg kind of *principled reasoning*. You also get reference to character and virtue, and to what people actually do in real situations that require moral evaluation and moral action. Thus, if you ask people to describe real moral dilemmas they have recently faced, or to describe the most important or the biggest dilemma they *ever* faced, the vast majority of moral problems described have to do with relationships—not with abstract notions of right and wrong, or with seemingly remote issues such as whether to steal a drug for a dying person.

Some researchers further suggest that Kohlberg's moral dilemmas are perhaps too verbal and too abstract for children. They ask that the child understand and keep in mind complex situations involving several actors; they require the manipulation of a variety of elements and circumstances; and often they don't provide enough information (but if they did, they would be even more complex). As a result, it appears that the Kohlberg dilemmas underestimate children's moral reasoning. When questions are made simpler, or when children and adolescents are observed in naturalistic settings, researchers sometimes find evidence of very sophisticated moral reasoning at very young ages. For example, children as young as 6 or 7 are likely to consider the actor's intentions in judging the severity of an act, report Darley and Shultz (1990). Also, they often take into account other factors, such as whether an authority permits the act to occur (Tisak, 1993). Thus, children will judge an act more harshly if it intentionally causes harm, or if the consequences could have been fore-

seen, than if the action's harm is unintentional and could not have been expected. Similarly, preschoolers, like older children, readily differentiate between lies and the truth, and judge lies as being less moral than the truth (Bussey, 1992). Says Buzzelli (1992), even preschoolers are not really "premoral." "As early as the second year of life, children begin to use standards in evaluating their own behavior and the behavior of others" (p. 48).

Too Male-Centered Reasoning that Kohlberg's abstract dilemmas were not very meaningful for most people, and even less meaningful for women, Gilligan (1982) examined morality by interviewing 29 pregnant women while they were actually facing the very real moral dilemma of needing to make a decision about having an abortion. Her findings reveal that these women's moral judgments were less the *justice*-oriented judgments that adult males typically make in response to the Kohlberg stories, but they were judgments based on compassion and caring.

Women, notes Gilligan, appear to progress through three stages in their moral development. In the first stage, the woman is moved primarily by selfish concerns ("This is what I want . . . what I need . . . what I should do . . . what would be best for me"). In the second stage, she progresses through a period of increasing recognition of responsibility to others. And the final stage reflects a morality of "nonviolence." At this stage, the woman's decision is based on her desire to do the greatest good both for self and for others.

Gilligan's View of Male-Female Differences in Morality

If Gilligan's description of female moral development is accurate, it reflects some important differences between male and female morality. In contrast with Kohlberg's description of male moral progression from what are initially hedonistic (pain-pleasure) concerns toward a conventional, rule-regulated morality, Gilligan describes female morality as progressing from initial selfishness toward a recognition of social responsibility. Boys are perhaps more concerned with law and order than with caring and compassion. Women's is a morality of caring rather than of abstract justice.

Negative and Positive Duties Nunner-Winkler (1984) elaborates Gilligan's position by reference to Kant's (1797–1977) distinction between negative and positive moral duties: Negative duties are illustrated in rules such as "Do not kill" and "Do not steal." These rules are absolute and clear; you follow them or you do not. In contrast, positive duties are open-ended. They are reflected in rules such as "Be kind" and "Be compassionate." There are no boundaries or limits on positive duties. They don't specify how kind, to whom, how often, or when.

Negative duties, says Nunner-Winkler, reflect the justice orientation of males; females feel more obliged than males to fulfill positive duties, which relate more closely to caring and compassion.

Relevant Research Do women and men see the world differently, and make different moral judgments? Some research says yes. Finlay and Love (1998) analyzed men and women's justifications for their opinions regarding an incident of military intervention. The analysis clearly supports Gilligan's view that women are moved more by considerations of compassion and care. Men in this sample responded clearly to issues of social order, justice, and law. Similarly, Crandall and associates (1999) had men and women respond to two actual situations involving moral dilemmas—one in which two babies had been switched at birth, and another involving a custody dispute in a case of surrogate motherhood. Again, female judgments reflected a higher level of care than male judgments, which tended to reflect a higher justice orientation.

But note that both sexes are capable of, and do manifest, both sorts of moral judgments. Thus, in the Crandall and associates study, differences between the sexes were seldom very dramatic. In this study, both sexes tended to respond to the switched-babies scenario with caring and compassion. And both reflected primarily a justice orientation in their responses to the surrogate parent dilemma. Nevertheless, as noted, the women scored higher on care and lower on justice than did the men.

That males and females have somewhat different orientations to morality does not make one more "morally good" than the other. For example, research on altruism, cooperation, and other forms of prosocial behavior has found no significant sex differences (Muuss, 1988). Both males and females appear to be equally altruistic. But their altruism might well stem from fundamentally different orientations, reflecting very different moralities. Females may, as Gilligan suggests, be altruistic because of their concern for humanity; males may be just as altruistic because of their adherence to principles and ideals that stress the injustice of being unkind.

An important contribution of Gilligan's approach is that it underlines the need to be aware that many of our theories and conclusions in human development may not equally apply to males and females. In Gilligan's (1982) words, the sexes speak in a different voice. Neither voice is louder or better; they are simply different.

Implications: Improving Morality

Some of the most important implications of research on morality relate to the observation that individuals who operate at the lowest levels (hedonistic) are more likely to be delinquent than those who operate at higher levels. As Gibbs (1987) notes, the delinquent's behavior generally reflects immature moral reasoning and egocentricity. Individuals who operate at higher levels of morality are more likely to be honest and to behave in a generally moral way. Similarly, altruism and other forms of prosocial behavior in children are related to their level of moral development (Fabes et al., 1999). Research also clearly indicates that prosocial behavior is influenced by the adolescent's social context (Carlo et al., 1999). Accordingly, it should be possible to improve moral development and behavior.

School Influences Unfortunately, says Folsom (1998), schools aren't very concerned with the development of moral character: They "bifurcate" the intellect and the moral. They are geared to the pursuit of external knowledge, but they ignore the pursuit of inner knowledge—of self-knowledge. Yet there is considerable evidence that moral judgments and behaviors can be influenced by specific programs in schools (Stoll & Beller, 1993). And when teachers were asked whether they thought values and morals should be taught in schools, a resounding 95% said yes (Zern, 1997). When asked what values should be taught, teachers had little difficulty agreeing: More than 75% thought that values such as responsibility, respect, caring, honesty, and justice should be included in a school curriculum.

Teaching morality in schools sometimes takes the form of **values education**, where values and principles are taught directly; or of **values clarification programs**, which don't attempt to teach values so much as to encourage students to examine and develop their own sets of values. Specific techniques used in these programs include discussing moral questions and dilemmas, evaluating the ethical implications of human behavior, role-playing situations involving moral issues, modeling procedures, and direct teaching.

A comprehensive program designed to increase prosocial behavior among elementary schoolchildren is described by Battistich and colleagues (1991). This program includes activities in the school as well as in the home. Activities are geared toward developing prosocial values and interpersonal understanding, and make extensive use of cooperative learning and discussion of rationales for rules and reasons underlying moral behaviors. The authors report that after five years, program children engage in more spontaneous prosocial behavior in the classroom, have improved perspective-taking skills, and are better at resolving conflicts. They caution, however, that differences between program children and other comparable children are slight and often inconsistent. In addition, it isn't always easy to measure the effects of programs such as this.

Family Influences In addition to what schools and educators might attempt to do, the values and behav-

iors of parents are highly instrumental in determining the values of their children (Kochanska, Murray, & Coy, 1997). There are ways, argue Colby and Damon (1995), in which people's values and goals can be translated into extraordinary moral commitment. In a world where immorality is highly visible, if not highly rampant, much needs to be done. One approach is through parenting.

Research reveals a clear relationship between parenting styles and children's morality. Specifically, the internalization of moral rules is fostered by two things: (1) the frequent use of discipline that points out the harmful consequences of the child's behavior for others; and (2) frequent expression of parental affection (Hoffman, 1979). Most forms of parental discipline, Hoffman argues, contain elements of "power assertion" and "love withdrawal." That is, discipline usually involves at least the suggestion of the possibility of loss of parental love, as well as the potential for losing privileges, hearing threats, or receiving physical punishment. The main purpose of this "power assertion," according to Hoffman, is to get the child to stop misbehaving and pay attention. From the perspective of the child's developing morality, however, what is most important is that there now be an accompanying verbal component. The purpose of this verbal component is to influence the child cognitively and emotionally—perhaps by bringing about feelings of guilt or of empathy, and by enabling the child to foresee consequences. The verbal component might simply admonish ("Don't do that"); ideally, however, it should go beyond the admonishment to describe the consequences ("Don't do that because . . ." or "If you do that, the cat might . . ."). Further, as pointed out elsewhere, the most meaningful rationalizations for adolescents should be more abstract than those used with younger children. That is, they would stress values and principles rather than the objective consequences of the act. And to be most meaningful, rationalizations might be different for girls and boys, stressing social relationships, empathy, compassion, and caring for girls; and emphasizing legal rights, social order, and justice for boys.

The future of this world depends on the morality of our children. (See *Concept Summary*. See, also, *In the News and on the Web:* "Gang Murder.")

---

values education Instructional programs and strategies designed to teach specific values (notions of right and wrong), thereby promoting good behavior and developing good "character."

values clarification programs Programs designed to encourage learners to examine their personal beliefs about right and wrong, with a view to improving and clarifying their awareness of their own morality.

CONCEPT SUMMARY **Ideas and Findings in Moral Development**

Concept/Theory	Description/Explanations
Morality	• An aspect of human interactions or judgments that implies recognition of right and wrong, virtue, principles, ethics . . .
Carroll and Rest's four steps involved in moral behavior	• Moral sensitivity (recognizing a moral issue) • Moral judgment (deciding what *ought* to be done) • Moral motivation (making a plan according to values) • Moral action (implementing the plan)
Piaget's two stages	• Heteronomy (obedience-based morality reflecting authoritarian parent-child relationship) • Autonomy (self-determined principles, reflecting mutually respectful parent-child relationship)
Kohlberg's stages of moral development	• Describe progression from self-centered (egocentric morality), to greater concern with others in immediate context (parents and peers—obedience orientation), to eventual concern with more universal context (universal principles and values) • Level 1—Preconventional (Stage 1: obedience oriented; Stage 2: pain-pleasure driven) • Level 2—Conventional (Stage 3: good boy, nice girl morality; Stage 4: law-and-order orientation) • Level 3—Postconventional (Stage 5: morality of social contracts; Stage 6: universal ethical principles)
Contrasts between newer research and Kohlberg's views	• Less restricted models include consideration of practical implications of moral judgments; influence of culture; and influences of religions, faith, and laws • Use of more meaningful, real-life dilemmas • Recognition of gender differences
Some male-remale differences	• Some evidence suggests that male morality is more a morality of law and order, of justice, of right and wrong • In contrast, female morality may be more a morality of caring and compassion • Differences between genders aren't always very significant; both are capable of all sorts of moral judgments; both might be equally moral, equally altruistic, but for different reasons, and perhaps in different ways
Implications of research on morality	• Schools (values education) can affect children's morality; parental and other social influences are enormously important • Our future may depend on the extent to which we can direct school, cultural, and family influences toward the development of morality

Gang Murder

Reena Virk, described by her classmates as "plump and insecure," dreamed of being a nurse, a writer, an artist. Too, she dreamed of having friends, of fitting in; but, sadly, she had no friends. Still, on a Friday night, Reena, age 14, found herself at a party by the river, in the company of those with whom she had sought friendship. Someone stubbed a cigarette on Reena's forehead, provoking her into a fight with not one, but an entire group of girls. She was brutally beaten and left somewhere along the Gorge, a river that runs through Victoria on Vancouver Island. Later, at least one boy and one girl returned to finish the savage beating, breaking Reena's back, her legs, and her neck, and then throwing her into the gorge. Later that week, police became aware of rumors in city high schools about a girl having been killed. Subsequently Reena's body was discovered. Seven girls and one boy were charged. Six of the girls have now been convicted and sentenced; none were charged with murder, all were tried in juvenile court, and all are or soon will be free. The lone male assailant, Warren Glowatski, was found guilty of second-degree murder and sentenced to life with no parole for 7 years. As of this writing, more than 2 years after the attack, the seventh girl has yet to face trial.

M. Jimenez, "'Worst Nightmare' for slain girl's parents." *Edmonton Journal*, 25 November 1997, p. A3.

M. Shephard, "Four teens charged with torturing girl, 14: In two hours, hit 60 times with cigarettes." *Toronto Star*, 18 November 1999, p. 3.

To Do: Violence perpetrated by females, the popular media informs us, is becoming increasingly common. Is there evidence that this is true? Why might it be true? Or, if it isn't true, why might it *seem* to be true?

Resources: For practical information on crime prevention, see the U.S. Department of Justice's Justice for Kids and Youth website:

http://www.usdoj.gov/kidspage/

For additional readings, explore *InfoTrac College Edition*, your online library. Go to http://infotrac-college.com/wadsworth and use the passcode that came on the card with your book. Try these search terms: youth gangs, youth murder, youth crime prevention.

MAIN POINTS

A Period of Transitions

In many nonindustrial societies, progress from childhood to adulthood is marked by ritual and ceremony collectively known as rites of passage, often characterized by separation, training, initiation, and induction. Initiation procedures sometimes involve scarification and circumcision. Some writers claim that secondary schools serve as rites of passage.

Biological and Physical Changes of Adolescence

Puberty is sexual maturity, which results from pubescence. Pubescence is heralded by hormonal changes; its initiation is evident in dramatic changes in growth velocity (the growth spurt). Physical changes are highly evident in increments in height and weight, and changes in strength and motor performance. For a time in late childhood and early adolescence, girls are taller and heavier than boys. From childhood through adulthood, boys have relatively more fat-free mass than girls.

The changes of pubescence that make reproduction possible involve primary sexual characteristics (menarche, first menstruation; and spermarche, first ejaculation of semen). Other changes that are not directly linked to reproducing involve secondary sexual characteristics (axillary hair, breasts, and voice changes, for example).

Maturation occurred earlier in succeeding generations through much of the twentieth century, and continues to do so in developing countries (the secular trend, attributed largely to changes in nutrition). Early maturation appears to be advantageous for boys but less so for girls. Pubertal change is most stressful when it puts adolescents out of step with peers, especially if the change is not seen as an advantage. Common adolescent concerns include worries about the future, finances, school, appearance, feelings of inferiority, loneliness, the purpose of life, sex, the stability of the parents' marriage, and lack of time.

Nutrition and Eating Disorders

There is a greater need for nutrients during adolescence. Although obesity is the most common nutritional problem of adolescents in North America, concerns over appearance and weight are sometimes apparent in eating disorders such as anorexia nervosa (significant weight loss, refusal to maintain weight, distorted body image) and bulimia nervosa (recurrent eating binges, use of laxatives and diuretics, self-induced vomiting), which is more common than anorexia.

Causes of eating disorders involve interactions among psychological factors (depression; distorted body image), sociocultural factors (cultural values that overemphasize thinness), and family-based factors (family conflict; sexual abuse). Treatment is sometimes difficult (anorectics often don't recognize their problem; bulimics hide theirs) and relapses are common.

Intellectual Development in Adolescence

The intellectual development of adolescents may culminate in thought that is potentially completely logical, that is inferential, that deals with the hypothetical as well as with the concrete, that is systematic, and that results in the potential for being idealistic. Among other things, formal operations make possible a type of intense idealism that may be reflected in adolescents' frustration or rebellion, as well as in more advanced levels of moral orientation.

Five major changes in thinking characterize adolescence: Thought is now more abstract, more hypothetical, more metacognitive, more multidimensional, and more relativistic.

Information-processing views of development are concerned with three aspects of cognition: the acquisition of a knowledge base (grows with schooling and experience); the development of information-processing strategies (develop by increasing memory capacity and by acquiring better and more appropriate processing strategies); and the development of metacognitive skills (relate to awareness of what is involved in knowing and remembering).

Adolescent Egocentrism

Adolescent egocentrism describes a self-centeredness that often leads adolescents to believe all others in the immediate vicinity are highly concerned with their thoughts and behaviors. It may be manifested in the creation of the imaginary audience (a hypothetical collection of people assumed to be highly concerned about the adolescent's behavior) and the personal fable (a fantasy with themes stressing the individual's invulnerability and uniqueness).

Adolescents' reckless behavior may be linked to egocentrism, a tendency to underestimate the probability of unpleasant outcomes, sensation-seeking drives, a sense of invulnerability, and the influence of the peer culture. Some adolescents remain cautious.

Moral Development in Adolescence

Carroll and Rest describe four components of moral behavior: recognizing a moral problem (moral sensitivity), deciding what ought to be done (moral judgment), devising a plan of action according to ideals (moral motivation), and implementing the plan (moral action). Failure to act morally may be due to a deficiency in any one of these four components.

Piaget draws a parallel between understanding the rules governing games and moral development (from no understanding of rules to a final stage in which rules are understood as being arbitrary, useful, and changeable). His two stages of moral development are *heteronomy* (egocentric, obedience-based) and *autonomy* (self-determined). Kohlberg describes morality as a decision-making process that progresses through three levels: preconventional (concerned with self: pain, pleasure, obedience, punishment), conventional (concerned with the group, with being liked, with conforming), and postconventional (concerned with abstract principles, ethics, social contracts). Each level consists of two stages. Both of these theories describe a progression from a self-centered (egocentric) morality, to greater concern with others in the immediate context (parents and peers—obedience orientation), to eventual concern with more universal context (universal principles and values).

Critics of Kohlberg attempt to use less restricted models that look at the implications of moral judgments and at the influence of culture, religion, and laws. They also attempt to use more meaningful moral dilemmas and to recognize gender differences in moral reasoning and behavior. Gilligan suggests that males become progressively more concerned with law and order (a morality of justice); in con-

trast, women respond more to social relationships and to the social consequences of behavior (a morality of caring).

Various programs using indoctrination, role playing, moral discourse, cooperative learning, and modeling have been successful in increasing levels of moral judgment (and sometimes behavior). Parental discipline that points out the harmful consequences of a child's behavior for others, and the frequent expression of parental affection, are also important.

Focus Questions: Applications

1. *Is adolescence a universal phenomenon, or is it largely cultural?*
   - Using anthropological studies of primitive rites in other cultures, address the question: Is adolescence a universal phenomenon?
2. *What are the most important biological changes of adolescence?*
   - Did you mature early or late? Was the timing important? Why?
3. *What are the defining characteristics of anorexia nervosa? Of bulimia nervosa?*
   - Starvation is a serious Third-World problem; the reasons for this are clear. Overeating, anorexia, and bulimia are serious problems of the developed world. List several explanations for each of these problems.

4. *How does adolescent thinking change?*
   - Try to find at least one example of how your own thinking is more abstract, more hypothetical, more multidimensional, more relativistic, or more cognitive than that of a typical 10-year-old.
5. *How are adolescents egocentric?*
   - How does adolescents' willingness to take risks relate to egocentricity?
6. *Is being good or bad an inescapable part of our personalities?*
   - Invent a moral dilemma, and ask several people what they think the best resolution for it might be. Analyze their responses using Kohlberg's levels of morality.

Possible Responses to Thought Challenges

Thought Challenge, page 471

Yes, they are potentially of great consequence. All these changes are tied very closely to cultural definitions of physical attractiveness. (Increased production of the sebaceous glands is what results in teenage acne. And uneven growth rates may result in big noses, droopy ears, lopsided lips, etc.) And, as we saw in Chapter 10, for many children (and adolescents) physical attractiveness is critical in determining self-esteem.

Thought Challenge, page 475

That poorer nutrition should result in later menarche makes biological sense. Later menarche means delayed sexual maturation, which means that child-rearing begins later than it otherwise might. The result is that

the scant food resources available aren't diluted as much, thus increasing the group's chances of survival.

Thought Challenge, page 489

Yes, you do, although of course you might be wrong. The card tasks given to Bill and Laura are actually cards from the *Matching Familiar Figures Test* (Kagan, 1966), a measure of the tendency to be reflective or impulsive. Reflective individuals place a premium on being correct; they like to think before they answer (they *reflect*); impulsive individuals place a premium on reacting quickly (they are more *impulsive*). Research suggests, not surprisingly, that reflective individuals are more likely to score high on measures of metacognition—and are also more likely to achieve well in school (Palladino et al., 1997).

Thought Challenge, page 490

1. Both are egocentric, although their egocentrism takes different forms.

2. Both are often rebellious, the one trying to achieve a sort of physical independence, and the other, a social and emotional independence.

3. Both are often involved in acquiring, perfecting, or even relearning, physical skills—one practicing the gross motor skills of locomotion, of skipping and hopping, and other elegant movements (and perhaps some finer motor movements as well, as in picking things up, stacking them, and scribbling); and the other, practicing dancing and skiing and writing electronic love notes—or maybe just relearning to walk with some semblance of ease and nonchalance with those long feet and newly stretched appendages.

Key Terms

adolescence, 468
anovulatory, 474
attention span, 488
autonomy, 496
bystander apathy, 495
continuous society, 470
conventional level, 498
discontinuous society, 470
eating disorder, 479
endocrine glands, 473
filial piety, 499
gonads, 473

hedonistic, 498
heteronomy, 496
hormone, 473
imaginary audience, 490
information-processing
   strategies, 487
menarche, 473
Moral Judgment Interview, 497
morality, 495
personal fable, 491
postconventional level, 498
preconventional level, 498

primary sexual characteristics, 473
rite of passage, 468
secondary sexual characteristics,
   473
secular trend, 475
sensation seeking, 494
spermarche, 474
Sturm und Drang, 470
taboo, 468
values clarification programs, 502
values education, 502

Further Readings

Because primitive rites of passage are so widespread, and because they share several common characteristics, they may have some evolutionary significance. This is the theme of Weisfeld's fascinating account of adolescence among humans and primates.

Weisfeld, G. E. (1999). *Evolutionary principles of human adolescence.* New York: Basic Books.

Wolman's short book deals with many of the topics included in this chapter. Of special interest is his account of the biological nature of adolescence and of intellectual development during this period. Elkind's book, written as much for the layperson as for the professional, is an exceptionally readable account of the adolescent experience in contemporary society.

Wolman, B. B. (1998). *Adolescence: Biological and psychosocial perspectives.* Westport, Conn.: Greenwood Press.

Elkind, D. (1998). *All grown up and no place to go: Teenagers in crisis* (rev. ed.). Reading, Mass.: Addison-Wesley.

The three articles in Part III of the following book look specifically at moral development. Their sociological orientation presents a useful addition to the more cognitive orientation in *Of Children.*

Woodhead, M., D. Faulkner, & K. Littleton, eds. (1999). *Making sense of social development.* New York: Routledge.

Online Resources

For additional readings, explore *InfoTrac College Edition,* your online library. Go to http://infotrac-college.com/wadsworth and use the passcode that came on the card with your book. Try these search terms: morality adolescence, adolescent peer pressure, initiation rights, eating disorders.

I would that there were no age between ten and three-and-twenty, or that youth would sleep out the rest; for there is nothing in between but getting wenches with child, wronging the ancientry, stealing, fighting . . .

William Shakespeare, *The Winter's Tale, Act III, Scene 3*

Social and Emotional Development in Adolescence

Myrleen Ferguson Cate/PhotoEdit

CHAPTER 12

When I was writing the first draft of this book, I often visited my grandmother. She had a way of putting things in perspective— and me in my place.

One night when I was about to start this chapter on social and emotional development in adolescence, I found her sitting on her porch soaking her feet. "Wards off the arthritis," she said, and insisting that I take off my shoes and dip my feet next to hers in the hot brine, she added with hardly a pause, "Beats scrubbing floors in the convent."

She was often like that, my grandmother. Mischievous. She was trying to get my goat by bringing up an old transgression—the time I got caught in my girlfriend's dormitory room at the convent. Someone (I won't rat and say who it was) had snuck into the convent and used a rope to tie together all the room doorknobs. Then he rang the fire bell, and the girls couldn't open their doors, so they scrambled out the windows instead—many throwing out their stuffed toys to save their lives. I got caught crawling out of Céline's window, and all my excuses fell on deaf ears.

The choice they gave me was to accept expulsion from school, an appealing option my father didn't like, or to scrub the convent's dining room floor for two months.

FOCUS QUESTIONS

1. Is adolescence generally a time of strife, typically marked by parent-adolescent conflict?

2. How free of gender discrimination are the lives of adolescents?

3. What are the principal sexual beliefs and behaviors of typical adolescents?

4. How common and serious are teenage delinquency, drug abuse, and suicide?

⌐ THE SELF AND IDENTITY

Maybe, hot brine does feel pretty good between the toes. But scrubbing the convent floor wasn't all that bad. It made me the center of attention, which I didn't mind. Frankly, I was often lonely as an adolescent.

Loneliness in Adolescence

Hodapp and Mueller (1982) observe that infancy is perhaps the least lonely period of the entire life span. At no other time are we more likely to be surrounded by others intimately concerned with our comfort and well-being: mothers, fathers, sisters and brothers, grandparents, medical personnel, and assorted relatives.

In contrast, adolescence is perhaps the beginning of the loneliest period of our lives, for it is then, Sartre insists, that we begin to sense most keenly our terrible aloneness, our abandonment (see Chapter 13). Bright adolescents, argues Ellsworth (1999), may be especially susceptible to a kind of "existential dread"—a hopelessness and anguish that comes with the realization of our aloneness. As we are cast adrift from our parents, there is a fear that we will find nothing else upon which to anchor.

For a long time, say Cassidy and Berlin (1999), researchers thought that younger children don't feel loneliness, that feelings of aloneness don't invade their lives until adolescence. Recently, however, there has been a wealth of research on loneliness in children—and in adolescents. Much of this research has used loneliness questionnaires, such as Asher's *Loneliness and Social Dissatisfaction Scale for Children* (Asher et al., 1984).

Among other things, this research reveals that there are developmental changes in the sorts of things that make children feel lonely. As Parkhurst and Hopmeyer (1999) explain, toddlers and preschoolers, strongly tied as they are to parents and siblings, need their affection, their attention, and the reassurance of their presence. And their absence, or threatened absence, can bring fear and loneliness. Thus, being alone in a strange place can be a potent source of loneliness for a 4-year-old—and perhaps a source of fear as well.

For the elementary school child, friendships have become far more important. Now, being left alone is not nearly so distressing as finding that one has no friends, that there is no one willing to come over and play.

And for adolescents, for whom peers and romantic attachments may be the very center of the universe, loneliness can arise from rejection, from betrayal, from the inability to find intimacy either with groups or with individuals. We need to be socially connected, insists Larson (1999). Ethologists speculate that humans, and probably most other species of mammals, need to form and maintain social attachments. Not only do these contribute to safety and physical survival, but they also make reproduction possible. When our needs for social attachment aren't met, we feel lonely.

Maybe it is this need for connectedness, this fear of aloneness, that drives the adolescent so strongly to seek the company of others—this and one other thing: sexual drives. (That is not why I was in the convent that night!) Among the most important aspects of social adaptation are those that are directed by the hormonal changes of adolescence,

THOUGHT CHALLENGE: *Sometimes we need to be alone; we need solitude, argue Buchholz and Catton (1999). Even very young infants clearly signal their caretakers when they no longer want to be socially engaged—when they want to be left alone (Buchholz & Marben, 1999; Buchholz & Helbraun, 1999). Why is this not a contradiction of the assertion that we need to be socially connected, that we sometimes desperately fear and avoid loneliness?*

those that have to do with the mounting urges of sexual maturation. Recognition of our aloneness and of our sexuality—these two, taken together, might do much to clarify our understanding of adolescence and of humanity.

The Self

But the urge to escape loneliness, to establish social connections, is not all that drives adolescents. The need to understand, to discover, perhaps even to invent the self is also crucial. In fact, so important is the concept of self that, as Banaji and Prentice (1994) report, in the six years immediately preceding 1993, more than 5,000 articles were published on the self. More recently, the word *self* has appeared in some 40,522 entries indexed in the database PsychInfo in the four years preceding 2000.

As we saw in Chapter 10, self is a difficult and complex concept, not easily defined—which is probably why it has been redefined by so many hundreds of psychologists over the years. Few, however, have made the concept much clearer than did the alleged "father" of psychology, William James, more than a century ago. "A man's self," wrote James in the highly masculine jargon of those times, "is the sum total of all that he can call his" (1890, p. 291). In this definition, *self* is a *conscious* awareness of one's characteristics. As we saw in Chapter 10, notions of self also include important evaluative aspects. Thus we have notions of our selves as being good or bad. In other words, we have feelings of self-esteem (or *self-worth*).

The term *identity* is often used as though it were synonymous with *self*. In fact, however, the terms have somewhat different meanings in psychology. The term identity is most closely related to the writing of Erikson, who sees the concept as signifying a sort of wholeness, a sense of being that has its roots in childhood and reaches its greatest importance in adolescence. In Erikson's words, "The young person, in order to experience wholeness, must feel a progressive continuity between that which he has come to be during the long years of childhood and that which he promises to become in the anticipated future . . ." (1968, p. 87).

Put more simply, in Erikson's writings on adolescence, identity means individuals' notions about who they are and who they are becoming—their *self-definition*. And this sense of identity relates specifically to different areas of life. As is illustrated shortly, the adolescent's achievement of identity may be at different levels of development with respect to social relations, politics and ideology, or schooling and career development. One of the important tasks of adolescence is to develop a strong sense of identity in all, or most, of these areas.

Changing Notions of Self

My notions of what I am—my self-concept—are not the same today as they were when, at the age of 6, I stole molasses cookies in Aunt Lucy's kitchen. The self-concept develops, as does the rest of the child. In general, it becomes more abstract, less concrete. Montemayor and Eisen (1977) had 262 boys and girls from grades 4, 6, 8, 10, and 12 give 20 answers to the question, "Who am I?" When analyzing the responses, the authors found a progressive increase in the number of responses relating to basic beliefs, **values**, personal style, self-determination, and other abstract personal qualities. At the same time, there was a dramatic reduction in the number of responses relating to geographic area, citizenship, possessions, and physical attributes. For example, a typical 9-year-old boy's responses included: "I have brown eyes; I have brown hair; I have seven people in my family; I live on 1923 Pinecrest Drive." An 11-year-old girl offers somewhat less concrete notions of self: "I'm a human being; I'm a girl; I'm a truthful person; I'm a very good pianist," and a 17-year-old girl presents a highly abstract self-concept, based largely on interpersonal style and emotional states: "I am a human being; I am an individual; I don't know who I am; I am a loner; I am an indecisive person; I am an atheist" (pp. 317, 318).

But no matter how the child or the adolescent organizes notions of self, what people think of themselves—in other words, their notions of self-esteem—is critical.

---

values Judgments or beliefs about the desirability of certain behaviors or goals.

The Importance of Self-Esteem

We saw in Chapter 10 that high self-esteem is associated with happiness and with high levels of adjustment. In contrast, low self-esteem is often associated with depression and behavior problems. In adolescence, as Zimmerman and associates (1997) found following a review of related research, low self-esteem has been found to be linked with depression, substance use, delinquency, suicide, and poorer performance in school.

Research suggests that the self-esteem of adolescents can be described using one or sometimes a combination of four distinct trajectories. On one hand are youth whose self-esteem is consistently high; on the other are those who lack significantly in self-esteem. A third group includes those whose self-esteem is slowly rising. And a fourth is made up of those whose self-esteem is rapidly declining.

In a four-year longitudinal study involving more than 1,100 students in grades 6 through 10, Zimmerman and associates (1997) investigated some characteristics of individuals in each of these four groups, also looking at the implications of high and low, or of rising or declining self-esteem. It was reassuring that the largest group comprised those whose self-esteem was consistently high throughout the 4-year period; and the smallest group consisted of those with low-self esteem. About 20% of the group had moderately high and rising self-esteem; another 20% had steadily decreasing notions of self-worth.

Zimmerman and associates looked at the relationship between membership in each of these self-esteem categories and a variety of factors such as susceptibility to peer pressures, academic achievement, tolerance for deviance, and alcohol use and misuse. Their most important findings were that those with consistently high self-esteem, as well as those with moderately high but rising self-esteem, were, in their words, "developmentally healthier" at tenth grade than were those in the other two groups. These youths were significantly more resistant to peer pressure, had higher average grades, and reported less tolerance for deviant behavior or alcohol misuse. In contrast, those with the lowest self-esteem, or with rapidly declining self-esteem, fared significantly less well.

It is worth noting that while self-esteem is relatively stable for many adolescents, for others it may change in important ways over time. Adolescents whose self-esteem is increasing are at considerably less risk for negative developmental outcomes than are those whose self-esteem is rapidly declining.

Facets of the Self

It may be a little misleading and oversimplified to speak of self-esteem as though it were a simple trait psychologists can easily make reliable judgments about such as "It's consistently high"; "It's moderate but rising"; or "It's declining rapidly." In fact, because *self* is a multifaceted concept, there are notions of self in many different areas. And in some cases, the individual may have quite different estimates of the worth of each of these different facets of self.

The term *self-image* is used extensively in adolescent research to mean something very similar to self-esteem or self-worth. Thus the *Offer Self-Image Questionnaire*, a widely used instrument for assessing self-image, has teenagers report on their attitudes toward and feelings about themselves in several different areas (Offer, Ostrov, & Howard, 1981). Like Harter (1983), Offer assumes the adolescent has a multiplicity of selves that can be considered and evaluated separately.

▲ *Psychological self.* Reflects adolescents' emotions, their conceptions of their bodies, and their ability to control impulses.

▲ *Social self.* Consists of adolescents' perceptions of their relationships with others, as well as their morals and their goals.

▲ *Sexual self.* Reflects attitudes and feelings about sexual experiences and behavior.

▲ *Familial self.* Consists of adolescents' feelings and attitudes toward parents and other members of their family.

▲ *Coping self.* Reflects psychological adjustment and how effectively the adolescent functions in the outside world.

The Offer questionnaire investigates these five facets of self (see Table 12.1) by presenting adolescents with a series of statements (for example, "Being together with other people gives me a good

TABLE 12.1
Facets of Self in the *Offer Self-Image Questionnaire*

IMPORTANT ASPECTS OF SELF	RELEVANT SELF-EVALUATIVE QUESTIONS
Psychological self	Do I like my body? Am I in control of myself? What are my wishes? My feelings? My fantasies?
Social self	Am I friendly? Outgoing? Do people like me? What kind of morals do I have? What are my aspirations? Am I a loner?
Sexual self	How do I feel about sex? What do I think of pornography? Am I sexually attracted to others? Sexually attractive to them? Comfortable with my sexuality?
Familial self	How do I feel about my parents? Home? Siblings? Other relatives? Do I prefer to stay home? Do people at home like me? Need me? Want me?
Coping self	How effective am I? How well do I cope with what others demand? What school demands? What I demand? Am I well adjusted? Reasonably happy? How decisive am I?

feeling") and having them select one of six alternatives relating to how well the statement describes them (ranging from *describes me very well* to *does not describe me at all*). Each descriptor in the questionnaire is worded both positively and negatively.

The Offer questionnaire was developed more than 20 years ago (scoring procedures have changed since then) and has now been given to tens of thousands of adolescents. Results provide important data concerning the adolescent experience.

In a massive study, appropriate translations of the *Offer Self-Image Questionnaire* were administered to 5,938 adolescents in nine different countries (Australia, Bangladesh, Hungary, Israel, Italy, Taiwan, Turkey, former West Germany, and the United States) (Offer et al., 1988). One of the objectives was to compare adolescents' self-images in each of these countries, and arrive at a better understanding of what is universal about adolescence in today's world and what might be specific to given cultural contexts. Adolescents included in the study were both male and female, classified into two age groups: younger (ages 13–15) and older (ages 16–19).

The Universal Adolescent What is similar about adolescence in these countries? A surprising number of things. The "universal adolescent," to use Offer and associates' phrase, resembles most other adolescents in some ways with respect to each of the major facets of self-image.

▲ *Psychological.* The universal adolescent is usually happy and optimistic, and enjoys being alive.

▲ *Social.* The universal adolescent enjoys the company of others, is caring and compassionate, and places great value on school, education, and preparation for adult work.

▲ *Sexual.* The universal adolescent is confident about the sexual self, and willing to talk and think about sex.

▲ *Familial.* The universal adolescent expresses strongly positive feelings toward parents, a high degree of satisfaction with home lives, and good feelings about relationships at home.

▲ *Coping.* The universal adolescent expresses confidence in his or her ability to deal with life, and feels talented and able to make decisions.

The Context-Bound Adolescent But there are differences, too, across these cultures. Adolescents from Bangladesh, for example, were consistently lower on impulse control. Forty-two percent of the Bengali (Bangladesh) adolescents reported they were constantly afraid; many admitted feeling inferior to other people, as well as feeling sadder, lonelier, and more vulnerable. Why? Context seems the most plausible explanation. This was the poorest of the countries sampled. Lack of economic opportunities and adequate medical care coupled with widespread disease and starvation might well lead to feelings of vulnerability and fear.

Other cross-national differences included the very high value placed on vocational and educational goals by American adolescents and the very low value placed on them by Hungarian and Israeli teenagers—probably because vocational choice is a complex and important developmental task for American adolescents. For most Israeli and Hungarian adolescents, choices are more limited or are largely predetermined by society.

It is not surprising that there were marked differences in the sexual attitudes of adolescents from some countries. In particular, Turkish and Taiwanese adolescents reported extremely conservative sexual attitudes and behaviors—clear evidence of the extent to which such attitudes are influenced by cultures (see Table 12.2). Similarly, Israeli adolescents reported the most positive family relationships, again not very surprising given the emphasis on family and community.

Storm and Stress? In spite of the very real differences that exist among adolescents of different cultures and different backgrounds, recall that among the most consistent findings of the Offer and associates (1988) study was that most adolescents are usually happy and optimistic. Furthermore, most are happy with their families and their homes; they are caring and compassionate; and they are confident in their abilities to cope with life. And, as we just saw, far more of them have positive than negative self-esteem.

So is this period, as G. Stanley Hall believed, a period of Sturm und Drang (storm and stress)? Hall had argued that this would be the case for most adolescents in all cultures because the mood swings, the irritability, and the conflict of this period are related directly to a dramatic increase in sex hormones. Most psychologists no longer believe this to be true (Lerner & Galambos, 1998). If the Offer and associates (1988) cross-national study were to be summarized in a single paragraph, it might read something like this: Contrary to what has been a popular view of adolescence since G. Stanley Hall's pronouncements about the storm and stress of this period, adolescence throughout the world is predominantly a positive, nonturbulent, energetic, growth-filled period.

TABLE 12.2
Sexual Self: Sample Items Showing Consistent Cross-National Differences Across Age and Gender*

ITEM	PERCENT ENDORSEMENT								
	Australia	Bangladesh	Hungary	Israel	Italy	Taiwan	Turkey	United States	West Germany
Dirty jokes are fun at times.	82	33	39	78	69	43	19	78	69
I think that girls/boys find me attractive.	53	63	58	68	55	41	59	73	63
Sexually I am way behind.	20	26	11	10	7	33	19	24	11
Thinking or talking about sex scares me.	7	50	13	6	7	27	22	10	6
Sexual experiences give me pleasure.	67	44	65	72	67	22	49	74	67
Having a girl-/boyfriend is important to me.	69	77	68	75	76	52	74	73	82

*Items presented (1) were on a scale on which at least one country was consistently high (or low) in all four age-by-gender cells and (2) were consistently high (or low) for that country for that scale. Consistently high (or low) was defined in terms of being in the upper (or lower) third of nine countries in all four age-by-gender cells. Percentages shown are the average percent endorsement for that item for the country across four age-by-gender cells.

Source: From *The Teenage World: Adolescents' Self-Image in Ten Countries* by D. O. Offer, E. Ostrov, K. Howard, and R. Atkinson, 1988, New York: Plenum. Reprinted by permission of the author and publisher.

Still, about 15% of North American adolescents describe themselves as anxious, depressed, confused, and emotionally empty (Offer, Ostrov, & Howard, 1984). This percentage is, in fact, significantly higher than for preadolescents. As we see later, adolescents are at far greater risk of engaging in any number of behaviors with potentially negative outcomes: unsafe sex, alcohol and substance abuse, school dropout, delinquency, suicide—to name only the most obvious. Clearly, there can be some storm and stress in adolescence.

Identity Status in Adolescence

When there are storms in adolescence, these are sometimes related to turbulence that occasionally surrounds the development of identity, of a sense of wholeness and purpose, of which we spoke earlier.

The notion that one of the most important aspects of all development is that of a sense of personal identity (**identity versus role diffusion**) is central to Erik Erikson's theory (discussed in Chapter 2). The main developmental crisis facing the adolescent, says Erikson (1968), is the conflict between accepting, choosing, or discovering an identity and doubt concerning choice of identities—hence an **identity crisis**.

Resolution of adolescents' identity crises can take a variety of forms—the most common of which is the selection of an identity that conforms to societal norms and to individuals' expectations of themselves. Erikson points out that one of the major

Paul Chesley/Tony Stone Images

Much of adolescence, theorists inform us, serves as a moratorium—a hiatus between childhood and adulthood. During this period, the adolescent is free to experiment with various ways of thinking and being—various identities, some of which may be negative in that they appear to run counter to generally established and expected standards of conduct, behavior, or dress. These experimental identities are typically temporary and are quite normal.

social functions of prolonged adolescence is simply to serve as a breathing space (an **adolescent moratorium**, in his terms) during which adolescents can experiment with different roles in their quest for identity. Erikson is not particularly alarmed that some of these roles constitute what he terms **negative identities** (delinquency and other forms of rebellion, for example), because in most cases they are temporary, eventually giving way to more acceptable and happier identities.

---

identity versus role diffusion An Erikson developmental stage spanning adolescence, marked by a struggle to establish a strong sense of identity, of self.

identity crisis In Erikson's theory, the main developmental crisis of the adolescent—specifically, the conflict that can arise when faced with a choice among various available roles (identities). The crisis is often related to the fact that some of these roles may be irresponsible, immature, and socially unacceptable—but appealing; and some of them may be more mature, more focused, more socially sanctioned—and sometimes, though not always, less appealing.

adolescent moratorium Erikson's term for the social function of the hiatus between childhood and adulthood. The adolescent period is a moratorium in that it gives the person some time to experiment with various identities.

negative identities Erikson's expression for the rebellious, nonconformist, antiestablishment roles with which adolescents sometimes experiment.

While in the transition between childhood and adulthood, the adolescent's **identity status** typically changes as crises come and go, and as the adolescent explores various commitments. Building on Erikson's work, Marcia (1966, 1993) identifies four distinct types of identity status, based on whether the adolescent has undergone (or is currently undergoing) a crisis and on whether a commitment has been made to a specific identity.

Identity Diffusion Adolescents in a state of identity diffusion are characterized by a total lack of commitment, as well as no experience with an identity crisis. These are individuals whose political, social, and religious beliefs are ambiguous or nonexistent, and who have no vocational aspirations. Identity diffusion is common in early adolescence, but sometimes persists much later. Individuals who have not developed a mature sense of identity by late adolescence are sometimes recognizable as full-time fun seekers (what Marcia calls "playboys") or as disturbed individuals characterized by high anxiety, low self-esteem, and lack of self-confidence (Marcia, 1980).

Foreclosure Foreclosure is a strong commitment to an identity without having experienced a crisis. Foreclosure is clearly illustrated in instances where political, religious, and vocational decisions have been made for the adolescent and are accepted without question. This is often the case, for example, in close-knit religious or political communities where the roles and the beliefs of each person are determined by others. It is also the case when adolescents simply allow parents, or sometimes peers, to make important identity-related decisions for them. These adolescents do not go through an identity crisis. Their most striking characteristics appear to be high adherence to authoritarian values of obedience and respect for authority (Marcia, 1980).

Moratorium Individuals As we saw earlier, Erikson believed that an important function of adolescence is to serve as a time during which it isn't necessary to be fully committed to one lifestyle, one vocation, one set of beliefs—a **moratorium** during which the adolescent can explore the alternatives that might be available. Moratorium adolescents have vague, changing commitments; in this sense, they are in crisis. But it is a useful crisis for most adolescents, because in the absence of a moratorium during which to explore, there is a danger of premature commitment (as in the case of foreclosure) or of continuing lack of commitment (as in identity diffusion).

Identity Achieved Adolescents who have experienced a crisis (a moratorium) and made a choice (a commitment) are described as identity achieved. Marcia (1980) reports that adolescents who have achieved an identity are more independent, respond better to stress, have more realistic goals, and have higher self-esteem than adolescents in any of the other three categories. However, he also emphasizes that identities are never static or absolutely permanent. Even when the adolescent appears to have achieved an identity, further changes often occur. For example, some college students move in and out of identity crises before finally achieving a permanent commitment. (See Table 12.3.)

THOUGHT CHALLENGE: *Peter Pan had the following conversation with Mrs. Darling one day:**
> *Peter: "Would you send me to school?"*
> *Mrs. Darling (obligingly): "Yes."*
> *Peter: "And then to an office?"*
> *Mrs. Darling: "Very soon."*
> *Peter (passionately): "I don't want to go to school and learn solemn things. No one is going to catch me, lady, and make me a man. I want always to be a little boy and to have fun."*

Peter Pan's character has since given its name to a condition labeled Peter Pan syndrome. *Which identity status do you suppose might best describe someone with Peter Pan syndrome?*

*James Barrie, *Peter Pan.*

---

identity status According to Erikson's theory (extended by Marcia), the extent and manner in which the adolescent has experienced, is experiencing, has resolved, or is resolving, an identity crisis—hence describable in terms of crisis and commitment.

foreclosure Marcia's term for the adoption of a ready-made identity.

moratorium Marcia's term for an adolescent stage marked by crisis and by vague, changing commitments; a time of exploration before commitment.

TABLE 12.3
Marcia's Descriptions of Identity Status in Terms of Crisis and Commitment

STATUS	CRISIS*	COMMITMENT	CHARACTERISTICS
Identity diffusion	No crisis	No commitment	Ambiguous belief systems; no vocational commitment
Foreclosure	No crisis	Strong commitment	Commitment predetermined by political, social, or religious affiliation
Moratorium	Crisis	No commitment	Period of exploring alternatives
Identity achieved	Crisis finished	Commitment made	Adultlike acceptance of social, religious, political, or vocational alternatives

*A *crisis* is defined as a period of active and conscious decision making during which various alternatives are examined and evaluated. *Commitment* is acceptance of a combination of political, social, religious, or vocational alternatives. Level of crisis and commitment may be different in each of these areas.

Common Pattern of Identity Development Researchers usually ascertain adolescents' identity status either through interviews or using measures such as Grotevant and Adams's (1984) *Extended Objective Measure of Ego Identity Status.* This 64-item questionnaire looks at adolescents' religious, occupational, political, philosophical, and social commitments.

Research indicates that most adolescents progress through some or all of these identity statuses in similar ways. Thus early adolescence is generally characterized by identity diffusion (no crisis; no commitment). This period is followed by the moratorium (a period of crisis; exploration of alternatives). Finally, adolescents achieve identity (crisis finished; commitment made). Of course there are exceptions to this pattern, most notably foreclosure individuals, who bypass the identity crises of adolescence by adopting a ready-made identity.

Career Preparation and Identity Formation We treat adolescents, especially older adolescents, differently than we do younger children, note Hart and Yates (1996). We give them more responsibility, and we expect more responsible behavior of them. Why? In a nutshell, because they have developed more adult identities.

It's important to note that Marcia's description of identity formation assumes that identity develops independently in different areas such as those relating to careers, schooling, and social relations. Not all adolescents will have achieved the same level of adult-like responsibility in each of these areas at the same time. For example, an adolescent who is married and has a child has achieved an apparently high level of identity (and concomitant responsibility) with respect to social relations. But that same adolescent might be at a stage of identity diffusion or moratorium regarding schooling and career development. That is, she might still be considering various alternatives, experimenting with different identities, and trying to develop a sense of purpose and continuity.

During adolescence, identity relating to schools and careers is often more important than identity having to do with social status or political or religious ideologies. As Blustein (1997) notes, this is largely because in contemporary industrialized societies, young adults are typically expected to develop a career before assuming adult social roles or developing political ideologies. This becomes increasingly true as the average age of marrying and of having a first child increases into the 20s or later. Preparing for a career, on the other hand, is something that most adolescents begin to think about well before leaving school. It is, as Kracke (1997) notes, a singularly important choice in identity formation.

Identity problems in the area of career preparation and development have often been related to high unemployment rates. Youth, and especially those who leave school early, make up a disproportionate percentage of the unemployed, note Meeus, Dekovic, and Ledema (1997). For some, unemployment is a source of considerable distress that can be manifested in adjustment problems including serious unhappiness, depression, and loss of self-esteem. But these authors also found that the reaction of different individuals to unemployment varies considerably. For many, the experience doesn't entail obvious negative consequences.

Ethnic Identity Formation

Achieving an identity, as we saw, goes beyond making a vocational commitment. Identity formation means arriving at some consistent, unified notion of what the self is, of its roles and beliefs, its aspirations, its strengths and weaknesses.

Minority Group Problems Most adolescents in North American cultures have relatively clear role models of acceptable and appropriate identities. But this is often not the case for children from ethnic minority groups. For many of these children, role models are contradictory and confusing. Sometimes there are conflicts among the various messages minority group children receive; often, too, there is prejudice. The North American First Nation (North American Indian) adolescent, explains Moran (1999), is uncertain about whether to identify with Native culture or with white culture. Schooling pressures may pull in one direction, parents in another. If the adolescent identifies too closely with the white culture, peers might label him "Whitey"; if he identifies too obviously with native culture he may be rejected by white society, and many doors leading to better employment or higher education may be closed to him.

So, too, with Chinese Canadians, report Lay and Verkuyten (1999), whose responses to the "Who am I?" questionnaire, a measure of identity formation, show considerable ambivalence. Self-perception, Lay and Verkuyten point out, is closely tied to group membership. But when you're uncertain about which group you belong to, your self-perception can be very unclear.

Ethnic identity confusion can be an enormous problem for African Americans, probably the most studied of all ethnic minority groups in North America. Wyatt (1999) points out that there has often been a sort of *invisibility* associated with being black in the United States. It's an invisibility caused partly by the stereotypes dominating the majority's perception of the minority—stereotypes that, for example, see blacks as "dangerous to themselves and to others" (Wyatt, p. 802). Stereotypes camouflage and hide the individual; when you look at a person and see only the stereotype, you can't see the person. Hence the individual becomes invisible. This, to put it mildly, can complicate the process of self-discovery.

The Meaning of Ethnic Identity Ethnic identity formation is a complex and difficult procedure. There is overwhelming agreement that it's fundamentally important; but there isn't so much agreement about exactly what it is or how it can be measured or studied. That it's important is evident in a variety of studies demonstrating that a strong sense of ethnic identity is positively related to measures of happiness and psychological well-being as well as to self-esteem, optimism, and achievement. And strong ethnic identity is negatively related to depression and loneliness (Roberts, 1999). Quintana and Vera (1999) also found that a strong sense of ethnic identity serves as a sort of buffer against prejudice. When you know clearly who you are, and when you are proud of who you are, prejudicial actions seem more invalid and less important.

Phinney (1990) reports that the phrase *ethnic identity* is not defined in about two-thirds of all studies of ethnic identity. Where it is defined, reference is usually made to *feelings* of belonging to an ethnic group, to *sharing* important things with the group (for example, language, values, beliefs), to *knowledge* about the group's history and characteristics, and to a strong sense of *self-identification*. Problems of ethnic identity formation, explains Brotman (1999), arise when two "opposing polarities demand the subject's allegiance at the same moment" (p. 418).

Paths to Ethnic Identity The minority group adolescent has at least four options regarding identity formation (Phinney & Devich-Navarro, 1997): assimilation, separation, marginalization, or biculturalism.

Assimilation occurs when the adolescent adopts the roles and norms of the majority culture

---

ethnic identity A person's perception of the strength of his or her connection to an ethnic group. Includes feelings and preferences relating to belongingness as well as knowledge and sharing of cultural values and history.

and rejects those of the minority group. This is the alternative that schools traditionally emphasized. And as we saw in Chapter 7, in spite of (or maybe because of) the increasingly multicultural nature of North American societies, there are many who advocate that English should be the only language taught in schools. Because ethnic identity is often closely tied with language, this position clearly encourages assimilation.

Marginalization occurs when the adolescent chooses to live within the majority culture but ends up only on the *margin*, an outcast, often rejected by both groups. Marginalization reflects unsuccessful ethnic identity formation, as well as unsuccessful assimilation. Rebellion and gang membership are common among marginalized youth, for whom the pressures and the confusion that surround identity formation are sometimes overwhelming.

Separation involves rejecting the dominant culture and instead embracing the values, norms, and lifestyles of the minority group. Separation may be manifested in separatist sentiment and sometimes even in militant actions.

Biculturalism describes a situation in which the adolescent attempts to adopt an identity that reflects identifying features of both the majority and the minority group. Many researchers in this area favor a bicultural approach to identity formation.

Research suggests that both parents and schools are centrally involved in successful biculturalism. For example, Quintana and Vera (1999) found the highest ethnic identity scores among children whose parents discussed ethnic topics with their chil-

dren—topics such as ethnic pride, prejudice, history, and cultural knowledge. Their sample included African, Japanese, and Mexican American youth and their parents. And multicultural education—that is, education that reflects an understanding and appreciation of different cultures and languages, and that accommodates the needs of children from different backgrounds—can do much to promote ethnic identity formation.

PARENTS AND PEERS

The development of self does not occur in a vacuum, as a consideration of ethnic identity so clearly illustrates. It occurs in a specific context, a niche characterized by a wealth of interactions and influences. Those occurring with peers and parents are among the most important.

Changing Relationships with Parents

Developmental psychologists generally agree that one of the things that happens throughout childhood and especially at adolescence is an emotional distancing of child from parents (Grotevant, 1994). At the risk of oversimplifying, we can thus describe the socialization of the adolescent in three stages based on changing relationships with parents. The first, a *preadolescent stage*, is marked by the child's high social, emotional, and physical dependence on parents, and is characterized by low conflict. The second, spanning early adolescence, involves increasing independence—that is, increasing emotional distancing—and sometimes increasing conflict as well. And the third, beginning in later adolescence, is marked by declining conflict and the achievement of relative independence.

Despite the near universality of the adolescent's emotional distancing from parents, it would be misleading to assume that adolescents and parents eventually end up far apart emotionally. The *emotional distancing* that occurs is relative: That is, adolescents are somewhat more emotionally independent from their parents than are preadolescents. Nevertheless, adolescents and parents typically remain very closely attached. This attachment, Grotevant (1994) explains, serves as a buffer for

---

assimilation In sociology, a term referring to the process by which members of ethnic minority groups adopt the cultural trappings of the dominant group, discarding those of the minority.

marginalization A sociological term referring to a condition in which minority group members have been unsuccessful in becoming part of the dominant cultural group, but have removed themselves from effective membership in the minority group. Hence they are out of one group (the minority group), but only on the fringe (margin) of the other.

separation In sociology, refers to actively rejecting the values and norms of the dominant group and embracing those of one's ethnic minority group.

biculturalism A process whereby an individual attempts to adopt roles and identities that reflect more than one cultural reality—typically both the majority and the minority group to which the individual belongs.

adolescents, protecting them from some of the stresses and anxieties of adjusting to a complex world. In addition, continued strong attachment to parents has repeatedly been shown to be closely related to the development of positive self-image. In a study of 167 adolescents, O'Koon (1997) found not only that strong attachments to parents continued right into late adolescence (and presumably beyond), but that those adolescents who were most attached to their parents were also, on average, those with the highest self-esteem.

Parenting Adolescents The transition from childhood to adulthood is not only a question of emotional distancing but also one of earning or being assigned adult responsibilities, notes Brannen (1996). However, contemporary industrialized societies often give young people conflicting messages concerning both their rights and their responsibilities. As we have seen, in these *continuous* societies there typically isn't a single accepted age at which a child becomes adult—nor a single act or event ensuring that status. Thus, adolescents may be allowed to vote at one age, to purchase alcohol or tobacco at another, to get married at yet a different age, perhaps to go to war at yet another. These contradictions don't simplify the task of parenting adolescents.

Much of parenting involves protecting children from their own immaturity. For young children, whose immaturity is clearly reflected in their dependence, this role poses little conflict. But for adolescents, whose immaturity is less (and who, in most cases, don't easily recognize their immaturity), parenting is a far more difficult function. Yet, as Glasgow and associates (1997) point out following an investigation of the effect of parenting styles on adolescents, it's clear that the importance of parenting doesn't decline as children become adolescents. Their study corroborates the often replicated finding that, at least in North America, *authoritative* parenting presents clear advantages over other parenting styles—and especially over *permissive indifferent* (or *neglectful*) parenting.

Parenting adolescents involves more than simply protecting them from their immaturity. It also includes providing basic resources and care, guiding and supporting development (providing opportunities for intellectual, social, emotional, and spiritual growth; fostering self-esteem), and advocacy (supporting and helping adolescents in relation to institutions or groups such as schools and employers). As we saw in Chapter 8, authoritative and even authoritarian parents are likely to at least attempt to provide all these dimensions of care; permissive parents, especially if they are neglectful rather than indulgent, are not.

Parent-Adolescent Conflict For centuries, parents, philosophers, and other sages have often complained that youth is rebellious and noncompliant, and that parenting is a difficult and thankless job. There are several reasons why today's parents might have more justification for these complaints.

1. The period of adolescence has lengthened in all industrialized countries. In the days of our great-foreparents, many youngsters made a swift transition from childhood to work and to domestic responsibilities—and consequently to emotional and financial independence. Now most adolescents attend schools and postsecondary institutions through their teen years and often well beyond. And many remain economically dependent on the family for all or much of that time. This situation has led to greater uncertainty about the responsibilities of parents.

2. In industrialized countries, the world changes rapidly, becomes increasingly complicated, and presents many competing sources of information and values. Parents are often confused about how best to prepare adolescents for entry into an increasingly complicated and rapidly changing world.

3. There are now more dangers to worry about—high-risk and potentially harmful activities, substances, and influences (such as drugs, radical cults, and fast automobiles).

4. Increases in family breakup and increased mobility of family members have led to an erosion of the family, so that parents of adolescents have fewer sources of advice or support.

Partly because of the responsibilities and difficulties of parenting adolescents, and partly because of the changing roles and relationships of parents and adolescents, this period frequently involves conflict. The greatest conflict occurs in early adolescence (during puberty) and often declines in later adolescence. The reasons for this, suggest Paikoff and Brooks-Gunn (1991), is that conflict typically arises because the changing needs and interests of the adolescent require a readjustment in the family system. Once this adjustment has been made, conflict declines. And where it doesn't, then perhaps the adolescent becomes an **early home leaver**.

Early Home Leavers

There are, of course, a vast number of reasons why an adolescent might be an early home leaver or a **late home leaver**. Clearly, parent-adolescent conflict is not the principal reason why children leave home. In fact, some evidence shows that where parent-adolescent relationships are warmest and most positive, adolescents find it easier to leave home, and even to move farther away geographically (Sherrod, 1996). And in some cases, where relations have been conflicted and strained, adolescents remain close, almost as though they had not quite finished their growing up. Still, one of the better predictors of children leaving home early, reports Tang (1997), is the structure of the family. Specifically, after an analysis of nearly 10,000 cases of early (before age 18), on-time (between ages 18 and 24), and late (after age 25) home leavers, Tang found that those most likely to leave home early were from nonbiological or nonintact families. This may be partly because of greater caregiver-adolescent conflict in these families; it might also be because attachments might not be as close. (See *Across Cultures:* "Street Children.")

Peer Groups in Adolescence

It would be misleading to suggest that parents and their adolescents are typically in conflict. In fact, as Smetana (1995) points out, some important areas of parent-child interaction are seldom the basis of conflict. For example, parents and their adolescents typically agree about most larger moral issues, almost as if children had adopted their parents' moral beliefs and made them their own. Where there is conflict, notes Smetana, it typically has to do with interpersonal relations—most often with sibling relationships or with peer relationships. It is hardly surprising that Bibby and Posterski (1992), following their survey of nearly 4,000 adolescents, ascribe "turbulence on the home front" to conflict over peer relationships. In this survey, freedom and friendship ranked first and second in importance; family life was a distant ninth, but was still selected by 60% of respondents as "very important" (see Figure 12.1).

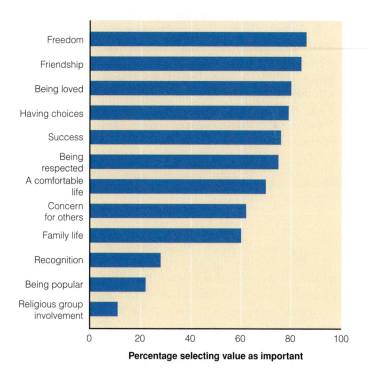

FIGURE 12.1 Percentage of Canadian adolescents selecting each value as "very important." Values were presented as "terminal" or "end-state"—as something desirable and worth striving for, for the future. Source: R. W. Bibby and D. C. Posterski, *Teen trends: A nation in motion*, Toronto: Stoddart Publishing Co., 1992, p. 15. Reprinted by permission of Stoddart Publishing Co., Ltd.

early home leaver For research purposes, often defined as someone who leaves home before age 18 (the typical age of high school graduation).

late home leaver For research purposes, someone who leaves home after the age of 24.

Street Children

Buzz "Hey, I don't got no last f----- name" might be 16 years old—he thinks. "Could be somethin' else, man," he says. "Like birthdays suck anyway."

He's not sure how long he's been on the street. When asked where he sleeps, he shrugs. "Depends on the weather. Depends if I got a place," he says.

Buzz is a street child. The term *street children* describes children who spend most of their time away from home. Researchers often distinguish between "home-based" homeless children, many of whom have at least some contact with their families, and "street-based" children, who have essentially no family contact. Many street children, like Buzz, lose track of time in their unstructured lives. They can't remember how long they've been on the street. Often, they can't even tell you clearly everything they did just yesterday (le Roux & Smith, 1998c).

Buzz is one of the estimated 30 to 170 million street children in the world (Scanlon et al., 1998). The enormous range in estimates shows just how hard it is to count street children. Besides, street children are viewed as a problem and an embarrassment in many countries; not everyone is willing to admit that the problem even exists. In most countries, street children are seen as deviant, as criminals, as dangerous, or at least as a nuisance (le Roux & Smith, 1998a). In some countries, they are thrown into jail to get them off the streets; in others, they are simply killed—sometimes by self-appointed "death squads." For example, a study in Brazil uncovered 457 murders of street children in a 7-month period; there is no

There are an estimated 30 to 170 million street children in the world.

Michael Newman/PhotoEdit

way of knowing how many murders were not uncovered (Unger et al., 1998).

Street children are a worldwide phenomenon. In the United States, an estimated 750,000 to 1.5 million adolescents run away or are ejected from their homes each year. Not all become permanently homeless, but many do. Who are they? What do they do? Why do they run from home?

In Third World countries, reports le Roux (1996a), street children are mostly boys, most of whom have left their homes

(continued on next page)

It's clear that during adolescence, peer relationships become even more important than they were in preadolescence. In all cultures, explains Schneider (1999), children appear motivated to become competent in both knowledge and in social interactions that will pave their way to *belonging* to the group. At adolescence, the urge to belong becomes stronger, more urgent. Not only does the peer group satisfy emotional needs, but it is an important source of information and opportunity for socialization. The adolescent peer group is, in many ways, like a separate culture that eases transition from childhood to adulthood.

Common North American Peer Groups Adolescent peer groups vary in size, interests, social backgrounds, and structure. They might consist of two or three like-sexed persons (buddies, pals, best friends), larger groups of like-sexed individuals, or couples. Yet another type of peer group comprises persons of both sexes who "hang out" together. In addition, there are gangs—close-knit groups of

ACROSS CULTURES

Street Children (continued)

for good. In more developed countries, street children are as likely to be girls. In Unger and associates' (1998) study of U.S. street children, numbers of girls and boys were almost equal.

Street children leave home for a variety of reasons. In Third World countries, they are often victims of what is sometimes labeled *economic violence*: Poverty, unemployment, population growth, and urban migration all contribute to growing numbers of street children. In more developed countries, conflict with parents, physical and sexual abuse, and parental separation or divorce are often implicated. So too is the young adolescent's greater propensity for sensation seeking and risk taking. But street children aren't always society's dropouts, explain le Roux and Smith (1998b). Although many have low self-esteem, and many are fleeing (rather than facing) problems, only a relatively small percentage have significant emotional or behavioral problems.

The risks the street child faces are considerable. They include risks to physical health, often associated with drug use (some studies indicate that about 80% of street children regularly use drugs, often inhalants); risks to sexual health (unprotected sex, anal sex, commercial sex, rape, and pregnancy are all common); risks to mental health (difficult to determine); and risks of violence and even extermination (Scanlon et al., 1998).

Many street children are running away from something—or being driven away. But for many, life on the street has its own attractions. Unfortunately, many of these attractions are high risk and illegal. One study of 245 street children in

California (ages 12 to 15) revealed very high rates of high-risk and problem behaviors: more than one-third were associated with gangs; almost half were involved in illegal activities including prostitution, drug dealing, theft, and assault

In much of the world, there is now increasing emphasis on doing things *for* street children, rather than *to* them. Assistance programs sometimes attempt to provide them with medical and health information and care; often, attempts are made to reunite them with their families (Scanlon et al., 1998). But in many parts of the world, they are still detained or imprisoned—or driven off the streets, or even killed.

To Think About: I have a relative who, by our definitions, has been a street child since he dropped out of school—or was invited to leave—for the last time in ninth or tenth grade. Technically, he continues to live at home and to take money from his parents. But he spends all his days and most of his nights hanging out with an amorphous group on the street. Mostly they sit on blankets on a busy street asking passersby for money. Sometimes one of them plays a guitar. Usually they have at least one dog with them.

This relative is now 22 years old. He is sometimes a charming, well-spoken, handsome lad. When he deigns to answer his parents' concerns, he insists he has no interest in doing anything else with his life.

Do you think anything can, or should, be done for (or to) this relative?

individuals distinguished by their conflict with authority (more about gangs later). Most adolescents belong to several groups at the same time. Indeed, friends (who are typically part of the peer groups) are the adolescent's most common source of enjoyment (Bibby & Posterski, 1992).

All North American high schools, Brown and colleagues (1993) note following a survey of six different U.S. schools, appear to have six distinct peer groups (or "crowds"): For example, there are "jocks," students committed to athletics and not overly focused on academics, but nevertheless interested in pleasing teachers and in getting acceptable grades. Their interest in drugs is generally limited to alcohol. The jocks are one of two "elite" peer groups; the other is the "populars," students who are more strongly committed to academics than the jocks, but who are also "moderately" interested in drug use and in delinquent behavior.

At the opposite end of the scale in social status are a group labeled "outcasts" and made up of "loners" and "nerds"—children who are socially awkward and inept, and whose social status is very low. The outcast group also includes other smaller groups such as "druggies," "greasers," and others who are heavily involved in drug use or delinquency, and who are often rebellious in school and society. The values and behavior of the outcast group stand in sharp contrast to those of the "brains," who are strongly focused on academic achievement, value close relationships with parents and authority, and carefully avoid drugs and delinquency.

Finally, the largest peer group is composed of "normals." Brown and colleagues (1993) note that these children tend to avoid deviant activities but are not clearly or strongly enough focused on any other activity to be identified as belonging to another distinct group (see Figure 12.2).

Perhaps the most revealing finding of the Brown investigation is that parents play a critical role in determining their children's most likely peer affiliations. Not only are parents instrumental in shaping their children's social skills and values, but they also exercise considerable influence over peer choice through their selection of neighborhoods in which to live as well as through their selection of schools, school programs, and leisure activities (such as sports). Brown and colleagues (1993) report that some specific parenting practices—such as monitoring the adolescent's activities, encouraging achievement (academic or athletic), and being involved in joint decision making with the adolescent—are closely reflected in adolescent behaviors and values, especially regarding things like academic achievement and drug use.

The influence of parents on adolescents may also be evident in the observation that brains tended to be overrepresented among children living in intact families, and that children from stepfamilies or one-parent families were underrepresented among brains but overrepresented among druggies. As Brown and associates (1993) put it, "Parenting practices and family background characteristics cannot determine a teenager's crowd affiliation, but their influence should not be discounted" (p. 478).

Peer Acceptance and Rejection The positive effects of peer acceptance and the negative effects of rejection are clear. As we saw in Chapter 10, peer rejection has been linked with emotional problems, school problems, child victimization, loneliness, and other unhappy eventualities. In contrast, peer acceptance, reflected in friendships and popularity, has been linked with much happier developmental outcomes.

Classification	Description
Popular	Socially competent; academically oriented; moderately involved in drugs and delinquency
Jock	Focused on athletics; drug involvement limited to alcohol; interested in acceptable grades and good relations with parents and teachers
Brain	Strong focus on academic achievement; close relationships with teachers; pointed avoidance of drugs and delinquency
Normal	Largest group; the "average"; avoid deviant activities; no overriding focus on drugs or achievement
Druggie	Strong focus on drugs; delinquency; inattentive to school and authority
Outcast	"Loners" and "nerds"; low social competence, low self-image; low involvement in deviant behavior; average or above-average academic achievement

Normal 19%
Druggie 6%
Brain 9%
Outcast 18%
Jock 7%
Popular 11%
Mixed or unclassified 30%

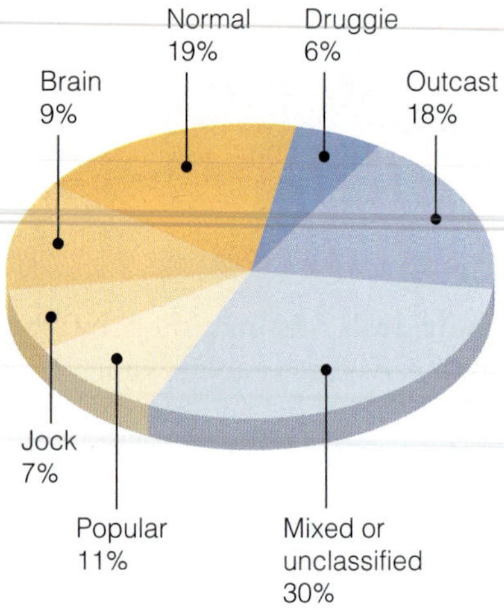

FIGURE 12.2 "Crowds" in the typical U.S. high school. These six groups accounted for 70% of the 3,781 students who were rated in a study of six high schools. Source: Based on Brown et al., 1993.

In adolescence, peer rejection is often implicated in school dropouts, delinquency, or other forms of social maladjustment (Miller-Johnson et al., 1999). This of course doesn't mean that peer rejection *causes* these developmental outcomes. It might be equally reasonable to suppose that the factors responsible for the outcomes are the very factors that cause children to be rejected by peers in the first place.

The characteristics of adolescents who are well liked by their peers are similar to the qualities of well-liked school-age children described in Chapter 10. Adolescents who are friendly, sociable, cheerful, and active—as opposed to hostile, withdrawn, and unsociable—are most liked by their peers.

Solitude

Still, in spite of their insistent need for the companionship of friends and peers, adolescents spend about a fourth of their *waking* hours alone, reports Larson (1999). In fact, on average, they spend *more*, rather than *less*, time alone as they move from childhood into adolescence. And most of the time, they do so voluntarily rather than because they have no friends, or because other circumstances force them to be alone.

Is **solitude** good or bad for the adolescent? The question is probably too simple for a complex issue, but Bucholz and Catton (1999) argue that aloneness is necessary for human growth. Even infants need to be alone, to rest from interacting with their caregivers, say Buchholz and Helbraun (1999). Children and adults are no different. When they sense the need to be alone, they withdraw from the group. Significantly, Larson (1997) found a positive relationship between time spent alone by adolescents and measures of their contentment and psychological well-being—providing the adolescent didn't spend an inordinate amount of time in solitude. In his study of 483 children from fifth through ninth grade, he found that the best-adjusted youngsters

Adolescent peer groups tend to consist of individuals of similar ages. Adolescents who are friendly and outgoing are most liked by their peers.

© Wartenberg/Picture Press/Corbis

were those who spent an intermediate amount of time alone.

Common sense has sometimes suggested that adolescent girls spend significantly more time than boys in conversation, and correspondingly less time in solitude. As is often her habit, common sense is again only half right. Following a survey of more than 2,000 seventh and ninth grade boys and girls, Smith (1997) reports that girls do, indeed, spend more time in conversation than do boys. But they also spend more time alone. That is one gender difference common sense might not have been gifted enough to see; are there others?

solitude A state of aloneness. Sometimes forced on those who have no friends and who cannot, or will not, buy companionship. Also, a state chosen by those who simply prefer to be alone, at least part of the time.

▛ GENDER STEREOTYPES AND DIFFERENCES

Perhaps there are other gender differences. But if we're to be informed clearly in this area, we'll have to look to science rather than to common sense.

Science tells us, first, what common sense already knew: Probably the most salient of all human characteristics are those that indicate membership in one of two categories: male or female. As biological categories, male and female are relatively easily identified and defined. But at another level, these are psychological and sociological categories. And here, science struggles a little more.

These psychological and sociological categories, science tells us, are evident in the sometimes dramatic (and sometimes very subtle) differences in the behaviors that are expected of males and females—hence that are considered masculine or feminine. These differences in behavior, together with the attitudes and personality characteristics associated with them, are what define gender roles (sex roles). Gender refers specifically to the psychological characteristics typically associated with biological sex. Thus there are two sexes, male and female, and two corresponding genders, masculine and feminine. Bem (1974) also argues that there are individuals who share relatively equally the characteristics of both genders, and labels these individuals androgynous. The learning of sex-appropriate behavior (of gender roles) is referred to as gender typing. Explanations of gender typing are presented in Chapter 8.

Common Gender-Role Stereotypes

Very early in life, children begin to learn about the behaviors their culture finds acceptable and desirable for their sex. For example, in North America, boys might learn to play with toy trucks and guns, to be interested in wrestling and play fighting, and to engage in boisterous, loud sports. Girls might learn to play with dolls and houses, to be interested in arts and books, and to like to cook and sew. As we saw in Chapter 8, both the toys they select and those their parents select for them tend to be "sex typed." These, and many other activities and interests, are aspects of the **sexual stereotypes** that characterize our societies.

Sexual stereotypes are firmly established and typically unquestioned beliefs about male-female differences. In some cases, they are superficial and trivial; in others, they are more fundamental. Some might reflect basic, undeniable anatomical differences; others are influenced more by context. For example, Biernat (1993) found that children typically judged that males were taller in photographs showing a male and female pair of *equal height*. However, when the photographs were of a male and female pair of seventh-grade children, the girl tended to be judged taller. Here is an example of a sexual stereotype that reflects actual experience and is, in fact, accurate. Unfortunately, not all stereotypes are accurate. Nor are all just.

Stereotypes are clearly evident in the workplace, for example, where gender-linked beliefs held by both men and women often determine not only which jobs will be available for either sex but also which jobs will be gladly accepted by one or the other (Ridgeway, 1997). In general, North American sexual stereotypes associate the male figure with active, work-oriented, and positively evaluated activities, and the female figure with more passive, home-oriented, and less positively evaluated roles (Williams, Satterwhite, & Best, 1999). Not surprisingly, Morrison and Rosales-Ruiz (1997) found that male adolescents were more likely than females to hold these stereotypes. However, in some respects, sexual stereotypes are biased *against* men, note Fiebert and Meyer (1997) following a survey of sexual stereotypes of college students. For example, women are seen as more caring, more nurturant, and less aggressive than men.

Gender-Role Preference: The Sex-Change Question

"If you woke up tomorrow and discovered that you were a girl (boy), how would your life be different?" Tavris and Baumgartner (1983) asked a group of

---

sexual stereotype A preconceived and typically unexamined belief about gender differences and gender roles.

American children. "Terrible," "A catastrophe," "I would immediately commit suicide" were some typical boys' answers. But girls responded quite differently: "Great," "Now I can do what I want," "Now I can be happy."

When Intons-Peterson (1988) replicated this study five years later, using the same question, there were no surprises. Boys still responded negatively to the thought of becoming female. They saw girls as more passive, weaker, more restricted in their activities, more emotional, and burdened by menstruation. And although most girls were content with their gender, many responded positively to the thought of being male. They saw males as more active, less constrained, better able to travel and to develop a career.

When Intons-Peterson (1988) compared responses of Swedish and American adolescents (ages 11, 14, and 18), she found the same patterns in both cultures. Males were still seen as hard-driving, aggressive, "macho"; females were seen as less aggressive, gentler. Of interest, however, is that differences tended to be less extreme in Sweden than in the United States. Intons-Peterson attributes this to the Swedish government's explicit family-based social program aimed at equalizing the sexes. And these gender stereotypes and preferences are more apparent for the 18-year-olds than for the younger group, especially in Sweden. This might be evidence that attempts to eradicate sex stereotypes and to achieve greater gender equality are having an effect.

Gender Differences

Gender stereotypes reflect widely held beliefs about gender. Some of these, especially if they have to do with biological differences, may well be accurate; and others, especially those relating to psychological differences, may well be dead wrong.

Biological Differences We know, for example, that there are some real biological and physical differences related to anatomical sex. Some are obvious: Males are taller and heavier than females (except for a brief period in late childhood); females mature approximately two years earlier than males; beginning from puberty, male blood pressure is higher than that of females; female heart rate is between two and six beats higher than that of males; fat-free mass in males is relatively higher than in females, as is metabolic rate; and among males, physical energy is greater, recuperative time is less, and muscle fatigue is slower.

In many ways, however, males are the weaker sex—even from the very beginning. About 50% more sperm bear the male (Y) than the female (X) sex chromosome; but there aren't 150 male infants born for every 100 females, because the male sperm is more fragile. And so it continues throughout life. At birth, there are about 105 males for every 100 females, but males are more vulnerable to most infections and diseases, so that by adolescence, numbers of males and females surviving are approximately equal; by age 65, there are almost 150 females living for every 100 males (U.S. Bureau of the Census, 1998).

Not only are males more fragile and less long-lived, but they are also more prone to learning, speech, and behavior disorders, greatly overrepresented among the retarded and the mentally disordered, and more prone to bed-wetting, night terrors, and hyperactivity (Blum, 1997).

Psychological Differences Biological differences between the sexes are generally clear; psychological differences are far less obvious and less certain.

In an early review and summary of much of the important research in this area, Maccoby and Jacklin (1974) had concluded that there are clear differences between the sexes in four areas: verbal ability (favoring females); visual/spatial ability (favoring males); mathematical ability (favoring males); and aggressiveness (lower among females).

But at least some of these gender differences no longer seem as apparent now as they did in 1974—evidence, perhaps, that they resulted mainly from socialization; and evidence, too, of rapidly changing cultural contexts.

Verbal Ability For example, the once-apparent greater verbal ability of females relative to males no longer appears very general, is usually very small, and is not apparent at early ages. In fact, in a large-scale survey of cognitive abilities among young adolescents, Rosen (1995) found no significant differences between boys and girls on measures of verbal ability. Similarly, Robinson and associates (1996) found no gender differences in verbal measures for high-ability preschoolers.

Visual/Spatial Ability Males often do better than females in tests of visual/spatial ability, beginning even in the preschool period (Livesey & Intili, 1996), and these differences appear to be general across a variety of cultures. For example, Amponsah and Krekling (1997) found significant, and highly similar, gender differences on measures of spatial/visual ability among adults in Ghana and Norway. Tests of spatial ability require the subject to visualize three-dimensional objects and be able to rotate or otherwise manipulate them mentally. For example, a three-dimensional block design test is often used with young children. There isn't a great deal of information about the importance of spatial ability, although some researchers argue that this gender difference may be related to differences in mathematics achievement. It is also apparent in map-reading skills.

Mathematics and Science There is some evidence that males perform better than females in mathematical skills, beginning in early elementary school (Davenport et al., 1998). The same appears to be true for physical sciences such as chemistry and physics, with gender differences in these subjects *increasing* after adolescence; but it is not the case for life sciences (Burkam, Lee, & Smerdon, 1997).

In mathematics, differences are most evident at the highest levels of mathematics achievement, where males consistently outnumber females. Hedges and Friedman (1993) report that there are about twice as many males as females in the top 5% in tests of mathematical ability—and about six times more in the top 1%. It is interesting that gender differences in mathematics and science are much smaller in the earlier years. Possibly, some of these differences result from girls often taking different math courses in high school, suggest Davenport et al. (1998). This in turn may be related

to different, culturally influenced, interests and vocational aspirations. For example, Hyde and Jaffee (1998) suggest that gender stereotypes about the different interests and abilities of boys and girls may lead teachers and parents to treat them differently and to expect different things of them. Thus research suggests that girls participate less than boys in science laboratory activities (Jovanovic & King, 1998). But when courses are modified to encourage active female participation, gender differences can be reduced (Burkam, Lee, & Smerdon, 1997).

Significantly, in the same way that gender differences in verbal performance have declined—and in many cases, completely disappeared—so too have differences in mathematics performance (Hyde, Fennema, & Lamon, 1990).

Aggression As we saw in Chapter 10, males are generally more aggressive than females (Windle & Windle, 1995). Recall, however, that this conclusion applies primarily to overt aggression—that is, to physical and verbal aggression. There is now evidence that females may be equally aggressive, but in relational aggression (social aggression) rather than overt aggression (Galen and Underwood, 1997). Overt aggression seeks to do physical harm; its methods include kicking, punching, pushing, and breaking or ripping off extremities. Social aggression seeks to do harm by disrupting peer relations; its methods include ridicule, exclusion, contempt, disdain, and vicious gossip.

Gender differences in overt aggression appear to have a biological as well as a cultural basis. For example, physical aggression has been shown to be related to the male sex hormone, testosterone. But because aggression is strongly influenced by culture, gender differences in aggression are sometimes very different in different sociocultural contexts (Mead, 1935).

A Conclusion Studies of gender differences in academic achievement reveal some small and declining differences, largely explainable by culturally based interests and opportunities. The studies do not provide data that would be sufficient for making inferences about specific individuals. Gender differences in height and strength are far more significant and far more stable. So are gender differences in career accessibility and in earning power, as well as in social attitudes toward careers and roles most appropriate for males and females (Lobel & Shavit, 1997). Not only are psychological gender differences very small, but they may not be very important. It might be far more useful to try to understand how interests and abilities develop and interact.

SEXUALITY AND ADOLESCENT PREGNANCY

A common sexual stereotype, note Baldwin and Baldwin (1997), is that males are more interested in sex *for purely physical reasons* than are females. However, science has not yet determined whether this stereotype is accurate. What science does indicate is that beginning early in adolescence and continuing until it doesn't matter any more, most males and females are very much interested in sex.

In psychology, sex is many things. To begin with, of course, it is simply a category—male or female—that is usually easily defined in biological terms. Sex is also a psychoanalytic concept which, in Freud's writings, becomes the source of energy that motivates all of us from birth to death.

Sex is also more than a psychoanalytic term or a biological dichotomy. It can mean (as it does in this section) nothing more or less complicated than the physical union between male and female (and other variations), with its accompanying desires and fantasies.

Sexual Beliefs and Behavior

There have been some major changes in sexual attitudes and behavior in recent decades. These are reflected in three areas: male-female difference evident in standards of conduct, attitudes toward sexual behavior, and age of sexual initiation.

The Double Standard The old sexual double standard has largely crumbled in many industrialized societies. This standard said, basically, "Boys will be boys; but girls, well, they should behave." In the 1950s, when Kinsey and associates (1948, 1953) first began to research sexual activity, the standard was in full force. At that time, most males reported experiencing orgasm before marriage, but only 30% of females reported doing so. By the mid-1960s, incidence of premarital intercourse among females had risen to about 40%—still some distance shy of males' reported 60% (Packard, 1968). By the 1980s, however, the numbers were about equal at around 75% or 80% (Darling, Kallen, & Van Dusen, 1984). By the 1990s, percentages for females had increased even more to around 80% to 85% (Chase-Lansdale & Brooks-Gunn, 1994) (see Figure 12.3). Now, most surveys of sexual behavior find little difference between male and female incidence of intercourse, although, there is some evidence that teenagers may now be *less* sexually active (for example, McCabe & Cummins, 1998).

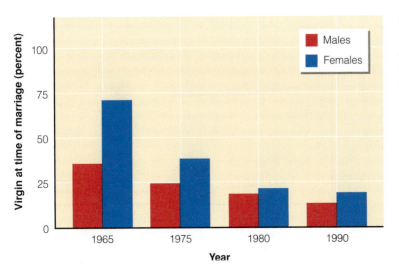

FIGURE 12.3 One manifestation of the sexual revolution: the decline in percentage of people who claim to be virgins at the time of marriage—a more dramatic revolution for women than for men.

Attitudes toward Sexuality In recent decades, attitudes toward sexuality have changed dramatically. These changes are reflected not only in the demise of the double standard but also in an increased openness about sexuality and in a wider acceptance of nonmarital sex. This does not mean that sex has become totally casual and matter-of-fact among today's adolescents. In fact, the vast majority of teenagers do not think it is appropriate to have intercourse when dating casually, but more than half believe it proper when in love and dating only one person (Roche & Ramsbey, 1993). For most adolescents, the critical factor is whether the partners have a caring and committed relationship. The new standard holds that sexual activity is permitted for both sexes providing there is affection between partners. It's a standard that appears to be shared both by adults and adolescents. For example, Bibby (1995) reports that only about 20% of adults think nonmarital sex is always or almost always wrong. However, a striking 85% think extramarital sex is always or almost always wrong. And the percentage of 18- to 35-year-olds who approve of extramarital sex *dropped* from 28% to 11% (Figure 12.4) between 1975 and 1995 (Bibby, 1995).

Age of Initiation Average age of sexual initiation has also declined significantly since the days of our grandparents. A study of more than 600 Italian adolescents found that about a third of the girls and a fourth of the boys had had sexual intercourse before age 15 (Zani, 1991). Smith (1997) reports similar findings for the United States, as do Cooksey, Rindfuss, and Guilkey (1996). The average age of first intercourse in the United States appears to be between 16 and 17 for men and between 17 and 18 for women, with significant numbers having first intercourse well before then (Boyer, 1998).

Early initiation of sexual activity is linked with numerous risks, including a higher probability of having multiple sex partners and a correspondingly higher risk of acquiring a sexually transmitted disease (more about these shortly), as well as higher rates of pregnancy (Kellogg, Hoffman, & Taylor, 1999). Unfortunately, very young age of sexual initiation, especially among women, is often involuntary. Boyer (1998) reports a survey in which 74% of the women who had experienced sexual intercourse before age 14 had done so involuntarily.

Among the most obvious antecedents of sexual activity are the biological changes of pubescence.

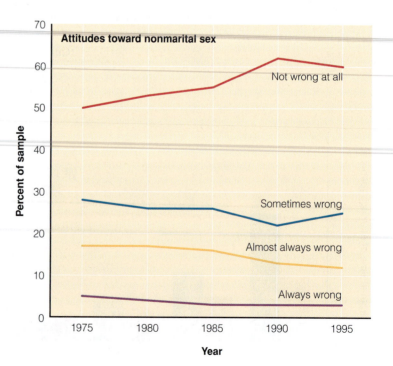

FIGURE 12.4 Increasing approval of *nonmarital* sex, 1975 through 1995, for 18- to 35-year-olds. In contrast, approval of *extramarital* sex has actually decreased during this 20-year period. Source: R. W. Bibby (1995). *The Bibby report: Social trends Canadian style.* Toronto, Ont.: Stoddart. Reprinted by permission.

Changes in hormone levels affect sexual arousal directly; in addition, changes in secondary sexual characteristics, such as breast enlargement in the girl or lowering of the boy's voice, may serve as important sexually linked stimuli. Other important factors linked to age of first sexual intercourse include some specific events and behaviors, including parental divorce, drug use, and age of dating (Dorius, Heaton, & Steffan, 1993). Peers also influence whether an adolescent is likely to engage in sexual intercourse. Significantly, adolescents typically overestimate the amount of sexual activity engaged in by their peers, and underestimate the age of first intercourse (Roche & Ramsbey, 1993; Zani, 1991). (See Figure 12.5.)

Masturbation The most common form of sexual outlet for adolescent males and females is masturbation. Although contemporary attitudes toward masturbation are that it is normal, pleasurable, and harmless, some adolescents continue to feel guilty and ashamed about masturbating. Males masturbate more frequently than females, and often have more liberal attitudes toward the acceptability of masturbation (Elkind, 1998).

For males, first ejaculation (spermarche), sometimes through a nocturnal emission or through masturbation or intercourse, is usually the first sign of pubescence. But unlike the girls' menarche, for boys it is often a secretive affair. Zani (1991) notes that because of males' reluctance to admit ignorance or innocence in sexual matters, most do not seek information.

Adolescent Pregnancy

Estimates suggest that there are as many as 12 million sexually active teenagers in the United States— 7 million males and 5 million females. Of the 5 million or so sexually active females, approximately 1 million become pregnant each year (see *At a Glance:* "Births to Unmarried Teenagers," and Figure 12.6). Teenagers account for 13.1% of all births in the United States; they also account for more than 20% of all abortions (U.S. Bureau of the Census, 1998).

Who gets pregnant? Why? What are the outcomes and implications of teenage pregnancy?

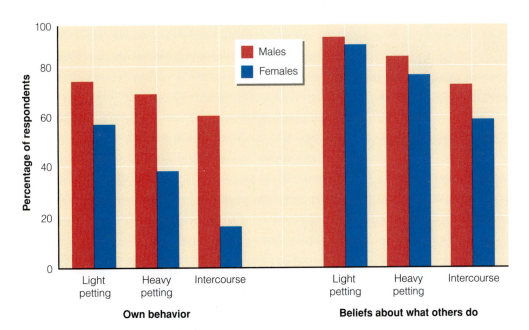

FIGURE 12.5 Teenagers' (ages 18 or 19) reported sexual behavior and their beliefs about what others do when dating and in love. Source: Based on data reported by J. P. Roche & T. W. Ramsbey (1993). *Premarital sexuality: A five-year follow-up study of attitudes and behavior by dating stage.* Adolescence 28: 67–80.

AT A GLANCE

Births to Unmarried Teenagers

The number of infants being born to unmarried women has increased enormously. In the United States in 1970, about 1 in 10 births (10.7%) was to an unmarried mother; by 1995 the proportion had climbed to about 1 in 3 (32%). Figures are similar in Canada, where 63.6% of all births in 1997 were to married women, 25.9% were to never-married women, and the others were to women classified as widowed, divorced, or separated. Unmarried teen mothers (ages 15–19) account for nearly a third of all births to unmarried women in the United States (30.8%). About one third of all teen pregnancies end in induced abortions. In Canada, 25% of teen mothers were single in 1974; by 1994, 81% were single (*Canada Yearbook, 1999*). (Figure 12.6)

David Young-Wolff/Tony Stone Images

In North America, between one-quarter and one-third of all births are to unmarried women, one-third of whom are teenagers.

FIGURE 12.6 Rise in births to unmarried U.S. teenage mothers (15 to 19), 1970–1995. Source: U.S. Bureau of the Census (1996, p. 80; 1998, p. 81).

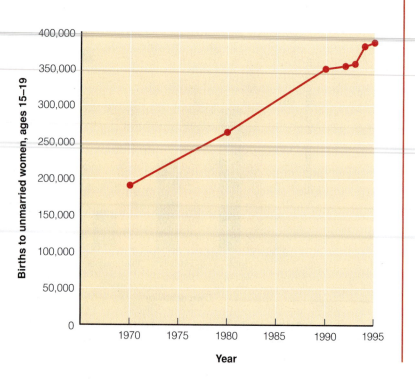

Who Gets Pregnant? It's important to note that although teenage pregnancies, by definition, involve teen mothers, it is misleading and inaccurate to treat the situation as though it were solely a teen problem. In fact, notes Males (1993a), in 69% of all teenage births where the mother is a teenager, the father is an adult. Even in cases where mothers are younger than 15, more than half the fathers are adults.

Teenage pregnancies are not restricted to any particular social, economic, religious, or ethnic group. However, in the United States, pregnancies are about twice as common among black compared to white teenagers (U.S. Bureau of the Census, 1998). Teenage pregnancies are also more common in economically depressed areas (Wilcox et al., 1996). Some have speculated that teenage pregnancy often leads to dropping out of school, to poverty, and to eventual dependence on social assistance. Not so, argues Gordon (1996) following a survey of pregnant or at-risk girls in an inner-city high school. The pattern is more often that the girls are poor to begin with. Many also have low academic skills. These two factors, argues Gordon, appear to result in pregnancy more often than pregnancy results in poverty. In fact, in Gordon's sample, most of the pregnant girls *wanted* to be pregnant.

Compared with married mothers of the same age, socioeconomic status, and religious background, unmarried teenage mothers often have lower educational and occupational status, more often come from broken homes, are more likely to have been sexually abused, and are more likely to engage in other high-risk behaviors such as drinking and abusing drugs (Macleod, 1999). Many are likely to have had initial intercourse at lower than average ages (Kellogg, Hoffman, & Taylor, 1999). And most, of course, had unprotected sex. In a survey of 2,029 college women who came to a university health center for pregnancy tests, Sawyer, Pinciaro, and Anderson-Sawyer (1998) found that some 37% had not used any form of contraception. And of those who had used condoms, 29% reported that the device had torn or slipped off.

Why Teenagers Get Pregnant The vast majority of teenage pregnancies are unplanned. Some suggest that one reason for increasing rates of teenage pregnancy is the relaxation of social attitudes toward sexual activity and unmarried childbirth. Because pregnancy no longer brings shame and humiliation, there is less pressure, on both boys and girls to prevent conception.

A raft of psychological factors might also motivate sexual intercourse, leading to pregnancy: loneliness and alienation that are often part of life in socially and economically depressed surroundings; the girl's wish to "get back" at overprotective parents; the boy's wish to establish the "macho" image that some male societies still reinforce.

Then there is the adolescent's egocentrism—the personal fable that stresses the special invulnerability of the teenager, premised on the belief that "It won't happen to me." This, coupled with the adolescent's sensation-seeking tendencies, may account for some teenage pregnancies. Of course, the more mature the teenagers, the more likely they are to use contraception. Thus the earlier the sexual initiation, the more likely the teenager is to become pregnant.

Perhaps most important, the majority of teen pregnancies occur accidentally and because of ignorance or misinformation concerning sex and contraception. A large percentage of teenagers don't use contraception, and many have multiple sex partners. And when they drink, the probability of these higher-risk behaviors occurring increases significantly (Santelli et al., 1998). Holland and Britain have very similar rates of teenage sexual activity, reports McKee (1999). Yet Britain has the highest teen pregnancy rate of Western Europe, and Holland's rate of teen pregnancy is only about 14% that of Britain. The reason, says McKee, is much wider use of contraception in Holland.

Many teenagers don't know where to get birth control information. And of those who have adequate information, many are only intermittently sexually active. For them, the cost of the safest birth control methods makes their use prohibitive. In addition, using an IUD (intrauterine device), oral contraceptives, or a diaphragm requires the cooperation of a physician. As a result, of those who do employ contraception, many are forced to use the least reliable methods: withdrawal, rhythm (attempting to time intercourse to coincide with the woman's cyclical periods of infertility), and condoms.

Implications of Teen Pregnancy Pregnancy for an unmarried teenager often poses a serious developmental crisis. Of the 10 most common reasons for seeking mental health services in a large high school, pregnancy-related issues was number one (Jepson, Juszczak, & Fisher, 1999).

Many teenage pregnancies result in a dramatic disruption of the mother's education and career plans (Trad, 1999). Teenage pregnancy and delivery also carry much higher health risks, both for mother and infant. Moreover, the economic and social conditions in which most teenage mothers are forced to live, and the emotional stresses associated with these conditions—as well as with child-rearing—can be a heavy burden. It is well known that divorce rates for teenage marriages are much higher than for marriages occurring later.

Teenage pregnancy has disadvantages not only for the mother but also for her offspring. Teenage parents tend to be less socially competent than their non-pregnant peers. They manifest higher levels of stress and are less sensitive to the needs of their infants. One study that compared child-rearing knowledge and attitudes of adolescent mothers with those of older mothers found that the teenage mothers were not only significantly lower on measures of parenting knowledge but also scored higher on indicators of authoritarian parenting (Camp, 1995). Teenage childbearing also has economic disadvantages, which often disappear over time. But as Furstenberg, Brooks-Gunn, and Chase-Lansdale (1989) put it, "The children of teenage mothers, however, are distinctly worse off throughout childhood than the offspring of older childbearers" (p. 313).

The implications of teenage parenthood are clearly more direct and more applicable for mothers and children than for fathers, a great many of whom are not involved in pregnancy-related decisions nor in child-rearing later—and most of whom are not teenagers (Males, 1993b). However, school dropout rates are higher for teenage fathers even when they do not marry the mother (Marsiglio, 1986).

Clearly, these observations and conclusions don't apply to all teenage parents. Many are sensitive, caring, and competent parents. Unfortunately, the probability that this will be the case, given their relative immaturity and lack of experience and information, is not overwhelmingly high.

Pregnancy Prevention and Abstinence Programs
Not all teenage mothers are economically disadvantaged, have inadequate job skills, and raise children who experience developmental problems. But many do. And given the staggering economic, psychological, and social costs of adolescent parenthood, the United States Public Health Service (since 1981) has funded a variety of pregnancy prevention programs. Most of these programs are offered in middle schools through family life and sex education courses. Their objectives are to decrease adolescent pregnancy by changing sexual attitudes and sexual behavior. For legal—and sometimes moral—reasons, many are abstinence programs that do not permit discussion of contraception or abortion. Others offer free access to contraception, provide information about sexuality and contraception, and attempt to influence sexual attitudes and expand adolescents' life options.

Sex education, pregnancy prevention programs, and providing contraceptives in schools remain controversial. When McKay (1996) surveyed parents to determine their attitudes toward sex education courses, he found that more than 90% of respondents either agreed very strongly or disagreed very strongly with the idea of providing sex education for students. Some parents fear that sex education and easy access to contraception may serve to increase adolescent sexual behavior and to foster values that run counter to those of the family and the community. Because of this, and because of the danger of sexually transmitted diseases, many parents advocate sexual abstinence programs. However, adolescents are not always highly motivated to participate in such courses, especially when the program content contradicts their values and behaviors. Gordon (1996) argues that if these programs are to succeed with adolescents, course developers must recognize that the problem is not adolescent sexual activity but teenage pregnancy.

Research suggests that the more multifaceted approaches to pregnancy prevention can be successful. For example, a comprehensive 4-year program in Kansas resulted in significant reductions in sexual activity among both males and females, an increase in the use of condoms, and a reduction in pregnancy rates ("Teen pregnancy prevention a success," 1999).

Different rationales underlie abstinence programs, explains Blinn-Pike (1999). These are typically used as arguments to convince teenagers that they should postpone sexual activity. Interestingly, the most effective of these rationales may be those based on fear. Blinn-Pike (1999) surveyed 697 students from 20 schools, who claimed that they had not had sex. The author reports that the most common reason for abstinence among these 414 girls and 282 boys (mean age 14.56 years) was fear of AIDS. The second most common reason was fear of getting someone pregnant or of becoming pregnant. The third was fear of getting some other disease. Thus, fear-based rationales were most common. The least common reasons for abstinence were not knowing where to get birth control information or devices and not having enough money to buy them.

Homosexuality

As we saw in Chapter 8, forming gender identity (or sexual identity—the learning that one is permanently male or female) and learning gender-appropriate interests and behaviors are important processes occurring in childhood. As Yelland and Grieshaber (1998) put it, there is considerable pressure on children to "get it right." Those who don't get it right are generally in for a hard time.

There is a basic difference between sexual (or gender) identity, which has to do with recognizing that one is male or female, and **sexual orientation**, which relates to emotional, sexual, or romantic attraction to one or the other sex, or to both. In fact, psychologists recognize three different kinds of sexual orientation. By far the most common is **heterosexual orientation**, attraction to the opposite sex. Less common is **homosexual orientation**, attraction to someone of the same sex. **Bisexual orientation** refers to attraction to both males and females.

Some children get their gender identity "right" (in the sense that it corresponds to anatomical sex) but discover, often in adolescence, that their sexual orientation is different—that it is homosexual or, less often, bisexual. It's not certain how common bisexual and homosexual orientations are. As Kagan and Gall (1998) point out, estimates of homosexuality are highly unreliable. One common guess is that about 5% of the population is homosexual.

Until 1973, homosexuality was considered a mental disorder, and was so labeled and described by the American Psychiatric Association. Accordingly, it was a highly stigmatized condition that often remained hidden, or for which individuals so oriented sought therapy. It's now clear, however, that sexual orientation cannot ordinarily be altered (Kagan & Gall, 1998).

Attitudes toward homosexuality have changed considerably in the past several decades. In Canada, for example, 28% of a large representative, 1975, sample considered homosexuality "not wrong at all" or "sometimes wrong." By 1995, those numbers had risen to 48%. Significantly, however, even in 1995, 52% of this same sample considered homosexuality always or almost always wrong. Clearly, despite increasing acceptance of homosexuality, considerable social stigma and disapproval remain.

Such attitudes present serious problems for adolescents who, while trying to cope with the identity issues that confront all adolescents, must also come to terms with their sexual orientation. "Compared to the development of a heterosexual identity, a norm requiring little conscious thought or effort," write Fontaine and Hammond (1996), "the attempt to develop a healthy and viable bi- or homosexual identity is a draining, secretive, anxiety-producing, and lonely task for adolescents" (p. 819). This is one reason, they claim, that research has often found these youngsters are more in need of counseling support. Many are overwhelmed by social and emotional isolation and loneliness.

---

sexual orientation Refers to an individual's customary and enduring attraction to persons of one, or occasionally both, genders.

heterosexual orientation Describes a customary and enduring attraction to persons of the opposite sex.

homosexual orientation Refers to an individual's customary and enduring romantic and sexual attraction to persons of the same gender.

bisexual orientation Defined by a person's customary and enduring romantic attraction to persons of either gender.

Relatively little is known about the causes of homosexuality, or about the formation of homosexual identity. Kagan and Gall suggest that the orientation probably results from a complex interaction of genetic and social factors. What *is* known is that sexual orientation doesn't appear to be a matter of conscious choice. When the adolescent begins to sense an unexpected sexual orientation, considerable confusion, uncertainty, and anguish may result. Fontaine and Hammond (1996) describe six relatively common stages through which the homosexual adolescent may pass in the process of achieving a healthy sexual identity (see Table 12.4). Understanding these stages may be especially important for teachers, counselors, and parents.

Sexually Transmitted Diseases

There are more than two dozen known **sexually transmitted diseases (STDs)**—also known as *venereal diseases.* Among the most common are chlamydia, gonorrhea, and herpes. Less common are syphilis and AIDS, although both of these are increasing. Reported yearly cases of syphilis in the United States almost doubled between 1980 and 1990 (134,000 cases reported in 1990 compared with 69,000 in 1980). Numbers appear to be decreasing once more (53,000 cases in 1996; U.S. Bureau of the Census, 1998). Canada reports a similar decline (from 2,376 cases in 1987 to 799 cases in 1996; *Canada Yearbook*, 1999). Significantly, STD rates are more than twice as high among teenage girls than would be predicted on the basis of rates among teenage boys. The reason for this, suggests Males (1993b), is the high rate of intercourse between adult males and teenage females.

Chlamydia Chlamydia may be the most common of the STDs, although the dramatic increase in infec-

sexually transmitted diseases (STDs) Also called *venereal diseases;* any of several dozen diseases transmitted primarily through sexual intercourse (for example, gonorrhea, herpes, chlamydia, and AIDS).

TABLE 12.4
Stages of Sexual Identity Formation for Bi- and Homosexual Adolescents

STAGE	POSSIBLE FEELINGS AND BEHAVIORS	COUNSELING INTERVENTIONS
1. Confusion	Feeling "different," same-sex attractions, dreams, fantasies	Provide support, suggest readings, explore strengths, discourage premature self-labeling.
2. Comparison	Continued sense of being different, strong same-sex attractions, anxiety about fitting in, isolation, shame	As in stage 1; also help youth in exploring fears, anxieties, and shame; and in identifying positive role models.
3. Tolerance	Active seeking out of others with same orientation, living double life, denial of sexuality	As in stages 1 and 2; also maintain supportive relationship with adults, discourage inappropriate sexuality with adults, and encourage gay activities.
4. Acceptance	Increased contact with peers with same sexual orientation, severe loneliness/alienation if peers not available, may be scapegoated	As in stages 1–3; also encourage safer sex, explore coming-out issues, affirm self-worth.
5. Pride	Us/them attitude, belief in superiority of own orientation, anger at prejudice	As in stages 1–4; also offer support, self-acceptance and pride, encourage relating with supportive heterosexuals.
6. Synthesis	Rejoining supportive heterosexuals, increased empathy, renewed emphasis on social roles	Support efforts to better understand self.

Source: Adapted from J. H. Fontaine & N. L. Hammond (1996). Counseling issues with gay and lesbian adolescents. *Adolescence*, 31: 817–830. Adapted with permission of Libra Publishers, Inc.

tion rates could be a function of better screening procedures (division of STD Prevention, 1995). This disease was seldom seen until very recently and still goes largely undetected. Estimates are that as many as 1 of every 10 sexually active women has chlamydia. In 1996, 50% more cases of chlamydia than of gonorrhea were reported (U.S. Bureau of the Census, 1998). Chlamydia is now one of the leading causes of infertility among women (Roberts, 1996).

In most women (approximately 80%) chlamydia presents no symptoms in its early stages; this is also the case for about 20% of infected men. In later stages, abdominal pain may cause the victim to seek medical help, but by then the woman is often infertile. Chlamydia can be treated easily and effectively with antibiotics.

Gonorrhea Gonorrhea has declined dramatically since 1980, when more than 1 million cases were reported in the United States, but is still a highly common STD at about 326,000 reported cases in the United States in 1996 (U.S. Bureau of the Census, 1998). Symptoms in the male usually include a discharge from the penis and pain during urination. Symptoms in the female are more subtle and often go unnoticed. The disease can usually be treated simply and effectively with penicillin and related drugs. Like some other sexually transmitted diseases, it can sometimes be prevented by using a condom or simply by washing the genitals thoroughly after intercourse.

Genital Herpes Genital herpes is caused by a virus and remains incurable, although the virus can remain inactive for a long time. An estimated 500,000 new cases are reported each year. The disease is believed to be contagious only when lesions are present (look like tiny cold sores; commonly found on the penis and scrotum in males and on the vulva, vagina, and cervix in females). Newer drugs are effective in control of symptoms.

AIDS Acquired immunodeficiency syndrome (AIDS) is a sexually transmitted disease caused by the human immunodeficiency virus (HIV)—an organism that appears to mutate rapidly, thereby increasing the difficulty of treating it. At present, AIDS is incurable and fatal. It is transmitted through the exchange of body fluids, principally blood and semen. Largely for that reason, AIDS has been most common among four high-risk groups: intravenous drug users who often share needles; homosexual males who engage in anal intercourse; hemophiliacs who have been exposed to the virus through blood transfusions; and certain groups of Haitians who engage in rituals involving blood exchange. As of 1997, in the United States 620,077 cases had been reported. In 1996 there were more than 39,000 AIDS deaths (U.S. Bureau of the Census, 1998; see Figure 12.7). Worldwide, an estimated 33.6 million people are infected with HIV; 50% of them are in eastern and southern Africa, where live some 95% of the world's 11 million children who have been orphaned by the AIDS deaths of their parents ("Eleven million children," 1999). In fact, as many as 1 out of every 10 people in South Africa—some 4 million people—have already been infected by the AIDS virus (Selsky, 2000).

Because there may be as much as a 10-year lag between exposure to the virus and development of symptoms, reported cases reflect what was happening 10 years ago. Still, more people have now died of AIDS than were killed in wars in the entire twentieth century ("Eleven million children," 1999). And while homosexual as well as drug-related transmission is still highly common, heterosexual transmission has become the norm throughout most of the world—as it is in Africa—and is expected to become more common in North America. In fact, relative incidence of AIDS among women in the United States has increased dramatically. Between 1981 and 1986, for example, only 7% of reported cases were female; but in 1997, nearly 22% of all new cases were female (U.S. Bureau of the Census, 1998).

Adolescents appear to be relatively well informed about AIDS and how it is transmitted; and as many as 84% claim they have changed their sexual behavior because of fear of AIDS (Bibby, 1995). As we saw, fear of AIDS was the most often cited reason for sexual abstinence among Blinn-Pike's (1999) sample of teenagers. Significantly, however, almost a third of all U.S. women (ages 15 to 29) who were sexually active with two or more partners in the past 12 months reported that their partners never used condoms, or used them less than half the time. (See *In the News and on the Web:* "HIV Supercarrier.")

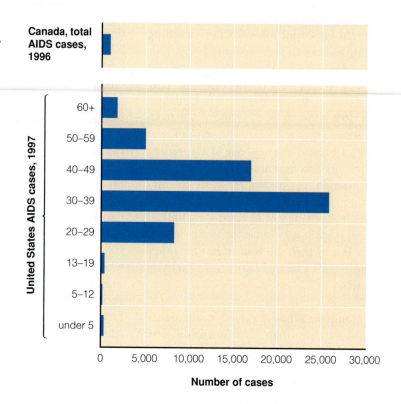

FIGURE 12.7 AIDS cases reported in the United States, 1997, by age; and total AIDS cases reported in Canada, 1996. Source: U.S. Bureau of the Census, 1998, p. 147 and *Canada Yearbook, 1999*, p. 134.

Other STDs Among other STDs is **acute pelvic inflammatory disease (PID)**, a complication that can result from diseases such as gonorrhea or chlamydia. It is a major health problem, affecting more than 1 million U.S. women per year (Quan, 1994). Resulting inflammation of the cervix and fallopian tubes can lead to infertility or tubal pregnancies, especially following repeated infections. In one study of 1,309 women who had been diagnosed as having acute pelvic inflammatory disease, 12.1% were found to be infertile. Of the others who did become pregnant, 7.8% had tubal pregnancies (Westrom, 1994).

Genital warts are also sexually transmitted. They are caused by a virus and affect about 1 million people in the United States each year. They are not usually dangerous, and can be removed. Sexual transmission is also the leading cause of hepatitis B, of which there were more than 10,000 cases

in the United States in 1996 (U.S. Bureau of the Census, 1998).

THE TURMOIL TOPICS

A large majority of adolescents pass exuberantly through the teen years, enjoying their increased powers of mind and body, successfully overcoming or avoiding the turmoil that besets their less fortunate peers. But for others, perhaps some 15% who describe themselves as anxious or confused or depressed, adolescence can be a turbulent and troubled time. Clearly, the turmoil topics—delinquency, gangs, drugs, suicide—relate only to the minority. But they are an important minority.

Delinquency

Delinquency is a legal rather than a scientific category. A *delinquent* is a juvenile who has been appre-

---

acute pelvic inflammatory disease A sexually transmitted disease (STD) that frequently results from other STDs such as gonorrhea. Also termed *salpingitis* or *endometritis*, pelvic inflammatory disease affects about 1 million women a year and is often associated with infertility and tubal pregnancies.

delinquency A legal category defined as the apprehension and conviction of a juvenile for some legal transgression.

IN THE NEWS AND ON THE WEB

HIV Supercarrier

AP/Wide World Photos

Hundreds of high school students attending Jamestown High in Jamestown, New York, have discovered that they might be infected with HIV. These include all the girls who had sex with Nushawn Williams. There were 28 of them, Nushawn admitted (and dozens more elsewhere). But what's different about Jamestown is that it's just a small town (34,000 residents). So when new HIV cases began to show up, one after another, the county medical commissioner became suspicious—and traced the cases back to Nushawn Williams. He may be what the medical profession refers to as a *super transmitter* who carries a particularly virulent mutation of the virus. Chances of infection are enormously higher with such individuals. Currently, at least 9 of the 28 girls who had sex with Williams are known to be infected; the youngest was only 13 when she was with Williams. These 9 girls are thought to have exposed at least another 70 sex partners to the virus. They, in turn, might have exposed dozens more. The final count remains unknown.

D. Lauter, "Man infects 9 with AIDS virus in semirural NY." *Los Angeles Times*, 28 October 1997, p. 1.

M. Mandel, "Terror comes to town." *Edmonton Sun*, 2 November 1997, p. News 10.

To Think About: A special court order was obtained to release Nushawn Williams's identity and to circulate his photograph among potential victims. Under what circumstances, if any, do you think authorities should be permitted to take such action? How about in the case of convicted sex offenders who have served their sentences?

Resources: For a frequently updated website dealing with all aspects of HIV and AIDS including not only incidence and treatment but also links to a wide variety of other AIDS- and HIV-related sites, see the *AIDS VIRTUAL LIBRARY* at

http://planetq.com/aidsvl/

Another useful Web source is

http://www.critpath.org/aric/aricinc.htm

For additional readings, explore *InfoTrac College Edition*, your online library. Go to http://infotrac-college.com/wadsworth and use the passcode that came on the card with your book. Try these search terms: AIDS adolescents, AIDS transmissions, safe sex.

---

hended and convicted for transgression of established legal rather than moral laws. Adults in similar situations are called criminals rather than delinquents.

When delinquency is defined in this manner, surveys of its prevalence can be based directly on police and legal records. These records indicate a tremendous increase in the delinquency rate in recent decades. Adolescents and younger children commit almost as many crimes as people over 25 (U.S. Bureau of the Census, 1998). However, many of the offenses for which juveniles are apprehended and brought to court are *status* offenses—for example, truancy, running away, sexual promiscuity, underage drinking, or driving without a license. This means they are related directly to age and don't exist as adult offenses. Nevertheless, 31% of all *serious* crimes committed in the United States in 1996 were committed by those under 18 (see *At a Glance:* "Gangs, Violence, and Delinquency," and Table

Gangs, Violence, and Delinquency

Random and unprovoked violence, sometimes perpetrated by gangs and sometimes by individuals, is as frightening as it is unpredictable. Violence that is not random, but based on allegiance to ideology and on hatred of identifiable groups (as is the case for some racist groups), is no less terrifying. Although the number of delinquency cases dealt with by U.S. courts has not changed very much in recent years (in the United States, 1.05 million cases in 1975 and 1.71 million in 1995), incidence of violent juvenile offenses in the United States increased from 67,000 cases in 1982 to 142,000 cases in 1996. For violent offenses, males outnumber females by approximately 7 to 1. As a result, more than 80% of all juveniles held in custody in 1995 were male.

TABLE 12.5
Number and Types of Delinquency Cases Disposed of by U.S. Juvenile Courts in 1995

All delinquency offenses	1,714,000
Violent offenses	142,000
Criminal homicide	3,000
Forcible rape	7,000
Robbery	40,000
Aggravated assault	93,000
Property offenses	623,000
Burglary	140,000
Larceny	419,000
Motor vehicle theft	53,000
Arson	10,000
Delinquency offenses	949,000
Simple assault	205,000
Vandalism	122,000
Drug law violations	159,000
Obstruction of justice	110,000
Other*	353,000

*Includes such crimes as stolen property offenses, trespassing, weapons offenses, other sex offenses, liquor law violations, disorderly conduct, and miscellaneous offenses.
Source: Adapted from U.S. Bureau of the Census (1998), p. 226.

12.5). And in a large-scale survey of self-reported delinquency (as opposed to delinquency defined by police records) in an affluent Canadian city, investigators found that more than half of all high school students had engaged in some form of delinquent behavior in the past year (Paetsch & Bertrand, 1999). True, the most common of these behaviors were relatively minor incidents of slapping, punching, or kicking someone. However, at least once during the preceding year, a full 28% had brought a weapon to school (the most common weapon was illegal knives). Ten percent of the males in this sample had actually threatened someone with a weapon.

A number of factors appear to be related to delinquency, but because most studies that have investigated delinquency simply indicate correlations, identifying its specific causes is impossible. Age, for example, is related to delinquency; but we have no evidence that it causes delinquency. Other related but not necessarily causal factors include social class, intelligence, peers, parents, personality, and sex.

Social Class Research on the relationship between social class and delinquency is ambiguous and inconclusive. Although the lower classes, as well as some racial subgroups, are greatly overrepresented among delinquent groups, it is by no means clear that there are, in fact, many more delinquents among these groups. Due to the nature of law enforcement systems, their often unconscious prejudices, and their consequently greater likelihood of recognizing and apprehending delinquents among minority and lower-class groups, it is hardly surprising that more of these adolescents are classified as delinquents. At the same time, to the extent that delinquency is a form of rebellion that is sometimes motivated by the desire for material possessions, it is reasonable to expect that more of the poorer adolescents would be delinquent. Furthermore, lower-class parents tend to look to the police for help with their children; middle-class parents go to therapists. Finally, as Hagan (1998) points out, in middle-class families, sons engaging in delinquent behaviors are less likely to continue engaging in criminal activities as adults than are the sons in lower-class families. One reason for this, suggests Hagan, is that these families are better able to protect their sons if they are apprehended, and they are better able to access services that might help them.

Intelligence A large body of evidence links delinquency with lower-than-average measured intelligence. This is not direct evidence that lower intelligence causes delinquency. However, lower intelligence is sometimes associated with being old for one's grade, which has been associated with delinquency (Loeber et al., 1998). Also, as Quay (1987) notes, lower measured intelligence often reflects lower verbal ability, which puts children at a disadvantage in social interaction as well as in school. Consequently, these children are more likely to get into trouble with teachers, school administrators, parents, and perhaps friends as well.

Peers Peer groups, particularly in the form of gangs, can also contribute to delinquent behavior. As we saw earlier, groups often tend to form on the basis of shared interests and characteristics. Thus, the more aggressive boys often seek the company of others who are also aggressive. But, as Cairns and associates (1998) point out, aggression doesn't ordinarily exclude a boy from membership in most groups and force him to seek the company of others who might have deviant inclinations. In contrast, aggressiveness in girls is more likely to lead to social rejection.

Like other peer groups, the delinquent gang reinforces its dominant values and serves as a model for translating these values into actual behaviors. Lindstrom (1996) describes this as a "spreading effect." His investigations indicate that not all youths are equally affected by their peers; but that some are, in effect, more susceptible than others. Correctional institutions for juveniles, which comprise primarily delinquent peer groups, may be one example of peer influence on delinquent behavior. Not surprisingly, more than half of all admissions to most correctional institutions are, in fact, readmissions.

Parents The father is perhaps the most influential parent with respect to juvenile delinquency. Fathers of delinquent boys are often more severe, more punitive, more prone to alcoholism, more rejecting, and more likely to have engaged in delinquent behavior themselves (Peiser & Heaven, 1996). At the same time, many parents of delinquent adolescents are likely not to have monitored or disciplined their children closely while they were growing up. Steinberg and Avenevoli (1998) studied students from nine high schools in Wisconsin and Northern California, looking specifically at the relationship between delinquency and two variables: parental permissiveness and *school disengagement*—defined as the extent to which children were involved in schoolwork and concerned about their progress. Both variables were significant predictors of deviant behavior. Especially noteworthy is the authors' finding that children who were seriously involved in part-time employment were more likely to engage in delinquent acts. This may be because these teenagers also tended to be less engaged in school.

There is evidence, too, that father absence may be related to delinquency (Amato & Keith, 1991). Some speculate that father absence may contribute to delinquency in sons, perhaps by failure to provide adequate male models, perhaps as a function of protest against female domination, or perhaps simply because of inadequate supervision. Girls, too, appear to be more prone to delinquency in father-absent homes or where the mother is viewed as cold and rejecting (Kroupa, 1988).

Personality Many studies have looked at the possibility that delinquency is at least partly a function of the individual's personality characteristics. Results are generally inconclusive although there is some evidence that high impulsivity (low impulse control), high need for stimulation (danger-seeking orientation), and low self-esteem are related to delinquency (St. C. Levy, 1997). With respect to low self-esteem, we noted earlier that delinquents typically think less well of themselves than do nondelinquent adolescents.

Sex The incidence of delinquency is about four times higher among boys than girls. This may be partly explained by the male's greater aggressiveness. Traditionally, delinquency among males has involved more aggressive transgressions; girls were apprehended more often for sexually promiscuous behavior, shoplifting, and related activities. Evidence indicates this pattern is now changing, as more girls become involved in aggressive delinquent acts, including breaking and entering, car theft, and even assault. Drug-related offenses also account for an increasing number of detentions. In a study of female delinquency, Caspi and colleagues (1993) found highest risk for delinquency among girls who matured earliest. Early-maturing girls were far more likely to know—and be friends with—delinquent boys than were girls who matured later.

In summary, a complex set of psychological and social forces impinge on the potential delinquent, although no single factor can reliably predict delinquent behavior. Social class, age, sex, home background, intelligence, personality, relationship with the father, and peer influences are all implicated, but these don't give a complete picture. Clearly, many adolescents from the most deprived backgrounds are not delinquents, and many from apparently superior environments are.

Adolescent Gangs

Matti Baranovski was sitting on a park bench near his home with a couple of his pals when a group of about 10 masked individuals approached them, asking for cigarettes and money ("Teens charged in," 1999). When Matti asked why he and his friends were being bothered, group members kicked him to death. An autopsy indicated he died of blunt trauma to the head; he had no other injuries. Two youths stand accused of murder; police hope to arrest a third; a fourth has fled the country ("Two in court," 1999).

What happened to Matti and his friends is known as **swarming**. In a recent 6-month period, there have been 485 reported swarmings in Matti's city (Toronto, Canada, population about 4.4 million). Police have set up an antiswarming task force.

Gang violence, and especially youth gang homicides, have become increasingly prevalent in recent years (Howell, 1999). Sociologists define a **gang** as a group that forms spontaneously, that interacts face-to-face, and that becomes aware of its group membership through conflict with some other group or, perhaps more often, with some representatives of established society. A gang may consist of different numbers of individuals from a wide variety of backgrounds and locales, although it typically includes a fairly homogeneous group of people who at least live close to one another and who often attend the same school. But most important, a group does not become a gang until it comes into conflict with something external. It is hardly surprising, then, that the word *gang* has always been closely associated with juvenile delinquency, truancy, rebelliousness, and violence.

Who Joins Gangs, and Why Gangs are primarily composed of adolescent males, although there is evidence of increasing numbers of girl gangs. Girl gangs, report Esbensen, Deschenes, and Winfree (1999), engage in much the same range of illegal activities as do boy gangs, and have very similar attitudes and perceptions of their gangs. Members of gangs are often children who had a previous history of antisocial behavior, sometimes reflected in conduct disorders, problems in school, and problems at home and in the community, report Lahey and associates (1999) following an investigation of 347 boys in a public school system. In addition, in many cities, gang members belong to ethnic minorities, tend to be from poorer families, and often live with only one parent. Lack of parental supervision is also a strong predictor of gang membership.

Analysis of data from the Seattle Social Development project, a longitudinal study including children from a wide range of backgrounds, reveals much the same risk factors for gang membership (Hill et al., 1999). Specifically, children from poorer neighborhoods where many other youths are typically in trouble, those living with one parent, poorer school achievers, and those who have easy access to **marijuana** and other drugs are most likely to become gang members.

---

swarming Current term used to describe acts of violence or intimidation motivated primarily by robbery and committed by at least three people acting as a gang.

gang A small group that interacts frequently face-to-face and that defines itself through conflict—sometimes with other gangs, sometimes with established authority, often with both.

marijuana A substance derived from the hemp plant. When smoked, it ordinarily induces a pleasant emotional state.

As gang members age, they typically drop out of the gang but often continue and even increase their involvement in illegal activities. For them, the gang is just another step in the further development of antisocial behavior (Lahey et al., 1999). Members who drop out are replaced by younger members, so that many gang members are school-age. As a result, gangs pose a real danger in many schools. Some communities and school systems respond to the problem aggressively; many react only when there is a crisis. One highly aggressive program implemented in Dallas, Texas, involves strict enforcement of curfew and truancy regulations and saturation patrols of troubled areas. The program has resulted in significant reduction in gang violence (Fritsch, Caeti, & Taylor, 1999).

Gang Violence Of special current concern are gangs whose members engage in violent behaviors with little or no apparent provocation, often simply because of an apparent taste for violence and mayhem. Some British soccer riots and the occasional school-holiday violence seen in some North American resort areas are examples of this kind of violence, as is swarming of the kind described earlier. Also of concern is gang violence premised on fundamental beliefs and principles that are focused against specific groups or institutions. Members of these gangs are clearly racist; their dream is of an all-white society; their music is counterculture, frenetic, and anarchistic; their dress, hairstyles, and makeup are intended to shock and outrage; and violence is their modus operandi. And, contrary to what had traditionally been the case, gang violence is not restricted to male gangs. It is also perpetrated by females, although to a lesser extent (Deschenes & Esbensen, 1999).

Violence among delinquent gangs is often an expression of a new identity that gang members adopt. Adolescents who join small, highly cohesive, counterculture groups are provided with a set of beliefs and principles that are sometimes very well articulated. Their allegiance to the gang is not only a rejection of family, school, and dominant cultural values but also an embracing of the values and of the individuals in their new community.

Drugs

But not all adolescents who are dissatisfied, disillusioned, hungry for violence, or in need of the community of groups join gangs. A significant number of the severely dissatisfied drop out of society in other ways—such as through use of drugs. Lest another stereotype be fostered, we need to point out that not all who use drugs are dissatisfied and anxious to drop out. Among drug users you will find both the adventurous and the timid, the weak and the strong, the deluded and the rational. Some drug users may be trying to drop out, to find happier realities, to ease pains and hungers that have no names; others may simply be trying to intensify the experience of what is already a good life. Adolescents, as should be clear by now, don't always make the best choices. Unfortunately, it's more difficult to protect them from their immaturity when they are so insistently blind to it.

Patterns of Use The most commonly abused drugs in North America are classified in Table 12.6. The U.S. Bureau of the Census (1998) reported declines between 1974 and 1996 in use of hallucinogens, tranquilizers, marijuana, and even cigarettes. However, there are some indications that alcohol use and abuse has increased during this time. (See *At a Glance:* "Changing Patterns of Drug Use," and Figure 12.8.)

Some Definitions The American Psychiatric Association (APA) distinguishes among a number of drug-use terms. **Drug abuse** refers primarily to the "recreational" use of drugs, and is not considered a disorder unless it impairs social or occupational functioning. **Drug dependence** is a disorder ordinarily resulting from the repeated use of drugs, and manifested in a strong desire to continue taking the drug—either for the pleasant sensations that might result or to escape feelings of withdrawal.

The APA distinguishes between **physiological dependence**, commonly called *addiction*, where the

---

drug abuse The continued use of drugs in spite of persistent physical, social, psychological, or occupational problems that result.

drug dependence Condition marked by a preoccupation with obtaining a drug, a compulsion to use it, and relapse following attempts to cease using it.

physiological dependence Commonly called addiction; refers to physiological changes following drug use such that stopping use leads to withdrawal symptoms.

TABLE 12.6
Classification of the Most Frequently Abused Drugs

CLASS	EXAMPLES
Narcotics	Opium
	Morphine
	Heroin
	Codeine
	Methadone
Sedatives (downers)	Barbiturates (Phenobarbital, Seconal, Nembutal)
	Tranquilizers (Valium, Librium, Vivol)
	Rohypnol, GHB (the date-rape drugs)
	Alcohol
Stimulants (uppers)	Cocaine
	Crack
	Amphetamines (Benzedrine, Dexedrine, Methedrine)
Hallucinogens (psychoactive, psychotropic, psychedelic, psychomimetic)	LSD
	PCP
	Mescaline
	Psilocybin
	Marijuana
Inhalants	Glue
	Paint thinner
	Aerosol sprays
	Solvents
Unclassified (or sometimes classified as stimulant)	Nicotine
"Designer" Drugs	Any of a combination of chemicals and drugs, often manufactured by amateur chemists

desire to continue taking the drug is at least partly organically based (for example, not taking it will lead to unpleasant physiological reactions), and **psychological dependence**, sometimes called *habituation*, where the desire to continue taking the drug has to do mainly with its psychological rather than its physiological effects. **Drug tolerance** refers to changes occurring in the user so that with the passage of time, he or she requires more of the drug to produce the desired effect.

Widiger and Smith (1994) make the important point that there are no infallible rules for identifying clearly when drug use is a problem for a given indi-

psychological dependence Sometimes called habituation; refers to a strong desire to continue using a drug.

drug tolerance Physiological changes following drug use that lead to higher doses of the drug being required to achieve the same effect.

vidual. The APA's *Diagnostic and Statistical Manual* (DSM-IV) recognizes that drug use and abuse exist on a continuum marked by increasing lack of control (*dyscontrol* is the term employed). To some extent, whether drug use constitutes abuse depends on the drug, the organism, and the context. Thus, use of certain drugs that are toxic or likely to have serious adverse consequences is probably abuse. Use of drugs by young children or adolescents may be abuse, because of the possibility that drug use will interfere with important aspects of development and adjustment. And use of drugs in inappropriate contexts (at work, in school) is also more likely to be abuse. (See *Across Cultures:* "Born-with-Two-Teeth and Bobby Thom Have a Smoke.")

Who Uses Drugs?   Researchers have sometimes assumed that there is a drug-use continuum that reflects psychological health and adjustment: At the

Changing Patterns of Drug Use

In the 1960s, social prophets loudly trumpeted their fears that drugs were taking over the lives of adolescents, that people in coming decades would witness drug-related social upheavals and political catastrophes that could scarcely be imagined. But in recent decades we have seen a decline in the use of drugs in most categories. There are some indications, however, that use of tobacco and cannabis (marijuana and hashish) may again be increasing. One large-scale Canadian survey found that 28% of 7th graders (12 or 13 years old) used tobacco. Nearly a third of all Canadian 19-year-olds smoke (about 75% of them every day) (*Canadian Yearbook, 1999*). (See Figure 12.8.)

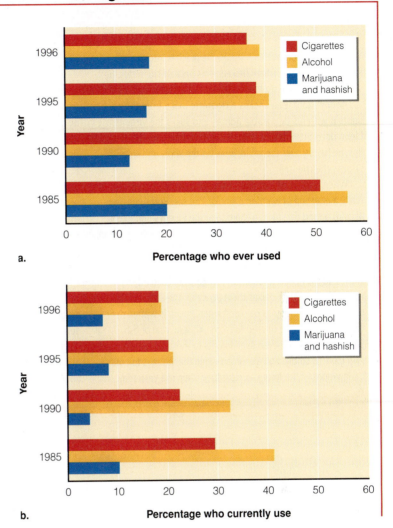

a.

b.

FIGURE 12.8a and b Percent of U.S. adolescents (ages 12 to 17) reporting use of three drugs, 1985 through 1996. Source: U.S. Bureau of the Census (1998), p. 151.

most positive extreme is the drug abstainer; at the most negative extreme, the frequent drug user or the addict; and in between are infrequent users who occasionally experiment with drugs. However, a longitudinal study conducted by Shedler and Block (1990) contradicts this view. The study compared the psychological characteristics of drug abstainers, drug experimenters, and drug users. As expected, drug users were found to be the least well adjusted, the most impulsive, and the most likely to suffer from emotional problems. But the abstainers were not the best adjusted of the three groups; the drug experimenters were. In Shedler and Block's (1990) words, "The picture of the abstainer that emerges is

of a relatively tense, overcontrolled, emotionally constricted individual who is somewhat socially isolated and lacking in interpersonal skills" (p. 618).

Other research has also found that frequent drug users often appear to have been relatively maladjusted as children, and especially to have had low self-esteem. (Luthar & Cushing, 1997). Many have been abused as children, and have a family history of drug abuse, including alcoholism (Chassin et al., 1999).

Prior use of tobacco is also a strong predictor of later drug use (Wu & Anthony, 1999), as is the age at which children first try drugs. A number of studies also provide convincing evidence that those who experiment at the youngest ages are those most

ACROSS CULTURES

Born-with-Two-Teeth and Bobby Thom Have a Smoke

When Bobby Thom wants a smoke, he reaches into the left sleeve of his T-shirt, where he keeps his pack of cigarettes. He saw Marlon Brando do that once in a movie. He thinks it's cool.

Bobby Thom then shakes a cigarette loose from the pack, lights it with his disposable lighter, and sucks the Virginia blend deep into his lungs. Now, cigarette dangling from his lips, he bends over the table, lines up the shot, and smoothly strokes the cue ball.

When Born-with-Two-Teeth Wants a Smoke . . . well, it isn't really a question of wanting a smoke. You see, Born-with-Two-Teeth is a medicine man, a shaman of the Stoneys. Tobacco is not just something you burn and inhale like you might chew on the stalk of a meadow plant or suck on a wild hazelnut. Tobacco is something to enrich a man's dreams, to give him visions, to move him to trances. Tobacco smoked jointly by those who are angry makes them peaceful. The sick and diseased can sometimes be cured when smoke is wafted over them. Gods who are offered tobacco will send rain or fish. Sometimes they will even send infants to those who are barren. And tobacco smoked by a shaman when the moon is full may bring visions of the future so clear they seem like yesterday.

Tobacco is holy. One has to be careful with its use.

Tobacco, says Dobkin de Rios (1984), served as a hallucinogenic drug in the New World long before European contact. It was used extensively by the Mayans, the Aztecs, and the Incas, by many other native tribes in what is now Mexico, and by the Plains Indians of North America. But it was not used as a pastime or as recreation—as rapidly became common among Europeans once the drug had been introduced there.

Some botanists speculate that the tobacco smoked by native North and South Americans was far more powerful than the blends commonly used today (see, for example, Heiser, 1969). There is evidence, nevertheless, that traces of certain hallucinogenic substances are still present in today's commercial tobaccos (see Dobkin de Rios, 1984).

To Think About: To what extent are people's reactions to drugs shaped by cultures? What factors are involved in determining the acceptability, availability, and legality of drugs? What sorts of changes in acceptability, availability, and legality might be desirable? How could they be brought about?

likely to become problem drug users (Gfroerer & Epstein, 1999; Dishion, Capaldi, & Yoerger, 1999). Also, not surprisingly, the *opportunity* to use drugs is highly correlated with actual use. In this connection, Van Etten and Anthony (1999) report that 51% of U.S. residents have apparently had an opportunity to try marijuana, 23% have been offered cocaine, 14% hallucinogens, and 5% heroin.

Reasons for Drug Use Experimentation with drugs is primarily an adolescent phenomenon. And when teenagers are asked about their decisions to use or not to use drugs, they seldom refer to morality, social convention, or even parents or the law. Even nonusers claim that the decision is a matter of personal choice dictated by prudence and not by morality. One of the most important factors in making that personal decision is the individual's perception of dangers associated with a drug. Frequent

drug users are most likely to discount a drug's harmfulness. However, the most frequent reason for *not* using a drug relates to its perceived risks. Danseco, Kingery, and Coggeshall (1999) report that U.S. youth who don't use marijuana, for example, typically cite one of four different areas of risk that affects their behavior: the possibility of physical harm, parental disapproval, peer disapproval, and fear of being arrested.

In the same way that fear of peer disapproval can prevent one adolescent from trying a drug, it might influence another to try a drug. Dinges and Oetting (1993) surveyed more than 100,000 junior high and high school students. Among other things, they found that adolescents who used a specific drug almost invariably had friends who also used the same drug. In their words, "Drug-using friends are a necessary condition in the evolution of drug use" (p. 263).

Some argue that the reasons for first using (and not necessarily eventually abusing) drugs often have to do with a simple urge to experiment. However, Perkonigg's (1999) research indicates that drug use isn't nearly as transient a phenomenon as this view might imply. Following a longitudinal study of 1,228 adolescents, the author reports that for marijuana users the probability of continued use, and of heavier use, is high. This finding provides some support for the so-called **gateway drug-use theory**, the belief that early use of drugs like alcohol and nicotine serves, in a sense, as a gateway to the use of other drugs. However, the fact that early use of tobacco or alcohol is predictive of later use of other drugs does not indicate that these drugs *cause* the user to need other drugs. Their predictive value is probably tied up with the effects of a host of other psychological and environmental influences. Use of drugs is most likely to become misuse, Segal (1997) suggests, among individuals with poor self-esteem who also experience the strong pressures of a peer drug culture, and who are not reared in a growth-fostering environment (parental neglect, abuse, and alcoholism; poverty; inadequate schooling; and so on). The type of drugs experimented with is also very important. Some drugs have a higher potential for physiological and psychological dependence than others (heroin and freebase cocaine, or crack, for example). In addition, genetics may well be involved in the nature and intensity of the individual's reaction.

Implications of Teenage Drug Use It is clearly unrealistic to expect that adolescents will not experiment with drugs. The vast majority will have puffed on a cigarette or sipped somebody's alcoholic drink well before adolescence. In adolescence, not to drink occasionally—and perhaps not to smoke cigarettes or try marijuana—would, in many instances, not be socially normal. Those who are most in danger, Dishion, Capaldi, and Yoerger (1999) point out, are those who begin to experiment with these drugs at the earliest ages.

The short-term implications of drug abuse among adolescents are sometimes painfully obvious. Alcohol, for example, is implicated in a staggering number of fatal teenage automobile accidents. Less dramatic—but no less real—drug abuse may be reflected in poorer school achievement, dropping out of school, failure to adjust to the career and social demands required for transition to young adulthood, deviance, and criminality. Also, drug and alcohol abuse can have serious health consequences (Aarons et al., 1999).

The long-term implications of teenage drug abuse also include possible negative health consequences. The medical consequences of drugs such as nicotine and alcohol are well known. In addition, as Stacy and Newcomb (1999) report following a 13-year longitudinal study, adolescent drug use is a significant predictor of adult drug-use problems, especially of multidrug problems. Teenagers who use large amounts of drugs are more likely to leave school early, to adopt adult roles less successfully, and to have failed attempts in careers and marriages.

Following is a brief look at some commonly abused drugs.

Marijuana Marijuana, whose active ingredient is **tetrahydrocannabinol (THC)**, is derived from hemp, a tall annual plant with male and female forms. It is variously known as hashish, bhang, grass, ganja, charas, marijuana, muta, grefa, muggles, pot, reefer, gauge, stick, Acapulco Gold, Panama Red, Panama Gold, Thai stick, jive, Indian, Jamaican, tea, weed, and dope. It is ordinarily smoked, although it can also be eaten or drunk. Its main psychological effect is a pleasant emotional state. If taken in sufficient doses and in sufficiently pure forms, it may evoke the same types of hallucinogenic reactions sometimes associated with stronger drugs like LSD.

Whether marijuana is physiologically addictive remains controversial. While some users experience difficulty and distress when they try to stop, some researchers believe there is no convincing evidence that it is addictive (Royal College of Psychiatrists, 1987). Others point out that an apparently strong

---

gateway drug-use theory The observation that certain drugs such as tobacco, alcohol, and marijuana are typically used first (usually in the order mentioned) before other "stronger" drugs, in a sense serving as a gateway to use of other drugs.

tetrahydrocannabinol (THC) The active ingredient in marijuana and related substances (of the *cannabis* family).

dependence does develop among some users; and that it appears to be stronger among adolescents than among adults, and stronger among females than among males (Kandel, 1998).

The physiological effects of marijuana use depend largely on the dosages and the frequency of use. Minor cardiovascular changes (increased heart rate, for example) are common even with very low doses. The respiratory system may be adversely affected with prolonged use and heavier doses (marijuana produces more tars than tobacco, and these contain a higher concentration of certain cancer-causing agents).

LSD LSD-25 (*D-lysergic acid diethylamide tartrate*) is the most powerful hallucinogen known. Because it is a synthetic chemical, it can be made by anyone who has the materials, the equipment, and the knowledge. The most common street name for LSD-25 is acid; others, sometimes reflecting the various forms it can take, are barrels, California sunshine, blotter, cube, domes, flats, wedges, purple haze, jellybeans, bluecaps, frogs, microdots, and window-pane. Its use appears to have declined recently (from 1.9% being current users in 1979 to only .6% in 1996; U.S. Bureau of the Census, 1998).

LSD-25 (ordinarily referred to simply as LSD) is usually taken orally, commonly in the form of a white, odorless, tasteless powder. Its effects vary widely from one person to another, as well as from one occasion to another for the same person. The predominant characteristic of an LSD experience (called an "acid trip") is the augmented intensity of sensory perceptions. An acid trip is occasionally accompanied by hallucinations, some of which may be mild; others may be sufficiently frightening to lead to serious mental disturbance in the user even after the immediate effects of the drug have worn off.

Alcohol Alcohol, the most commonly used and abused drug in contemporary society, is a central nervous system depressant. In relatively moderate doses, its primary effect is to suppress inhibition, which is why many individuals who have consumed

---

LSD-25 (d-lysergic acid diethylamide tartrate) A particularly powerful hallucinogenic drug; an inexpensive, easily made, synthetic chemical that can sometimes have profound influences on human perception. In everyday parlance it is often referred to as "acid."

alcohol behave as though they had taken a stimulant. In less moderate doses, the individual progresses from being "high" or "tipsy" to intoxication. Literally, to be intoxicated is to be poisoned. Behavioral symptoms of varying degrees of intoxication may include impaired muscular control, delayed reflexive reactions, loss of coordination and balance, impaired vision, uncertain speech, faintness, nausea, amnesia (blackouts), and, in extreme cases, paralysis of heart and lung muscles sometimes leading to death.

Alcohol is physiologically addictive, although prolonged or excessive consumption is generally required before symptoms of physical addiction are present. Signs of psychological dependency (a strong desire to continue taking the drug) may appear considerably sooner. One of the major physiological effects of alcohol is its contribution to cirrhosis of the liver—one of the 10 leading causes of death in the United States. In addition, it is implicated in more than half of all motor vehicle deaths, many of which involve adolescents.

Alcohol consumption among adolescents is widespread. Most surveys report that extremely few teenagers have not tried alcohol at least once (U.S. Bureau of the Census, 1998). In a nationwide U.S. survey, 52% of high school seniors reported getting drunk in the past year (Johnston, O'Malley & Bachman, 1995). Close to 20% of adolescents aged 14 to 17 are considered problem drinkers.

Why do adolescents drink? There are clearly many reasons, including social pressure, experimentation, insecurity, and other personal problems, as well as simply for the sensation of being tipsy, high, or drunk. Why do adolescents want to get drunk? To feel good, have fun, celebrate, let off steam, cheer up, forget worries, feel less shy, and impress friends, they claim (Brown & Finn, 1982). But when they are asked about their actual behaviors and feelings when they are drunk, although a large number do "feel good" and "laugh a lot," a significant number fall asleep, feel unhappy, cry, damage property, and get into fights—and approximately a third occasionally get sick.

When is alcohol consumption by adolescents deviant or a problem? Is it a problem only when the adolescent gets into trouble? Does it become a problem when alcohol consumption becomes habitual or excessive, or when it interferes with normal social or physical functioning? Or is it always a problem because the behavior is generally illegal? There are no easy answers.

Cocaine Cocaine is ordinarily a white powder derived from coca leaves. Also known as coke, big "C," snow, gold dust, stardust, flake, Bernice, or Corinne, it is most commonly inhaled vigorously through the nostrils, although it can also be injected.

In moderate doses, the primary effect of cocaine, like that of other stimulants, is one of euphoria and high energy. In higher doses, it can lead to hallucinations and sometimes convulsions. For some decades it was widely believed that cocaine is nonaddictive and largely harmless. It is now considered to be extremely addictive and dangerous (Cheung, Erickson, & Landau, 1991). Indications are that it may be as addictive as heroin (Ringwalt & Palmer, 1989).

Cocaine is sometimes purified to produce crack (freebase cocaine), which has a more profound effect on the user. Some users mix it with heroin and inject it intravenously (called a speedball). Crack appears to be particularly attractive to adolescents, for several reasons. First, it is far cheaper than cocaine. Second, its effects are almost instantaneous and intensely euphoric. And third, so much glamour and misinformation has surrounded the so-called recreational use of cocaine that many adolescents think there is nothing to fear.

Crack is easily and quickly manufactured by cooking down ordinary powdered cocaine with bicarbonate of soda (or mixing it with some petroleum product such as ammonia). Small pieces of the resulting off-white, rocklike, moldy-smelling solid are then chopped up and smoked, usually in a water pipe. The euphoric effect or "rush" occurs within 5 to 10 seconds and is far more intense than that associated with inhaling ordinary cocaine—because the concentrations of cocaine reaching the brain are many times higher than when cocaine is inhaled. Consequently, there is a far higher risk of overdos-

ing with crack, of experiencing convulsions, or even of dying. Many users of crack experience an overwhelming compulsion to use it again as soon as possible, even after using it only once. The use of crack is also associated with psychological changes, most commonly involving strong feelings of paranoia. Many users also become violent, and some commit suicide.

Other Drugs Other drugs used by some adolescents include various hallucinogens such as STP and MDA (methyl amphetamines), PCP (phencyclidene), inhalants, various barbiturates and other milder tranquilizers, and a range of new molecular variations of these and other chemicals (such as "ecstasy"), sometimes collectively labeled "designer drugs." Drugs such as *ecstasy* are also sometimes called "club drugs" because of their popularity in clubs—especially in teen dance clubs or at other music events such as *raves* (all-night teen dance sessions). Also of current interest are **Rohypnol** and **GHB**, the so-called date-rape drugs (see *In the News and on the Web:* "Date-Rape"). Of these, alcohol is still the drug of choice, both among adolescents and adults (see Table 12.7 for some symptoms of drug use and abuse).

Suicide

Suicide, the deliberate taking of one's own life, is final—an end that people seek when they can see only two choices: life as it is now or death. Evidently, they prefer to die.

Suicide is not a pleasant topic; it so violently contradicts our implicit belief in the goodness of life. Consequently, a powerful social stigma is associated with the act, and the event is often glossed over by both the information media and the attending physician. As a result, we hear only about suicides of people we have known (and sometimes not even then), or of particularly prominent people (not

---

cocaine A stimulant drug, ordinarily inhaled as a white powder, the primary effects of which are feelings of euphoria. Possible effects also include hallucinations. In some forms (freebase or as what is called "crack" or "rock"), its effects are more immediate and more intense, and its use leads more readily to psychological dependence.

Rohypnol A "date-rape" drug, so called because it leaves victims helpless and suffering from amnesia. Colorless, odorless, and illegal.

GHB The drug *gamma hydroxybutyric acid*, which, especially when combined with alcohol, causes prolonged amnesia and physical helplessness. One of the "date-rape" drugs.

IN THE NEWS AND ON THE WEB

Date Rape

Paul Lesniak's ex-wife woke up partially naked one morning, totally disoriented, late for an appointment, and unable to remember anything since early the previous evening. At the suggestion of a friend, she sought medical assistance. The doctor ordered a blood test; traces of Rohypnol—the "rape" drug—were found, and police were notified. In Lesniak's home they found traces of Rohypnol in juice; e-mail correspondence relating to the purchases of Rohypnol from an address in Paris ($15 U.S. for 20 tablets); and about 20 pages of stories about sex slaves. Paul Lesniak has been charged with administering a noxious substance, aggravated assault, sexual assault, overcoming resistance, and four other counts of assault.

Rohypnol is a powerful tranquilizer—odorless, colorless, tasteless, and illegal in North America. It can easily be mixed into a drink, and it leaves victims helpless. It, along with another drug, GHB (gamma hydroxybutyric acid), has been implicated in a large number of recent rape cases—hence the name "date-rape" drugs. Rohypnol is also known as *roofie*, or *roche*. When combined with alcohol, both Rohypnol and GHB cause prolonged periods of amnesia, often making it difficult for victims to identify their attackers.

K. Powell, "Man drugged, assaulted wife, jury told." *Edmonton Journal*, 7 December 1999, p. B1.

 Resources: Comprehensive information on drug abuse and abuse prevention, as well as on specific drugs and a host of related topics, can be found at the National Institute for Drug Abuse website:

http://165.112.78.61/NIDAHome1.html

For additional readings, explore *InfoTrac College Edition*, your online library. Go to http://infotrac-college.com/wadsworth and use the passcode that came on the card with your book. Try these search terms: Rohypnol, date rape, GHB.

---

always those either), or of people who commit the act so flagrantly that it compels attention.

For many years, there were few scientific investigations into the causes of suicide or into the problems and personalities of those who deliberately choose their time and method of departure. Now suicidology is a growing field, with dozens of new investigations published each year. These studies are typically either **epidemiological studies** (concerned with distribution and frequency of suicide), or **clinical studies** (concerned with the characteristics, symptoms, and thought process of suicidal individuals). Following are some important findings from this research.

Rates and Distribution Epidemiological studies reveal that the suicide rate in the United States is about 12 per 100,000. Few children under the age of 15 commit suicide. Suicide rates increase slowly from adolescence, peaking at above age 65 for white males and at around ages 45 to 55 for white females; peaks are at younger ages for African Americans and their rates are also lower (U.S. Bureau of the Census, 1998). The most dramatic recent increase in suicide rates is among those age 15 to 19, where suicide rates nearly doubled between 1970 and 1990 (U.S. Bureau of the Census, 1996). Interesting to note, suicide rates are consistently higher in the New World countries (Canada, the United States, Australia, and New Zealand) than they are in Old World countries (England, Wales, Scotland, Northern Ireland, and Ireland). And, for some unexplained reason, the most advanced countries—that is, those with the highest life expectancies and the lowest infant mortality rates—have had the highest recent increases in youth suicide rates (Cantor et al.,

---

epidemiological studies Research that looks at the distribution patterns and frequency of diseases and other related conditions.

clinical studies Investigations concerned with the primary symptoms and the normal course of diseases and related conditions.

TABLE 12.7
Symptoms of Drug Use and/or Abuse

DRUG	SIGNS AND EARLY SYMPTOMS	LONG-TERM SYMPTOMS
Narcotics	Medicinal breath Traces of white powder around nostrils (heroin is sometimes inhaled) Red or raw nostrils Needle marks or scars on arms Long sleeves (or other clothing) at inappropriate times Physical evidence may include cough syrup bottles, syringes, cotton swabs, and spoon or cap for heating heroin	Loss of appetite Constipation
Sedatives	Symptoms of alcohol consumption with or without odor Poor coordination and speech Drowsiness Loss of interest in activity	Withdrawal symptoms when discontinued Possible convulsions
Stimulants	Excessive activity Irascibility Argumentativeness Nervousness Pupil dilation Dry mouth and nose with bad breath Chapped, dry lips Scratching or rubbing of nose Long periods without sleep Loss of appetite Mood shifts Changes in friends "Hangover" symptoms	Loss of appetite Possible hallucinations and psychotic reactions
Hallucinogens, marijuana	Odor on breath and clothing	None definite
LSD, PCP, MDA, STP	Animated behavior or its opposite Bizarre behavior Panic Disorientation	Possible contribution to psychoses Recurrence of experiences after immediate effects of drug
Inhalants	Odor of glue, solvent, or related substance Redness and watering of eyes Appearance of alcoholic intoxication Physical evidence of plastic bags, rags, glue, or solvent containers	Disorientation Brain damage

1996). (See *At a Glance:* "Adolescent Suicide," and Figure 12.9.)

Sex Differences At all age levels, more females than males attempt suicide, but about five or six times more males are successful. More than 25,000 males committed suicide in the United States in 1994, com-pared with slightly more than 6,000 females. Some have argued that this is because males who attempt suicide are more serious about wanting to die than are females. It may also be because the more violent and instantaneous methods employed by males (for example, guns in 66% of all cases) do not provide much opportunity for help. In contrast, the slower

Adolescent Suicide

Adolescent suicide rates are alarmingly high. Suicide is now the second leading cause of death for Canadian teenagers age 15 to 19, at a rate of about 13 per 100,000. (*Canada Yearbook, 1999*). In the United States, it is the third most frequent cause of death for that age group (after accidents and homicides). Suicide rates for young males, though not for females, have risen dramatically in the United States—from below 6 to more than 10 per 100,000 between 1970 and 1993. In 1995, suicide rates for white males age 15 to 24 approached 25 per 100,000 (U.S. Bureau of the Census, 1998).

Males typically use more violent methods such as guns; female methods are more passive and protracted and sometimes less successful (for example, poison).

Suicide is among the top three causes of adolescent deaths in North America.

FIGURE 12.9 Suicide rates per 100,000 population by race for U.S. youth, age 15 to 24. Source: U.S. Bureau of the Census (1998), p. 104.

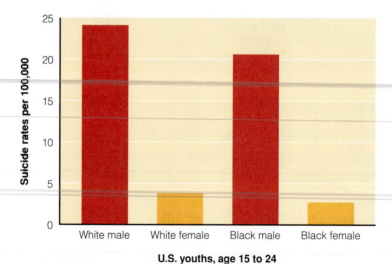

and more passive methods most often employed by females (such as poisoning, which is used about a third of the time) often allow time for rescue.

Suicidal Ideation and Action Researchers often distinguish between those who successfully complete suicide (completors), those who attempt but are unsuccessful (attempters), and those who simply think about it (ideators). Researchers suggest that for many, there is a natural progression from ideation (thinking about the possibility of committing suicide) to forming a plan, and finally to attempting suicide (Kessler, Borges, & Walters, 1999).

Longitudinal investigations reveal a strong tendency for those who have attempted suicide to attempt again. In one 10-year follow-up of 150 suicide attempters who had been released from a clinic, 25% later reattempted suicide, and 12% completed the act—almost the same number as died naturally during that period (Tejedor et al., 1999). Another study of 180 adolescent suicide attempters also found that 25 percent had reattempted within 5 years—the vast majority within 6 months (Goldston et al., 1999). Suicide attempters are especially difficult to help, explains Ottino (1999), partly because of very high drop-out rates from help programs.

Psychological Explanations Gust-Brey and Cross (1999) describe a large variety of proposed theories to account for suicide, including

▲ *Biological theories.* Suicide is due to bad genes, psychiatric disorders, biochemical changes of adolescence, and the like.

▲ *Psychoanalytic theories.* Suicidal adolescents are those whose unconscious death wish is exaggerated by deficient ego development during this critical period; suicide is internal conflict or aggression *directed toward oneself.*

▲ *Psychological stress theory.* Suicide results from a perceived inability to cope with stress associated with rapid and demanding life changes.

▲ *Sociological theories.* Social norms sometimes sanction suicide by giving the adolescent the opportunity to die for the group; alternatively, groups sometimes exclude the adolescent, thus causing depression and leading to suicide.

▲ *Social learning theories.* Suicidal behavior is suggested by the behaviors and attitudes of friends, family, or other important people; imitation and social contagion are important contributors.

▲ *Cognitive theory.* Lack of effective problem-solving skills when faced with situations of high stress leads to hopelessness and suicide.

▲ *Ecological theory.* Suicide results from the combined interaction of environmental, individual, and social factors.

Henry and associates (1993) suggest that of these theories, the most useful may be the ecological approach because it takes into account most of the explanations included in other theories. Thus, rea-

sons for adolescent suicide can include a range of family-based problems (Bronfenbrenner's microsystem), such as death in the family, parental abuse or alcohol use, suicide by other family members, and inability to satisfy parental expectations. They can also include wider social problems (meso-, exo-, or macrosystems). For example, Henry and colleagues (1993) report that suicide rates are about 10 times higher among Native American youth, perhaps partly because of economic, social, and even cultural factors associated with hopelessness. Similarly, suicide rates were significantly higher in North America during the depression of the 1930s (Gust-Brey & Cross, 1999). Henry and associates suggest that in the same way, certain characteristics of contemporary societies—such as high mobility, family instability, lack of intergenerational cohesiveness, poor economic conditions, high unemployment, and expensive and sometimes inaccessible postsecondary education—might all contribute to a greater likelihood of suicide.

Clinical Studies: Individual Explanations Although adolescent suicide might result from the combined effects of these various factors, it is often precipitated by a single event such as the death of a parent or friend, fear of pregnancy, rejection by a close friend, or arrest (Gutierrez, King, & Ghaziuddin, 1996). Overall, however, the single best predictor of adolescent suicide is clearly depression. Laederach and associates (1999) studied 148 adolescents who were in a hospital following an attempted suicide. A large percentage of them met the criteria for diagnosis of a major affective (emotional) disorder, with depression as the major symptom. Many also had other serious problems.

Other precipitation factors sometimes include conflict-filled family relationships, failure in school, a history of sexual abuse and assault, drug-abuse problems (sometimes, specifically, the difficulty of obtaining a drug like heroin), and problems relating to homosexual identity (Yoder, 1999; Gust-Brey & Cross, 1999; Renaud et al., 1999).

Adolescent suicide, like most adult suicides, rarely occurs without warning. The most common warning is one or more unsuccessful attempts at suicide. Other warning signs include statements such as, "I wish I were dead," "Nobody would miss me if I weren't here," and "I wish I'd never been born."

Suicide is still the solution of an isolated few. Most of us choose to wait for death and hope that it will be a long time in coming. And for most adolescents, life is only occasionally turbulent and stressful; generally, it abounds with joy and excitement.

⬛ ENDING ON A HIGHER NOTE

Suicide would not have been a pleasant note upon which to end this chapter. Nor would it have been realistic. Indeed, closing the chapter with the "turmoil topics," as we have, is misleading.

It bears repeating that the adolescents whose lives are described among these last pages are not "average" adolescents. Average adolescents are more joyful than sad, more exuberant than depressed, more confident than self-deprecating. They like order more than chaos, purpose more than dissipation, junk food more than drugs.

And they laugh and smile a lot more than they cry.

That's ending on a higher note.

MAIN POINTS

The Self and Identity

Loneliness is an emotional reaction to loss or threatened loss of important social relationships. Its existence underlines the importance of social interaction in adolescence.

Self refers to the individual's perceptions of individual characteristics; *identity* refers to a sense of wholeness, of purpose, of continuity; *self-esteem* refers to subjective evaluations of individual worth (to how much we like ourselves, what we think we are worth).

Adolescents in different countries share characteristics such as general happiness and optimism, caring and concern for others, confidence and openness about sexual matters, positive feelings toward the family, and confidence in their ability to deal with life. However, they are also different in predictable ways regarding things such as confidence, feelings of vulnerability, values placed on educational and vocational goals, and sexual attitudes. Contrary to Hall's belief, adolescence is not a period of storm and stress for most of the world's adolescents.

According to Erikson, the major developmental task of adolescence is to develop a sense of identity (a notion of self reflected in commitments). Marcia describes four possible identity statuses of adolescents, including *identity diffusion* (no commitment and no identity crisis), *foreclosure* (strong commitment to parent- or religion-determined identity), *moratorium individuals* (active exploration of alternatives, sometimes negative); and *identity achieved* (commitment following the crises of the moratorium).

Ethnic identity formation refers to *feelings* (of belonging to an ethnic group), to *sharing* (language, values, beliefs), to *knowledge* (for example, about history, traditions), and to a strong sense of *self-identification*. Ethnic identity formation is sometimes difficult for ethnic minority adolescents, and may result in *assimilation* (loss of ethnic identity), *marginalization* (failed assimilation resulting in rejection); *separation* (active, sometimes militant rejection of mainstream culture) or *biculturalism* (attempt to retain aspects of both the minority and the dominant culture).

Parents and Peers

Adolescent social development generally involves increasing independence from parents (emotional distancing) and increasing allegiance to peers, although most teenagers have good relations with their parents. Parenting remains very important, although the tasks of protecting children from their immaturity sometimes become more difficult.

Parent-adolescent conflict is not universal, and seldom involves questions of morality. Children of nonintact families are most likely to be early home leavers. Some become street children, a high percentage of whom engage in high-risk and illegal activities.

High school peer groups include those labeled *normal* (largest group, nondeviant), *popular* (socially competent, academically successful); *jock* (focused on sports); *brain* (focused on academics); *druggie* (focused on drugs); and *outcast* (rejected, loners, low self-esteem).

Gender Stereotypes and Differences

Gender roles define masculine and feminine interests and behaviors; *gender stereotypes* are fixed, unexamined beliefs we have about people based on their gender (male stereotype: typically more active, aggressive, powerful, than female, who is more nurturant, more passive). Some research indicates a clear preference for the male role and more negative evaluations of the female role by both males and females.

Males are physically more fragile (higher mortality rates and much lower life expectancies). They have traditionally been more aggressive, and females have been more submissive and nurturant. Gender differences in verbal and mathematical ability are small and inconsistent and are better explained by culturally determined interests and opportunities rather than by basic genetically ordained differences. More males score at the extreme ends of most measures of ability.

Sexuality and Adolescent Pregnancy

The sexual revolution among adolescents is reflected in an increase in the number of adolescents reporting sexual intercourse before marriage, a greater increase in sexual activity among females than among males, earlier age of sexual initiation, and very high rates of unplanned adolescent pregnancy. Teenage parents are more likely to divorce than are people who marry later. Also, their marriages are more often associated with depression, suicide, infant mortality, child neglect, and other signs of inadequate parenting.

Homosexuality, one of three possible sexual orientations (hetero- and bisexuality are the other two) can present serious sexual identity formation problems for adolescents, partly because of the social stigma attached to the orientation, as well as lack of clear role models.

The most common sexually transmitted diseases (STDs) are gonorrhea, herpes, chlamydia, and PID (pelvic inflammatory diseases). Syphilis, and AIDS are rarer. Gonorrhea, chlamydia, syphilis, and PID can normally be cured with drugs; herpes can be controlled but not cured; AIDS, which is most common among homosexual males, intravenous drug users, and hemophiliacs, is fatal.

The Turmoil Topics

Delinquency is a legal category defined by juvenile apprehension and conviction of a legal transgression. Related factors include social class, sex, intelligence, self-esteem, family background, and peer influences. A small minority of adolescents become members of countercultural and sometimes violent gangs.

Drug abuse refers to the recreational use of drugs. *Drug dependence* is manifested in a strong desire to continue taking a drug. It may be *physiological* (desire to take the drug is partly organically based; also termed addiction) or it may be *psychological* (the urge to continue taking the drug is related mainly to its psychological effects; termed habituation). Predictors of the likelihood of drug abuse among teenagers include earlier maladjustment; drug use among peers or parents; delinquency; stressful life changes; parental neglect, abuse, or abandonment; and low self-esteem.

Suicide is an uncommon end, although its frequency among adolescents has doubled in recent decades. More boys successfully attempt suicide. Although adolescent suicides are often precipitated by a single event (such as the death of a friend, pregnancy, parental divorce, or arrest), few occur without warning. Depression, family and relationship problems, or serious loss or failure are predictive of suicide.

Focus Questions: Applications

1. *Is adolescence generally a time of strife, typically marked by parent-adolescent conflict?*
   - Using library resources and illustrating your arguments with personal experience, examine the proposition that adolescence is a period of "Sturm und Drang."

2. *How free of gender discrimination are the lives of adolescents?*
   - Answer the sex-change question (honestly): "If you woke up tomorrow and discovered that you were a girl (boy), how would your life be different?" Now examine your answer for evidence of sexual stereotypes and gender biases.

3. *What are the principal sexual beliefs and behaviors of typical adolescents?*
   - Debate the following proposition: Teenagers should not be discouraged from having sex, but should be provided with sex education and contraception.

4. *How common and serious are teenage delinquency, drug abuse, and suicide?*
   - Outline a drug abuse prevention program that takes into consideration each of the principal factors potentially involved in drug abuse.

Possible Responses to Thought Challenges

Thought Challenge, page 510

Loneliness and aloneness (or solitude) are different conditions. Loneliness is a *negative* emotion that results from not having important social connections, or from the threat or fear that they will be ruptured. Aloneness is solitude, the physical state of not being in the presence of others—or, at least, of not being immediately engaged in social interaction. Aloneness is essentially a neutral state, although it can be either negative or positive depending on our immediate needs and wishes.

Thought Challenge, page 516

Peter Pan syndrome is marked by an unwillingness to grow up, to accept the normal responsibilities of adulthood—to make a commitment. Hence it describes either *identity diffusion* (no crisis, no commitment) or the *moratorium* (ongoing crisis, no commitment).

Because crises are stressful, disturbing, and must ordinarily be resolved, Peter Pan syndrome describes someone in the first of these stages, *identity diffusion*—without either crisis or commitment, just having fun, much like the child Peter always wants to be.

Thought Challenge, page 527

Yes, it does. It might not mean that you will be more likely to obey—unless, perhaps, you are less likely to disobey a female than a male. When Nass, Moon, and Green (1997) tested undergraduate students using computers whose only gender clue was either a male or a female voice, both male and female students readily ascribed gender stereotypes *to the machine*. A female voice in your car makes you think of *her* as feminine. No doubt. Whether that's good or bad is another thought challenge.

Key Terms

acute pelvic inflammatory disease (PID), **538**

adolescent moratorium, **515**

assimilation, **519**

biculturalism, **519**

bisexual orientation, **535**

clinical studies, **550**

cocaine, **549**

delinquency, **538**

drug abuse, **543**

drug dependence, **543**

drug tolerance, **544**

early home leaver, **521**

epidemiological studies, **550**

ethnic identity, **518**

foreclosure, **516**

gang, **542**

gateway drug-use theory, **547**

GHB, **549**

heterosexual orientation, **535**

homosexual orientation, **535**

identity crisis, **515**

identity status, **516**

identity versus role diffusion, **515**

late home leaver, **521**

LSD-25 (d-lysergic acid diethy-lamide tartrate), **548**

marginalization, **519**

marijuana, **542**

moratorium, **516**

negative identities, **515**

physiological dependence, **543**

psychological dependence, **544**

Rohypnol, **549**

separation, **519**

sexual orientation, **535**

sexual stereotype, **526**

sexually transmitted diseases (STDs), **536**

solitude, **525**

swarming, **542**

tetrahydrocannabinol (THC), **547**

values, **511**

Further Readings

The following collection of articles presents a highly authoritative and insightful look at loneliness in children. Of special relevance for this chapter is Part IV, which deals specifically with loneliness in adolescence:

Rotenberg, K. J. & S. Hymel, eds. (1999). *Loneliness in childhood and adolescence.* New York: Cambridge University Press.

Offer and associates submitted a self-image questionnaire to nearly 6,000 teenagers in 10 different countries. The result is a fascinating look at the thoughts and attitudes of teenagers around the world:

Offer, D. O., E. Ostrov, K. Howard, & R. Atkinson, (1988). *The teenage world: Adolescents' self-image in ten countries.* New York: Plenum Press.

The Woodhead, Faulkner, and Littleton collection deals with many topics of relevance to this chapter. Note especially Chapter 3, which looks at friendships during adolescence:

Woodhead, M., D. Faulkner, & K. Littleton, eds. (1999). *Making sense of social development.* New York: Routledge.

Dean's book presents an in-depth look at the lives of poor, unwed, African American teenage mothers in a rural area of southern Louisiana. It provides important insights on how cultures and environmental conditions interact to influence decisions:

Dean, A. L. (1997). *Teenage pregnancy: The interaction of psyche and culture.* Hillsdale, N.J.: The Analytic Press.

The following collection looks at the variety of risk behaviors adolescents are susceptible to, including drugs, alcohol, and early sexual activity:

Jessor, R., ed. (1998). *New perspectives on adolescent risk behavior.* New York: Cambridge University Press.

 Online Resources

For additional readings, explore *InfoTrac College Edition,* your online library. Go to http://infotrac-college.com/wadsworth and use the passcode that came on the card with your book. Try these search terms: adolescent sexual abstinence, adolescent drug use, adolescent suicide, adolescent stress, street children.

When I am dead, I hope it may
   be said
"His sins were scarlet, but his books
   were read."

Hilaire Belloc, *On His Books*

The End

Had you been standing behind me these past months, looking over my shoulder, you surely would have thought I was writing this book. You would have been at least partly wrong—I think. Because it seems to me that books are only partly from the minds and guts of their authors. A large part of them must come from somewhere else, because it's not until a book has set itself down on paper that it really exists. Before then, it could have taken a thousand other forms. But from the moment it is recorded, it has its own definite shape and substance.

The life of a child is something like a book. It too can take any number of shapes and directions, and no one knows precisely what that form will be until it happens. But quite unlike a book, as the life of a child unfolds and takes form and substance, it never irrevocably possesses that form. It changes constantly. That is the undeniable truth of human development.

Sometimes we forget that. One night not very long ago, as I staggered through a dimly lit hallway in our house, I met a tall stranger who, it seemed, grumbled something mean under his breath. I jumped back in sudden fright, curling my toes, raising my hands, and covering my head in some unconscious and primitive defensive gesture.

But it was only my 14-year-old son who had muttered a greeting, and who now lurched toward his bedroom, all arms and legs and long, scrawny neck. I had forgotten that he has become taller than I am and that his voice now rumbles from hidden places in his chest.

He is not a stranger at all, this son. Nor are my other two children, but sometimes I wonder who they will become, even who they are.

It's easy for me to sit here in this booklined workplace and compose such humanistic phrases as "There is no average child," "It is the whole infant with whom we are concerned," and "A child is an incredibly complex little organism." But it is something else to be faced with the whole infant, the nonaverage child, and the incredibly complex organism all at once and in the flesh—and not just for a brief passing glance in a hallway but for an uninterrupted period of years.

As I look at my children, I cannot help thinking that they are what I have undertaken to describe in this book. And I now know so much more clearly than before that there is no average child, that the whole process of attempting to set down in static words a thing that is at once as dynamic and as elusive as a child "in progress" necessarily robs both child and process of their dynamism.

To repeat that this is so makes it no less so. But perhaps it does make us more aware of what concerns us: That a child, like an adult, is never just being, but always becoming. The small insight I have gained from trying to relate what I have written to my children is this: When all the layers that make up the chapters and sections of this book have been bound together and the painting of children finally rendered, it will still bear only a faint resemblance to its subjects. For the subjects of the process of becoming do not stop and pose; by their very nature they continue to move forever.

A SUMMARY

This book explores the movement of children from the beginning through adolescence, divided into 12 chapters. Here is what each of those chapters said.

Chapter 1: Studying the Child

Child development studies the progressive adaptation of mythical "average children," although we know that children are neither average nor mythical; they are real and individual. Our beliefs about children reflect our social and cultural contexts; our methods are those of science.

Chapter 2: Theories of Development

Theories direct our investigations and shape our beliefs about what is important. What is important, you ask? Early emotional experiences and especially child/parent relationships, says Freud. Social competence, insists Erikson. Consequences, the behaviorists inform us. The ability to symbolize and to anticipate the outcomes of our behavior, says Bandura. Biology, the brain, and our genes, claim the biologically oriented psychologists. Language, culture, and social/historical context, Vygotsky asserts. The ecology of human interaction, thinks Bronfenbrenner.

Chapter 3: Conception, Heredity, and Environment

The fact that there is a you or a me is largely a matter of fortune. It could have been another ovum; it could have been any one of many millions of other sperm cells. In each case, the result would have been someone else. Or would it?

What you and I are continually becoming is not solely a function of the intricate arrangement of DNA molecules that our parents passed on to us (that they, in turn, got from their parents, and so on, so that there exists in a remote sense a common pool of genes for all of us). What we are is also a matter of where we have been at different times in our lives, and of who the people around us have been—of our contexts.

Chapter 4: Prenatal Development and Birth

We begin as a microscopic speck in one of our mother's fallopian tubes. Through the next 266 days, this indistinct glob of cells changes into the form and functions that make up newborns. And although these changes are ordered, systematic, and highly predictable, they are nevertheless subject to external influences such as drugs, illnesses, malnutrition, and other stressors. And then we are born. And just about everybody loves us!

Chapters 5 and 6: Development through Infancy

As infants, we discover our hands, our feet, and our parents; and we learn that blankets are for chewing. Later we are initiated into the wonderful secrets of language, and we learn that there are things to cry and laugh about, and things, we could never have dreamed of. And if we continue to be lucky, just about everybody still loves us a lot. We mean something!

Chapters 7 and 8: Development through the Preschool Period

In early childhood, we learn mystical, magical things that dazzle our senses and our minds. A new logic invades our thinking—egocentric, perception dominated, and intuitive, but nevertheless the germ of a finer, more advanced logic. As preschoolers, our world enlarges. The microsystems of our ecology are no longer defined only by parents and siblings; now they include peers and playmates and caregivers and teachers. Sometimes we have to struggle a little to be loved. Some of us pretend we don't care all that much. But deep down, we do.

Philip and Karen Smith/Tony Stone Images

A child in the process of becoming is a dynamic and elusive being, not easily captured and reduced to printed words on textbook pages. The subject does not stop and pose; it moves forever.

Chapters 9 and 10: Development through the Early School Years

Through middle childhood, we expand our powers of mind and body, refining our thinking, expanding our knowledge base, honing our language and social skills. And perhaps as our construction of reality becomes more sophisticated, we begin to forget a little of the magic and the mystery that filled our younger lives. But not all of it, for we are still in those sweet childish days, when every day is like 20. Now our lives are filled with buddies, and love is a remote abstraction. Being really liked is enough.

Chapters 11 and 12: Development through Adolescence

Finally we become adolescents, newly aware of the power of our logic, egocentric and full of our *selves*, smitten with a sense of competence and invulnera-

bility, imbued with a wonderful conviction that we are very special. Then bang! puberty strikes, sending hormones raging through our veins, and we are driven even further from our childish games as we struggle to invent the many meanings of love. We teeter uncertainly on the brink of adulthood—sometimes torn and confused, sometimes angry and rebellious, sometimes hungry to try everything that life has to offer before it's too late, desperate to gather our rosebuds while we may. And sometimes, as adolescents we just sleep in for a surprisingly long time.

Of "Average Children" and of Other Children

At every step in the chronology that composes this text, something was said about the physical, cognitive, social, and emotional development of the "average child." Even the exceptional children we spoke about were sometimes treated as averages too. But at every step, you were urged to keep in mind that the average we refer to is an invention. To emphasize this, in boxes scattered here and there in *Of Children*, we looked as well at children in other contexts, whose lives are sometimes dramatically different from yours or mine. But sadly, we couldn't reveal many details of these other lives. Still, we have tried hard not to rob children of their individuality, not to strip the magic from the processes and the outcomes of development.

That part of the story has now been told. There remains only the attempt to bring the various layers and pieces into a cohesive whole to provide a richer, more accurate, more complete, and more human picture of children in the process of becoming.

⌐ TWO OTHER VIEWS

Who are you? Who am I? Is the *I* who is sitting here thinking about who he is—and wondering who the blazes *you* are—different from the *I* who questioned my grandmother's fertile theories? Was *I* the same *me* when, as an adolescent, I let my fantasies gleam in my eyes, causing my uncle to fire me? Was the *I* who went to school as a freshly scrubbed 6-year-old the same person who graduated from college many years later? Who is my *self*, and what is it; how did it become what it is?

Perhaps we still can't answer the question of personal identity, a question that has plagued philosophers, psychologists, theologians, grandmothers, and all manner of thinkers since thinking began. But two useful answers are often given—both intuitive and highly subjective, but no less meaningful. The first asserts there is an unidentifiable something about the self that continues from the dawning awareness of a personal identity until the oblivion of psychotic disorder, memory loss, or death destroys all sense of existence. The other answer does not contradict the first, but simply extends it: It maintains that the self is continually developing, despite the individual's feeling of a single and unique personal identity throughout life.

As we saw in Chapter 2, the self and its development are primary concerns of humanistic psychol-

ogy; they are also major concerns of existential philosophy. Each of these orientations can add to our appreciation of the phenomena of development. Taken together, they present something of a finishing touch for the portrait that has been attempted in this text.

Humanism

Recall that **humanism** is a concern for humans, for humanity, for the development and expression of humanness. Humanism exalts the individual and glorifies the self. The concepts of paramount concern to the humanistic psychologist include notions such as self-structure, self-concept, self-image, self-understanding, self-acceptance, self-enhancement, self-realization, and self-actualization. Humanism sees the development of self (self-actualization) as the goal toward which all humans should strive.

The process of self-actualization is the act of becoming whatever one has the potential to become through one's own efforts; it is the process of actualizing—of making potential actual. But it is not a static goal like some mountaintop we struggle toward. Rather, it is a process, an ongoing activity; we never reach the ruddy stop!

Put another way, self-actualization is simply the process of development. We could have substituted different terms in this text to make this clearer. For example, instead of speaking of development, we might have spoken of self-actualization or of the development of self. And, instead of referring to the identity crises of adolescents, who cannot easily determine whether they are child or adult, we could have referred to problems of self-knowledge and self-definition and self-discovery during the transition from childhood to adulthood. Also, we could have tied our discussion of the factors that impede and accelerate and shape development to a consideration of self-enhancement or changing self-structure or contributions to self-esteem. The picture that would have emerged might have been a more integrated

---

humanism A philosophical and psychological orientation primarily concerned with the worth of humans as individuals and processes that augment their human qualities.

one, for we would constantly have been speaking of the self. It would also have been a more realistic picture that dealt more with real children than with a hypothetical "average child," for the self belongs solely to the individual; there is no "average" self. To speak of the average self is to distort the concept miserably. At the same time, our portrait would probably have been a more global, less precise, and less informative study of the child.

Existentialism

To complete our description of children, we might consider concepts of **existentialism**, which are similar to those of humanistic psychology. From Jean-Paul Sartre we borrow a description of the human condition—cynical and pessimistic, but one that enables us to understand better the direction of development, particularly in its nearly adult stages. From Martin Buber we borrow ideas from a philosophy of what he terms personalism, which is only a short distance from humanism.

Jean-Paul Sartre's existential picture of people and of the forces that move them can be described by three words: anguish, **abandonment**, and despair. These words summarize the human condition: They are both the facts of existence and its consequences. We are forever in anguish because we are constantly forced to make decisions and yet have no guides for these decisions. There is no guarantee that anything we do is correct, for there is no God, Sartre informs us; and without a God all action must be justified by its effects on others. Such resolution is a tremendous

Does self-actualization ever become self-realization? Does the adolescent ever know that the child has grown up? Does the adult? The old person?

Ryan McVay/PhotoDisc

and terrible responsibility, and its consequence is deep and undying anguish. We have also been abandoned, and abandonment is an indescribably lonely feeling. We have been abandoned not merely by others but in a general sense, without purpose and with no a priori values—abandoned and not only free to make choices but also required to make them. So we despair because we are free but without hope, because to will something is not necessarily to achieve it, and because when we die all our efforts may have been in vain.

This is *atheistic existentialism*, which is described here as a contrast to the more optimistic reflections of Martin Buber. Buber (1958, 1965) tells us that there are four main evils in the modern world, and that the effect of each of these evils is to highlight the importance of the human self. The first of these evils is our terrible loneliness, and loneliness has long been recognized by existentialists as a central concept. Existence as a self is essentially a lonely experience, because the self always belongs only to the individual; it can never be shared completely. Therefore, we are always alone.

Buber's second evil is the never-ending drive for technological progress, the individual's worth lessening with the increasing importance of machines and science and technology.

existentialism A philosophical/psychological orientation that stresses *existence* (the facts of existence, the purpose of existence, the realities of existence) rather than *essence* (the substance of the human being, the basic nature of the human organism).

abandonment The existential dilemma. An atheistic-existential concept referring to an intense feeling that results from the realization that we have been abandoned on earth with no purpose and no knowledge of where we come from or where we are going.

The third evil stems from a basic human duality, the good-versus-evil dichotomy—the id warring with the superego. Life is forever a struggle to know what is good and bad and, even more difficult, to be good rather than bad.

Finally, Buber contends that the individual is being degraded by the state. The conglomerate, impersonal, and faceless entities that define states, says Buber, are incompatible with the uniqueness and personal worth of the individual.

The result of these evils is summarized in a single existentialist (and humanistic) term: **alienation**. To be alienated is to be separated from, to be a stranger to. We are alienated from ourselves, from others, and from our environment. In short, we have been uprooted from the relationships that we should have

---

alienation A condition or emotion resulting from being turned away from, estranged, shunned, separated from, or excluded with respect to important human relationships and interactions.

with all three: our private self, those who surround us, and our environment. Accordingly, the greatest evil that besets us, social animals that we are, is alienation; and the greatest good is the opposite of alienation: love, not only of the self but also of and from others.

Buber's philosophy is seldom pessimistic, for it asserts strongly that through love, our salvation, our happiness, and our consequent self-actualization can be achieved. Love, says Buber, is a question of relationships—what he terms the *I-Thou relationship*. In the I-Thou relationship the object or person being related to is not being used selfishly; the relationship is mutual, there is dialogue as opposed to monologue, and people say and do what they honestly mean rather than what is merely convenient or socially appropriate.

If the process of human development has a goal—if it ever ceases to be a process of becoming—then its goal must surely be a capacity to feel great love, and the reward for having reached that state must surely be great happiness.

GLOSSARY

This glossary defines the most important terms and expressions used in this text. In each case the meaning given corresponds to the usage in the text. For more complete definitions, consult a standard psychological dictionary.[1]

abandonment The existential dilemma. An atheistic-existential concept referring to an intense feeling that results from the realization that we have been abandoned on earth with no purpose and no knowledge of where we come from or where we are going. (See *alienation.*)

abortion A miscarriage occurring usually before the twentieth week of pregnancy when the fetus ordinarily weighs less than 1 pound.

accommodation The modification of an activity or an ability that a child has already learned, to conform to environmental demands. Piaget's description of development holds that assimilation and accommodation are the means by which an individual interacts with the world and adapts to it. (See *assimilation.*)

acquired immunodeficiency syndrome (AIDS) An incurable and fatal disease, transmitted through the exchange of body fluids, caused by HIV (*human immunodeficiency virus*).

active correlation Scarr and McCartney's label for the observation that people often deliberately select, or try to shape, environments to conform to genetic predispositions—a phenomenon that accounts for genotype-environment correlation.

acute pelvic inflammatory disease A sexually transmitted disease (STD) that frequently results from other STDs such as gonorrhea. Also termed *salpingitis* or *endometritis*, pelvic inflammatory disease affects about 1 million women a year and is often associated with infertility and tubal pregnancies.

---

[1] Some of these definitions are taken from the glossary in Guy R. Lefrançois (2000). *Psychology for Teaching,* 10th ed. Belmont, Calif.: Wadsworth; and from Guy R. Lefrançois (1999) *The Lifespan*, 6th ed. Belmont, Calif.: Wadsworth, 1999. Used by permission.

adaptation The process whereby an organism changes in response to the environment. Such changes are assumed to facilitate interaction with that environment. Adaptation plays a central role in Piaget's theory. (See *accommodation, assimilation.*)

adolescence A general term signifying the period from the onset of puberty to adulthood, typically including the teen years (13 to 19). (See *puberty.*)

adolescent moratorium Erikson's term for the social function of the hiatus between childhood and adulthood. The adolescent period is a moratorium in that it gives the person some time to experiment with various identities.

Adult Attachment Interview (AAI) A questionnaire developed by Main designed to uncover parents' recollections of their relationships with their own caregivers when they were children.

affect synchrony Descriptive label for the matching of emotional states, a phenomenon often evident in mother-infant interactions. Sometimes described as a sort of dance: One moment, infant leads, mother follows; then perhaps mother leads, infant follows.

affiliative behaviors Behaviors that indicate wanting to interact with or do things with someone; for example, smiling, looking at, laughing, and giving things to. May be contrasted with attachment, which is a more powerful emotional bond evident in seeking to be close, clinging, wanting to be picked up, putting the head in the lap, snuggling, and so on.

AFP test A screening test designed to detect the likelihood of a fetal neural tube defect by revealing the presence of *alphafetoprotein* in the mother's blood.

afterbirth The placenta and other membranes that are expelled from the uterus following the birth of a child.

aggression Forceful action intended to dominate or intimidate, including actions such as insisting, asserting, intruding, or being angry or even violent. (See *violence.*)

aggressive-rejected Category of children who are rejected primarily because of their high aggression. (See *withdrawn-rejected.*)

alienation A condition or emotion resulting from being turned away from, estranged, shunned, separated from, or excluded with respect to important human relationships and interactions.

allele Each of the two corresponding forms of a gene, one being inherited from each parent.

altricial Born with highly undeveloped motor capacities. Requiring a relatively lengthy period of care. (See *precocial*.)

Alzheimer's disease A disease associated with old age (but also occurring as young as 40), marked by progressive loss of memory and brain function, and eventual death.

amniocentesis A procedure whereby amniotic fluid is removed from a pregnant woman by means of a hollow needle. Subsequent analysis of this fluid may reveal chromosomal aberrations (Down syndrome, for example) and other fetal problems.

amniotic fluid A clear or straw-colored fluid in which the fetus develops in the uterus.

anal-retentive Freudian term for a personality type described as stingy, hoarding, selfish, and linked with fixation or regression at the anal stage of development.

anal stage The second of Freud's psychosexual stages of development, beginning at approximately 8 months and lasting until around 18 months, and characterized by children's preoccupation with physical anal activities.

androgynous Characterized by a balance of masculine and feminine characteristics.

anencephalic A condition in which parts, or all, of the brain are missing.

animistic thinking Attributing lifelike qualities to inanimate objects. In Piaget's theory, young preschoolers are sometimes described as using animistic thinking.

anorexia nervosa A medical condition not due to any detectable illness, primarily affecting adolescent girls and involving a loss of 15% to 25% of ideal body weight. It usually begins with dieting and ends when the patient is unwilling or unable to eat normally.

anovulatory Literally, occurring without ovulation. Characteristic of a girl's first menstrual periods.

anoxia A condition in which there is an insufficient supply of oxygen to the brain.

Apgar scale Widely used standardized evaluation procedure for newborns that looks at their heart rate, respiration, muscle tone, color, and reflexive responses.

apnea A temporary paralysis or collapse of throat muscles during sleep. Victims typically awaken at once and again breathe normally. Apnea is involved in about 5% of all insomnia complaints. Severe apnea can endanger life.

arousal As a physiological concept, arousal refers to changes in functions such as heart rate, respiration rate, electrical activity in the cortex, and electrical conductivity of the skin. As a psychological concept, arousal refers to degree of alertness, awareness, vigilance, or wakefulness. Arousal varies from very low (coma or sleep) to very high (panic or high anxiety).

artificial insemination An artificial breeding procedure often used in animal husbandry and sometimes with humans. This procedure eliminates the necessity for a physical union between a pair of opposite-sex individuals.

assimilation (1) In Piaget's theory, the act of incorporating objects or aspects of objects to previously learned activities. To assimilate is, in a sense, to ingest or to use something that is previously learned; more simply, the exercising of previously learned responses. (2) In sociology, a term referring to the process by which members of ethnic minority groups adopt the cultural trappings of the dominant group, discarding those of the minority. (See *accommodation*.)

associative play A form of social play in which children sometimes share toys, but each child plays independently without mutually accepted goals or rules.

attachment A strong emotional bond that seems to have its roots in powerful biological tendencies. Parent-infant attachment is important for healthy infant development.

attention deficit hyperactivity disorder (ADHD) A disorder marked by excessive general activity for the child's age, attention problems, high impulsivity, and low frustration tolerance.

attention span A measure of the capacity to hold more than one item in consciousness at one time.

authoritarian parenting A highly controlling, dogmatic, obedience-oriented parenting style in which there is little recourse to reasoning and no acceptance of children's autonomy.

authoritative parenting A moderately controlling parenting style in which value is placed on independence and reasoning, but in which parents impose some regulations and controls.

autistic disorder A serious childhood mental disorder usually apparent by 30 months, characterized by social unresponsiveness, poor or nonexistent communication skills, and bizarre behavior.

autobiographical memory A type of declarative (conscious, long-term) memory consisting of knowledge about personal experiences, tied to specific times and places—hence personal *episodes*; also called *episodic memory*. (See *explicit memory, semantic memory*.)

autonomous A classification, based on the *Adult Attachment Interview*, marked by predominantly positive and highly consistent recollections of relationships with parents.

autonomy Piaget's label for the second stage of moral development, marked by a reliance on internal standards as guides for behaving and for judging morality. (See *heteronomy*.)

autonomy versus shame and doubt The second Erikson stage, about ages 18 months to 2 or 3 years, when the preschooler faces the challenge of developing a sense of mastery and control (autonomy) but has to give up some of the security of relying on parents.

autosomes All chromosomes in mature sperm and ova other than the sex chromosome. Each of these cells therefore contains 22 autosomes.

axon Elongated, trunklike extension of a nerve cell. Nerve impulses are ordinarily transmitted from the nerve cell outward along the axon.

Babinski reflex A reflex present in newborn children but disappearing later in life. The toes fan out as a result of being tickled in the center of the soles of the feet. Normal adults curl their toes inward rather than fanning them outward.

basic gender understanding An early stage in the development of gender awareness in which the infant recognizes that there are two different genders and that he is a boy or she is a girl.

basic needs Unlearned physiological requirements of the human organism; specifically, the needs for food, drink, and sex.

Bayley Scales Standardized scales used to measure infant development, reflecting extent to which infant has acquired motor and mental skills expected at specific ages.

behavior modification A general term for the application of behavioristic principles (primarily principles of operant conditioning) in systematic and deliberate attempts to change behavior.

behavioral genetics The branch of genetics whose goal is to understand the functions, the identity, and the interactions of genes that are relevant to behavior.

behaviorism A general term used to describe approaches to learning and development that are concerned primarily with the observable, objective components of behavior (such as stimuli and responses).

biculturalism A process whereby an individual attempts to adopt roles and identities that reflect more than one cultural reality—typically both the majority and the minority group to which the individual belongs.

bilingual education Use of more than one language in a classroom. In North America, typically means instructing in English part of the time and using a language other than English the rest of the time.

birth The process whereby the fetus, the placenta, and other membranes are separated from the mother's body and expelled. (See *labor.*)

birth cohort A group of individuals who have in common the fact that they were born within the same range of time.

bisexual orientation Defined by a person's customary and enduring romantic attraction to persons of either gender.

body mass index (BMI) The ratio of height to weight, computed by dividing weight in kilograms by the square of height in meters. Normal BMI is between about 20 and 27 (somewhat higher with increasing age). Indexes above and below these cutoffs indicate obesity or excessive thinness.

bonding failure A biologically oriented phrase to indicate the failure of a bond to form between a mother and infant, usually as a result of not being exposed to each other during a critical period. The concept has limited applicability to humans.

Bradley method A method of prepared childbirth emphasizing relaxation training and tuning in to the mother's body to find what is most comfortable.

brain proliferation Expression used to describe the rapid development of a staggering number of increasingly complex neural connections in the first two years of life.

brain stem Brain structure at top of spinal cord, involved mainly in functions essential for physiological survival (respiration, heart action, temperature control).

Brazelton Neonatal Behavioral Assessment Scale (NBAS) A wide-ranging assessment scale for newborns that looks at many different reflexes and several dozen different types of behaviors.

breech birth An abnormal presentation of the fetus at birth: buttocks first rather than head first.

bulimia nervosa Significant preoccupation with body shape and weight manifested in recurrent episodes of binge eating often accompanied by self-induced vomiting, use of laxatives or diuretics, strict fasting, or vigorous exercise.

bulletin boards An Internet phenomenon whereby groups who share specific interests can *post* and read information, advice, and propaganda relevant to their interests, typically anonymously.

bullying Repeatedly and habitually attempting to inflict pain, to terrorize, or to intimidate. Can be verbal or physical.

bystander apathy The well-researched tendency of many people not to intervene even when they witness perpetration of some horrendous act.

canalization Waddington's term to describe the extent to which genetically determined characteristics are resistant to environmental influences. A highly canalized trait (such as hair color) remains unchanged in the face of most environmental influences; less highly canalized characteristics (such as manifested intelligence) are highly influenced by the environment.

case studies A research technique in the social sciences in which investigators do an in-depth analysis of only one case (or individual), or a small number of them.

cataracts Opaque coating over the lens of the eye, causing partial or sometimes total blindness.

cathartic model Expression of the Freudian notion that certain experiences or events can serve to release pent-up negative tendencies, serving a purifying or purging function.

cell body The main part of a cell, containing the nucleus.

cephalocaudal Referring to the direction of development beginning with the head and proceeding outward toward the tail. Early infant development is cephalocaudal because children acquire control over their heads before acquiring control over their limbs.

cerebellum Brain structure at base of skull, at the rear of the brain stem, closely involved in coordinating motor activity and maintaining balance.

cerebral cortex Outer covering of the cerebrum, only about one-eighth inch thick.

cerebral hemispheres The two opposite halves of the cerebrum. In adults, their functions overlap but are not exactly duplicated.

cerebral palsy Label for a collection of congenital problems associated with brain damage and manifested in motor problems of varying severity, and occasionally in other problems such as convulsions or behavior disorders. (See *significant developmental motor disability.*)

cerebrum Most highly developed part of the brain. A wrinkled mass of brain tissue whose principal functions relate to sensation, thinking, speech, and other higher mental processes.

cervix The small circular opening to the womb (uterus) that dilates considerably during birth to permit passage of the baby.

cesarean delivery A common surgical procedure in which the fetus is delivered through an incision in the mother's abdomen and uterus.

chat groups An Internet phenomenon whereby pairs or groups of individuals, typically unidentified or using pseudonyms, can communicate with one another in real time by computers.

chlamydia A highly common STD, especially among women, often asymptotic (without apparent symptoms), especially in its early stages, and therefore often undetected and unreported. A common cause of infertility among women.

chorion Part of the placenta, the flat membrane on the inside of the uterus, to which the umbilical cord is attached. (See *chorionic villus sampling; placenta.*)

chorionic villus sampling (CVS) A procedure in which samples of the membrane lining the uterus are used to permit prenatal diagnosis of potential birth defects.

chromosomal disorders Chromosomal errors sometimes evident in the presence or absence of extra chromosomes or portions thereof.

chromosome A microscopic body in the nucleus of all human and plant cells containing the genes—the carriers of heredity. Each mature human sex cell (sperm or ovum) contains 23 chromosomes, each containing countless numbers of genes. (See *genes.*)

chronosystem Bronfenbrenner's term for his recognition that important aspects of environments (of ecologies) change over time.

class In logic, an abstraction signifying a collection of items (for example, people, ideas, things) that share one or more identifiable characteristics (for example, the class of blue things; or the class of blue things that are also hairy).

classical conditioning Also called learning through stimulus substitution, because it involves the repeated pairing of two stimuli so that a previously neutral (conditioned) stimulus eventually comes to elicit the same response (conditioned response) that was previously evoked by the first stimulus (unconditioned stimulus). This type of conditioning was first described by Pavlov.

clinical studies Investigations concerned with the primary symptoms and the normal course of diseases and related conditions.

cocaine A stimulant drug, ordinarily inhaled as a white powder, the primary effects of which are feelings of euphoria. Possible effects also include hallucinations. In some forms (freebase or as what is called "crack" or "rock"), its effects are more immediate and more intense, and its use leads more readily to psychological dependence.

cognition Mental processes such as thinking, knowing, and remembering. Theories of cognition attempt to explain intellectual development and functioning.

colic Infant disorder characterized by excessive crying, often following feeding. May occasionally, but not always, be due to intense abdominal pain resulting from muscular spasms.

comorbidity A medical term for the frequent co-occurrence of a number of conditions. For example, profound mental retardation often includes visual or other sensory problems as comorbidities.

compensation A logical rule relating to the fact that certain changes can compensate for opposing changes, thereby negating their effect. For example, as a square object becomes longer, it also becomes thinner. Increases in length compensate for decreases in width. These changes combine to negate any actual changes in mass.

compensatory preschool programs Preschool education programs that attempt to make up for early disadvantages in the lives of some children. The best known of these programs in the United States is Project Head Start. (See *Project Head Start.*)

concept A collection of perceptual experiences or ideas related by virtue of their possessing common properties.

conception The beginning of life. Also called *fertilization*, conception occurs with the union of a sperm cell with an egg cell.

conceptualization The forming of concepts (ideas or meanings); an intellectual process leading to thinking and understanding.

concordance A measure of the probability that both individuals of a twin pair will share the same characteristic. A concordance rate of 50% for schizophrenia means that half of all individuals who have a schizophrenic identical twin would also be expected to be schizophrenic.

concrete operations The third of Piaget's four major developmental stages, lasting from age 7 or 8 to approximately 11 or 12, characterized primarily by children's ability to deal with concrete problems and objects, or objects and problems easily imagined in a tangible sense.

conditioned response (CR) A response that is elicited by a conditioned stimulus. A conditioned response resembles its corresponding unconditioned response. The two are not identical, however.

conditioned stimulus (CS) A stimulus that elicits no response—or elicits a global response initially, but as a result of being paired with an unconditioned stimulus and its response, acquires the capability of eliciting that same response. For example, a stimulus that is always present at the time of a fear reaction may become a conditioned stimulus for fear.

conditioning A term used to describe a simple type of learning whereby certain behaviors are determined by the environment. (See *classical conditioning, operant conditioning.*)

conduct disorder An emotional disorder evident in persistent and significant violation of rules and laws, and of others' basic rights, often manifested in excessive aggression, vandalism, theft, and deceitfulness.

confluence model Zajonc's term for the hypothesis that various factors such as family size, birth order, and family spacing interact to determine the intellectual climate of the home, and have a profound influence on the intellectual development of children.

congenital Present at birth, although not necessarily inherited. For example, a birth defect would be congenital if it is due to the influence of drugs, and *genetic* if it is a condition determined by genetic makeup. It might also be *multifactorial.*

conscience An internalized set of rules governing an individual's behavior.

consciousness Awareness of one's self and surroundings; awareness of one's existence; awareness of one's awareness.

conservation A Piagetian term implying that certain quantitative attributes of objects remain unchanged unless something is added to or taken away from them. Such characteristics of objects as mass, number, area, and volume are capable of being conserved.

context That which surrounds and influences. In psychology, the term is used to include the totality of environmental and circumstantial influences on development and behavior.

contextual model A developmental model that emphasizes the importance of the individual's interaction with environmental context. It looks at the historical period in which individuals are raised, as well as at the unique experiences they have.

continuous society A society that doesn't clearly demarcate passage from one major life stage to the next. (See *discontinuous society*.)

control group Consists of subjects who are not experimented with but who are used as comparisons to the experimental group to ascertain whether the outcomes were affected by the experimental procedure.

conventional level Kohlberg's second level of morality, reflecting a desire to establish and maintain good relations with others (law and order; obedience).

convergent thinking Guilford's expression for thinking that leads to a unique, correct solution, in contrast with *divergent thinking*, which leads to the production of a wide variety of solutions.

Cooley's approach to self-worth The belief that evaluation of our self reflects what we think others think of us. (See *James's approach to self-worth*.)

correlation A mathematical measure of a relationship among variables. It is usually expressed as a number ranging from +1.00 (a perfect positive relationship) through 0 (no relationship) to −1.00 (a perfect inverse relationship).

correlational fallacy The apparently logical but often false assumption that if two events are related (correlated), one causes the other.

crack Name given to the drug that results when cocaine is "cooked down" with bicarbonate of soda to produce freebase cocaine (also called rock). It is usually smoked rather than snorted and produces a much stronger and more immediate rush than cocaine.

creativity Generally refers to the capacity of individuals to produce novel or original answers or products. The term *creative* is an adjective that can be used to describe people, products, or processes.

critical period The period during which an appropriate stimulus must be presented to an organism for imprinting to occur.

cross-sectional study A technique in the investigation of child development that involves observing and comparing different subjects at different age levels. A cross-sectional study would compare 4- and 6-year-olds by observing two groups of children at the same time, one group consisting of 6-year-old children and the other of 4-year-old children. A longitudinal study would require that the same children be examined at the age of 4 and again at age 6.

crystallized abilities Cattell's term for intellectual abilities that are highly dependent on experience (verbal and computational skills and general information, for example). These abilities may continue to improve well into old age. (See *fluid abilities*.)

culture Signifies the customs, beliefs, achievements, art, and literature that are particular to a distinct group of people.

cyclic movements Expression used to describe the young infant's spontaneous, regularly recurring body movements.

cytomegalovirus (CMV) A herpes virus affecting the salivary glands; can be transmitted from mother to infant during birth. An important cause of mental retardation and deafness.

defense mechanism A relatively irrational and sometimes unhealthy method used by people to compensate for their inability to satisfy their basic desires and to overcome the anxiety accompanying this inability.

deferred imitation Imitating people or events in their absence. Deferred imitation is assumed by Piaget to be critical to developing language abilities.

delinquency A legal category defined as the apprehension and conviction of a juvenile for some legal transgression.

delivery The second stage of labor, beginning with the baby's head emerging (in a normal delivery) at the cervical opening and terminating with the birth of the child.

dendrites Hairlike tendrils found on a neuron's cell body; their function is to receive neural impulses.

deoxyribonucleic acid (DNA) A substance assumed to be the basis of all life, consisting of four chemical bases arranged in an extremely large number of combinations. The two strands of the DNA molecule that compose genes are arranged in the form of a double spiral (helix). These double strands are capable of replicating themselves as well as crossing over from one strand of the spiral to the other and forming new combinations of their genetic material. The nuclei of all cells contain DNA molecules.

dependent variable The variable that may or may not be affected by manipulations of the independent variable in an experimental situation. (See *independent variable, variable*.)

development The total process whereby individuals adapt to their environment. Development includes growth, maturation, and learning.

developmental arithmetic disorder A learning disability evident in specific problems in developing arithmetic skills in the absence of other problems such as mental retardation. Sometimes labeled *dyscalculia*.

developmental coordination disorder A childhood motor skills disorder not associated with brain damage or cerebral palsy, often evident in difficulties in learning or in carrying out motor tasks.

developmental psychology That aspect of psychology concerned with the development of individuals.

developmental quotient (DQ) Score reflecting infant development, based largely on infants' acquisition of expected motor and mental skills.

developmental reading disorder A learning disability manifested in reading problems of varying severity; sometimes evident in spelling difficulties. Also labeled *dyslexia* or *specific reading disability*.

developmental tasks Sequential, age-related developmental milestones usually evident in new abilities or changes in attitudes or interests. Although many developmental tasks are common across cultures, some are specific to particular cultures.

developmental theory Psychological theory concerned with systematic changes that define human development. Child developmental theories deal with changes from birth to adolescence; life-span developmental theories deal with the entire span of life (birth to death).

developmental timetables Lists of observable developmental achievements with information concerning the average ages at which children normally attain these achievements. Such timetables are often used as instruments to assess the relative development of individual children.

developmentally delayed Term used to describe apparent cognitive or adaptive deficits in children below age 3 or sometimes 5, or even as old as 9. Recommended term because of problems in identifying both the existence and the causes of apparent deficits at very young ages.

diabetes Disease associated with deficient secretion of insulin resulting in abnormally high sugar levels in the blood and urine. Some forms are linked with a recessive gene.

diary description A method of child study that records sequential descriptions of a child's behavior at predetermined intervals (daily or weekly, for example). Sometimes useful for arriving at a better understanding of general developmental patterns.

diethylstilbestrol (DES) A drug once widely prescribed to lessen the probability of miscarriages. It has been linked with medical problems in offspring.

difficult infants A type of temperament characterized by irregularity with respect to things like eating, sleeping, and toilet functions; withdrawal from unfamiliar situations; slow adaptation to change; and intense as well as negative moods.

dilation and curettage (D&C) A surgical procedure that involves scraping the walls of the uterus. It is occasionally necessary after birth if all of the placenta has not been expelled.

dilation and effacement of the cervix The first stage of labor, during which the cervix dilates until, having reached a diameter of about 10 cm. (4 in.), it is large enough to permit passage of the fetus.

direct reinforcement Reinforcement that occurs as a direct consequence of a behavior—like getting paid to work. (See *vicarious reinforcement*.)

discontinuous society A society, typically *traditional* or *preindustrial*, that clearly marks passage from one major life stage to the next. Puberty rites are the hallmark of discontinuous societies.

disinhibitory effect The appearance of previously suppressed deviant behavior as a function of observing a model.

dismissing An *Adult Attachment Interview* classification reflected in fragmentary, poorly detailed adult recollections of childhood relationships with parents, often overidealized but devoid of specific memories.

disorganized/disoriented Describes infants whose attachment behaviors toward caregivers are confused, unclear, and sometimes contradictory.

distinct society A metaphor used to describe the Canadian cultural scene where, theoretically, two distinct cultures coexist with neither being assimilated to the other as would be the case in a melting pot society. (See *melting pot societies*.)

doctrine of the tabula rasa The belief, associated with John Locke and with behaviorists such as Watson, that children are born with no (or few) predetermined characteristics, tendencies, or habits. Developmental outcomes are thought to result primarily from the effects of experience.

dominant gene The gene (carrier of heredity) that takes precedence over all other related genes in genetically determined traits. Because all genes in the fertilized egg normally occur in pairs of corresponding genes (termed *alleles*—one from the male and one from the female), the presence of a dominant gene as one member of the pair of genes means that the hereditary characteristic it controls will be present in the individual. (See *recessive gene, allele*.)

dominant inheritance The expression of traits related to a dominant allele. Occurs in individuals who are homozygous for the dominant form of the allele (have inherited identical *dominant* forms of the allele) and in individuals who are heterozygous for that trait (have inherited competing dominant and recessive forms of the allele). (See *allele*.)

double-blind procedure An experimental method in which neither subjects nor experimenters involved in data collection or analysis are aware of which subjects are members of experimental groups and which are not. Double-blind procedures are used as a safeguard against experimenter and subject bias.

double helix The natural state of DNA molecules; essentially, two spiraling, intertwining chains of corresponding molecules.

doula A birth assistant. May be involved before, during, and after birth. Sometimes plays a role similar to that of a caring partner.

Down syndrome The most common chromosomal birth defect, related to the presence of an extra twenty-first chromosome (technically labeled *trisomy 21*) and sometimes evident in mild to severe mental retardation.

drug abuse The continued use of drugs in spite of persistent physical, social, psychological, or occupational problems that result.

drug dependence Condition marked by a preoccupation with obtaining a drug, a compulsion to use it, and relapse following attempts to cease using it.

drug tolerance Physiological changes following drug use that lead to higher doses of the drug being required to achieve the same effect.

drugs Chemical substances that have marked physiological and sometimes psychological effects on living organisms.

dynamic systems approaches Approaches that emphasize the dynamic (changing) nature of human development, and that view development as a complex and highly variable interaction of processes involving all aspects of development. Often based on complex mathematical models.

dyslexia A form of learning disability manifested in reading problems of varying severity. Dyslexia may be evident in spelling errors that are erratic rather than consistent.

early home leaver For research purposes, often defined as someone who leaves home before age 18 (the typical age of high school graduation).

Early Infancy Temperament Questionnaire (EITQ) A questionnaire, often used in research, designed to allow caregivers to systematize their perceptions of their infants in order to classify their infants' temperaments.

easy infants A temperament type marked by high regularity in eating, sleeping, and so on; high interest in novel situations; high adaptability to change; and a preponderance of positive moods, as well as low or moderate intensity of reaction.

eating disorder A clinical disorder, as defined by the American Psychiatric Association, involving a serious disturbance in eating habits. The two principal eating disorders are anorexia nervosa and bulimia nervosa. (See *anorexia nervosa, bulimia nervosa.*)

ecological validity An expression sometimes used to refer to the fact that psychological phenomena are highly dependent on environmental factors. For example, cultural, social, and other systems affect our behavior. A generalization is said to be ecologically valid to the extent that it takes environmental circumstances into account.

ecology The study of the interrelationships between organisms and their environment. In developmental psychology, ecology relates to the social context in which behavior and development occur.

ectopic pregnancy A pregnancy in which the zygote implants and develops anywhere outside the uterus—most often in a fallopian tube (a *tubal pregnancy*), though sometimes elsewhere as well.

egg cell (See *ovum.*)

ego The second stage of the human personality, according to Freud. It is the rational, reality-oriented level of human personality, which develops as children become aware of what the environment makes possible and impossible, and therefore serves as a damper to the id. The id tends toward immediate gratification of impulses as they are felt, whereas the ego imposes restrictions that are based on environmental reality. (See *id, superego.*)

egocentric Adjective based on Latin words for *self* (*ego*) and *center*. Literally, it describes a self-centered behavior, attitude, or personality characteristic. Although egocentrism often has negative connotations of selfishness, it is simply descriptive rather than evaluative when applied to children's perception of the world. For example, egocentric perception is characterized by an inability to assume an objective point of view.

ejaculation Seminal emission. The sudden and usually forceful discharge of semen, a liquid containing sperm, by the male.

elaborated language code A phrase used by Bernstein to describe the language of middle- and upper-class children. Elaborated language codes are grammatically correct, complex, and precise. (See *restricted language code.*)

elaborating A long-term memory process involving changing or adding to material or making associations to make remembering easier. (See *organizing, rehearsing.*)

Electra complex A Freudian stage occurring around the age of 4 or 5 years, when a girl's sexual feelings lead her to desire her father and to become jealous of her mother. (See *Oedipus complex.*)

electrodermal response (EDR) A measure of changes in the skin's electrical conductivity. With increasing arousal (emotion), minute increases in perspiration result in increased skin conductivity. Hence EDR (also termed *galvanic skin response* or *GSR*) is a physiological measure of arousal (emotion).

elementary mental functions In Vygotsky's system, simple, unlearned behaviors like reflexes. Present in both animals and human infants.

eliciting effect That type of imitative behavior in which the observer does not copy the model's responses but simply behaves in a related manner. (See *inhibitory effect, disinhibitory effect, modeling effect.*)

embryo The prenatal organism between 2 and 8 weeks after conception.

embryonic period The second stage of prenatal development, lasting from the end of the second week through the eighth week after conception.

emergentism An explanation that describes language learning as a gradual learning process involving social interaction, where understanding of grammar emerges step by step rather than being prewired.

emitted response A response not elicited by a known stimulus but simply emitted by the organism. An emitted response is an operant.

emotional abuse Child maltreatment that causes emotional and psychological rather than physical harm (for example, shaming, ridiculing, ignoring, or humiliating children). A form of "mental cruelty" to children.

emotional disorder Also termed *behavior disorder*, a classification used to include a wide range of nonphysical exceptionalities ranging from relatively minor behavior problems to serious mental disorders such as autism or schizophrenia (including ADHD).

emotional display rules Implicit, socially accepted rules that tell us when it is appropriate to display emotion, how it should be displayed, and what other people's emotional displays mean. (See *prosocial display rules; self-protective display rules.*)

emotional intelligence A type of emotional competence reflected in high levels of emotional self-knowledge and self-control, as well as the ability to discern and empathize with others' emotional states.

emotions The *feeling* or *affective* component of human behavior; an individual's responses to the occurrence of events relating to important goals.

empathy The mental apprehension of another's feelings and state of mind.

encoding Change into a form that can be represented in memory.

endocrine glands Ductless glands, such as the pituitary, the adrenals, and the gonads, that secrete hormones directly into the bloodstream. Centrally involved in regulating growth as well as sexual maturation and sexual behavior.

English as a second language (ESL) Common phrase to describe educational programs designed to develop English proficiency among those whose first language is not English.

entity theory of intelligence Dweck's label for the belief that ability is a fixed, unchanging entity. Associated with performance goals—that is, with doing well in order to be judged positively by others. (See *incremental theory of intelligence.*)

environment The significant aspects of an individual's surroundings. All the experiences and events that influence development, including the prenatal environment, social interactions, health, education, and so on.

epidemiological studies Research that looks at the distribution patterns and frequency of diseases and other related conditions.

epigenesis The developmental unfolding of genetically influenced characteristics.

epigenetic landscape Waddington's graphic analogy used to clarify the relationship between genetic and environmental forces.

episiotomy A small cut made in the vaginal opening to facilitate the birth of a child. An episiotomy prevents the tearing of membranes and ensures that once the cut has been sutured, healing will be rapid and complete.

equilibration A Piagetian term for the process by which we maintain a balance between assimilation (using old learning) and accommodation (changing behavior; learning new things). Equilibration is essential for adaptation and cognitive growth.

ethnic identity A person's perception of the strength of his or her connection to an ethnic group. Includes feelings and preferences relating to belongingness as well as knowledge and sharing of cultural values and history.

ethologists Scientists who study the behavior of animals (including humans) in their natural habitats.

ethology The science of animal behavior. Involves the study of animal forms (including humans) in their natural environments.

eugenics A form of genetic engineering that selects specific individuals for reproduction. Applying eugenics to humans raises a number of serious moral and ethical questions. It is widely accepted and practiced with animals, however.

event sampling A method of child study in which specific behaviors are observed and recorded and unrelated behaviors are ignored.

exceptionality A category used to describe physical, social, or intellectual abilities and performance that are significantly above or below average.

existentialism A philosophical/psychological orientation that stresses *existence* (the facts of existence, the purpose of existence, the realities of existence) rather than *essence* (the substance of the human being, the basic nature of the human organism).

exosystem Interactions between a system in which a child is involved (microsystem) and another system that does not ordi-

narily include the child (father's relationships with employers, for example).

experiment A procedure for scientific investigation requiring manipulation of some aspects of the environment to determine what the effects of this manipulation will be.

experimental group A group of subjects who undergo experimental manipulation. The group to which something is done in order to observe its effects. (See *control group.*)

explicit memory *Declarative,* conscious, long-term memory, in contrast with implicit (or nondeclarative) memory. May be either semantic or episodic. (See *autobiographical memory, semantic memory.*)

extended family A large family group consisting of parents, children, grandparents, and occasionally uncles, aunts, cousins, and so on. (See *nuclear family.*)

external orientation A tendency to attribute the outcomes of behavior to factors outside the individual, hence not under the individual's control (such as luck or the difficulty of a task). (See *attribution theory, internal orientation, learned helplessness, locus of control, mastery-oriented.*)

extinction In operant conditioning, the cessation of a response as a function of the withdrawal of reinforcement.

Fagan Test of Infant Intelligence A nonverbal, individual intelligence test for use with infants, useful for screening infants at risk for mental retardation.

failure to thrive (FTT) Infants' failure to gain weight at a normal rate (within the bottom 3% of the population) for no apparent organic reason. Also called *maternal deprivation syndrome* because maternal absence or neglect may be implicated.

fallopian tube One of two tubes that link the ovaries and the uterus. Fertilization (conception) ordinarily occurs in the fallopian tubes. From there the fertilized egg cell moves into the uterus and attaches to the uterine wall.

familial causes Relating to mental retardation, environmental causes often associated with lower socioeconomic levels, including unstimulating environments and malnutrition.

fast mapping Describes learning that occurs extraordinarily rapidly—typically after only one or two exposures. Often used to describe the process by which young children learn the meanings of words.

fat-free mass The major constituent of the human body, consisting largely of organs, muscles, and bone (which in turn consist primarily of water).

fat mass Made up mostly of white adipose tissue (fat cells). Accounts for an average of about 30% of body weight in adult females and about 15% in adult males.

feral children Wild children; children allegedly abandoned by their parents and raised by wild animals.

fertilization The union of sperm and ovum; the beginning of life.

fertilized ovum stage (also called *germinal stage*) The first stage of prenatal development, beginning with fertilization and lasting until the end of the second week of intrauterine development.

fetal alcohol syndrome (FAS) A collection of symptoms in newborns associated with maternal alcohol consumption during pregnancy and sometimes evident in varying degrees of neurological, mental, and physical problems.

fetal erythroblastosis A medical condition in the newborn marked by lack of red blood cells. Can be fatal if sufficiently serious and not attended to in time.

fetal period The final stage of prenatal development, which begins at the end of the eighth week after conception and lasts until the baby's birth.

fetoscopy A surgical procedure that allows the physician to see the fetus while obtaining samples of tissue for determining its status.

fetus An immature child in the uterus. Fetal development begins eight weeks after conception and lasts until the birth of the baby.

filial piety A fundamental virtue in many oriental cultures. In effect, the premise that people should always, under all circumstances and at all ages, display the highest devotion and complete obedience to their parents, and that the welfare of parents always comes first. My kids are occidental.

fine motor development The development of motor skills involving relatively small (fine) body movements such as learning to grasp or to scribble with a pencil.

fixation A Freudian term for the arresting of development at an immature developmental stage. Thought to be evident in personality characteristics and emotional disorders relating to the earlier stage.

flexibility A factor tapped by production measures of divergent thinking (of creativity). Evident in the ability or propensity to switch from one class of responses or solutions to another. (See *fluency, originality.*)

fluency A factor thought to be involved in creativity, evident in the production of a large number of responses or solutions in a problem situation. (See *flexibility, originality.*)

fluid abilities Cattell's term for intellectual abilities that seem to underlie much of our intelligent behavior and are not highly affected by experience (general reasoning, attention span, memory for numbers). Fluid abilities are more likely to decline in old age than are crystallized abilities. (See *crystallized abilities.*)

fontanels Six gaps, detectable as soft spots, in the skull of a newborn.

foreclosure Marcia's term for the adoption of a ready-made identity.

formal operations The last of Piaget's four major developmental stages. It begins around the age of 11 or 12 and lasts until about 14 or 15. It is characterized by children's increasing ability to use logical thought processes.

fragile X syndrome A sex-linked primarily male disorder that increases with the mother's age and is often manifested in mental retardation.

fraternal (dizygotic) twins Twins whose genetic origins are two different ova and who are therefore no more alike genetically than any other pair of siblings. (See *identical twins.*)

frustration An affective (emotional) reaction to the inability to gratify one's desires.

g Spearman's abbreviation for general intelligence, a notion based on his observation that people who do well on one kind of intelligence test also tend to do well on others, as though there is some general mental ability that affects performance in all areas. (See *general factor theory, special abilities theory.*)

gametes Mature sex cells. In humans, the egg cell (ovum) and the sperm cell.

gang A small group that interacts frequently face-to-face and that defines itself through conflict—sometimes with other gangs, sometimes with established authority, often with both.

gateway drug-use theory The observation that certain drugs such as tobacco, alcohol, and marijuana are typically used first (usually in the order mentioned) before other "stronger" drugs, in a sense serving as a gateway to use of other drugs.

gaze following The human tendency to look where others are looking, presumably based on the assumption that if someone else is looking or—even more—if many people are looking simultaneously, there must surely be something worth looking at. Gaze following is readily apparent in infants beginning around 9 to 12 months.

gender A social construct defined in terms of the characteristics generally associated with biological sex in a given culture. Thus there is a *masculine* and a *feminine* gender.

gender constancy Refers to the developing child's realization that gender is permanent and unchangeable.

gender identity The recognition, which begins in early childhood, that one is male or female, coupled with an understanding of the meaning and permanence of maleness and femaleness.

gender identity disorder Label for the relatively rare condition in which individuals don't feel comfortable with their anatomical sex—where they feel themselves to *be* the other sex, and have strong preferences for that alternative.

gender roles The particular combination of attitudes, behaviors, and personality characteristics that a culture considers appropriate for the individual's anatomical sex—what is considered masculine or feminine. Also termed *sex roles.*

gender schema theory A cognitive gender-typing theory that recognizes that elements of both cognitive explanations (the child's growing understanding of the nature and meaning of gender) and social learning explanations (the influence of models and reinforcements) are useful to account for the shaping of gender roles.

gender schemas Knowledge about the characteristics associated with being male and female.

gender typing Learning behavior according to the sex of the individual. The term refers specifically to the acquisition of masculine behavior for a boy and feminine behavior for a girl.

general factor theory A theory of intelligence based on the assumption that there is a basic, underlying quality of intellectual functioning that determines *intelligence* in all areas. This quality is sometimes labeled *g*. (See *special abilities theory.*)

generalizability The extent to which conclusions can be applied (generalized) from one situation to others; the generality of conclusions.

generativity versus self-absorption The Erikson stage spanning middle adulthood, marked by a need to be productive and useful to society despite tendencies to be highly concerned with the self.

genes The carriers of heredity—of which we have perhaps 70,000 or 100,000. (See *dominant gene, recessive gene.*)

genetic counseling Medical/psychological assistance with decisions regarding the initiation or termination of pregnancy when there are known or suspected genetic risks involved.

genetics The science that studies heredity.

genital herpes An incurable sexually transmitted viral disease that usually includes sometimes painful or itchy lesions in the genital area.

genital stage The last of Freud's stages of psychosexual development, beginning around the age of 11 and lasting until around 18. It is characterized by involvement with normal adult modes of sexual gratification.

genome The complete set of genetic instructions contained in our genes.

genotype Our inherited chromosomal or genetic makeup.

germinal period The first two weeks of prenatal development.

gestation period The period of time between conception and birth (typically 266 days for humans).

GHB The drug *gamma hydroxybutyric acid*, which, especially when combined with alcohol, causes prolonged amnesia and physical helplessness. One of the "date-rape" drugs. (See *Rohypnol.*)

gist memory Describes the remembering of main ideas and central themes, rather than details. Much of our memory appears to be *gist memory.* We remember the gist of something and generate the details.

gonads Sexual endocrine glands. Testes in the male; ovaries in the female.

gonorrhea A relatively common STD, most strains of which are easily treated with antibiotics. Usually results in painful urination and a mucuslike discharge in males, but is not so easily detected in women.

grand mal Label sometimes used for the more severe forms of epilepsy. Sometimes used to refer specifically to the seizures that accompany this form of epilepsy. (See *petit mal.*)

gross motor development The development of motor skills involving large (gross) bodily movements such as walking or throwing a ball.

growth Ordinarily, such physical changes as increasing height or weight.

growth velocity A measure of how rapidly an individual gains height and weight—for example, kilograms per year.

habituation To become accustomed to as a function of repetition. Habituation is evident when the organism no longer responds as it would to a novel stimulus.

hedonistic Relating to the pain-pleasure principle, to the tendency to seek pleasure and avoid pain.

heredity The transmission of physical and personality characteristics and predispositions from parent to offspring.

heritability An estimate, often expressed as a percentage, of the extent to which variations in a characteristic are determined by the individual's genetic makeup (genotype).

hermaphrodite Individual having both male and female reproductive organs, often with ambiguous external genitalia. The condition is sometimes corrected anatomically shortly after birth, but is nevertheless frequently associated with gender identity problems later.

heteronomy Piaget's label for the first stage of moral development, marked by reliance on outside authority. (See *autonomy.*)

heterosexual orientation Describes a customary and enduring attraction to persons of the opposite sex.

heterozygous Having inherited different forms of corresponding alleles for a gene. (See *homozygous.*)

higher mental functions In Vygotsky's system, learned behaviors such as are evident in thinking and speaking. Highly dependent on language.

homeostasis A term used in theories that deal with organic, physiological, social, and other systems (hence *general systems theory*) to signify the apparent tendency of these systems to maintain a beneficial stability or balance among and within their functioning parts.

homosexual orientation Refers to an individual's customary and enduring romantic and sexual attraction to persons of the same gender.

homozygous Having inherited identical forms of alleles for a gene. (See *heterozygous.*)

hopeful monsters Deacon's label for explanations that resort to what is sometimes termed Deus ex machina—"God from a machine." Such explanations rely on an assumed but unprovable entity, organ, or feature to explain what cannot easily be explained otherwise.

horizontal décalage Literally, a displacement or gap. Piaget's term for the observation that certain skills or understandings that clearly apply to a variety of situations are sometimes treated as though they apply in only a few specific instances. Horizontal décalage is a gap *within* a stage (hence *horizontal* rather than *vertical*). It is evident in the wide range of ages between the acquisition of the first conservation (conservation of mass, for example) and the last (conservation of area or volume).

hormone Substance secreted by an endocrine gland (such as testosterone or estrogen) into the bloodstream and carried to some part of the body where it has a specific effect.

human immunodeficiency virus (HIV) The presumed cause of *acquired immunodeficiency syndrome (AIDS);* a virus that appears to be able to mutate rapidly, and whose control has proven difficult. (See *acquired immunodeficiency syndrome.*)

humanism A philosophical and psychological orientation primarily concerned with the worth of humans as individuals and processes that augment their human qualities.

Huntington's disease An inherited neurological disorder characterized by neural degeneration, typically beginning between the ages of 20 and 40 and usually leading to death.

hurried child Expression coined by Elkind for children whose parents are so eager for them to learn and to accomplish that they "rush" them through childhood, dragging them from one lesson or school to another, scarcely giving them time to pause and play and just be children.

hypothesis An assumption, prediction, or tentative conclusion that may be tested through the application of the scientific method.

id One of the three levels of the human personality, according to Freudian theory. The id is defined as all the instinctual urges to which humans are heir and is the source of all human motives. A newborn child's personality, according to Freud, is all id.

identical (monozygotic) twins Twins whose genetic origin is a single egg. Such twins are genetically identical. (See *fraternal twins.*)

identification A general term referring to the process of assuming the goals, ambitions, mannerisms, and so on of another person—of identifying with that person. (See *imitation.*)

identity In Erickson's theory, a term closely related to self. To achieve identity is to arrive at a clear notion of who one is. It includes the goals, values, and beliefs to which the individual is committed. One of the important tasks of adolescence is to select and develop a strong sense of identity.

identity crisis In Erikson's theory, the main developmental crisis of the adolescent—specifically, the conflict that can arise when faced with a choice among various available roles (identities). The crisis is often related to the fact that some of these roles may be irresponsible, immature, and socially unacceptable—but appealing; and some of them may be more mature, more focused, more socially sanctioned—and sometimes, though not always, less appealing.

identity diffusion Marcia's term for an adolescent state devoid of commitment or identity crisis; common in early adolescence.

identity status According to Erikson's theory (extended by Marcia), the extent and manner in which the adolescent has experienced, is experiencing, has resolved, or is resolving, an identity crisis—hence describable in terms of crisis and commitment. (See *identity crisis.*)

identity versus role diffusion An Erikson developmental stage spanning adolescence, marked by a struggle to establish a strong sense of identity, of self. (See *identity.*)

imaginary audience An expression of adolescent egocentrism; an imagined collection of all who might be concerned with the adolescent's self and behavior.

imaginative play (also called *pretend play*) Activities that include make-believe games, daydreaming, imaginary playmates, and other forms of pretending; highly prevalent during the preschool years. (See *sensorimotor play, social play.*)

imitation The complex process of learning through observation of a model.

immature birth A miscarriage occurring sometime between the 20th and 28th weeks of pregnancy and resulting in the birth of a fetus weighing between 1 and 2 pounds.

implicit memory Refers to unconscious, nonverbalizable effects of experience such as might be manifested in acquired motor skills or in classical conditioning. Also termed *nondeclarative memory.* (See *autobiographical memory, explicit memory, semantic memory.*)

imprinting An instinct-like type of learning that occurs shortly after birth in certain species and that is seen in the "following" behavior of young ducks or geese.

incidental mnemonics Nonsystematic, *incidental* approaches to remembering sometimes used by young children, such as paying attention.

inclusion The practice of placing students in need of special services in the regular classroom rather than segregating them. Also termed *inclusive education,* or *mainstreaming.*

incongruity hypothesis The supposition that infant fear reactions result from a discrepancy between reality and what the infant has learned to expect.

incremental theory of intelligence Dweck's label for the belief that ability is malleable through work and effort. Associated with mastery goals—that is, with increasing personal competence. (See *entity theory of intelligence.*)

independent variable The variable in an experiment that can be manipulated to observe its effect on other variables. (See *dependent variable, variable.*)

individuation The recognition of one's own individuality.

industry versus inferiority Erikson's label for a developmental period spanning middle childhood, characterized by emphasis on interaction with peer.

infancy A period of development that begins a few weeks after birth and lasts until approximately 2 years of age.

infanticide The killing of an infant.

infantile amnesia A mysterious but apparently universal human phenomenon evident in the fact that most people do not remember events of infancy or of the early preschool period.

inflections Morphemes that alter the meanings of words. Thus *dog* consists of a single morpheme, whereas *dogs* consists of two morphemes: DOG and the inflection S.

information-processing approach A psychological orientation that attempts to explain cognitive processes such as remembering, decision making, or problem solving. This orientation is primarily concerned with how information is acquired and stored (acquisition of a knowledge base), as well as the development of cognitive strategies and notions of the self as a processor of information (metacognition).

inhibitory effect The suppression of deviant behavior as a result of observing a model.

initiative versus guilt The third of Erikson's stages (2 or 3 to 6 years), marked by a developing sense of self and of responsibility, and a greater independence from parents.

inner speech Vygotsky's final stage in the development of speech, attained at around age 7, and characterized by silent "self-talk," the stream-of-consciousness flow of verbalizations that give direction and substance to our thinking and behavior. Inner speech is involved in all higher mental functioning.

insecure-avoidant Describes infants who are anxiously attached to a caregiver, who show little signs of distress when that person leaves, and who initially avoid reestablishing contact when the person returns.

insecure-resistant Describes infants who are profoundly upset when the principal caregiver leaves and who often display anger when that person returns.

instinct A complex, species-specific, relatively unmodifiable pattern of behaviors such as migration or nesting in some birds and animals.

integrity versus despair Erikson's label for the last developmental stage in the life span, marked by a need to make sense of one's life despite increasing tendencies toward despair in the face of old age and imminent death.

intelligence A property measured by intelligence tests. Seems to refer primarily to the capacity of individuals to adjust to their environment.

intelligence quotient (IQ) A way of describing intelligence by assigning it a number. May be arrived at by giving tests to estimate mental age, and then multiplying the ratio of mental to chronological age by 100. Average IQ is therefore 100.

intention Relating to conscious, deliberate purposefulness. The ability to form intentions is central to guiding behavior, and is also the basis of morality.

interaction A condition that exists when two or more forces influence each other, sometimes in very complex ways; also relates to how two or more forces act together (*coact*) to affect certain outcomes.

internal orientation A tendency to attribute the outcomes of behavior to factors within the individual's control (such as effort or ability). (See *external orientation, learned helplessness, locus of control, mastery oriented.*)

internalizing actions Piaget's expression for the mental representation of events, their characteristics, their relationships, and their consequences. The expression recognizes that the infant's early thinking is closely tied to real actions. Our thinking is potentially more abstract, more symbolic, more removed from the concrete.

intimacy and solidarity versus isolation Erikson's label for the developmental stage that spans early adulthood, marked by the need to develop close, caring relationships with others.

intracytoplasmic sperm injection (ICSI) Microassisted fertilization. Involves the mechanical insertion of sperm into ova in the laboratory.

introjection Freudian term for the unconscious process of adopting as part of one's own belief system the inferred attitudes, beliefs, desires, and so on, of significant other persons—especially of parents.

intuitive thinking A Piagetian stage (ages 4 to 7) in which thought is based on immediate comprehension rather than logical processes. Also characterized by difficulties in class inclusion, egocentricity, and marked reliance on perception.

James's approach to self-worth The belief that notions of self-esteem are a direct function of the difference between perceived self and self-ideal. (See *Cooley's approach to self-worth.*)

Klinefelter's syndrome Results from the presence of an extra X chromosome in a male child; marked by the presence of both male and female secondary sexual characteristics.

knock-outs Custom-made genetic probes consisting of a DNA sequence that has been altered so as to block the synthesis of a specific protein in a target gene. Also termed *null mutants.*

knowledge base All that is in memory. Information-processing approaches to learning and development look at the nature and construction of the knowledge base, at strategies for adding material to, or retrieving from, the knowledge base, and at the knower's awareness of self as knower.

kwashiorkor An infant nutritional deficiency disease related primarily to lack of protein; marked by stunting, listlessness, apathy, failure to thrive, and sometimes death. Physical symptoms often include swollen bellies and feet, and loss of hair.

labor The process during which the fetus, placenta, and other membranes are separated from the woman's body and expelled. The termination of labor is usually birth.

Lamaze method A method of natural childbirth based on a variety of breathing and relaxation exercises designed to remove, or at least reduce, the need for anesthetics and other medical intervention.

language Spoken language consists of complex arrangements of sounds that have accepted referents and can therefore be used for communication among humans, and to represent and invent meanings. Some languages, such as American Sign Language (ASL), are based on gestures and signs rather than sounds. ASL also permits communication as well as the representation and invention of concepts.

language acquisition device (LAD) Chomsky's label for the prewired neurological something in our brains that corresponds to grammar and explains how we can learn, understand, and use language.

lanugo Downy, soft hair that covers the fetus. Lanugo grows over most of a fetus's body sometime after the fifth month of pregnancy and is usually shed during the seventh month. However, some lanugo is often present at birth, especially on the infant's back.

latchkey children Label for children who return (from schools, playground, gym, or wherever) to caretakerless homes. So called because parents sometimes hang their home keys around children's necks so that they are less likely to lose them.

late home leaver For research purposes, someone who leaves home after the age of 24.

latency stage The fourth of Freud's stages of psychosexual development, characterized by the development of the superego (conscience) and by loss of interest in sexual gratification. This stage is assumed to last from the age of 6 to 11 years.

lateralization The specialization of brain functions so that one hemisphere becomes more involved than the other in certain functions. Lateralization occurs in infancy and early childhood.

learned helplessness Personality characteristic evident in a tendency to attribute outcomes to causes over which the person has no control. (See *mastery-oriented.*)

learning Includes all changes in behavior that are due to experience. Does not include temporary changes brought about by drugs or fatigue or changes in behavior resulting simply from maturation or growth.

learning disability Significant impairment in a specific skill or ability in the absence of a general depression in ability to learn (mental retardation).

Leboyer method A method of prepared childbirth emphasizing birthing conditions rather than preparation of the mother (for example, birth occurs in a softly lit room, and the infant is immersed in a lukewarm bath and later placed directly on the mother's abdomen).

libido A general Freudian term denoting sexual urges. The libido is assumed to be the source of energy for sexual urges. Freud considered these urges the most important force in human motivation.

locomotor abilities Abilities involved in self-propelled motion; hence essential for moving oneself from one position or location to another (crawling or walking, for example, for those who—unlike kings, queens, and infants—don't have personal bearers).

long-term memory Memory that lasts from minutes to years and that involves rehearsal and organization.

longitudinal study A research technique in the study of child development that observes the same subjects over a long period of time. (See *cross-sectional study.*)

LSD-25 (d-lysergic acid diethylamide tartrate) A particularly powerful hallucinogenic drug; an inexpensive, easily made, synthetic chemical that can sometimes have profound influences on human perception. In everyday parlance it is often referred to as "acid."

lunar month The length of a complete moon cycle—from full moon to full moon, for example; hence, 28 days.

macrosystem All interactive social systems that define a culture or subculture.

magical thinking Phrase used to describe a type of thinking, often characteristic of preschoolers and young children, that is not entirely logical or scientifically valid, but rather inventive and surprising and sometimes bizarre—hence *magical.*

magnetic resonance imaging Popularly referred to as an MRI, a powerful medical diagnostic tool that makes use of computer-enhanced images of magnetic fields in the body to reveal details about physical and neurological structure and functioning. Highly useful in brain and memory research.

mainstreaming The practice of placing students in need of special services in regular classrooms rather than segregating them. Also called *inclusive education.*

marginalization A sociological term referring to a condition in which minority group members have been unsuccessful in becoming part of the dominant cultural group, but have removed themselves from effective membership in the minority group.

Hence they are out of one group (the minority group), but only on the fringe (margin) of the other.

marijuana A substance derived from the hemp plant. When smoked, it ordinarily induces a pleasant emotional state.

marker genes Genes whose presence on a chromosome is associated with a known characteristic.

mastery-oriented Personality characteristic marked by a tendency to attribute the outcomes of behavior to factors under personal control. (See *learned helplessness.*)

maturation A developmental process defined by changes that are relatively independent of a child's environment. Although the nature and timing of maturational changes are assumed to result from genetic predispositions, their manifestation is at least partly a function of the environment.

mature birth The birth of an infant between the 37th and 42nd weeks of pregnancy.

mean length of utterance (MLU) Average number of morphemes per utterance.

mechanistic model A model in human developmental psychology based on the belief that it is useful to view human beings in terms of their reactive, *machinelike* characteristics.

mediators Those whose function it is to act as peacemakers, to intervene between disputing parties. In schools, teachers often act as mediators. In some cases, older children and adolescents are trained to serve as mediators.

medical neglect Child maltreatment where caregivers fail to provide adequate medical care to children in need—sometimes through carelessness, ignorance, or poverty; sometimes for religious reasons.

meiosis The division of a single sex cell into two separate cells, each consisting of 23 chromosomes rather than 23 pairs of chromosomes. Meiosis therefore results in cells that are completely different, whereas mitosis results in identical cells.

melting pot societies Geographical or political entities composed of a variety of cultures that are gradually assimilated to the dominant culture. The result is that individual cultures are no longer identifiable, and the dominant culture becomes a *macroculture.*

memory Relates to the storage of the effects of experience. May be evident in the ability to recognize or to recollect previous experiences, or in changes in behavior as a result of experience.

memory strategies Systematic plans or procedures designed to improve the likelihood of remembering. The most common adult memory strategies are *organization*, *grouping*, *rehearsing*, and *elaboration.*

menarche A girl's first menstrual period, an event that transpires during pubescence.

Mendelian genetics The study of heredity through an examination of the characteristics of parents and offspring. (See *molecular genetics.*)

menopause Cessation of menustruation.

menses A monthly discharge of blood and tissue from the womb of a mature female. The term refers to menstruation.

mental age A measure or estimate of intellectual functioning expressed in terms of age. Thus an average 7-year-old has a mental age of 7.

mental retardation A global term referring to the mental state of individuals whose intellectual development is significantly slower than that of normal children and whose ability to adapt to their environment is consequently limited.

mentors Individuals engaged in a one-to-one teaching/learning relationship in which teachers serve not only as a source of information, but also as important models with respect to values, beliefs, philosophies and attitudes.

mesosystem Interactions among two or more microsystems (for example, family and school).

meta-analysis A research technique involving careful, systematic analysis of all or most of the relevant studies that have looked at a research question in an attempt to arrive at conclusions far more general and reliable than those based on the results of a single study.

metacognition Knowledge about knowing. As we grow and learn, we develop notions of ourselves as learners. Accordingly, we develop strategies that recognize our limitations and allow us to monitor our progress and take advantage of our efforts.

metamemory The knowledge that we develop about our own memory processes—knowledge about how to remember rather than simply about our memories.

metaneeds Maslow's term for higher needs. In contrast to basic needs, metaneeds are concerned not with physiological but with psychological functions. They include the need to know truth, beauty, justice, and to self-actualize. Also termed *growth needs*.

methylmercury Mercury compound that tends to accumulate in fatty tissue, and that is associated with birth deformities and malformations in offspring.

microsystem Defined by immediate, face-to-face interactions in which everybody affects everybody (for example, child and parent.)

midwife In many jurisdictions, a licensed professional, generally female but occasionally male, who assists in childbirth—but who is generally neither a doctor nor a nurse.

mild retardation Mild cognitive deficits, usually defined in terms of an IQ range between 50 and about 70. Also termed *educable*, children with mild retardation are capable of achievement at about the sixth-grade level, and of adequate social adaptation.

Minimata disease Disease linked with the presence of methylmercury. Affects prenatal development, typically causing severe deformations, mental retardation, blindness, and even death.

misattribution An error of interpretation, relatively common in studies of infants and animals, in which the researcher makes incorrect assumptions about the meanings of certain reactions or behaviors, for example attributing them to motives characteristic of adult humans.

mitosis The division of a cell into two identical cells. Occurs in body cells as opposed to sex cells.

model A pattern for behavior that can be copied by someone else.

modeling effect Imitative behavior involving the learning of a novel response. (See *eliciting effect, inhibitory effect, disinhibitory effect.*)

moderate retardation A degree of mental retardation defined in terms of an IQ range between 35 or 40 and 50 or 55. Can achieve at about the second-grade level, and can profit from training in social and occupational skills.

molecular genetics The study of genetics based on the structure of chromosomes. (See *Mendelian genetics.*)

monozygotic Resulting from a single egg. Twins and higher multiples whose origins are the division of a single fertilized ovum are genetically identical.

Moral Judgment Interview A procedure for determining stage and level of moral reasoning. Uses stories illustrating moral dilemmas developed by Lawrence Kohlberg.

morality The ethical aspect of human behavior. Morality is intimately bound to the development of an awareness of acceptable and unacceptable behaviors. It is therefore linked to what is often called conscience.

moratorium Marcia's term for an adolescent stage marked by crisis and by vague, changing commitments; a time of exploration before commitment.

moro reflex The generalized startle reaction of a newborn infant. It characteristically involves throwing out the arms and feet symmetrically and then bringing them back in toward the center of the body.

morphemes Combinations of phonemes that make up the meaningful units of a language.

mother-infant bonding The emotional bond that exists between mother and infant.

motivation Our reasons for behaving. What initiates behavior, directs it, and accounts for its cessation.

multicultural education Educational procedures and curricula that are responsive to the different cultures and languages of students, with the goal of assuring that all children experience high-quality education.

multiculturalism Having to do with many cultures.

multifactorial Affected by or resulting from the combined or interactive effects of more than one factor—for example, the combined effects of genes and environments.

muscular dystrophy (MD) A degenerative muscular disorder, most forms of which are genetic, usually manifested in an inability to walk and sometimes fatal.

mutagens Substances capable of causing changes in genetic material. (See *teratogens.*)

mutations Changes in genetic material as a result of a mutagen (agent such as x-rays or certain drugs capable of altering genetic codes).

myelin sheath Fatty covering that surrounds nerves and nerve cells, protecting them and enhancing neural transmission.

nativism A hopeful monster type of explanation for language learning, like Chomsky's, which assumes that language learning depends on a preexisting neurological organ or pattern in the brain corresponding to a universal language grammar.

natural childbirth Childbirth with little or no use of drugs such as painkillers.

naturalistic observation The study of children in natural settings; an investigation in which the observation has little effect on the behavior of those observed. (See *nonnaturalistic observation*.)

nature-nurture controversy A very old argument in psychology about whether genetics (nature) or environment (nurture) is more responsible for determining development. Also called the heredity-environment question.

need Ordinarily, a lack or deficiency in the organism. Needs may be unlearned (for example, the need for food and water) or learned (the need for money or prestige).

negative correlation A relationship where increases or decreases in one variable are associated with opposite changes in another.

negative identities Erikson's expression for the rebellious, non-conformist, antiestablishment roles with which adolescents sometimes experiment.

negative reinforcement A stimulus that, when removed from the situation, increases the probability of occurrence of the response that precedes it. A negative reinforcer is usually an unpleasant or noxious stimulus that is removed when the desired response occurs.

neonatal abstinence syndrome (NAS) Neonatal symptoms associated with the mother's use of narcotics that has resulted in the newborn also being addicted. Severe cases may be fatal.

neonate A newborn infant. The neonatal period terminates when birth weight is regained.

nerves Bundles of related neurons that function to relay messages (impulses) between the central nervous system and sensory and body systems. Some nerves can be very long; others, very short.

neural pruning The process by which unused neural connections and brain cells atrophy and die.

neural tube defects Spinal cord defects often linked with recessive genes, sometimes evident in failure of the spine to close (spina bifida) or in the absence of portions of the brain.

neurons Nerve cells, the basic building blocks of the human nervous system. Each neuron consists of a cell body, axon, and dendrites.

niche-picking Scarr and McCartney's term for the active selection of environments highly compatible with personal interest, skills, and other personal characteristics.

non-Duchenne smile A smile, typical of a young infant, that involves the lower part of the face rather than the upper cheeks. Genuinely happy adults are more likely to manifest *Duchenne* smiles.

nonnaturalistic observation The study of children using questionnaires or interviews (clinical investigations) or when the environment is manipulated or changed (experimental investigations). (See *naturalistic observation*.)

norm An average or standard way of behaving. Cultural norms, for example, refer to the behaviors expected of individuals who are members of that culture.

normal curve A mathematical function represented in the form of a symmetrical bell-shaped curve that illustrates how a large number of naturally occurring or chance events are distributed.

nuclear family A family consisting of a mother, a father, and their offspring. (See *extended family*.)

object concept Piaget's expression for a child's understanding that the world is composed of objects that continue to exist quite apart from the child's immediate perception of them.

observational learning Learning through imitation.

obstetrics A sophisticated medical term for midwifery; the medical art and science of assisting women who are pregnant, both during pregnancy and at birth.

Oedipus complex A Freudian concept denoting the developmental stage (around 4 years) when a boy's increasing awareness of sexual feelings leads him to desire his mother and envy his father. (See *Electra complex*.)

onlooker play Consists of child watching others play but not actively participating.

ontogeny Systematic changes that occur in the lives of individuals. Changes that define life-span development. (See *phylogeny*.)

operant The label used by B. F. Skinner to describe a response not elicited by any known or obvious stimulus. Most significant human behaviors appear to be operant. Such behaviors as writing a letter or going for a walk are operants, if no known specific stimulus elicits them.

operant conditioning A type of learning in which the probability of a response changes as a result of reinforcement. Much of the experimental work of B. F. Skinner investigates the principles of operant conditioning.

operation Piaget's term for mental activity. An operation is a thought process characterized by certain rules of logic. Preoperations are more intuitive and egocentric, and less logical.

operational thought A Piagetian developmental stage beginning around the age of 7 or 8. Specifically, an operation is a thought that is governed by certain rules of logic.

oppositional defiant disorder An emotional disorder evident in open defiance of authority and serious displays of anger and hostility that cause the individual significant social, academic, or occupational problems.

oral-aggressive Freudian label for personality characterized as loud, obnoxious, demanding, and thought to be associated with fixation at or regression to the oral stage of development.

oral stage The first stage of psychosexual development, lasting from birth to approximately 8 months of age. The oral stage is characterized by preoccupation with the immediate gratification of desires. This is accomplished primarily through the oral regions, by sucking, biting, swallowing, playing with the lips, and so on.

organic causes With respect to mental retardation, physiological or biological causes including genetic conditions or maternal diseases, drugs, and radiation.

organismic model A model in human development that assumes people are active rather than simply reactive, and they are therefore more like biological organisms than like machines.

organizing A memory strategy involving grouping and relating material to maintain it in long-term memory. (See *elaborating, rehearsing.*)

orienting response The initial response of humans and other animals to novel stimulation. Also called the orienting reflex or orientation reaction. Components of the orienting response include changes in EEG patterns, respiration rate, heart rate, and galvanic skin response.

originality A measure of creativity evident in the production of novel (unexpected or statistically rare) responses or solutions in a problem situation. (See *flexibility, fluency.*)

otitis media A highly common childhood disease of the middle ear, sometimes accompanied by prolonged hearing loss, the main medical symptom of which is fluid in the middle ear. May be associated with language problems.

ovary A female organ (most women have two of them) that produces ova (egg cells).

overregularization The misuse of grammatical rules, often because they are applied to irregular forms. (Saying "I eated," or "I broked it," for example.)

overt aggression Visible, outwardly manifested form of aggression that includes a range of possible forceful human actions intended to dominate, to frighten, perhaps even to hurt physically. One extreme form of overt aggression is violence. (See *aggression, violence.*)

ovum (plural, **ova**) The sex cell produced by a mature female approximately once every 28 days. When mature it consists of 23 chromosomes, as opposed to all other human body cells (somatoplasm), which consist of 23 *pairs* of chromosomes. It is often referred to as an egg cell. (See *sperm cell.*)

oxytocin A hormone that brings about contractions and leads to childbirth. Synthetic oxytocin is often used to induce labor.

palmar reflex The grasping reflex that newborn infants exhibit when objects are placed in their hands.

parallel play A form of play in which children play side by side but individually, sharing neither activities nor rules.

parentese (Also called *child-directed speech* or *motherese*) Describes the characteristics of parental speech when interacting with language-learning infants and preschoolers. Characterized by simpler, shorter, more repetitive utterances, often with exaggerated intonations, and by a preponderance of nouns.

passive correlation Scarr and McCartney's label for the observation that genetically influenced parental characteristics sometimes determine important aspects of a child's environment—thus explaining some of the correlation often observed between genotype and environments.

peak experience Label introduced by Maslow to describe an intensely moving and unforgettable experience that has a profound effect on an individual's life. Peak experiences might involve what are interpreted by the individual as supernatural experiences, profound mystical revelations, startling insights, and other events closely related to the process of self-actualization. (See *self-actualization.*)

pedophiles Literally, lovers of children. Describes a category of sexual deviance where sexual gratification is tied to activities involving children.

peer group A group of equals. Peer groups may be social groups, age groups, intellectual groups, or work groups. Young children's peer groups are usually age and grade mates.

perception Reaction to and interpretation of physical stimulation (sensation). A conceptual process dependent on activity of the brain.

permissive parenting A parenting style that may be characterized as "laissez-faire." Permissive parents are nonpunitive and undemanding. Their children are autonomous rather than obedient and, as such, are responsible for their own decisions and actions.

personal fable An expression of adolescent egocentrism marked by the elaboration of fantasies, the hero of which is the adolescent.

personality The set of characteristics that we typically manifest in our interactions with others. It includes all the abilities, predispositions, habits, and other qualities that make each of us different.

pervasive developmental disorder A disorder first manifested in infancy or childhood, evident in delayed or abnormal development especially in social skills, communication, and emotional maturity. May take the form of autism or childhood schizophrenia.

petit mal Label for the milder forms of epilepsy, not characterized by major seizures, and often controllable with drugs. (See *grand mal.*)

phallic stage The third stage of Freud's theory of psychosexual development. It begins at about the age of 18 months and lasts to the age of approximately 6 years. During this stage children become concerned with their genitals and may show evidence of the much-discussed complexes labeled Oedipus and Electra. (See *Electra complex, Oedipus complex.*)

phenomenology An approach concerned primarily with how individuals view their own world. Its basic assumption is that each individual perceives and reacts to the world in a unique manner, and that it is this phenomenological worldview that is important in understanding an individual's behavior.

phenotype Manifest characteristics related to genetic makeup.

phenylketonuria (PKU) A genetic disorder associated with the presence of two recessive genes.

phoneme The simplest unit of language, consisting of a single sound such as a vowel.

phonology The phonemes or sounds of a language.

phylogeny Changes that occur in a species over generations. Evolutionary changes. (See *ontogeny.*)

physical abuse Child victimization defined mainly in terms of actual physical injury, as might result from excessive beating or "shaken baby syndrome."

physical neglect Most common form of child maltreatment. Involves failure to provide for children's needs (failure to provide nourishment, shelter, clothing).

physiological dependence Commonly called addiction; refers to physiological changes following drug use such that stopping use leads to withdrawal symptoms.

placenta A flat, thick membrane attached to the inside of the uterus during pregnancy and to the developing fetus. The placenta connects the mother and the fetus by means of the umbilical cord, through which the fetus receives nourishment.

placenta previa A condition in which the placenta detaches from the uterine wall prior to the birth of the infant, leading to anoxia and fetal distress, in the absence of rapid intervention.

polychlorinated biphenyls (PCBs) Group of chemicals, such as dioxin, that may be associated with miscarriage and deformities in offspring.

polygenic determination The determination of genetically based characteristics as a function of the interaction of groups of genes.

positive correlation A relationship where increases or decreases in one variable are associated with corresponding increases or decreases in another.

positive reinforcement A stimulus that increases the probability of a response recurring as a result of being added to a situation after the response has occurred. It usually takes the form of a pleasant stimulus (reward) that results from a specific response.

positron emission tomography Also referred to as *PET scan*, a medical diagnostic technique, as well as a research tool, which can be used to provide computer-enhanced images of body structures and also of neurological functioning. A powerful tool in brain and memory research.

postconventional level Kohlberg's third level of morality, reflecting an understanding of social contract and more individualistic principles of morality.

postmature birth The birth of an infant after the 42nd week of pregnancy.

postpartum depression A form of depression that affects about 10% of all women and begins shortly after childbirth. In some cases, postpartum depression can be serious and dangerous, but it usually ameliorates and disappears with time.

posttraumatic stress disorder (PTSD) A serious emotional disorder that is attributed to a stressful event (or a series of such events), but that doesn't appear until after the event. A possible consequence of armed conflict, for example, or of early sexual abuse. Possible symptoms include fatigue, depression, loss of appetite, and obsessive thoughts.

pragmatics In reference to language development, implicit rules that tell children when and how to speak.

precocial In biology, refers to birds and animals whose motor capacities are highly developed at or within a short time of birth. (See *altricial*.)

preconcept The label given to a preconceptual child's incomplete understanding of concepts, resulting from an inability to reason correctly about related classes. (See *preconceptual thought*.)

preconceptual thought In Piaget's system, a substage of preoperational thought, beginning around 2 and lasting until 4. It is so called because children have not yet developed the ability to classify and therefore have an incomplete understanding of concepts. (See *preconcept*.)

preconventional level The first of Kohlberg's three levels of moral development, based on hedonistic or obedience-oriented judgments.

preimplantation diagnosis A fetal diagnostic technique in which fertilization typically occurs in vitro and a cell from the fertilized ovum is removed and examined for abnormalities prior to implantation in the mother.

premature birth The birth of a baby between the 29th and 36th weeks of pregnancy. A premature baby weighs somewhere between 2 and 5 pounds and is less likely to survive if less than 2 pounds.

prenatal diagnosis Assessment of the unborn, typically aimed at detecting the presence of disorders and abnormalities.

preoccupied Parents who, on the *Adult Attachment Interview*, show evidence of being highly preoccupied with, and emotional about, their childhood relationships, but who cannot provide a very coherent description of these relationships.

preoperation Piaget's label for a thought that is not limited by ordinary rules of logic. Preoperations tend to be unstable, idiosyncratic, perception dominated, and egocentric.

preoperational thought The second of Piaget's four major stages, lasting from about 2 to 7 or 8 years. It consists of two substages: intuitive thinking and preconceptual thinking. (See *intuitive thinking, preconceptual thought*.)

primary circular reaction An expression used by Piaget to describe a simple reflex activity (such as thumb-sucking) that serves as a stimulus for its own repetition. (See *secondary circular reaction, tertiary circular reaction*.)

primary sexual characteristics Changes of sexual maturation involved in the production of offspring (for example, the ability of the testes to produce sperm and of the ovaries to produce ova).

primitive social play An early form of social play involving "shared meaning" rather than shared rules; for example, infant "peek-a-boo" games or toddler "chase" games.

process disorders A type of learning disability that involves a deficit in a basic psychological process such as perceiving, remembering, or paying attention. In practice, process disorders are difficult to separate from other specific learning disabilities such as developmental reading or arithmetic disorder. (See *developmental arithmetic disorder, developmental reading disorder*.)

prodigy Somebody who displays exceptional talent for something at an early age.

production measures Tests that require testees to *produce* or *invent* responses rather than being allowed to select or calculate them. Commonly used as measures of creativity.

productiveness The quality of language that allows its users to *produce* an almost unlimited range of meanings simply by combining words and using pauses, intonations, and so on, in different ways.

profound mental retardation A degree of mental retardation defined in terms of a measured IQ below 20 or 25 and marked by limited motor development and a need for nursing care.

Project Head Start A large-scale, federally funded preschool program in the United States, conceived as part of the war on poverty. It is designed to overcome some of the disadvantages associated with economic and social deprivation in early life and, in a sense, to give children a head start.

prolapsed cord A condition that sometimes occurs during birth when the umbilical cord becomes lodged between the infant's body and the birth canal, cutting off the infant's supply of oxygen. The effect may be brain damage of varying severity, depending on the length of time until delivery following prolapsing of the cord.

prone On the belly; a sleep position. Or sometimes not a sleep position.

prosocial display rules A rule of emotional expression implying that there are certain things one should and should not say and do to please others, and not hurt their feelings—for instance, profusely expressing thanks for unattractive and useless gifts. (See *emotional display rules, self-protective display rules.*)

protein A molecule made up of chains of one or more amino acids. In a sense, proteins are the basis of organic life.

proximodistal Literally, from near to far. Refers to a developmental progression in which central organs develop before external limbs and in which the infant acquires control over muscles closer to the center of the body before acquiring control over those more peripheral.

psychoanalytic General label for Freudian theory. Also used to describe clinical or therapeutic procedures based on Freudian ideas, and especially on ideas related to the subconscious.

psycholinguists People who study the relationship between language (linguistics) and development, thinking, learning, and behaving (psychology).

psychological birth trauma The supposed shocking effects of the transition from the comforts of the womb to the cold, cruel world, evident in our abiding, albeit subconscious, desire to return to the safety of the womb—especially in times of great stress.

psychological dependence Sometimes called habituation; refers to a strong desire to continue using a drug.

psychology The science that examines human behavior (and that of animals as well).

psychometric intelligence Psychometrics has to do with measuring psychological functioning. Hence psychometric intelligence is a label for approaches that describe or define intelligence in terms of its measurement.

psychosexual A term used to describe psychological phenomena based on sexuality. Freud's theories are psychosexual in that they attribute development to sexually based forces and motives.

psychosexual development A Freudian term describing child development as a series of stages that are sexually based.

psychosocial development A term used by Erikson to describe human development as a sequence of stages involving the resolution of crises that are primarily social.

puberty Sexual maturity following pubescence.

pubescence Changes of adolescence leading to sexual maturity.

pull-out program A school program, sometimes used in language immersion classes or for children with special needs, in which the child is removed from the regular classroom for special instruction and experiences.

punishment Involves either the presentation of an unpleasant stimulus or the withdrawal of a pleasant stimulus as a consequence of behavior. Punishment should not be confused with negative reinforcement, because punishment does not increase the probability of a response occurring; rather, it is intended to have the opposite effect.

pupillary reflex An involuntary change in the size of the pupil as a function of brightness or darkness. The pupillary reflex is present in neonates.

questionnaires Sequences of carefully structured questions. Questionnaires are often used in social science research.

quickening The name given to the first movements of the fetus in utero. Quickening does not occur until after the fifth month of pregnancy.

radiography The use of x-rays; occasionally used as a tool in prenatal diagnosis.

rapid eye movement (REM) sleep A stage of sleep characterized by rapid eye movements. Most of our dreaming occurs during REM sleep, which accounts for approximately 25% of an adult's sleep time and as much as 50% of an infant's.

reaction range All the possible outcomes for a particular characteristic given variations in the nature and timing of environmental influences.

recessive gene A gene whose characteristics are not manifest in the offspring unless it happens to be paired with another recessive gene. When a recessive gene is paired with a dominant gene, the characteristics of the dominant gene will be manifest.

recessive inheritance The expression of traits related to a recessive allele. Occurs in individuals who are homozygous for the recessive form of the allele (have identical recessive alleles for the gene in question).

reflex smiling Also termed *spontaneous smiling*, the earliest form of infant smile, reflecting bursts of cortical activity rather than contentment or social reactivity. (See *social smiling, selective social smile.*)

reflexes Simple, unlearned, genetically based, unconscious, and largely unavoidable reactions to specific stimuli—such as blinking the eye in response to a puff of air.

regression A psychoanalytic (Freudian) expression for the phenomenon of reverting to some of the activities and preoccupations of earlier developmental stages. Evident in abnormal personality characteristics and emotional disorders.

rehearsing A memory process involving repetition, important in maintaining information in short-term memory and transferring it to long-term memory. (See *elaborating, organizing*.)

reinforcer A reinforcing stimulus. The effect of a reinforcer is reinforcement —an increase in the probability of a response recurring. (See *negative reinforcement, positive reinforcement, reward*.)

relational aggression A form of aggression that seeks to harm people by disrupting their social relations (also called *social aggression*). The methods of relational aggression are ridicule, social exclusion, rumor mongering, malicious teasing, contempt, and disdain. (See *aggression, violence, overt aggression*.)

releaser A biological term for the stimulus that first gives rise to instinct-like behaviors such as the "following" behavior of newly hatched chicks. In this case, the *releaser* is generally the mother hen.

reliable A measure is reliable to the extent that it measures accurately whatever it measures.

replicability A crucial quality of valid scientific or experimental procedures. A procedure is said to be replicable when it can be repeated and the results of so doing are identical (or highly similar) with each repetition.

reprimands Expressions of disapproval commonly used as a form of mild punishment. Often verbal ("You're not supposed to. . ."), but also nonverbal (an admonishing finger, for example).

respondent Used by Skinner in contrast to the term *operant*. A respondent is a response elicited by a known specific stimulus. Unconditioned responses of the type referred to in classical conditioning are examples of respondents.

response Any organic, muscular, glandular, or psychic process that results from stimulation.

response-cost A form of punishment involving the loss of a previously earned reward.

restricted language code A term used by Bernstein to describe the language typical of the lower-class child. Restricted language codes are characterized by short and simple sentences, general and relatively imprecise terms, idiom and colloquialism, and incorrect grammar. (See *elaborated language code*.)

retrospective studies Studies that attempt to identify causes and precursors of current situations by looking at preceding historical conditions.

reversibility A logical property manifested in the ability to reverse or undo activity either empirically or conceptually. An idea is said to be reversible when a child can imagine its opposite, and realize that certain logical consequences follow from doing so.

reward An object, stimulus, event, or outcome that is perceived as pleasant and may therefore be reinforcing.

Rh(D) immunization Process in which the introduction of the Rh(D) factor into the blood of someone who doesn't already possess this factor leads to the formation of antibodies to counteract the D factor. These antibodies can be fatal to someone with the Rh(D) factor.

Rh factor A blood protein found in some individuals but not others. When present in the fetus's blood but not in the mother's, it can cause birth complications. (See *Rh(D) immunization*.)

ritalin A stimulant drug of the amphetamine family designed to sedate rather than stimulate children diagnosed with hyperactivity. Also a relatively common street drug that is combined with the drug *talwin* to produce what is sometimes known as "poor man's heroin," with the street name *R and T's*.

rites of passage Ritualistic ceremony marking the passage from childhood to adulthood in many societies.

Rohypnol A "date-rape" drug, so called because it leaves victims helpless and suffering from amnesia. Colorless, odorless, and illegal. (See *GHB*.)

role taking A role is a part or a character played by an actor. In psychology, role taking implies assuming the character of others in the sense of being able to understand and empathize with their emotions. (See *empathy*.)

rubber-band hypothesis Stern's comparison of human intelligence to a rubber band, the original length of which is genetically determined. The final length of the band is determined by the interaction of environmental forces with the band's elasticity.

sample A subset of a population. A representative selection of individuals with similar characteristics drawn from a larger group.

scaffolding A Vygotskian concept to describe the various types of support that teachers/upbringers need to provide for children if they are to learn. Scaffolding often takes the form of directions, suggestions, and other forms of verbal assistance and is most effective if it involves tasks within the child's zone of proximal growth. (See *zone of proximal development*.)

schema (also scheme) The label used by Piaget to describe a unit in cognitive structure. It usually labels a specific activity: the looking scheme, the grasping scheme, the sucking scheme.

science An approach and an attitude toward knowledge that emphasize objectivity, precision, and replicability. Also, one of several related bodies of knowledge.

scripts Our knowledge of what goes with what and in what sequence. Scripts are a part of cognitive structure that deals with the routine and the predictable.

secondary circular reaction Infant responses that are circular in the sense that the response serves as a stimulus for its own repetition and secondary because the responses do not center on the child's body, as do primary circular reactions. (See *primary circular reaction, tertiary circular reaction*.)

secondary sexual characteristics Changes of pubescence that accompany maturation of the sexual organs (for example, growth of facial hair, development of breasts, voice changes).

secular trend The trend toward earlier maturation.

securely attached Describes infants who are strongly and positively attached to a caregiver, who are distressed when that person leaves, and who quickly reestablish contact when the person returns.

selective social smile Smiling in response to social stimuli that the infant can identify as familiar. (See *reflex smiling; social smiling*.)

self The *I*. Also the *me* and the *myself*. Notions of our *self*. The subject of our own consciousness. (See *self-concept*.)

self-actualization The process or act of becoming oneself, developing one's potentiality, achieving an awareness of one's identity, fulfilling oneself. The term *actualization* is central to humanistic psychology.

self-concept The ideas an individual has of him- or herself. Notions of the self reflect what we think others think of us; our own estimates of what we are, relative to what we would like to be; and our estimates of our competence and "goodness" in various important areas.

self-efficacy Describes our estimates of our personal effectiveness. The most efficacious individuals are those who deal most effectively with a variety of situations, especially those that are ambiguous or stressful.

self-esteem The evaluative aspect of our concepts of self. What we think of ourselves. Our *self-image*. Our opinions about the relative worth of our different characteristics.

self-protective display rules An emotional expression rule motivated by the desire to save face, not to suffer, to project a desired image—such as not crying even when it really hurts. (See *emotional display rules, prosocial display rules*.)

self-referent thought Ideas or thoughts that have to do with the self and, specifically, with self-knowledge. Self-referent thoughts are often evaluative; they deal with our personal estimates of how effective we are in our dealings with the world and with others. (See *self-efficacy*.)

semantic memory A type of declarative (conscious, long-term) memory consisting of stable knowledge about the world, principles, rules, and procedures, and other verbalizable aspects of knowledge, including language. (See *autobiographical memory*.)

semantics The component of language that relates to meaning or significance of sounds.

sensation The physical effect of stimulation; a physiological process dependent on activity of the senses.

sensation seeking A personality trait reflected in an eagerness to take risks for the sensations involved. A high sensation-seeking drive might be evident in activities such as driving motorcycles, automobile racing, ice climbing, or using drugs.

sensitive parenting Phrase used to describe parenting characterized by a high degree of sensitivity to infant (and child) moods and emotions, and an ability to adjust parenting behaviors to these. Associated with *authoritative parenting*. Sensitive parenting is closely related to secure infant attachments and to positive developmental outcomes.

sensitive period A period during which specific experiences have their most pronounced effects—for example, the first six months of life, during which an infant forms strong attachment bonds to the mother or caregiver.

sensorimotor period The first stage of development in Piaget's classification. It lasts from birth to approximately age 2 and is so called because children understand their world primarily through their activities toward it and sensations of it.

sensorimotor play (also called *practice play*) Activity involving the manipulation of objects or execution of activities simply for the sensations that are produced. (See *play, imaginative play, social play*.)

sensory memory The simple sensory recognition of stimuli (also called *short-term sensory memory*). Sensory memory requires no cognitive processing and does not involve conscious awareness.

separation In sociology, refers to actively rejecting the values and norms of the dominant group and embracing those of one's ethnic minority group.

sequential designs Research strategies that involve taking a sequence of samples at different times of measurement in order to reduce or eliminate biases that may result from confounding the effects of age with influences relating to the time of testing and the subject's birth cohort.

severe mental retardation A level of mental retardation defined in terms of an IQ range between 20 or 25 and 35 or 40. The individual can learn to communicate and, with systematic training, take care of simple hygiene.

sex cells Sperm and ovum. Mature sex cells each contain 23 chromosomes rather than 23 pairs and are different from each other. (See *somatic cells*.)

sex chromosome A chromosome contained in sperm cells and ova responsible for determining the sex of the offspring. Sex chromosomes produced by the female are of one variety (X); those produced by the male may be either X or Y. At fertilization (the union of sperm and ovum), an XX pairing will result in a girl; an XY pairing will result in a boy. Hence the sperm cell is essentially responsible for determining the sex of the offspring.

sexual abuse A form of maltreatment in which the victim is forced—physically or by virtue of the abuser's status and power— to submit to sexual behaviors.

sexual latency A Freudian developmental period during which sexual interest is dormant (latent). Assumed to last from about ages 6 to 11.

sexual orientation Refers to an individual's customary and enduring attraction to persons of one, or occasionally both, genders. (See *heterosexual orientation; homosexual orientation; bisexual orientation*.)

sexual stereotype A preconceived and typically unexamined belief about gender differences and gender roles.

sexually transmitted diseases (STDs) Also called *venereal diseases*; any of several dozen diseases transmitted primarily through sexual intercourse (for example, gonorrhea, herpes, chlamydia, and AIDS).

shaken baby syndrome The effects of violent shaking of an infant. Essentially a whiplash-related brain injury, typically with retinal damage sometimes leading to blindness or other physical disability, or death.

short-term memory Information that lasts from a few seconds to a minute, requiring limited cognitive processing. It defines our immediate consciousness. Also termed *primary memory* or *working memory*.

sickle-cell anemia A blood-cell disorder associated with a recessive allele, far more common among blacks than whites.

significant developmental motor disability A collection of symptoms manifested early in life, evident primarily in motor problems, associated with brain damage, and commonly labeled "cerebral palsy." Can vary in severity from barely detectable to severe paralysis. (See *cerebral palsy*.)

slow-to-warm-up infants An infant temperament type marked by low activity level, high initial withdrawal from the unfamiliar; slow adaptation to change; and a somewhat negative mood, with moderate or low intensity of reaction.

social cognition The realization that others have feelings, motives, intentions, and so on; knowledge of the emotions of others.

social play Activity that involves interaction between two or more children and that frequently takes the form of games with somewhat defined rules. (See *play, sensorimotor play, imaginative play*.)

social referencing Using others' reactions as a norm or reference point to guide one's personal reactions. Thus a young child's response to a strange situation might be heavily influenced by the parent's apparent reaction.

social smiling The second phase in the development of smiling, initially occurring in response to auditory and visual stimuli that are social in nature, like the caregiver's voice. (See *reflex smiling; selective social smile*.)

socialization The complex process of learning those behaviors that are appropriate within a given culture as well as those that are less appropriate. The primary agents of socialization are home, school, and peer groups.

sociogram A pictorial or graphic representation of the social structure of a group.

sociological Related to sociology, the study of the origin of and relationships among social groups and social phenomena.

solitary play Nonsocial child play that a child undertakes alone. It is the most common form of play before age 2.

solitude A state of aloneness. Sometimes forced on those who have no friends and who cannot, or will not, buy companionship. Also, a state chosen by those who simply prefer to be alone. At least part of the time.

somatic cells Also called body cells; all cells in our body other than sex cells. Normal somatic cells each contain 23 pairs of chromosomes. All our body cells normally contain identical genetic information. (See *sex cells*.)

special abilities theory A theory of intelligence based on the assumption that intelligence consists of several separate factors (for example, numerical, verbal, memory) rather than a single underlying factor common to performance in all areas. (See *g, general factor theory*.)

special needs Global term that includes all who need special training, equipment, or services to reach their full human potential. What is often termed *special education* is also *special needs education* or education for those with *special needs*.

specimen description A method of child study in which detailed specific instances of a child's behavior are recorded. Useful for in-depth studies of individual children.

sperm cell The sex cell produced by a mature male. Like egg cells (ova), sperm cells consist of 23 chromosomes rather than 23 *pairs* of chromosomes.

spermarche A boy's first ejaculation, often a nocturnal event. (See *menarche*.)

stages Identifiable phases in the development of human beings. Such developmental theories as Jean Piaget's are referred to as stage theories because they describe behavior at different developmental levels.

standard deviation A mathematical measure of the distribution of scores around their mean (average). In a *normal distribution*, about 68% of all scores fall within 1 standard deviation of the mean; 95% fall within 2 standard deviations of the mean.

STDs (See *sexually transmitted diseases*.)

stereotype Denotes a fixed, firm, relatively unexamined belief typically generalized to a class of superficially similar situations or individuals.

stimulus (plural *stimuli*) Any change in the physical environment capable of exciting a sense organ.

stranger anxiety Fear reactions in the presence of unknown people; seldom seen in infants until the middle of their first year, after which some babies begin to "make strange."

stress A force exerted on an individual, often related to change or to high environmental demands; sometimes associated with high arousal.

stunting Severe growth retardation, defined as more than 2 standard deviations below average height relative to normal children of the same age. (See *wasting*.)

Sturm und Drang Literally, storm and stress (German). G. Stanley Hall's expression to describe what he thought was the confusion, the turmoil, the stresses, the difficulties of the adolescent period.

successful intelligence Sternberg's view that intelligence involves a balance between selecting and shaping environments and adaptation to achieve personal goals.

sucking reflex The automatic sucking response of a newborn child when the oral regions are stimulated. Nipples are particularly appropriate for eliciting the sucking reflex.

sudden infant death syndrome (SIDS) Unexplained and unexpected infant death. The leading cause of infant death between the ages of 1 month and 1 year (not really a cause, because the *cause* remains unknown; rather, a *label*).

superego The third level of personality according to Freud. It defines the moral or ethical aspects of personality and is in constant conflict with the id. (See *ego, id*.)

supermale syndrome A chromosomal disorder affecting males with two y chromosomes (hence XYY), sometimes, though not always, linked with greater than average height, lower intelligence, and higher impulsivity.

supine On the back; a sleep position. Or sometimes just a way to look at clouds.

surrogate mothers Surrogates are substitutes. In assisted reproduction, a surrogate mother is a woman who carries a child for someone else.

survival reflex One of several reflexes in the newborn that are closely linked to physical survival—for example, the breathing reflex and the sucking reflex.

swarming Current term used to describe acts of violence or intimidation motivated primarily by robbery and committed by at least three people acting as a gang.

symbolic models Nonhuman models such as movies, television programs, oral and written instructions, or religious, literary, musical, or folk heroes.

synapses Connections between neurons. A synapse is formed whenever the gap between neurons (the *synaptic cleft*) is bridged by an impulse. (See *synaptic cleft*.)

synaptic cleft Space between terminal buttons at ends of axons and dendrites of adjoining neurons. A gap that must be bridged if neural transmission is to occur. (See *synapse*.)

syncretic reasoning A type of semilogical reasoning characteristic of the classification behavior of very young preschoolers. In syncretic reasoning, objects are grouped according to egocentric criteria, which are subject to change from one object to the next. In other words, children do not classify on the basis of a single dimension but change dimensions as they classify.

syntax The grammar of a language, consisting of the set of implicit or explicit rules that govern the combinations of words composing a language.

taboo A prohibition imposed by social custom; a behavior widely accepted as forbidden and inappropriate by a culture.

Tay-Sachs disease A fatal genetic enzyme disorder that can be detected before birth, but that cannot yet be prevented or cured.

telegraphic speech Speech of infants and young children that compresses meaning into short utterances, typically consisting of only two words.

temperament The biological basis of personality—its hereditary components. The expression *infant temperament* refers to infants' characteristic emotional responses.

teratogens Drugs and other substances that cause fetal defects.

tertiary circular reaction Infant responses that are circular in the sense that the response serves as the stimulus for its own repetition, but the repeated response is not identical to the first response. This last characteristic, the altered response, distinguishes a tertiary circular reaction from a secondary circular reaction. (See *primary circular reaction, secondary circular reaction*.)

testes Spherical male organs in mammals, of which there are normally two. Produce sperm, but, strangely, are termed eggs (*huevos*) in Spanish.

tests of divergent thinking Creativity tests. Usually open-ended, *production* tests designed to measure factors such as fluency, flexibility, and originality.

tetrahydrocannabinol (THC) The active ingredient in marijuana and related substances (of the *cannabis* family).

theory An organized, systematic explanation of observations useful for explaining and for predicting.

theory of mind The intuitive notions children have about the existence and characteristics of their own and others' minds. A theory of mind allows a child to predict and explain behavior by relating it to mental states such as beliefs and intentions.

theory of multiple intelligences Howard Gardner's belief that human intelligence consists of 7—or perhaps 8 or even 10—distinct and largely unrelated areas of talent or capability: logical-mathematical, linguistic, musical, spatial, bodily-kinesthetic, interpersonal, and intrapersonal—and perhaps naturalist, spiritual, and existential.

time-lag study A developmental study in which subjects of one age are compared to other groups who are also the same age, but at a different point in time (for example, comparing 12-year-olds in 1995 with 12-year-olds in 1990 and in 1985).

time-out A form of punishment in which the transgressor is removed from ongoing (and presumably rewarding) activities.

time sampling A method of child observation in which behavior is observed during specific time intervals, frequently with the aim of recording instances or frequency of specific behaviors.

toddler General term with imprecise age boundaries. Often used to encompass the end of infancy and beginning of the preschool period—about ages 18 to 30 months.

trait Any distinct, consistent quality in which one person can be different from another. (See *types*.)

transductive reasoning The type of semilogical reasoning that proceeds from particular to particular, rather than from particular to general or from general to particular. One example of transductive reasoning is the following: (1) Cows give milk. (2) Goats give milk. (3) Therefore, goats are cows.

transitional objects Blankets, teddy bears, or other objects that children focus affection and attention on while in transition between a state of high parental dependency and the development of a more independent self.

transverse presentation A crosswise presentation of the fetus at birth.

trauma An injury or nervous shock. Traumatic experiences are usually intense and unpleasant.

triadic friendships A grouping of three very close friends. More common among girls than boys.

triarchic theory of successful intelligence Sternberg's model of successful intelligence as involving analytical, creative, and practical abilities. (See *successful intelligence*.)

trisomy 21 (See *Down syndrome*.)

trust versus mistrust The first of Erikson's stages (to age 2), marked by a conflict between the infant's need to develop trust and an urge to remain dependent.

Turner's syndrome A chromosomal abnormality in which a female child is born with a missing sex chromosome (one rather than two X's); characterized by underdeveloped secondary sexual characteristics that can sometimes be improved with injections of estrogen before puberty.

types Any of several groupings of personality traits. *Extraversion* for example, is a personality type that includes traits such as boldness, outgoingness, assertiveness, sociability. (See *trait*.)

ultrasound A diagnostic technique in medicine that uses high-frequency sound waves to provide images of internal body structures. Ultrasound recordings are used extensively to evaluate the condition of the fetus.

umbilical cord A long, thick cord attached to what will be the child's navel at one end and to the placenta at the other. It transmits nourishment and oxygen to the growing fetus from the mother.

unconditioned response (UR) A response elicited by an unconditioned stimulus.

unconditioned stimulus (US) A stimulus that elicits a response before learning. All stimuli capable of eliciting reflexive behaviors are examples of unconditioned stimuli. For example, food is an unconditioned stimulus for the response of salivation.

under-5 mortality rate (U5MR) Death rate for children under 5 who are born alive. U5MR is used by the United Nations as an indicator of how well nations treat their children.

unresolved An *Adult Attachment Interview* category marked by incoherent and disintegrated recollections of childhood relationships, characterized as well by significant and unresolved emotional issues having to do with parents.

uterus A relatively sophisticated term for the womb.

valid A measure is said to be valid to the extent that it measures what it is intended to measure. (See *reliable*.)

values Judgments or beliefs about the desirability of certain behaviors or goals.

values clarification programs Programs designed to encourage learners to examine their personal beliefs about right and wrong, with a view to improving and clarifying their awareness of their own morality.

values education Instructional programs and strategies designed to teach specific values (notions of right and wrong), thereby promoting good behavior and developing good "character."

variable A property, measurement, or characteristic that is susceptible to variation. In psychological experimentation, such qualities of human beings as intelligence and creativity are referred to as variables. (See *dependent variable, independent variable*.)

V-chip A Canadian-designed technological device which, when installed in a television set, blocks reception of programs that have specific codes. The codes are ratings that reflect whether programs are designed specifically for children, whether they contain violence, sex, fear-inducing elements, and so on.

vegetative reflexes Reflexes pertaining to the intake of food (for example, swallowing and sucking).

version The act of turning. In obstetrics, refers to turning the child in the uterus to facilitate birth.

vicarious reinforcement Reinforcement that results from observing someone else being reinforced. In imitative behavior, observers frequently act as though they are being reinforced when in fact they are not being reinforced; rather, they are aware, or simply assume, that the model is being reinforced. (See *direct reinforcement*.)

villi Tiny, tentacle-like growths emanating from the fertilized egg, allowing it to attach itself to the uterine wall to what will become the placenta.

violence An extreme form of aggressiveness, implying physical action and real or possible physical harm to people or objects. (See *aggression*.)

visual acuity Sharpness and clarity of vision. Visual acuity is often expressed by Snellen ratings, in which 20/20 vision is considered average (the individual can see as well at 20 feet as individuals with normal vision). Vision can be poorer than 20/20 (for example, 20/40 when the individual sees as clearly at 20 feet as people with normal vision see at 40) or better (for example, 20/15, when the individual sees as well at 20 feet as average people do at 15).

visual-vestibular sense Describes sensation relating to sensing and maintaining balance, involving both the inner ear and vision.

visually impaired Technically, those who, with corrected vision in their best eye, can see at 20 feet what normal people see at 200 feet. An expression for *legal blindness*.

wasting Defined as more than 2 standard deviations below average weight for average children of that age—hence in the bottom 2.27% of the population. (See *stunting*.)

Whorfian hypothesis In its extreme form, the belief that language is essential for thinking, that thinking does not occur in its absence. In its more moderate form, the belief that language *influences* thinking.

withdrawn-rejected Category of children who are rejected mainly because they are timid, withdrawn, socially awkward. (See *aggressive-rejected*.)

X chromosome One of two types of sex chromosomes, produced by both males and females. It is the only sex chromosome produced by females. An XX pairing of chromosomes determines that the offspring will be female.

X-linked Refers to genes that appear only on the X sex chromosome. Typically used to describe certain genetic defects that, because they are on the X chromosome, are far more common in males than in females.

Y chromosome One of two types of sex chromosomes, produced only by the male (who also produces X chromosomes). An XY pairing determines that the offspring will be male.

zone of proximal development Vygotsky's phrase for the individual's current potential for further intellectual development, a capacity not ordinarily measured by conventional intelligence tests. He suggests that hints and questions might help in assessing this zone.

zygote A fertilized egg cell (ovum). A zygote is formed from the union of a sperm cell and an egg cell; it normally contains 46 chromosomes (a full complement).

BIBLIOGRAPHY

AAMD Ad Hoc Committee on Terminology and Classification (1992). *Mental retardation: Definition, classification, and systems of support* (9th ed.). Washington, DC: American Association on Mental Retardation.

Aaron, J., Zaglul, H., & Emery, R. E. (1999). Posttraumatic stress in children following acute physical injury. *Journal of Pediatric Psychology, 24,* 335–343.

Aarons, G. A., Brown, S. A., Coe, M. T., Myers, M. G., Garland, A. F., Ezzet-Lofstram, R., Hazen, A. L., & Hough, R. L. (1999). Adolescent alcohol and drug abuse and health. *Journal of Adolescent Health, 24,* 412–421.

Abecassis, J. (1993). De Henri Wallon a Jerome Bruner, continuité ou discontinuité? Enfance, 47, 47–57.

Abel, E. L. (1984). Fetal alcohol syndrome and fetal alcohol effects. New York: Plenum Press.

Abel, E. L. (1998). *Fetal alcohol abuse syndrome.* New York: Plenum.

Abell, S. C., Horkheimer, R., & Nguyen, S. E. (1998). Intellectual evaluations of adolescents via human figure drawings: An empirical comparison of two methods. *Journal of Clinical Psychology, 54,* 811–815.

Aber, J. L., Belsky, J., Slade, A., & Crnic, K. (1999). Stability and change in mothers' representations of their relationship with their toddlers. *Developmental Psychology, 35,* 1038–1047.

Abood, D. A., & Chandler, S. B. (1997). Race and the role of weight, weight change, and body dissatisfaction in eating disorders. *American Journal of Health Behavior, 21,* 21–25.

Abraham, R. (1999). Emotional intelligence in organizations: A conceptualization. *Genetic, Social, & General Psychology Monographs, 125,* 209–224.

Abram, M. J., & Dowling, W. D. (1979). How readable are parenting books? *The Family Coordinator, 28,* 365–368.

Abramsky, L. (1994). Counselling prior to prenatal testing. In L. Abramsky & J. Chapple (Eds.), *Prenatal diagnosis: The human side.* New York: Chapman and Hall.

Abramson, L. (1991). Facial expressivity in failure to thrive and normal infants: Implications for their capacity to engage in the world. Merrill-Palmer Quarterly, 37, 159–182.

Abravanel, E., & Ferguson, S. A. (1998). Observational learning and the use of retrieval information during the second and third years. *Journal of Genetic Psychology, 159,* 455–476.

Abroms, I. F., & Panagakos, P. G. (1980). The child with significant developmental motor disability (cerebral palsy). In A. P. Scheiner & I. F. Abroms (Eds.), The practical management of the developmentally disabled child. St. Louis: C. V. Mosby, 145–166.

Acker, A. (1986). Children of the volcano. Toronto: Between the Lines.

Acker, M. M., & O'Leary, S. G. (1996). Inconsistency of mothers' feedback and toddlers' misbehavior and negative affect. *Journal of Abnormal Child Psychology, 24,* 703–714.

Acock, A. C., & Kiecolt, K. J. (1989). Is it family structure or socioeconomic status? Family structure during adolescence and adult adjustment. *Social Forces, 68,* 553–571.

ACOG practice bulletin. Vaginal birth after previous cesarean delivery. Number 2, October 1998. Clinical management guidelines for obstetrician-gynecologists, (1999). American College of Obstetricians and Gynecologists. *International Journal of Gynaecology and Obstetrics, 64,* 201–208.

ACOG Technical Bulletin. (1988). Human Immune Deficiency Virus Infections. Number 123. Washington, D.C., December.

Acredolo, L. P., & Hake, J. L. (1982). Infant perception. In B. B. Wolman (Ed.), *Handbook of developmental psychology.* Englewood Cliffs, N.J.: Prentice-Hall.

Adair, J. G., Sharpe, D., & Huynh, C. (1989). Hawthorne control procedures in educational experiments: A reconsideration of their use and effectiveness. *Review of Educational Research, 59,* 215–228.

Adams, R. E., Jr., & Passman, R. H. (1979). Effects of visual and auditory aspects of mothers and strangers on the play and exploration of children. *Developmental Psychology, 15,* 269–274.

Adams, R. E., Jr., & Passman, R. H. (1981). The effects of preparing two-year-olds for brief separations from their mothers. *Child Development, 52,* 1068–1070.

Adams, R. E., Jr., & Passman, R. H. (1983). Explaining to young children about an upcoming separation from their mother: When do I tell them? *Journal of Applied Developmental Psychology, 4,* 35–42.

Adams, R. J., & Courage, M. L. (1998). Human newborn color vision: Measurement with chromatic stimuli varying in excitation purity. *Journal of Experimental Child Psychology, 68,* 22–34.

Adegoke, A. A. (1993). The experience of spermarche (the age of onset of sperm emission) among selected adolescent boys in Nigeria. *Journal of Youth and Adolescence, 22,* 201–209.

Adler, P. A., & Adler, P. (1998). *Peer power: Preadolescent culture and identity.* New Brunswick, NJ: Rutgers University Press.

Adolph, K. E. (1997). Learning in the development of infant locomotion. *Monographs of the Society for Research in Child Development, 62,* 1–140.

Agarwal, D. K., Agarwal, A., Singh, M., Satya, K., Agarwal, S., & Agarwal, K. N. (1998). Pregnancy wastage in rural Varanasi: Relationship with maternal nutrition and sociodemographic characteristics. *Indian Pediatrics, 35,* 1071–1079.

Agmon, S., & Schneider, S. (1998). The first stages in the development of the small group: A psychoanalytic understanding. *Group Analysis, 31,* 131–156.

AIDS kids beat odds against survival. (1994). *Edmonton Journal,* April 17, C7.

AIDS virus strain beats pill; scientists scramble for new cure. (1989). *Edmonton Journal,* March 15, A2.

AIDS will kill 4M women by 2000: WHO. (1993). *Edmonton Journal,* September 8, p. A12.

Ainsworth, L. L. (1984). Contact comfort: A reconsideration of the original work. *Psychological Reports, 55,* 943–949.

Ainsworth, M. D. S. (1973). The development of infant-mother attachment. In B. M. Caldwell & H. N. Ricciuti (Eds.), *Review of child devel-*

opment research (Vol. 3). Chicago: University of Chicago Press.

Ainsworth, M. D. S. (1979). Infant-mother attachment. *American Psychologist, 34*, 932–937.

Ainsworth, M. D. S., Blehar, M. C., Waters, E., & Wall, S. (1978). Patterns of attachment. Hillsdale, N.J.: Lawrence Erlbaum.

Ajuriaguerra, J. (1988). L'enfant dans l'histoire: problèmes psychologiques. *Psychiatrie de l'Enfant, Jul*, 417–442.

Alarcon, M., Plomin, R., Fulker, D. W., Corley, R., & DeFries, J. C. (1998). Multivariate path analysis of specific cognitive abilities data at 12 years of age in the Colorado Adoption Project. *Behavior Genetics, 28*, 255–264.

Albers, S. M. (1998). The effect of gender-typed clothing on children's social judgments. *Child Study Journal, 28*, 137–159.

Albert, R. S., & Runco, M. A. (1986). The achievement of eminence: A model based on a longitudinal study of exceptionally gifted boys and their families. In R. J. Sternberg & J. E. Davidson (Eds.), Conceptions of giftedness. New York: Cambridge University Press.

Alcock, J. (1984). Animal behavior: An evolutionary approach (3rd ed.). Sunderland, Mass.: Sinauer.

Aldis, O. (1975). Play fighting. New York: Academic Press.

Allen, R. E., & Oliver, J. M. (1982). The effects of child maltreatment on language development. Child Abuse and Neglect, 6, 299–305.

Allen, R. E., & Wasserman, G. A. (1985). Origins of language delay in abused infants. Child Abuse and Neglect, 9, 335–340.

Allison, P. D., & Furstenberg, F. F., Jr. (1989). How marital dissolution affects children: Variations by age and sex. Developmental Psychology, 25, 540–549.

Allison, S., Pearce, C., Martin, G., Miller, K., & Long, R. (1995). Parental influence, pessimism and adolescent suicidality. *Archives of Suicide research, 1*, 229–242.

Almqvist, K., & Hwang, P. (1999). Iranian refugees in Sweden: Coping processes in children and their families. *Childhood, 6*, 167–188.

Als, H., Tronick, E., Lester, B. M., & Brazelton, T. B. (1979). Specific neonatal measures: The Brazelton Neonatal Behavior Assessment Scale. In J. D. Osofsky (Ed.), Handbook of infant development. New York: John Wiley.

Alvy, K. T. (1987). Parent training: A social necessity. Studio City, Calif.: Center for the Improvement of Child Caring.

Amato, P. R., & Keith, B. (1991). Parental divorce and the well-being of children: A meta-analysis. *Psychological Bulletin, 110*, 26–46.

American Psychiatric Association. (1987). Diagnostic and statistical manual of mental disorders (3rd ed., revised). Washington, D.C.: American Psychiatric Association.

American Psychiatric Association. (1994). *Diagnostic and statistical manual of mental disorders (DSM-IV),* (4th ed) Washington, DC : American Psychiatric Association.

Ames, C. (1992). Classrooms: Goals, structures, and student motivation. *Journal of Educational Psychology, 84*, 261–271.

Ammerman, R. T. (1990). Predisposing child factors. In R. T. Ammerman & M. Hersen (Eds.), *Children at risk: An evaluation of factors contributing to child abuse and neglect.* New York: Plenum.

Ampollini, P., Marchesi, C., Gariboldi, S., Cella, P., Bertacca, S. G., Borghi, C., & Maggini, C. (1999). The Parma high school epidemiological survey: Eating disorders. *Journal of Adolescent Health, 24*, 158–159.

Amponsah, B., & Krekling, S. (1997). Sex differences in visual-spatial performance among Ghanaian and Norwegian adults. *Journal of Cross-Cultural Psychology, 28*, 81–92.

Anastasi, A. (1958). Heredity, environment, and the question "how?" *Psychological Review, 65*, 197–208.

Anastasiow, N. (1984). Preparing adolescents in child bearing: Before and after pregnancy. In M. Sugar (Ed.), *Adolescent parenthood.* New York: SP Medical and Scientific Books, 141–158.

Andersen, R. E., Crespo, C. J., Bartlett, S. J., Cheskin, L. J., & Pratt, M. (1998). Relationship of physical activity and television watching with body weight and level of fatness among children: Results from the third national health and nutrition examination survey. *Jama: Journal of the American Medical Association, 279*, Mar 1998, 938–942.

Anderson, D. R., & Bryant, J. (1983). Research on children's television viewing: The state of the art. In J. Bryant & D. R. Anderson (Eds.), Children's understanding of television: Research on attention and comprehension. New York: Academic Press, 331–355.

Anderson, J. A. (1983). Television literacy and the critical viewer. In J. Bryant & D. R. Anderson (Eds.), Children's understanding of television: Research on attention and comprehension. New York: Academic Press, 297–327.

Anderson, J. R. (1980). *Cognitive psychology and its applications.* San Francisco: W. H. Freeman.

Anisfeld, M. (1991). Review: Neonatal imitation. *Developmental Review, 11*, 60–97.

Anthony, E. J. (Ed.). (1975). *Exploration in child psychiatry.* New York: Plenum Press.

Anthony, E. J. (1987). Children at high risk for psychosis growing up successfully. In E. J. Anthony & B. J. Cohler (Eds.), *The invulnerable child.* New York: Guilford Press.

Anthony, E. J., & Koupernik, C. (Eds.). (1974). *The child in his family: Children at psychiatric risk* (Vol. 3). New York: John Wiley.

Appel, L. F., Cooper, R. G., McCarrell, N., Sims-Knight, Y., Yussen, S. R., & Flavell, J. H. (1972). The development of the distinction between perceiving and memorizing. *Child Development, 43*, 1365–1381.

Arbuthnot, J. (1975). Modification of moral judgment through role playing. *Developmental Psychology, 11*, 319–324.

Ariès, P. (1962). *Centuries of childhood: A social history of family life* (R. Baldick, trans.). New York: Alfred A. Knopf. (Originally published 1960.)

Arlin, P. K. (1975). Cognitive development in adulthood: A fifth stage? *Developmental Psychology, 11*, 602–606.

Armen, J. C. (1974). *Gazelle boy.* New York: Universe Books. (Translated by S. Hardman from L'enfant sauvage du grand désert. Neuchâtel: Delachaux & Niestlé.)

Armstrong, C. A., Sallis, J. F., Alcaraz, J. E., Kolody, B., & McKenzie, T. L. (1998). Children's television viewing, body fat, and physical fitness. *American Journal of Health Promotion, 12*, 363–368.

Arnett, J. (1990). Contraceptive use, sensation seeking, and adolescent egocentrism. *Journal of Youth and Adolescence, 19*, 171–182.

Arnett, J. (1992). Reckless behavior in adolescence: A developmental perspective. *Developmental Review, 12*, 339–373.

Aronfreed, J. (1968). *Conduct and conscience.* New York: Academic Press.

Artiles, A. J., Barreto, R. M., Pena, L., & McClafferty, K. (1998). Pathways to teacher learning in multicultural contexts: A longitudinal case study of two novice bilingual teachers in urban schools. *Rase: Remedial and Special Education, 19*, 70–90.

Asher, S. R. (1983). Social competence and peer status: Recent advances and future directions. *Child Development, 54*, 1427–1434.

Asher, S. R., Hymel, S., & Renshaw, P. (1984). Loneliness in children. *Child Development, 55*, 1456–1464.

Askew, S., & Ross, C. (1988). *Boys don't cry: Boys and sexism in education.* Philadelphia, Penn.: Open University Press.

Aslin, R. N., & Smith, L. B. (1988). Perceptual development. *Annual Review of Psychology, 39*, 435–473.

Aslin, R. N., Jusczyk, P. W., & Pisoni, D. B. (1997). Speech and auditory processing during infancy: Constraints on and precursors to language. In D. K. Kuhn & R. S. Siegler (Eds.), *Handbook of child psychology: Vol. 2. Cognition, perception, and language* (5th ed.). New York: Wiley.

Aslin, R. N., Pisoni, D. P., & Jusczyk, P. W. (1983). Auditory development and speech perception in infancy. In M. H. Haith & J. J. Campos (Eds.), *Handbook of child psychology* (2nd ed.): *Infancy and developmental psychology.* New York: John Wiley.

Asp, E., & Garbarino, J. (1988). Integrative processes at school and in the community. In T. D. Yawkey & J. E. Johnson (Eds.), *Integrative processes and socialization: Early to middle childhood.* Hillsdale, N.J.: Lawrence Erlbaum.

Astington, J. W., (1991). Intention in the child's theory of mind. In D. Frye & C. Moore (Eds.), *Children's theories of mind: Mental states and social understanding.* Hillsdale N.J.: Lawrence Erlbaum.

Atkinson, R. C., & Shiffrin, R. M. (1972). The control of short-term memory. *Scientific American, 225*, 82–90.

Atlas, R. S., &Pepler, D. J. (1998). Observations of bullying in the classroom. *Journal of Educational Research, 92*, 86–99.

Aubrey, C. (1993). An investigation of the mathematical knowledge and competencies which young children bring into school. *British Educational Research Journal, 19*, 27–41.

Ayoub, C. C., Deutsch, R. M., & Maraganore, A. (1999). Emotional distress in children of high-conflict divorce: The impact of marital conflict and violence. *Family & Conciliation Courts Review, 37*, 297–314.

Babad, E. Y. (1985). Some correlates of teachers' expectancy bias. *American Educational Research Journal, 22*, 175–183.

Babaeva, J. D. (1999). A dynamic approach to giftedness: Theory and practice. *High Ability Studies, 10*, 51–68.

Babrick, H. P., Babrick, P. O., & Wittlinger, R. P. (1975). Fifty years of memory for names and faces: A cross-sectional approach. *Journal of Experimental Psychology, 104*, 54–75.

Babson, S. G., Pernoll, M. L., Benda, G. I., & Simpson, K. (1980). Diagnostics and management of the fetus and neonate at risk: A guide for team care (4th ed.). St. Louis: C. V. Mosby.

"Baby shakers are rarely prosecuted: tough to make charges stick, say forensic experts." (1999, Nov. 19)*Edmonton Journal*, p. B1.

Backstrom, K. (1992). Children's rights and early childhood education. *International Journal of Early Childhood, 24,* 22–27.

Bailey, D. B. Jr., Hatton, D. D., & Skinner, M. (1998). Early developmental trajectories of males with fragile X syndrome. *American Journal on Mental Retardation, 103,* 29–39.

Baillargeon, R. (1987). Object permanence in 3- and 4-month-old infants. *Developmental Psychology, 23,* 655–664.

Baillargeon, R. (1992). The object concept revisited. In Visual Perception and Cognition in Infancy: Carnegie-Mellon Symposia on Cognition, Vol. 23. Hillsdale, N.J.: Lawrence Erlbaum.

Baillargeon, R., & DeVos, J. (1991). Object permanence in young infants: Further evidence. *Child Development, 62,* 1227–1246.

Baird sounds off at Snell. (1994, Oct. 20). *Gateway,* p. 3.

Bajaj, J. S., Misra, A., Rajalakshmi, M., & Madan, R. (1993). Environmental release of chemicals and reproductive ecology. *Environmental Health Perspectives, 2,* 125–130.

Baker, D. P. (1993). Compared to Japan, the U.S. is a low achiever . . . really: New evidence and comment on Westbury. *Educational Researcher, 22,* 18–20.

Baker, L., & Lyen, K. (1982). Anorexia nervosa. *Current Concepts in Nutrition, 11,* 139–149.

Baker, R. L., & Mednick, B. R. (1984). Influences on human development: A longitudinal perspective. Boston: Kluwer-Nijhoff Publishing.

Bakwin, H. (1949). Psychologic aspects of pediatrics. Journal of Pediatrics, 35, 512–521.

Baldry, A. C., & Farrington, D. P. (1998). Parenting influences on bullying and victimization. *Legal & Criminological Psychology, 3,* 237–254.

Baldwin, J. D., & Baldwin, J. I. (1997). Gender differences in sexual interest. *Archives of Sexual Behavior, 26,* 181–210.

Balke, E. (1992). Children's rights and the world summit for children. *International Journal of Early Childhood, 24,* 2–7.

Balow, B. (1980). Definitional and prevalence problems in behavior disorders of children. *School Psychology, 8,* 348–354.

Baltes, M. M., & Silverberg, S. B. (1994). The dynamics between dependency and autonomy: Illustrations across the lifespan. In D. L. Featherman, R. M. Lerner, & M. Perlmutter (Eds.), *Life-span development and behavior* (Vol. 12). Hillsdale, NJ: Erlbaum.

Banaji, M. R., & Prentice, D. A. (1994). The self in adolescence. *Annual Review of Psychology, 45,* 297–332.

Bancroft, R. (1976). Special education: Legal aspects. In P. A. O'Donnell & R. H. Bradfield (Eds.), Mainstreaming: Controversy and consensus. San Rafael, Calif.: Academic Therapy Publications

Bandura, A. (1969). *Principles of behavior modification.* New York: Holt, Reinhart & Winston.

Bandura, A. (1977). Social learning theory. Englewood Cliffs, N.J.: Prentice-Hall.

Bandura, A. (1981). Self-referent thought: A developmental analysis of self-efficacy. In J. H. Flavell & L. Ross (Eds.), Social cognitive development: Frontiers and possible futures. Cambridge: Cambridge University Press.

Bandura, A. (1986). Social foundations of thought and action: A social cognitive theory. Englewood Cliffs, N.J.: Prentice-Hall.

Bandura, A. (1989a). Regulation of cognitive processes through perceived self-efficacy. *Developmental Psychology, 25,* 729–735.

Bandura, A. (1993). Perceived self-efficacy in cognitive development and functioning. *Educational Psychologist, 28,* 117–148.

Bandura, A. (1997). *Self-efficacy: The exercise of control.* New York: W. H. Freeman.

Bandura, A. (Ed.) (1995). *Self-efficacy in changing societies.* New York : Cambridge University Press.

Bandura, A., & Walters, R. (1963). Social learning and personality development. New York: Holt, Rinehart & Winston.

Bandura, A., Pastorelli, C., Barbaranelli, C., Caprara, G. V., & Gian, V. (1999). Self-efficacy pathways to childhood depression. *Journal of Personality and Social Psychology, 76,* 258–269.

Bandura, A., Ross, D., & Ross, S. A. (1963). Vicarious reinforcement and imitative learning. *Journal of Abnormal and Social Psychology, 67,* 601–607.

Banerjee, M. (1997). Hidden emotions: preschoolers' knowledge of appearance-reality and emotion display rules. *Social Cognition, 15,* 107–132.

Banks, M. S. (1980). The development of visual accommodation during early infancy. *Child Development, 51,* 646–666.

Baran, S. J., Chase, L. J., & Courtright, J. A. (1979). Television drama as a facilitator of prosocial behavior: "The Waltons." Journal of Broadcasting, 23, 277–285.

Baranowski, T., Smith, M., Hearn, M. D., Lin, L. S., Baranowski, J., Doyle, C., Resnicow, K., & Wang, D. T. (1997). Patterns in children's fruit and vegetable consumption by meal and day of the week. *Journal of the American College of Nutrition, 16,* 216–223.

Baris, M. A., & Garrity, C. B. (1997). Co-parenting post-divorce: Helping parents negotiate and maintain low-conflict separations. In W. K. Halford & H. J. Markman (Eds.). *Clinical handbook of marriage and couples interventions.* Chichester, England: John Wiley.

Barnett, W. S. (1992). Benefits of compensatory preschool education. *Journal of Human Resources, 27,* 279–312.

Barnett, W. S. (1993). Benefit-cost analysis of preschool education: Findings from a 25–year follow-up. *American Journal of Orthopsychiatry, 63,* 500–508.

Barr, O. (1999). Genetic counselling: A consideration of the potential and key obstacles to assisting parents adapt to a child with learning disabilities. *Mental Handicap, 27,* 30–36.

Barr, R. G. (1998). Crying in the first year of life: Good news in the midst of distress. *Child: Care, Health & Development, 24,* 425–439.

Barrett, G. V., & Depinet, R. L. (1991). A reconsideration of testing for competence rather than for intelligence. *American Psychologist, 46,* 1012–1024.

Barry, H. III & Schlegel, A. (Eds.). (1980).Cross-cultural samples and codes. Pittsburgh: University of Pittsburgh Press.

Bartoshuk, L. M., & Beauchamp, G. K. (1994). Chemical senses. *Annual Review of Psychology, 45,* 419–449.

Basadur, M., & Hausdorf, P. A. (1996). Measuring divergent thinking attitudes related to creative problem solving and innovation management. *Creativity Research Journal, 9,* 21–32.

Basseches, M. (1984). Dialectical thinking and adult development. Norwood, N.J.: Ablex.

Bates, E. (1976). The emergence of symbols. New York: Academic Press.

Bates, E., Bretherton, I., Shore, D., & McNew, S. (1981). Names, gestures, and objects: The role

of context in the emergence of symbols. In K. E. Nelson (Ed.), Children's language (Vol. 3), New York: Gardner Press.

Bates, E., Thal, D., Whitesell, K., Fenson, L., & Oakes, L. (1989). Integrating language and gesture in infancy. *Developmental Psychology, 25,* 1004–1019.

Bates, J. E. (1989). Concepts and measures of temperament. In G. A. Kohnstamm, J. E. Bates, & M. K. Rothbart (Eds.), *Temperament in Childhood.* New York: John Wiley.

Battachi, M. W. (1993). Une contribution à la psychologie des émotions: L'enfant humilié. *Enfance, 47,* 21–26.

Battistich, V., Watson, M., Solomon, D. I., Schaps, E., & Solomon, J. (1991). The child development project: A comprehensive program for the development of prosocial character. In W. M. Kurtines & J. L. Gewirtz, (Eds.), *Handbook of moral behavior and development* (Vol 3: Application), Hillsdale, N.J.: Lawrence Erlbaum.

Baum, C. G., & Forehand, R. (1984). Social factors associated with adolescent obesity. *Journal of Pediatric Psychology, 9,* 293–302.

Baumrind, D. (1967). Child care practices anteceding three patterns of pre-school behavior. *Genetic Psychology Monographs, 75,* 43–88.

Baumrind, D. (1977). Some thoughts about child-rearing. In S. Cohen & T. J. Comiskey (Eds.), Child development: Contemporary perspectives. Itasca, Ill.: F. E. Peacock.

Baumrind, D. (1989). Rearing competent children. In W. Damon (Ed.), *Child development today and tomorrow,* San Francisco: Jossey-Bass.

Baumrind, D. (1993). The average expectable environment is not good enough: A response to Scarr. *Child Development, 64,* 1299–1317.

Baxter, G., & Beer, J. (1990). Educational needs of school personnel regarding child abuse and/or neglect. *Psychological Reports, 67,* 75–80.

Bayley, N. (1969). Bayley scales of infant development. New York: Psychological Corp.

Bayley, N. (1993). *Bayley Scales of Infant Development* (2nd ed.). New York: The Psychological Corporation.

Beatty, P. (1991). Forward. *The Journal of Drug Issues, 21,* 1–7.

Beck, C. T. (1996). A meta-analysis of the relationship between postpartum depression and infant temperament. *Nursing Research, 45,* 225–230.

Becker, A. E., Grinspoon, S. K., Klibanski, A., Herzog, D. B. (1999). Current concepts: Eating disorders. *New England Journal of Medicine, 340,* 1092–1098.

Becker, G. S. (2000). Cracking the genetic code: Competition was the catalyst. *Business Week,* 08/14/2000, Issue 3694, p. 26.

Becker, J. C, Liersch, R., Tautz, C., Schlueter, B., & Andler, W. (1998). Shaken Baby Syndrome: Report on four pairs of twins. *Child Abuse & Neglect, 22,* 931–937.

Beckwith, L., & Rodning, C. (1991). Intellectual functioning in children born preterm: Recent research. In L. Okagaki & R. J. Sternberg (Eds.), Directors of development: Influences on the development of children's thinking. Hillsdale, N.J.: Lawrence Erlbaum.

Beckwith, L., Cohen, S. E., & Hamilton, C. E. (1999). Maternal sensitivity during infancy and subsequent life events relate to attachment representation at early adulthood. *Developmental Psychology, 35,* 693–700.

Beckwith, R. T. (1991). The language of emotion, the emotions, and nominalist bootstrapping.

In D. Frye & C. Moore (Eds.), Children's theories of mind: Mental states and social understanding. Hillsdale N.J.: Lawrence Erlbaum.

Beer, J. M., Arnold, R. D., & Loehlin, J. C. (1998). Genetic and environmental influences on MMPI factor scales: Joint model fitting to twin and adoption data. *Journal of Personality and Social Psychology, 74*, 818–827.

Beilin, H. (1992). Piaget's enduring contribution to developmental psychology. *Developmental Psychology, 28*, 191–204.

Bekaroglu, M., Soylu, C., Soylu, N., & Bilici, M. (1997). Bipolar affective disorder associated with Klinefelter's syndrome: A case report. *Israel Journal of Psychiatry and Related Science, 34*, 308–310.

Bell, C. S., & Battjes, R. (1985). Prevention research: Deterring drug abuse among children and adolescents. NIDA Research Monograph 63. Rockville, Md.: National Institute on Drug Abuse.

Bellamy, C. (1996). *The state of the world's children: 1996.* New York: Oxford University Press.

Bellamy, C. (1996b). About the Convention. *The Progress of Nations, 1996.* New York: UNICEF.

Bellamy, C. (1999a). *The state of the world's children:1999.* New York: Oxford University Press.

Bellamy, C. (1999b). Commentary: Six Billionth Baby. *The Progress of Nations, 1999.* New York: UNICEF.

Belsky, J. (1980). Child maltreatment: An ecological integration. *American Psychologist, 35*, 320–335.

Belsky, J. (1981). Early human experience: A family perspective. *Developmental Psychology, 17*, 3–23.

Belsky, J. (1997). Variation in susceptibility to environmental influence: An evolutionary argument. *Psychological Inquiry, 8*, 182–186.

Belsky, J. (1999). Interactional and contextual determinants of attachment security. In J. Cassidy & P. R. Shaver (Eds.), *Handbook of attachment: Theory, research, and clinical applications,* New York, NY: Guilford Press.

Belsky, J. (1999). Quantity of nonmaternal care and boys' problem behavior/adjustment at ages 3 and 5: Exploring the mediating role of parenting. *Psychiatry: Interpersonal & Biological Processes, 62*, 1–20.

Belsky, J., & Hsieh, K. H. (1998). Patterns of marital change during the early childhood years: Parent personality, coparenting, and division-of-labor correlates. *Journal of Family Psychology, 12*, 511–528.

Belsky, J., & Rovine, M. J. (1988). Nonmaternal care in the first year of life and the security of infant-parent attachment. Child Development, 59, 157–167.

Belsky, J., Lerner, R. M., & Spanier, G. B. (1984). The child in the family. Reading, Mass.: Addison-Wesley.

Bem, S. (1981). Gender schema theory: A cognitive account of sex typing. *Psychological Review, 88*, 354–364.

Bem, S. L. (1974). The measurement of psychological androgyny. *Journal of Consulting and Clinical Psychology, 42*, 155–162.

Bem, S. L. (1989). Genital knowledge and gender constancy in preschool children. *Child Development, 60*, 649–662.

Benasich, A. A., & Brooks-Gunn, J. (1996). Maternal attitudes and knowledge of child-rearing: Associations with family and child outcomes. *Child Development, 67*, 1186–1205.

Benoit, D., & Parker, K. C. (1994). Stability and transmission of attachment across three generations. *Child Development, 65*, 1444–1456.

Benthin, A., Slovic, P., & Severson, H. (1993). A psychometric study of adolescent risk perception. *Journal of Adolescence, 16*, 153–168.

Bentley, K. S., & Fox, R. A. (1991). Mothers and fathers of young children: Comparison of parenting styles. *Psychological Reports, 69*, 320–322.

Berdine, W. H., & Blackhurst, A. E. (Eds.). (1985). An introduction to special education (2nd ed.). Boston: Little, Brown.

Bereiter, C. (1991). Implications of connectionism for thinking about rules. *Educational Researcher, 20*, 10–16.

Bereiter, C., & Engelmann, S. (1966). Teaching disadvantaged children in the preschool. Englewood Cliffs, N.J.: Prentice-Hall.

Berg, B., & Turner, D. (1993). MTV unleashed: Sixth graders create music videos based on works of art. *Techtrends, 38*, 28–31.

Berg, W. K., & Berg, K. M. (1987). Psychophysiological development in infancy: State, startle, and attention. In J. D. Osofsky (Ed.), *Handbook of infant development.* New York: John Wiley.

Berkovic, S. F., & Scheffer, I. E. (1997). Genetics of human partial epilepsy. *Current Opinion in Neurology, 10*, 110–114.

Berkowitz, M. W., Oser, F., & Althof, W. (1987). The development of sociomoral discourse. In W. M. Kurtines & J. L. Gewirtz (Eds.), Moral development through social interaction. New York: John Wiley.

Berman, H. (1999). Stories of growing up amid violence by refugee children of war and children of battered women living in Canada. *Image—The Journal of Nursing Scholarship, 31*, 57–63.

Berman, T., Douglas, V. I., & Barr, R. G. (1999). Effects of methylphenidate on complex cognitive processing in attention-deficit hyperactivity disorder. *Journal of Abnormal Psychology, 108*, 90–105.

Berndt, T. J. (1979). Developmental changes in conformity to peer and parents. *Developmental Psychology, 15*, 608–616.

Berndt, T. J. (1988). The nature and significance of children's relationships. In R. Vasta (Ed.), *Annals of child development* (Vol. 5). Greenwich, Conn.: JAI Press.

Berndt, T. J. (1989). Friendships in childhood and adolescence. In W. Damon (Ed.), Child development today and tomorrow. San Francisco: Jossey-Bass.

Berndt, T. J. (1999). Friends' influence on students' adjustment to school. *Educational Psychologist, 34*, 15–28.

Berndt, T. J., Cheung, P. C., Lau, S., Hau, K. T., & Lew, W. J. F. (1993). Perceptions of parenting in Mainland China, Taiwan, and Hong Kong: Sex differences and societal differences. *Developmental Psychology, 29*, 156–164.

Berne, E. (1964). Games people play. New York: Grove Press.

Bernstein, B. (1958). Social class and linguistic development: A theory of social learning. *British Journal of Sociology, 9*, 159–174.

Bernstein, B. (1961). Language and social class. *British Journal of Sociology, 11*, 271–276.

Bertalanffy, L. von. (1950). The theory of open systems in physics and biology. *Science, 111*, 23–29.

Bertenthal, B. I., & Campos, J. J. (1990). A systems approach to the organizing effects of self-produced locomotion during infancy. In

C. Rovee-Collier & L. P. Lipsitt (Eds.), Advances in infancy research (Vol. 6), Norwood, N.J.: Ablex.

Betz, P., Puschel, K., Miltner, E., Lignitz, E., & Eisenmenger, W. (1996). Morphometrical analysis of retinal hemorrhages in the shaken baby syndrome. *Forensic Science International, 78*, 71–80.

Beunen, G., & Malina, R. M. (1988). Growth and physical performance relative to the timing of the adolescent spurt. *Exercise and Sport Sciences Review, 16*, 503–540.

Beyth-Marom, R., Austin, L., Fischhoff, B., Palmgren, C., & Jacobs-Quadrel, M. (1993). Perceived consequences of risky behaviors: Adults and adolescents. *Developmental Psychology, 29*, 549–563.

Bibby, R. W. (1995). *The Bibby report: Social trends Canadian style.* Toronto, Ont.: Stoddart.

Bibby, R. W., & Posterski, D. C. (1985). *The emerging generation: An inside look at Canada's teenagers.* Toronto: Irwin Publishing.

Bibby, R. W., & Posterski, D. C. (1992). *Teen trends: A nation in motion.* Toronto: Stoddart Publishing Co.

Biederman, J., Faraone, S. V., Mick, E., Williamson, S, Wilens, Timothy E., Spencer, T. J. Weber, W., Jetton, J., Kraus, I., Pert, J., & Zallen, B. (1999). Clinical correlates of ADHD in females: Findings from a large group of girls ascertained from pediatric and psychiatric referral sources. *Journal of the American Academy of Child & Adolescent Psychiatry, 38*, 966–975.

Biernat, M. (1993). Gender and height: Developmental patterns in knowledge and use of an accurate stereotype. *Sex Roles, 29*, 691–713.

Bijou, S. W. (1989a). Behavior analysis. In R. Vasta (Ed.), Annals of child development (Vol. 6). Greenwich, Conn.: JAI Press.

Bijou, S. W. (1989b). Psychological linguistics: Implications for a theory of initial development and a method for research. In H. W. Reese (Ed.), Advances in child development and behavior. New York: Academic Press.r2

Bijou, S. W., & Sturges, P. S. (1959). Positive reinforcement for experimental studies with children—Consumables and manipulatables. *Child Development, 30*, 151–170.

Biller, H. B. (1982). Fatherhood: Implications for child and adult development. In B. B. Wolman and others (Eds.), *Handbook of developmental psychology.* Englewood Cliffs, N.J.: Prentice-Hall.

Binder, A. (1988). Juvenile delinquency. *Annual Review of Psychology, 39*, 253–282.

Bishop, J. E., & Waldholz, M. (1990). Genome: The most astonishing scientific adventure of our time—the attempt to map all the genes in the human body. New York: Simon & Schuster.

Black, C., & DeBlassie, R. R. (1985). Adolescent pregnancy: Contributing factors, consequences, treatment, and plausible solutions. *Adolescence, 78*, 281–290.

Blinn-Pike, L. (1999). Why abstinent adolescents report they have not had sex: Understanding sexually resilient youth. *Family Relations: Interdisciplinary Journal of Applied Family Studies, 48*, 295–301.

Bloch, H. A., & Niederhoffer, A. (1958). The gang: A study in adolescent behavior. New York: Philosophical Library.

Block, J. H. (1983). Differential premises arising from differential socialization of the sexes:

Some conjectures. *Child Development, 54,* 1335–1354.

Bloom, L. (1973). One word at a time: The use of single word utterances before syntax. The Hague: Mouton.

Bloom, L., Beckwith, R., Capatides, J. B., & Hafitz, J. (1988). Expression through affect and words in the transition from infancy to language. In P. B. Baltes, D. L. Featherman, & R. M. Lerner (Eds.), Life-span development and behavior (Vol. 8), Hillsdale, N.J.: Lawrence Erlbaum.

Blum, D. (1997). *Sex on the brain: The biological differences between men and women.* New York: Viking.

Blum, K., Noble, E. P., Sheridan, P. J., Montgomery, A., Ritchie, T., Jagadeeswaran, P., Nogami, H., Briggs, A. H., & Cohn, J. B. (1990). Allelic association of human dopamine D receptor gene in alcoholism. *Journal of the American Medical Association, 263,* 2055–2060.

Blumberg, M. L. (1974). Psychopathology of the abusing parent. *American Journal of Psychotherapy, 28,* 21–29.

Blustein, D. L. (1997). The role of work in adolescent development. *Career Development Quarterly, 45,* 381–389.

Bodmer, W., & McKie, R. (1995). *The book of man: The human genome project and the quest to discover our genetic heritage.* New York: Scribner.

Boekaerts, M (1997). Self-regulated learning: A new concept embraced by researchers, policy makers, educators, teachers, and students. *Learning & Instruction, 7,* 161–186.

Boero, D. L., Volpe, C., Marcello, A., Bianchi, C., & Lenti, C. (1998). Newborns crying in different contexts: Discrete or graded signals? *Perceptual & Motor Skills, 86,* 1123–1140.

Boldizar, J. P. (1991). Assessing sex typing and androgyny in children: The Children's Sex Role Inventory. *Developmental Psychology, 27,* 505–515.

Bolton, P. J. (1983). Drugs of abuse. In D. F. Hawkins (Ed.), Drugs and pregnancy: Human teratogenesis and related problems. London: Churchill Livingstone, 128–154.

Bombar, M. L., & Littig, L. W. Jr. (1996). Babytalk as a communication of intimate attachment: An initial study in adult romances and friendships. *Personal Relationships, 3,* 137–158.

Bonta, B. D. (1997). Cooperation and competition in peaceful societies. *Psychological Bulletin, 121,* 299–320.

Boone, D. E. (1995). A cross-sectional analysis of WAIS-R aging patterns with psychiatric inpatients: Support for Horn's hypothesis that fluid cognitive abilities decline. *Perceptual and Motor Skills, 81,* 371–379.

Booth, A. (1999). Causes and consequences of divorce: Reflections on recent research. In R. A. Thompson & P. R. Amato (Eds.), *The postdivorce family: Children, parenting, and society.* Thousand Oaks, CA, USA: Sage.

Borg, M. G. (1998). The emotional reaction of school bullies and their victims. *Educational Psychology, 18,* 433–444.

Borg, M. G. (1999). The extent and nature of bullying among primary and secondary schoolchildren. *Educational Research, 41,* 137–153.

Boring, E. G. (1923). Intelligence as the tests test it. *New Republic, 35,* 35–37.

Borkowski, J. G., Milstead, M., & Hale, C. (1988). Components of children's metamemory: Implications for strategy generalization. In

F. E. Weinert & M. Perlmutter (Eds.), Memory development: Universal changes and individual differences. Hillsdale, N.J.: Lawrence Erlbaum.

Bornstein, M. H. (1979). Effects of habituation experience on posthabituation behavior in young infants: Discrimination and generalization among colors. *Developmental Psychology, 15,* 348–349.

Bornstein, M. H., & Marks, L. E. (1982, January). Color revisionism. *Psychology Today,* 64–72.

Bornstein, M. H., Haynes, O. M., Pascual, L., Painter, K. M., & Galperín, C. (1999). Play in two societies: Pervasiveness of process, specificity of structure. *Child Development, 70,* 317–331.

Bosworth, K., Espelage, D. L., Simon, T. R. (1999). Factors associated with bullying behavior in middle school students. *Journal of Early Adolescence, 19,* 341–362.

Bottoms, B. L., Shaver, P. R., Goodman, G. S., & Qin, J. (1995). In the name of God: A profile of religion-related child abuse. *Journal of Social issues, 51,* 85–111.

Bottoms, S. F., Paul, R. H., Mercer, B. M., MacPherson, C. A., Caritis, S. N., Moawad, A. H., Van Dorsten, J. P., Hauth, J. C., Thurnau, G. R., Miodovnik, M., Meis, P. M., Roberts, J. M., McNellis, D., & Iams, J. D. (1999). Obstetric determinants of neonatal survival: Antenatal predictors of neonatal survival and morbidity in extremely low birth weight infants. *American Journal of Obstetrics and Gynecology, 180,* 665–669.

Bouchard, T. C., Tremblay, A., Despries, J. P., Nadeau, A., Lupien, P. J., Theriault, G., Dussault, J., Moorjani, S., Pinault, S., & Fournier, G. (1990). The response to longterm overfeeding in identical twins. *New England Journal of Medicine, 322,* 1477–1488.

Bouchard, T. J., Jr., & McGue, M. (1981). Familial studies of intelligence: A review. *Science, 212,* 1055–1059.

Boukydis, C. F. Z., & Lester, B. M. (1998). Infant crying, risk status and social support in families of preterm and term infants. *Early Development & Parenting, 7,* 31–40.

Boulton, M. J. (1993). Proximate causes of aggressive fighting in middle-school children. *British Journal of Educational Psychology, 63,* 231–244.

Boulton, M. J. (1996). A comparison of 8- and 11-year-old girls' and boys' participation in specific types of rough-and-tumble play and aggressive fighting: Implications for functional hypotheses. *Aggressive Behavior, 22,* 271–287.

Boulton, M. J. (1999). Concurrent and longitudinal relations between children's playground behavior and social preference, victimization, and bullying. *Child Development, 70,* 944–954.

Bower, T. G. R. (1971). The object in the world of the infant. *Scientific American, 225,* 30–38.

Bower, T. G. R. (1977). The perceptual world of the child. Cambridge, Mass.: Harvard University Press.

Bower, T. G. R. (1989). The rational infant: Learning in infancy. New York: W. H. Freeman.

Bowlby, J. (1940). The influence of early environment. *International Journal of Psychoanalysis, 21,* 154–178.

Bowlby, J. (1953). Some pathological processes set in train by early mother-child separation. *Journal of Mental Science, 99,* 265–272.

Bowlby, J. (1958). The nature of the child's tie to his mother. *International Journal of Psychoanalysis, 39,* 350–373.

Bowlby, J. (1969). Attachment and loss: Vol. 1. Attachment. New York: Basic Books.

Bowlby, J. (1979). The making and breaking of affectional bonds. London: Tavistock Publications.

Bowlby, J. (1980). Attachment and loss: Vol. 3. Loss, sadness and depression. New York: Basic Books.

Bowlby, J. (1982). Attachment and loss: Vol. 1. Attachment (2nd ed.). London: Hogarth Press.

Bowman, B. (1993). Early childhood education. In L. Darling-Hammond (Ed.), Review of Research in Education (Vol. 19). Washington, D.C.: American Educational Research Association.

Bowman, J. (1997). The management of hemolytic disease in the fetus and newborn. *Seminars in Perinatology, 21,* 39–44.

Bowman, J. M. (1990). Maternal blood group immunization. In R. D. Eden, F. H. Boehm, & M. Haire (Eds.), Assessment and care of the fetus: Physiological, clinical, and medicolegal principles. Norwalk, Conn.: Appleton & Lange.

Boyatzis, C. J., Chazan, E., & Ting, C. Z. (1993). Preschool children's decoding of facial emotions. *Journal of Genetic Psychology, 154,* 375–382.

Boyd, G. A. (1976). Developmental processes in the child's acquisition of syntax: Linguistics in the elementary school. Itasca, Ill.: F. E. Peacock.

Boyer, C. B. (1998). Sexually transmitted diseases (STDs). In J. Kagan & S. B. Gall, (Eds.). *The Gale encyclopedia of childhood and adolescence.* Detroit, MI: Gale Publishing.

Bradley, R. A., & Hathaway, M. (1996). *Husband coached childbirth* (4th rev. ed.). New York: Bantam, Doubleday, Dell.

Bradley, R. H., Whiteside, L., Mundfrom, D. J., Casey, P. H., Kelleher, K. J., & Pope, S. K. (1994). Contribution of early intervention and early caregiving experiences to resilience in low-birthweight, premature children living in poverty. *Journal of Clinical Child Psychology, 23,* 425–434.

Bradshaw, G. L., & Anderson, J. R. (1982). Elaborative encoding as an explanation of levels of processing. *Journal of Verbal Learning and Verbal Behavior, 21,* 165–174.

Braet, C., Mervielde, I., & Vandereycken, W. (1997). Psychological aspects of childhood obesity: A controlled study in a clinical and nonclinical sample. *Journal of Pediatric Psychology, 22,* 59–71.

Braine, L. G., Pomerantz, E., Lorber, D., & Krantz, D. H. (1991). Conflicts with authority: Children's feelings, actions, and justifications. *Developmental Psychology, 27,* 829–840.

Brainerd, C. J. (1978). *Piaget's theory of intelligence.* Englewood Cliffs, NJ: Prentice-Hall.

Brannen, J. (1996). Discourses of adolescence: Young people's independence and autonomy within families. In J. Brannen & M. O'Brien (Eds.), *Children in families: research and Policy,* Washington: Falmer Press.

Bransford, J. D. (1979). Human cognition: Learning, understanding and remembering. Belmont, Calif.: Wadsworth.

Brantner, J. P., & Doherty, M. A. (1983). A review of time-out: A conceptual and methodological analysis. In S. Axelrod & J. Apsche (Eds.),

The effects of punishment on human behavior. New York: Academic Press.

Braun, C. (1976). Teacher expectations: Sociopsychological dynamics. *Review of Educational Research, 46,* 185–213.

Brazelton, T. B., Nugent, J. K., & Lester, B. M. (1987). Neonatal behavioral assessment scale. In J. D. Osofsky (Ed.), *Handbook of infant development.* New York: John Wiley.

Brazelton, T. D. (1973). Neonatal behavioral assessment scale. Philadelphia: J. B. Lippincott.

Breast milk prevents disease. (1984). Glimpse, Vol. 6, No. 2.

Bremer, J., & Rauch, P. K. (1998). Children and computers: Risks and benefits. *Journal of the American Academy of Child & Adolescent Psychiatry, 37,* 559–560.

Brendt, R. L., & Beckman, D. A. (1990). Teratology. In R. D. Eden, F. H. Boehm, & M. Haire (Eds.), Assessment and care of the fetus: Physiological, clinical, and medicolegal principles. Norwalk, Conn.: Appleton & Lange.

Brennan, K. A. (1999). Searching for secure bases in attachment-focused group therapy: Reaction to Kilmann et al. *Group Dynamics, 32,* 148–151.

Brenner, J., & Mueller, E. (1982). Shared meaning in boy toddler's peer relations. *Child Development, 53,* 380–391.

Bretherton, I. (1991). Intentional communication and the development of an understanding of mind. In D. Frye & C. Moore (Eds.), Children's theories of mind: Mental states and social understanding. Hillsdale N.J.: Lawrence Erlbaum.

Bretherton, I. (1997). Bowlby's legacy to developmental psychology. *Child Psychiatry and Human Development, 28,* 33–43.

Brewer, K. R., & Wann, D. L. (1998). Observational learning effectiveness as a function of model characteristics: Investigating the importance of social power. *Social Behavior and Personality, 26,* 1–10.

Brewin, C. R., Andrews, B., & Gotlib, I. H. (1993). Psychopathology and early experience: A reappraisal of retrospective reports. *Psychological Bulletin, 113,* 82–98.

Brick, P., & Roffman, D. M. (1993). "Abstinence, no buts" is simplistic. *Educational Leadership, 51,* 90–92.

Brisk, M. E. (1991). Toward multilingual and multicultural mainstream education. *Journal of Education, 173,* 114–129.

British Medical Association, (1998). *Human Genetics: Choice and Responsibility.* New York: Oxford University Press.

Britner, P. A., & Phillips, D. A. (1995). Predictors of parent and provider satisfaction with child day care dimensions: A comparison of center-based and family child day care. *Child Welfare, 74,* 1135–1168.

Britton, B. K., Stimson, M., Stennett, B., & Guelgoez, S. (1998). Learning from instructional text: Test of an individual-differences model. *Journal of Educational Psychology, 90,* 476–491.

Broadbent, D. E. (1952). Speaking and listening simultaneously. *Journal of Experimental Psychology, 43,* 267–273.

Brockmeyer, N. (1999). German-Austrian guidelines for HIV-therapy during pregnancy—status: May/June 1998—common statement of the Deutsche AIDS-Gesellschaft (DAIG) and the Osterreichische AIDS-esellschaft (OAG). *European Journal of Medical Research, 4,* 35–42.

Broderick, P. (1986). Perceptual motor development in children's drawing skill. In C. Pratt, A. F. Garton, W. E. Tunmer, & A. R. Nesdale (Eds.), Research issues in child development. Boston: Allen & Unwin.

Brody, G. H. (1998). Sibling relationship quality: Its causes and consequences. *Annual Review of Psychology, 49,* 1–24.

Brody, J. (1988). Cocaine: Litany of fetal risks grows. New York Times, C1, C8.

Brody, L. E., & Mills, C. J. (1997). Gifted children with learning disabilities: A review of the issues. *Journal of Learning Disabilities, 30,* 282–296.

Bronfenbrenner, U. (1970). Two worlds of childhood: U.S. and U.S.S.R. New York: Russell Sage Foundation.

Bronfenbrenner, U. (1977a, May). Nobody home: The erosion of the American family. *Psychology Today,* 41–47.

Bronfenbrenner, U. (1977b). Is early intervention effective? In S. Cohen & T. J. Comiskey (Eds.), Child development: Contemporary perspectives. Itasca, Ill.: F. E. Peacock.

Bronfenbrenner, U. (1979). The ecology of human development. Cambridge, Mass.: Harvard University Press.

Bronfenbrenner, U. (1989). Ecological systems theory. In R. Vasta (Ed.), Annals of child development (Vol. 6). Greenwich, Conn.: JAI Press.

Bronfenbrenner, U. (1998). The ecology of developmental processes. In R. M. Lerner (Ed.), *Handbook of child psychology: Vol I. Theoretical models of human development.* (5th ed.). New York: Wiley.

Bronfenbrenner, U., Belsky, J., & Steinberg, L. (1977). Day care in context: An ecological perspective on research and public policy. In Policy issues in daycare. Washington, D.C.: U.S. Department of Health, Education, & Welfare.

Bronson, G. W. (1971). Fear of the unfamiliar in human infants. In H. R. Schaffer (Ed.), The origins of human social relations. London: Academic Press.

Bronson, G. W. (1972). Infants' reactions to unfamiliar persons and novel objects. *Monographs of the Society for Research in Child Development,* 37, No. 3.

Bronstein, P., Clauson, J., Stoll, M. F., & Abrams, C. L. (1993). Parenting behavior and children's social, psychological, and academic adjustment in diverse family structures. *Family Relations, 42,* 268–276.

Bronstein, P., Clauson, J., Stoll, M. F., & Abrams, C. L. (1993). Parenting behavior and children's social, psychological, and academic adjustment in diverse family structures. *Family Relations, 42,* 268–276.

Brooks, J. B. (1981). The process of parenting. Palo Alto, Calif.: Mayfield.

Brooks-Gunn, J., & Furstenberg, F. F., Jr. (1989). Adolescent sexual behavior. *American Psychologist, 44,* 249–257.

Brophy, J. E., & Good, T. L. (1974). Teacher-student relationships: Causes and consequences. New York: Holt, Rinehart & Winston.

Brotman, S. (1999). Ethnic and lesbian; Understanding identity through the life-history approach. *Affilia: Journal of Women and Social Work, 14,* 417–439.

Brower, R. (1999). Dangerous minds: Eminently creative people who spent time in jail. *Creativity Research Journal, 12,* 3–13.

Brown, B. B., Mounts, N., Lamborn, S. D., & Steinberg, L. (1993). Parenting practices and peer group affiliation in adolescence. *Child Development, 64,* 467–482.

Brown, J. L. (1964). States in newborn infants. *Merrill-Palmer Quarterly, 10,* 313–327.

Brown, J., & Finn, P. (1982). Drinking to get drunk: Findings of a survey of junior and senior high school students. *Journal of Alcohol and Drug Education, 27,* 13–25.

Brown, K., Covell, K., & Abramovitch, R. (1991). Time course and control of emotion: Age differences in understanding and recognition. *Merrill-Palmer Quarterly, 37,* 273–287.

Brown, M. C. J., & Guest, J. F. (1999). Economic impact of feeding a phenylalanine-restricted diet to adults previously untreated phenylketonuria. *Journal of Intellectual Disability Research, 43,* 30–37.

Brown, M. H. (1991). Innovations in the treatment of bulimia: Transpersonal psychology, relaxation, imagination, hypnosis, myth, and ritual. *Journal of Humanistic Education and Development, 30,* 50–60.

Brown, R. (1973). A first language: The early stages. Cambridge, Mass.: Harvard University Press.

Browne Miller, A. (1990). The day care dilemma. New York: Plenum Press.

Brownell, C. A., & Carriger, M. S. (1998). Collaborations among toddler peers: Individual contributions to social contexts. In M. Woodhead, D. Faulkner, & K. Littleton (Eds.), *Making sense of social development..* New York: Routledge.

Brownell, C. A., & Carriger, M. S. Collaborations among toddler peers: Individual contributions to social contexts. In M. Woodhead, D. Faulkner, & K. Littleton (Eds.) (1998), *Cultural worlds of early childhood.* New York: Routledge.

Brownell, K. D., & Wadden, T. A. (1984). Confronting obesity in children: Behavioral and psychological factors. *Pediatric Annals, 13,* 473–480. r3

Bruchkowsky, M. (1991). The development of empathic cognition in middle and early childhood. In R. Case et al., (Eds.), The mind's staircase: Exploring the conceptual underpinnings of children's thought and knowledge. Hillsdale, N.J.: Lawrence Erlbaum.

Bruck, M., & Ceci, S. J. (1999). The suggestibility of children's memories. *Annual Review of Psychology, 50,* 419–439.

Bruck, M., Ceci, S. J., Francoeur, E., & Barr, R. J. (1995). "I hardly cried when I got my shot!": Influencing children's reports about a visit to their pediatrician.

Bruner, J. S. (1957). On Perceptual readiness. *Psychological review, 64,* 123–152.

Bruner, J. S. (1964). The course of cognitive growth. *American Psychologist, 19,* 1–15.

Bruner, J. S. (1977). Early social interaction and language acquistion. In H. R. Schaffer (Ed.), Studies in mother-infant interaction. London: Academic Press.

Bruner, J. S. (1978). Learning the mother tongue. Human Nature, September, 43–49.

Bruner, J. S. (1983). Child's talk. New York: W. W. Norton.

Bruner, J. S. (1985). Models of the learner. *Educational Researcher, 14,* 5–8.

Bruner, J. S. (1997). Comment on "Beyond competence." *Cognitive Development, 12,* 341–343.

Bryan, T. L., Georgiopoulos, A. M., Harms, R. W., Huxsahl, J. E., Larson, D. R., & Yawn, B. P. (1999). Incidence of postpartum depression in Olmsted County, Minnesota. A population-based retrospective study. *Journal of Reproductive Medicine, 44,* 351–358.

Bryant, B. K. (1992). Conflict resolution strategies in relation to children's peer relations. *Journal of Applied Developmental Psychology, 13,* 35–50.

Buber, M. (1958). I and thou. New York: Charles Scribner's.

Buber, M. (1965). The knowledge of man (M. Friedman, Ed.). New York: Harper & Row.

Buchanan, C. M., Eccles, J. S., & Becker, J. B. (1992). Are adolescents the victims of raging hormones: Evidence for activational effects of hormones on moods and behavior at adolescence. *Psychological Bulletin, 111,* 62–107.

Buchanan, T. A. , & Kjos, S. L. (1999). Gestational diabetes: Risk or myth? *Journal of Clinical Endocrinology and Metabolism, 84,* 1854–1857.

Buchholz, E. S. & Catton, R. (1999). Adolescents' perceptions of aloneness and loneliness. *Adolescence, 34,* 203–213.

Buchholz, E. S., & Helbraun, E. (1999). A psychobiological developmental model for an "alonetime" need in infancy. *Bulletin of the Menninger Clinic, 63,* 143–158.

Buchholz, E. S., & Korn-Bursztyn, C. (1993). Children of adolescent mothers: Are they at risk for abuse? *Adolescence, 28,* 361–382.

Buchholz, E. S., & Marben, H. (1999). Neonatal temperament, maternal interaction, and the need for "alonetime." *American Journal of Orthopsychiatry, 69,* 9–18.

Buckingham, D. (1998). Doing them harm? Children's conceptions of the negative effects of television. In K. Swan, C. Meskill, & S. DeMaio (Eds.), *Social learning from broadcast television.* Creskill, NJ: Hampton.

Buis, J. M., & Thompson, D. N. (1989). Imaginary audience and personal fable: A brief review. *Adolescence, 24,* 773–781.

Bulik, C. M., Sullivan, P. F., Joyce, P. R., Carter, F. A., & McIntosh, V. V. (1998). Predictors of 1–year treatment outcome in bulimia nervosa. *Comprehensive Psychiatry, 39,* 206–214.

Bullies drive teen to suicide. (1994, Dec. 6), *Edmonton Sun,* p. 24.

Bullinger, A. (1985). The sensorimotor nature of the infant visual system: Cognitive problems. In V. L. Shulman, L. C. R. Restaino-Baumann & L. Butler (Eds.), The future of Piagetian theory: The neo-Piagetians. New York: Plenum Press.

Bullock, J. R. (1993). Children's loneliness and their relationships with family and peers. *Family Relations, 42,* 46–49.

Bullock, J. R. (1994). Children without friends: Who are they and how can teachers help? *Childhood Education, 69,* 92–96.

Bullock, M. (1985). Animism in childhood thinking: A new look at an old question. *Developmental Psychology, 21,* 217–225.

Bullough, V. L. (1981). Age at menarche: A misunderstanding. *Science, 213,* 365–366.

Bunyan, N. (1999, Dec. 04). Fathering twins at 13 'a nice shock,' boys says. *The National Post,* Toronto, p. A1.

Burkam, D. T., Lee, V. E., & Smerdon, B. A. (1997). Gender and science learning early in high school: Subject matter and laboratory experiences. *American Educational Research Journal, 34,* 297–331.

Burman, E. (1999). Morality and the goals of development. In M. Woodhead, D. Faulkner, & K. Littleton (Eds.), *Making sense of social development.* New York: Routledge.

Burnett, B. B. (1993). The psychological abuse of latency age children: A survey. *Child Abuse and Neglect: The International Journal, 17,* 441–454.

Burns, A., Dunlop, R., & Taylor, A. (1997). Children and parental divorce: The meaning of small effects. *Australian Psychologist, 32,* 136–138.

Burns, B., & Lipsitt, L. P. (1991). Behavioral factors in crib death: Toward an understanding of the sudden infant death syndrome. *Journal of Applied Developmental Psychology, 12,* 159–184.

Burr, D. C., Morrone, M. C., & Fiorentini, A. (1996). Spatial and temporal properties of infant colour vision. In Vital-Durand, F., Atkinson, J., & Braddick, O. J. (Eds.), *Infant vision.* New York: Oxford Univeristy Press.

Bush calls for unprecedented increase in Head Start program. (1992). *The Monterey Herald,* January 22, p. 3A.

Bushnell, E. W., & Boudreau, J. P. (1993). Motor development and the mind: The potential role of motor abilities as a determinant of aspects of perceptual development. *Child Development, 64,* 1005–1021.

Buss, A. H., & Plomin, R. (1985). Temperament: Early developing personality traits. Hillsdale, N.J.: Lawrence Erlbaum.

Buss, K. A., & Goldsmith, H. H. (1998). Fear and anger regulation in infancy: Effects on the temporal dynamics of affective expression. *Child Development, 69,* 359–374.

Bussey, K. (1992). Lying and truthfulness: Children's definitions, standards, and evaluative reactions. *Child Development, 63,* 129–137.

Butler, E. R. (1993). Alcohol use by college students: A rites or passage ritual. *NASPA Journal, 31,* 48–55.

Butler, J. R., & Burton, L. M. (1990). Rethinking teenage childbearing: Is sexual abuse a missing link? *Family Relations, 39,* 73–80.

Buzzelli, C. A. (1992). Young children's moral understanding: Learning about right and wrong. *Young Children, 47,* 48–53.

Byrne, B. M., & Shavelson, R. J. (1987). Adolescent self-concept: Testing the assumption of equivalent structure across gender. *American Educational Research Journal, 24,* 365–385.

Cairns, R. B. (1998). The emergence of developmental psychology. In P. H. Mussen (Ed.), Handbook of child psychology (4th ed.) (Vol. 1): History, theory, and methods (W. Kessen, Ed.). New York: John Wiley, 41–102.

Cairns, R. B., & Valsiner, J. (1984). Child psychology. *Annual Review of Psychology, 35,* 553–577.

Cairns, R. B., Cairns, B. D., Rodkin, P., & Xie, H. (1998). New directions in developmental research: Models and methods. In R. Jessor (Ed.), *New perspectives on adolescent risk behavior.* New York: Cambridge University Press.

Cairns, R. B., Gariepy, J. L., & Hood, K. E. (1990). Development, microevolution, and social behavior. *Psychological Review, 97,* 49–65.

Caldwell, B. (1991). Educare: New product, new future. *Journal of Developmental and Behavioral Pediatrics, 12,* 199–205.

Caldwell, B. M. (1980). Balancing children's rights and parents' rights. In R. Haskins & J. J. Gallagher (Eds.), Care and education of young children in America: Policy, politics and social science. Norwood, N.J.: Ablex.

Caldwell, B. M. (1989). Achieving rights for children: Role of the early childhood profession. *Childhood Education, 66,* 4–7.

Caldwell, J. C. (1986). Routes to low mortality in poor countries. *Population and Development Review, 12,* 171–214.

Calfee, R. (1981). Cognitive psychology and educational practice. In D. C. Berliner (Ed.), Review of Research in Education (Vol. 9). Washington, D. C.: American Educational Research Association.

California Assessment Program. (1982). Survey of sixth grade school achievement and television viewing habits. Sacramento: California State Department of Education.

Camp, B. W. (1995). Maternal characteristics of adolescent mothers and older mothers of infants. *Psychological Reports, 77,* 1152–1154.

Campbell, F. A., & Ramey, C. T. (1990). The relationship between Piagetian cognitive development, mental test performance, and academic achievement in high-risk students with and without early educational intervention. *Intelligence, 14,* 293–308.

Campbell, F. A., Helms, R., Sparling, J. J., & Ramey, C. T. (1998). Early-childhood programs and success in school: The Abecedarian study. In W. S. Barnett & S. S. Boocock (Eds.), *Early care and education for children in poverty: Promises, programs, and long-term results. SUNY series, youth social services, schooling, and public policy / SUNY series, early childhood education: Inquiries and insights.* Albany, NY: State University of New York

Campbell, S. B., & Cohn, J. F. (1991). Prevalence and correlates of postpartum depression in first-time mothers. *Journal of Abnormal Psychology, 100,* 594–599.

Campfield, L. A., Smith, F. J., & Burn, P. (1998). Strategies and potential molecular targets for obesity treatment. *Science, 280,* 1383–1387.

Canada Yearbook 1999. Ottawa, Ontario: Minister of Industry, Communications Division, Statistics Canada, 1998.

Candy, T. R., Crowell, J. A., & Banks, M. S. (1998). Optical, receptoral, and retinal constraints on foveal and peripheral vision in the human neonate. *Vision Research. 38,* 3857–70.

Canning, P. M., & Lyon, M. E. (1991). Misconceptions about early child care, education and intervention. *Journal of Child and Youth Care, 5,* 1–10.

Cantor, C. H., Leenaars, A. A., Lester, D., Slater, P. J., et al. (1996). Suicide trends in eight predominantly English-speaking countries. 1960–1989. *Social Psychiatry and Psychiatric Epidemiology, 31,* 363–373.

Caprara, G. V., Scabini, E., Barbaranelli, C., Pastorellil, C.l, Regalia, C., & Bandura, A. (1998). Impact of adolescents' perceived self-regulatory efficacy on familial communication and antisocial conduct. *European Psychologist, 3,* 125–132.

Capron, C., Vetta, A. R., Duyme, M., & Vetta, A. (1999). Model fitting is no substitute for learning. *Cahiers de Psychologie Cognitive, 18,* 263–285.

Caregiver-parent relationships in daycare: A review and re-examination

Carey, E. J. B., Miller, C. L., & Widlak, F. W. (1975). Factors contributing to child abuse. *Nursing Research, 24,* 293–295.

Carey, S. T. (1987). Reading comprehension in first and second languages of immersion and Francophone students. *Canadian Journal for Exceptional Children, 3,* 103–108.

Carey, W. B. (1989). Introduction: Basic issues. In W. B. Carey & S. C. McDevitt (Eds.), Clinical and educational applications of temperament research. Berwyn, Penn.: Swets North America.

Carlo, G., Fabes, R. A., Laible, D., & Kupanoff, K. (1999) Early adolescence and prosocial/moral behavior II: The role of social and contextual influences. *Journal of Early Adolescence, 19,* 133–147.

Carlson, P., & Anisfeld, M. (1969). Some observations on the linguistic competence of a two-year-old child. *Child Development, 40,* 572–574.

Carmichael, B., Pembrey, M., Turner, G., & Barnicoat, A. (1999). Diagnosis of fragile-X syndrome: The experiences of parents. *Journal of Intellectual Disability research, 43,* 47–53.

Carroll, D. W. (1986). Psychology of language. Monterey, Calif.: Brooks/Cole.

Carroll, J. L., & Rest, J. R. (1982). Moral development. In B. B. Wolman and others (Eds.), *Handbook of developmental psychology.* Englewood Cliffs, N.J.: Prentice-Hall.

Cartwright, D. S., Tomson, B., & Schwartz, H. (1975). Gang delinquency. Monterey, Calif.: Brooks/Cole.

Case, R. (1991). General and specific views of the mind, its structure and its development. In R. Case, et al., (Eds.), The mind's staircase: Exploring the conceptual underpinnings of children's thought and knowledge. Hillsdale, N.J.: Lawrence Erlbaum.

Case-Smith, J., Bigsby, R., & Clutter, J. (1998). Perceptual-motor coupling in the development of grasp. *American Journal of Occupational Therapy, 52,* 102–110.

Casler, L. (1961). Maternal deprivation: A critical review of the literature. *Monograph of the Society for Research in Child Development, 26* (2).

Caspi, A., Lynam, D., Moffitt, T. E., & Silva, P. A. (1993). Unraveling girls' delinquency: Biological, dispositional, and contextual contributions to adolescent misbehavior. *Developmental Psychology, 29,* 19–30.

Cassidy, J., & Berlin, L. J. (1999). Understanding the origins of loneliness: Contributions of attachment theory. In K. J. Rotenberg & S. Hymel (Eds.), *Loneliness in childhood and adolescence.* New York: Cambridge University Press.

Castles, A., Adams, E. K., Melvin, C. L., Kelsch, C., & Boulton, M. L. (1999a). Effects of smoking during pregnancy. Five meta-analyses. *American Journal of Preventive Medicine, 16,* 208–215.

Castles, A., Datta, H., Gayan, J., & Olson, R. K. (1999). Varieties of developmental reading disorder: Genetic and environmental influences. *Journal of Experimental Child Psychology, 72,* 73–94.

Cattell, R. B. (1971). Abilities: Their structure, growth, and action. Boston: Houghton Mifflin.

Caughy, M. O., DiPietro, J. A., & Strobino, D. M. (1994). Day care participation as a protective factor in the cognitive development of low-income children. *Child Development, 65,* 457–471.

Ceci, S. J. (1991). How much does schooling influence general intelligence and its cognitive components? A reassessment of the evidence. *Developmental Psychology, 27,* 703–722.

Center for Disease Control (1992). Vigorous physical activity among high school students—United States, 1990. *Morbidity and Mortality Weekly Report, 41,* 33–36.

Chapman, P. L., & Mullis, R. L. (1999). Adolescent coping strategies and self-esteem. *Child Study Journal, 29,* 69–77.

Charlesworth, W. R. (1996). Co-operation and competition: Contributions to an evolutionary and developmental model. *International Journal of Behavioral Development, 19,* 25–38.

Charlton, T., Gunter, B., & Coles, D. (1998). Broadcast television as a cause of aggression? Recent findings from a naturalistic study. *Emotional & Behavioural Difficulties, 3,* 5–13.

Chase, N. F. (1975). A child is being beaten. New York: Holt, Rinehart & Winston.

Chase-Lansdale, P. L., & Brooks-Gunn, J. (1994). Correlates of adolescent pregnancy and parenthood. In C. B. Fisher & R. M. Lerner (Eds.), *Applied developmental psychology.* New York: McGraw-Hill.

Chase-Lansdale, P. L., Brooks-Gunn, J., & Paikoff, R. L. (1991). Research and programs for adolescent mothers: Missing links and future promises. *Family Relations, 40,* 396–403.

Chasnoff, I. Burns, W., Schnoll, S., & Burns, K. (1985). Cocaine use in pregnancy. *New England Journal of Medicine, 313,* 666–669.

Chasnoff, I. J. (1986). Perinatal addiction: Consequences of intrauterine exposure to opiate and nonopiate drugs. In I. J. Chasnoff (Ed.), Drug use in pregnancy: Mother and child.Boston: MTP Press.

Chasnoff, I. J. (1986/1987). Cocaine and pregnancy. *Childbirth Educator,* 37–42.

Chassin, L., Pitts, S. C., DeLucia, C., & Todd, M. A. (1999) Longitudinal study of children of alcoholics: Predicting young adult substance use disorders, anxiety, and depression. *Journal of Abnormal Psychology, 198,* 106–119.

Chassin, L., Rogosch, F., & Barrera, M. (1991). Substance use and symptomatology among adolescent children of alcoholics. Journal of *Abnormal Psychology, 4,* 449–463.

Chatoor, I., Ganiban, J., Colin, V., Plummer, N., & Harmon, R. J. (1998). Attachment and feeding problems: A reexamination of nonorganic failure to thrive and attachment insecurity. *Journal of the American Academy of Child & Adolescent Psychiatry, 37,* 1217–1224.

Chechik, G., Meilijson, I., & Ruppin, E. (1998). Synaptic pruning in development: A computational account. *Neural Computation, 10,* 1759–1777.

Cheng, Pui-wan. (1993). Metacognition and giftedness. *Gifted Child Quarterly, 37,* 105–112.

Cherney, S. S., Fulker, D. W., & Hewitt, J. K. (1997). Cognitive development from infancy to middle childhood. In R. J. Sternberg & E. L. Grigorenko (Eds.), *Intelligence, heredity, and environment.* New York: Cambridge University Press.

Cherry, E. C. (1953). Some experiments on the recognition of speech with one and two ears. *Journal of the Acoustical Society of America, 25,* 975–979.

Chess, S., & Thomas, A. (1989a). Temperament and its functional significance. In S. I. Greenspan & G. H. Pollock (Eds.), The course of life: Vol II. Early Childhood. Madison, Conn.: International Universities Press.

Chess, S., & Thomas, A. (1989b). The practical application of temperament to psychiatry. In W. B. Carey & S. C. McDevitt (Eds.), Clinical and educational applications of temperament

research. Berwyn, Penn.: Swets North America.

Chester, R. D. (1992). Views from the mainstream: Learning disabled students as perceived by regular education classroom teachers and by non-learning disabled secondary students. *Canadian Journal of School Psychology, 8,* 93–102.

Cheung, Y. W., Erickson, P. G., & Landau, T. C. (1991). Experience of crack use: Findings from a community-based sample in Toronto. *Journal of Drug Issues, 21,* 121–140.

Chez, R. A., & Chervenak, J. L. (1990). Nutrition in pregnancy. In R. D. Eden, F. H. Boehm, & M. Haire (Eds.), Assessment and care of the fetus: Physiological, clinical, and medicolegal principles. Norwalk, Conn.: Appleton & Lange.

Chi, M. T. H. (1978). Knowledge structure and memory development. In R. Siegler (Ed.), *Children's thinking: What develops?* NJ: Erlbaum.

Chi, M. T. H., & Glaser, R. (1980). The measurement of expertise: Analysis of the development of knowledge and skill as a basis for assessing achievement. In E. L. Baker & E. S. Quellmal (Eds.), Educational testing and evaluation: Design, analysis and policy. Beverly Hills, Calif.: Sage.

Chilman, C. S. (1983). Remarriage and step-families: Research results and implications. In E. D. Macklin & R. H. Rubin (Eds.), Contemporary families and alternative lifestyles: Handbook on research and theory. Beverly Hills, Calif.: Sage.

China fears sexual imbalance. (1983). *Edmonton Journal,* March 14, p. D-4.

Chipman, S. F. (1988). Far too sexy a topic. *Educational Researcher, 17,* 46–49.

Chiu, L. H. (1993). Self-esteem in American and Chinese (Taiwanese) children. *Current Psychology: Research & Reviews, 11,* 309–313.

Chlamydia—More common than gonorrhea. (1988). Folio. Edmonton, Alberta: University of Alberta, Nov. 24., p. 6.

Chomsky, N. (1957). Syntactic structures. The Hague: Mouton.

Chomsky, N. (1965). Aspects of the theory of syntax. Cambridge, Mass.: M.I.T. Press.

Chomsky, N. (1972). *Language and mind* (Enl. ed.) New York: Harcourt Brace Jovanovich.

Chou, Kee-Lee. (1998). Effects of age, gender, and participation in volunteer activities on the altruistic behavior of Chinese adolescents. *Journal of Genetic Psychology, 159,* 195–201.

Christopher, F. S., & Roosa, M. W. (1990). An evaluation of an adolescent pregnancy prevention program: Is "Just say no" enough? *Family relations, 39,* 68–72.

Christopherson, V. A. (1988). The family as a socialization context. In T. D. Yawkey & J. E. Johnson (Eds.), Integrative processes and socialization: Early to middle childhood. Hillsdale, N.J.: Lawrence Erlbaum.

Chugani, H. T., & Phelps, M. E. (1986). Maturational changes in cerebral function in infants determined by FGG positron emission tomography. *Science, 231,* 840–843.

Chumlea, W. C. (1982). Physical growth in adolescence. In B. B. Wolman and others (Eds.), *Handbook of developmental psychology.* Englewood Cliffs, N.J.: Prentice-Hall.

Churchill, J. A. (1965). The relationship between intelligence and birth weight in twins. *Neurology, 15,* 341–347.

Claes, M., & Simard, R. (1992). Friendship characteristics of delinquent adolescents.

International Journal of Adolescence and Youth, 3, 287–301.

Clarizio, H. F., & Yelon, S. L. (1974). Learning theory approaches to classroom management: Rationale and intervention techniques. In A. R. Brown & C. Avery (Eds.), Modifying children's behavior: A book of readings. Springfield, Ill.: Charles C. Thomas.

Clark, H. H., & Clark, E. V. (1977). Psychology and language: An introduction to psycholinguistics. New York: Harcourt Brace Jovanovich.

Clarke-Stewart, K. A. (1984). Day care: A new context for research and development. In M. Perlmutter (Ed.), The Minnesota symposia on child psychology: Vol. 17. Parent-child interaction and parent-child relations in child development. Hillsdale, N.J.: Lawrence Erlbaum.

Clarke-Stewart, K. A. (1989). Infant day care: Maligned or malignant? *American Psychologist, 44,* 266–273.

Clarke-Stewart, K. A., Gruber, C. P., & Fitzgerald, L. M. (1994). *Children at home and in day care.* Hillsdale, NJ: Erlbaum.

Clarkson, M. G., & Berg, W. K. (1983). Cardiac orienting and vowel discrimination in newborns: Crucial stimulus parameters. *Child Development, 54,* 162–171.

Clausen, J. A. (1975). The social meaning of differential physical and sexual maturation. In S. E. Ragastin & G. H. Elder (Eds.), Adolescence in the life cycle: Psychological change and social context. New York: John Wiley.

Clement, P. F. (1997). *Growing pains: Children in the industrial age, 1850–1890.* New York: Twayne Publishers.

Clements, S. D. (1966). Minimal brain dysfunction in children: Terminology and identification (NINDB Monograph No. 3). Washington, D.C.: U.S. Department of Health, Education, & Welfare.

Clifford, B. R., Gunter, B., & McAleer, J. (1995). *Television and children: Program evaluation, comprehension, and impact.* Hillsdale, N.J.: Erlbaum.

Clitheroe, H. C. Jr., Stokols, D., & Zmuidzinas, M. (1998). Conceptualizing the context of environment and behavior. *Journal of Environmental psychology, 18,* 103–112.

Cobb, E. (1977). The ecology of imagination in childhood. New York: Columbia University Press.

Coghlan, D., Milner, M., Clarke, T., Lambert, I., McDermott, C., McNally, M., Beckett, M., & Matthews, T. (1999). Neonatal abstinence syndrome. *Irish Medical Journal, 92,* 232–233.

Cohen, S. (1993/1994). Television in the lives of children and their families. *Childhood Education, 70,* 103–104.

Cohen, Y. A. (1964). The transition from childhood to adolescence. Chicago: Aldine.

Colborn, T., vom Saal, F. S., & Soto, A. M. (1993). Developmental effects of endocrine-disrupting chemicals in wildlife and humans. *Environmental Health Perspectives, 101,* 378–384.

Colby, A., & Damon, W. (1995). The development of extraordinary moral commitment. In M. Killen & D. Hart (Eds.), *Morality in everyday life: Developmental perspectives.* New York: Cambridge University Press.

Colby, A., & Kohlberg, L. (1984). Invariant sequence and internal consistency in moral judgment stages. In W. M. Kertines & J. L. Gerwirtz (Eds.), Morality, moral behavior,

and moral development. New York: John Wiley.

Cole, P. M. (1986). Children's spontaneous control of facial expression. *Child Development, 57,* 1309–1321.

Cole, P. M., Usher, B. A., & Cargo, A. P. (1993). Cognitive risk nd its association with risk for disruptive behavior disorder in preschoolers. *Journal of Clinical Child Psychology, 22,* 154–164.

Collett, J., & Serrano, B. (1992). Stirring it up: The inclusive classroom. New Directions for Teaching and Learning, 49, 35–48.

Collins, A., Brown, J. S., & Newman, S. E. (1989). Cognitive apprenticeship: Teaching the craft of reading, writing, and mathematics. In L. B. Resnick (Ed.), *Knowing, learning, and instruction: Essays in honor of Robert Glaser.* Hillsdale, N.J.: Lawrence Erlbaum.

Collins, P. L. (1997). Prematurity. In G. G. Ashmead, & G. B. Reed (Eds.), *Essentials of maternal fetal medicine.* New York: Chapman & Hall.

Collins, W. A. (1983). Interpretationand inference in children's television viewing. In J. Bryant & D. R. Anderson (Eds.), Children's understanding of televison: Research on attention and comprehension. New York: Academic Press, 125–150.

Collins, W. A. (1991). Shared views and parent-adolescent relationships. *New Directions for Child Development, 51,* 103–110.

Collins, W. A., & Gunnar, M. R. (1990). Social and personality development. *Annual Review of Psychology, 41,* 387–416.

Collins, W. A., & Russell, G. (1991). Mother-child and father-child relationships in middle childhood and adolescence: A developmental analysis. *Developmental Review, 11,* 99–136.

Collins, W. A., Wellman, H., Keniston, A. H., & Westby, S. D. (1978). Age-related aspects of comprehension and inference from a televised dramatic narrative. *Child Development, 49,* 389–399.

Coloroso, B. (1994). *Kids are worth it : giving your child the gift of inner discipline .* Toronto : Somerville House.

Compton's Online Encyclopedia, (2000), http://www.optonline.com/comptons/

Condon, W. S., & Sander, L. W. (1974). Neonate movement is synchronized with adult speech: Interactional participation and language acquisition. *Science, 183,* 99–101.

Connell, B. (1985). A new man. In The English Curriculum, ILEA. London: English Centre Publication. Cook, T. D., Appleton, H.,

Conner, R. F., Shaffer, A., Tamkin, G., &Weber, S. J. (1975). "Sesame Street"revisited. New York: Russell Sage Foundation.

Conrad, P. (1997). Public eyes and private genes: Historical frames, news constructions, and social problems. *Social Problems, 44,* 139–154.

Conti-Ramsden, G., & Jones, M. (1997). Verb use in specific language impairment. *Journal of Speech and Hearing Research, 40,* 1298–1313.

Cooke, B. (1991). Family life education. *Family Relations, 40,* 3–13.

Cooksey, E. C., Rindfuss, R. R., & Guilkey, D. K. (1996). The initiation of adolescent sexual and contraceptive behavior during changing times. *Journal of Health and Social Behavior, 37,* 59–74.

Coolbear, J., & Benoit, D. (1999). Failure to thrive: Risk for clinical disturbance of attachment? *Infant Mental Health Journal, 20,* 87–104.

Cooley, C. H. (1902). *Human nature and the social order.* New York: Charles Scribner's.

Cooper, S. H. (1998). Changing notions of defense within psychoanalytic theory. *Journal of Personality, 66,* 947–964.

Coopersmith, S. (1967). The antecedents of self-esteem. San Francisco: W. H. Freeman.

Corbin, C. B. (1980). The physical fitness of children: A discussion and point of view. In C. B. Corbin (Ed.), *A textbook of motor development.* Dubuque, Iowa: Wm. C. Brown.

Corbin, C. B., & Pangrazi, R. P. (1992). Are American children and youth fit? *Research Quarterly for Exercise and Sport, 62,* 96–106.

Corsaro, W. A. (1997). *The sociology of childhood.* Thousand Oaks, Cal.: Pine Forge Press.

Cortada, J. M., Milsark, I., & Richards, C. S. (1990). Genetic counseling issues in the use of DNA analysis for Duchenne/Becker muscular dystrophy. In B. A. Fine, E. Getting, K. Greendale, B. Leopold, & N. W. Paul (Eds.), Strategies in genetic counseling: Reproductive genetics and new technologies, White Plains, N.Y.: March of Dimes Birth Defects Foundation.

Cote, J. E., & Levine, C. (1988). A critical examination of the ego identity status paradigm. *Developmental Review, 8,* 147–184.

Cotton, S., Crowe, S. F., & Voudouris, N. (1998). Neuropsychological profile of Duchenne Muscular Dystrophy. *Child Neuropsychology, 4,* 110–117.

Coulter, D. (1993). Alberta students lag behind Asians in math: North American youths spend too much time on sports, socializing, study shows. *Edmonton Journal,* October 25, p. A5.

Coulter, D. L. (1993). Epilepsy and mental retardation: An overview. *American Journal on Mental Retardation, 98,* 1–11.

Courage, M. L., & Adams, R. J. (1990). Visual acuity assessment from birth to three years using the acuity card procedures: Cross-sectional and longitudinal samples. *Optometry and Vision Science, 67,* 713–718.

Court to decide right of surrogate mother, (1992, Jan. 24). *Monterey Herald,* p. A8.

Coustan, D. R. (1990). Diabetes mellitus. In R. D. Eden, F. H. Boehm, & M. Haire (Eds.). Assessment and care of the fetus: Physiological, clinical, and medicolegal principles. Norwalk, Conn.: Appleton & Lange.

Coustan, D. R., & Mochizuki, T. K. (1998). *Handbook for prescribing medications during pregnancy* (3rd ed.). New York: Lippincott-Raven.

Cox, A. J., & Leon, J. L. (1999). Negative schizotypal traits in the relation of creativity to psychopathology. *Creativity Research Journal, 12,* 25–36.

Cox, T. C., Jacobs, M. R., Leblanc, A. E., & Marshman, J. A. (1983). Drugs and drug abuse: A referencetext. Toronto: Addiction Research Foundation.

Crandall, C. S., Tsang, J. A., Goldman, S., & Pennington, J. T. (1999). Newsworthy moral dilemmas: Justice, caring, and gender. *Sex Roles, 40,* 187–209.

Cratty, B. J. (1978). Perceptual and motor development in infants and children(2nd ed.). Englewood Cliffs, N.J.:Prentice-Hall.

Creasy, R. K. (1988). Preterm labor and delivery. In R. K. Creasy & R. Resnik (Eds.), Maternal-fetal medicine; Principles and practice. Philadelphia: W. B. Saunders.

Creasy, R. K. (1990). Preterm labor. In R. D. Eden, F. H. Boehm, & M. Haire (Eds.), Assessment and care of the fetus: Physiological, clinical, and medicolegal principles. Norwalk, Conn.: Appleton & Lange.

Crick, N. R. (1996). The role of relational aggression, overt aggression, and prosocial behavior in the prediction of children's future social adjustment. *Child Development, 67,* 2317–2327.

Crick, N. R., & Bigbee, M. A. (1998). Relational and overt forms of peer victimization: A multiinformant approach. *Journal of Consulting & Clinical Psychology, 66,* 337–347.

Crick, N. R., Casas, J. F., & Mosher, M. (1997). Relational and overt aggression in preschool. *Developmental Psychology, 33,* 579–588.

Crisp, A. H., Palmer, R. L., & Kalucy, R. S. (1976). How common is anorexia nervosa: A prevalence study. *British Journal of Psychiatry, 128,* 549–554.

Crockett, L. J., & Petersen, A. C. (1987). Pubertal status and psychosocial development: Findings from the Early Adolescence Study. In R. M. Lerner & T. T. Foch (Eds.), Biological-psychosocial interactions in early adolescence: A life-span perspective. Hillsdale, N.J.: Lawrence Erlbaum.

Crockett, L. J., Losoff, M., & Petersen, A. C. (1984). Perceptions of the peer group and friendship in early adolescence. *Journal of Early Adolescence, 4,* 155–181.

Crouter, A. C., McHale, S. M., & Bartko, W. T. (1993). Gender as an organizing feature in parent-child relationships. In R. A. Pierce & M. A. Black (Eds.), *Life-span development: A diversity reader.* Dubuque, Iowa: Kendall/Hunt.

Crowell, J. A., & Feldman, S. S. (1991). Mothers' working models of attachment relationships and mother and child behavior during separation and reunion. *Developmental Psychology, 27,* 597–605.

Crowley, P. A. (1983). Premature labour. In D. F. Hawkins (Ed.), Drugs and pregnancy: Human teratogenesis and related problems. New York: Churchill Livingstone, 155–183.

Crystal, D. S., Watanabe, H., & Chin, W. (1997). Intolerance of human differences: A cross-cultural and developmental study of American, Japanese, and Chinese children. *Journal of Applied Developmental Psychology, 18,* 149–167.

Culbertson, J. L. (1991). Child advocacy and clinical child psychology. *Journal of Clinical Child Psychology, 20,* 7–10.

Cummins, J. (1986). Empowering minority students: A framework for intervention. Harvard *Educational Review,56,* 18–36.

Cummins, J. (1999). Alternative paradigms in bilingual education research: Does theory have a place? *Educational Researcher, 28,* 26–32.

Cummins, J., & Swain, M. (1986). Bilingualism in education: Aspects of theory, research and practice. London: Taylor & Fry.

Curtiss, S. (1977). Genie: A psycholinguistic study of a modern-day wild child. New York: Academic Press.

Cusack, R. (1984). Dietary management of obese children and adolescents. *Pediatric Annals, 13,* 455–464.

Cutting, A. L., & Dunn, J. (1999). Theory of mind, emotion understanding, language, and family background: Individual differences and interrelations. *Child Development, 70,* 853–865.

Czeizel, A. E., Hegedus, S., & Timar, L. (1999). Congevnital abnormalities and indicators of germinal mutations in the vicinity of an acry-

lonitrile producing factory. *Mutation Research, 427,* 105–123.

Cziko, G. A. (1992). The evaluation of bilingual education. *Educational Researcher, 21,* 10–15.

Dalton, K. (1980). Depression after childbirth. Oxford: Oxford University Press.

Damerow, P. (1998). Prehistory and cognitive development. In J. Langer & M. Killen (Eds.), *Piaget, evolution, and development. The Jean Piaget symposium series.* Mahwah, NJ: Erlbaum.

Damon, W., & Colby, A. (1987). Social influence and moral change. In W. M. Kurtines & J. L. Gewirtz (Eds.), Moral development through social interaction. New York: John Wiley.

Danilewitz, D., & Skuy, M. (1990). A psychoeducational profile of the unmarried mother. *International Journal of Adolescence and Youth, 2,* 175–184.

Danseco, E. R., Kingery, P. M., & Coggeshall, M. B. (1999). Perceived risk of harm from marijuana use among youth in the USA. *School Psychology International, 20,* 39–56.

Dansky, J. L. (1980). Make-believe: A mediator of the relationship between play and associative fluency. *Child Development, 51,* 576–579.

Danto, E. A. (1998). The ambulatorium: Freud's free clinic in Vienna. *International Journal of Psycho-Analysis, 79,* 287–300.

Darley, J. M., & Shultz, T. R. (1990). Moral rules: Their content and acquisition. *Annual Review of Psychology, 41,* 525–556.

Darley, J. M., & Zanna, M. P. (1982). Making moral judgments. *American Scientist, 70,* 515–521.

Darling, C. A., Kallen, D. J., & Van Dusen, J. E. (1984). Sex in transition, 1900–1980. *Journal of Youth and Adolescence, 13,* 385–394.

Darwin, C. (1877). A biographical sketch of an infant. *Mind, 2,* 285–294.

Das, J. P., & Dash, U. N. (1990). Schooling, literacy and cognitive development: A study in rural India. In C. K. Leong & B. S. Randhawa (Eds.), Understanding literacy and cognition: Theory, research, and application. New York: Plenum Press.

Dasen, P. R. (Ed.). (1977). Piagetian psychology: Cross-cultural contributions. New York: Gardner Press.

Davenport, E. C. Jr., Mark, L. D., Haijiang, K., Shuai, D., Se-Kang, K., & Nohoon, K. (1998). High school mathematics course-taking by gender and ethnicity. *American Educational Research Journal, 35,* 497–514.

David, C. B., & David, P. H. (1984). Bottle feeding and malnutrition in a developing country: The "bottle-starved" baby. *Journal of Tropical Pediatrics,* Vol. 30.

Davies, M., Stankov, L., & Roberts, R. D. (1998). Emotional intelligence: In search of an elusive construct. *Journal of Personality & Social Psychology, 75,* 989–1015.

Davis, C., Katzman, D. K., & Kirsh, C. (1999). Compulsive physical activity in adolescents with anorexia nervosa: A psychobehavioral spiral of pathology. *Journal of Nervous & Mental Disease, 187,* 336–342.

Davis, S. M., & Harris, M. B. (1982). Sexual knowledge, sexual interests, and sources of sexual information of rural and urban adolescents from three cultures. *Adolescence, 17,* 471–492.

Davydov, V. V. (1995). The influence of L. S. Vygotsky on education theory, research, and practice. *Educational Researcher, 24,* 12–21.

Davydov, V. V. (1998). The concept of developmental teaching. *Journal of Russian and East European Psychology, 36,* 11–36.

Davydova, E. Y., Gorbachevskaya, N. L., Yakupova, L. P, & Iznak, A. F. (1999). Age-specific changes in phonological and visual memory in boys and girls aged six to twelve. *Human Physiology, 25,* 134–139.

Dawkins, R. (1976). The selfish gene. New York: Oxford University Press.

Day, N. L., Zuo, Y., Richardson, G. A., Goldschmidt, L., Larkby, C. A., & Cornelius, M. D. (1999). Prenatal alcohol use and offspring size at 10 years of age. *Alcoholism: Clinical and Experimental Research, 23,* 863–869.

De Fiorini, L. G. (1998). The feminine in psychoanalysis: A complex construction. *Journal of Clinical Psychoanalysis, 7,* 421–439.

de Haan, M., & Nelson, C. A. (1997). Recognition of the mother's face by six-month-old infants: A neurobehavioral study. *Child Development, 68,* 187–210.

de Jonge, J. (1995). The theological roots of violence in families. *Journal of Psychology and Christianity, 14,* 26–37.

de Mey, L., Baartman, H. E. M, & Schulze, H. J. (1999). Ethnic variation and the development of moral judgment of youth in Dutch society. *Youth & Society, 31,* 54–75.

de Winter, M., Baerveldt, C., & Kooistra, J. (1999). Enabling children: Participation as a new perspective on child-health promotion. *Child: Care, Health, and Development, 25,* 15–25.

Deacon, T. W. (1997). *The symbolic species: The co-evolution of language and the brain.* New York: W. W. Norton.

Deal, L. V., & Haas, W. H. (1996). Hearing and the development of language and speech. *Folia Phoniatrtica et Logopedica, 48,* 111–116.

Dean, A. L. (1997). *Teenage pregnancy: The interaction of psyche and culture.* Hillsdale, NJ: The Analytic Press.

Dean, A. L., Ducey, S. J., & Malik, M. M. (1997). *Teenage pregnancy: The interaction of psyche and culture.* Hillsdale, NJ: The Analytic Press.

DeCasper, A. J., & Fifer, W. P. (1980). Of human bonding: Newborns prefer their mother's voices. *Science, 208,* 1174–1175.

DeCharms, R. (1972). Personal causation training in the schools. *Journal of Applied Social Psychology, 2,* 95–113.

Deep, A. L., Lilenfeld, L. R., Plotnicov, K. H., Pollice, C., & Kaye, W. H. (1999). Sexual abuse in eating disorder subtypes and control women: The role of comorbid substance dependence in bulimia nervosa. *International Journal of Eating Disorders, 25,* 1–10.

Deiner, P. L. (1999). *Resources for educating children with diverse abilities: Birth through eight.* Fort Worth, Tex: Harcourt Brace.

DeLissovoy, V. (1973). Child care by adolescent parents. *Children Today,* July, 22–25.

deMause, L. (1974). The evolution of childhood. In L. deMause (Ed.), The history of childhood. New York: Psychohistory Press.

deMause, L. (1975, April). Our forebears made childhood a nightmare. *Psychology Today,* 85–88.

Dement, W. C. (1974). Some must watch while some must sleep. San Francisco: Newman.

Demo, D. H. (1993). The relentless search for effects of divorce: Forging new trails or tumbling down the beaten path. *Journal of Marriage and the Family, 55,* 42–45.

DeMyer, M. K., Barton, S., DeMyer, W. E., Norton, J., Allen, J., & Steele, R. (1973). Prognosis in autism: A follow-up study. *Journal of Autism and Childhood Schizophrenia, 3,* 199–246.

Denham, S. A. (1993). Maternal emotional responsiveness and toddlers' social-emotional competence. *Journal of Child Psychology and Psychiatry and Allied Disciplines, 34,* 715–728.

Denham, S. A. (1997). "When I have a bad dream mommy holds me": Preschoolers' conceptions of emotions, parental socialization, and emotional competence. *International Journal of Behavioral Development, 20,* 301–319.

Denham, S. A., & Holt, R. W. (1993). Preschooler's likeability as cause or consequence of their social behavior. *Developmental Psychology, 29,* 271–275.

Dennis, M., Lockyer, L., Lazenby, A. L., Donnelly, R. E., Wilkinson, M., & Schoonheyt, W. (1999). Intelligence patterns among children with high-functioning autism, phenylketonuria, and childhood head injury. *Journal of Autism and Developmental disorders, 29,* 5–17.

Dennis, W. (1941). The significance of feral man. *American Journal of Psychology, 54,* 425–432.

Dennis, W. (1951). A further analysis of reports of wild children. *Child Development, 22,* 153–158.

Dennis. W. (1960). Causes of retardation among institutional children: Iran. *The Journal of Genetic Psychology, 96,* 47–59.

Denver Developmental Materials: Catalog of screening and training materials. (1990) P. O. Box 6919, Denver Colo., 80206–0919.

deRegt, R. H., Minkoff, H. L., Feldman, J., & Schwartz, R. H. (1986). Relation of private or clinic care to the Cesarean birth rate. *The New England Journal of Medicine, 315,* 619–625.

Deschenes, E. P., & Esbensen, F. A. (1999). Violence and gangs: Gender differences in perceptions and behavior. *Journal of Quantitative Criminology, 15,* 63–96.

Desor, J. A., Maller, O., & Greene, L. S. (1978). Preference for sweet in humans: Infants, children and adults. In J. M. Weiffenbach (Ed.), Taste and development: The genesis of sweet preference. Bethesda, Md.: National Institute of Dental Research, DHEW Publication 77–1068.

Deuel, R. K. (1992). Motor skill disorders. In S. R. Hooper, G. W. Hynd, & R. E. Mattison, (Eds.), Developmental disorders: Diagnostic criteria and clinical assessment. Hillsdale, N.J.: Lawrence Erlbaum.

DeVries, M. W. (1989). Difficult temperament: A universal and culturally embedded concept. In W. B. Carey & S. C. McDevitt (Eds.), Clinical and educational applications of temperament research. Berwyn, Penn.: Swets North America.

DeVries, M. W., & Sameroff, A. J. (1984). Culture and temperament: Influences on infant temperament in three East African societies. *American Journal of Orthopsychiatry, 54,* 83–96.

DeVries, R. (1997). Piaget's social theory. *Educational Researcher, 26,* 4–18.

Diamond, M. C. (1998). *Magic trees of the mind: How to nurture your child's intelligence, creativity, and healthy emotions.* New York : Dutton.

Diaz, R. M. (1983). Thought and two languages: The impact of bilingualism on cognitive development. In E. W. Gordon (Ed.), Review of Research in Education (Vol. 10). Washington, D.C.: American Educational Research Association.

Dick-Read, G. (1972). *Childbirth without fear: The original approach to natural childbirth* (4th ed.) (H. Wessel & H. F. Ellis, Eds.). New York: Harper & Row.

Diefenbach, D. L. (1997). The portrayal of mental illness on prime-time television. *Journal of Community Psychology, 25,* 289–302.

Diener, C. I., & Dweck, C. S. (1980). An analysis of learned helplessness: II. The processing of success. *Journal of Personality and Social Psychology, 39,* 940–952.

Dietz, W. H. (1995). Childhood obesity. In L. W. Y. Cheung & J. B. Richmond (Eds.), *Child health, nutrition, and physical activity.* Champaign, Il.: Human Kinetics.

DiLalla, L. F., & Watson, M. W. (1988). Differentiation of fantasy and reality: Preschoolers' reactions to interruptions in their play. *Developmental Psychology, 24,* 286–291.

Dill, F., & McGillivray, B. (1992). Chromosome anomolies. In J. M. Friedman, F. J. Dill, M. R. Hayden, & B. C. McGillivray (Eds.), Genetics, Baltimore: Williams & Wilkins.

Diller, L. H. (1999). Attention-deficit-hyperactivity disorder. *New England Journal of Medicine, 340,* 1766.

Dinges, M. M. & Oetting, E. R. (1993). Similarity in drug use patterns between adolescents and their friends. *Adolescence, 28,* 253–266.

Dinkmeyer, D., & McKay, G. (1976). Systematic training for effective parenting (S.T.E.P.). Circle Pines, Minn.: American Guidance Service.

DiPietro, J. A., Hodgson, D. M., Costigan, K. A., & Johnson, T. R. (1996). Fetal antecedents of infant temperament. *Chid Development, 67,* 2568—83.

Dishion, T. J., Capaldi, D. M., & Yoerger, K. (1999) Middle childhood antecedents to progressions in male adolescent substance use: An ecological analysis of risk and protection. *Journal of Adolescent Research, 14,* 175–205.

Dix, T. (1991). The affective organization of parenting: Adaptive and maladaptive processes. *Psychological Bulletin, 110,* 3–25.

D'Lugoff, M. I., & Baker, D. J. (1998). Case study: Shaken baby syndrome—one disorder with two victims. *Public Health Nursing, 15,* 243–249.

Dobkin de Rios, M. (1984). Hallucinogens: Cross-cultural perspectives. Albuquerque: University of New Mexico Press.

Doby, J. (1980). Firstborn fallacies. *Science, 80,* 4–10.

Doman, G. J. (1984). How to multiply your baby's intelligence. Garden City, N.Y.: Doubleday.

Domingo, R. A., & Goldstein-Alpern, N. (1999). "What dis?" and other toddler-initiated, expressive language-learning strategies. *Infant-Toddler Intervention, 9,* 39–60.

Donaldson, M. (1978). Children's minds. London: Fontana/Croom Helm.

Donate-Bartfield, E., & Passman, R. H. (1985). Attentiveness of mothers and fathers to their baby's cries. *Infant Behavior and Development, 8,* 385–393.

Donnelly, B. W., & Voydanoff, P. (1991). Factors associated with releasing for adoption among adolescent mothers. *Family Relations, 40,* 404–410.

Donovan, C. M. (1980). Program planning for the visually impaired child. In A. P. Scheiner & I. F. Abroms (Eds.), The practical management of the developmentally disabled child. St. Louis: C. V. Mosby, 280–289.

Dorian, B. J. & Garfinkel, P. E. (1999). The contributions of epidemiologic studies to the etiology and treatment of eating disorders. *Psychiatric Annals, 29,* 187–192.

Dorius, G. L., Heaton, T. B., & Steffan, P. (1993). Adolescent life events and their association with the onset of sexual intercourse. *Youth and Society, 25,* 3–23.

Douvan, E. (1997). Erik Erikson: Critical times, critical theory. *Child Psychiatry and Human Development, 28,* 15–21.

Dreher, B. B. (1997). Montessori and Alzheimer's: A partnership that works. *American Journal of Alzheimer's Disease, 12,* 138–140.

Drewett, R. F., Corbett, S. S., & Wright, C. (1999). Cognitive and educational attainments at school age of children who failed to thrive in infancy: A population-based study. *Journal of Child Psychology and Psychiatry and Allied Disciplines, 40,* 551–561.

Dreyer, P. H. (1982). Sexuality during adolescence. In B. B. Wolman (Ed.), *Handbook of developmental psychology.* Englewood Cliffs, N.J.: Prentice-Hall.

Drugan, A., Johnson, M. P., & Evans, M. I. (1990). Amniocentesis. In R. D. Eden, F. H. Boehm, & M. Haire (Eds.), Assessment and care of the fetus: Physiological, clinical, and medicolegal principles. Norwalk, Conn.: Appleton & Lange.

Drummond, W. J. (1991). Adolescent relationships in a period of change: A New Zealand perspective. *International Journal of Adolescence and Youth, 2,* 275–286.

Dubas, J. S., & Petersen, A. C. (1993). Female pubertal development. In M. Sugar (Ed.), *Female adolescent development.* New York: Brunner/Mazel.

Duberman, L. (1975). The reconstituted family: A study of remarried couples and their children. Chicago: Nelson-Hall.

Dubner, A. E., & Motta, R. W., (1999). Sexually and physically abused foster care children and posttraumatic stress disorder. *Journal of Consulting & Clinical Psychology, 67,* 367–373.

Duffty, P., & Bryan, M. H. (1982). Home apnea monitoring in "near-miss" Sudden Infant Death Syndrome (SIDS) and in siblings of SIDS victims. *Pediatrics, 70,* 69–74.

Dugger, J. M., & Dugger, C. W. (1998). An evaluation of a successful alternative high school. *High School Journal, 81,* 218–228.

Duncan, S., & Fiske, D. W. (1977). Face-to-face interaction: Research methods and theory. Hillsdale, N.J.: Erlbaum.

Dunn, J. (1988). The beginnings of social understanding. Cambridge, Mass.: Harvard University Press.

Dunn, J. (1998). Young children's understanding of other people: Evidence from observations within the family. In M. Woodhead, D. Faulkner, & K. Littleton (Eds.). *Cultural worlds of early childhood.* New York: Routledge.

Dunn, L, Kontos, S., & Potter, L. (1996). Mixed-age interactions in family child care. *Early Education and Development, 7,* 349–366.

Dunphy, D. C. (1963). The social structure of urban adolescent peer groups. *Sociometry, 26,* 230–246.

Durkin, K. F., & Bryant, C. D. (1999). Propagandizing pederasty: A thematic analysis of the on-line exculpatory accounts of unrepentant pedophiles. *Deviant Behavior, 20,* 103–127.

Duskin Feldman, R. (1982). *Whatever happened to the quiz kids? Perils and profits of growing up gifted*. Chicago: Chicago Review Press.

Dweck, C. S. (1975). The role of expectations and attributions in the alleviation of learned helplessness. *Journal of Personality and Social Psychology, 31*, 674–685.

Dweck, C. S. (1986). Motivational processes affecting learning. *American Psychologist, 41*, 1040–1048.

Dweck, C. S., & Reppucci, N. D. (1973). Learned helplessness and reinforcement responsibility in children. *Journal of Personality and Social Psychology, 25*, 109–116.

Dybing, E., & Sanner, T. (1999). Passive smoking, sudden infant death syndrome (SIDS) and childhood infections. *Human and Experimental Toxicology, 18*, 202–205.

d'Ydewalle, G., & Van de Poel, M. (1999). Incidental foreign-language acquisition by children watching subtitled television programs. *Journal of Psycholinguistic Research, 28*, 227–244.

Eacott, M. J. (1999). Memory for the events of childhood. *Current Directions in Psychological Science, 8*, 46–49.

Eagle, M. (1997). Contributions of Erik Erikson. *Psychoanalytic Review, 84*, 337–347.

Early Childhood Research Quarterly. Vol 10(2), Jun 1995, 249–259.

Early Education & Development. Vol 9(3), July 1998, 239–259.

Eastman, P., & Barr, J. L. (1985). Your child is smarter than you think. London: Jonathan Cape.

Eccles, J. S., & Jacobs, J. E. (1986). Social forces shape math attitudes and performance. *Signs, 11*, 367–389.

Eckerman, C. O., & Whatley, J. L. (1975). Infants' reactions to unfamiliar adults varying in novelty. *Developmental Psychology, 11*, 562–566.

Eckland, B. K. (1977). Darwin rides again. *American Journal of Sociology, 82*, 693–697.

Eddowes, E. A., & Ralph, K. S. (1998). *Interactions for development and learning: Birth through eight years*. Upper Saddle River, NJ: Merrill.

Eden, R. D., Blanco, J. D., Tomasi, A., & Gall, S. A. (1990). Maternal-fetal infection. In R. D. Eden, F. H. Boehm, & M. Haire (Eds.), Assessment and care of the fetus: Physiological, clinical, and medicolegal principles. Norwalk, Conn.: Appleton & Lange.

Edmonton (Alberta) Public School Board. (1978). Learning disability, Fall, No. 7.

Egeland, B., & Stroufe, L. (1981). Attachment and early maltreatment. *Child Development, 52*, 44–52.

Egeland, B., & Vaughn, B. (1981). Failure of "bond formation" as a cause of abuse, neglect, and maltreatment. *American Journal of Orthopsychiatry, 51*, 78–84.

Egeland, J. A., Gerhard, D. S., Pauls, D. L., Sussex, J. N., Kidd, K. K., et al. (1987). Bipolar affective disorders linked to DNA markers on chromosome 11. *Nature, 325*, 783–787.

Eibl-Eibesfeldt, I. (1989). *Human ethology*. Hawthorne, NY: Aldine de Gruyter.

Eiger, M. S., & Olds, S. W. (1987). The complete book of breastfeeding. New York: Workman.

Eilers, R. E., & Minifie, F. D. (1975). Fricative discrimination in early infancy. *Journal of Speech and Hearing Research, 18*, 158–167.

Eilers, R. E., & Oller, D. K. (1988). Precursors to speech. In R. Vasta (Ed.), Annals of child development (Vol. 5). Greenwich, Conn.: JAI Press.

Eisenberg, L. (1998). Nature, niche, nurture: The role of social experience in transforming genotype into phenotype. *Academic Psychiatry, 22*, 213–222.

Eisenberg, N. (1990). Prosocial development in early and mid-adolescence. In R. Montemayor, G. R. Adams, & T. P. Gullotta (Eds.), Advances in adolescent development: Vol. 2. From childhood to adolescence: A transitional period? Newbury Park, Calif.: Sage Publications.

Eisenberg, N., Miller, P. A., Shell, R., McNalley, S., & Shea, C. (1991). Prosocial development in adolescence: A longitudinal study. *Developmental Psychology, 27*, 849–857.

Eisenberg, R. B. (1976). Auditory competence in early life. Baltimore: University Park Press.

Eisenberg-Berg, N., & Hand, M. (1979). The relationship of preschoolers' reasoning about prosocial moral conflicts to prosocial behavior. *Child Development, 50*, 356–360.

Elder, G. H., Jr. (1974). Children of the great depression. Chicago: University of Chicago Press.

Elder, G. H., Jr. (1979). Historical change in life patterns and personality. In P. B. Baltes & O. G. Brim, Jr. (Eds.), Life span development and behavior (Vol. 2). New York: Academic Press.

Elder, G. H., Jr., Nguyen, T. Van, & Caspi, A. (1985). Linking family hardship to children's lives. *Child Development, 56*, 361–375.

"Eleven million children orphaned already by AIDS, mostly in Africa." (1999). *Edmonton Journal*, Dec. 2, p. A3.

Elias, G., & Broerse, J. (1996). Developmental changes in the incidence and likelihood of simultaneous talk during the first two years: A question of function. *Journal of Child Language, 23*, 201–217.

Elkind, D. (1967). Egocentrism in adolescence. *Child Development, 38*, 1025–1034.

Elkind, D. (1981a). The hurried child: Growing up too fast too soon. Reading, Mass.: Addison-Wesley.

Elkind, D. (1981b). Understanding the young adolescent. In L. D. Steinberg (Ed.), The life cycle: Readings in human development. New York: Columbia University Press.

Elkind, D. (1987). Miseducation: Preschoolers at risk. New York: Alfred A. Knopf.

Elkind, D. (1987). Superkids and super problems. *Psychology Today, 21*, 60–61.

Elkind, D. (1996). Inhelder and p;iaget on adolescence and adulthood: A postmodern appraisal. *Psychological Science, 7*, 216–220.

Elkind, D. (1998). *All grown up and no place to go: Teenagers in crisis* (Rev. ed.). Reading, Mass: Addison-Wesley.

Elkind, D., & Bowen, R. (1979). Imaginary audience behavior in children and adolescents. *Developmental Psychology, 15*, 38–44.

Elkington, J. (1986). The poisoned womb. Harmondsworth, Middlesex, England: Penguin Books.

Elliott, G. C. (1982). Self-esteem and self-presentation among the young as a function of age and gender. Journal of Youth and Adolescence, 11, 135–142.

Ellsworth, J. (1999). Today's adolescent: Addressing existential dread. *Adolescence, 34*, 403–408.

Elster, A. B., Lamb, M. E., & Tavare, J. (1987). Association between behavioral and school problems and fatherhood in a national sample of adolescent youths. *Journal of Pediatrics, 1211*, 932–936.

Emery, A. E. H. (1984). Introduction—The principles of genetic counseling. In A. E. H. Emery & I. Pullen (Eds.), Psychological aspects of genetic counseling. New York: Academic Press.

Emery, A. E., & Mueller, R. F. (1992). Elements of medical genetics (8th ed.). Edinburgh & London: Churchill Livingstone.

Emery, R. E. (1989). Family violence. *American Psychologist, 44*, 321–328.

Endsley, R. C., & Bradbard, M. R. (1981). Quality day care: A handbook of choices for parents and caregivers. Englewood Cliffs, N.J.: Prentice-Hall.

Engle, R. W., Tuholski, S. W., Laughlin, J. E., & Conway, A. R. A. (1999). Working memory, short-term memory, and general fluid intelligence: A latent-variable approach. *Journal of Experimental Psychology: General, 128*, 309–331.

Enright, R., Shukla, D., & Lapsley, D. (1980). Adolescent egocentrism—sociocentrism in early and late adolescence. *Adolescence, 14*, 687–695.

Epling, W. F., Pierce, W. D., & Stefan, L. (1983). A theory of activity-based anorexia. *International Journal of Eating Disorders, 3*, 27–45.

Erickson, G., & Farkas, S. (1991). Prior experience and gender differences in science achievement. Alberta *Journal of Educational Research, 37*, 225–239.

Erickson, J. D., & Bjerkedal, T. (1981). Down's syndrome associated with father's age in Norway. *Journal of Medical Genetics, 18*, 22–28.

Erickson, M. T. (1987). Behavior disorders of children and adolescents. Englewood Cliffs, N.J.: Prentice-Hall.

Erickson, M. T. (1992). Behavior disorders of children and adolescents (2nd ed.). Englewood Cliffs, N.J.: Prentice Hall.

Erikson, E. H. (1956). The problems of ego identity. *Journal of the American Psychoanalytic Association, 4*, 56–121.

Erikson, E. H. (1959). Identity and the life cycle: Selected papers. From *Psychological Issue Monograph Series*, 1. New York: International Universities Press.

Erikson, E. H. (1961). The roots of virtue. In J. Huxley (Ed.), The humanist frame. New York: Harper & Row.

Erikson, E. H. (1968). Identity, youth and crisis. New York: W. W. Norton.

Erin, J. K., & Koenig, A. J. (1997). The student with a visual disability and a learning disability. *Journal of Learning Disabilities, 30*, 309–320.

Ernst, C., & Angst, J. (1983). Birth order: Its influence on personality. New York: Springer-Verlag.

Eronen, S., & Nurmi, Jari-Erik. (1999). Social reaction styles, interpersonal behaviours and person perception: A multi-informant approach. *Journal of Social & Personal Relationships, 16*, 315–333.

Erwin, E. J., & Kontos, S. (1998). Parents' and kindergarten teachers' beliefs about the effects of child care. *Early Education and Development, 9*, 131–146.

Erwin, P. (1993). Friendship and peer relationships in children. New York: John Wiley.

Erwin, P. (1998). *Friendship in childhood and adolescence*. New York; Routledge.

Esbensen, F. A., Deschenes, E. P., & Winfree, L. T. Jr. (1999). Differences between gang girls and gang boys: Results from a multisite survey. *Youth & Society, 37,* 27–53.

Estanol, V. B., Huerta, D. E., & Garcia, R. G. (1997). Cien anos del signo Babinski. *Revista de Investigacion Clinica, 49,* 141–144.

Etheridge chose 'musical' Crosby despite problems. (2000, Jan. 10). *The National Post,* Toronto, p. A3.

Ethical standards for research with children. (1973). SRCD Newsletter, Winter, 3–4.

Evans, R. I. (1989). Albert Bandura: The man and his ideas—a dialogue. New York: Praeger.

Eveleth, P. B., & Tanner, J. M. (1976). Worldwide variation in human growth. Cambridge, England: Cambridge University Press.

Evers-Kiebooms, G., & Decruyenaere, M. (1998). Predictive testing for Huntington's disease: A challenge for persons at risk and for professionals. *Patient Education and Counseling, 35,* 15–26.

Evra, J. V. (1990). Television and child development. Hillsdale, N.J.: Lawrence Erlbaum.

Evra, J. V. (1998). *Television and child development* (2nd ed.). Mahwah, NJ: Erlbaum.

Eysenck, H. J., & Kamin, L. (1981). Intelligence: The battle for the mind. London: Macmillan.

Fabes, R. A., Carlo, G., Kupanoff, K., & Laible, D. (1999) Early adolescence and prosocial/moral behavior I: The role of individual processes. *Journal of Early Adolescence, 19,* 5–16.

Fabes, R. A., Eisenberg, N., Jones, S., Smith, M., Guthrie, I., Poulin, R., Shepard, S., & Friedman, J. (1999). Regulation, Emotionality, and Preschoolers' socially competent peer interactions. *Child Development, 70,* 432–442.

Fabricius, W. V., & Wellman, H. M. (1993). Two roads diverged: Young children's ability to judge distance. *Child Development, 64,* 399–419.

Fagan, J. F. (1992). *Fagan Test of Infant Intelligence.* Cleveland, Oh: Infantest Corporation.

Fagan, J. F., III. (1974). Infant color perception. *Science, 183,* 973–975. Fantz, R. L. (1963). Pattern vision in newborn infants. *Science, 140,* 296–297.

Fagan, J., Piper, E., & Moore, M. (1986). Violent delinquents and urban youths. *Criminology, 24,* 439–468.

Fagot, B. (1997). Attachment, parenting, and peer interactions of toddler children. *Developmental Psychology, 33,* 489–499.

Faith, M. S., Johnson, S. L., & Allison, D. B. (1997). Putting the behavior into the behavior genetics of obesity. *Behavior Genetics, 27,* 423–439.

Famuyiwa, O. O., & Akinyanju, O. O. (1998). Burden of sickle cell anaemia on families of patients. *International Journal of Social Psychiatry, 44,* 170–180.

Fandal, A. W., Sciarillo, W., & Burgess, D. (1981). The newly abbreviated and revised Denver Developmental Screening Test. *Journal of Pediatrics, 99,* 995–999.

Fantz, R. L. (1963). Pattern vision in newborn infants. *Science, 140,* 269–297.

Fantz, R. L. (1965). Visual perception from birth as shown by pattern selectivity. *Annals of the New York Academy of Science, 118,* 793–814.

Faraone, S. V, Biederman, J., Weiffenbach, B., Keith, T., Chu, M. P., Weaver, A., Spencer, T. J., Wilens, T. E., Frazier, J., Cleves, M., & Sakai, J. (1999). Dopamine D-sub-4 gene 7–repeat allele and attention deficit hyperactivity disorder. *American Journal of Psychiatry, 156,* 768–770.

Farbman, A. I. (1994). The cellular basis of olfaction. *Endeavour, 18,* 2–8.

Farleger, D. (1977, July). The battle over children's rights. *Psychology Today,* 89–91.

Farver, J. M. (1992). An analysis of young American and Mexican children's play dialogues: Illustrative study 3. In C. Howes, O. Unger, & C. C. Matheson, (Eds.), The collaborative construction of pretend: Social pretend play functions. New York: State University of New York Press.

Farver, J. M., & Howes, C. (1993). Cultural differences in American and Mexican mother-child pretend play. *Merrill-Palmer Quarterly, 39,* 344–358. r6

Fasick, F. A. (1988). Patterns of formal education in high school as rites de passage. *Adolescence, 23,* 457–471.

Feagans, L. V., & Proctor, A. (1994). The effects of mild illness in infancy on later development: The sample case of the effects of otitis media (middle ear effusion). In C. B. Fisher & R. M. Lerner (Eds.), *Applied developmental psychology.* New York: McGraw-Hill.

Feingold, A. (1992). Sex differences in variability in intellectual abilities: A new look at an old controversy. *Review of Educational Research, 62,* 61–84.

Feinstein, C., & Reiss, A. L. (1998). Autism: The point of view from fragile X studies. *Journal of Autism and Developmental Disorders, 28,* 393–405.

Feldman, D. H. (1989). Creativity: Proof that development occurs. In W. Damon (Ed.), Child development today and tomorrow. San Francisco: Jossey-Bass.

Feldman, R., Greenbaum, C.W., & Yirmiya, N. (1999). Mother-infant affect synchrony as an antecedent of the emergence of self-control. *Developmental Psychology, 35,* 223–231.

Felton, B. (2000, Jan. 9). Hard choices as the disabled age. *The New York times,* Section 3, Pp. 1, 8, 9.

Felton, G. M., Pate, R. R., Parsons, M. A., Ward, D. S., Saunders, R. P., Trost, S., & Dowda, M. (1998). Health risk behaviors of rural sixth graders. *Research in Nursing & Health, 21,* 475–485.

Fenson, L. (1987). The developmental progression of play. In A. W. Gottfried & C. C. Brown (Eds.), Play interactions: The contribution of play materials and parental involvement to children's development. Lexington, Mass.: D. C. Heath.

Fernandes, O., Sabharwal, M., Smiley, T., Pastuszak, A., Koren, G., & Einarson, T. (1998). Moderate to heavy caffeine consumption during pregnancy and relationship to spontaneous abortion and abnormal fetal growth: A meta-analysis. *Reproductive Toxicology, 12,* 435–444.

Feuerstein, R. (1979). The dynamic assessment of retarded performers: The learning potential assessment device, theory, instruments, and techniques. Baltimore: University Park Press.

Fiebert, M. S., & Meyer, M. W. (1997). Gender stereotypes: A bias against men. *Journal of Psychology, 131,* 407–410.

Field, T. M. (1987). Coping with separation stress by infants and young children. In T. M. Field, P. M. McCabe, & N. Schneiderman (Eds.), Stress and coping. Hillsdale, N.J.: Lawrence Erlbaum.

Field, T., Mai, W., Goldstein, S., Perry, S., & Parl, S. (1988). Infant day care facilitates preschool social behavior. *Early Childhood Research Quarterly, 3,* 341–359.

Filiano, J. J., & Kinney, H. C. (1994). A perspective on neuropathologic findings in victims of the sudden infant death syndrome: The triple-risk model. *Biology of the Neonate, 65,* 194–197.

Fine, M. A. (1993). Current approaches to understanding family diversity: An overview of the special issue. *Family Relations, 42,* 235–237.

Fine, M. A., Coleman, M., & Ganong, L. H. (1998). Consistency in perceptions of the step-parent role among step-parents, parents and stepchildren. *Journal of Social & Personal Relationships, 15,* 810–828.

Finkelhor, D., & Dziuba-Leatherman, J. (1994). Victimization of children. *American Psychologist, 49,* 173–183.

Finkelhor, D., and associates (Eds.) (1986). A source-book on child sexual abuse. Beverly Hills, Calif.: Sage.

Finlay, B., & Love, G. D. (1998). Gender differences in reasoning about military intervention. *Psychology of Women Quarterly, 22,* 481–485.

Fischer, C. S., Hout, M., Jankowski, M. S., Lucas, S. R., Swidler, A., & Voss, K. (1996). *Inequality by design: Cracking the bell curve myth.* Princeton, NJ: Princeton University Press.

Fischer, G., Jagsch, R., Eder, H., Gombas, W., Etzersdorfer, P, Schmidl-Mohl, K., Schatten, C., Weninger, M., & Aschauer, H. N. (1999). Comparison of methadone and slow-release morphine maintenance in pregnant addicts. *Addiction, 94,* 231–239.

Fischer, K. W., & Bidell, T. R. (1998). Dynamic development of psychological structures in action and thought. In W. Damon (editor-in-chief: R. M. Lerner, volume editor), *Handbook of child psychology: Vol. 1. Theoretical models of human development* (5th ed.). New York: Wiley.

Fischer, K. W., & Pipp, S. L. (1984). Development of the structures of unconscious thought. In K. Bowers & D. Meichenbaum (Eds.), The unconscious reconsidered. New York: John Wiley.

Fischer, K. W., & Rose, S. P. (1996). Dynamic growth cycles of brain and cognitive development. In R. W. Thatcher & G. R. Lyon (Eds.), *Developmental neuroimaging: Mapp;ing the development of brain and behavior.* San Diego, Ca.: Academic Press.

Fischer, K. W., & Silvern, L. (1985). Stages and individual differences in cognitive development. *Annual Review of Psychology, 36,* 613–648.

Fisher, E. M. C. (1997). The contribution of the mouse to advances in human genetics. In Hall, J. C., & Dunlap, J. C. (Eds.), *Advances in genetics: Incorporating molecular genetic medicine.* San Diego, Ca: Academic Press.

Fisher-Thompson, D., Sausa, A. D., & Wright, T. F. (1995). Toy selection for children: Personality and toy request influence. *Sex Roles, 33,* 239–255.

Fishkin, J., Keniston, K., & MacKinnon, C. (1973). Moral reasoning and political ideology. *Journal of Personality and Social Psychology, 27,* 109–119.

Fishman, G. G. (1999). Knowing another from a dynamic systems point of view: The need for a multimodal concept of empathy. *Psychoanalytic Quarterly, 68,* 376–400.

Fiske, S. T. (1993). Social cognition and social perception. *Annual Review of Psychology, 44,* 155–194.

Flannery, K. A., & Liederman, J. (1995). Is there really a syndrome involving the co-occurrence of neurodevelopmental disorder, talent, non-right handedness and immune disorder among children? *Cortex, 31,* 503–515.

Flavell, J. H. (1982). On cognitive development. *Child Development, 53,* 1–10.

Flavell, J. H. (1985). Cognitive development (2nd ed.). Englewood Cliffs, N.J.: Prentice-Hall.

Flavell, J. H. (1996). Piaget's legacy. *Psychological Science, 7,* 200–203.

Flavell, J. H. (1999). Cognitive development: Children's knowledge about the mind. *Annual Review of Psychology, 50,* 21–45.

Flynn, J. R. (1987). Massive IQ gains in 14 nations: What IQ tests really measure. *Psychological Bulletin, 101,* 171–191.

Fogel, A. (1984). Infancy: Infant, family, and society. St. Paul, Minn.: West.

Fogel, A., Toda, S., & Kawai, M. (1988). Mother-infant face-to-face interaction in Japan and the United States: A laboratory comparison using 3–month-old infants. *Developmental Psychology, 3,* 398–406.

Folsom, C. (1998). From a distance: Joining the mind and moral character. *Roeper Review, 20,* 265–270.

Fong, L., & Wilgosh, L. (1992). Children with autism and their families: A literature review. *Canadian Journal of Special Education, 8,* 43–54.

Fontaine, J. H., & Hammond, N. L. (1996). Couseling issues with gay and lesbian adolescents. *Adolescence, 31,* 817–830.

Food and Nutrition Board. (1990). Nutrition during pregnancy. Washington, D.C.: National Academy Press.

Food and Nutrition Board, Subcommittee on the Tenth Edition of the RDAs. (1989). *Recommended dietary allowances* (10th ed.) Washington, DC: National Academy Press.

Fordham, K., & Stevenson-Hinde, J. (1999). Shyness, friendship quality, and adjustment during middle childhood. *Journal of Child Psychology & Psychiatry & Allied Disciplines, 40,* 757–768.

Fouts, R. S. (1987). Chimpanzee signing and emergent levels. In G. Greenberg & E. Tobach (Eds.), Cognition, language and consciousness: Integrative levels. Hillsdale, N.J.: Lawrence Erlbaum.

Fox, N. A., Calkins, S. D., & Bell, M. A. (1994). Neural plasticity and development in the first two years of life: Evidence from cognitive and socioemotional domains of research. *Development and psychopathology, 6,* 677–696.

Fox, N. A., Kimmerly, N. L., & Schafer, W. D. (1991). Attachment to mother/attachment to father: A meta-analysis. *Child Development, 62,* 210–225.

Fox, R. A. (1990). Assessing parenting of young children. Bethesda, Md.: Center for Nursing Research of the National Institutes of Health. (Contract 1 RO1 NRO1609O1A1)

France-Kaatrude, A., & Smith, W. P. (1985). Social comparison, task motivation, and the development of self-evaluative standards in children. *Developmental Psychology, 21,* 1080–1089.Frankenburg, W. K.,

Franco, P., Szliwowski, H., Dramaix, M., & Kahn, A. (1999). Decreased autonomic responses to obstructive sleep events in future victims of sudden infant death syndrome. *Pediatric Research, 46,* 33–39.

Franke, P., Schwab, S. G., Knapp, M., Gaensick, M., Delmo, C., Zill, P., Trixler, M., Lichtermann, D., Hallmayer, J., Wildenauer,

D. B., & Maier, W. (1999). DAT1 gene polymorphism in alcoholism: A family-based association study. *Biological Psychiatry, 45,* 652–654.

Frankenburg, W. K., & Dodds, J. B. (1992). *Denver II* (2nd ed.). *Training Manual.* Denver, Co: Denver Developmental Materials.

Frankenburg, W. K., Fandal, A. W., Sciarillo, W., & Burgess, D. (1981). The newly abbreviated and revised Denver Developmental Screening Test. *Journal of Pediatrics, 99,* 995–999.

Franklin, J. T. (1985). Alternative education as substance abuse prevention. *Journal of Alcohol and Drug Education, 30,* 12–23.

Franzen, U., & Gerlinghoff, M. (1997). Parenting by patients with eating disorders: Experiences with a mother-child group. *Eating Disorders: The Journal of Treatment and Prevention, 5,* 5–14.

Frazier, A., & Lisonbee, L. K. (1950). Adolescent concerns with physique. *School Review, 58,* 397–405.

Frederickson, N. L., & Furnham, A. F. (1998). Sociometric-status-group classification of mainstreamed children who have moderate learning difficulties: An investigation of personal and environmental factors. *Journal of Educational Psychology, 90,* 772–783.

Freese, J., Powell, B., & Steelman, L. C. (1999). Rebel without a cause or effect: Birth order and social attitudes. *American Sociological Review, 64,* Apr. 1999, 207–231.

Freud, A. (1946). The ego and the mechanisms of defense (C. Baines, Trans.). New York: International Universities Press.

Freyberg, J. T. (1973). Increasing the imaginative play of urban disadvantaged kindergarten children through systematic training. In J. L. Singer (Ed.), The child's world of make-believe. New York: Academic Press.

Frick, P. J., Christian, R. E. & Wooton, J. M. (1999). Age trends in association between parenting practices and conduct problems. *Behavior Modification, 23,* 106–128.

Fridell, S. R., Zucker, K. J., Bradley, S. J., & Maing, D. M. (1996). Physical attractiveness of girls with gender identity disorder. *Archives of Sexual Behavior, 25,* 17–31.

Fried, M. N., & Fried, M. H. (1980). *Four rituals in eight cultures.* New York: W. W. Norton.

Fried, P. A. (1986). Marijuana and human pregnancy. In I. J. Chasnoff (Ed.), Drug use in pregnancy: Mother and child. Boston, Mass.: MTP Press.

Fried, S. B. (1998). An undergraduate course in American popular psychology. *Teaching of Psychology, 25,* 38–40.

Friedman, J. M. (1992). Teratogenesis and mutagenesis. In J. M. Friedman, F. J. Dill, M. R. Hayden, & B. C. McGillivray (Eds.), Genetics. Baltimore: Williams & Wilkins.

Friedman, J. M., & McGillivray, B. (1992). Genetic paradigms in human disease. In J. M. Friedman, F. J. Dill, M. R. Hayden, & B. C. McGillivray (Eds.), Genetics. Baltimore: Williams & Wilkins.

Friedman, J. M., & Polifka, J. E. (1996). *The effects of drugs on the fetus and nursing infant.* Baltimore, Md.: Johns Hopkins Univeristy Press.

Friedman, J. M., Dill, F. J., Hayden, M. R., & McGillivray, B. C. (1992). Genetics. Baltimore: Williams & Wilkins.

Friedman, J. M., Dill, F., & Hayden, M. R. (1992). Nature of genetic material. In J. M. Friedman, F. J. Dill, M. R. Hayden, & B. C. McGillivray

(Eds.), Genetics. Baltimore: Williams & Wilkins.

Friedman, L. (1989). Mathematics and the gender gap: A meta-analysis of recent studies on sex differences in mathematical tasks. *Review of Educational Research, 59,* 185–213.

Frisch, R. E., & Revelle, R. (1970). Height and weight at menarche and a hypothesis of critical body weights and adolescent events. *Science, 169,* 397–398.

Fritsch, E. J., Caeti, T. J., & Taylor, R. W. (1999). Gang suppression through saturation patrol, aggressive curfew and truancy enforcement: A quasi-experimental test of the Dallas anti-gang initiative. *Crime & Delinquency, 45,* 122–139.

Frye, D. (1991). The origins of intention in infancy. In D. Drye & C. Moore (Eds.), Children's theories of mind: Mental states and social understanding. Hillsdale N.J.: Lawrence Erlbaum.

Fuligni, A. J., & Eccles, J. S. (1993). Perceived parent-child relationships and early adolescents' orientation toward peers. *Developmental Psychology, 29,* 622–632.

Funakoshi, M., Goto, K., & Arahata, K. (1998). Epilepsy and mental retardation in a subset of early onset 4q35–facioscapulohumeral muscular dystrophy. *Neurology, 50,* 1791–1794.

Furrow, D., Nelson, K., & Benedict, H. (1979). Mother's speech to children and syntactic development: Some simple relationships. *Journal of Child Language, 6,* 423–442.

Furst, R. T., Johnson, B. D., Dunlap, E., & Curtis, R. (1999). The stigmatized image of the "crack head": A sociocultural exploration of a barrier to cocaine smoking among a cohort of youth in New York City. *Deviant Behavior, 20,* 153–181.

Furstenberg, F. F., Jr., Brooks-Gunn, J., & Chase-Lansdale, L. (1989). Teenaged pregnancy and childbearing. *American Psychologist, 44,* 313–320.

Furth, H. (1980). Piagetian perspectives. In J. Sants (Eds.), Developmental psychology and society. London: Macmillan, 142–168.

Gabrieli, J. D. E. (1998). Cognitive neuroscience of human memory. *Annual Review of Psychology, 49,* 87–115.

Gaddis, A., & Brooks-Gunn, J. (1985). The male experience of pubertal change. *Journal of Youth and Adolescence, 14,* 61–72.

Gagne, R. M., & Briggs, L. J. (1983). Principles of instruction design (3rd ed.). New York: Holt, Rinehart & Winston.

Galef, B. G., Jr. (1991). A contrarian view of the wisdom of the body as it relates to dietary self-selection. *Psychological Review, 98,* 218–223.

Galen, B. R., & Underwood, M. K. (1997). A developmental investigation of social aggression among children. *Developmental Psychology, 33,* 589–600.

Gall, S. A. (1996). St. Louis, Mo.: Mosby.

Galler, J. R. (Ed.). (1984). Human nutrition: A comprehensive treatise: Vol. 5. Nutrition and behavior. New York: Plenum.

Galler, J. R., & Ramsey, F. (1989). A follow-up study of the influence of early malnutrition on development: Behavior at home and at shool. *Journal of the American Academy of Child and Adolescent Psychiatry, 28,* 254–261.

Galton, F. (1896). Hereditary genius: An enquiry into its laws and consequences. London: Macmillan.

Gamble, T. J., & Zigler, E. (1986). Effects of infant day care: Another look at the evidence. *American Journal of Orthopsychiatry, 56,* 26–42.

Ganong, L., Coleman, M., Fine, M., & Martin, P. (1999). Stepparents' affinity-seeking and affinity-maintaining strategies with stepchildren. *Journal of Family Issues, 20,* 299–327.

Garbarino, J., & Crouter, A. (1977). The human ecology of child maltreatment: A conceptual model for research. *Journal of Marriage and the Family, 39,* 721–735.

Garcia, E. E. (1993). Language, culture, and education. In L. Darling-Hammond (Ed.), Review of Research in Education (Vol. 19). Washington, D.C.: American Educational Research Association.

Gardner, H. (1983). *Frames of mind: The theory of multiple intelligences.* New York: Basic Books.

Gardner, H. (1997). Six afterthoughts: Comments on "Varieties of intellectual talent." *Journal of Creative Behavior, 31,* 120–124.

Gardner, H. (1998). Are there additional intelligences? The case for naturalist, spiritual, and existential intelligences. In J. Kane (Ed.), *Education, information, and transformation.* Englewood Cliffs, NJ: Prentice-Hall.

Gardner, H., & Hatch, T. (1989). Multiple intelligences go to school: Educational implications of the theory of multiple intelligences. *Educational Researcher, 18,* 4–10.

Gardner, M. K. (1985). Cognitive psychological approaches to instructional task analysis. In W. W. Gordon (Ed.), Review of Research in Education (Vol. 12), Washington, D. C.: American Educational Research Association, 157–196.

Gargan, T. J. (1997). "Current concepts: Turner's syndrome": Comments. *New England Journal of Medicine, 336,* 1526–1527.

Garmezy, N. (1976). Vulnerable and invulnerable children: Theory, research, and intervention. Master lecture on developmental psychology, American Psychological Association.

Garnier, H. E., Stein, J. A., & Jacobs, J. K. (1997). The process of dropping out of high school: A 19-year perspective. *American Educational Research Journal, 34,* 395–419.

Garvey, C. (1977). Play. Cambridge, Mass.: Harvard University Press.

Gaskins, S. (1999). Children's daily lives in a Mayan village. In A. Göncü (Ed.), *Children's engagement in the world: Sociocultural perspectives.* New York: Cambridge University Press.

Gathercole, S. E. (1998). The development of memory. *Journal of Child Psychology & Psychiatry & Allied Disciplines, 39,* 3–27.

Gaudin, J. M., Jr. (1993). *Child neglect: A guide for intervention. The User Manual Series.* National Center on Child Abuse and Neglect. Washington, DC: Westover Consultants.

Gavazzi, S. M., Alford, K. A., & McKenry, P. C. (1996). Culturally specific programs for foster care youth: The sample case of an African American rites of passage program. *Family Relations: Journal of Applied Family & Child Studies, 45,* 166–174.

Gaynor, J. L. R., & Runco, M. A. (1992). Family size, birth-order, age-interval, and the creativity of children. *Journal of Creative Behavior, 26,* 108–118.

Ge, X., Conger, R. D., & Elder, G. H. Jr. (1996). Coming of age too early: Pubertal influences on girls' vulnerability to psychological distress. *Child Development, 67,* 3386–3400.

Geiger, B. (1996). *Fathers as primary caregivers.* Westport, Conn: Greenwood Press.

Gelles, R. J. (1979). Violence toward children in the United States. In R. Bourne & E. H. Newberger (Eds.), Critical perspectives on child abuse. Lexington, Mass.: D. C. Heath.

Gelman, R. (1978). Cognitive development. *Annual Review of Psychology, 29,* 297–332.

Gelman, R. (1982). Basic numerical abilities. In R. J. Sternberg (Ed.), Advances in the psychology of human intelligence (Vol. 1). Hillsdale, N.J.: Lawrence Erlbaum.

Gelman, R., & Gallistel, C. R. (1978). The young child's understanding of number. Cambridge, Mass.: Harvard University Press.

Gelman, S., Collman, P., & Maccoby, E. (1986). Inferring properties from categories versus inferring categories from properties: The case of gender. *Child Development, 57,* 396–404.

Genesee, F. (1985). Second language learning through immersion: A review of U.S. programs. *Review of Educational Research, 55,* 541–546.

"Gentle giant" stabs boy for taunts. (1994), Dec. 6. *Edmonton Sun,* p. 24.

Gerber, M. (1958). The psycho-motor development of African children in the first year and the influence of maternal behavior. *Journal of Social Psychology, 47,* 185–195.

Gerbner, G. (1972). Violence in television drama: Trends and symbolic functions. In G. A. Comstock & E. A. Rubenstein (Eds.), Television and social behavior (Vol. 1). Washington, D.C.: U.S. Government Printing Office.

Gerbner, G., & Gross, L. (1980). The violent face of television and its lessons. In E. L. Palmer & A. Dorr (Eds.), Children and the faces of television. New York: Academic Press.

Gesell, A. (1925). The mental growth of the preschool child. New York: Macmillan.

Getzels, J. W., & Jackson, P. W. (1962). Creativity and intelligence. New York: John Wiley.

Gewirtz, J. L. (1965). The course of infant smiling in four child-rearing environments in Israel. In B. M. Foss (Ed.), Determinants of infant behavior 3. London: Methuen.

Gfroerer, J. C., & Epstein, J. F. (1999). Marijuana initiates and their impact on future drug abuse treatment need. *Drug & Alcohol Dependence, 54,* 229–237.

Ghosh, D., & Pradhan, S. (1998). "Extensor toe sign" by various methods in spastic children with cerebral palsy. *Journal of Child Neurology, 13,* 216–220.

Gianino, A., & Tronick, E. Z. (1988). The mutual regulation model: The infant's self and interactive regulation coping and defense. In T. Field, P. McCabe, & N. Schneiderman (Eds.), Stress and coping. Hillsdale, N.J.: Lawrence Erlbaum.

Gibbs, J. C. (1987). Social processes in delinquency: The need to facilitate empathy as well as sociomoral reasoning. In W M. Kurtines & J. L. Gewirtz (Eds.), Moral development through social interaction. New York: John Wiley.

Gibson, E. J., & Walk, R. D. (1960). The "visual cliff." *Scientific American, 202,* 64–71.

Gibson, K. (1996). The ontogeny and evolution of the brain, cognition, and language. In A. Lock & C. R. Peters (Eds.), *Handbook of human symbolic evolution.* Oxford, Eng.: Clarendon Press/Oxford University Press.

Gibson-Cline, J. (Ed.) (1996). *Adolescence: From crisis to coping: A thirteen nation study.* Boston: Butterworth/Heinemann.

Gil, D. G. (1970). Violence against children: Physical child abuse in the United States. Cambridge, Mass.: Harvard University Press.

Gillespie, C. (1998). *Your pregnancy: Month by month.* New York: Harper Perennial.

Gilligan, C. (1982). In a different voice: Psychological theory and women's development. Cambridge, Mass.: Harvard University Press.

Gilligan, C., Ward, J. V., Taylor, J. M., & Bardige, B. (1988). Mapping the moral domain. Cambridge, Mass.: Harvard University Press.

Gilmore, D. H., & Aitken, D. A. (1989). Specific diagnostic techniques. In M. J. Whittle & J. M. Connor (Eds.), Prenatal diagnosis in obstetric practice. Boston: Blackwell Scientific Publications.

Giraudo, S. Q., Billington, C. J., & Levine, A. S. (1998). Feeding effects of hypothalamic injection of malanocortin 4 receptor ligands. *Brain research, 809,* 302–306.

Gitomer, D. H., & Pellegrino, J. W. (1985). Developmental and individual differences in long-term memory retrieval. In R. F. Dillon (Ed.), Individual differences in cognition (Vol. 2). New York: Academic Press.

Glasgow, K. L., Dornbusch, S. M., Troyer, L., Steinberg, L., & Ritter, P. L. (1997). parenting styles, adolescents' attributions, and educational outcomes in nine heterogeneous high schools. *Child Development, 68,* 507–529.

Glass, J. (1998). Gender liberation, economic squeeze, or fear of strangers: Why fathers provide infant care in dual-earner families. *Journal of Marriage & the Family, 60,* 821–834.

Glick, P. C. (1989). Remarried families, stepfamilies, and stepchildren: A brief demographic profile. *Family Relations,* 38, 24–27.

Goelman, H., Shapiro, E., & Pence, A. R. (1990). Family environment and family day care. *Family Relations, 39,* 14–19.

Golbus, M. S. (1982). Future uses of fetoscopy. In H. Galjaard (Ed.), The future of prenatal diagnosis. London: Churchill Livingstone, 128–132.

Gold, M. S. (1989). Drugs of abuse: A comprehensive series for clinicians (Vol. 1). Marijuana. New York: Plenum Press.

Gold, R. (1986). Failure on Piagetian tasks: Misinterpretation of the question? In C. Pratt, A. F. Garton, W. E. Tunmer, & A. R. Nesdale (Eds.), Research issues in child development. Boston: Allen & Unwin.

Goldberg, S. (1983). Parent-infant bonding: Another look. *Child Development, 54,* 1355–1382. r7

Goldenberg, C. (1992). The limits of expectations: A case for case knowledge about teacher expectancy effects. *American Educational Research Journal, 29,* 517–544.

Goldfield, B. A., & Reznick, J. S. (1996). Measuring the vocabulary spurt: A reply to Mervis and Bertrand. *Journal of Child Language, 23,* 241–246.

Goldgaber, D., Lerman, M. I., McBride, O. W., Saffiotti, U., & Gajdusek, D. C. (1987). Characterization and chromosomal localization of a DNA encoding brain amyloid of Alzheimer's disease. *Science, 235,* 877–880.

Goldsmith, H. H. (1983). Genetic influences on personality from infancy to adulthood. *Child Development, 54,* 331–355.

Goldsmith, J. (1990a). Childbirth wisdom: From the world's oldest societies. Brookline, Mass.: East-West Health Books.

Goldsmith, J. P. (1990b). Neonatal morbidity. In R. D. Eden, F. H. Boehm, & M. Haire (Eds.), Assessment and care of the fetus: Physiological, clinical, and medicolegal principles. Norwalk, Conn.: Appleton & Lange.

Goldston, D. B., Sergent D. S., Reboussin, D. M., Reboussin, B. A., Frazier, P. H., & Kelley, A. E. (1999). Suicide attempts among formerly hospitalized adolescents: A prospective naturalistic study of risk during the first 5 years after discharge. *Journal of the American Academy of Child & Adolescent Psychiatry, 38*, 660–671.

Goldwater, E. (1998). What do men fear? *Modern Psychoanalysis, 23*, 211–224.

Goode, E. T. (1985). Medical aspects of the bulimic syndrome and bulimarexia. *Transactional Analysis Journal, 15*, 4–11.

Goodwin, R. (1980). Two decades of research into early language. In J. Sants (Ed.), Developmental psychology and society. London: Macmillan, 169–218.

Gordon, C. P. (1996). Adolescent decision making: A broadly theory and its application to the prevention of early pregnancy. *Adolescence, 31*, 561–584.

Gordon, E. W., & Armour-Thomas, E. (1991). Culture and cognitive development. In L. Okagaki & R. J. Sternberg (Eds.), Directors of development: Influences on the development of children's thinking. Hillsdale, N.J.: Lawrence Erlbaum.

Gordon, T. (1975). P.E.T.: Parent effectiveness training. New York: New American Library.

Gordon, T. (1976). P.E.T. in action. New York: Bantam Books.

Gottesman, I. I. (1974). Developmental genetics and ontogenetic psychology: Overdue detente and propositions from a matchmaker. In A. Pick (Ed.), Minnesota symposia on child psychology, 12, 55–80.

Gottesman, I. I., & Shields, J. (1982). The schizophrenic puzzle. New York: Cambridge University Press.

Gottlieb, G. (1992). Individual development and evolution: The genesis of novel behavior. Oxford: Oxford University Press.

Gottman, J. M. (1977). Toward a definition of social isolation in children. *Child Development, 48*, 513–517.

Gottman, J. M., & Mettetal, G. (1987). Speculations about social and affective development: Friendship and acquaintanceship through adolescence. In J. M. Gottman & J. Parker (Eds.), Conversations of friends. New York: Cambridge University Press.

Gottman, J. M., Guralnick, M. J., Wilson, B., & Swanson, C. C. (1997). What should the focus of emotion regulation in children be? A nonlinear dynamic mathematical model of children's peer interaction in groups. *Development and Psychopathology, 9*, 421–452.

Gould, S. J. (1981). The mismeasure of man. New York: W. W. Norton.

Gowers, S.G., & North, C. (1999). "Family functioning and adolescent anorexia nervosa": Reply. *British Journal of Psychiatry, 175*, 89–90.

Graham, J. M., Jr. (1985). The effects of alcohol consumption during pregnancy. In M. Marois (Ed.), Prevention of physical and mental congenital defects. New York: Alan R. Liss.

Graham, M. J., Larsen, U., & Xu, X. (1999). Secular trend in age at menarche in China: A case study of two rural counties in Anhui Province. *Journal of Biosocial Science, 31*, 257–267.

Graillon, A., Barr, R. G., young, S. N., Wright, J. H., & Hendricks, L. A. (1997). Differential response to intraoral sucrose, quinine and corn oil in crying human newborns. *Physiology and Behavior, 62*, 317–325.

Grant, J. P. (1992). The state of the worlds children: 1992. New York: Oxford University Press.

Grant, J. P. (Executive Director of the United Nation's Children's Fund, UNICEF). (1986). The state of the world's children: 1986. New York: Oxford University Press.

Grattan, M. P., DeVos, E., Levy, J., & McClintock, M. K. (1992). Asymmetric action in the human newborn: Sex differences in patterns of organization. *Child Development, 63*, 273–289.

Gray, P., & Feldman, J. (1997). Patterns of age mixing and gender mixing among children and adolescents at an ungraded democratic school. *merrill-Palmer Quarterly, 43*, 67–86.

Green, J. A., Gustafson, G. E., & McGhie, A. C. (1998). Changes in infants' cries as a function of time in a cry bout. *Child Development, 69*, 271–279.

Green, J. M. (1994). Women's experiences of prenatal screening and diagnosis. In L. Abramsky, & J. Chapple, (Eds.), *Prenatal diagnosis: The human side.* New York: Chapman and Hall.

Green, K. D., Forehand, R., Beck, S. J., & Vosk, B. (1980). An assessment of the relationship among measures of children's social competence and children's academic achievement. *Child Development, 51*, 1149–1156.

Greenacre, P. (1959). Play in relation to creative imagination. *Psychoanalytic Studies of the Child, 14*, 61–80.

Greenberg, B. S., & Brand, J. E. (1993). Television news and advertising in schools: The "Channel One" controversy. *Journal of Communication, 43*, 143–151.

Greenberg, D. E. (1996). The object permanence fallacy. *Human Development, 39*, 117–131.

Greene, J. (1975). Thinking and language. London: Methuen.

Greene, K., Rubin, D.L., Hale, J. L., & Walters, L. H. (1996). The utility of understanding adolescent egocentrism in designing health promotion messages. *Health Communication, 8*, 131–152.

Greene, S. (1999). Child development: Old themes, new directions. In M. Woodhead, D. Faulkner, & K. Littleton (Eds.), *Making sense of social development..* New York: Routledge.

Greenfield, P. M., & Savage-Rumbaugh, E. S. (1993). Comparing communicative competence in child and chimp: The pragmatics of repetition. *Journal of Child Language, 20*, 1–26.

Greenspan, S. I., & Lieberman, A. F. (1989). A quantitative approach to the clinical assessment of representational elaboration and differentiation in children two to four. In S. I. Greenspan & G. H. Pollck (Eds.), The course of life: Vol II. Early Childhood. Madison, Conn.: International Universities Press.

Gregory, R. L. (1973). *Eye and brain: The psychology of seeing* (2nd ed.). New York: McGraw-Hill.

Gregory, S., & Bates, J. E. (1999). Early behavior problems as a predictor of later peer group victimization: Moderators and mediators in the pathways of social risk. *Journal of Abnormal Child Psychology, 27*, 191–201.

Grieser, D. L., & Kuhl, P. K. (1988). Maternal speech to infants in a tonal language: Support for universal prosodic features in motherese. *Developmental Psychology, 24*, 14–20.

Grieshaber, S. (1998). Constructing the gendered infant. In N. Yelland (Ed.), *Gender in early childhood*: New York: Routledge

Griffin, S. (1985). Eating issues and fat issues. *Transactional Analysis Journal, 15*, 30–36.

Griffiths, M. (1997). Friendship and social development in children and adolescents: The impact of electronic technology. *Educational & Child Psychology, 14*, 25–37.

Griffiths, M. (1997). Video games and aggression. *Psychologist, 10*, 397–401.

Griffiths, M. D. (1991). Amusement machine playing in childhood and adolescence: A comparative analysis of video games and fruit machines. *Journal of Adolescence, 14*, 53–73.

Grindstaff, C. F. (1988). Adolescent marriage and childbearing: The long-term economic outcome, Canada in the 1980s. *Adolescence, 23*, 45–58.

Gronlund, N. E., & Holmlund, W. S. (1958). The value of elementary school sociometric status scores for predicting a pupil's adjustment in high school. *Educational Administration and Supervision, 44*, 255–260.

Groome, L. J., Swiber, M. J., Atterbury, J. L., Bentz, L. S., & Holland, S. B. (1997). Similarities and differences in behavioral state organization during sleep periods in the perinatal infant before and after birth. *Child Development, 68*, 1–11.

Grossman, H. (1995). *Special education in a diverse society*. Boston: Allyn & Bacon.

Grossman, J. J. (Ed.). (1983). Manual on terminology and classification in mental retardation, 1983 revision. Washington, D.C.: American Association on Mental Deficiency.

Grotevant, H. D. (1994). Assessment of parent–adolescent relationships. In C. B. Fisher & R. M. Lerner (Eds.), *Applied developmental psychology*. New York: McGraw-Hill.

Grotevant, H. D., & Adams, G. R. (1984). Development of an objective measure to assess ego identity in adolescence; Validation and replication. *Journal of Youth and Adolescence, 13*, 419–438.

Grotevant, M. D., Scarr, S., & Weinberg, R. A. (1977). Intellectual development in family constellations with adopted and natural children: A test of the Zajonc and Markus model. Paper presented at a meeting of the Society for Research in Child Development, New Orleans.

Grotpeter, J. K., & Crick, N. R. (1996). Relational aggression overt aggression and friendship. *Child Development, 67*, 2328–2338.

Grow, L. J. (1979). Early childrearing by young mothers: A research study. New York: Child Welfare League of America.

Grych, J. H., & Clark, R. (1999). Maternal employment and development of the father-infant relationship in the first year. *Developmental Psychology, 35*, 893–903.

Guesry, P. (1998). The role of nutrition in brain development. *Preventive Medicine, 27*, 189–194.

Guidubaldi, J., & Cleminshaw, H. (1985). Divorce, family health, and child adjustment. *Family Relations, 34*, 35–41.

Guilford, J. P. (1950). Creativity. *American Psychologist, 5*, 444–454.

Guilford, J. P. (1959). Three faces of intellect. *American Psychologist, 14*, 469–479.

Gullone, E., & King, N. J. (1997). Three-year follow-up of normal fear in children and adolescents aged 7 to 18 years. *British Journal of Developmental Psychology, 15,* 97–111.

Gunnar, M. R., Larson, M. C., Hertsgaard, L., Harris, M. L., & Brodersen, L. (1992). The stressfulness of separation among nine-month-old infants: Effects of social context variables and infant temperament. *Child Development, 63,* 290–303.

Gunter, B., & McAleer, J. L. (1990). Children and television. The one-eyed monster? New York: Routledge.

Gustafson, G. E., &Harris, K. L. (1990). Women's responses to young infants' cries. *Developmental Psychology, 26,* 144–152.

Gustafsson, J. E., & Undheim, J. O. (1992). Stability and change in broad and narrow factors of intelligence from ages 12 to 15. *Journal of Educational Psychology, 84,* 141–149.

Gust-Brey, K., & Cross, T. (1999). An examination of the literature base on the suicidal behaviors of gifted students. *Roeper Review, 22,* 28–35.

Gutierrez, P., King, C. A., & Ghaziuddin, N. (1996). Adolescent attitudes about death in relation to suicidality. *Suicide and Life-Threatening Behavior, 26,* 8–18.

Hack, M., & Fanaroff, A. A. (1999). Outcomes of children of extremely low birthweight and gestational age in the 1990's. *Early Human Development. 53,* 193–218.

Hack, M., Breslau, N., Aram, D., Weissman, B., Klein, N., & Borawski-Clark, E. (1992). The effect of very low birth weight and social risk on neurocognitive abilities at school age. *Journal of Developmental and Behavioral Pediatrics, 13,* 412–420.

Hack, M., Taylor, H. G., Klein, N., Eiben, R., Schatschneider, C., & Mercuri-Minich, N. (1994). School-age outcomes in children with birth weights under 750 g. *New England Journal of Medicine, 331,* 753–759.

Hack, M., Weissman, B., Breslau, N., Klein, N., Borawski-Clark, E., & Fanaroff, A. A. (1993). Health of very low birth weight children during their first eight years. *Journal of Pediatrics, 122,* 887–892.

Hagan, J. (1998). Life course capitalization and adolescent behavioral development. In R. Jessor (Ed.), *New perspectives on adolescent risk behavior.* New York: Cambridge University Press.

Hagopian, L. P., Fisher, W. W., & Legacy, S. M. (1994). Schedule effects of noncontingent reinforcement on attention-maintained destructive behavior in identical quadruplets. *Journal of Applied Behavior Analysis, 27,* 317–325.

Hague, W. J. (1991). Kohlberg's legacy—More than ideas: An essay review. *The Alberta Journal of Educational Research, 37,* 277–294.

Haith, M. M. (1980). Rules that babies look by: The organization of newborn visual activity. Hillsdale, N.J.: Lawrence Erlbaum.

Haith, M. M. (1986). Sensory and perceptual processes in early infancy. *Journal of Pediatrics, 109,* 158–171.

Haith, M. M. (1993). Preparing for the 21st century: Some goals and challenges for studies of infant sensory and perceptual development. *Developmental Review, 13,* 354–371.

Haith, M. M. (1998). Who put the cog in infant cognition? Is rich interpretation too costly? *Infant Behavior and Development, 21,* 167–179.

Hakuta, K., & D'Andrea, D. (1992). Some properties of bilingual maintenance and loss in Mexican background high-school students. *Applied Linguistics, 13,* 72–99.

Hakuta, K., & Garcia, E. E. (1989). Bilingualism and education. *American Psychologist, 44,* 374–379.

Halamek, L. P. (1997). Fetal and neonatal injury as a consequence of maternal substance abuse. In D. K. Stevenson & P. Sunshine (Eds.), *Fetal and neonatal brain injury: Mechanisms, management, and the risks of practice.* New York: Oxford University Press.

Halasz, G. (1996). The rights of the child in psychotherapy. *American Journal of Psychotherapy, 50,* 285–297.

Halberstadt-Freud, H. C. (1998). Electra vs Oedipus: Femininity reconsidered. *International Journal of Psycho-Analysis, 79,* 41–56.

Hall, G. S. (1891). The contents of children's minds on entering school. *Paediatric Seminars, 1,* 139–173.

Hall, G. S. (1916). Adolescence (2 vols.). New York: Appleton-Century-Crofts.

Hall, J. C., & Dunlap, J. C. (Eds.) (1997).*Advances in genetics: Incorporating molecular genetic medicine.* San Diego, Ca: Academic Press.

Hall, K., Bowman, H., & Myers, J. (1999). Metacognition and reading awareness among samples of nine-year-olds in two cities. *Educational Research, 41,* 99–107.

Hall, W. G., & Oppenheim, R. W. (1987). Developmental psychobiology: Prenatal, perinatal, and early postnatal aspects of behavioral development. *Annual Review of Psychology, 38,* 91–128.

Hallahan, D. P. & Kauffman, J. W. (1999). *Introduction to learning disabilities* (2nd ed.). Boston : Allyn and Bacon.

Hallahan, D. P., & Kauffman, J. M. (1986). *Exceptional children: Introduction to special education* (3rd ed.). Englewood Cliffs, N.J.: Prentice-Hall.

Hallahan, D. P., & Kauffman, J. M. (1991). *Exceptional children: Introduction to special education* (4th ed.). Englewood Cliffs, N.J.: Prentice Hall.

Hallahan, D. P., & Kauffman, J. M. (1997). *Exceptional learners : introduction to special education* (7th ed.). Boston: Allyn and Bacon.

Halonen, J. S., & Passman, R. H. (1978). Pacifiers' effects upon play and separations from the mother for the one-year-old in a novel environment. Infant Behavior and Development, 1, 70–78.

Halpern, C. T., Udry, J.R., Campbell, B., & Suchindran, C. (1999). Effects of body fat on weight concerns, dating, and sexual activity: A longitudinal analysis of Black and White adolescent girls. *Developmental Psychology, 35,* 721–736.

Hamner, T. J., & Turner, P. H. (1985). Parenting in contemporary society. Englewood Cliffs, N.J.: Prentice-Hall.

Hampson, J., & Nelson, K. (1993). The relation of maternal language to variation in rate and style of language acquisition. *Journal of Child Language, 20,* 313–342.

Hampsten, E. (1991). Settler's children: Growing up on the Great Plains. Norman: The University of Oklahoma Press.

Hanawalt, B. (1993). *Growing up in medieval London.* New York: Cambridge University Press.

Handyside, A. H. (1991). Preimplantation diagnosis by DNA amplification. In M. Chapman,

G. Grudzinskas, & T. Chard (Eds.), The embryo: Normal and abnormal development and growth. New York: Springer-Verlag.

Hanke, W., Kalinka, J., Florek, E., & Sobala, W. (1999). Passive smoking and pregnancy outcome in central Poland. *Human and Experimental Toxicology, 18,* 265–271.

Hanley, R. (2000, Jan. 5). Man is freed after serving 18 months in baby's death. *The Washington Post, P. A21.*

Hanna, E., & Meltzoff, A. N. (1993). Peer imitation by toddlers in laboratory, home, and day-care contexts: Implications for social learning and memory. *Developmental Psychology, 29,* 701–710.

Hanson, I. C., Antonelli, T. A., Sperling, R. S., Oleske, J. M., cooper, E., Culnane, M., Fowler, M. G., Kalish, L. A., Lee, S. S., McSherry G., Mofenson, L., & Shapiro, D. E. (1999). Lack of tumors in infants with perinatal HIV-! Exposure and fetal/neonatal exposure to zidovudine. *JAIDS: Journal of Acquired Immune Deficiency Syndromes, 20,* 463–467.

Hardyment, C. (1983). *Dream babies: Three centuries of good advice on child care.* New York: Harper and Row.

Hare, J. W. (Ed.). (1989). Diabetes complicating pregnancy: The Joslin Clinic Method. New York: Alan R. Liss.

Hargrove, L. J., & Poteet, J. A. (1984). Assessment in special education: The education evaluation. Englewood Cliffs, N.J.: Prentice-Hall.

Harju, B. L., & Eppler, M. A. (1997). Achievement motivation, flow and irrational beliefs in traditional and nontraditional college students. *Journal of Instructional Psychology, 24,* 147–157.

Harland, D. (Ed.). (1989). Children on the front line: The impact of apartheid, destabilization and warfare on children in Southern and South Africa, New York: United Nations Children's Fund.

Harlow, H. F. (1959). Love in infant monkeys. *Scientific America, 200,* 68–70.

Harris, D. (1963). *Children's drawings as measures of intellectual maturity.* New York: Harcourt.

Harris, J. R. (1998). *The nurture assumption: Why children turn out the way they do.* New York: The Free Press.

Harris, P. L., & Gross, D. (1988). Children's understanding of real and apparent emotion. In J. W. Astington, P. L. Harris, & D. R. Olson (Eds.), Developing theories of mind. New York: Cambridge University Press.

Harris, T. (1972). I'm ok—You're ok. New York: Avon Books.

Harris, Y. R., & Hamidullah, J. (1993). Maternal and child utilization of memory strategies. *Current Psychology: Research and Reviews, 12,* 81–94.

Harrison, L. (1985). Effects of early supplemental stimulation programs for premature infants: Review of the literature. *Maternal-Child Nursing Journal, 14,* 69–90.

Hart, D., & Yates, M. (1996). The interrelation of self and identity in adolescence; A developmental account. In *Annals of Child Development, 12,* 207–242.

Harter, S. (1983). Developmental perspectives on the self-system. In P. H. Mussen (Ed.), *Handbook of child psychology* (4th ed.) (Vol. 4): Socialization, personality, and social development (E. M. Hetherington, Ed.). New York: John Wiley.

Harter, S. (1985a). Processes underlying the construct, maintenance and enhancement of the self-concept in children. In J. Suls & A.

Greenwald (Eds.), Psychological perspectives on the self (Vol. 3). Hillsdale, N.J.: Lawrence Erlbaum.

Harter, S. (1985b). The Self-Perception Profile for Children: Revision of the Perceived Competence Scale for Children, Manual. Denver: University of Denver.

Harter, S. (1987). The determinants and mediational role of global self-worth in children. In N. Eisenberg (Ed.), Contemporary topics in developmental psychology. New York: Wiley.

Harter, S. (1988). Developmental processes in the construction of self. In T. D. Yawkey, G. R. Adams, & J. E. Johnson (Eds.), Integrative processes and socialization: Early to middle childhood. Hillsdale, NJ: Erlbaum.

Harter, S. (1990). Processes underlying adolescent self-concept formation. In R. Montemayor, G. R. Adams, & T. P. Gullotta (Eds.), Advances in adolescent development: Vol. 2. From childhood to adolescence: A transitional period? Newbury Park, Calif.: Sage.

Hartup, W. W. (1978). Children and their friends. In H. McGurk (Ed.), Issues in childhood social development. London: Methuen.

Hartup, W. W. (1983). Peer relations. In P H. Mussen (Ed.), Handbook of child psychology (4th ed.) (Vol. 4): Socialization, personality, and social development (E. M. Hetherington, Ed.). New York: John Wiley, 103–196.

Hartup, W. W. (1989). Social relationships and their developmental significance. American Psychologist, 44, 120–126.

Hartwell, E. A. (1998). Use of Rh Immune globulin: ASCP practice parameter. American Society of Clinical Pathologists. American journal of Clinical Pathology, 110, 281–292.

Harvey, A. R., & Rauch, J. B. (1997). A comprehensive Afrocentric rites of passage program for black male adolescents. Health & Social Work, 22, 30–37.

Haselager, G. J. T., Hartup, W. W., van Lieshout, C. F. M., & Riksen-Walraven, J. M. A. (1998). Similarities between friends and nonfriends in middle childhood. Child Development, 69, 1198–1208.

Haskins, R. (1989). Beyond metaphor: The efficacy of early childhood education. American Psychologist, 44, 274–282.

Haslett, B. B., & Samter, W. (1997). Children communicating: The first 5 years. Mahwah, NJ: Erlbaum.

Hass, A. (1979). Teenage sexuality: A survey of teenage sexual behavior. New York: Macmillan.

Hauser, R. M., & Sewell, W. H. (1985). Birth order and educational attainment in full sibships. American Journal of Educational Research Journal, 22, 1–23.

Havighurst, R. J. (1972). Developmental tasks and education. New York: D. McKay.

Havighurst, R. J. (1979). Developmental tasks and education (4th ed.). New York: D. McKay.

Havighurst, R. J. (1982). The world of work. In B. B. Wolman (Ed.), Handbook of developmental psychology. Englewood Cliffs, N.J.: Prentice-Hall.

Hay, D. F. (1981). Multiple functions of proximity-seeking in infancy. Child Development, 51, 636–645.

Hay, D. F., Stimson, C. A., & Castle, J. (1991). A meeting of minds in infancy: Imitation and desire. In D. Frye & C. Moore (Eds.), Children's theories of mind: Mental states and social understanding. Hillsdale N.J.: Lawrence Erlbaum.

Hayden, M. R. (1992). DNA diagnosis. In J. M. Friedman, F. J. Dill, M. R. Hayden, & B. C. McGillivray (Eds.), Genetics. Baltimore: Williams & Wilkins.

Hayes, C. D., Palmer, J. L., & Zaslow, M. J. (Eds.). (1990). Who cares for America's children? Child care policy for the 1990's. Washington, D.C.: National Academy Press.

Hayes, D. S., & Casey, D. M. (1992). Young children and television: The retention of emotional reactions. Child development, 63, 1423–1436.

Hayes, K. J., & Hayes, C. (1951). Intellectual development of a home-raised chimpanzee. Proceedings of the American Philosophical Society, 95, 105–109.

Hazen, N. L., & Lockman, J. J. (1989). Skill and context. In J. J. Lockman & N. L. Hazen (Eds.), Action in social context: Perspectives on early development. New York: Plenum Press.

Health Guide: Pregnancy: Pregnancy Tests. (1999, Nov. 04). Internet: http://www.health-center .com/eopoEnglish/family/pregnancy/tests .htm

Hebb, D. O. (1966). A textbook of psychology (2nd ed.). Philadelphia: W. B. Saunders.

Hecht, D. B., Inderbitzen, H. M., & Bukowski, A. L. (1998). The relationship between peer status and depressive symptoms in children and adolescents. Journal of Abnormal Child Psychology, 26, 153–160.

Hedges, L. V., & Friedman, L. (1993). Gender differences in variability in intellectual abilities: A reanalysis of Feingold's results. Review of Educational Research, 63, 94–105.

Heinicke, C. M., Guthrie, D., & Ruth, G. (1997). Marital adaptation, divorce, and parent-infant development: A prospective study. Infant Mental Health Journal, 18, 282–299.

Heinonen, O. P., Slone, D., & Shapiro, S. (1983). Birth defects and drugs in pregnancy. Boston: John Wright.

Heinzen, T. E. (1991). A paradigm for research in creativity. The Creative Child and Adult Quarterly, 16, 164–174.

Heisel, B. E., & Retter, K. (1981). Young children's storage behavior in a memory for location task. Journal of Experimental Child Psychology, 31, 250–364.

Heiser, C. B., Jr. (1969). Nightshades: The paradoxical plants. San Francisco: W. H. Freeman.

Held, R. (1993). What can rates of development tell us about underlying mechanisms? In C. E. Granrud (Ed.), Visual preception and cognition in infancy. Hillsdale, NJ: Erlbaum.

Henderson, G., & Henderson, B. B. (1984). Mending broken children: A parent's manual. Springfield, Ill.: Charles C. Thomas.

Henderson, R. H. (1999). Immunization: Going the extra mile. Progress of nations, 1999. New York: UNICEF.

Hendrick, H. (1997). Constructions and reconstructions of British childhood: An interpretative survey, 1800 to the present. In A. James & A. Prout (Eds.), Constructing and reconstructing childhood: Contemporary issues in the sociological study of childhood. Washington, D.C.: Falmer Press.

Henington, C., Hughes, J. N., Cavell, T. A., & Thompson, B. (1998). The role of relational aggression in identifying aggressive boys and girls. Journal of School Psychology, 36, 457–477.

Henker, B., & Whalen, C. K. (1989). Hyperactivity and attention deficits. American Psychologist, 44, 216–223.

Henry, C. S., Stephenson, A. L., Hanson, M. F., & Hargett, W. (1993). Adolescent suicide and families: An ecological approach. Adolescence, 28, 291–308.

Henshaw, A., Kelly, J., & Gratton, C. (1992). Skipping's for girls: Children's perceptions of gender roles and gender preferences. Educational Research, 34, 229–235.

Hernandez, D. J. & Myers, D. E. (1993). America's children: Resources from family, government, and the economy. New York: Russell Sage Foundation.

Herrnstein, R. J., & Murray, C. (1994). The bell curve: Intelligence and class structure in American life. New York: Free Press.

Hershkowitz, I., & Elul, A. (1999). The effects of investigative utterances on Israeli children's reports of physical abuse. Applied Developmental Science, 3, 28–33.

Hertz, R., & Ferguson, F. I. T. (1996). Childcare choice and constraints in the United States: Social class, race and the influence of family views. Journal of Comparative Family Studies, 27, 249–280.

Herzog, D. B., Dorer, D. J., Keel, P. K., Selwyn, S. E., Ekeblad, E. R., Flores, A. T., Greenwood, D. N., Burwell, R. A., & Keller, M. B. (1999). Recovery and relapse in anorexia and bulimia nervosa: A 7.5–year follow-up. Journal of the American Academy of Child & Adolescent Psychiatry, 38, 829–837.

Herzog, E., & Sudia, C. (1970). Boys in fatherless homes. Washington, D.C.: U.S. Department of Health, Education, & Welfare.

Hess, G. C. (1990). Sexual abstinence, a revived option for teenagers. Modern Psychology, 1, 19–21.

Hess, L. J., Dohrman, K., & Huneck, B. (1997). Communication begins at birth: Are infants at-risk for delays identified early enough? Infant-Toddler Intervention, 7, 111–122.

Hesse, E. (1999). The adult attachment interview: Historical and current perspectives. In J. Cassidy & P. R. Shaver, (Eds) Handbook of attachment: Theory, research, and clinical applications. New York: The Guilford Press.

Hetherington, E. M., Cox, M., & Cox, R. (1979). Play and social interaction in children following divorce. Journal of Social Issues, 35, 26–49.

Hetherington, E. M., Stanley-Hagen, M., & Anderson, E. R. (1989). Marital transitions: A child's perspective. American Psychologist, 44, 303–312.

Higbee, K. L. (1977). Your memory: How it works and how to improve it. Englewood Cliffs, N.J.: Prentice-Hall.

Hill, K. G., Howell, J. C., Hawkins, J. D., & Battin-Pearson, S. R. (1999). Childhood risk factors for adolescent gang membership: Results from the Seattle Social Development Project. Journal of Research in Crime & Delinquency, 36, 300–322.

Hillman, L. S. (1991). Theories and research. In C. A. Corr, H. Fuller, C. A. Barnickol, & D. M. Corr (Eds.), Sudden infant death syndrome: Who can help and how. New York: Springer.

Hinde, R. A. (1983). Ethology and child development. In P. H. Mussen (Ed.), Handbook of child psychology (4th ed.) (Vol. 2): Infancy and developmental psychobiology (M. M. Haith & J. J. Campos, Eds.). New York: John Wiley, 27–94.

Hinde, R. A. (1989). Ethological and relationship approaches. In R. Vasta (Ed.), Annals of child development (Vol. 6). Greenwich, Conn.: JAI Press.

Hindelang, M. J. (1981). Variations in sex-race-age-specific incidence of offending. *American Sociological Review, 46,* 461–474.

Hirsch, B. J., & Dubois, D. L. (1991). Self-esteem in early adolescence: The identification and prediction of contrasting longitudinal trajectories. *Journal of Youth and Adolescence, 20,* 53–72.

Ho, D. Y. F. (1987). Fatherhood in Chinese culture. In M. E. Lamb (Ed.). The father's role: Cross-cultural perspectives.Hillsdale, N.J.: Lawrence Erlbaum.

Hodapp, R. M., & Mueller, E. (1982). Early social development. In B. B. Wolman and others (Eds.), Handbook of developmental psychology. Englewood Cliffs, N.J.: Prentice-Hall.

Hodges, E. V. E., & Perry, D. G. (1999). Personal and interpersonal antecedents and consequences of victimization by peers. *Journal of Personality & Social Psychology, 76,* 677–685.

Hoek, D., van den Eeden, P., & Terwel, J. (1999). The effects of integrated social and cognitive strategy instruction on the mathematics achievement in secondary education. *Learning & Instruction, 9,* 427–448.

Hofer, M. A. (1981). The roots of human behavior: An introduction to the psychobiology of early development. San Francisco: W. H. Freeman.

Hofferth, S. L. (1992). The demand for and supply of child care in the 1990s. In A. Booth (Ed.), *Child care in the 1990's: Trends and consequences.* Hillsdale, NJ: Erlbaum.

Hoff-Ginsberg, E. (1998). The relation of birth order and socioeconomic status to children's language experience and language development. *Applied psycholoinguistics, 19,* 603–629.

Hoffman, E. (1998). Peak experiences in childhood: An exploratory study. *Journal of Humanistic Psychology, 38,* 109–120.

Hoffman, L. W. (1991). The influence of the family environment on personality: Accounting for sibling differences. *Psychological Bulletin, 110,* 187–203.

Hoffman, M. L. (1975). Developmental synthesis of affect and cognition and its implications for altruistic motivation. *Developmental Psychology, 11,* 607–622.

Hoffman, M. L. (1976). Empathy, role-taking, guilt, and development of altruistic motives. In T. Likona (Ed.), Moral development: Current theory and research. New York: Holt, Rinehart & Winston.

Hoffman, M. L. (1978). Empathy: Its developmental and prosocial implications. In C. B. Keasey (Ed.), Nebraska symposium on motivation (Vol. 25). Lincoln: University of Nebraska Press.

Hoffman, M. L. (1979). Development of moral thought, feeling, and behavior. *American Psychologist, 34,* 958–966.

Hoge, R. D. (1988). Issues in the definition and measurement of the giftedness construct. *Educational Researcher, 17,* 12–66.

Hoge, R. D., & Renzulli, J. S. (1993). Exploring the link between giftedness and self-concept. *Review of Educational Research, 63,* 449–465.

Holahan, C. K. (1996). Lifetime achievement among the Terman gifted women. *Gifted and Talented International, 11,* 65f-71.

Holbrook, R. H. Jr., Givson, R. N., El-Sayed, Y. Y., & Seidman, D. S. (1997). Fetal responses to asphyxia. In D. K. Stevenson & P. Sunshine (Eds.), *Fetal and neonatal brain injury: Mechanisms, management, and the risks of practice.* New York: Oxford University Press.

Holbrook, R. H., Jr.; Laros, R. K., Jr.; & Creasy, R. K. (1988). Evaluation of a risk-scoring system for prediction of preterm labor. *American Journal of Perinatology, 6,* 62.

Holland, A. J., Hall, A., Murray, R., Russell, G. F. M., & Crisp, A. H. (1984). Anorexia nervosa: A study of 34 twin pairs and one set of triplets. *British Journal of Psychiatry, 145,* 414–419.

Holmes, C. S., Yu, Z., & Frentz, J. (1999). Chronic and discrete stress as predictors of children's adjustment. *Journal of Consulting & Clinical Psychology, 67,* 411–419.

Holmes, R. H., & Rahe, R. H. (1967). The social readjustment rating scale. *Journal of Psychosomatic Research, 11,* 213–218.

Holstein, C. B. (1976). Irreversible, stepwise sequence in the development of moral judgment: A longitudinal study of males and females. *Child Development, 47,* 51–61.

Hommers, W. (1997). Integration of Kohlbergian information in punishment. *European Review of Applied Psychology/Revue Européenne de Psychologie Appliquée, 47,* 31–36.

Hooper, S. R. (1992). The classification of developmental disorders: An overview. In S. R. Hooper, G. W. Hynd, & R. E. Mattison, (Eds.), Developmental disorders: Diagnostic criteria and clinical assessment. Hillsdale, N.J.: Lawrence Erlbaum.

Hoorn, J. V., Scales, B., Nourot, P. M., & Alward, K. R. (1999). *Play at the center of the curriculum* (2nd ed.). Upper Saddle River, NJ: Prentice Hall.

Horn, J. (1983). The Texas Adoption Project. *Child Development, 54,* 268–275.

Horn, J. L. (1976). Human abilities: A review of research and theory in the early 1970s. In M. R. Rosenzweig & L. W. Porter (Eds.), Annual review of psychology (Vol. 27). Palo Alto, Calif.: Annual Reviews.

Horn, J. L., & Donaldson, G. (1980). Cognitive development in adulthood. In O. G. Brim, Jr., & J. Kagan (Eds.), Constancy and change in human development. Cambridge, Mass.: Harvard University Press.

Horns, P. N., Ratcliffe, l. P., Leggett, J. C., & Swanson, M. S. (1996). Pregnancy outcomes among active and sedentary primiparous women. *Journal of Obstetric, Gynecologic, and Neonatal Nursing, 25,* 49–54.

Horton, D. L., & Mills, C. B. (1984). Human learning and memory. *Annual Review of Psychology, 35,* 361–394.

Hough, K. J., & Erwin, P. G. (1997). Children's attitudes toward violence on television. *Journal of Psychology, 131,* 411–415.

Howard, C. R., & Lawrence, R. A. (1999). Drugs and breastfeeding. *Clinics in Perinatology, 26,* 447–478.

Howe, M. L., & Courage, M. L. (1993). On resolving the enigma of infantile amnesia. *Psychological Bulletin, 113,* 305–326.

Howell, J. C. (1999). Youth gang homicides: A literature review. *Crime & Delinquency, 45,* 208–241.

Howes, C., & Segal, J. (1993). Children's relationships with alternative caregivers: The special case of maltreated children removed from their homes. *Journal of Applied Developmental Psychology, 14,* 71–81.

Howes, C., Galinsky, E., & Kontos, S. (1998). Child care caregiver sensitivity and attachment. *Social Development, 7,* 25–36.

Hsu, L. Y. F. (1986). Prenatal diagnosis of chromosome abnormalities. In A. Milunsky (Ed.), Genetic disorders and the fetus (2nd ed.). New York: Plenum Press.

Hubel, D. H. (1988). *Eye, brain, and vision.* New York; Scientific American Library.

Hubel, D. H., & Wiesel, T. N. (1970). The period of susceptibility to the physiological effects of unilateral eye closure in kittens. *Journal of Physiology, 206,* 419–436.

Huesmann, L. R., & Eron, L. D. (1986b). The development of aggression in children of different cultures: Psychological processes and exposure to violence. In L. R. Huesmann & L. D. Eron (Eds.), Television and the aggressive child: A cross-national comparison. Hillsdale, N.J.: Lawrence Erlbaum.

Huesmann, L. R., & Eron, L. D. (Eds.) (1986a). Television and the aggressive child: A cross-national comparison. Hillsdale, N.J.: Lawrence Erlbaum.

Huesmann, L. R., Eron, L. D., Lefkowitz, M. M., & Walder, L. O. (1984). The stability of aggression over time and generations. *Developmental Psychology, 20,* 1120–1134.

Hughes, C., Dunn, J., & White, A. (1988). Trick or Treat? Uneven understanding of mind and emotion and executive dysfunction in "hard-to-manage" preschoolers. *Journal of Child Psychology and Psychiatry, 39,* 981–994.

Hughes, F. P. (1990). Children, play, and development. Boston: Allyn & Bacon.

Hughes, F. P. (1999). *Children, play, and development* (3rd ed.). Boston: Allyn & Bacon.

Hughes, R., Tingle, B. A., & Sawin, D. B. (1981). Development of empathic understanding in children. *Child Development, 52,* 122–128.

Hull, M., Joyce, D., Turner, G., & Wardle, P. (1997). *Undergraduate obstetrics and gynaecology* (3rd ed.). Oxford: Butterworth-Heinemann.

Human Resources Development Canada (1999). *Readiness to learn, child development and learning outcomes: Potential measures of readiness to learn.* Hull, Quebec, Canada: Applied Research Branch.

Hunt, C. E. (1991). Sudden infant death syndrome: The neurobehavioral perspective. *Journal of Applied Developmental Psychology, 12,* 185–188.

Hunt, E., & Agnoli, F. (1991). The Whorfian hypothesis: A cognitive psychology perspective. *Psychological Review, 98,* 377–389.

Hunt, J. McV. (1961). Intelligence and experience. New York: The Ronald Press.

Hurlock, E. B. (1964). *Child development* (4th ed.). New York: McGraw-Hill.

Hurrelman, K. (1990). Parents, peers, teachers and other significant partners in adolescence. *International Journal of Adolescence and Youth, 2,* 211–236.

Husen, T., & Tuijnman, A. (1991). The contribution of formal schooling to the increase in intellectual capital. *Educational Researcher, 20,* 17–25.

Huston, A. C., & Wright, J. C. (1983). Children's processing of television: The informative functions of formal features. In J. Bryant & D. R. Anderson (Eds.), Children's understanding of television: Research on attention and comprehension. New York: Academic Press, 35–68.

Huston, A. C., Watkins, B. Q., & Kunkel, D. (1989). Public policy and children's television. *American Psychologist, 44,* 424–433.

Huston, A. C., Wright, J. C., Rice, M. L., Kerkman, D., & St. Peters, M. (1990). Development of television viewing patterns in early childhood: A longitudinal investigation. *Developmental Psychology, 26*, 409–420.

Huston, A., McLoyd, V. C., & Coll, C. G. (1997). Poverty and behavior: The case for multiple methods and levels of analysis. *Developmental Review, 17*, 376–393.

Hutchinson, J. (1991). What crack does to babies. *American Educator, 15*, 31–32.

Hutt, S. J., Lenard, H. G., & Prechtl, H. F. R. (1969). Psychophysiology of the newborn. In L. P. Lipsitt & H. W. Reese (Eds.), Advances in child development and behavior. New York: Academic Press.

Hyde, J. S. (1986). Understanding human sexuality (3rd ed.). New York: McGraw-Hill.

Hyde, J. S., & Jaffee, S. (1998). Perspectives from social and feminist psychology. *Educational Researcher, 27*, 14–17.

Hyde, J. S., Fennema, E., & Lamon, S. J. (1990). Gender differences in mathematics performance. A meta-analysis. *Psychological Bulletin, 107*, 139–155.

Hyde, S., & Linn, M. C. (1986). The psychology of gender: Advances through meta-analysis. Baltimore: Johns Hopkins University Press.

Iacono, T. A., Chan, J. B., & Waring, R. E. (1998). Efficacy of a parent-implemented early language intervention based on collaborative consultation. *International Journal of Language and Communication Disorders, 33*, 281–303.

Ialongo, N. S., Vaden-Kiernan, N., & Kellam, S. (1998). Early peer rejection and aggression: Longitudinal relations with adolescent behavior. *Journal of Developmental & Physical Disabilities, 10*, 199–213.

Iennarella, R. S., Chisum, G. M., & Bianchi, J. (1986). A comprehensive treatment model for pregnant chemical users, infants and families. In I. J. Chasnoff (Ed.), Drug use in pregnancy: Mother and child. Boston: MTP Press.

Ijzendoorn, M. H. Van (1993). Intergenerational transmission of parenting: A review of studies in nonclinical populations. *Developmental Review, 12*, 76–99.

Ikomi, A., Matthews, M., Kuan, A. M., & Henson, G. (1998). The effect of physiological urine dilution on pregnancy test results in complicated early pregnancies. *British Journal of Obstetrics and Gynaecology, 105*, 462–465.

Ikonen, P. (1998). On phallic defense. *Scandinavian Psychoanalytic Review, 21*, 136–150.

Imbesi, L. (1999). The making of a narcissist. *Clinical Social Work Journal, 27*, 41–54. Indiana U. School of Medicine, Dept of Psychiatry, Indianapolis, IN, USA.

Individuals with Disabilities Education Act of 1997. Public Law No. 105–17, 111 stat. 37–157. 20 U.S.C. 1400.

Ingram, D. (1991). A historical observation on "Why 'Mama' and 'Papa'?" *Journal of Child Language, 18*, 711–713.

Inhelder, B., & Piaget, J. (1958). The growth of logical thinking from childhood to adolescence. New York: Basic Books.

Inoff-Germain, G.; Arnold, G. S.; Nottelmann, E. D.; Susman, E. J.; Cutler, G. B., Jr.; & Chrousos, G. P. (1988). Relations between hormone levels and observational measures of aggressive behavior of young adolescents in family interactions. *Developmental Psychology, 24*, 129–139. Inst of Psychiatry, SGDP Ctr, London, England UK.

Intons-Peterson, M. J. (1988). Gender concepts of Swedish and American youth. Hillsdale, N.J.: Lawrence Erlbaum.

Isabell, B. J., & McKee, L. (1980). Society's cradle: An anthropological perspective on the socialisation of cognition. In J. Sants (Ed.), Developmental psychology and society. London: Macmillan, 327–365.

Itoga, S., Nomura, F., Harada, S., Tstsumi, M., Takase, S., & Nakai, T. (1999). Mutations in the exons and exon-intron junction regions of human cytochrome P-4502E1 gene and alcoholism. *Alcoholism: Clinical and Experimental Research, 23*, 29S-32S.

Izard, C. E. (1977). Human emotions. New York: Plenum.

Izard, C. E., & Malatesta, C. Z. (1987). Perspectives on emotional development I: Differential emotions theory of early emotional development. In J. D. Osofsky (Ed.), Handbook of infant development (2nd ed.). New York: Wiley.

Izenberg, N., & Lieberman, D. A. (1998). The Web, communication trends, and children's health: Part 4: How children use the Web. *Clinical Pediatrics, 37*, 335–340.

Jacklin, C. N. (1989). Female and male: Issues of gender. *American Psychologist, 44*, 127–133.

Jackson, J. F. (1993). Multiple caregiving among African Americans and infant attachment: The need for an emic approach. *Human Development, 36*, 87–102.

Jacobson, J. L., & Jacobson, S. W. (1990). Methodological issues in human behavioral teratology. In C. Rovee-Collier & L. P. Lipsitt (Eds.), Advances in infancy research (Vol. 6), Norwood, N.J.: Ablex.

Jacobson, J. L., & Wille, D. E. (1984). Influence of attachment and separation experience on separation distress at 18 months. *Developmental Psychology, 20*, 477–484.

Jacobson, S. W., Fein, G. G., Jacobson, S. W., & Kagan, J. (1979). Interpreting "imitative" responses in early infancy. *Science, 205*, 215–217.

Jacobson, J. L., Schwartz, P. M., & Dowler, J. K. (1985). Neonatal correlates of exposure to smoking, caffeine, and alcohol. *Infant and Behavior Development, 7*, 253–265.

Jacobvitz, R. S., Wood, M. R., & Albin, K. (1991). Cognitive skills and young children's comprehension of television. *Journal of Applied Developmental Psychology, 12*, 219–235.

Jacopini, G. A., D'Amico, R., Frontali, M., & Vivona, G. (1992). Attitudes of persons at risk and their partners toward predictive testing. In G. Evers-Kiebooms, J. P. Fryns, J. J. Cassiman, & H. Van den Berghe (Eds.), Psychosocial aspects of genetic counseling. New York: John Wiley.

Jaffke, F. (1996). *Work and play in early childhood*. Edinburgh: Floris Books.

Jagodzinska, M. (1997). Memory in young children: Passive or active? *Polish Psychological Bulletin, 28*, 3–18.

Jahnke, H. C., & Blanchard-Fields, F. (1993). A test of two models of adolescent egocentrism. *Journal of Youth and Adolescence, 22*, 313–326.

Jain, A., Belsky, J., & Crnic, K. (1996). Beyond fathering behaviors: Types of dads. *Journal of Family Psychology, 10*, 431–442.

Jain, A., & Belsky, J. (1997). Fathering and acculturation: Immigrant Indian families with young children. *Journal of Marriage & the Family, 59*, 873–883.

Jalongo, M. R., & Isenberg, J. P. (2000). *Exploring your role: A practitioner's introduction to early childhood education*. Upper Saddle River, NJ: Merrill.

James, A., & Prout, A. (1997). A new paradigm for the sociology of childhood? Provenance, promise and problems. In A. James & A. Prout (Eds.), *Constructing and reconstructing childhood: Contemporary issues in the sociological study of childhood*. Washington, D.C.: Falmer Press.

James, W. (1890). *The principles of psychology*. New York: Holt, Rinehart & Winston.

James, W. (1892). *Psychology: The briefer course*. New York: Henry Holt.

Janke, J. (1999). The effect of relaxation therapy on preterm labor outcomes. *Journal of Obstetric, Gynecologic, and Neonatal Nursing, 28*, 255–263.

Jean, S. S., Pape, J. W., Verdier, R. I., Reed, G. W., Hutto, C., & Johnson, W. D. Jr. (1999). The natural history of human immunodeficiency virus 1 infection in Haitian infants. *Pediatric Infectious Disease Journal, 18*, 58–63.

Jean-Gilles, M., & Crittenden, P. M. (1990). Maltreating families: A look at siblings. *Family Relations, 39*, 323–329.

Jeffery, H. E., Megevand, A., & Page, H. D. (1999). Why the prone position is a risk factor for sudden infant death syndrome. *Pediatrics, 104*, 263–269.

Jelliffe, D. B., & Jelliffe, E. F. (1990). Growth monitoring and promotion in young children: Guidelines for the selection of methods and training techniques. New York: Oxford University Press.

Jenkins, R. (1995). Midwifery — a matter of politics. In Murphy-Black, T. (Ed.), *Issues in midwifery*. New York: Churchill Livingstone.

Jensen, A. R. (1968). Social class, race, and genetics: Implications for education. *American Educational Research Journal, 5*, 1–42.

Jensen, W. A., et al. (1979). *Biology*. Belmont, Calif.: Wadsworth.

Jepson, L., Juszczak, L., & Fisher, M. (1999). Mental health care in a high school based health service. *Adolescence, 33*, 1–15.

Jersild, A. T. (1963). The psychology of adolescence (2nd ed.). New York: Macmillan.

Jessor, R. (Ed.) (1998). *New perspectives on adolescent risk behavior*. New York: Cambridge University Press.

Johnson, B., & Morse, H. (1968). *Injured children and their parents. Children, 15*, 147–152.

Johnson, D. W., & Johnson, R. T. (1994). *Learning together and alone: Cooperative, competitive, and individualistic learning* (4th ed.). Boston: Allyn & Bacon.

Johnson, H. R., Myhre, S. A., Ruvalcaba, R. H. A., Thuline, H. C., & Kelley, V. C. (1970). Effects of testosterone on body image and behavior in Klinefelter's syndrome: A pilot study. *Developmental Medicine and Child Neurology, 12*, 454–460.

Johnson, J. E., & McGillicuddy-Delisi, A. (1983). Family environment factors and children's knowledge of rules and conventions. *Child Development, 54*, 218–226.

Johnson, J. E., Christie, J. F., & Yawkey, T. D. (1999). *Play and early childhood development* (2nd Ed.). New York: Longman.

Johnson, J. G., Cohen, P., Brown, J., Smailes, E., & Bernstein, D. P. (1999). Childhood maltreatment increases risk for personality disorders during early adulthood. *Archives of General Psychiatry, 56*, 600–606.

Johnson, J. H. (1986). Life events as stressors in childhood and adolescence. Beverly Hills, Calif.: Sage.

Johnson, M. H. (1998). The neural basis of cognitive development. In D. Kuhn & R. S. Siegler

(Eds.), *Handbook of child psychology: Vol. 2. Cognition, perception, and language.* New York: Wiley.

Johnson, M. K., Bransford, J. D., & Solomon, S. (1973). Memory for tacit implications of sentences. *Journal of Experimental Psychology, 98,* 203–205.

Johnson, R. D. (1962). Measurements of achievement in fundamental skills of elementary school children. *Research Quartery, 33,* 94–103.

Johnson, S. A., & Green, V. (1993). Female adolescent contraceptive decision making and risk taking. *Adolescence, 28,* 81–96.

Johnson, S. A., & Green, V. (1993). Female adolescent contraceptive decision making and risk taking. *Adolescence, 28,* 81–96.

Johnston, J. R. (1994). High-conflict divorce. *Future of Children, 4,* 165–182.

Johnston, L. D., O'Malley, P. M., & Bachman, J. G. (1995). *National survey results on drug use from the monitoring the Future study, 1975–1973.* NIH Pub. No. 94–3810. Rockville, MD: National Institute on Drug Abuse.

Jones, A. (1997). Issues relevant to therapy with adoptees. *Psychotherapy, 34,* 64–68.

Jones, E. F., and associates, (1986). Teenage pregnancy in industrialized countries. New Haven, Conn.: Yale University Press.

Jones, J. (1995). Institutional abuse: Understanding domination from the inside looking out. *Early Child Development and Care, 113,* 85–92.

Jones, M. C. (1957). The later careers of boys who are early- or late-maturing. *Child Development, 28,* 113–128.

Jones, M. C. (1965). Psychological correlates of somatic development. *Child Development, 36,* 899–911.

Jones, M. C. (1974). Albert, Peter, and John B. Watson. *American Psychologist, 29,* 581–583.

Jordan, N. H. (1993). Sexual abuse prevention programs in early childhood education: A caveat. *Young Children, 48,* 76–79.

Jorgensen, S. R. (1991). Project taking charge: An evaluation of an adolescent pregnancy prevention program. *Family Relations, 40,* 373–380.

Journal of Child Psychology & Psychiatry & Allied Disciplines. Vol 39(8),

Jovanovic, J., & King, S. S. (1998). Boys and girls in the performance-based science classroom: Who's doing the performing? *American Educational Research Journal, 35,* 477–496.

Joy, L. A., Kimball, M., & Zabrack, M. L. (1977). Television exposure and children's aggressive behavior. Paper presented at the annual meeting of the Canadian Psychological Association, Vancouver, B.C.

Juffer, F., van Ijzendoorn, M. H., & Bakermans-Kranenburg, M. J. (1997). Intervention in transmission of insecure attachment: A case study. *Psychological Reports, 80,* 531–543.

Julieboe, M. F., Malicky, G. V., & Norman, C. (1998). Metacognition of young readers in an early intervention programme. *Journal of Research in Reading, 21,* 24–35.

Justice, E. (1985). Categorization as a preferred memory strategy: Developmental changes during elementary school. *Developmental Psychology, 21,* 1105–1110.

Juvonen, J. (1991). Deviance, perceived responsibility, and negative peer reactions. *Developmental Psychology, 27,* 672–681.

Kagan, J. (1966). Reflection-impulsivity: The generality and dynamics of conceptual tempo. *Journal of Abnormal Psychology, 71,* 17–24.

Kagan, J. (1976). Emergent themes in human development. *American Scientist, 64,* 186–196.

Kagan, J. (1978, August). The parental love trap. *Psychology Today,* 54–61, 91.

Kagan, J. (1992). Yesterday's premises, tomorrow's promises. *Developmental Psychology, 28,* 990–997.

Kagan, J. (1997). Temperament and the reactions to unfamiliarity. *Child Development, 68,* 139–143.

Kagan, J., & Gall, S. B. (Eds.). (1998) *The Gale encyclopedia of childhood and adolescence.* Detroit, Mi: Gale Publishing.

Kagan, J., & Snidman, N. (1991). Temperamental factors in human development. *American Psychologist, 46,* 856–862.

Kagan, J., Kearsley, R. B., & Zelazo, P. R. (1977). The effects of infant day care on psychological development. *Educational Quarterly, 1,* 109–142.

Kagan, J., Snidman, N., & Arcus, D. (1998). Childhood derivatives of high and low reactivity in infancy. *Child Development, 69,* 1483–1493.

Kahn, K., Tollman, S. M., Garenne, M. & Gear J. S. (1999).Who dies from what? Determining cause of death in South Africa's rural northeast. *Tropical Medicine & International Health, 4,* 433–41.

Kahne, J. (1996). The politics of self-esteem. *American Educational Research Journal, 33,* 3–22.

Kaiser, P. (1996). Relationships in the extended family and diverse family forms. In A. E. Auhagen & M. von Salisch (Eds.), *The diversity of human relationships.* New York: Cambridge University Press.

Kaitz, M., Meschulach-Sarfaty, O., Auerbach, J., & Eidelman, A. (1988). A reexamination of newborn's ability to imitate facial expressions. *Developmental Psychology, 24,* 3–7.

Kalamas, A. D., & Gruber, M. L. (1998). Electrodermal responses to implied versus actual violence on television. *Journal of General Psychology, 125,* 31–37.

Kaler, S. R., & Freeman, B. J. (1994). Analysis of environmental deprivation; Cognitive and social development in Romanian orphans. *Journal of Child Psychology and Psychiatry and Allied Disciplines, 35,* 769–781.

Kampen, D. Van (1999). Genetic and environmental influences on pre-schizophrenic personality: MAXCOV-HITMAX and LISREL analyses. *European Journal of Personality, 134,* 63–80.

Kandall, S. R., Gaines, J., Habel, L., et al. (1993). Relationship of maternal substance abuse to subsequent sudden infant death syndrome in offspring. *Journal of Pediatrics, 123,* 120–126.

Kandel, D. (1998). Persistent themes and new perspectives on adolescent substance use: A life-span perspective. In R. Jessor (Ed.), *New perspectives on adolescent risk behavior.* New York: Cambridge University Press.

Kandel, D. B., & Logan, J. A. (1984). Patterns of drug use from adolescence to young adulthood: I. Period of risk for initiation, continued use, and discontinuation. *American Journal of Public Health, 74,* 660–666.

Kant, I. (1977; original in 1797). Die Metaphysic der Sitten. Frankfurt: Suhrkamp.

Kaplan, L. J. (1984). Adolescence: The farewell to childhood. New York: Simon & Schuster.

Kasof, J. (1993). Sex bias in the naming of stimulus persons. *Psychological Bulletin, 113,* 140–163.

Kato, T. (1970). Chromosome studies in pregnant rhesus monkeys macaque given LSD-25. *Diseases of the Nervous System, 31,* 245–250.

Katsuragi, S., Kunugi, H., Sano, A., Tsutsumi, T., Isogawa, K., Nanko, S., & Akiyoshi, J. (1999). Association between serotonin transporter gene polymorphism and anxiety-related traits. *Biological Psychiatry, 45,* 368–370.

Katz, L. F., & Gottman, J. M. (1997). Buffering children from marital conflict and dissolution. *Journal of Clinical Child Psychology, 26,* 157–171.

Katzmarzyk, P. T., Malina, R. M., Song, T. M. K., & Bouchard, C. (1998). Television viewing, physical activity, and health-related fitness of youth in the Quebec Family Study. *Journal of Adolescent Health, 23,* 318–325.

Kaufman, A. S., Kaufman, J. C., Chen, T.H., & Kaufman, N. L. (1996). Differences on six Horn abilities for 14 age groups between 15–16 and 75–94 years. *Psychological Assessment, 8,* 161–171.

Kaukiainen, A., Bjoerkqvist, K., Lagerspetz, K., Oesterman, K., Salmivalli, Cl, Rothberg, S., & Ahlbom, A. (1999). The relationships between social intelligence, empathy, and three types of aggression. *Aggressive Behavior, 25,* 81–89.

Kavale, K. A., Forness, S. R., & Lorsbach, T. C. (1991). Definition for definitions of learning disabilities. *Journal of Learning Disabilities, 14,* 257–266.

Kavale, K.,& Forness, S. (1985). The science of learning disabilities. San Diego, Calif.: College-Hill Press.

Kaye, K. (1977). Toward the origin of dialogue. In H. R. Schaffer (Ed.), Studies in mother-infant interaction. London: Academic Press.

Kazdin, A. E. (1989). Developmental psychopathology: Current research, issues, and directions. *American Psychologist, 44,* 180–187.

Keating, D. (1990). Adolescent thinking. In S. Feldman & G. Elliott (Eds.), *At the threshold; The developing adolescent.* Cambridge, MA: Harvard University Press.

Keel, P. K., Fulkerson, J. A., & Leon, G. R. (1997). Disordered eating precursors in pre- and early adolescent girls and boys. *Journal of Youth and Adolescence, 26,* 203–217.

Kegan, R. (1982). The evolving self: Problem and process in human development. Cambridge, Mass.: Harvard University Press.

Kelley, H. H. (1992). Common-sense psychology and scientific psychology. *Annual Review of Psychology, 43,* 1–23.

Kellogg, N. D., Hoffman, T. J., & Taylor, E. R. (1999). Early sexual experiences among pregnant and parenting adolescents. *Adolescence, 34,* 293–303.

Kempe, R. S., & Kempe, C. H. (1984). The common secret: Sexual abuse of children and adolescents. New York: W. H. Freeman.

Kendall-Tackett, K. A., Williams, L. M., & Finkelhor, D. (1993). Impact of sexual abuse on children: A review and synthesis of recent empirical studies. *Psychological Bulletin, 113,* 164–180.

Kendall-Tackett, K. A., Williams, L. M., & Finkelhor, D. (1993). Impact of sexual abuse on children: A review and synthesis of recent empirical studies. *Psychological Bulletin, 113,* 164–180.

Kennedy, D., & Koren, G. (1998). Valproic acid use in psychiatry: Issues in treating women of reproductive age. *Journal of Psychiatry and Neuroscience, 23,* 223–228.

Kennell, J. H., Trause, M. A., & Klaus, M. H. (1975). Evidence for a sensitive period in the human mother. *Parent-Infant Interaction* (Ciba Foundation Symposium, new series) 33, 87–102.

Kent, L., Evans, J., Paul, M., & Sharp, M. (1999). Comorbidity of autistic spectrum disorders in children with Down syndrome. *Developmental Medicine and Child Neurology, 41,* 153–158.

Kessen, W. (1965). The child. New York: John Wiley.

Kessen, W. (1975). Childhood in China. New Haven, Conn.: Yale University Press.

Kessler, R. C., Borges, G., & Walters, E. E. (1999). Prevalence of and risk factors for lifetime suicide attempts in the National Comorbidity Survey. *Archives of General Psychiatry, 56,* 617–626.

Khan, K., & Chang, J. (1997). Neonatal abstinence syndrome due to codeine. *Archives of Disease in Childhood Fetal and Neonatal Edition, 76,* F59–60.

Kiesler, S., & Kraut, R. (1999). Internet use and ties that bind. *American Psychologist, 54f,* 783–784.

Kim, K., & Smith, P. K. (1999). Family relations in early childhood and reproductive development. *Journal of Reproductive & Infant Psychology, 17,* 133–148.

Kinsey, A. C., Pomeroy, W. B., & Martin, C. E. (1948). *Sexual behavior in the human male.* Philadelphia: W. B. Saunders.

Kinsey, A. C., Pomeroy, W. B., Martin, C. E., & Gebhard, P. H. (1953). *Sexual behavior in the human female.* Philadelphia: W. B. Saunders.

Kirby, J. R., & Das, J. P. (1990). A cognitive approach to intelligence: Attention, coding, and planning. Canadian *Psychology, 31,* 320–331.

Kirk, S. (1979). Educating exceptional children (3rd ed.). Boston: Houghton Mifflin.

Kirsh, S. J. (1998). Seeing the world through Mortal Kombat-colored glasses: Violent video games and the development of a short-term hostile attribution bias. *Childhood, 5,* 177–184.

Klaus, M. H., & Kennell, H. H. (1983). The beginnings of parent-infant attachment. St. Louis: C. V. Mosby. (Originally published as Maternal-infant bonding, 1980.)

Klaus, M. H., Kreger, N., McAlpine, W., Steffa, M., & Kennell, J. (1972). Maternal attachment: Importance of the first post-partum days. *New England Journal of Medicine, 286,* 460–463.

Klein, M., & Stern, L. (1971). Low birth weight and the battered child syndrome. *American Journal of Diseases 1, 22,* 15–18.

Klein, P. D. (1997). Multiplying the problems of intelligence by eight: A critique of Gardner's theory. *Canadian Journal of Education, 22,* 377–394.

Kleinginna, P. R., Jr., & Kleinginna, A. M. (1988). Current trends toward convergence of the behavioristic, functional, and cognitive perspectives in experimental psychology. *The Psychological Record, 38,* 369–392.

Kline, S. M. (1985). Achieving weight gain with anorexia and bulimic clients in a group setting. *Transactional Analysis Journal, 15,* 62–67.

Kloza, E. M. (1990). Low MSAFP and new biochemical markers for Down syndrome: Implications for genetic counselors. In B. A. Fine, E. Gettig, K. Greendale, B. Leopold, & N. W. Paul (Eds.), Strategies in genetic counseling: Reproductive genetics and new technologies, White Plains, N.Y.: March of Dimes Birth Defects Foundation.

Knoblauch, K., Bieber, M., & Werner, J. S. (1996). Assessing dimensionality in infant colour vision. In Vital-Durand, F., Atkinson, J., & Braddick, O. J. (Eds.), *Infant vision.* New York: Oxford Univeristy Press.

Knuppel, R. A., & Angel, J. L. (1990). Diagnosis of fetal-maternal hemorrhage. In R. D. Eden, F. H. Boehm, & M. Haire (Eds.), Assessment and care of the fetus: Physiological, clinical, and medicolegal principles. Norwalk Conn.: Appleton & Lange.

Knutson, J. F. (1978). Child abuse as an area of aggression research. *Journal of Pediatric Psychology, 3,* 20–27.

Kochanska, G. (1997). Mutually responsive orientation between mothers and their young children: Implications for early socialization. *Child Development, 68,* 94–112.

Kochanska, G. (1997). Mutually responsive orientation between mothers and their young children: Implications for early socialization. *Child Development, 68,* 94–112.

Kochanska, G., Clark, L. A., & Goldman, M. A. (1997). Implications of mothers' personality for their parenting and their young children's development outcomes. *Journal of Personality, 65,* 387–420.

Kochanska, G., Murray, K., & Coy, K. C. (1997). Inhibitory control as a contributor to conscience in childhood: From toddler to early school age. *Child Development, 68,* 263–277.

Kogan, N. (1983). Stylistic variation in childhood and adolescence: Creativity, metaphor, and cognitive style. In P. H. Mussen (Ed.), *Handbook of child psychology* (4th ed.) (Vol. 3): Cognitive development (J. H. Flavell & E. M. Markman, Eds.). New York: John Wiley, 630–706.

Kohlberg, L. A. (1964). Development of moral character and moral ideology. In M. L. Hoffman & L. W. Hoffman (Eds.), *Review of Child Development Research* (Vol. 1). New York: Russell Sage Foundation.

Kohlberg, L. A. (1966). Cognitive-development analysis of children's sex-role concepts and attitudes. In E. Maccoby (Ed.), The development of sex differences. Stanford, Calif.: Stanford University Press.

Kohlberg, L. A. (1969). Stage and sequence: The cognitive-developmental approach to socialization. In D. Gosslin (Ed.), *Handbook of socialization theory and research.* Chicago: Rand McNally.

Kohlberg, L. A. (1978). Revisions in the theory and practice of moral development. *New Directions for Child Development, 2,* 83–87.

Kohlberg, L. A. (1980). The meaning and measurement of moral development. Worcester, Mass.: Clark University Press.

Kohlberg, L. A., & Candee, D. (1984). The relationship of moral judgment to moral action. In W. M. Kurtines & J. L. Gewirtz (Eds.), Morality, moral behavior, and moral development. New York: John Wiley.

Kohlberg, L. A., & Ryncarz, R. A. (1990). Beyond justice reasoning: Moral development and consideration of a seventh stage. In C. N. Alexander & E. J. Langer, (Eds.), Higher stages of human development: Perspectives on adult growth. New York: Oxford University Press.

Kolata, G. B. (1978). Behavioral teratology: Birth defects of the mind. *Science, 202,* 732–734.

Kondro, W. (1992). Canada: Controversy over Royal Commission on Reproductive Technologies. *Lancet, 340,* 1214–1215

Konner, M. (1982). Biological aspects of the mother-infant bond. In C. Parks & J. Stevenson-Hinde (Eds.), The place of attachment in human behavior. New York: Basic Books.

Kontos, S., Howes, C., & Galinsky, E. (1996). Does training make a difference to quality in family child care? *Early Childhood Research Quarterly, 11,* 427–445.

Kopp, C. B., & Brownell, C. A. (1991). The development of self: The first 3 years. *Developmental Review, 11,* 195–196.

Kopp, C. B., & Kaler, S. R. (1989). Risk in infancy: Origins and implications. *American Psychologist, 44,* 224–230.

Kopp, C. B., & Parmelee, A. H. (1979). Prenatal and perinatal influences on infant behavior. In J. D. Osofsky (Ed.), *Handbook of infant development.* New York: John Wiley.

Korbin, J. E. (1981). "Very few cases": Child abuse and neglect in the People's Republic of China. In J. E. Korbin (Ed.), Child abuse and neglect: Cross-cultural perspectives. Berkeley: University of California Press.

Kotch, J. B. (1993). Morbidity and death due to child abuse in New Zealand. *Child Abuse and Neglect: The International Journal, 17,* 233–247.

Kotelchuck, M. (1976). The infant's relationship to the father: Experimental evidence. In M. Lamb (Ed.), The role of the father in child development. New York: John Wiley.

Koutsouvanou, E. (1993). Television and child language development. *International Journal of Early Childhood, 25,* 27–32.

Kovacs, M. (1989). Affective disorders in children and adolescents. *American Psychologist, 44,* 209–215.

Kozulin, A. (1990). Vygotsky's psychology: A biography of ideas. New York: Harvester Wheatsheaf.

Kracke, B. (1997). Parental behaviors and adolescents' career exploration. *Career Development Quarterly, 45,* 341–350.

Kraut, R., Patterson, M., Lundmark, V., Kiesler, S., Mukophadhyay, T., & Scherlis, W. (1998). Internet paradox: A social technology that reduces social involvement and psychological well-being? *American Psychologist, 53,* 1017–1031.

Krcmar, M., & Greene, K. (1999). Predicting exposure to and uses of television violence. *Journal of Communication, 49,* 24–45.

Krew, M. A., & Gill, P. (1997). Antepartum and intrapartum fetal infection. In G. G. Ashmead, & G. B. Reed (Eds.), *Essentials of maternal fetal medicine.* New York: Chapman & Hall.

Kropp, P. (1998). *I'll be the Parent, You be the Kid.* New York: Random House.

Kroupa, S. E. (1988). Perceived parental acceptance and female juvenile delinquency. *Adolescence, 23,* 143–155.

Kuczynski, L., & Kochanska, G. (1995). Function and content of maternal demands: Developmental significance of early demands for competent action. *Child Development, 66,* 616–628.

Kuhn, D. (1972). Mechanisms of change in the development of cognitive structures. *Child Development, 43,* 833–844.

Kuhn, D. (1984). Cognitive development. In M. H. Bornstein & M. E. Lamb (Eds.), Developmental psychology: An advanced textbook. Hillsdale, N.J.: Lawrence Erlbaum, 133–180.

Kumar, V. K., Kemmler, D., & Holman, E. R. (1997). The Creativity Styles Questionnaire-Revised. *Creativity Research Journal, 10,* 51–58.

Kumin, L., Councill, C., & Goodman, M. (1999). Expressive vocabulary in young children with Down syndrome: From research to treatment. *Infant-Toddler Intervention, 9,* 87–100.

Kunz, C., Rodriguez-Palmero, M., Koletzko, B., & Jensen, R. (1999). Nutritional and biochemical properties of human milk, Part I: General aspects, proteins, and carbohydrates. *Clinics in Perinatology, 26,* 307–333.

Kupetz, B. N. (1993). Reducing stress in your child's life. *PTA Today, 18,* 10–12.

Kurdek, L. A. (1993). Issues in proposing a general model of the effects of divorce on children. *Journal of Marriage and the Family, 55,* 39–41.

Kurtines, W., & Grief, E. B. (1974). The development of moral thought: Review and evaluation of Kohlberg's approach. *Psychological Bulletin, 81,* 453–470.

Kuziel-Perri, P., & Snarey, J. (1991). Adolescent repeat pregnancies: An evaluation study of a comprehensive service program for pregnant and parenting black adolescents. *Family Relations, 40,* 381–385.

Kuzyk, B. (1993). Breast-feeding is best for babies. Edmonton Sun, September 2, p. 38.

Kwok, S. K., Ho, P. C. P., Chan, A. K. H., Ghandi, S. R., et al. (1996). Ocular defects in children and adolescents with severe mental deficiency. *Journal of Intellectual Disability Research, 40,* 330–335.

La Greca, A. M., & Stone, W. L. (1993). Social anxiety scale for children-revised: Factor structure and concurrent validy. *Journal of Clinical Child Psychology, 22,* 17–27.

Labbok, M. H. (1999). Health sequelae of breast-feeding for the mother. *Clinics in Perinatology, 26,* 491–503.

Labouvie-Vief, G. (1986). Modes of knowledge and the organization of development. In M. L. Commons, L. Kohlberg, F. A. Richards, & J. Sinnott (Eds.), *Beyond formal operations 3: Models and methods in the study of adult and adolescent thought.* New York: Praeger.

Labudova, O., Fang-Fircher, S., Cairns, N., Moenkemann, H., Yeghiazaryan, K., & Lubec, G. (1998).Brain vasopressin levels in Down Syndrome and Alzheimer's Disease. *Brain Research, 806,* 55–59.

Lachenmeyer, J. R., & Muni-Brander, P. (1988). Eating disorders in a nonclinical adolescent population: Implications for treatment. *Adolescence, 23* (90), 303–312. r10

Ladame, F., & Jeanneret, O. (1982). Suicide in adolescence: Some comments on epidemiology and prevention. *Journal of Adolescence, 5,* 355–366.

Ladd, G. W. (1999). Peer relationships and social competence during early and middle childhood. *Annual Review of Psychology, 50,* 333–359.

Laederach, J., Fischer, W., Bowen, P., & Ladame, F. (1999). Common risk factors in adolescent suicide attempters revisited. *Crisis, 20,* 15–22.

Lagercrantz, H., & Slotkin, T. A. (1986). The "stress" of being born. *Scientific American, 254,* 100–107.

Lahey, B. B., Gordon, R. A., Loeber, R., Stouthamer-Loeber, M., & Farrington, D. P. (1999). Boys who join gangs: A prospective study of predictors of first gang. *Journal of Abnormal Child Psychology, 27,* 261–276.

Laitinen-Krispijn, S., Van der Ende, J., Hazebroek-Kampschreur, A. A. J. M, & Verhulst, F. C. (1999). Pubertal maturation and the development of behavioural and emotional problems in early adolescence. *Acta Psychiatrica Scandinavica, 99,* 16–25.

Lam, T. C. L. (1992). Review of practices and problems in the evaluation of bilingual education. *Review of Educational Research, 62,* 181–203.

Lamanna, M. A., & Reidmann, A. (1994). Marriages and families: Making choices and facing change (5th ed.). Belmont, Calif.: Wadsworth.

Lamaze, F. (1972). *Painless childbirth: The Lamaze method.* New York: Pocket Books.

Lamb, M. E. (1980). The development of parent-infant attachments in the first two years of life. In F. A. Pedersen (Ed.), The father-infant relationship: Observational studies in the family setting. New York: Praeger, 21–42.

Lamb, M. E. (1997). The role of the father in child development (3rd. ed.). New York : Wiley.

Lamb, M. E., & Elster, A. B. (1985). Adolescent mother-infant-father relationships. *Developmental Psychology, 21,* 768–773.

Lamb, M. E., Easterbrooks, M. A., & Holden, G. W. (1980). Reinforcement and punishment among preschoolers: Characteristics, effects and correlates. *Child Development, 51,* 1230–1236.

Lamb, M. E., Frodi, M., Hwang, C., & Frodi, A. M. (1983). Effects of paternal involvement on infant preferences for mothers and fathers. *Child Development, 54,* 450–458.

Lamb, M. E., Keterlinus, R. D., & Fracasso, M. P. (1992). Parent-child relationships. In M. H. Bornstein & M. E. Lamb (Eds.), *Developmental psychology: An advanced textbook.* Hillsdale, NJ: Erlbaum

Lambert, W. E. (1975). Culture and language as factors in learning and education. In A. Wolfgang (Ed.), Education of immigrant students. Toronto: Ontario Institute for Studies in Education.

Lamson, S. R. (1995). Media violence has increased the murder rate. In C. Wekesser (Ed.), *Violence in the media.* San Diego, CA: Greenhaven Press.

Landesman, S., & Ramey, C. (1989). Developmental psychology and mental retardation: Integrating scientific principles with treatment practices. *American Psychologist, 44,* 409–415.

Landine, J., & Stewart, J. (1998). Relationship between metacognition, motivation, locus of control, self-efficacy, and academic achievement. *Canadian Journal of Counselling, 32,* 200–212.

Landow, R. W., & Glenwick, D. S. (1999). Stress and coping in homeless children. *Journal of Social Distress & the Homeless, 8,* 79–93.

Landry, R. (1987). Additive bilingualism, schooling, and special education: A minority group perspective. *Canadian Journal for Exceptional Children, 3,* 109–114.

Lane-Garon, P. S. (1998). Developmental considerations: Encouraging perspective taking in student mediators. *Mediation Quarterly, 16,* 201–217.

Lang, P. (1999). Counselling, counselling skills and encouraging pupils to talk: Clarifying and addressing confusion. *British Journal of Guidance & Counselling, 27,* 23–33.

Langford, P. E. (1997). Separating judicial from legislative reasoning in moral dilemma interviews. *Child Development, 68,* 1105–1116.

Langkamp, D. L., Kim, Y., & Pascoe, J. M. (1998). Temperament of preterm infants at 4 months of age: Maternal ratings and perceptions. *Journal of Developmental and Behavioral Pediatrics, 19,* 391–396.

Langlois, J. H., & Roggman, L. A. (1990). Attractive faces are only average. *Psychological Science, 1,* 115–121.

Langlois, J. H., & Stephan, C. W. (1981). Beauty and the beast: The role of physical attractiveness in the development of peer relations and social behavior. In S. S. Brehm, S. M. Kassin, & F. X. Gibbons (Eds.), Developmental social psychology. New York: Oxford University Press.

Langlois, J. H., Ritter, J. M., Roggman, L. A., & Vaughn, L. S., (1991). Facial diversity and infant preferences for attractive faces. *Developmental Psychology, 27,* 79–84.

Langlois, J. H., Roggman, L. A., & Rieser-Danner, L. A. (1990). Infants' differential social responses to attractive and unattractive faces. *Developmental Psychology, 26,* 153–159.

Langs, R., Badalamenti, A. F., & Savage-Rumbaugh, S. (1996). Two mathematically defined expressive language stgstructures in humans and chimpanzees. *Behavioral Science, 41,* 124–135.

Langton, J. (1997, Dec. 1). American doctors selling made-to-order embryos. *The Daily Telegraph* (London), p. 6.

Lansford, J. E., & Parker, J. G. (1999). Children's interactions in triads: Behavioral profiles and effects of gender and patterns of friendships among members. *Developmental Psychology, 35,* 80–93.

Lapsley, D. K. (1990). Continuity and discontinuity in adolescent social cognitive development. In R. Montemayor, G. R. Adams, & T. P. Gullotta (Eds.), Advances in adolescent development: Vol. 2. From childhood to adolescence: A transitional period? Newbury Park, Calif.: Sage.

Larson, R. W. (1997). The emergence of solitude as a constructive domain of experience in early adolescence. *Child Development, 68,* 80–93.

Larson, R. W. (1999). The uses of loneliness in adolescence. In K. J. Rotenberg & S. Hymel (Eds.), *Loneliness in childhood and adolescence.* New York: Cambridge University Press.

Larson, R., & Ham, M. (1993). Stress and "Storm and Stress" in early adolescence: The relationship of negative events with dysphoric affect. *Developmental Psychology, 29,* 130–140.

Laszlo, J. I. (1986). Development of perceptual motor abilities in children from 5 years to adults. In C. Pratt, A. F. Garton, W. E. Tunmer, & A. R. Nesdale (Eds.), Research issues in child development. Boston: Allen & Unwin.

Latané, R., & Darley, J. M. (1970). The unresponsive bystander: Why doesn't he help? New York: Appleton-Century-Crofts.

Lay, C., & Verkuyten, M. (1999). Ethnic identity and its relation to personal self-esteem: A comparison of Canadian-born and foreign born Chinese adolescents. *Journal of Social Psychology, 139,* 288–300.

Lazar, I., Darlington, R., Murray, H., Royce, J., & Snipper, A. (1982). Lasting effects of early education: A report from the Consortium for Longitudinal Studies. *Monographs of the*

Society for Research in Child Development, 47, no. 195.

Lazarus, R. S. (1993). From psychological stress to the emotions: A history of changing outlooks. *Annual Review of Psychology, 44,* 1–21.

Le monde au chevet de l'enfance menacee. (1990, September 29). *Le Monde,* p. 15.

le Roux, J. (1996a). The worldwide phenomenon of street children: Conceptual analysis. *Adolescence, 31,* 965–971.

le Roux, J., & Smith, C. S. (1998a). Is the street child phenomenon synonymous with deviant behavior? *Adolescence, 33,* 915–925.

le Roux, J., & Smith, C. S. (1998b). Public perceptions of, and reactions to, street children. *Adolescence, 33,* 901–913.

le Roux, J., & Smith, C. S. (1998c). Psychological characteristics of South African street children. *Adolescence, 33,* 891–899.

Leaper, C., Anderson, K. J., & Sanders, P. (1998). Moderators of gender effects on parents' talk to their children: A meta-analysis. *Developmental Psychology, 34,* 3–27.

Leask, S. J., & Crow, T. J. (1997). How far does the brain lateralize? An unbiased method for determining the optimum degree of hemispheric specialization. *Neuropsychologia, 35,* 1381–1387.

Leboyer, F. (1975). *Birth without violence.* New York: Random House.

Leclerc, G., Lefrançois, R., Dube, M., Hebert, R., & Gaulin, P. (1998). The self-actualization concept: A content validation. *Journal of social Behavior and Personality, 13,* 69–84

Ledoux, S., Choquet, M., & Manfredi, R. (1993). Associated factors for self-reported binge eating among male and female adolescents. *Journal of Adolescence, 16,* 75–91.

Lee, B. C. P., Kuppusamy, K., Grueneich, R., El-Ghazzawy, O., Gordon, R. E., Lin, W., & Haacke, M. (1999). Hemispheric language dominance in children demonstrated by functional magnetic resonance imaging. *Journal of Child Neurology, 14,* 78–82.

Lee, K. (1992). Pattern of night waking and crying of Korean infants from 3 months to 2 years old and its relation with various factors. *Journal of Developmental and Behavioral Pediatrics, 13,* 326–330.

Lee, V. E., Brooks-Gunn, J., & Schnur, E. (1988). Does Head Start work? A 1-year follow-up comparison of disadvantaged children attending Head Start, no preschool, and other preschool programs. *Developmental Psychology, 24,* 210–222.

Leferink, K. (1998). Sportswissenschaft, Fachbereich Erziehungwiss, Berlin, Germany. Private and public in the lives of chronic schizophrenic patients. *Psychiatry: Interpersonal & Biological Processes., 61,* 147–162.

Lefkowitz, M., Eron, L., Walder, L., & Huesmann, L. R. (1972). Television violence and child aggression: A follow-up study. In G. A. Comstock & E. A. Rubinstein (Eds.), Television and social behavior (Vol. 3). Washington, D.C.: U.S. Government Printing Office.

Lefrançois, G. R. (1967). Jean Piaget's developmental model: Equilibration-through-adaptation. *Alberta Journal of Educational Research, 13,* 161–171.

Lefrançois, G. R. (1968). A treatment hierarchy for the acceleration of conservation of substance. *Canadian Journal of Psychology, 22,* 277–284.

Lefrançois, G. R. (1973). *Of children: An introduction to child development.* Belmont, Calif.: Wadsworth.

Lefrançois, G. R. (1983). *Psychology* (2nd ed.). Belmont, Calif.: Wadsworth.

Lefrançois, G. R. (2000). *Psychology for teaching: The bear is not a choir boy.* Belmont, Cal.: Wadsworth/ITP.

Legerstee, M. (1991). Changes in the quality of infant sounds as a function of social and nonsocial stimulation. *First Language, 11,* 327–343.

Leibel, R. L. (1997). And finally, genes for human obesity. *Nature Genetics, 16,* 218–220.

Leinbach, M. D., & Fagot, B. I. (1986). Acquisition of gender labels: A test for toddlers. *Sex Roles, 15,* 655–667.

Leiter, J., & Johnsen, M. C. (1997). Child maltreatment and school performance declines: An event-history analysis. *American Educational Research Journal, 34,* 563–589.

Lemery, K. S., Goldsmith, H. H., Klinnert, M. D., & Mrazek, D. A. (1999). Developmental models of infant and childhood temperament. *Developmental Psychology 35,* 189–204.

Lendon, C. L., Ashall, F., & Goate, A. M. (1997). Exploring the etiology of Alzheimer disease using molecular genetics. *Jama: Journal of the American Medical Association, 277,* 825–831.

Lenneberg, E. H. (1969). On explaining language. *Science, 164,* 635–643.

Leon, M. (1992). The neurobiology of learning. *Annual Review of Psychology, 43,* 377–398.

Lepore, S. J., & Sesco, B. (1994). Distorting children's reports and interpretations of events through suggestion. *Applied Psychology, 79,* 108–120.

Lerner, R. M. (1985). Individual and context in developmental psychology: Conceptual and theoretical issues. In J. R. Nesselroade & A. Von Eye (Eds.), Individual development and social change: Explanatory analysis (pp. 155–188). New York: Academic Press.

Lerner, R. M. (1987). The concept of plasticity in development. In J. J. Gallagher & C. T. Ramey (Eds.), The malleability of children. Baltimore: Brookes.

Lerner, R. M. (1991). Changing organism-context relations as the basic process of development: A developmental contextual perspective. *Developmental Psychology, 27,* 27–32.

Lerner, R. M., & Galambos, N. L. (1998). Adolescent development: Challenges and opportunities for research, programs and policies. *Annual Review of Psychology, 49,* 413–446.

Lerner, R. M., & Korn, S. J. (1972). The development of body-build stereotypes in males. *Child Development, 43,* 908–920.

Lerner, R. M., & Shea, J. A. (1982). Social behavior in adolescence. In B. B. Wolman and others (Eds.), Handbook of developmental psychology. Englewood Cliffs, N.J.: Prentice-Hall.

Lerner, R. M., (1993). The demise of the nature-nurture dichotomy. *Human Development, 36,* 119–124.

Lerner, R. M., Lerner, J. V., Winelle, M., Hooker, K., Lenez, K., and others. (1986). Children and adolescents in their contexts: Tests of the goodness of fit model. In R. Plomin & J. Dunn (Eds.), The study of temperament: Changes, continuities and challenges. Hillsdale, N.J.: Lawrence Erlbaum.

Leslie, A. M. (1988). Some implications of pretense for mechanisms underlying the child's theory of mind. In J. W. Astington, P. L. Harris, & D. R. Olson (Eds.), Developing the-

ories of mind. New York: Cambridge University Press.

Lesser, H. (1977). Television and the preschool child: A psychological theory of instruction and curriculum development. New York: Academic Press.

LeTendre, G. K. (1999). The problem of Japan: Qualitative studies and international educational comparisons. *Educational Researcher, 28,* 38–45.

Levine, J. M., Resnick, L. B., & Higgins, E. T. (1993). Social foundations of cognition. *Annual Review of Psychology, 44,* 585–612.

Levine, M. P., Smolak, L., & Schermer, F. (1996). Media analysis and resistance by elementary school children in the primary prevention of eating problems. *Eating Disorders: The Journal of Treatment and Prevention, 4,* 310–322.

Levine, R. A. (1987). Women's schooling, patterns of fertility, and child survival. *Educational Researcher, 16,* 21–27.

Levitt, M. J., Guacci, N., & Coffman, S. (1993). Social network relations in infancy: An observational study. *Merrill-Palmer Quarterly, 39,* 233–251.

Levy, G. D. (1993). Introduction: An integrated collection on early gender-role development. *Developmental Review, 13,* 123–125.

Levy, G. D., & Fivush, R. (1993). Scripts and gender: A new approach for examining gender-role development. *Developmental Review, 13,* 126–146.

Lewin, R. (1975, September). Starved brains. *Psychology Today,* 29–33.

Lewis, M., & Lee-Painter, S. (1974). An interactional approach to the mother-infant dyad. In M. Lewis & L. A. Rosenblum (Eds.), The effect of an infant on its caregiver. New York: John Wiley.

Lewis, M., Sullivan, M. W., & Vasen, A. (1987). Making faces: Age and emotion differences in the posing of emotional expressions. *Developmental Psychology, 23,* 690–697.

Li, C., Nuttall, R. L., & Zhao, S. (1999). A test of the Piagetian water-level task with Chinese students. *Journal of Genetic Psychology, 160,* 369–380.

Liben, L. (1975). Perspective-taking skills in young children: Seeing the world through rose-colored glasses. Paper presented at the meeting of the Society for Research in Child Development, Denver, April.

Liberty, C., & Ornstein, P. A. (1973). Age differences in organization and recall: The effects of training in categorization. *Journal of Experimental Child Psychology, 15,* 169–186.

Lieberman, A. B. (1987). Giving birth. New York: St. Martin's Press.

Lieberman, M., Doyle, A. B., & Markiewicz, D. (1999). Developmental patterns in security of attachment to mother and father in late childhood and early adolescence: Associations with peer relations. *Child Development, 70,* 202–213.

Liebert, R. M., & Schwartzberg, N. S. (1977). Effects of mass media. In M. R. Rosenzweig & L. W. Porter (Eds.), Annal review of psychology (Vol. 28). Palo Alto, Calif: Annual Reviews.

Lieblich, A. (1982). *Kibbutz Makom: Report from an Israeli kibbutz.* London: Andre Deutsch.

Liggins, G. C. (1988). The onset of labor: An historical review. In C. T. Jones (Ed.), Research in perinatal medicine (VII): Fetal and neonatal development. Ithaca, N.Y.: Perinatology Press.

Liljestrom, R. (1982). The family in China yesterday and today. In R. Liljestrom, E. Noren-Bjorn, G. Schyl-Bjurman, B. Ohrn, L. H. Gustasfsson, & O. Lofgren (Eds.), Young children in China. Clevedon, Avon, England: Multilingual Matters Ltd.

Lillard, A. (1998). Playing with a theory of mind. In O. Saracho and B. Spodek (Eds.), *Multiple perspectives on play in early childhood education.* Albany, NY: SUNY Press.

Lindberg, A. C., Kelland, A., & Nicol, C. J. (1999). Effects of observational learning on acquisition of an operant response in horses. *Applied Animal Behaviour Science, 61,* 187–199.

Lindstrom, P. (1996). Family interaction, neighbourhood context and deviant behaviour: A research note. *Studies on Crime and Crime Prevention, 5,* 113–119.

Linich, M. (1999). Beyond constructivism in the life sciences. In J. A. Chambers (Ed), *Selected papers from the 10th International Conference on College Teaching and Learning. (pp. 99–108).* Jacksonville, FL: Florida Community College.

Linker, J. S., Stolberg, A. L., & Green, R. G. (1999). Family communication as a mediator of child adjustment to divorce. *Journal of Divorce & Remarriage, 30,* 83–97.

Linn, M. C., & Hyde, J. S. (1989). Gender, mathematics, and science. *Educational Researcher, 18,* 17–27.

Lipschitz, D. S., Winegar, R. K., Nicolaou, A. L., Hartnick, E., Wolfson, M., & Southwick, S. M. (1999). Perceived abuse and neglect as risk factors for suicidal behavior in adolescent inpatients. *Journal of Nervous & Mental Disease. 187,* 32–39.

Lipsitt, L. P. (1982). Infant learning. In T. M. Field, A. Huston, H. C. Quay, L. Troll, & G. E. Finley (Eds.), Review of human development. New York: John Wiley.

Lipsitt, L. P., Engen, T., & Kaye, H. (1963). Developmental changes in the olfactory threshold of the neonate. *Child Development, 34,* 371–376.

Liu, D. T. (1991). Introduction and historical perspectives. In D. T. Liu (Ed.), A practical guide to chorion villus sampling. New York: Oxford University Press.

Livesey, D. J., & Intili, D. (1996). A gender difference in visual-spatial ability in 4-year-old children: Effects on performance of a kinesthetic acuity task. *Journal of Experimental Child Psychology, 63,* 436–446.

Lobel, T. E., & Shavit, T. (1997). Targets' and perceivers' occupation and gender as determinants of social judgments. *Social Behavior & Personality, 25,* 339–343.

Locke, J. (1699). *Some thoughts concerning education* (4th ed.). London: A. & J. Churchills.

Lockhart, A. S. (1980). Motor learning and motor development during infancy and childhood. In C. B. Corbin (Ed.), A textbook of motor development. Dubuque, Iowa: Wm. C. Brown.

Lockwood, G. M. (1997). Donating life: Practical and ethical issues in gamete donation. In F. Shenfield & C. Sureau (Eds.), *Ethical dilemmas in assisted reproduction.* London: Parthenon.

Loeber, R., Farrington, D. P., Stouthamer-Loeber, M., & Van Kammen, W. B. (1998). Multiple risk factors for multiproblem boys: Co-occurrence of delinquency, substance use, attention deficit, conduct problems, physical aggression, covert behavior, depressed mood, and shy/withdrawn behavior. In R. Jessor (Ed.), New perspectives on adolescent risk

behavior. New York: Cambridge University Press.

Loehlin, J. C. (1985). Fitting heredity-environment models jointly to twin and adoption data from the California Psychological Inventory. *Behavior Genetics, 15,* 199–221.

Loehlin, J. C., Horn, J. M., & Willerman, L. (1997). Heredity, environment and IQ in the Texas Adoption Project. In R. J. Sternberg & E. L. Grigorenko (Eds.), *Intelligence, heredity, and environment.* New York: Cambridge University Press.

Loehlin, J. C., Willerman, L., & Horn, J. M. (1988). Human behavior genetics. *Annual Review of Psychology, 39,* 101–133. Long, L., & Long, T. (1983). The handbook for latchkey children and their parents. New York: Arbor House.

Lohman, D. F. (1993). Teaching and testing to develop fluid abilities. *Educational Researcher, 22,* 12–23.

Long, V. O. (1991). Gender role conditioning and women's self-concept. *Journal of Humanistic Education and Development, 30,* 19–29.

Loo, S. K., Teale, P. D., & Reite, M. L. (1999). EEG correlates of methylphenidate response among children with ADHD: A preliminary report. *Biological Psychiatry, 45,* 1657–1660.

Lookabaugh, S. L., & Fu, V. R. (1992). Children's use of inanimate transitional objects in coping with hassles. *Journal of Genetic Psychology, 153,* 37–46.

Looney, M. A., & Plowman, S. A. (1990). Passing rates of American children and youth on the FITNESS-GRAM criterion-referenced physical fitness standards. *Research Quarterly for Exercise and Sport, 61,* 215–223.

Lorenz, K. (1952). King Solomon's ring. London: Methuen.

Louden, W., & Hunter, J. (1999). One hundred children: Baseline assessment of literacy in the early years of education. *Journal of Research in Reading, 22,* 89–94.

Lourenco, O., & Machado, A. (1996). In defense of Piaget's theory: A reply to 10 common criticisms. *Psychological Review, 103,* 143–164.

Love, H., & Walthall, J. E. (1977). A handbook of medical, educational, and psychological information for teachers of physically handicapped children. Springfield, Ill.: Charles C. Thomas.

Lowenthal, B. (1997). Useful early childhood assessment: Play-based, interviews and multiple intelligences. *Early Child Development & Care, 129,* 43–49.

Lowery, C. R., & Settle, S. A. (1985). Effects of divorce on children: Differential impact of custody and visitation patterns. *Family Relations, 34,* 455–463.

Lozoff, B. (1989). Nutrition and behavior. *American Psychologist, 44,* 231–236.

Lucas, A., & St. James-Roberts, I. (1998). Crying, fussing, and colic behaviour in breast- and bottle-fed infants. *Early Human Development, 53,* 9–18.

Luke, C. (1988). *Television and your child: A guide for concerned parents.* Toronto: Kagan & Woo.

Lummaa, Vi., Vuorisalo, T., Barr, R. G., & Lehtonen, L. (1998). Why cry? Adaptive significance of intensive crying in human infants. *Evolution & Human Behavior, 19,* 193–202.

Lupart, J. L., & Pyryt, M. C. (1996). "Hidden gifted" students: Underachiever prevalence and profile. *Journal for the Education of the Gifted, 20,* 36–53.

Luthar, S. S., & Cushing, G. (1997). Substance use and personal adjustment among disadvantaged teenagers: A six-month prospective study. *Journal of Youth and Adolescence, 26,* 353–372.

Lynn, D. B. (1974). The father: His role in child development. Monterey, Calif.: Brooks/Cole.

Lynn, D. B. (1979). Daughters and parents: Past, present and future. Monterey, Calif.: Brooks/Cole.

Lyon, M., Chatoor, I., Atkins, D., Silber, T., Mosimann, J., & Gray, J. (1997). Testing the hypothesis of the multidimensional model of anorexia nervosa in adolescents. *Adolescence, 32,* 101–113.

Macas, E., Imthurn, B., Borsos, M., Rosselli, M., Maurer-Major, E., & Keller, P. J. (1998). Impairment of the developmental potential of frozen-thawed human zygotes obtained after intracytoplasmic sperm injection. *Fertility and Sterility, 69,* 630–635.

Maccoby, E. E., & Jacklin, C. N. (1974). The psychology of sex differences. Stanford, Calif.: Stanford University Press.

Maccoby, E. E., & Jacklin, C. N. (1980). Sex differences in aggression: A rejoinder and reprise. *Child Development, 51,* 964–980.

Maccoby, E. E., & Martin, J. A. (1983). Socialization in the context of the family: Parent-child interaction. In E. M. Hetherington (Ed.), *Handbook of child psychology:* (Vol. 4). *Socialization, personality, and social development* (4th ed.). New York: Wiley.

Macfarlane, A. (1975). Olfaction in the development of social preferences in the human neonate. In Proceedings of CIBA Foundation Symposium, Parent-infant interaction. Amsterdam: Elsevier.

Mackey, M. C. (1998). Women's evaluation of the labor and delivery experience. *Nursing Connections, 11,* 19–32.

Macleod, C. (1999). The "causes" of teenage pregnancy: Review of South African research: Part 2. *South African Journal of Psychology, 29,* 8–16.

Macmillan, D. L., Keogh, B. K., & Jones, R. L. (1986). Special educational reasearch on mildly handicapped learners. In M. C. Wittrock (Ed.), *Handbook of research on teaching* (3rd ed.). New York: Macmillan.

MacQueen, G. M., Rosebush, P. I., & Mazurek, M. E. (1998). Neuropsychiatric aspects of the adult variant of Tay-Sachs disease. *Journal of Neuropsychiatry and Clinical Neurosciences, 10,* 10–19.

MacWhinney, B. (1998). Models of the emergence of language. *Annual Review of Psychology, 49,* 199–227.

Madak, P. R., & Berg, D. H. (1992). The prevention of sexual abuse: An evaluation of "Talking about Touching." *Canadian Journal of Counselling, 26,* 29–40.

Madonna, P. G., Van Scoyk, S., & Jones, D. P. (1991). Family interactions within incest and nonincest families. *American Journal of Psychiatry, 148,* 46–49.

Madsen, M. C. (1971). Developmental and cross-cultural differences in the cooperation and competitive behavior of young children. *Journal of Cross-Cultural Psychology, 2,* 365–371.

Madsen, M. C., & Lancy, D. F. (1981). Cooperative and competitive behavior: Experiments related to ethnic identity and urbanization in Papua, New Guinea. *Journal of Cross-Cultural Psychology, 12,* 389–409.

Maeki-Torkko, E. M., Jaervelin, M. R., Sorri, M. J., Muhli, A. A., & Oja, H. F. V. (1998). Aetiology and risk indicators of hearing impairments in a one-year birth cohort for 1985–86 in Northern Finland. *Scandinavian Audiology, 27*, 237–247.

Magnus, K. B., Cowen, E. L., Wyman, P. A., Fagen, D. B., & Work, W. C. (1999). Correlates of resilient outcomes among highly stressed African-American and White urban children. *Journal of Community Psychology, 27*, 473–488.

Magnusson, D., & Backteman, G. (1978). Longitudinal stability of person characteristics: Intelligence and creativity. *Applied Psychological Measurement, 2*, 481–490.

Main, E. K. (1999). Reducing cesarean birth rates with data-driven quality improvement activities. *Pediatrics, 103*, 374–383.

Main, M. (1995). Recent studies in attachment. In S. Goldberg, R. Muir, & J. Kerr (Eds.), *Attachment theory: Social, developmental, and clinical perspectives.* Hillsdale, N.J.: Analytic Press.

Main, M. (1995). Recent studies in attachment: Overview, with selected implications for clinical work. In S. Goldberg & R. Muir (Eds.), *Attachment theory:*

Main, M. (1996). Introduction to the special section on attachment and psychopathology: 2. Overview of the field of attachment. *Journal of Consulting & Clinical Psychology, 64*, 237–243.

Main, M., & Solomon, J. (1986). Discovery of an insecure, disorganized/disoriented attachment pattern: Procedures, findings, and implications for the classification of behavior. In M. Yogman & T. B. Brazelton (Eds.), *Affective development in infancy.* Norwood, NJ: Ablex.

Males, M. (1993a). Schools, society, and "teen" pregnancy. *Phi Delta Kappan, 74*, 566–568.

Males, M. (1993b). School-age pregnancy. Why hasn't prevention worked? *Journal of School Health, 63*, 429–432.

Malina, R. M. (1990). Physical growth and performance during the transitional years (9 to 16). In R. Montemayor, G. R. Adams, & T. P. Gullotta (Eds.), Advances in adolescent development: Vol. 2. From childhood to adolescence: A transitional period? Newbury Park, Calif.: Sage.

Malina, R. M., & Bouchard, C. (1988). Subcutaneous fat distribution during growth In C. Bouchard & F. E. Johnston (Eds.), Fat distribution during growth and later health outcomes. New York: Liss.

Malina, R. M., & Bouchard, C. (1991). *Growth, maturation, and physical activity.* Champaign, IL: Human Kinetics Books.

Malloy, M. H., & Freeman, D. H. Jr. (1999). Sudden infant death syndrome among twins. *Archives of Pediatrics and Adolescent medicine, 153*, 736–740.

Malpas, T. J., & Darlow, B. A. (1999). Neonatal abstinence syndrome following abrupt cessation of breastfeeding. *New Zealand Medical Journal, 112*, 12–13.

Mandich, M., Simons, C. J., Ritchie, S., Schmidt, D., & Mullett, M. (1994). Motor development, infantile reactions and postural responses of preterm, at-risk infants. *Developmental Medicine and Child Neurology, 36*, 397–405.

Mandler, J. M. (1984). Representation and recall in infancy. In M. Moscovitch (Ed.), Infant memory. New York: Plenum Press.

Manios, Y., Kafatos, A., & Mamalakis, G. (1998). The effects of a health education intervention initiated at first grade over a 3 year period: Physical activity and fitness indices. *Health Education Research, 13*, 593–606.

Manning-Orenstein, G. (1998). A birth intervention: The therapeutic effects of Doula support versus Lamaze preparation on first-time mothers' working models of caregiving. *Alternative Therapies in Health and Medicine, 4*, 73–81.

Manuck, S. B., Flory, J. D., Ferrell, R. E., Dent, K. M., Mann, J. J., & Muldoon, M. F. (1999). Aggression and anger-related traits associated with a polymorphism of the tryptophan hydroxylase geme. *Biological Psychiatry, 45*, 603–614.

March, J. S., Parker, J. D. A., Sullivan, K., & Stallings, P. (1997). The Multidimensional Anxiety Scale for Children (MASC): Factor structure, reliability, and validity. *Journal of the American Academy of Child & Adolescent Psychiatry, 36*, 554–565.

Marcia, J. E. (1966). Development and validation of ego-identity status. *Journal of Personality and Social Psychology, 3*, 551–558.

Marcia, J. E. (1980). Identity in adolescence. In J. Adelson (Ed.), *Handbook of adolescent psychology.* New York: Wiley.

Marcia, J. E. (1993). The relational roots of identity. In J. Kroger (Ed.), *Discussions on ego identity.* Hillsdale, NJ: Erlbaum.

Marcia, J. E., & Friedman, M. L. (1970). Ego identity status in college women. *Journal of Personality, 39*, 249–269.

Marjoribanks, K. (1997). Ordinal position, family environment, and status atttainment among Australian young adults. *Journal of Social Psychology, 137*, 398–399.

Marks, C., Fethers, K., & Mindel, A. (1999). Management of women with recurrent genital herpes in pregnancy in Australia. *Sexually Transmitted Infections, 75*, 55–57.

Markson, L. & Bloom, P. (1997). Evidence against a dedicated system for word learning in children. *Nature, 385*, 813–815.

Marlatt, G. A., Baer, J. S., Donovan, D. M., & Kivlahan, D. R. (1988). Addictive behaviors: Etiology and treatment. *Annual Review of Psychology, 39*, 223–252.

Marsh, H. W. (1989). Sex differences in the development of verbal and mathematics constructs: The high school and beyond study. *American Educational Research Journal, 26*, 191–225.

Marsh, H. W., & Holmes, I. W. MacDonald (1990). Multidimensional self-concepts: Construct validation of responses by children. *American Educational Research Journal, 27*, 89–117.

Marsiglio, W. (1986). Teenage fatherhood: High school accreditation and educational attainment. In A. B. Elster & M. E. Lamb (Eds.), *Adolescent fatherhood.* Hillsdale, N.J.: Lawrence Erlbaum.

Marston, A. R., Jacobs, D. F., Singer, R. D., Widaman, K. F., & Little, T. D. (1988). Characteristics of adolescents at risk for compulsive overeating on a brief screening test. *Adolescence, 23*, 288–302.

Martin, C. L. (1993). New directions for investigating children's gender knowledge. *Developmental Review, 13*, 184–204.

Martin, C. L., & Halverson, C. F. (1987). The role of cognition in sex role acquisition. In D.l B. Carter (Ed.), *Current conceptions of sex roles and sex typing: Theory and research.* New York: Praeger.

Martin, G., & Waite, S. (1994). Parental bonding and vulnerability to adolescent suicide. *Acta Psychiatrica Scandinavica, 89*, 246–254.

Martin, H. (1976). The abused child. Cambridge, Mass.: Ballinger.

Martin, N., & Jardine, R. (1986). Eysenck's contributions to behaviour genetics. In S. Modgil & C. Modgil (Eds.), Hans Eysenck: Consensus and controversy. Philadelphia: Falmer.

Martinez-Pons, M. (1997). The relation of emotional intelligence with selected areas of personal functioning. *Imagination, Cognition & Personality, 17*, 3–13.

Martinsen, O. (1997). The construct of cognitive style and its implications for creativity. *High Ability Studies, 8*, 135–158.

Mascolo, M. F., & Fischer, Kurt W. (1999). The development of representation as the coordination of component systems of action. In I. E. Sigel (Ed.), *Development of mental representation: Theories and applications.* Mahwah, NJ: Lawrence Erlbaum.

Mascolo, M. F., Fischer, K. W., & Neimeyer, R. A. (1999). The dynamic codevelopment of intentionality, self, and social relations. In J. Brandstaedter & R. M. Lerner (Eds.), *Action & self-development: Theory and research through the lift span.* Thousand Oaks, CA: Sage

Masi, W., & Scott, K. (1983). Preterm and full-term infants' visual responses. In T. F. Sostek & A. Sostek, (Eds.), Infants born at risk: Physiological, perceptual and cognitive process. New York: Grune and Stratton.

Maslow, A. H. (1970). Motivation and personality (2nd ed.). New York: Harper & Row.

Mason, M. A., & Mauldon, J. (1996). The new stepfamily requires a new public policy. *Journal of Social Issues, 52*, 11–27.

Mason, W. A., & Kenney, M. D. (1974). Redirection of filial attachments in rhesus monkeys: Dogs as mother surrogates. *Science, 183*, 1209–1211.

Masters, J. C. (1979). Interpreting "imitative" responses in early infancy. *Science, 205*, 215.

Masters, W. H., Johnson, V. E., & Kolodny, R. C. (1988). Crisis: Heterosexual behavior in the age of AIDS. New York: Grove Press.

Masur, E. F. (1993). Transitions in representational ability: Infants' verbal, vocal, and action imitation during the second year. *Merrill-Palmer Quarterly, 39*, 437–455.

Mattson, S. (1998). Maternal-child health in Zimbabwe. *Health Care for Women International, 19*, 231–242.

Maxim, G. W., (1993). The very young (4th ed.). Columbus, Ohio: Merrill. Mazur, A. (1977). On Wilson's sociobiology. *American Journal of Sociology, 83*, 697–700.

Mayer, N. K., & Tronick, E. Z. (1985). Mother's turn-giving signals and infant turn-taking in mother-infant interaction. In T. M. Field & N. A. Fox (Eds.), Social perception in infants. Norwood, N.J.: Ablex.

Mazzocco, M. M. M., Baumgardner, T., Freund, L. S., & Reiss, A. L. (1998). Social functioning among girls with fragile X or Turner syndrome and their sisters. *Journal of Autism and Developmental Disorders, 28*, 509–517.

McBride, B. A., & Darragh, J. (1995). Interpreting the data on father involvement: Implications for parenting programs for men. *Families in Society, 76*, 490–497.

McBrien, C., & Dagenbach, D. (1998). The contributions of source misattributions, acquiescence, and response bias to children's false memories. *American Journal of Psychology, 111*, 509–528.

McCabe, M. P. (1991). Influence of creativity and intelligence on academic performance. *The Journal of Creative Behavior, 25*, 116–122.

McCabe, M. P., & Cummins, R. A. (1998). Sexuality and quality of life among young people. *Adolescence, 331*, 761–773.

McCall, R. B., Applebaum, M. I., & Hogarty, F. S. (1973). Developmental changes in mental test performance. *Monographs of the Society for Research in Child Development, 38*, No. 150.

McCartney, K., & Howley, E. (1992). Parents as instruments of intervention in home-based preschool programs. In L. Okagaki & R. J. Sternberg (Eds.), Directors of development: Influences on the development of children's thinking. Hillsdale, N.J.: Lawrence Erlbaum.

McCartney, K., & Jordan, E. (1990). Parallels between research on child care and research on school effects. *Educational Researcher, 19*, 21–27.

McCartney, K., Bernieri, F., & Harris, M. J. (1990). Growing up and growing apart. A developmental meta-analysis of twin studies. *Psychological Bulletin, 107*, 226–237.

McCartney, K., Scarr, S., Rocheleau, A., Phillips, D., Abbott-Shim, M., Eisenberg, M., Keefe, N., Rosenthal, S., & Rah, J. (1997). Teacher-child interaction and child-care auspices as predictors of social outcomes in infants, toddlers, and preschoolers. *Merrill-Palmer Quarterly, 43*, 426–450.

McCarty, M. E., & Ashmead, D. H. (1999). Visual control of reaching and grasping in infants. *Developmental psychology, 35*, 620–631.

McClelland, D. C. (1973). Testing for competence rather than for "intelligence." *American Psychologist, 28*, 1–14.

McClelland, D., Constantian, C. S., Regalado, D., & Stone, C. (1978, June). Making it to maturity. *Psychology Today*, 42–53, 114.

McClure, F. H., & Teyber, E. (1996). Attention-deficit/hyperactivity disorder: Case illustration of Timmy: An 8-year-old biracial child. In H. McClure & E. Teyber (Eds.), *Child and adolescent therapy: A multicultural-relational approach*. Ft. Worth, TX: Harcourt Brace.

McCormick, L. H. (1997). Treatment with buspirone in a patient with autism. *Archives of Family Medicine, 6*, 368–370.

McCormick, M., Shapiro, S., & Starfield, B. (1984). High-risk young mothers: Infant motality and morbidity in four areas in the United States, 1973–1978. *American Journal of Public Health, 74*, 18–23.

McCune, L. (1993). The development of play as the development of consciousness. *New Directions for Child Development, 59*, 67–80.

McDill, E. L., & Natriello, G. (1998). The effectiveness of the Title I compensatory education program: 1965–1997. *Journal of Education for Students Placed at Risk (Jespar), 3*, 317–335.

McFarland, R. B. (1998). Improvements in parenting are real. *Journal of Psychohistory, 25*, 237–239.

McGillivray, B., & Hayden, M. R. (1992). Single gene alterations. In J. M. Friedman, F. J. Dill, M. R. Hayden, & B. C. McGillivray (Eds.), Genetics. Baltimore: Williams & Wilkins.

McGraw, M. B. (1943). The neuromuscular maturation of the human infant. New York: Columbia University Press.

McGroarty, M. (1992). The societal context of bilingual education. *Educational Researcher, 21*, 7–9, 24.

McIlroy, A. (1993). Test can predict Alzheimer's victims. *Edmonton Journal*, September 18, p. B-1.

McKay, A. (1996). Rural parents' attitudes toward school-based sexual health education. *The Canadian Journal of Human Sexuality, 5*, 15–23.

McKay, J., Sinisterra, L., McKay, A., Gomez, H., & Lloreda, P. (1978). Improving cognitive ability in chronically deprived children. *Science, 200*, 270–278.

McKay, M. M. (1994). The link between domestic violence and child abuse: Assessment and treatment considerations. *Child Welfare, 73*, 29–39.

McKee, M. (1999). Sex and drugs and rock and roll. *British Medical Journal, 318*, 1300–1301.

McKim, M. K., Cramer, K. M., Stuart, B., & O'Connor, D. L. (1999). Infant care decisions and attachment security: The Canadian Transition to Child Care Study. *Canadian Journal of Behavioural Science, 31*, 92–106.

McKusick, V. A. (1998). *Mendelian inheritance in man: A catalog of human genes and genetic disorders* , Vol. 1, 2, 3. (12th ed.). Baltimore: Johns Hopkins University Press.

McLaughlin, C. R., Hull, J. G., Edwards, W. H., Cramer, C. P., & Dewey, W. L. (1993). Neonatal pain: A comprehensive survey of attitudes and practices. *Journal of Pain and Symptom Management, 8*, 7–16.

Mcloyd, V. C. (1998). Socioeconomic disadvantage and child development. *American Psychologist, 53*, 185–204.

McNeil, D. (1970). The acquisition of language: The study of developmental psycholinguistics. New York: Harper & Row.

McNeil, M. C., Polloway, E. A., & Smith, J. D. (1984). Feral and isolated children: Historical review and analysis. *Education and Training of the Mentally retarded, 19*, 70–79.

Mead, M. (1935). *Sex and temperament in three primitive societies*. New York: New American Library.

Meadow, R. (1999). Unnatural sudden infant death. *Archives of Disease in Childhood, 8*, 7–14.

Mednick, S. A. (1962). The associative basis of the creative process. *Psychological Review, 69*, 220–232.

Medoff-Cooper, B., Carey, W. B., & McDevitt, S. C. (1993). The Early Infancy Temperament Questionnaire. *Journal of Developmental and Behavioral Pediatrics, 14*, 230–235.

Meeus, W., Dekovic, M., & Ledema, J. (1997). Unemployment and identity in adolescence; A social comparison perspective. *Career Development Quarterly, 45*, 368–380.

Mehanni, M., Kiberd, B., McDonnell, M., O'Regan, M., & Mathews, T. (1999). Reduce the risk of cot death guidelines. The effect of a revised intervention programme. National Sudden Infant Death Register, Dublin. *Irish Medical Journal, 92*, 266–269.

Meighan, M., Davis, M. W., Thomas, S. P., & Droppleman, P. G. (1999). Living with postpartum depression: The father's experience. *MCN, American Journal of Maternal Child Nursing, 24*, 202–208.

Melican, G. J., & Feldt, L. S. (1980). An empirical study of the Zajonc-Marcus hypothesis for achievement test scores declines. *American Educational Research Journal, 17*, 5–19.

Meline, C. W. (1976). Does the medium matter? *Journal of Communication, 26*, 81–89.

Meltzoff, A. N. (1988). Infant imitation after a 1–week delay: Long-term memory for novel acts and multiple stimuli. *Developmental Psychology, 24*, 470–476.

Meltzoff, A. N., & Moore, M. K. (1983). Newborn infants imitate adult facial gestures. *Child Development, 54*, 702–709.

Meltzoff, A. N., & Moore, M. K. (1989). Imitation in newborn infants: Exploring the range of gestures imitated and the underlying mechanisms. *Developmental Psychology, 25*, 954–962.

Meltzoff, A. N., Gopnik, A., & Repacholi, B. M. (1999). Toddlers' understanding of intentions, desires, and emotions: Explorations of the dark ages. In P. D. Zelazo, J. W. Astington, & D. R. Olson (Eds.), *Developing theories of intention: Social understanding and self-control* Mahwah, NJ: Lawrence Erlbaum.

Meneese, W. B., Yutrzenka, B. A., & Vitale, P. (1992). An analysis of adolescent suicidal ideation. *Current Psychology: Research & Reviews, 11*, 51–58.

Mennella, J. A., & Beauchamp, G. K. (1996). The early development of human flavor preferences. In E. D. Capaldi (Ed.), *Why we eat what we eat: The psychology of eating*. Washjington, DC: American Psychological Association.

Mennella, J. A., & Beauchamp, G. K. (1997). The ontogeny of human flavor perception. In G. K. Beauchamp & L. Bartoschuk (Eds.), *Tasting and smelling. Handbook of perception and cognition* (2nd ed.). San Diego: Academic Press.

Mercer, C. D. (1990). Learning disabilities. In N. G. Haring & L. McCrmick (Eds.), Exceptional children and youth (5th ed.). Columbus, Ohio: Merrill.

Merrell, K. W., & Wolfe, T. M. (1998). The relationship of teacher-rated social skills deficits and ADHD characteristics among kindergarten-age children. *Psychology in the Schools, 35*, 101–110.

Mesibov, G. B., & Van Bourgondien, M. E. (1992). Autism. In S. R. Hooper, G. W. Hynd, & R. E. Mattison, (Eds.), Developmental disorders: Diagnostic criteria and clinical assessment. Hillsdale, N.J.: Lawrence Erlbaum.

Meskill, C. (1998). Commercial television and the limited English proficient child: Implications for language development. In K. Swan, C. Meskill, & S. DeMaio (Eds.), *Social learning from broadcast television*. Creskill, NJ: Hampton.

Messinger, D. S., Fogel, A., & Dickson, K. L. (1999). What's in a smile? *Developmental Psychology, 35*, 701–708.

Meyer, W. J. (1985). Summary, integration, and prospective. In J. B. Dusek (Ed.), Teacher expectancies. Hillsdale, N.J.: Lawrence Erlbaum.

Mielke, K. W. (1983). Formative research on appeal and comprehension in 3–2–1 CONTACT. In J. Bryant & D. R. Anderson (Eds.), Children's understanding of television: Research on attention and comprehension (pp. 241–264). New York: Academic Press.

Miles, H. L. (1997). Anthropomorphism, apes, and language. In R. W. Mitchell, N. S. Thompson, & H. L. Miles (Eds.), *Anthropomorphism, anecdotes, and animals*. SUNY series in philosophy and biology. Albany, N.Y.: State University of New York Press.

Miller, B. C., & Dyk, P. H. (1991). Community of caring effects on adolescent mothers: A program evaluation case study. *Family Relations, 40,* 386–395.

Miller, C. E., Edwards, J. G., Shipley, C. F., & Best, R. B. (1990). Assessment of routine amniocentesis for unexplained maternal serum alpha-fetoprotein elevations. In B. A. Fine, E. Getting, K. Greendale, B. Leopold, & N. W. Paul (Eds.), Strategies in genetic counseling: Reproductive genetics and new technologies. White Plains, N.Y.: March of Dimes Birth Defects Foundation.

Miller, G. A. (1956). The magical number seven, plus or minus two: Some limits on our capacity for processing information. *Psychological Review, 63,* 81–97.

Miller, G. A. (1999). On knowing a word. *Annual Review of Psychology, 50,* 1–19.

Miller, J. M. Jr., & Boudreaux, M. C. (1999). A study of antenatal cocaine use-chaos in action. *American Journal of Obstetrics and Gynecology, 180,* 1427–1431.

Miller, L. B., & Bizzell, R. P. (1983). Long-term effects of four preschool programs: Sixth, seventh, and eighth grades. *Child Development, 54,* 727–741.

Miller, S. A. (1981). Certainty and necessity in the understanding of Piagetian concepts. Paper presented at the Society for Research in Child Development meetings, Boston, April.

Miller-Johnson, S., Coie, J. D., Maumary-Gremaud, A., Lochman, J., & Terry, R. (1999). Relationship between childhood peer rejection and aggression and adolescent delinquency severity and type among African American youth. *Journal of Emotional & Behavioral Disorders, 7,* 137–146.

Minister of Supply and Services Canada (1989). Canada Yearbook (1990). Ottawa: Statistic Canada.

Mitchell, S. A. (1999). Attachment theory and the psychoanalytic tradition: Reflections on human rationality. *Psychoanalytic Dialogues, 9,* 85–107.

Mix, K. S., Levine, S. C., & Huttenlocher, J. (1999). Early fraction calculation ability. *Developmental Psychology, 35,* 164–174.

Miyawaki, K., Strange, W., Verbrugge, R., Liberman, A. M., Jenkins, J. J., & Fujimura, O. (1975). An effect of linguistic experience: The discrimination of r and l by native speakers of Japanese and English. *Perception & Psychophysics, 18,* 331–340.

Mobley, C. E. (1996). Assessment of health knowledge in preschoolers. *Children's Health Care, 25,* 11–18.

Moerk, E. L. (1991). Positive evidence for negative evidence. *First Language, 11,* 219–251.

Moffitt, A. R. (1971). Consonant cue perception by 20–24 week old infants. *Child Development, 42,* 717–731.

Mom had son's sperm removed before he died. (1999, Oct. 2, Cold Springs, Nevada, AP). *Edmonton Sun,* p. 41.

Mom, 60, delivers healthy girl. (1994, Feb. 22, Jerusalem, AP). *Edmonton Sun,* p. 18.

Monachesi, E. D., & Hathaway, S. R. (1969). The personality of delinquents. In J. N. Butcher (Ed.), MMPI: Research developments and clinical applications. New York: McGraw-Hill, 207–219.

Montemayor, R., & Eisen, M. (1977). The development of self-conceptions from childhood to adolescence. *Developmental Psychology, 13,* 314–319.

Montemayor, R., & Flannery, D. J. (1990). Making the transition from childhood to early adolescence. In R. Montemayor, G. R. Adams, & T. P. Gullotta (Eds.), Advances in adolescent development: Vol. 2. From childhood to adolescence: A transitional period? Newbury Park, Calif.: Sage.

Montemayor, R., & Van Komen, R. (1980). Age segregation of adolescents in and out of school. *Journal of Youth and Adolescence, 9,* 371–381.

Montessori, M. (1912). The Montessori method. New York: Frederick A. Stokes.

Montgomery, R. L., Haemmerlie, F. M., & Zoellner, S. (1996). The "imaginary audience," self-handicapping, and drinking patterns among college students. *Psychological Reports, 79,* 783–786.

Monto, M. A. (1996). Lamaze and Bradley childbirth classes: Contrasting perspectives toward the medical model of birth. *Birth, 23,* 193–201.

Moore, C., & Frye, D. (1991). The acquisition and utility of theories of mind. In D. Frye & C. Moore (Eds.), Children's theories of mind: Mental states and social understanding. Hillsdale N.J.: Lawrence Erlbaum.

Moore, R. C. (1986). Childhood's domain: Play and place in child development. London: Croom Helm.

Moorjhani, J. D., Jacob, E. A., & Nathawat, S. S. A comparative study of intelligence and creativity in hearing impaired and normal boys and girls. *Indian Journal of Clinical Psychology, 25,* 200–205.

Moran, J. R. (1999). Measuring bicultural ethnic identity among American Indian adolescents: A factor analytic study. *Journal of Adolescent Research, 99,* 405–427.

Morand, D. A. (1999). Family size and intelligence revisited; The role of emotional intelligence. *Psychological Reports, 84,* 643–649.

Morande, G., Celada, J., Casas, J. J. (1999). Prevalence of eating disorders in a Spanish school-age population. *Journal of Adolescent Health, 24,* 212–219.

Moray, N. (1959). Attention and dichotic listening: Affective cues and the influence of instruction. *Quarterly Journal of Experimental Psychology, 11,* 56–60.

Morelock, M. J. (1996). On the nature of giftedness and talent: Imposing order on chaos. *Roeper Review, 19,* 4–12.

Morgan, H. (1999). *The imagination of early childhood education.* Westport, Ct: Bergin & Garvey.

Morgane, P. J., Austin-LaFrance, R., Bronzino, J., Tonkiss, J., Diaz-Cintra, S., Cintra, L., Kemper, T., & Galler, J. R. (1993). Prenatal malnutrition and development of the brain. *Neuroscience & Biobehavioral Reviews, 17,* 91–128.

Moriarty, A. (1990). Deterring the molester and abuser: Pre-employment testing for child and youth care workers. *Child and Youth Care Quarterly, 18,* 59–65.

Morin, S. F. (1988). AIDS: The challenge to psychology. *American Psychologist, 43,* 838–842.

Morrill, C. M., Leach, J. N., Shreeve, W. C., Radenaugh, M. R. & Linder, K. (1991). Teenage obesity: An academic issue. *International Journal of Adolescence and Youth, 2,* 245–250.

Morris, A. M., Williams, J. M., Atwater, A. E., & Wilmore, J. H. (1982). Age and sex differences in motor performance of 3 through 6 year old children. *Research Quarterly for Exercise and Sport, 534,* 214–221.

Morrison, E., Starks, K., Hyndman, C., & Ronzio, N. (1980). Growing up sexual. New York: Van Nostrand Reinhold.

Morrison, K., & Rosales-Ruiz, J. (1997). The effect of object preferences on task performance and stereotypy in a child with autism. *Research in Developmental Disabilities, 18,* 127–137.

Morrison, T. G., McCleod, L. D., Morrison, M. A., Anderson, D., et al. (1997). Gender stereotyping, homonegativity, and misconceptions about sexually coercive behavior among adolescents. *Youth and Society, 28,* 351–382.

Morsink, C. V. (1985). Learning disabilities. In W. H. Berdine & A. E. Blackhurst (Eds.), An introduction to special education (2nd ed.). Boston: Little, Brown.

Morton, J., & Johnson, M. H. (1991). CONSPEC and CONLERN: A two-process theory of infant face recognition. *Psychological Review, 98,* 164–181.

Moskowitz, B. A. (1978). The acquisition of language. *Scientific American, 239,* 92–108.

Mott, F. L. (1991). Developmental effects of infant care: The mediating role of gender and health. *Journal of Social Issues, 47,* 139–158.

Mowat, F. (1952). People of the deer. New York: Little, Brown.

Moyle, E. (1999, Dec. 9). Cheerleading parents may be hurting kids: Damned with praise? *Edmonton Sun, Express,* p. 46.

Moynahan, E. D. (1973). The development of knowledge concerning the effect of categorization upon free recall. *Child Development, 44,* 238–245.

Mueller, C. M., & Dweck, C. S. (1998). Praise for intelligence can undermine children's motivation and performance. *Journal of Personality and Social Psychology, 75,* 33–52.

Mueller, R. F., & Young, I. D. (1998). *Emery's elements of medical genetics* (10th ed.). New York: Churchill Livingstone.

Mulcahy, B. F. (1991). Developing autonomous learners. *Alberta Journal of Educational Research, 37,* 385–397.

Mulhern, R. K., & Passman, R. H. (1979). The child's behavioral pattern as a determinant of maternal punitiveness. *Child Development, 15,* 417–423.

Mulhern, R. K., Jr., & Passman, R H. (1981). Parental discipline as affected by the sex of the parent, the sex of the child, and the child's apparent responsiveness to discipline. *Developmental Psychology, 17,* 604–613.

Mullin, J. B. (1992). Children prenatally exposed to cocaine and crack: Implications for schools. *B. C. Journal of Special Education, 16,* 282–289.

Mullis, R. L., Youngs, G. A., Jr., Mullis, A. K., & Rathge, R. W. (1993). Adolescent stress: Issues of measurement. *Adolescence, 28,* 280–290.

Munson, K. J., & Crosbie, J. (1998). Effects of response cost in computerized programmed instruction. *Psychological Record. 48,* 233–250.

Murphy-Brennan, M. G., & Oei, T. P. (1999). Is there evidence to show that fetal alcohol syndrome can be prevented? *Journal of Drug Education, 29,* 5–24.

Murphy-Cowan, T. & Stringer, M. (1999). Physical punishment and the parenting cycle: A survey of Northern Irish parents. *Journal of Community & Applied Social Psychology, 9,* 61–71.

Murray, J., Henjum, R., & Freeze, R. (1992). Analysis of male and female experiences with abuse in family of origin. *Canadian Journal of Special Education, 8*, 90–100.

Muuss, R. E. (1975). Theories of adolescence (3rd ed.). New York: Random House.

Muuss, R. E. (1988). Carol Gilligan's theory of sex differences in the development of moral reasoning during adolescence. *Adolescence, 23*, 229–243.

Myers, P. I., & Hammill, D. D. (1990). Learning disabilities: Basic concepts, assessment practices, and instructional strategies (4th ed.). Austin, Tex.: Pro-Ed.

Naglieri, J. A. (1988). *DAP; draw a person: A quantitative scoring system.* New York: Harcourt.

Nahas, V. L., Hillege, S., & Amasheh, N. (1999). Postpartum depression. The lived experiences of Middle Eastern migrant women in Australia. *Journal of Nurse-Midwifery, 44*, 65–74.

Naka, M. (1999). The acquisition of Japanese numerical classifiers by 2–4–year-old children: The role of caretakers' linguistic inputs. *Japanese Psychological Research, 41*, 70–78.

Narváez, D., & Rest, J. (1995). The four components of acting morally. In W. M. Kurtines, & J. L. Gewirtz, (Eds.), *Moral development: An introduction.* Boston: Allyn & Bacon.

Nashelsky, M. B., & Dix, J. D. (1995). The time interval between lethal infant shaking and onset of symptoms. A review of the shaken baby syndrome literature. *American Journal of Forensic Medicine and Pathology, 16*, 154–157.

Nass, C., Moon, Y., & Green, N. (1997). Are machines gender neutral? Gender-stereotypic responses to computers with voices. *Journal of Applied Social Psychology, 27*, 864–876.

National Center for Education Statistics (1995). *Approaching kindergarten: A look at preschoolers in the United States.* Washington, DC: U.S. Department of Education, Office of Educational Research and improvement.

National Center for Health Statistics. (1987). Advance report of final natality statistics, 1985. Monthly vital statistics report (Vol. 36). Washington, D.C.: National Center for Health Statistics.

Nazzi, T., Bertoncini, J., & Mehler, J. (1998). Language discrimination by newborns: Towards an understanding of the role of rhythm. *Journal of Experimental Psychology: Human Perception and Performance, 24*, 756–766.

Neal, J. H. (1983). Children's understanding of their parents' divorces. In L. A. Kurdek (Ed.), Children and divorce: New directions for child development. San Francisco: Jossey-Bass, 3–14.

Nealis, J. T. (1983). Epilepsy. In J. Umbriet (Ed.), Physical disabilities and health impairment: An introduction (pp. 74–85). Columbus, Ohio: Charles E. Merrill.

Neiger, B. L., & Hopkins, R. W. (1988). Adolescent suicide: Character traits of high-risk teenagers. *Adolescence, 23*, 468–475.

Neihart, M. (1999). Systematic risk-taking. *Roeper Review, 21*, 289–292.

Neinstein, L., & Harvey, F. (1998). Effect of low urine specific gravity on pregnancy testing. *Journal of American College Health, 47*, 138–139.

Nelle, M., Kraus, M., Bastert, G., & Linderkamp, O. (1996). Effects of Leboyer childbirth on left- and right systolic time intervals in healthy term neonates. *Journal of Perinatal Medicine, 24*, 513–520.

Nelson, C. A. (1998). The nature of early memory. *Preventive Medicine: An International Journal Devoted to Practice and Theory, 27*, 172–179.

Nelson, J. K. (1998). The meaning of crying based on attachment theory. *Clinical Social Work Journal, 26*, 9–22.

Nelson, K. (1993). Events, narratives, memory: What develops? In C. A. Nelson (Ed.), *Memory and affect in development: The Minnesota Symposia on Child Psychology* (Vol. 26). Hillsdale, NJ: Erlbaum.

Nelson, K. E. (1989). Strategies for first language teaching. In M. L. Rice & R. L. Schiefelbusch (Eds.), Teachability of language. Baltimore: Brookes.

Nesbitt, W. (1993). Self-esteem and moral virtue. *Journal of Moral Education, 22*, 51–54.

Nesca, M. (1997). Seeking a middle ground on the recovered memories controversy. *American Journal of Forensic Psychology, 15*, 3–22.

Neugarten, B. L. (1993). Robert J. Havighurst (1900–1991): Obituary. *American Psychologist, 48*, 1290–1291.

Neuman, S. B. (1991). Literacy in the television age: The myth of the TV effect. Norwood, N.J.: Ablex.

Nevskaya, A. A., Leushina, L. I., & Bondarko, V. M. (1998). Visual impairment and the formation of concrete visual thinking in infants in the first year of life. *Human Physiology, 24*, 275–280.

New, M. J. C., Stevenson, J., & Skuse, D. (1999). Characteristics of mothers of boys who sexually abuse. *Child Maltreatment: Journal of the American Professional Society on the Abuse of Children, 4*, 21–31.

Newburg, D. S. (1999). Human milk glycoconjugates that inhibit pathogens. *Current Medicinal Chemistry, 6*, 117–127.

Newcomb, A. F., Bukowski, W. M., & Pattee, L. (1993). Children's peer relations: A meta-analytic review of popular, rejected, neglected, controversial, and average sociometric status. *Psychological Bulletin, 113*, 99–128.

Newcomb, A. F., Bukowski, W. M., & Pattee, L. (1993). Children's peer relations: A meta-analytic review of popular, rejected, neglected, controversial, and average sociometric status. *Psychological Bulletin, 113*, 99–128.

Newcomb, M. D., & Bentler, P. M. (1988). Consequences of adolescent drug use: Impact on the lives of young adults. Newbury Park, Calif.: Sage.

Newcomb, M. D., & Bentler, P. M. (1989). Substance use and abuse among children and teenagers. *American Psychologist, 44*, 242–248.

Newcombe, N., & Fox, N. A. (1994). Infantile amnesia: Through a glass darkly. *Child Development, 65*, 31–40.

Newman, L. F., & Buka, S. L. (1991). Clipped wings: The fullest look yet at how prenatal exposure to drugs, alcohol, and nicotine hobbles children's learning. *American Educator, 15*, 27–30, 33, 42.

Newsweek, January 6, 1969, p. 37.

Nicolopoulou, A. (1993). Play, cognitive development, and the social world: Piaget, Vygotsky, and beyond. *Human Development, 36*, 1–23.

Nielsen Television Index: Report on television usage. (1984). Hackensack, N.J.: A. C. Nielsen Co.

Nightingale, E. O., & Wolverton, L. (1993). Adolescent rolelessness in modern society. *Teacher's College Record, 94*, 472–486.

Nolan, E. E., Volpe, R. J., Gadow, K. D., & Sprafkin, J. (1999). Developmental, gender, and comorbidity differences in clinically referred *Journal of Emotional & Behavioral Disorders, 7*, 11–20.

Norcia, A. M., & Tyler, C. W. (1985). Spatial frequency sweep VEP: Visual acuity during the first year of life. *Vision Research, 25*, 1399–1408.

Noren Bjorn, E. (1982). Welcome to the preschool. In R. Liljestrom, E. Noren-Bjorn, G. Schyl-Bjurman, B. Ohrn, L. H. Gustasfsson, & O. Lofgren (Eds.), Young children in China. Clevedon, Avon, England: Multilingual Matters Ltd. Nov 1998, 1083–1095.

Nucci, L. P., & Turiel, E. (1978). Social interactions and the development of social concepts in preschool children. *Child Development, 49*, 400–407.

Nucci, L., Guerra, N., & Lee, J. (1991). Adolescent judgments of the personal, prudential, and normative aspects of drug use. *Developmental Psychology, 27*, 841–848.

Nunner-Winkler, G. (1984). Two moralities? A critical discussion of an ethic of care and responsibility versus an ethic of rights and justice. In W. M. Kurtines & J. L. Gewirtz (Eds.), Morality, moral behavior, and moral development. New York: John Wiley.

Oatley, K. (1992). Best laid schemes: The psychology of emotions. New York: Cambridge University Press.

Oatley, K., & Jenkins, J. M. (1992). Human emotions: Function and dysfunction. *Annual Review of Psychology, 32*, 55–85.

Oberklaid, F., Sanson, A., Pedlow, R., Prior, M. (1993). Predicting preschool behavior problems from temperament and other variables in infancy. *Pediatrics, 91*, 113–120.

O'Brien, M. (1996). Child-rearing difficulties reported by parents of infants and toddlers. *Journal of Pediatric Psychology, 21*, 433–446.

O'Connor, T. G., Deater-Deckard, K., Fulker, D., Rutter, M., & Plomin, R. (1998). Genotype-environment correlations in late childhood and early adolescence: Antisocial behavioral problems and coercive parenting. *Developmental Psychology, 34*, 970–981.

Oden, M. (1968). The fulfillment of promise: 40–year follow-up of the Terman gifted group. In R. S. Albert (Ed.), Genius and eminence: The social psychology of creativity and exceptional achievement. New York: Oxford University Press (1983).

Oden, S. (1988). Alternative perspectives on children's peer relationships. In T. D. Yawkey & J. E. Johnson (Eds.), Integrative processes and socialization: Early to middle childhood. Hillsdale, N.J.: Lawrence Erlbaum.

Offer, D., & Offer, J. (1975). From teenage to young manhood: A psychological study. New York: Basic Books. Offer, D. O.,

Offer, D. O., Ostrov, E., & Howard, K. (1981). *The adolescent: A psychological self-protrait.* New York: Basic Books.

Offer, D. O., Ostrov, E., Howard, K., & Atkinson, R. (1988). *The teenage world: Adolescents' self-image in ten countries.* New York: Plenum.

Ohuche, R. O., & Otaalam, B. (Eds.) (1981). *The African child and his environment.* New York: Pergamon Press.

Okonkwo, R. U. N. (1997), Moral development and culture in Kohlberg's theory: A Nigerian (Igbo) evidence. *Ife Psychologia: an International Journal, 5*, 117–128.

O'Koon, J. (1997). Attachment to parents and peers in late adolescence and their relationship with self-image. *Adolescence, 32,* 471–482.

O'Leary, K. D., Kaufman, K., Kass, R. E., & Drabman, R. S. (1974). The effects of loud and soft reprimands on the behavior of disruptive students. In A. R. Brown & C. Avery (Eds.), *Modifying children's behavior: A book of readings.* Springfield, Il.: Charles C. Thomas.

Olson, D. R. (1986). The cognitive consequences of literacy. *Canadian Psychology, 27,* 109–121.

Olson, D. R., Astington, J. W., & Zelazo, P. D. (1999). Introduction: Actions, intentions, and attributions. In P. D. Zelazo, J. W. Astington, & D. R. Olson (Eds.), *Developing theories of intention: Social understanding and self-control* Mahwah, NJ: Lawrence Erlbaum.

Olweus, D. (1997). Bully/victim problems in school: Knowledge base and an effective intervention program. *Irish Journal of Psychology, 18,* 170–190.

Ondis, G. W., Gibson-Cline, J., Dragoon, M., & Jones, C. (1996). Continental United States. In J. Gibson-Cline (Ed.), *Adolescence: From crisis to coping: A thirteen-nation study.* Boston: Butterworth/Heinemann.

Oppawsky, J. (1999). Psychosomatic reactions of very young children to divorce: Elective mutism, tic and Erl-Koenigs syndrome. *Journal of Divorce & Remarriage, 30,* 71–84.

Opper, S. (1977). Concept development in Thai urban and rural children. In P. R. Dasen (Ed.), Piagetian psychology: Cross-cultural contributions. New York: Gardner Press.

O'Reilly, A. W., & Bornstein, M. H. (1993). Caregiver-child interaction in play. *New Directions for Child Development, 59,* 55–66.

Ormond, K. E. (1997). Update and review: Maternal serum screening. *Journal of Genetic Counseling, 6,* 395–417.

Ornstein, P. A., Baker-Ward, L., & Naus, M. J. (1988). The development of mnemonic skill. In F. E. Weinert & M. Perlmutter (Eds.), Memory development: Universal changes and individual differences. Hillsdale, N.J.: Lawrence Erlbaum.

Oster, H., Daily, L., & Goldenthal, P. (1989). Processing facial affect. In A. W. Young & H. D. Ellis (Eds.), Handbook of research on face processing. Amsterdam: North Holland.

Ostrov, E., Howard, K. (1981). The adolescent: A psychological self-portrait. New York: Basic Books. Offer, D. O.,

Ostrov, E., Howard, K. (1984). Patterns of adolescent self-image. San Francisco: Jossey-Bass. Offer, D. O.,

Ostrov, E., Howard, K., & Atkinson, R. (1988). The teenage world: Adolescents' self-image in ten countries. New York: Plenum Press.

Ottino, J. (1999). Suicide attempts during adolescence: Systematic hospitalization and crisis treatment. *Crisis, 20,* 41–48.

Overton, W. F. (1973). On the assumptive base of the nature-nurture controversy: Additive versus interactive conceptions. *Human Development, 16,* 74–89.

Ozturk, M., & Ozturk, O. M. (1990). Thumbsucking and falling asleep. *Turkish Journal of Pediatrics, 32,* 161–174.

Paardekooper, B., de Jong, J. T. V. M., & Hermanns, J. M. A. (1999). The psychological impact of war and the refugee situation on South Sudanese children in refugee camps in Northern Uganda: An exploratory study. *Journal of Child Psychology and Psychiatry and Allied Disciplines, 40,* 529–536.

Packard, V. (1968). *The sexual wilderness.* New York: Pocket Books.

Packard, V. (1983). Our endangered children: Growing up in a changing world. Boston: Little, Brown.

Padilla, A. M. (1991). English only vs. bilingual education: Ensuring a language-competent society. *Journal of Education, 173,* 38–51.

Paetsch, J. J., & Bertrand, L. D. (1999). Victimization and delinquency among Canadian Youth. *Adolescence, 34,* 351–367.

Page, E. B., & Grandon, G. M. (1979). Family configuration and mental ability. Two theories contrasted with U.S. data. *American Educational Research Journal, 16,* 257–272.

Paikoff, R. L., & Brooks-Gunn, J. (1991). Do parent-child relationships change during puberty? *Psychological Bulletin, 110,* 47–66.

Painter, K. (1997). A brief history of the AIDS epidemic. *USA Today,* Sept. 09.

Paley, V. G. (1984). Boys and girls: Superheroes in the doll corner. Chicago: University of Chicago Press.

Paley, V. G. (1986). Mollie is three: Growing up in School. Chicago: University of Chicago Press.

Paley, V. G. (1997). *The girl with the brown crayon.* Cambridge, MA: Harvard University Press.

Palladino, P., Poli, P., Masi, G., & Marcheschi, M. (1997). Impulsive-reflective cognitive style, metacognition, and emotion in *Perceptual & Motor Skills., 84,* 47–57.

Pallas, A. M., Natriello, G., & McDill, E. L. (1989). The changing nature of the disadvantaged population: Current dimensions and future trends. *Educational Researcher, 18,* 16–22.

Palmlund, I., Apfel, R., Buitendijk, S., Cabau, A., & Forsberg, J. G. (1993). Effects of diethylstilbestrol (DES) medication during pregnancy: From a symposium at the 10th International Congress of ISPOG. *Journal of Psychosomatic Obstetrics and Gynecology, 14,* 71–89.

Pangrazi, R. P., & Corbin, C. B. (1993). Physical fitness: Questions teachers ask. *Journal of Physical Education, Recreation & Dance, 64,* 14–19.

Pape, K. E., Kirsch, S. E., Galil, A., White, M. A., & Chipman, M. (1994). Neuromuscular approach to the motor deficits of cerebral palsy: A pilot study. *Journal of Pediatric Orthopaedics, 13,* 628–633.

Papousek, M. & von Hofacker, N. (1998). Persistent crying in early infancy: A nontrivial condition of risk for the developing mother-infant relationship. *Child: Care, Health & Development, 24,* 395–424.

Paris, S. G., & Lindauer, B. K. (1976). The role of inference in children's comprehension and memory for sentences. *Cognitive Psychology, 8,* 217–227.

Paris, S. G., & Lindauer, B. K. (1982). Cognitive development in infancy. In B. B. Wolman and others (Eds.), Handbook of developmental psychology. Englewood Cliffs, N.J.: Prentice-Hall.

Park, K. A., Lay, K. L., & Ramsay, L. (1993). Individual differences and developmental changes in preschoolers' friendship. *Developmental Psychology, 29,* 264–270.

Parke, R. D. (1970). The role of punishment in the socialization process. In R. A. Hoppe, G. A. Milton, & E. C. Simmel (Eds.), Early experiences and the process of socialization. New York: Academic Press.

Parke, R. D. (1979). Perspectives on father-infant interaction. In J. D. Osofsky (Ed.), Handbook of infant development. New York: John Wiley.

Parke, R. D., MacDonald, K. B., Burks, V. M., Carson, J., Bhavnagri, N., et al. (1989). Family and peer systems: In search of linkages. In K. Kreppner & R. M. Lerner (Eds.), Family systems of life span development. Hillsdale, N.J.: Lawrence Erlbaum.

Parker, J. G., & Asher, S. R. (1993). Friendship and friendship quality in middle childhood: Links with peer group acceptance and feelings of loneliness and social dissatisfaction. *Developmental Psychology, 29,* 611–621.

Parkhurst, J. T., & Hopmeyer, A. (1999). Developmental change in the sources of loneliness in childhood and adolescence: Constructing a theoretical model. In K. J. Rotenberg & S. Hymel (Eds.), *Loneliness in childhood and adolescence.* New York: Cambridge University Press.

Parnes, S. J., & Harding, H. E. (Eds.). (1961). A source-book for creative thinking. New York: Charles Scribner's.

Parten, M. B. (1932). Social participation among preschool children. *Journal of Abnormal Social Psychology, 27,* 243–270.

Pasley, K., Dollahite, D. C., & Ihinger-Tallman, M. (1993). Bridging the gap: Clinical applications of research findings on the spouse and stepparent roles in remarriage. *Family Relations, 42,* 315–322.

Pasquet P., Biyong, A. M., Rikong-Adie, H., Befidi-Mengue, R., Garba, M. T., & Froment, A. (1999). Age at menarche and urbanization in Cameroon: current status and secular trends. *Annals of Human Biology, 26,* 89–97.

Passino, A. W., Whitman, T. L., Borkowski, J. G., Schellenbach, C. J., Maxwell, S. E., Keogh, D., & Rellinger, E. (1993). Personal adjustment during pregnancy and adolescent parenting. *Adolescence, 28,* 67–79.

Passman, R. H. (1974). The effects of mothers and security blankets upon learning in children (Should Linus bring his blanket to school?). Paper presented at the American Psychological Association Convention, New Orleans, September.

Passman, R. H. (1976). Arousal reducing properties of attachment objects: Testing the functional limits of the security blanket relative to the mother. *Developmental Psychology, 12,* 468–469.

Passman, R. H. (1977). Providing attachment objects to facilitate learning and reduce distress: Effects of mothers and security blankets. *Developmental Psychology, 12,* 25–28.

Passman, R. H. (1987). Attachments to inanimate objects: Are children who have security blankets insecure? *Journal of Consulting and Clinical Psychology, 55,* 825–830.

Passman, R. H., & Adams, R. E. (1982). Preferences for mothers and security blankets and their effectiveness as reinforcers for young children's behaviors. *Journal o Child Psychology and Psychiatry, 23,* 223–236.

Passman, R. H., & Erck, T. W. (1978). Permitting maternal contact through vision alone: Films of mothers for promoting play and locomotion. *Developmental Psychology, 14,* 512–516.

Passman, R. H., & Halonen, J. S. (1979). A developmental survey of young children's attachments to inanimate objects. *The Journal of Genetic Psychology, 134,* 165–178.

Passman, R. H., & Longeway, K. P. (1982). The role of vision in maternal attachment: Giving 2-year-olds a photograph of their mother during separation. *Developmental Psychology, 18,* 530–533.

Passman, R. H., & Weisberg, P. (1975). Mothers and blankets as agents for promoting play and exploration by young children in a novel environment: The effects of social and nonsocial attachment objects. *Development Psychology, 11*, 170–177.

Patton, J. M., Prillaman, D., & Tassel-Baska, J. V. (1990). The nature and extent of programs for the disadvantaged gifted in the United States and Territories. *Gifted Child Quarterly, 34*, 94–96.

Patton, J. R., & Polloway, E. A. (1990). Mild mental retardation. In N. G. Haring & L. McCormick (Eds.), Exceptional children and youth (5th ed.). Columbus, Ohio: Merrill.

Pavlov, I. P. (1927). Conditioned reflexes. London: Oxford University Press.

Pawlak, C., Pascual-Sanchez, T., Raee, P., Fischer, W., & Ladame, F. (1999). Anxiety disorders, comorbidity, and suicide attempts in adolescence: A preliminary investigation. *European Psychiatry, 14*, 132–136.

Pazulinec, R., Meyerrose, M., & Sajwaj, T. (1983). Punishment via response cost. In S. Axelrod & J. Apsche (Eds.), The effects of punishment on human behavior. New York: Academic Press.

Peakman, T. C., & Page, M. J. (1998). Recombinant products for medical use. In T. M. Cox, & J. Sinclair (Eds.), *Molecular biology in medicine,* Malden, Ma.: Blackwell Science.

Pearce, J. C. (1977). Magical child: Rediscovering nature's plan for our children. New York: Bantam Books.

Pearl, R., Bryan, T., & Herzog, A. (1990). Resisting or acquiescing to peer pressure to engage in misconduct: Adolescents' expectations of probable consequences. *Journal of Youth and Adolescence, 19*, 43–55.

Pearson, D. W., & Copland, S. A. (1999). The management of hypertension in a diabetic pregnancy. *Diabetes/Metabolism Research Reviews, 15*, 146–151.

Pearson, J. L., & Ferguson, L. R. (1989). Gender differences in patterns of spatial ability, environmental cognition, and math and English achievement in late adolescence. *Adolescence, 24*, 421–431.

Pease-Alvarez, L., & Hakuta, K. (1992). Enriching our views of bilingualism and bilingual education. *Educational Researcher, 2*, 4–6.

Pederson, D. R., Gleason, K. E., Moran, G., & Bento, S. (1998). Maternal attachment representations, maternal sensitivity, and the infant-mother attachment relationship. *Developmental Psychology, 34*, 925–933.

Pediatric Nutrition Handbook (4th ed.). (1997). Elk Grove Village, Illinois: American Academy of Pediatrics.

Peiser, N. C., & Heaven, P. C. L. (1996). Family influences on self-reported delinquency among high school students. *Journal of Adolescence, 19*, 557–568.

Pellegrini, A. D., Bartini, M., & Brooks, Fr. (1999). School bullies, victims, and aggressive victims: Factors relating to group affiliation and victimization in early adolescence. *Journal of Educational Psychology, 91*, 216–224.

Penner, L. A., Thompson, J. K., & Coovert, D. L. (1991). Size overestimation among anorexics: Much ado about very little? *Journal of Abnormal Psychology, 100*, 90–93.

Pepler, D., Craig, W. M., & O'Connell, P. (1999). Understanding bullying from a dynamic systems perspective. In A. Slater & D. Muir (Eds.), *The Blackwell reader in development psychology.* Malden, M.A: Blackwell.

Pergament, E. (1990). Reproductive genetics in the 21st century: Fact and fantasy. In B. A. Fine, E. Getting, K. Greendale, B. Lepold, & N. W. Paul (Eds.), Strategies in genetic counseling: Reproductive genetics and new technologies, White Plains, N.Y.: March of Dimes Birth Defects Foundation.

Perkins, D., Jay, E., & Tishman, S. (1993). Introduction: New conceptions of thinking. *Educational Psychologist, 28*, 1–5.

Perkonigg, A. (1999). Patterns of cannabis use, abuse and dependence over time; Incidence, progression and stability in a sample of 1,228 adolescents. *Addiction, 94*, 1633–1648.

Perl, M. A., Mandic, M. L., Primorac, L., Klapec, T., & Perl, A. (1998). Adolescent acceptance of different foods by obesity status and by sex. *Physiology & Behavior, 65*, 241–245.

Perlmutter, M. (1980). Development of memory in the preschool years. In R. Greene & T. D. Yawkey (Eds.), Childhood development. Westport, Conn.: Technomic Publishing.

Perner, J. (1991). On representing that: The asymmetry between belief and desire in children's theory of mind. In D. Frye & C. Moore (Eds.), Children's theories of mind: Mental states and social understanding. Hillsdale N.J.: Lawrence Erlbaum.

Perry, P., Pasnak, R., & Holt, R. W. (1992). Instruction on concrete operations for children who are mildly mentally retarded. *Education and Training in Mental Retardation, 27*, 273–281.

Peskin, H. (1973). Influence of the developmental schedule of puberty on learning and ego functioning. *Journal of Youth and Adolescence, 2*, 273–290.

Petersen, A. C. (1988). Adolescent development. *Annual Review of Psychology, 39*, 583–607.

Peterson, C., & Peterson, R. (1986). Parent-child interaction and daycare: Does quality of daycare matter? *Journal of Applied Developmental Psychology, 7*, 1–15.

Peterson, G. W., Leigh, G. K., & Day, R. D. (1984). Family stress theory and the impact of divorce on children. *Journal of Divorce, 7*, 1–20.

Petrovich, O. (1999). Preschool children's understanding of the dichotomy between the natural and the artificial. *Psychological Reports, 84*, 3–27.

Pett, M. A., Wampold, B. E., Turner, C. W. & Vaughan-Cole, B. (1999). Paths of influence of divorce on preschool children's psychosocial adjustment.

Peverly, S. T. (1991). Problems with the knowledge-based explanation of memory and development. *Review of Educational Research, 61*, 71–93.

Phares, V. (1992). Where's poppa? The relative lack of attention to the role of fathers in child and adolescent psychopathology. *American Psychologist, 47*, 656–664.

Phillips, D., McCartney, K., & Scarr, S. (1987). Childcare quality and children's social development. *Developmental Psychology, 23*, 537–543.

Phinney, J. (1990). Ethnic identity in adolescents and adults: A review of research. *Psychological Bulletin, 108*, 499–514.

Phinney, J., & Devich-Navarro, M. (1997). Variations in bicultural identification among African American and Mexican American adolescents. *Journal of Research on Adolescence, 7*, 3–32.

Piaget, J. (1923). Le langage et la pensée chez l'enfant. London: Kegan Paul.

Piaget, J. (1932). The moral judgment of the child. London: Kegan Paul.

Piaget, J. (1951). Play, dreams and imitation in childhood. New York: W. W. Norton.

Piaget, J. (1954). The construction of reality in the child. New York: Basic Books.

Piaget, J. (1960). *The child's conception of the world.* London: Routledge.

Piaget, J. (1961). The genetic approach to the psychology of thought. *Journal of Educational Psychology, 52*, 275–281.

Piaget, J., & Garcia, R. (1991). Toward a logic of meanings. Hillsdale N.J.: Lawrence Erlbaum.

Pianta, R. C., & Ball, R. M. (1993). Maternal social support as a predictor of child adjustment in kindergarten. *Journal of Applied Developmental Psychology, 14*, 107–120.

Piazze, J. J., Anceschi, M. M., Maranghi, L., Brancato, V., Marchiani, E., & Cosmi, E. V. (1999). Fetal lung maturity in pregnancies complicated by ionsulin-dependent and gestational diabetes: A matched cohort study. *European Journal of Obstetrics, Gynecology, and Reproductive Biology, 83*, 145–150.

Pilkington, L. R., White, J., & Matheny, K. B. (1997). Perceived coping resources and psychological birth order in school-aged children. *Individual Psychology: Journal of Adlerian Theory, Research and Practice, 53*, 42–57.

Pill, C. J. (1990). Stepfamilies: Redefining the family. *Family Relations, 39*, 186–193.

Pilon, B. (1999, Dec. 26). Invisible victims: Relief agencies have ignored the plight of Serbia's Gypsies. *Edmonton Sun*, p. 72.

Pinabel, F., Gorwood, P., & Ades, J. (1997). The impact of oestradiol on ages at onset in schizophrenia reevaluated through Klinefelter syndrome. *Schizophrenia research, 23*, 269–270.

Pinchbeck, I., & Hewitt, M. (1973). Children in English society (Vol. II): From the eighteenth century to the Children Act of 1948. London: Routledge & Kegan Paul.

Pines, M. (1966). Revolution in learning: The years from birth to six. New York: Harper & Row.

Pines, M. (1975). In praise of the "invulnerables." APA Monitor, December, 7.

Pines, M. (1978, September). Invisible playmates. *Psychology Today*, 38–42, 106.

Pines, M. (1979, January). Superkids. *Psychology Today*, 53–63.

Pines, M. (1982, February). Baby, you're incredible. *Psychology Today*, 48–53.

Pinyerd, B. J. (1994). Infant cries: Physiology and assessment. *Neonatal Network, 13*, 15–20.

Pipes, P. L., Bumbals, J., & Pritkin, R. (1985). Collecting and assessing food intake information. In P. L. Pipes (Ed.), Nutrition in infancy and childhood. St. Louis: Times-Mirror/Mosby.

Pipp, S., & Haith, M. M. (1984). Infant visual responses: Which metric predicts best? *Journal of Experimental Child Psychology, 38*, 373–399.

Pitcher, E. G., & Schultz, L. H. (1983). Boys and girls at play: The development of sex roles. New York:

Plomin, R. (1987). Developmental behavioral genetics and infancy. In J. D. Osofsky (Ed.), *Handbook of infant development* (2nd ed.). New York: John Wiley.

Plomin, R. (1989). Environment and genes: Determinants of behavior. *American Psychologist, 44*, 105–111.

Plomin, R., DeFries, J. C., McClearn, G. E., & Rutter, M. (1997). *Behavioral genetics.* New York: Freeman

Plomin, R., Fulker, D. W., Corley, R., & DeFries, J. C. (1997). Nature, nurture, and cognitive development from 1 to 16 years: A parent-offspring study. *Psychological Science, 8,* 442–447.

Pogrebin, L. C. (1980). *Growing up free: Raising your child in the 80's.* New York: McGraw-Hill.

Pogue-Geile, M. F., & Rose, R. J. (1985). Developmental genetic studies of adult personality. *Developmental Psychology, 21,* 547–557.

Polansky, J. M., Buki, L. P., Horan, J. J., Ceperich, S. D., & Burows, D. D. (1999). The effectiveness of substance abuse prevention videotapes with Mexican American adolescents. *Hispanic Journal of Behavioral Sciences, 21,* 186–198.

Polivy, J., & Herman, C. P. (1985). Dieting and binging. A causal analysis. *American Psychologist, 40,* 193–201.

Pollack, A. (2000). Supercomputers Track Human Genome. *New York Times,* 08/28/2000, Vol. 149 Issue 51495, pC1, 0p, 1.

Pollitt, E., Haas, J., & Levitsky, D. (Eds.). (1989). International conference on iron deficiency and behavioral development. *American Journal of Clinical Nutrition,* Vol. 50, No. 3.

Pollock, L. (1983). *Forgotten children.* New York: Cambridge University Press.

Polson, B., & Newton, M. (1984). Not my kid: A family's guide to kids and drugs. New York: Arbor House.

Poole, D., & White, L. (1991). Effects of question repetition on the eyewitness testimony of children and adults. *Developmental psychology, 27,* 975–986.

Pope, A. W., Bierman, K. L., & Mumma, G. H. (1991). Aggression, hyperactivity, and inattention-immaturity: Behavior dimensions associated with peer rejection in elementary school boys. *Developmental Psychology, 27,* 663–671.

Pope, H. G., Hudson, J. I., Jurgelun-Todd, D., & Hudson, M. S. (1984). Prevalence of anorexia nervosa and bulimia in three student populations. *International Journal of Eating Disorders, 2,* 75–85.

Popkewitz, T. S. (1998). Dewey, Vygotsky, and the social administration of the individual: Constructivist pedagogy as systems of ideas in historical spaces. *American Educational Research Journal, 35,* 535–570.

Porath, M. (1996). Affective and motivational considerations in the assessment of gifted learners. *Roeper Review, 19,* 13–17.

Porerelli, J. H., Thomas, S., Hibbard, S., & Cogan, R. (1998). Defense mechanisms development in children, adolescents, and late adolescents. *Journal of Personality Assessment, 71,* 411–420.

Potts, R., & Swisher, L. (1998). Effects of televised safety models on children's risk taking and hazard identification. *Journal of Pediatric Psychology, 23,* 157–163.

Powell, K. (1999). Man drugged, assaulted wife, jury told. *Edmonton Journal,* Dec. 7, p. B1.

Powell, M. B. (1991). Investigating and reporting child sexual abuse: Review nd recommendations for clinical practice. *Australian Psychologist, 26,* 77–83.

Power, C., Lake, J. K., & Cole, T. J. (1997). Body mass index and height from childhood to adulthood in the 1958 British Birth Cohort.

American Journal of Clinical Nutrition, 66, 1094–1101.

Pozzulo, J. D., & Lindsay, R. C. L. (1998). Identification accuracy of children versus adults: A meta-analysis. *Law & Human Behavior, 22,* 549–570.

Prado, W. (1958). Appraisal of performance as a function of the relative-ego-involvement of children and adolescents. Unpublished doctoral dissertation, University of Oklahoma.

Praeger. Plomin, R. (1987). Developmental behavioral genetics and infancy. In J. D. Osofsky (Ed.), *Handbook of infant development* (2nd ed.). New York: John Wiley.

Preemies' diet seen key to progress. (1988). *Edmonton Journal,* Feb. 1, p. C1.

Preis, S., Jancke, L., Schmitz-Hillebrecht, J., & Steinmetz, H. (1999). Child age and planum temporale asymmetry. *Brain and Cognition, 40,* 441–452.

Premack, A. J., & Premack, D. (1972). Teaching language to an ape. *Scientific American, 227,* 92–99.

Premack, D. (1965). Reinforcement theory. In D. Levine (Ed.), Nebraska Symposium on Motivation (Vol. 13). Lincoln: University of Nebraska Press.

Pressley, M., Forrest-Pressley, D., & Elliott-Faust, D. J. (1988). What is strategy instructional enrichment and how to study it: Illustrations from research on children's prose memory and comprehension. In F. E. Weinert & M. Perlmutter (Eds.), Memory development: Universal changes and individual differences. Hillsdale, N.J.: Lawrence Erlbaum.

Preyer, W. (1888–1889). The mind of the child (2 vols.). New York: Appleton Century. (First published in German, 1882.)

Provine, R. R., & Westerman, J. A. (1979). Crossing the midline: Limits of early eye-hand behavior. *Child Development, 50,* 804–814.

Prytula, R. E., Oster, G. D., & Davis, S. F. (1977). The "rat rabbit" problem: What did John B. Watson really do? *Teaching of Psychology, 4,* 44–46.

Pungello, E. P., & Kurtz-Costes, B. (1999). Why and how working women choose child care: A review with a focus on infancy. *Developmental Review, 19,* 31–96.

Purdue U, Dept of Psychological Sciences, West Lafayette, IN, USA.

Putallaz, M., & Gottman, J. M. (1981). An interactional model of children's entry into peer groups. *Child Development, 52,* 986–994.

Quan, M. (1994). Pelvic inflammatory disease: Diagnosis and management. *Journal of the American Board of Family Practice, 7,* 110–123.

Quas, J. A., Goodman, G. S., Bidrose, S., Pipe, M., Craw, S., & Ablin, D. S. (1999). Emotion and memory: Children's long-term remembering, forgetting, and suggestibility. *Journal of Experimental Child Psychology, 72,* 235–270.

Quay, H. C. (1987). Intelligence. In H. C. Quay (Ed.), *Handbook of juvenile delinquency.* New York: JohnWiley, 106–117.

Quintana, S. M., & Vera, W. M. (1999). Mexican-American children's ethnic identity, understanding of ethnic prejudice, and parental ethnic socialization. *Hispanic Journal of Behavioral Sciences, 21,* 387–405.

Rabin, A. I., & Beit-Hallahmi, B. (1982). *Twenty years later: Kibbutz children grown up.* New York: Springer.

Rall, J. E. (1998). Where are the genes specifying mental illness? *Journal of Nervous and Mental Disease, 186,* 722–723.

Ramey, C. T. & Campbell, F. A. (1994). Poverty, early childhood education, and academic competence: The Abecedarian experiment. In A. C. Huston (Ed), *Children in poverty: Child development and public policy.* Cambridge, England: Cambridge University Press.

Ramey, C. T., & Blair, C. (1996). Intellectual development and the role of early experience. In D. K. Detterman (Ed), *The environment. Current topics in human intelligence,* Vol. 5. (pp. 59–67). Norwood, NJ: Ablex.

Ramey, C. T., & Landesman R. S. (1998). Prevention of intellectual disabilities: Early interventions to improve cognitive development. *Preventive Medicine: an International Devoted to Practice & Theory, 27,* 224–232.

Randall, V. (1997). Gifted girls: What challenges do they face: A summary of the research. *Gifted Child Today, 20,* 42–50.

Randhawa, B. S. (1991). Gender differences in academic achievement: A closer look at mathematics. *Alberta Journal of Educational Research, 37,* 241–257.

Rank, O. (1929). The trauma of birth. New York: Harcourt Brace & World.

Ranney, M. D. (1991). SIDS and parents. In C. A. Corr, H. Fuller, C. A. Barnickol, & D. M. Corr (Eds.), Sudden infant death syndrome: Who can help and how. New York: Springer.

Raver, C. C., Blackburn, E. K., Bancroft, M., & Torp, N. (1999). Relations between effective emotional self-regulation, attentional control, and low-income preschoolers' social competence with peers. *Early Education & Development, 10,* 333–350.

Ray, W. Z., & Ravizza, R. (1985). Methods toward a science of behavior and experience (2nd ed.). Belmont, Calif. Wadsworth.

Ray, William J. (1997). *Methods toward a science of behavior and experience* (5th ed.). Pacific Grove: Brooks/Cole.

Rayburn, W., Wilson, G., Schreck, J., Louwsma, G., & Hamman, J. (1982). Prenatal counseling: A state-wide telephone service. *Obstetrics and Gynecology, 60,* 243–246.

Rayna, S., Sinclair, H., & Stambak, M. (1989). Infants and physics. In H. Sinclair, M. Stambak, I. Lezine, S. Rayna, & M. Verba (Eds.), Infants and objects: The creativity of cognitive development. New York: Academic Press.

Rebok, G. W., & Balcerak, L. J. (1989). Memory self-efficacy and performance differences in young and old adults: The effect of mnemonic training. *Developmental Psychology, 25,* 714–721.

Recommended Dietary Allowances (9th ed.). 1980. Washington, D.C.: National Academy of Sciences.

Redmond, M. (1985). Attitudes of adolescent males toward adolescent pregnancy and fatherhood. *Family Relations, 34,* 337–342.

Reid, L. D., & Carpenter, D. J. (1990). Alcohol-abuse and alcoholism. In L. D. Reid (Ed.), Opioids, bulimia, and alcohol abuse & alcoholism. New York: Springer-Verlag.

Reiss, I. L. (1966). The social context of premarital sexual permissiveness. New York: Holt, Rinehart & Winston.

Reissland, N. (1988). Neonatal imitation in the first hour of life: Observations in rural Nepal. *Developmental Psychology, 24,* 464–469.

Renaud, J., Brent, D. A., Birmaher, B., Chiappetta, L. & Bridge, J. (1999). Suicide in adolescents with disruptive disorders. *Journal of the American Academy of Child & Adolescent Psychiatry, 38,* 846–851.

Renzulli, J. S. (1986). The three-ring conception of giftedness: A developmental model for creative productivity. In R. J. Sternberg & J. E. Davidson (eds.), *Conceptions of giftedness.* Cambridge: Cambridge University Press.

Renzulli, J. S., Reis, S. M., & Smith, L. H. (1981). *The revolving door identification model.* Mansfield Center, Conn.: Creative Learning Press.

Report of the Surgeon General's Workshop on Breastfeeding and Human Lactation, (1984). Rockville, MD: US Department of Health and Human Services.

Reschly, D. J. (1990). Adaptive behavior. In A. Thomas & J. Grimes (Eds.), Best practices in school psychology (2nd ed.). Washington, D.C.: National Association of School Psychologists.

Reschly, D. J. (1992). Mental retardation: Conceptual foundations, definitional criteria, and diagnostic operations. In S. R. Hooper, G. W. Hynd, & R. E. Mattison, (Eds.), Developmental disorders: Diagnostic criteria and clinical assessment. Hillsdale, N.J.: Lawrence Erlbaum.

Rescorla, L. (1991). Early academics: Introduction to the debate. *New Directions for Child Development, 53,* 5–11.

Reyna, V. F. (1996). Conceptions of memory development with implications for reasoning and decision making. *Annals of Child Development, 12,* 49–86.

Reynolds, A. J., & Temple, J. A. (1998). Extended early childhood intervention and school achievement: Age thirteen findings from the Chicago Longitudinal Study. *Child Development, 69,* 231–246.

Reynolds, P. (1989). Childhood in crossroads: Cognition and society in South Africa. Grand Rapids, Mich.: Wm. B. Eerdmans.

Reyome, N. D. (1993). A comparisonof the school performance of sexually abused, neglected and non-maltreated children. *Child Study Journal, 23,* 17–38.

Reznick, J. S., Corley, R., & Robinson, J. (1997). A longitudinal twin study of intelligence in the second year. *Monographs of the society for research in child development, 62,* Whole No1.

Rheingold, H. L. (1985). Development as the acquisition of familiarity. *Annual Review of Psychology, 36,* 1–17.

Rheingold, H. L., & Cook, K. V. (1975). The contents of boys' and girls' rooms as an index of parents' behavior. *Child Development, 46,* 459–463.

Ricci, C. M., & Beal, C. R. (1998). Child witnesses: Effect of event knowledge on memory and suggestibility. *Journal of Applied Developmental Psychology, 19,* 305–317.

Ricciuti, H. N. (1991). Malnutrition and cognitive development: Research-policy linkages and current research directions. In L. Okagaki & R. J. Sternberg (Eds.), Directors of development: Influences on the development of children's thinking. Hillsdale, N.J.: Lawrence Erlbaum.

Ricco, R. B. (1993). Revising the logic of operations as a relevance logic: From hypothesis testing to explanation. *Human Development, 36,* 125–146.

Rice, B. (1982, February). The Hawthorne defect: Persistence of a flawed theory. *Psychology Today,* 71–74.

Rice, M. (1983). The role of television in language acquisition. *Developmental Review, 3,* 211–224.

Rice, M. L. (1989). Children's language acquisition. *American Psychologist, 44,* 149–156.

Richards, L. N., & Schmeige, C. J. (1993). Problems and strengths of single-parent families: Implications for practice and policy. *Family Relations, 42,* 277–285.

Richardson, G. A., Hamel, S. C., Goldschmidt, L., & Day, N. L. (1999). Growth of infants prenatally exposed to cocaine/crack: comparison of a prenatal care and a no prenatal care sample. *Pediatrics, 104,* e18.

Ridgeway, C. L. (1997). Interaction and the conservation of gender inequality: Considering employment. *American Sociological Review, 62,* 218–235.

Ridley-Johnson, R., Surdy, T., & O'Laughlin, E. (1991). Parent survey on television violence viewing: Fear, aggression, and sex differences. *Journal of Applied Developmental Psychology, 12,* 63–71.

Rierdan, J. (1999). Internet-depression link? *American Psychologist, 54,* 781–782.

Ringler, N. M., Kennell, J. H., Jarvella, R., Navojosky, B. J., & Klaus, M. H. (1975). Mother to child speech at two years: Effects of early post-natal contact. *Journal of Pediatrics, 86,* 141–144.

Ringwalt, C. L., & Palmer, J. H. (1989). Cocaine and crack users compared. *Adolescence, 24,* 851–859.

Ritts, V., Patterson, M. L., & Tubbs, M. E. (1992). Expectations, impressions, and judgments of physically attractive students: A review. *Review of Educational Research, 62,* 413–426.

Rizzo, T. A., Metzger, B. E., Dooley, S. L., & Cho, N. H. (1997). Early malnutrition and child neurobehavioral development: Insights from the study of children of diabetic mothers. *Child Development, 68,* 26–38.

Roazen, P. (1975). Freud and his followers. New York: Alfred A. Knopf.

Roberts, D. F., & Bachan, C. M. (1981). Mass communication effects. *Annual Review of Psychology, 32,* 307–356.

Roberts, K. P., & Lamb, M. E. (1999). Children's responses when interviewers distort details during investigative interviews. *Legal & Criminological Psychology, 4,* 23–31.

Roberts, R. B. (1996). *Sexually transmitted diseases.* Internet: http://edcenter.med.cornell .edu/PathophysiologyCases/STDs/STD04 .html

Roberts, R. E. (1999). The structure of ethnic identity of young adolescents from diverse ethnocultural groups. *Journal of Early Adolescence, 19,* 301–323.

Robertson, S. S. (1993a). Mechanism and function of cyclicity in spontaneous movement. In W. P. Smotherman & S. R. Robinson (Eds.), *Behavior of the fetus.* Caldwell, NJ: Telford.

Robertson, S. S. (1993b). Oscillation and complexity in early infant behavior. *Child Development, 64,* 1022–1035.

Robinshaw, H. M. (1996). The pattern of development from non-communicative behaviour to language by hearing impaired and hearing infants. *British Journal of Audiology, 30,* 177–198.

Robinson, A., & Clinkenbeard, P. R. (1998). Giftedness: An exceptionality examined. *Annual Review of Psychology, 49,* 117–139.

Robinson, N. M., Abbott, R. D., Berninger, V. W., & Busse, J. (1996). Structure of abilities in

math-precocious young children: Gender similarities and differences. *Journal of Educational Psychology, 88,* 341–352.

Robinson, S. (1989). Caring for childbearing women: The interrelationship between midwifery and medical responsibilities. In S. Robinson & A. M. Thomson (Eds.), Midwives, research and childbirth (Vol. 1). New York: Chapman and Hall.

Robison, L. M., Sclar, D. A., Skaer, T. L., & Galin, R. S. (1999). National trends in the prevalence of attention-deficit/hyperactivity disorder and the prescribing of methylphenidate among school-age children: 1990–1995. *Clinical Pediatrics, 38,* 209–217.

Robson, L. G., & Hughes, S. M. (1996). The distal limb environment regulates MyoD accumulation and muscle differentiation in mousechick chimaeric limbs. *Development, 122,* 3899–3910.

Rochat, P. (1989). Object manipulation and exploration in 2– to 5–month-old infants. *Developmental Psychology, 25,* 871–884.

Roche, A. F., Lipman, R. S., Overall, J. E., & Hung, W. (1979). The effects of stimulant medication on the growth of hyperkinetic children. *Pediatrics, 63,* 847–850.

Roche, J. P., & Ramsbey, T. W. (1993). Premarital sexuality: A five-year follow-up study of attitudes and behavior by dating stage. *Adolescence, 28,* 67–80.

Roche, J. P., & Ramsbey, T. W. (1993). Premarital sexuality: A five-year follow-up study of attitudes and behavior by dating stage. *Adolescence, 28,* 67–80.

Rock, A. M. L., Trainor, L. J., & Addison, T. L. (1999). Distinctive messages in infant-directed lullabies and play songs. *Developmental Psychology, 35,* 527–534.

Rodeck, C. H. (1982). Fetal blood sampling. In H. Galjaard (Ed.), The future of prenatal diagnosis. London: Churchill Livingstone, 85–92.

Rodgers, B. (1996). Social and psychological well-being of children from divorced families: Australian research findings. *Australian Psychologist, 31,* 174–182.

Rodgers, B. (1997). Children and parental divorce: The meaning of small effects—A reply. *Australian Psychologist, 32,* 139–142.

Rodney, H. E., & Mupier, R. (1999). The impact of parental alcoholism on self-esteem and depression among African-American adolescents. *Journal of Child & Adolescent Substance Abuse, 8,* 55–71.

Rodriguez-Palmero, M., Koletzko, B., Kunz, C., & Jensen, R. (1999). Nutritional and biochemical properties of human milk, Part II: Lipids, micronutrients, and bioactive factors. *Clinics in Perinatology, 26,* 335–359.

Roethlisberger, S. J., & Dickson, W. J. (1939). Management and the worker. Cambridge, Mass.: Harvard University Press.

Roffwarg, H. P., Muzio, J. N., & Dement, W. C. (1966). Ontogenetic development of the human sleep-dream cycle. *Science, 152.* 604–619.

Rogers, C. R. (1951). Client-centered therapy: Its current practice, implications, and theory. Boston: Houghton Mifflin.

Rolison, M. A., & Medway, F. J. (1985). Teachers' expectations and attributions for student achievement: Effects of label, performance pattern, and special education intervention. *American Educational Research Journal, 22,* 561–573.

Romans, S. M., Roeltgen, D. P., Kushner, H., & Ross, J. L. (1997). Executive function in girls with Turner's syndrome. *Developmental Psychology, 13*, 23–40.

Romig, C. A., & Bakken, L. (1990). Teens at risk for pregnancy: The role of ego development and family processes. *Journal of Adolescents, 13*, 195–199.

Roosa, M. W. (1991). Adolescent pregnancy programs collection: An introduction. *Family Relations, 40*, 370–372.

Roscoe, B., & Kruger, T. L. (1990). AIDS: Late adolescents' knowledge and its influence on sexual behavior. *Adolescence, 25*, 39–48.

Rose, N. C., Palomaki, G. E., Haddow, J. E., Goodman, D. B., & Mennuti, M. T. (1994). Maternal serum alpha-fetoprotein screening for chromosomal abnormalities: A prospective study in women aged 35 and older. *American Journal of Obstetrics and Gynecology, 170*, 1073–1078.

Rose-Krasnor, L. (1997). The nature of social competence: A theoretical review. *Social Development, 6*, 111–135.

Rosen, M. (1995). Gender differences in structure, means and variances of hierarchically ordered ability dimensions. *Learning and Instruction, 5*, 37–62.

Rosenak, D., Diamant, Y. Z., Yaffe, H., & Hornstein, E. (1990). Cocaine: Maternal use during pregnancy and its effect on the mother, the fetus, and the infant. *Obstetrical and Gynecological Survey, 45*, 348–357.

Rosenblatt, R. (1984). Children of war. New York: Anchor Books.

Rosengren, K. E., & Windahl, S. (1989). Media matter: TV use in childhood and adolescence. Norwood, N.J.: Ablex.

Rosenkoetter, L. I. (1999). The television situation comedy and children's prosocial behavior. *Journal of Applied Social Psychology, 29*, 979–993.

Rosenkoetter, L. I., Huston, A. C., & Wright, J. C. (1990). Television and the moral judgment of the young child. *Journal of Applied Developmental Psychology, 11*, 123–137.

Rosenthal, R., & Jacobson, L. (1968a). Pygmalion in the classroom: Teacher expectations and pupils' intellectual development. New York: Holt, Rinehart & Winston.

Rosenthal, R., & Jacobson, L. (1968b). Teacher expectations for the disadvantaged. *Scientific American, 218*, 19–23.

Rosenthal, T. L., & Zimmerman, B. J. (1972). Modeling by exemplification and instruction in training conservation. *Developmental Psychology, 6*, 392–401.

Rosenzweig, M. R. (1984). Experience and the brain. *American psychologist, 39*, 365–376.

Rosett, H. L., & Sander, L. W. (1979). Effects of maternal drinking on neonatal morphology and state regulation. In J. D. Osofsky (Ed.), Handbook of infant development. New York: John Wiley, 809–836.

Ross, A. O. (1980). Psychological disorders of children: A behavioral approach totheory, research, and therapy (2nd ed.). New York: McGraw-Hill.

Ross, H. S. (1982). Establishment of social games among toddlers. *Developmental Psychology, 18*, 509–518.

Rotenberg, K. J. & Hymel, S. (Eds.) (1999). Loneliness in childhood and adolescence. New York: Cambridge University Press.

Rotenberg, K. J., & Eisenberg, N. (1997). Developmental differences in the understanding of and reaction to others' inhibition of emotional expression. *Developmental Psychology, 33*, 526–537.

Rothstein, E. (1980). The scar of Sigmund Freud. *New York Review of Books*, October 9, 14–20.

Rousseau, J. J. (1911). Emile, or on education (Barbara Foxley, Trans.). London: Dent. (Originally published, 1762.)

Rovee-Collier, C. (1996). Shifting the focus from what to why. *Infant Behavior and Development, 19*, 385–400.

Rovee-Collier, C. K. (1987). Learning and memory in infancy. In J. D. Osofsky (Ed.), Handbook of infant development. New York: John Wiley.

Rovee-Collier, C. K. (1999). The development of infant memory. *Current Directions in Psychological Science, 8*, 80–85.

Rovee-Collier, C. K., & Hayne, H. (1987). Reactivation of infant memory: Implications for cognitive development. In H. W. Reese (Ed.), *Advances in child development and behavior* (Vol. 20). New York: Academic Press.

Rovee-Collier, C. K., Sullivan, M. W., Enright, M. L., Lucas, D., & Fagen, J. W. (1980). Reactivation of infant memory. *Science, 208*, 1159–1161.

Rowan, A. B., Foy, D. W., & Rodriguez, N. (1994). Postraumatic Stress Disorder in a clinical sample of adults sexually abused as children. *Child Abuse and Neglect: The International Journal, 18*, 151–161.

Rowan, J. (1998). Maslow amended. *Journal of Humanistic Psychology, 38*, 81–92.

Rowen, L., Mahairas, G., & Hood, L. (1997). Sequencing the human genome. *Science, 278*, 605–607.

Royal College of Psychiatrists. (1987). Drug scenes: A report on drugs and drug dependence by the Royal College of Psychiatrists. London: Gaskell Press.

Royer, J. M., Cisero, C. A., & Carlo, M. S. (1993). Techniques and procedures for assessing cognitive skills. *Review of Educational Research, 63*, 201–243.

Rozhon, T. (2000, Jan. 9) Fido is meeting the Coop board and learning to beg. *The New York Times*, Section 1, Pp. 1, 39).

Rubin, J. Z., Provenzano, J. J., & Luria, Z. (1974). The eye of the beholder: Parent's views on sex of newborns. *American Journal of Orthopsychiatry, 44*, 512–519.

Rubin, K. H., Maioni, T. L., & Hornung, M. (1976). Free play behaviors in middle- and lower-class preschoolers: Parten and Piaget revisited. *Child Development, 47*, 414–419.

Rubin, Z. (1980). Children's friendships. Cambridge, Mass.: Harvard University Press.

Ruff, H. A., & Saltarelli, L. M. (1993). Exploratory play with objects: Basic cognitive processes and individual differences. *New Directions for Child Development, 59*, 5–16.

Ruffman, T., Olson, D. R., Ash, T., & Keenan, T. (1993). The ABCs of deception: Do young children understand deception in the same way as adults? *Developmental Psychology, 29*, 74–87.

Ruiselova, Z. (1998). Relationships with parents and teachers in connection with pubertal maturation timing in girls. *Studia Psychologica, 40*, 277–281.

Rumbaugh, D. M. (1998). Austin H. Riesen (1913–1996). *American Psychologist, 53*, 60–61.

Rumbaugh, D. M., & Savage-Rumbaugh, E. S. (1996). Biobehavioral roots of language: Words, apes, and a child. In B. M. Velichkovsky & D. M. Rumbaugh, (Eds.), *Communicating meaning: The evolution and development of language*. Mahwah, NJ: Lawrence Erlbaum.

Rumbelow, H. (1999, Dec. 6). Weighty women are in better shape than men. *The London Times*, P. News 7.

Rumsey, J. M. (1998). Brain imaging of reading disorders. *Journal of the American Academy of Child & Adolescent Psychiatry, 37*, 12.

Runco, M. A. (1986a). Maximal performance on divergent thinking tests by gifted, talented, and nongifted children. *Psychology in the Schools, 23*, 308–315.

Runco, M. A. (1986b). Flexibility and originality in children's divergent thinking. *The Journal of Psychology, 120*, 345–352.

Runco, M. A. (1996). Personal creativity: Definition and developmental issues. *New Directions for Child Development, 72*, 3–27.

Runco, M. A., & Albert, R. S. (1986). Exceptional giftedness in early adolescence and intrafamilial divergent thinking. *Journal of Youth and Adolescence, 15*, 335–344.

Russ, S. W. (1996). Development of creative processes in children. *New Directions for Child Development, 72*, 31–42.

Rycek, R. F., Stuhr, S. L., McDermott, J., Benker, J., & Schwartz, M. D. (1998). Adolescent egocentrism and cognitive functioning during late adolescence. *Adolescence, 33*, 745–749.

Rymer, R. (1993). Genie: A scientific tragedy. New York: Harper Perennial.

Saarni, C. (1997a). Coping with aversive feelings. *Motivation & Emotion, 21*, 45–63.

Saarni, C. (1997b). Emotional competence and self-regulation in childhood. In P. Salovey & D. J. Sluyter (Eds.), *Emotional development and emotional intelligence: Educational implications*. New York, NY: Basicbooks.

Saarni, C. (1999). *The development of emotional competence*. New York, NY: The Guilford Press.

Saarnio, D. A. (1993). Scene memory in young children. *Merrill-Palmer Quarterly, 39*, 196–212.

Sabatino, D. A. (1991). A fine line: When discipline becomes child abuse. Blue Ridge Summit, Pa.: TAB Books.

Sachs, M. (1984). The fat girl. New York: Dutton.

Sachweh, S. (1998). Granny darling's nappies: Secondary babytalk in German nursing homes for the aged. *Journal of Applied Communication Research, 26*, 52–65.

Sagan, C. (1977). *The dragons of Eden*. New York: Ballantine Books.

Sagi, A., van Ijzendoorn, M. H., Scharf, M., & Joels, T. (1997). Ecological constraints for intergenerational transmission of attachment. *International Journal of Behavioral Development, 20*, 287–299.

Sagi, A., van Ijzendoorn, M. H., & Koren-Karie, N. (1991). Primary appraisal of the strange situation: A cross-cultural analysis of preseparation episodes. *Developmental Psychology, 27*, 587–596.

Sagov, S. E., Feinbloom, R. I., Spindel, P., & Brodsky, A. (1984). Home births: A practitioner's guide to birth outside the hospital. Rockville, Md.: Aspen Systems Corporation.

Saidla, D. D. (1992). Children's rights regarding physical abuse. *Journal of Humanistic Education and Development, 31*, 73–83.

Sakihara, H. (1998). A developmental study of letter copying in preschool children: Evaluation from the viewpoint of segmentation/construction. *Japanese Journal of Educational Psychology, 46*, 212–220.

Salomon, G., Perkins, D. N., & Globerson, T. (1991). Partners in cognition: Extending human intelligence with intelligent technologies. *Educational Researcher, 20,* 2–9.

Sameroff, A. J. (1968). The components of sucking in the human newborn. *Journal of Experimental Child Psychology, 6,* 607–623.

Sander, T., Ladehoff, M., Samochoziec, J., Finckh, U., Rommelspacher, H., & Schmidt, L. G. (1999). Lack of an allelic association between polymorphisms of the dopamine D2 receptor gene and alcohol dependence in the German population. *Alcoholism: Clinical and Experimental Research, 23,* 578–581.

Sandler, J., & Freud, A. (1984). Discussions in the Hampstead Index on "The Ego and the Mechanisms of Defense": XIV. Conclusion. *Bulletin of the Hampstead Clinic, 7,* 219–229.

Santelli, J. S., Brener, N. D., Lowry, R., Bhatt, A., & Zabin, L. S. (1998). Multiple sexual partners among U.S. adolescents and young adults. *Family Planning Perspectives, 30,* 271–275.

Santonastaso, P., Ferrara, S., & Favaro, A. (1999). Differences between binge eating disorder and nonpurging bulimia nervosa. *International Journal of Eating Disorders, 25,* 215–218.

Santos, I. S., Victora, C. G., Huttly, S., & Morris, S. (1998). Caffeine intake and pregnancy outcomes: A meta-analytic review. *Cadernos de Saude Publica, 14,* 523–530.

Sasco, A. J., & Vainio, H. (1999). From in utero and childhood exposure to parental smoking to childhood cancer: A possible link and the need for action. *Human and Experimental Toxicology, 18,* 192–201.

Saudino, K. & McManus, I. C. (1998). Handedness, footedness, eyedness and earedness in the Colorado Adoption Project. *British Journal of Developmental Psychology, 16,* 167–174.

Savage-Rumbaugh, E. S., Murphy, J., Sevcik, R. A., Brakke, K. E., Williams, S. L., & Rumbaugh, D. M. (1993). Language comprehension in ape and child. *Monographs of the Society for Research in Child Development, 58,* 1–222.

Savin-Williams, R. C., & Small, S. A. (1986). The timing of puberty and its relationship to adolescent and parent perceptions of family interactions. *Developmental Psychology, 22,* 342–347.

Sawyer, R. G., Pinciaro, P. J., & Anderson-Sawyer, A. (1998). Pregnancy testing and counseling: A university health center's 5–year experience. *Journal of American College Health, 46,* 221–225.

Scanlon, T. J., Tomkins, A., Lynch, M. A., & Scanlon, F. (1998). Street children in Latin America. *British Medical Journal, 316,* 1596–1561.

Scarr, S. (1985). Constructing psychology: Making facts and fables for our times. *American Psychologist, 40,* 499–512.

Scarr, S. (1993). Biological and cultural diversity: The legacy of Darwin for development. *Child Development, 64,* 1333–1353.

Scarr, S. (1997). Why child care has little impact on most children's development. *Current Directions in Psychological Science, 6,* 143–148.

Scarr, S. (1998). American child care today. *American Psychologist,.53,* 95–108.

Scarr, S. (1999). Freedom of choice for poor families. *American Psychologist, 54,* 144–145.

Scarr, S., & Eisenberg, M. (1993). Child care research: Issues, perspectives, and results. *Annual Review of Psychology, 44,* 613–644.

Scarr, S., & McCartney, K. (1983). How people make their own environments: A theory of genotype-environment effects. *Child Development, 54,* 424–435.

Scarr, S., & Salapatek, P. (1970). Patterns of fear development during infancy. *Merrill-Palmer Quarterly, 16,* 56–90.

Scarr, S., & Weinberg, R. A. (1983). The Minnesota Adoption Studies: Genetic differences and malleability. *Child Development, 54,* 260–267.

Scarr-Salapatek, S., & Williams, M. L. (1973). The effects of early stimulation on low-birth weight infants. *Child Development, 44,* 94–101.

Schacter, D. L., Norman, K. A., & Koutstaal, W. (1998). The cognitive neuroscience of constructive memory. *Annual Review of Psychology, 49,* 289–318.

Schaefer, C. E. (1969). Imaginary companions and creative adolescents. *Developmental Psychology, 1,* 747–749.

Schaffer, H. R. (1966). The onset of fear of strangers and the incongruity hypothesis. *Journal of Child Psychology and Psychiatry, 7,* 95–106.

Schaffer, H. R. (1984). The child's entry into a social world. New York: Academic Press.

Schaffer, H. R., Collis, G. M., & Parsons, G. (1977). Vocal interchange and visual regard in verbal and preverbal children. In H. R. Schaffer (Ed.), *Studies in mother-infant interaction.* London: Academic Press.

Schaie, K. W. (1965). A general model for the study of developmental problems. *Psychological Bulletin, 64,* 92–107.

Schanler, R. J., Hurst, N. M., & Lau, C. (1999). The use of human milk and breastfeeding in premature infants. *Clinics in Perinatology, 26,* 379–398.

Schardein, J. L. (1985). Chemical induced birth defects. New York: Marcel Dekker.

Schave, D., & Schave, B. (1989). Early adolescence and the search for self: A developmental perspective. New York: Praeger.

Scher, J., & Dix, C. (1983). Will my baby be normal? Everything you need to know about pregnancy. New York: Dial Press.

Schiefelbusch, R. L., & McCormick, L. (1981). Language and speech disorders. In J. M. Kauffman & D. P. Hallahan (Eds.), Handbook of Special Education. Englewood Cliffs, N.J.: Prentice-Hall.

Schlegel, A., & Barry, H., III (1980). Adolescent initiation ceremonies: A cross-cultural code. In H. Barry III & A. Schlegel (Eds.), *Cross-cultural samples and codes.* Pittsburgh: University of Pittsburgh Press.

Schlegel, A., & Barry, H., III. (1991). Adolescence: An anthropological inquiry. New York: Free Press.

Schmidt, L. A., & Fox, N. A. (1998). Fear-potentiated startle responses in temperamentally different human infants. *Developmental Psychobiology, 32,* 113–120.

Schmidt, M. (1995). Anglo Americans and sexual child abuse. In L. A. Fontes (Ed.), *Sexual abuse in nine North American cultures: Treatment and prevention,* Thousand Oaks, CA: Sage.

Schmidt-Hellerau, C. (1997). Libido and lethe: Fundamentals of a formalised conception of metapsychology. *International Journal of Psycho-Analysis, 78,* 683–697.

Schneider, B. H. (1999). Cultural perspectives on children's social competence. In M. Woodhead, D. Faulkner, & K. Littleton (Eds.), *Making sense of social development..* New York: Routledge.

Schneider, D. J. (1991). Social cognition. *Annual Review of Psychology, 42,* 527–561.

Schneider, W., & Sodian, B. (1997). Memory strategy development: Lessons from longitudinal research. *Developmental Review, 17,* 442–461.

Schneider, W., Borkowsky, J. G., Kurtz, B. E., & Kerwin, K. (1986). Metamemory and motivation: A comparison of strategy use in German and American children. *Journal of Cross-Cultural Psychology, 17,* 315–336.

Schneider, W., Schlagmueller, M., & Vise, M. (1998). The impact of metamemory and domain-specific knowledge on memory. *European Journal of Psychology of Education, 13,* 91–103.

Schneider-Rosen, K., Braunwald, K. G., Carlson, V., & Cicchetti, D. (1985). Current perspectives in attachment theory: Illustration from the study of maltreated infants. In I. Bretherton & E. Waters (Eds.), Growing points of attachment theory and research. Monographs of the Society for Research in Child Development, 50, No. 209.

Schoonhoven, R., Lamore, P. J. J., de Laat, J. A. P. M., & Grote, J. J. (1999). The prognostic value of electrocochleography in severely hearing-impaired infants. *Audiology, 38,* 141–154.

Schumer, F. (1983). Abnormal psychology. Lexington, Mass.: D. C. Heath.

Schunk, D. H. (1984). Self-efficacy perspective on achievement behavior. *Educational Psychologist, 19,* 48–58.

Schupf, N., Kapell, D., Nightingale, B., Rodriguez, A., Tycko, B., & Mayeux, R. (1998). Earlier onset of Alzheimer's disease in men with Down syndrome. *Neurology, 50,* 991–995.

Schutte, N. S., Malouff, J. M., Hall, L. E., Haggerty, D. J., Cooper, J. T., Golden, C. J., & Dornheim, L. (1998). Development and validation of a measure of emotional intelligence. *Personality & Individual Differences, 25,* 167–177.

Schwartz, D., McFadyen-Ketchum, S., A., Dodge, K. A., Pettit, G. S., & Bates, J. E. (1998). Peer group victimization as a predictor of children's behavior problems at home and in school. *Development & Psychopathology, 10,* 87–99.

Schwartzman, H. B. (1987). A cross-cultural perspective on child-structured play activities and materials. In A. W. Gottfried & C. C. Brown (eds.), Play interactions: The contribution of play materials and parental involvement to children's development. Lexington, Mass.: D. C. Heath.

Scott, D. G. (1998). Rites of passage in adolescent development: A reappreciation. *Child & Youth Care Forum, 27,* 317–335.

Scott, J. A., & Binns, C. W. (1999). Factors associated with the initiation and duration of breastfeeding; A review of the literature. *Breastfeeding Review, 7,* 5–16.

Scott, L. L. (1999). Prevention of perinatal herpes: Prophylactic antiviral therapy? *Clinical Obstetrics and Gynecology, 42,* 174–175.

Scragg, R. K., Mitchell, E. A., Stewart, A. W., Ford, R. P., Taylor, B. J., Hassall, I. B., Williams, S. M., & Thompson, J. M. (1996). Infant room-sharing and prone sleep position in sudden infant death syndrome. New Zealand Cot Death Study Group. *Lancet, 347,* 7–12.

Sears, R. R. (1984). Patterns of child rearing. In S. A. Mednick, M. Harway, & K. M. Finello (Eds.), *Handbook of longitudinal research*